AF194431

Economics

for Cambridge IGCSE™ and O Level

EXAM PREPARATION AND PRACTICE

George Vlachonikolis

Shaftesbury Road, Cambridge CB2 8EA, United Kingdom

One Liberty Plaza, 20th Floor, New York, NY 10006, USA

477 Williamstown Road, Port Melbourne, VIC 3207, Australia

314–321, 3rd Floor, Plot 3, Splendor Forum, Jasola District Centre, New Delhi – 110025, India

103 Penang Road, #05–06/07, Visioncrest Commercial, Singapore 238467

Cambridge University Press & Assessment is a department of the University of Cambridge.

We share the University's mission to contribute to society through the pursuit of education, learning and research at the highest international levels of excellence.

www.cambridge.org
Information on this title: www.cambridge.org/9781009817967

First published 2026
20 19 18 17 16 15 14 13 12 11 10 9 8 7 6 5 4 3 2 1

Printed in Malaysia by Vivar Printing

A catalogue record for this publication is available from the British Library

ISBN 978-1-009-81796-7 Exam Preparation and Practice with Digital Access (2 Years)
ISBN 978-1-009-81795-0 Digital Exam Preparation and Practice (2 Years)
ISBN 978-1-009-81794-3 Exam Preparation and Practice – eBook

Additional resources for this publication at www.cambridge.org/9781009817967

Some texts and case studies in this book have been taken from the *Economics for Cambridge IGCSE™ and O Level Coursebook*.

Cambridge International Education material in this publication is reproduced under licence and remains the intellectual property of Cambridge University Press & Assessment.

....

2025 Cambridge Dedicated Teacher Awards

Our **Cambridge Dedicated Teacher Awards** are an opportunity to show appreciation for the incredible work teachers do every day.

Thank you to everyone who nominated this year; we have been inspired and moved by all of your stories. Well done to all of our nominees for your dedication to learning and for inspiring the next generation of thinkers, leaders and innovators.

Congratulations to our winners!

Global Winner

Sub-Saharan Africa

Portia Dzilah
Pakro-Adjinase St. James Anglican Basic School, Ghana

East Asia

Yun Xie
Yew Wah International Education School of Shanghai Lingang, China

Europe

Oleksandr Zhuk
Zaporizhzhia Special Comprehensive Boarding Xchool, Dzherelo, Ukraine

Latin America

Eduardo Pérez
Instituto Técnico Guaimaral, Colombia

North America

Isabel de Feria
Marjory Stoneman Douglas Elementary, USA

Middle East and North Africa

Farrukh Saleem
Pakistan International School Jeddah English Section, Saudi Arabia

Pakistan

Adnan Ahmed Usmani
Bahria Town School and College, Pakistan

South Asia

Sakina Bharmal
The Galaxy School - Wadi, India

Southeast Asia & Pacific

Polly Neville
Denla British School Bangkok, Thailand

For more information about our dedicated teachers and their stories, go to **dedicatedteacher.cambridge.org**

CAMBRIDGE

Contents

Digital questions for all chapters can be found online at Cambridge GO. For more information on how to access and use your digital resource, please see inside front cover.

> How to use this series

This suite of resources supports students and teachers following the Cambridge IGCSE™, IGCSE (9–1), and O Level Economics syllabuses (0455/0987/2281) for examination from 2027. All of the components in the series are designed to work together and help students develop the necessary knowledge and skills for this subject.

With clear language and style, they are designed for international students.

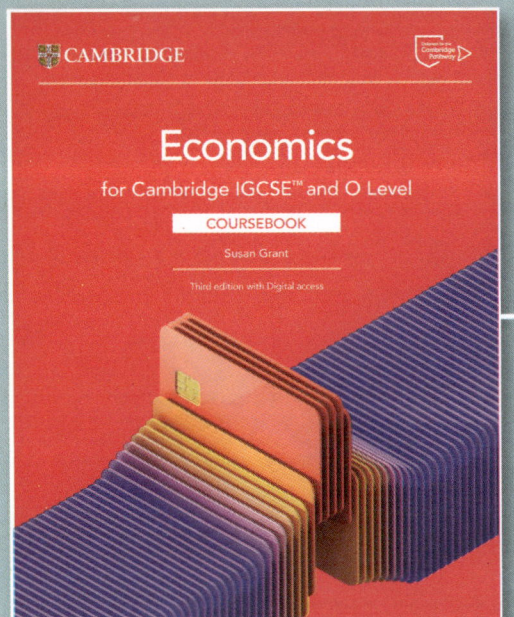

The coursebook is designed for students to use in class with guidance from the teacher. It offers complete coverage of the Cambridge IGCSE™, IGCSE (9–1) and O Level Economics syllabuses (0455/0987/2281). The coursebook contains in-depth explanations of economics concepts, a variety of independent and group activities, engaging new features and images to help students make real-world connections.

A digital version of the coursebook is included with the print version, and available separately. It includes access to video content to further support students' learning, as well as simple tools for students to use in class or for self-study.

The workbook provides further practice of all the skills presented in the coursebook and is ideal for use in class or as homework. It provides engaging activities, worked examples and opportunities for students to evaluate sample answers so they can put into practice what they have learnt.

A digital version of the workbook is included with the print version. It includes simple tools for students to use in class or for self-study, as well as downloadable templates to complete some of the activities.

The digital teacher's resource provides everything teachers need to deliver the course. It is packed full of useful teaching notes and lesson ideas, with suggestions for differentiation to support and challenge students, ideas for formative assessment, overcoming common misconceptions and language support.

The digital teacher's resource contains downloadable resource sheets and worksheets.

All answers are available on Cambridge GO.

The exam preparation and practice resource provides dedicated support for students in preparing for their final assessments. Hundreds of questions in the book and accompanying digital resources will help students to check that they understand, and can recall, syllabus concepts. To help students to show what they know in an exam context, a specially developed checklist of exam skills with corresponding questions, and practice questions, is also included. Self-assessment and reflection features support students to identify any areas that need further practice. This resource should be used alongside the coursebook, throughout the course of study, so students can most effectively increase their confidence and readiness for their exams.

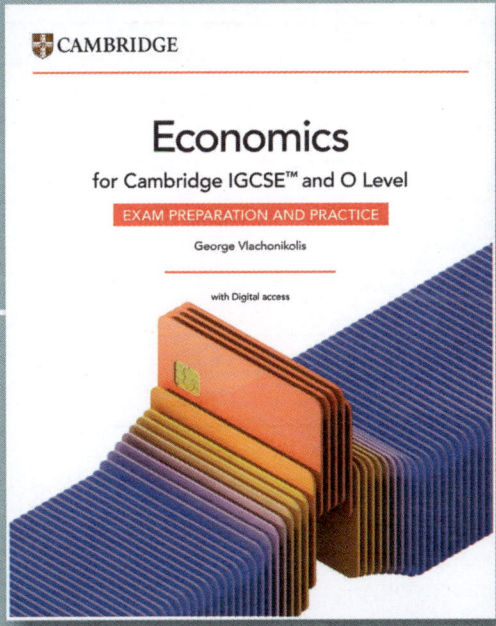

> How to use this book

This book will help you to check that you **know** the content of the syllabus and practise how to **show** this understanding in an exam. It will also help you be cognitively prepared and in the **flow**, ready for your exam. Research has shown that it is important that you do all three of these things, so we have designed the Know, Show, Flow approach to help you prepare effectively for exams.

Know You will need to consolidate and then recall a lot of syllabus content.

Show You should demonstrate your knowledge in the context of a Cambridge exam.

Flow You should be cognitively engaged and ready to learn. This means reducing test anxiety.

Please note that you should complete all the tasks in this book in your notebook.

Exam skills checklist

Category	Exam skill
Understanding the question	Recognise different question types
	Understand command words
	Mark scheme awareness
Providing an appropriate response	Understand connections between concepts
	Keep to time
	Know what a good answer looks like
Developing supportive behaviours	Reflect on progress
	Manage test anxiety

This **Exam skills checklist** helps you to develop the awareness, behaviours and habits that will support you when revising and preparing for your exams. For more exam skills advice, including understanding command words and managing your time effectively, please go to the **Exam skills chapter**.

Know

The full syllabus content of your Cambridge IGCSE and O Level Economics course is covered in your Cambridge coursebook. This book will provide you with different types of questions to support you as you prepare for your exams. You will answer **Knowledge recall questions** that are designed to make sure you understand a topic, and **Recall and connect questions** to help you recall past learning and connect different concepts.

KNOWLEDGE FOCUS

Knowledge focus boxes summarise the topics that you will answer questions on in each chapter of this book. You can refer back to your Cambridge coursebook to remind yourself of the full detail of the syllabus content.

Knowledge recall question

Testing yourself is a good way to check that your understanding is secure. These questions will help you to recall the core knowledge you have acquired during your course, and highlight any areas where you may need more practice. They are indicated with a blue bar with a gap, at the side of the page. We recommend that you answer the Knowledge recall questions just after you have covered the relevant topic in class, and then return to them at a later point to check you have properly understood the content.

≪ RECALL AND CONNECT 1 ≪

To consolidate your learning, you need to test your memory frequently. These questions will test that you remember what you learned in previous chapters, in addition to what you are practising in the current chapter.

UNDERSTAND THIS TERM

These list the important vocabulary that you should understand for each chapter. Definitions are provided in the glossary of your Cambridge coursebook.

Show

Exam questions test specific knowledge, skills and understanding. You need to be prepared so that you have the best opportunity to show what you know in the time you have during the exam. In addition to practising recall of the syllabus content, it is important to build your exam skills throughout the year.

EXAM SKILLS FOCUS

This feature outlines the exam skills you will practise in each chapter, alongside the Knowledge focus. They are drawn from the core set of eight exam skills, listed in the exam skills checklist. You will practise specific exam skills, such as understanding command words, within each chapter. More general exam skills, such as managing test anxiety, are covered in the Exam skills chapter.

Exam skills question

These questions will help you to develop your exam skills and demonstrate your understanding. To help you become familiar with exam-style questioning, these questions follow the style and use the language of real exam questions, and have allocated marks. They are indicated with a solid red bar at the side of the page.

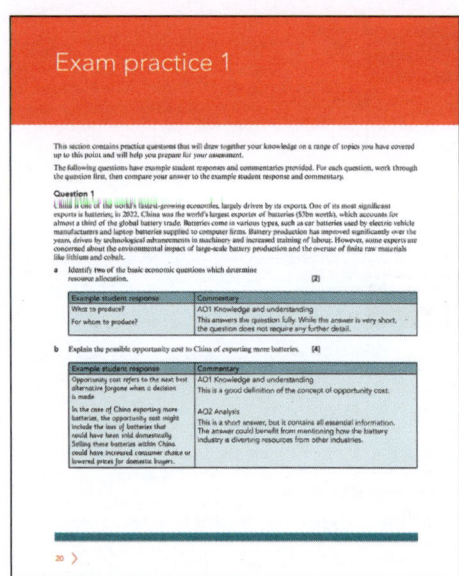

Looking at sample answers to past paper questions helps you to understand what to aim for.

The **Exam practice** sections in this resource contain example student responses and examiner-style commentary showing how the answer could be improved (both written by the authors).

Some of the older past paper questions in this resource reflect the type of questions that appeared in previous exam papers and may therefore differ slightly from those you will experience in your upcoming examinations

Flow

Preparing for exams can be stressful. One of the approaches recommended by educational psychologists to help with this stress is to improve behaviours around exam preparation. This involves testing yourself in manageable chunks, accompanied by self-evaluation. You should avoid cramming, and build in more preparation time. This book is structured to help you do this.

Increasing your ability to recognise the signs of exam-related stress and working through some techniques for how to cope with it will help to make your exam preparation manageable.

REFLECTION

This feature asks you to think about the approach that you take to your exam preparation, and how you might improve this in the future. Reflecting on how you plan, monitor and evaluate your revision and preparation will help you to do your best in your exams.

SELF-ASSESSMENT CHECKLIST

These checklists return to the Learning intentions from your coursebook, as well as the Exam skills focus boxes from each chapter. Checking in on how confident you feel in each of these areas will help you to focus your exam preparation. The 'Show it' prompts will allow you to test your rating. You should revisit any areas that you rate 'Needs more work' or 'Almost there'.

Now I can	Show it	Needs more work	Almost there	Confident to move on

Increasing your ability to recognise the signs of exam-related stress and working through some techniques for how to cope with it will help to make your exam preparation manageable. The **Exam skills chapter** will support you with this.

Syllabus assessment objectives for Cambridge IGCSE and O Level Economics

You should be familiar with the Assessment Objectives from the syllabus, as you will need to show evidence of these requirements in your responses. The assessment objectives for this syllabus are:

Assessment objective	Cambridge IGCSE weighting
AO1: Knowledge and understanding	43%
AO2: Analysis	47%
AO3: Evaluation	10%

Digital questions

Extra digital questions, in the form of **Multiple choice** and **Flip cards**, for all chapters can be found online at Cambridge GO. For more information on how to access and use your digital resource, please see inside the front cover.

- Provides lots of additional practice to reinforce knowledge and understanding

- Gives instant feedback to support autonomy over your own learning

- Encourages self-assessment to understand your strengths and weaknesses

- User-friendly design to help with easy navigation

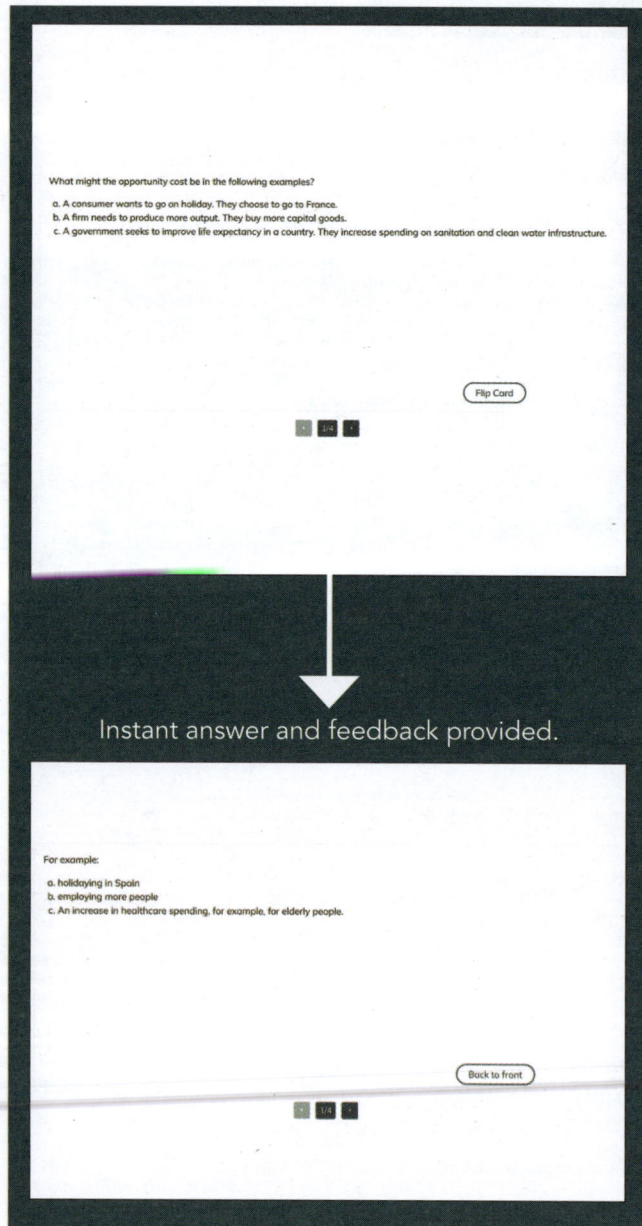

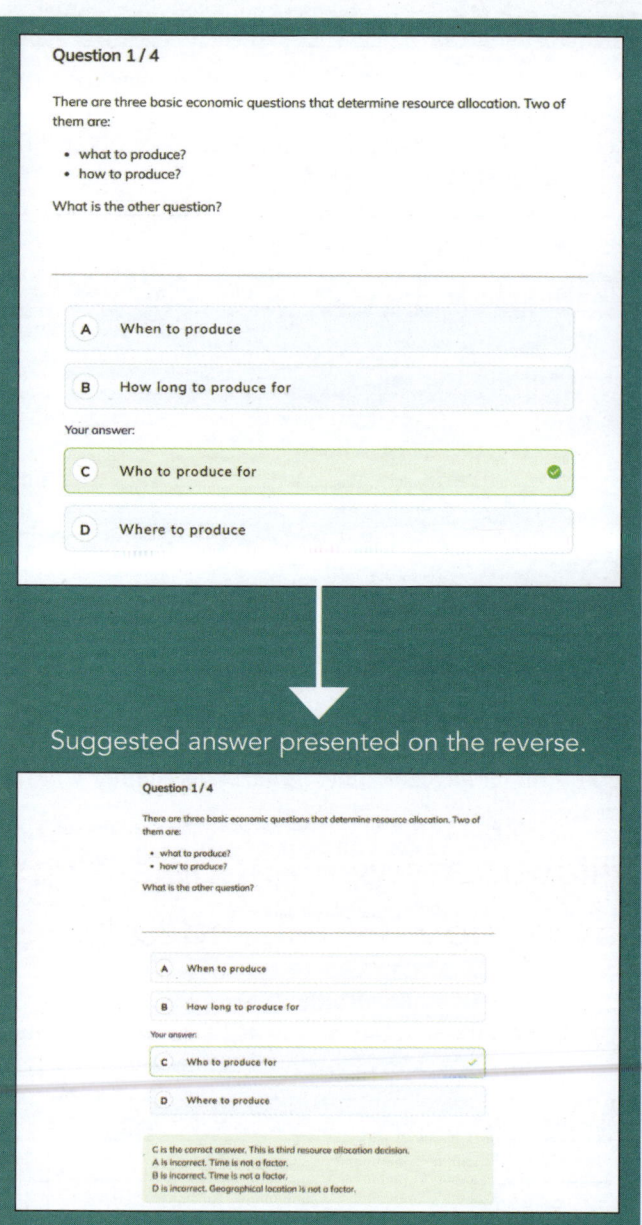

Exam skills

by Lucy Parsons

What's the point of this book?

Most students make one really basic mistake when they're preparing for exams. What is it? It's focusing far too much on learning 'stuff' – that's facts, figures, ideas, information – and not nearly enough time practising exam skills.

The students who work really, really hard but are disappointed with their results are nearly always students who focus on memorising stuff. They think to themselves, 'I'll do practice papers once I've revised everything.' The trouble is, they start doing practice papers too late to really develop and improve how they communicate what they know.

What could they do differently?

When your final exam script is assessed, it should contain specific language, information and thinking skills in your answers. If you read a question in an exam and you have no idea what you need to do to give a good answer, the likelihood is that your answer won't be as brilliant as it could be. That means your grade won't reflect the hard work you've put into revising for the exam.

There are different types of questions used in exams to assess different skills. You need to know how to recognise these question types and understand what you need to show in your answers.

So, how do you understand what to do in each question type?

That's what this book is all about. But first a little background.

Meet Benjamin Bloom

The psychologist Benjamin Bloom developed a way of classifying and valuing different skills we use when we learn, such as analysis and recalling information. We call these thinking skills. It's known as Bloom's Taxonomy and it's what most exam questions are based around.

If you understand Bloom's Taxonomy, you can understand what any type of question requires you to do. So, what does it look like?

Bloom's Taxonomy of thinking skills

Increasing difficulty

Evaluation → **Passing judgement** on something

Synthesis → **Putting together knowledge**, understanding, application and analysis **to create something new**

Analysis → **Taking apart** information or data in order to **discover relationships**, motives, causes, patterns and connections

Application → **Using knowledge** and understanding in **new and different circumstances**

Understanding → **Distinguishing between two similar ideas** or things by using knowledge to **recognise the difference**

Knowledge → **Recalling, memorising and knowing**

The key things to take away from this diagram are:

- Knowledge and understanding are known as lower-level thinking skills. They are less difficult than the other thinking skills. Exam questions that just test you on what you know are usually worth the lowest number of marks.

- All the other thinking skills are worth higher numbers of marks in exam questions. These questions need you to have some foundational knowledge and understanding but are far more about how you think than what you know. They involve:

  - Taking what you know and using it in unfamiliar situations (application).

  - Going deeper into information to discover relationships, motives, causes, patterns and connections (analysis).

  - Using what you know and think to create something new – whether that's an essay, long-answer exam question a solution to a maths problem, or a piece of art (synthesis).

  - Assessing the value of something, e.g. the reliability of the results of a scientific experiment (evaluation).

In this introductory chapter, you'll be shown how to develop the skills that enable you to communicate what you know and how you think. This will help you achieve to the best of your abilities. In the rest of the book, you'll have a chance to practise these exam skills by understanding how questions work and understanding what you need to show in your answers.

Every time you pick up this book and do a few questions, you're getting closer to achieving your dream results. So, let's get started!

Exam preparation and revision skills

What is revision?

If you think about it, the word 'revision' has two parts to it:

- re – which means 'again'

- vision – which is about seeing.

So, revision is literally about 'seeing again'. This means you're looking at something that you've already learned.

Typically, a teacher will teach you something in class. You may then do some questions on it, write about it in some way, or even do a presentation. You might then have an end-of-topic test sometime later. To prepare for this test, you need to 'look again' or revise what you were originally taught.

Step 1: Making knowledge stick

Every time you come back to something you've learned or revised you're improving your understanding and memory of that particular piece of knowledge. This is called **spaced retrieval**. This is how human memory works. If you don't use a piece of knowledge by recalling it, you lose it.

Everything we learn has to be physically stored in our brains by creating neural connections – joining brain cells together. The more often we 'retrieve' or recall a particular piece of knowledge, the stronger the neural connection gets. It's like lifting weights – the more often you lift, the stronger you get.

However, if you don't use a piece of knowledge for a long time, your brain wants to recycle the brain cells and use them for another purpose. The neural connections get weaker until they finally break, and the memory has gone. This is why it's really important to return often to things that you've learned in the past.

Great ways of doing this in your revision include:

- Testing yourself using flip cards – use the ones available in the digital resources for this book.

- Testing yourself (or getting someone else to test you) using questions you've created about the topic.

- Checking your recall of previous topics by answering the Recall and connect questions in this book.

- Blurting – writing everything you can remember about a topic on a piece of paper in one colour. Then, checking what you missed out and filling it in with another colour. You can do this over and over again until you feel confident that you remember everything.

- Answering practice questions – use the ones in this book.

- Getting a good night's sleep to help consolidate your learning.

The importance of sleep and creating long-term memory

When you go to sleep at night, your brain goes through an important process of taking information from your short-term memory and storing it in your long-term memory.

This means that getting a good night's sleep is a very important part of revision. If you don't get enough good quality sleep, you'll actually be making your revision much, much harder.

Step 2: Developing your exam skills

We've already talked about the importance of exam skills, and how many students neglect them because they're worried about covering all the knowledge.

What actually works best is developing your exam skills at the same time as learning the knowledge.

What does this look like in your studies?

- Learning something at school and your teacher setting you questions from this book or from past papers. This tests your recall as well as developing your exam skills.

- Choosing a topic to revise, learning the content and then choosing some questions from this book to test yourself at the same time as developing your exam skills.

The reason why practising your exam skills is so important is that it helps you to get good at communicating what you know and what you think. The more often you do that, the more fluent you'll become in showing what you know in your answers.

Step 3: Getting feedback

The final step is to get feedback on your work.

If you're testing yourself, the feedback is what you got wrong or what you forgot. This means you then need to go back to those things to remind yourself or improve your understanding. Then, you can test yourself again and get more feedback. You can also congratulate yourself for the things you got right – it's important to celebrate any success, big or small.

If you're doing past paper questions or the practice questions in this book, you will need to mark your work. Marking your work is one of the most important things you can do to improve. It's possible to make significant improvements in your marks in a very short space of time when you start marking your work.

Why is marking your own work so powerful? It's because it teaches you to identify the strengths and weaknesses of your own work. When you look at the mark scheme and see how it's structured, you will understand what is needed in your answers to get the results you want.

This doesn't just apply to the knowledge you demonstrate in your answers. It also applies to the language you use and whether it's appropriately subject-specific, the structure of your answer, how you present it on the page and many other factors. Understanding, practising and improving on these things are transformative for your results.

The most important thing about revision

The most important way to make your revision successful is to make it active.

Sometimes, students say they're revising when they sit staring at their textbook or notes for hours at a time. However, this is a really ineffective way to revise because it's passive. In order to make knowledge and skills stick, you need to be doing something like the suggestions in the following diagram. That's why testing yourself and pushing yourself to answer questions that test higher-level thinking skills are so effective. At times, you might actually be able to feel the physical changes happening in your brain as you develop this new knowledge and these new skills. That doesn't come about without effort.

The important thing to remember is that while active revision feels much more like hard work than passive revision, you don't actually need to do nearly as much of it. That's because you remember knowledge and skills when you use active revision. When you use passive revision, it is much, much harder for the knowledge and skills to stick in your memory.

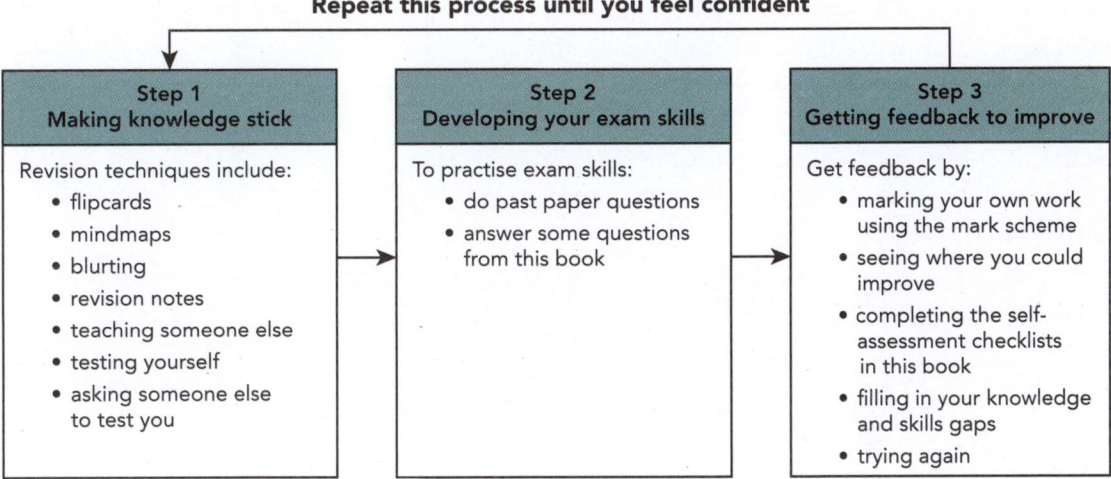

Repeat this process until you feel confident

Step 1 Making knowledge stick	Step 2 Developing your exam skills	Step 3 Getting feedback to improve
Revision techniques include: • flipcards • mindmaps • blurting • revision notes • teaching someone else • testing yourself • asking someone else to test you	To practise exam skills: • do past paper questions • answer some questions from this book	Get feedback by: • marking your own work using the mark scheme • seeing where you could improve • completing the self-assessment checklists in this book • filling in your knowledge and skills gaps • trying again

How to improve your exam skills

This book helps you to improve in eight different areas of exam skills, which are divided across three categories. These skills are highlighted in this book in the Exam skills focus at the start of each chapter and developed throughout the book using targeted questions, advice and reflections.

1 **Understand the questions: what are you being asked to do?**

- Know your question types.
- Understand command words.
- Work with mark scheme awareness.

2 **How to answer questions brilliantly**

- Understand connections between concepts.
- Keep to time.
- Know what a good answer looks like.

3 **Give yourself the best chance of success**

- Reflection on progress.
- How to manage test anxiety.

Understand the questions: what are you being asked to do?

Know your question types

In any exam, there will be a range of different question types. These different question types will test different types of thinking skills from Bloom's Taxonomy.

It is very important that you learn to recognise different question types. If you do lots of past papers, over time you will begin to recognise the structure of the paper for each of your subjects. You will know which types of questions may come first and which ones are more likely to come at the end of the paper. You can also complete past paper questions in the Exam practice sections in this book for additional practice.

You will also recognise the differences between questions worth a lower number of marks and questions worth more marks. The key differences are:

- how much you will need to write in your answer
- how sophisticated your answer needs to be in terms of the detail you give and the depth of thinking you show.

Types of questions

1   Multiple-choice questions

Multiple-choice questions are generally worth smaller numbers of marks. You will be given several possible answers to the question, and you will have to work out which one is correct using your knowledge and skills.

There is a chance of you getting the right answer with multiple-choice questions even if you don't know the answer. This is why you must **always give an answer for multiple-choice questions** as it means there is a chance you will earn the mark.

Multiple-choice questions are often harder than they appear. The possible answers can be very similar to each other. This means you must be confident in how you work out answers or have a high level of understanding to tell the difference between the possible answers.

Being confident in your subject knowledge and doing lots of practice multiple-choice questions will set you up for success. Use the resources in this book and the accompanying online resources to build your confidence.

This example of a multiple-choice question is worth one mark. You can see that all the answers have one part in common with at least one other answer. For example, palisade cells is included in three of the possible answers. That's why you have to really know the detail of your content knowledge to do well with multiple-choice questions.

Which two types of cells are found in plant leaves?

A   Palisade mesophyll and stomata

B   Palisade mesophyll and root hair

C   Stomata and chloroplast

D   Chloroplast and palisade mesophyll

2 Questions requiring longer-form answers

Questions requiring longer-form answers need you to write out your answer yourself.

With these questions, take careful note of how many marks are available and how much space you've been given for your answer. These two things will give you a good idea about how much you should say and how much time you should spend on the question.

A rough rule to follow is to write one sentence, or make one point, for each mark that is available. You will get better and better at these longer form questions the more you practise them.

In this example of a history question, you can see it is worth four marks. It is not asking for an explanation, just for you to list Lloyd George's aims. Therefore, you need to make four correct points in order to get full marks.

> What were Lloyd George's aims during negotiations leading to the
> Treaty of Versailles? [4]

3 Essay questions

Essay questions are the longest questions you will be asked to answer in an exam. They examine the higher-order thinking skills from Bloom's Taxonomy such as analysis, synthesis and evaluation.

To do well in essay questions, you need to talk about what you know, giving your opinion, comparing one concept or example to another, and evaluating your own ideas or the ones you're discussing in your answer.

You also need to have a strong structure and logical argument that guides the reader through your thought process. This usually means having an introduction, some main body paragraphs that discuss one point at a time, and a conclusion.

Essay questions are usually level-marked. This means that you don't get one mark per point you make. Instead, you're given marks for the quality of the ideas you're sharing as well as how well you present those ideas through the subject-specific language you use and the structure of your essay.

Practising essays and becoming familiar with the mark scheme is the only way to get really good at them.

Understand command words

What are command words?

Command words are the most important words in every exam question. This is because command words tell you what you need to do in your answer. Do you remember Bloom's Taxonomy? Command words tell you which thinking skill you need to demonstrate in the answer to each question.

Two very common command words are **describe** and **explain**.

When you see the command word 'describe' in a question, you're being asked to show lower-order thinking skills like knowledge and understanding. The question will either be worth fewer marks, or you will need to make more points if it is worth more marks.

The command word 'explain' is asking you to show higher-order thinking skills. When you see the command word 'explain', you need to be able to say how or why something happens.

You need to understand all of the relevant command words for the subjects you are taking. Ask your teacher where to find them if you are not sure. It's best not to try to memorise the list of command words, but to become familiar with what command words are asking for by doing lots of practice questions and marking your own work.

How to work with command words

When you first see an exam question, read it through once. Then, read it through again and identify the command word(s). Underline the command word(s) to make it clear to yourself which they are every time you refer back to the question.

You may also want to identify the **content** words in the question and underline them with a different colour. Content words tell you which area of knowledge you need to draw on to answer the question.

In this example, command words are shown in red and underlined with content words in **blue and bold**:

1   a   Explain **four** reasons why **governments** might **support business start-ups**.   [8]

    Adapted from Cambridge IGCSE Business Studies (0450)
    Q1a Paper 21 June 2022

Marking your own work using the mark scheme will help you get even better at understanding command words and knowing how to give good answers for each.

Work with mark scheme awareness

The most transformative thing that any student can do to improve their marks is to work with mark schemes. This means using mark schemes to mark your own work at every opportunity.

Many students are very nervous about marking their own work as they do not feel experienced or qualified enough. However, being brave enough to try to mark your own work and taking the time to get good at it will improve your marks hugely.

Why marking your own work makes such a big difference

Marking your own work can help you to improve your answers in the following ways:

1   Answering the question

Having a deep and detailed understanding of what is required by the question enables you to answer the question more clearly and more accurately.

It can also help you to give the required information using fewer words and in less time, as you can avoid including unrelated points or topics in your answer.

2   Using subject-specific vocabulary

Every subject has subject-specific vocabulary. This includes technical terms for objects or concepts in a subject, such as mitosis and meiosis in biology. It also includes how you talk about the subject, using appropriate vocabulary that may differ from everyday language. For example, in any science subject you might be asked to describe the trend on a graph.

Your answer could say it 'goes up fast' or your answer could say it 'increases rapidly'. You would not get marks for saying 'it goes up fast', but you would for saying it 'increases rapidly'. This is the difference between everyday language and formal, scientific language.

When you answer lots of practice questions, you become fluent in the language specific to your subject.

3 Knowing how much to write

It's very common for students to either write too much or too little to answer questions. Becoming familiar with the mark schemes for many different questions will help you to gain a better understanding of how much you need to write in order to get a good mark.

4 Structuring your answer

There are often clues in questions about how to structure your answer. However, mark schemes give you an even stronger idea of the structure you should use in your answers.

For example, if a question says:

'Describe and explain **two** reasons why…'

You can give a clear answer by:

- Describing reason 1
- Explaining reason 1
- Describing reason 2
- Explaining reason 2

Having a very clear structure will also make it easier to identify where you have earned marks. This means that you're more likely to be awarded the number of marks you deserve.

5 Keeping to time

Answering the question, using subject-specific vocabulary, knowing how much to write and giving a clear structure to your answer will all help you to keep to time in an exam. You will not waste time by writing too much for any answer. Therefore, you will have sufficient time to give a good answer to every question.

How to answer exam questions brilliantly

Understand connections between concepts

One of the higher-level thinking skills in Bloom's Taxonomy is **synthesis**. Synthesis means making connections between different areas of knowledge. You may have heard about synoptic links. Making synoptic links is the same as showing the thinking skill of synthesis.

Exam questions that ask you to show your synthesis skills are usually worth the highest number of marks on an exam paper. To write good answers to these questions, you need to spend time thinking about the links between the topics you've studied before you arrive in your exam. A great way of doing this is using mind maps.

How to create a mind map

To create a mind map:

1 Use a large piece of paper and several different coloured pens.

2   Write the name of your subject in the middle. Then, write the key topic areas evenly spaced around the edge, each with a different colour.

3   Then, around each topic area, start to write the detail of what you can remember. If you find something that is connected with something you studied in another topic, you can draw a line linking the two things together.

This is a good way of practising your retrieval of information as well as linking topics together.

Answering synoptic exam questions

You will recognise questions that require you to make links between concepts because they have a higher number of marks. You will have practised them using this book and the accompanying resources.

To answer a synoptic exam question:

1   **Identify the command and content words**. You are more likely to find command words like **discuss** and **explain** in these questions. They might also have phrases like 'the connection between'.

2   **Make a plan for your answer**. It is worth taking a short amount of time to think about what you're going to write in your answer. Think carefully about what information you're going to put in, the links between the different pieces of information and how you're going to structure your answer to make your ideas clear.

3   **Use linking words and phrases in your answer**. For example, 'therefore', 'because', 'due to', 'since' or 'this means that'.

Here is an example of an English Literature exam question that requires you to make synoptic links in your answer.

1   Discuss **Carol Ann Duffy's exploration of childhood** in her poetry.

    Refer to **two** poems in your answer.   [25]

Content words are shown in blue; command words are shown in red.

This question is asking you to explore the theme of childhood in Duffy's poetry. You need to choose two of her poems to refer to in your answer. This means you need a good knowledge of her poetry, and to be familiar with her exploration of childhood, so that you can easily select two poems that will give you plenty to say in your answer.

Keep to time

Managing your time in exams is really important. Some students do not achieve to the best of their abilities because they run out of time to answer all the questions. However, if you manage your time well, you will be able to attempt every question on the exam paper.

Why is it important to attempt all the questions on an exam paper?

If you attempt every question on a paper, you have the best chance of achieving the highest mark you are capable of.

Students who manage their time poorly in exams will often spend far too long on some questions and not even attempt others. Most students are unlikely to get full marks on many questions, but you will get zero marks for the questions you don't answer. You can maximise your marks by giving an answer to every question.

Minutes per mark

The most important way to keep to time is knowing how many minutes you can spend on each mark.

For example, if your exam paper has 90 marks available and you have 90 minutes, you know there is 1 mark per minute.

Therefore, if you have a 5 mark question, you should spend five minutes on it.

Sometimes, you can give a good answer in less time than you have budgeted using the minutes per mark technique. If this happens, you will have more time to spend on questions that use higher-order thinking skills, or more time on checking your work.

How to get faster at answering exam questions

The best way to get faster at answering exam questions is to do lots of practice. You should practise each question type that will be in your exam, marking your own work, so that you know precisely how that question works and what is required by the question. Use the questions in this book to get better and better at answering each question type.

Use the 'Slow, Slow, Quick' technique to get faster.

Take your time answering questions when you first start practising them. You may answer them with the support of the textbook, your notes or the mark scheme. These things will support you with your content knowledge, the language you use in your answer and the structure of your answer.

Every time you practise this question type, you will get more confident and faster. You will become experienced with this question type, so that it is easy for you to recall the subject knowledge and write it down using the correct language and a good structure.

Calculating marks per minute

Use this calculation to work out how long you have for each mark:

Total time in the exam / Number of marks available = Minutes per mark

Calculate how long you have for a question worth more than one mark like this:

Minutes per mark × Marks available for this question
= Number of minutes for this question

What about time to check your work?

It is a very good idea to check your work at the end of an exam. You need to work out if this is feasible with the minutes per mark available to you. If you're always rushing to finish the questions, you shouldn't budget checking time. However, if you usually have time to spare, then you can budget checking time.

To include checking time in your minutes per mark calculation:

(Total time in the exam − Checking time) / Number of marks available
= Minutes per mark

Know what a good answer looks like

It is much easier to give a good answer if you know what a good answer looks like.

Use these methods to know what a good answer looks like:

1 **Sample answers** – you can find sample answers in these places:

    • from your teacher

    • written by your friends or other members of your class

    • in this book.

2 **Look at mark schemes** – mark schemes are full of information about what you should include in your answers. Get familiar with mark schemes to gain a better understanding of the type of things a good answer would contain.

3 **Feedback from your teacher** – if you are finding it difficult to improve your exam skills for a particular type of question, ask your teacher for detailed feedback. You should also look at their comments on your work in detail.

Give yourself the best chance of success

Reflection on progress

As you prepare for your exam, it's important to reflect on your progress. Taking time to think about what you're doing well and what could be improved brings more focus to your revision. Reflecting on progress also helps you to continuously improve your knowledge and exam skills.

How do you reflect on progress?

Use the Reflection feature in this book to help you reflect on your progress during your exam preparation. Then, at the end of each revision session, take a few minutes to think about the following:

	What went well? What would you do the same next time?	What didn't go well? What would you do differently next time?
Your subject knowledge		
How you revised your subject knowledge – did you use active retrieval techniques?		
Your use of subject-specific and academic language		
Understanding the question by identifying command words and content words		
Giving a clear structure to your answer		
Keeping to time		
Marking your own work		

Remember to check for silly mistakes – things like missing the units out after you carefully calculated your answer.

Use the mark scheme to mark your own work. Every time you mark your own work, you will be recognising the good and bad aspects of your work, so that you can progressively give better answers over time.

When do you need to come back to this topic or skill?

Earlier in this section of the book, we talked about revision skills and the importance of spaced retrieval. When you reflect on your progress, you need to think about how soon you need to return to the topic or skill you've just been focusing on.

For example, if you were really disappointed with your subject knowledge, it would be a good idea to do some more active retrieval and practice questions on this topic tomorrow. However, if you did really well you can feel confident you know this topic and come back to it again in three weeks' or a month's time.

The same goes for exam skills. If you were disappointed with how you answered the question, you should look at some sample answers and try this type of question again soon. However, if you did well, you can move on to other types of exam questions.

Improving your memory of subject knowledge

Sometimes students slip back into using passive revision techniques, such as only reading the coursebook or their notes, rather than also using active revision techniques, like testing themselves using flip cards or blurting.

You can avoid this mistake by observing how well your learning is working as you revise. You should be thinking to yourself, 'Am I remembering this? Am I understanding this? Is this revision working?'

If the answer to any of those questions is 'no', then you need to change what you're doing to revise this particular topic. For example, if you don't understand, you could look up your topic in a different textbook in the school library to see if a different explanation helps. Or you could see if you can find a video online that brings the idea to life.

You are in control

When you're studying for exams it's easy to think that your teachers are in charge. However, you have to remember that you are studying for your exams and the results you get will be yours and no one else's.

That means you have to take responsibility for all your exam preparation. You have the power to change how you're preparing if what you're doing isn't working. You also have control over what you revise and when: you can make sure you focus on your weaker topics and skills to improve your achievement in the subject.

This isn't always easy to do. Sometimes you have to find an inner ability that you have not used before. But, if you are determined enough to do well, you can find what it takes to focus, improve and keep going.

What is test anxiety?

Do you get worried or anxious about exams? Does your worry or anxiety impact how well you do in tests and exams?

Test anxiety is part of your natural stress response.

The stress response evolved in animals and humans many thousands of years ago to help keep them alive. Let's look at an example.

The stress response in the wild

Imagine an impala grazing in the grasslands of east Africa. It's happily and calmly eating grass in its herd in what we would call the parasympathetic state of rest and repair.

Then the impala sees a lion. The impala suddenly panics because its life is in danger. This state of panic is also known as the stressed or sympathetic state. The sympathetic state presents itself in three forms: flight, fight and freeze.

The impala starts to run away from the lion. Running away is known as the flight stress response.

The impala might not be fast enough to run away from the lion. The lion catches it but has a loose grip. The impala struggles to try to get away. This struggle is the fight stress response.

However, the lion gets an even stronger grip on the impala. Now the only chance of the impala surviving is playing dead. The impala goes limp, its heart rate and breathing slows. This is called the freeze stress response. The lion believes that it has killed the impala so it drops the impala to the ground. Now the impala can switch back into the flight response and run away.

The impala is now safe – the different stages of the stress response have saved its life.

What has the impala got to do with your exams?

When you feel test anxiety, you have the same physiological stress responses as an impala being hunted by a lion. Unfortunately, the human nervous system cannot tell the difference between a life-threatening situation, such as being chased by a lion, and the stress of taking an exam.

If you understand how the stress response works in the human nervous system, you will be able to learn techniques to reduce test anxiety.

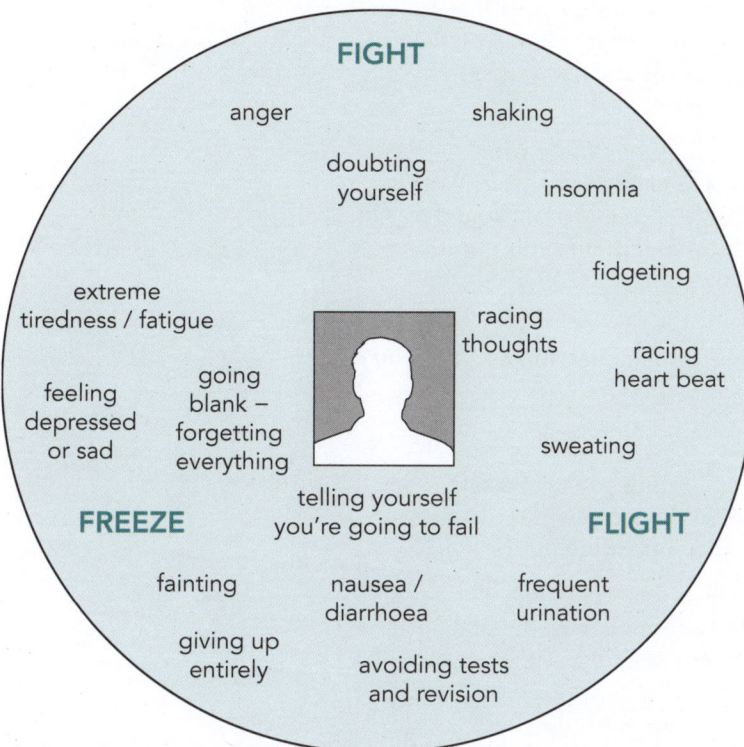

The role of the vagus nerve in test anxiety

The vagus nerve is the part of your nervous system that determines your stress response. Vagus means 'wandering' in Latin, so the vagus nerve is also known as the 'wandering nerve'. The vagus nerve wanders from your brain, down each side of your body, to nearly all your organs, including your lungs, heart, kidneys, liver, digestive system and bladder.

If you are in a stressful situation, like an exam, your vagus nerve sends a message to all these different organs to activate their stress response. Here are some common examples:

- **Heart** beats faster.
- **Kidneys** produce more adrenaline so that you can run, making you fidgety and distracted.
- **Digestive system** and **bladder** want to eliminate all waste products so that energy can be used for fight or flight.

If you want to feel calmer about your revision and exams, you need to do two things to help you move into the parasympathetic, or rest and repair, state:

1 Work with your vagus nerve to send messages of safety through your body.

2 Change your perception of the test so that you see it as safe and not dangerous.

How to cope with test anxiety

1 Be well prepared

Good preparation is the most important part of managing test anxiety. The better your preparation, the more confident you will be. If you are confident, you will not perceive the test or exam as dangerous, so the sympathetic nervous system responses of fight, flight and freeze are less likely to happen.

This book is all about helping you to be well prepared and building your confidence in your knowledge and ability to answer exam questions well. Working through the knowledge recall questions will help you to become more confident in your knowledge of the subject. The practice questions and exam skills questions will help you to become more confident in communicating your knowledge in an exam.

To be well prepared, look at the advice in the rest of this chapter and use it as you work through the questions in this book.

2 Work with your vagus nerve

The easiest way to work with your vagus nerve to tell it that you're in a safe situation is through your breathing. This means breathing deeply into the bottom of your lungs, so that your stomach expands, and then breathing out for longer than you breathed in. You can do this with counting.

Breathe in deeply, expanding your abdomen, for the count of four; breathe out drawing your navel back towards your spine for the count of five, six or seven. Repeat this at least three times. However, you can do it for as long as it takes for you to feel calm.

The important thing is that you breathe out for longer than you breathe in. This is because when you breathe in, your heart rate increases slightly, and when you breathe out, your heart rate decreases slightly. If you're spending more time breathing out overall, you will be decreasing your heart rate over time.

3 Feel it

Anxiety is an uncomfortable, difficult thing to feel. That means that many people try to run away from anxious feelings. However, this means the stress just gets stored in your body for you to feel later.

When you feel anxious, follow these four steps:

1 Pause.

2 Place one hand on your heart and one hand on your stomach.

3 Notice what you're feeling.

4 Stay with your feelings.

What you will find is that if you are willing to experience what you feel for a minute or two, the feeling of anxiety will usually pass very quickly.

4 Write or talk it out

If your thoughts are moving very quickly, it is often better to get them out of your mind and on to paper.

You could take a few minutes to write down everything that comes through your mind, then rip up your paper and throw it away. If you don't like writing, you can speak aloud alone or to someone you trust.

Other ways to break the stress cycle

Exercise and movement	Being friendly	Laughter
• Run or walk. • Dance. • Lift weights. • Yoga. Anything that involves moving your body is helpful.	• Chat to someone in your study break. • Talk to the cashier when you buy your lunch.	• Watch or listen to a funny show on TV or online. • Talk with someone who makes you laugh. • Look at photos of fun times.
Have a hug	**Releasing emotions**	**Creativity**
• Hug a friend or relative. • Cuddle a pet e.g. a cat. Hug for 20 seconds or until you feel calm and relaxed.	It is healthy to release negative or sad emotions. Crying is often a quick way to get rid of these difficult feelings so if you feel like you need to cry, allow it.	• Paint, draw or sketch. • Sew, knit or crochet. • Cook, build something.

If you have long-term symptoms of anxiety, it is important to tell someone you trust and ask for help.

Your perfect revision session

1 Intention

What do you want to achieve in this revision session?
- Choose an area of knowledge or an exam skill that you want to focus on.
- Choose some questions from this book that focus on this knowledge area or skill.
- Gather any other resources you will need e.g. pen, paper, flashcards, coursebook.

2 Focus

Set your focus for the session
- Remove distractions from your study area e.g. leave your phone in another room.
- Write down on a piece of paper or sticky note the knowledge area or skill you're intending to focus on.
- Close your eyes and take three deep breaths, with the exhale longer than the inhale.

3 Revision

Revise your knowledge and understanding
- To improve your knowledge and understanding of the topic, use your coursebook, notes or flashcards, including active learning techniques.
- To improve your exam skills, look at previous answers, teacher feedback, mark schemes, sample answers or examiners' reports.

4 Practice

Answer practice questions
- Use the questions in this book, or in the additional online resources, to practise your exam skills.
- If the exam is soon, do this in timed conditions without the support of the coursebook or your notes.
- If the exam is a long time away, you can use your notes and resources to help you.

5 Feedback

Mark your answers
- Use mark schemes to mark your work.
- Reflect on what you've done well and what you could do to improve next time.

6 Next steps

What have you learned about your progress from this revision session? What do you need to do next?
- What did you do well? Feel good about these things, and know it's safe to set these things aside for a while.
- What do you need to work on? How are you going to improve? Make a plan to get better at the things you didn't do well or didn't know.

7 Rest

Take a break
- Do something completely different to rest: get up, move or do something creative or practical.
- Remember that rest is an important part of studying, as it gives your brain a chance to integrate your learning.

> Unit 1

The basic economic problem

1 The nature of the basic economic problem

KNOWLEDGE FOCUS

In this chapter you will answer questions on:

- 1.1 Finite resources and infinite wants
- 1.2 Resource allocation decisions
- 1.3 Economic goods and free goods

EXAM SKILLS FOCUS

In this chapter you will:

- show that you understand the 'define' command word and answer a define question.

In this chapter, the focus is on the command word 'define', which means to give a precise meaning. When asked to define a term, ensure your explanation is concise – typically one or two sentences. While providing an example is not essential, it can sometimes enhance your definition. Writing clearly and concisely is a key skill in economics, where many important concepts need to be communicated. The questions in this chapter will help you practise this skill by encouraging you to define terms like 'scarcity' and the 'basic economic problem'. Practising defining terms will help build your confidence in offering clear and accurate definitions.

1.1 Finite resources and infinite wants

REFLECTION

Learning is often described as a 'change in long-term memory'. It is worth spending a few minutes thinking about how you might use this exam preparation and practice resource to improve your learning. You might like to think about:

- When will you use this resource? Will you use it at the same time every week?
- How will you use this resource in relation to your lessons? Will you use it alongside your lessons, or once you have completed a particular topic?
- Where will you use this resource? Will you use this resource at school during a study session, or at home?

1   Give some examples of people's wants.

2   Give some examples of resources.

3
> The **scarcity** of **resources** means that societies have to make difficult choices about allocation. The competing demands of individuals and firms puts the **basic economic problem** into sharp focus.

    a   Define the 'basic economic problem'. [2]

    b   Define 'resources'. [2]

    c   Define 'scarcity'. [2]

1.2 Resource allocation decisions

1   What is the difference between a want and a need?

2   What are the **three** fundamental economic questions?

3   Complete Table 1.1. You should decide which of the three fundamental economic questions the middle column relates to.

Table 1.1: Fundamental economic questions

	Question	Key resource allocation decision
a	Should a car manufacturer focus on developing electric vehicles?	
b	Should governments in Asia provide free education for all citizens?	
c	Should urban and rural populations have equal access to clean water?	
d	Should artificial intelligence be used to handle a greater number of healthcare appointments?	
e	Should more agricultural land be dedicated to growing biodiesel instead of palm oil?	
f	Should construction firms use the cheapest materials to build houses?	

1.3 Economic goods and free goods

1   List some goods that do **not** require resources to make them.

2

> In Switzerland, clean mountain air and stunning alpine views are **free goods** enjoyed by all, while its famous chocolates and premium watches are highly sought after **economic goods**. This mix highlights the country's unique offering.

    Define 'free good'.   [2]

3   Define 'economic good'.   [2]

REFLECTION

Being able to define terms quickly in simple and precise language requires a solid understanding of the concepts, which you should acquire in class and through consolidation of notes outside of class. But, to some extent, it also requires repetitive practice and some element of rote learning. In order to support this, you can break down complex ideas into smaller, easier-to-remember parts as well as using everyday examples. You could also keep a glossary to record your definitions prior to revision.

Think about the following:

- How can I incorporate breaking down complex ideas into my study routine to better understand and define terms?
- Where can I find reliable information or examples to support my understanding of key terms?

SELF-ASSESSMENT CHECKLIST

Let's revisit the Knowledge focus and Exam skills focus for this chapter.
Decide how confident you are with each statement.

Now I can	Show it	Needs more work	Almost there	Confident to move on
define and give examples of the basic economic problem	Write a short description of the basic economic problem.			
explain the concept of scarcity	Define the term 'scarcity'.			
give examples of the basic economic problem in the context of consumers, workers, producers/firms, governments	Describe a real-life situation where resources are limited and choices must be made.			
explain the key resource allocation decisions answering the three basic economic questions of what to produce, how to produce and for who to produce	List **two** examples for each of the three fundamental economic questions.			
explain the difference between economic goods and free goods	List examples of economic goods and free goods.			
show that I understand the 'define' command word and answer a define question.	Describe what the 'define' command word means.			

2 Factors of production

KNOWLEDGE FOCUS

In this chapter you will answer questions on:

- 2.1 The factors of production
- 2.2 Rewards for the factors of production
- 2.3 Causes of changes in the quantity and quality of the factors of production

EXAM SKILLS FOCUS

In this chapter you will:

- show that you understand the purpose of a short answer question
- show that you understand what the assessment objective of AO1 Knowledge and understanding means with regards to microeconomics.

You will be faced with different question types during your exam. A short answer question is typically worth fewer marks than an extended response question. The question may contain an indication of how many points should be made, such as asking for '**one** reason' or '**two** consequences'. Follow the mark allocation; if a question asks for '**one** reason,' providing two won't earn extra marks. Using a simple structure like 'Point + Explanation' can help improve clarity and maximise marks.

Short answer questions assess the first assessment objective: AO1 Knowledge and understanding. Assessment objectives are a set of statements that outline what skill(s) you need to demonstrate in your response to the question. The command words of 'define', 'state' and 'identify' are checking your AO1 Knowledge and understanding skills. In these cases, you should demonstrate knowledge and understanding of economic definitions, formulas and concepts using precise economic terminology.

2.1 The factors of production

≪ RECALL AND CONNECT 1 ≪

a What is the basic economic problem?

b How does the concept of scarcity relate to factors of production?

UNDERSTAND THESE TERMS

- enterprise
- entrepreneur

1 List the **four** factors of production.

2 Match the term with its correct definition.

Term			Definition	
a	Land		i	Human effort used in production
b	Labour		ii	Human-made goods used in production
c	Capital		iii	Risk-taking and key decision-making in business
d	Enterprise		iv	Natural resources used in production

3 Match the term with the correct example.

Term			Example	
a	Land		i	Tools, vehicles, office buildings
b	Labour		ii	Project managers, entrepreneurs, investors
c	Capital		iii	Forests, rivers, mineral deposits
d	Enterprise		iv	Teachers, construction workers, dentists

4 What is the difference between enterprise and an entrepreneur?

5 What is the difference between labour and capital?

6

In Guyana, large rainforests and fertile agricultural land are seen as valuable land resources, while its gold-mining equipment and modern machinery serve as essential capital goods. Guyana is one of the fastest-growing economies in the world, demonstrating its diverse and expanding potential.

a Define the term 'land' in economics. [2]

b Define 'capital goods'. [2]

2.2 Rewards for the factors of production

1   Fill in the missing word using **one** of the terms from the word box.

profits   payments   prizes

Rewards to the factors of production are the _____ made for the use of the factors.

2   Fill in the missing words using **two** of the terms from the word box.

income   transfers   earnings   output

The rewards or factor payments can also be called factor _____ and factor _____.

3   Match the term with the correct reward.

Term	
a	Land
b	Labour
c	Capital
d	Enterprise

Reward	
i	Rent
ii	Profit
iii	Interest
iv	Wages

2.3 Causes of changes in the quantity and quality of the factors of production

1   Complete Table 2.1, using suitable examples. The first row has been completed for you.

Table 2.1: Changes in the quantity and quality of factors of production

	An increase in quantity	An increase in quality
Land	• Reforestation • Land reclamation	• Irrigation • Use of fertilisers
Labour	a	b
Capital	c	d
Enterprise	e	f

For Question 2, make sure you use the information in the scenario in your answer.

2

In recent years, Guyana has experienced significant oil discoveries. However, the country faces some development challenges. First, nearly half of nationals with tertiary education leave the country, contributing to a high emigration rate. Second, the basic literacy and numeracy rates across its workers will need to be improved to ensure that the workforce can effectively support the growing oil industry and meet its increasing demand for skilled labour.

Explain **two** ways in which Guyana can increase its labour resource. [4]

REFLECTION

How should you prepare for these sorts of short AO1 Knowledge and understanding questions?

There is no real substitute for extra reading. The more you read, the more you will become more familiar with economic vocabulary and improve your capacity to identify key information that could be useful for a question like this. As you read, challenge yourself to identify economic theories and consider using a highlighter pen to mark important ideas, statistics and concepts that may be useful in your responses. For example, while reading about a country's economic policy, ask yourself:

- What economic concepts are being applied here?
- Are there any terms I don't understand?
- Is there anything specific that I want to remember from this article?

Highlighting will not only keep you engaged with the content but will help you to quickly refer back to crucial details when needed. For these reasons, it is always important to read exam case studies with a highlighter pen.

- How much reading do you do outside of class?
- Do you read with a highlighter pen to hand?

SELF-ASSESSMENT CHECKLIST

Let's revisit the Knowledge focus and Exam skills focus for this chapter. Decide how confident you are with each statement.

Now I can	Show it	Needs more work	Almost there	Confident to move on
define the factors of production: land, labour, capital and enterprise	Explain the difference between each of the factors of production.			
identify the rewards to the factors of production: rent, wages, interest and profit	List the different rewards to each of the factors of production.			

CONTINUED

Now I can	Show it	Needs more work	Almost there	Confident to move on
analyse the causes of changes in the quantity and quality of the factors of production	Describe **three** ways in which a country could increase the quantity or quality of its factors of production.			
understand the purpose of a short answer question	Explain the difference between a short answer question and a multiple-choice question.			
understand what the assessment objective of AO1 Knowledge and understanding means with regards to microeconomics.	Give an oral explanation to a fellow student of what AO1 Knowledge and understanding means.			

3 Opportunity cost

KNOWLEDGE FOCUS

In this chapter you will answer questions on:

- 3.1 The meaning of opportunity cost
- 3.2 Influence of opportunity cost on decision-making

EXAM SKILLS FOCUS

In this chapter you will:

- show that you understand the 'state' command word and answer a state question
- show that you can spend a proportionate amount of time on short answer questions.

The command word 'state' means express in clear terms. State questions are checking the assessment objective AO1 Knowledge and understanding only, which focuses on demonstrating knowledge of syllabus content, recalling of facts or applying formulae. Sometimes, a state question may simply require a definition.

The sorts of short answer questions that we have looked at so far are often referred to as low-mark questions, which typically do not require lengthy answers. With this in mind, it is usually beneficial to keep your responses concise while ensuring that you cover the essential information. Since these questions are worth fewer marks, you should spend less time on them than on the higher-mark questions.

To manage your time effectively, consider the total marks and duration of the exam. For example, Paper 2 – Structured Questions has 80 marks and lasts two hours, meaning you have approximately 1.5 minutes per mark. However, since all questions require reading case studies, you may need to adjust this slightly. As a general guideline:

- 2-mark questions should take around three minutes
- 4-mark questions should take around six minutes.

3.1 The meaning of opportunity cost

≪ RECALL AND CONNECT 1 ≪

a What are the factors of production?

b What is the reward for each factor of production?

c Why are factors of production considered scarce?

d How does scarcity force choices when using factors of production?

UNDERSTAND THIS TERM

- opportunity cost

1 How does the concept of opportunity cost link to the basic economic problem?

Note that both questions below require you to state what is meant by the term 'opportunity cost'. However, they also require you to select some economic information from the case study as well. This checks whether you can apply the concept of opportunity cost to a new context.

Make a note of the amount of time it takes you to answer each of the Exam skills questions in this chapter.

2

> Anaya has saved $1 000 from her part-time job. Her cousin, Meera, suggests that she spends the money to buy some jewellery and clothes. Anaya chooses, instead, to save the money in a high-interest bank account.

State, using an example from the data, what is meant by the term 'opportunity cost'. [2]

3

> Jordan, an aspiring artist, is gifted $300 by their parents for their birthday. They are torn between purchasing a digital drawing tablet or treating themself to a spa day. After some thought, Jordan chooses to buy the drawing tablet, investing in their creative ambition.

State, using an example from the data, what is meant by the term 'opportunity cost'. [2]

3.2 Influence of opportunity cost on decision-making

1 What might be the opportunity cost in each of the following situations?

   a   A person wanting to travel buys a plane ticket to Australia.
   b   A business decides to invest in new technology rather than hiring more workers.
   c   A government chooses to fund public transport.
   d   A farmer plants wheat instead of corn.

2 Complete Table 3.1 with a possible opportunity cost of each decision.

   The first row has been done for you.

Table 3.1: Opportunity costs

	Opportunity cost	Example
Consumer	Opportunity cost of buying a cup of coffee	• Making one at home • Buying a cup of tea
	Opportunity cost of buying a rain jacket	• Getting wet • Buying an umbrella
Firms	Opportunity cost of investing in new technology	a
	Opportunity cost of reducing production	b
Workers	Opportunity cost of working two jobs	c
	Opportunity cost of moving abroad	d
Government	Opportunity cost of building a new hospital	e
	Opportunity cost of increasing defence spending	f

3

In 2024, luxury car manufacturer Aston Martin announced its intent to borrow £100m in order to support its future business strategy. Having seen profits fall over two years, the firm plans to use the funds to speed up the process of producing electric cars and expand its product line by moving away from traditional petrol vehicles.

Explain, using your own example, how the influence of opportunity cost affects decision-making at Aston Martin.   [4]

REFLECTION

You should have made a note of how long it has taken you to answer the Exam skills questions in this chapter.

You have answered some 2-mark and 4-mark questions now, which should help you estimate your writing speed. Reflecting on the time you spent on these questions can also give you a sense of how efficiently you are managing your exam time.

- Did you find it easy to recall the key concepts, or did you need to spend more time thinking about your responses?
- How could you improve your time management in future practice sessions?

SELF-ASSESSMENT CHECKLIST

Let's revisit the Knowledge focus and Exam skills focus for this chapter. Decide how confident you are with each statement.

Now I can	Show it	Needs more work	Almost there	Confident to move on
define opportunity cost	Define the term 'opportunity cost'.			
give examples of opportunity cost in different contexts	Identify examples of opportunity cost in your own life.			
explain the influence of opportunity cost on decisions made by consumers, workers, producers/firms and governments when allocating their resources	Identify the trade-offs each group faces when choosing between alternatives.			
understand the 'state' command word and answer a state question	Describe what the 'state' command word means.			
spend a proportionate amount of time on short answer questions.	Write the answer to a 4-mark question in six minutes or less.			

4 Production possibility curve diagrams

KNOWLEDGE FOCUS

In this chapter you will answer questions on:

- 4.1 Production possibility curves
- 4.2 Points under, on and beyond a PPC
- 4.3 Movements along a PPC
- 4.4 Shifts of a PPC

EXAM SKILLS FOCUS

In this chapter you will:

- show that you understand the 'explain' command word and answer an explain question
- show that you understand the importance of drawing diagrams in economics questions.

The command word 'explain' means set out purposes or reasons / make the relationships between things clear / say why and/or how and support with relevant evidence. In exams, 'explain' is typically used in short answer questions, which are often worth 2 or 4 marks. In such questions, it is important to use linking phrases such as 'because', 'this means that', 'as a result' or 'therefore' to show clear connections between ideas. Simply stating a fact is not enough, because your answer must show the reasoning behind it. You will consider its use here in short answer questions only.

Economics heavily relies on diagrams to simplify and analyse complex scenarios. Throughout your studies, you have encountered many key diagrams, not just PPCs. In exams, some questions will explicitly ask you to include a diagram. When this is the case, it is essential to do so in order to achieve full marks. However, even when a question does not specifically require a diagram, including one can often strengthen your explanation and demonstrate a clearer understanding of economic concepts. Mark schemes for longer answer questions (6 or 8 marks) often reward well-integrated diagrams, so using them effectively can help you to achieve higher marks.

4.1 Production possibility curves

UNDERSTAND THIS TERM

- production possibility curve (PPC)

1 Draw a PPC for a country that makes two goods: coffee and durian fruit.

2 Describe what a PPC is and explain its shape using the diagram you drew for Question 1.

4.2 Points under, on and beyond a PPC

1 Complete Table 4.1. For each description, decide whether it would be illustrated on a PPC with a point under, on or beyond the PPC.

Table 4.1: Points under, on and beyond a PPC

	Description	Under, on or beyond
a	A country is producing at its maximum capacity for both goods.	
b	A country is producing fewer goods than it could, with some resources left unused.	
c	A country is trying to produce more than its resources will allow.	
d	A country is using all of its resources to make one good (there is no production of the other good).	
e	A country has a large portion of its labour force unemployed.	

2 Fill in the missing words using the terms in the word box.

increase	efficient	capacity	resources	idle	maximum

A point on the PPC represents an _____ use of _____. It shows the economy is operating at full _____, using all available resources to their _____ potential. A point under the PPC suggests that some resources remain _____, and the economy could _____ production without needing additional resources.

4.3 Movements along a PPC

≪ RECALL AND CONNECT 1 ≪

a   Define the term 'opportunity cost'.

b   A farmer chooses to plant coffee instead of durian fruit. What is the opportunity cost of this decision?

In this explain question, try to provide a clear and concise answer by breaking down the key concepts. The question also asks you to use a diagram to support your explanation. Ensure that you refer to your diagram in your answer.

1

Algeria is a country that produces an enormous amount of hydrocarbons, such as petroleum and natural gas, which together account for more than 95% of the country's exports. However, the government is trying to diversify into new sectors such as tourism.

Explain, using a production possibility curve (PPC) diagram, how the reallocation of resources from hydrocarbons to tourism can affect Algeria's production possibilities and the opportunity cost involved.   **[4]**

4.4 Shifts of a PPC

≪ RECALL AND CONNECT 2 ≪

a   What are the four factors of production?

b   What are some of the ways in which the quantity or the quality of the factors of production can increase?

1 An economy splits its resources between making electrical goods and agricultural goods. Identify which items in the word box will lead to a leftwards shift of the PPC and which will lead to a rightwards shift of the PPC. Complete Table 4.2.

a natural disaster	training programmes
population decline	discovery of a new natural resource
a decrease in profit taxes for firms	an increase in emigration numbers

Table 4.2: Leftwards and rightwards shifts of the PPC

Leftwards	Rightwards

2 Draw a PPC that illustrates this news story:

'South Korean birth rate falls below 0.8 births per woman.'

3

Costa Rica is a country in Central America known for its important agricultural sector, with coffee, bananas and pineapples being key exports. In recent years, however, the government has invested heavily in renewable energy sources, particularly in wind and solar power. This focus towards green energy is helping Costa Rica expand its production capabilities and reduce its reliance on traditional methods of energy generation.

a Explain the difference between a movement along the PPC and a shift of a PPC. [4]

b Explain, using a production possibility (PPC) diagram, how Costa Rica's PPC is likely to shift as a result of its focus on green energy. [4]

REFLECTION

When answering PPC questions, you should consider how effectively you have addressed the 'explain' command word by providing a clear connection between your diagram and your written response.

Questions to consider:

- Did the diagram support your answer and align with the scenario given?
- Did you clearly link your explanation to the key features of the PPC?
- Could you improve your ability to integrate diagrams into your answers?

SELF-ASSESSMENT CHECKLIST

Let's revisit the Knowledge focus and Exam skills focus for this chapter.
Decide how confident you are with each statement.

Now I can	Show it	Needs more work	Almost there	Confident to move on
define a production possibility curve (PPC)	Define a production possibility curve (PPC).			
draw a PPC	Draw a PPC for a country that only produces cars (manufactured good) and coffee (agricultural good).			
interpret points under, on and beyond a PPC	Describe what the various points on a PPC diagram mean.			
analyse movements along a PPC	A country only produces cars and coffee, and coffee prices double. State which good's production is increasing and which is decreasing.			
analyse the causes and consequences of shifts in a PPC in terms of an economy's growth	Explain, with a diagram, why a PPC might shift to the left or right.			
understand the 'explain' command word and answer an explain question	Answer the question: Explain **two** reasons why a country's PPC might shift to the left.			
show that I understand the importance of drawing diagrams in economics questions.	Answer the question: Using a diagram, explain the impact of reallocating resources from capital to consumer goods.			

Exam practice 1

This section contains practice questions that will draw together your knowledge on a range of topics you have covered up to this point and will help you prepare for your assessment.

The following questions have example student responses and commentaries provided. For each question, work through the question first, then compare your answer to the example student response and commentary.

Question 1

China is one of the world's fastest-growing economies, largely driven by its exports. One of its most significant exports is batteries; in 2022, China was the world's largest exporter of batteries ($3bn worth), which accounts for almost a third of the global battery trade. Batteries come in various types, such as car batteries used by electric vehicle manufacturers and laptop batteries supplied to computer firms. Battery production has improved significantly over the years, driven by technological advancements in machinery and increased training of labour. However, some experts are concerned about the environmental impact of large-scale battery production and the overuse of finite raw materials like lithium and cobalt.

a   Identify **two** of the basic economic questions that determine resource allocation. [2]

Example student response	Commentary
What to produce?	AO1 Knowledge and understanding
For whom to produce?	This answers the question fully. While the answer is very short, the question does not require any further detail.

b   Explain the possible opportunity cost to China of exporting more batteries. [4]

Example student response	Commentary
Opportunity cost refers to the next best alternative forgone when a decision is made.	AO1 Knowledge and understanding This is a good definition of the concept of opportunity cost.
In the case of China exporting more batteries, the opportunity cost might include the loss of batteries that could have been sold domestically. Selling these batteries within China could have increased consumer choice or lowered prices for domestic buyers.	AO2 Analysis This is a short answer, but it contains all the essential information. The answer could benefit from mentioning how the battery industry is diverting resources from other industries.

c Analyse **two** reasons why batteries are considered economic goods. [6]

Example student response	Commentary
Batteries can be considered economic goods for two main reasons: (1) scarcity of resources and (2) the opportunity cost of their production. Batteries require finite raw materials such as lithium and cobalt. The text tells us that raw materials are limited – and that they are also essential for other technologies like laptops and electric vehicles. This scarcity makes batteries economic goods because the resources needed to produce them are not freely available. Producing batteries involves trade-offs since these materials are not only in short supply but are also crucial for manufacturing other devices. Because these resources are scarce and not freely accessible, batteries are considered economic goods.	AO1 Knowledge and understanding There is no definition of the key concept 'economic good', but the rest of the answer shows a strong implied understanding. AO2 Analysis The structure of this answer is good in the sense that the student highlights two clear reasons and leaves a line break between the two paragraphs. However, the analysis of the second point is essentially just a repeat of the first. The answer could be improved by potentially linking to the environmental impact and using that as a further example of opportunity cost, since resources used to address these impacts could be directed elsewhere.

d Discuss whether 'the technological advance in machinery and increased training of labour' will continue to shift China's PPC to the right. [8]

Example student response	Commentary
A production possibility curve (PPC) shows the maximum possible output combinations of two goods or services that an economy can produce given its factors of production. Technological advancements in machinery can increase productivity, enabling the country to produce more goods with the same amount of resources. This would shift the PPC to the right, reflecting an increase in the economy's productive capacity. However, the impact of technology on the PPC may be limited if it is not widely implemented across other industries. Increased training of labour can enhance workers' skills, leading to higher productivity and better use of available resources. This would also shift the PPC to the right as the economy becomes more efficient at producing goods and services. However, the impact of labour training is dependent on the amount of time and money spent on the training.	AO1 Knowledge and understanding and AO2 Analysis The answer outlines two clear lines of argument. The general economic theory part of this answer is effective; it explains how both factors link to a country's factors of production and the impact on output. The biggest issue, however, is that the answer is very generic. This means that it does not relate to the case study well. It never talks about China, nor about anything specific to do with battery making. AO3 Evaluation The evaluative sections are too short. For example, the student explains that the impact of technology 'could be limited' but does not explain why or offer any development of this point.

Now that you have read the example student response to the previous question, here is a similar practice question which you should attempt.

Question 2

Analyse the significance of a point under the PPC and a point beyond the PPC. [6]

The allocation of resources

5 The role of markets in allocating resources

KNOWLEDGE FOCUS

In this chapter you will answer questions on:

- 5.1 How markets work
- 5.2 The role of buyers and sellers

EXAM SKILLS FOCUS

In this chapter you will:

- show that you understand the importance of using examples when answering economic questions.

In economics, using examples in your answers is very important. This is because examples help to illustrate abstract concepts in real-world situations, making your response clearer and more convincing. When explaining economic theories, an example can show that you understand not just the theory but also how it works in practice. Sometimes in revision, it can also be useful to think of your own examples or to research different case studies from current affairs or historical contexts.

5.1 How markets work

UNDERSTAND THIS TERM

- market

1 Fill in the missing words using the terms in the word box.

> advertisements   goods   internet   exchange
>
> markets   buyers   traded

In economics, the term 'market' means any arrangement that allows

_____ and services to be _____. For example, it may include a

furniture manufacturer making contact with potential _____ of its chairs

by placing _____ in magazines. Many _____ are now online.

Online banking allows customers and their banks to _____ payments and

services over the _____.

Text taken from Grant: Economics for Cambridge IGCSE™ and O Level, Coursebook

2 Identify **four** examples of a market from the following list:

A An e-commerce platform

B A family dinner

C A public beach

D A community event selling handmade goods

E A stock exchange

F A roadside stall selling fresh fruit

G A volunteer cleanup

H A conversation

5.2 The role of buyers and sellers

≪ RECALL AND CONNECT 1 ≪

Using your own examples, explain how the concept of opportunity cost can influence the decisions of consumers and firms.

UNDERSTAND THESE TERMS

- consumers
- firm
- raw materials

1 Complete Table 5.1. For each statement, identify whether the role belongs to a **buyer** or a **seller**.

Table 5.1: Buyer or seller?

	Description	Buyer or seller
a	Chooses between competing options on sale in the market	
b	Offers discounts to attract more customers	
c	Provides goods to meet customers' needs	
d	Decides to purchase a product based on quality and price	
e	Creates demand by requesting a specific service frequently	

2

The global demand for non-dairy milks like soy and oat has increased in recent years. This has been particularly evident in Western countries due to the popularity of plant-based lifestyles, environmental awareness and ethical concerns about animal welfare. As a result, supermarkets now offer a variety of plant-based milk options, innovating with flavours and ingredients to attract health-conscious and environmentally aware consumers.

Explain, using examples, **two** roles of a seller in markets. [4]

REFLECTION

In your response to this Exam skills question, you were asked to explain two roles of a seller in markets using an example. You should reflect on how well you explained the roles of a seller, and whether you found suitable excerpts from the text to use as examples.

- Did you find it easy to separate and explain two distinct roles?
- How did you identify the passage in the text that you would use?
- Was your example relevant in the sense that it clearly demonstrated the role of the seller?

SELF-ASSESSMENT CHECKLIST

Let's revisit the Knowledge focus and Exam skills focus for this chapter.
Decide how confident you are with each statement.

Now I can	Show it	Needs more work	Almost there	Confident to move on
define a market	Define a market.			
give examples of markets	List **three** real-world examples of markets.			
explain the roles of buyers and sellers	Create a list of the different roles of buyers and sellers in markets.			
understand the importance of using examples when answering economic questions.	Answer the question: Explain **two** roles of the buyer in a market of your choosing.			

6 Demand

KNOWLEDGE FOCUS

In this chapter you will answer questions on:

- 6.1 Individual and market demand
- 6.2 Movements along a demand curve
- 6.3 Shifts of a demand curve

EXAM SKILLS FOCUS

In this chapter you will:

- show that you understand the 'draw' command word and answer a draw question.

The command word 'draw' in an exam means to produce a clear and accurate diagram, often without needing a ruler (to save time). Some questions may only require you to draw a diagram; other questions will ask you to draw a diagram and explain the diagram.

It is essential to draw the diagram large enough to ensure clarity. Avoid rubbing out too much, as this can make your work illegible. If the diagram becomes too unclear, it is better to start over to maintain neatness and precision.

6.1 Individual and market demand

≪ RECALL AND CONNECT 1 ≪

Describe the role of a buyer in the market.

UNDERSTAND THESE TERMS

- demand
- market demand

1 Suppose three people are interested in buying luxury watches. Person A is willing to pay up to $200 000, Person B up to $150 000, and Person C up to $100 000.

   a If the price of the watch is set at $120 000, who will buy it?

   b What would happen to market demand if the price dropped to $90 000?

   c How does joining of individual demand curves form the market demand curve?

   d Why is it important for sellers to understand market demand rather than just individual demand?

2 Table 6.1 shows the demand schedule for pizzas from a takeaway pizza shop.

Table 6.1: Demand schedule for takeaway pizzas

Price ($)	Quantity demanded
20	50
16	70
12	90
8	130
4	190

Use Table 6.1 to draw the demand curve for takeaway pizza.

REFLECTION

As we saw in earlier chapters, you will often need to draw a diagram (such as a demand curve) in support of answers. When drawing a diagram, you must ensure that you have included all its important elements. Here is a list of things you need to remember when drawing a demand curve:

- The axes must be labelled (Price and Quantity).
- The demand curve should be drawn as a downward sloping line, preferably drawn straight.
- The demand curve must be labelled D.

Sometimes you might also be asked to draw, or plot, a demand curve from data onto a set of grid squares. In this case, make sure you use the correct scale on the grid squares you are given.

- How comfortable are you with plotting coordinates on grid squares?

6.2 Movements along a demand curve

UNDERSTAND THESE TERMS

- extension in demand
- contraction in demand

1 Using the demand curve you drew for Question 2 in Section 6.1:

a Calculate the change in quantity demanded when the price falls from $16 to $8.

b Calculate the change in quantity demanded when the price rises from $8 to $12.

c Draw an extension along the demand curve.

2

For the past ten years, Singapore has been ranked the world's most expensive city to live in, largely due to high rental prices and land scarcity. The city has a population of 5.4 million and so finding affordable housing is always challenging. However, in late 2024, Singapore's private home prices fell for the first time in five quarters; the market showed a 1.1% decrease in the average house price compared to the previous quarter.

Draw a demand curve to illustrate the impact of a 'decrease in the average house price' on the demand for houses in Singapore. [4]

REFLECTION

Review your answer to Question 1 in Section 6.2 and go through the diagram checklist below.

Diagram checklist:

- Are the axes labelled?
- Is the demand curve labelled?
- Do you have an arrow to show the direction of movement between the two prices?
- Have you plotted (with dotted lines) the price and quantity?
- Have you accurately labelled the changes to price and quantity?

How confident are you in being able to able to draw fully labelled diagrams?

6.3 Shifts of a demand curve

UNDERSTAND THESE TERMS

- normal goods
- substitute
- complement

1   Consider the list of factors in the word box below. Each factor will lead to either an increase in demand or a decrease in demand for takeaway pizza.

a rise in average income	the season changes to summer
the price of a substitute (takeaway pasta or frozen pizza) rises	the price of a complement (soft drinks, garlic bread) falls
the price of a substitute falls	
a rise in the number of a health-conscious consumers	

Complete Table 6.2 by putting each factor into the relevant column. Assume that takeaway pizza is a normal good.

Table 6.2: Shifts in demand for takeaway pizza

Demand increase	Demand decrease

2   Draw a demand curve diagram that shows the demand for a product decreasing.

3

Boosted by interest in health and fitness during the COVID-19 pandemic, there has since been a significant increase in demand for home fitness equipment and wearable technology in countries like India and Malaysia. Consumers are prioritising at-home workouts and, as a result, products like treadmills, resistance bands and fitness trackers have become increasingly popular. This trend highlights a growing awareness of personal health and wellness in the region.

a   Explain the difference between a movement along and a shift of the demand curve.   [4]

b   Explain, using a diagram, the impact of 'the COVID-19 pandemic' on the demand curve for home fitness equipment.   [4]

SELF-ASSESSMENT CHECKLIST

Let's revisit the Knowledge focus and Exam skills focus for this chapter.
Decide how confident you are with each statement.

Now I can	Show it	Needs more work	Almost there	Confident to move on
define demand	Define the term 'demand'.			
recognise the link between individual and market demand	Explain the link to another student.			
draw and interpret the demand diagram	Draw a demand curve diagram and label all the elements clearly. Then swap with another student and peer-assess each other's diagrams.			
explain the causes of extensions and contractions in demand	Define the terms 'extension' and 'contraction' in relation to demand curves.			
draw diagrams that illustrate movements along a demand curve	Draw a demand curve for hot chocolate that illustrates the impact of a price rise for the product.			
analyse the causes of increases and decreases in demand	List **three** reasons demand might increase or decrease for a hot chocolate drink.			
draw diagrams that illustrate shifts of the demand curve	Draw a diagram that illustrates how the demand curve for hot chocolate changes during winter months.			
understand the 'draw' command word and answer a draw question.	Answer a 4-mark draw question.			

7 Supply

KNOWLEDGE FOCUS

In this chapter you will answer questions on:

- 7.1 Individual and market supply
- 7.2 Movements along a supply curve
- 7.3 Shifts of a supply curve

EXAM SKILLS FOCUS

In this chapter you will:

- show that you understand some of the connections between concepts from previous chapters
- show that you understand what point-based marking is.

The concept of supply is closely connected to the concept of demand. Therefore, you should look to revise the Chapter 7 content in conjunction with the Chapter 6 content. They are similar in many ways (such as the definitions) but different in many ways too (such as the factors that cause a shift in the curves). Therefore, it is easy to get muddled between the two. Throughout this chapter, you will be prompted to consider the links with Chapter 6.

Mark schemes can help you understand how marks are awarded. In this chapter, you should review a past paper mark scheme for short answer questions with the command words 'state', 'define' and 'explain' in order to see how marks are awarded in a point-based marking system. This is where each correct term or explanation is awarded a specific number of marks. Knowing this will help you to practise giving clear answers that meet the marking criteria, which should improve your exam technique.

7.1 Individual and market supply

≪ RECALL AND CONNECT 1 ≪

Describe the role of a seller in the market.

UNDERSTAND THESE TERMS

- supply
- market supply

1 Table 7.1 shows the supply schedule for the daily supply of organic apples from an orchard.

Table 7.1: Supply schedule for organic apples

Price ($) per apple	Quantity supplied
2.25	8000
2.00	7000
1.75	6000
1.50	5000
1.25	4000

Use Table 7.1 to draw the supply curve for organic apples

2 Name some of the main features of a supply curve.

7.2 Movements along a supply curve

≪ RECALL AND CONNECT 2 ≪

a What might cause an extension in demand for oil?

b What might cause a contraction in demand for baby wipes?

UNDERSTAND THESE TERMS

- extension in supply
- contraction in supply

1   Using your supply curve from Question 1 in Section 7.1, complete the following tasks:

   a   Calculate the change in quantity supplied when the price rises from $1.50 to $2.00.

   b   Calculate the change in quantity supplied when the price falls from $2.00 to $1.75.

   c   Draw an extension along the supply curve.

2   Explain why a rise in price leads to an extension in the quantity supplied but a contraction in the quantity demanded.

For a short answer question like Question 3, marks are awarded using a point-based marking system. A certain number of marks (two) will be allocated for an accurate and well-labelled diagram. Additional marks (two) will be given for a clear explanation. To maximise your score, ensure that both elements are completed.

3

> Recent falls in hotel prices in Bali have affected hotel availability.
> As prices drop, many hotel owners have reduced their offerings or delayed new developments.

Draw a supply curve to illustrate the impact of 'recent falls in hotel prices' on the supply of affordable accommodation in Bali.   [4]

7.3 Shifts of a supply curve

≪ RECALL AND CONNECT 3 ≪

   a   Give **three** factors that would lead to an increase in demand for running trainers.

   b   Give **three** factors that would lead to a decrease in demand for sunscreen.

1   Consider the list of factors in the word box below. Each factor will lead to either an increase in supply or a decrease in supply for fresh flowers.

Complete Table 7.2 by putting each factor into the relevant column.

> favourable weather conditions   government subsidies
>
> increase in production costs   labour shortages
> (e.g. fertiliser)
>   technological advancements leading
> disease or pest outbreak   to more efficient farming methods

Table 7.2: Changes in supply of fresh flowers

Supply increase	Supply decrease

2 Draw a supply curve diagram that shows the supply for a product rising.

Before you complete Question 3, review some past paper mark schemes to see how marks are awarded using a point-based marking system for short answer questions like these.

3

In recent years, growing citrus fruit such as oranges has become difficult work. Climate challenges such as droughts and extreme temperatures, as well as the spread of various diseases, have made it harder to maintain a steady supply. By contrast, many farmers worldwide are now switching to quinoa production. Quinoa is a more resilient crop than citrus because it is more adaptable to different climates and soils.

a Define 'supply'. [2]

b State **two** reasons why the supply curve for citrus fruits such as oranges has shifted leftwards. [2]

c Explain, using a diagram, what is likely to have happened to the global supply curve for quinoa. [4]

REFLECTION

Throughout this chapter, you have been asked to make connections between the supply curve and the previous chapter on the demand curve. Hopefully, you have noticed some patterns between the two. On the surface, they may appear very different – firms versus consumers, and the upward-sloping supply curve versus the downward-sloping demand curve. However, there are key similarities, such as definitions and explanations of movements along the curve. Take a moment now to reflect on these links:

- How do the definitions vary?
- What similarities are there when explaining the movements along the supply and demand curves?
- How do the factors that shift the supply curve compare to those that shift the demand curve?

Connections between topics can be made across the Cambridge IGCSE and O Level Economics syllabuses. The next most obvious occasion will be with the concepts of price elasticity of demand (PED) and price elasticity of supply (PES).

How might you create an organiser to illustrate and record these cross-syllabus links?

SELF-ASSESSMENT CHECKLIST

Let's revisit the Knowledge focus and Exam skills focus for this chapter.
Decide how confident you are with each statement.

Now I can	Show it	Needs more work	Almost there	Confident to move on
define supply	Define the term 'supply'.			
recognise the link between individual and market supply	Explain the link between individual and market supply to another student.			
explain the causes of extensions and contractions in supply	Explain the difference between extensions and contractions in supply to another student.			
draw a diagram to illustrate a movement along a supply curve	Draw a supply curve to show a contraction along the curve.			
analyse the causes of shifts in the supply curve	List **three** reasons the supply curve might increase or decrease for coffee beans.			
draw diagrams that illustrate shifts of a supply curve	Draw the supply curve for coffee bean production during the winter months.			
understand some of the connections between concepts from previous chapters	Explain **two** differences and **two** similarities between demand and supply curves.			
understand what point-based marking is.	Create a revision timetable in which you revisit key concepts regularly over time, sometimes approaching them in different ways or alongside other related topics.			

8 Price determination

KNOWLEDGE FOCUS

In this chapter you will answer questions on:

- 8.1 The price mechanism
- 8.2 Market equilibrium
- 8.3 Market disequilibrium

EXAM SKILLS FOCUS

In this chapter you will:

- show that you understand the 'analyse' command word and answer an analyse question
- show that you understand what the assessment objective of AO2 Analysis means.

The command word 'analyse' means to examine in detail in order to show meaning, and identify elements and the relationship between them. It involves breaking down economic data or issues and exploring how different elements are connected. It requires interpreting written, numerical or diagrammatic information and applying economic theory to explain what is happening. Analysis requires building a clear chain of reasoning, where each point logically follows from the last. It is crucial to explain the links in between thoroughly. This command word is often associated with 4-mark or 6-mark questions that ask you to analyse one or two reasons behind an economic event.

The 'analyse' command word is obviously linked closely to AO2 Analysis. AO2 Analysis goes beyond the basic knowledge required in AO1 Knowledge and understanding (which focuses on recalling facts and definitions). AO2 Analysis requires you to select, organise and interpret data, and apply economic theory to different forms of information such as written, numerical, diagrammatic or graphical data. AO2 Analysis is all about identifying and developing links between economic factors and then using logical reasoning to explain how they interact. AO2 Analysis involves a deeper level of thinking than AO1 Knowledge and understanding.

8.1 The price mechanism

≪ RECALL AND CONNECT 1 ≪

a   What are the three fundamental economic questions?

b   A country produces textiles and tech-based goods. Consumers shift their preferences away from fast fashion towards more internet-enabled devices. Use a PPC diagram to illustrate how resources will move automatically as a result of the changes to consumer preferences.

1   Read the scenario in Question (b) in the Recall and connect box again. In this question you will explain the reallocation from fast fashion to tech-based goods in a bit more detail, according to the price mechanism.

Complete Tables 8.1 and 8.2 using the terms in the word boxes. This will highlight the various steps of the price mechanism.

a

fall in profit   fall in price   firms produce less

Table 8.1: Reallocation away from textiles

Decrease in demand for textiles
↓

i

↓

ii

↓

iii

↓
Reduce number of workers and capital employed

b

firms produce more   rise in profit   rise in price

Table 8.2: Reallocation towards tech-based goods

Increase in demand for tech-based goods
↓

i

↓

ii

↓

iii

↓
Increase number of workers and capital employed

REFLECTION

Activities like Question 1 will help to strengthen your analytical skills. Analysis requires you to build clear chains of reasoning that progress from one point to another. Many students make the mistake of jumping from A to Z without addressing the important steps in between. Unfortunately, this approach means that statements are often made without support. High quality analysis requires justified reasoning.

- What strategies can you use to avoid making statements without support and instead focus on building a well-supported argument?

Now try to utilise the skill of building a chain of reasoning in your answer to an Exam skills question (Question 2).

2

Vietnam is a major producer of textiles, particularly for the fast fashion industry, but it is also becoming a significant player in tech-based production, including electronics and internet-enabled devices. As global consumer preferences shift away from fast fashion and toward more technology products, demand for these tech-based goods is driven by Vietnamese consumers as well as international markets. As a result, Vietnam should reallocate more resources toward tech manufacturing, while still maintaining its strong textile sector.

Analyse how the price mechanism answers the basic economic questions of 'what to produce' and 'for whom to produce'? [6]

8.2 Market equilibrium

UNDERSTAND THESE TERMS

- market equilibrium
- market price
- equilibrium price
- equilibrium quantity

1 a Look at the demand and supply schedules for a product in Table 8.3.
Identify the market equilibrium price.

Table 8.3: Demand and supply schedules

Price ($)	Quantity demanded	Quantity supplied
30	12 000	14 500
25	14 000	14 000
20	16 000	13 500
15	19 500	13 000
10	25 000	12 500

b Draw a supply and demand diagram using the data in Table 8.3 and show the
equilibrium price.

8.3 Market disequilibrium

UNDERSTAND THESE TERMS

- market disequilibrium
- surplus
- shortage

1 Complete the following explanation about market disequilibrium using the terms
in the word box.

> market   change   disequilibrium   equilibrium
>
> supply   demanded

A market is in _____ when there is an imbalance between demand

and _____. In this case, the _____ price will not be the

market _____ price. There will be a difference between the quantity

_____ and the quantity supplied. There will be pressure for the price

to _____.

2

Twenty years ago, in 2005, the government of Kenya introduced a high market price for milk in order to try to protect local dairy farmers. The market price was set above the equilibrium price, which led to an increase in milk prices for consumers. As a result, while farmers benefitted from higher prices, some consumers struggled with the higher costs and there was a surplus of milk that could not be sold at the new price.

Analyse how the government setting of a market price that is too high or too low can result in market disequilibrium. [6]

REFLECTION

As you come across more analyse questions, it is important to develop an awareness of mark scheme expectations. In this regard, some useful strategies might be: review several analyse questions from past papers, read through the relevant mark schemes and highlight the recurring elements. You should find that while the content may change, the assessment criteria tend to remain consistent.

- How can you find past papers and mark schemes to support your preparation?
- How often will you set aside time to review past papers and reflect on the recurring patterns in mark schemes?

Regular practice and reflection on these patterns can significantly improve your analysis skills.

SELF ASSESSMENT CHECKLIST

Let's revisit the Knowledge focus and Exam skills focus for this chapter. Decide how confident you are with each statement.

Now I can	Show it	Needs more work	Almost there	Confident to move on
explain how the price mechanism answers the basic resource allocation questions	Explain how increased demand for electric vehicles will lead to a reallocation of resources.			
define market equilibrium	Identify the equilibrium price and quantity from a schedule or a diagram. You could use Figure 8.7 from the coursebook.			
interpret equilibrium price and quantity in a market using demand and supply schedules	Create your own demand and supply schedules and highlight the equilibrium price and quantity.			

CONTINUED

Now I can	Show it	Needs more work	Almost there	Confident to move on
draw and interpret equilibrium price and quantity using demand and supply curves	Create your own demand and supply diagram and label the equilibrium price and quantity.			
define market disequilibrium	Explain the difference between market equilibrium and disequilibrium.			
interpret disequilibrium prices and quantities in a market using demand and supply schedules	Calculate the surplus or shortage at different prices using Table 8.3 from the coursebook.			
draw and interpret disequilibrium prices and quantities using demand and supply curves	Draw a market disequilibrium diagram (shortage).			
explain shortages and surpluses	Define both shortages and surpluses.			
understand the 'analyse' command word and answer an analyse question	Find an analyse past paper question. Complete it and then self-mark against the mark scheme.			
understand what the assessment objective of AO2 Analysis means.	Verbally explain to another student what AO2 Analysis means.			

9 Price changes

KNOWLEDGE FOCUS

In this chapter you will answer questions on:

- 9.1 Causes of price changes
- 9.2 The consequences of changes in demand
- 9.3 The consequences of changes in supply
- 9.4 The consequences of changes in demand and supply

EXAM SKILLS FOCUS

In this chapter you will:

- show that you understand what a good answer looks like
- show that you can label diagrams accurately.

Understanding what makes a good answer is important because it helps you to structure your own responses clearly and logically. In the context of price changes, with supply and demand diagrams, a good answer shows a clear progression of thought that links the shifts in demand or supply to the resulting changes in price and quantity. By following a structured approach, such as identifying the initial change, the surplus or shortage, the price adjustment, movement along the supply curve and the new equilibrium, you ensure that all key points are addressed with clear reasoning.

Likewise, accurately labelling diagrams is essential for demonstrating your understanding of economic concepts alongside your analysis. This is particularly the case in price changes with supply and demand diagrams, where curves are beginning to shift. Accurate labels will help to ensure that your analysis is easy to follow, highlighting key elements like the initial equilibrium, shifts in curves, and changes in price and quantity.

9.1 Causes of price changes

≪ RECALL AND CONNECT 1 ≪

a   What is demand?

b   What is supply?

c   What is market demand?

d   What is market supply?

e   Why is the demand curve downward sloping?

f   Why is the supply curve upward sloping?

1   Table 9.1 outlines scenarios related to the gems and jewellery market. Complete the table. For each scenario, identify whether it affects the demand curve or the supply curve and explain why. The first one has been done for you.

Table 9.1: Effects on the demand and supply curves

Scenario	Demand or supply	Explanation
The government reduces tax rates on firms' profits	Supply	Lower tax rates encourage greater investment and production
An increase in average income	a	b
Changing fashion trends to more sustainable alternatives to jewellery	c	d
Unseasonal rains affect the production of gemstones in mining regions	e	f
Government imposes stricter mining regulations, increasing costs of production	g	h
A major festival season boosts consumer spending	i	j

2   Decide whether each of the following statements is true or false.

a   A price change occurs only when demand changes.

b   An increase in supply shifts the supply curve left.

c   Market conditions must change for a price change to occur.

d   When demand rises, the equilibrium price is expected to rise also.

9.2 The consequences of changes in demand

1   Figure 9.1 shows a decrease in demand for a product. Most of the labels have been removed. Complete Figure 9.1 by labelling the diagram.

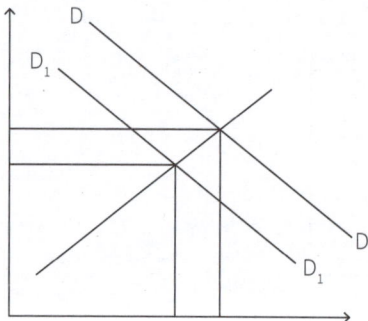

Figure 9.1: The effect of a decrease in demand

In an exam, it is likely that you would need to write a chain of analysis that supports any movement in a diagram. To support your analysis, you can break the process of price changes into five steps. The focus is on demand shifts.

- Step 1: Identify the initial change – determine whether demand is increasing or decreasing. Then, shift the curve accordingly.

- Step 2: Identify the shortage/surplus – assess whether there is now a surplus or shortage at the original price.

- Step 3: Identify the adjustment in price – a shortage will lead to upwards pressure on price, while a surplus will lead to downwards pressure on price.

- Step 4: Movement along the supply curve – identify whether the demand curve shift results in an extension or a contraction along the supply curve.

- Step 5: Identify the new equilibrium point – find the new equilibrium price and quantity.

Use this five-step process to help you answer Question 2.

2   India is one of the largest economies in the world. The gems and jewellery industry is an important part of the economy; some estimates state that it contributes up to 7% of the country's GDP and 15% of its exports. The sector is booming. In 2015, the average income in India was around $1 500 per year, but ten years later it has nearly doubled to $3 000, reflecting the country's growing economic prosperity.

Explain the likely price change in jewellery in India as a result of 'the country's growing economic prosperity'.   [4]

REFLECTION

How did identifying the steps in the price change process help you better understand the relationship between shifts in demand and supply?

9.3 The consequences of changes in supply

1 Figure 9.2 shows a decrease in supply for a product. Most of the labels have been removed. Complete Figure 9.2 by labelling the diagram.

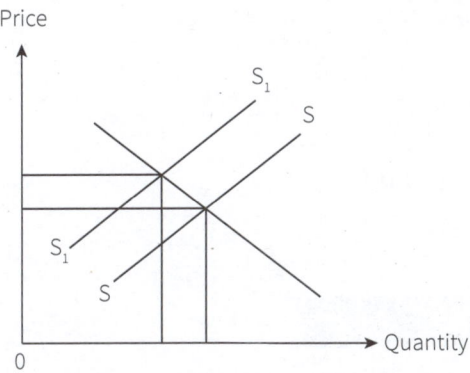

Figure 9.2: The effect of a decrease in supply

REFLECTION

Before trying the next question, please read the answer provided. This is meant as a WAGOLL (What A Good One Looks Like). WAGOLLs are useful because they provide students with a clear example of what is expected in terms of structure, content and level of detail. After reading the WAGOLL, think about:

- Did it help you understand how to convey the different steps involved in analysing price changes?
- What aspects of the answer do you think are most important to include in your own response?

2 In 2024, the Indian government announced that it is working to support producers in the mining sector by providing subsidies for mining activities and setting up evacuation infrastructure. These policies aim to make it more affordable to extract and process gemstones. As a result, the jewellery industry could benefit from more competitive pricing in both domestic and global markets.

Explain the likely price change in jewellery in India as a result of the government subsidies. [4]

WAGOLL

The Indian government's subsidies for the mining sector are likely to reduce the costs of production for jewellery sellers. As a result, the supply curve for jewellery will shift to the right. At the original price, there is now a surplus. This surplus puts downward pressure on prices, leading to an extension along the demand curve. Eventually, a new equilibrium is reached at a lower price (and greater quantity) of jewellery sold.

Now assume that a government in another country is increasing the tax rates on mining firms. Before you write your answer to Question 3, use the five-step process (see Section 9.2) to build your own high-level chain of analysis. Then, using the WAGOLL (What A Good One Looks Like) for Question 2 as a guide, write your answer to Question 3.

3   Explain the likely price change in jewellery as a result of the government taxes on mining firms.

[4]

9.4 The consequences of changes in demand and supply

≪ RECALL AND CONNECT 2 ≪

a   List **three** factors that would lead to a shift in the demand for apples.

b   List **three** factors that would lead to a shift in the supply for apples.

1   Read the passage below and answer the questions that follow.

> It is possible for both supply conditions and demand conditions to change at the same time. When this happens, the impact on the market depends on both the size and direction of the changes. The effect on price will be determined by the relative strength of shifts in demand and supply.

a   What **two** market conditions can change at the same time?

b   What **two** factors determine the impact of these changes on the market?

c   What does the effect on price depend on?

2   Complete Table 9.2 by identifying the likely price change as a result of different demand and supply changes. The first row has been done for you.

Table 9.2: Price changes

	Demand curve	Supply curve	Price change
a	Large increase	Small increase	Increase
b	Small increase	Large increase	
c	Large decrease	Small decrease	
d	Small decrease	Large decrease	

3   Figure 9.3 shows a small increase in the demand for a product at the same time as a large increase in supply of that product. Most of the labels have been removed. Complete Figure 9.3 by labelling the diagram.

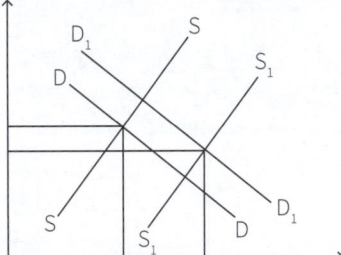

Figure 9.3: The effect of supply increasing more than demand

REFLECTION

You have had the opportunity to relabel three diagrams in this chapter. Accurate labelling helps reinforce your understanding and makes your analysis easier to follow.

- Are you confident in identifying shifts, equilibrium points and price/quantity changes on your diagrams now?
- What can you do to improve your accuracy in labelling these key elements?

4   An apple orchard is facing a unique situation. Health-conscious trends mean that apples have become a popular snack choice among consumers. There is also a large increase in demand from juice manufacturers and food processors, driven by a larger focus on natural ingredients. At the same time, the orchard has seen a small increase in its crop yield this year. After investing in an improved irrigation system, output has increased by just under 2%.

Explain the likely price change in apples as a result of the 'unique situation' described.   [4]

a   Read the answer provided to Question 4 below. This answer is not fully complete and could be improved. You should think why the response is weak. For example, you could consider:

- Does the answer clearly explain the relationship between the changes in demand and supply and the price change?
- Does it describe the size and direction of the shifts in enough detail?

Student answer:

Demand increases and supply increases. However, the increase in supply is smaller and so prices are likely to rise.

b   After considering these points, rewrite the answer to Question 4 to make it clearer and more detailed.

SELF-ASSESSMENT CHECKLIST

Let's revisit the Knowledge focus and Exam skills focus for this chapter.
Decide how confident you are with each statement.

Now I can	Show it	Needs more work	Almost there	Confident to move on
analyse how changes in demand and supply can cause price changes	Use the five-step process (see Section 9.2) to explain why an increase in supply will lead to a fall in price for a product.			
use demand and supply diagrams to illustrate how changes in demand and supply affect price	Draw a demand and supply diagram, showing both curves shifting to different extents.			
analyse the consequences of price changes	Explain the impact on consumers if prices rise.			
understand what a good answer looks like	Explain the main features of a good answer to another student.			
label diagrams correctly.	Ask another student or a teacher to take a diagram from any of the first nine chapters in the coursebook and remove all the labels. Relabel the diagram.			

10 Price elasticity of demand (PED)

KNOWLEDGE FOCUS

In this chapter you will answer questions on:

- 10.1 What is price elasticity of demand (PED)?
- 10.2 Calculating PED
- 10.3 Influences on PED
- 10.4 Changes in PED
- 10.5 Significance of PED for decision-making

EXAM SKILLS FOCUS

In this chapter you will:

- show that you understand the 'calculate' command word and answer a calculate question
- show that you understand what case-study-based questions are.

Calculate questions require you to work out answers from given facts, figures or information. These questions are typically worth 2 marks, and you should focus on completing the calculation and providing your final answer (there is no need for a written explanation). As you will see, you will earn full marks for the correct answer, but even if your answer is incorrect, you might still earn partial marks – for example, if you state the correct formula or use the correct method but make a mistake in the calculation. Given this, it is helpful to state the formulae (for example, the PED formula) and to show your working.

Case-study-based questions in Paper 2 – Structured Questions require you to read a small case study and then answer questions that are based on that content. In these questions, you must refer to the case study to support your answers. This means using the information provided (whether it is written text, data, diagrams or tables) to justify your analysis. Your answers should be grounded in the case study details and should clearly demonstrate how the information provided applies to the question you are answering.

10.1 What is price elasticity of demand (PED)?

≪ RECALL AND CONNECT 1 ≪

a What are some synonyms (alternative words) for 'elasticity'?

b What is market demand?

c Draw a demand curve.

1 Define 'price elasticity of demand'. [2]

2 State the formula for price elasticity of demand. [2]

10.2 Calculating PED

UNDERSTAND THESE TERMS

- elastic demand
- inelastic demand
- perfectly elastic demand
- perfectly inelastic demand
- unitary elastic demand

Calculate questions are typically worth 2 marks. You will earn full marks for the correct answer, but even if your answer is incorrect, you might still earn partial marks for showing your working or stating the formula you plan to use. As you work through the calculate questions in this chapter, ensure that you get into the habit of showing your working clearly.

1 Read the following scenarios and answer the questions.

a The price of a packet of stickers rises from $2 to $2.20. As a result, sales fall by 2.5%.

Calculate the PED value.

b A car company wants to increase sales by reducing the price of its car. The average price reduction is 12%. As a result, the company sees its biggest ever jump in sales. Sales rise by 30%.

Calculate the PED value.

c The PED value of Product X is –0.5. If the price rises by 20%, calculate the impact on the quantity demanded.

d Draw a demand curve that illustrates the type of PED associated with Product X in Question (c).

2

Jonjo is a small-business owner in Nairobi, Kenya. He owns a small stall, in a busy street market, selling SIM cards and other accessories for smartphones. Over the past week, he noticed that his sales were lower than usual. Jonjo has limited control over the price of the SIM cards due to agreements with his suppliers, but he managed to reduce the price by 5% in the hope of boosting sales. Last week, Jonjo sold 200 SIM cards. As a result of the price change, this week's sales rise to 240 SIM cards.

    a   Calculate the PED value for SIM cards on Jonjo's stall.   **[2]**

    b   Draw a demand curve that illustrates the type of PED that is being described in the text.   **[4]**

REFLECTION

After completing a few of these calculation questions, take a moment to pause. How did it go?

In the future, you need to be confident in showing your working and completing the calculation efficiently within a short time frame. Reflect on how you approached the task and think about areas where you can improve for next time.

10.3 Influences on PED

≪ RECALL AND CONNECT 2 ≪

    a   What is a substitute good?

    b   Provide an example of **two** goods with a substitute relationship.

    c   How does the price change of a substitute affect demand for a product?

    d   What is a complement?

    e   Provide an example of **two** goods with a complementary relationship.

    f   How does the price change of a complement affect demand for a product?

1   The word box contains different factors that are associated with more price elastic or more price inelastic demand. Complete Table 10.1 by sorting each factor into the appropriate column based on how it is likely to influence PED.

large availability of substitutes	small proportion of income
necessity product	habitual purchase
long time horizon	non-essential (luxury) product

Table 10.1: Price elasticity of demand

More price elastic in demand	More price inelastic in demand
a	b
c	d
e	f

2 Identify **two** reasons why a small pack of headache tablets might be considered price inelastic in demand.

3 Identify **two** reasons why the purchase of a takeaway coffee might be considered price elastic in demand.

10.4 Changes in PED

1 a Define the term 'revenue'.

 b State the formula for revenue.

2 a Draw a perfectly inelastic demand curve.

 b If the price rises for the product in Question 2(a), what happens to the firm's revenue?

3 a Draw a perfectly elastic demand curve.

 b If the price rises for the product in Question 3(a), what happens to the firm's revenue?

 c The price of a SIM card falls from $2 to $1.90. As a result, sales rise from 200 to 240 units.

 Calculate the change in revenue for the firm.

10.5 Significance of PED for decision-making

1 Read the scenarios below. Complete Table 10.2 by:

- matching each scenario to the correct economic agent: consumers, workers, firms or government
- deciding whether the scenario applies to elastic or inelastic demand.

The first two scenarios have been done for you.

Scenarios:

a Prices are unlikely to go up because demand would contract significantly, reducing revenue.

b A tax on sugary foods generates substantial tax revenue since demand does not contract by much.

c Higher wages can be negotiated without fear of significant job losses because sales are stable regardless of price.

d Price cuts are the only way to generate more sales.

e High prices are charged even though the quality of service does not improve. There are few alternatives.

f A subsidy on public transport significantly increases usage.

g A focus on building brand loyalty to make demand for a product less responsive to price changes.

h Workers face reduced bargaining power for wages as firms can easily replace them.

Table 10.2: Price elasticity of demand for different economic agents

	Elastic demand	Inelastic demand
Consumers	**a** Prices are unlikely to go up because demand would contract significantly, reducing revenue.	i
Workers	ii	iii
Firms	iv	v
Government	vi	**b** A tax on sugary foods generates substantial tax revenue since demand does not contract by much.

2 Decide whether each of the following statements is true or false.

a If a government wants to raise tax revenue, it will be more successful if demand is inelastic.

b A firm may try to make their product more elastic though the use of a special design or slogan to encourage brand loyalty.

c A firm selling a highly addictive good should increase prices in order to increase revenue.

3

> Sarah is a visiting economist in Kuala Lumpur, Malysia. After studying data on consumer behaviours at Jalan Alor, the city's famous food market, she estimates that the PED for any single restaurant on the street is approximately 3.5. Sarah's findings could have significant implications for pricing strategies, consumer choices and the livelihoods of workers in the market.

Analyse the impact of Sarah's estimated PED value on consumers and workers at Jalan Alor food market. [6]

REFLECTION

There have been two longer case-study-based questions in this chapter: Jonjo and Sarah. Take a moment to reflect on the advice given about case-study-based questions.

• Did you effectively use the information provided in the case studies?

• Did you incorporate a specific example?

In the future, what steps can you take to make sure you include relevant examples from the case study to strengthen your analysis?

SELF-ASSESSMENT CHECKLIST

Let's revisit the Knowledge focus and Exam skills focus for this chapter. Decide how confident you are with each statement.

Now I can	Show it	Needs more work	Almost there	Confident to move on
define price elasticity of demand (PED)	Define price elasticity of demand.			
calculate price elasticity of demand	Answer questions about PED.			
interpret the significance of the PED value: perfectly inelastic, inelastic, unitary elastic, elastic, perfectly elastic	Explain the difference between a PED of –0.5 and –2.			
draw and interpret demand curve diagrams to show PED	Draw a demand curve for each of the **five** scenarios: perfectly inelastic, inelastic, unitary elastic, elastic, perfectly elastic.			
analyse the main influences on whether demand is elastic or inelastic	List **three** factors that would mean a product is more likely to be price inelastic in demand.			
explain the relationship between PED and the amount spent by consumers and revenue raised by firms	Explain whether a firm selling an inelastic good should raise price or lower price.			
discuss the implications of PED for decision-making by consumers, workers, producers/ firms and government	State **one** impact on each economic agent of an elastic demand.			
understand the calculate' command word and answer a calculate question	Explain to another student what the command word 'calculate' means.			
show that I understand what 'case-study based' questions are.	List **two** things to remember when answering questions based on case studies.			

11 Price elasticity of supply (PES)

KNOWLEDGE FOCUS

In this chapter you will answer questions on:

- 11.1 What is price elasticity of supply (PES)?
- 11.2 Calculating PES
- 11.3 Influences on PES

EXAM SKILLS FOCUS

In this chapter you will:

- show that you understand why planning your answer is necessary
- show that you understand some of the connections between concepts from previous chapters.

Planning your answer means giving some thought to your answer before you write it. You might even create a small plan before you write your full answer. Planning is not for everyone, however; some students might prefer just going straight into an answer without planning. The benefit with that approach is that it saves time. On the other hand, planning helps you to keep your focus on the exam question. For some students it can also help reduce the stress of not knowing what the next step of your answer is while writing it.

The concept of price elasticity of supply (PES) is closely connected to the concept of price elasticity of demand (PED). Therefore, you should look to revise the Chapter 11 content in conjunction with the Chapter 10 content. They are similar in many ways, such as the formulae, but different in many ways too, such as the factors affecting the elasticity value. Therefore, it is easy to get muddled between the two.

11.1 What is price elasticity of supply (PES)?

≪ RECALL AND CONNECT 1 ≪

a What is market supply?

b Draw a supply curve.

c What is the definition for price elasticity of demand (PED)?

d What is the formula for PED?

UNDERSTAND THIS TERM

- price elasticity of supply (PES)

With command words like 'define' and 'state' (that we have looked at in previous chapters), the aim is to provide a short, clear and concise answer without unnecessary elaboration. The focus is on delivering the requested information directly and accurately. Therefore, it is reasonable to assume that you do not need to plan answers to such questions.

1 Define 'price elasticity of supply'. [2]

2 State the formula for price elasticity of supply. [2]

11.2 Calculating PES

UNDERSTAND THESE TERMS

- elastic supply

- inelastic supply

- perfectly inelastic supply

- perfectly elastic supply

- unitary elastic

1 Read the following scenarios and answer the questions.

a The price of a 1 kg bag of grapes rises from $8 to $9.20. As a result, the number of extra bags that are supplied increases by 3%. Calculate the PES value.

b The price of a popular smartphone accessory (a phone cover) rises from $15 to $15.30. As a result, suppliers quickly increase the market supply by 10%. Calculate the PES value.

c The market price for a branded hoodie decreases from $40 to $35. As a result, the suppliers reduce output by 12.5%. Calculate the PES value.

d The PES value of Product Y is 0.4. If the price rises by 10%, calculate the impact on the quantity supplied.

2 Draw the diagrams that represent:

a perfectly inelastic supply

b perfectly elastic supply.

REFLECTION

PED and PES are related concepts. There are many similarities between the two ideas.

- In what ways does understanding price elasticity of demand complement your knowledge of price elasticity of supply?

- Can you identify specific examples that reinforced your learning?

3

Jeanie is a small-scale coffee farmer in rural Burundi, growing high-quality Arabica coffee beans. Due to growing global demand, the price of her product is rising by 25%. Although Jeanie would like to increase her supply to take advantage of the higher prices, she faces limitations. For example, Jeanie cannot increase her supply quickly because coffee plants take three to four years to mature. Currently, she harvests about 800 kg of coffee beans per month and, in the foreseeable future, she can only realistically increase this by 20 kg.

a Calculate the PES value for Jeanie's coffee production. [2]

b Draw a supply curve that illustrates the type of PES that is being described in the text. [4]

11.3 Influences on PES

1 The numbers in Table 11.1 are the PES values for different products. Complete the table, by matching each value with the correct classification in the word box, to indicate the type of elasticity it represents.

| price elastic | price inelastic | perfectly price inelastic | unitary elasticity |

Table 11.1: PES values

0	0.5	1	2.5
a	b	c	d

2 Complete Table 11.2, by categorising the factors in the word box under the headings 'Price elastic supply' or 'Price inelastic supply'.

quick manufacturing process	short time taken	storable
crafted by hand	simple design	easily spoiled
relies on very scarce materials		

Table 11.2: Influences on PES

Price elastic supply	Price inelastic supply
a	b
c	d
e	f
g	

For longer answer questions that are worth a higher number of marks, it is helpful to plan your response. Planning will help you to address all parts of the question and stay focused. Without planning, you risk straying off-topic and not fully answering the question.

Look at the question first. Then, spend one or two minutes planning your answer by highlighting key words and identifying the main elements. Finally, create bullet points to outline your answer's structure before writing it out in full. Try this method for Question 3.

3

The global shipbuilding industry operates on long timelines due to the complex design and construction processes required for each ship. Production speed is limited by factors such as labour availability and material sourcing. For example, the industry relies on high-skilled labour, requiring expertise in areas such as engineering, design and construction. Likewise, shipbuilding depends on scarce materials such as specialised metals and high-quality woods, which are essential for ensuring durability.

Analyse **two** reasons why shipbuilding is seen as price inelastic in supply. [6]

REFLECTION

Planning does not need to be time-consuming; keep it quick and simple, using notes or bullet points. You still need to write your answer fully, so do not spend too much time on the plan.

- How successful was your planning?
- How long did it take?
- In what ways do you think that taking the time to plan benefited you once you were writing the answer?

4

The clothing manufacturing industry is famous for its 'fast fashion', which implies that firms can rapidly increase production in response to rising demand. For example, brands can ask their designers to quickly look at current trends through social media and consumer feedback and create new ideas. Then, they can use their suppliers to quickly source affordable fabrics and materials, often using synthetic materials that are cheaper and easier to produce.

Analyse **two** reasons why clothes manufacturing is seen as price elastic in supply.

[6]

SELF-ASSESSMENT CHECKLIST

Let's revisit the Knowledge focus and Exam skills focus for this chapter. Decide how confident you are with each statement.

Now I can	Show it	Needs more work	Almost there	Confident to move on
define price elasticity of supply (PES)	Explain the term 'price elasticity of supply'.			
calculate price elasticity of supply (PES)	State the PES formula.			
draw and interpret supply curve diagrams to show different PES	Draw an inelastic supply curve and an elastic supply curve.			
interpret the significance of the PES value: perfectly inelastic, inelastic, unitary elastic, elastic, perfectly elastic	Create a number line that has the PES coefficients running from 0 to +10 and insert the classifications of inelastic and elastic onto it.			
analyse the main influences on whether supply is elastic or inelastic	Explain why agricultural goods are considered to be price inelastic in supply but manufactured goods are not.			
understand why planning my answer is necessary	Make a plan before answering your next Exam skills question.			
understand some of the connections between concepts from previous chapters.	Make a mind map of some of the connections between other chapters (not just Chapters 10 and 11).			

12 Market economic system

KNOWLEDGE FOCUS

In this chapter you will answer questions on:

- 12.1 Different economic systems
- 12.2 Market economic system
- 12.3 Arguments for and against the market economic system

EXAM SKILLS FOCUS

In this chapter you will:

- show that you understand the 'discuss' command word and answer a discuss question
- show that you understand how to read a mark scheme so that you can improve the quality of your own answers.

The command word 'discuss' means to write about issue(s) or topic(s) in depth in a structured way. It involves presenting a reasoned analysis that considers both sides of an economic argument, using relevant economic information and clear, logical reasoning to evaluate the case study at hand. Discuss questions are often associated with 6-mark and 8-mark longer answer questions.

Students often report that they do not understand why marks are awarded or not awarded for their answers. Therefore, knowing what a mark scheme looks like, and the language it uses, is an important step in becoming more familiar with understanding how to write successful answers. It also helps with self-assessment and with preparing effectively. The mark scheme for 8-mark discuss questions are level-based marking. In this approach, answers are evaluated according to specific levels of performance. Each level corresponds to a range of marks based on the quality and depth of the response.

12.1 Different economic systems

UNDERSTAND THESE TERMS

- economic system
- planned economic system
- market economic system
- mixed economic system

1   Read the statements in Table 12.1. Decide which sort of economic system – planned, market or mixed – they refer to. Complete the table.

Table 12.1: Planned, market and mixed economic systems

	Statement	Planned, market or mixed
a	The price of a loaf of bread is determined by how much consumers demand and the market supplies.	
b	Private companies produce cars but the government builds the roads.	
c	Farmers do not own land and the government decides how much rice each farm must produce annually.	
d	Government-funded public schools co-exist alongside private schools.	
e	All workers are assigned jobs by the government and wages are determined by the state.	
f	An entrepreneur starts a new hairdressing business and sets a price based on what competitors charge.	

12.2 Market economic system

≪ RECALL AND CONNECT 1 ≪

a How are the following questions likely to be answered in a market economic system?

    i   What is produced?

    ii   How is output produced?

    iii Who gets the products produced?

b In a market economic system, resources move towards those products for which demand is rising and away from those that are becoming less popular.

  Draw a demand and supply diagram that shows the demand for avocados increasing.

c Draw a PPC diagram that shows a reallocation of resources towards avocados and away from DVD players.

UNDERSTAND THESE TERMS

- public sector
- privatisation

1 Fill in the missing words using the terms in the word box.

> entrepreneurs   consumers   demand   preferences   profits
>
> incentives   penalties   costs   benefits

The market economic system is driven by the _____ of competition, which provides _____ with choice and encourages firms to meet consumer _____. Competition incentivises firms to operate efficiently by minimising _____ and responding to consumer _____. The system rewards _____ who adapt to market signals with high _____, while penalising those who fail to adjust. This combination of _____ and _____ fosters innovation and efficiency.

2 Give **two** examples of public sector businesses, and **two** examples of privately owned businesses.

3 Give **two** examples of capital-intensive industries, and **two** examples of labour-intensive industries.

12.3 Arguments for and against the market economic system

UNDERSTAND THESE TERMS

- market failure
- free rider

1 Decide whether each of the following statements about the advantages of the market economic system is true or false.

   a In the market economic system, resources adapt quickly to changes in consumer demand.

   b In the market economic system, competitive pressure reduces quality and discourages innovation.

   c In the market economic system, consumers, firms and workers have freedom of choice in what to buy, what to produce and who to work for.

   d In the market economic system, firms are rewarded even if they continue to produce goods with falling demand.

2 Explain **two** ways in which the market economic system can lead to market failure.

An 8-mark discuss question, like the one in Question 3, is level-based marked. In this approach, answers are evaluated according to specific levels of performance rather than a simple point-per-mark system. Each level corresponds to a range of marks based on the quality and depth of the response. This means that the overall quality of the response will be considered when determining which level to award. Top level answers should accurately discuss and consider two sides of an economic argument, clearly and logically analysing and evaluating economic information, issues and situations.

3

By 1989, Poland was falling behind many Western European economies, and its average wage was just $1 850. The legacy of central planning was visible in Poland's structural characteristics:

- State ownership: Most businesses were government-run, with private ownership forbidden.

- Lack of competition: Those government-run businesses did not face any competitive pressure in markets.

- Guaranteed incomes: Salaries were similar, and workers could not be fired, discouraging entrepreneurship.

- Central planning: Output targets were set by the government, regardless of consumer demand.

- Inefficient agriculture: Poland had a large, low-productivity agricultural sector with very little technological investment.

In the early 1990s, Poland implemented large-scale economic reforms in order to support its transition to a market economic system.

Discuss whether there are disadvantages of a market economy system. [8]

REFLECTION

Reflect on your ability to answer discuss questions. Remember: these are marked using a level-based system, so the overall quality of your reasoning, structure and balance is important.

- Did you evaluate both sides of the argument?
- Did you present those arguments with clear and logical chains of reasoning?
- Did you use the information in the case study?

Also, think about how familiarising yourself with mark schemes helped you understand how answers are graded and how this awareness can improve the quality and structure of your responses.

SELF-ASSESSMENT CHECKLIST

Let's revisit the Knowledge focus and Exam skills focus for this chapter. Decide how confident you are with each statement.

Now I can	Show it	Needs more work	Almost there	Confident to move on
define a market economic system	Explain the difference between a market economic system and a planned economic system.			
discuss the arguments for and against the market economic system	List **three** advantages and **three** disadvantages of the market economic system.			
understand the 'discuss' command word and answer a discuss question	Answer the question: Discuss the advantages of the market economic system.			
understand how to read a mark scheme so that you can improve the quality of your own answers.	Find a mark scheme for the specimen papers or a past paper. Read it and summarise your findings.			

13 Market failure

KNOWLEDGE FOCUS

In this chapter you will answer questions on:

- 13.1 What is market failure?
- 13.2 Causes and consequences of market failure
- 13.3 Other consequences of market failure

EXAM SKILLS FOCUS

In this chapter you will:

- explore the use of flashcards to help you remember key terms
- show that you can understand the level of depth required.

Economics is a subject full of new vocabulary, and Chapter 13, in particular, has a lot of new key terms to learn. Flashcards are a great tool to help you remember these terms effectively; they allow you to test yourself on definitions, concepts and examples. By regularly reviewing your flashcards, you can improve your recall of important economic terms as well as identifying which areas you need to focus on more.

You should, by now, be becoming familiar with the depth you go need to go into in your answers. There are two guides to this. One is the command words used, and the other is the number of marks awarded. You should, for example, provide more depth on an analyse question with 6 marks than an explain question with 4 marks.

13.1 What is market failure?

≪ RECALL AND CONNECT 1 ≪

a What is the market economic system?

b How does the price mechanism (in the market economic system) work to allocate resources?

1 Read the scenarios in Table 13.1. For each one, decide whether it represents an example of market failure or not. Complete the table.

Table 13.1: Market failure

	Scenario	Is it market failure?
a	A technology firm refuses to invest in renewable energy research because it is more profitable to continue producing non-renewable energy sources.	
b	A factory reduces its production of electric cars because consumer demand is low.	
c	A public park is left to deteriorate because there is no incentive for private companies to maintain it.	
d	An oil company invests heavily in developing a new oil field in an area known for its outstanding natural wildlife	
e	The price of ice cream increases over the summer months and temperatures rise.	

13.2 Causes and consequences of market failure

UNDERSTAND THESE TERMS

- third parties
- social benefits
- social costs
- private benefits
- private costs
- external benefits
- external costs

- information failure
- merit goods
- demerit goods
- public good
- private good
- monopoly
- price fixing

REFLECTION

There are a lot of new terms to remember from this chapter. Make flashcards for the words in the Understand these terms box.

Flashcards are a great way to revise because they help break down complex terms into simple definitions, making it easier to test yourself and reinforce your memory through active recall.

- How could you use flashcards to memorise key examples of market failure?
- Which terms related to market failure do you find most challenging, and how can flashcards help you focus on these?

1   Read the statements in Table 13.2 and decide which market failure in the word box is being described. The first one has been done for you.

public goods	merit goods	demerit goods	high external costs
	information failure	monopoly power	price fixing

Table 13.2: Types of market failure

	Statement	Type of market failure
a	The total costs to society outweigh the benefits.	High external costs
b	A non-rival and non-excludable good, which cannot be provided by private firms due to free riders.	
c	It is more harmful to consumers than they realise.	
d	There is one firm in the market and this leads to high prices for consumers, as they have no alternative.	
e	The seller encourages the buyer to upgrade their product even though there is little benefit to be gained.	
f	The consumption of this good is much more beneficial to the buyer than they realise.	
g	A handful of large firms in the market collude with each other to keep price above the market equilibrium.	

2   A large firm produces industrial chemicals such as dyes, solvents and cleaning solutions in a large factory located in a rural area near a river. The firm disposes of its chemical waste directly into the river, causing significant harm to wildlife and making the water unsafe for human consumption.

a From this scenario, identify the following:

    i private costs

    ii external costs

    iii social costs.

b Explain how the scenario leads to market failure.

3

A large healthcare company operates a state-of-the-art hospital in an urban area, offering critical care and advanced medical treatments. The facility enhances the quality of life, increases life expectancy and reduces the prevalence of disease in the local population. Additionally, its focus on public health initiatives, for example, vaccination drives and health education, contributes to a more productive society.

a From this scenario, identify the following:

    i private benefits

    ii external benefits

    iii social benefits.

b Explain how the scenario leads to market failure.

4

UK government expenditure on street lighting exceeded £1bn ($1.35bn) for the first time during the 2023/24 fiscal year. To many, this is an extraordinary amount of money – especially at a time when the government is cutting subsidies to support older people with heating costs and reducing healthcare benefits. Nevertheless, some economists believe that there is no other option for them, attempting to have street lights provided by private firms would simply result in market failure.

a Define 'market failure'. [2]

b State, using an example from the text, what is meant by the term 'opportunity cost'. [2]

c Explain the economists' belief that 'street lights provided by private firms would simply result in market failure'. [4]

REFLECTION

In Question 4, there were two 2-mark questions and one 4-mark question.

- Were you confident with the depth you need to go into for your answers to each of the questions?
- Did you spend a proportionate amount of time on each type of question?

Question 5 is a 6-mark analyse question. Remember to adjust your approach for this type of question, as it differs from the previous question.

5

In Country A, a monopoly in the telecommunications sector controls the market for internet services. The company charges excessively high prices for its services, leaving many consumers unable to afford reliable internet access. In addition, the monopoly misleads consumers by falsely advertising faster speeds and better service than it provides. Unfortunately, customers have no option but to accept the poor quality service and inflated prices.

Analyse **two** consequences of the market failures being described in the text.   [6]

13.3 Other consequences of market failure

≪ RECALL AND CONNECT 2 ≪

a Look at the PPC diagram in Figure 13.1. Which point will lead to greater long-term growth and why?

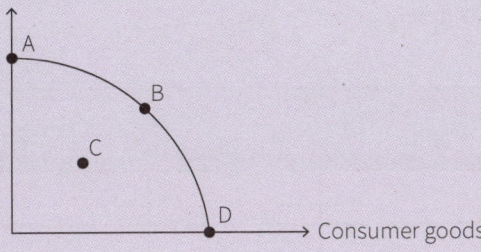

Figure 13.1: PPC with different points of resource allocation

b How would you adapt the PPC diagram to show the impact of having more capital goods?

1 Complete Table 13.3 by sorting the following examples into the table, to show whether they are examples of geographical immobility or occupational immobility:

- A worker in manufacturing has been completing the same task for 20 years
- Someone without the relevant qualifications to work in a different field
- High cost of moving to another region
- A person has caregiving responsibilities that prevent them from relocating

Table 13.3: Geographical and occupational immobility

Geographical immobility	Occupational immobility

2 Explain why geographical immobility of labour can lead to market failure.

3 Complete the following text using the terms in the word box.

> investment   private   profits   resources   capital   government

Short-termism is the idea that _____ sector firms are more interested in making quick _____ than planning for the future. Such a short-sighted approach can result in a lack of _____, and not enough _____ are allocated to producing _____ goods. As a result, a _____ may have to stimulate private sector investment.

Text taken from Grant: Economics for Cambridge IGCSE™ and O Level, Coursebook

SELF-ASSESSMENT CHECKLIST

Let's revisit the Knowledge focus and Exam skills focus for this chapter. Decide how confident you are with each statement.

Now I can	Show it	Needs more work	Almost there	Confident to move on
define market failure	Define market failure.			
explain key terms associated with market failure: public goods, merit goods, demerit goods, private benefits, external benefits, social benefits, private costs, external costs, social costs, monopoly	Create some flashcards with definitions of each of the key terms on them.			
explain the causes of market failure relating to public goods, merit goods, demerit goods, external costs, external benefits and abuse of monopoly power	Write a brief description of each of the causes of market failure and identify a real-world example.			
analyse the consequences of market failure	Answer the question: Explain **two** consequences of demerit goods.			

CONTINUED

Now I can	Show it	Needs more work	Almost there	Confident to move on
explore the use of flashcards to help remember key terms	Create some flashcards based on content from this chapter. Use them to revise at the completion of this topic.			
understand the level of depth required.	Explain to another student the difference in depth required for 2-mark, 4-mark and 6-mark questions.			

14 Mixed economic system

KNOWLEDGE FOCUS

In this chapter you will answer questions on:

- 14.1 What is a mixed economic system?
- 14.2 Arguments for and against the mixed economic system
- 14.3 Government intervention to address market failure

EXAM SKILLS FOCUS

In this chapter you will:

- show that you understand the 'identify' command word and answer an identify question
- show that you can find key information a text.

The command word 'identify' simply means to name, select or recognise key information. Identify questions are associated with short answer questions, typically worth 2 marks. Your response should be short and concise.

You will need to read a lot of text both while revising for the exam and when taking the exam itself. Economics includes both qualitative data and quantitative data. Within the information text in the exam paper, there will be useful evidence (and clues) that can help support your main chains of analysis. Ensure you always have a highlighter pen with you to identify key words.

14.1 What is a mixed economic system?

≪ RECALL AND CONNECT 1 ≪

Read the following text:

> The fundamental problem of scarcity requires choices to be made. The choices that are made are determined by a country's economic system. The economic system identifies the means by which decisions can be made relating to the three resource allocation questions.

Now consider some of the key terms from that text.

a State what is meant by the term 'scarcity'.

b Explain how an opportunity cost arises when choices are made.

c Identify the three resource allocation questions.

1 Complete the following sentence:

A mixed economic system is an economy in which …

2 Describe the main features of a mixed economy.

14.2 Arguments for and against the mixed economic system

≪ RECALL AND CONNECT 2 ≪

a Using examples, define a merit good.

b Using examples, define a demerit good.

c Using examples, define a public good.

1 Read through the scenario text and identify **three** advantages and **three** disadvantages of mixed economic systems. You should highlight key passages. Then, complete Table 14.1 by summarising each point in just a few words.

It is argued that a mixed economic system allows the government to maintain essential services that benefit society, even if those services would be unprofitable for the private sector. A mixed economic system encourages the consumption of merit goods through subsidies and discourages the consumption of demerit goods via taxes or regulation. Public goods such as street lighting are provided, and vulnerable groups are supported with basic necessities and income redistribution.

However, government intervention can lead to inefficiency and an even greater misallocation of resources. For example, taxes and subsidies may distort prices, and public sector monopoly power in some areas might reduce innovation and competition. In addition, vulnerable groups may over-rely on government support, discouraging work.

Table 14.1: Advantages and disadvantages of mixed economic systems

Advantage	Disadvantage
a	b
c	d
e	f

REFLECTION

Using a pen to highlight key words is a highly effective strategy. You may want to use facts, figures or quotes from a text to support your response. Alternatively, as seen in Question 1, it could be a simple matter of highlighting important ideas, which you can then summarise.

- How might highlighting key points and summarising help you improve the clarity of your analysis during an exam?

14.3 Government intervention to address market failure

UNDERSTAND THESE TERMS

- nationalisation (nationalise)
- quota
- subsidy

1   a   Draw a maximum price diagram.

b   Identify the change in price and the shortage that is created.

2   a   Draw a minimum price diagram.

b   Identify the change in price and the surplus that is created.

3   a   Draw a subsidy diagram in the case of elastic demand.

b   Identify the change in price and change in quantity demanded.

4   a   Draw a subsidy diagram in the case of inelastic demand.

b   Identify the change in price and change in quantity demanded.

5   Complete Table 14.2, which focusses on some of the advantages and disadvantages of maximum prices. Fill in the blanks (either Advantage/disadvantage).

Table 14.2: Advantages and disadvantages of maximum prices

Advantage/disadvantage	Explanation
Increase affordability	a
b	Prevents producers from charging excessively high prices in markets where consumers have limited options, for example, monopolies.
Leads to an informal market	c
d	If the price is set below the equilibrium, demand may exceed supply.

6   Create your own table to explain some of the advantages and disadvantages of minimum prices.

7   Complete Table 14.3, which focusses on some of the advantages and disadvantages of subsidies. Fill in the blanks (either Advantage/disadvantage).

Table 14.3: Advantages and disadvantages of subsidies

Advantage/disadvantage	Explanation
Supports merit goods	a
b	They ensure that essential goods and services, for example, food, are affordable for low-income households.
High cost	c
d	Artificially low prices can lead to overconsumption or inefficiency, if they support uncompetitive firms.

8   Create your own table to explain some of the advantages and disadvantages of indirect taxes.

9   Table 14.4 explains how government interventions affect consumers, firms and government.

Complete Table 14.4, selecting which policy is being described from the terms in the word box.

> privatisation   nationalisation   quotas
>
> regulation   direct provision of goods and services

Table 14.4: Effects of government interventions on consumers, firms and government

Policy	Consumers	Firms	Government
a	Keeps prices low	Increases the costs of compliance	High administrative burden
b	Lower prices	Increases competition	Gains revenue from asset sales
c	Affordable prices	Less competition	Control of industry
d	Ensures availability at low prices	Reduces market opportunities	High government spending
e	Higher prices	Restricts output	Reduces waste and supports environmental sustainability

10

> Venezuela, a country in South America, has long struggled with incredibly high price increases (known as hyperinflation). In a bid to prevent food prices from rising further and to protect essential goods for low-income households, the government has a history of implementing maximum price controls on items like eggs, rice and even certain meats. Over the past three decades, government policies like this have played a significant role in shaping food access for Venezuela's population.

a   Identify **two** reasons a government might **not** want to use a subsidy to lower food prices.   [2]

b   Discuss the advantages and disadvantages of the Venezuelan government using maximum prices to address market failure.   [8]

REFLECTION

The command word 'identify' simply means to name, select or recognise key information. For identify questions, your response should be brief and direct, focusing on providing the key points without additional explanation. In Question 10(a), when you were asked to identify reasons, you needed to consider specific factors that might prevent a government from using subsidies.

- How can repetitive practice with this type of question help you to become more efficient in recognising and pinpointing relevant information quickly?

SELF-ASSESSMENT CHECKLIST

Let's revisit the Knowledge focus and Exam skills focus for this chapter. Decide how confident you are with each statement.

Now I can	Show it	Needs more work	Almost there	Confident to move on
define a mixed economic system and discuss its advantages and disadvantages	Explain the disadvantages of a market economic system and a planned economy.			
define a maximum price, draw and interpret a diagram showing a maximum price and analyse its advantages and disadvantages	Explain the purpose of a maximum price policy to another student.			
define a minimum price, draw and interpret a diagram showing a minimum price and analyse its advantages and disadvantages	Draw a diagram to show the impact of a minimum price policy.			
define indirect taxation, draw and interpret a diagram showing the effect of an indirect tax and analyse its advantages and disadvantages	State **three** advantages of using indirect taxes.			
define a subsidy and draw and interpret a diagram showing the effect of a subsidy	Draw a diagram to show the impact of a subsidy.			

CONTINUED

Now I can	Show it	Needs more work	Almost there	Confident to move on
define regulation and analyse its advantages and disadvantages	List **two** disadvantages of regulation in markets.			
define privatisation and analyse its advantages and disadvantages	Find an example of privatisation in your own country. List **two** advantages of privatisation.			
define nationalisation and analyse its advantages and disadvantages	Find an example of nationalisation in your own country. List **two** advantages of nationalisation.			
define direct provision of goods and services and analyse its advantages and disadvantages	List **three** goods/services that are directly provided in your country.			
define quotas and analyse their advantages and disadvantages	Explain the purpose of a quota to another student.			
understand the 'identify' command word and can answer an identify question	Complete two identify questions from past papers.			
find key information in a text.	Find a news article about recent economic events. Highlight the key information from the article and then summarise the article to another student.			

Exam practice 2

This section contains practice questions that will draw together your knowledge on a range of topics you have covered up to this point and will help you prepare for your assessment.

The following question has example student responses and commentaries provided. For each part of the question, work through the question first, then compare your answer to the example student response and commentary.

Question 1

Thailand is a development success story, having rapidly transformed from an economy dominated by agriculture into a more market-based system focused on secondary sector industries and exports. For example, Thailand is currently one of the world's largest exporters of toothpaste, a product with inelastic demand. Since the start of the 21st century, Thailand's population has grown significantly, increasing from 63 million to 73 million people. This population growth, combined with rising incomes and urbanisation, has influenced both production and consumption patterns in the country.

a Identify **two** influences on price elasticity of demand. [2]

Example student response	Commentary
Whether the good is a necessity. Whether the price of the good is a low percentage of income.	AO1 Knowledge and understanding This question assesses AO1 Knowledge and understanding only and so short, succinct sentences are appropriate. This is a good answer, although other responses would have been suitable too, such as 'number of substitute goods' or 'brand loyalty'.

b Explain what a merit good is and why toothpaste might be considered a merit good. [4]

Example student response	Commentary
A merit good is a product that the government considers consumers do not fully appreciate the benefits of, and so which will be under-consumed if left to market forces.	AO1 Knowledge and understanding This short answer contains all essential information about what a merit good is, so shows good knowledge and understanding. AO2 Analysis However, the question also asks the student to explain why toothpaste should be considered a merit good. This requires application. The student has not completed this part of the question and is unlikely to gain any AO2 Analysis marks.

c   Analyse, using a demand and supply diagram, how an increase in population would affect the market for toothpaste.   [6]

Example student response	Commentary
If the population rises then the demand for toothpaste will increase, shifting the demand curve to the right. This is because most people buy toothpaste as a necessity, and so if there are more people in Thailand then there are more consumers in the toothpaste market. As population rises, the quantity demanded rises. 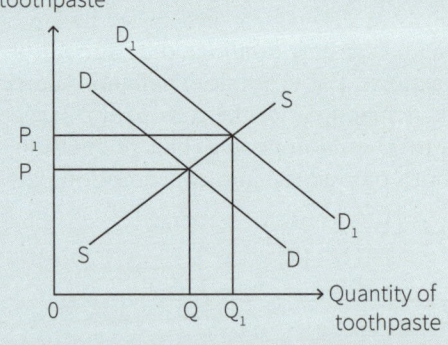	AO1 Knowledge and understanding The student has drawn a well-labelled market equilibrium diagram. AO2 Analysis The student has shifted the demand curve on the diagram (correctly). The student uses excellent terminology to explain the initial shift in demand, followed by a clear explanation of the reasons for this, with reference to the case study about population increase. The student correctly identifies that sales have increased but perhaps could have also mentioned the price change.

d   Discuss whether consumers will benefit from a market economic system providing consumer goods such as toothpaste.   [8]

Example student response	Commentary
A market economic system is an economic system where supply and demand determine the allocation of resources. One benefit of a market economy is that competition drives efficiency and innovation in producing consumer goods like toothpaste. For example, in the USA, various toothpaste brands compete by offering better whitening formulas and cavity protection, encouraging product improvements. In addition, consumers can select from different toothpaste options based on their needs. However, market economies can lead to inequalities in access to essential goods. Lower-income individuals may struggle to afford high-quality toothpaste, as firms prioritise profit over low prices.	AO1 Knowledge and understanding and AO2 Analysis The answer shows a clear understanding of what the market economic system is. It also outlines two benefits. Both points could have been developed more. The student could write more about why competition drives efficiency and innovation. In addition, the student could write more about the different needs of consumers. The question does not say that the answer needs to be restricted to a discussion about toothpaste; other examples of consumer goods could have been used. AO3 Evaluation The evaluative section is too brief. It also needs developing in terms of depth and range. First, the student should explain why firms prioritise profit. Second, the student should try to present an additional aspect of evaluation that offers a distinct view. For example, a merit good like toothpaste is likely to be under-consumed in a market economy.

Use the guidance in the commentaries in this section to help you as you answer Question 2.

Question 2

Write an improved answer to Question 1(d).

The following question has example student responses and commentaries provided. For each part of the question, work through the question first, then compare your answer to the example student response and commentary.

Question 3

Cotton is a primary sector product with a total global export value of just over $20 billion. While its global value may seem small, cotton is an important source of income and employment for some countries. In Benin, for example, cotton accounts for a quarter of all exports. By contrast, cotton represents just 0.2% of Turkey's exports, despite Turkey being one of the world's largest cotton producers. The Turkish government uses subsidies to support its cotton industry. These subsidies help to influence the price elasticity of supply and to reduce the price for buyers. These subsidies are partially funded through indirect taxes – such as the Special Consumption Tax (SCT) – which is imposed on fuel and natural gas.

a   Identify **two** influences on price elasticity of supply.   [2]

Example student response	Commentary
Whether the good can be stored or not.	AO1 Knowledge and understanding
Whether the good takes a long time to grow.	This question assesses AO1 Knowledge and understanding only.
	The second answer is quite specific to agricultural goods, and it may have been better to write 'length of time to produce' (rather than 'grow').

b   Explain the role of buyers and the role of sellers in the cotton market.   [4]

Example student response	Commentary
Buyers play a key role in the market by choosing between competing options, such as selecting cotton products based on factors like quality and price. They create demand for a product by choosing how to spend their money.	AO1 Knowledge and understanding The role of a buyer is correctly identified. The role of a seller is mentioned but lacks detail.
Sellers simply sell their products to buyers.	AO2 Analysis The points about buyers are developed sufficiently and there is some alignment with the case study about cotton. Further detail on the role of sellers would improve the answer.

c   Analyse, using a demand and supply diagram, how the price of cotton might be affected by a subsidy. **[6]**

Example student response	Commentary
Subsidies should lead to a decrease in price. This is because it is now cheaper to make cotton. The firm passes on the cost saving and consumers have a lower price to pay. 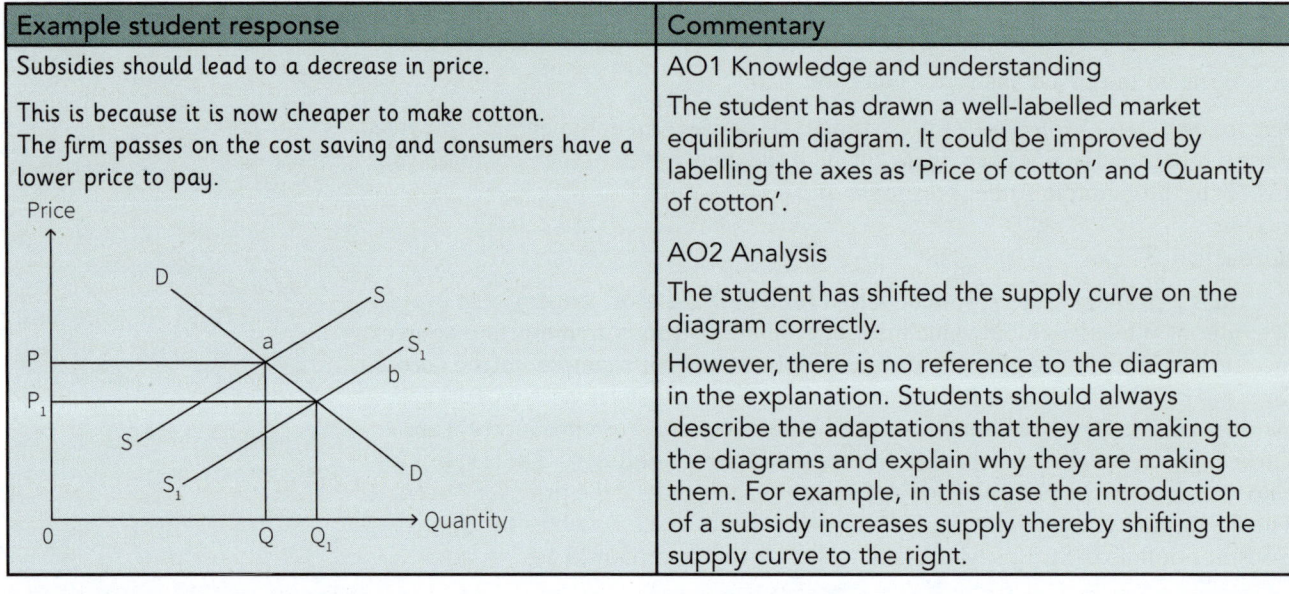	AO1 Knowledge and understanding The student has drawn a well-labelled market equilibrium diagram. It could be improved by labelling the axes as 'Price of cotton' and 'Quantity of cotton'. AO2 Analysis The student has shifted the supply curve on the diagram correctly. However, there is no reference to the diagram in the explanation. Students should always describe the adaptations that they are making to the diagrams and explain why they are making them. For example, in this case the introduction of a subsidy increases supply thereby shifting the supply curve to the right.

d   Discuss whether or not the Turkish government should use an indirect tax on fuel and natural gas to raise tax revenue. **[8]**

Example student response	Commentary
An indirect tax is a tax imposed on goods and services, which is paid by producers but passed on to consumers through higher prices. One advantage of taxing gas is that it provides the Turkish government with a stable source of revenue, helping fund subsidies on cotton but also public goods like street lights. Street lights cannot be provided by the free market due to the free-rider problem, so government intervention is required. Increased tax revenue can also be used to improve infrastructure projects and merit goods like healthcare. However, an indirect tax on fuel and natural gas can lead to higher costs for consumers, making transport and heating more expensive. This can disproportionately affect lower-income households. Another advantage is that higher natural gas prices may encourage people to use energy more efficiently. This means that they might use less gas. This leads to a shift in the demand curve for natural gas and less will be consumed. However, if natural gas demand is inelastic, consumers may not significantly reduce consumption.	AO1 Knowledge and understanding and AO2 Analysis The answer shows a clear understanding of what indirect taxes are. The student did not use an indirect tax diagram. This may have been useful to illustrate their points. In the first paragraph, the student spends too much time talking about public goods and other areas that the government could spend their money on. This is not the topic of the question. The question asks about the advantages and disadvantages of imposing an indirect tax, rather than where should the government spend its money. AO3 Evaluation The evaluative section is too brief. The two sections only amount to three sentences. The student must develop these points more.

Use the guidance in the commentaries in this section to help you as you answer Question 4.

Question 4

Write an improved answer to Question 3(d).

> Unit 3

Microeconomic decision makers

15 Money and banking

KNOWLEDGE FOCUS

In this chapter you will answer questions on:

- 15.1 Money
- 15.2 Banking

EXAM SKILLS FOCUS

In this chapter you will:

- show that you can recognise the progress you are making
- learn to reduce test anxiety by taking part in revision with others.

As you work through this course, your skills and understanding will grow as you apply familiar concepts to new scenarios, even if progress feels uneven at times. Improvement comes with consistent practice – just as athletes perfect their skills through repetition, like footballers practising penalties or dancers refining their routines. This consistent effort helps build confidence over time.

One way to reduce test anxiety is to make revision more engaging. Studying with a partner can make the process both more enjoyable and more effective than revising alone.

15.1 Money

UNDERSTAND THESE TERMS

- money
- central bank
- commercial bank

1   Complete Table 15.1 to indicate which of the following is an accepted form of money.

Table 15.1: Forms of money

	Form of money?	Yes or no
a	Coins	
b	Company shares	
c	Bank deposits	
d	Electronic money	
e	Banknotes	
f	Gift cards	
g	Loyalty points	

2   List **three** characteristics of money.

3   List **three** functions of money.

When you answer Question 4, make sure that you comment on the data from the scenario in your answer.

4

> In recent years, large retail firms such as Amazon and Walmart have increased their use of digital gift cards. These cards can be used like money within that company, but they cannot be redeemed elsewhere. In late 2024, during the holiday season, nearly two-thirds of US shoppers reported using digital gift cards as part of their regular spending.

Explain **two** functions of money that digital gift cards fulfil.   [4]

REFLECTION

This chapter has a lot of new content. Therefore, it will be important to consolidate your understanding effectively. One way to do this is revising with other students – perhaps even forming a study group. Think about working through the next section (Section 15.2) together with another student and then asking each other the questions.

- Is there another student you can work with?
- What are the best sorts of activities you could be doing together?

15.2 Banking

UNDERSTAND THESE TERMS

- central bank
- commercial bank
- interest
- liquidity

1   Complete Table 15.2. Add a description to each of the functions of commercial banks. The first one has been done for you.

Table 15.2: Functions of commercial banks

	Function	Description
a	Accepting deposits	Provides a safe place for customers to store their money
b	Providing loans	
c	Enabling payments	
d	Offering credit services	

2   Explain why a commercial bank charges a higher interest rate to borrowers than savers.

3   Complete Table 15.3. Add a description to each of the functions of central banks. The first one has been done for you.

Table 15.3: Functions of central banks

	Function	Description
a	Banker to the government	Collects tax revenue into government accounts and makes payments for government expenditures
b	Monetary policy	
c	Lender of last resort	
d	Issues bank notes	
e	Controls the banking system	

4   Explain what the 'independence of central banks' means and why it is advantageous.

5

Itaú Unibanco is the one of the largest commercial banks in Brazil. The bank made large profits in the third quarter of 2024 and, as a result, they announced that they would look to make more loans in 2025. Itaú has been careful about who it lends to, cutting back on risky loans. This strategy has helped lower the number of people falling behind on payments. Analysts think this cautious approach will help the bank grow even more in the future.

a   State what is meant by a commercial bank. [2]

b   Explain **two** important roles of commercial banks like Itaú Unibanco to the Brazilian economy. [4]

REFLECTION

Remember to make time to recognise and celebrate the progress you are making as you work through this course. Hopefully, in this chapter the structure of the questions is familiar, even if the content was different.

- How has your ability to approach different types of questions improved as you have progressed through this chapter?
- Can you identify any specific strategies that helped you?

SELF-ASSESSMENT CHECKLIST

Let's revisit the Knowledge focus and Exam skills focus for this chapter. Decide how confident you are with each statement.

Now I can	Show it	Needs more work	Almost there	Confident to move on
explain the forms, functions and characteristics of money	List **three** forms, **three** functions and **three** characteristics of money.			
analyse the role and importance of central banks and commercial banks	List **three** roles of a commercial bank and **three** roles of a central bank.			
recognise the progress I am making	Keep a diary of all the work you have completed so far.			
learn to reduce test anxiety by taking part in revision with others.	Create a revision activity that is enjoyable for another student to complete.			

16 Households

KNOWLEDGE FOCUS

In this chapter you will answer questions on:

- 16.1 Influences on households' spending
- 16.2 Influences on households' saving
- 16.3 Influences on households' borrowing

EXAM SKILLS FOCUS

In this chapter you will:

- show that you can present knowledge clearly and coherently
- have an opportunity to write answers to a series of questions under time limits.

It is important to write clearly and use appropriate terms in your answers. Each point should flow logically from the previous one. In longer answer questions, it is crucial to explain the points you make rather than simply stating them. Always remember to demonstrate your reasoning. The activities in this chapter are designed to help you develop these skills.

Exams are time-limited. Therefore, at some point, every student needs to practise writing their answers under fixed timed limits. In the first few attempts, you should monitor the time you take and, if necessary, looks for ways you can write more efficiently in the future.

16.1 Influences on households' spending

UNDERSTAND THESE TERMS

- consumer durables
- wealth
- disposable income
- rate of interest

1   What is a normal good and what is an inferior good?

2   Explain what happens to the demand for normal goods and inferior goods when income falls.

3   Draw a demand curve diagram for an inferior good when incomes rise.

4   List **three** main items of expenditure for households.

5   List **three** examples of consumer durables.

6   Decide whether each of the following statements is true or false.

   a   High-income households tend to spend a higher proportion of their income, and total expenditure, on food and clothing than low-income households.

   b   High-income households spend more, both in total and as a proportion of their income, on luxury items, consumer durables, entertainment and services, than low-income households.

   c   Households without children are likely to spend a higher proportion of their income on leisure activities and eating out than households with children.

   d   Younger people often spend a lower proportion of their income on clothing and entertainment than older people.

7   Consider the scenarios in Table 16.1. Decide whether each one will cause households' spending to rise or fall.

Table 16.1: Changes in households' spending

	Scenario	Households' spending rise or fall
a	Rate of interest decreases	
b	People feel more optimistic about their future career prospects and income	
c	Income tax rates rise	
d	Greater availability of credit	

Try to write the answer to Question 8 under timed conditions. If you can, aim to write your answer in 12 minutes.

8

> In the winter months of 2024, Japan's household spending fell by 1.3% compared to the year before. Reports suggest that spending trends remained weak due to rising prices and warm weather, which reduced demand for seasonal items. However, economists were optimistic. Wage growth data was showing that higher wages in 2025 could eventually encourage consumers to spend more, while the central bank (the Bank of Japan) was happy to keep interest rates at just 0.25%.

Discuss whether household spending in Japan is likely to increase in the near future.

[8]

REFLECTION

If you did not complete your answer in the 12-minute limit, then you should consider strategies that might enable you to achieve this.

- How can you write more efficiently?
- Do you remember that 8-mark discuss questions are level marked (see Chapter 12)? If not, you could look back at the guidance in Chapter 12.

16.2 Influences on households' saving

« RECALL AND CONNECT 1 «

a   List **two** functions of a commercial bank.

b   What is the rate of interest?

1   List **three** reasons to save.

2   List **three** ways to encourage saving.

3   Explain how the factors in Table 16.2 might affect households' savings.

Table 16.2: Factors that affect households' saving

	Factor	Explanation
a	Interest rates rise	
b	Consumer confidence rises	
c	National income rises	

4

> Savings rates in Asia are typically higher than those in other regions. For example, Singapore's savings rate is often above 40%, Japan's is around 30% and the Philippines's is about 25%. Part of the reason for this is culture, and part of it is government-mandated saving programmes. By contrast, the USA has a low savings rate. A large portion of US consumer spending is driven by credit. Many Americans also accumulate wealth through housing or stock investments instead of saving cash, and are supported by a larger social safety net.

a State what is meant by the term 'savings rate'. [2]

b Explain **two** influences on household savings in the USA. [4]

16.3 Influences on households' borrowing

UNDERSTAND THIS TERM

- mortgage

To give a strong explanation, it is important to include a reason to support your point. A good way to do this is by using the word 'because' to show cause and effect. Use the task below to practise developing deeper explanations.

1 Complete these sentences:

a Rate of interest. A rise in the rate of interest is likely to reduce borrowing because …

b Confidence. The more confident people are about the future, the more likely they are to borrow money. This is because …

c Age. People in their 20s and 30s may borrow relatively large amounts. This is because …

d Income. Low-income households may sometimes have a greater need to borrow; however, they are likely to experience greater difficulty in getting a loan. This is because …

REFLECTION

Try to incorporate more exercises like the one in Question 1 into your revision. It will force you remember not just what happens but why it happens.

- How can explaining the reasons behind key concepts improve your understanding of the material?

2

Japan's borrowing trends are influenced by its ageing population, cultural attitudes and monetary policy. Despite extremely low or even negative interest rates, borrowing has slowed because Japanese households are traditionally cautious with debt, preferring to save. With nearly 30% of the population over 65, Japan faces a tricky puzzle in trying to stimulate household spending.

Analyse the relationship between an ageing population and household borrowing in Japan. **[4]**

REFLECTION

At the start of the chapter, it was noted that exams are time-limited and therefore – at some point – every student needs to practise writing their answers under fixed timed limits.

- Did you put yourself under timed constraints when answering Question 2? If so, how did it go?

You do not need to complete every assignment under timed conditions – sometimes it is better to take the time to think carefully about your structure and whether or not you have fulfilled all of the marking criteria. However, timed practice should be a key part of your revision.

- How will you ensure that timed practice becomes a regular part of your exam preparation?

SELF-ASSESSMENT CHECKLIST

Let's revisit the Knowledge focus and Exam skills focus for this chapter. Decide how confident you are with each statement.

Now I can	Show it	Needs more work	Almost there	Confident to move on
analyse the influences on households' spending, saving and borrowing	List **three** influences that affect households' spending, **three** influences on households' saving and **three** influences on households' borrowing.			
present knowledge clearly and coherently	Produce a brief plan for the question: Discuss what is the most important factor influencing Japan's high household saving rate. **[8]**			
have an opportunity to write answers to a series of questions under time limits.	Complete a full past paper question under timed conditions. Reflect on ways to write more efficiently.			

17 Workers

KNOWLEDGE FOCUS

In this chapter you will answer questions on:

- 17.1 Factors affecting an individual's choice of occupation
- 17.2 Wage determination and the reasons for differences in wages
- 17.3 Effects of changes in demand and supply in the labour market
- 17.4 Mobility of labour
- 17.5 Division of labour

EXAM SKILLS FOCUS

In this chapter you will:

- show that you can interpret information in tables
- show that you can reduce test anxiety by including breaks in your revision.

A wide variety of information can be provided in tables. These tables may appear in multiple-choice questions in Paper 1 – Multiple Choice or in longer-form questions in Paper 2 – Structured Questions. It is important to check carefully what the headings for the columns and rows are showing. If a table is used, then it is likely that the table is showing you something that could be useful for your answer.

It is normal to get anxious over performance and progress. One reason this happens is because you get tired. It is important that you build breaks into your work schedule. Quite often, having a break and then coming back to a question when you are feeling fresher can help you think more clearly.

17.1 Factors affecting an individual's choice of occupation

≪ RECALL AND CONNECT 1 ≪

a   What does the term 'reward to a factor of production' mean?

b   What is the reward for labour?

c   List **three** labour-intensive industries.

UNDERSTAND THESE TERMS

- earnings
- wage rate

1   Identify the type of wage factor based on its description in Table 17.1.

| commission | wages | overtime | bonuses |

Table 17.1: Wage factors

	Wage factor	Description
a		Payment earned for work or services, typically paid on a daily or weekly basis
b		Paid to the workers who work longer hours than the standard working week
c		An extra payment, often paid to workers who produce as a reward for finishing a project ahead of time, meeting a specific sales target or securing a profitable contract
d		A payment often given to salespeople to reward them for the quantity of goods or services that they sell

2   How is the term 'earnings' related to the forms of payment in Table 17.1?

3   Assume that earnings stay constant. List **three** non-wage factors that would influence an individual's choice of occupation.

17.2 Wage determination and the reasons for differences in wages

UNDERSTAND THESE TERMS

- wage differential
- trade union
- collective bargaining
- industrial action
- strike
- national minimum wage (NMW)

1 Complete Table 17.2. You should use brief descriptions to fill in the missing details. Two entries have been provided for you.

Table 17.2: Reasons for differences in wages

	Brain surgeon	Miner
Qualifications required	High	a
Training time	b	c
Industry sector	d	Primary
Number of available individuals	e	f
Essential or non-essential product	g	h

2 Complete the following explanation of why brain surgeons get paid more than miners. Use your answers in Table 17.2 to fill in the missing words.

The supply of brain surgeons is _____ relative to the demand for

their services. This is due to the _____ level of qualifications required,

including advanced medical degrees. The training time is _____,

often taking over a decade to complete. The number of available individuals is

_____, but brain surgery is considered an _____ service, as it

addresses critical health needs.

The supply of miners is _____ relative to the demand for their services.

This is because the qualifications required are _____, usually requiring

no formal education. The training time is _____, typically involving

a few weeks of on-the-job training. The number of available individuals is

_____, but mining is often considered a _____ service since many of the materials obtained through mining, such as metals and minerals, can be substituted or recycled.

3 Draw a minimum wage diagram.

4 Explain the impact of a minimum wage on wages and the quantity of workers demanded.

5

Table 17.3: Selected data from South Korea, by gender

	Men	Women
Literacy rate (%)	99.2	98.4
Mean years in education (years)	13.1	12.0
Labour force participation (%)	79.0	56.0
Trade union membership (%)	11.6	11.6

South Korea's gender wage gap is one of the largest among high-income countries. On average, women earn only about 69% of men's wages. The argument is often made that the gender wage gap cannot solely be explained by differences in education or literacy. For example, caregiving responsibilities in South Korea often fall on women. This is a cultural norm and it includes caregiving for the elderly (ageing population) as well as children.

Analyse, using the table, **two** likely reasons for the differences in wages between men and women in South Korea. [6]

REFLECTION

Now that you have seen a table of data used in the context of a question, reflect on how well you were able to integrate the data into your response.

- Did you enhance the depth and accuracy of your economic arguments by using the data from the table?

17.3 Effects of changes in demand and supply in the labour market

≪ RECALL AND CONNECT 2 ≪

a List **three** factors that would shift the demand curve for melons.

b List **three** factors that would shift the supply curve for melons.

c Explain the impact on price if there is relatively small rightwards shift in demand at the same time as a large increase in supply due to a bumper harvest.

UNDERSTAND THIS TERM

- mobility of labour

1 Complete Table 17.4. For each of the following scenarios, decide whether the demand curve for labour or the supply curve for labour is shifting and determine what the impact on wages is. The first row has been completed for you.

Table 17.4: Impact of shifts in supply and demand curves for labour

	Scenario	Demand or supply	Wage rise or fall
a	A rise in labour productivity	Demand increase	Rise
b	A decrease in the working age population		
c	A technological advancement that automated work		
d	A rise in the price of capital goods		
e	An improvement in the non-wage benefits of a job		

2 Draw a labour market diagram that would illustrate the impact of the following newspaper headlines:

a 'The robots are taking all our jobs!'

b 'A surge in solar panel sales leads to job creation in the sustainable sector'

3

Table 17.5: Selected data from Mexico (figures correct as of 20 December 2024)

Minimum wage / month	$430
Average wage for a factory worker / month	$980
Trade union membership among factory workers	90%
Birth rate	1.8 births per woman

The automotive sector is one of Mexico's most significant industries, making up 3.6% of the nation's gross domestic product (GDP) and 22% of all exports. The industry employs over one million people nationwide. However, there is growing concern among workers about the potential for new tariffs on car exports to the USA, which could destabilise demand. Additionally, the rise of automation in manufacturing processes is leading to fears about job displacement.

a Define 'minimum wage'. [2]

b Explain, using a diagram, the likely impact on an automotive factory worker's wage if capital goods become cheaper. [4]

c Discuss whether automotive factory workers in Mexico should be concerned about their wages over the next ten years. [8]

17.4 Mobility of labour

UNDERSTAND THIS TERM

- mobility of labour

1 Explain the difference between geographical immobility and occupational immobility of labour.

2 List **three** causes of geographical immobility of labour.

3 List **three** possible solutions to improving the geographic mobility of labour.

4 List **three** primary sector industries.

5 Complete these sentences about primary sector workers:

   a People working in the primary sector may be less well paid than those who work in secondary and tertiary sectors. This is because …

   b People working in the primary sector also tend to be more occupationally immobile. This is because …

   c One solution to the problem of occupational immobility is to provide targeted training and education programmes. This would help because …

17.5 Division of labour

≪ RECALL AND CONNECT 3 ≪

Using a PPC diagram, explain the likely impact on potential growth of division of labour.

1 Complete Table 17.6 with the advantages and disadvantages of division of labour.

Table 17.6: Advantages and disadvantages of division of labour

Advantage	Disadvantage
a	b
c	d
e	f

2

> In the past, car factories widely adopted the principle of division of labour to reduce their production costs and increase efficiency. This system was highly effective in increasing output and making cars more affordable in the early and mid-20th century. However, in recent years, the appeal of factory line work has diminished. Many workers today are less inclined to take on repetitive, physically demanding roles. Instead, they prefer jobs that offer more variety or creativity or higher levels of skill development. As a result, car manufacturers are facing challenges in attracting employees, and automation is increasingly being used to fill the gap.

a   Define 'division of labour'.   [2]

b   Explain **two** reasons why costs might **not** decrease as a result of division of labour.   [4]

c   Analyse **two** reasons why fewer people are deciding to become factory workers.   [6]

REFLECTION

There was a lot of content in this chapter. Well done for working through it. Consider the importance of taking rest breaks during revision and think about taking your own break now.

- How do you think short periods of rest can improve your focus and retention when working intensively?

SELF-ASSESSMENT CHECKLIST

Let's revisit the Knowledge focus and Exam skills focus for this chapter. Decide how confident you are with each statement.

Now I can	Show it	Needs more work	Almost there	Confident to move on
analyse the wage and non-wage factors that influence an individual's choice of occupation	List **three** reasons that you might choose to become a teacher.			
discuss, using demand and supply diagrams, the influences on wage determination: demand and supply of labour, trade unions and their relative bargaining power, government policy	Draw a labour market diagram and illustrate the impact of an increase in demand.			
explain the reasons for differences in wages	Explain why a cardiologist is paid more than a cleaner.			

CONTINUED

Now I can	Show it	Needs more work	Almost there	Confident to move on
discuss how the reasons for differences in wages influence the wages of workers	Write a brief explanation why lead actors get paid more than extras (background characters) in movies.			
explain the causes and consequences of changes in the occupational and geographical mobility of labour	Explain the difference between the two concepts.			
define the division of labour (worker specialisation)	Describe the meaning of 'division of labour'.			
discuss the advantages and disadvantages of division of labour	List **two** advantages and disadvantages of division of labour			
interpret information in tables	Research on the internet to find some tabular (economic) data. Summarise your conclusions from the data to another student.			
reduce test anxiety by including breaks in my revision.	Take a break now!			

18 Firms

KNOWLEDGE FOCUS

In this chapter you will answer questions on:

- 18.1 Different types of firms
- 18.2 Mergers of firms
- 18.3 Economies and diseconomies of scale

EXAM SKILLS FOCUS

In this chapter you will:

- show that you read widely, beyond the core reading
- show that you understand the need to be precise with terminology.

Reading widely beyond the core materials helps you develop a deeper understanding of economic concepts by exposing you to more diverse perspectives and real-world applications. In particular, it allows you to build your own real-world examples. In Chapter 18, real-world examples are particularly useful because it means you can picture the type of firm being talked about – whether it's a retail firm like Starbucks or a streaming service like Netflix. In addition, reading widely demonstrates your commitment to learning and enhances your ability to analyse complex issues from multiple angles, which supports your answers to the longer discuss questions.

By now you will probably have realised how important it is to use clear and precise terminology as a key part of providing high-quality answers. In this chapter, for example, knowing the difference between the different types of mergers and the different types of economies of scale is critical.

18.1 Different types of firms

≪ RECALL AND CONNECT 1 ≪

a What is the difference between the market economic system and a mixed economic system?

b What is the role of a producer?

UNDERSTAND THESE TERMS

- industry
- primary sector
- secondary sector
- tertiary sector

1 Complete Table 18.1 by sorting the following examples of firms into the categories of primary, secondary or tertiary.

- **Rio Tinto** – Mining and extraction of minerals
- **FedEx** – Courier and delivery services
- **Netflix** – Entertainment and streaming services
- **Saudi Aramco** – Oil and gas production
- **Toyota** – Manufacturing of automobiles
- **Samsung** – Electronics and appliances manufacturing
- **Boeing** – Aircraft manufacturing
- **Forestry England** – Timber and forest management
- **Hilton Hotels** – Hospitality and tourism services

Table 18.1: Examples of primary, secondary and tertiary firms

Primary	Secondary	Tertiary
a	b	c
d	e	f
g	h	i

2 Explain the difference between a private sector firm and a public sector firm.

3 List **two** examples of public sector firms in your country.

4   Decide whether each of the following statements is true or false.

   a   In a market economic system, most firms are owned by the government and run in the interests of the whole country.

   b   In a mixed economic system, firms can belong to both the private and public sectors.

   c   Public sector firms are typically owned by entrepreneurs pursuing their own interests, such as profit.

5

Starbucks is a US firm that operates the largest coffee shop chain and one of the most recognisable brands in the world. Headquartered in Seattle, the firm operates more than 35 000 stores across 80 countries. However, not everyone is a fan – many people prefer going to smaller independent coffee shops. Interestingly, Starbucks has a minimal presence across the continent of Africa. Even in Ethiopia, a country known as the birthplace of coffee and renowned for its rich coffee culture, the market is characterised by small traditional coffee houses rather than big-name franchises.

   a   Explain **two** advantages of small firms to the consumer.　　　　　　**[4]**

   b   Explain **two** advantages of large firms to business owners.　　　　　**[4]**

REFLECTION

In this section, a lot of real-world firms have been mentioned. Do you know them all?

- How much current affairs reading are you doing?
- Could you be doing more?

The exam questions should provide the information you need about a firm, and so it is not essential that you learn detailed case studies about firms. However, staying updated on current events and familiarising yourself with a variety of businesses can help provide context and a deeper understanding, making it easier to apply economic concepts in real-world scenarios.

18.2 Mergers of firms

UNDERSTAND THESE TERMS

- horizontal merger
- vertical merger
- vertical merger backwards
- vertical merger forwards
- conglomerate merger

1   Complete Table 18.2 by identifying which type of merger is being described.

Table 18.2: Mergers of firms

	Description	Type of merger
a	A car manufacturer merges with a coffee shop	
b	A car manufacturer merger with a tyre manufacturer	
c	A coffee shop merges with another coffee shop	
d	A farm merges with a takeaway sandwich shop	

2   List **two** advantages and **two** disadvantages of a horizontal merger.

3   List **two** advantages and **two** disadvantages of a vertical merger.

4   List **two** advantages and **two** disadvantages of a conglomerate merger.

REFLECTION

It is easy to get confused with the terminology in the topic. However, repetition helps reinforce key concepts and encourages you to practise using clear and precise terminology, which is essential for answering questions accurately. By consistently identifying the advantages and disadvantages of different types of mergers, you can develop a more structured approach to analysing each one. This approach helps to develop the skill of using clear and precise language, helping you to gain a deeper understanding of the implications of each merger type. We will use the same approach with different types of economies of scale later in the chapter.

- How confident are you in identifying the advantages and disadvantages of different types of mergers after this sort of activity?

5   Jeanie is a small-scale coffee farmer in rural Burundi, growing high-quality Arabica coffee beans. She harvests about 800 kg of coffee beans per month. Her friend Rosa owns a small coffee shop nearby, which doubles as a roastery and a community hub. Rosa suggests that the two entrepreneurs merge their businesses, believing there will be significant advantages.

a   Identify the type of merger being described.   [2]

b   Discuss the likely advantages and disadvantages of the merger.   [8]

REFLECTION

This question might have been easier to answer if you had come across a real-world merger beforehand. By reading widely, you can encounter diverse examples of mergers and gain insights into how they work in practice. Building your own real-world examples from a wider selection of sources will help you connect theory to reality.

- How can you record any real-world examples that you read about?

18.3 Economies and diseconomies of scale

UNDERSTAND THIS TERM

- long run

1 Match the term with its correct definition.

Term		Definition	
a	Internal economies of scale	i	Lower long run average total cost resulting from an industry growing in size
b	Internal diseconomies of scale	ii	Higher long run average total cost arising from an industry growing too large
c	External economies of scale	iii	Lower long run average total cost resulting from a firm growing in size
d	External diseconomies of scale	iv	Higher long run average total cost arising from a firm growing too large

2 Draw the diagram for internal economies of scale.

3 Draw the diagram for internal diseconomies of scale.

4 Draw the diagram for external economies of scale.

5 Draw the diagram for external diseconomies of scale.

6 a If a restaurant increases in size, list **two** internal economies of scale that it might achieve.

b If a supermarket increases in size, list **two** internal diseconomies of scale that it might incur.

c If the electric vehicle manufacturing industry grows in size, list **two** external economies of scale that firms in the industry might experience.

d If the baking industry grows in size, list **two** external diseconomies of scale that firms in the industry might experience.

REFLECTION

Any question on economies of scale is potentially tricky because you could confuse the type of economy of scale that you are meant to be talking about. Yet, mark schemes reward accuracy in your response. Repetitive practice will help reinforce your understanding and accuracy.

- How can you ensure that you accurately identify the correct type of economy of scale when answering a question?
- What strategies can you use to avoid confusing different types of economies of scale in your response?

SELF-ASSESSMENT CHECKLIST

Let's revisit the Knowledge focus and Exam skills focus for this chapter.
Decide how confident you are with each statement.

Now I can	Show it	Needs more work	Almost there	Confident to move on
explain the difference between primary, secondary and tertiary sector firms	Name **two** firms in each sector.			
explain the difference between private sector firms and public sector firms	State the differences in objectives and ownership of both types of firm.			
discuss the advantages and disadvantages of small and large firms	List **two** advantages and **two** disadvantages of a firm staying small.			
define the different types of mergers: horizontal, vertical and conglomerate	Give a (real or fictional) example of each type of merger.			
discuss the advantages and disadvantages of mergers	Answer the question: Discuss whether horizontal mergers are always beneficial for the firm. **[8]**			
discuss how internal and external economies and diseconomies of scale can affect a firm/industry as the scale of production changes	Explain the difference between all four types of economy of scale.			
draw and interpret average total cost (ATC) diagrams to illustrate economies and diseconomies of scale	Draw **one** diagram to illustrate internal economies of scale and **one** diagram to illustrate external diseconomies of scale.			
read widely, beyond the core reading	Keep a record of real-world examples from your reading.			
understand the need to be precise with terminology.	Ask another student to test you on the definitions of key words from this chapter.			

19 Firms and production

KNOWLEDGE FOCUS

In this chapter you will answer questions on:

- 19.1 Demand for factors of production
- 19.2 Labour-intensive and capital-intensive production
- 19.3 Production and productivity

EXAM SKILLS FOCUS

In this chapter you will:

- practise answering more questions with the command word 'explain'
- show that you understand how to answer multiple-choice questions (MCQs).

'Explain' is a commonly used command word. As we have seen, the command word means to outline the reasons behind a concept and how they are connected, supporting your response with relevant evidence. It is worth practising these types of questions many times.

Learning how to succeed with multiple-choice questions (MCQs) is vitally important. After all, Paper 1 – Multiple Choice is an entire MCQ paper. Throughout this chapter, you will be encouraged to create your own MCQs. Creating your own MCQs is a useful activity because it helps you understand the structure of questions, strengthens your ability to identify key concepts and improves your critical thinking skills.

19.1 Demand for factors of production

≪ RECALL AND CONNECT 1 ≪

a   What are the **four** factors of production?

b   Explain the difference between the long run and the short run.

c   List **two** factors that influence the demand for labour.

d   Draw a diagram to show the impact of an increase in the demand for labour on wages.

UNDERSTAND THIS TERM

- corporate income (corporation) tax

1   Complete Table 19.1 to explain how the following factors are likely to affect the demand for capital goods.

Table 19.1: Demand for capital goods

	Factor	Explanation
a	Interest rates	
b	Government tax on firms' profits	
c	Economic growth	
d	Business confidence	

2   Complete Table 19.2 to explain how the following factors are likely to affect the demand for land.

Table 19.2: Demand for land

	Factor	Explanation
a	Fertility of land	
b	City centre land	
c	Proximity to water	

3   Explain how technological advancements can lead to an increase in the demand for capital goods but a decrease in the demand for land.

19.2 Labour-intensive and capital-intensive production

« RECALL AND CONNECT 2 «

a   Explain what is meant by capital-intensive and labour-intensive production.

b   What internal economies of scale are related to capital and labour?

1   Look at the industries in the word box below. Decide whether they are capital intensive or labour intensive. Then complete Table 19.3.

> automobile manufacturing   hospitality   agriculture
>
> aerospace engineering   textiles   oil production

Table 19.3: Capital-intensive and labour-intensive industries

Capital intensive	Labour intensive
a	b
c	d
e	f

Question 2 includes two multiple-choice questions (MCQs). When answering MCQs, it is important to read the question carefully to understand exactly what is being asked. When approaching MCQs, one helpful tip is to identify the obvious wrong answers first. Eliminate those answers from your thinking before choosing the best option from the remaining choices. The first question has been completed for you.

2   a   What is an advantage of capital-intensive production?

   A   Production can be flexible.

   B   Products are standardised.   ✓

   C   It is appropriate for low-scale production.

   D   There may be high maintenance costs.

In Question 2a, option D is clearly wrong because it describes a disadvantage rather than an advantage. From the remaining choices, A and C are ruled out because they are advantages of labour-intensive production rather than capital-intensive production.

   b   What is a disadvantage of labour-intensive production?

   A   It can reduce unit costs through automation.

   B   There is a risk of breakdown.

   C   It is appropriate for low-scale production.

   D   There is a risk of human error.

3

Saudi Arabia has been awarded the men's football World Cup for 2034. The kingdom plans to spend tens of billions of dollars on construction projects related to the World Cup as part of its Vision 2030 initiative that aims to modernise Saudi society and economy.

The construction industry is traditionally associated with labour-intensive practices, such as a high number of workers for tasks such as building, plumbing and electrical installation. Interestingly, however, the global construction robotics market is rapidly expanding. Driven by a push for efficiency and safety, Saudi Arabia is at the forefront of the trend. State subsidies for robotics companies mean that major construction projects like the World Cup and NEOM – its grand urban development project – will come to rely more on advanced technology.

a Explain **two** factors influencing the demand for capital goods in Saudi Arabia. [4]

b Analyse **two** disadvantages of the construction industry being labour-intensive. [6]

REFLECTION

Take a pause here. Can you create a multiple-choice question (MCQ) based on the content from this section?

There are plenty of opportunities for you to practise answering MCQs – these can be found at the end of every chapter in the coursebook and additional MCQs are also provided as part of this book, found online at Cambridge GO.

When you are completing Paper 1 – Multiple Choice, it is okay to move on and come back to tricky questions later. Just make sure that you answer all the questions before the end of the exam. Time management is also important. For Paper 1, you should spend roughly 1.5 minutes per question because you only have 60 minutes in which to answer 40 MCQs.

- How do you feel about answering MCQs?
- Do you think creating your own MCQs can help you solidify your understanding and improve your exam performance?

19.3 Production and productivity

1 Explain the difference between production and productivity.

2

A large soft-drinks company factory produces 800 000 cans a day (24 million a month). The factory improves its production methods and starts to produce 1 million cans a day (30 million a month).

a   Calculate the percentage increase in production.

b   Calculate the firm's change in production over the course of a year.

c   Give **two** factors that could have caused this change.

3

A bakery employs 8 workers. They can normally make 1 040 loaves of bread a day. However, for the past few weeks, they can only produce 720 loaves of bread a day.

a   Calculate the bakery's rate of labour productivity before and after the change.

b   Give **two** factors that could have caused this change.

4

The Olive Tree bakery is a beloved family-owned bakery located in Thessaloniki, Greece. For the past 12 years, it has been producing traditional Greek bread, pastries and cakes using manual labour and basic kitchen equipment. In recent months, the bakery has experienced an increase in demand due to the growing popularity of the area among tourists, as well as local residents seeking premium, handmade baked goods. As a result, the owners, Yorgos and Manolis, decide to invest in new equipment.

a   Identify **two** ways that a government can seek to increase
business investment.   [2]

b   Explain the likely impact of Yorgos and Manolis's decision 'to invest
in new equipment' on the bakery's productivity.   [4]

REFLECTION

Take a pause here. Can you create another multiple-choice question (MCQ) based on the content from this section?

As you write your own MCQ, think about the key concepts you have learned and how they connect to the material. Reflect on why you chose each potential answer and what might make one option more correct than the others.

•   How does this process help you identify areas that might need more review?

SELF-ASSESSMENT CHECKLIST

Let's revisit the Knowledge focus and Exam skills focus for this chapter. Decide how confident you are with each statement.

Now I can	Show it	Needs more work	Almost there	Confident to move on
analyse the influences on the demand for factors of production	List **two** reasons for the demand for capital goods to rise, and **two** reasons for the demand for land to rise.			
analyse the reasons for adopting labour-intensive production or capital-intensive production	Explain why the manufacturing sector is associated with capital-intensive production.			
discuss the advantages and disadvantages of different forms of production	Create a table with a list of advantages and disadvantages for labour-intensive production.			
explain the difference between production and productivity	Explain the difference between production and productivity.			
explain the influences on production and productivity	Explain how capital investment and government policies can affect both.			
analyse the effects of changes in investment on productivity	Discuss the specific ways that investment can influence productivity with another student.			
practise answering more questions with the command word 'explain'	Find some questions from a past paper with the 'explain' command word, and complete them.			
understand how to answer multiple-choice questions (MCQs).	Create **three** MCQs based on the content from this chapter and share them with another student.			

20 Firms' costs, revenue and objectives

KNOWLEDGE FOCUS

In this chapter you will answer questions on:

- 20.1 Calculating the costs of production
- 20.2 Calculating revenue and the influence of sales on revenue
- 20.3 Objectives of firms

EXAM SKILLS FOCUS

In this chapter you will:

- practise answering more questions with the command word 'calculate'.

In this chapter, you will encounter many questions presenting firms' costs and revenues in a tabular format. From these tables, you will be required to carry out various calculations. As mentioned in Chapter 10, always write the formula first before performing the calculation.

20.1 Calculating the costs of production

1 Match the type of cost to its correct definition.

Type of cost	
a	Total cost (TC)
b	Fixed cost (FC)
c	Variable cost (VC)

Definition	
i	The full amount that has to be spent on the factors of production used to produce a product
ii	Costs that change with output
iii	Costs that do not change with output in the short run

2 Explain how you would convert any of the costs in Question 1 into averages. For example, how do you get calculate average fixed costs from fixed costs?

3 If a company has total fixed costs of $1 000 and produces 200 units of output, calculate the average fixed cost.

4 Draw **one** diagram that shows total costs, variable costs and fixed costs.

5 Draw another diagram that shows average total costs, average variable costs and average fixed costs.

6 A manufacturing firm in Sweden makes table tennis bats. Their cost schedule for the year is shown in Table 20.1. Complete Table 20.1 by inserting the missing values.

Table 20.1: Cost schedule for a manufacturing firm

Output	Total costs ($)	Fixed costs ($)	Variable costs ($)	Average total costs ($)
0	a	100 000	N/A	N/A
25 000	b	c	1 000 000	d
50 000	e	f	2 000 000	g
75 000	h	i	3 000 000	j
100 000	k	l	4 000 000	m

7 Ade and Zinnia are chicken farmers in Ghana. They have relatively low operating costs, which are shown in Table 20.2.

Table 20.2: Operating costs

Output	Fixed costs	Variable costs
0	$2 000	N/A
1 000	$2 000	$400
2 000	$2 000	$800
3 000	$2 000	$1 200
4 000	$2 000	$1 600
5 000	$2 000	$2 000

a   Calculate Ade and Zinnia's total costs if they produce 3 000 chickens. **[2]**

b   Calculate Ade and Zinnia's average total costs if they produce 4 000 chickens. **[2]**

c   Define 'fixed costs'. **[2]**

d   Identify **two** types of fixed costs for a business in the agricultural sector. **[2]**

e   Explain how changes in output affect fixed costs and average fixed costs. **[4]**

20.2 Calculating revenue and the influence of sales on revenue

« RECALL AND CONNECT 1 «

a   What is a demand schedule?

b   How can you calculate revenue from data in a demand schedule?

UNDERSTAND THESE TERMS

- total revenue
- average revenue

1   What is the relationship between average revenue and price?

2   The table tennis bat manufacturer firm in Sweden has the revenue schedule shown in Table 20.3. Complete the table by inserting the missing values.

Table 20.3: Revenue schedule

Quantity sold	Average revenue (price) ($)	Total revenue ($)
1	120	a
2	120	b
3	120	c
4	120	d
5	120	e
6	120	f

3   Describe how changes in sales affect average revenue and total revenue.

4   a   Ade and Zinnia, the Ghanian chicken farmers, can only charge $1.10 for each chicken. Calculate the total revenue they will make if they sell 3 000 chickens at this price.

    b   Using Table 20.2 from earlier in this chapter, calculate Ade and Zinnia's profit (total revenue – total costs) from producing and selling 3 000 chickens.

REFLECTION

When working on calculate questions, it can be helpful to break down the calculation into smaller steps. By clearly showing each stage, you reduce the chance of making mistakes and make your process easier to follow.

Time management is also important. If you find yourself stuck on a calculation, it is often best to move on to the next question and return to the tricky question later, rather than spending too much time on one issue.

- How will breaking down calculations into smaller steps and managing your time help you to feel more confident in answering calculate questions during exams?

20.3 Objectives of firms

≪ RECALL AND CONNECT 2 ≪

a   List **two** different types of mergers.

b   List **two** advantages of a merger.

1   Complete Table 20.4 by identifying either the business objective or its description.

Table 20.4: Business objectives

Business objective	Description
Profit maximisation	a
Growth	b
c	Ensuring the firm can cover its costs and remain in the market during challenging conditions
d	Prioritising affordable products and minimising social and environmental harm, often as a government or ethical private sector goal

2   Let's look back at our two businesses from this chapter.

a   The Swedish table tennis bat manufacturer is profitable. However, all its profits go directly into supporting community table tennis groups across the globe.

Identify this type of business objective.

b   Ade and Zinnia only managed to produce 3 000 chickens this year, making them very little profit overall. Other new firms are entering the market and threatening to reduce their profit still further.

Identify what business objective they are likely to have now.

SELF-ASSESSMENT CHECKLIST

Let's revisit the Knowledge focus and Exam skills focus for this chapter.
Decide how confident you are with each statement.

Now I can	Show it	Needs more work	Almost there	Confident to move on
define key terms: total cost (TC), average total cost (ATC), fixed cost (FC), average fixed cost (AFC), variable cost (VC) and average variable cost (AVC)	Explain the difference between fixed costs and variable costs. Explain how you get average values from total values.			
calculate total cost, average total cost, fixed cost, average fixed cost, variable cost and average variable cost	State the formulae for ATC, AFC and AVC.			
draw and interpret diagrams that show how changes in output can affect costs of production	Draw FC, AFC, VC and TC diagrams.			
define total revenue (TR) and average revenue (AR)	Explain how you get average revenue from total revenue.			
calculate total revenue and average revenue	State the formulae for both.			
explain the influence of sales on revenue	Describe the relationship between sales and revenue.			
discuss the objectives of firms including survival, social welfare, profit maximisation and growth	Find real-life examples of firms with each of these business objectives.			
practise answering more questions with the command word 'calculate'.	Practise calculating TC, ATC, FC, AFC, VC and AVC using data from the tables in the coursebook or the workbook.			

21 Types of markets

KNOWLEDGE FOCUS

In this chapter you will answer questions on:

- 21.1 Competitive markets
- 21.2 Monopoly markets

EXAM SKILLS FOCUS

In this chapter you will:

- practise answering more questions with the command word 'discuss'
- show that you can create mnemonics to support revision.

'Discuss' is a commonly used command word. It requires you to evaluate different perspectives on an issue. This involves presenting arguments for and against, weighing up the evidence and offering a well-rounded conclusion. It is important to practise answering discuss questions, and in this chapter there are two more for you to try.

A mnemonic is a memory aid that helps people remember information more easily. It often involves associating complex information with a simple word, phrase, acronym or image that is easier to recall. This chapter will encourage you to create your own mnemonics to support recall.

21.1 Competitive markets

« RECALL AND CONNECT 1 «

a What is the mixed economic system?

b List **two** advantages of small firms.

UNDERSTAND THESE TERMS

- market structure

- competitive market

1 Complete Table 21.1 to describe why the presence of the following barriers to entry might make it hard for new firms to enter a market.

Table 21.1: Barriers to entry

	Barrier to entry	Description
a	Brand loyalty	
b	Patents	
c	Government licencing	

2 Competitive markets have several characteristics. Identify the correct characteristics from the list below:

a High barriers to entry / Low barriers to entry

b Lots of small firms in the market / One large firm in the market

c Price maker / Price taker

3 Consider the following areas: choice, price, profit and quality. Identify whether each category will be high or low if there is a large number of firms competing with one another and explain why.

Table 21.2: Impact of competitive markets

	Area	High or low	Explanation
a	Choice		
b	Price		
c	Profit		
d	Quality		

REFLECTION

Mnemonics are effective for revision because they help simplify complex information into easy-to-remember chunks. For example, learning the different characteristics of competitive markets can be tricky. Therefore, you could create a mnemonic like this:

Firms No Power

- **F**irms (lots of firms in the market)
- **N**o (no barriers to entry)
- **P**ower (firms have no power to set price)

Come up with your own mnemonic.

- Can you design a mnemonic for remembering the advantages and disadvantages of competitive markets?
- Do you think that creating mnemonics, such as the one above, will support your own learning effectively?

Discuss questions ask you to explore the different sides of an issue. Start by identifying a couple of contrasting perspectives and then use examples from the case study to support your points. Make sure you are clear about why each argument matters in relation to the question being asked.

Remember that 8-mark discuss questions are marked using a level-based marking system, not a point-based marking system. This means your answer is not rewarded simply for listing separate points. Instead, you will be assessed on how well you develop your ideas and how clearly you evaluate both sides of the argument. For an answer to be awarded the top level, it should include the following:

- There is a reasoned discussion that accurately examines both sides of the economic argument, making use of economic information and clear and logical analysis to evaluate economic issues and situations.

- One side of the argument may have more depth than the other, but, overall, both sides of the argument are considered and developed.

- There is thoughtful evaluation of economic concepts, terminology, information and/or data appropriate to the question.

- The discussion may also point out the possible uncertainties of alternative decisions and outcomes.

4

In India, the demand for affordable home appliances, such as refrigerators and washing machines, has been rising rapidly due to increasing urbanisation and a growing number of middle-income households. The production of home appliances relies heavily on the division of labour in large-scale manufacturing facilities. The Indian home appliance market is highly competitive, with many firms vying for market share, including both domestic and international brands. Many families save for months or even years to purchase these essential items.

Discuss whether Indian consumers are likely to benefit from a 'highly competitive' market in home appliances.

[8]

21.2 Monopoly markets

« RECALL AND CONNECT 2 «

a   List **two** benefits of a large firm.

b   List **two** internal economies of scale.

c   List **two** internal diseconomies of scale.

UNDERSTAND THESE TERMS

- monopoly
- scale of production
- sunk costs

1   Write a short description of a monopoly market that includes the following words:

- single firm
- scale of production
- barriers to entry
- market share.

2   Complete Table 21.3. In each case, complete the sentence in the right-hand column. The first one has been done for you.

Table 21.3: Impact of monopoly markets

	Area	The impact of a monopoly market
a	Choice	The usual meaning of a monopoly is a sole supplier of a product, having 100% share of the market. Therefore, a monopoly does not provide consumers with a choice of which firm to buy from.
b	Price	In a monopoly, the lack of competition gives the firm significant market power. Therefore, …
c	Profit	With no competition, a monopoly can set prices above the cost of production. Therefore, …
d	Quality	A monopoly may not feel the competitive pressure to innovate or improve its products. Therefore, …

3

> The demand for electricity in South Africa has been steadily rising over the past few decades. Approximately 95% of the electricity used in South Africa is produced by Eskom, a state-owned company that controls nearly all of the country's power generation and distribution. The presence of this monopoly has raised concerns about high electricity prices and inconsistent service, especially as many households struggle with the rising cost of living. While Eskom's large-scale infrastructure enables it to meet the demand, the lack of competition means consumers – both household and industry – have little choice but to rely on the single supplier for their increasing electricity needs.

a   Identify **two** characteristics of a monopoly. [2]

b   Explain **two** reasons why the 'demand for electricity in South Africa has been steadily rising over the past few decades'. [4]

c   Discuss whether South African consumers are likely to benefit from a 'single supplier for their increasing electricity needs'. [8]

REFLECTION

You have had the opportunity to practise two discuss exam questions in this chapter. Both questions focused on the impact on consumers. As mentioned earlier in this chapter, when answering discuss questions, it is important to explore the different sides of an issue. Remember that these questions are marked using a level-based marking system, which rewards balanced chains of reasoning and evaluation rather than simply listing points. In the case of consumers, this is relatively straightforward: they tend to benefit from low prices, higher quality and access to full information. A useful exercise would be to think more broadly – what kinds of benefits or drawbacks might a producer, a worker or a government experience in similar scenarios?

- How confident are you feeling with discuss questions now?

SELF-ASSESSMENT CHECKLIST

Let's revisit the Knowledge focus and Exam skills focus for this chapter. Decide how confident you are with each statement.

Now I can	Show it	Needs more work	Almost there	Confident to move on
explain the characteristics of a competitive market	Create a mnemonic to remember the characteristics of a competitive market.			
discuss the advantages and disadvantages of competitive markets	List **two** advantages and **two** disadvantages of competitive markets.			

CONTINUED

Now I can	Show it	Needs more work	Almost there	Confident to move on
explain the effect of having a high number of firms on price, quantity, choice and profit	Discuss a real-world example of a competitive market with another student and explain how it impacts on price, quantity, choice and profit.			
explain the characteristics of a monopoly market	Create a mnemonic to remember the characteristics of a monopoly market.			
discuss the advantages and disadvantages of a monopoly market	List **two** advantages and **two** disadvantages of a monopoly market.			
explain the effect of having only one firm on price, quantity, choice and profit	Discuss a real-world example of a monopoly with another student and explain how it impacts on these areas.			
practise answering more questions with the command word 'discuss'	Complete a past paper discuss question.			
create mnemonics to support my revision.	Create at least **three** more mnemonics for content in other chapters.			

Exam practice 3

This section contains practice questions that will draw together your knowledge on a range of topics you have covered up to this point and will help you prepare for your assessment.

The following question has example student responses and commentaries provided. For each part of the question, work through the question first, then compare your answer to the example student response and commentary.

Question 1

Morocco is the biggest car manufacturing hub in North Africa, with major international manufacturers like Renault, Peugeot (Stellantis) and Volkswagen operating there. The country has seen significant economic growth, driven in large part by high-value car exports to Europe. Despite this growth in income, household saving has remained relatively constant, at about 11% of disposable income. Morocco is still largely a cash-based economy, although alternative forms of money are becoming more popular.

In February 2025, Morocco suffered some disruption to production when the country's biggest trade unions called for the first nationwide strike in almost a decade.

a   Identify **two** characteristics of money. [2]

Example student response	Commentary
Coins Banknotes	AO1 Knowledge and understanding This answer is incorrect. The student has identified two forms of money but not two characteristics. The question asks for characteristics, which includes things like 'durable' and 'portable'.

b   Explain **two** possible causes of an increase in household saving. [4]

Example student response	Commentary
A rise in interest rates will increase the return from saving, encouraging households to save rather than spend or borrow. Low-income households usually save a low percentage of their income. Therefore, even if interest rates rise then we would still expect savings to be low among low-income households. The data says that 'savings have remained constant', which implies that the reward for saving may not be high enough. Interest rates may still be very low, even if they are rising.	AO1 Knowledge and understanding This answer demonstrates that the student has a good understanding of two key factors that affect household saving: interest rates and confidence. AO2 Analysis Likewise, the student develops their points in the context of the question effectively.

Example student response	Commentary
A fall in consumer confidence can lead to households choosing to save rather than spend. When people have job security and are confident about their incomes in the future, they are more likely to spend money. However, if the opposite is true (they have less job security or they expect wages to fall) then they are more likely to save in the short term. Of course, this depends on the inflation rate. If prices rise, then the purchasing power of money is reduced and savings become worth less in real terms. Therefore, households may not decide to increase their level of saving because they are worried about doing so in times of high inflation.	One of the downsides to this answer is that it is too long. Four-mark questions should be answered quickly so that the student has enough time to answer the other (higher-mark) questions effectively as well. The student has probably spent too much time on this question. Another downside is that the student has spent a lot of time explaining the circumstances in which the theory may not hold. However, the command word 'explain' does not require this. The part about inflation is unnecessary and does not support the answer at all.

c   Analyse the role of trade unions in influencing workers' wages.   [6]

Example student response	Commentary
Trade unions play a significant role in influencing workers' wages through bargaining with firms. They negotiate for higher wages, aiming to improve the income of workers, often using strikes to increase their bargaining power. For example, in Morocco 'the country's biggest trade unions called for the first nationwide strike in almost a decade', presumably in the hope that it might be able to successfully negotiate a wage increase for its members. Additionally, trade unions seek to improve working conditions and secure other benefits such as healthcare or pensions, which can indirectly enhance workers' financial security. Trade unions can also exert pressure on the government to raise the national minimum wage or reduce the retirement age, further influencing the wages of workers in certain sectors.	AO1 Knowledge and understanding This answer demonstrates that the student has a good understanding of the key concepts. AO2 Analysis This is a good, well-developed answer. However, the student could still provide a clearer explanation of how trade unions directly influence wage negotiations in specific industries or sectors, rather than just discussing general actions like strikes. They could also use a labour market diagram. The student could use demand and supply analysis in the labour market to develop their answer further.

d   Discuss the advantages and disadvantages of using division of labour in an industry like car manufacturing.   [8]

Example student response	Commentary
Division of labour in car manufacturing can be good because it allows workers to focus on their tasks, which makes them faster. This can lead to lower costs because workers can do their jobs faster. Also, the company can produce more cars faster, which is good for business.	AO1 Knowledge and understanding and AO2 Analysis The answer is overly simplistic and does not explore the topic in depth. Saying that something is 'good for business' without further development is meaningless. Instead, the student should have written about higher productivity rates, lower production costs and a high-level profit for the firm.

Example student response	Commentary
On the other hand, division of labour can also be bad because workers might get bored doing the same task over and over again. It can also make workers less skilled overall, as they only focus on one thing. This means that if they ever need to do something else, they might not be able to. Lastly, if one part of the production line breaks down, it can slow down the whole process, leading to delays. So, division of labour has some benefits, but it also has a few downsides.	The technical language is missing. The student suggests that the workers will be faster, but it would be better to focus on productivity or the rate of production. Again, the student could link here to falling total costs, and could even draw a diagram to show that prices might fall. The answer does not include any real-life examples or specific details related to car manufacturing. For instance, it could mention specific tasks in a car factory or how companies like Renault or Volkswagen use division of labour in their production lines. AO3 Evaluation The answer is still too superficial. It mentions that workers might get bored or that breakdowns can affect production, but it does not explain the broader effects, such as reduced productivity, or the impact on worker motivation or quality control.

Now that you have read the example student response to the previous question, here is a similar practice question which you should attempt. Use the guidance in the commentaries in this section to help you as you answer the question.

Question 2

a   Identify **two** forms of money.   [2]

b   Explain **two** reasons why household borrowing may change as a result of ngo.   [1]

The following question has example student responses and commentaries provided. For each part of the question, work through the question first, then compare your answer to the example student response and commentary.

Question 3

Italy is one of the largest economies in the world. In 2024, its GDP grew by nearly 1%, outperforming many other European countries. Growth in 2025 is expected to remain at a similar level.

Italy is home to some of the world's oldest commercial banks, including Banca Monte dei Paschi di Siena (MPS) and UniCredit, as well as one of the world's oldest airlines – Alitalia. Both banking and air travel (key tertiary industries) remain highly competitive.

The banking industry is experiencing a recent boom, and there has been a rise in the amount of money borrowed from the banks. This has led to an increase in demand for financial services and, in turn, a rise in wages for bank workers. Many economists believe this could encourage greater investment in the economy, which has struggled with low productivity for the past two decades.

Alitalia, however, did not share the same success. Originally a government-owned national airline from its founding in 1946, it was privatised in 2009 but struggled to remain profitable. After years of financial losses, Alitalia ceased operations in 2021.

In 2022, its assets were transferred to ITA Airways, a joint venture between the Italian government and Lufthansa Group. It is hoped that this merger will help ITA achieve economies of scale.

In 2023, ITA posted their financial results:

- 15m passengers

- Total revenue of €2.4bn (€2 400m)

- Total loss of €5m

a Calculate ITA's average revenue per passenger in 2023. [2]

Example student response	Commentary
Average revenue = total revenue / number of passengers Average revenue = 2.400m / 15m = €160	AO1 Knowledge and understanding This answer is correct. It is also good practice that the student included their working.

b Identify **two** influences that could affect household borrowing in Italy. [2]

Example student response	Commentary
Interest rates Confidence levels Income	AO1 Knowledge and understanding This is a satisfactory answer (although the student only needed to include two factors).

c Explain **one** way in which airlines might benefit from economies of scale. [2]

Example student response	Commentary
Airlines can benefit from economies of scale by purchasing aircraft in bulk, which allows them to negotiate lower prices with manufacturers. This reduces the average cost per plane, helping the airline lower overall costs of operation.	AO1 Knowledge and understanding The answer could perhaps be improved with a definition of economies of scale at the start. However, this is still a very strong answer.

d Draw a diagram to show the effect of 'a recent boom' on the wages of bank workers. **[4]**

Example student response	Commentary
A boom increases demand for banking services (e.g. loans, investments). This increases the demand for bank workers, shifting the demand curve from D to D_1. The increased demand leads to higher wages (moving from W to W_1) and possibly an increase in employment (moving from Q to Q_1). 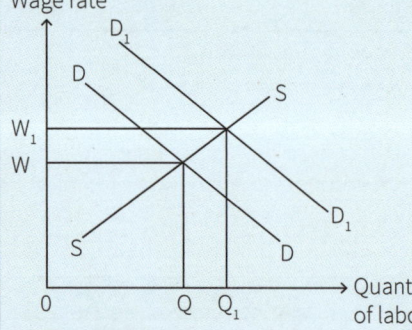	AO1 Knowledge and understanding and AO2 Analysis The student has drawn a well-labelled labour market equilibrium diagram. The student also explains their diagram very well, although a written explanation is not necessarily required here as the command word is 'Draw'.

e Analyse the relationship between investment and productivity. **[4]**

Example student response	Commentary
Productivity is the rate of output per worker or per machine. The case study says that 'Italy has struggled with low productivity for the past two decades', so productivity is starting from a low base. Investment is the purchase of capital by firms. The case study says that 'many economists believe this could encourage greater investment'. Therefore, we are expecting investment to increase. An increase in investment should lead to an increase in productivity.	AO1 Knowledge and understanding and AO2 Analysis This answer has some correct points but lacks depth and there is not a clear explanation of the relationship between investment and productivity. For example, the answer states that investment should increase productivity but does not explain how. A strong response would mention that investment in capital (for example, new machinery, technology or worker training) makes production more efficient, allowing workers to produce more output in the same amount of time.

f   Discuss whether competition between airlines is always advantageous.   **[6]**

Example student response	Commentary
Competition in the airline industry has both advantages and disadvantages. On the positive side, competition encourages airlines to become more efficient by adopting the latest technology and reducing wasteful spending. This leads to lower costs of production which, in turn, allows airlines to offer cheaper ticket prices. Air travel is then more affordable for consumers and could increase the quantity demanded, leading to higher total revenue and profits for the firm. Furthermore, competition forces airlines to improve service quality, such as offering better in-flight experiences or more convenient flight schedules. On the other hand, competition can be bad because if there are too many airlines, they will all struggle. If they have to advertise a lot, it costs them more money. Some airlines might even shut down because they can't handle the competition. Also, big airlines don't have to compete much because people already like them.	AO1 Knowledge and understanding and AO2 Analysis The first half of this answer is very good. It provides a strong analysis of the advantages of competition in the context of air travel. The contextualised analysis that reads 'competition forces airlines to improve service quality, such as offering better in-flight experiences or more convenient flight schedules' is particularly strong. AO3 Evaluation The second half of this answer is less impressive. It makes general statements without explaining why or how. And there is a real lack of technical vocabulary such as economic concepts like 'economies of scale', 'profit margins' or 'market share'.

Now that you have read the example student response to the previous question, here are some similar practice questions for parts (a) and (f) which you should attempt. Use the guidance in the commentaries in this section to help you as you answer the questions.

Question 4

a   Calculate ITA's average cost per passenger in 2023.   **[2]**

f   Discuss whether air travel is best served by a monopoly.   **[6]**

> Unit 4

Government and the macroeconomy

22 Government macroeconomic intervention

KNOWLEDGE FOCUS

In this chapter you will answer questions on:

- 22.1 Macroeconomic aims of government

- 22.2 Possible conflicts between macroeconomic aims

EXAM SKILLS FOCUS

In this chapter you will:

- show that you can interpret and comment on line graphs

- show that you understand how scaffolding can support better answers.

Both Paper 1 – Multiple Choice and Paper 2 – Structured Questions may include data sets presented in a variety of ways. The most common are line graphs. The more you practise interpreting graphs, the more confident and the more skilled you will become in answering questions that are related to data graphs. There will be opportunity to answer two questions related to line graphs in this chapter.

Scaffolding means breaking down complex information into manageable steps, allowing you to build a chain of analysis gradually. It is a helpful process to follow when revising. In this chapter, there is a scaffolded activity to help support answers to longer answer questions.

22.1 Macroeconomic aims of government

≪ RECALL AND CONNECT 1 ≪

a Use a demand and supply diagram to illustrate why prices may rise as a result of demand changes.

b Use a demand and supply diagram to illustrate why prices may rise as a result of supply changes.

UNDERSTAND THESE TERMS

- economic growth
- actual economic growth
- potential economic growth
- inflation
- balance of payments

1 Complete Table 22.1 by identifying the macroeconomic aim for each of the descriptions in the table. The first one has been done for you.

Table 22.1: Macroeconomic aims

	Description	Macroeconomic aim
a	An increase in this would lead to an increase in living standards.	Economic growth
b	An increase in this would lead to an increasing waste of resources.	
c	This is required in order to help people get out of poverty.	
d	This ensures greater economic certainty and prevents the country's products from losing international competitiveness.	
e	This is required in order to prevent global heating and also to protect the planet for future generations.	
f	If this gets out of control then it would lead to high levels of external debt (borrowing from foreign lenders or international organisations, for example, the IMF or World Bank).	

2 Use Table 22.2 to identify which countries have achieved the usual macroeconomic aims in 2024.

Table 22.2: Economic indicators in three countries in 2024

	Economic growth rate (%)	Unemployment rate (%)	Inflation rate (%)	% of population in absolute poverty
Netherlands	0.8	3.7	3.3	0.1
Nicaragua	4.6	4.8	8.4	3.9
Nigeria	2.7	4.0	34.6	30.9

3 Decide whether each of the following statements is true or false.

a Many governments in the world have an inflation target of 0.2%.

b Most governments would seek to have a trade surplus where export revenue is greater than import expenditure.

c A significant gap between the rich and those experiencing poverty can cause social unrest.

d Environmental sustainability can only be achieved by reducing economic growth.

Line graphs are widely used in economics. They show how one or more variables change, usually over time. When examining a line graph, first check what is shown on the axes and then look for trends. Think about whether that is what you expected to see.

4

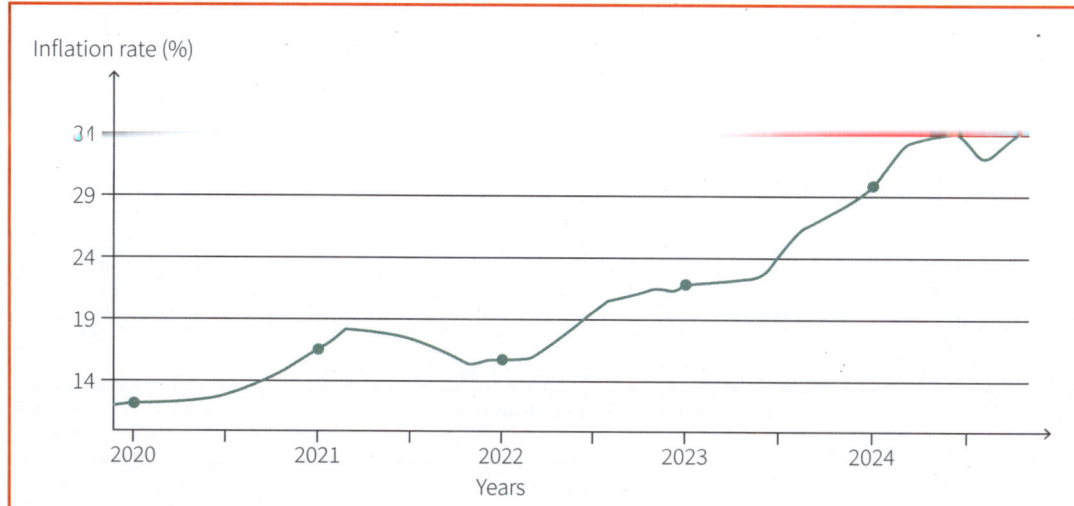

Figure 22.1: Nigeria's inflation rate, 2020–2024

Nigeria is the largest economy in Africa. It is an export-led economy in the sense that exports are over 10% of its GDP. Figure 22.1 shows Nigeria's inflation rate over the five-year period 2020–2024. At the start of 2024, the central bank stated that it wanted to reduce inflation back down to 21%. At the end of 2024, however, inflation was recorded at 34.6%.

a   Define 'inflation rate'. [2]

b   Calculate the percentage point change in the inflation rate between the start of 2020 and the end of 2024. [2]

c   Identify **two** roles of a central bank. [2]

d   Explain **two** reasons for the decision of Nigeria's central bank to 'reduce inflation back down'. [4]

REFLECTION

How confident did you feel in interpreting this line graph? Look back at your answer to Questions 4(b) and 4(d). How could you have improved your answers?

22.2 Possible conflicts between macroeconomic aims

Question 1 is a scaffolded activity. For each part of Question 1, you should follow the same order:

- Identify what the government's macroeconomic aim will be.
- Then describe the conflict between the two economic aims.

1   a   In the areas of unemployment and inflation:

    i   Identify what the government's macroeconomic aim will be.

    ii   Describe the conflict between the two economic aims.

  b   In the areas of growth and the environment:

    i   Identify what the government's macroeconomic aim will be.

    ii   Describe the conflict between the two economic aims.

  c   In the areas of unemployment and the balance of payments:

    i   Identify what the government's macroeconomic aim will be.

    ii   Describe the conflict between the two economic aims.

To help with answering Question 2(d), Figure 22.1 has been repeated below.

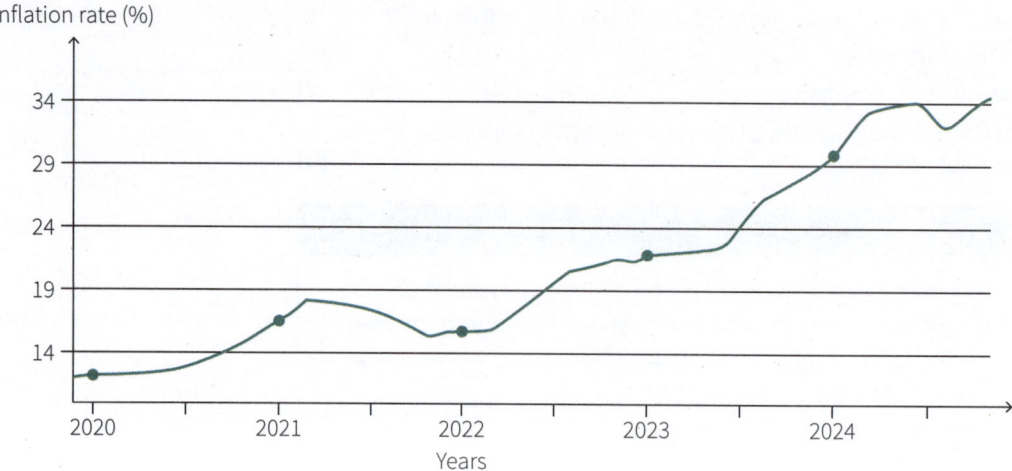

Figure 22.1: Nigeria's inflation rate, 2020–2024

2

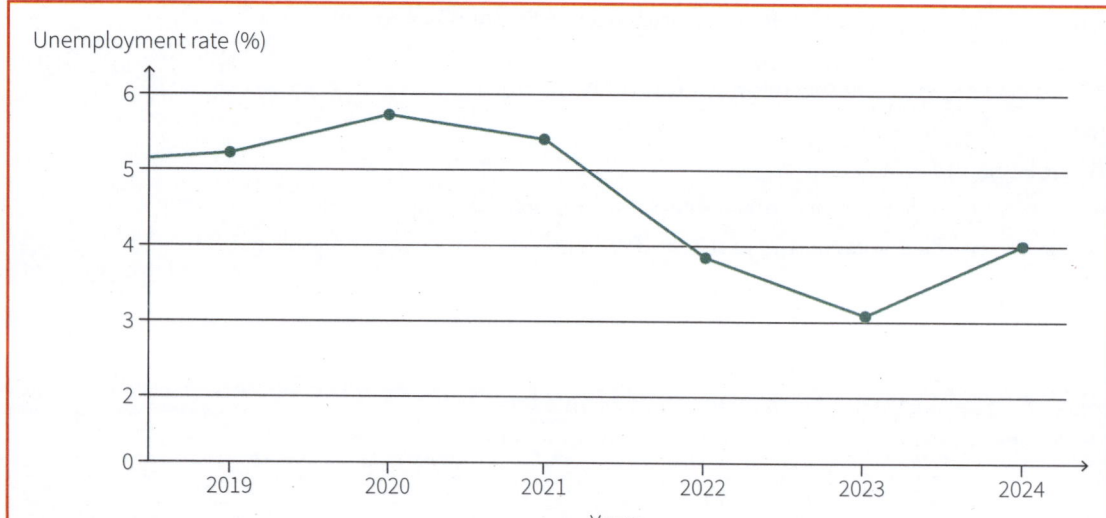

Figure 22.2: Nigeria's unemployment rate, 2019–2024

At the start of 2023, the global unemployment rate was 4.9% while Nigeria's unemployment rate was significantly lower at 3.1%. By the end of 2023, however, unemployment had increased to 4.0%. Around that time, the government indicated that efforts were being made to reduce joblessness, particularly among young people.

a   Define 'unemployment rate'. [2]

b   Calculate, using Figure 22.2, the percentage point decline in the unemployment rate between 2022 and 2023. [2]

c   State **two** reasons to reduce the unemployment rate. [2]

d   Analyse, using Figures 22.1 and 22.2, the relationship between unemployment and inflation in Nigeria 2020–2024. [4]

SELF-ASSESSMENT CHECKLIST

Let's revisit the Knowledge focus and Exam skills focus for this chapter. Decide how confident you are with each statement.

Now I can	Show it	Needs more work	Almost there	Confident to move on
explain the macroeconomic aims of economic growth, full employment/low unemployment, stable prices/low inflation, balance of payments stability, redistribution of income and environmental sustainability	Create a mnemonic to remember all the macroeconomic aims.			
analyse the reasons behind the choice of aims	Explain why countries tend to seek stable prices and full employment.			
explain the criteria that governments may set for meeting each aim	Create a table showing the broad targets for each macroeconomic aim.			
discuss the possible conflicts between macroeconomic aims	Create a network diagram to show the conflicts. Place 'macroeconomic aims' in the middle, branching out to **six** main aims, and then use arrows to demonstrate conflicts with other aims.			
interpret and comment on line graphs	Explore websites such as Trading Economics or Macrotrends. Describe various data sets that you find to another student.			
understand how scaffolding can support better answers.	Explain what scaffolding is to another student.			

23 Fiscal policy

KNOWLEDGE FOCUS

In this chapter you will answer questions on:

- 23.1 Government budget
- 23.2 Reasons for government spending
- 23.3 Taxation
- 23.4 Fiscal policy and policy measures
- 23.5 Effects of fiscal policy on government macroeconomic aims

EXAM SKILLS FOCUS

In this chapter you will:

- show that you understand how interleaving can support better answers
- show that you understand what the assessment objective of AO1 Knowledge and understanding means with regards to macroeconomics.

Learning is often described as a 'change in long-term memory'. Metacognition means that students try to understand more about how they learn and the most effective ways to improve their long-term memory. An important part of metacognition is where students revisit a particular concept in their learning, sometimes approaching it from a different perspective, in order to improve their understanding. This is known as 'interleaving'.

Chapter 2 considered the assessment objective AO1 Knowledge and understanding from a microeconomic perspective. However, AO1 Knowledge and understanding is relevant across all question types and is therefore also associated with short answer questions in macroeconomics. For example, command words such as 'define', 'state' and 'identify' are designed to assess your AO1 Knowledge and understanding skills. In responses to questions with these command words, you should show accurate knowledge and understanding of macroeconomic key terms (such as GDP, inflation and unemployment) using precise and appropriate economic vocabulary.

23.1 Government budget

UNDERSTAND THESE TERMS

- government budget
- government budget deficit
- government budget surplus

1 In each of the following cases, determine whether the government has a budget surplus or a budget deficit and calculate the size of the surplus or deficit.

   a In 2023/24, the UK government raised approximately $1.39 trillion from taxes. This is equivalent to $20,506 per person in the UK. In the same period, government spending was approximately $1.52 trillion.

   b In the year 2024/25, the federal government of Canada spent $543bn while taking $495bn in tax revenues.

   c In 2023/24, the German government expenditure was $942bn. Tax revenue was $879bn.

2 Explain why many developed countries run a budget deficit.

23.2 Reasons for government spending

≪ RECALL AND CONNECT 1 ≪

a What is a mixed economic system?

b Why might a government need to provide public goods such as street lights?

c Why might a government need to provide merit goods such as healthcare?

REFLECTION

How easy was it to remember the definitions from previous chapters? Revisiting concepts from previous chapters is a process called interleaving. Pedagogical research tells us that learning new information, waiting for a period of time to elapse and then trying to retrieve that information again, helps to reinforce your long-term memory.

- How could you embed interleaving into your revision routine?

UNDERSTAND THIS TERM

- national debt

1 As mentioned in Section 23.1, the UK government spent $1.52 trillion in the year 2023/24. The top five areas of UK government spending are given in Table 23.1. Explain why the UK government might have chosen to spend in these areas.

Table 23.1: Top five areas of UK government spending

	Area	Reason
a	Social security including state pensions and benefits	
b	Healthcare	
c	Education	
d	Debt repayments	
e	National defence	

2 Norway and Chile have the highest total expenditures on education, as a percentage of GDP (6.6% and 6.5% respectively) anywhere in the world. Explain the likely impact on their economies as a result.

3 Greece is a country that spends more money on debt repayments (20% of its budget) than healthcare (10% of its budget). Explain the likely impact on its economy as a result.

23.3 Taxation

≪ RECALL AND CONNECT 2 ≪

a Draw a demand and supply diagram for cars.

Assume that the government now increases income tax for workers. Show how that affects the price of cars.

b Draw a demand and supply diagram for cars.

Assume that the government now cuts corporation tax for firms, encouraging them to invest. Show how that affects the price of cars.

1 Match the type of tax to its correct definition.

	Type of tax		Definition
a	Progressive	i	Taxes on expenditure
b	Regressive	ii	Tax that takes the same percentage of the income or wealth of all taxpayers
c	Proportional	iii	Tax that takes a larger percentage of the income or wealth of the rich
d	Direct	iv	Taxes on income and wealth
e	Indirect	v	Tax that takes a larger percentage of the income or wealth of those living in poverty

2 In the UK, three of the largest sources of tax revenue are income tax, VAT (sales tax) and corporation tax.

Read the descriptions in Table 23.2 and decide whether they are direct or indirect, and whether they are progressive, regressive or proportional.

Table 23.2: Sources of tax revenue

	Description	Direct or indirect	Progressive, regressive or proportional
a	Income tax: a tax on all forms of income. Tax rates rise as workers earn more money; bands range from 0% to 45%.		
b	VAT: a tax on the sale of goods and services. VAT is a flat tax rate of 20% but that means lower-income households end up paying a higher percentage of their income on VAT.		
c	Corporation tax: a tax on business profits. As long as the firm makes more than £250 000 it will pay a flat 25% tax rate.		

3

In 2023/24, government tax revenue in Italy amounted to approximately $1.05 trillion, while government spending came to around $1.21 trillion USD. This is the 30th year in a row that Italy has recorded a budget deficit, and its national debt stands at well above $3 trillion. Prime Minister Giorgia Meloni has suggested that she will try to reverse the budget position during her tenure. In late 2024, she announced that her government would seek to raise more taxes from households and firms in order to repay national debt quicker, saying that '[the tax rises] will require sacrifices from everyone'.

a Apart from repaying 'national debt quicker', explain **two** other reasons for a government to raise tax rates. [4]

b Analyse the impact of tax rises on Italian consumers and firms. [6]

23.4 Fiscal policy and policy measures

UNDERSTAND THESE TERMS

- fiscal policy
- expansionary fiscal policy
- contractionary fiscal policy

1   Look back at your budget calculations for the UK, Canada and Germany from Question 1 in Section 23.1. Then, read the following fictional newspaper headlines. For each:

- Decide whether the headline describes an expansionary or contractionary fiscal policy.

- Recalculate the budget position based on the new information.

a   'UK government increases tax rates to highest level in twenty years, bringing in $50bn more tax revenue'

b   'Canada plans new $10bn stimulus investment into green technology despite deficit'

c   'Germany cuts public expenditure by $20bn at the same time as raising tax rates in order to receive a further $45bn'

23.5 Effects of fiscal policy on government macroeconomic aims

≪ RECALL AND CONNECT 3 ≪

a   How would a decrease in income tax rates affect household expenditure?

b   How would an increase in corporate income tax rates affect the demand for capital goods?

c   How would a decrease in corporate income tax rates affect the demand for labour?

1   Complete Table 23.3 by describing how an increase in income tax rates would affect the macroeconomic aims. The first row has been completed for you.

Table 23.3: Effects of an increase in income tax rates on macroeconomic aims

	Macroeconomic aim	Effect
a	Economic growth	Slow down – because household expenditure would decrease.
b	Unemployment	
c	Inflation	
d	Redistribution of income	
e	Environmental stability	

2   How could contractionary fiscal policy lead to an increase in the inflation rate?

3   How could expansionary fiscal policy lead to an increase in the unemployment rate?

4

> Japan is a country that has been associated with expansionary fiscal policy in recent years. In 2024, Japan's government approved a $250bn stimulus package to address economic challenges such as rising prices and an ageing population. The three key aims of the stimulus are: (1) to support industries like AI and semiconductors; (2) to provide benefits and energy subsidies to lower-income households; and (3) to raise the minimum salary threshold for income tax.

a   Define 'expansionary fiscal policy'.   [2]

b   Discuss whether expansionary fiscal policies, like Japan's, will always enable a government to achieve its macroeconomic aims.   [8]

SELF-ASSESSMENT CHECKLIST

Let's revisit the Knowledge focus and Exam skills focus for this chapter. Decide how confident you are with each statement.

Now I can	Show it	Needs more work	Almost there	Confident to move on
define the government budget, deficit and surplus	Create a multiple-choice question for another student that has the terms budget, deficit and surplus as answer choices.			
calculate the size of a government budget deficit or surplus	Find some data for a country of your choice and calculate the size of their budget surplus or deficit.			
explain the main areas of government spending	List **three** main areas of government spending.			
analyse the reasons for and effects of government spending	Give **three** reasons for increasing government spending.			
analyse the reasons for taxation: raising revenue, discouraging consumption of demerit goods, reducing imports, redistributing income, influencing total demand, encouraging environmental sustainability	Give **three** reasons for increasing tax rates.			

CONTINUED

Now I can	Show it	Needs more work	Almost there	Confident to move on
explain the different classifications of tax: progressive, regressive, proportional, direct and indirect	Explain the difference between direct and indirect taxes.			
analyse the impact of taxation on consumers, workers, firms/producers, government and the economy	Create a flashcard on the impact of a tax rate change on different economic agents.			
define fiscal policy	Describe what fiscal policy means.			
analyse taxes and government spending changes in the form of fiscal policy measures	Outline the difference between expansionary and contractionary fiscal policy.			
discuss how fiscal policy measures may enable a government to achieve its macroeconomic aims	Explain **two** reasons why fiscal policy may not have the impact that was intended.			
understand how interleaving can support better answers	Create a revision timetable in which you can revisit previous material.			
understand what the assessment objective of AO1 Knowledge and understanding means with regards to macroeconomics.	Create a short macroeconomic question for another student that only assesses AO1 Knowledge and understanding.			

24 Monetary policy

KNOWLEDGE FOCUS

In this chapter you will answer questions on:

- 24.1 Money supply and monetary policy
- 24.2 Monetary policy measures
- 24.3 Effects of monetary policy on government macroeconomic aims

EXAM SKILLS FOCUS

In this chapter you will:

- show that you understand the 'describe' command word and answer a describe question
- practise the skill of writing efficiently.

The command word 'describe' means to state the points of a topic / give characteristics and main features. In this chapter, you will mainly be asked to describe some data. In doing so, ensure that you focus on outlining the key features only. When describing, you do not need to include any analysis or interpretation – just present the facts such as changes over time, patterns or notable values.

Many students report that they feel like they do not have sufficient time in an exam. One of the reasons for this is that they spend too long on questions that are worth a relatively low number of marks. In essence, they are writing too much information that is unnecessary. During this chapter, you should aim to spend an appropriate amount of time writing your answers. In particular, pay attention to the describe questions. Remember, with describe questions, you do not need to offer an explanation.

24.1 Money supply and monetary policy

« RECALL AND CONNECT 1 «

a Define money.

b List **three** forms of money.

c List **three** functions of money.

d List **three** characteristics of money.

UNDERSTAND THESE TERMS

- monetary policy
- foreign exchange rate

1 In which of the following ways could a central bank increase the money supply?

A Printing more money

B Raising tax rates

C Buying back government bonds

D Encouraging commercial banks to lend more

E Lowering the reserve requirement for commercial banks

F Increasing minimum wage

2 Which of the following would be considered monetary policy?

A Increasing the money supply

B Decreasing tax rates

C Decreasing interest rates

D Encouraging investment by offering subsidies

E Influencing the foreign exchange rate

F Increasing minimum wage

24.2 Monetary policy measures

« RECALL AND CONNECT 2 «

a What is the difference between a central bank and a commercial bank?

b Apart from monetary policy, name **two** roles of central banks.

c Apart from interest rates, list **two** factors affecting household savings.

d Apart from interest rates, list **two** factors affecting household borrowing.

1 Table 24.1 shows some interest rates from around the world at the end of 2024. Explain **one** reason for differences in interest rates between different countries.

Table 24.1: Interest rates (end of 2024)

Country	Interest rate
Japan	0.25%
Switzerland	0.5%
USA	4.75%
South Africa	7.75%
Egypt	27.75%
Argentina	40.45%

Before you attempt to answer the question below, here is a simple four-point checklist for describing graphical data:

- State what each axis represents, for example, time on the x-axis, value on the y-axis.

- Describe the overall trend, for example, increasing, decreasing, fluctuating.

- Note any significant points or changes, for example, peaks, troughs, sharp increases.

- If relevant, mention time frames or comparisons between different data points.

2

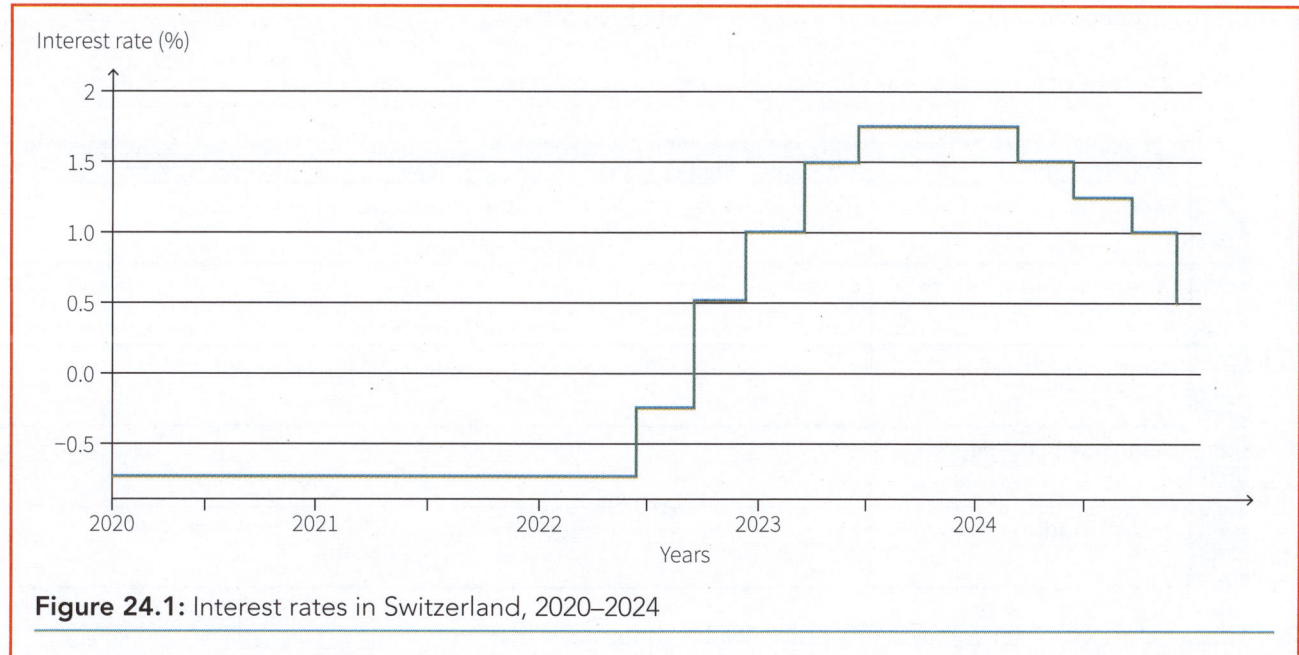

Figure 24.1: Interest rates in Switzerland, 2020–2024

Describe the changes to Switzerland's monetary policy in the period 2020–2024.   [2]

REFLECTION

If you used the four-point checklist to help you answer Question 2, reflect now on how it went.

- Did you find it easy to stick to the key points, or did you find yourself adding unnecessary details?
- Were you able to stay focused on just describing, without going into explanations?
- If you found this difficult, what might help you stay on track for next time?

24.3 Effects of monetary policy on government macroeconomic aims

UNDERSTAND THESE TERMS

- expansionary monetary policy
- contractionary monetary policy

1 Complete Table 24.1 by describing how a decrease in interest rates would affect the macroeconomic aims. The first row has been completed for you.

Table 24.1: Effects of a decrease in interest rates on macroeconomic aims

	Macroeconomic aim	Effect
a	Economic growth	Rise – because household expenditure would increase.
b	Unemployment	
c	Inflation	
d	Balance of payments	
e	Redistribution of income	

2 How could contractionary monetary policy lead to an increase in economic growth?

3 How could expansionary monetary policy lead to an increase in environmental sustainability?

4 Describe the relationship between interest rates and foreign exchange rates.

5

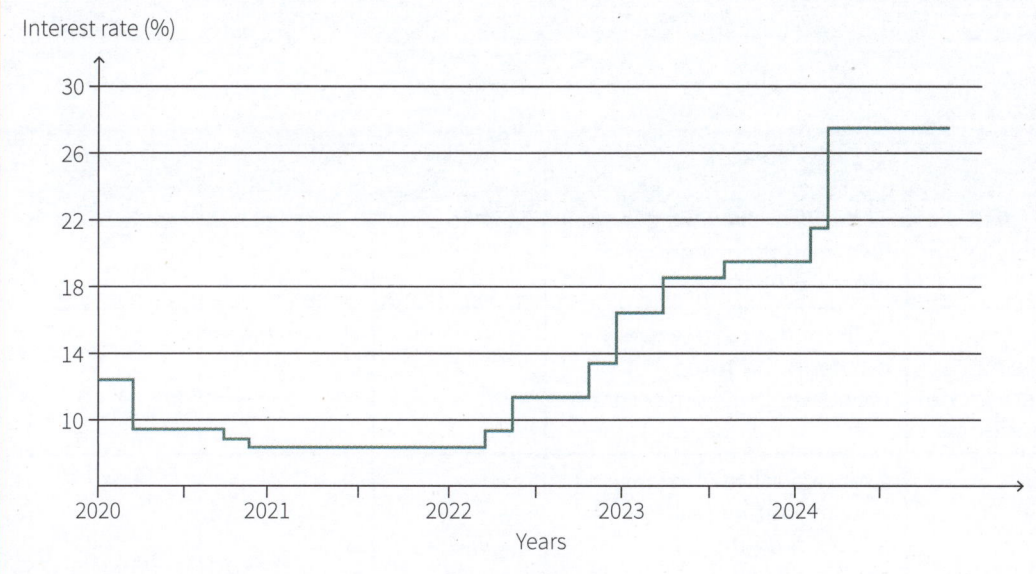

Figure 24.2: Interest rates in Egypt, 2020–2024

According to its website, the Central Bank of Egypt (CBE) aims to 'achieve monetary and banking system soundness and price stability, within the context of the general economic policy of the state'. At the end of 2024, the inflation rate in Egypt had reached 23.7%, well above the central bank's target rate of 7.0% (±2 percentage points). In November 2024, the CBE left its interest rate unchanged at a record high of 27.25% for the eighth consecutive month.

a   Describe the changes to Egypt's monetary policy in the period 2020–2024. **[2]**

b   Discuss whether increasing interest rates, like in Egypt, will always enable a government to achieve its macroeconomic aims. **[8]**

REFLECTION

In the Exam skills question (Question 5), there was one short describe question and one much longer discuss question. One way students might struggle with time management is by spending too much time on the first part, providing unnecessary detail, and not leaving enough time for the longer discuss question.

- On a scale of 1 to 5 (with 5 being totally confident), how confident are you in writing efficiently?

- If you feel you could still improve, what strategies could help you manage your time better for future questions?

SELF-ASSESSMENT CHECKLIST

Let's revisit the Knowledge focus and Exam skills focus for this chapter. Decide how confident you are with each statement.

Now I can	Show it	Needs more work	Almost there	Confident to move on
define money supply and monetary policy	Describe the meaning of monetary policy.			
explain monetary policy measures: changes in money supply, interest rate and foreign exchange rate	Identify the differences between the three monetary policy measures.			
discuss the effect of monetary policy on government macroeconomic aims	Create a table showing how monetary policy affects growth, price stability and employment.			
understand the 'describe' command word and answer a describe question	Explain to another student what the command word 'describe' means.			
practise the skill of writing efficiently.	Go back through some of your previous answers from other chapters and try to edit your work by removing unnecessary sentences.			

25 Supply-side policy

KNOWLEDGE FOCUS

In this chapter you will answer questions on:

- 25.1 What is supply-side policy?
- 25.2 Supply-side policy measures
- 25.3 Effects of supply-side policy measures on government macroeconomic aims

EXAM SKILLS FOCUS

In this chapter you will:

- explore the importance of the affective domain of learning.

The affective domain of learning means how you feel when you are studying. It is important to pay attention to how you are feeling. Monitoring your emotions while you learn can help you to identify sources of stress and, as a result, help you to find potential solutions.

25.1 What is supply-side policy?

≪ RECALL AND CONNECT 1 ≪

a Draw a diagram showing an increase in supply.

b List **three** factors that might shift the supply curve to the right.

c What is a demand-side policy?

UNDERSTAND THIS TERM

- supply-side policy

25.2 Supply-side policy measures

≪ RECALL AND CONNECT 2 ≪

a What is privatisation?

b Why should privatisation lead to a decrease in costs of production?

UNDERSTAND THIS TERM

- deregulation

1 Explain why deregulation should lead to an increase in total supply.

2 Find the following supply-side policies in the word search.

education	infrastructure	reforms	taxes
deregulation	incentives	privatise	

P	V	R	I	E	P	D	G	R	L	O	R	S	I
E	D	U	C	A	T	I	O	N	E	S	I	D	F
S	S	T	A	M	O	L	U	D	E	U	S	E	R
H	C	E	T	V	S	X	S	A	U	I	M	R	A
I	P	R	I	V	A	T	I	S	E	N	R	E	E
R	F	O	S	R	U	E	D	X	A	O	O	G	E
L	A	M	G	U	F	A	R	C	U	E	F	U	C
F	O	E	R	M	W	N	I	O	F	S	E	L	A
I	N	C	E	N	T	I	V	E	S	B	R	A	V
D	A	E	G	D	L	E	D	T	C	V	W	T	S
E	I	T	A	X	E	S	R	U	A	I	A	I	E
C	T	N	A	I	O	F	R	S	E	G	X	O	T
V	S	T	R	E	R	I	G	E	R	U	A	N	U
E	R	U	T	C	U	R	T	S	A	R	F	N	I

REFLECTION

A word search can sometimes be a valuable pedagogical tool, helping to reinforce key vocabulary and concepts while promoting memory recall. The aim of this word search is to familiarise you with specific supply-side policies to support key term recognition and retention.

In addition, word searches can help to tap into the affective domain. Quick interactive challenges can help reduce the monotony of traditional study methods.

- How do you think engaging with key vocabulary through activities like word searches can help improve your understanding and recall of economic concepts?
- Was it fun?

25.3 Effects of supply-side policy measures on government macroeconomic aims

1   Complete Table 25.1 by describing how an increase in education spending might affect the government's macroeconomic aims. The first row has been completed for you.

Table 25.1: Effects of an increase in education spending on macroeconomic aims

	Macroeconomic aim	Effect
a	Economic growth	Can boost skills of workers, leading to higher productivity and long-term economic growth
b	Unemployment	
c	Balance of payments	
d	Redistribution of income	

2 State **two** disadvantages of education spending as a supply-side policy.

3 Complete Table 25.2 by describing how an increase in infrastructure spending might affect the government's macroeconomic aims.

Table 25.2: Effects of an increase in infrastructure spending on macroeconomic aims

	Macroeconomic aim	Effect
a	Economic growth	
b	Unemployment	
c	Inflation	
d	Balance of payments	

4 State **two** disadvantages of infrastructure spending as a supply-side policy.

5

> Over the past few decades, a series of labour market reforms in the USA have shaped the country's labour market. These include maintaining a low minimum wage. The USA has one of the lowest minimum wages among high-income countries (the federal minimum wage has been $7.25 per hour since 2009). In addition, the USA has also introduced policies that make it easier for firms to hire and fire workers and to reduce the influence of trade unions. As a result, trade union membership has been in decline for decades; only about 10% of workers in the private sector are unionised. While some US politicians have attempted to challenge these labour market reforms, many economists argue that they are crucial to achieve the economy's macroeconomic aims.

a Define 'labour market reforms'. [2]

b Discuss whether the labour market reforms described in the text are likely to help the economy achieve its macroeconomic aims. [8]

SELF-ASSESSMENT CHECKLIST

Let's revisit the Knowledge focus and Exam skills focus for this chapter.
Decide how confident you are with each statement.

Now I can	Show it	Needs more work	Almost there	Confident to move on
define supply-side policy	Describe the meaning of supply side policy.			
explain supply-side policy measures: education and training, infrastructure spending, labour market reforms, lower direct taxes and improving incentives to work and invest, deregulation, privatisation and subsidies	Create flashcards with the different types of supply-side policies on them.			
discuss the effects of supply-side policy on government macroeconomic aims	Create a table showing how supply-side policy affects growth, price stability and employment.			
explore the importance of the 'affective' domain of learning.	Start a study journal in which you note down your feelings as you study.			

26 Economic growth

KNOWLEDGE FOCUS

In this chapter you will answer questions on:

- 26.1 How economic growth is measured
- 26.2 Causes and consequences of economic growth
- 26.3 Causes and consequences of recession
- 26.4 Policies to promote economic growth

EXAM SKILLS FOCUS

In this chapter you will:

- have opportunities to research real-world examples.

Researching real-world examples can be useful. If you are familiar with different scenarios (for example, a country where recession was caused by a fall in business confidence), this will help you answer a question on a new scenario about a country in a similar situation. In this chapter, the questions are about two countries – but you will be encouraged to look at the experiences of other countries as well

26.1 How economic growth is measured

UNDERSTAND THESE TERMS
- gross domestic product (GDP)
- nominal GDP
- real GDP

1 Complete the following text using the terms in the word box.

output	calculate	adjusted	constant	economic
prices	inflation	misleading	accurate	growth

When governments _____ GDP, they usually first measure it in terms of
nominal GDP. Nominal GDP is GDP in terms of the _____ operative
at that time. In other words, nominal GDP has not been _____ for
_____. For this reason, nominal GDP figures may give a _____
impression of what is happening to the output of a country over time.
For example, if prices rise by 20% in a year, there will be a 20% rise in nominal
GDP even if _____ does not change. To get an _____ picture of
a country's output and assess its _____ _____, economists adjust
nominal GDP by taking out the effects of inflation. They do this by multiplying
nominal GDP with the price index in the base year, divided by the price index in
the current year. This gives a figure for GDP at _____ prices referred to as
real GDP.

Text taken from Grant: Economics for Cambridge IGCSE™ and O Level, Coursebook

2

> In 2024, the nominal GDP of Country A is $2.0 trillion. Over twelve months
> it rises to $2.2 trillion. The inflation rate over the same time is 5%. This is
> above the target rate.

a Calculate Country A's real GDP for 2025.
b Comment on your result.

3 In Country B, real GDP is $530bn. The population is 70m. Calculate real GDP
per head.

26.2 Causes and consequences of economic growth

1 What is meant by the term 'economic growth rate'?

2 Look at Figure 26.1.

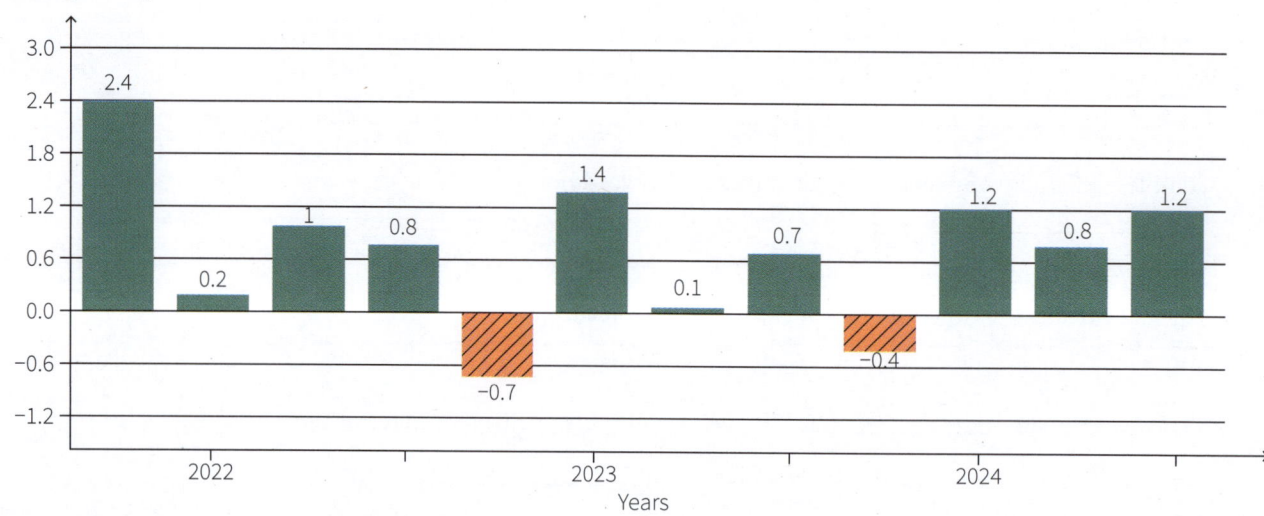

Figure 26.1: GDP quarterly growth rate, Thailand, 2022–2024

a Describe the data.

b Identify **one** reason why Thailand might see this seasonal pattern in its growth rate.

c Explain the relationship between economic growth rate and GDP, including a reason why GDP might increase even if the growth rate declines.

d Apart from tourism, list **two** reasons why the Thai economy might grow rapidly over the next three years.

3

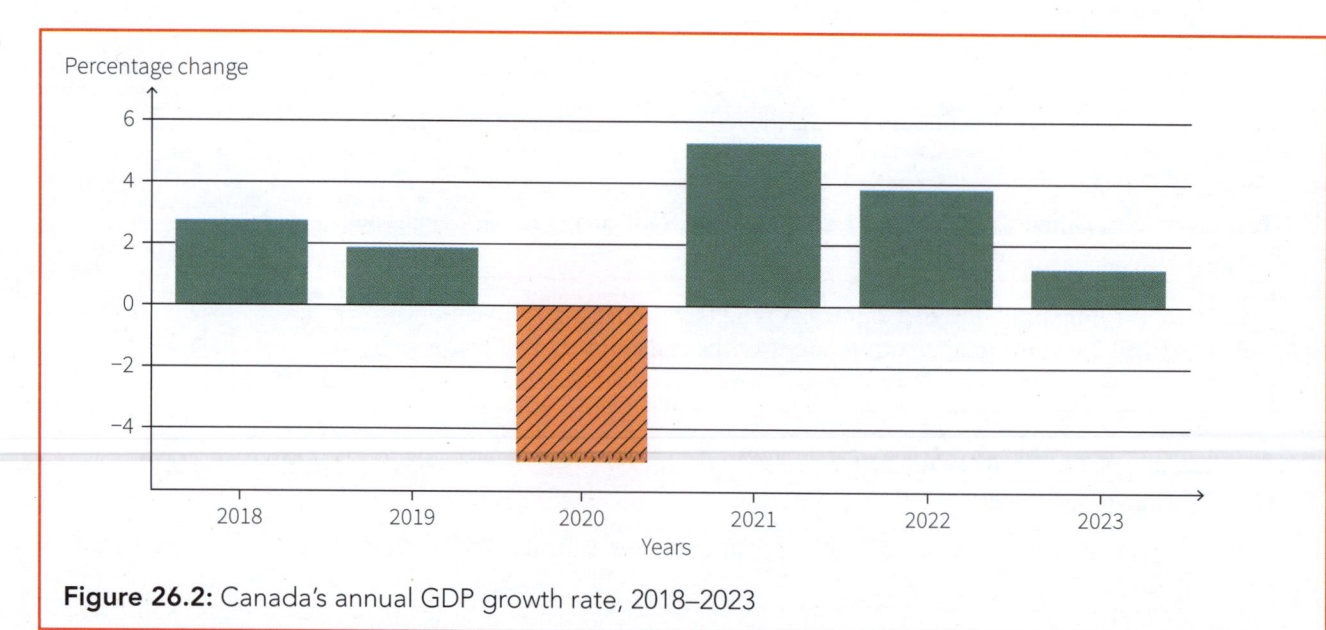

Figure 26.2: Canada's annual GDP growth rate, 2018–2023

At the end of 2024, Canada recorded a real GDP size of $2.2 trillion. Its population is a little over 40m. In 2024, Canada's annual GDP growth rate was 1.6%, only slightly higher than the previous year's figure. Many Canadians are becoming increasingly frustrated by a lack of serious growth and are urging the government to do more over the coming years.

a   Calculate Canada's real GDP per head in 2024.   [2]

b   Calculate Canada's real GDP in 2023.   [2]

c   Analyse **two** advantages of higher economic growth in Canada. [6]

REFLECTION

In the two preceding sections, you have looked at data on Thailand and Canada. The aim of this chapter is not to deepen your knowledge of either country specifically; rather, it is to help you practise interpreting economic data and drawing reasonable conclusions about a country's situation.
By engaging with real data and case studies, you are developing the ability to apply your knowledge flexibly to unfamiliar contexts – something that is essential in exam scenarios.

- How confident do you feel about interpreting economic data from an unfamiliar country and suggesting appropriate policy responses?
- What strategies could help you to improve your ability to draw conclusions from a combination of case studies and economic data?

26.3 Causes and consequences of recession

≪ RECALL AND CONNECT 1 ≪

a   What is an inferior good?

b   What is contractionary fiscal policy?

c   What is contractionary monetary policy?

UNDERSTAND THIS TERM

- recession

1   Decide whether each of the following statements is true or false.

a   A recession may be caused by a decrease in the quantity or quality of resources.

b   Contractionary fiscal policy may cause a recession.

c   If total demand in the economy rises, this might cause a demand-pull recession.

d   Inflation cannot occur at the same time as a recession.

2 Complete Table 26.1 by stating the negative consequences of a recession for different economic agents.

Table 26.1: Negative consequences of a recession for different economic agents

	Economic agent	Consequence
a	Consumer	
b	Worker	
c	Firm	
d	Government	

3 Explain **two** ways in which economic agents could benefit from a recession.

REFLECTION

Now is a perfect time to research your own case study. Find a country that has recently experienced a recession and identify the causes. Alternatively, you could research the causes of the Great Recession 2007/08.

- What did you learn from researching your own case study that could help you answer a future exam question on recession?

26.4 Policies to promote economic growth

When answering Questions 1 and 2, it would be useful to refer to the previous information in this chapter about Thailand and Canada.

To provide more practice answering questions in this topic, make sure you choose different ways of promoting growth to explain for Question 1 and Question 2.

1 Explain **two** ways that the Thai government could promote economic growth. **[4]**

2 Explain **two** ways that the Canadian government could promote economic growth. **[4]**

SELF-ASSESSMENT CHECKLIST

Let's revisit the Knowledge focus and Exam skills focus for this chapter. Decide how confident you are with each statement.

Now I can	Show it	Needs more work	Almost there	Confident to move on
define economic growth	Describe what economic growth means to another student.			

CONTINUED

Now I can	Show it	Needs more work	Almost there	Confident to move on
explain how economic growth is measured: real gross domestic product (GDP)	Explain how real GDP is calculated from nominal GDP.			
analyse the causes of economic growth: an increase in total demand, an increase in the quantity of resources or an increase in the quality of resources	Link the idea of economic growth to a PPC diagram.			
discuss the advantages and disadvantages of economic growth	List **three** advantages and **three** disadvantages of economic growth.			
define a recession	Explain what a recession is in terms of economic growth and time period.			
analyse the causes of a recession: a decrease in total demand, a decrease in the quantity of resources or a decrease in the quality of resources	Research why the Great Recession of 2007/08 happened.			
discuss the consequences of a recession for consumers, workers, producers/firms and the government	Explain why economic agents might benefit from a recession.			
discuss the range of policies available to promote economic growth and their effectiveness	Create a mind map showing different pro-growth policies available to Thai and/or Canadian governments.			
have opportunities to research real-world examples.	Find an example of a country that has recently seen a high level of economic growth and an example of a country that has experienced a recession.			

27 Employment and unemployment

KNOWLEDGE FOCUS

In this chapter you will answer questions on:

- 27.1 Employment, unemployment and full employment
- 27.2 Measurement of unemployment
- 27.3 Types and causes of unemployment
- 27.4 Consequences of unemployment
- 27.5 Policies to reduce unemployment

EXAM SKILLS FOCUS

In this chapter you will:

- show that you understand the 'give' command word and answer a give question
- show that you understand the assessment objective of AO3 Evaluation.

The command word 'give' means produce an answer from a given source or recall/memory. A relatively short answer is usually sufficient for a give question. It is associated with AO1 Knowledge and understanding. You will not be required to write any evaluative comments.

In economics, it is essential to not only understand and analyse information but also to critically evaluate the information, data and arguments being presented. The assessment objective AO3 Evaluation requires the ability to consider a range of potential outcomes of economic decisions, while acknowledging that these outcomes are often uncertain and influenced by a variety of unpredictable factors. By considering alternative perspectives you can demonstrate a deeper understanding of the complexities involved in economic analysis.

27.1 Employment, unemployment and full employment

≪ RECALL AND CONNECT 1 ≪

a   Draw a PPC diagram that shows an economy at full employment.

b   What does 'full employment' mean?

c   Why is full employment desirable?

UNDERSTAND THESE TERMS

- employment
- unemployment

27.2 Measurement of unemployment

UNDERSTAND THESE TERMS

- Labour Force Survey
- unemployment rate

1   What is meant by the term 'labour force'?

2   Give the formula for the unemployment rate.

3   a   Country A has a labour force of 32 million; 2.56 million are unemployed. Calculate the unemployment rate.

   b   Country B has 1 million people unemployed; the unemployment rate is 4%. Calculate the size of the labour force.

4   Decide whether each of the following statements is true or false.

   a   The Labour Force Survey asks whether you have been actively looking for work in the past month.

   b   The Labour Force Survey asks how much of your income you save.

   c   It is generally agreed that full employment means that the unemployment rate must equal zero.

   d   The Labour Force Survey only gives an approximation of unemployment for a country.

27.3 Types and causes of unemployment

1 Write a single sentence mini-scenario that demonstrates each type of unemployment below. The first one has been completed for you.

a Frictional: Alejandra just graduated and is applying for jobs in the engineering sector.

b Structural: _____

c Cyclical: _____

d Seasonal: _____

2 Match the type of unemployment with its correct definition.

Type of unemployment			Definition	
a	Frictional		i	Unemployment caused by a lack of total demand
b	Structural		ii	Unemployment caused by long-term changes in the pattern of demand and methods of production
c	Cyclical		iii	Temporary unemployment arising from workers being in between jobs
d	Seasonal		iv	Unemployment caused by a fall in demand at particular times of the year

3 Complete Table 27.1 by identifying the type of unemployment being described in each of the scenarios.

frictional	structural	cyclical	seasonal

Table 27.1: Types of unemployment

	Scenario	Type of unemployment
a	In early April, the weather improves and George comes to the end of his employment as a ski instructor.	
b	Priya quits her job in marketing in order to start a new job as a teacher, beginning in September.	
c	Luka cannot find work locally because he does not have any of the relevant qualifications for the jobs available.	
d	Tong struggles to find work because the economy is in recession and businesses are not hiring.	

27.4 Consequences of unemployment

≪ RECALL AND CONNECT 2 ≪

a Draw a PPC diagram that shows an economy with unemployment.

b Describe the relationship between mobility of labour and unemployment.

1 Complete Table 27.2 by stating the negative consequences of unemployment for different economic agents.

Table 27.2: Negative consequences of unemployment for economic agents

	Economic agent	Consequence
a	Consumer	
b	Worker	
c	Firm	
d	Government	

2 Explain **two** possible benefits of unemployment for an economy.

3

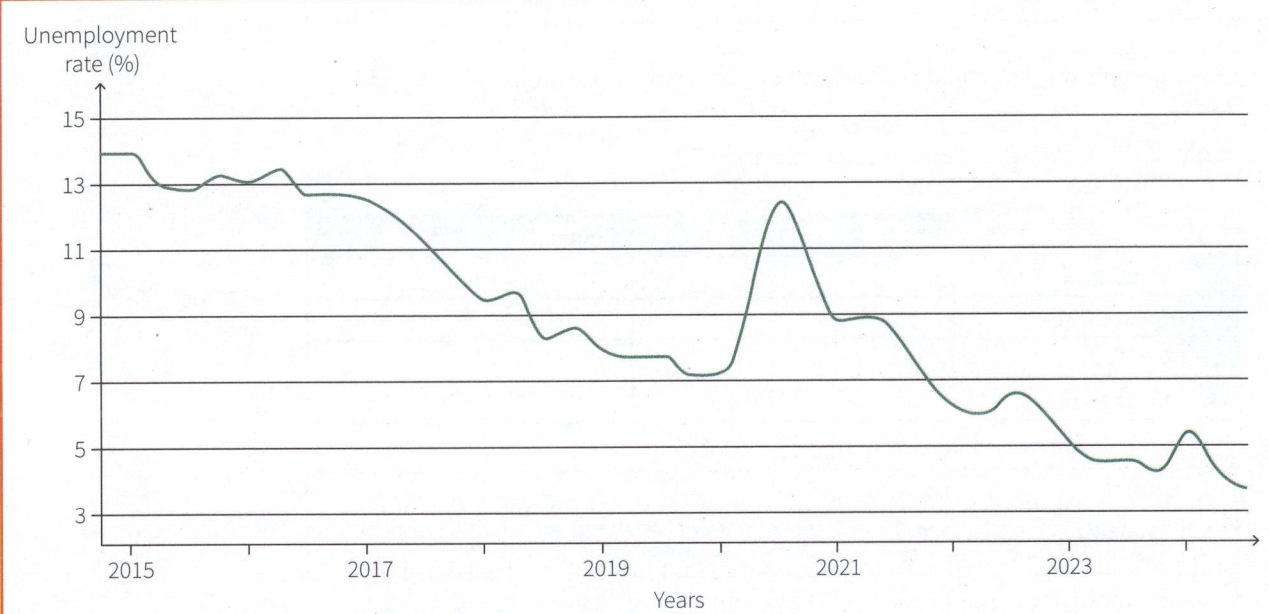

Figure 27.1: Unemployment rate in Jamaica, 2015–2023

Jamaica is an island nation in the Caribbean Sea. It has a population of 2.8 million. Over 50% of the Jamaican economy comes from the service sector, with tourism being the biggest driver. Over 4 million tourists visit Jamaica every year. The expanding tourism sector, combined with government tax reforms to encourage business investment, have led to a significant shift in the employment opportunities for Jamaicans.

a   Give the formula for calculating unemployment rate. [2]

b   Describe the trend in Jamaica's unemployment rate, 2015–2023. [2]

c   Analyse **two** possible consequences of falling unemployment on the Jamaican economy. [6]

REFLECTION

- When practising answering questions with the command word 'give', how did you ensure that your responses were simple and to the point?
- What strategies could you use to help with this?

27.5 Policies to reduce unemployment

« RECALL AND CONNECT 3 «

a   Explain how expansionary fiscal policy could create jobs.

b   Explain how expansionary monetary policy can create jobs.

c   Explain how supply-side policies like education programmes and infrastructure can help people to get jobs.

1   Give **two** policies that could reduce each of the types of unemployment listed in Table 27.3.

Table 27.3: Policies to reduce unemployment

		Policy 1	Policy 2
a	Frictional		
b	Structural		
c	Cyclical		
d	Seasonal		

2   In 2024, Botswana had an unemployment rate of 23.4%, meaning that at least two in every ten Batswana were unemployed. The economy of Botswana is one of the world's fastest growing economies, but this has not translated into stable employment opportunities. The country's largest industry – mining – contributes 35% of GDP but accounts for only 1% of jobs. Workers who lose their jobs in mining cannot easily find work elsewhere. Similarly, workers in other sectors, such as tourism and agriculture, also tend to find themselves out of work for long periods.

a   Give an example of structural unemployment and an example of
    seasonal unemployment from the data.   [2]

b   Discuss whether the government should spend more money on
    education programmes or reduce tax rates for businesses in non-seasonal
    industries like manufacturing.   [8]

REFLECTION

The requirement of AO3 Evaluation is most evident in 8-mark questions
like Question 2(b), where you need to consider both sides of the argument.
A high-quality evaluation will not only answer the question directly but will
also explore a range of potential outcomes for each economic decision.
For example, when discussing whether the government should spend more
on education or reduce tax rates for businesses, you need to assess the
benefits and drawbacks of each option, consider different stakeholders (such
as households, firms and governments) and recognise the uncertainty of
future outcomes.

- How well did you evaluate both sides of the argument?
- Did you explore the potential uncertainties and broader
  economic implications?

SELF-ASSESSMENT CHECKLIST

Let's revisit the Knowledge focus and Exam skills focus for this chapter.
Decide how confident you are with each statement.

Now I can	Show it	Needs more work	Almost there	Confident to move on
define employment, unemployment and full employment	Explain the difference between employment, unemployment and full employment.			
explain how unemployment is measured	State the formula for unemployment rate.			
analyse the causes and types of unemployment: frictional, structural, cyclical and seasonal	Give definitions for the **four** different types of unemployment.			
discuss the consequences of unemployment for the individual, producers/ firms, the government and the economy	List **one** negative impact of unemployment on each economic agent.			

CONTINUED

Now I can	Show it	Needs more work	Almost there	Confident to move on
discuss policies to reduce unemployment and their effectiveness	Explain how fiscal policy and monetary policy can be used to decrease unemployment.			
understand the 'give' command word and answer a 'give' question	Answer a past paper question that has 'give' as the command word.			
understand the assessment objective of AO3 Evaluation.	Explain to another student what AO3 Evaluation means.			

28 Inflation

KNOWLEDGE FOCUS

In this chapter you will answer questions on:

- 28.1 What are inflation and deflation?
- 28.2 Measurement of inflation and deflation
- 28.3 Causes of inflation
- 28.4 Consequences of inflation
- 28.5 Policies to control inflation

EXAM SKILLS FOCUS

In this chapter you will:

- show that you can refer to data effectively in your answer
- understand that eye strain can affect the quality of your revision.

Referring to data effectively in your answer is crucial in Economics exams because it demonstrates your ability to apply theoretical concepts to real-world situations. In this chapter, you will have the opportunity to consider graphical data as well as tabular data. By referencing data, you show that you understand how economic concepts work in a given context and can use quantitative information to support your arguments.

Eye strain can occur when you are studying for long hours. It happens when your eyes are working too hard (reading or staring at a screen) and can lead to discomfort, headaches and difficulty concentrating – all of which can negatively impact your revision. When your eyes are tired, it becomes harder to concentrate. This can cause you to miss important details or make mistakes, slowing down your progress. To reduce eye strain during revision, you should adjust screen settings, study in well-lit areas and take frequent breaks to stretch and reset your focus. The 20-20-20 rule is that every 20 minutes, you should take a 20-second break and look at something 20 feet (6 metres) away. This helps relax the muscles in your eyes and reduces strain.

28.1 What are inflation and deflation?

≪ RECALL AND CONNECT 1 ≪

a Why do prices rise?

b Why do prices fall?

UNDERSTAND THESE TERMS

- inflation
- deflation
- disinflation

1 Consider Figure 28.1 and decide whether each of the following statements is true or false.

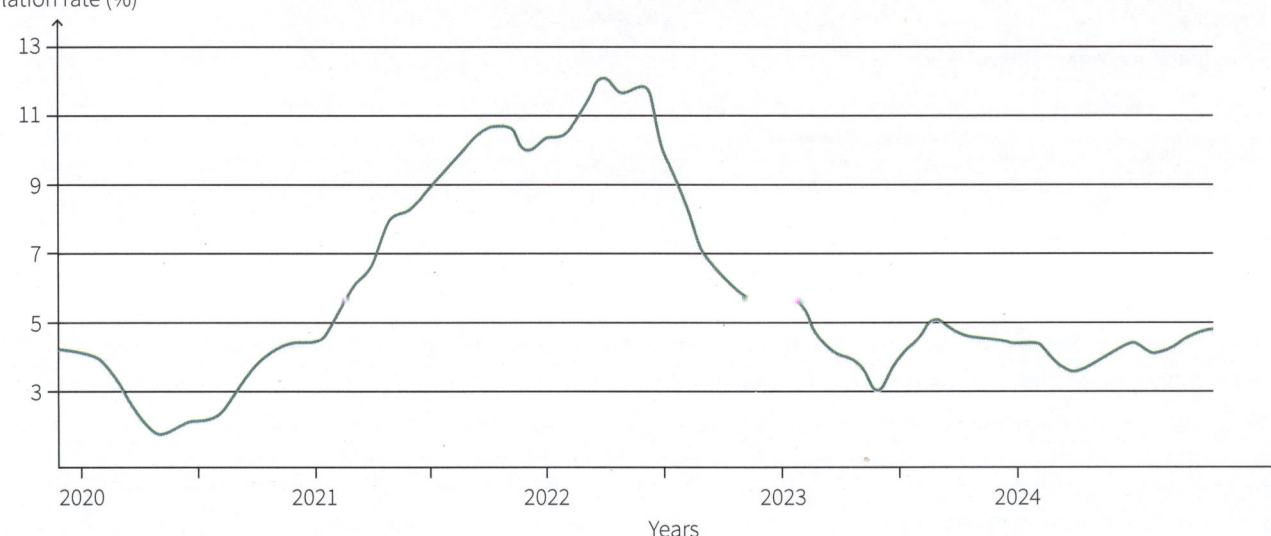

Figure 28.1: Brazil's inflation rate, 2020–2024

a Brazil has seen inflation throughout the time period.

b There is period of deflation immediately after the inflation rate peak (12.1%) in April 2022.

c Prices in 2024 are higher than they were in 2022.

d Deflation is big problem in Brazil.

28.2 Measurement of inflation and deflation

UNDERSTAND THIS TERM

- consumer price index (CPI)

1 There are several stages in constructing a price index. Expand on each of these stages in Table 28.1. The first row has been completed for you.

Table 28.1: Constructing a price index

	Stage	Description
a	Select a basket of goods	Government conducts household surveys to identify the range of goods and services that are most commonly bought by typical households
b	Select a base year	
c	Find out price changes	
d	Find out typical household spending	
e	Construct a weighted price index	

2 a In the construction of Brazil's CPI, explain why fuel might have a higher weighting than restaurant meals.

  b In the construction of Brazil's CPI, explain why DVD prices are unlikely to be measured but smartphone prices are.

3

For a long time, Brazil has been associated with high levels of inflation. Table 28.2 shows the country's CPI at the start of the 21st century.

Table 28.2: Brazil's CPI, 2000–2004

Year	2000	2001	2002	2003	2004
Brazil CPI (base year: 1993)	1 600	1 680	2 040	2 220	2 400

a   Calculate the annual inflation rate in 2001.

b   Calculate the annual inflation rate in 2004.

c   Given that 1993 is the base year and yet by the year 2000 – just 7 years later – CPI is at 1 600 points, what does this tells us about inflation in Brazil in the late 1990s?

28.3 Causes of inflation

≪ RECALL AND CONNECT 2 ≪

a   With reference to the price mechanism, explain how an increase in demand can lead to an increase in price.

b   With reference to the price mechanism, explain how an increase in supply can lead to a decrease in price.

UNDERSTAND THESE TERMS

- cost-push inflation
- demand-pull inflation

1   Complete Table 28.3. Consider the scenarios in the table and decide whether they are examples of demand-pull inflation or cost-push inflation. In the final two rows, add your own scenarios.

Table 28.3: Demand-pull and cost-push inflation

	Scenario	Demand-pull / Cost-push
a	The price of oil increases globally, leading to higher production costs.	
b	A natural disaster disrupts availability of various goods, leading to a rise in prices.	
c	Lower interest rates lead to a spike in credit-fuelled consumption.	
d	A shortage of raw materials leads to an increase in production costs.	
e	The government increases its spending on large infrastructure projects.	
f		Demand-pull
g		Cost-push

28.4 Consequences of inflation

≪ RECALL AND CONNECT 3 ≪

a   What is the link between inflation and the measurement of real GDP?

b   How might inflation affect cyclical unemployment?

UNDERSTAND THESE TERMS

- menu costs
- shoe-leather costs

Question 1 is a good example to check your ability to refer to data in your answer. Ensure that you use Figure 28.1 to help you answer Question 1 and Table 28.2 to help you answer Question 2.

1   Explain the likely impact of the inflation rates in Brazil (2020–2024) on Brazilian savers and borrowers.   [4]

2   Explain the likely impact of the inflation rates in Brazil at the start of the 21st century on consumers and firms.   [4]

28.5 Policies to control inflation

≪ RECALL AND CONNECT 4 ≪

a   What policies can a government use to stimulate growth?

b   What policies can a government use to reduce unemployment?

In Question 1, make sure that you refer to Table 28.4 in your answer.

1

Brazil has long been associated with high inflation, but its neighbour, Argentina, has faced even more severe inflationary challenges. For example, in recent years, inflation in Argentina has reached nearly 300%. In 2023, Javier Milei became the new President of Argentina. He vowed to reduce inflation to more manageable levels through a strong combination of contractionary fiscal and monetary policies.

Table 28.4: Selected data, Argentina (2024)

Economic measure	2024 value
Inflation rate	166%
Interest rate	32%
Unemployment rate	6.2%
Economic growth rate	−1.6%

Discuss whether contractionary fiscal policy or contractionary monetary policy is likely to be more effective at reducing inflation in Argentina.   **[8]**

REFLECTION

Data allows you to ground abstract economic theories in actual information, enabling you to assess their relevance and impact. In the previous question about Argentina, referring to specific data like the inflation rate of 166%, the interest rate of 32% and the economic growth rate of −1.6% allows you to demonstrate how these figures would influence the effectiveness of contractionary fiscal and monetary policies. Without data, your answer may appear generic.

•   Were you able to use the data in your answer effectively?

SELF-ASSESSMENT CHECKLIST

Let's revisit the Knowledge focus and Exam skills focus for this chapter.
Decide how confident you are with each statement.

Now I can	Show it	Needs more work	Almost there	Confident to move on
define inflation and deflation	Explain the difference between the terms 'inflation' and 'deflation'.			
explain how inflation is measured using the consumer price index (CPI)	Describe the different stages of constructing the CPI.			
analyse the causes of inflation: demand-pull and cost-push	Explain the difference between demand-pull and cost-push inflation.			
discuss the consequences of inflation for consumers, workers, producers/firms and the economy	Identify **one** impact of inflation on each of the different economic agents.			
discuss the range of policies available to control inflation and their effectiveness	Create a mind map with different policies that a country like Brazil could use to reduce the price level.			
refer to data effectively in my answer	Find some data on a country of your choice and practise writing descriptive sentences about what the data shows.			
understand that eye strain can affect the quality of my revision.	Create a revision plan that includes regular screen breaks and rest periods to reduce eye strain.			

Exam practice 4

This section contains practice questions that will draw together your knowledge on a range of topics you have covered up to this point and will help you prepare for your assessment.

The following question has example student responses and commentaries provided. For each part of the question, work through the question first, then compare your answer to the example student response and commentary.

Question 1

In July 2024, the unemployment rate in Australia rose to 4.2%, the highest level in two years. The disappointing news came despite Australia generally reporting better economic data. Annual GDP growth figures over the last three years have been strong (2.1% in 2022, 4.3% in 2023 and 3.0% in 2024) and inflation has also fallen from a high of 7.8% in October 2023 to 2.8% in July 2024.

The recent unemployment data will likely harm business confidence and there may be renewed calls for the government to reduce direct tax rates on individuals and firms. The highest income tax rate in Australia is 45%, which is much higher in comparison to 37% in the USA and just 24% in Singapore.

a State **two** types of unemployment. [2]

Example student response	Commentary
Frictional unemployment	AO1 Knowledge and understanding
Cyclical unemployment	This answer is correct.

b Explain **two** reasons why inflation may fall when there is an increase in total demand. [4]

Example student response	Commentary
First, inflation may fall when there is an increase in total demand. In Australia, this happened when inflation fell from 'a high of 7.8% in October 2023 to 2.8% in July 2024', despite strong economic growth over the same period. This can happen if the increase in total supply exceeds the rise in demand. For example, if there is an improvement in productivity, firms can produce more goods with the same or fewer resources, which can lead to lower production costs and more goods being available in the market. This could offset the upward pressure on prices from higher demand.	AO1 Knowledge and understanding and AO2 Analysis The student demonstrates a very strong understanding of economic theory. In addition, there is an effective link back to the data, with good use of a quotation. The layout of the answer makes it very clear where the first reason ends and where the second reason starts.
Second, a reduction in the costs of production (such as a decrease in raw material costs or a stronger exchange rate) can help firms to lower their prices even when demand is rising. As a result, even with higher demand, inflation might not increase significantly, or it could even fall.	

c Analyse the potential consequences of unemployment for the individual, the government and the economy. [6]

Example student response	Commentary
Unemployment is undesirable for the individual because it means they do not get paid. Unemployment is undesirable for the government because they will need to pay more money in unemployment benefits. Unemployment is undesirable for the economy because it means there is less total demand in the economy, causing a recession.	AO1 Knowledge and understanding and AO2 Analysis The student correctly identified potential consequences of unemployment on all three parties. However, the response could be more detailed. In terms of the individual, for example, unemployment affects not only income but also psychological well-being, job skills and future employability. The government might also experience other issues like a loss in tax revenue, a rise in public debt and potential social unrest. These additional effects would enrich the answer.

d Discuss whether lower taxes on firms will benefit the economy. [8]

Example student response	Commentary
There are several advantages of lower taxes. Lower taxes on firms directly increase the profits of firms, leaving them with more money to invest. In Australia, 'the recent unemployment data will likely harm business confidence' and so it seems like firms are unlikely to invest unless the government chooses the lower taxes. If they do, firms could become more productive and, ultimately, more competitive. Likewise, when taxes are reduced, firms have more funds available for investment in capital and technology. This could stimulate economic growth as firms expand their operations and increase their productivity. Finally, lower taxes can reduce the cost of production for firms, potentially allowing them to lower prices for consumers. This reduction in prices could ease inflationary pressures. Firms may see more revenue, which they could use to reinvest and then expand in scale. There are also several disadvantages. For example, firms may choose to keep the additional profits rather than reinvest them. If firms do not reinvest, the anticipated increase in economic growth and productivity may not materialise. Lower taxes on firms would also lead to a reduction in government revenue. This could limit the government's ability to fund public services such as education and healthcare.	AO1 Knowledge and understanding and AO2 Analysis There is a lot of good analysis in this answer. However, the second paragraph doesn't offer much to advance the first paragraph. It reads like a repeat of the same chain of analysis. It would be better to develop the first point from a different perspective, perhaps looking at the possibility for the firm to sell more exports. AO3 Evaluation The evaluation in this answer is good. The student covers a range of points but the final section on MNCs, in particular, is strong as it shows a real depth and nuance to the evaluation.

Example student response	Commentary
Finally, lower taxes might attract MNCs to operate in Australia. This can bring some benefits, such as increased investment and employment in the short term. Australia currently has an unemployment rate of 4.2% so there is some room for improvement. However, it might also lead to domestic firms being crowded out or losing market share. Additionally, MNCs may repatriate profits back to their home countries rather than reinvesting them locally, which could limit the long-term benefits to the domestic economy.	

Now that you have read the example student response to the previous question, here are some similar practice questions for parts (b), (c) and (d) which you should attempt. Use the guidance in the commentaries in this section to help you as you answer the questions.

Question 2

b   Explain **two** reasons why a decrease in unemployment is often accompanied by an increase in inflation. [4]

c   Analyse the potential consequences of inflation for the individual, the government and the economy. [6]

d   Discuss whether lower taxes on individuals are good for the economy. [8]

The following question has example student responses and commentaries provided. For each part of the question, work through the question first, then compare your answer to the example student response and commentary.

Question 3

Table 1: Japan fact file December 2024

Unemployment rate	2.4%
Inflation rate	3.6%
Interest rate	0.25%
Economic growth	2.8% (Oct–Dec 2024)

Japan faced significant economic challenges between 2022 and 2024, including slow economic growth, high inflation and rising government debt. For example, Japan experienced some of its highest inflation rates in over 40 years, reaching 3.6% in late 2024. This had a major impact on consumers, workers and firms. The central bank – the Bank of Japan – raised interest rates accordingly to support the government's macroeconomic aims. Interest rates in 2024 stood at 0.25% (the highest level since 2008).

Japan also faced a recession in late 2023, arguably caused by a decline in the quality of factors of production. Supply-side policies, such as labour market reforms and deregulation, were introduced to try to reduce unemployment, but their success was varied. The government also took steps to change tax rates in the country and reduce the budget deficit. In 2023, Japan's budget deficit narrowed by 5.4% due to increased tax revenues.

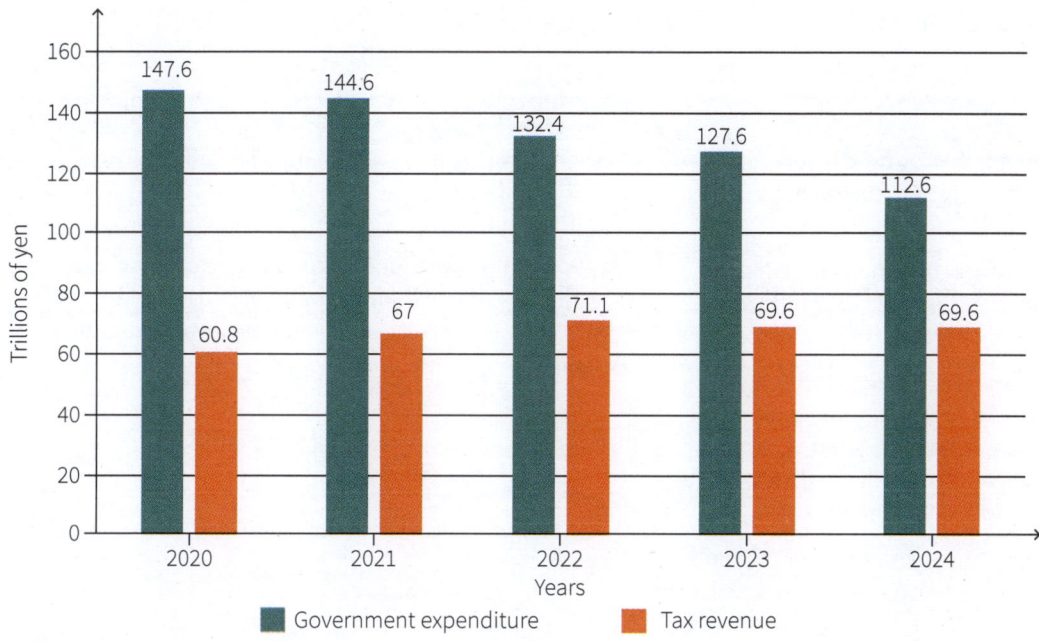

Figure 1: Japan's public finances (2020–2024)

a Calculate Japan's budget deficit or surplus in 2023. [2]

Example student response	Commentary
Budget deficit / surplus = tax revenue – government expenditure 69.6 – 127.6 = –58 trillion yen deficit	AO1 Knowledge and understanding This answer is correct. The working is clearly laid out. It is helpful that the student has added the units/currency and stated that it is a budget deficit.

b Identify **two** reasons for taxation. [2]

Example student response	Commentary
To fund public goods. To redistribute income.	AO1 Knowledge and understanding This answer is correct.

c Explain **one** way in which high inflation rates affect firms in Japan. [2]

Example student response	Commentary
High inflation increases Japanese firms' production costs as the prices of raw materials and wages rise. This can reduce their profit, forcing them to either increase prices (which may lower consumer demand) or cut costs, potentially leading to reduced investment and unemployment.	AO1 Knowledge and understanding This is a really good answer. The student links the inflation well to the impact on firms (reduced profit). However, there is no real application to the case study. The question says how high inflation rates affect firms **in Japan**. For example, a good linking sentence might be added at the end, such as: 'This was clearly seen in Japan where firms struggled with rising costs between 2022 and 2023, contributing to the recession in late 2023.'

d Explain how a decline in the quality of factors of production can contribute to a recession. **[4]**

Example student response	Commentary
A decline in the quality of factors of production can contribute to a recession by reducing overall productivity and economic output. A recession is defined as six-month period of negative economic growth. As stated in the text, Japan 'faced a recession in late 2023'. For example, if Japanese workers (labour) lack necessary skills due to poor education or training, productivity falls, leading to lower efficiency and reduced economic growth. High structural unemployment may also weaken consumer spending, reducing total demand. Equally, outdated or poorly maintained machinery and infrastructure (capital goods) lower production efficiency, increasing costs and reducing competitiveness. Japanese firms may struggle to expand, leading to slower growth and potential job losses.	AO1 Knowledge and understanding and AO2 Analysis This is good answer. The student correctly identifies two factors of production (labour and capital goods) and develops two chains of analysis to explain why a decline in the factors of production might cause a recession.

e Analyse the relationship between contractionary monetary policy and inflation. **[4]**

Example student response	Commentary
Contractionary monetary policy measures such as a decrease in government spending and a rise in tax rates, can help a government achieve its macroeconomic aim of low inflation. For example, decreased government spending on infrastructure and public services reduces total demand, leading to a fall in the price level. Likewise, in times of high inflation, the government may increase taxes or reduce spending to lower total demand.	AO1 Knowledge and understanding and AO2 Analysis Unfortunately, the student has confused fiscal policy and monetary policy. The student is writing about fiscal policy, but the focus should instead be on the impact of monetary tools like interest rates or money supply. The student shows a good understanding of how total demand can affect the price, however, and may receive some marks for that part of the answer.

f   Discuss whether supply-side policies can reduce unemployment in Japan.   [6]

Example student response	Commentary
Supply-side policies might help reduce unemployment in Japan, but they are not always effective. On one hand, policies like better education and training can make Japanese workers more skilled, so they can get jobs more easily. Cutting taxes for businesses might encourage them to hire more people. However, these policies take a long time to work. If there's not enough demand in the economy, firms won't hire even if workers are well trained. Also, cutting taxes would be difficult for the Japanese government because they already have a large budget deficit, and this would only make it wider. If the Japanese government decreased benefits then this might force people to take jobs, but it could also make life harder for those who are unemployed. Overall, supply-side policies can help reduce unemployment, but they aren't a quick fix and might not work alone. Supply-side policies are expensive, and Japan already has a large budget deficit, as shown in the graph.	AO1 Knowledge and understanding and AO2 Analysis The answer would be improved if the student focussed more on the supply-side policies that are mentioned in the case, such as labour market reform and deregulation. Statements like 'policies like better education and training can make workers more skilled, so they can get jobs more easily' need more development. In this case, the student should have linked to the concept of structural unemployment. In addition, they could have given an example of training that may have fulfilled a specific skills gap in the Japanese economy. AO3 Evaluation There is an effective link back to the case study in terms of identifying that Japan already has a large budget deficit. There is no need to repeat the same point twice, though. The evaluation could also benefit from more technical vocabulary; for example, highlighting the difference between structural unemployment and cyclical unemployment. Overall, this answer lacks depth. The points are mostly assertion rather than analysis and the student would benefit from asking themselves 'what are the implications?' at every stage.

Question 4

Write an improved answer to Question 3(e).

> Unit 5

Economic development

29 Living standards

KNOWLEDGE FOCUS

In this chapter you will answer questions on:

- 29.1 Indicators of living standards
- 29.2 Comparing living standards and income distribution

EXAM SKILLS FOCUS

In this chapter you will:

- have the opportunity to practise the key skill of analysis, which is one of the assessment objectives
- show that you understand how thinking aloud can support metacognition.

The assessment objective AO2 Analysis requires you to select, organise and interpret economics data and information. This involves applying economic analysis to various types of data, including written, numerical, diagrammatic and graphical. In this chapter, you will see two sets of Exam skills questions: those that have no context and those that do. In the second set, you should think about how the content shapes your analysis. Are there any clues in the data or case study that help you interpret what is going on? What relationships can you identify between the figures or the events described? Good analysis is not just about repeating facts; it is about making sense of them in a logical and structured way.

Metacognition has been shown to be an effective way to improve your own learning. One strategy that is frequently used as part of a wider metacognitive strategy is 'thinking aloud'. Like it sounds, this means that you will verbally talk about your thought processes as you are conducting a task.

29.1 Indicators of living standards

≪ RECALL AND CONNECT 1 ≪

a   What is real GDP per head?

b   Why would a high real GDP value per head suggest high living standards?

UNDERSTAND THIS TERM

- Human Development Index (HDI)

1   The Human Development Index (HDI) is known as a composite indicator. What does that mean?

2   List the **three** components of HDI.

Before you write your answer to each of the following questions, talk aloud about how you plan to write it. You could even talk aloud as you are writing the answer, too.

3   Identify **two** limitations of using real GDP per head as an indicator of living standards. [2]

4   Identify **two** limitations of using HDI as an indicator of living standards. [2]

5   Discuss whether a high real GDP per head will always lead to a high HDI. [8]

REFLECTION

Talking through your ideas (even if just to yourself) can help you plan more clearly and avoid common errors. For example, it might help you remember that an identify question only needs a brief response while a discuss question requires a more developed answer.

- How did thinking aloud help (or not help) your understanding and planning of these questions?
- Will you use this strategy again in future revision or assessments? Why or why not?

29.2 Comparing living standards and income distribution

Table 29.1: Selected countries HDI

Country	HDI
Singapore	0.95
Spain	0.91
Saudi Arabia	0.87
Sri Lanka	0.78
South Africa	0.71
Senegal	0.52
Sierra Leone	0.47

1   Describe the differences in living standards according to the data in Table 29.1.

2   List some of the reasons for differences in living standards between countries.

Unlike in the Exam skills questions in Section 29.1, Question 3 below requires you to analyse economic issues using the information available. In this case, it requires you to identify the key differences between living standards in two countries.

You can choose to think aloud as you plan your answer, but also make sure that your analysis is structured and focused on key differences, rather than just summarising the data.

3

Table 29.2: Selected data for Singapore and Sierra Leone, 2021

	Real GDP per capita	HDI
Singapore	$89 400	0.95
Sierra Leone	$440	0.47

Located on the west coast of Africa, Sierra Leone is associated with one of the most valuable exports in the world: diamonds. And yet, it is one of the poorest countries in the world. Income inequality is significant, with a large portion of the population living in poverty and lacking access to wealth-building opportunities.

With a population of just 5.7 million people and a total land area of 750 square kilometres, Singapore is one of the richest counties in the world and it has a highly educated workforce. It specialises in finance, technology and trade.

Analyse possible reasons for differences in living standards between countries like Sierra Leone and Singapore.   [6]

REFLECTION

Remember, effective analysis is about making meaningful connections and drawing conclusions based on the information you have.

- How could you improve your analysis skills for future questions?

SELF-ASSESSMENT CHECKLIST

Let's revisit the Knowledge focus and Exam skills focus for this chapter.
Decide how confident you are with each statement.

Now I can	Show it	Needs more work	Almost there	Confident to move on
explain indicators of living standards: real gross domestic product (GDP) per head and the Human Development Index (HDI) and its components	Explain the difference between the two indicators of living standards.			
discuss the advantages and disadvantages of real GDP per head and HDI as indicators of living standards	List **two** advantages of using each indicator of living standards.			
analyse the reasons for differences in living standards and income distribution within and between countries	Research the causes of differences in living standards for any **two** countries (not Singapore or Sierra Leone) in Table 29.1.			
have the opportunity to practise the key skill of analysis, which is one of the assessment objectives	Explain what AO2 Analysis means to another student.			
show that I understand how thinking aloud can support metacognition.	Write down what you am thinking before you attempt your next long answer question.			

30 Poverty

KNOWLEDGE FOCUS

In this chapter you will answer questions on:

- 30.1 The difference between absolute poverty and relative poverty
- 30.2 Causes of poverty
- 30.3 Policies to alleviate poverty and redistribute income

EXAM SKILLS FOCUS

In this chapter you will:

- show that you understand the importance of regular self-testing
- develop empathy for the real-world impact of economic issues such as poverty.

It is important that you avoid leaving revision until the exam is close. Instead, aim for a longer period before the exam for preparation. In addition, you should increase the volume of testing opportunities. In this chapter, you will have the opportunity to practise several more explain questions and a discuss question, which should give you some idea of the frequency of testing that you should aim for.

Having empathy for the scenarios you will read in this chapter can improve your learning experience by fostering a deeper understanding of the real-world implications of economic theories. In economics, it is sometimes too easy to just look at data and figures and not think about the human situation at the end. However, when you connect emotionally with the experiences of individuals or communities affected by economic issues, you are more likely to engage with the material on a personal level, and this will help you to retain key concepts.

30.1 The difference between absolute poverty and relative poverty

UNDERSTAND THESE TERMS

- absolute poverty
- relative poverty
- vicious circle of poverty

1 Read the following statements. Are they describing a situation of absolute poverty or relative poverty?

   a Reuben lives on less than $2 a day, struggles to afford basic food and has no access to clean drinking water.

   b Sienna earns less than 50% of the median income in her country, making it difficult for her to afford a reliable internet connection and make the most of her leisure time.

   c Scarlett lives in a wealthy urban area but, month to month, she is struggling to meet her car repayments and the rent for a neglected apartment in her neighbourhood.

   d Alphonso and his family live in a remote village where they lack access to shelter, basic healthcare and sufficient clothing for the harsh winters.

2 In this activity, read the journal entry of someone living in poverty. Highlight any examples that indicate absolute poverty or relative poverty. Create a table with two columns: one for absolute poverty and one for relative poverty. Write down the evidence you underlined in the correct column.

'I don't have a lot of money left until next week when I'm supposed to get my next payment. I have a bit of cash and some money on a pre-paid card. I'm planning to buy the cheapest things we need: bread, milk for my children and maybe some rice if it's not too expensive.

I hesitated to apply for the government's social welfare programme but, after my partner lost their seasonal work, we didn't have much choice. It's better than nothing. However, I won't get any money for a while because there's a delay in the system. In the meantime, I will borrow from my sister just to buy firewood and basic food.'

REFLECTION

Empathy encourages you to consider the human side of statistics and theories, making it easier to grasp the complexities behind economic content. In addition, it can motivate you to explore solutions more thoughtfully, enhancing critical thinking and encouraging a well-rounded perspective in your studies.

- How did reading this journal entry make you feel?
- How can considering the human side of economic issues influence your approach to thinking about real-world problems in your studies?

30.2 Causes of poverty

« RECALL AND CONNECT 1 «

a   What is unemployment?

b   List **three** types of unemployment.

c   Why do some people earn less than others?

1   Complete Table 30.1 by filling in the blank cells with either a factor that causes poverty or an explanation of why that factor leads to poverty. The first row has been completed for you.

Table 30.1: Explanations for poverty

	Factor	Explanation
a	Age	Elderly individuals may lack income if they have no savings or pension.
b	Low wages	
c		Medical expenses and inability to work reduce income, leading to financial hardship.
d		Without a job, people lose their primary source of income, leading to financial hardship.
e	Environmental factors	

2

Haiti is a country in the Caribbean Sea. According to the World Bank, over a third (36.6%) of Haiti's 12m population live on less than $2.15 a day. Haiti has one of the highest rates of income inequality worldwide, as well as an HDI of just 0.55. Haiti is extremely vulnerable to natural disasters – notable earthquakes hit the country in 2010 and 2021.

Explain **two** factors that might cause Haiti's high prevalence of poverty.   **[4]**

30.3 Policies to alleviate poverty and redistribute income

« RECALL AND CONNECT 2 «

a   What is a minimum wage?

b   Draw a minimum wage diagram.

c   What is a progressive tax?

d   Identify a disadvantage of raising progressive tax rates.

1 a Explain how increasing the minimum wage can alleviate poverty and redistribute income.

b Explain how increasing progressive tax rates can alleviate poverty and redistribute income.

2 Poverty in India remains a major challenge despite the country's rapid economic growth in the 21st century. According to the UN, India lifted 270 million people out of extreme poverty between 2005 and 2015. Today, poverty in India is concentrated in just five states; these states account for nearly two-thirds of all poverty in the country. As India continues to grow economically, there are ongoing federal government efforts to improve education, healthcare and social welfare programmes in these regions.

Discuss whether government policies are likely to be effective in alleviating poverty in India over the next decade. [8]

SELF-ASSESSMENT CHECKLIST

Let's revisit the Knowledge focus and Exam skills focus for this chapter. Decide how confident you are with each statement.

Now I can	Show it	Needs more work	Almost there	Confident to move on
define and explain the difference between absolute poverty and relative poverty	Create a flashcard with the terms 'absolute poverty' and 'relative poverty' on one side and their definitions on the other.			
analyse the causes of poverty: unemployment, low wages, illness, age and environmental factors	Research the main causes of regional poverty in India.			
discuss the policies to alleviate poverty and redistribute income: promoting economic growth, improved education, improved healthcare provision, more generous state benefits, progressive taxation and national minimum wage	Answer the question: Discuss whether it would be more effective to raise the minimum wage or to raise progressive tax rates in Haiti, in order to alleviate poverty. [8]			
understand the importance of regular self-testing	Create a revision schedule that has a self-assessment check built into it.			
develop empathy for the real-world impact of economic issues such as poverty.	Look through previous chapters and try to connect emotionally with some of the stories.			

31 Population

KNOWLEDGE FOCUS

In this chapter you will answer questions on:

- 31.1 Factors that affect population growth
- 31.2 The effects of changes in the size and structure of populations

EXAM SKILLS FOCUS

In this chapter you will:

- recognise how to respond to a quotation in a question
- show that you can manage test anxiety by using a reward approach.

A common way to assess understanding of an economic concept is to ask students to respond to a quotation. Students can find this tricky. However, it is important to remember that all exam questions must be based on content in the syllabus. Therefore, you should always think: which part of the syllabus am I being assessed on now? In addition, the command words will still be the same and the number of marks for the question will indicate the depth that you need to write to. So, you can continue to follow the advice you have been given for other types of question.

It can be useful to follow a reward approach. After you successfully complete a revision task, why not reward yourself? This can be a playing a small game or a walk around the local park.

31.1 Factors that affect population growth

UNDERSTAND THESE TERMS

- death rate
- net migration
- immigration
- emigration
- net migration rate

1　**Table 31.1:** Net migration rates for selected countries, 2023

Country	Net migration rate
New Zealand	+4.8
Iceland	+2.7
Estonia	–2.7
Zimbabwe	–2.9

a　What do the net migration rates in Table 31.1 indicate about migration trends in these countries?

b　Suggest **two** reasons why New Zealand and Iceland have positive net migration rates.

c　Suggest **two** reasons why Estonia and Zimbabwe have negative net migration rates.

d　The birth rate in Zimbabwe is 27.3 births per 1 000. Its death rate is 8.9 deaths per 1 000. Using all this information, describe the likely changes to Zimbabwe's population over the next decade.

2　Decide whether each of the following statements is true or false.

a　High economic growth always leads to a high birth rate.

b　A net negative migration rate is sometimes referred to as 'brain drain'.

c　War and natural disaster will lead to a short-term increase in the death rate.

d　All governments aim to have net positive migration.

3

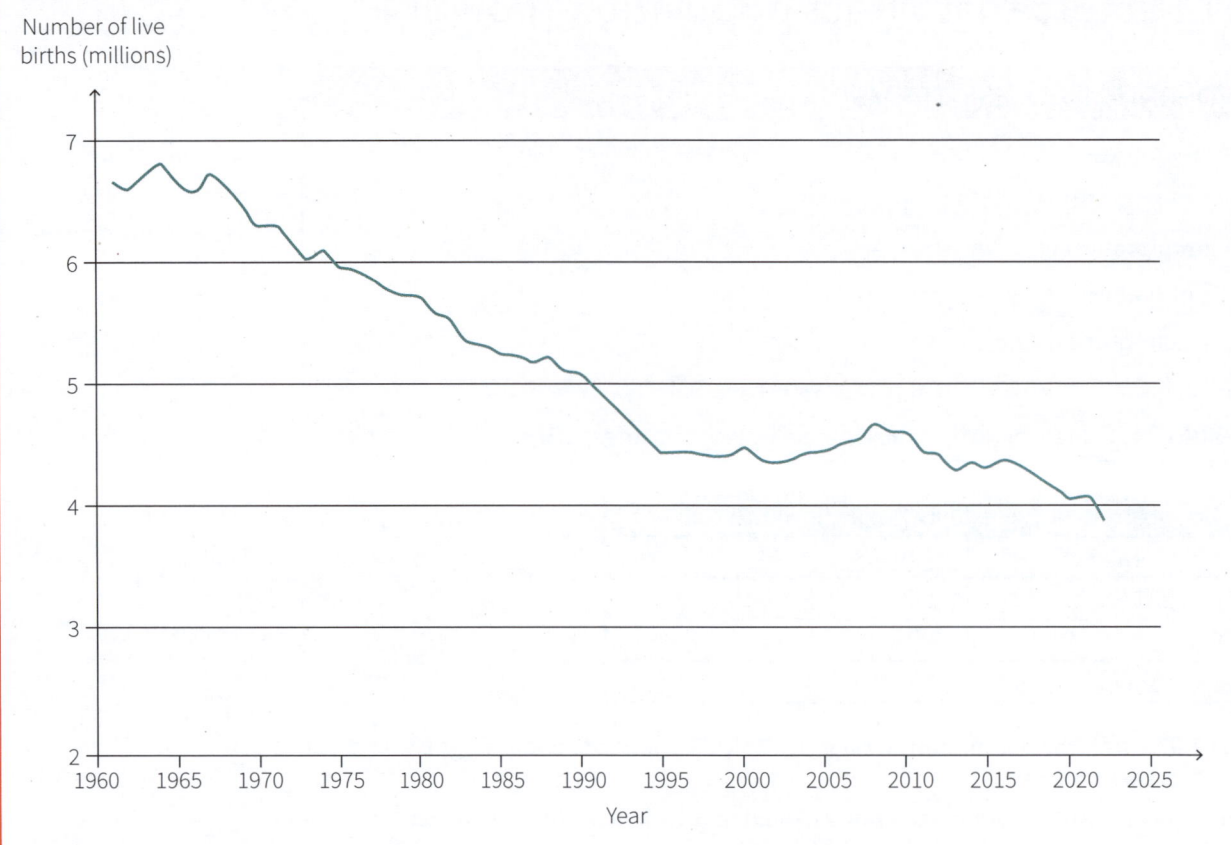

Figure 31.1: Number of live births in EU countries per year, 1962–2022

In 2022, 3.9 million babies were born in the European Union. This represents a birth rate of just 8.7 births per 1 000 people, far lower than birth rates in Africa (32.3 per 1 000) and Asia (15.3 per 1 000). While birth rates vary across European countries, the overall trend is clear: Europe's birth rate has been declining steadily since 1960. In 1960, there were 6.7 million new babies, in 1990 there were 5.1 million new babies, and in 2022, the total went below 4 million for the first time. Figure 31.1 shows the number of live births in EU countries over a 60-year period.

a Calculate the percentage change in the number of live births in the European Union between 1960 and 2022. **[2]**

b Explain **two** reasons why birth rates can vary between countries. **[4]**

REFLECTION

Well done on completing this section. Before moving on, take a moment to reflect: what did you find most challenging in this section, and what helped you to stay focused or make progress?

If you have worked hard and feel you have earned it, this might also be a good time for a quick reward, like a short walk or a break doing something you enjoy.

31.2 The effects of changes in the size and structure of populations

≪ RECALL AND CONNECT 1 ≪

a How does household spending change with age?

b How does household saving change with age?

c Name **two** state benefits that elderly people might receive.

1 Explain the concept of an 'optimum population'.

2 Complete Table 31.2, listing the advantages and disadvantages of increases in population size.

Table 31.2: Advantages and disadvantages of increases in population size

Advantage	Disadvantage

3 Decide whether each of the following statements is true or false.

    a An increasing population always leads to an improvement in living standards.

    b Immigration directly causes unemployment by reducing the number of available jobs.

    c Population growth could result in more investment and the adoption of new technologies.

    d A declining population could improve environmental sustainability and resource conservation.

4 Explain how a declining population could reduce pressure on housing but increase pressure on businesses.

In Question 5, a quotation is used. When tackling questions with quotations, always link your answer back to the key message of the quotation. Use the quotation as a starting point to frame your analysis, showing how it connects to the broader economic concepts or impacts being discussed.

5

> 'In 2050, Spain will have the oldest population in the world,' said the former director of the UN population division. The average life expectancy in Spain is 83.6. Combined with its low birth rate (see Figure 31.1), Spain is seeing the average age of its population rise quickly. In 2025, nearly 10 million Spaniards were over the age of 65. The total population is just 48 million. Economists around the world have been vocal about the impact this is likely to have on the country's future economic growth and government policies.

Discuss whether having 'the oldest population in the world' will impact Spain's economic growth and government policies. [8]

REFLECTION

Questions will frequently use the wording from the case study; however, they may or may not use quotation marks to highlight this fact. Nevertheless, the advice remains the same: the question must connect back to a specific part of the syllabus. Ensure that you understand the context of the question and also connect the quotation to the real-world consequences for a country's economy.

- How well did you connect the quotation to the real-world consequences for a country's economy?

SELF-ASSESSMENT CHECKLIST

Let's revisit the Knowledge focus and Exam skills focus for this chapter. Decide how confident you are with each statement.

Now I can	Show it	Needs more work	Almost there	Confident to move on
define birth rate, death rate, net migration, immigration and emigration	Explain the difference between net positive migration and net negative migration.			
explain how birth rates, death rates and net migration rates can vary between countries	Research the data for your own country and try to explain the reasons for them.			
explain the concept of optimum population	Describe the meaning of 'optimum population' in your own words.			
discuss the effects of increases and decreases in population size and changes in the age and gender distribution of population	Answer the question: Explain **two** possible impacts of a rising population in Nigeria (the country with the highest birth rate in the world).			
recognise how to respond to a quotation in a question	Look at some past paper questions and highlight whether the questions have picked up on the wording from the case study.			
manage test anxiety by using a reward approach.	Think about treating yourself to a small reward now.			

32 Differences in economic development between countries

KNOWLEDGE FOCUS

In this chapter you will answer questions on:

- 32.1 Economic development
- 32.2 Causes of international differences in economic development
- 32.3 Consequences of international differences in economic development

EXAM SKILLS FOCUS

In this chapter you will:

- show that you understand how to create your own questions in order to improve metacognition.

An effective strategy that can support learning is to create your own questions. Creating questions is a high-order thinking skill. It engages your working memory in the short term but also supports your long-term memory too. In this chapter, you are encouraged to create your own questions and to use them as part of a self-questioning process.

32.1 Economic development

《 RECALL AND CONNECT 1 《

a What is HDI?

b What is better for a country: high HDI or low HDI?

UNDERSTAND THIS TERM

• economic development

1 Explain the difference between economic growth and economic development.

32.2 Causes of international differences in economic development

《 RECALL AND CONNECT 2 《

a Using examples, describe the difference between primary, secondary and tertiary sectors.

b What does productivity mean?

c List **two** reasons why productivity might rise.

d How will high productivity affect living standards?

When writing about the causes of international development, it is important that you do not just repeat the same chains of analysis about the causes of economic growth. Growth is about total output of the economy, whereas development is about living standards. Therefore, your chain of analysis must end with a comment about living standards.

1 Complete the flow diagram to build a chain of analysis showing how a rise in savings can lead to better living standards.

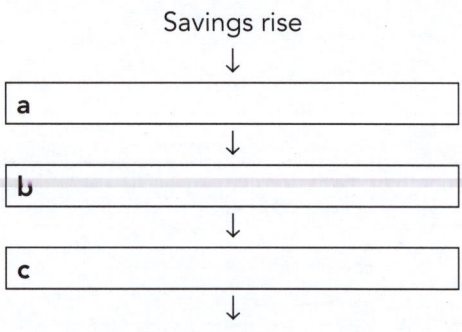

2 Complete the following text using the terms in the word box.

> national   export   rise   sudden   manufactured
>
> decreases   volatility   faster   weather

Countries that _____ a narrow range of goods, particularly primary

goods, can be adversely affected by large _____ in demand or supply.

This is because primary products often experience significant price _____

due to factors like _____ conditions. A _____ drop in prices can

decrease _____ income and living standards. By contrast, the demand for

_____ goods and services tends to grow _____ than the demand

for primary products as global incomes rise. As a result, living standards tend to

_____ faster in these countries.

3 Explain why differences in natural resources causes differences in development between countries.

4 Explain why differences in population growth causes differences in development between countries.

REFLECTION

You should spend some time practising answering other variations of questions like Questions 3 and 4. The focus of any question in this area can be changed easily to a different cause, for example: Explain why differences in healthcare causes differences in development between countries.

In the next section, you could simply reframe the question to ask about 'consequences' rather than 'causes'.

- Can you create your own questions?
- How do you think creating your own questions could help you better understand this topic and prepare for the exam?

32.3 Consequences of international differences in economic development

1 Complete Table 32.1 by describing the consequence of low development on the following areas of an economy. The first row has been completed for you.

Table 32.1: Consequences of low development

	Area of an economy	Consequence of low development
a	Population growth	High growth due to lack of access to family planning healthcare
b	Education	
c	Natural resources (environment)	
d	Savings	

It is important that you write about the consequences of low development for this question, rather than the causes.

2

Table 32.2: Selected data of Niger's economy, 2023

GDP	$17bn
Primary sector share of GDP	42%
HDI	0.394
Life expectancy	62 years
Birth rate	45 birth per 1 000 people

Niger is a country in West Africa. Its economy is largely based on its primary sector: gold mining and agriculture. It has one of the highest birth rates in the world (which is set to double in 17 years) and yet it has one of the lowest HDI rankings in the world.

a Calculate the value of Niger's primary sector output in 2023. [2]

b Discuss whether Niger's large primary sector and high population growth are more of a hinderance than help to its economic development. [8]

SELF-ASSESSMENT CHECKLIST

Let's revisit the Knowledge focus and Exam skills focus for this chapter.
Decide how confident you are with each statement.

Now I can	Show it	Needs more work	Almost there	Confident to move on
discuss the causes of economic development between countries	Research the main causes of Niger's lack of economic development.			
explain the consequences of differences in income (real GDP), population growth, proportion of workers employed in different sectors, saving, investment, levels of education and healthcare	Explain the impact of low economic development on national income and productivity.			
understand how to create my own questions in order to improve metacognition.	Write **two** explain questions based on content from this chapter.			

Exam practice 5

This section contains practice questions that will draw together your knowledge on a range of topics you have covered up to this point and will help you prepare for your assessment.

The following question has example student responses and commentaries provided. For each part of the question, work through the question first, then compare your answer to the example student response and commentary.

Question 1

Canada has a population of around 40m people. It is a high-income country with a high standard of living. The country is, however, facing several economic challenges including concerns about its population size and structure. For example, its birth rate has recently hit a record low at just 10 births per 1 000 people. To address these concerns, the government has implemented policies to encourage greater inward migration, which has partially offset those population concerns. In recent years, Canada has experienced consistently high levels of net migration. The country had a net migration of 460 000 people in 2022 and 434 000 people in 2023.

One significant economic challenge is poverty, with 9.9% of Canadians struggling with severe poverty. Poverty is particularly widespread among people with disabilities, single-parent families, individuals living alone and immigrants.

a Define 'net migration'. [2]

Example student response	Commentary
Net migration is when people move in and out of a country. If more people come in than leave, net migration is positive.	AO1 Knowledge and understanding This answer doesn't clearly define net migration in economic terms. A better definition should mention that net migration is the difference between immigration (inflows) and emigration (outflows).

b Explain the effects of **two** changes in the size or structure of the population for a high-income country like Canada. [4]

Example student response	Commentary
A rich country like Canada may experience an ageing population. This is partly due to a falling death rate (caused by a high level of healthcare) and a declining birth rate (caused by an increasing life expectancy). A decreasing population means that the country is likely to see a decreasing labour force size, which would lead to a leftwards shift of the PPF.	AO1 Knowledge and understanding and AO2 Analysis. While this answer describes the ageing population well, the question is asking for 'effects of **two** changes' in population size or structure, not just causes. Therefore, the first paragraph could be improved, as: 'One key change in a high-income country like Canada is an ageing population. As more people live longer due to better healthcare and lower death rates, the proportion of elderly people rises. This is likely to reduce the size of the working-age population, which may slow economic growth.' Similarly, the second point about a declining labour force should be developed to economic consequences beyond just a PPF shift.

c Analyse how improved education and more generous state benefits could help to alleviate poverty. [6]

Example student response	Commentary
Poverty is a condition where people's income is too low to enable them to meet their basic needs. The data suggest that '9.9% of Canadians' are struggling with poverty despite the fact that Canada is a rich, developed country. Government spending on education could help to alleviate poverty. Education helps to provide people with new skills and to improve their existing skills. Therefore, it can increase the job prospects and earning potential of those experiencing poverty and their children. This can help to break households out of a poverty cycle. While education programmes can take time to implement, in the long term this can be a very effective policy. Providing more generous state benefits can also be effective because the elderly, and some sick and disabled people, may not be able to work and may not have any savings to support them. Giving them benefits, or raising the benefits they receive, may enable them to avoid absolute poverty. The data suggests that 'poverty is particularly widespread among people with disabilities, single-parent families, individuals living alone and immigrants', so giving these vulnerable groups more generous benefits could seem to affect this specific problem directly.	AO1 Knowledge and understanding and AO2 Analysis There is a good definition of poverty in terms of low income and the inability to meet basic needs. In addition, there is a good explanation of how education improves skills, increases job prospects and breaks the poverty cycle. The student states that more generous benefits can help people who cannot work, but perhaps should explain how this reduces poverty in both the short and long term. For example, state benefits increase disposable income, which can help people afford necessities and increase demand in the economy, potentially creating jobs.

d Discuss whether a high level of real GDP per head always means that living standards are high in a country. [8]

Example student response	Commentary
High levels of real GDP per head are normally associated with a high HDI. The data does not tell us what Canada's HDI is, but it does say that 'Canada is a high-income country with a high standard of living'. If people are wealthy then it follows that they should buy more goods and services. This will increase total demand and create jobs for others. This increases the standard of living for people who now have a new job or a higher income. In addition, if people are spending more money then it follows that the government will collect more tax revenue. This is because the government will collect tax revenue from sales taxes, as well as direct taxes like income tax.	AO1 Knowledge and understanding and AO2 Analysis Much of the economic theory is correct but it needs more depth. For example, the student mentions that increased spending leads to job creation, but then does not explain how (e.g. increased total demand boosting production and employment). Also, higher tax revenue doesn't automatically mean better living standards – it depends on how the government spends the tax revenue.

Example student response	Commentary
However, money is not necessarily evenly distributed across the country. The data tells us that '9.9% Canadians are struggling with severe poverty'. Presumably, this is because the government is not using its tax revenue on policies to improve living standards – especially for disabled people and immigrants. It is possible that some people in low-income countries actually have a better living standard than everyone who lives in Canada. It is also the case that environmental conditions are better in some developing countries. Canada is known for its oil exploration and there are vast areas of Canada that have toxic water reserves as a result of their oil industry. This has been bad for wildlife but also indigenous people.	AO3 Evaluation The same point is true for the evaluation section. The student mentions that income inequality exists, but then asserts that 'the government is not using its tax revenue' effectively without evidence or alternative explanations (e.g. structural unemployment, automation). A better argument would discuss why redistribution policies might fail rather than just assuming poor government spending. The environmental argument is underdeveloped. It could be improved with a comparison to a different country.

Now that you have read the example student response to the previous question, here are some similar practice questions for parts (b) and (c) which you should attempt. Use the guidance in the commentaries in this section to help you as you answer the questions.

Question 2

b Explain the effects of **two** changes in the size or structure of population for a low-income country. [4]

c Analyse how improved progressive taxes and increasing national minimum wage could help to alleviate poverty. [6]

The following question has example student responses and commentaries provided. For each part of the question, work through the question first, then compare your answer to the example student response and commentary.

Question 3

Table 1: Ethiopia fact file, 2023

Indicator	Value
HDI	0.492
Real GDP per head	$1 272
Annual economic growth rate	7.9%
Unemployment rate	18.9%

Ethiopia has seen significant demographic and economic changes over the past two decades. In 2000, the population was approximately 67.4 million, and yet by 2023 it had grown to about 128.7 million. This rapid population increase presents both opportunities and challenges for the country.

Despite being one of Africa's fastest-growing economies, with growth rates between 8% and 11% annually before 2016, Ethiopia faces persistent poverty issues. In 2023, real GDP per head was just $1 272, and a quarter of the population lives in absolute poverty (below $2.15 a day). Its HDI is just 0.492.

Table 2: Selected countries birth rate and poverty rate, 2023

Country	Birth rate (births per 1 000 people)	Poverty rate (% of population in poverty)
Ethiopia	30.3	25% (absolute poverty)
Niger	46.6	41% (absolute poverty)
Turkey	11.2	13.5% (relative poverty)
Canada	10.0	9.9% (relative poverty)

Ethiopia has seen its birth rate fall by 50% since the 1990s, but it is still high compared to more economically developed countries. In 2023, there were 30.3 births per 1 000 people. Such a high birth rate can lead to a larger workforce in the future, potentially boosting economic growth. However, it also demands increased investment in education, healthcare and infrastructure to support the growing population.

a   Calculate the percentage change in Ethiopia's population between 2000 and 2023. [2]

Example student response	Commentary
The data suggests that 'in 2000, the population was approximately 67.4 million, and yet by 2023 it had grown to about 128.7 million'. Percentage change is $\left(\frac{new - old}{old}\right) \times 100$ $\left(\frac{128.7 - 67.4}{128.7}\right) \times 100 = 47.63\%$	AO1 Knowledge and understanding This formula is correct and so the student might receive some marks. However, the student has divided by the wrong value. The correct answer is 90.95%.

b   Identify **two** causes of poverty. [2]

Example student response	Commentary
Unemployment Low wages	AO1 Knowledge and understanding This is correct.

c   Explain **one** disadvantage of using real GDP per head as an indicator of living standards. [2]

Example student response	Commentary
One disadvantage of using real GDP as an indicator of living standards is that it does not account for income distribution. A country may have a high real GDP, but if wealth is concentrated among a small percentage of the population, many people may still experience poverty and a low standard of living. For example, Ethiopia's economy has grown significantly, yet a quarter of the population lives in absolute poverty and its HDI is just 0.492. This shows that GDP alone does not reflect inequalities in wealth and well-being.	AO1 Knowledge and understanding This is a really good answer. The student has probably included more detail than required for a 2-mark question, so an improvement would be to answer in a more concise way, which would allow them more time to answer other questions.

d Explain **two** advantages of using the HDI to compare living standards between countries. **[4]**

Example student response	Commentary
The Human Development Index (HDI) compares living standards between countries by considering three key indicators: income, healthcare, education. By looking at three areas rather than just one (like real GDP per head), this gives a more rounded view of living standards. Each country is given an HDI score between 0 and 1, which allows for comparison. Countries are then categorised as very high, high, medium or low HDI, with a higher HDI indicating a higher standard of living.	AO1 Knowledge and understanding and AO2 Analysis The answer includes a list of the three key indicators and also explains why HDI is useful. It states that looking at multiple factors gives a more rounded view of living standards and mentions the HDI scoring and classification elements. However, it lacks specific details in terms of defining each indicator correctly and then explaining why that factor is a useful measure for living standards.

e Analyse the relationship between a high birth rate and the level of poverty. **[4]**

Example student response	Commentary
In the short run, a higher birth rate means more children, increasing the dependency ratio. This can reduce disposable income for households and as the data says, 'it also increases the demands [on the government] of investment in education, healthcare and infrastructure to support the growing population'. In addition, more women may temporarily leave the workforce to care for children, reducing the labour force and potentially slowing economic productivity. The data says that 'Ethiopia still has a high birth rate compared to more economically developed countries'. However, certain industries like baby products, education and childcare services may experience increased demand, creating jobs and reducing unemployment. In the long run, as these children grow up, they enter the workforce. This 'can lead to a larger workforce in the future, potentially boosting economic growth'. A larger working population may encourage investment in industries such as housing, education, and infrastructure. However, a sustained high birth rate could lead to overpopulation, straining resources and worsening poverty.	AO1 Knowledge and understanding and AO2 Analysis The student has structured their answer like an evaluative question. This will not necessarily lower their marks, but it is unnecessary. The answer might benefit from a clearer explanation of how a high birth rate affects the government's budget and resource allocation in more detail. The student has used quotes from the case study well to justify the analysis throughout. However, the answer is too focussed on Ethiopia. Table 2 allows for a much wider analysis of other countries, including higher income countries like Turkey and Canada. The student should use Table 2 more effectively in the answer.

f Discuss whether population growth is the main cause of differences in economic development between countries. [6]

Example student response	Commentary
Yes, population growth can be a major cause of differences in economic development. A larger workforce in the future can potentially boost economic growth. More people also means more demand for goods and services, which can drive economic growth. No, population growth is not the only factor. Resources like natural resources and access to capital are more important. Even countries with high populations may not develop economically if they don't have access to resources or infrastructure. For example, countries like Ethiopia have high birth rates but remain underdeveloped due to lack of access to resources and poor governance. Also, governance and political stability matter a lot more. Overall, population growth can affect development, but it is also about how resources and policies are managed. High population growth can be a problem if it leads to overpopulation and strains resources, but could boost a country's economy if managed well.	AO1 Knowledge and understanding and AO2 Analysis The analysis needs more depth. The line 'a larger workforce in the future can potentially boost economic growth' is taken directly from the case study but it is not developed at all. The student should explain why population growth can lead to higher productivity and economic growth. AO3 Evaluation The comment 'also, governance and political stability matter a lot more' adds nothing to the answer. It is not supported with references to the data or the use of economic theory.

Question 4

Write an improved answer to Questions 3(d) and 3(f).

> Unit 6

International trade and globalisation

33 Specialisation and free trade

KNOWLEDGE FOCUS

In this chapter you will answer questions on:

- 33.1 Specialisation by country
- 33.2 Free trade

EXAM SKILLS FOCUS

In this chapter you will:

- improve your understanding of a synoptic question.

Synoptic questions assess your understanding of links between different topics. In this chapter, you will see some Exam skills question that use one case study to assess a range of areas – not just content related to this chapter. Synoptic questions can draw on a range of economic topics. Think about which are the most appropriate microeconomic or macroeconomic concepts to use in your answer.

33.1 Specialisation by country

≪ RECALL AND CONNECT 1 ≪

a Explain what specialisation means in the context of division of labour.

b What is meant by structural unemployment?

UNDERSTAND THIS TERM

- specialisation by country

1   Match the country with its largest export (what it specialises in). The first one – Iceland – has been done for you.

Country		Largest export	
a	Iceland	i	Financial services
b	Luxembourg	ii	Fishing
c	China	iii	Oil
d	Qatar	iv	Copper
e	Zambia	v	Manufactured goods

2   Using the example of Iceland specialising in fishing, explain the basis for specialisation by a country in terms of the best resource allocation and/or low-cost production.

3   Answer Question 2 again, using another country of your choice for the example.

4   Complete Table 33.1 by listing some of the advantages and disadvantages of specialisation to different economic agents.

Table 33.1: Advantages and disadvantages of specialisation

	Advantage	Disadvantage
Consumers	a	b
Workers	c	d
Firms	e	f

5

Angola is a relatively large country on the west coast of sub-Saharan Africa. With access to vast offshore oil reserves, Angola produces around 1.6m barrels of oil per day. Oil makes up 90% of the country's exports (worth around $50bn). Oil prices are determined by global forces of demand and supply, so Angola has little price-setting power of its own. Despite its apparent riches, Angola still has high levels of poverty, income inequality and unemployment.

a   Explain the different between poverty and income inequality. [4]

b   Explain, using a diagram, how 'prices are determined by global forces of demand and supply'. [4]

c   Analyse **two** reasons why, despite its 'vast offshore oil reserves', Angola's specialisation in oil has **not** had a positive impact on the economy. [6]

REFLECTION

The case study about Angola provided a rich context for discussing several interconnected economic issues: natural resource dependence (economic development), oil prices (microeconomics) and domestic challenges such as poverty, income inequality and unemployment (macroeconomics). It is a good example of a set of synoptic questions.

Synoptic questions are designed to assess your ability to apply your knowledge across a range of topics. In Question 5, you were asked to think not just about the content specific to the topic (for example, specialisation) but also how it links to other economic areas, such as the macroeconomic objectives. This required you to use both development and macroeconomic concepts in a single response. By practising more Exam skills questions (see Section 33.2), you can better demonstrate your understanding of how different aspects of economics are interconnected and how policies or events in one area can affect others.

- How do you feel about linking different economic concepts when answering synoptic questions?
- Which areas of economics do you find easiest or most challenging to apply in synoptic questions, and why?

33.2 Free trade

UNDERSTAND THIS TERM

- free trade

1   How are the concepts of specialisation and free trade related? Fill in the missing words using the terms in the word box.

export	import	restrictions	buy	free
movement	specialise	production	governments	

Free trade is international trade without any _____. When countries

_____, they have to trade. The large-scale _____ of the goods

and services they specialise in will mean that they want to _____ some

of them. They will also have to _____ those products that their citizens are willing and able to _____ but their countries are not producing.

If there is free trade, _____ will not be using any measures to stop the

_____ _____ of exports and imports.

2   Complete Table 33.2 by listing some of the advantages and disadvantages of free trade to different economic agents.

Table 33.2: Advantages and disadvantages of free trade

	Advantage	Disadvantage
Consumers	a	b
Workers	c	d
Firms	e	f

3   Decide whether each of the following statements is true or false.

a   Governments have nothing to gain from free trade.

b   Governments never use measures to stop the free movement of exports and imports.

c   Most countries in the world today have free trade on all their goods and services.

d   Free trade may make it difficult for new firms to grow to a size where they can take advantage of economies of scale.

4

In 2024, Timor-Leste became the 166th and most recent member of the World Trade Organization, thus signalling its commitment to free trade. Timor-Leste is a low-income country in South-east Asia. Its main exports are oil (worth around $113m), coffee ($19m) and scrap iron ($0.9m). Timor-Leste is considered one of the world's most vulnerable countries to climate change and its government is focused on developing sustainable industries to reduce dependence on oil exports. The country is working to improve infrastructure as well as providing subsidies to agricultural and tourism sectors.

a   Define 'subsidy'.   [2]

b   Analyse the relationship between economic growth and environmental sustainability.   [6]

c   Discuss whether a low-income country like Timor-Leste has anything to gain from free trade.   [8]

SELF-ASSESSMENT CHECKLIST

Let's revisit the Knowledge focus and Exam skills focus for this chapter.
Decide how confident you are with each statement.

Now I can	Show it	Needs more work	Almost there	Confident to move on
define specialisation by country	Explain the difference between specialisation by country and specialisation by worker.			
analyse the basis for specialisation by country in terms of best resource allocation and/or lowest-cost production	Explain why Qatar is specialised in oil production.			
discuss the advantages and disadvantages of specialisation	List **three** advantages and **three** disadvantages of specialisation.			
define free trade	Describe the meaning of free trade.			
discuss the advantages and disadvantages of free trade	List **three** advantages and **three** disadvantages of free trade.			
improve my understanding of a synoptic question.	Explain to another student what 'synoptic' means.			

34 Globalisation and trade restrictions

KNOWLEDGE FOCUS

In this chapter you will answer questions on:

- 34.1 What is globalisation?
- 34.2 Causes and effects of changes in globalisation
- 34.3 Multinational companies
- 34.4 Types of trade restrictions
- 34.5 Reasons for trade restrictions
- 34.6 Consequences of trade restrictions

EXAM SKILLS FOCUS

In this chapter you will:

- show that you understand what non-examples are
- engage in active retrieval such as word searches, speed quizzes and matching games.

Non-examples are the opposite of examples. They serve to clarify what a concept is not. Non-examples actually prevent confusion by highlighting characteristics that differentiate similar concepts, helping you to avoid common misconceptions. In this chapter, you will have the opportunity to identify both examples and non-examples from a list. Studying non-examples encourages deeper thinking, as it forces you to understand why something does not belong in the category.

Active retrieval is a revision technique that involves actively stimulating your memory by retrieving information from your long-term memory, rather than passively reviewing notes or textbooks. It is effective for revision because it strengthens your ability to recall key terms under exam conditions, so improving retention and understanding. In this chapter, you will complete one word search, one speed quiz and one matching game; these activities are designed to support your learning by encouraging quick retrieval of key terms.

34.1 What is globalisation?

UNDERSTAND THIS TERM

- globalisation

1 Which **two** of the following four statements would be considered a satisfactory definition of globalisation?

   A Globalisation is the process by which firms develop international influence or start operating on an international scale.

   B Globalisation is the spread of Western values and lifestyles across the world.

   C Globalisation is the complete elimination of all national borders, resulting in a single unified global economy.

   D Globalisation is the increasing interconnectedness and interdependence of economies across the world through trade, technology and travel.

2 Which **four** of the following characteristics would be good examples of a globalised country?

   A High level of trade

   B High unemployment rate

   C High numbers of multinational companies in the country

   D High level of migration

   E High economic growth rate

   F High level of foreign investment

   G High level of specialisation in tertiary sector

   H High level of trade restrictions

34.2 Causes and effects of changes in globalisation

≪ RECALL AND CONNECT 1 ≪

a What does specialisation by country mean?

b What is net migration?

c How does globalisation affect both specialisation by country and net migration?

1   It can be easy to mistake *causes* of globalisation for *consequences* of globalisation. Look at the list below and decide whether each one is a cause or an effect of globalisation. Then complete Table 34.1. The first row has been completed for you.

reduced transport costs	specialisation
increase in competition in markets	increased level of migration
increase in international trade	removal of trade restrictions
advances in communications	rise of multinational companies

Table 34.1: Causes and consequences of globalisation

Cause of globalisation	Consequence of globalisation
Reduced transport costs	Increase in competition in markets
a	b
c	d
e	f

2   Explain how reduced transport costs lead to globalisation.

3   Explain how globalisation leads to increased competition in markets.

34.3 Multinational companies

UNDERSTAND THIS TERM

- multinational company (MNC)

1   a   Identify whether the statements in Table 34.2 are **examples of advantages** of multinational companies (MNCs) to the host or home country, or if they are **non-examples** (misconceptions or indirect effects).

Table 34.2: Advantages of multinational companies

	Statement	Example of advantage, or non-example
i	MNCs create job opportunities by setting up operations in the host country.	
ii	MNCs always pay higher taxes to the host country.	
iii	MNCs guarantee long-term economic stability in the host country.	
iv	MNCs repatriate profits from foreign markets, contributing to the home country's economic growth.	

b   Identify whether the statements in Table 34.3 are **examples of disadvantages** of MNCs to the host or home country, or if they are **non-examples** (misconceptions or indirect effects).

Table 34.3: Disadvantages of multinational companies

	Statement	Example of disadvantage, or non-example
i	MNCs never contribute to the local economy of the host country.	
ii	MNCs exploit local labour in the host country by paying low wages or imposing poor working conditions.	
iii	MNCs contribute to environmental degradation in the host country by cost cutting instead of using sustainable practices.	
iv	MNCs never increase wages for domestic workers in the host country.	

REFLECTION

- How helpful are you finding thinking about non-examples in your revision?
- Would it be useful to apply to other topics as well?

2

> Coca-Cola is one of the most recognisable brands in the world. It has factories across the continent of Africa, including two in Tanzania. Coca-Cola Kwanza, a branch of the larger Coca-Cola company, operates two bottling factories in Tanzania; it employs over 700 individuals and has annual sales exceeding 30m units (or \$80m). Over the last decade or so, Coca-Cola Kwanza has contributed significantly to the local economy.

Analyse **two** benefits to Tanzania of an MNC, like Coca-Cola, operating in the country. [6]

34.4 Types of trade restrictions

≪ RECALL AND CONNECT 2 ≪

a List the **four** components of the current account on the balance of payments.

b Explain the impact on the current account if a country uses trade restrictions successfully.

1 Find the following terms in the word search.

tariff	quota	embargo	subsidy

F	A	D	Y	I	M	A	E
F	F	I	R	A	T	Q	M
I	R	S	U	S	A	U	B
S	D	S	Y	D	R	F	A
U	Q	U	O	T	A	F	R
G	B	O	M	B	E	B	G
S	U	B	S	I	D	Y	O
E	M	G	I	O	A	U	Q

2 Complete Table 34.4, using the terms in the word box to identify which type of trade restriction is being described.

| tariff | quota | embargo | subsidy |

Table 34.4: Types of trade restriction

	Description	Type
a	A ban on imports or exports	
b	A tax on imports	
c	A limit placed on imports or exports	
d	A payment by a government to a domestic firm to reduce the price	

3 Explain how tariffs and subsidies can be used to reduce imports. [4]

REFLECTION

In this section (Section 34.4), you had the opportunity to complete a couple of active retrieval tasks (the word search and matching game) before the Exam skills question. The intention was to reinforce some key terms before you embarked on a question that required more detailed explanations.

- Did you find the tasks helpful?
- How could creating your own retrieval tasks enhance your revision process?

34.5 Reasons for trade restrictions

UNDERSTAND THESE TERMS

- infant (sunrise) industries
- declining (sunset) industries
- strategic industries
- dumping

In this section, there is a quick quiz of six questions. Try to answer the questions using as few words as possible, to practise answering low-mark questions efficiently.

1 Name **three** types of industries that a government might try to protect.

2 Why may dumping by foreign firms harm a country's consumers?

3 What type of unemployment may be avoided if declining industries are protected?

4 How can trade restrictions improve economic growth?

5 What is the link between tariffs and tax revenue?

6 How can trade restrictions improve environmental sustainability?

34.6 Consequences of trade restrictions

UNDERSTAND THIS TERM

- trade war

1 Table 34.5 lists one-word descriptions of the various consequences of trade restrictions. Develop these points further by providing explanations for each consequence.

Table 34.5: Consequences of trade restrictions

	Consequence	Explanation
a	Prices	
b	Competition	
c	Inefficiency	
d	Retaliation	
e	Choice	
f	Dependency	

2 Explain **two** reasons why the use of tariffs might lead to inflation in a country. **[4]**

SELF-ASSESSMENT CHECKLIST

Let's revisit the Knowledge focus and Exam skills focus for this chapter.
Decide how confident you are with each statement.

Now I can	Show it	Needs more work	Almost there	Confident to move on
define globalisation	Explain what globalisation is to another student.			
explain the causes and consequences of changes in globalisation	Name **two** causes and **two** consequences of globalisation.			
explain the role of multinational companies (MNCs)	Describe the benefits of a MNC to the host country.			

CONTINUED

Now I can	Show it	Needs more work	Almost there	Confident to move on
explain the types of trade restrictions/methods of protection: tariffs, import quotas, subsidies and embargoes	Create flashcards with the definitions of all **four** types of trade restrictions.			
discuss the reasons for trade restrictions	List **three** reasons for a government to use trade restrictions.			
discuss the consequences of trade restrictions	List **three** consequences of using trade restrictions.			
understand what non-examples are	List **three** non-examples of trade restrictions.			
engage in active retrieval such as word searches, speed quizzes and matching games.	Choose a topic you have recently studied and test yourself without notes. Try to recall key facts, definitions or steps in a process by writing them down from memory.			

35 Foreign exchange rates

KNOWLEDGE FOCUS

In this chapter you will answer questions on:

- 35.1 What is a foreign exchange rate?
- 35.2 Reasons for buying and selling foreign currencies
- 35.3 Determination of a foreign exchange rate in foreign exchange markets
- 35.4 Effects of changes in foreign exchange rates

EXAM SKILLS FOCUS

In this chapter you will:

- learn to test your understanding of topics that you find challenging
- practise using a scaffolded chain of analysis to write clear, structured answers.

Foreign exchange rates are a topic that students often say they find very tricky. However, the more you test your knowledge of any topic, the stronger your understanding is likely to become. It is straightforward to find new sources of information for the topic of exchange rates because they are changing all the time. You can use questions in this chapter as the basis for new questions to test yourself.

In Chapter 22, you used a scaffolded activity to help explain the macroeconomic conflicts that can arise between various government policies. In this chapter, you will use a scaffolded activity to help build a chain of analysis with regards to the impact of exchange rates on key economic indicators such as inflation and unemployment. When you come to write your answer, this should demonstrate that you can select, organise and interpret economics data and information, which is an important aspect of the assessment objective AO2 Analysis.

35.1 What is a foreign exchange rate?

1 Define the term 'foreign exchange rate'.

2 **a** Complete the following statements about the foreign exchange rate of US dollars to Japanese yen:

   i An exchange rate of $1 = 150 ¥ means that one US dollar is worth _____ Japanese yen.

   ii A $25 book would cost _____ Japanese yen.

   iii A microwave costing 13 500 yen would cost _____ US dollars.

   b Complete the following statements about the foreign exchange rate of euros to Indian rupee:

   i An exchange rate of €1 = ₹90 means that one euro is worth _____ Indian rupees.

   ii A €50 pair of jeans would cost _____ Indian rupees.

   iii An Indian painting costing 18 000 Indian rupees would cost _____ euros.

35.2 Reasons for buying and selling foreign currencies

UNDERSTAND THESE TERMS

- workers' remittances
- foreign direct investment (FDI)

1 Complete Table 35.1 by listing **three** reasons why people would want to buy Japanese yen and **three** reasons reason why people would want to sell it.

Table 35.1: Reasons for buying and selling Japanese yen

	Buy yen	Sell yen
a		
b		
c		

2   Read each scenario in Table 35.2. For each one, decide whether it causes an increase or decrease in the demand curve or the supply curve for the currency.

Table 35.2: Changes in the demand or supply curve for currency

	Scenario	Demand or supply	Shift to the right or left
a	Speculators expect the currency to appreciate and buy it.		
b	Central bank sells its currency to lower its value.		
c	Export demand falls as a result of changing trends.		
d	Migrant workers living in this country send remittances to their families abroad.		
e	Foreign workers choose to invest and buy more capital goods.		

35.3 Determination of a foreign exchange rate in foreign exchange markets

≪ RECALL AND CONNECT 1 ≪

a   What does market equilibrium mean?

b   In general terms, how are price changes caused by changes in demand and supply?

UNDERSTAND THESE TERMS

- floating exchange rate
- appreciation
- depreciation
- hot money flows

For Question 1(a), make sure you refer to Figure 35.1 in your answer.

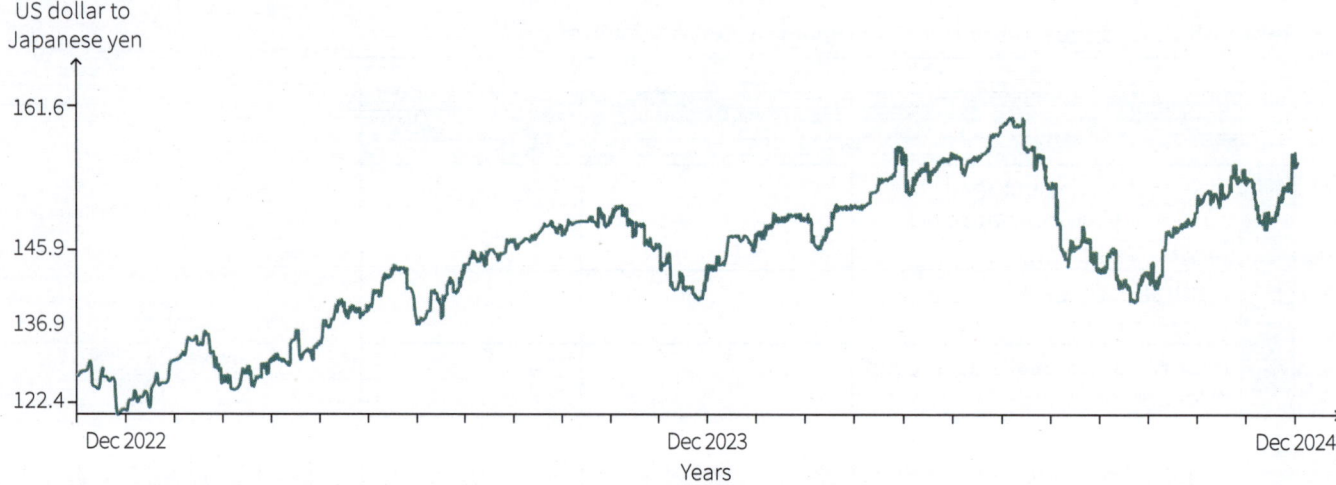

Figure 35.1: The value of US dollars in terms of Japanese yen, 2022–2024

    a   Describe the change in the value of the US dollar in terms of Japanese yen in the period 2022–2024.   **[2]**

    b   Explain **two** possible causes of this exchange rate change.   **[4]**

REFLECTION

Finding exchange rate data is straightforward. Find current exchange rate graphs like the one shown in Figure 35.1 online. Adapt the questions in this section to the graphs that you find, and practise answering them.

- How confident do you feel in interpreting exchange rate graphs and explaining possible reasons behind changes?
- What would help you improve further?

35.4 Effects of changes in foreign exchange rates

1   Complete Table 35.3 and Table 35.4 to build chains of analysis about the possible consequences of a change in foreign exchange rates. Use the terms in the word boxes for support.

    a

total demand rises   export prices fall   demand for exports rises

Table 35.3: Chain of analysis for depreciation leading to increased employment

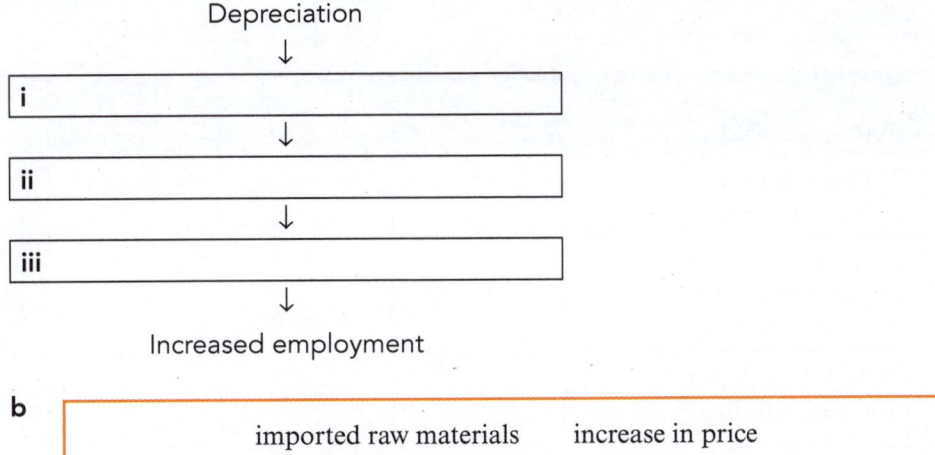

b

| imported raw materials | increase in price |
| increased costs of production | import prices rise |

Table 35.4: Chain of analysis for depreciation leading to higher inflation

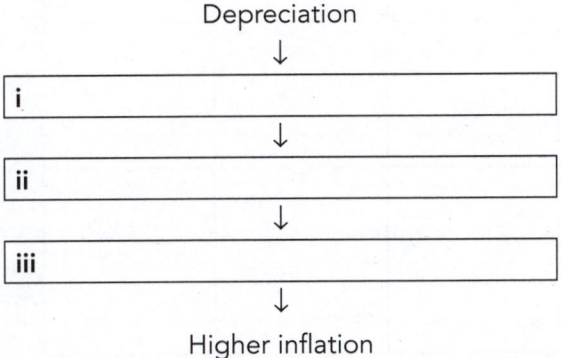

Using the same scaffolding technique, write a full answer to Question 2.

2   Analyse why an appreciation of a currency might increase unemployment but reduce inflation.   [6]

REFLECTION

The aim of using a scaffolded activity like Questions 1 and 2 was to help you to organise your thoughts in a logical order.

•   How useful did you find the scaffolding in thinking about your answer?

SELF-ASSESSMENT CHECKLIST

Let's revisit the Knowledge focus and Exam skills focus for this chapter.
Decide how confident you are with each statement.

Now I can	Show it	Needs more work	Almost there	Confident to move on
define a foreign exchange rate	Describe the meaning of a foreign exchange rate.			
explain the reasons for buying and selling foreign currencies	List **three** reasons why the demand for a currency might increase.			
analyse how a foreign exchange rate is determined in foreign exchange markets	Explain the difference between currency appreciation and depreciation.			
discuss the consequences of changes in foreign exchange rates	Analyse how a depreciation of the currency affects the macroeconomic aims of government.			
learn to test my understanding of topics that I find challenging	Identify **three** different ways you could test your knowledge of foreign exchange rates.			
practise using a scaffolded chain of analysis to write clear, structured answers.	Answer the question: Analyse why a depreciation of a currency might increase growth and reduce unemployment. **[6]**			

36 Current account of the balance of payments

KNOWLEDGE FOCUS

In this chapter you will answer questions on:

- 36.1 Structure of the current account of the balance of payments
- 36.2 Causes and consequences of current account deficit
- 36.3 Causes and consequences of current account surplus
- 36.4 Policies to achieve balance of payments stability

EXAM SKILLS FOCUS

In this chapter you will:

- show that you can manage distribution of your time
- congratulate yourself for the progress you have made.

It would be a good idea to answer a whole past paper under timed conditions. This would provide you with useful practice and could help you to identify any topics that you still need to go over again. It would also help you to check whether you can divide up your time appropriately.

In this last chapter, do not forget to congratulate yourself. Positive reinforcement during revision can help reduce test anxiety by boosting confidence; it can help you to feel more capable and prepared. Instead of stressing over mistakes, congratulating yourself helps to shift your mindset to focus on the things you are doing well.

36.1 Structure of the current account of the balance of payments

≪ RECALL AND CONNECT 1 ≪

a Use a demand and supply diagram to illustrate the concept of a surplus.

b What is a budget surplus?

c What is a budget deficit?

UNDERSTAND THESE TERMS

- balance of payments
- trade in goods
- trade in goods deficit
- trade in goods surplus
- primary income
- secondary income
- current account balance

1 Match the key term with its definition.

Term	
a	Trade in goods
b	Trade in services
c	Primary income
d	Secondary income
e	Balance of payments

Definition	
i	Income earned by people working in different countries and investment income that comes into and goes out of the country
ii	Transfers between residents and non-residents of money, goods or services, not in return for anything else
iii	The value of exported services and the value of imported services
iv	The record of a country's economic transactions with other countries
v	The value of exported goods and the value of imported goods

2 Consider the scenarios in Table 36.1. Decide whether each scenario would be recorded on the balance of payments as 'trade in goods', 'trade in services', 'primary income' or 'secondary income'. The first row has been completed for you.

Table 36.1: Components of the current account

	Scenario	Component
a	Interest on savings held abroad	Primary income
b	Exports of cars overseas	
c	Migrants send their earnings overseas	
d	Multinational firm sends its profit overseas	
e	Receipt of foreign aid from a donor country	
f	Using the financial services from a foreign firm	
g	Import steel and other metals from abroad	

3 Consider the balance of payments for fictional countries: Country A in Table 36.2 and Country B in Table 36.3. Calculate their balance of payments position and state whether the current account has a surplus or a deficit.

a

Table 36.2: Country A's current account balance

Component	Value ($m)
Trade in goods	−13 200
Trade in services	+14 000
Primary income	−300
Secondary income	−700
Current account balance	

b

Table 36.3: Country B's current account balance

Component	Value ($m)
Exports of goods	540 000
Imports of goods	380 000
Exports of services	200 000
Imports of services	210 000
Primary income	−50 000
Secondary income	−80 000
Current account balance	

You should have noticed that the data has been presented differently for the countries. For example, more data has been given for Country B. The signs have also been omitted from the export and import rows, which means that you will need to remember to subtract import values and add export values. Did you remember to do this?

36.2 Causes and consequences of current account deficit

1   Consider the scenarios in Table 36.4. Decide whether each scenario is likely to worsen the current account position.

Table 36.4: The current account position

	Scenario	Likely to worsen the current account
a	The exchange rate appreciates	
b	Country receives a large amount of foreign aid	
c	A rise in domestic income	
d	A rise in trade restrictions on foreign importers	

2   Explain why an increase in the domestic inflation rate might worsen the current account, but an increase in productivity might not.

3   Country A has experienced a current account deficit due to a lack of international competitiveness. Trade in exported goods, in particular, has decreased sharply.

Give **three** possible impacts on the country's macroeconomic aims.

4

> The USA is the largest economy in the world, but it has a current account deficit of nearly $1 trillion ($944 billion). The country's current account has been in deficit since the 1980s, but it has grown significantly since 2020 and hit a record high in 2024. Economists differ in their opinions about the root cause of the deficit – some say that it is the strong value of the dollar; others that it is the result of low productivity but they generally agree that it is a major drag on economic growth.

a   Describe the relationship between a current account deficit and economic growth.   [2]

b   Explain **two** possible causes of the USA's large current account deficit.   [4]

36.3 Causes and consequences of current account surplus

≪ RECALL AND CONNECT 2 ≪

a   What is specialisation?

b   List **two** advantages and **two** disadvantages of specialisation to a country.

1   Explain why high investment income earned abroad might improve a country's current account but high incomes at home might not.

2 Country B enjoys a large current account surplus, driven by its specialisation in primary sector goods such as oil and gas. This specialisation ensures a consistent surplus in its trade in goods.

Give **three** possible impacts on the country's macroeconomic aims.

3

China is the second-largest economy in the world and has a significant current account surplus of nearly $300 billion. The country's current account surplus has persisted throughout the first quarter of the 21st century, except for some fluctuation in 2020 due to global economic disruption. There is general agreement among economists that China's low production costs – particularly in manufacturing – and high quality of finished products have boosted its current account position. The only question is whether China's current surplus will continue to be as beneficial to its macroeconomic aims as it has been so far.

a Describe the relationship between low production costs and a current account surplus. [2]

b Explain **two** possible consequences of China's large current account surplus on its economy. [4]

REFLECTION

This was the last Exam skills question of this exam preparation and practice resource. Well done for getting this far! For further practice, you should complete a full past paper under timed conditions.

- Paper 1 – Multiple Choice: 40 multiple-choice questions to be completed in 60 minutes.
- Paper 2 – Structured Questions: A series of case-study-based questions worth 80 marks, to be completed in 2 hours (120 minutes).

We have suggested pacing yourself at 1.5 minutes per mark. However, remember that you will need some time to read the case studies in Paper 2 – Structured Questions. This time can probably be saved from the shorter 2-mark questions. However, make sure that you leave yourself enough time to answer the longer 6-mark and 8-mark questions thoroughly.

- When will you be able to complete a full past paper?
- How will you ensure that you will manage your time effectively in an exam?

36.4 Policies to achieve balance of payments stability

≪ RECALL AND CONNECT 3 ≪

a List **three** types of trade restrictions.

b Explain the difference between monetary policy and fiscal policy.

1 The government of Country A seeks to reduce its current account deficit. Complete Table 36.5 by explaining how the policy might help to reduce a current account deficit. The first row has been completed for you.

Table 36.5: Policies to reduce a current account deficit

	Policy	Explanation
a	Exchange rate adjustment	Devaluing the currency can make exports cheaper and imports more expensive.
b	Fiscal policy	
c	Monetary policy	
d	Protectionism	
e	Supply-side policies	

2 The government of Country B seeks to reduce its current account surplus. Explain **two** ways it does so by completing the following statements.

a If a government wants to reduce a current account surplus, it could use expansionary fiscal policy. For example, a cut in income tax rates. This will …

b It could also reduce its use of trade restrictions like import tariffs. This will …

REFLECTION

You're there! Celebrate your efforts. Recognising your achievements can make the process feel more rewarding and less overwhelming, motivating you to continue studying.

- How will you celebrate?

SELF-ASSESSMENT CHECKLIST

Let's revisit the Knowledge focus and Exam skills focus for this chapter. Decide how confident you are with each statement.

Now I can	Show it	Needs more work	Almost there	Confident to move on
describe the components of the current account of the balance of payments	List the **four** major components of the current account of the balance of payments.			

CONTINUED

Now I can	Show it	Needs more work	Almost there	Confident to move on
calculate deficits and surpluses on the current account of the balance of payments	Practise some calculation questions.			
analyse the causes of current account deficits and surpluses	Find out why the UK has such a large current account deficit, and why Norway has such a large current account surplus.			
analyse the consequences of current account deficits and surpluses	Answer this question: Analyse **two** consequences of a current account deficit to Country A. **[6]**			
discuss the range of policies available to achieve balance of payments stability and their effectiveness	Answer this question: Discuss whether it would be better for the USA to use tariffs or contractionary fiscal policy to reduce its current account deficit. **[8]**			
show that I can manage distribution of my time	Complete a full past paper under timed conditions.			
congratulate myself for the progress I have made.	Do something to celebrate.			

Exam practice 6

This section contains practice questions that will draw together your knowledge on a range of topics you have covered up to this point and will help you prepare for your assessment.

The following question has example student responses and commentaries provided. For each part of the question, work through the question first, then compare your answer to the example student response and commentary.

Question 1

Since the late 1970s, Chile has become an increasingly globalised economy. It has privatised several state-owned industries, reduced trade restrictions like quotas, and deregulated markets to encourage more foreign direct investment and MNC activity. In 2023, Chile had the third highest real GDP per head ($17 800) in South America.

There are concerns, however, that Chile has an incredibly high current account deficit of more than $11.8 billion (−3.6% of GDP) and the value of its currency – the Chilean peso – is losing value. In January 2022, US$1 bought 700 Chilean pesos. In January 2025, US$1 bought 1 000 Chilean pesos. Many economists have started to wonder whether Chile should rethink its economic strategies and could even begin to impose tariffs on imports.

a   Define 'globalisation'.   **[2]**

Example student response	Commentary
Globalisation is interconnectedness between economies.	AO1 Knowledge and understanding This is not a good definition. Globalisation must be defined as a process and as an end-state. For example, globalisation is the process by which the world becomes increasingly interconnected through trade and other links.

b   Explain **two** reasons for foreigners to buy the Chilean peso.   **[4]**

Example student response	Commentary
Foreigners may buy the Chilean peso to pay for Chilean exports such as copper, fruits and wine. When countries import goods from Chile, they need to purchase pesos to complete the transaction, increasing demand for the currency. Foreigners may buy the Chilean peso to invest in Chilean firms or infrastructure projects. When foreign investors purchase assets like land, firms or shares in Chile, they need to convert their own currency into pesos to facilitate the investment.	AO1 Knowledge and understanding and AO2 Analysis This is a good answer. The student identifies two reasons but also develops them in accordance with the question about the Chilean peso. Other reasons could have included: • speculation • government intervention in currency markets • workers' remittances.

c   Analyse how imposing tariffs on imports may benefit a country like Chile.   [6]

Example student response	Commentary
Imposing tariffs on imports could be one way to address many of Chile's challenges. Tariffs would make imports more expensive, which in turn could help to reduce demand for foreign goods. This would potentially improve the country's current account balance and decrease its reliance on imports. This might also support domestic industries, especially if Chile wants to protect its strategic sectors or infant industries from foreign competition. Reducing the outflow of foreign currency through imports could help prevent further depreciation of the peso, stabilising its value in the international market. In addition, tariffs could encourage consumers to shift from buying imported goods to locally produced alternatives, fostering economic growth and potentially reducing unemployment in certain sectors. If consumers continue to buy imported goods, then at least the government will collect more tax revenue, and this can be spent on public goods and merit goods, which might increase living standards in Chile further.	**AO1 Knowledge and understanding and AO2 Analysis** This is a very good answer. The student demonstrates an excellent understanding of the topic in the question (tariffs) but also uses the context of Chile to support their answer. Chile has very specific issues like a large current account deficit and a depreciating currency, both of which can be improved by tariffs.

d   Discuss whether high economic growth in a country might lead to a current account deficit in its balance of payments.   [8]

Example student response	Commentary
A high economic growth rate in a country might result in a deficit on its current account for several reasons. As incomes rise, consumers are likely to buy more imports, especially if domestic products cannot meet their increased demand. Additionally, as firms expand and grow, they may switch from selling to foreign markets to focusing more on the growing home market, reducing exports. Firms may also import more raw materials and capital goods to support the production process, further increasing imports. Moreover, economic growth could lead to inflation, which might reduce the country's international price competitiveness, making exports more expensive and less attractive to foreign buyers. This could also contribute to a worsening current account deficit. However, it depends on the specific policies adopted – whether they are export-led policies or protectionist policies like tariffs.	**AO1 Knowledge and understanding and AO2 Analysis** The first half of this answer is very good. The student identifies several reasons why high economic growth might result in a current account deficit. These points are developed, although they could have been applied more to the context of Chile. **AO3 Evaluation** The evaluative section is quite poor. The one-sentence remark 'it depends on' would not be sufficient to receive many marks. Like analysis, evaluative comments need to be developed and justified. For example, the student could have developed the export-led argument more. If there is increased demand for goods and services abroad, this might improve the current account. Such economic growth might also encourage more investment, leading to an improvement in the quality of domestically produced goods, making them more competitive globally and potentially lowering prices.

Question 2

Write an improved answer to Questions 1(a) and (d).

The following question has example student responses and commentaries provided. For each part of the question, work through the question first, then compare your answer to the example student response and commentary.

Question 3

Table 1: Jordan fact file

	2022	2023
Balance of trade in goods and services	–$9.3bn	–$6.7bn
Net primary income	–$0.5bn	–$0.4bn
Net secondary income	X	$5.3bn
Current account balance	–$3.8bn	Y

Jordan is a small country in the Middle East. Its currency is the Jordanian dinar. Over the years, the country has started to specialise in chemical products, particularly in areas such as fertilisers and pharmaceuticals. The country's chemical industry now makes up approximately 40% of its exports. However, Jordan still faces challenges in terms of balancing its current account. In 2022, the balance of trade in goods and services stood at –9.3 billion USD. In 2023, it had improved slightly to –6.7 billion USD, and this had helped to reduce the deficit on the current account.

Table 2: Selected countries current account balance and inflation rate, 2023

	Current account balance (% of GDP)	Annual inflation rate
Germany	+5.6%	5.9%
Japan	+3.8%	3.1%
Chile	–3.6%	7.58%
Argentina	–3.2%	211.4%

Jordan's main trading partner is the United States, which accounts for 21% of its exports. Jordan enjoys a favourable exchange rate against the US dollar and, in 2001, the country further strengthened its ties with the USA by signing a free trade agreement, which has significantly boosted trade between the two nations. However, despite these advantages, Jordan still ranks relatively poorly in terms of its overall free trade compared to the rest of the world.

a   Define 'foreign exchange rate'.   [2]

Example student response	Commentary
Foreign exchange rate is the price of one country's currency in terms of another currency, and it determines how much one currency is worth relative to another. In this case, how much one US dollar is worth in terms of Jordanian dinar.	AO1 Knowledge and understanding This is a correct answer. The student has written a short but clear statement.

b Calculate the values for X and Y on Jordan's current account. [2]

Example student response	Commentary
X = 6.0 Y = −1.8	AO1 Knowledge and understanding These answers are correct, but it would have been better if the student had shown their workings so that it is clear how they got to these answers.

c Identify **two** types of trade restrictions. [2]

Example student response	Commentary
Indirect taxes Subsidies	AO1 Knowledge and understanding This is partially correct, but it could be clearer. Indirect taxes can be considered a form of trade restriction if they are applied to imported goods (i.e. a tariff). Subsidies could also be provided to domestic producers to make their goods cheaper in comparison to imports. However, these are not common types of trade restrictions, so it would have been better to list tariffs and quotas.

d Explain **one** advantage and **one** disadvantage of specialisation to a country like Jordan. [4]

Example student response	Commentary
Specialisation is when a country concentrates on producing a limited number of goods and services that they are best at producing. In this case, the case study says that Jordan 'has started to specialise in chemical products', which 'now make up approximately 40% of its exports'. One advantage is that specialisation can enable the firms in the country that concentrate on producing the product to develop skills and techniques in its production. This would raise the quality of the product. This may increase the international competitiveness of those products further and stimulate exports. A second advantage is that if firms specialise, they can produce the product on a large scale and this may enable them to take advantage of economies of scale, such as buying and technical economies. Firms can also buy their raw materials from specialist firms that are producing high-quality raw materials at low costs.	AO1 Knowledge and understanding and AO2 Analysis The student has not answered the question fully. The question asks for one advantage and one disadvantage. Unfortunately, the student offered two advantages only. While these are both well-developed points, this answer cannot receive full marks because it does not fully answer the question.

e Analyse the relationship between a country's current account balance and its inflation rate. [4]

Example student response	Commentary
A country's current balance and its inflation rate are often closely linked. A current account surplus is often associated with a high level of international competitiveness. This means there is a high demand for exports, which in turn leads to an appreciation of the currency. The strong currency then helps to keep inflation low because imported raw materials are much cheaper. This is not an automatic relationship and demand pressures can lead to an increase in the price level, but the examples of Germany and Japan (from the data) tend to prove the point. Likewise, a current account deficit can weaken the currency, making imports more expensive. This can push up inflation.	AO1 Knowledge and understanding and AO2 Analysis This answer demonstrates an understanding of the relationship between the two variables. The student identifies that a current account surplus is often linked to international competitiveness, and then explains the impact on the exchange rate. The second paragraph is shorter, but it still offers a relatively clear and concise explanation. There is some application to the data – with references to Germany and Japan – but the answer could be improved by also applying the theory to the deficit examples in the data, such as Chile, Argentina or Jordan.

f   Discuss whether reducing a deficit on the current account of the balance of payments will increase living standards in a country like Jordan.   **[6]**

Example student response	Commentary
Reducing a deficit on the current account will definitely increase living standards. When the country has less of a deficit, the government will be able to spend more on things like education and healthcare. This helps people because they have better access to services. When the current account improves, the country's economy becomes stronger and people can get better jobs. Also, if there is no deficit, there is no need to borrow money, so the country will have less debt and more money to spend.	AO1 Knowledge and understanding and AO2 Analysis The answer provides a superficial link between reducing the current account deficit and living standards without any specific detail or reasoning. It looks like a major misconception as well. For example, the statement 'when the country has less of a deficit, the government will be able to spend more on things like education and healthcare' sounds like the student is confusing a current account deficit with a fiscal deficit. There is no reference to Jordan. The question requires for the answer to be written in the context of a country like Jordan. AO3 Evaluation The answer is poorly structured and does not address different aspects of the question. There is no balance between when reducing the deficit could improve living standards and when it might not. There is, simply, no evaluation. There could be other factors like economic policies, global economic conditions or domestic issues that influence living standards. Also, the answer ignores potential trade-offs or challenges in reducing a current account deficit, such as the need for austerity measures or the impact on consumption and investment.

Now that you have read the example student response to the previous question, here are some similar practice questions for parts (c) and (d) which you should attempt before trying to write an improved answer to part (f). Use the guidance in the commentaries in this section to help you as you answer the questions.

Question 4

a   Identify **two** benefits of a free trade agreement to Jordan's producers.   [2]

b   Explain **one** advantage and **one** disadvantage of multinational companies (MNCs) to a country that hosts them.   [4]

Question 5

Write an improved answer to Question 3 (f).

Las tecnologías de la información y la comunicación en España

La colección Historia nace con el propósito de difundir entre la comunidad académica los resultados más relevantes de nuevas investigaciones, con la intención de convertirse en una de las colecciones universitarias de referencia en el panorama historiográfico actual.

Comité científico de la colección

Dirección
Carmen Sanz Ayán
Universidad Complutense de Madrid/Real Academia de la Historia, España

Secretaría
Alejandra Franganillo Álvarez
Universidad Complutense de Madrid, España

Asesoría
Mafalda Soares D'Acunha
CIDEHUS- Universidad de Évora, Portugal

Juan Pablo Fusi Aizpurúa
Real Academia de la Historia, España

Béatrice Perez
Universidad de la Sorbona-Paris IV, Francia

Miguel Luque Talaván
Universidad Complutense de Madrid, España

Marcella Aglietti
Universidad de Pisa, Italia

Antonio Pizzo
Escuela Española de Historia y Arqueología en Roma.Consejo Superior de Investigaciones Científicas, Italia

Allyson M. Poska
Universidad de Mary Washington, Estados Unidos

David Hernández de la Fuente
Universidad Complutense de Madrid, España

Cristina Jular Pérez-Alfaro
Centro de Ciencias Humanas y Sociales-Consejo Superior de Investigaciones Científicas, España

Enrique Moradiellos
Universidad de Extremadura, España

Luis Perdices de Blas
Universidad Complutense de Madrid, España

Christopher F. Laferl
Universidad de Salzburgo, Austria

Paloma Cuenca Muñoz
Universidad Complutense de Madrid, España

Juan Carlos Díez Fernández-Lomana
Universidad de Burgos, España

Las tecnologías de la información y la comunicación en España

Ángel Calvo Calvo

EDICIONES
COMPLUTENSE

PRIMERA EDICIÓN: FEBRERO 2024

© 2024, de los textos: Ángel Calvo Calvo

© 2024, Ediciones Complutense
Pabellón de Gobierno
Isaac Peral s/n
28015 Madrid, España
913 941127
info.ediciones@ucm.es
http://www.ucm.es/ediciones-complutense

ISBN: 978-84-669-3824-2
Depósito Legal: M-30339-2023

Diseño de cubiertas de la colección: Koln Studio

Imagen de cubierta: «Nuevas tecnologías (1994)» © 2024, Carlos Casariego, VEGAP, Madrid. Facilitada por el Archivo Histórico Fotográfico de Telefónica.

Impresión
Solana e Hijos Artes Gráficas
San Alfonso, 26 Bº La Fortuna
28917 Leganés (Madrid)

Ediciones Complutense es miembro de Unión de Editoriales Universitarias Españolas (UNE) y está asociado a Cedro.

Ediciones Complutense garantiza un riguroso proceso de selección y evaluación de los trabajos que publica.

A Mayte, Julia, Pablo y Marc

Índice

Prólogo

JAVIER NADAL

Director General de Telecomunicaciones entre 1985 y 1995

El libro que tenemos delante es una nueva obra de Ángel Calvo que trata de los avatares del sector español de la industria TIC durante las dos décadas finales del siglo pasado. El autor tiene una dilatada experiencia académica e investigadora en la materia y ha realizado publicaciones relevantes sobre historia de la economía industrial y, en particular, sobre telecomunicaciones y el sector electrónico en España.

En esta ocasión no ha tratado de hacer una historia global del periodo, sino exponer casos concretos y significativos que ilustran las motivaciones de los protagonistas, los objetivos planteados y los resultados obtenidos. Ha tenido acceso a fuentes primarias relevantes y dispone de testimonios orales de algunos protagonistas que le han permitido iluminar aquellos casos singulares elegidos. Con ese material de partida, ha seleccionado una decena de esos momentos y los relata con la metodología de casos. Los episodios son casos separados, pero no son totalmente independientes, lo que permite que, de su lectura conjunta, aflore el hilo conductor de aquellas décadas cruciales en las que se fraguó la revolución tecnológica en la que todavía nos encontramos.

Leer un libro es siempre una experiencia personal, en buena medida intransferible. Sobre todo, si trata de una materia relacionada con la trayectoria vital del lector, como es mi caso. Vaya por delante que los diferentes episodios que nos presenta el profesor Calvo y que constituyen la materia del libro me parecen todos ellos relevantes y cumplen el objetivo previsto por el autor. Comprendo y aplaudo el modo como los agrupa, como los relaciona entre sí y las conclusiones que obtiene.

Dicho lo anterior, con el riesgo de ser repetitivo respecto a lo que el propio autor ha escrito con mayor autoridad que yo, me gustaría trasmitir las sensaciones que la lectura del texto me ha generado, resituando cada una de las diez historias en el contexto mental que yo conservo de aquellos años. Tal vez añada algún matiz al conjunto.

Cuando en 1971, Intel lanzó al mercado el primer microprocesador, Gordon Moore ya había enunciado su famosa 'Ley' según la cual la tecnología permitiría duplicar cada dos años, durante las décadas siguientes, el número de transistores por unidad de superficie de un chip, haciendo crecer exponencialmente la potencia de procesamiento y reduciendo sistemáticamente los precios. Así se inició la carrera que ha revolucionado al mundo desde entonces. Las empresas y profesionales del sector electrónico español estuvieron muy atentos a estos avances y se esforzaron para mantenerse en sintonía con los tiempos. Con la debida modestia de un país de tipo medio, es preciso reconocer que tanto la Universidad como la industria electrónica del país hicieron su trabajo de manera razonable.

En 1978, el sector industrial electrónico de España comprendía tres subsectores: electrónica de consumo, electrónica profesional y componentes. Según los datos de la patronal electrónica (ANIEL), su capacidad de producción anual alcanzó aquel año 167.000 millones de pesetas corrientes, cubriendo el 68% de la demanda interna y exportando el 15% de su producción. Generaba unos 55.000 puestos de trabajo y tenía una razonable capacidad de I+D de la que se ocupaban alrededor de 1.800 profesionales. Había además un pequeño, pero significativo, sector productor de *software* que acababa de constituir su propia patronal (SEDISI). La producción conjunta de ambos rondaba el 2% del PIB nacional. No era un sector grande, estaba equipado razonablemente, contaba con profesionales bien preparados y tenía un futuro prometedor. Pero tenía ineficiencias y debilidades bien conocidas y detectadas por sus protagonistas y el Gobierno.

En aquella época los países punteros aspiraban a participar en el liderazgo de las tecnologías clave y a no ser dependientes de tecnologías exteriores. Procuraban hacerlo a través de empresas nacionales o de empresas extranjeras instaladas en el país. La existencia de un tejido industrial propio integrado en los mercados internacionales se consideraba esencial para fomentar, difundir y protagonizar la nueva cultura tecnológica en la sociedad.

El sector español no era homogéneo. Determinadas áreas de actividad consideradas estratégicas, como la informática o la microelectrónica, mostraban lagunas importantes que se consideraba necesario cubrir a través de la instalación industrial en España de empresas multinacionales punteras. Entre 1980 y 1990, los gobiernos de UCD y del PSOE desplegaron una gran actividad negociadora que se visibilizó en una docena de acuerdos firmados con las principales multinacionales de informática, microelectrónica y fibra óptica.

Esta faceta negociadora de los gobiernos de la Transición y su motivación queda muy bien retratada por Ángel Calvo a través de tres interesantes casos en los que no solo participó el Gobierno, por la parte española, sino que le acompañó de manera muy activa la Compañía Telefónica Nacional de España (entonces cabecera de un importante Grupo Industrial), para constituir un consorcio europeo sobre microelectrónica, para atraer la instalación de una planta de chips de AT&T o conseguir la autosuficiencia en el abastecimiento de fibra óptica, respectivamente.

Los enormes esfuerzos desplegados por los Ministerios de Industria para conseguir la instalación de multinacionales en España no eran contradictorios con el objetivo de lograr que alguna de las iniciativas de empresas nacionales se convirtiera en una multinacional de su especialidad. Era una misión complicada a la que se dedicaron muchos esfuerzos desde el principio.

Dos de los casos desarrollados en el libro son buenos ejemplos de estos esfuerzos. El primero de ellos se refiere al Grupo electrónico del INI, sobre el que se diseñaron diferentes estrategias de reestructuración hasta desembocar en la consolidación de Indra como mayor multinacional tecnológica de matriz española. El segundo tiene que ver con la *joint venture* de Telefónica y Fujitsu para crear una empresa conjunta en Málaga con ambición de presencia internacional que sin embargo, a lo largo del tiempo, evolucionó hacia una filial 100% de la empresa japonesa.

En la década de los 80, mientras estaban vigentes las políticas tecnológicas citadas de desarrollo nacional o nacionalista, se estaba fraguando en occidente un cambio de 180° en la orientación estratégica mundial, para orientar la economía hacia un mercado global y abandonar la estrechez de las naciones. Era la vuelta del liberalismo que privatizó las empresas públicas y abrió todos los sectores a la competencia, incluidos los históricos monopolios de los servicios públicos. El éxito internacional de las políticas liberalizadoras de las telecomunicaciones en la década de los 90, junto a la sorpresiva irrupción de Internet y la no menos sorpresiva explosión de la telefonía móvil, dieron la primera prueba de la capacidad disruptiva de las tecnologías de la información.

El cambio fue de tal magnitud, que la propia industria de las telecomunicaciones sufrió las consecuencias en sus cimientos. Era una industria con una base tecnológica importante pero desarrollada sobre un modelo nacional en el que cada país tenía su propio campeón. De pronto el paradigma cambió. El mercado se hizo mundial, la 'guerra fría' había terminado e, incluso, países antes proscritos, como China, participaron en la globalización. La deslocalización se impuso sin restricciones y los grandes actores industriales de las telecomunicaciones europeas sufrieron lo indecible.

El segundo capítulo del libro se centra precisamente en este escenario. España tenía desde 1926 su propio campeón que era la Standard Eléctrica, filial de la IT&T, nacida como brazo industrial de la CTNE cuando el modelo imperante en el mundo era el servicio telefónico prestado en monopolio e integrado verticalmente con la industria productora de equipos. El impacto de los cambios operados en la década de los 90 sobre este Grupo empresarial fueron tremendos, tanto en términos de la pérdida de masa laboral como en la transformación de sus mercados tradicionales. Los tres casos que desarrolla Ángel Calvo en este capítulo son muy expresivos de la magnitud de esta reconversión, mostrando: 1) la transformación de la Standard Eléctrica en la empresa ALCATEL-SESA al entrar a formar parte de la multinacional Alcatel; 2) el impacto que las políticas de deslocalización causaron a la propia Alcatel con posterioridad; y 3) el caso específico de los problemas de supervivencia que sufrió una empresa del Grupo (CITESA de Málaga).

La lista de diez casos se completa con dos análisis complementarios sobre una misma empresa. Se trata de Amper, empresa privada de origen familiar, creada en 1971 Durante una etapa posterior estuvo participada por Telefónica, para luego conocer diferentes etapas con otros socios importantes. Lo más significativo de esta empresa es su capacidad de adaptación y supervivencia como empresa multinacional con tecnología propia.

Los diez casos pueden ser leídos e interpretados como piezas únicas y separadas, pero también pueden considerarse piezas de un puzle más amplio, del que faltan otras muchas por conocer. Ojalá que la publicación de este libro anime a otros académicos e investigadores de la economía industrial a publicar nuevos trabajos rigurosos de esta interesante etapa de nuestra historia que nos ayuden a conocernos mejor y a aprender de nuestros errores y nuestros aciertos del pasado.

Ahora es el momento de felicitar a Ángel Calvo por el resultado alcanzado, agradecerle por su decisión de escribir el libro y además, en mi caso, agradecerle por hacerme el honor de pedirme un prólogo.

Madrid, Agosto de 2023

Presentación

Equiparándola a integración, el World Bank (2002) define la globalización, a grandes rasgos, como la integración mundial de las economías y las sociedades, resultado de la reducción de los costes de transporte, la disminución de las barreras comerciales, la comunicación más rápida de las ideas, el aumento de los flujos de capital y la intensificación de las presiones de mitigación.

En este contexto, nuestro mundo se desliza hacia la Cuarta Revolución Industrial o Industria 4.0, que echa sus raíces en los conocimientos y sistemas de las anteriores, en particular en las capacidades digitales de la Tercera Revolución Industrial, e incluye tecnologías tales como la inteligencia artificial y la robótica, la fabricación aditiva, las bio y neurotecnologías, la realidad virtual y aumentada, los nuevos materiales, las tecnologías energéticas, así como ideas y capacidades cuya existencia ignoramos (Schwab y Davis 2018; Johnson y Markey-Towler 2020). La Tercera Revolución Industrial consiste en la aplicación creciente y generalizada de la tecnología de la información en la mayoría de las sociedades industriales avanzadas y su extensión a los países en desarrollo. En otros términos, puede definirse como la integración de ordenadores y comunicaciones y el uso creciente de la electrónica tanto en los procesos industriales como en el comercio (Khan 1987, 114-116). Ordenadores y comunicaciones conforman la base de las Tecnologías de la Información y la Comunicación, a las que nos referiremos por su sigla (TIC).

Mejor definidos, los adelantos tecnológicos consisten en la combinación de procesos, instrumentos y redes. En particular, comprenden la digitalización de la información (texto, cifras, sonido, imágenes fijas, imágenes en movimiento) y la subsiguiente capacidad de transmitir mayores volúmenes de información a alta velocidad. Incluyen asimismo la inteligencia artificial y la incorporación de interfaces «inteligentes» y de posibilidades de interacción a los productos y servicios de información. Utilizan los satélites de comunicación, de potencia y accesibilidad muchísimo mayores, junto a la fibra óptica a bajo precio, nuevas tecnologías de transmisión inalámbrica y técnicas de conexión e intercambio y, finalmente, las redes informáticas para la investigación, en particular Internet (UNESCO 2001).

Lo esencial de esa definición se recoge en un informe del Consejo de Europa (Council of Europe 1997, 613). El organismo se refería a la explosión de la comunicación electrónica como la conjunción de cinco factores principales: la digitalización de los datos; la miniaturización, que favorece el uso intensivo de componentes electrónicos; la compresión de datos; el uso de sistemas de transmisión óptica de banda ancha y la aparición de nuevos componentes de *software* o soporte lógico en su denominación alternativa. Como resultado, la línea divisoria entre el procesamiento de datos y la comunicación, entre la electrónica de ocio y los medios de comunicación, es cada vez más tenue.

De acuerdo con la panorámica trazada por los grandes organismos internacionales, las TIC crecieron de forma muy dinámica ya que la tasa de adopción en el mundo durante los dos decenios 1994-2014 superó la de cualquier otra tecnología anterior. El rápido crecimiento en las capacidades de los componentes y las redes de las TIC impulsaron una innovación de igual rapidez en la tecnología y los servicios.

Su naturaleza de tecnologías con fines generales proporciona a las TIC tres rasgos especialmente importantes para el desarrollo económico y social: una mayor eficiencia en los procesos económicos y sociales; una mejora de la eficacia de la cooperación entre los distintos interesados y un aumento del volumen y la variedad de información a disposición de las personas, las empresas y los gobiernos (Naciones Unidas 2014, 3-4)[1].

Para la corriente mayoritaria del pensamiento las TIC son la espina dorsal de la economía, la sociedad y la vida cotidiana de las personas en el mundo actual[2]. Según el análisis de algunos especialistas (Mansell et al. (ed.) 1995, 83-108), como nuevo patrón o estructura de la economía, las TIC no solo impactan por entero en las industrias y servicios, sino también a la totalidad de funciones dentro de estas industrias y servicios. No solo la producción,

---

[1] TIC como tecnología de uso general teorizada por el economista Paul David (1991, 315–348), recogida por Bresnahan y Trajtenberg (1995, 83-108) y comentada por Liao (2016, 10-25) y Garrido (2009).

[2] Limitamos una ingente bibliografía a un solo título de alta representatividad (OECD 2003, 9).

sino también el diseño, la distribución y el *marketing* se ven profundamente afectados por las TIC.

El debate internacional se centra hoy en las vías de fomentar el uso productivo e inclusivo de las TIC, en su calidad de tecnología de uso general. ¿Basta con expandir las infraestructuras o se requiere crear marcos legales, institucionales y de políticas orientadas al desarrollo de las naciones? (Conferencia de las Naciones Unidas sobre Comercio y Desarrollo 2005).

Desde el punto de vista semántico, la expresión Tecnologías de la Información y la Comunicación se hizo esperar. En 1982, la Comisión Europea usaba el término genérico «tecnología de la información» pero en algunos programas desglosaba campos diferentes sin adscribirlos a un concepto común. Así, por ejemplo, aludía al proyecto ESPRIT como instrumento de promover la I+D europea en la tecnología de la información en especial, sin dejar de desgranar por separado en otro momento la microelectrónica, la tecnología de los programas informáticos, el procesamiento avanzado de la información, la burocracia y la fabricación integrada de ordenadores (Joint Research Center 1982, 3; EU Commission 1982).

En los documentos también aparecía el vocablo «tecnologías informáticas» («informatics technologies»), que abarcaba la microelectrónica avanzada, el procesamiento avanzado de la información, la tecnología de *software*, la automatización de oficinas y la fabricación flexible integrada en el ordenador (Committee on Energy and Research on the communications 1982, 14) .

La primera conceptualización de las TIC se debe a académicos y entidades especializadas. IGI Global señaló en 1988 que la convergencia de la industria de las telecomunicaciones con las industrias de la informática y la radiodifusión dio lugar a una definición más amplia de las tecnologías de la información y las comunicaciones (IGI Global 1988). Hall y Preston (1988) acuñaron el término de industrias de Nueva Tecnología de la Información (NTI), en las que incluían las tecnologías (mecánica, eléctrica, electromagnética y electrónica) de grabado, transmisión, tratamiento y distribución de información, originadas en el siglo XIX y soporte de la cuarta ola Kondratieff. Con los años, el término tendió a perder adjetivaciones. En las discusiones de la Ronda Uruguay (1994) se hablaba de «Information Technology Industry» (Hearings 1994, 164). La Organización de Cooperación y Desarrollo Económicos (OCDE) acabó por asimilar el sector de las TIC a la industria de equipos y a los servicios relacionados con la radiodifusión, la informática y las telecomunicaciones, todos los cuales capturan y muestran información electrónicamente (United Nations, Economic and Social Council, E/CN.3/2004/16, 30 de enero de 2004, 2).

En el límite superior de la cronología que hemos adoptado, parece oportuno presentar una visión general que nos sitúe ante las grandes líneas de debate. En el manual por excelencia de la TIC –el de Oxford– aparecen cuatro temas, que aspiran a ser de utilidad para los responsables políticos y para quienes trabajan en ese campo.

El tema 1 –la economía del conocimiento–, que incluye las aportaciones sobre el paradigma de las TIC, hace hincapié en la dinámica de la «nueva» economía, centrándose en las dimensiones económicas y políticas de la convergencia de la televisión, la informática e Internet, y en el papel cambiante de la política y la reglamentación nacionales e internacionales. El segundo tema –dinámica organizativa, estrategia y diseño– aborda el consenso. Se centra en las formas en que los implicados negocian la introducción y el uso de las aplicaciones de las TIC y en el potencial de diversas estrategias para lograr el consenso sobre las necesidades de los usuarios y el diseño de la tecnología. El tercer tema –gobernanza y democracia– se propone hacer una evaluación crítica del modo en que las TIC articulan con las relaciones de poder con respecto a las instituciones y los individuos. Las TIC se examinan en función de la medida en que se movilizan para mejorar la participación democrática y apoyar los movimientos sociales. El cuarto tema –cultura, comunidad y nuevas alfabetizaciones mediáticas– reafirma el compromiso de entender la relación entre la tecnología y el cambio social como una relación de determinación mutua y, por lo tanto, una que depende crucialmente de las acciones de los individuos y las instituciones en el mundo moderno.

A la hora de adoptar un marco guía, este estudio recoge el término de macro o hipersector de las Tecnologías de la Información y la Comunicación (HTIC), definido como «el conjunto de actividades de investigación, desarrollo, fabricación, integración, instalación, comercialización y mantenimiento de componentes, subconjuntos, productos y sistemas físicos y lógicos, fundamentados en la tecnología electrónica». La definición incluye «la explotación de servicios basados en dichas tecnologías, así como la producción y difusión de contenidos soportados electrónicamente y las aplicaciones de Internet» (Banegas 2002, 184).

Este volumen reúne diversas investigaciones sobre la problemática y se estructura en tres grandes apartados. El primero, de índole más general, pretende sentar los fundamentos y en esta tarea aborda los fundamentos, a saber, materiales y componentes.

El segundo se refiere al torbellino en el que se vieron envueltas las telecomunicaciones en las dos décadas finales del siglo XX, uno de cuyos componentes primordiales lo protagonizó el paso de la conmutación electromecánica a la electrónica. El tercer apartado se centra en el análisis de las telecomunicaciones, electrónica e informática en la era digital.

Una característica común a todos ellos es la índole interdisciplinar y transversal, de honda raíz platónica, después desplazada por el fraccionamiento en dominios de especialización disciplinaria y, finalmente, convertida en eje de la actividad intelectual. En otras palabras, persigue la descripción y análisis de las transformaciones tanto del conocimiento y la tecnología en sí como del entramado institucional en el que han surgido y desarrollado a lo largo del tiempo (Klein 1990, 17-19, 620).

En términos generales, combina la tecnología en su realidad de sistema, una acepción primordial en la obra excepcional elaborada por Thomas P. Hughes (1983) y cultivada por Melvin Kranzberg (1986, 544-560), con la aproximación desde la historia económica y empresarial, propia de Nathan Rosenberg (1994).

En su conjunto, la obra tiene una perspectiva comparada, de notable potencial de modelización y tipificación, que arrancó en la historia social en los años sesenta y no se asentó hasta una década después (Welskopp 2010, 1-17). Los niveles de comparación adoptados son diversos e incluyen entre otros términos la dimensión geográfica tanto distante como próxima, así como la sectorial y cronológica.

El segundo rasgo distintivo tiene que ver con el predominio de lo narrativo, plenamente justificado por el desconocimiento que se tiene de los hechos básicos. También desde el punto de vista metodológico, se utiliza el estudio de caso como herramienta ampliamente reconocida por su potencial de explicación (Jones 2018). Desfilan por estas páginas un nutrido grupo de empresas, la mayoría en calidad de protagonistas de subsectores distintos. Algunas cobran rabiosa actualidad en estos tiempos convulsos en los que la escasez de semiconductores en Europa y otras regiones del mundo han llevado a la Comisión Europea a proponer un amplio conjunto de medidas para reforzar el frágil ecosistema de semiconductores de la UE, la European Chips Act. Pienso en AT&T Microelectrónica de España, cuya fábrica de Tres Cantos ha vuelto a ocupar las páginas de la prensa, aupada por el Proyecto de Interés Común Europeo de semiconductores o el PERTE español de microchips, como lo hizo en el momento de su difícil gestación. Y cómo olvidar el chip de código abierto "sargantana", diseñado en España y rutilante promesa de acabar con la dependencia tecnológica de Europa.

Unas han emergido del olvido absoluto –ES2, por ejemplo– en el mundo académico mientras que otras se habían labrado un puesto desde muy antiguo. Unas terceras, de todos conocidas como es el caso de Indelec, apenas se habían ganado unas líneas en estudios más generales.

La cronología abarca las dos décadas finales del siglo XX y los primeros años del XXI. Algunos de estos aspectos se recogen más adelante en su lugar específico y si se señalan aquí es para darles mayor énfasis.

El tercer eje gira en torno a la variedad de fuentes utilizadas, que incluyen las primarias de procedencia diversa –las propias empresas, la administración o las instituciones–, la fuente oral, la hemeroteca y la bibliografía secundaria. Dar con ellas ha sido siempre una aventura y, en ocasiones, un verdadero milagro.

En versiones preliminares, los textos han sido presentados en reuniones científicas internacionales. Por lo general, han sido revisados por evaluadores independientes y algunos han visto la luz en revistas especializadas españolas y extranjeras. Pero lo que es esencial es que sobre ellos el autor conserva plenos derechos. En su práctica totalidad, han sido ampliados, pulidos, reforzados con nuevos documentos y reestructurados para adecuarlos al formato de libro. En esta tarea se han impuesto como fundamentales la homogeneización de criterios y las obligadas referencias cruzadas. La acumulación de materiales y la extensa relectura de los manuscritos han propiciado la reflexión sobre los problemas primordiales. Aquí hay materia larga para llorar. No caben lágrimas; tan solo inteligencia.

Todo libro es fruto de un trabajo colectivo y este no escapa a la norma. Las numerosas personas y entidades que han contribuido de una u otra manera a hacer realidad esta obra quedan recogidas en diversos lugares de forma precisa y adecuada al nivel de su participación. No obstante, algunas merecen asomarse aquí por su apoyo sostenido y aliento generoso. Mi reconocimiento pone en escena dos personajes clave de la aventura que explico en estas páginas –Luis Solana Madariaga y Javier Nadal– junto a los nombres de Jesús Banegas y Luis Méndez en el ámbito profesional y de Alfonso Herranz en el académico.

Luis Solana me ha favorecido con la memoria de su mandato en la Compañía Telefónica Nacional de España, que él mismo bautizó con el nombre de Telefónica. Los numerosos encuentros –personales o a distancia– mantenidos con él siempre se han nutrido de su pasión por la historia y han estado presididos por el respeto hacia mi trabajo. Desde sus puestos de responsabilidad en

Telefónica, Javier Nadal ha alentado y respaldado mi esfuerzo por esclarecer el pasado de las telecomunicaciones en España.

En su conjunto, el estudio se adscribe al Observatori Centre d'Estudis Jordi Nadal d'Història Econòmica del Departament d'Història Econòmica, Institucions, Política i Economia Mundial, Facultat d'Economia i Empresa (Universitat de Barcelona). Agradezco a sus responsables el apoyo que prestan a mi labor, que gana con ello anclaje y proyección académica.

Referencias

Banegas, Jesús. 2002. *La nueva economía española: impactos de las tecnologías de la información y la comunicación en la economía y la sociedad.* Madrid: Universidad Complutense de Madrid, 2 (cortesía del autor).

Bresnahan, Timothy F. y Trajtenberg, Manuel. 1995. «General Purpose Technologies Engines of Growth». *Journal of Econometrics*, 65, 83-108.

Committee on Energy and Research on the communications. 1982. *European parliament Working Documents, 1982 –1983.* Doc. 1-682/82, 15 de octubre.

Council of Europe Parliamentary Assembly Staff. 1997. Scientific and technical aspects of the new information and communication technologies, Report of M. Frey. Estrasburgo: Council of Europe, 613.

David, Paul A. «General – purpose Engines, Investment and Productivity Growth: from the Dynamo Revolution to the Computer Revolution». En *Technology and Investment — Crucial Issues for the '90s*, editado por Deiaco, Enrico et al. Londres: Pinter.

EU Commission. 1982. *Communication from the Commission to the Council on laying the foundations for a European strategic programme of research and development in information technology: the pilot phase.* COM (82) 486 final/2, 13 de agosto.

Garrido, Celso. 2009. *La innovación en los servicios: aspectos generales y los casos de los servicios de telecomunicaciones, turismo y bancario.* Santiago de Chile: Comisión Económica para América Latina y el Caribe (CEPAL), Naciones Unidas.

Hall, Peter y Preston, Pascal. 1988. *The Carrier Wave: New Information Technology and the Geography of Innovation, 1846-2003.* Boston MA: Unwin Hyman.

Hugues, Thomas P. 1983. *Networks of Power: Electrification in Western Society, 1880-1930.* Boulder CO: Westview Press.

IGI Global. 1988. *What is ICT Industry*. Hershey: IGI Global.

Johnson, Nicholas y Markey-Towler, Brendan. 2020. *Economics of the Fourth Industrial Revolution: Internet, Artificial Intelligence and Blockchain*. Londres y Nueva York: Routledge.

Joint Research Center. *1982 Annual Status report*. Bruselas-Luxemburgo: Commission of the European Communities.

Jones, Geoffrey. 2018. *Varieties of Green Business: Industries, Nations and Time*. Cheltenham R.U. y Northampton MA: Edward Elgar.

Khan, Rahat N. 1987. «The third industrial revolution: an economic overview». *Impact of science on society*, 146, 114-116.

Klein, Julie T. 1990. *Interdisciplinarity: History, theory, and practice*. Detroit: Wayne State University Press.

Kranzberg, Melvin. 1986. «Technology and History: 'Kranzberg's Laws'». *Technology and Culture* 27, n°.3: 544-560.

Liao, Hailin. 2016. «ICT as a general-purpose technology: The productivity of ICT in the United States revisited». *Information Economics and Policy*, 36, septiembre, 10-25.

Mansell, Robin et al. (ed.) 2007. *The Oxford Handbook of Information and Communication Technologies*. Oxford: Oxford University Press.

Naciones Unidas. 2014. *Tecnologías de la información y las comunicaciones para un desarrollo social y económico incluyente*. Informe del Secretario General, E/CN.16/2014/3. GE.14-50218 (S) 270314 310314, 3-4.

Rosenberg, Nathan. 1994. *Exploring the black box: technology, economics and history*. Nueva York: Cambridge University Press.

Schwab, Klaus y Davis, Nicholas. 2018. *Shaping the Future of the Fourth Industrial Revolution: A guide to building a better world*. Londres: Penguin UK.

Welskopp, Thomas. 2010. «Comparative History». En *European History Online* Mainz: Institute of European History. http://www.ieg-ego.eu/welskoppt-2010-en URN:urn:nbn:de:0159-20100921414

World Bank. 2002. *Globalization, Growth and Poverty: Building an Inclusive World Economy*. Washington y Nueva York: World Bank y Oxford University Press.

I. LOS FUNDAMENTOS: COMPONENTES Y MATERIALES

1. Los componentes de la Tercera Revolución Industrial: AT&T Microelectrónica de España

1. Introducción

La industria de los semiconductores se distingue por su naturaleza muy específica. Produce tecnología de vanguardia en entornos empresariales impredecibles bajo los principios de «más pequeño, más rápido y más barato». En sus inicios, las empresas del ramo controlaban todo el proceso de producción –desde el diseño hasta la fabricación–. En un momento de su expansión, empezó la transición a una creciente delegación de la producción a otras empresas del sector, principalmente empresas de fabricación (*foundries*) que brindaban atractivas opciones de subcontratación. La índole cíclica de la industria de los semiconductores situaba a las empresas de este compuesto químico ante constantes auges y descensos en la demanda de productos. Como resultado del alto coste de entrada y de la elevada intensidad de capital, los principales protagonistas de la operación forjaban alianzas para repartir los costes y la creación de fabricantes sin fábrica. Al mismo tiempo, muchos pequeños fabricantes de circuitos integrados *chips* dependían cada vez más de un número reducido de grandes empresas con plantas de producción propias, que alcanzaban un considerable poder de negociación en la industria. Esta se enfrentó así a la amenaza de los sustitutos, con notables variaciones según el segmento (Pricewaterhouse Coopers EU Services 2013, 21)[1].

Históricamente, la industria electrónica mundial se ha caracterizado por el predominio de regiones no europeas. En los primeros años del siglo XXI,

---

[1] Véase también Used (1982, 18-20).

los fabricantes de Asia, en especial de China, que habían sustituido el anterior empuje de Japón, encabezaban la distribución mundial de la industria electrónica. Europa quedaba relegada a la tercera posición como productora mundial.

Si retrocedemos en el tiempo, la industria electrónica europea de la década de 1980 estaba dominada por las tres grandes potencias industriales: Alemania, Reino Unido y Francia. A este grupo le seguía Italia en una posición destacada de un gran conjunto de países de características muy diversas por tamaño de sus economías, en el que estaban presentes los pequeños –Holanda, Suecia, Suiza y Bélgica– y los intermedios, como España (Zysman y Borrus 1994, 141-167) (Gráfico 1).

Figura 1. Producción de la industria electrónica de
Europa occidental, 1988 (millones de dólares)

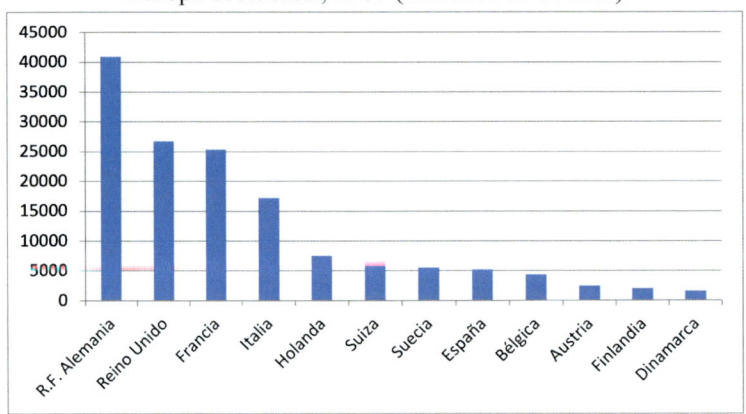

Fuente: Elaborado a partir de VVAA (1984), p. 134.

Más atrás todavía, a mediados de la década de 1970, la industria mundial de semiconductores estaba dominada por EE. UU. A partir de entonces, se dieron dos fenómenos complementarios: el descenso del peso del país líder y el ascenso paralelo de Japón (Anexo 1). Por su parte, Europa imitó a EE. UU. en su trayectoria descendente[2]. En Europa, el consumo creció sobre todo en la segunda mitad de la década de 1980, después de unos años de curvas casi planas (Gráfico 2).

---

[2] El poderoso Ministerio de Comercio Internacional e Industria (MITI) japonés calificó la industria de los semiconductores «el arroz de la industria» (Rogers y Larsen 1986, 199).

Gáfico 2. Consumo de semiconductores en Europa (miles de millones de dólares)

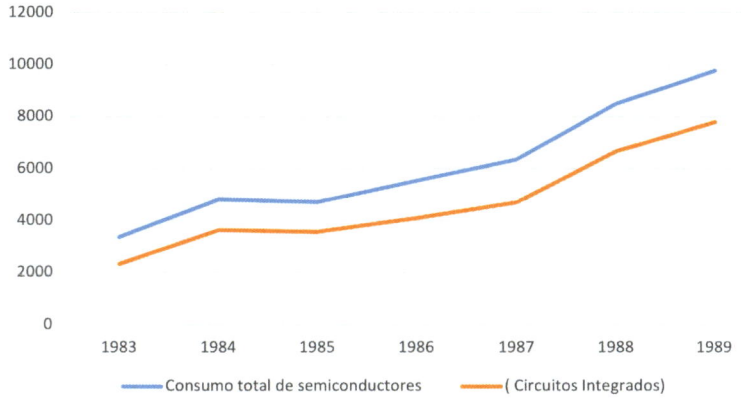

Fuente: Elaboración a partir de DataquestEurope, 1991.

España ocupaba posiciones modestas en Europa Occidental como productor en esta rama de la industria –5,5% del total, lejos de Alemania y Reino Unido (UK)–, y como consumidor, con un 6% (Anexo 1). Esta nación mediterránea iba a la zaga de los principales países occidentales y era el principal mercado de semiconductores de un grupo de categoría regional, que incluía a los países del sur y del centro de Europa (Suiza, Austria, Portugal, Grecia, Turquía y Malta). Varios de los principales fabricantes de telecomunicaciones, procesamiento de datos y electrónica de consumo localizaron sus plantas en España, atraídos por los bajos salarios y el suelo barato (Dataquest 1990, 15). Se configuró, así, una demanda local de componentes electrónicos.

2. España en la industria electrónica

En España, la industria resolvió sus necesidades de diversas maneras, entre ellas la subcontratación de componentes. Por ejemplo, Citesa adquirió a los Standard Telecommunications Laboratories el circuito integrado STL70, resultado del proyecto Regular Loop destinado a terminales telefónicos. El principal centro de investigación de IT&T asumió así un desarrollo optimizado para los requisitos técnicos de España, que redujo el coste del circuito de conversación total (chip más circuitería discreta adicional) y aumentó la eficiencia en la fabricación. En realidad, el proyecto obedeció a un bosquejo cooperativo: diseño en los laboratorios de Standard Telecommunications Laboratories en Harlow (Inglaterra); prototipos del transductor T800 construidos por Kirk Standard Electric en Dinamarca; primera fabricación del circuito integrado de conversación de tecnología bipolar STL 70 en IT&T Intermetall (Alemania); prototipos con teclados de multifrecuencia de IT&T en Corinth (Estados Unidos) o teclados de pulsos diseñados en STL. En este marco de asignación de tareas, Citesa aportó el diseño de los requisitos de la red española al desarrollo común. El circuito integrado de conversación de tecnología bipolar STL70 junto con el transductor electroacústico T800 de bobina móvil, un desarrollo del mismo proyecto, fueron la base años después del teléfono TEIDE (Méndez s.f.).

Las primeras iniciativas en microelectrónica sucumbieron a la incertidumbre y a la ineptitud del Gobierno en la primera fase de la transición democrática tras la larga dictadura franquista. Así ocurrió con la misión técnica a Silicon Valley, corazón de la alta tecnología, que impulsó un plan de la AMI norteamericana para establecerse en suelo español. Un destino similar corrió el proyecto de fabricación de chips con Motorola, pionera de las comunicaciones electrónicas, como socio tecnológico. La CTNE intentó asimilar el *know-how* enviando técnicos al centro de diseño de esta multinacional en Suiza, pero a pesar de los avances y la buena puesta a punto, la multinacional declinó ofertas por el poco atractivo del mercado español según el sentir de la empresa. En términos comparativos, American Micro Systems impulsó un proyecto similar en Austria y uno de los negociadores de Motorola, Pistorio, creó en Italia la Società Generale Semiconduttori (SGS), innovadora empresa conjunta entre Olivetti y Telettra SpA a la que se alude en otro apartado (Calvo 2014, 297; Henderson 2002, 169)[3]. Se asoció con AT&T en las tecnologías de circuitos bipolares y se fusionó con Thomson en 1987, creando uno de los dos grandes bloques de la industria europea del silicio, junto al eje centroeuropeo Philips-Siemens, piezas claves junto a STC y Bull de un clúster europeo (Hagedoorn y Schakenraad 1992, 163-190). Fuerte contraste con Italia, dedicada a la cultura del campeón nacional en un contexto de predominio en el mercado mundial[4]. Tampoco prosperó un preacuerdo de la operadora

[3]   American Microsystems, Inc. de California y Voest-Alpine AG, el grupo industrial estatal austriaco, fundaron en 1981 la empresa conjunta Austria Mikro Systeme International (AMS). Al principio, esta se especializó en la fabricación de productos estándar, pero los problemas financieros pronto se enseñorearon de la empresa. En 1986, se racionalizó y reestructuró para centrarse en sus conocimientos de tecnología de señal mixta (McClean (ed.) 1996, 3-3).

[4]   Conversación del autor con Juan Mulet Melià, Barcelona, 16 de mayo de 2013. La multinacional Motorola tenía cinco centros de diseño en Europa: East Kilbride (Escocia), Ginebra

CTNE y el INI con la americana Silicon Valley Supertex, en la vanguardia de los chips de energía inteligentes para paneles de visualización junto con Texas Instruments (*Popular Science*, noviembre de 1985, 86) y muy interesada en la infraestructura del Centro Nacional de Microelectrónica, para fabricar en España chips de alto voltaje para bienes de consumo. Desde la CTNE, Solana se inclinó por una ubicación equilibrada de las tecnologías de vanguardia para las fábricas en todo el territorio español. Uno de los emplazamientos que se barajó fue Barcelona, como contrapeso a los proyectos de AT&T y Fujitsu en Madrid y Málaga, respectivamente[5]. Sin duda, el sector público, representado por el Gobierno, y el INI tomaron parte en los primeros proyectos para crear una empresa conjunta con el TCA, pero este camino se cerró[6].

España alcanzó varias alianzas internacionales en el sector de la microelectrónica, patrocinadas por el Gobierno, instituciones públicas y em-

---

(Suiza), Munich (Alemania), Toulouse y Burdeos (Francia). Motorola –la cuarta en toda la industria de los semiconductores por ingresos después de NEC, Toshiba e Intel y en 2003 la 19ª entre las empresas multinacionales por volumen de inversión en I+D– fue pionera en la introducción del primer microprocesador de 32 bits (MC68020), que contiene 200.000 transistores (Fletcher 2013, 129). Su sección de semiconductores representaba aproximadamente el 30% de sus ventas; un tercio de sus ingresos totales se generaba fuera de los Estados Unidos y se había destinado a I+D el 7,6-8,3% de sus ingresos (Dataquest 1989, 215). Como sabemos, poco antes del final de la década de 1980, la CTNE se apoyó en AMPER para crear la empresa conjunta de telefonía móvil Telcel Motorola (Calvo 2014, 242; Forsgren 2013, 19; Historia oral de Pasquale Pistorio entrevistado por Doug Fairbairn, 26 de abril de 2010; *EE Times,* 25, 3, 2005; Queisser 1990, 165; Roche 1992, 186-187). Sobre grupos estratégicos y redes interempresariales véase Duysters y Hagedoorn (1995, 359-381).

5   Telefónica, *Libros de Actas del Consejo de Administración (LACA),* 28 de octubre de 1987. Telefónica comparó el proyecto con una empresa punta en el «chip de energía inteligente», sin duda Supertex, con el de AT&T (*Popular Science*, noviembre de 1985, 85; *El País*, 15 de octubre de 1987). El proyecto contemplaba crear un centenar y medio de puestos de trabajo y destinar el grueso de la producción al mercado exterior (*Cinco Días*, 2 de junio de 1987; *Tiempo*, 15/6/1987). Estrategia descentralizadora de IBM (Thakur et al. 1997, 304). IBM abrió un Centro de Desarrollo de Software internacional en Barcelona (MBDoT, 28 de octubre de 1987; Smidt y Wever 2012, 39). Telefónica apoyó con 40 millones de dólares el proyecto Everest, dentro de ESPRIT, para desarrollar herramientas para probar chips (Telefónica, *Acta del Comité Directivo* (ACD), 30 de enero de 1991; *Libros de Actas del Comité Directivo de Telefónica (LACD),* 30 de enero de 1991). Telefónica, *Acta del Comité Directivo* (ACD), 30 de enero de 1991. Telefónica I+D estaba empeñada en el diseño de circuitos de comunicaciones con un número muy elevado de celdas de memoria. El grupo de ingeniería microelectrónica de la Universidad de Cantabria, que trabajaba en tests de circuitos integrados desde 1980, estudió inicialmente los sistemas BIST, para realizar el test de circuitos digitales VLSI. Como resultado de estos tests obtuvo contratos con Telefónica I+D y Alcatel-SESA a mediados de la década de 1980 y por esa vía tuvo acceso al Proyecto ESPRIT de la Unión Europea Everest, en tareas lideradas por Siemens AG y Philips BV (Bracho 1999, 54-55).

6   Acuerdo AT&T-Compañía Telefónica Nacional de España, 26 de julio de 1984, (Archivo Histórico del INI).

presas. California Micro Devices (CMD), fabricante de componentes electrónicos de alto rendimiento a través de sus divisiones de Thin Film, ASIC y Microcircuitos, acordó con Telefónica la creación de una filial denominada California Micro Devices, España. CMD debía proporcionar tecnología, formación y unos dos millones de dólares de inversión para un tercio aproximado de la propiedad. CMD comercializaría sus componentes a clientes militares y civiles, aeroespaciales, médicos, informáticos y de comunicaciones; los productos vendidos en España debían atender las necesidades de la defensa española[7].

El mercado español tenía un tamaño similar al austriaco, alrededor de un cuarto del tamaño del grupo total, con la mayoría de los usuarios de los segmentos de consumo, telecomunicaciones y EDP (*European Semiconductor Consumption History and Forecast 1985-1995*, 9). Tras un periodo de inercia de los conservadores, el gobierno socialista español de turno concibió estrategias para impulsar las actividades de producción e investigación con el objetivo de incorporar al país a la corriente principal de la revolución electrónica y potenciar la economía para ganar competitividad. Lo hizo segmentando el mercado según el nivel tecnológico. De esta manera, para cruzar la frontera, los planes implicaban la asociación con líderes tecnológicos multinacionales, mientras que para la tecnología menos sofisticada se recurría a socios tecnológicos nacionales. Desde la empresa, el monopolio de la telefonía, ante el reto del inevitable cambio tecnológico, tenía justo el puesto de avanzada con iniciativas en el campo de la microelectrónica. Personalidades y asociaciones del sector habían sido empujadas en la misma dirección con poco éxito.

---

[7] ASIC (Application Specific Integrated Circuit) o Circuito Integrado de Aplicación Específica, creado en 1971, es un único chip de silicio que integra toda o la mayor parte de la funcionalidad electrónica de un producto (Anexo 2). La gran penetración de los ASICs – la quinta parte del mercado mundial de circuitos integrados a principios de los años 90– se debió a dos claves primordiales: uso de bibliotecas según la metodología de diseño «*semicustom*» y alto grado de madurez de las herramientas de diseño, cuyo primer objetivo fue proporcionar al diseñador la seguridad de éxito al primer intento mediante un simulador, evitando las costosas repeticiones (Fundación Cotec 1980, 9-10 y 16-17). CMD (1980) unió los activos de Capsco Sales (1976), una compañía de película delgada, y en 1982, estableció Custom MOS Arrays (CMA), que diseñó, fabricó y comercializó ICs basados en células HCMOS y *gate arrays* en el rango de 200 a 2.000 puertas antes de fusionarse en 1986 con CMA en una nueva firma. Componentes: componentes pasivos de película delgada para ensamblajes híbridos/arreglos de puertas/ICS basados en células/y sustratos de cabezales de impresión sin impacto, así como ASIC (Dataquest 1088, 136 137). CMD ofrece un caso típico de fraude con varios ardides de contabilidad, incluyendo ventas e ingresos ficticios (un tercio de los 45 millones de dólares de ingresos de la compañía en 1994 eran espurios) (Securities Exchange Commission 1999; MacDonald 2000; Jones 2011).

La confluencia de todos los esfuerzos se tradujo en un plan de acción general –Plan Electrónico e Informático Nacional (PEIN)– y proyectos empresariales concretos. El mayor significaba atraer inversiones y tecnología de la gigantesca multinacional estadounidense AT&T en una empresa conjunta, con fábrica e instalaciones de investigación ubicadas en España, una práctica inusual de AT&T. Tanto la CTNE como pionera en la introducción de la microelectrónica y cliente natural de la producción como el Estado como palanca del sector aportaron recursos financieros, apoyo e infraestructura para hacer posible la empresa más avanzada en circuitos integrados altamente sofisticados (Calvo 2016; Majó 1997).

También hubo otras realizaciones en el mismo subsector de la electrónica, entre las que destaca la participación en la empresa europea conjunta European Silicon Structures como vía de acceso a un material básico para las TIC[8]. En pocas palabras de uno de los protagonistas, CTNE utilizó su enorme poder adquisitivo y de inversión para hacer política industrial (Cohen 2007, 213–227)[9, 10].

A continuación se examina una de las dos iniciativas más destacadas en la tecnología de los semiconductores, crucial para la competencia y el progreso en las TIC en su calidad de núcleo de las telecomunicaciones, los ordenadores, los bienes de consumo y otros sistemas electrónicos (Hobday 1989, 155-186).

3. La apuesta por el acceso a los componentes básicos: AT&T

Sin duda, una de las realizaciones estrella impulsadas por la operadora monopolista CTNE en la década de 1980 fue fruto de la cooperación con una líder mundial del sector: la multinacional norteamericana AT&T.

En el contexto de la convergencia entre informática y electrónica, cobró especial significado el pacto entre la AT&T y la CTNE para la fabricación en España de circuitos integrados o chips. La feroz competencia entre numero-

---

[8]   En 1985, CTNE compró la participación del INI en SECOINSA por 2.160 millones (*El País*, 23 de marzo de 1985).

[9]   En su sentido amplio, el concepto de política industrial combina, bajo la misma etiqueta, políticas comerciales, tecnológicas y competitivas y el alcance de las políticas es tanto horizontal como vertical. En cambio, el concepto de política industrial en Francia se utiliza principalmente para las políticas sectoriales de la industria manufacturera: las que moldean la especialización industrial.

[10] Conversación con Luis Solana, Madrid, 8 de marzo de 2016.

sos gobiernos europeos por atraerse al mismo socio añadió nuevos elementos al acuerdo[11].

El programa socialista se comprometía a potenciar industrias estratégicas utilizando empleo del sector público para frenar la creciente dependencia exterior e impulsar la competitividad de la economía española, afrontando la incertidumbre de la transferencia tecnológica desde multinacionales históricamente poco proclives a ceder tecnología[12]. Hasta entonces, los propósitos de definir una política de promoción de la industria electrónica autóctona no habían pasado de tentativas fallidas[13]. De este substrato abonado con redoblados bríos emanaron unas directrices que incitaban a considerar el ciclo industrial completo de los circuitos microelectrónicos –concepción, diseño, fabricación y utilización de componentes– asunto prioritario para el desarrollo tecnológico e industrial nacional y a emprender acciones para fomentarlos. En la rama específica de los circuitos a medida (*custom design*), las directrices recomendaban promover centros de diseño y atraer empresas extranjeras en solitario o en colaboración con españolas, primando las iniciativas de mayoría española. Sobre la Dirección General de Electrónica e Informática recaía la responsabilidad de ejecutar esa política, que aceptaba el dominio selectivo de las multinacionales en la transferencia de tecnología y se comprometía a aportar recursos complementarios para garantizar la asimilación de la nueva tecnología y su desarrollo. Tal dominio sin embargo excluía los equipos para defensa y telecomunicaciones[14].

[11] Solana exhibía el «pequeño placer personal de haber ganado por la mano a la señora Thatcher, que siempre es algo que tiene sus componentes de atractivo»: *DSCD*, 10 de octubre de 1984, 6.498-6.526. Los chips aparecían en la documentación del III Plan de Desarrollo con el apelativo de «bloquecitos» (Comisaría del Plan de Desarrollo Económico y Social 1971, 101). No ha dejado rastro documental el inicio de las negociaciones con AT&T que los biógrafos atribuyen a Salvador Sánchez Terán durante su mandato en la CTNE (Azulgaray 2003, 51; González 2017, 323).

[12] El Programa socialista de 1982 señalaba explícitamente (11-12) el impulso de una industria electrónica nacional competitiva. El presidente González conocía la incertidumbre inherente a un acuerdo con AT&T (Castells et al. 1986). Está teorizado que las multinacionales no siempre desean transferir tecnología.

[13] Declaraciones de un alto responsable del Gobierno expresan un pesimismo desesperado ante una situación deplorable: «En microelectrónica, no tenemos industria ni investigadores capaces de hacer un dispositivo que funcione» (Entrevista a M. Pereda, *Actualidad Electrónica*, 1986, on-line). Declaración como sector preferente en 1974 y actuación posterior, recogida en Buesa y Molero (1986, 2) y en el controvertido estudio de De Diego (1995, 138-143).

[14] *Directrices* (1983); *El País*, 7 de enero de 1983. Joan Majó, con dilatada experiencia en el sector como inversor (Telesincro) y representante del asociacionismo profesional (ANIEL), fue nombrado director general: Entrevista a Joan Majó i Cruzate (JMiC). Resulta curiosa la

El pilar de la política electrónica fue el Plan Electrónico e Informático Nacional (PEIN) de 1984, con el que el gobierno conjugaba todas las palancas de su modelo de relanzamiento industrial, es decir, la industria, el asociacionismo profesional y, fundamental, una parte sustancial de la demanda. Era un plan con cinco líneas de actuación: fomento de la utilización de la informática en la Administración pública; estímulo de la asociación con las multinacionales para cubrir selectivamente la demanda interior; promoción por el sector público de las aplicaciones en oficinas, enseñanza y telecomunicaciones, en estrecha relación con la demanda de Telefónica, entonces en expansión; vinculación de las compras de la Administración al mayor esfuerzo inversor de los proveedores en el país y fomento de un desarrollo autónomo a través de ayudas a la investigación[15].

En el terreno de la microelectrónica, el PEIN contemplaba una segmentación del mercado por niveles de tecnología. En el más sofisticado, terreno exclusivo de las multinacionales, una planta fabricaría y ensamblaría circuitos integrados *custom*, aceptando el papel subordinado del capital español. En el de menor nivel, actuaría una empresa con mayoría de capital español a partir de Piher, respaldada por un centro de investigación. En la senda intervencionista apuntada, el gobierno español impulsó diversos proyectos en sectores punteros de la industria, especialmente en informática y electrónica de consumo y profesional. La fórmula implicaba la reorganización de las empresas electrónicas del INI para crear en su seno un *holding* a partir de una fórmula idéntica si bien con distintos protagonistas: un núcleo industrial nacional y una multinacional, de preferencia europea, como socio tecnológico. Sobre este particular se vuelve en otro capítulo[16].

referencia (Lázaro 1983, 131-144) a una reconversión en la industria electrónica. Los chips a medida o personalizados satisfacían los mismos requerimientos que un traje hecho a medida (Cane 1987, 37); la prensa norteamericana los acogió como la nueva ola de la industria europea (*New York Times*, 1 de agosto de 1988).

[15] Un excelente análisis del PEIN (Buesa y Molero 1986). El PEIN, que seguía en parte las orientaciones de la CTNE, con cuyo presidente Majó tenía buena sintonía, gozó de buena acogida por el sector privado (IBM, SESA), si bien la primera alertaba contra el excesivo proteccionismo estatal.

[16] JMiC, Proyectos con IBM, J2T, Olivetti, Thomson, Nixdorf, HP y General Electric (Archivo SEPI, 223, 614). Thomson sería socio tecnológico del grupo autóctono Piher en restructuración, que en una primera etapa realizaría el diseño de productos fabricados en el exterior; socios alternativos: la británica Ferranti y Philips (Archivo SEPI, 547, 01662, 26 de julio de 1984). Planes de un subholding del INI con Isel, Equipos Electrónicos, Experiencias Industriales, Piher y Enosa y Telesincro, filial de SECOINSA y pendiente de un acuerdo con Bull (*El País*, 23 de marzo de 1985).

La CTNE tenía reservado un protagonismo indiscutible. Impelida por la demanda de equipos de conmutación digital y transmisión de datos, llevaba la delantera con iniciativas como la creación de un Centro de diseño de circuitos integrados, especializado en la gama de alta complejidad. Su misión radicaba en cubrir las necesidades de la compañía sin dar por ello la espalda a la penuria de las empresas de electrónica (CTNE, *Informe Anual* 1982, 30).

Por el lado norteamericano, AT&T afrontaba una nueva configuración del mercado interior con la estrategia de expansión mundial tras su desmembramiento forzado. Su política de alianzas la llevó a unir fuerzas con IBM para desarrollar la industria de microchips a partir del grupo de investigación Sematech y a pertrecharse frente a la industria japonesa, bien respaldada por el gobierno e imbuida de la colaboración en consorcios. Lo propio hizo con Mitsubishi y NEC. AT&T ambicionaba reforzar su implantación competitiva en Europa, a través del ahorro de inversión, minimización de riesgos, captura de subvenciones públicas y privilegios por localización, sin excluir el recurso a mercados con costes inferiores de mano de obra. Un paso fue su alianza en minoría con Philips (APT) y otro su acuerdo con Olivetti, ambos en la electrónica de consumo, campo hasta el momento excluido de su intervención. En este sentido, los chips a la medida pretendían convertirse en la punta de lanza en el mercado español de microcircuitos (Malerba 1985, 222; Roche 1992, 189; Entrevista a W. J. Warwick, *ABC*, 18 de abril de 1988, 48)[17].

El proceso de creación de la empresa española bien merece atención pormenorizada, más allá de los apuntes escuetos, espigados en fuentes dispersas. El largo camino se inició hacia finales de 1983 con negociaciones a tres bandas entre la CTNE y la Dirección General de Electrónica e Informática, de un lado, y AT&T International y AT&T Technology (antes Western Elec-

---

[17]   Philips, una de las grandes empresas europeas más globalizadas, dependía fuertemente del mercado europeo (Van Appledoorn 1999). A diferencia de los acuerdos AT&T-Telefónica, los alcanzados con NEC atañían al intercambio de diseño CAD (AT&T) por tecnología lógica (chips de ordenador) de NEC (Ostry y Nelson 1995, 54). AT&T fracasó frente a Siemens en su proyecto de empresa conjunta con una filial de la italiana STET (*Business Week*, 10 de abril de 1994). Francia vetó a APT la compra de CGCT, dueña del 16% en el mercado francés de equipos de conmutación. Expansión mundial de AT&T Microelectronics y estructuración en divisiones por grandes regiones: Fletcher (2013, 101). Considerada campeona de las alianzas pero ajena inicialmente a la diferencia de valores respecto a su socio Olivetti, AT&T adoptó un bajo perfil público para evitar una sensación de dominio, personal autóctono para subrayar el entorno local y una identidad predominantemente europea (Huber y Glick 1993, 315); ejemplos de trasvase de capital humano de la matriz a la filial española los ofrecen la manager Anne Kingsbury y los ingenieros George Foyo, de origen cubano, y el colombiano Héctor Ruiz-Puyana, director del centro de diseño; directivos autóctonos: Valentín Rodríguez, director general de la planta.

tric), de otro lado. Fueron contactos llevados con la máxima discreción y sigilo por miedo a cualquier filtración en asunto tan delicado. AT&T presentó un plan de negocio, al que la CTNE planteó objeciones y propuestas relacionadas con el mercado, el calendario, la tributación y el grado de participación en la nueva empresa. La multinacional admitió contrarrestar con exportaciones las correcciones de demanda a la baja en el mercado español a fin de mantener el nivel de ocupación de la fábrica planeada. Además, se mostró proclive a acelerar el inicio de la fabricación y a aceptar el plan de amortizaciones así como el pago del impuesto de sociedades en España. La modificación de la estructura del capital de la nueva sociedad por aumento de la participación de AT&T en trece puntos sobre el 67% previsto y la consiguiente reducción de la participación de la CTNE llevarían consigo el recorte del pago por transferencia de tecnología en una cuantía de 15 millones de dólares. Irremediablemente, el gobierno español debía dar su aquiescencia al esquema de financiación y al ritmo de los reembolsos. Los objetivos cruciales de Telefónica eran el logro de un centro de diseño y el acceso a la tecnología punta, actualizada al ritmo de la invención, aspecto trascendental en productos de corto ciclo de vida[18].

En el paso siguiente quedaron definidas las características generales de una *joint venture* en España para fabricar circuitos integrados diseñados para una aplicación de la tecnología más sofisticada –inicialmente de 1,75 micras pero gradualmente modificados al compás del avance tecnológico. Asimismo, se fijaron como características de la mano de obra el nivel previsible de empleo en la fábrica, el grado de cualificación, la nacionalidad y el adiestramiento en EE. UU. A continuación, las conversaciones se encaminaron a lograr un acuerdo de principio sobre mecanismos de transferencia de tecnología y de garantía de calidad y actualidad, fechas de aportación de capital y de recepción de la subvención, derechos de minorías, garantía del mercado aportado por AT&T y aspectos legales. AT&T sometió un borrador de acuerdo a Telefónica, que, por su parte, se había asesorado con el Stanford Research Institute (SRI), destacada

---

[18] Telefónica conocía la relativamente baja repercusión sobre el empleo en relación con el esfuerzo inversor realizado: los puestos de trabajo creados –unos 700, 100 menos que en la planta de Orlando–, el 28% titulados superiores. Algunas cifras: capital social, subvenciones y créditos oficiales: 65, 60 y 75 millones de dólares; ayudas de 200 millones de ptas. para formación en EE. UU., clasificación de industria de interés preferente; terrenos e infraestructura para 120.000 m². AT&T exigía el desembolso de la subvención previo al del capital y un calendario (Noam 1992, 256); *LACA*, 29 y 25 de abril de 1984. En el marco del predominio de FDI norte-norte, España era el mayor receptor de FDI norte-sur en Europa; la subvención de España a AT&T disputaba el primer puesto a las de Italia e Irlanda entre las mayores concedidas en Europa a multinacionales (Froot 2008, 219). Thomsen, de Technology Systems, situaba a España en el buen camino tecnológico (*LACA*, 30 de enero de 1985).

consultora mundial en tecnologías avanzadas, algunas de cuyas conclusiones en materia de tecnología pretendía verter en la negociación. La documentación no deja traslucir dudas sobre la marca o intangibles, no otros que los de AT&T, a la vez que sobre el protagonismo indiscutible de la CTNE, por parte española, como adelantada en las políticas y factor de demanda (Anexo 3)[19].

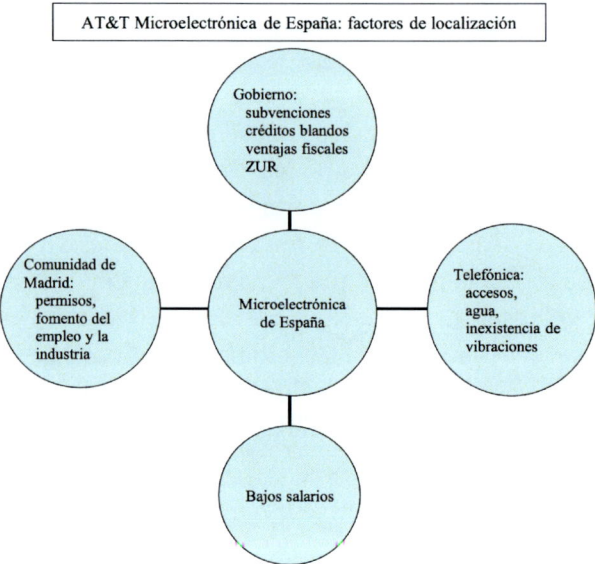

Fuente: Elaboración a partir del texto.

Las negociaciones, coronadas por el acuerdo suscrito a finales de julio de 1984 con las bendiciones oficiales, se orientaron a la concreción de los detalles de la operación. El gobierno comprometió el 60% de la inversión total en subvenciones y créditos blandos, convencido de la necesidad de

[19] El SRI, en territorio de Silicon Valley y asesor del Reino Unido, rechazó como obsoleta la tecnología inicialmente propuesta por AT&T (*El País,* 1 de diciembre de 1987; Fletcher (2013, 102) señala la fabricación de 1,25 micras –una micra equivale a una millonésima parte de una pulgada– (Castells 1999a, 68-69). Calendario: inicio de la fabricación a finales de 1986; plena capacidad en 1990; ventas de 220 millones de dólares en 1990 y 290 en 1993, 58% para exportación; tasa de rentabilidad del 24%; periodo de recuperación del capital: diez años; clasificación de industria de interés preferente: *LACA,* 25 de abril de 1984. La producción se orientaba al mercado europeo y norteamericano, dejando un resquicio para otros como el chino, donde la CTNE planeaba una fábrica de aparatos telefónicos; el alcance del mercado cautivo interno –especialmente los proveedores de la operadora– se redujo a un quinto del total (*El País,* 1 de diciembre de 1987; 31 de agosto de 1985). Hubo recelos por la exclusión del INI pero AT&T, como sus homólogas, anteponía acuerdos con los accionistas de la CTNE a otros con el Instituto, plenamente estatal (JMiC).

incorporar conocimiento antes que capital (Infograma)[20]. A punto de finalizar el año, subsistían sin cerrar puntos centrales, entre ellos la fiscalidad, la transferencia de tecnología y la base del *royalty*[21]. El preacuerdo de 1985 topó temporalmente con recelos, dificultades administrativas relacionadas con la tramitación de las licencias y autorizaciones para exportar tecnología en el caso estadounidense y con la asunción de obligaciones derivadas del contrato por parte del gobierno español. AT&T, recelosa de las tentaciones nacionalizadoras del gobierno socialista, pidió un compromiso de no nacionalizar la empresa (Entrevista JMiC). El escollo fundamental en las calificadas de «tortuous negotiations» (*New York Times*, 5 de diciembre de 1985) residía en motivos geoestratégicos y políticos, a saber, la exigencia norteamericana de sometimiento a su política de seguridad frente al bloque soviético como condición indispensable para dar vía libre a las inversiones de AT&T frente a la alternativa del Reino Unido (NATO Archives)[22]. Supe-

---

[20] Para el conjunto del apartado véase Adanero et al. (2006, 551-566). Desde 1978, un Reino Unido en declive preconizaba el desarrollo de la microelectrónica desde el gobierno y la industria con recurso a las multinacionales. El SRI recomendó fragmentar la industria de semiconductores en dos tipos de compañías: las productoras de bienes estándar en serie y las especializadas y verticalmente integradas (SRI, *Informe*, 1979, Thatcher Archives). Ericsson diversificó sus socios tecnológicos: Texas Instruments para microelectrónica y HP para sistemas operativos de soporte (Ericsson, *Annual Report*, 1995, 8).

[21] Archivo SEPI (INI). Se añadía a la lista un posible documento marco permanente al margen de los acuerdos específicos relativos a la nueva empresa, pagos a terceros y reclamaciones de estos, legislación aplicable y precio de venta de las exportaciones de la empresa española (*LACA*, 28 de noviembre de 1984); en las negociaciones participaron Luis Lada, Víctor Goyenechea y Enrique Lucas.

[22] Reivindicación del carácter vanguardista del acuerdo en la electrónica, compartida por el gobierno y Telefónica (*LACA*, 26 de agosto de 1984). Majó, ya ministro, vio un efecto llamada y lo calificó como «el más importante proyecto para el inicio de la nueva sociedad», enmarcado en la sustitución de un modelo industrial intensivo en energía por otro intensivo en tecnología (*DSCD*, 1984, 213, 6.471; JMiC). Tras algún conato infructuoso por obtener financiación de la Comisión Asesora de Investigación Científica y Técnica (CAICYT), la AT&T exploró planes conjuntos (Sánchez Miñana, Congreso de los diputados, 23 de octubre de 1984). Dentro de la competencia por atraer la inversión, la Comunidad de Madrid se involucraba a través de las licencias administrativas para la fábrica y, sobre todo, por una política anticrisis de impulso al empleo y a la industria; la Generalitat se involucró en menor medida, según Majó. El proyecto con AT&T alentó la creación de un parque tecnológico con el apoyo inicial del Instituto Madrileño de Desarrollo, fundado en 1984. El Parque Industrial de Tecnología Avanzada se destinó a albergar industrias innovadoras, con acceso a un centro de empresas, centro de encuentros e incubadora de empresas. La Comunidad de Madrid otorgó a AT&T Microelectrónica subvenciones que consistieron en cesión de terreno, obras de acceso y de acondicionamiento de la zona, provisión de valla y obras de suministro de agua, energía eléctrica, combustibles y saneamiento (*Boletín Oficial de la Asamblea de Madrid*, 69, 1 de diciembre de 1988). La existencia de universidades figuraba en la lista de condiciones exigidas por las multinacionales, junto a buenas comunicaciones y conexio-

radas las complicaciones, a finales del primer trimestre de 1986 la CTNE tenía expedita la vía para cerrar en EE. UU. un acuerdo con AT&T que culminaría con la creación en España de una nueva empresa con el nombre de AT&T Microelectrónica de España (AT&TME)[23].

Faltaba resolver la ubicación de la planta, decisión que competía a AT&T, y precisar las condiciones de la transferencia de tecnología. Madrid, Cataluña y Andalucía se reivindicaron como las aspirantes más sólidas. El director general de Electrónica e Informática del Ministerio de Industria, Joan Majó, negó cualquier indicación al respecto. La CTNE priorizó comunicaciones y entorno, disponibilidad de agua e inexistencia de vibraciones (*LACA*, 30 de mayo de 1984).

Volvió a reproducirse la pugna entre comunidades autónomas deseosas de dar cobijo al proyecto, al estilo de las que se dieron con la llegada de las grandes del automóvil –Ford y General Motors– a España. Pronto se eliminó la

nes con Europa. Por el acuerdo de colaboración entre el CSIC y AT&T, el Centro Nacional de Microelectrónica de Barcelona (1984) podría disponer de tecnologías desarrolladas por AT&T, entre ellas la CMOS, nótese, de dos micras (*ComputerWorld*, 8 de octubre de 1993). CAICYT promovió en 1984 un Programa especial de I+D en microelectrónica. Del total de 31.845 millones de pesetas del Plan Nacional de I+D (PN I+D) (1988-1991), a las tecnologías de la producción y las telecomunicaciones les correspondió el 41% y de este porcentaje el 13% a la microelectrónica (CICYT 1992, 8). El Grupo Activador de la Microelectrónica en España (GAME), de financiación conjunta – la CE, el Gobierno Español y el Plan de Plan Nacional de I+D (España Comisión Interministerial de Ciencia y Tecnología 1992, 42), lanzó su primera acción especial en 1990 en el marco del programa europeo ESPRIT y del PN de I+D y el PEIN, con el objetivo prioritario de reforzar la integración de la investigación en microelectrónica en las actividades industriales; los circuitos integrados de aplicación específica captaron la mitad de los fondos (Sánchez Izquierdo 1982, 106-106); *Política científica*, 23, 1990, 14-16; *El País,* 7 de junio de 1990 y 24 de noviembre de 1990. Miembros de los comités GAME: José Antonio Martín-Pereda, presidente del Comité GAME; Fernando Aldana Mayor, Universidad Politécnica de Madrid; Santiago Álvarez Pérez, COPRECI, FAGOR; Dave Broster, Commission European Community; Luis Castañer Muñoz, Universidad Politécnica de Cataluña; Javier Díez Roncero, Centro para el Desarrollo Tecnológico Industrial; José Ramón García Martínez, Fundación COTEC, Proyecto GAME; Eloy Gómez Gutiérrez, Consultor; Francisco Ibáñez, Commission European Community; Manuel Lázaro de la Fuente, Ministerio de Industria y Energía; Agustín Morales Bueno, Centro para el Desarrollo Técnológico Industrial; Juan Mulet Meliá, Fundación COTEC; Manuel Poza Martínez, Alcatel; Luis Prieto Cuerdo, Ministerio de Industria y Energía; Francisco Serra Mestres, Centro Nacional de Microelectrónica (Fundación Cotec 1998, 7).

23 *LACA*, 6 de marzo de 1985. Solana rechazaba esperar a la última tecnología posible antes de abrir fábricas y reivindicaba la oportunidad que se presentaba de obtener la tecnología más avanzada del mundo. En efecto, en España iban a producirse chips de 1,75 micras antes que en ningún país de Europa y la fábrica estaría ligada a los laboratorios de AT&T con la posibilidad de seguir desarrollando la tecnología al mismo ritmo que la Universidad de Stanford descubriera nuevos productos: Intervención de Luis Solana Madariaga, Cortes Generales, *Diario de sesiones del Senado*, Comisiones, 93, 14 de febrero de 1986, 25-26.

candidatura andaluza por razones de índole técnica y de infraestructura por lo que la batalla se libró entre los gobiernos de Jordi Pujol y Joaquín Leguina. La Generalitat de Cataluña pugnó por radicar en Barcelona la primera industria de circuitos integrados (chip) de alta sofisticación. Joan Hortalá, *conseller* de Industria de la Generalitat, se pronunció en público contra la instalación de AT&T en Madrid, lamentó la decisión de la multinacional AT&T y escudó la candidatura de Barcelona. A favor de la capital de la Generalitat jugaban factores de localización –las mejores comunicaciones internacionales y la existencia de un gran puerto industrial–, de capacidad acumulada –mayor tradición empresarial, la disponibilidad de personal cualificado en electrónica y la instalación en Bellaterra del Centro de Investigación Microelectrónica–, sin olvidar los físicos –la mayor estabilidad sísmica[24].

El País Vasco, Asturias y Madrid fueron las zonas más afectadas por la destrucción de empleo en la reconversión; Cataluña, Madrid y País Vasco figuraban como principales receptoras de inversión en los planes de las ZUR (Fernández 1988, 191-200). La Comunidad de Madrid apostaba por potenciar zonas aquejadas de un grave problema de desindustrialización, que incluían Villaverde, Móstoles, Coslada, Arganda del Rey y San Sebastián de los Reyes. Estas áreas fueron excluidas por la Administración central. El secreto obedecía, sin duda, a las prevenciones ante la opinión pública por los problemas de contaminación de suelo y agua causados por las industrias de nuevas tecnologías, que tenían antecedentes en Silicon Valley, finalmente convertida en una zona de elevadísima contaminación.

---

[24] *El País*, 7 de noviembre de 1984; Hortalà negó cualquier batalla personal entre los responsables de las comunidades autónomas catalana y madrileña respecto al tema: *La Vanguardia*, 9 de noviembre de 1984. En cuanto al emplazamiento de la fábrica, secreto inicialmente, AT&T y CTNE coincidían en sus preferencias por Madrid (Entrevista JMiC). La Dirección de Electrónica e Informática, ante la imposibilidad de localizar en Cataluña las tres grandes empresas por crear, centró su táctica en atraer a Hewlett Packard y en el Centro de Microelectrónica, empeño en el que tuvo éxito. El gobierno negaba favoritismos, aunque reconocía preferencias por zonas especialmente castigadas, estériles en ocasiones frente a las pretensiones de las multinacionales, determinantes cuando General Electric impuso Cartagena relegando Asturias, pese a inconvenientes y carencias en infraestructuras (Carlos Solchaga, Congreso de los diputados, 147, 16 de noviembre de 1988, 8.610). Anteriormente, Solchaga presentó una serie de consideraciones sobre la planta de la AT&T en España como centro de tecnología avanzada en microelectrónica. Un ejemplo de la competición de las Comunidades autónomas por atraer capital multinacional y de la consideración de las multinacionales como un «bien escaso» lo presenta la alarma por «llegar tarde» y quedarse con los restos, expresada por el Consejero de Industria, Comercio y Turismo (Zapatero González) en las Cortes de Aragón (*Diario de Sesiones de las Cortes de Aragón*, 009 de Plenos (III Legislatura), 218).

Tras barajar diversas opciones, AT&T escogió la Zona de Urgente Reindustrialización (ZUR) de Tres Cantos, localidad creada por la empresa pública homónima al norte de Madrid, atractiva por las ventajas fiscales y de localización (Brierly 1993, 274-275; Doiro, Fernández y González 2005). Tres Cantos fue planificada bajo la inspiración del urbanismo racionalista con el bloque abierto y la zonificación funcional como elementos más representativos. Sin embargo, la incertidumbre del final de la dictadura de Franco y la crisis económica de los años 70 obstaculizaron su gestación y desarrollo. Durante años, presentaba un aire fantasmal e incluso, en 1991, al segregarse de Colmenar Viejo, tan solo contaba con 15.431 habitantes (Molinero 2011, 223)[25]. Asimismo, un contrato de cesión de tecnología con AT&T daba acceso a los técnicos de la operadora a las herramientas de diseño de la norteamericana para la fabricación específica de semiconductores. La CTNE afrontaba así el doble reto de capacitar al personal en las nuevas tecnologías y de entrar en un mercado pujante[26].

Hacia finales de 1985, pergeñado ya el nombre, la ubicación y la envergadura de la inversión en la empresa, John M. Nemecek, vicepresidente de AT&T, mantuvo entrevistas en Madrid con el ministro de Industria, Joan Majó, y el presidente de la Comunidad, Joaquín Leguina. La reunión con Joan Majó sirvió para ir concretando detalles del acuerdo todavía pendientes. Básicamente, faltaba por articular legalmente las ayudas concedidas por la Administración española, lo que implicaba homologarlas con la legislación comunitaria, obvio en un proceso de integración de España ya muy avanzado[27].

---

[25] Algunos especialistas (Menéndez de Luarca, 1986) sitúan la decisión en un contexto de desvirtuación de la política de reindustrialización de la capital, cuyo origen se remonta a la inscripción de manera forzada del polígono de Tres Cantos en la ZUR de Madrid. Algún incidente –carga de agua de un gran estanque de la factoría para apagar un fuego forestal, orden de devolverla por su alta toxicidad (*El País*, 22 de septiembre de 1988)– y los malentendidos suscitados por la falta de transparencia de AT&T Microelectrónica de España contribuyeron a enrarecer el clima de entendimiento (Moliní 1989, 450-453). Como contrapartida, en 1990 AT&T encargó un Proyecto de Reforestación del Área externa de los terrenos de AT&T Microelectrónica España en Tres Cantos para la recuperación de la vegetación natural en el área externa de su factoría.

[26] Telefónica, *Memoria,* 1985, 156; *LACA,* 24 de febrero de 1988 (Todd 1990, 94). La visita a España del presidente de AT&T, Charles L. Brown, impulsor de AT&T en el exterior, adquirió tonos de acontecimiento oficial (*LACA*, 29 de enero y 26 de marzo de 1986). General Motors impuso también a su filial española restricciones de transferencias.

[27] El alto ejecutivo de la multinacional norteamericana, que estuvo acompañado en su periplo madrileño por el consejero delegado de la Compañía Telefónica Nacional de España, Diego Martínez Boudes, negó retrasos significativos en el proceso de negociación. Nemecek aseguró, sin embargo, que el acuerdo con España no tenía relación alguna con el ingreso del país en el COCOM (Comité de Control de Exportaciones) (*El País*, 28 de septiembre de 1985).

AT&T inauguró en el verano de 1986 su nuevo centro de diseño, acordado con Telefónica. Según el presidente de AT&T Microelectrónica de España, John M. Nemecek, era «también el centro de diseño de Telefónica», cuyos terminales estarían interconectados. Contradecía así a quienes afirmaban que la implantación de este centro de diseño impedía de hecho la posibilidad de acceder a los ingenieros de Telefónica a tecnología de punta de la compañía estadounidense. El centro de diseño de AT&TME ofrecía a los clientes la posibilidad de acceder a los sistemas más avanzados de la compañía norteamericana para la realización específica de semiconductores utilizando los diseños por ordenador (CAD). La máxima autoridad de AT&T Microelectrónica de España recalcó el compromiso de mantener «las adaptaciones precisas y las inversiones que sean precisas» en los productos de la factoría española (*El País*, 2 de julio de 1986).

En opinión de algunos especialistas, el proyecto de AT&T contenía más una orientación tecnológica que una mera inversión industrial, orientación que debía plasmarse en el centro de diseño de circuitos *custom* a cargo de la CTNE. Sin embargo, al desgajarse dicho centro del proyecto la capacidad de la parte española para asimilar el *know how* de AT&T quedó limitada a la vertiente productiva. Se aplicó el programa fuente, es decir, las restricciones impuestas por AT&T en la transferencia de tecnología bajo clave secreta, que impedían al socio español acceder con plenitud al *know-how* (Buesa y Molero 1986, 14)[28].

Hasta finales de 1988, AT&T había invertido 22.000 millones de pesetas, en torno a los dos tercios de la suma comprometida. La subvención recibida hasta 1988 por la AT&T, en el marco de las ayudas aprobadas por la ZUR de Madrid, ascendía a 3.280 millones de pesetas, y esta subvención había sido pagada en su totalidad por la Administración central (Consejero de Economía (Royo), *Diario de Sesiones de la Asamblea de Madrid*, 242, 14 de octubre de 1988, 4.774).

---

[28] AT&T unía tecnología avanzada, experiencia en calidad y *management* pero atravesaba problemas financieros (*Network World*, 21 de abril de 1986, 6). El diseño del primer chip por técnicos españoles en conexión con equipos del centro de vanguardia de AT&T en EE. UU. (*LACA*, 28 de enero de 1987; Queisser 1990, 142) cabe interpretarlo como transferencia controlada de conocimiento sin revelar claves. Según testimonios cualificados, el tamaño de esta operación superó con creces la idea de Telefónica, limitada a poder abastecerse en España de circuitos *custom*. No obstante, la planta se concibió para atender también circuitos de catálogo destinados al mercado mundial, entre otros, memorias, microprocesadores y microcircuitos para móviles (Entrevista del autor a Juan Mulet, 16 de mayo de 2013).

Para algunos hubo transferencia efectiva de tecnología y de conocimiento en la dirección del proyecto y su realización (diseño de la fábrica, desarrollo de una infraestructura gerencial, gestión de recursos humanos), junto con el reclutamiento, contratación y adiestramiento de la mano de obra, casi un tercio femenina y en su mayoría local (*Hispanic Engineer & IT* 1993, 23).

Cabe preguntarse si había alternativas en Europa. Las iniciativas europeas en la gama submicrónica llegaron con retraso. La Joint European Submicron Silicon Initiative (JESSI) para reconstruir la competitividad europea mediante un programa de desarrollo de la microelectrónica y su integración en sistemas se postergó hasta 1992. Con todo, no faltaron algunas actuaciones previas en el terreno regulatorio[29]. En la vertiente industrial destaca la sociedad paneuropea European Silicon Structures, sobre la que se detiene otro capítulo.

Tabla 5. Total de proveedores de CBIC MOS por ingresos (millones de dólares)

	1987	1988	1989	Ranking 1989
Mietec	27	29	34	1
Texas Instruments	5	12	30	2
VLSI Technology	15	22	29	3
Austria Mikro Systeme	15	19	27	4
MEDL	5	12	19	5
SGS-Thomson	2	3	19	6
European Silicon Structures	6	12	17	7
Siemens	15	15	17	8
IMP Europe	2	7	11	9
LSI Logic	4	7	11	10

Fuente: Elaboración a partir de *Dataquest Annuary 1991*.

---

[29] Cabe citar la Proposal for a Council Regulation (EEC) concerning Community actions in the field of microelectronic technology (COM (80) 421 final, 1 September 1980 and COM (80) 421 final/2, 10 October 1980).

Conclusión y epílogo

Las realizaciones industriales de la década de 1980 examinadas guardaban diferencias notables respecto a las precedentes. En sustancia, cabe calificarlas como actuaciones intensivas en capital que requerían escasa creación de empleo si bien este debía ser de elevada cualificación. Respondían a la segmentación de la producción (fabricación de un solo componente y no el producto entero), a políticas de reindustrialización fuertemente influenciadas por orientaciones estatales basadas en el equilibrio territorial, distantes, por tanto, de las proclives al *cluster*.

El punto de vista del país de origen evidencia una inversión horizontal o producción en el extranjero de la misma línea de productos que en casa. Desde la óptica del país receptor, se trata de la suma de sustitución de importaciones, aumento de exportación e inversión con iniciativa mixta público-privada condicionada por la condición mixta de la empresa concernida. La transferencia de tecnología resulta ser de índole vertical por implicar un movimiento desde un país avanzado a otro más atrasado.

Difícilmente se puede negar a la concepción de esas políticas y actuaciones señaladas una clarividencia notable, pero, aun alejadas del perfil faraónico que algunos les atribuyen, no dieron los resultados apetecidos. Desde la vertiente del servicio, especialistas como López sí reconocen a la CTNE claras ventajas competitivas en calidad del servicio a un coste competitivo.

A juicio de algunos (Noam 1992), España se convirtió en la principal base industrial de AT&T en Europa gracias a la integración de centro de diseño y fábrica con alta productividad, un aspecto de gran relevancia. La orientación al mercado exterior perduró ya que a mediados de la década de 1990 en él se colocaba tres cuartos de la producción de AT&T Microelectrónica de España y la factoría madrileña no tardó en embarcarse en planes de modernización[30]. Posiblemente sean estos proyectos lo que fueron tomados como una segunda fábrica de centrales electrónicas 5ESS, que costó 100 millones de dólares

---

[30] AT&T Microelectronics planeó invertir 700 millones de dólares en una nueva planta de chips en Madrid. Las conversaciones con la Administración española sobre el tema de las compensaciones que esta estaría dispuesta a otorgar a cambio de la apertura de la fábrica fueron positivas, aunque no se alcanzó ningun compromiso. AT&T Microelectronics confirmó la inversion de 18.000 millones en la fábrica de Tres Cantos (*Cinco Días*, 16 de noviembre de 1995).

y empezó a producir en 1991 (The AT&T Consent Decree's Manufacturing Restriction U.S. Government Printing Office, 1991, 505)[31].

La brillante trayectoria no parecía augurar un final decepcionante. Telefónica canjeó su participación en AT&TME para entrar discretamente en AT&T Network Systems International, proveedora de *software* y *hardware* de las operadoras europeas. El polígono de Tres Cantos llegó a concentrar medio centenar largo de empresas, grandes empleadoras de la economía informacional. No obstante, el balance de la actuación arrojaba abundantes sombras –«carencias y dificultades»– por más que el sistema telefónico hubiera avanzado y mejorado. En transferencia de tecnología, los resultados se vieron sometidos a las trabas impuestas por AT&T, que impedían al socio español acceder con plenitud al *know-how*. Respecto a la creación de empleo, la repercusión fue relativamente baja en relación con el esfuerzo inversor realizado, si bien la calidad mejoró gracias a los programas de formación, subordinados en ocasiones a otras prioridades. Así sucedió en 1994 con la solicitud de una ayuda de 52 millones de pesetas para financiar parcialmente la actuación en los Laboratorios Bell[32].

El esfuerzo tecnológico en la industria española, entendido como porcentaje del gasto en I+D/valor añadido industrial, que estaba estancado en los 70', experimentó un leve incremento en la década siguiente. Si se mira a la economía española en su conjunto, las exportaciones de productos de alta

---

[31]   En la noticia de la primera central digital de AT&T para telefonía pública instalada en España (Barcelona) no aparecía lugar de fabricación (*La Vanguardia*, 23 de diciembre de 1989). En 1990, el plan de compras de Telefónica concedía a AT&T una participación del 8,7%, correspondiente a un total de 244.924 líneas digitales del sistema ESS-5 –probado en la red desde 1988–. por un importe de 19.715 millones de pesetas (*El País*, 9 de agosto de 1989; *Computer Business Review*, 28 de febrero de 1989). AT&T Microelectrónica España llevó cabo una experiencia de diseño e implantación de un nuevo sistema de gestión del rendimiento (Fernández 1996, 311-325). La empresa contó con gerentes muy cualificados. Entre ellos destaca el actual comisionado para el plan de inversión en microelectrónica Jaime Martorell Suárez, conocido como fundador de empresas en EE. UU. y España y como director de Motorola y Ono. Se incorporó a AT&T Microelectrónica en 1987 como director general de productos MOS (semiconductores complementarios de óxido metálico) y, al año siguiente, fue nombrado consejero delegado de Amper (*ComputerWorld*, 24 de mayo de 2022; *Cinco Días*, 28 de mayo de 2022). AT&T y la fabricante (*foundry*) europea ES2 fabricaron circuitos integrados clave para el éxito del registrador electrónico MORE (Modernización de Registradores Electromecánicos), un desarrollo aplicado a las centrales telefónicas analógicas preexistentes, que tantos frutos reportó a la CTNE (Calvo 2022, 43).

[32]   En 1998, el ministerio de Industria y Energía y AT&T Microelectrónica de España, S.A llegaron a un acuerdo suscrito el 7 de diciembre de 1998 pero el Tribunal Supremo ratificó la denegación de subvención (Tribunal Supremo, Sala Tercera de lo Contencioso-Administrativo, 20 de mayo de 2004). AT&T Microelectrónica España motor del Polígono de Tres Cantos (Egea y Fernández 1993).

tecnología, bienes altamente intensivos en investigación y desarrollo, entre 1988-2000 mantuvieron una desesperante estabilidad, sin rebasar nunca el 8% sobre las exportaciones. La modesta posición de España en la industria electrónica europea no varió sustancialmente y la cobertura de la balanza tecnológica se mantuvo baja, signo de dependencia persistente. A despecho de logros de cierto relieve en la I+D, la dependencia tecnológica persistió en el tiempo y hasta se encastró en el sistema. El carácter oligopólico del sistema mundial se impuso a las políticas y aspiraciones de los países periféricos.

En última instancia, el relato de la interactuación pública y privada en un sector industrial concreto se trueca primordialmente en la narración de las vicisitudes de los conatos por la implantación de un modelo industrial intensivo en tecnología como vía única de recuperar la competitividad de la economía española.

Pese a algunos logros parciales, AT&T Microelectrónica de España representa una tentativa fallida de situar a España en la industria de semiconductores. A mediados de la década de 1990, AT&T Microelectrónica atravesaba por un proceso de expansión de su capacidad productiva que pretendía concretarse en una inversión total de 250.000 millones de pesetas en cinco años y 125.000 millones más en cuatro años para tareas de I+D. Algo más de 18.000 millones de pesetas invertidos entre 1995 y 1997 se dedicarían a la modernización y reconversión de la planta de Tres Cantos para trabajar con tecnología de 0,35 micras (*ComputerWorld*, 24 de noviembre de 1995).

Pero la estrategia de Lucent Technologies dio un vuelco. Esta compañía diseñaba, fabricaba y vendía circuitos integrados (CI), sistemas de alimentación electrónica y componentes optoelectrónicos para aplicaciones de comunicaciones. También vendía estos componentes a otros fabricantes de sistemas de comunicaciones y computadoras. La compañía ofrecía productos de CI críticos para las comunicaciones, aplicaciones, incluidos los procesadores de señales digitales (DSP) para teléfonos celulares digitales y los circuitos integrados específicos para aplicaciones de células estándar (ASIC). En el ejercicio económico de 1996, más de la mitad de la producción de microelectrónica de la empresa se vendió a clientes distintos de la empresa. Poco antes de finalizar el año 1996, la compañía se desprendió de sus operaciones para el diseño y la fabricación de placas de circuitos impresos y placas base (Lucent Technologies, *Annual Report* 1996, 6-7)[33].

---

[33] Más tarde, Lucent Technologies decidió integrar su negocio de microelectrónica, que incluía las divisiones de optoelectrónica y de circuitos integrados, en una compañía independiente, que debía iniciar sus actividades como el principal proveedor de semiconductores

AT&T Microelectrónica de España, S.A. acordó una escisión total consistente en la extinción por disolución sin liquidación de AT&T Microelectrónica de España, S.A. y la división de su patrimonio en dos bloques transmitidos respectivamente a dos sociedades anónimas unipersonales de nueva creación, que adoptarían a continuación una nueva denominación social. Lucent Technologies Microelectrónica, S.A. pasaba a llamarse Communications Sytems & Technology España, S.A. y Sinat Iberia, S.A. Gis Holding España, S.A. *(El Mundo del Siglo Veintiuno,* 14 de febrero de 1996).

El cambio de estrategia arrastró a sus previsiones en España[34]. Lucent Technologies había planeado convertir sus fábricas de Network Systems y Microelectrónica de Tres Cantos (Madrid) en el centro mundial de competencia de redes inteligentes, la base sobre la que se sustenta la gestión de las autopistas de la comunicación *(El País,* 12 de junio de 1996). En 1996, AT&T emprendió la segregación y la fábrica de circuitos integrados de Tres Cantos pasó a formar parte del grupo Lucent Technologies y se extinguió para pasar a operar con el nombre de Lucent Technologies Microelectrónica España S.A. Hacia 1998, Lucent dedicó a la fábrica de microelectrónica tres cuartas partes de los 300 millones de dólares invertidos en los últimos dos años en España, y el resto lo destinó a la planta que producía centros de atención de llamadas, situada también en Tres Cantos *(ComputerWorld,* 4 de febrero de 1998).

Al cabo de cuatro años, albergaba planes de centrarse en negocios básicos, lo que implicó la escisión de la actividad de semiconductores, junto a la integración en una nueva compañía, denominada Agere Systems y cuyo 48 % cotizaba en la Bolsa de Nueva York, en tanto que el 52% restante de Agere se mantenía bajo control de Lucent. Esta pensaba mantener en Tres Cantos sus actividades destinadas al desarrollo de sistemas para operadoras de telecomunicaciones. Incuso había planes de inversión en marcha como lo atestigua la compra de material a la californiana Adaptec destinado a la sala blanca de Lucent Technologies Microelectrónica España S.A. En ese momento, Lucent daba empleo en España a cerca de 1.500 personas, repartidas entre una fábri-

---

para el sector de las telecomunicaciones, con una facturación superior a los 680.000 millones de pesetas (*Computerworld*, 24 de julio de 2000; *Compound Semiconductor*, 20th July 2000).

[34] En el año fiscal 1994, AT&T Microelectrónica tuvo una facturación de 185,2 millones de dólares el 95% de la producción se vendió fuera de AT&T, y el 75% se destinó a Europa. Se excluía fusionar las actividades de producción de AT&T Microelectronics y AT&T Network Systems en España, debido a la diferencia en su línea de negocio y mercados (*Computer Business Review*, 13 de diciembre de 1995).

ca, varios centros de desarrollo tecnológico y departamentos de operaciones, ventas y soporte técnico (*ABC*, 29 de junio de 2001)[35].

El emplazamiento de la locomotora que supuso un revulsivo para la zona, atrajo proveedores e inversiones de otras multinacionales en Tres Cantos –Airbus, GSK, Merck, Netflix, Cuatro, Danone, Siemens, Nivea, Línea Directa, GMV–; acabó mutando en una fábrica de placas solares fotovoltaicas de la petrolera BP (*El Confidencial*, 25 de enero de 2020).

Anexo 1. Industria de semiconductores. Producción mundial (%)

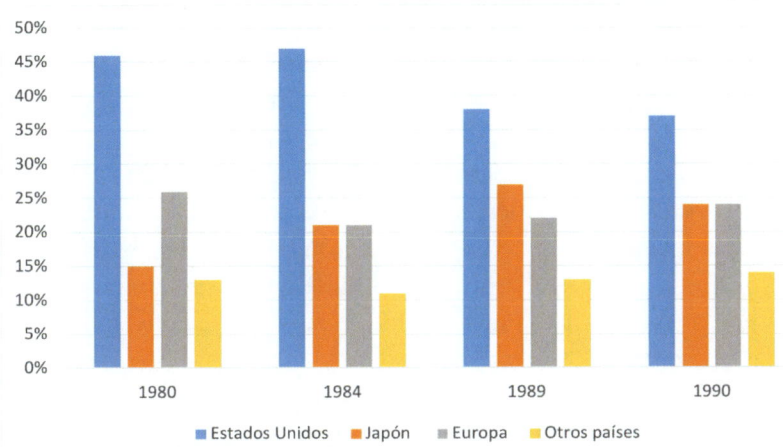

Fuente: Elaboración a partir de VVAA, *El sector*, 1984.

Anexo 2. Ciclo de desarrollo de un ASIC

El procedimiento de desarrollo de un ASIC *semicustom* es bastante simple y está totalmente descentralizado: el fabricante de ASICs distribuye sus bibliotecas a los usuarios finales o a centros de diseño locales (distribuidores o centros de diseño independientes). Estos realizan la totalidad del diseño funcional y eléctrico del chip y, con frecuencia, el diseño geométrico de la interconexión final, verificando mediante simulación la coincidencia exacta entre la funcionalidad y las especificaciones del producto.

Una parte importante de este diseño es la definición del plan de pruebas con la ayuda de la herramienta correspondiente y que será utilizado por el

---

[35] Extinción: *Boletín Oficial del Registro Mercantil*, 117, 20 de junio de 1996.

fabricante para comprobar todos los chips que se fabriquen. El paso siguiente consiste en el envío de la descripción al fabricante, quien la somete a una revisión automática en sus instalaciones; define la geometría de la interconexión final y fabrica algunos prototipos que envía al usuario para la verificación de su funcionalidad antes de iniciar la producción. El plazo desde que el fabricante recibe el diseño hasta que envía los prototipos suele ser del orden de un mes. Los ASICs necesitan un juego de máscaras (equivalente a los moldes) específico para cada diseño, preparar equipos de pruebas, y realizar otros trabajos iniciales, que servirán también para la producción. El coste de este «utillaje» se denomina NRE (costes de ingeniería no recurrentes). El ciclo de diseño termina una vez el usuario comprueba el funcionamiento correcto de los prototipos en una preserie del producto, y se pasa a producción.

Aun con estas facilidades, para la mayoría de las empresas sigue sin tener sentido adquirir estas herramientas y formar personal técnico que las utilice: desde compañías pequeñas del sector electrónico hasta las ajenas al mismo con mayor motivo. Sin embargo, este tipo de empresas, que a menudo no tienen siquiera en plantilla ningún técnico en electrónica convencional, son el grupo más numeroso de usuarios de ASICs.

Los usuarios habituales –compañías pequeñas del sector electrónico y otras ajenas al mismo– acceden a la tecnología ASIC a través de los centros de diseño locales, que cuentan con las herramientas necesarias y personal especializado. En España existían varios de estos centros, tanto públicos como privados, donde el usuario potencial podía asesorarse sobre la forma más eficaz de aplicar ASICs en su producto y contratar con ellos su diseño.

El proceso de elaboración de la especificación consiste fundamentalmente en una serie de reuniones entre el responsable del producto en la empresa y un experto del centro de diseño, donde uno plantea necesidades y el otro dice cómo podrían satisfacerse y evalúa su coste correspondiente. Por lo general, cuando el producto es factible con un ASIC, el usuario va descubriendo a lo largo del proceso de especificación otras posibilidades que no veía al principio. El resultado de este proceso es un documento de especificaciones que define con exactitud las funciones deseadas y una oferta en firme con los costes del ASIC o la electrónica que las realizará. Si la especificación es correcta, el éxito del proyecto está prácticamente asegurado. Fuente: Elaborado a partir de Fundación Cotec (1998, 16-17).

Anexo 3. Memorándum de Acuerdo entre AT&T y Telefónica

El Memorándum de Acuerdo entre AT&T y Telefónica, firmado el 30 de julio de 1984, estableció las bases para la constitución de una sociedad española dedicada al diseño, fabricación y venta de circuitos integrados según una participación accionarial del 80% y 20%, respectivamente. En primer lugar, AT&T consideraba a la sociedad española parte integrante de su capacidad conjunta de circuitos integrados y, por consiguiente, la equiparaba a las restantes fábricas de AT&T en el acceso a la tecnología y mercados mundiales de AT&T Technologies. Por su parte, Telefónica debía prestar plena colaboración y apoyo para asegurar el éxito de la nueva empresa. Esta tendría capacidad para diseñar circuitos CMOS (Complementary Metal Oxide Semiconductor), específicos (CUSTOM) así como para fabricar productos CMOS tanto específicos como de catálogo, utilizando reglas de diseño de 1,75 micras. Las instalaciones incluirían la fabricación de obleas así como el montaje y prueba de los dispositivos encapsulados. Un conjunto de acuerdos requerirían el voto favorable del 82 % del capital desembolsado con la finalidad de proteger determinados derechos de la minoría. Tales acuerdos incluían la transformación, fusión, reducción del número de consejeros por debajo de diez, aprobación de los términos y condiciones de cualquier contrato de transferencia de tecnología que sea incompatible con las estipulaciones sobre tecnología del Memorandum de Acuerdo. Además, se introducían en los estatutos estipulaciones para proteger al accionista minoritario en los casos de introducción de cambios importantes en la naturaleza del negocio o de disolución antes de transcurridos siete años desde el comienzo de la fabricación.

AT&T se comprometía a proveer mercados para la producción de la nueva fábrica según una norma que dejaba por fijar los porcentajes del primer año y los reducía a cero a partir del sexto año. A partir del segundo año y hasta el quinto, los porcentajes irían en cantidades decrecientes, es decir, 95%, 75%, 55% y 15%, respectivamente. AT&T asumía la gestión y colocación de los remanentes de producción en el resto de Europa y otros mercados extranjeros.

A su vez, concedería derecho personal, no exclusivo e intransferible a la utilización de la tecnología necesaria para la realización del diseño y fabricación de circuitos CMOS inicialmente de 1,75 micras. Proporcionaría además la información sobre diseño asistido por ordenador (CAD) y la capacitación y asistencia técnica oportuna para el cumplimiento de los objetivos. AT&T Technologies proporcionaría los avances tecnológicos y las herramientas para lograr reglas de diseño más evolucionadas.

El pago de la nueva empresa en concepto de tecnología transferida –y de la potencial hasta 1,25 micras– se cifraba en 10 millones de dólares USA y en 200.000 dólares por cada año que se suministrase información CAD y un royalty del 6% sobre las ventas netas totales, importaciones procedentes de AT&T Technologies excluidas.

La inversión prevista alcanzaba los 200 millones de dólares, de los que el 26% corresponderían a AT&T y el 6% a Telefónica, en concordancia con las aportaciones de cada socio a un capital total estimado en 65 millones de dólares. AT&T se reservaba determinar los «estrictos criterios técnicos» para la localización de la fábrica, presentar varias zonas que cumplieran estos requisitos y decidir, en último extremo, la localización exacta de la fábrica, por encima de la predilección del gobierno. Cuando la planta se encontrara en plena producción, el personal empleado rondaría las 700 personas, en un 97% de nacionalidad española y, en una mitad aproximada, compuestas de técnicos e ingenieros cualificados. Curiosamente, el detalle de personal previsto para 1993 cifraba en 61 el de diseño y en 612 el de fabricación.

Los requisitos para el emplazamiento de la fábrica eran de diversa índole. Requisitos técnicos: treinta acres de terreno (121.406 m²) (una quinta parte para la planta fabril y el resto en derredor para carreteras de acceso, futura ampliación, así como zona intermedia de aislamiento para asegurar el control de las vibraciones).

El terreno debía tener una carga admisible de 3.000 PSF mínimo y un coeficiente de rigidez de 1.000 KSF mínimo para proporcionar la estabilidad necesaria. Se precisaba un servicio primario de electricidad de 60.000 KW provenientes de fuentes distintas de suministro y una fuente sobrante de 3 millones de galones diarios de agua potable (11,34 millones de litros). El agua había de tener menos de 300 partes por millón (ppm.) de partículas en suspensión y disueltas. Idéntico volumen –11,34 millones de litros diarios– de aguas negras mezcladas con efluentes, en instalación industrial de tratamiento de aguas residuales *in situ*, ajustándose a las normas vigentes en EE. UU. Gas natural o instalación equivalente en fueloil. Ausencia de vibraciones, de forma que el nivel medio de densidad espectral energética de los niveles de vibraciones del entorno del emplazamiento en g2/Hz (densidad de energía espectral), no debía superar los 100 db de la escala de frecuencias de 0-100HA en las tres principales direcciones. Otros requisitos atañían a medios de transporte, mano de obra y clima social. Los de accesibilidad consistían en la proximidad (hasta treinta minutos de viaje) a un aeropuerto internacional con vuelos regulares a EE.UU. y otros países europeos durante todo el año al igual que proximidad a los principales centros de consumo de España respecto al centro de diseño. Se requería asimismo ambiente de trabajo agradable, calidad de vida, conflictos laborales mínimos, tradición de trabajo estable y poco absentismo. Mención expresa se hacía de la disponibilidad de industrias y servicios de mantenimiento (talleres mecánicos, troquelado, aire acondicionado y en particular, de ordenadores). Finalmente, no faltaba la alusión a los medios de procurar la fácil adaptación para el personal norteamericano y de ofrecer vivienda y servicios adecuados para una comunidad norteamericana en el extranjero. Fuente: Elaborado a partir de Respuesta del Gobierno – secretario de estado, Madrid, 25 de marzo de 1985– sobre acuerdo de la CTNE con la AT&T de Estados Unidos, *Boletín Oficial de las Cortes Generales*, Senado, 3 de abril de 1985, 5.658-5.660.

Fuentes primarias

Actas del consejo de administración de la CTNE (*LACA*), Madrid.
Actas del comité ejecutivo de la CTNE (*ACE*), Madrid.
Archivo del Congreso de los Diputados, Madrid.
Archivo SEPI (INI), Madrid.
Archivo Margaret Thatcher.
NATO Archives.
Securities Exchange Commission, US.

Fuentes orales

Computer History Museum, Mountain View, USA.
Entrevistas del autor a Luis Solana, Barcelona, 9/7/2013 y 4/1/2015.
Entrevista del autor a Joan Majó, Barcelona, 17/9/2015.
Entrevista del autor a Juan Mulet Melià, Barcelona, 16/5/2013.
«Interview with Pasquale Pistorio», *EE Times,* 25, 3, 2005.
Juan Mulet Melià, conversación con el autor, Barcelona.

Luis Solana, conversación con el autor, Madrid, 8/3/2016.

Oral History of Pasquale Pistorio Interviewed by Doug Fairbairn.

Referencias

Azulgaray, Juan José. 2003. *Personajes de mi vida.* Madrid: Encuentro.

Amatori, Franco y Colli, Andrea. 2013. *Business History: Complexities and Comparisons.* Londres: Routledge.

Adanero, José Luis et al. 2006. *Crónicas y Testimonios de las Telecomunicaciones Españolas.* Madrid: Colegio Oficial de Ingenieros de Telecomunicación.

Bernstein, Michael A. y Adler, David E. (eds.). 1994. *Understanding American Economic Decline.* Cambridge MA: Cambridge University Press.

Bonno, Gérard. «Des puces sur mesure», *L'Observateur*, [1986]: 82, on-line.

Bracho, Salvador. 1999. *La ingeniería microelectrónica ante el cambio de milenio.* Santander: Ed. Universidad de Cantabria.

Brierly, William et al. 1993. *Business Cultures in Europe.* Abingdon: Routledge.

Brooke, Peter A. y Penrice, Daniel. 2009. A *Vision for Venture Capital: Realizing the Promise of Global Venture Capital and Private Equity.* Boston MA: UPNE.

Buesa, Mikel y Molero, José. 1986. *La intervención estatal en la remodelación del sistema productivo español.* Madrid: Facultad de CCEE y Empresariales.

Calvo, Ángel. *Standard Eléctrica y la industria de las telecomunicaciones en España, 1877-1975.* Barcelona: Ariel.

Calvo, Ángel. 2022. *La revolución de la electrónica en las telecomunicaciones españolas. Tecnología, Estado y empresas.* Chisinau: Generis.

Campbell, Katharine. 2003. *Smarter Ventures: A Survivor's Guide to Venture Capital.* Londres: Pearson Education.

Cane, Alan. 1987. «ES2 Moves Bespoke Chips Towards Off-the-Peg Prices». *Financial Times,* 10 de junio: 37.

Castells, Manuel. 1986. *Nuevas tecnologías, economía y sociedad en España.* Madrid: Alianza.

Castells, Manuel. 1999a. *La era de la información: economía, sociedad y cultura,* volumen 1. Madrid: Siglo XXI.

Castells, Manuel. 1999. *Information technology, globalization and social development.* Ginebra: United Nations Research Institute for Social Development.

Cohen, Elie. 2007. «Industrial Policies in France: The Old and the New». *Journal of Industry, Competition and Trade.* 7, 213–227. https://doi.org/10.1007/s10842-007-0024-8.

Collins, Timothy M. y Doorley, Thomas L. 1994. *Teaming Up for the '90s: A Guide to International Joint Ventures and Strategic Alliances.* Homewood IL: McGraw-Hill School Education Group.

Comisaría del Plan de Desarrollo Económico y Social. 1971. *III Plan de desarrollo 1972-1975: Telecomunicaciones y correos.* Madrid: Imprenta Nacional Del Boletín Oficial.

Cowhey, Peter F. y Aronson, Jonathan D. 1993. *Managing the World Economy: The Consequences of Corporate Alliances*, Nueva York: Council on Foreign Relations.

Daim, Tugrull U. et al. (eds.). 2014. *Technology Development: Multidimensional Review for Engineering and Technology Managers.* Cham: Springer.

Dataquest. 1990. *European semiconductor consumption forecast 1983-1995.* San José: Dataquest.

Dataquest. 1987. *IC Startups 1987: The Next Generation.* San José: Dataquest.

Dataquest. 1989. *Worldwide Semiconductor Companies.* San José: Dataquest.

Dataquest. 1988. *A decade of semiconductor companies.* San José: Dataquest.

Dataquest. 1991. *Semiconductors Europe.* San José: Dataquest.

De Diego, Emilio. 1995. *Historia de la industria en España: la electrónica y la informática.* Madrid: EOI.

Directrices para la elaboración de un Plan Nacional de la Industria Electrónica. 1983. Madrid: Ministerio de Industria.

Doiro, Manuel; Fernández, Francisco J. y González, Beatriz. 2005. «Cooperación en innovación tecnológica: un análisis comparado». En *Cities in competition. XV Spanish-Portuguese Meeting of Scientific Management (261-271).* Sevilla: Universidad de Sevilla.

Dosi, Giovani. 2000. *Innovation, Organization and Economic Dynamics: Selected Essays.* Cheltenham: Edward Elgar.

Dubocage, Emmanuelle y Rivaud-Danset, Dorothée. 2002. «The development of venture capital in Europe». En Mayumana, Seichi y Vanderbrink, Donna (eds.). The developmen of capital markets adn their governance, *Tokyo Clup Papers*, n°6: 69-113

Dunning, John H. 2001. «The eclectic (OLI) paradigm of international production: Past, present and future». *International Journal of the Economics of Business* 8 (2): 173-190.

Duysters, Geert y Hagedoorn, John. 1995. «Strategic groups and inter-firm networks in international high-tech industries». *Journal of management studies*, Volume 32, n°3: 359-381.

Egea, Mónica y Fernández, Donato. 1993. *Tres Cantos: 20 años de historia*. Madrid: Inciativas y Publicaciones.

España Comisión Interministerial de Ciencia y Tecnología. 1992. *Memoria de actividades del Plan Nacional de I+D durante 1991, Resumen del cuatrienio 1988-1991 y perspectivas futuras: Memoria aprobada por el Consejo de Ministros*. Madrid: Ministerio de Educación.

ERT. 1985. *Changing Scales: A Review prepared for the European Roundtable of Industrialists*. París: ERT.

Etxezarreta, Miren. 1991. *La Reestructuración del capitalismo en España, 1970-1990*. Barcelona: Icaria.

European Communities Commission. 1989. *Strategic partnering and local employment initiatives*. Luxemburgo: OOPEC.

Fernández, Aladino. 1988. «La reconversión industrial en España». *ERIA*, 17: 191-200.

Fernández, Vicente. 1996. «Diseño e implantación de un nuevo sistema de gestión del rendimiento». En Ordóñez, Miguel (coord.). *Modelos y experiencias innovadoras en la gestión de los recursos humanos*. Barcelona: Gestión 2000, 311-325.

Fletcher, André. 2013. *Profile of the Worldwide Semiconductor Industry: Market Prospects to 1997*. Oxford: Elsevier.

ESPRIT. 1991. *Progress and results 1990/91*. Luxemburgo: Commission of the European Communities.

Fagen, Richard R. (ed.). 1979. *Capitalism and the State in U.S.-Latin American Relations*. Stanford: Stanford University Press.

Faulhaber, Gerald R. y Tamburini, Gualtiero. 2012. *European Economic Integration: The Role of Technology*. Nueva York: Springer.

Forester, Thomas. 1989. *High-Tech Society: The Story of the Information Technology Revolution*. Cambridge MA: MIT Press.

Forsgren, Mats. 2013. *Theories of the Multinational Firm: A Multidimensional Creature in the Global Economy*. Cheltenham-Nueva York: Edward Elgar.

Friedrichs, Günter y Schaf, Adam (eds.). 1982. *Microelectronics and society for better or for worse: a report to the Club of Rome*. Nueva York: Pergamon.

Friend, Julius W. 1998. *The Long Presidency: France in the Mitterrand Years, 1981-1995*. Boulder CO: Westview Press.

Froot, Ken A. (ed.). 2008. *Foreign Direct Investment*. Chicago: University of Chicago Press.

Fundación Cotec. 1998. *Soluciones microelectrónicas (ASICS) para todos los sectores industriales*. Madrid: Fundación Cotec.

González, Carlos. 2017. *Salvador Sánchez-Terán: Un político de la transición*. Madrid: ACCI.

Guile, Bruce R. 1987. *Technology and Global Industry: Companies and Nations in the World Economy*. Washington: National Academies Press.

Hagedoorn, John y Schakenraad, Jos. 1992. «Leading companies and networks of strategic alliances in information technologies». *Research policy*, vol. 21, nº2: 163-190.

Henderson, Jeffrey. 2002. *Globalisation of High Technology Production*. Londres-Nueva York: Routledge.

Hill, Charles W. L. et al. 2016. *Strategic Management: Theory: An Integrated Approach*. Boston MA: Cengage Learning.

Hobday, Michael. 1989-1990. «The European Semiconductor Industry: Resurgence and Rationalization». *Journal of Common Market Studies*, 155, 28, 2: 155-186.

Huber, George P. y Glick, William H. 1993. *Organizational Change and Redesign: Ideas and Insights for Improving Performance*. Nueva York: Oxford University Press.

Hussein, Kassim y Menon, Anand (eds.). 2002. *The European Union and National Industrial Policy*. Londres: Routledge.

Johanson, Jan y Vahlne, Jan-Erik. 2009. «The Uppsala internationalization process model revisited: From liability of foreignness to liability of outsidership». *Journal of International Business Studies* 40 (9): 1.411-1.431.

Jones, Phil L. y Buckley, Anne. 1989. *Electronics Computer Aided Design*. Manchester: Manchester University Press.

Jones, Michael J. 2011. *Creative Accounting, Fraud and International Accounting Scandals*. Chichester: John Wiley & Sons.

Kabene, Stéfane M. 2010. *Human Resources in Healthcare, Health Informatics and Healthcare Systems*. Nueva York: Idea Group Inc.

Khanna, Dan M. 1997. *The Rise, Decline, and Renewal of Silicon Valley's High Technology Industry*. Nueva York: Garland.

Klincewicz, Krzysztof. 2005. *Strategic Alliances in the High-tech Industry*. Berlín: Logos Verlag.

Langlois, Richard N. y Steinmueller, William E. 2000. «Strategy and circumstance: the response of American firms to Japanese competition in semiconductors, 1980-1995». *Strategic Management Journal* 21: 1.163-1.173.

Lázaro, Manuel. 1983. «La reconversión en la industria *electrónica*». *Economía Industrial*, 232: 131-144.

Leuenberger, Theodor y Weinstein, Martin E. 2012. *Europe, Japan and America in the 1990s: Cooperation and Competition*. Berlín: Springer.

Lipnack, Jessica y Stamps, Jeffrey. 1993. *The TeamNet Factor: Bringing the Power of Boundary Crossing Into the Heart of Your Business*. Essex: Wiley.

McClean, Bill (ed.). 1996. *European Company Profiles 1996. A Worldwide Survey of IC Manufacturers and Suppliers*. Scottsdale: Integrated Circuit Engineering Corporation.

MacDonald, Elizabeth. 2000. «Regulators seek to penalize auditors who missed fraud». *Wall Street Journal*, febrero: 19.

Malerba, Franco. 1985. *The Semiconductor Business*. Madison: University of Wisconsin Press.

Majó, Joan. 1997. *Chips, cables y poder*. Barcelona: Planeta.

Marchipont, Jean-François. 1997. *La stratégie industrielle de l'Union européenne. Conséquences et enjeux*. París: Éditions Continent Europe.

Meister, Jeanne C. 2001. *Building a learning organization: 7 lessons to involve your CEO*, San José: iUniverse.

Méndez, Félix. s.f. *Equipos terminales utilizados en España hasta final del siglo xx*. Volumen 2, Félix Méndez, 481 (cortesía del autor).

Menéndez de Luarca, José R. 1986. *Tres Cantos. En busca de la trama perdida*. Madrid: Centro de Información y Documentación de la Consejería de Ordenación del Territorio.

Molinero, Fernando. 2011. *España en la Unión Europea: Un cuarto de siglo de mutaciones territoriales*. Madrid: Casa de Velázquez.

Moliní, Fernando. 1986. «Costes, beneficios y oportunidades de la localización de ATT Microelectrónica en Madrid». En: *Descentralización productiva y movilidad industrial en la Comunidad de Madrid*, edirado por Méndez, Ramón y Moliní,

Fernando. (eds.), Madrid: Consejería de Trabajo, Comercio e Industria de la Comunidad, 106-125.

Moliní, Fernando. 1989. *Geografía, Desarrollo y medio ambiente en las concentraciones tecnológicas y en Soria. Un análisis territorial de la calidad de vida.* Tesis doctoral. Madrid: Universidad Autónoma de Madrid.

Morán, José M. y Lada, Luis. «Los planes de Telefónica». *El País,* 2 de mayo de 1984.

Mosakowski, Phil. «Recent trends in start-up activity». *Solid State Technology,* agosto, 1990, [sp].

Mytelka, Lynn K. 1990. *Strategic Partnerships: States, Firms, and International Competition.* Londres: Pinter.

Noam, Eli. 1992. *Telecommunications in Europe.* Nueva York: Oxford University Press.

Office of Microelectronics and Instrumentation. 1985. *A Competitive assessment of the U.S. semiconductor manufacturing equipment industry.* Washington: G.P.O.

Ostry, Sylvia y Nelson, Richard R. 1995. *Techno-Nationalism and Techno-Globalism.* Washington: Brookings Institution.

Ozawa, Terutomo. 1974. *Japan's Technological Challenge to the West, 1950–1974: Motivation and Accomplishment.* Cambridge: MIT Press.

Pérez, Carlota. 1985. «Microelectronics, long waves and world structural change: Nueva perspectives for developing countries». *World Development* 13, n°.3: 441-463.

Pouderoux, Noël. «La micro-électronique européenne face aux Etats-Unis». *Le Monde diplomatique,* 22 de diciembre de 1968.

Pricewaterhouse Coopers EU Services. 2013. *Comparison of European and non-European regional clusters in KETs. The case of semiconductors.* Bruselas: European Union.

Robin Saxby. 2012. Interviewed by Dane Elliot and Doug Fairbairn, *Oral History of Sir Robin Saxby,* Mountain View, California, 16 de octubre.

Roche, Edward M. 1992. *Managing Information Technology in Multinational Corporations.* Nueva York: Macmillan.

Rogers, Everett M. y Larsen, Judith K. 1986. *La fiebre del Silicón Valley.* Barcelona: Reverté.

Sánchez Izquierdo, Jesús. 1982. «Promoción de la microelectrónica en España». *Economía industrial,* 225-226: 106-106.

Sandholtz, Wayne. 1992. *High-Tech Europe: The Politics of International Cooperation.* Berkeley: University of California Press.

Smidt, Marc y Wever, Egbert. 2012. *The Corporate Firm in a Changing World Economy: Case Studies in the Geography of Enterprise.* Abingdon: Routledge.

Thakur, Manab et al. 1997. *International Management: Concepts and Cases.* Nueva Delhi: McGraw-Hill.

The AT&T Consent Decree's Manufacturing Restriction. 1991. *Hearing Before the Subcommittee on Antitrust, Monopolies, and Business Rights of the Committee on the Judiciary, United States Senate, One Hundred Second Congress, First Session, May 21, 1991*, vol. 4. Washington: G.P.O.

Todd, Daniel. 1990. *The World Electronics Industry.* Londres: Routledge.

Van Appledoorn, Bastiaan. 1999. *Transnational Capitalism and the Struggle over European Order.* Florencia: EUI.

US Congress. 1991. *Competing economies: America, Europe, and the Pacific Rim.* Washington: DIANE Publishing.

Used, Enrique. «La industria de los semiconductores». *Economía industrial*, 225-226, 1982, 18-20.

Vasudeva, P. K. 2006. *International Marketing.* Nueva Delhi: Excel Books.

VVAA. 1984. *El sector electrónico español ante la entrada en la CEE.* Madrid: Editorial Instituto de Empresa.

Wedgwood, C. G. (ed.). 2013. *European Electronics Directory 1994: Systems and Applications.* Oxford: Elsevier.

Weinstein, Joshua I. 2009. «The Market in Plato's Republic». *Classical Philology* 104: 439–458.

Yin, Robert K. 1993. «Applications of case study research». *Applied Social Research Series*, vol. 34. Londres: Sage.

Zysman, John y Borrus, Michael. 1994. «From failure to fortune?: European electronics in a changing world economy». *The annals of the American Academy of Political and Social Science,* vol. 531, enero: 141-167.

2. Los componentes. Alianzas internacionales por la autosuficiencia en la electrónica: la paneuropea European Silicon Structures

1. Introducción

Hasta mediados del siglo XX, la electrónica estuvo orientada al consumo. Esa línea temporal divisoria marca el inicio del protagonismo de los bienes electrónicos de inversión –fundamentalmente equipos de radio, sistemas de comunicación y radar[1]. Crecimientos anuales del 15% dieron a la electrónica profesional una holgada posición predominante en el segmento del sector. Con el aumento de la complejidad de la electrónica, el desarrollo y fabricación de componentes alcanzaron la madurez y dieron lugar a empresas especializadas. Desde entonces, la carrera por la integración de más funciones electrónicas en menor espacio no se detuvo. La integración de componentes electrónicos a gran escala permitió a Intel Corporation la introducción de las primeras memorias de circuitos integrados en 1971. Con la invención del microprocesador los ordenadores dieron un extraordinario giro hacia la extensión de su uso gracias a la gran reducción de costes (Banegas 2002, 187-189).

La fabricación de circuitos integrados requiere un gran número de operaciones complejas, pero los circuitos son baratos, ya que la mayoría de esas operaciones son repetitivas. Cada oblea de silicio procesada se corta en cientos de dados. Para algunas de las operaciones más lentas y costosas, se fabrican decenas de miles de circuitos simultáneamente. Con este elevado número, la industria puede tolerar rendimientos relativamente bajos (Circuits Multi-Projets 2005, 7).

---

[1] Para una panorámica general, véase Watson 2016.

Los semiconductores pueden fabricarse con diferentes tecnologías de proceso. Desde mediados de la década de 1970, los dos procesos dominantes fueron el bipolar (la tecnología original utilizada para producir circuitos integrados) y el CMOS (complementario de óxido metálico y silicio). Los primeros se distinguían por su alta velocidad y los segundos por su bajo consumo de energía y su alta capacidad de integrar más elementos en un solo circuito. Mientras que los semiconductores bipolares se utilizaban mucho en los grandes sistemas informáticos, los CMOS se convirtieron en predominantes, sobre todo en los dispositivos utilizados en los ordenadores personales. En la década de 1990, maduraron tecnologías avanzadas especialmente adecuadas para las aplicaciones de semiconductores más orientadas a los sistemas. Para las aplicaciones de señal mixta, se desarrollaron tecnologías BiCMOS que combinaban las ventajas de las tecnologías bipolares y de las tecnologías CMOS (STMICROELECTRONICS N, 20-F, June 29, 1998).

Nos proponemos analizar una empresa conjunta, fruto de una alianza estratégica bajo el paraguas de instituciones supranacionales en vistas a potenciar la unificación y armonización del mercado.

Las alianzas estratégicas mundiales son acuerdos comerciales de cooperación entre empresas competidoras reales o potenciales de varios países, que comprenden desde empresas conjuntas hasta acuerdos contractuales a corto plazo sobre un aspecto concreto, como, por ejemplo, el desarrollo de un nuevo producto. Desde el punto de vista de la gestión, las alianzas estratégicas tienen como objetivos entrar en un mercado extranjero, compartir los costos fijos y los riesgos asociados al desarrollo de nuevos productos y procesos, ayudar a las empresas a transferir competencias complementarias y establecer normas técnicas (Porter y Fuller 1986, 366-373; Hill et al. 2016, 269-270). En las alianzas estratégicas verticales las empresas comparten algunos de sus recursos y capacidades desde diferentes estadios (*stages*) de la cadena de valor en busca de ventajas comparativas. En las horizontales, las empresas comparten algunos de sus recursos y capacidades desde el mismo estadio de la cadena de valor en busca de ventajas comparativas (Hill et al. 2016, 284-285).

En un marco más general, las empresas encuentran en las alianzas internacionales flexibilidad para responder a las condiciones cambiantes del mercado, vías eficaces para ampliar la escala de las operaciones junto con inversiones en nuevas instalaciones y fusiones y adquisiciones (M&A, por sus siglas inglesas). Las fuerzas motrices que las impulsan abarcan la economía de costes en la producción y la investigación y el desarrollo, el fortalecimiento de la presencia en el mercado y el acceso a activos intangibles.

La dependencia de los objetivos de los diferentes socios hace que las coaliciones tecnológicas pueden generar resultados imprevistos. La mayor cercanía a la competencia impone una mayor preocupación por el impacto en la cadena de valor agregado y vínculos más formales entre los socios, incluidas estructuras más sólidas como empresas conjuntas y adquisiciones (Oosterveld y Nueno 1987, 12).

Durante las dos últimas décadas del siglo xx, la intensificación de la competencia en los mercados abiertos obligó a las empresas a adoptar medidas que les permitieran hacer frente a los nuevos desafíos en condiciones óptimas. Una de las respuestas fueron las alianzas estratégicas internacionales, que se convirtieron en una práctica habitual en la lucha por la competitividad y dieron lugar a resultados muy diferentes. El componente sectorial y geográfico dejó huella en la plasmación de las alianzas, de tal manera que, en algunas industrias, como la de tecnología avanzada, superaron holgadamente las fusiones y adquisiciones y en el caso de Europa, en el que se centra este apartado, predominó lo establecido con los Estados Unidos en lo intraeuropeo.

La dimensión del fenómeno ha obligado a los expertos a revisar sus ideas preconcebidas sobre la internacionalización de las empresas para incluirla en sus modelos, como lo ha hecho la escuela de Uppsala, inicialmente muy condicionada por su lealtad a los procesos industriales de la Europa nórdica. Uniéndose al paradigma de la OLI de Dunning (2001) reconoce la relevancia de las empresas conjuntas y las alianzas estratégicas como una forma de internacionalización (Dunning 2001; Johanson y Vahlne 2009).

Este capítulo pretende recuperar una de esas alianzas forjadas en Europa, que tiene el incentivo de desviarse de la práctica predominante porque es una empresa con socios exclusivamente europeos. Lo hace desde la perspectiva de un país periférico en la economía mundial y desde el estatus especial de al menos uno de los socios en el monopolio. Por último, se ajusta a la metodología del estudio de casos, que tiene por objeto profundizar en la complejidad de los procesos y fenómenos[2].

La investigación responde a la necesidad de un enfoque alternativo para el análisis de la industria, de especial importancia para las industrias basadas en la alta tecnología más convulsa –un marco centrado en las redes complicadas de relaciones y que tenga en cuenta las múltiples configuraciones posibles de

---

[2] Yin (1993, 59) define el estudio de caso como una investigación empírica sobre «un fenómeno contemporáneo dentro de su contexto de vida real y aborda una situación en la que los límites entre el fenómeno y el contexto no son claramente evidentes».

creación y entrega de valor, no solo el típico escenario de proveedor y cliente (Klincewicz 2005, 17-18).

En cuanto a su estructura, un primer apartado examina la creación de European Silicon Structures como una alianza estratégica en la industria europea de los semiconductores. Los apartados dos y tres plantean el caso de España, y, dentro de él, el papel de la demanda con el ejemplo de Telefónica; un último apartado presenta las principales conclusiones.

2. Una alianza estratégica en la industria europea de semiconductores: European Silicon Structures

El estudio de caso –European Silicon Structures (ES2)– aparece, pues, como una iniciativa formada bajo el paraguas de instituciones supranacionales para promover la unificación y armonización del mercado. En los años 80 la Comunidad Europea preparó el fin de sus barreras comerciales internas, fechado para principios de la siguiente década. En la telemática la región pasó de los campeones nacionales a la estrategia de cooperación, posible porque varios países se enfrentaron simultáneamente a un problema de escala. Por otra parte, las acciones de jóvenes empresas casi inexistentes algunos años antes estaban en auge (Sandholtz 1992, 20; *Fortune*, 27 de abril de 1987)[3].

Gráfico 1. Alianzas interempresariales en la industria electrónica mundial

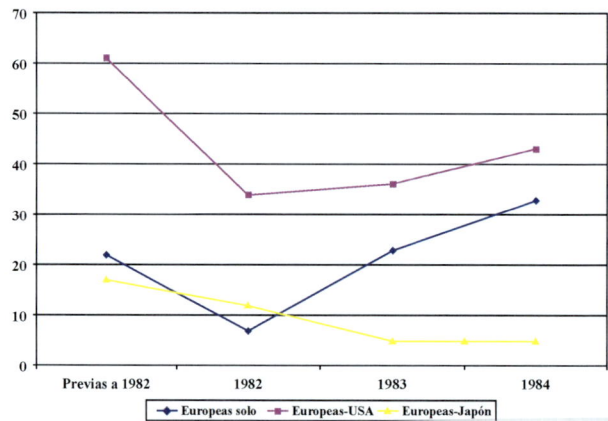

---

[3] Analistas pioneros destacaron el retraso europeo en su conjunto y el francés, en particular Pouderoux (1968, 22).

La tipología de la cooperación internacional en la industria electrónica sufrió un cambio importante en su aspecto geográfico. A partir de 1982, el predominio de las alianzas interempresariales entre socios estadounidenses y europeos se mantuvo. Sin embargo, se abrió camino una tendencia hacia el establecimiento de alianzas entre socios europeos exclusivamente, que disminuyó el peso de las forjadas con socios estadounidenses y japoneses (Gráfico 1).

A partir de 1993, el auge de la demanda mundial de semiconductores retó la capacidad de las plantas de fabricación y redujo el suministro de obleas fabricadas por las empresas de diseño. La negativa de los países asiáticos a nuevas inversiones en la fabricación de semiconductores forzó la integración en la fabricación de obleas. Las empresas de diseño sin fábrica tuvieron que asumir buena parte de la inversión en fabricación o afrontar costes de transacción crecientes si dependían exclusivamente de otras empresas para obtener obleas. La inversión directa tomó la forma de adquisición de instalaciones de fabricación y de creación de empresas conjuntas de fabricación y capital. Por otra parte, varias empresas cerraron contratos con fabricantes y algunas siguieron dependiendo de los contratos de mercado al contado para las obleas (Ó Uallacháin 1997, 217-237).

Como característica importante, Europa presentaba una endeble industria electrónica autóctona, cebo de la industria de los semiconductores, a su vez giro motor de la electrónica. A ello se añadía una ausencia de cultura de gestión, circunstancia agravada por la falta de correspondencia entre el tremendo énfasis en la ciencia y la tecnología y la producción y la comercialización. En contrapartida, Europa llegó a contar con una fuerte capacidad de I+D, especialmente en la investigación aplicada tanto básica como financiada con fondos públicos, a la vez que una fuerte base industrial. Los políticos y la élite empresarial europea consideraban que la innovación tecnológica duradera y la asunción de riesgos en un clima socioeconómico favorable eran las mejores esperanzas para sobrevivir en la competencia mundial (Papers 1985, 82; Forester 1987, 289)[4].

---

[4]   El *think tank* Roundtable of European Industrialists juzgó crucial abolir las normas nacionales que se oponen al libre comercio en la CE y los monopolios de telecomunicaciones restantes, así como eliminar todos los obstáculos a las fusiones y adquisiciones transfronterizas y extender los programas de investigación de la CE más allá de la etapa precompetitiva (Dataquest 1991, 104). La fortaleza en I+D y en la base industrial se plasmaron en agrupaciones de éxito con diferentes fortalezas y especializaciones. Europa logró destacar en sectores con marcadas interdependencias con la microelectrónica, entre ellos la indus-

El dominio del mercado de semiconductores por los productos normalizados o los chips de productos básicos permitió cierta diferenciación en la velocidad y en el control de calidad, una peculiaridad de los japoneses[5]. El aumento de los costes de I+D y las crecientes inversiones de capital obligaron a las empresas a aumentar sus ventas para resarcirse de los gastos. A pesar de que los costes marginales de los chips eran muy bajos y estaban en disminución, y de los reiterados sobrantes competitivos en esta industria altamente cíclica, la omnipresencia de los chips en las TIC obligó a las grandes empresas a una integración vertical hacia circuitos integrados más potentes. Sobrevinieron tres procesos relevantes para comenzar con la reestructuración en la conexión orientada a la investigación en el caso de Philips y Siemens y la fusión entre la italiana SGS con la sección de semiconductores de la francesa Thomson. Otro movimiento fue la creciente búsqueda de subvenciones y protección del gobierno. El tercero fue la superación del mercado de productos básicos mediante la formación de una nueva empresa (Faulhaber y Tamburini 2012, 109).

Los planes para una nueva empresa europea en la industria de los semiconductores se fundamentaban en varios supuestos, como la tendencia del mercado y su propia naturaleza. El tipo de tecnología CMOS de circuitos integrados en series cortas se ajustaba exactamente a las necesidades del cliente para ayudar a aumentar la competitividad por la vía de acortar el tiempo de desarrollo, aumentar la funcionalidad y el rendimiento o reducir los costes. En un escenario de crecimiento muy rápido del mercado europeo de circuitos CMOS a medida, se esperaba que podría triplicarse con creces en el periodo 1985-1988 para obtener 1.440 millones de dólares en 1991. Era posible un aumento de los circuitos totalmente personalizados desde los 120 millones de dólares de 1984 hasta los 1.000 millones de dólares de 1991. La nueva empresa intentaría cubrir no menos del 10 % para prototipos y pequeños volúmenes, un mercado que ascendía a 110 millones de dólares en 1991.

---

tria aeroespacial, la automoción, la seguridad, la industria y la medicina (Dornbusch 2018, 1-37).

[5]   En la década de 1980, los fabricantes japoneses de semiconductores comenzaron a dominar el mercado mundial con tres tipos sucesivos de memorias dinámicas de acceso aleatorio (*dynamic random access memories*, o DRAM) de capacidad creciente. A continuación, la cuota de Japón en el mercado mundial de semiconductores comenzó a declinar gradualmente (Okada 2006, 39-103).

Los clientes europeos necesitaban una electrónica de procesamiento de datos profesional, industrial y especializada cimentada en series de circuitos de preferencia con tiempos de diseño y fabricación muy breves para acortar el proceso de producción. Satisfacer esta necesidad específica fue una diferenciación significativa frente a las orientadas de preferencia a las grandes series de las empresas estadounidenses y japonesas. La experiencia en compiladores de silicio de alta tecnología prometía dar velocidad de diseño y de fabricación de prototipos y derivar pequeñas series de una tecnología innovadora[6].

Para entonces, Europa tenía alrededor de la décima parte de la producción mundial de semiconductores. La CEE emprendió un conjunto de proyectos de investigación y desarrollo (programas ESPRIT, BRITE y RACE). Entre ellos destacaba el programa mediterráneo de orientación civil EUREKA y, en el contexto del mismo, se disponía a involucrarse en otros, que implicaban una cooperación a gran escala entre empresas de varios países en las primeras fases del proceso que lleva de la investigación a la aplicación industrial. Se trataba de los proyectos de diversa envergadura EUROCIM, MEGA entre Philips y Siemens, European Silicon Structures-ES2 y EUROLASER, con costes de unos 30, unos 2.000, 94 y unos 80 millones de ecus, respectivamente. La Comisión estudiaba diversas formas de lograr que los inversores y los bancos aceptasen estos riesgos. Un ejemplo era la creación de sociedades de inversión (EUROTECH CAPITAL) para financiar con fondos propios los proyectos emprendidos en una fase muy temprana del desarrollo de un producto o proceso (Cowhey y Aronson 1993, 157; European Commission, Press Releases, 31 de octubre de 1986, 2).

EUREKA era uno de los varios programas con alto grado de riesgo que implicaba una cooperación masiva entre empresas en las primeras etapas del proceso que conducía desde la investigación a la aplicación industrial. En uno de sus componentes ideológicos el proyecto perseguía erigir un contrapeso del plan de Reagan para la Iniciativa de Defensa Estratégica (SDI), una defensa con misiles espaciales (Friend 1998, 228; *Business Week*, 3.108-3.121, 1989, 158)[7]. Otros defendían el carácter netamente civil de EUREKA, entre

---

6   La planta estaría equipada con un enmascarador electrónico. El 80% de todo el equipo europeo se fabricó en series inferiores a 5.000 piezas (Informe PRS Ciencia y Tecnología, 8 de noviembre de 1985, 40)

7   El presidente francés François Mitterrand, que conoció *in situ* la organización de Silicon Valley, fue una fuente de inspiración de una tecnología común europea y se reunió con los líderes de los chips informáticos y los sistemas de información (*Le Monde*, 28 de diciembre de 1985; *The New York Times*, 26 de marzo de 1984).

los que se alineaba Hubert Curien, expresidente del CNES, la agencia espacial de Francia y uno de los asesores de Mitterand (*New Scientist*, 4 de julio de 1985).

Siete participantes del primer programa EUREKA de 1985 ayudaron a establecer una puesta en marcha paneuropea en el marco de la iniciativa francesa, denominada European Silicon Structures, o, abreviado, ES2. Su objetivo era la producción de prototipos o pequeñas series –menos de 50.000 unidades– de circuitos completos personalizados. La nueva empresa tenía la misión de formar a los diseñadores de las empresas clientes, asistirlos en su trabajo, proporcionarles herramientas de diseño y, finalmente, ofrecer un servicio de embalaje y pruebas (Forester 1989, 13; Mytelka 1990, 110; Sandholtz 1992). Esta nueva apuesta fue posible gracias a la suma de una idea original unida a la transferencia de conocimientos técnicos y de gestión acumulados por el trío fundador en varias empresas europeas y estadounidenses del sector, el respaldo financiero y el apoyo político del Estado[8]. Por otra parte, ofrece uno de los escasos ejemplos de resistencia europea al dominio norteamericano (Sautter 1987).

Lo que podría calificarse de primera fase de siembra y aprendizaje se puso en 1979 con el establecimiento de Eurotechnique, una asociación entre el ahora grupo Saint Gobain, que tenía una participación mayoritaria del 51%, y la californiana National Semiconductor Corporation, deseosa de establecerse en Europa, que inspiró el modelo y aportó las tecnologías y el equipo (*Electronics*, 57, 1984, 62; Sandholtz 1992, 81). La dependencia tecnológica y territorial fue una fase de aprendizaje de transición que condujo a la autonomía europea. Esta primera fase del *spin-off* se cierra con la creación en 1988 de GEMPLUS, que conocerá un auge deslumbrante[9].

[8]　En su plan primigenio, ES2 perseguía suministrar o explotar todos los recursos de procesamiento de datos, en particular los compiladores de silicio, necesarios para diseñar rápidamente circuitos completos a medida (excluyendo matrices de compuertas y células estándar) desde París, Londres y Munich antes del 1 de enero de 1986, para probar los circuitos correspondientes en dos semanas y luego producirlos internamente en series de hasta unas diez mil piezas a precios competitivos (*West Europe Report. Science and Technology* 1985. Noviembre, 35-41).

[9]　En 1981 tenía 383 empleados. Tras el abandono de Saint-Gobain en 1982, solo MATRA y Thomson (asociadas con Harris y Motorola, respectivamente) siguieron siendo los pilares del plan francés de componentes. Los poderes públicos decidieron confiar a Thomson la toma de control de Eurotechnique. El director de la nueva unidad era un antiguo ingeniero del LETI, también formado en los EE. UU. –departamento de I+D de los laboratorios BELL y más tarde director de TEXAS INSTRUMENT Francia. La producción y la fuerza de trabajo se expandieron (Daviet 1999, 33-40). National Semiconductor mutó en Silicon Valley Analog (SVA) y en sección de Texas Instruments.

El cerebro genuino de ES2 fue el ingeniero francés y gerente cosmopolita altamente cualificado Jean-Luc Grand-Clement, que se apoyó en un equipo de Thomson en Rousset. Grand-Clement contactó con el miembro de la élite empresarial Robert R. Heikes, jefe de las operaciones de la National Semiconductor Corporation en Europa y América Latina (*Business Week*, 2.901-2.913, 1985, 84; Daviet 1999, 33-40)[10]. Ambos atrajeron consecutivamente a Robert W. Wilmot, presidente del fabricante británico de computadoras ICL Ltd., y a una firma de capital riesgo con sede en Londres, Advent, la rama extranjera de TA Associates de Boston, el mayor grupo de Estados Unidos en su especie[11]. Varios de ellos intervinieron en proyectos anteriores. Heikes y Grand-Clement, respectivamente director general y gerente general de Motorola Europe y Glasgow, tomaron parte en un proyecto de planta de semiconductores en Malta. Motorola enseñó a Grand-Clement «la importancia de tener una financiación sólida y una estrategia clara desde el principio»[12].

Dado que se necesitaba una gran suma −50 millones de dólares− para construir la compañía y equipar la planta y los laboratorios de investigación, los fundadores concibieron una empresa paneuropea, más compleja que las anteriores empresas bilaterales simples[13]. Advent inyectó la primera

---

[10] Ingeniero de la École Nationale Supérieure de Télécommunications, se incorporó a Eurotechnique y, dentro de la electrónica, a CIT-Alcatel; destacó como fundador de L'Occitane de la electrónica (*Le Monde*, 4 de septiembre de 1985 y 28 de marzo de 1987).

[11] Cuando Grand-Clement, antiguo directivo de Motorola Europa, se puso en contacto con Saxby, el secretario de este le dijo «Hay un francés al teléfono, y suena un poco como el inspector Clouseau» (Saxby 2012). Algunas fuentes añaden otros capitales-riesgo (Technoventures y Euroventures, fundados en 1984 por un grupo europeo −Asea, Fiat, 3M, Olivetti, Bosch y Volvo- (Lipnack y Stamps 1993, 124)− y respaldado por una serie de gigantes, entre ellos Pirelli y Saint-Gobain (*Fortune*, 27 de abril de 1987), Four Seasons/Alfa-Laval, el Fondo Fjarde AP, SFP y otros (Schroder Ventures: *Investors Chronicle*, 86, 1988, 81) a Advent (*PRS Report Science & Technology*, 8 de noviembre de 1985, 39; *Les Échos*, 5 de abril de 1995). Advent aparece a veces como coordinador de la financiación y Robb Wilmot como principal impulsor en ES2 (*Investors Chronicle*, 75, 1986, 61). Wilmot provenía de una estancia de dieciséis años en Texas Instruments Inc. y de su cargo de presidente ejecutivo de International Computers Limited (ICL) (1984) y, en última instancia, de director general de su filial británica (*PRS Report Science & Technology*, 8 de noviembre de 1985, 40; *The New York Times*, 24 de octubre de 1990). Wilmot comentó en 1987: «Puede que no esté lejos el día en que cueste menos diseñar un chip a medida que comprar un coche de segunda mano» (*Semiconductor International*, 12, 1-6, 1987, 76).

[12] Heike indicó que Malta extraía sus ventajas del dumping laboral −una escala salarial comparativamente baja− combinada con las preferencias del mercado común; las negociaciones continuaron en 1974 (*Industrialization: Motorola Semiconductors*, 1973 October 1, Wikeleaks, 1973VALLET01930_b; 1974 April 10, 1974VALLET00677_b).

[13] La gran prensa destacaba ese carácter de primera sociedad verdaderamente europea (*Le Monde*, 28 de marzo de 1987). Acuerdo franco-italiano orientado a la exportación Sesco-

mitad de un millón de dólares en capital inicial, ofreció sus oficinas en los primeros días y ES2 finalmente recaudó cerca de 100 millones de dólares en inversiones corporativas, capital de riesgo y subvenciones (Campbell 2003, 59)[14]. La situación en 1985 era la siguiente: las dos principales empresas europeas de capital de riesgo, Advent (Londres y Bélgica) y Techno-Venture Management en Munich, así como Alpha Associates en Francia, Orange Nassau en Holanda y Four Seasons en Suecia, habían aportado 4 millones de dólares. Los inversionistas industriales y las instituciones financieras de seis países europeos debían proporcionar los 61 millones de dólares restantes, en cantidades iguales con exclusión de cualquier fuente no europea. La estructura de capital planeada otorgaba el control –el 60 %– a los grandes fabricantes y las «instituciones» a partes iguales, a la vez que reservaba la cuarta parte para los fundadores y el personal y el 15 % restante para el capital riesgo[15]. En la Tabla 1 se muestran las operaciones financieras posteriores en varios años.

sem-Mistral (Pouderoux 1968, 22). Rod Attwooll confesó que la implicación de unos dependía de la de los otros. «Todos por separado dijeron que invertirían si X lo hacía, y prometieron hablar con X. Mientras tanto, pasaban las semanas y los meses. Al final, los metimos a todos en una habitación de un hotel de Bruselas y les dijimos que se pusieran a hablar entre ellos». En retrospectiva, la fabricación de silicio con dinero de capital riesgo resultaba una tarea difícil (Campbell 2003, 59).

[14] Insistencia en la ambición del programa: 65 millones de dólares para empezar, o 100 millones de dólares en cinco años para una instalación completa (*PRS Report Science & Technology*, 8 noviembre de 1985, 40). Las fuentes difieren en los datos: 46 millones de dólares según *Fortune*, 27 de abril de 1987. Advent sembró ES2 con unos 5 millones de dólares; capital inicial de 60 millones de dólares (*The Economist*, 303, 1987, 71); 60 millones de dólares reunidos de ocho empresas europeas (entre ellas, la italiana Olivetti, la sueca Saab, la británica British Aerospace y la holandesa Philips) (*The Scientist*, 28 de noviembre de 1988). Los desembolsos de capital riesgo se multiplicaron por 6,4 en 1978-1986. La capitalización de ES2 en 1988 era de 44 millones de dólares, similar a la de Matra Harris y Mietec. ES2 contaba con el mayor respaldo de capital riesgo visto hasta entonces fuera de EE. UU. (*Electronics*, 59, 1986). Algunos estudiosos consideraron que la empresa era «una apuesta ambiciosa –algunos dirían que insensata– para crear el primer diseñador y desarrollador de circuitos integrados con sede en Europa en un momento en el que un exceso mundial de chips de silicio estaba causando estragos en la industria» (Brooke y Penrice 2009, 66).

[15] Four Seasons se propuso presentar el proyecto a una serie de grupos financieros de inversión de Suecia, entre ellos Folksam y Aktiv (*PRS Report Science & Technology*, 8 de noviembre de 1985, 36). El proyecto no incluía a países dinámicos como Irlanda, entonces en vías de volverse un Silicon Valley en Europa, como afirmaba el Gobierno (*Public Papers of the Presidents of the United States*, Reagan, Ronald. 1986, 801).

Tabla 1. Socios de la European Silicon Structures, según fechas de entrada

Fecha	Financiación	Millones de dólares
1985	Advent, London; Techno-Venture Management Corp.	5
Diciembre de 1985	Brown Boveri y CIE (Suiza); Ing. C. Olivetti & Co. (Italia); Philips NV (Holanda); Saab-Scandia AB (Suecia)	25
Enero de 1986	British Aerospace Plc	5
Noviembre de 1986	Banque Internationale, Luxembourg	9
Junio de 1988	Aérospatiale SA (Francia) Bull SA; Telefónica SA; Telfin Oy	

Fuente: Elaborado a partir de Dataquest, junio de 1988, 205:
Computer Business Review, 29 de junio de 1989.

La estructura de ES2 se forjó durante la más terrible recesión de la industria de los semiconductores en el pasado (Cowhey y Aronson 1993, 157; *The New York Times*, 1 de agosto de 1988). Como rasgo principal, la ES2 revistió un complejo desarrollo legal, que permitió introducirse como empresa local en los diversos países en los que se implantó (Buckley y Dunning 1994, 256; *PRS* 1988, 11-12)[16]. Las fronteras nacionales seguían siendo un problema que requería, incluso dentro de Europa occidental, licencias de exportación, así como la documentación habitual para el transporte. Al carecer de un estatuto jurídico europeo para una empresa paneuropea, ES2 se constituyó en Luxemburgo como sociedad matriz de varias filiales en cada país en el que se pretendía implantar, una sociedad de cartera con filiales nacionales[17]. La composición del consejo de administración que aparece en el Anexo 1 muestra la presencia de fundadores, financieros y algunos ejecutivos del sector, entre

---

[16] En Alemania se estableció como ES2 GmbH (Wedgwood ed. 2013, 146); en el Reino Unido como ES2 Limited, y en Holanda como ES2 Netherlands B.V. Los diseños propios de chips realizados por el *software* de ES2 fueron traducidos por sus ordenadores en instrucciones de grabado para las máquinas de haz de electrones Able 150, de 4 millones de dólares, fabricadas por la Perkin-Elmer Corporation; también fue tomada como un «fabricante de chips sin país» (*The New York Times*, 1 de agosto de 1988); otros la consideraron de orientación geocéntrica (Vasudeva 2006, 48) y el curso The case of European Silicon Structures, SUNY Buffalo State College, ECO 434, 1-16; más correctamente, la tidó de «empresa con muchos países» (*The Scientist*, 28 de noviembre de 1988).

[17] *The Scientist,* 28 de noviembre de 1988.

ellos el franco-internacional Bernard Pruniaux, formado en Francia, capacitado en los EE.UU. y en activo en su país de origen. La situación en 1994 cambió con la llegada de nuevos nombres[18].

Presentaba una estructura descentralizada, ya que su planta de producción, montaje y ensayo estaba situada en el Centro Tecnológico de Rousset, cerca de Aix-en-Provence, y una de las secciones intensivas en tecnología –diseño de soporte lógico– se hallaba en el Reino Unido. En este sentido, su nacimiento coincidió con una primera fase de agrupación de microelectrónica o tecnópolis en la ciudad de Rousset, caracterizada por la aparición de una «red» de microelectrónica en la región de Bouches-du-Rhône cuando el Gobierno se propuso entrar en la industria de la microelectrónica a través de empresas públicas y empresas mixtas con socios tecnológicos norteamericanos (Dang y Longhi 2009, 126.). Para la mayoría aplastante Rousset era la capital de un Silicon Valley provenzal con la cuarta parte de la microelectrónica francesa. El Instituto Milken de EE. UU. identificó ocho ingredientes clave en la creación de *clusters* de alta tecnología para comenzar a cobrar importancia, con la presencia de centros e instituciones de investigación civil y militar de vanguardia. Combinados con una red de empresarios y capitalistas de riesgo como segundo elemento notable, se traducen en una rápida adopción de la tecnología. Los seis componentes restantes abarcan una fuerza de trabajo capacitada y formada; los efectos indirectos de la tecnología de las industrias de alta tecnología cercanas; la disponibilidad de capital de riesgo; la alta calidad del lugar y dos elementos

---

[18] Pruniaux: Ingeniero en electrónica (Toulouse), dos años en Leti (Grenoble CENG), un cuatrienio en los Laboratorios Bell (Nueva Jersey) le permitieron adquirir una sólida experiencia técnica en semiconductores. En las instalaciones francesas de Texas Instrument (Niza), fue pionero en la técnica de reducción de las dimensiones de los chips, aumentando el rendimiento y el coste. Como director industrial en Eurotechnique, una empresa conjunta de St. Gobain y National Semiconductor (1979), contribuyó tempranamente a lanzar el clúster de microelectrónica en Rousset. Se jubiló en 2008 en Atmel (Letter to Steve Laub, president and chief executive officer at Atmel Corporation: EX-10.10 2 f51611exv10w10.htm EXHIBIT 10.10, 17 October 2008). Jean Pierre Demange era vicepresidente y director de ES2 para el sur de Europa; el director general era Manfred Koslar, desarrollador del ordenador de señales. Situación en 1994: los directores generales W. Koepf y Bernard Pruniaux; director de investigación y director técnico Eric Detoullin; director de producto Eric Detoullin y Lucien Brau; director de compras Jean Louis Palazzo; director de *marketing* y director de publicidad Christian Fleutelot (licenciado en la École centrale de Lyon y postgrado en microelectrónica; ingeniero de calidad MATRA defensa en 1986-1988); director de ventas Jean Yves Lesaux (Wedgwood ed. 2013, 36). Dos ejemplos de la movilidad de los técnicos en las grandes empresas: Lucien Brau (Eurotechnique y Texas Instrument), director de operaciones de back-end en European Silicon Structures; Christian Dupuy (Motorola) creó las capacidades de ingeniería de producto y de diseño analógico en European Silicon Structures.

favorables relacionados con los bajos costes: el coste de la vida y el de hacer negocios, entre ellos los bajos precios del suelo (*Strategy+business*, 1 de julio de 2001)[19]. Tras descartar Sofía-Antipolis como emplazamiento, la planta de Rousset fue construida sobre el modelo de las unidades americanas de Santa Clara y Salt Lake City. La tecnología procedía de los Estados Unidos, país en que se había formado el personal, incluido el cargo de mayor responsabilidad[20].

La puesta en marcha se hizo de forma gradual. Igual que muchas empresas de la industria de los semiconductores, ES2 fue al principio una empresa «sin fábrica» o sin planta, orientada a los avances tecnológicos en la empresa de diseño de microchips pero subcontratando sus productos antes de que comenzara la fabricación. La planta de producción de Rousset, inaugurada en 1987 (*Journal de l'année*, 1988, 265), comenzó a ensamblar y probar circuitos; el procesamiento de obleas de silicio se siguió realizando en Exel Microelectronics en California bajo una fórmula de subcontratación[21]. En su calidad de alianza horizontal, ES2 trató de alcanzar rápidamente economías de escala y masa crítica para labrarse un nicho rentable de pequeñas series de producción en el mercado de semiconductores de 5.000 millones de dólares en la región. Se eligió una tecnología punta de haz electrónico (un proceso de escritura directa de diseños en obleas de silicio con una máquina de haz electrónico) y una forma que le permitió reducir drásticamente –más de la mitad– el tiempo de entrega de un prototipo de chips y el precio de sus competidores, a saber, los norteamericanos y los japoneses (*PRS* 1988, 11-12; Saxby 2012; Campbell 2003, 59; *Business International* 33, 1986,

---

[19] El aprendizaje era posible en el centro principal de la Universidad, cerca de la fábrica (Meister 2001, 159).

[20] La elección de esta ubicación se basó en la existencia de la central eléctrica de carbón, muy rentable tras la crisis energética de 1973. También se deseaba reavivar una región en relativo declive. El centro francés de investigación de estas tecnologías, el LETI (Laboratorio de Electrónica e Informática), se estableció en Grenoble en 1967 bajo la égida de la CEA (Comisión Francesa de Energía Atómica) (Daviet 1999, 33-40). ES2 llevó a cabo actuaciones colaborativas como, por ejemplo, la fabricación en su laboratorio de París de dispositivos experimentales consistentes en una serie de estructuras MOS utilizando el proceso de 2 micras, que fueron facilitados por el Centre de Développement des Technologies Avancées de Argel (Bentarzi 2011, 99).

[21] En febrero de 1986, Exar Integrated Circuits, una empresa pública de California, adquirió Exel Microelectronics por 5,5 millones de dólares. Exel operaba una subsidiaria de Exar y mantenía una planta independiente y personal de I+D (*Dataquest* 1988, 209). STMicroelectronics gestionaba una planta de fabricación en Rousset, junto a otras en Europa, Estados Unidos, el Mediterráneo y Asia-Pacífico (*STM*, 31 de diciembre de 1997; 29 de junio de 1998, 4).

241)[22]. Sorprendentemente, entre los futuros clientes de ES2 se perdió a las dos compañías electrónicas dominantes y, en cierto modo, antagonistas en Europa, Thomson y Siemens[23].

Thomson y SGS recalcan que sus movimientos para acometer este sector fueron el resultado de sus propios análisis de mercado y estaban siendo considerados mucho antes de que se anunciara la creación de ES2. Thomson, moviéndose para atacar este sector como resultado de los propios análisis, ofreció a Siemens bloquear el mercado con una empresa conjunta para fabricar los circuitos a medida. Después de la negativa de los alemanes, Thomson buscó llegar al mercado con el apoyo técnico de los ingleses y los norteamericanos[24].

El plan de negocios se frustró porque la máquina litográfica de haz electrónico tenía una décima parte del rendimiento de las especificaciones y no se cumplieron las ventajas en cuanto a los precios. En realidad, el plan técnicamente factible y diferenciador puso a la ES2 fuera de la fabricación de chips convencionales y en un nicho compartido entre los circuitos digitales programables FPGAs y los mercados semi y totalmente personalizados de varias empresas. En 1991, los principales proveedores europeos, que a menudo se concentran en nichos de mercado y circuitos integrados para aplicaciones específicas, son, junto con ES2: ABB-Hafo (Suecia); Austria Microsysteme (Austria); GEC Plessey Semiconductors (UK); Matra-Harris Semiconducteurs (Francia); Mietec (Bélgica) y Telefunken (Alemania). Las empresas no

---

[22] VLSI Technology Inc., una empresa californiana de 125 millones de dólares fundada en 1979, especializada en complejos ASIC y ASSP de alto rendimiento, era una de las principales competidoras de ES2. El mercado internacional la llevó a la intervención con tecnología propia. ES2 fue uno de los primeros compradores de la máquina Aeble 150, ya que adquirió la tercera fabricada por Perkin Elmer y la instaló por primera vez en Exel en octubre de 1986, asumiendo los diseños del ASIC desde abril siguiente (*Electronic Engineering*, 60, 733-738, 23). Compass Design Automation, Inc., filial de VLSI, suministró *software* y librerías de diseño al amplio mercado comercial del ASIC y de la automatización del diseño electrónico. Grand-Clement consideraba que el mercado de las matrices de puertas estaba dominado por «una metodología anticuada y un torpe y áspero enfoque» (*Profiles* 1998, 2-446).

[23] Siemens, comprometida en el proyecto europeo Mega al pasar a la producción en serie de chips de un megabit en colaboración con Toshiba, fingió relegar a SGS-Thomson con la irritación tanto de esta empresa franco-italiana como del gobierno francés. SGS-Thomson reivindicó su liderazgo en el nicho de la tecnología del chip de memoria programable borrable (EPROM) y un lugar para las tres empresas por igual (Sandholtz 1992, 293); Siemens, «Japan and the USA in the lead – Siemens aims to catch up», consultado en https://new.siemens.com/global/en/company/about/history/news/4mbit-dram.html.

[24] Bonno (on-line); *Electronics*, 59, 1986.

europeas incluían, entre otras, AMD (USA); Analog Devices (USA); Fujitsu (Japón); Matsushita (Japón); and Mitsubishi (Japón) (Fletcher 2013, 168)[25].

Debido a la estrechez del mercado europeo, ES2 pagó un precio para superar los peores aspectos de la fragmentación con un alto coste de coordinación de la empresa colaboradora (Guile 1987, 103).

Posiblemente, la razón más fuerte de la decepción estaba en la concepción, una especie de trampa: una empresa de nicho tenía ventajas para la expansión pero también problemas por los estrictos límites del mercado. En 1987, ES2 se situaba en el cuarto lugar como proveedor de circuitos integrados basados en células y dos años depués su cuota de mercado europea de semiconductores era de 0,2% con 17 millones de dólares de ventas. La empresa paneuropea se clasificó en los mercados de diferentes productos como sigue: centésima décima sexta en el ranking mundial de empresas europeas de semiconductores de 1989 con 18 millones de dólares, trigésimo quinta en el MOS (semiconductor de óxido metálico) digital europeo, trigésimo tercera en el CMOS (semiconductor complementario de óxido metálico) europeo, vigésimo primera en la lógica MOS europea, décimo novena en el MOS ASIC (Application specific integrated cicuits) y cuadragésimo segunda en el circuito integrado europeo. 17 millones de dólares de ingresos para el ASIC en 1989 dieron a ES2 un 1,44% de los ingresos totales europeos del mercado ASIC (Harding 1991, 83; Dataquest 1990, *passim*; Dataquest, 1991, 6)[26].

ES2 reorganizó su estructura corporativa, salió del mercado europeo y trabajó para insertarse en redes más amplias. Respaldada por capital de riesgo de EE.UU., creó United Silicon Structures, o US2 (Tabla 2), una filial norteamericana de poco éxito, que se ahogó en problemas financieros y de gestión (Wedgwood 2013, 329)[27]. En octubre de 1987 ES2 compró una empresa de *software* y diseño en Japón llamada Best para convertirla en una agencia de ventas de productos de ES2 en dicho país. Más allá de estos planes, quería formar una nueva empresa de producción bajo el nombre de Japan Silicon Structures y las siglas de JS2[28]. ES2 se alió a Development Co. en una empre-

---

[25] LSI Logic Corp., VLSI Technology Inc. y Taiwan Semiconductor Manufacturing Co. Ltd. (*EE Times Europe*. January 9, 2014).

[26] ASICs representaban un quinto de los circuitos integrados consumidos en Europa. ASIC es una tecnología para diseñar, producir y probar CI a satisfacción de los usuarios (United *States Committee on Science, Space, and Technology*, 1989, 764).

[27] A Robin Saxby le encomendaron alcanzar la rentabilidad en US2 a la que también se unió Tim O'Donnell (Finlay 2000, 655; Saxby 2012 [sp]).

[28] *Dataquest,* June 1988, 207; *Business Week*, 1989, 3.094-3.097, 102.

sa conjunta, European CAD Developments Ltd., especializada en actividades de investigación y desarrollo en los mercados de automatzación del diseño elecrónico (EDA) y ASIC[29]. Más tarde, planeó su expansión mediante la vinculación con los Estados Unidos y una empresa líder de Alemania Occidental, este segundo país de enorme significado por tratarse de un no copropietario.

La senda de ES2 se relacionaba notablemente con Lattice Logic, una empresa *spin-off* propietaria de un sistema automático de Diseño Asistido por Ordenador (CAD) original para trazar circuitos integrados en el estilo de la matriz de entradas. En primer lugar, desde 1985 ES2 fue cliente del pionero compilador de silicio de Lattice Logic, como fue el caso de varias empresas clave, incluyendo Ferranti Ltd., que permitía a los diseñadores producir diseños totalmente a medida y optimizados[30].

En segundo lugar, ES2 fortaleció su capacidad gerencial y técnica con la incorporación de los directores fundadores Irene Buchanan y John Gray a la división de *software*, el segundo como VP de tecnología de diseño[31]. En tercer lugar, ES2 eliminó dependencias externas con la adquisición de su antiguo proveedor Lattice Logic en 1987 (Dodgson 1989, 84; Dataquest 1991, 105).

ES2 formalizó varios acuerdos de colaboración con empresas europeas, japonesas y norteamericanas, en ocasiones con una clara división de funciones, cuyo detalle puede apreciarse en la Tabla 2.

---

[29] European Cad Developments se registró el 8 de enero de 1990 en Londres y se disolvió (*Moody's OTC Industrial News Reports*, 20, 1989, 1870; Dataquest 1991, 105).

[30] Por su parte, SOLO 2000 se basaba en la familia de herramientas CAD integradas de SDA Systems e incorporaba macrobloques compilados (Dataquest, junio de 1988, 205). ES2 firmó contratos para los programas SOLO I000' y SOLO 1200 y para el programa Qudos QUICKCHIP PLUS, y ya se habían tomado medidas para el suministro a instituciones académicas (*Journal of Semicustom ICs*, 7-8, 1989, 45). European Silicon Structures usó el CAD SUN 3/SOLO 1400 para el diseño, análisis y simulación de un filtro de tecnología FSK 1.2u. ES2 proporcionó material para actividades educativas en Essex a través del Consorcio de la Universidad de Londres (Jones y Buckley 1989, 16).

[31] John Gray, profesor de informática, puso en marcha Lattice Logic con dos graduados de doctorado cuando en 1980 dejó la Universidad de Edimburgo (Ibbett 1997); fue aclamada como una de las empresas autóctonas más interesantes de Silicon Glen (*Business Herald*, 28 de abril de 1986, 15). Irene Buchanan, John Gray y Tom Kean fundaron en 1989 Algotronix, pionera en el uso de chips FPGA. Conexión japonesa: Lattice concedió la licencia de su diseño y tecnología de 64 KSRAM a Seiko Epson/S-MOS (*Dataquest*, October 1986, 28).

Tabla 2. Acuerdos mundiales de ES2 con empresas

Socio	Año	Propósito
Etec Systems*		Desarrollo de la tecnología para la personalización de la matriz de entrada de escritura directa
Jenoptik		Desarrollo de la técnica LIGA o litografía con radiación de sincrotrón, galvanoplastia y moldeado de plástico
Compass Design Automation		Compass proporcionará a sus clientes acceso a las Máquinas de Riesgo Avanzado
Siemens		Permitió a ES2 producir chips con el proceso CMOS de 0,5 micrones de Siemens
Phoenix V SLI		Especialización: United Silicon Structures hará los prototipos y VLSI los volúmenes
Cascade Design Automation		Para proporcionar una tecnología de proceso de 0,7 micrones usando las herramientas de diseño de Cascade y la tecnología de proceso ES2
Lattice Logic	1985	Exportar el compilador de Lattice a Europa
Solomon Design Associates (SDA) Systems	1986	Comercializar la familia de diseño de SDA Systems en Europa y usarlos en varios centros de diseño
Philips-Elcoma-Texas Instruments	1986	Cooperar en la biblioteca de células estándar del Sistema de Células
Exel	1986	Subcontratación de la producción en la planta de Exel
Philips-Texas Instruments	1987	Fabricación de la Célula de Sistema: TI y Philips suministrarán piezas de volumen y ES2 proporcionará prototipos y cantidades pequeñas
Sun Microsystems	1987	Para unificar el sistema de diseño SOLO 2000 v.i.s.i. de ES2 con la estación de trabajo Sun-3
Mitsui&Co. Ltd	1988	Especialización: Mitsui diseño de los ASICs y ES2 fabricación de los productos en pequeños lotes
Development Co.	1990	I+D en los mercados de diseño de la EDA y la ASIC

Fuente: Elaboración propia.
* El acuerdo con Etec Systems se denominó Eubeam y el de
Development Co. European CAD Developments Ltd.

ES2 fue uno de los integrantes de los diversos proyectos –ESPRIT, más general y JESSI, más específico–, comenzando por el IDPS, coordinado por Philips International, para proporcionar a la industria informática europea la base de un servicio completo para diseñar y producir en diversas fundiciones sistemas integrados sobre el silicio. El resto de los participantes fueron Bull S.A., Francia; GEC Marconi Electronic Devices Ltd., Reino Unido y Robert Bosch GMBH, Alemania (*CORDIS*, Publications Office of the European Union). Otros dos fueron 5075IDPS Sistema integrado de diseño y producción con Philips International, Robert Bosch, SGS-Thomson Microelectronics, Siemens, Plessey, STC-ICL y Bull, y el proyecto lógico conjunto 5080JPL Philips International, con Plessey, Siemens-Nixdorf, Telefunken Electronic SGS-Thomson Microelectronic, Mietec y Matra-MHS (ESPRIT 1991, 99-100).

European Silicon Structures se sumó a la Iniciativa Tecnológica en BiC-MOS para Aplicaciones (TIBIA), coordinada por Nederlandse Philips Bedrijven BV. Su objetivo era satisfacer las necesidades de componentes de la industria de equipos electrónicos para tecnologías de circuitos integrados bipolares y BiCMOS en la gama de 0,7-0,5 micras, junto con el diseño y la experiencia en CAD para explotar la tecnología. Participaron diecisiete instituciones científicas y diez fabricantes (Anexo 2), entre ellas algunas empresas y centros españoles (*Cordis*, 21 de junio de 1994). Las voces críticas reconocían al programa el gran éxito de aumentar la colaboración transeuropea financiada por la CE, sensible por otra parte a la reducción de la financiación (US Congress, 1991 225-226).

Los programas de investigación europeos trataron de proporcionar una coordinación central a las empresas nacionales europeas y una plataforma para adoptar un enfoque más proactivo en la elaboración de normas para Europa y el mundo (Dataquest's eighth annual European Semiconductor Industry Conference, Munich, 1989, 8).

ES2 tuvo unos ingresos de 19,3 millones de dólares en 1989, un 45% más que el año anterior pero sustancialmente por debajo de la previsión de 100 millones de dólares en cinco años hecha por sus fundadores y se situó en el número uno entre los participantes en los programas de tecnología paneuropeos[32].

---

[32] US Congress (1991, 225). En 1986, Siemens, Philips y Thomson comenzaron a discutir un proyecto sucesor del Mega, que se llamaría Joint European Submicron Silicon Initiative (JESSI). Las propuestas iniciales contemplaban un plan de ocho años con un presupuesto de 3 a 4 mil millones de marcos para desarrollar y diseñar tecnologías de última generación

Como reconoció Saxby, ES2 recaudó un «cargamento de dinero con mucho éxito, tenía una idea fantástica, fracasó en la implementación de la ingeniería, luego se quedó sin dinero… y fue comprada por ATMEL», una empresa californiana que buscaba una base de fabricación europea convertida en líder mundial en el diseño, fabricación y comercialización de semiconductores avanzados (Campbell 2003, 59; Saxby 2012; *Le Monde*, 10 de septiembre de 1995)[33].

European Silicon Structures demostró sus dotes para ajustarse a los requerimientos de la clientela. En el ejemplo que conocemos, el de la empresa Circuits Multi-Projet (CMP), lo consiguió con una combinación de formalidad, presteza e innovación tecnológica. En 1987, ES2 fabricó varias tiradas de circuitos para cuatro proyectos de CMP con un total de 87 circuitos mientras que las otras corrieron a cargo de Matra-Harris-Semi-Conducteurs. A partir de la tirada de CMP C87-3, CMP ejecutó sistemáticamente un comprobador de reglas de diseño en cada circuito antes de la fabricación. A finales de 1986 se estableció un nuevo conjunto de reglas de diseño de CMP que se utilizó para las reglas de diseño del ES2. En 1989, ES2 procesó cinco series de cinco proyectos, reagrupando una cantidad de 92 circuitos, con una reducción del plazo de entrega respecto a 1988 en una semana. En 1991 ES2 participó en 14 proyectos para fabricar un total de 137 circuitos añadiendo una nueva tecnología –CMOS 1.2 micras DLM– a las existentes. En 1994, utilizó la tecnología CMOS de 0,7 micras (Circuits Multi-Projets, 2005 10-13)[34].

de circuitos integrados (Hart 2018, 216). El estratégico JESSI, una iniciativa para restablecer la competitividad europea en microelectrónica, fue uno de los proyectos de colaboración más ambiciosos lanzados en el marco de EUREKA junto con la Televisión de Alta Definición dominada por Alemania (Kassim y Menon (eds.) 2002, 233; Marchipont 1997, 115). Fue considerado el primo ascendente del JESSI, ambos con chips (Leuenberger y Weinstein (eds.) 2012, 28).

[33] Atmel and Virage Logic Grow Partnership for 0.13-micron SoC Designs, *JPR Newswire*, January 21, 2003. En palabras de Saxby, «la visión de la ES2 no pudo hacerse realidad. Y realmente necesitaban un cambio de estrategia empresarial, que consistía en olvidarse de la máquina de haz electrónico y volverse más convencional». Advanced Technology-Memory&Logic (ATMEL), fundada por dos miembros de la familia Perlegos y fondos privados T.C., se especializó en el diseño, fabricación y comercialización de productos analógicos y de alta velocidad (Dataquest, junio de 1988, 113). ES2 vendió la división de CAD a Cadence, donde O'Donnell ayudó a integrar esa división.

[34] A lo largo de veintiséis años –1981 a 2004– CMP realizó proyectos con quince fundiciones y según medio centenar de tecnologías (Circuits Multi-Projets, 2005 101).

3. España y la microelectrónica

El mercado de semiconductores en el conjunto de Europa se multiplicó por 1,5 entre 1980-1986. Las prospecciones lo situaban en una cifra que multiplicaba por 3,3 la de 1980. Entre 1978 y 1989 estuvo permanentemente dominado por la industria norteamericana, que, sin embargo, fue perdiendo cuota de mercado frente al asceso del Japón.

España ocupaba posiciones discretas en Europa Occidental como productor en la industria de los semiconductores –5,5% del total, lejos de Alemania y el Reino Unido (UK)–, y como consumidor, con un 6% (Gráfico 2). Recordemos que este país del sur de Europa estaba a la zaga de los principales países occidentales y era el principal mercado de semiconductores de un grupo de categoría regional, que incluía a los países del sur y del centro (Suiza, Austria, Portugal, Grecia, Malta y Turquía) (Gráfico 3). Varios de los principales fabricantes de telecomunicaciones, procesamiento de datos y electrónica de consumo habían instalado plantas en España, atraídos por los bajos salarios y suelo barato (Dataquest 1990, 15)[35].

Gráfico 2. Mercado total de semiconductores en Europa,
1990 (millones de dólares)

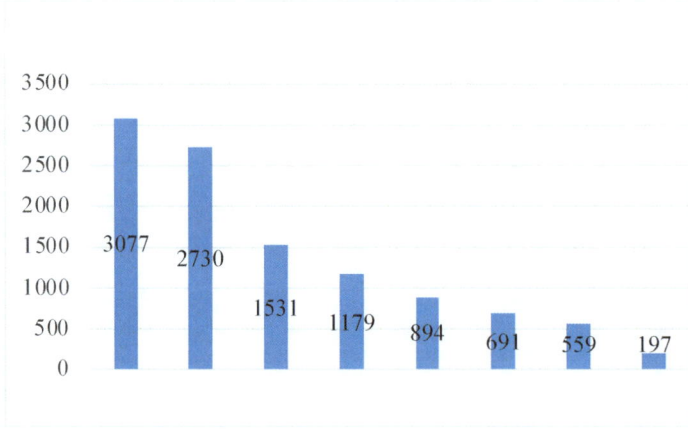

Fuente: Elaboración a partir de Dataquest (septiembre 1991).

---

[35] Portugal, Grecia, Malta y Turquía tenían el 1,67; 0,42; 0,21 y 0,12%, respectivamente, en relación a las cuatro grandes potencias europeas.

Gráfico 3. Mercado de semiconductores en países no centrales de Europa, 1990
(millones de dólares)

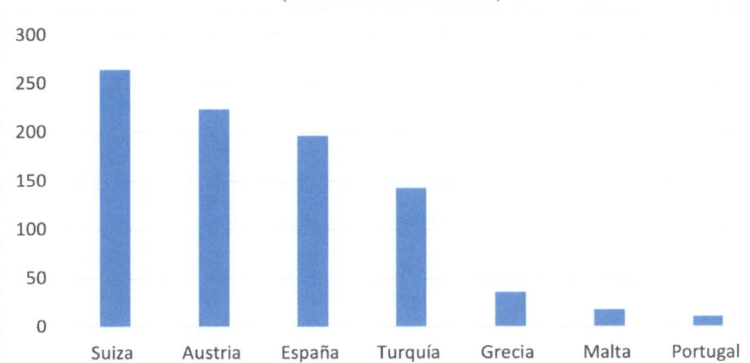

Fuente: Elaboración a partir de Dataquest (septiembre 1991).

Permítasenos reiterar aquí argumentos ya esgrimidos. En España, las primeras iniciativas relativas a la microelectrónica sucumbieron a la incertidumbre y a la ineptitud gubernamental en la primera fase de la transición democrática, después de una prolongada dictadura franquista. Así ocurrió con la misión técnica a Silicon Valley, corazón de la alta tecnología, que impulsó un plan de la norteamericana AMI para establecerse en suelo español. Un destino similar corrió el proyecto de fabricar chips con Motorola como socio tecnológico. La CTNE intentó asimilar el *know-how* enviando técnicos al centro de diseño de Motorola en Suiza, pero a pesar de los avances y la buena puesta a punto, la multinacional declinó ofertas por el poco atractivo del mercado español según el sentir de la empresa. Un fuerte contraste con Italia, dedicada a la cultura del campeón nacional en un contexto de predominio en el mercado mundial[36]. Tampoco prosperó un preacuerdo con la norteamericana Supertex

---

[36] Juan Mulet Melià, conversación con el autor, Barcelona, 16 de mayo de 2013. La multinacional Motorola tenía cinco centros de diseño en Europa: East Kilbride (Escocia), Ginebra (Suiza), Munich (Alemania), Toulouse y Burdeos (Francia) (Fletcher 2013, 129). Motorola –la cuarta en toda la industria de los semiconductores por ingresos después de NEC, Toshiba e Intel y en 2003 la 19ª entre las empresas multinacionales por volumen de inversión en I+D– fue pionera en la introducción del primer microprocesador de 32 bits (MC68020), que contiene 200.000 transistores (Fletcher 2013, 129). Su sección de semiconductores representaba aproximadamente el 30% de sus ventas; un tercio de sus ingresos totales se generaba fuera de los Estados Unidos y se había asignado a la I+D el 7,6-8,3% de sus ingresos (Dataquest 1989, 215). Poco antes de acabar la década de 1980, AMPER creó con Motorola la empresa conjunta de telefonía móvil Telcel —con un 65% de participación de Motorola y un 35% de Amper con un ambicioso plan de inversión industrial y garantías de cogestión. La clave de bóveda la puso la adjudicación de un concurso de ofertas abierto

de Silicon Valley, muy interesada en la infraestructura del Centro Nacional de Microelectrónica, para fabricar chips de alto voltaje para bienes de consumo en España. Según Solana, se inclinó por una ubicación justa en todo el territorio español de las tecnologías de vanguardia para las fábricas, uno de los sitios que se barajaban fue Barcelona, como compensación por los proyectos de AT&T y Fujitsu en Madrid y Málaga[37]. Sin la menor duda, el sector público, representado por el Gobierno y el INI, apareció en los primeros planes para crear una empresa conjunta con AT&T, pero este camino se bloqueó[38].

España fue escenario de varias alianzas internacionales en la industria de la microelectrónica, patrocinadas por el Gobierno, instituciones públicas y empresas. California Micro Devices (CMD), fabricante de componentes electrónicos de alto rendimiento a través de sus divisiones de Thin Film, ASIC y Microcircuitos, acordó con Telefónica formar California Micro Devices Spain. Esta filial debía proveer tecnología y entrenamiento y cerca de 2 millones de dólares e inversión para cerca de un tercio de la titularidad. CMD se encargaría de comercializar sus componentes a clientes militares y civiles, aeroespaciales, médicos, informáticos y de comunicaciones; los productos vendidos en España debían servir a las necesidades de la defensa española[39].

por Telefónica, tras derrotar a Ericsson (Banegas (inédito), 9-12; Calvo 2020, 165-202; Forsgren 2013, 19), *Oral History of Pasquale Pistorio Interviewed by Doug Fairbairn*, 20 de abril de 2010; «Interview with Pasquale Pistorio». *EE Times*, 25, 3, 2005; Queisser 1990, 165; Roche 1992, 186-187.

[37] *Libros de Actas del Consejo de Administración de Telefónica (LACA)*, 28/10/1987; la CTNE comparó el proyecto con una empresa, sin duda Supertex, que se dedicaba al «chip de energía inteligente», con la de AT&T (*Popular Science*, noviembre de 1985, 85; *El País*, 15 de octubre de 1987). A partir de 1986, IBM emprendió una descentralización en etapas sucesivas: transferencia de autoridad a las filiales nacionales; separación de estas en dos grupos según un esquema de magnitud y velocidad de crecimiento del mercado (Francia, Italia y Alemania/resto de Europa) desde el centro de París (Thakur et al. 1997, 304). IBM abrió un Centro de Desarrollo de Software internacional en Barcelona (*LACA*, 28 de octubre de 1987; Smidt y Wever 2012, 39). Ya conocemos la aportación de Telefónica al proyecto Everest para desarrollar herramientas de prueba de chips (*Libros de Actas del Comité Directivo de Telefónica (LACD)*, 30 de enero de 1991; Telefónica, *Acta del Comité Directivo* (ACD), 30 de enero de 1991).

[38] «Acuerdo AT&T-Compañía Telefónica Nacional de España». 26 de julio de 1984, Archivo Histórico del INI.

[39] *TechMonitor*, 6 de abril de 1988. CMD (1980) unió los activos de Capsco Sales (1976), una compañía de películas delgadas, y en 1982 estableció Custom MOS Arrays (CMA), que diseñaba, fabricaba y comercializaba CI y gate arrays basados en células de HCMOS en el rango de 200 a 2.000 puertas antes de fusionarse en 1986 con CMA en una nueva firma. Componentes: componentes pasivos de película delgada para ensamblajes híbridos/matrices de compuertas/conjuntos de CI basados en células y sustratos de cabezales de impresión sin impacto, así como ASIC (Dataquest 1988, 135-137). CMD ofrece un caso típico de

Retomaremos aspectos ya señalados en otro lugar. El mercado español tenía un tamaño similar al austriaco, alrededor de un cuarto del tamaño del grupo total, con la mayoría de los usuarios de los segmentos de consumo, telecomunicaciones y EDP (*European Semiconductor Consumption History and Forecast 1985-1995,* 9). En este país, el Gobierno socialista de turno, tras un tiempo de inercia de los conservadores, concibió planes para impulsar las actividades de producción e investigación con el fin de introducir al país en la corriente principal de la revolución electrónica y potenciar la economía para aumentar la competitividad. Lo hizo segmentando el mercado según el nivel tecnológico. De esta manera, para pasar a la vanguardia los planes implicaban la asociación con líderes tecnológicos multinacionales, mientras que para la tecnología menos sofisticada se recurría a socios tecnológicos nacionales. Desde la empresa, el monopolio de teléfonos, ante el reto del inevitable cambio tecnológico, tenía justo la forma de avanzar con iniciativas en el campo de la microelectrónica. Las personalidades y asociaciones del sector habían sido empujadas en la misma dirección con poco éxito.

La confluencia de todos los esfuerzos desembocó en un plan de acción general –Plan Electrónico e Informático Nacional, PEIN– y proyectos empresariales concretos. Como se señala en el capítulo específico, el principal consistía en atraer inversiones y tecnología de la gigantesca multinacional estadounidense AT&T en una empresa conjunta llamada AT&T Microelectrónica de España, con fábrica e instalaciones de investigación ubicadas en España, una práctica inusual de AT&T. Tanto la CTNE como pionera en la introducción de la microelectrónica y cliente natural de la producción como el Estado como palanca del sector aportaron recursos financieros, apoyo e infraestructura para hacer posible la empresa más avanzada en circuitos integrados altamente sofisticados (Calvo 2016; Majó 1997).

Esta no fue la única iniciativa de la CTNE en el sector, sino que combinó esta empresa conjunta con otras de características diferentes. Conviene recordar una vez más, en pocas palabras dichas por uno de los protagonistas, que la CTNE utilizó su enorme poder adquisitivo y de inversión para hacer política industrial[40].

---

fraude con una docena o más trucos contables, incluyendo ventas ficticias y reconocimiento ficticio de ingresos (un tercio de los 45 millones de dólares de ingresos de la compañía en 1994 eran espúreos) (Securities Exchange Commission 1999; MacDonald 2000; Jones 2011 [sp]). La compañía fue engullida por ON Semiconductor en busca de tamaño y escala para competir con éxito (*Onsemi*, 14 de diciembre de 2009).

[40] Conversación del autor con Luis Solana. Madrid: 8 de marzo de 2016.

La CTNE era una empresa clave en la economía nacional debido a la abultada cifra de abonados –8,5 millones– o usuarios (varios millones), empleo –61.500– y ventas –380.000 miles de millones de pesetas–. Su decisivo peso también se derivaba de las grandes inversiones anuales – 180.000 millones – y su inmovilizado neto de 1,3 billones de pesetas (Morán y Lada 1984).

Como también queda apuntado en otro lugar, el monopolio semipúblico español puso en marcha un plan cuatrienal que pretendía reestructurar la industria y los servicios de telecomunicaciones con una inversión colosal de unos 800.000 millones de pesetas, la mitad de los cuales se destinaron a la red telefónica. El crecimiento cuantitativo se unió a la modernización de los equipos con tecnología electrónica y semieléctrica y al inicio de la adopción de la fibra óptica[41].

En el marco del plan de inversiones de la CTNE, las asociaciones con empresas que poseían conocimientos parecían inevitables. Debido a la aplicación del plan, la inversión efectiva de la CTNE en 1985 casi se duplicó en comparación con la del año anterior[42].

La CTNE se unió el 26 de diciembre al grupo inicial de siete empresas de alta tecnología involucradas en European Silicon Structures para desarrollar y fabricar una forma de circuitos integrados y poner ese producto de alta tecnología al alcance de las pequeñas empresas: Bosch, British Aerospace, Olivetti, Saab Scania, Bull, Philips y Brown Boveri[43]. Estos socios eran clientes y proveedores de información sobre mercados y tecnología al mismo tiempo que receptores de capacitación sobre las posibles aplicaciones de los productos de ES2. Se unieron a los tres grandes objetivos estratégicos, quizás el más importante de los cuales era la expectativa de que los productos y la tecnología de ES2 ejercieran de catalizadores de la innovación a largo plazo. La inversión también buscaba la rentabilidad y el acceso a una instalación de fabricación de silicio de vanguardia a un costo y nivel de riesgo bajos[44]. En este

---

[41] Más de dos millones de líneas y enlaces urbanos equivalentes a unas 700.000 líneas; 56 km de fibra óptica (*El País*, 23 de octubre de 1983).

[42] Comparecencia, *DSCD*, 10 de octubre de 1984, 6.498-6.526 (*The Telefonica Group*, 1985, 40).

[43] *Le Monde*, 28 de diciembre de 1985. Algunas fuentes excluyeron a Bosch, señalado como miembro de Saab-Scania Combitech, una filial electrónica del grupo automotor y aeroespacial sueco, y añadieron a Advent, una empresa de capital de riesgo. British Aerospace consideró que la empresa European Silicon Structures representaba un nuevo e importante enfoque de la colaboración europea en una industria de alta tecnología vital (*British Business*, 20, 1986, 3).

[44] *MBDoT*, 18 de diciembre de 1985; Telefónica, *Memoria, Balance Social 1984-1985*, 156. Con anterioridad ya se ha señalado la fundición de los chips personalizados.

grupo de sello europeo, la CTNE era la única empresa de telecomunicaciones por su fundación, su sede, su centro de investigación y su fábrica.

La operadora participó con el 5% de las acciones de la empresa paneuropea ES2, el máximo tolerado a los participantes en el proyecto para evitar cualquier otra presión (*PRS* 1985, 40)[45]. Al presentarlo en el mercado español, la CTNE dijo que estaba destinado a servir a los circuitos de mercado personalizados y de fabricación en Europa en términos y precios más bajos que los prototipos existentes. El papel de Telefónica se resumía en tutelar la introducción en España de estos componentes a través de Comelta y Semiconductores S. A., especializada en la distribución y comercialización de componentes electrónicos. Por otro lado, Telefónica debía proporcionar asesoramiento técnico a ambas empresas, completar las solicitudes de diseño y ofrecer cursos de formación precisos.

Tabla 3. Vista comparativa de los perfiles de AT&T y ES2

	AT&T Microelectrónica de España	ES2
Ciudad/País	Madrid, España	Rousset, France
Productos	CBIC customs	CBIC, Arrays, Custom mil
Tecnología de procesos	CMOS M2	CMOS M2
Mínimo Ancho de línea	1.25	0.80
Tamaño de la oblea	6	5
Capacidad máx. Capacidad de la oblea	14,000	1,000
S. Q. en capacidad de arranque (4 semanas)	383,320	19020
Sala limpia (pies cuadrados)	25,000	0
Clase de sala limpia	1	10/1
Origen del propietario	USA	Paneuropea
Estructura del mercado	Merchant	Merchant

Fuente: Elaboración propia a partir de European Fab Database
CBIC: Circuitos integrados basados en células. Un dispositivo ASIC que se hace a medida utilizando un juego completo de máscaras y que utiliza la colocación automática de células y el encaminamiento automático.

---

[45] Telefónica aportó 2,5 millones de dólares y poseía 45.000 acciones del total en manos de socios españoles, también compuestos por los principales bancos –Banesto, Bilbao, Hispano, Santander y Urquijo-Unión- (*MBDOT*, 26 de noviembre de 1986). La prensa redujo la contribución de España al 4% (*El País*, 19 de noviembre de 1986).

Desde una visión comparativa, la participación de Telefónica en Microelectrónica de España y ES2 presenta varias diferencias importantes. Las más puramente técnicas, contenidas en la Tabla 3, indican que no compitieron en el mismo mercado ya que ES2 se basó en series cortas y AT&T en largas[46]. Entre otras muy notables se encuentran algunas relacionadas con la escala, la naturaleza de la Alianza, la forma de financiación, el papel de la CTNE en la empresa conjunta y la representación territorial de la iniciativa. Microelectrónica de España es el resultado de un acuerdo bilateral entre el monopolio semipúblico Telefónica y la multinacional AT&T bajo la importante dirección política de los gobiernos por varias razones, entre ellas la económica y geoestratégica. A diferencia de lo que ocurrió con ES2, el Gobierno español ayudó a Microelectrónica de España con subvenciones, recursos financieros y fiscales, así como con infraestructuras como contrapartida de la localización de la actividad productiva de Microelectrónica de España y su fiscalidad en territorio español. Microelectrónica de España fue un caso de atracción de IED frente al capital de exportación en el de ES2. El mercado integrado para ES2 y los mercados nacionales e internacionales españoles para MEdE fue la fórmula adoptada. La integración de Telefónica en el proyecto tuvo un carácter subordinado a pesar de la aparente igualdad de participación, a juzgar por la ausencia casi total de españoles en la gestión de ES2[47]. MEdE era una empresa conjunta con participación desigual de los socios y, por lo tanto, con diferentes niveles de control sobre la empresa por parte de los miembros.

---

[46] Característica destacada por *Le Monde*, 28 de diciembre de 1985.

[47] Como excepción, Carlos A. López Barrio ha sido presidente del Comité de Socios Estratégicos de ES2 y miembro del Consejo de Administración de esta empresa. López Barrio era Catedrático de Tecnología Electrónica de la Universidad Politécnica de Madrid y Director del Laboratorio de Sistemas Integrados (Departamento de Ingeniería Electrónica) (Kabene 2010, 344).

Tabla 4. Los diez principales proveedores mundiales de CBIC
MOS Digital por ingresos (millones de dólares)

Proveedores	Ingresos			
	1987	1988	1989	Ranking 1989
VLSI Technology	15	22	29	1
Austria Mikro Systeme	13	16	24	2
Texas Instruments	5	12	24	3
European Silicon Structures	6	12	17	4
MEDL	5	11	17	5
Siemens	15	15	17	6
SGS-Thomson	2	3	15	7
AT&T	6	9	10	8
Harris Semiconductor	4	8	10	9
Honeywell/Atmel	0	0	10	10

Fuente: Dataquest, enero de 1991.

Gráfico 4. Los 10 principales provedores de MOS CBIC digitales
según ingresos, 1987-1989 (millones de dólares).

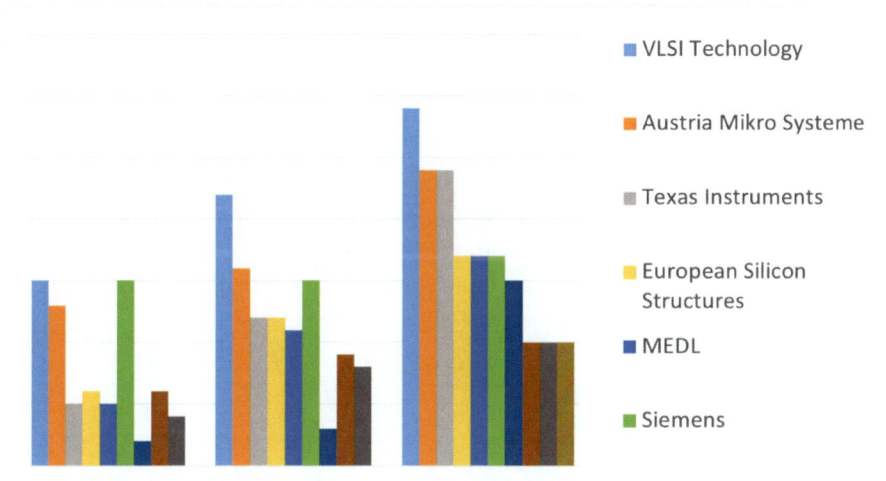

Fuente: Elaboración propia a partir de Dataquest, enero de 1991.

4. Conclusión

En el transcurso de las dos últimas décadas del siglo XX, la agudización de la competencia obligó a las empresas a adoptar medidas que les permitieran afrontar los nuevos retos en condiciones óptimas. Una modalidad de respuesta fueron las alianzas estratégicas internacionales. En este capítulo se ha abordado como estudio de caso una de las forjadas en Europa, que tiene la peculiaridad de apartarse de la práctica imperante al ser impulsada por socios exclusivamente europeos.

Los gobiernos europeos deseosos de promover industrias competitivas en sus respectivos países, las elites empresariales y la voracidad del capital unieron sus fuerzas en proyectos industriales de alta tecnología en el marco de la creación de un mercado único. Sin duda, uno de los más característicos fue el encarnado por ES2, una iniciativa paneuropea en el campo de la microelectrónica y los semiconductores. Los resultados distaron mucho de las ambiciones de los planes iniciales, pero muy posiblemente, dejaron huella en la configuración de las características diferenciales de la industria europea con respecto a la norteamericana y la japonesa.

Puso a prueba la capacidad europea −insuficiente, por otro lado− para movilizar recursos de diverso tipo, buscar alternativas, coordinar esfuerzos fronteras afuera de los países y llegar a acuerdos sobre una problemática de importancia capital cual es la independencia tecnológica respecto a otras potencias mundiales. En los márgenes del eje central del proyecto, España desempeñó un papel de participante secundario mediante la participación de la CTNE, monopolio de las telecomunicaciones a punto de desaparecer como tal para ajustarse a las normas comunitarias. La CTNE utilizó en general su poder de compra y de inversión como herramienta de política industrial, pero a diferencia de este camino, en el caso estudiado −European Silicon Structures− lo empleó como medio de acción colectiva internacional, aspecto no siempre puesto de relieve de forma conveniente.

Anexo 1. Junta Directiva de European Silicon Structures, 1988

Nombre	Cargo	Empresa anterior	Cargo anterior
J.L. Grand-Clement	CEO/MngDir	Motorola	VP Europe Group
Pierre Lesieur	VPFin/Admin	Motorola	Dir Finance
Rod Attwooll	VP/DirOps	Texas Instrument	Mng Dir Bedford
Bernard Pruniaux	VP/Mfg	Thomson CSF	Dir Opns
John Gray	VP/DirS/ WTech	Lattice Logic	Founder/Mng Dir
J.P. Demange	VP/DirS.Europe	National	Dir Strat Mktg
H.P. Friedrich	VP/DirCentra Europe	N/A	Mng Dir
Francis Courrèges	WfrFabMgr	Sierra Semicond	Prod Eng Mgr
Eric Demoulin	DirTechnology	Thomson CSF	Dir MOS Tech

Fuente: Elaboración a partir de Dataquest, junio de 1988, 205.

Anexo 2. Participantes en la Iniciativa Tecnológica en BiCMOS para Aplicaciones (TIBIA)

Empresas

Semiconductores Investigación y Diseño, Tres Cantos España; Telefónica I+D, España; Alcatel Bell Manufacturing Company, Bélgica; Alcatel SEL AG, Alemania; GEC Plessey Semiconductors PLC, Reino Unido; Philips Consumer Electronics B.V., Holanda; SGS Thomson Microelectronics SA, Francia; SGS-Thomson Microelectronics SrL, Italia; Siemens AG, Alemania; Temic Telefunken Microelectronic GMBH, Alemania.

Instituciones científicas

Centro Nacional de Microelectrónica, Bellaterra, España; Centre National d'Études des Télécommunications (CNET); Commissariat à l'Énergie Atomique (CEA) y Centre d'Études de Grenoble, Francia; Delft Institute of Microelectronics & Submicrontechnology, Holanda; École Polytechnique Fédérale de Lausanne, Suiza; Industrial Microelectronics Center y Linkoeping University (Suecia); Instituto de Engenharia de Sistemas e Computadores, Portugal; Inter University Microelectronics Center, Bélgica; National Technical University of Athens, Grecia; Siemens Entwicklungszentrum fuer Mikroelektronik, Austria; Technical Research Centre of Finland, Finlandia; Technische Universitaet Berlin, Alemania; Tecnopolis Csata Novus Ortus; NMRC, University College Cork y University of Dublin, Irlanda; SCRL y Università di Catania, Italia (*Cordis*, 21 de junio de 1994).

Fuentes primarias

Archivo Histórico del INI, Madrid.
Securities Exchange Commission, US.
Telefónica, *Actas del Consejo de Administración*, Madrid.
Telefónica, *Actas del Comité Directivo*, Madrid.

Fuentes orales

Computer History Museum, Mountain View, USA.
Jesús Banegas, Conversaciones con el autor, 2020.
Juan Mulet Melià, Conversación con el autor, Barcelona
Luis Solana, Conversación con el autor. Madrid: 8 de marzo de 2016.
Oral History of Pasquale Pistorio Interviewed by Doug Fairbairn.

Referencias

Banegas, Jesús. 2002. *La nueva economía española: impactos de las tecnologías de la información y la comunicación en la economía y la sociedad.* Madrid: Universidad Complutense de Madrid (cortesía del autor).

Banegas, Jesús. «Memorias Profesionales» [manuscrito inédito (cortesía del autor)], recogidas en Banegas, Jesús. 2023. *Memorias de un tiempo feliz.* Madrid: Bubok, 115-187.

Bernstein, Michael A. y Adler David E. (eds.) 1994. *Understanding American Economic Decline.* Cambridge MA: Cambridge University Press.

Bentarzi, Hamid. 2011. *Transport in Metal-Oxide-Semiconductor Structures.* Berlín: Springer.

Bonno, G. «Des puces sur mesure». *L'Observateur* [1986]: 82.

Brooke, Peter A. y Penrice, Daniel A. 2009. *Vision for Venture Capital: Realizing the Promise of Global Venture Capital and Private Equity.* Boston: UPNE.

Calvo, Ángel. 2020. «Tecnología autóctona y oligopolio en el sector de las telecomunicaciones: Amper, 1980-2003». *Revista de Historia Industrial* 29(79), julio: 165-202.

Calvo, Ángel. 2014. *Standard Eléctrica y la industria de las telecomunicaciones en España, 1877-1975.* Barcelona: Ariel.

Campbell, Katharine. 2003. *Smarter Ventures: A Survivor's Guide to Venture Capital.* Londres: Pearson Education.

Circuits Multi-Projets. 2005. *Annual Report 2005.*

Collins, Timothy M. y Doorley, Thomas L. 1994. *Teaming Up for the '90s: A Guide to International Joint Ventures and Strategic Alliances.* Homewood IL: McGraw-Hill School Education Group.

Cowhey, Peter F. y Aronson, Jonathan D. 1993. *Managing the world economy: the consequences of corporate alliances.* Nueva York: Council on Foreign Relations Press.

Daim, Tugrul U. et al. (eds.). 2014. *Technology Development: Multidimensional Review for Engineering and Technology Managers.* Cham: Springer.

Dang, Rani Jeanne y Longhi, Christian. 2009. «Clusters and Cluster Strategies: The Case of the 'Secure Communicating Solutions' Competitiveness Cluster». *Revue d'économie industrielle*, 4, n°.128: 121-152.

Dataquest. 1991. *Semiconductors Europe.* San José: Dataquest.

Dataquest. 1990a. *European Semiconductor Market Share Estimates Final 1989.* San José: Dataquest.

Dataquest. 1990b. *European semiconductor consumption forecast 1983-1995.* San José: Dataquest.

Dataquest. 1991. *A European Semiconductor Industry Service Report.* San José: Dataquest.

Dataquest. 1988. *A decade of semiconductor companies.* San José: Dataquest.

Dataquest. 1987. *IC Startups 1987: The Next Generation* San José: Dataquest.

Dataquest. 1989. *Worldwide Semiconductor Companies.* San José: Dataquest.

Daviet, Sylvie. 1999. «Micro-électronique en Provence. Une redéfinition de l'industrie par le territoire». *Méditerranée*, 92: 33-40.

Dodgson, Mark. (ed.) 1989. *Technology Strategy and the Firm: Management and Public Policy.* Nueva York: Longman.

Dornbusch, Fraunhofer. 2018. *Global competition in microelectronics industry from a European perspective: Technology, markets and implications for industrial policy.* Leipzig: Fraunhofer, marzo: 1-37.

Dosi, Giovani. 2000. *Innovation, Organization and Economic Dynamics: Selected Essays.* Cheltenham: Edward Elgar.

Dubocage, Emmanuelle y Rivaud-Danset, Dorothée. 2002. *The development of venture capital in Europe*, on-line. En Masuyama, Seichi y Vander Drink, Donna (eds). *Development of capital markets and their governance. Toky Club Papers*, n°16: 69-113

Dunning, John H. 2001. «The eclectic (OLI) paradigm of international production: Past, present and future». *International Journal of the Economics of Business* 8 (2): 173-190.

ESPRIT. 1991. *Progress and results 1990/91.* Luxemburgo: Commission of the European Communities.

Fagen, Richard R. (ed.) 1979. *Capitalism and the State in U.S.-Latin American Relations.* Stanford: Stanford University Press.

Faulhaber, Gerald R. y Tamburini, Gualtiero. 2012. *European Economic Integration: The Role of Technology.* Nueva York: Springer.

Forester, Tom. 1989. *High-Tech Society. The Story of the Information Technology Revolution.* Cambridge MA. MIT Press.

Forsgren, Mats. 2013. *Theories of the Multinational Firm. A Multidimensional Creature in the Global Economy.* Cheltenham: Edward Elgar.

Friedrichs, Günter y Schaf, Adam. (eds.) 1982. *Microelectronics and society for better or for worse, a report to the Club of Rome.* Nueva York: Pergamon.

Friend, Julius W. 1998. *The Long Presidency, France in the Mitterrand Years, 1981-1995.* Boulder CO: Westview Press.

Guile, Bruce R. 1987. *Technology and Global Industry, Companies and Nations in the World Economy.* Washington: National Academies Press.

Harding, Byron. 1991. «European Semiconductor Market Overview», *Dataquest's European Semiconductor Industry Conference*, Dataquest, Marbella, 66-89.

Hart, Jeffrey A. 2018. *Rival Capitalists: International Competitiveness in the United States, Japan, and Western Europe.* Ithaca y Londres: Cornell University Press.

Hill, Charles W. L, et al. 2016. *Strategic Management, Theory, An Integrated Approach.* Boston MA: Cengage Learning.

Hussein Kassim y Anand, Menon (eds.) 2002. *The European Union and National Industrial Policy*. Londres: Routledge.

Johanson, Jan y Vahlne, Jan-Erik. 2009. «The Uppsala internationalization process model revisited: From liability of foreignness to liability of outsidership». *Journal of International Business Studies* 40 (9): 1.411-1.431.

Jones, Michael J. 2011. *Creative Accounting, Fraud and International Accounting Scandals*. Chichester: John Wiley & Sons.

Jones, Phil L. y Buckley, Anne. 1989. *Electronics Computer Aided Design*. Manchester: Manchester University Press.

Kabene, Stéfane M. 2010. *Human Resources in Healthcare, Health Informatics and Healthcare Systems*. Nueva York: Idea Group Inc.

Khanna, Dan M. 1997. *The Rise, Decline, and Renewal of Silicon Valley's High*. Nueva York: Garland.

Klincewicz, Krzysztof. 2005. *Strategic Alliances in the High-tech Industry*. Berlín: Logos Verlag.

Langlois, Richard N. y Steinmueller, Edward. 2000. «Strategy and circumstance: the response of American firms to Japanese competition in semiconductors, 1980-1995». *Strategic Management Journal* 21: 1.163-1.173.

Leuenberger, Theodor y Weinstein, Martin E., 2012. *Europe, Japan and America in the 1990s, Cooperation and Competition*. Berlín: Springer.

Lipnack, Jessica y Stamps, Jeffrey 1993. *The Team Net Factor, Bringing the Power of Boundary Crossing Into the Heart of Your Business*. Essex: Wiley.

MacDonald, Elizabeth 2000. «Regulators seek to penalize auditors who missed fraud». *Wall Street Journal*, 19 de febrero.

Majó, Joan. 1997. *Chips, cables y poder*. Barcelona: Planeta.

Marchipont, Jean-François. 1997. *La stratégie industrielle de l'Union européenne. Conséquences et enjeux*. París: Éditions Continent Europe.

Meister, Jeanne C. 2001. *Building a learning organization, 7 lessons to involve your CEO*. San José: iUniverse.

Morán, José M. y Lada, Luis. 1984. «Los planes de Telefónica». *El País*, 2 de mayo.

Mosakowski, P. M. 1990. «Recent trends in start-up activity». *Solid State Technology*, agosto [sp].

Mytelka, Lynn K. 1990. *Strategic Partnerships, States, Firms, and International Competition*. Londres: Pinter.

Office of Microelectronics and Instrumentation. 1985. *A Competitive assessment of the U.S. semiconductor manufacturing equipment industry*. Washington: U.S. G.P.O.

Okada, Yoshitaka. 2006. «Decline of the Japanese Semiconductor Industry: Institutional Restrictions and the Disintegration of Techno-Governance». En *Struggles for Survival*, editado por Okada, Yoshitaka. Tokyo: Springer. https://doi.org/10.1007/4-431-28916-X_3

Ó Uallacháin, Breandan. 1997. «Restructuring the American Semiconductor Industry: Vertical Integration of Design Houses and Wafer Fabricators». *Annals of the Association of American Geographers*, 87, n°. 2: 217-237.

Ozawa, Terutomo. 1974. *Japan's Technological Challenge to the West, 1950–1974, Motivation and Accomplishment*. Cambridge: MIT Press.

Papers Commissioned for a Workshop on the Federal Role in Research and Development. 1985. Washington: National Academies Press.

Pérez, Carlota. 1985. «Microelectronics, long waves and world structural change, New perspectives for developing countries». *World Development* 13, n°.3: 441-463.

Porter, Michael E. y Fuller, Mark B. 1986. «Coalitions and Global Strategy». En *Competition in Global Industries*, editado por Porter, Michael E. Boston MA: Harvard Business Press, 366-373.

Poudroux, Noël. 1968. «La micro-électronique europeenne face aux États-Unis». *Le Monde diplomatique*, 22 de diciembre.

Profiles. 1998. *A Worldwide Survey of IC Manufacturers and Suppliers*, 2-446.

PRS. 1988, *Report Science & Technology, Europe & Latin America*, 26 de enero.

Sandholtz, Wayne. 1992. *High-Tech Europe. The Politics of International Cooperation*. Berkeley: University of California Press.

Sautter, Chistian. 1987. *Les dents du géant: le Japon à la conquête du monde*. París: Olivier Orban.

Saxby, Robin. 2012. Interviewed by Dane Elliot and Doug Fairbairn, *Oral History of Sir Robin Saxby*. Mountain View, California, 16 de octubre.

Smidt, Marc de y Wever, Egbert. 2012. *The Corporate Firm in a Changing World Economy, Case Studies in the Geography of Enterprise*. Abingdon: Routledge.

Thakur, Manab et al. 1997. *International Management, Concepts and Cases*. Nueva Delhi: McGraw-Hill.

United States Committee on Science, Space, and Technology. 1989. *Europe 1992 and Its Effects on U.S. Science, Technology, and Competitiveness: Hearings*, U.S.

House of Representatives, One Hundred First Congress, First Session, May 16, 17, vol. 4.

US Congress. 1991. *Competing economies, America, Europe, and the Pacific Rim*. Washington: DIANE Publishing.

Vasudeva, P. K. 2006. *International Marketing*. Nueva Delhi: Excel Books.

Watson, J. 2016, *Mastering Electronics*, Londres: Macmillan International Higher Education: Londres.

Wedgwood, C. G. (ed.) 2013. *European Electronics Directory 1994, Systems and Applications*. Oxford: Elsevier.

Wedgwood, C. G. 2013. *International Electronics Directory '90: The Guide to European Manufacturers, Agents and Applications*. Londres: Elsevier.

Weinstein, Joshua I. 2009. «The Market in Plato's *Republic*». *Classical Philology*, 104: 439–458.

Yin, Robert K. 1993. *Applications of case study research. Applied Social Research Series*, vol. 34. Londres: Sage.

3. La tecnología avanzada en el sector público: la división electrónica del INI

1. Introducción

La profunda y en todos los sentidos devastadora recesión mundial de los últimos años ha revitalizado un debate ya existente desde antiguo sobre el diferente impacto de las crisis en cuanto a ritmo, magnitud y forma en que se tomaron las decisiones de reestructuración de sectores industriales, reflejo del diverso estado del desarrollo económico y de las características institucionales, en particular el papel del estado y el sistema de relaciones industriales (Eurofound 2015; Rose et al. 2000, 601-625)[1].

En este sentido, el análisis de las características diferenciales de las empresas de alta tecnología se ha visto a veces afectado por prejuicios sobre la intervención estatal. El capítulo recupera el debate central sobre el modelo de crecimiento y las características de las empresas estatales y su eficiencia relativa, que alcanzó su punto álgido durante los años ochenta y comienzos de la década siguiente pero que todavía sigue vivo[2].

---

[1] En sus *Directrices sobre ayudas estatales de salvamento y de reestructuración de empresas en crisis* de 1994, modificadas en 1999 y 2004, y prorrogadas hasta octubre de 2012, la Comisión Europea consideraba en crisis una empresa condenada a desaparecer a corto o medio plazo sin una intervención del estado (Comisión Europea 2014, 3 y 5).

[2] Vickers y Yarrow (1988), Pestieau y Tulkens (1993) y Martin y Parker (1997), entre una extensa bibliografía recopilada por Argimón, Artola y González-Páramo (1997, 5-6). A modo de ejemplo, Bös (1986) y (1988, 409-414) analizó varias preguntas clave: las interdependencias con la economía privada; ajuste a precios monopolistas en el sector privado, así como a mercados racionados; gerentes de empresas públicas y relaciones sindicales; maximización de la producción o ingresos, recursos energéticos e índices de precios.

Una investigación en treinta países europeos durante el periodo comprendido entre 2010 y 2016 concluye que las empresas estatales (SOE) no son positivas ni negativas en sí para el crecimiento. El efecto de crecimiento de las empresas públicas mejora significativamente con la calidad institucional del país (Szarzec, Dombi y Matuszak 2021, 1-20). Por el contrario, otros encuentran un rendimiento inferior de las SOEs con respecto a las empresas privadas y, concretamente, una tendencia a ser menos rentables que las empresas de propiedad privada. Sin embargo, parecen depender más de la deuda para sus necesidades financieras y, por tanto, están mejor apalancadas. Además, las empresas públicas son más intensivas en mano de obra y tienen mayores costes laborales (Phi et al. 2019).

Estudios de la European Commission (2016, 1-2) introducen en el debate los factores geográficos y sectoriales y señalan que en la UE, la rentabilidad de las empresas públicas en sectores de red clave como la energía y los ferrocarriles se mantuvo positiva y bastante estable a lo largo de la crisis, aunque con diferencias a nivel nacional y subsectorial. En los nuevos Estados miembros, con una mayor presencia del sector público en varios sectores económicos, el rendimiento de las empresas privadas superó, en la mayoría de los casos, sustancialmente al de las empresas públicas. Sin embargo, la rentabilidad de estas últimas parece haber resistido mejor la crisis. La gobernanza de las empresas públicas es importante para su rendimiento.

Algo similar, por otro lado, ha sucedido con el interminable debate académico sobre la reestructuración de las empresas estatales, relanzado en su día con la transición de la planificación central a las economías de mercado, para muchos el mayor experimento social en los tiempos modernos, cebado por la oleada de privatizaciones al abrigo del consenso de Washington y llevado a ignición por el creciente peso de algunas BRICS o economías emergentes (Hare y Turley 2013; Radygin y Entov 2012, 4-30; Abramov et al. 2017, 1-23; OECD 2009)[3].

---

[3] Más allá de reseñar los principales defensores de la empresa pública –Vickers y Yarrow (1988); Martin y Parker (1997) y, más recientemente, Mazzucato (2013)–, resulta inviable incluir aquí ni siquiera un resumen de la bibliografía sobre el debate en torno a la pretendida ineficiencia de la empresa pública, por lo que remitimos a un estudio específico: Hernández (2004), 13-21. Un recorrido histórico sobre las corrientes dominantes, en Musacchio y Lazzarini (2014). Una organización africana especializada atribuía al estado las funciones de instaurar un entorno regulatorio junto a una política de competencia apropiados y de proporcionar servicios dentro de un marco de existencia de otros alternativos con voluntad de garantizar el nivel más apropiado posible en la participación del sector privado (Parliamentary Monitoring Group 2000).

Un debate, por cierto, que en España tuvo abundantes ramificaciones, algunas desde aportaciones de evidencia empírica[4].

Puede merecer la pena considerar particularmente para nuestro caso la controversia sobre la privatización desde un enfoque interdisciplinario, que tiene aportaciones notables. En España, el debate se basó a menudo en contribuciones que colocaron la tecnología avanzada en el centro, mientras que al mismo tiempo destacaron el papel del estado y los riesgos de la dependencia tecnológica[5].

Sin duda por razones de visibilidad, el estudio de la reconversión industrial llevada a cabo en España se ha centrado en los aspectos generales de las políticas de reconversión, a veces a cargo de protagonistas destacados de esos procesos[6], y en sectores energéticos y de equipo pesado. Las industrias avanzadas de Tercera Revolución Industrial han quedado, si no olvidadas, sí, al menos, marginadas de la atención de los estudiosos. Este aserto se refiere en particular a las tecnologías de la información y la comunicación, cuyo interés, sin embargo, ha aumentado entre los investigadores de historia empresarial (Haigh 2001)[7].

[4] Recogidas a satisfacción por Hernández (2004), 13-21. Resulta esclarecedora la reproducción del debate en el Parlamento español y la confrontación entre la posición conservadora –el Estado óptimo se asimila al Estado mínimo– y la del gobierno, en manos del partido socialista, que subrayaba la realidad de la competencia oligopólica, la información asimétrica e imperfecta en los mercados, la importante fuente de ganancia de las economías externas y la frecuencia de las economías de escala (Ministro de Industria y Energía (Eguiagaray Ucelay), *Diario de Sesiones*, Congreso de los Diputados, Pleno y Diputación Permanente, 161, 4/7/1995, Comunicación del Gobierno sobre la política del sector público empresarial, 8.575).

[5] Entre una larga lista, véase Buesa y Molero (1986); Molero (1988) y López (1992, 30-55).

[6] Aranzadi (1987), 162-163 y (1989), 258-261; Aranzadi et al. (1983), 317-325; Boyer (2004), 239-304; Fernández Marugán (1992), 135-194; García (1989), 262-276; Guerra y Tezanos (1992); Solchaga (2017).

[7] La historia empresarial es uno de los enfoques más relevantes seguidos por James Cortada, que trata la historia de la computación (Cortada, 1996a y 1996b), y predomina en Batiz-Lazo y Boyns (2004, 225-232) y Batiz-Lazo (2009, 1-27). De gran relevancia son los enfoques interdisciplinarios: la historia de las empresas de informática se une con el desarrollo de tecnologías clave de la informática en Campbell-Kelly et al. (2014); Akera (2008) mezcla la historia de los negocios con varios géneros históricos: la biografía y la historia institucional de la ciencia; finalmente, Riordan y Hoddeson (1997) y Reid (2001) resumen la historia de la ingeniería electrónica y la historia empresarial de la industria electrónica y el circuito integrado. IBM domina ampliamente en las monografías dedicadas a empresas individuales. La visión general del desarrollo de la empresa, basada en fuentes de archivo (Pugh, 1994), se centra en las relaciones entre las posiciones de mercado de IBM, las tecnologías y la dinámica interna. Dos monografías dedicadas a compañías individuales distintas de IBM son las de Campbell-Kelly (1989) sobre ICL y de Norberg (2005) sobre dos de las primeras empresas nuevas en la industria –Eckert Mauchly Computer Co. Enginee-

Este capítulo pretende atenuar esta situación injusta y examinar la reestructuración de las empresas del sector público en España, centrándose en el *holding* de las Tecnologías de la Información y la Comunicación (TIC) del Instituto Nacional de Industria (INI)[8].

Los temas tratados se refieren a la reestructuración en un sector clave con empresas intensivas en I+D. En cuanto a la metodología, el capítulo describe los cambios que han tenido lugar en el sector de las TIC en dos aspectos relacionados: estrategia y estructura organizativa. De naturaleza preponderantemente descriptiva, conjuga la historia industrial pero también el *management* estratégico, utiliza fuentes primarias tanto de origen público como privado, a la vez que se nutre de informes y estudios de grandes organizaciones internacionales. Así pues, pertenece a la categoría de un estudio de caso, contextualizado dentro de un debate más amplio sobre privatización y reestructuración en Europa occidental.

El capítulo se estructura en cuatro grandes apartados, que comprenden la introducción, una presentación del sector público de las tecnologías de la información y la comunicación, la reestructuración del sector público de las TIC y el nacimiento del grupo Inisel, llamado a ejercer un papel importante en el futuro por su protagonismo en la creación de Indra.

Antes de avanzar, conviene sentar una serie de consideraciones preliminares sobre el contenido y ámbito del tema tratado en aras del mejor seguimiento del relato. En primer lugar, la información y la comunicación corresponden a industrias y empresas que usan de forma intensiva tecnologías punta, singularmente la electrónica (Mohr et al. 2009, 9). En cuanto al tamaño, en la industria electrónica española predominaron las pequeñas y medianas unidades, como se verá oportunamente[9].

---

ring Research Associates–. que se fusionaron para formar UNIVAC. Un intento de superar la visión periodística dominante en la historia de Microsoft: Fisher et al. (1983); desde la economía evolutiva: Lechman (2015); Garretsen y Brakman (2005). Un análisis según la metodología del muestreo –casi dos centenares de respuestas a cuestionarios, obtenidas en las tres regiones españolas que concentran el grueso de la industria electrónica (Madrid, Cataluña y País Vasco)– y desde la óptica de los clusters: Rama y Holl (2009), 182-204.

[8] Avances de algunos resultados fueron presentados en el Seminario de la UCM, 2017 y en la sesión «Industrialización, desindustrialización y reindustrialización en España». XII Congreso de AEHE. Lecciones de la historia reciente», ambos organizados por José L. García Ruiz y Jesús Mª Valdaliso a quienes agradezco la favorable acogida de mi aportación. A esta me remito para una mayor elaboración teórica sobre la política industrial y referencias más amplias a la bibliografía existente. Una versión preliminar fue publicada en Calvo (2019), 142-179.

[9] Solo había una en la lista de las cincuenta mayores en 1982, una de las veinticinco mayores en 1992 y cinco de las cien mayores (Buesa 1994, 12).

Respecto a las precisiones terminológicas, de acuerdo con la OCDE, las empresas estatales o SOE, se caracterizan por el control significativo mantenido por el estado a través de la propiedad total, mayoritaria o minoritaria significativa. Tal definición comprende las empresas que son propiedad del gobierno central o federal, así como las empresas estatales de los gobiernos regionales y locales (Sturesson et al. 2015, 8)[10].

En este sentido, el valor de las empresas estatales en el área de la OCDE rebasaba los 2 trillones de dólares y el empleo superaba los 6 millones de personas. Pero su importancia viene determinada no solo por el peso que tienen en la economía productiva (promedio del 2.5% del empleo nacional), sino también por estar altamente concentradas en sectores estratégicos de los que dependen grandes porciones de la economía privada. Significativamente, la mitad de las empresas estatales por valor operan en las industrias de red (telecomunicaciones, gas y electricidad, transporte y servicios postales) (OECD 2014).

El carácter estratégico del sector impone una fuerte intervención del estado en sus diversas facetas de regulador, diseñador e inspirador de las políticas, inversor directo y comprador de productos. En este último aspecto, conviene recordar los porcentajes superiores al 70% del mercado total en el equipo de comunicación y menores en ordenadores y equipo de oficina propios de los grandes países desarrollados, con la sola excepción de EE. UU. (Locksley 1983, 74).

Parece apropiado dibujar el marco europeo en un contexto global donde EE. UU. y Japón controlaban cada vez más las claves. En la producción mundial, la industria electrónica europea ocupaba posiciones importantes en equipos de telecomunicaciones, informática médica, equipos profesionales y soporte lógico y servicios. La participación en el mercado europeo de 13.000 empresas europeas de tecnología de la información de todos los tamaños sumó ocho puntos porcentuales entre 1984 y 1989 desde el 47%. A nivel de empresa, Philips y Thomson se encontraban entre los seis fabricantes de electrónica de consumo más grandes del mundo, y SGS Thomson figuraba como número dos a nivel mundial por memorias no volátiles. Sin embargo, la balanza comercial europea se mantuvo fuertemente negativa, con una tasa de cobertura global de alrededor de tres cuartos del total. Solo cuatro empresas europeas figuraban entre las 20 principales del mercado mundial de semi-

---

[10] Vale la pena señalar que la definición común para una empresa pública es aquella que ha emitido valores a través de una oferta pública inicial y se cotiza en el mercado de valores.

conductores en 1985: Philips (6ª), Siemens (15ª), Thomson (17ª) y SGS (2°) (Anexo 1). En Francia, Thomson adquirió el norteamericano Mostek[11].

En cuanto al sentido comparativo, cabe destacar algunas similitudes y diferencias con otros países europeos. El caso italiano parece ser el más sugerente para llevar a cabo este ejercicio, dada la existencia de un organismo público (IRI) que, por otro lado, inspiró a la dictadura de Franco en España para crear el INI. Respecto a las similitudes, encontramos la existencia de un monopolio de telecomunicaciones en manos de la Compañía Telefónica Nacional de España (CTNE) y STET, en España e Italia, respectivamente. Las diferencias apuntan a varios aspectos. En primer lugar, debe subrayarse el gran impulso dado en Italia al sector de la electrónica después de la crisis del petróleo de 1973, mucho antes de los esfuerzos de España, aunque estuvo limitado por un respaldo público inadecuado a la I+D. En segundo lugar, el apoyo a la integración vertical debería ser destacado al menos en una doble dirección. La división electrónica de IRI quedó bajo el control del operador italiano STET para explotar los vínculos con las telecomunicaciones, también controladas por STET. El IRI se hizo cargo igualmente de la Società Generale Semiconduttori (SGS), la compañía italiana más grande en el campo de los componentes electrónicos, afectada por la crisis tras la retirada del grupo fundador de EE. UU. Esta transacción diferencia entre los dos países, ya que el sector electrónico del INI español carecía de un subsector de componentes, considerado como básico por el gobierno y que padecía ineficiencias en el tamaño, la tecnología y la estructura financiera de las empresas[12]. Algunos de los elementos mencionados, particularmente a nivel de la empresa, apuntan a ciertas peculiaridades interesantes que Francia presentó, en el marco de un viaje de ida y vuelta a nacionalizaciones/privatizaciones. Más allá, una de las peculiaridades de Francia fue la existencia de laboratorios públicos de I+D[13].

---

[11] M. André Rouvière (Gard – SOC), «Question écrite» *Journal Officiel du Sénat*, 4 de diciembre de 1986, 1,670; Réponse du ministère de l'Industrie, *Journal Officiel du Sénat*, 14 de mayo de 1987, 760. Philips, Siemens, STC y Bull eran las integrantes del clúster europeo (Hagedoorn y Schakenraad 1992, 163-190).

[12] Baumol (1980); Kumar (1994), 60-109; había nueve empresas de componentes electrónicos, una de las cuales, Piher, con cuatro filiales (Ministerio de Industria y Energía 1983, 163-164 y 170-173). En 1993, el mercado de componentes electrónicos ascendió a 168.000 millones de pesetas, equivalente al 14% del mercado total, 15 puntos porcentuales menos que diez años antes.

[13] Laboratorios públicos de I+D: C.E.T.-C.N.S. y C.E.A.-L.E.T.I. SGS-Thomson, por ejemplo, una empresa nacional, fue considerada un gran éxito de la microelectrónica francesa porque nació en el sector público: Dominique Strauss-Kahn, Ministre d'Économie, Finances et Industrie (Sénat de la France, 11 de diciembre de 1997; 26 de abril de 1989,

2. Las tecnologías de la información y la comunicación en el INI

A comienzos de la década de 1980, España figuraba entre los países europeos en que el estado mantenía una presencia fuerte en la economía, si bien inferior a la media de la CE[14].

El INI fomentó las Sociedades de Desarrollo Industrial (SODI), en las que controlaba un mínimo del 51% del capital social, y en las que participaban las cajas de ahorro y, en algún caso, instituciones financieras privadas y diputaciones provinciales. Las SODIs, cuyo origen se remonta a 1972, alcanzaron 130.000 millones de pesetas en inversiones durante el decenio 1976-1985[15].

Las políticas de ajuste del sector público forman parte de la reconversión más amplia llevada a cabo bajo el mandato de gobiernos socialistas en la década de 1980, en su mayoría como medida por la entrada en la EC, que se tradujo en crecimientos importantes de la economía, a costa de mantener un alto nivel de desempleo. Los datos disponibles muestran que el crecimiento anual del PIB desde 1979 a 1996 solo superaba el 3% entre 1987 y 1990, mientras que en el periodo anterior, de 1961 a 1978, el crecimiento del PIB superó el 3% en todos los años (Carreras y Tafunell 2004)[16]. Unos ocho centenares de empresas en once sectores contemplaba la Ley de Reconversión y Reindustrialización de 1984, con una pérdida estimada de 830.000 empleos (Burgess 2004, 25-26).

De la mano de Luis Carlos Croissier en el INI, el gobierno impulsó la recuperación del prestigio de las empresas públicas; precisamente lo que había solicitado el ministro de Industria en su discurso motejado como la «solchaguina». En segundo término, promovió la privatización de numerosas empre-

---

398). SGS-Thomson esperaba beneficiarse de una importante ayuda pública (región PACA, DATAR, Fondo Europeo) para instalar una nueva planta de semiconductores cerca de Aix-en-Provence (Sénat de la France, 5 de diciembre de 1995, 3.840). Mientras Thomson-S.G.S estaba transfiriendo las producciones al sudeste asiático y los Estados Unidos, anunció la eliminación de miles de empleos en Europa, como Siemens y Philips pronosticaron por su parte. Thomson fue comprado por el Grupo Lagardère (*L'Économiste*, 24 de octubre de 1996.

[14] Empresas de propiedad estatal/PIB en 1982: CE: 14,1%; España: 6,8% (Dehesa 1993, 131).

[15] *El País*, 31 de mayo de 1983 y 5 de abril de 1986. Esta política permite recuperar el debate sobre el sector público en España; en este sentido, y a título de ejemplo, Sánchez (2009, 1-27) afirma que la empresa pública no redujo las diferencias regionales.

[16] Bliss y Braga De Macedo (1990, 193) afirman que el ajuste redundó en un crecimiento significativo de la economía, a costa de mantener un alto nivel de desempleo; ver también Prados (2017).

sas del grupo público en los que ciertos especialistas apuntan como «proceso dual» de privatizaciones en el INI, que parecía haber esperado la participación activa del capital financiero autóctono y del de multinacionales extranjeras[17].

En sucesivas transformaciones, el sector productivo público español se agrupó en tres *holdings*: el Grupo del Instituto Nacional de Industria (INI), que se dividió a su vez en dos *subholdings* y abarcaba las industrias básicas y estratégicas; el Grupo INH, que congregaba al sector de hidrocarburos (petróleo, gas y petroquímica) y el Grupo Patrimonio, que reunía empresas de servicios y banca (Aceña y Comín 1991, 539)[18].

No está de más recordar aspectos ya apuntados. La electrónica había llegado tardía y tímidamente a España, coincidiendo con los albores de la transición democrática. Parte de los esfuerzos procedieron del sector público a través del INI y de forma indirecta a través de CTNE[19]. En años sucesivos, los propósitos de desarrollar los sectores de tecnología de punta y de la electrónica se quedaron cortos. A inicios del nuevo milenio, la producción electrónica española representaba el 5,5% de la europea, 3,5 puntos porcentuales por debajo del peso que tenía en el mercado europeo. En cuanto a la inversión en TIC con relación al PIB, España se situaba por debajo de la media de la UE de los 27 y de los 15 e incluso por debajo de Portugal y países del Este (Lawlor, Rigby y Smith 2005, 55-56; Sieber y Valor 2008, 30). Si consideramos el modesto lugar que ocupaba la electrónica europea en el mercado mundial podremos concluir la escasa relevancia de la española.

La apuesta del INI por las tecnologías de la información y la comunicación (TIC) arrancó en la década de 1970 a través de empresas –generalmente

---

[17]   Ese «proceso dual» de privatizaciones en el INI habría comenzado por una reestructuración financiera y seguido con una venta a compradores agraciados por la operación (Heywood 1999, 171).

[18]   La creación de un *subholding* que englobara a sus empresas de informática y electrónica fue concebida bajo el mandato de Croissier en el INI y con la orientación inicial de asemejarlo a los ya creados en el sector eléctrico y alimentario (*El País*, 23 de marzo de 1985). Para un análisis de la reestructuración del sector público véase Parker (2002), 200.

[19]   La actividad del INI cobró gran importancia para la base industrial militar española, ya que tuvo un papel destacado en la creación y el mantenimiento de varias empresas de defensa, la reestructuración de arsenales antiguos y establecimientos militares que necesitaban transformaciones profundas. El desarrollo de la industria autóctona se resintió de las importaciones de productos para la modernización del material militar desde mediados de la década de 1950 gracias a acuerdos con los Estados Unidos, pese a que el INI jugó un papel destacado en la consolidación de algunas de las firmas que eventualmente se convertirían en contratistas principales de defensa en una etapa posterior (Duch-Brown y Fonfría 2014, 1).

vinculadas a la industria militar y algunas filiales de compañías extranjeras–. que incorporaban la electrónica a la tecnología de uso tradicional y mediante creación o adquisición de otras nuevas.

En la primera categoría, la histórica Experiencias Industriales (EISA), nacida en 1921, se especializó en la producción militar y se integró en el Programa Naval de la Armada; Empresa Nacional de Óptica (ENOSA), creada en 1951 con orientación a la óptica militar, llegó a la electrónica a través de las tecnologías de visión pasiva. En la segunda categoría, Equipos Electrónicos, S. A. (EESA), fundada en 1971 por la francesa Thomson, fue adquirida por el INI en 1978 para reforzar el mercado de la defensa dentro de las telecomunicaciones y electrónica de municionamiento (Molas-Gallart 1992, 64).

Por su parte, en el área de servicios informáticos surgió la Empresa Nacional de Innovación (ERIA, 1973), mientras que la Sociedad Española de Construcciones e Industria (SECOINSA) fue la gran empresa del *hardware* informático, fruto de la alianza tecnológica-industrial-financiera con la japonesa Fujitsu, la operadora CTNE y un grupo bancario español (Infograma)[20].

Tabla 1. Evolución histórica de las empresas de la industria
electrónica en España y los procesos de fusión

Empresa	Año de creación	Campo	Propiedad	Propiedad posterior
Experiencias Industriales (EISA)	1921	Sistemas de artillería y equipos de control para el transporte	EISA	-
Empresa Nacional de Óptica (ENOSA)	1951	Óptica de defensa	INI	-
Equipos Electrónicos S. A. (EESA)	1971	Óptica de defensa	Thomson	INI (1978)
ERIA	1973	Servicios IT		

[20] El grupo de bancos estaba formado por el Hispanoamericano, Bilbao, Urquijo, Central, Santander, Vizcaya, Popular y Banesto (Calvo 2014, 222-224). El INI sustituyó a José Solís, hombre de consenso entre Fujitsu y los socios españoles, por Santiago Rodríguez Miranda; la dirección del sector fue encomendada a José Luis Niño, hasta entonces director de ingeniería (*El País,* 8 de mayo de 1979). A continuación de un periodo de marginación de la política industrial de defensa, en los primeros años de la década de 1980 el gobierno español, muy pendiente de las alianzas militares occidentales, empezó a dirigir su atención a ese sector olvidado (Latham y Hooper 2013, 147).

Empresa	Año de creación	Campo	Propiedad	Propiedad posterior
SECOINSA	1975	*Hardware* informático	Fujitsu, CTNE y bancos españoles	Telefónica
Estudios y Realizaciones de Diseño Informatizados (ERDISA)	1981	Diseño y fabricación asistidos por ordenador (CAD)	INI, Control Data Ibérica	-
AEREA		*Software*	INI	-
ICuatro		Equipo médico eléctrico	INI	-
Isel	1981	Proceso integral de sistemas electrónicos e informáticos	Grupo Inisel y ENDESA, a través de ENHER	-
Pesa				-
Telesincro	1963	Ordenadores, terminales periféricos, pantallas e impresoras	Joan Majó	Entrada de Bull (40%)
Inisel	1985	Electrónica profesional	Fusión de EESA y EISA	-
Gyconsa	1991	equipo de defensa	Inisel/Hughes	Indra/Hughes
SADIEL	1984	Sociedad para promoción de inversiones	ERIA 10%	-

Empresa	Año de creación	Campo	Propiedad	Propiedad posterior
Empresa Nacional de Ingeniería y Tecnología (INITEC)	1964	Servicios de ingeniería	INI	1999: Técnicas Reunidas y Westinghouse, que vendió el 25% a Dragados Industrial
DEFEX	1972	Promoción y exportación de bienes y servicios españoles de defensa	BAZAN, CASA, EISA, ENOSA y Santa Bárbara (51%)	-
MICROCARE (USA)	1956	Sistemas de limpieza de precisión en electrónica y en industrias de acabado de metales	ENISA 33%	-
SELESMAR	1980	Radares marinos y sistemas anticolisión ARPA	Segnalamento Marittimo ed Aereo (Florencia)	EISA 20%
Eritel	1991	*Software* para ordenadores	Telefónica (39%) y el INI (51%) a través de ENTEL y ERIA	-
Indra	1993	Tecnologías de información y control	INISEL (66,6%) y CESELSA (33,3%)	2/3 Inisel y 1/3 Ceselsa.

Fuente: Elaboración propia a partir del texto.

Gráfico 1. La división electrónica del NI, 1984 (millones de pesetas)

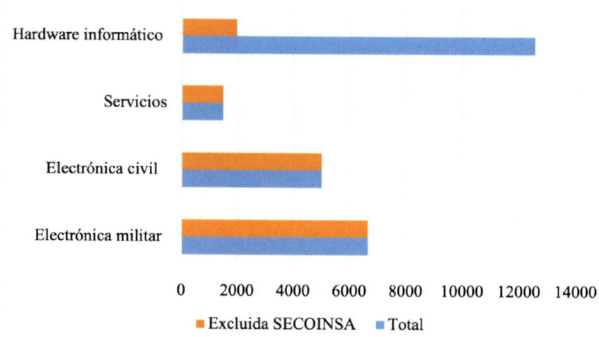

Fuente: Elaboración a partir de *Reorganización de empresas electrónicas del INI. Creación de un holding en el sector electrónico-informático del INI,* Archivo del INI.

En su primer quinquenio de vida, el grupo de empresas de la división alcanzó un crecimiento medio acumulativo del 32% en ventas, 150 en *cash*-flow y 6 en empleo. Si tomamos un solo año, en 1982, las ventas alcanzaron 17.518 millones de pesetas y la plantilla 3.166 personas. Las actividades de I+D se cifraban en gastos por 1.002 millones de pesetas, equivalentes al 5,7% sobre ventas y en un crecimiento del 70%. El personal de I+D se situaba en 252 personas, 8% sobre el total de la plantilla, el 54% de ellos titulados superiores[21].

Hay que situarse en 1984, año para el que existe un diagnóstico y diversas recetas del propio INI. La División de Electrónica e Informática (DEeI) de este organismo se componía de un conjunto de diez empresas públicas o mixtas, pertenecientes a tres grandes áreas, de las que estaban excluidas la electrónica de consumo y la de componentes (Infograma). En ese momento, la División tenía un volumen de ventas de 25.576 millones de pesetas, de los cuales el 15,83% le correspondía a la exportación, la cartera de pedidos se situaba en 26.275 millones de pesetas, las aplicaciones totales de I+D en 1.193 (el 5,04% sobre las ventas) y el empleo en 3.581 personas[22]. Los prin-

---

[21] Antonio Alabau, *BIT,* abril de 1983, 93.

[22] *Reorganización de empresas electrónicas del INI. Creación de un holding en el sector electrónico-informático del INI* (Archivo del INI). Conocemos detalles de alguna empresa en particular. Eisa empleaba en su departamento de I+D 49 personas en 1983, casi la cuarta parte de las cuales eran titulados superiores; al mismo se habían destinado 220 millones de ptas., el 6% ventas (la mayoría aplastante para desarrollo y confección de prototipos y los

cipales clie1ntes eran diversos organismos del sector de defensa nacional (Anexos 2 y 3)[23].

En cuanto a la estructura productiva, el área de la informática encabezaba la actividad de la División con el 45% de la facturación, seguida de la electrónica para la defensa con el 30%, mientras que a la electrónica profesional civil le correspondía el restante 25%, en cada caso en porcentajes aproximados (Gráfico 1). Algunas de estas empresas de la División eran líderes en sus áreas respectivas, como sucedía con el equipamiento para televisión, con la electromedicina y con las comunicaciones digitales, si bien aquí bajo un liderazgo subsidiario dado que la propiedad industrial del producto pertenecía a un accionista de la empresa que lo desarrollaba[24].

La política seguida por el INI ya desde 1983 consistió en la «reducción de las pérdidas y la formación de un grupo industrial rentable y competitivo»[25]. En consecuencia, la fase expansiva que vivió la división electrónica en los primeros años de la década de 1980 dio un giro brusco a continuación. No lo veían así los responsables de la división, que esgrimían a favor de sus razones el aumento del volumen de actividad en términos de facturación en un 25%, una notable orientación exportadora –la cuarta parte del volumen de facturación– y un apreciable nivel de gasto –7% de sus ventas aproximadamente– en I+D o inversiones en tecnología.

restantes 11 millones para inversiones materiales en equipos de laboratorio); en cuanto al origen, 79 millones de ptas. procedían de la financiación externa (CAYCIT y CDTI, principalmente); en EISA, que atravesaba por una etapa de consolidación del alto nivel de ventas, el inmovilizado inmaterial – propiedad industrial– representaba el 22% del material, cifrado en 1.554.193.675 (EISA 1984).

23 *Reorganización de empresas electrónicas del INI. Creación de un holding en el sector electrónico-informático del INI,* Archivos INI. Cuatro años antes, el capital social de la división era de 3.266 millones de ptas. Sus ventas fueron de 7.688 y sus gastos de I+D 351; su plantilla era de 2.646 empleados (*BIT*, 16, mayo-junio de 1981, 8-12).

24 Comparecencias en relación con el Plan Electrónico e Informático Nacional del director de la División Electrónica e Informática del INI, Rodríguez Cortezo (*DSCD*, 226, 23 de octubre de 1984, 7.090-7.093); Rodríguez Cortezo hizo en otro apartado una referencia expresa a ETESA, dedicada a equipamientos para televisión profesional. Por número, la división representó el 5% del total de empresas del INI (*Informe anual sobre la gestión del sector público en 1985*, Congreso de los Diputados, 27 de junio de 1990, 109).

25 *El País*, 13 de agosto de 1988. El Partido Socialista, en el gobierno, se manifestaba contrario radicalmente a un comportamiento errático de la empresa pública propio de los años anteriores, causa de graves daños a esa empresa pública, y partidario de una estrategia explícita para lograr la mejor implantación y la más conveniente en los diferentes subsectores de la electrónica y la informática (Intervención de Eugenio Triana (Grupo Socialista), *DSCD*, 226, 23 de octubre de 1984, 7.090-7.093).

Vinculado a mercado e inversión, la I+D tenía la doble faceta de su incremento y su naturaleza estratégica. El gasto de la División por este concepto sextuplicó con creces entre 1979 y 1984 pasando de 184 a 1.193 millones pesetas. Esto sucedía en un país, España, cuya industria realizaba un esfuerzo tecnológico que apenas llegaba al 0,3% del PIB, muy por debajo de los países del entorno. Según las mismas fuentes, el conjunto de las empresas de la División iba a terminar el ejercicio de 1984 muy cerca del punto de equilibrio y en situación óptima para obtener beneficios en el siguiente[26].

Un argumento esgrimido en contra de las acusaciones de repliegue se refería a la estrategia de diversificación de la actividad y de los mercados, junto a la búsqueda de mayor cualificación en un sector dinámico, amenazado por la obsolescencia. La decisión de aplicar la informática y la electrónica a la productividad industrial se había plasmado en la creación de una empresa conjunta con el socio tecnológico Control Data con el nombre de Estudios y Realizaciones de Diseño Informatizados (ERDISA), filial de AEREA. La empresa se enmarcaba en la política de desarrollo corporativo orientada al aprovechamiento de nuevas ideas y oportunidades de mercado –conocido como células de generación de nuevas actividades–; en especial de aquellas con un mayor valor añadido nacional[27].

El INI se apoyaba en la aportación de SECOINSA a la fabricación del sistema Tesys, un desarrollo tecnológico de la CTNE y nodo de la red de transmisión de datos española, para considerarse a la vanguardia tecnológica mundial en ese campo. A la actividad de AEREA, empresa de *software* de la División, se debía el desarrollo de un lenguaje de programación, objeto de un convenio de exportación con una de las multinacionales americanas más importantes del soporte lógico y que había conseguido penetrar en el mercado mundial. La División se planteaba también estar en nuevos campos, dando prioridad a la enseñanza asistida por ordenador y a la robótica. Pero significativamente para su posicionamiento en el mercado, en este campo, la División

---

[26] Comparecencias en relación con el Plan Electrónico e Informático Nacional del director de la División Electrónica e Informática del INI Rodríguez Cortezo (*DSCD*, 226, 23 de octubre de 1984, 7.090-7.093). Comparecencia del señor director general de electrónica y nuevas tecnologías (*Diario de Sesiones del Senado*, 111, 19 de noviembre de 1991, 31-34).

[27] *El País*, 7 de diciembre de 1983; *Spanish Economic News Service*, 38, 1-51, 9: ERDISA tenía un capital social de 60 millones de pesetas (*El País*, 7 de diciembre de 1983); se encargaba de desarrollar nueva tecnología y productos CAD al servicio de las industrias locales, a la vez que de promocionar y comercializar productos y servicios CAD existentes. El INI, a través de Eria y Enisa, y Control Data se dividieron la participación a partes iguales (*Computers in Mechanical Engineering*, 2, 1983, 84).

aspiraba no tanto a fabricar robots, pese a disponer de tecnología propia, sino a ofrecer al país una capacidad de ingeniería en robótica[28].

A la reivindicación de la expansión, de la diversificación y de la pugna por estar a la vanguardia se añadía la estrategia de internacionalización de las actividades. En un grupo de tamaño relativamente reducido, dicha estrategia pasaba no solo por la mencionada exportación sino también por el establecimiento de cabezas de puente o núcleos de expansión en los mercados con mayor potencial. Estos eran básicamente tres, que, en su diversidad incluían los Estados Unidos de América, la Comunidad Económica Europea (CEE) e Iberoamérica. En el primero la División contaba con dos cabezas de puente, inicios de dos actuaciones y perspectivas de una tercera. En la CEE, más en concreto en Holanda por razones fiscales, el INI planeaba establecer una empresa mixta de *software* en alianza tecnológica con un grupo francés y a partir de una empresa propia. En cuanto a Latinoamérica, ya un mercado importante, la intención era crear una plataforma, a la sazón en Argentina, a cuyo fin se estaban estableciendo relaciones institucionales con el gobierno de dicho país[29].

El INI siguió apostando por un grupo empresarial español fortalecido, consolidado, estable a largo plazo y con capacidad de asegurar, a solas o en alianzas, la participación nacional en la industria y los servicios europeos. En palabras de su presidente, la propia dinámica empresarial imponía, sin embargo, adoptar medidas de desinversión o de participación en determinados negocios. El cumplimiento de su misión como agente en la consolidación de un núcleo duro de capital nacional en Europa exigía niveles de eficiencia mínimos, a la vez que métodos de gestión adecuados (Salas 1991).

Más tarde prosiguieron los recortes, que la oposición no dejó de echar en cara al gobierno. En ese sentido, las inversiones del ministerio de Industria y Energía (MINER) en I+D sufrieron una contracción importante del 13%,

---

[28] Comparecencias en relación con el Plan Electrónico e Informático Nacional del director de la División Electrónica e Informática del INI Rodríguez Cortezo (*DSCD*, 226, 23 de octubre de 1984, 7.090-7.093).

[29] Para EEUU señalaba actuaciones en el campo de equipos para prueba de microprocesadores: Comparecencias en relación con el Plan Electrónico e Informático Nacional del director de la División Electrónica e Informática del INI Rodríguez Cortezo (*DSCD*, 226, 23 de octubre de 1984, 7.090-7.093). Como actividad anterior en la informática en Argentina, la monopolista semipública CTNE se había adjudicado la concesión de la construcción y puesta en servicio de la primera red pública de informática del país y se había implantado en el tejido industrial a través de una empresa local –Microsistemas S. A.–, presente en el mercado de los micro y monousuarios y con un departamento de compras y *software* en EEUU (Calvo 2016, 250-251).

equivalente a unos 7.000 millones de pesetas[30]. El gobierno contrarrestó los ataques esgrimiendo la plena vigencia del Plan Electrónico e Informático Nacional durante casi un decenio y el lanzamiento del Plan de Actuación Tecnológica Industrial (PATI). Este, adscrito a una política industrial, consistía en un plan trienal para 1991-1993 de carácter horizontal con el objetivo único de lograr un aumento notable del esfuerzo tecnológico de la industria española en sectores diversos –siderurgia, calzado, textil y bienes de equipo. Se plasmaba en planes específicos, entre los que figuraba el de la industria electrónica e informática. Su cifra en el año inicial se fijaba en un 0,42% del PIB y en un 0,57 % en el final.

En total, el gobierno esperaba movilizar fondos públicos por una suma algo superior a 150.000 millones de pesetas. Los fondos procederían de cuatro fuentes distintas: el propio presupuesto del MINER en forma de subvenciones; créditos blandos del Centro para el Desarrollo Tecnológico e Industrial (CDTI); recursos canalizados a las empresas españolas por programas europeos tanto comunitarios como extracomunitarios y otras aportaciones públicas de diferentes orígenes y modalidades, entre ellas fondos procedentes de presupuestos de comunidades autónomas o de la Administración[31]. En realidad, entre 1991 y 1994, el MINER destinó 23.000 millones de pesetas, en forma de subvenciones directas a las empresas, a financiar desarrollos de nuevos productos o bien a mejoras de los procesos productivos. En una reedición del PATI para el periodo 1994-1996, el gobierno planeaba destinar a I+D 28.000 millones de pesetas en forma de subvenciones a las empresas. Con todo, el propio ministro del ramo reconocía el bajo nivel de la inversión en I+D en el contexto de los países desarrollados (*Desarrollo Tecnológico* 6, enero de 1994, 11-12 y 50)[32].

---

[30] Triana (1991), 8-9; Intervención del senador Unceta Antón, *Diario de Sesiones del Senado*, 111, 19 de noviembre de 1991, 31-34.

[31] Comparecencia del señor director general de electrónica y nuevas tecnologías, *Diario de Sesiones del Senado*, 111, 19 de noviembre de 1991, 31-34. Respecto a las comunidades autónomas y a título de ejemplo, el plan de competitividad de la industria catalana contemplaba cuatro ámbitos de actuación preferentes –internacionalización, investigación y tecnología, servicios a las empresas, reequilibrio industrial y territorial–, que se repartían el grueso de los 44.150 millones de ptas. con el que estaba dotado (Mosconi et al. 2001). Conviene recordar que la política europea supranacional de promoción de la I+D respondió al fracaso de las políticas nacionales (Kassim y Menon 2002, 228).

[32] Habría que añadir el Plan de calidad industrial.

3. La reestructuración del sector público de las TIC

Volviendo al sector que nos ocupa en los años iniciales de la década de 1980, la realidad dejó lugar a muy pocas dudas. En SECOINSA el INI inyectó 5.000 millones de pesetas en capital en 1983, con efecto positivo en la cuenta de resultados al reducir los números rojos. Pero al refuerzo financiero le sucedió la desinversión con la venta de la participación en SECOINSA a Telefónica, su principal cliente. Lo que en el INI era un cierre de compuertas se convertía en la CTNE, momentáneamente al menos, en exponente de una política firme de reindustrialización del país, de integración de la actuación de la operadora y ocasión para relanzar la actividad industrial, esta vez en alianza con la multinacional Fujitsu, aspecto que merece un estudio aparte y que tendremos ocasión de ver en el capítulo correspondiente[33].

Otra pieza importante era Telesincro. En 1980, la francesa Bull, otra de las pertenecientes al cluster de la electrónica europea, pactó con el INI iniciar una fase de fabricación de productos propios en Telesincro, acuerdo que se tradujo en exportaciones por valor de 4.300 millones de pesetas. Ambos socios planeaban ampliar la colaboración con un acuerdo tecnológico e industrial para potenciar el desarrollo de Telesincro, reforzada por la entrada de Bull (Sánchez 2020, 394). Esta, líder en la informática europea, aspiraba a enraizar aún más su presencia en España desbordando ese marco mediante una participación minoritaria en una empresa española. Por su parte, la Administración española pretendía acceder a un futuro programa informático europeo que reforzara la competitividad europea frente a la supremacía de EE. UU. y Japón. En 1984, la empresa francesa y el gobierno español convinieron que Bull, ahora nacionalizada, entraría como socio minoritario en el capital de la española Telesincro. Antes debía finalizarse la valoración de la empresa mixta SECOINSA –matriz de Telesincro–, materializarse la toma del 60% del capital por parte de Fujitsu (el 40% restante quedaría en poder de Telefónica) y quedar resuelto a nivel jurídico el pase de Telesincro al INI (*El País*, 6 de mayo de 1985). El pacto contemplaba la posible entrada de un tercer socio nacional. El plan de empresa acordado entre el INI y Bull preveía unas inversiones de 1.000 millones de pe-

---

[33] En palabras de Luis Solana, «política firme de reindustrialización del país, en la que todos los grupos de empresas con participación pública están inmersos y comprometidos» y parte de una pionera política de Telefónica que tendía a potenciar un sector de TIC al integrar la voz, la imagen y los datos (*El País*, 23 de marzo de 1985). El precio a pagar por Telefónica al INI por la compra de las acciones del Instituto en SECOINSA se fijó en 1.411 millones de pesetas, equivalentes al importe total, de 2.234 millones de pesetas, menos los pagos que el INI debería efectuar a Telefónica por Telesincro, ISEL y Digi Power (*El País*, 26 de julio de 1985).

setas en 1986-1988, dotando a Telesincro de una nueva fábrica y de un centro de investigación y desarrollo de nueva creación, que estaría inicialmente compuesto por 25 ingenieros y técnicos de alto nivel. El presupuesto de este centro se cifraba para 1988 en un 8% de la cifra de negocios de la compañía (*El País*, 23 de marzo y 23 de junio de 1986).

Conforme a los planes, Telesincro e Isel debían integrarse en un subgrupo de informática y electrónica defensiva y profesional, que incluiría asimismo EESA, EISA, Piher y ENOSA.

En una primera fase, la fusión de EESA y EISA dio lugar a Inisel, que se convirtió en cabecera de grupo –aspecto sobre el que volveremos–, clave de la electrónica de defensa y una de las empresas significativas de la electrónica europea[34].

Gráfico 2. Principales magnitudes del grupo Inisel
(monetarias en millones de pesetas)

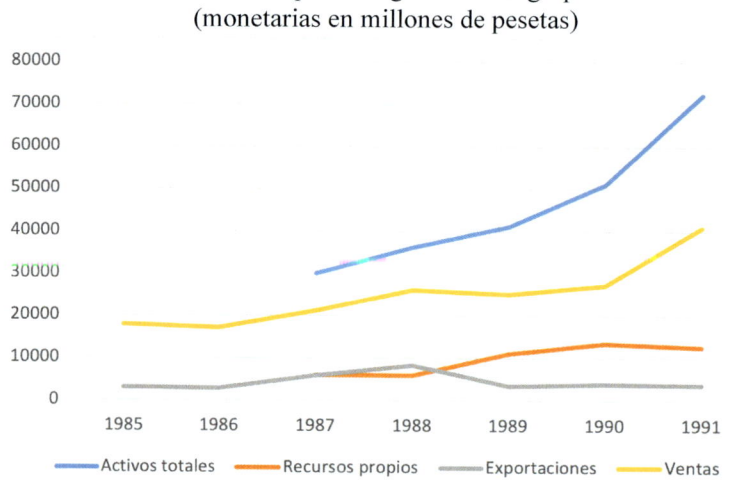

Fuente: Elaboración a partir de Grupo Inisel (1991) y Karl (1994), 97.

Los años iniciales de la segunda mitad de la década de 1980 fueron de una relativa atonía para Inisel. Crecieron los activos totales junto con los recursos propios y, con un pequeño desfase de un año, las ventas, a cuenta del mercado interior (Gráfico 2).

---

[34] INISEL, *Memoria anual*, 1992; *El País*, 10 de marzo de 1989; *ABC*, 10 de noviembre de 1988. La creación de Inisel es un hecho repetidamente reflejado en la bibliografía internacional (Gummett y Stein (ed.) 2014, 206; Featherstone y Kazamias 2014, 181; Wilson 2013, 186). Fabrie (1987, 19) recoge pormenores importantes de la empresa.

A Inisel no le faltaron, incluso, episodios de internacionalización en la modalidad primordial de alianzas industriales y tecnológicas. Inisel fue la responsable industrial y contratista principal en España para equipar las estaciones terrestres del satélite militar de observación Helios, un proyecto europeo con un coste estimado de 160.000 millones de pesetas, liderado por Francia (79%) y con una participación de Italia (14%) y de España (7%). La acción del gobierno español fue fundamental aquí. Primero, al incitar a Inisel para que participase en un programa de defensa internacional y formase un consorcio internacional con otras tres empresas europeas –AEG (Alemania), Ferranti (Reino Unido) y la FIAR de Marconi (Italia)–, para impulsar el radar de a bordo del European Fighter Aircraft (EFA) con el objetivo de desarrollar su base tecnológica. El consorcio confió a una empresa, Eurofighter, la misión de coordinar y subcontratar todas las actividades del proyecto. En segundo lugar, al apoyar a Inisel en el sellado de una alianza en el campo de la guerra electrónica con la compañía italiana Elettronica, que consistía en el 51% de la compañía española ELT, S.A., especializada en este sector y controlada por la compañía italiana mencionada anteriormente. En una situación en que el gasto en defensa mundial tendía a disminuir, los esfuerzos de cooperación cobraron suma importancia. Por su parte, las aspiraciones de la industria norteamericana para hacerse un hueco en el mercado europeo abonaban el terreno a dicha colaboración interempresarial. Ahí radican los ingredientes de la alianza estratégica «puntual» entre la multinacional estadounidense Hughes e Inisel, concebida en dos fases. La primera consistía en un triple movimiento accionarial –entrada de Hugues como socio minoritario en el capital de ENOSA, del grupo Inisel–, de transferencia de tecnología punta en el campo de la optrónica de ENOSA a Hughes, y de fabricación en España de un nuevo lanzador de misiles TOW, esta vez a cargo de Inisel con aporte tecnológico de la socia. El acuerdo se completaba con el desarrollo conjunto de armamento nuevo –un misil anticarro– que se fabricaría en España. Con estas premisas, Inisel se asoció con Hughes Aircraft Company Missile Systems Group en la empresa de riesgo compartido Gyconsa SA (Guiado y Control SA), en la que retuvo una participación minoritaria del 49%. El objetivo era desarrollar el programa Aries, más tarde sustituido por el MACAM (Misil Avanzado Contra-Carro de Alcance Medio)[35]. En la guerra antiaérea, España se sumó en

---

[35] MACAM-Archivado 9/2003, 2-3; Ceselsa-Inisel *Informe anual*, 1992, 11; Molas-Gallart (1992), 70. El nuevo misil debería competir con el proyecto europeo Trigat (Alemania, Francia y Reino Unido), abandonado por España a finales de 1989 (*El País*, 11 de mayo de 1991). En 1992, Gyconsa SA recibió del gobierno español un contrato de 20 millones de

junio al consorcio EUROSAM, formado por las empresas Aérospatiale (Francia) y Selenia (Italia) para llevar a cabo el costoso programa Aster de misiles antiaéreos. Este acuerdo general iba acompañado por la celebración de un contrato que contemplaba el intercambio financiero, técnico e industrial entre el grupo español Inisel y los dos socios de EUROSAM[36].

La División Electrónica e Informática del INI se reforzó con la incorporación de empresas nuevas –Sociedad Andaluza para el Desarrollo de la Informática y la Electrónica (SADIEL), DIGIPOWER y PESA Inc., por citar las más destacadas–. Entre 1980-1984 el crecimiento acumulativo medio del grupo de empresas fue del 32% en ventas, 150% en *cash-flow* y 6% en empleo.

Hacia el final de la década de 1970, el INI creó una nueva dirección para coordinar las actividades en los campos de la ingeniería, electrónica e informática. Ahí se encuentra el fermento de la nueva y agresiva Empresa Nacional de Ingeniería y Tecnología (INITEC), que prestaba servicios generales de ingeniería en el mercado nacional e internacional, incluidas centrales nucleares, térmicas convencionales e hidroeléctricas.

Fuera de España, INITEC vendió su tecnología y *know-how* a América del Sur, Europa, Medio Oriente y África. Más tarde fue sometida a un proceso de ajuste, que se encaminaba hacia la consolidación económica antes de ser vendida a Westinghouse y Técnicas Reunidas en el último año de la década[37]. A

---

dólares para suministrar un nuevo lanzador ligero para los misiles españoles TOW 2B y desarrollar un sistema antitanque de tercera generación, MACAM, contrato valorado en 4.85 millones. En 1997, ENOSA contrató con Kuwait el suministro de su lanzador ligero TOW (MACAM-Archived 9/2003, 2-3). En el ejemplo de España, entre 1985 y 1993 la participación del gasto militar en el PIB se redujo en un punto porcentual –del 2,2% al 1,2%; entre 1982 y 1993, el porcentaje respecto al total del Presupuesto mermó a menos de la mitad –de un 11,5% a un 5,1% (Canales y Elices 1994, 107).

[36]   La cuota de Inisel en el desarrollo de este programa se fijó en 1.500 millones de francos (*Le Monde,* 16 y 22 de junio de 1991). Dentro de los planes de la OTAN de un despliegue de fuerzas rápidas (Cleland et al. 1993, 38/2).

[37]   Muller (1991), 104; Tribunal de Cuentas (2007), 15. Se produjeron varios recortes de empleos, primero bajo la propiedad pública, en 1987, que afectaron a quinientos trabajadores, y durante el proceso de privatización, con una reducción de 189 por medio de despidos voluntarios y jubilación anticipada (*El País,* 9 de diciembre de 1987). Dos mil expertos en más de veinte campos y experiencias diferentes evaluados en cientos de proyectos colocaron a INITEC en un lugar destacado entre las empresas de ingeniería españolas (*Información comercial española,* 564-568, 1980, 245). El desplome drástico de la demanda de productos energéticos (especialmente los servicios para centrales nucleares) condujo en 1988 a un proceso de ajuste, impulsando otros productos con contenido tecnológico innovador, ya sea derivado de actividades tradicionales o nuevas. En 1989, la inversión de INITEC en I+D ascendió a 245 millones de pesetas y se centró principalmente en proyectos y programas en el campo de la energía, el medio ambiente y los nuevos productos, así como una política de transferencia de tecnología y cooperación. Tecnología Internacional (*Boletín Oficial de*

partir de entonces, esta última y ERIA, SECOINSA, ENOSA, EESA y EISA junto a otras similares actuarían de forma integrada. Además de esta restructuración, el INI se hizo con la mayoría en SECOINSA. A continuación, en 1980, el INI emprendió la tercera fase de su reorganización interna, que significó la creación de un Comité financiero, el aumento de las seis divisiones ya existentes desde 1979 con nueve más y la supresión de las direcciones de sector que aún subsistían. En este contexto se sitúa la creación por el INI de una División de Tecnologías de la Información y la Comunicación (TIC) con la misión de potenciar y coordinar la presencia de sus empresas en el sector, iniciada en la década de 1970.

La estructura participativa de la División de las TIC obedecía a un esquema complejo según tres niveles de dependencia y un juego de relaciones interempresas muy diverso. El primer y segundo nivel incluían empresas de la primera hora y de las que dependía el resto –EESA, EISA, ENOSA, SECOINSA y ERIA, empresa esta última de tamaño mediano y que vendía primordialmente a la industria y los servicios, con un poco más de la tercera parte del total (Anexo 4)[38]–. La división se completaba con un cuarteto de empresas formado por la empresa mixta DEFEX (EISA y ENOSA con el 10%), la norteamericana MICROCARE (33% de la Empresa Nacional de Innovación (ENISA), SELESMAR (20% de EISA) y SADIEL (10% ERIA) e ICuatro.

Esta última, especializada en electromedicina y equipamientos electromédicos, con una fuerte presencia en el mercado internacional, especialmente en los países en vías de desarrollo, mercados naturales conforme a la consideración de la empresa. Se trataba de mercados psicológicamente cercanos, según la expresión de la escuela de Uppsala, dos países latinoamericanos – Bolivia y Chile–, cuatro países africanos –Gabón, Congo, Marruecos y Mauritania–, aparte de la Unión Soviética[39].

---

las Cortes Generales-Congreso de los Diputados, 89, 12 de septiembre de 1990, 200). El análisis de la privatización queda fuera de este estudio (*Consejo Consultivo de Privatizaciones* 1999, 103).

[38] La estructura de los costes de producción estaba dominada por los costes de personal, que rebasaban ligeramente la mitad de los totales (ERIA, *Informe anual*, 1989). En 1985, participó en dos nuevas empresas y realizó unas inversiones cercanas a los 3.000 millones de pesetas, que generaron unos 250 puestos de trabajo: *El País*, 31 de mayo de 1983 y 5 de abril de 1986. En 2017, el Consejo de Administración de SEPI acordó solicitar al Consejo de Ministros autorización para la disolución voluntaria de la controvertida DEFEX, actuando COFIVACASA como liquidadora única.

[39] *Reorganización de empresas electrónicas del INI. Creación de un holding en el sector electrónico-informático del INI*, 223, 614, 01927 (Archivo Histórico del INI, 14 –21 de mayo de 1985; Cantoni, Falciasecca y Pelosi 2011, 610). MICROCARE: 33% de la ENISA, que sir-

La primera, DEFEX, era una empresa mixta de capital público y privado al 51/49%. Como asociación de empresas estaba respaldada por los ministerios de Comercio, Defensa y Exteriores y tenía como cometido promover la industria española de defensa en las exportaciones a todo el mundo. Los servicios incluían la formación, el material de defensa, soporte logístico y servicio, revisión y mantenimiento para una amplia gama de productos de defensa y acuerdos de financiación. DEFEX coordinaba programas de formación con financiación pública y privada para potenciar las exportaciones. La estrategia se orientaba a extenderse donde las industrias españolas eran más competitivas y al Tercer mundo. Tenía dos secciones: la comercial, comprometida en la promoción de productos de defensa, y la financiera encargada de arreglar la financiación bancaria para países compradores de productos españoles de defensa (Fabrie 1987, 11).

Por su parte, EISA vendía el grueso de su producción en el mercado interior y tenía como principal cliente el Cuartel general de la Armada (Anexos 2 y 3).

El proceso de formación de un consorcio español de *software* como parte de la reestructuración de las actividades industriales del sector electrónico autóctono sufrió diversos retrasos. Tras superar dudas y posturas no coincidentes, Telefónica y el INI alcanzaron un acuerdo para reestructurar el sector de las telecomunicaciones con la implicación de las empresas respectivas de ambos grupos. El acuerdo giraba en torno al eje de la doble necesidad de concentrar los grupos industriales para propiciar la especialización y de evitar el solapamiento a la vez que de redimensionar la industria en un intento de ganar competitividad.

En el marco de la política de reordenación del sector electrónico e informático impulsada desde el ministerio de Industria, Comercio y Turismo, Inisel vendió a Telefónica el 44% de ENTEL y compró la totalidad de acciones de Ceninsa, hasta el momento integrada en la dirección general del patrimonio. Con estas dos inversiones que totalizan 4.500 millones de pesetas el grupo Inisel se convirtió en accionista mayoritario en la nueva Eritel que debía

vió como canal para crear Incipresa, empresa fabricante de equipos de protección contra incendios, en asociación con la multinacional alemana Preussag (80%) como matriz de la participante directa Pefripesa y la empresa pública Sodiga (*El País,* 1 de marzo de 1985). ICuatro durante 1990 exportó equipos hospitalarios a cuatro países latinoamericanos –Perú (5.000 millones de pesetas), México (1.200), Argentina (8.000) y Brasil (1800)–; uno africano –Uganda (650)– y uno europeo –Turquía (2.500)–: ICuatro, *Informe anual,* (1990). ICuatro tenía en plantilla diecisiete personas, en su mayoría administrativos y secretarias (11); tan solo cinco eran titulados superiores (ICuatro, *Informe anual,* 1990).

surgir de la fusión entre la División y ENTEL y a la que debía incorporarse Ceninsa (Inisel, *Informe anual*, 1990).

En efecto, en 1991, Telefónica y el INI sumaron los activos de sus filiales respectivas ENTEL y de ERIA según la modalidad de la integración[40]. El capital comprometido se cifraba en unos 10.000 millones de pesetas, del que Inisel (INI) aportaba el 51%, Telefónica el 39% y varios bancos y la francesa Cap Gemini el restante 10% (Telefónica, *Memoria,* 1990, 26; Lane (1997, 279); Boix (1998, 105-130); *Tecnología militar*, 1990, 12, 5 y 75).

De tal empeño, un tanto intricado, nació Eritel, controlada mayoritariamente por el INI mediante Inisel, con el cometido de desarrollar algo tan fundamental en las TIC como *software* para aplicaciones informáticas. De esta forma, dentro del Grupo Inisel la rama de aplicaciones civiles adquirió un mayor peso relativo y brindó al grupo mayores opciones para hacer frente a la recesión internacional de la industria de la defensa[41].

Eritel desplegó su actividad en torno a cinco líneas de actuación. La primera se refería a consultoría en su doble faceta de organización y sistemas de información. Tenía como finalidad el asesoramiento de las empresas sobre la utilización y los servicios derivados del uso de las tecnologías de la información en la mejora de la rentabilidad de los negocios. A su vez, la compañía agrupaba la amplia variedad de servicios en dos grandes ámbitos. La segunda línea comprendía la integración de sistemas, una actividad estratégica que consistía en suministrar soluciones llave en mano en las que Eritel asumía por entero desde la fase de diseño hasta la de implantación como primer contratista y único interlocutor con el cliente. En tercer lugar, la ingeniería de sistemas se centraba en el diseño, desarrollo e implantación de aplicaciones y sistemas de información automatizados para las empresas y organizaciones, a la búsqueda de aumentos de la productividad de los desarrollos, minimiza-

---

[40] Los acuerdos de fusión entre Eria y Entel que daban lugar a la nueva Eritel se materializaron ya a nivel operativo en 1990 si bien su ejecución formal se completó al año siguiente (Inisel, *Informe anual*, 1990; Eritel, *Memoria de 1991*, Archivo Histórico del INI; *Actas del Consejo de Telefónica*, 20/12/1989; *AEC*, 11/7/1990; Telefónica, *Memoria,* 1989, 17-19; Comparecencia del señor Presidente de la Compañía Telefónica Nacional de España, don Luis Solana Madariaga, *Diario de Sesiones del Senado*, 93, 14/2/1986, 1-26; *Expansión*, 1 de febrero de 2015). La creación de Eritel fue presentada como el mayor acontecimiento de esos años (*Jane's Defence Weekly*, 17, 1992, 1.034); se publicitó como una «integración para la calidad», una empresa de dimensión y experiencia, altamente cualificada (2.000 profesionales) «proveedor oficial del *software* de sistemas de comunicación e información a la familia olímpica» y «aliado estratégico» de sus clientes (*La Vanguardia*, 13 de mayo y 17 de junio de 1991).

[41] Inisel, *Informe anual*, 1990.

ción de los errores y disminución del coste total. A través de su cuarta línea, el Centro de cálculo-*facilities management*, Eritel contaba con una infraestructura y un equipamiento informático al servicio de la gestión de un centro de esta índole. La línea de formación iba dirigida a difundir las posibilidades de las tecnologías de la información en la mejora de la gestión y rentabilidad empresarial entre directivos de las empresas, organizaciones y simples usuarios (Eritel, *Informe anual*, 1991, 13-17).

Telefónica y el INI mantuvieron un tenaz pulso por el control de la nueva gran empresa, debido a la índole estratégica de sus respectivas filiales y al elevado capital comprometido. El proceso de fusión arrastró la incorporación al grupo Telefónica de Maptel y Ecotel, especializadas en cartografía digital y medición de audiencia, respectivamente. La consolidación del sector público avanzó con un acuerdo entre Inisel y Ceselsa, que allanó el camino a la fusión en una única unidad empresarial y, más delante, a la creación de la nueva tecnológica INDRA. El acuerdo de diciembre de 1991 con Ceselsa para la integración de ambas sociedades, que se esperaba formalizar a lo largo de 1992, era consecuencia del convencimiento de ambos grupos de la necesidad de conformar proyectos industriales en la electrónica española con capacidad financiera y tecnológica propia para poder competir en los mercados nacionales e internacionales. En una nueva línea de avance, un cruce accionarial entre Sainco e Inisel intercambiaba el 6% del capital de la segunda por el 18% de la primera. La operación suponía la entrada inicial de capital privado en el grupo Inisel a través de una participación financiera, que iba acompañada por una alianza estratégica con actuaciones concretas en áreas operativas y aportes a las capacidades industriales compartidas entre las participantes (Grupo Inisel, *Informe* 1991, 1)[42].

4. Integración y concentración del sector público de las TIC en España: criterios, alternativas y propuesta de reorganización

Los movimientos descritos invitan a analizar con un poco de detalle los entresijos de la restructuración de las empresas electrónicas del INI y de la crea-

---

[42] Presión del Ministerio de Industria para acelerar la fusión y oposición de Telefónica a integrar las actividades de *software* de comunicaciones (*ABC*, 11 de junio de 1989); dificultades e interrupciones (*El País*, 25 de marzo de 1990).

ción de un *holding* con recursos financieros propios y planes de autofinancia-ción.

Fue un proceso escalonado que desembocó en una nueva empresa de cabecera, producto de la absorción de EISA por EESA y la adquisición del resto de empresas de la División –ENOSA, EISA, ICuatro, ISEL, PESA y Telesincro– que se tornaban filiales, aprovechando ventajas fiscales. El objetivo era múltiple. Para empezar, perseguía racionalizar la presencia del INI en la industria electrónica en respuesta a la necesidad de una mayor coordinación y mejor definición de estrategias en el mercado preciso de la defensa. Además, propugnaba integrar las capacidades de I+D para optimizar los recursos, limitar la dispersión de las acciones y obtener economías de escala sin olvidar la racionalización de actuaciones básicas –inversiones, comercialización y recursos humanos–. Finalmente, buscaba la cohesión en actividades dispersas en campos relevantes como el de la automatización industrial, a la vez que la asignación más coherente de mercados, evitando duplicidad de acciones y escenarios de autocompetencia[43].

No olvidemos que el sector electrónico se distinguía por una gran velocidad de cambio tecnológico unida a una fuerte competencia de la industria internacional. El fuerte crecimiento de la División hizo aflorar problemas no entrevistos en el momento de su creación, esencialmente la estructura no adecuada a las necesidades.

Recogiendo aspectos apuntados antes, la División del INI tenía como misión coordinar las empresas cuyo tamaño relativamente pequeño obligaba a optimizar recursos y potencialidades en mercados, inversiones, I+D y personal, entre otros aspectos. En mercados porque la adquisición de tecnologías afines y la extensión lógica de las actividades por parte de las distintas compañías había dado lugar a un solapamiento de productos. Los láseres coincidían en EISA y ENOSA, las consolas de presentación de datos en EESA y EISA por desarrollos para aviación civil y programas navales, respectivamente, mientras que EESA y PESA compartían radares por desarrollos para aviación civil y para aplicaciones destinadas a la infantería, así como transmisiones de televisión. Por lo demás, la automatización industrial o robótica en diversas empresas abría la posibilidad de nuevos solapamientos, que solo la integración podía evitar. La necesidad de optimización se extendía a las inversiones porque el uso de nuevas tecnologías por las diversas empresas

---

[43] «Reorganización de empresas electrónicas del INI. Creación de un holding en el sector electrónico-informático del INI», *Archivo Histórico del INI*, 14 y 21 de mayo de 1985.

requería crecidas sumas, en ocasiones duplicadas y fuera del alcance del conjunto.

Si uno se atiene a los criterios, la División electrónica e informática del INI perseguía objetivos varios con la reestructuración. Incluían racionalizar la oferta procedente de las diversas empresas del grupo; la complementariedad tecnológica y especialización; el aprovechamiento de recursos y capacidades comunes a fin de optimizar su utilización y permitir el acceso compartido a medios inasequibles a una iniciativa individual, así como la coordinación de acciones de proyección internacional que garantizasen su viabilidad. Cerraban la larga lista la agilidad y unidad de decisión en los mecanismos de realización de inversiones, lanzamiento de nuevas actividades, acción comercial, compras, aprovechamiento de recursos humanos, junto a la asignación de recursos en función de las necesidades derivadas de una estrategia conjunta.

La falta de integración de las empresas provocaba pérdida de economías de escala, duplicación de actividades y recursos y dispersión del esfuerzo en unidades pequeñas. El logro de esas economías de escala era asimismo posible por medio de la coordinación de las compras, acción que en 1984 había permitido ahorrar 500 millones de pesetas.

Las alternativas barajadas consistían en una sociedad de cartera o en una empresa cabecera y accionista única o mayoritaria en el resto de empresas. La sociedad de cartera, contemplada en un proyecto de la División fechado en noviembre de 1984, se justificaba en razones de optimización de las aplicaciones de tecnología y en la existencia de actividades específicas que habría de realizar SECOINSA en el campo de la informática, razones inexistentes una vez SECOINSA perteneciera al INI. En su contra iba el inconveniente del coste, acrecentado al quedar excluida SECOINSA del grupo. La opción que contemplaba la empresa de cabecera se fundamentaba en la existencia de dos empresas de envergadura y actividad equiparables, a saber EESA y EISA. Permitía aprovechar los recursos existentes en ella para alcanzar los objetivos y sacar provecho de la homogeneización en mercados y dimensión conseguida con la salida de SECOINSA de la División.

En cuanto a la propuesta de reorganización, la alternativa de la empresa cabecera como matriz del *holding* contemplaba la fusión EESA-EISA según dos criterios básicos. El primero aunaba dimensión similar entre ambas, complementariedad de sus mercados respectivos, fuerte dependencia de un mismo cliente y perspectivas comunes de futuro. El segundo traducía el impulso gubernamental al desarrollo de una industria de defensa nacional, campo al que las citadas empresas aportaban casi un tercio de su cifra de negocios. Las diferencias entre ellas se compensaban con la complementariedad, visible en la orientación más mecánica de EESA y más electrónica de EISA. El objetivo giraba en torno a evitar duplicaciones y conseguir tamaño.

Si consideramos el contenido de la integración, debía mantenerse la doble localización industrial de las plantas de EESA y EISA con optimización de su relativa especialización. También debía unificarse el resto de actividades funcionales en aras de una mayor eficacia y de asignación más racional de recursos.

Por su parte, interesaba unificar los respectivos departamentos de I+D, acción con efectos positivos sobre el grave problema de contratación de personal técnico con destino a la planta de Aranjuez, ciudad en la que EISA ocupaba la segunda posición entre las grandes empresas detrás de la Fábrica Española de Magnetos. Convenía también generar desarrollos en microelectrónica en respuesta a necesidades futuras. En lo relativo a gestión, el *holding* debía dotarse de una estructura capaz de vertebrar y coordinar el acceso a grandes áreas de negocio en un marco multiempresa. Estas incluían en lugar destacado defensa y robótica y se completaban con otras varias, entre ellas televisión, electromedicina, ingeniería y servicios informáticos. El *holding* debía adquirir capacidad de coordinación en áreas como planificación, tecnología, compras y recursos humanos. La racionalización debía extenderse a la asignación de mercados y actividades del conjunto de las empresas.

De las dos posibilidades abiertas para la integración EEISA-EISA –fusión y absorción– la óptima era la segunda por los beneficios fiscales: mantenimiento del derecho a la compensación de pérdidas en el impuesto de sociedades al salvaguardarse la sociedad y bonificación de hasta el 99% prevista en la ley 76/1980 para fusiones de empresas de interés nacional (*BOE*, 9, 10 de enero de 1981, 517-519).

A ello se añadían motivos organizativos, como la reducción del número de unidades ejecutivas y administrativas –según informaba la división–. Una vez elegida la absorción como forma de integración, decidir la sociedad absorbente y la disuelta dependía de los menores costes fiscales. En ese sentido, EESA debía absorber a EISA para mantener el derecho de compensación por pérdidas existentes en EESA, cifrado en 88 millones de pesetas.

En cuanto al esquema general de financiación, el *holding* se creaba a través de dos tipos de operaciones, a saber, la transferencia por el INI de participaciones directas en empresas y las «compras del *holding* a las demás empresas de sus participaciones en compañías indirectas». Así, los desembolsos a realizar tenían un doble origen: uno propio de la acción de compra y otro fiscal. La adquisición de participaciones de empresas, o sea la compra de acciones de ISEL y PESA en poder de ENOSA y ERIA, debería ser soportada por el *holding*, a excepción de los costes fiscales derivados de una operación mercantil de compra, que debería ir a cargo del INI.

Queda una referencia a las etapas. El *holding* debía constituirse en tres sucesivas: absorción de EISA por EESA, adquisición por parte de la absorbente de las sociedades participadas indirectamente por el INI –ENOSA, ERIA y PESA en ISEL– y compra de las directas –ENOSA, ERIA y TELESINCRO–.

En la primera etapa, el coste fiscal de la ampliación de capital en EESA para adquirir el patrimonio de EISA, previa disolución de esta, ascendía a 4 millones de pesetas, honorarios incluidos; la segunda etapa exigía al *holding* desembolsos de 98,3 millones de pesetas para las compras de las participaciones indirectas del INI en PESA e ISEL, que se cubrirían por autofinanciación en la cuantía de 98 millones de pesetas y por desembolso del INI de la pequeña cantidad restante en concepto de coste fiscal y honorarios. La tercera etapa zanjaba la cesión del INI al *holding* de su cartera de valores en las participadas directas ENOSA y ERIA, valoradas conjuntamente en 612 millones de pesetas. Junto a ello, implicaba la ampliación de patrimonio del *holding* por adquisición de TELESINCRO, de la participación de SECOINSA en ISEL y de las acciones del INI en ERIA a través de INITEC. Dicha ampliación de patrimonio debía cubrirse vía ampliación de capital con unos costes fiscales en torno a 40 millones de pesetas. El coste total a cubrir por el INI se elevaba a 60 millones de pesetas en efectivo, 98 en forma de autofinanciación y un traspaso de cartera de valores del INI por 3.657 millones de pesetas.

Tabla 2. Reordenación de la división de electrónica del INI (millones de pesetas.)

	Inversión financiera	Coste fiscal; honorarios	Financiación total
Absorción de EISA por EESA	2.562	4	2.566
Adquisición indirecta ISEL y PESA	98	0	98
Adquisición directa ENOSA, TELESA y ERIA	1.111	40	1.151
Totales	3.771	44	3.815

Fuente: Elaboración propia a partir de Archivo Histórico del INI.

La reducción de costes fiscales indujo a descartar el procedimiento de integrar las dos empresas y a crear en su lugar una sociedad, heredera de los patrimonios de ambas. Esta nueva empresa, ya con el posible nombre de EESA-EISA a fin de preservar los dos nombres comerciales, debía adquirir las participaciones accionariales en ese momento correspondientes al INI en las empresas directas ENOSA (100% del capital) y ERIA (61,8%), así como en las indirectas PESA (75%) e ISEL (84,5%). Por su parte, en el *holding* debían integrarse TELESINCRO, las participaciones de SECOINSA en ISEL y las de INITEC en ERIA.

La Asesoría jurídica del INI se decantaba por el *holding*, que requería la aprobación del gobierno a la totalidad de la operación por la importancia y la normativa del INI en vigor así como el respeto de la legislación vigente –ley de sociedades y régimen fiscal de fusiones – y del Estatuto de los Trabajadores. La Asesoría presentó los motivos y elementos básicos de la propuesta de la creación del *holding*. Según este órgano, el estudio del director de la División de electrónica informática se fundamentaba en razones jurídicas, centradas en la falta de personalidad jurídica y la complejidad de las participaciones financieras en la composición de la división. El órgano asesor negaba al sistema organizativo vigente, es decir la división, eficacia para desarrollar proyectos multiempresa especialmente en mercados exteriores, al carecer de personalidad jurídica. La complejidad del organigrama mencionado restaba oportunidades al ejercicio de un control efectivo y a la asignación ponderada de recursos entre las empresas según fueran estas directas, indirectas o participadas indirectas[44].

5. Nacimiento y evolución del grupo Inisel

Inisel presentó al INI una propuesta de plan organizativo en la que matizaba el organigrama presentado para aprobación en octubre de 1985 y, sobre todo, justificaba tal organigrama incluyendo además definiciones de funciones o actividades a desarrollar en las principales unidades en el nuevo organigrama o en el contexto de las definiciones de funciones o actividades.

Inisel recogió las sugerencias hechas en su momento por la Dirección de estructura y política de directivos. En la nueva propuesta se contemplaban hasta siete objetivos principales a alcanzar en la vertiente organizativa. En

[44] Asesoría jurídica (1985).

esencia, suponían la creación de un grupo industrial sometido a una estrategia y acción empresarial común con unidad jerárquica y organizativa flexible para responder a mercados emergentes y muy cambiantes, compuesto por unidades operativas de gestión aligeradas de funciones no ejecutivas y con unidades directivas y de mando claramente definidas[45].

El esquema organizativo contenido en la propuesta se atenía básicamente al que figuraba en la anterior y consistía en la creación de tres gerencias operativas, una dirección económico financiera común, un comité ejecutivo, un comité directivo, una dirección de planificación técnica y prospectiva, una dirección de recursos humanos y una unidad de política corporativa. En detalle, las tres gerencias operativas de Inisel debían agrupar las actividades de Inisel (EESA) y EISA y regular las relaciones operativas con las empresas del grupo industrial de operaciones industriales, de sistemas militares y aeroespaciales y de sistemas civiles. La dirección económico financiera común en Inisel (EESA) complementariamente a sus misiones en Inisel debía asumir las funciones de control económico, seguimiento y supervisión de las empresas del grupo industrial en las áreas económicas y aquellas otras que el INI realizaba desde estas empresas. El comité ejecutivo estaría presidido por el presidente ejecutivo de Inisel y del mismo eran además miembros los gerentes y el director económico financiero. El comité directivo, con idéntico presidente, estaría formado por los restantes miembros del comité ejecutivo y los representantes de las empresas integradas en el grupo (*Propuesta plan organizativo Inisel y su grupo industrial*, Archivo Histórico del INI, 21/11/1985).

En la propuesta figuraban también los organigramas y breves descripciones de funciones o de actividades a desarrollar por las principales unidades. Finalmente se señalaba un plan para la implementación de la organización propuesta. La Dirección de estructura y política de directivos señaló como

---

[45] Comprendían los siguientes: 1) crear desde un principio un grupo industrial basado en una estrategia y acción empresarial común; 2) establecer con carácter urgente una unidad jerárquica y organizativa de Inisel sin esperar a la finalización del proceso jurídico que fuera desarrollando los procedimientos comunes internos; 3) establecer unidades operativas de gestión con alta capacidad ejecutiva claramente identificadas con objetivos particulares y cuentas de pérdidas y ganancias singulares; 4) adecuar la estructura a las necesidades organizativas y de filosofía de actuación que imponen la variedad de mercados y tecnologías en que se había de trabajar y cuyas diferencias eran muy profundas; 5) limitar al máximo las unidades no ejecutivas; 6) fijar muy claramente las unidades directivas y de mando así como su ámbito y 7) establecer una estructura de organización muy dinámica y agresiva capaz de adaptarse y absorber el considerable potencial de crecimiento y el papel protagonista que le correspondía en una serie de mercados emergentes y muy cambiantes (*Propuesta plan organizativo Inisel y su grupo industrial*, Archivo Histórico del INI, 21/11/1985).

sugerencia principal que aun cuando cada gerencia se dedicase a un negocio diferente parecería necesario coordinar la política comercial: esa función se asignó aunque no figurase específicamente en la descripción de funciones a la Dirección de planificación técnica. El esquema contenido en el informe deslindaba las funciones de los tres negocios de Inisel y contaba con un reducido número de unidades centrales. En cualquier caso, tal como se preveía en el plan de implementación, debía desarrollarse convenientemente la descripción de funciones de las principales unidades para definir con suficiente claridad el funcionamiento operativo[46].

En definitiva, Inisel se configuró como un conglomerado dinámico y diversamente articulado de empresas dedicadas al diseño de sistemas de electrónica profesional en los ámbitos civil y militar. Su objetivo genérico era consolidar una posición competitiva, fuerte y sostenida en los mercados nacionales e internacionales en sistemas electrónicos e informáticos de control y para la gestión con especial acento en los caracterizados por su alto contenido de integración y uso de tecnologías avanzadas (Grupo Inisel, *Informe* 1991, 1; Ballart 2001, 124)[47]. Inisel estaba regida por una presidencia ejecutiva, responsable de la asesoría jurídica y de la secretaría del Consejo y la dirección de planificación técnica, por un lado, y de la política corporativa y direcciones de recursos humanos y económico financiera, por el otro. El Grupo quedaba integrado por ENYSA, ICuatro, PESA con su filial PESA Miami, ISEL, Telesincro y FRIASA con su filial ERDISA. Su línea de productos se componía de productos militares, sistemas para la defensa, equipos espaciales, sistemas civiles y electrónica industrial. A su vez, los primeros incluían municionamiento, comunicaciones tácticas, direcciones de tiro, electrónica submarina y misiles; los segundos agrupaban aviónica, radares, guerra electrónica, sistemas automáticos de medida y sistemas de transmisión de datos; los terceros, estaciones terrenas y equipamiento de satélites; los últimos comprendían automatización industrial y control de procesos industriales. Su clientela se componía predominantemente de grandes empresas privadas y públicas de fuerte componente tecnológico (*Boletín informativo*, Grupo INISEL, diciembre 1985, 4).

Inisel llevó a cabo un diagnóstico de la situación del grupo –«definición del problema» en términos del presidente– como paso previo a una reorien-

---

[46] *Propuesta plan organizativo Inisel y su grupo industrial*, Archivo Histórico del INI, 21/11/1985.

[47] La gran prensa internacional aireaba: «the Inisel concern is building an automated factory to make electronic equipment, in cooperation with France and Italy» (*New York Times*, 23 de marzo de 1986).

tación estratégica. El diagnóstico reveló una situación demasiado dispersa, desorganizada y con excesivas líneas de negocio poco claras. De ahí surgía una orientación consensuada a la reordenación, especialmente atendiendo a que el sector estaba concentrándose a gran velocidad a nivel mundial (Ballart 2001, 125).

Gráfico 3. Inisiel: volumen de negocio por área de actividad

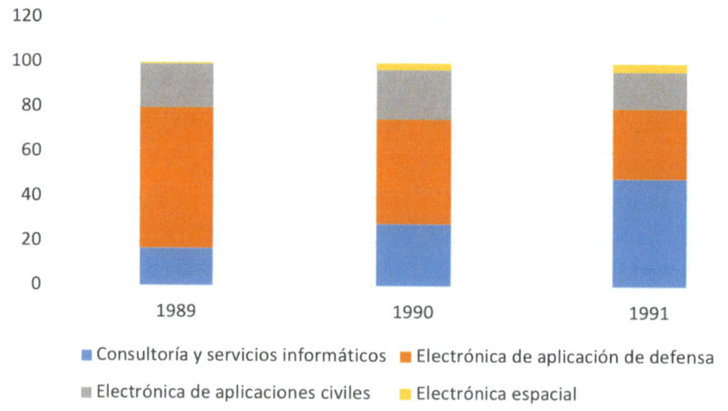

Fuente: Elaboración a partir de Grupo Inisel (1991).

Inisel no tardó en forjar una política de alianzas y toma de posiciones estratégicas. Entre otras destacan el acuerdo suscrito en 1990 con el grupo Abengoa-Sainco para unificar intereses así como el refuerzo de su papel en el segmento de guerra electrónica con el acuerdo de compra de la mayoría accionarial de ELT España. En paralelo, aceleró las negociaciones con otros potenciales socios industriales para líneas de negocio específicas al objeto de completar sus capacidades con nuevos productos y de asegurar el acceso a nuevos mercados. Por otra parte, compró a través de su filial DISEL el 50% de ACD, empresa que estaba controlada en su totalidad por Sainco y que se dedicaba a la actividad de sistemas de control de energía. Además, tuvo lugar el lanzamiento de SAES como empresa tecnológica especializada dentro del segmento de negocio de electrónica submarina. Inisel proyectaba la participación de un socio industrial que complementara sus actividades tanto desde el punto de vista tecnológico como en la apertura de mercados y ampliación de producto (Inisel, *Informe anual*, 1990).

Gráfico 4. Estructura del Grupo Inisel. Participación (%)

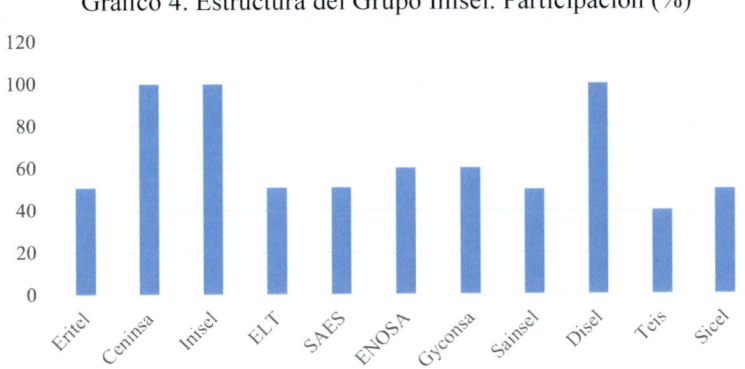

Fuente: Elaboración a partir de Grupo Inisel (1991).

En 1991, el grupo Inisel se componía de once unidades empresariales, en su mayoría dedicadas a electrónica de aplicación en defensa y en proporción menor a electrónica civil. La participación de la matriz en las mismas oscilaba entre un 40% en el caso de Teis, un 50/51% en los de Eritel, ELT, SAES, Sainsel y Sicel, un 60% en los de ENOSA y Gyconsa y la totalidad en los de Ceninsa y DISEL (Gráfico 4) (Grupo Inisel, *Memoria*, 1991).

Inisel fue sometida a cambios importantes en la estructura organizativa, base de alteraciones en los sistemas de trabajo del grupo de empresas. El relevo generacional en el equipo directivo se basó en la promoción interna de profesionales jóvenes pero con conocimientos tecnológicos específicos en sustitución de personal directivo de avanzada edad, apenas orientado al mercado y con bajas opciones de reciclaje. Respecto a los cambios en los sistemas de trabajo, Inisel se inclinó a centrarse en los resultados, desarrollando mecanismos de coordinación más ágiles e implantando un sistema de *reporting* mensual, priorizando la satisfacción del cliente. En otras palabras, orientaba a los directivos de la empresa a definir objetivos concretos y a sistematizar mecanismos de seguimiento operativo que midiesen los logros. Llevaba aparejado el replanteamiento selectivo de las actividades en las que participaba Inisel, con la consiguiente renuncia a ciertas líneas de negocio para centrar los esfuerzos en otras (Ballart 2001, 129).

A finales de 1992, de la concentración de los esfuerzos empresariales realizada en el sector español de las tecnologías de la información, nació Ceselsa-Inisel. La alianza del sector público y de la iniciativa privada dio como resultado un grupo español con vocación de reafirmar su liderazgo como suministrador de productos y sistemas basados en la integración de las nuevas tecnologías de la electrónica, informática y comunicaciones con el fin de consolidar una oferta de soluciones en sistemas integrados de control, gestión y comunicaciones[48]. Se trataba de un verdadero grupo industrial y de servicios con cuatro áreas estratégicas de negocio, a saber, defensa y tecnologías duales, la predominante; consultoría y servicios informáticos; automatización, control y comunicaciones, y espacio. Dentro de ellas, Ceselsa-Inisel compartía algunas líneas de negocio con socios españoles y extranjeros que respaldaban el desarrollo estratégico del grupo a través de la aportación de nuevos mercados y de tecnologías complementarias. Ceselsa-Inisel empleaba un total de 5.000 personas de las que un 68% eran técnicos titulados o de alta especialización. El área de defensa y tecnologías duales estaba formada por diez empresas –Inisel, ENOSA, ELT, SAES, GYCONSA, SAINSEL, Electrónica ENSA, AISA, Giravions Dorand Industries y Aeronautical Systems Designers Ltd.– con cuatro grandes líneas de negocio –detección mando y control; control de armas y equipos, sistemas de aplicación aeronáutica y sistemas navales–. Los programas y actuaciones más relevantes de área se centraron en armamento diverso –sistemas de misiles, MACÁM, programa EFA, nuevo avión de combate europeo, guerra electrónica, simuladores de control de tráfico aéreo y submarino de carácter militar y civil–.

Por su parte, el área estratégica de espacio se estructuraba en torno a Inisel Espacio, que aglutinaba todas las actuaciones del grupo Ceselsa-Inisel, organizadas en tres líneas de negocio: sistemas de comunicaciones vía satélite, de control de vehículos espaciales y de observación de tierra. Las principales actuaciones se plasmaron en tres Centros de control, recepción, tratamiento y explotación de imágenes –de control de satélites de Hispasat, los centros de recepción de imágenes y de tratamiento y explotación de imágenes del satélite Helios–, en el proyecto CISAT (Configuración inicial de comunicaciones por satélite, mediante la utilización de la carga gubernamental de Hispasat) y en la participación en programas de la Agencia Espacial Europea (ESA)[49].

---

[48] Estructura accionarial de Ceselsa-Inisel: Teneo, 60%, Pérez Nievas 20%, Sainco 7%, BBV 4%, Parisbas 3% y Bolsa 6%. El acuerdo existente con Sainco para participar al 50% en la empresa Sainsel fue reforzado a finales de 1992 con objeto de especializarse en el segmento de sistemas navales para la defensa y de sistemas de combate, simuladores tácticos, para el sector civil (control de tráfico marítimo) (Ceselsa-Inisel, *Informe anual*, 1992, 10-11).

[49] Recogiso en Ceselsa-Inisel, *Informe anual*, 1992, 23.

El área estratégica de consultoría y servicios informáticos estaba formada por Eritel y la Central Informática, adquirida en su totalidad por la primera en 1992. Sus líneas de negocio eran tres: sistemas-soluciones, *outsourcing*-centro de cálculo y asistencia técnica. Los proyectos más significativos del área fueron los relativos a sistemas en diversos campos[50].

Ceselsa-Inisel transformó en seña de identidad el uso y la integración de tecnologías avanzadas en sistemas electrónicos e informáticos. La empresa aplicaba una serie de tecnologías de carácter horizontal, comunes a la mayoría de las áreas (electrónica digital y analógica, microelectrónica, microondas y radiofrecuencia, *software* en tiempo real, etcétera), junto a otras diferenciadas, tales como la ingeniería de sistemas. Ceselsa-Inisel basaba su estrategia en materia de I+D en ajustar el desarrollo tecnológico a las estrategias de negocio con énfasis en la ingeniería de sistemas como elemento diferenciador, optimizar las inversiones en tecnología gestionando el riesgo y la rentabilidad de los proyectos, maximizar las energías potenciales y el uso de las tecnologías horizontales y complementar el esfuerzo propio con una política de acuerdos tecnológicos industriales con otros grandes grupos empresariales. En 1992, las inversiones del grupo en I+D se cifraron en 3.200 millones de pesetas, equivalentes al 7,1% de la facturación, mientras que 375 técnicos titulados trabajaban en tareas de innovación dentro del grupo (Ceselsa-Inisel *Informe anual*, 1992, 13).

Como resultado de la integración de Ceselsa e Inisel se formó un mercado que en 1992 rebasaba ampliamente los 45.000 millones de pesetas, de las que cerca del 60% fueron a parar al mercado civil y el 40% restante al de defensa, un área en retroceso debido a la drástica caída de las inversiones en defensa en todo el mundo. La composición de las ventas por áreas de negocio era la siguiente: defensa 41,5%, consultoría y servicios informáticos 34,6, auto-

---

[50] Se trata de los sistemas siguientes: acceso múltiple a la comunicación e información del COOB92, sistema ATLAS para la gestión de circuitos de Telefónica de España; de comunicaciones del tren AVE Madrid-Sevilla; de diagnóstico y evaluación de programas de vuelo para Iberia; sistema integrado de representación gráfica de trenes para RENFE; diseño y construcción de los puntos de información y venta automática de los servicios telefónicos instalados en la Expo 92; de compensación y liquidación de valores para el Banco Central Hispano; de gestión de recursos tóxicos y peligrosos para la comunidad Valenciana; creación del Centro servidor de telecomunicaciones para la Junta de Andalucía; sistema integrado de contabilidad para Universidad de Barcelona; de gestión hospitalaria para la sanidad; sistema integrado de registro del estado civil de las personas y padrón electoral para Nicaragua; sistema presupuestario y contable para Ecuador y sistema de registro civil del ministerio del Interior, migración y justicia de Bolivia (Ceselsa-Inisel, *Informe anual*, 1992, 16).

matización, control y comunicaciones 20,6 y espacio 3,35%[51]. Primero como unidades empresariales separadas y finalmente como integradas, Ceselsa e Inisel intensificaron su estrategia de posicionamiento en los mercados internacionales, que generaban aproximadamente un 15% del volumen agregado de negocio. Los esfuerzos tuvieron una inmediata plasmación organizativa una vez alcanzada la integración. En efecto, el Grupo creó una dirección específica con la misión de desarrollar la actividad internacional dando servicio a las cuatro áreas estratégicas en las que se estructuraba el grupo. La dirección internacional tenía como objetivo prioritario la apertura de nuevos mercados para los productos, sistemas y servicios de la empresa. En 1992, las actuaciones más destacadas en el mercado internacional fueron los nuevos contratos para suministrar a cinco países sistemas de diverso tipo aplicables a los trasportes aéreos y terrestres[52].

Conclusión

Este capítulo analiza el componente nacional de las crisis y la reconversión industrial a partir de un estudio de caso, centrado en la División electrónica e informática del INI, una de las tres grandes reestructuraciones de las TIC en España, junto a las de los grupos privados de Telefónica e IT&T. Específica mente, estudia la relación entre tecnología punta y estructura organizativa, a la vez que ahonda en las diversas alternativas a esta relación en los sectores público y privado. El corte cronológico escogido se inscribe en la etapa de la globalización de la economía y comprende el periodo a caballo entre la preparación para la incorporación de España a la Unión Europea y su integración plena. Por consiguiente, implica un escenario nada estático, con las políticas

---

[51] La cifra de ventas de Ceselsa solo recoge el periodo económico de los ocho meses finales de 1992 (Ceselsa-Inisel, *Informe anual*, 1992, 11).

[52] Consistieron en la ejecución con destino a Portugal de sendos simuladores de tren para los ferrocarriles y de vuelo para el avión de combate F-16, la implantación de sendos sistemas de registro civil en Bolivia y Nicaragua, así como los sistemas de control de tráfico aéreo de tres aeropuertos (de Ámsterdam en Holanda, y de San Pedro de Sula y Roatán en Honduras). Estaban todavía en proyecto el desarrollo del simulador de vuelo del avión CN-235 y de los sistemas de control de tráfico vial para diversas ciudades indonesias (Mergati, Yakarta y Surabaya), además de la participación en los principales programas del nuevo avión de combate europeo (Nuevo EFA), en el desarrollo informático del ministerio de finanzas de Ecuador y en los principales programas de la agencia espacial Europea ESA (Ceselsa-Inisel, *Informe anual*, 1992, 13).

de reajuste previo, el sometimiento a las directrices europeas y el aprovechamiento de los planes de tipo horizontal y sectorial (Henderson 1991).

En uno de los campos de mayor impacto en la tecnología de vanguardia, la estrategia del grupo Ceselsa-Inisel en materia de I+D se puede resumir en torno a tres objetivos básicos. En primer lugar, pretendía ajustar el desarrollo tecnológico a las estrategias de negocio poniendo la ingeniería de sistemas como elemento diferenciador. En segundo lugar, buscaba optimizar las inversiones en tecnología gestionando el riesgo y la rentabilidad de los proyectos manteniendo el esfuerzo en I+D en cifras ajustadas a la disponibilidad de recursos de las empresas del grupo, maximizar las energías potenciales y el uso de las tecnologías horizontales. Finalmente, perseguía conjugar el propio desarrollo tecnológico con una eficaz política de acuerdos tecnológicos con otros grandes grupos empresariales (Ceselsa-Inisiel, 1992, 13).

La evidencia empírica muestra que no se trataba tanto de una reconversión previa a la privatización como obsequio a posibles compradores sino más bien de una reestructuración en búsqueda de competitividad para su permanencia en el sector público. Los procesos aquí descritos para definir el comportamiento del INI en el sector de las TIC parecen encajar de forma apropiada en los términos de consolidación de las empresas, búsqueda de economías de escala por competir en mercados abiertos e internacionalización.

Anexo 1. La industria mundial de los semiconductores: diez empresas principales, 1992

	Ingresos totales (millones de dólares)	Clasificación	Cuota (%)
NEC	4.774	1	8,00
Toshiba	4.579	2	7,67
Intel	4.019	3	6,73
Motorola	3.802	4	6,37
Hitachi	3.765	5	6,31
Texas Instruments	2.738	6	4,59
Fujitsu	2.705	7	4,53
Mitsubishi	2.303	8	3,86
Matsushita	2.037	9	3,41

Philips	2.022	10	3,39
Total World Revenue ($M)	59.694	–	100
			54,85

Fuente: Elaboración a partir de Dataquest, septiembre de 1992.

Anexo 2. Los mercados de Eisa

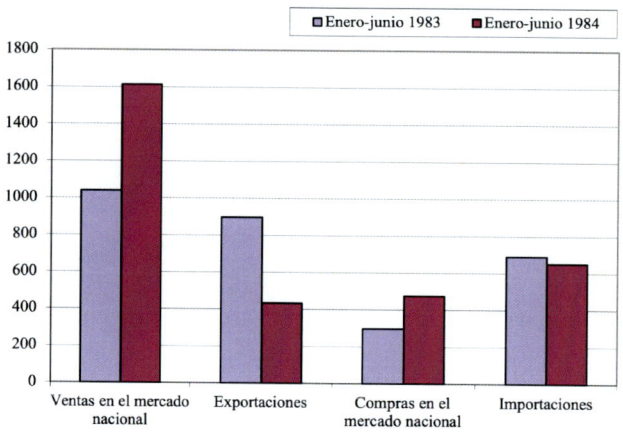

Fuente: Elaboración a partir de EISA, *Información correspondiente a 1983*, junio de 1984, 19.

Anexo 3. Clientes de EISA. Saldos, diciembre 1983

Clientes	Saldos, diciembre de 1983
Academia Artillería	0,9
Arsenal Naval Militar	0,3
Cuartel General Armada	872,1
Cuartel General Ejército	169,4
Dirección General Tráfico	85,0
División Acorazada	0,6
División I+D	2,5

Ejército Aire	1,8
Ministerio Industria y Energía	0,2
Ministerio Transportes y Comunicaciones	9,0
Parque Artillería Valladolid	0,9
Parque Central Artillería	4,1
Parque y Maestranza Artillería Madrid	0,2
Parque y Maestranza Artillería Sevilla	12,7
División Militar	0,5
U.J.T. y M. Rto. Mixto Artillería	0,1
Junta Energía Nuclear	2,2
RTV	0,6
RENFE	1,1
Astilleros Canarios S. A.	2,3
Astilleros Españoles	5,9
Auxini	0,3
CETME S.A.	1,5
CASA	10,5
ENISA	2,6
ENAGAS	0,2
Empresa Nacional Bazán	88,5
Empresa Nacional Bazán S. Fernando	49
Empresa Nacional Bazán Cartagena	4
Empresa Nacional Bazán El Ferrol	0,4
Empresa Nacional de Uranio	12,1
Empresa Nacional Sta. Bárbara	43,4
ERIA Systems	0,1
Gas y Electricidad	6,1
Hunosa	0,2
Unión Eléctrica de Canarias	2,4

Empresa Nacional Bazán: central (35,1).

Fuente: Elaboración a partir de EISA, *Información correspondiente a 1983*, 19.

Anexo 4.1. Perfil de ERIA

ERIA: estructura de los costes de producción (%)

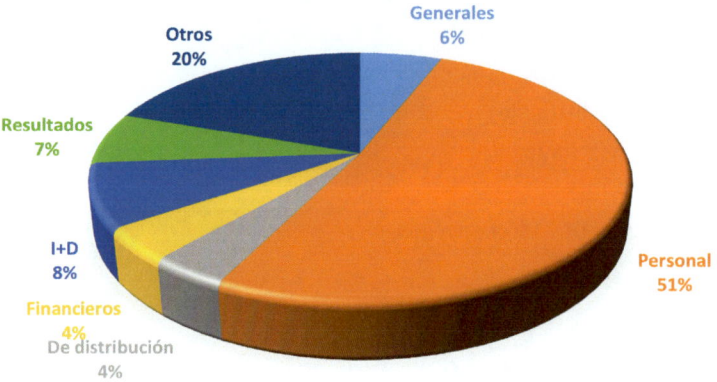

Fuente: Elaboración a partir de ERIA, *Informe(s) anual(es)*.

Anexo 4.2. Ventas totales y valor añadido, ERIA 1985-1989

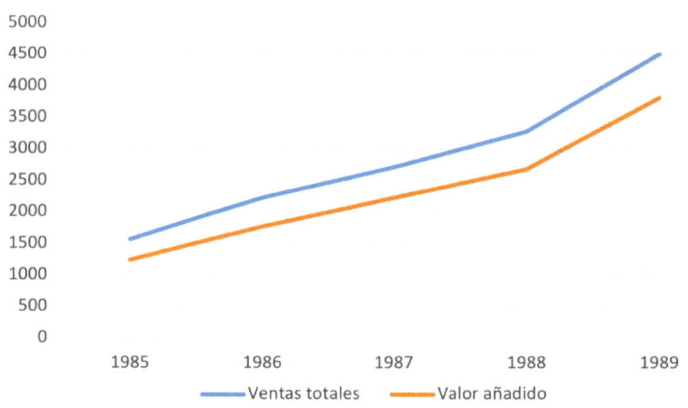

Fuente: Elaboración a partir de ERIA, *Informe(s) anual(es)*.

Anexo 4.3. ERIA: cifras significativas, 1989 (%)

Destino de las ventas por sectores económicos

Industria y servicios	34
Defensa aerospacial	9
Administración civil	25
Informática	6
Financiero	26
Subtotal	100

Estructura de los costes de producción

Generales	5,9
Personal	51,4
De distribución	4
Financieros	4,2
I+D	8,2
Resultados	6,7
Otros	19,6
Subtotal	100

Composición mano de obra

Hombres	62
Mujeres	38
Subtotal	100

Fuente: Elaboración a partir de ERIA, *Informe(s) anual(es)*.

Fuentes primarias

Archivo Histórico del INI, Madrid.
Archivo Histórico del Congreso de los diputados, Madrid.
Archivo Histórico del Senado, Madrid.
Telefónica, Madrid.

Hemeroteca (Referencias más frecuentes)

ABC, Madrid.
El País, Madrid.
La Vanguardia, Barcelona.
New York Times, Nueva York.

Referencias

Abramov, Alexander et al. 2017. «State-owned enterprises in the Russian market: Ownership structure and their role in the economy», *Russian Journal of Economics*, 3, 1, 1-23.

Aceña, Pablo M. y Comín, Francisco. 1991. *INI: 50 años de industrialización en España*, Madrid: Espasa Calpe.

Akera, Atsushi. 2008. *Calculating a Natural World: Scientists, Engineers, and Computers During the Rise of U.S. Cold War Research.* Cambridge MA: MIT Press.

Aranzadi, Claudio et al. 1983. «Una nota sobre ajuste y reindustrialización». *Papeles de economía española*, 15, 317-325.

Aranzadi, Claudio. 1987. «La crisis ha exigido una reorientación de los instrumentos financieros de promoción del INI». *Perspectivas del sistema financiero*, 20, 162-163.

Aranzadi, Claudio. 1989. «La política de desinversiones en el INI». *Papeles de economía española*, 38, 258-261.

Asesoría jurídica. 1985. *Nota sobre la propuesta de creación de un 'holding' en el sector electrónico informático del Instituto* [INI], Archivo Histórico del INI, 16/5.

Ballart, Xavier. 2001. *Innovación en la gestión pública y en la empresa privada.* Madrid: Ediciones Díaz de Santos.

Batiz-Lazo, Bernardo y Boyns, Trevor. 2004. «The Business and Financial History of Automation and Technological Change in 20th Century Banking». *Accounting Business and Financial History Journal*, 14, nº3: 225-232.

Baumol, William J. (ed.). 1980. *Public and Private Enterprise in a Mixed Economy: Proceedings of a Conference held by the International Economic Association in Mexico City.* Nueva York: MacMillan.

Bliss, Christopher J. y Braga De Macedo, Jorge. 1990. *Unity with Diversity in the European Economy: The Community's Southern Frontier.* Nueva York: Cambridge University Press.

Boix, Carles. 1998. *Political Parties, Growth and Equality. Conservative and Social Democratic Economic Strategies in the World Economy*. Cambridge: Cambridge University Press.

Bös, Dieter. 1988. «Introduction: Recent theories on public enterprise economics». *European Economic Review*, 32, 409-414.

Bös, Dieter. 1986. *Public Enterprise Economics: Theory and Application*. Ámsterdam y Nueva York: North-Holland.

Boyer, Miguel. 2004. «El segundo ajuste económico de la democracia española (diciembre de 1982 a julio de 1985)». En *Economía y economistas españoles*, vol. 8, dirigido por Fuentes Quintana, Enrique, Barcelona: Galaxia Gutenberg/Círculo de Lectores, 239-304.

Buesa, Mikel. 1994. «Movilidad y cambios en el liderazgo entre las grandes empresas industriales españolas (1982-1992)». *Documentos de Trabajo de la Facultad de Ciencias Económicas y Empresariales*, 15.

Buesa, Mikel y Molero, José. 1986. «La intervención estatal en la remodelación del sistema productivo: el caso de la industria electrónica española durante los años 80». *Documento de trabajo 8.619*. Madrid: Universidad Complutense.

Burgess, Katrina. 2004. *Parties and Unions in the New Global Economy*. Pittsburgh: University of Pittsburgh Press.

Calvo, Ángel. 2014. *Telecomunicaciones y el nuevo mundo digital en. España: la aportación de Standard Eléctrica*. Barcelona: Ariel/Fundación Telefónica.

Calvo, Ángel. 2016. *Historia de Telefónica: 1976-2000. Las telecomunicaciones en la España democrática*. Barcelona: Ariel/Fundación Telefónica.

Calvo, Ángel. 2019. «Consolidation and rationalization of the public companies in Spain: the information and communication technologies (ICT) holding». *Journal of Evolutionary Studies in Business*, 4, 1, enero-junio, 142-179.

Campbell-Kelly, Martin et al. 2014. *Computer: a history of the information machine*. Boulder CO: Westview Press.

Canales, Álvaro y Elices, Adolfo. 1994. «La contratación por el Ministerio de Defensa de armamento y material: las compensaciones económicas, industriales y tecnológicas». *Cuaderno de Estrategia*, 64, 103-117.

Cantoni, Virginio; Falciasecca, Gabriele y Pelosi, Giuseppe. 2011. *Storia delle telecomunicazioni*. Florencia: Firenze University Press.

Carreras, Albert y Tafunell, Xavier. 2004. *Historia económica de la España contemporánea*. Barcelona: Crítica.

Cleland, David I. et al. 1993. *Military Project Management Handbook*. Nueva York: McGraw-Hill.

Comisión Europea. 2014. «Directrices sobre ayudas estatales de salvamento y de reestructuración de empresas no financieras en crisis». *Diario Oficial de la Unión Europea*, 31 de julio, 3 y 5.

Consejo Consultivo de Privatizaciones. 1999. *Informe de actividades – 1999*. Madrid: CCP.

Cortada, James W. 1996a. *A Bibliographic Guide to the History of Computer Applications, 1950-1990*. Westport CT: Greenwood Press.

Cortada, James W. 1996b. *Second bibliographic guide to the history of computing, computers, and the information processing industry*. Westport CT: Greenwood Press.

Dehesa, Guillermo de la. 1993. «Las privatizaciones en España». *Moneda y Crédito*, 196, 131-133.

Disco, Cornelis y van der Meulen, Barend. 1998. *Getting New Technologies Together: Studies in Making Sociotechnical*. Berlín: Walter de Gruyter.

Duch-Brown, Nestor y Fonfría, Antonio. 2014. «The Spanish defence industry: an introduction to the special issue». *Defence and Peace Economics* 25, 1-6.

EISA. 1984. *Memoria 1983,* Archivo del INI, 346.3 (2ª).

Eurofound. 2015. *ERM Annual report 2014: Restructuring in the public sector.* Luxemburgo: Publications Office of the European Union.

European Commission. 2016. *State-Owned Enterprises in the EU: Lessons Learnt and Ways Forward in a Post-Crisis Context*. Luxemburgo: Publications Office of the European Union.

Fabrie, Robert. 1987. *World Support Base, Spain*. Washington: National Defense University.

Fernández de Pinedo, Emiliano. 2003. «Desarrollo, crisis y reconversión de la siderurgia española a través de una empresa vizcaína, AHV (1929-1996)». *Ekonomiaz*, nº 54: 28-51.

Fernández Marugán, Francisco. 1992. «La década de los ochenta. Impulso y reforma económica». En *La década del cambio: diez años de gobierno socialista 1982-1992*, coordinado por Guerra, Alfonso y Tezanos, José F., Madrid: Sistema, 135-194.

Fisher, Franklin M. et al. 1983. *IBM and the U.S. Data Processing Industry: An Economic History*. Nueva York: Praeger.

Freedman, Lawrence. 1999. *The Politics of British Defence 1979-98.* Houndmills: Macmillan.

García, José M. 1989. «El INI como grupo de negocios». *Papeles de Economía Española*, 38, 262-276.

Garretsen, Harry y Brakman, Steven. 2005. *Location and Competition.* Londres y Nueva York: Routledge.

Gummett, Philip y Stein, Josephine A. (ed.). 2014. *European Defence Technology in Transition.* Londres: Routledge.

Haigh, Thomas. 2001. «Inventing Information Systems: The Systems Men and the Computer, 1950-1968». *Business History Review*, 75, 1, 15-61.

Hagedoorn, John y Schakenraad, Jos. 1992. «Leading companies and networks of strategic alliances in information technologies». *Research policy*, 21, 163-190.

Hare, Paul y Turley, Gerard. 2013. *Handbook of the Economics and Political Economy of Transition.* Abingdon: Routledge.

Henderson, Jeffrey. 1991. *The Globalisation of high technology production: society, space, and semiconductors in the restructuring of the modern world.* Londres: Routledge.

Hernández, Pablo. 2004. *Empresa pública, privatización y eficiencia.* Madrid: Banco de España.

Heywood, Paul. 1999. *Politics and Policy in Democratic Spain-no Longer Different?* Londres: Frank Cass.

Karl, Wilfried. 1994. *Rüstungskooperation und Technologiepolitik als Problem der westeuropäischen Integration.* Wiesbaden: Springer-Verlag.

Kassim, Hussein y Menon, Anand. 2002. *The European Union and National Industrial Policy.* Nueva York: Routledge.

Kumar, Anjali. 1994. «Italy: IRI and Others, State Holding Companies and Public Enterprises in Transition». En *Patterns of a Network Economy*, editado por Johansson, Borje; Karlsson, Charlie y Westin, Lars. Berlín/Nueva York: Springer, 60-109.

Lane, Jan-Erik. 1997. *Public Sector Reform: Rationale, Trends and Problems.* Londres: Sage.

Latham, Andrew A. y Hooper, Nick. 2013. *The Future of the Defence Firm: New Challenges, New Directions.* Dordrecht: Springer.

Lawlor, Teresa; Rigby, Mike y Smith, Roger. 2005. *European Trade Unions: Change and Response.* Londres: Routledge.

Lechman, Ewa. 2015. *ICT Diffusion in Developing Countries: Towards a New Concept of Technological Takeoff.* Cham: Springer.

Locksley, Gareth. 1983. *The EEC telecommunications industry. Competition, concentration & competitiveness.* Bruselas: Commission of the European Communities.

Martin, Stephen y Parker, David. 1997. *The Impact of Privatisation: Ownership and corporate performance in the UK.* Londres: Routledge.

Mazzucato, Mariana. 2013. *The Entrepreneurial State: debunking public vs. private sector myths.* Londres: Anthem Press.

Ministerio de Industria y Energía. 1990. *Informe sobre la industria española.* Madrid: MINER.

Mohr, Jakki J. et al. 2009. *Marketing of High-technology Products and Innovations,* Upper Saddle River NJ: Pearson.

Molas-Gallart, Jordi. 1992. *Military Production and Innovation in Spain.* Harwood: Chur.

Molero José. 1988. «Foreign Technology and Local Innovation: Some Lessons from Spanish Defence Industry Experience». En *The Relations between Defence and Civil Technologies,* editado por Gummett, Philip y Reppy, Judith. NATO ASI Series, vol 46. Dordrecht: Springer.

Mosconi, Franco et al. 2001. *Política industrial y tecnológica II: documentos,* Volumen 2. Barcelona: Universitat Politècnica de Catalunya.

Muller, Harald. 1991. *How Western European Nuclear Policy is Made: Deciding on the Atom.* Nueva York: Palgrave Macmillan.

Musacchio, Aldo y Lazzarini, Sergio G. 2014. *Reinventing State Capitalism.* Cambridge: Harvard University Press.

Norberg, Arthur L. 2005. *Computers and Commerce: A Study of Technology and Management at Eckert Mauchly Computer Company, Engineering Research Associates, and Remington Rand, 1946-1957.* Cambridge MA: MIT Press.

OECD. 2009. *State-Owned Enterprises in China: Reviewing the Evidence.* París: OECD.

OECD. 2014. *The size and sectoral distribution of SOEs in OECD and partner countries.* París: OECD.

Parker, David. 2002. *Privatization in the European Union: Theory and Policy Perspectives.* Londres. Taylor & Francis.

Parliamentary Monitoring Group. 2000. *Restructuring of State-Owned Enterprises: briefing.* Ciudad del Cabo: Parliamentary Monitoring Group.

Pestieau, Pierre y Tulken, Henry. 1993. «Assessing and explaining the performance of public enterprises». *Finanz Archiv Journal,* 50, n°.3: 293-323.

Prados, Leandro. 2017. *Spain's Performance in Comparative Perspective. In: Spanish Economic Growth, 1850–2015.* Cham: Palgrave Macmillan.

Pugh, Emerson W. 1995. *Building IBM: Shaping an Industry and Its Technology.* Cambridge MA: MIT Press.

Radygin, Alexander y Entov, Revold. 2012. «Government failures: Theory and policy». *Voprosy Ekonomiki,* 12, 4-30.

Rama, Ruth y Holl, A. 2009. «Networking and R&D in domestic and FDI plants in Spanish electronics clusters». *International Journal of Strategic Business Alliances,* 1, 2, 182-204.

Reid, Tom R. 2001. *The Chip: How Two Americans Invented the Microchip and Launched a Revolution.* Nueva York: Random House.

Riordan, Michael y Hoddeson, Lillian. 1997. *Crystal Fire: The Birth of the Information Age.* Nueva York y Londres: W. W. Norton & Company.

Rose, Joseph B. et al. 2000. A comparative analysis of public sector restructuring in the U.S., Canada, Mexico, and the Caribbean». *Journal of Labor Research,* December, 21, n°.4: 601-625.

Sáez, Miguel Á. y Díaz Morlán, Pablo. 2009. *El puerto del acero: Historia de la siderurgia de Sagunto (1900-1984).* Madrid: Marcial Pons.

Salas, Javier. 1991. «Tribuna: El fortalecimiento del Grupo INI». *El País,* 26 de agosto.

Sánchez, Esther. 2020. «Los grandes proyectos de la industria francesa en España en tiempos de Mitterrand y González (1981-1986)». *Historia y política,* 44, 369-401

Sánchez, María del Carmen. 2009. «El papel de la empresa pública industrial en el desarrollo regional». *Revista Galega de Economía,* 18, 1, 1-27.

Szarzec, Katarzyna, Dombi, Ákos y Matuszak, Piotr. 2021. «State-owned enterprises and economic growth: Evidence from the post-Lehman period». *Economic Modelling,* 99, marzo 2021, n°.4: 1-20.

Sieber, Sandra y Valor, Josep. 2008. «El sector de las tecnologías de la información y comunicación en España en el contexto europeo: evolución y tendencias». Madrid: IESE.

Solchaga, Carlos. 2017. *Las cosas como son.* Madrid: Editorial Galaxia.

Sturesson, Jan et al. 2015. *State-Owned Enterprises. Catalysts for public value creation?* Londres: PWC.

Triana, Eugenio. 1991. «Plan de Actuación Tecnológico Industrial». *Política científica*, 29, 8-9.

Valdaliso, Jesús M. 2003. «Crisis y reconversión de la industria de construcción naval en el País Vasco». *Ekonomiaz*, cuarto trimestre, 52-67.

Vickers, John y Yarrow, George. 1988. *Privatization: an economic analysis.* Cambridge MA: MIT Press.

Wilson, Kenneth F. 2013. *West Europe.* Oxford: Elsevier.

Wood, Pia Ch. y Sorenson, David S. 2000. *International Military Aerospace Collaboration: Case Studies in Domestic and Intergovernmental Politics.* Farnham: Ashgate.

4. Los materiales de la Tercera Revolución Industrial: la fibra óptica en España

1. Introducción

Los especialistas internacionales, atentos al fenómeno de la globalización, se han preguntado una y otra vez por las manifestaciones de esta y, en concreto, por las razones del notable aumento de la inversión extranjera directa (IED) en los años finales de la década de los 80, liderado por grandes empresas (Graham y Krugman 1993, 28). ¿Repercutió sobre estas el potencial corolario de la globalización, es decir, la «retirada del Estado», la erosión de la soberanía económica del Estado nación por trasvase de muchos instrumentos tradicionales de la política económica nacional a las instituciones regionales y mundiales y de los mercados? (Cable 1995, 23-53).

La historiografía sobre la IED, en contraste con las «inversiones de cartera» en valores, y sobre sus principales ejecutoras, las compañías multinacionales, aumentó considerablemente desde la Segunda Guerra Mundial[1]. Pese a ello, numerosos estudiosos decepcionados con los logros reconocen que el consenso se circunscribe a reconocer la importancia creciente de la IED y el número igualmente creciente de multinacionales. No pocos que admiten la importancia de la IED y las multinacionales en la economía mundial hacen hincapié en las brechas de la investigación sobre el tema[2]. Lejos de conclusiones adecuadas y

---

[1] Entre los trabajos esenciales, destacamos el pionero de Mira Wilkins (1970), el de Buckley y Casson (1976) y el más reciente de Dunning y Lundan (2008). Para el conjunto del capítulo, véase Calvo (2020), 1-36.

[2] Lipsey (2002) niega a los estudios microeconómicos sobre el impacto de la IED en el crecimiento carácter de concluyentes a causa de su carencia de universalidad. Llamadas de

generalizadas, las posiciones sobre el efecto de las IED son objeto de encendido debate[3]. Hay quienes se preguntan acerca del influjo de las diferentes instituciones políticas en la IED (Jensen 2006).

Con el telón de fondo de las referencias internacionales, la estructura de ideas originaria sobre la envergadura de la IED en España durante la segunda mitad del siglo xx se ha fortalecido de forma apreciable con varias aportaciones recientes, que incluyen síntesis puestas al día del estado de la cuestión. Tales publicaciones ponen de relieve la dinámica general de expansión de las multinacionales en España, muy atentas a los alicientes de las políticas internas y propensas a privilegiar las empresas conjuntas y la contratación de mano de obra local, entre otras cuestiones (Álvaro y Puig 2015, 249-285 y 2016, 14-39).

La hipótesis de trabajo de la existencia de un armazón de profundas relaciones entre política industrial, política regional y las multinacionales requiere incorporar al marco teórico un variado número de aportaciones. Surgidas a lo largo de un amplio periodo de tiempo, ponen esencialmente el foco en los factores de localización y en los procesos de decisión de esta, a la vez que ayudan a poner en contexto las ideas de política regional e industrial al uso en aquella época (Alonso, 1964, 303-329; Alonso (1989), 246-247; Anderson, 2012; Chisholm, 1990, 137-164; Cuervo, 1978, pp.127-153; De la Dehesa, 2004; Kline y Moretti, 2014, 629-662; Krugman, 1992, 21-46; Hernández y Guillón, 2018, 24-33).

Considerando lo anterior, este capítulo aspira a proporcionar elementos para llenar ciertos vacíos relacionados con aspectos de la implicación empresarial mundial con una fracción de la IED mundial en las postrimerías del siglo xx e indaga en las causas de la implantación de las multinacionales de las tecnologías de la información y la comunicación en España, país del sur de Europa con un perfil similar a otro «país de cohesión» –Irlanda, el tigre celta– como destino de la IED[4]. Desde el lado del país anfitrión, el estudio se centra en los motivos

alerta de prominentes instituciones mundiales acerca de la inversión internacional de las multinacionales han contribuido recientemente a reavivar el debate. Un ejemplo lo proporciona el aviso del FMI de que el 40% de dicha inversión internacional obedece a ingeniería financiera tan solo interesada por la elusión fiscal mediante sociedades instrumentales o vacías (*Financial Times*, 8 de septiembre de 2019).

[3]   Los críticos no reconocen a la creciente entrada de IED en los países en desarrollo los estímulos económicos esperados (Stiglitz 2002; Rodrik 2006, 973–987); otros le achacan abiertamente explotar recursos y mano de obra barata, alimentar las tensiones y apoyar regímenes represivos (Klein 2000).

[4]   En Irlanda, los dos ramos más importantes para esta inversión fueron el de las TIC y el de los productos farmacéuticos/sanitarios. España e Irlanda se diferenciaron de los restantes países de la cohesión por el mal funcionamiento de su mercado de trabajo cuyo rendimien-

de las administraciones públicas –estatales y no estatales– para atraer capital extranjero y del papel contradictorio que ejercieron al competir entre ellas. La circunstancia de que, en ocasiones, España está ausente de las observaciones sobre la IED, posiblemente debido a su integración tardía en la Comunidad Económica Europea, acrecienta, sin duda, el interés del caso. Otro aliciente del estudio radica en la elección de un sector generalmente desdeñado por la investigación, más atenta a los avatares de otros en la región, entre ellos la industria naval gijonesa, o las empresas Hunosa y Ensidesa[5].

La investigación aborda los proyectos de creación y trayectoria de empresas conjuntas relacionadas con la fibra óptica en España. Se basa en fuentes cuantitativas y cualitativas de diversa naturaleza y procedencia, algunas de extraordinaria relevancia debido a su valor intrínseco y dificultad de acceso para los investigadores. Entre ellas descuellan las de la Compañía Telefónica Nacional de España (CTNE), junto a las de instituciones nacionales, regionales e internacionales.

El texto se estructura en cuatro apartados principales, que abordan sucesivamente la revolución de la fibra óptica y su extensión mundial, la estrategia de expansión de las multinacionales en España, la dependencia tecnológica respecto a las multinacionales en este país y la potencial alternativa del capital multinacional europeo.

2. La revolución de la fibra óptica y su extensión mundial

Hacia finales del siglo XX, un profundo y acelerado cambio tecnológico generó al menos media docena de avances capaces de crear nuevos productos y servicios y reducir los costes unitarios de los mensajes[6]. Las telecomunicaciones tuvieron como frente de avance el descubrimiento o utilización de nuevos materiales, idóneos para satisfacer las necesidades nuevas y crecientes de los consumidores.

---

to se deterioró en relación con la UE-15 durante el periodo 1974-86 (Barry 2004, 11-12; Grimes y Collins 2009, 45-67).

5   *El País*, 26 de octubre de 1983.

6   Strange (1996, 100-102) ofrece una buena síntesis: grandes mejoras en los sistemas de transmisión, aumentos de la capacidad de las conexiones gracias a las grandes centrales digitales, el teléfono celular o móvil, los satélites que circundan la tierra y el fax como sistema de comunicación más común para los usuarios empresariales; solo faltaría mencionar expresamente Internet para completar la lista de avances tecnológicos.

La transmisión de ingentes volúmenes de datos exigió soportes adecuados, el fundamental de los cuales resultó ser la fibra óptica, sustitutiva del cobre y que yuxtaponía los altos costes de investigación a economías de escala significativas (Hufbauer 1990, 186)[7]. Una mayor capacidad de transporte de voz, telemática e imágenes con menor peso y volumen unitario, así como una alta fiabilidad y cuantiosa reducción de costes en la fabricación le conferían una clara ventaja comparativa[8]. El nuevo material resultó clave por su elevado valor añadido y su idoneidad para la digitalización, en suma, para la infraestructura de las grandes redes de telecomunicaciones (Elion y Elion 1978, 213)[9].

Un sistema experimental de fibra óptica envió por primera vez señales en 1977. Al cabo de unos meses, General Telephone and Electronics (a 6 Mb/s), AT&T (a 45 Mb/s) y la Administración de Correos del Reino Unido (a 8,4 Mb/s) transmitieron tráfico telefónico en directo a través de fibras multimodo. Los sistemas de transmisión por fibra óptica en los últimos cuarenta y cinco años han atravesado por cuatro grandes eras: la era de la regeneración (1977-1995), la de los sistemas amplificados gestionados por dispersión (1995~2008), la de los sistemas coherentes amplificados (2008~actualidad) y

---

[7] La fibra óptica forma parte de los materiales de alto valor añadido ligado a su intenso contenido tecnológico, que incluyen también los paneles de pantallas de cristal líquido (LOD), vidrios fotovoltaicos y de protección contra las radiaciones.

[8] A la invención de la fibra óptica y los láseres en la década de 1960 le sucedieron diversos desarrollos –disminución de la atenuación en los años 70 por Corning and Glass y láseres semiconductores InGaAsP de modo único en los 80–, que permitieron aumentar la distancia de la transmisión, primero más allá de los 58 km de longitud y a continuación hasta los 130 (Mishra 2013, 1-7). A los esfuerzos de Corning Glass Works en los Estados Unidos se sumaron dos entidades de otros tantos países (Bell Laboratories, un consorcio de investigadores en el Reino Unido y Nippon Sheet Glass-Nippon Electric en Japón) (U.S. International Trade Commission 1988, 3/7).

[9] Algún órgano de prensa (*Le Monde*, 13 de octubre de 1982) resumía así para el gran público la capacidad extraordinaria del material: «millones de imágenes y sonidos en un "cabello" de sílice». Su importancia estratégica la hizo objeto de vigilancia por el Comité de control de las exportaciones de bienes sensibles al bloque soviético o COCOM, que se encontraba con el problema de la dispersión de la producción en numerosos países (*International Trade Reporter: Current reports*, 1994). Una nota negativa del imaginario colectivo: desde la ruptura de AT&T y la posterior carrera de otras compañías para ocupar el terreno de la larga distancia, la calidad del "sonido" de las conferencias había eliminado toda sensación de distancia. La fibra óptica que usan algunas de las nuevas compañías ha generado una recepción tan inquietantemente nítida que destruye toda sensación de separación entre uno y la persona que hay al otro lado de la línea. El sonido de su voz es como algo que te implantan en el cerebro, o como un CD diminuto que suena en el auricular de tu teléfono. A mi esa pérdida de la sensación de distancia me parece una tragedia» (S. Tesich, *Karoo*, 94).

la era de la multiplexación por división espacial (desde 2008) (Winzer, Neilson y Chraplyvy 2018, 24.190-24.239)[10].

En los cables, caracterizados por su elevado potencial de demanda, la fibra óptica revolucionó la tecnología dual del cobre y de los coaxiales a la vez que la economía de esta rama de las telecomunicaciones. En las comunicaciones submarinas en particular, el nuevo material garantizaba bajas pérdidas con baja dispersión cromática incluso con señales de altas frecuencias y de transmisión de señales digitales (Aditi 2012, 79-83; *Submarine Fiber Optic Communications Systems*, 3, 2, febrero, 1995, 8; RACE 1991, 58)[11]. Por su parte, dio un vuelco al tradicional predominio de los satélites en el tráfico mundial de las comunicaciones, en un contexto de crecimiento imparable del volumen total. La fibra óptica aventajaba a los satélites, incluso como tecnología aún en desarrollo, en la claridad e ininterrupción de la transmisión, inmunidad a los problemas de interferencia y en inexistencia o escasez de riesgos de seguridad. La amplitud del ancho de banda era suficiente como para una multitud de aplicaciones sofisticadas. En 1986, casi los cuatro quintos del tráfico transatlántico y el 95% del transpacífico se realizaban por satélite. Desde 1992, el coste por circuito de la fibra óptica submarina cayó por debajo del de los satélites. Enseguida se invirtió la tendencia: el uso de cables superó al de los satélites tanto en el Atlántico como en el Pacífico (IGI Consulting 1998, 35-37)[12].

En definitiva, enorme ancho de banda para transmitir cantidades enormes de datos y densidad de interconexión junto a mayor velocidad y baratura refrendaron la superioridad de la fibra óptica (Anexo 1).

---

[10] Las primeras pruebas de campo y el tráfico de producción de los sistemas de fibra óptica en otros países europeos se resumen en Moncalvo y Tosco (1983).

[11] Tres componentes: emisor y receptor ópticos y cable de fibra óptica; el láser sustituye a la electricidad en la transmisión: «Several advantages such as higher bandwidth, higher interconnection densities, and lower crosstalk,which is independent of data rate, inherent parallelism and immunity from electromagnetic interference. Several advantages such as higher bandwidth, higher interconnection densities, and lower crosstalk, crosstalk which is independent of data rate, inherent parallelism and immunity from electromagnetic interference» (Gambhir 2013, 99-104). Más información con menor peso y volumen unitario (Elion y Elion 1978, 213). El inicio de la segunda mitad de la década de 1980 señala la línea divisoria entre cables analógicos y ópticos. El talón de Aquiles de la fibra óptica radicaba en los riesgos por chispas e incendios y daños por rayos (*International Fiber Optics & Communications*, febrero de 1986, 27).

[12] En sus orígenes, el término «banda ancha» traducía una diferencia respecto al servicio de conexión telefónica y revestía dos características distintas: velocidad y encendido fijo. La primera era una burda medida de capacidad mientras que la segunda definía una integración relativamente perfecta en la vida del usuario (Bucher 2010, 18).

Gráfico 1. Mercado mundial de fibra óptica, 1982-1986 (miles millones de dólares)

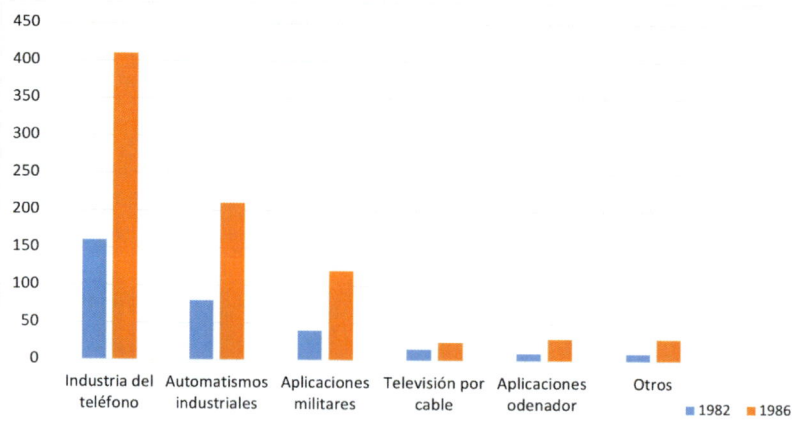

Fuente: Elaboración a partir de Elion y Elion (1978), 219.

La demanda mundial de fibra óptica creció con vigor a impulso sobre todo de las telecomunicaciones, precisamente la fracción con potencial de crecimiento considerablemente mayor. Las previsiones en el mercado de componentes de fibra óptica para mediados de los 80 arrojaban cifras que duplicaban con holgura las del inicio de la década (Gráfico 1). Se esperaba que en la segunda mitad de la década e inicios de la siguiente las cantidades se quintuplicaran, con oscilaciones en los años a caballo entre los dos milenios y un despegue importante a continuación (Hufbauer 1990, 186)[13].

Estas previsiones reposaban en la simple constatación del predominio aplastante de la transmisión de datos en el mercado competitivo local de las telecomunicaciones[14]. El crecimiento real fue impulsado por la demanda en alza del teléfono, la televisión por cable, el cable local y de larga distancia y los mercados submarinos[15]. En 1999, la capacidad de cable submarino interregional en todo el mundo se cifraba en 326,3 Gbps y se estimaba que la cifra se multiplicaría casi por nueve en 2003. En sectores de la industria

[13] La reapertura de cuatro plantas de CGW indicaba un retorno de la demanda en EE. UU. (*Fiber Optics Business Newsletter*, 2002, 16, 4, 2002, 1); se preveía un volumen de mercado por encima de los 3 billones de dólares hacia 1989, empujado también por la radio y la televisión (U.S. Industrial Outlook 1985, 29-4).

[14] *Fiber Optics Business Newsletter*, 1994, 8, 21, 1; en los componentes, destacaba la importancia del cable monomodo, de los transmisores y de los receptores (*Fiber Optics and Communications*, 15, 11, noviembre de 1992, 8).

[15] U. S. Department of Commerce 1994, 30-14; *Fiber Optics Weekly Update*, 2001, 21, 45, 1; *Fiber Optics Weekly Upate*, 26, 2, 1996, 2.

particulares, la expansión de la fibra óptica dio un gran empuje a los equipos de prueba, cuyo valor ascendía en 1992 a 365,9 millones de dólares, más del tercio de los cuales correspondía a EE.UU.[16].

Hagamos un breve alto en los rasgos distintivos que presentaba el mercado europeo de fibra óptica a mediados de los 80. Europa era el segundo consumidor de este material, con una cuota del 28% de la producción mundial, 32 puntos porcentuales por detrás de Norteamérica y 18 por delante de Asia (Figura 2). El Reino Unido, Francia y la República Federal de Alemania (Alemania) eran los mayores mercados de fibra óptica, cable y equipos anejos. Puestos mucho más modestos ocupaban otros países de Europa occidental, entre ellos, los tres nórdicos –Suecia, Dinamarca, y Noruega–, Benelux y, en particular, España[17].

Gráfico 2. Mercado mundial de fibra óptica en 1984 y estimación para 1989

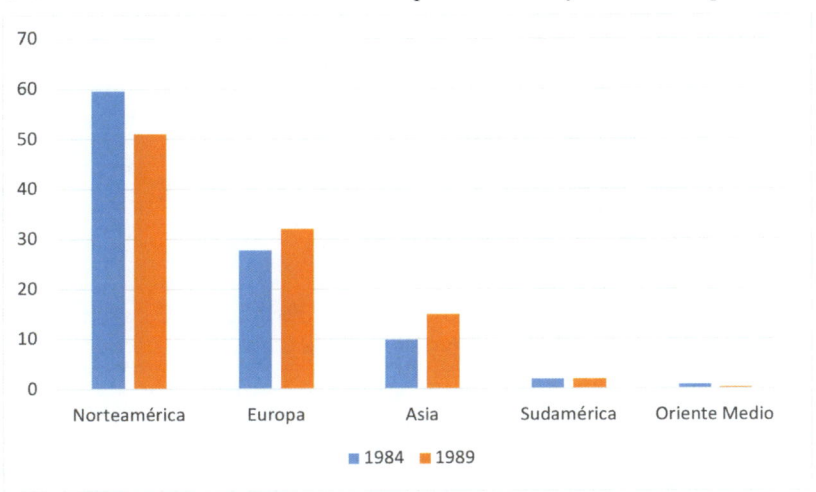

Fuente: Elaborado a partir de United States International
Trade Commission (1988), 10-1 y 10-3.

El desarrollo histórico de las comunicaciones europeas había creado una mezcolanza de diferentes estándares, redes y necesidades (Boucher 1986, 1)[18].

[16] *Fiber Optics Business Newsletter*, 1993, 7, 14, 15.

[17] United States International Trade Commission 1988, 10-1 y 10-3.

[18] Por lo general, los PTTs aplicaron políticas de compras que beneficiaban a unos cuantos proveedores en cada país y estos, a su vez, se repartían la fracción mayor del mercado. La CE estimaba entre el 70 y el 90% los porcentajes de contratos adjudicados por los mono-

En Europa occidental, a semejanza de Estados Unidos, las telecomunicaciones representaban el grueso del mercado para fibra óptica. En las conjeturas para el decenio de 1980, los expertos situaban a Europa en segunda posición y más pegada al líder, como muestra el Gráfico 2. Por más que breve, la pervivencia de los numerosos monopolios estatales o PTTs, responsables de las telecomunicaciones fronteras adentro de cada país, configuraba un escenario complejo y diverso.

Gráfico 3. Grandes productoras de fibra óptica en Europa según capacidad estimada, 1988 (km/año)

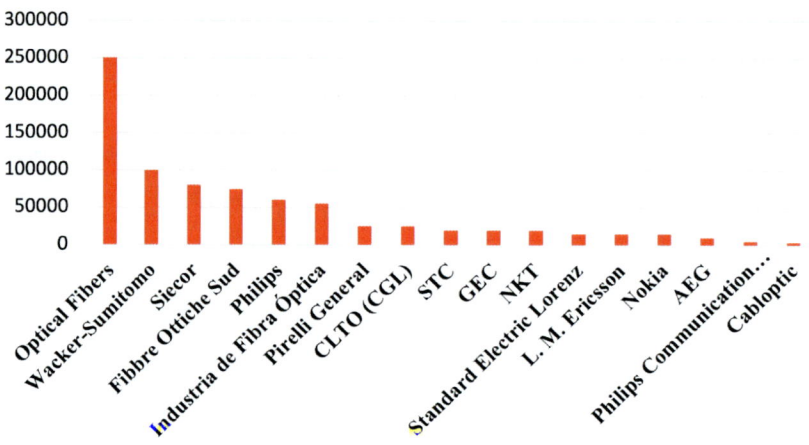

Fuente: Elaboración a partir de United States International Trade Commission (1988), 10-6.

Tabla 1. Productores europeos de cables

País	Compañías
Alemania	Felten & Guilleaume, Monette, E.I.W., Reinshagen Kabelwerke (G.M.), A.E.G. Kabelwerke, Siemens, Berkenhoff & Drebes (Thyssen Draht), Kabelmetal (Câbles de Lyon), Spiralglass Kabel, LAPP
Austria	Gebauer & Griller, Felten & Guilleaume, Kabel & Draht Werke
Bélgica	Opticable
Dinamarca	NKT
España	Cables de Comunicaciones, Standard Eléctrica (IT&T)

polios estatales a los productores nacionales (United States International Trade Commission 1989, 4/42).

Finlandia	Nokia Helikama Kaapeliteollisuus Oyòme
Francia	LTT Câbles de Lyon SAT Cable (SAT), SILEC (SAT), Câbles de Lyon, Precicâble (Pirelli), Acome, GORSE (Câbles de Lyon), Fileca, Filotex, (CGE– Câbles de Lyon), Cordons et Équipements (CEAC)
Holanda	NKF (Philips), Pope (Philips), De Regt Cables Twentsche Kabelfabrieken DRAKA (Philips)
Noruega	STK (IT&T), NORSK KABEL
Portugal	Cabelte Celcat (BICC) Avila
Reino Unido	Sterling Cables, B.I.C.C. Pilkington, S.T.C., A.E.I. Cables, Telephone Cables (GEC), Pirelli General, Raychem, Folhergill & Harvey
Suecia	Sieverts ASEA Kabel
Suiza	Cabloptic Huber & Suhner Daetwyler

Fuente: Elaboración a partir de Boucher (1986), 46.

Como evidencian el Gráfico 3 y la Tabla 1, abundaban los productores de fibra óptica, que se esparcían por Europa y tenían estructuras nacionales de mercado bien diversas. Mientras que en cinco casos – Bélgica, Dinamarca, Finlandia, Suecia y Suiza– solo existía una empresa productora implantada en el país, en otros cuatro –Alemania, Austria, Francia y Reino Unido– el mercado estaba fuertemente compartimentado. No obstante, poco menos de una veintena de empresas pertenecían al grupo de grandes y cuatro acaparaban casi dos tercios de la producción.

En este contexto de florecimiento de la industria, Europa debilitó su posición internacional en 1992, retroceso que compartió con Japón en beneficio de EE. UU. Cinco de los cuatro puntos porcentuales que Europa cedió en cuota de mercado respecto al año anterior y tres de Japón fueron a parar a EE. UU. (*Fiber Optics Weekly Update* 26 de febrero de 1993, 2-3).

En el inicio del nuevo milenio, la producción se concentraba en tres grandes áreas (Asia-Pacífico, EE. EU. y Europa Occidental). En 2003, ocho grandes proveedores– Corning, Furukawa-OFS, Sumitomo, Fujikura, YOFC (empresa conjunta con Draka), Pirelli, la holandesa Draka y Alcatel– junto con sus filiales, producían unos cuatro quintos del total mundial. Todos se organizaban según una integración vertical y operaban en un mercado fuertemente competitivo, liderado tecnológicamente por la pionera Corning and

Glass Works[19]. El sector no pudo rehuir los efectos devastadores del estallido de la burbuja tecnológica y acusó fuertes recortes de puestos de trabajo, ejemplificados por la pérdida de varios miles de empleos en la empresa líder (Hérisson 2001).

3. La estrategia de expansión de las multinacionales en España: Corning and Glass Works

La fibra óptica se introdujo en España con cierto retraso, una constante histórica habitual en muchas innovaciones. A modo de ejemplo: en 1986, datos oficiales europeos cifraban las conexiones digitales en el 13% total[20].

El inicio de los cables para comunicaciones ópticas se remonta a finales de la década del 70. Fueron introducidos por Standard Eléctrica (SESA), cuando oferta –muchos fabricantes mundiales de sistemas de telecomunicación– y demanda –Administraciones telefónicas– se orientaron hacia esta nueva tecnología. En su condición de filial de IT&T, SESA seguía los desarrollos tanto en fibras ópticas como en dispositivos luminosos semiconductores y equipos de transmisión para comunicaciones ópticas que se estaban llevando a cabo en los laboratorios ingleses de Standard Telephone and Cables (STC), también del grupo de la multinacional norteamericana. Asimismo, la filial española pudo conocer los trabajos para enlazar dos centrales londinenses, que dieron carta de naturaleza a la primera ruta comercial de comunicaciones ópticas de alta capacidad en el mundo (140 Mbitls)[21].

Las primeras realizaciones españolas pecaron de experimentación e incertidumbre y fueron determinadas en sustancia por el tamaño del mercado potencial. Dos ciudades –Madrid y Zaragoza– recibieron hasta cuatro enlaces experimentales –de 2, 8, 34 y 140 Mbps–, como anticipo de otros que debían repetirse en Madrid e instalarse en otros dos puntos extremos –Barcelona y

---

[19] Corning detentaba del 20 al 30% de la producción mundial; Furukawa entre 1-20 y Fijukira, Sumimoto y Pirelli entre 0-10 cada uno (Servicio de defensa de la competencia 2004, 8-9). DRAKA, participada mayoritariamente por Flint Holding y Parcom Ventures, era la matriz de un grupo de 59 empresas con actividades en Europa, América y Asia, dedicadas al desarrollo, producción y comercialización de sistemas de fibra de vidrio y cable. En España, DRAKA y sus filiales simultaneaban la producción y venta de cables de cobre y la venta de fibra óptica, así como de sistemas de video (Servicio de defensa de la competencia 2004, 3-4).

[20] Commission of the European Communities (1991), 25.

[21] Blanco-Vázquez 1990, 25-27.

Cádiz. Asimismo, estaba previsto un enlace de larga distancia entre Madrid y Barcelona con dieciséis fibras monomodo, así como la instalación de un prototipo de red de banda ancha en Salamanca con un centenar de abonados. A comienzos de 1981, SESA presentó el primer sistema comercial español de fibra óptica y, al año siguiente, instaló y puso el primer sistema español de transmisión digital de fibra óptica soportada por líneas de transporte de energía eléctrica de alta tensión. A ello se sumó la primera fibra óptica al aire libre con cable óptico fabricada en la factoría de cántabra de Maliaño[22].

En una segunda fase, al comienzo de los años 90, el Plan Foton de la operadora Telefónica proyectaba llevar la fibra óptica a 7,5 millones de hogares de ciudades de tamaño medio –125 con más de 50.000 habitantes– en el marco de la ampliación de la cadena de valor a nuevos productos. En 1994, 4,5 millones de viviendas dispusieron de acceso con fibra óptica mediante el cableado de treintaiséis poblaciones en las trece provincias más importantes del país[23].

En la ampliación del mercado pesaron con fuerza factores institucionales –la liberalización de las telecomunicaciones y la configuración territorial del Estado por comunidades autónomas–. En el País Vasco, el gobierno empezó a desarrollar en 1992 una red autonómica de fibra óptica bajo el nombre de Euskalnet, con un plan de extensión universal a partir de las tres capitales provinciales. Con la apertura del mercado y la adjudicación de la segunda licencia de telefonía a Retevisión, esta nueva operadora desplegó una base inicial de apenas 1.700 kilómetros de fibra óptica para conectar Madrid y Sevilla y para distintas comunicaciones internas en Madrid. A partir de ahí, concibió planes de expansión cuyo eje sería la comercialización de la red de Correos, a base de la instalación de fibra óptica en 2.000 oficinas, un soporte gubernamental de indudable valía[24].

---

[22] Las empresas eléctricas fueron pioneras en adoptar esta tecnología introducida en España por Standard Eléctrica (Hidroeléctrica Española, Unión Eléctrica Fenosa y Thermidor) (Standard Eléctrica 1983, 22).

[23] Roche y Bakis 1997, 150; *El País*, 3 de marzo de 1995; *Computerworld*, 16 de junio de 1995. El enlace entre Madrid y Barcelona permitiría, además de la extensa gama de transmisión de datos, capacidad para 50 canales de televisión por cable.

[24] *El País*, 12 de mayo de 1995. Los proyectos iniciales a largo plazo de CTNE en España comprendían tres cables interiores de fibra óptica, el más largo de los cuales era el de Cádiz (30 km, 8 fibras y 140 Mbps), mientras que el de Madrid era el más denso (5; 16 y 140), con doble de fibras que el de Barcelona (5; 8 y 140 Mbps) (Boucher 1986, 109). Entre las primeras instalaciones de fibra óptica se cuenta un tramo de gran tráfico en Madrid, no sin antes conocer la postura del gobierno en materia de tv por cable, y a continuación en las redes urbanas de tráfico denso (Madrid, Barcelona) hasta extenderse a las redes de abona-

En el largo plazo, España fomentó la producción de fibra óptica para salir del furgón de cola entre los países de Europa occidental (United States International Trade Commission 1988, 10-1 y 10-3). Recordemos que como responsable de la instalación de cables en su condición de operadora aún monopolista, la Compañía Telefónica Nacional de España (CTNE) usó su consabida amplia capacidad de compra, alimentada por cuantiosos recursos financieros no dependientes del presupuesto del Estado, con dos finalidades industriales paralelas y complementarias. Por un lado, se esforzó en atraer inversiones a suelo español en sectores punta y, por otro, impulsó proyectos colectivos de producción que suponían exportar capitales[25]. Se trataba de un ingrediente de la estrategia gubernamental de convertir a España en un centro de producción de alta tecnología, lejos de la ineficiente industria pesada española. Esta estrategia, con el punto de mira en las tecnologías más avanzadas de las telecomunicaciones, como la microelectrónica, la fibra óptica y la informática, cuajó en acuerdos con un socio tecnológico que ostentara el liderazgo mundial del sector correspondiente. Así se desgranaron acuerdos con multinacionales norteamericanas, europeas y japonesas, a la vez que se contemplaron otros, recogidos en la Tabla 2[26]. La operadora monopolista cerraba estos acuerdos en ocasiones con multinacionales ya establecidas en el territorio y en otras involucraban a no presentes todavía. Todos ellos perseguían un doble propósito, a saber, dar a Telefónica un impacto multinacional y atraer las nuevas tecnologías a España[27]. Generalmente, se inscribían en planes del Gobierno –como el Plan Electrónico e Informático– y contaban con el apoyo de la Administración, que aportaba recursos y ayudas. De esta manera, la CTNE se convertía en instrumento –«locomotora»– de la políti-

do en 1990. Según J. Agirre, el despliegue de la fibra óptica en el País Vasco se apoyó en gran medida en la red de la Erzaintza.

25 Conversación de Luis Solana Madariaga con el autor, Madrid, 8 marzo 2016 (Calvo 2016).

26 THM era una pequeña empresa de alto valor añadido, formada junto con Messerschmitt-Bolkow-Bohm (MBB) y Hormann y que luego pasó a denominarse TSC Telefónica de Seguridad y Comunicaciones S.A. y a ser participada en su totalidad por Telefónica de España S.A. (Sentencia, Madrid, 12 de diciembre de 1997; Castells 1986, 148 y 156; CTNE, Memoria, 1984, 39-40; *Telecommunication Journal*, 52, 7-12, 1985, 436; Calvo 1916, 246).

27 Castells 1986, 487; *New York Times*, 5 diciembre de 1985; Víctor Goyenechea en *Actualidad Económica*, 10 de febrero de 1986, 42; *Progreso*, 1988, 38. Las multinacionales perseguían penetrar los mercados europeos: AT&T, *Annual Report*, 1986. Para Castells (1986) la modernización de un país dependía primordialmente de cuatro eslabones perfectamente entrelazados: una investigación básica de calidad, una estructura importante de I+D, un tejido productor de nuevas tecnologías y una suficiente capacidad de absorción de esas nuevas tecnologías. La prensa subrayaba que los acuerdos de empresas conjuntas venían a rellenar huecos sin agredir al sector (*Hoja Oficial del lunes*, 22 de diciembre de 1985).

ca económica que aspiraba a hacer competitivas las empresas españolas para operar en mercados abiertos, asumiendo así parcelas del papel de Estado desde una posición de independencia financiera respecto al erario público[28].

Tabla 2. Proyectos industriales del Gobierno en España

Empresa española	Socio tecnológico	Producto
Thomson Española	J2T	vídeos
IBM España	IBM Co	ordenadores gama media
Hispano Olivetti	Olivetti	ordenadores personales
Nixdorf Computer S. A.	Nixdorf Computer	miniordenadores
Por crear	Hewlett Packard	periféricos ordenador y/o equipos instrumentación
General Electric Electro-medicina	General Electric	equipos de radiología

Fuente: Elaboración a partir de Archivo del INI.

A esa estrategia se sumaron filiales españolas de multinacionales enclavadas en sectores de tecnología avanzada, entre ellos el de las TIC, como muestra la Tabla 2. La gama de actividad, el grado de implicación de los socios y los objetivos específicos variaban según los casos. Así, el proyecto con IBM perseguía aumentar el grado de integración de la fabricación a partir de componentes propios mientras que el de Thomson entrañaba la participación española en el consorcio J2T.

En este punto se impone esclarecer la intensa pugna entre empresas por control del mercado en general y, más en concreto, el del *videocassette*. Acuciado por la competencia del sistema rival electromecánico VCR (*videocassette recorder*), JVC (Japan Victor Company) forjó acuerdos en 1978 con Thorn-EMI en el Reino Unido, con Telefunken en Alemania occidental y con Thomson en Francia. En este último país, el gobierno entró en liza y conminó a Thomson-Brandt a retirarse y buscar socios europeos. De ahí surgió el consorcio J2T como una empresa conjunta entre la japonesa JVC, Thorn-EMI y Telefunken bajo la denominación de J2T Holdings BV con sede en Holan-

---

[28] Luis Solana Madariaga, presidente de la CTNE, utilizaba con frecuencia la expresión «locomotora telefónica»; en una de sus intervenciones apuntaba: «Y pido al cielo que nadie plantee nunca que la Compañía Telefónica acabe colgada de los Presupuestos Generales del Estado, cuando justamente se está planteando una reducción del déficit público» (Solana Madariaga 1986, 7).

da–. El veto francés al acuerdo tuvo su respuesta en el veto alemán al pacto de Thomson-Brandt con la filial de Philips, Grundig AG. Inmediatamente, el grupo francés acordó adquirir las tres cuartas partes de las acciones de la maltrecha AEG-Telefunken en el negocio de la electrónica de consumo. Tres años transcurrieron antes de que se forjara el acuerdo J3T por el que los socios repartían la producción en tres fábricas, cada una especializada en un solo producto (Strange 2002, 301-303)[29].

La fibra óptica encontró en las redes de banda ancha un trampolín para su expansión. En Europa se dieron cinco grandes proyectos de banda ancha en Alemania; Italia; Francia (Biarritz) (Gerin 1984, 207-211); RU (Milton-Keynes) (Information Gatekeepers 1987, 216-218) y Dinamarca (Arhus), además de otros menores en Holanda, Suiza y Suecia. Fuera de Europa cabe reseñar el HI-OVIS (Japón), el Elie (Canadá) y otro en EE.UU. (Albella 1988, 191-192)[30]. A título de ejemplo, señalamos algunos detalles de los dos primeros.

Desde 1977, el organismo público alemán de correos Deutsche Bundespost mostró un vivo interés por la fibra óptica y sus aplicaciones. Seis años se hicieron esperar las pruebas de BiGFON (Red de Telecomunicaciones de Fibra Óptica Integrada de Banda Ancha) en Berlín y otras seis ciudades alemanas, que demostraron la viabilidad técnica de una red universal de fibra óptica. Todos los servicios de telecomunicaciones se transmitían a través de una única línea de abonado de fibra óptica. Tres años más se necesitaron para poner en marcha con el apoyo y la concertación del Senado de Berlín el proyecto BERKOM (BERliner KOMmunikations System) (Information Gatekeepers 1991, 280)[31].

---

[29] JVC se sirvió de J2T para eludir las restricciones a la importación de productos japoneses VCR impuestas por Francia y otros países europeos. La capacidad de decidir productos y procesos, proporcionar componentes y establecer criterios de productividad, otorgaba a JVC el control casi por completo de los niveles de coste de J2T (Doz y Hamel 1995, 21).

[30] Véase Information Gatekeepers Inc. (1994). Hacia finales de 1977, Telecom Italia Mobile culminó un programa de investigación conjunta de CGW y el Centro Studi e Laboratori Telecomunicazioni –que actuó de intermediario entre la multinacional norteamericana y Pirelli, como confiesa Basilio Catania, uno de los protagonistas–, con el tendido del primer cable de fibra óptica entre dos centrales telefónicas urbanas de Turín. La presencia de Pirelli señala la gran diferencia existente entre los casos de España e Italia en la industria de fibra óptica, un sector internacionalizado. Pirelli contaba con dos unidades de producción de este nuevo material: una en Sorocaba (Brasil) y otra en Battipaglia (Italia), esta en alianza con CGW (Pirelli & C. S p A, Rapporto Ambientale 2004, 39; Cantoni et al, 2011, 292). Finalmente, Pirelli, de espaldas a la diversificación, vendió Optical Tecnologies a Corning y sus sistemas ópticos a Cisco, por casi 5.000 millones de liras (La Repubblica, 28 de octubre de 2005).

[31] Telefónica Investigación y Desarrollo y la ETSI de Madrid presentaron sendas comunicaciones sobre monomodo/multimodo y ethernet a la Novena conferencia anual sobre comuni-

El programa nacional italiano de redes de fibra óptica a larga distancia se dio con retraso ya que no quedó definido hasta 1986 (Onida (a cuidado de) 1987, 266). Poco antes se lanzó el proyecto FIORE, basado en un acuerdo de cuatro años entre el PTT italiano, la Universidad de Florencia y Alcatel SIETTE. Tenía como objetivo primordial desarrollar y experimentar en la Universidad de Florencia servicios telemáticos avanzados a través de una red de área metropolitana (MAN) integrada de comunicación que explotara las tecnologías de fibra óptica y, parcialmente, de cable coaxial. En el proyecto FIORE se identificaron dos subredes diferentes, integradas desde el punto de vista físico en los mismos enlaces de transmisión: el subsistema de transmisión de datos, que proporcionaba rutas de alta velocidad entre sistemas de *hardware* y *software* no homogéneos, a través de la interconexión de LANs, y el subsistema videomático, que permitía establecer canales de vídeo de 6 MHz a mano completa sobre enlaces de fibra óptica, con interconexión al servicio público nacional de videoconferencia. Tras esta red urbana inicial basada en puentes de 2 Mbitts, el plan continuaba con la instalación de una MAN de alta velocidad basada en la arquitectura DODB. La implementación inicial de esta MAN en Florencia debía interconectar una serie de centros de investigación de la Universidad y del Consejo Nacional de Investigación (Information Gatekeepers 1991, 338).

En España, la Administración dejó ver signos de interés por la importancia y exigencias de los materiales avanzados de telecomunicaciones al iniciarse la década de 1980[32]. Radio Televisión Española realizó la conexión por cable de fibra óptica entre el centro nodal y la torre de comunicaciones y el control central de la M-30. La experiencia no estuvo exenta de problemas, como evidenciaron a mediados de 1983 frecuentes fallos de señal en la terminal de llegada, en realidad debidos a defectos de la fibra óptica[33].

Contemporáneas con las iniciativas del Gobierno, la CTNE emprendió realizaciones como la instalación y desarrollo de un sistema de transmisión por fibra óptica llamado TRACOF II para una central hidroeléctrica (SESA, *Memoria*, 1981, p. 10). En lo fundamental, la operadora monopolista vio en la red, el cable o la banda ancha la clave de las comunicaciones en los años fina-

caciones de fibra óptica y redes de área local a que se hace referencia.

[32] *Diario de Sesiones del Congreso de los diputados (DSCD)*, 11 Legislatura, 6, 16 de febrero de 1983, 269.

[33] La fibra procedía de Alemania y fue sustituida por fibra óptica norteamericana. Radio Televisión Española podía llegar a un acuerdo con Telefónica para trasladar la señal de televisión en la accidentada orografía de las Islas Canarias (*DSCD*, COMISIONES, 24 de octubre de 1984, 7186).

les del siglo XX. «Es la enorme autopista por la que circularán las relaciones de los seres humanos en el año 2000», zanjaba el presidente de la compañía, Luis Solana, decidido a apostar por las altas tecnologías[34]. Empeñada en una introducción gradual de la fibra óptica en su red, la CTNE consideró insustituible alcanzar acuerdos con empresas avanzadas en las tecnologías en rápida evolución para procurárselas. La decisión de Telefónica, alineada con los planes del gobierno español, obedeció a una política de diversificación de proveedores[35].

La exploración de posibles socios tecnológicos para la fabricación conjunta de fibra óptica en España apuntó hacia la líder Corning Glass Works (CGW), que, si bien tenía fábricas en Francia y RU así como proyectos en Alemania, carecía de presencia industrial en España. Rival de AT&T en el mercado mundial, CGW afrontaba los retos del crecimiento y del rendimiento para no sucumbir a envites hostiles e incluso a riesgos de desaparición (U.S. International Trade Commission 1988, 10/35; 86/405/EEC)[36]. En esa perspectiva, el mercado español no carecía de atractivos.

Para apreciar el alcance de la apuesta conviene definir el socio elegido. CGW consiguió en sus laboratorios los primeros productos de calidad para el mercado en 1970. Un cuatrienio más emplearía Ericsson en erigirse como competidora con *know-how* y tecnología apropiados para echar los cimientos de la fabricación y desarrollo de productos futuros[37].

Corning-Glass Works llevó a cabo una internacionalización intensa que se plasmó en una presencia con instalaciones de producción y oficinas en veintitrés países hacia mediados de la década de 1970 (Hill 1974, 32). A continuación, CGW desplegó una notable actividad inversora e inventora con el registro de patentes de proceso y producto en los principales países europeos y en el conjunto de Europa occidental a excepción de Irlanda, Grecia y Portu-

---

[34] *El País*, 28 de mayo de 1985. Telefónica se codeó con Corning Glass en actos internacionales sobre las nuevas tecnologías (Solana 1985, 17). La CTNE era presentada como «vitrine» de la política socialista de modernización industrial (*Le Monde*, 26 de febrero de 1985).

[35] *El País*, 8 de octubre de 1988.

[36] Las iniciativas de Corning Glass encontraban respaldo en los organismos europeos (Commission Decision of 14 July 1986 (IV/30.320), *Official Journal* L 236, *22/8/1986, 0030 – 0044*). CGW sí ofrecía a potenciales clientes españoles licencias de sus patentes al menos desde 1932 (*El Debate*, 10 de noviembre de 1932).

[37] Este trabajo preparatorio incluía desarrollar métodos de medición y tecnología de fibra y componentes, que se completaron con el diseño de sistemas de ensayo para la transmisión de datos y vídeo (Johansson y Lundstrom 1980, 74; *New Scientist*, 118, 1.611, 5 de mayo de 1988, 66). Véase también Munier (1976).

gal[38]. Cobijada en el baluarte de sus patentes y con una dilatada experiencia, Corning forjó una amplia gama de alianzas –empresas conjuntas y contratos de licencia– con importantes proveedores en los mercados europeos. Esta intensa actividad cooperativa se nutrió de los principios de especialización, complementariedad y desarrollo rápido de aplicaciones, minimizando las superposiciones y los riesgos de invasión entre ella misma y los interlocutores (Doz y Hamel 1995, 17; Maidment 1991, 98)[39].

En los años 70 abundaron los acuerdos cooperativos en Europa. En la primera mitad, Corning cerró cuatro de ellos con BICC Pie y The Plessey Company Pie en el Reino Unido[40], la Compagnie Générale d'Electricité (CGE) en Francia e Industrie Pirelli Spa en Italia. Al mismo tiempo, creó en Alemania una *joint venture* a partes iguales con Siemens AG, denominada Siecor Gmbh, y orientada al mercado europeo y norteamericano. De ella hablaremos más adelante. Ambas empresas concluyeron también un acuerdo de cooperación técnica, similar a los acuerdos de desarrollo en común en los otros tres países. En virtud de los mismos, sobre los socios europeos recayó el desarrollo de la tecnología necesaria para las fibras ópticas de cable, mientras la propia Cor-

---

[38] Las inversiones de Corning en I+D alcanzaban 8,02% de las ventas en 1998, 7,86% en 1999 y 7,56% en 2000; desde el punto de vista geográfico, se concentraban en EE. EU. y las telecomunicaciones constituían el destino prioritario (Corning Incorporated 2000, 43-44 y 51).

[39] Corning se alió con empresas provistas de capacidades complementarias para obtener una ventaja competitiva (Samsung) y con competidores para desarrollar nuevas tecnologías (Saint-Gobain) e involucró a sus propios proveedores en el desarrollo (Bidault 2012, 20). La empresa perseguía una penetración instantánea en el mercado y drenar nuevas tecnologías. En 1989, el nuevo nombre de Corning Inc. certificó la diversificación de sus productos (Corning Inc. 2006; UNCTAD 2006, 128). Corning, a semejanza de grandes empresas británicas y americanas, no se incorporó a la Convention Internationale des Glaceries, cartel integrado por la práctica totalidad de los fabricantes de Europa continental entre los que destacaba Saint-Gobain (Sánchez 2011, 3). Th. N. Cochran califica las empresas conjuntas de CGW los puntos fuertes ocultos de la empresa.

[40] Acuerdos en el RU: en 1981, sociedad colectiva al 50 % entre Corning Canada INC y BICC Plc, nuevo nombre de Callender's Cables Limited desde 1975, con el nombre de Optical Fibres para la producción y venta de fibras ópticas; sendos acuerdos de transferencia de *know-how* y de licencia de patente (1981) en favor de la empresa común; modificación de la sociedad colectiva y del acuerdo de *know-how* y de licencia de patente (1985); recisión del acuerdo de distribución de 6 de febrero de 1981. Esta pauta se repite en la República Federal de Alemania con acuerdos de *joint–venture* de abril de 1973 con el nombre de Siecor GmbH al 50 % entre Corning Glass Works y Siemens AG para el desarrollo, producción y venta de fibras ópticas y cables ópticos y acuerdo de licencia de enero de 1978 entre Corning Glass Works y Siemens AG por una parte y Siecor GmbH por la otra, ambos modificados en 1985; estatutos de Siecor Gesellschaft für Lichtwellenleiter GmbH & Co KG para fabricación de fibras ópticas; en 1985, rescisión del acuerdo de distribución y representación de ventas de 1 de abril de 1975 (*Official Journal* L 236, 22/08/1986, 0030 – 0044).

ning continuaba con el desarrollo de las fibras ópticas. Corning ofreció a sus socios la opción de obtener, en cualquier momento del periodo de duración de los acuerdos, una licencia de fabricación y venta exclusivas de fibras ópticas cubierta por sus respectivas patentes en los tres países europeos en que estaba presente industrialmente. Más tarde, CGE y Pirelli obtuvieron una licencia exclusiva como se preveía mientras que BICC y Siemens prefirieron concluir un acuerdo de empresa conjunta antes que obtener una licencia exclusiva. El ejercicio de las opciones de licencia o la creación de empresas comunes hicieron que caducaran todos los acuerdos de desarrollo en común[41].

En la segunda mitad de los años 70, Corning concluyó con sus socios europeos acuerdos de distribución exclusiva (pero no exclusivos con respecto a la propia Corning) para la venta de su producción propia en sus respectivos países. En el Reino Unido y en Alemania, Corning concedió dichos derechos a las recién citadas empresas comunes con BICC y Siemens[42]. Las dos décadas finales del siglo xx fueron fecundas en ampliaciones de esta estrategia de expansión. Corning forjó *joint ventures* en diversos campos y según tres variantes distintas de participación con predominio numérico de la modalidad del cincuenta por ciento[43]. En la estrategia de expansión, la búsqueda de rentas de localización tenía una importancia primordial.

La inmensa mayoría de socios de *joint–venture* de Corning en Europa eran los grandes fabricantes de cable, principales clientes de fibra óptica y proveedores, a su vez, de los usuarios (PTTs). Pese a su posición dominante en Europa occidental, su cobertura de patente variaba de un país a otro y algunos productores de fibra óptica prescindían de licencia de Corning por un doble motivo. El primero obedecía a la posibilidad de aprovisionarse de alguna rival japonesa –Sumitomo a General Pirelli en el RU y a Wacker Chemitronic, en Alemania occidental (Tabla 3)–. El segundo se explica por la aversión de Corning hacia los mercados pequeños que, como ocurría con la danesa NKT, no justificaban la negociación de un acuerdo de licencia. A estos nichos se

---

[41]   86/405/EEC: Commission Decision of 14 July 1986 relating to a proceeding under Article 85 of the EEC Treaty (IV/30.320 – optical fibres), (*Official Journal*, L 236, 22/08/1986 P. 0030 – 0044; Chaffee 2012, 139); Siedcor, a la que Porter (1983, 371) le dedicó una atención especial dentro de su análisis de Corning, creó la filial Fiberlan orientada al servicio de empresas (Mccarthy [saf], 13).

[42]   Commission Decision of 14 July 1986, IV/30.320, *Official Journal*, L 236, 22/8/1986 P. 0030 – 0044.

[43]   Se trata de Genencor con Genentech, Ciba-Corning con Ciba-Geigy, Cormetech con Mitsubishi y Eurokera con Saint Gobain; al 51/49%: American video con Asahi y Sony; al 50/47 Samsung-Corning con Samsung (Bidault 2012, 18).

asió AT&T para la venta de fibra óptica en otros mercados europeos. Aunque Corning pleiteó por trasgresión de patente de proceso contra Sumitomo en Estados Unidos y logró cerrar la producción de fibra de esta, la empresa no procedió con demandas similares en Europa[44].

Ese apego a las alianzas como vía de expansión al que se alude antes era añejo y, en alguna ocasión, España se había visto implicada en la estrategia. En 1921, Corning se unió con la vidriera francesa Saint Gobain en una *joint venture*, Société Le Pyrex, que obtuvo licencia para fabricar y vender Pyrex hasta en siete países europeos –Francia, Bélgica, Holanda, España, Portugal, Italia y Suiza–. Idéntico proceder se repitió con James A. Jobling Co. para producir Pyrex en Inglaterra. En 1955, Corning amplió su participación minoritaria al 32% en Le Pyrex, que cambió su nombre por el de Sovirel (Société des Verrières Industrielles Réunies du Loin) (Dyer y Gross 2001, 115 y 238).

Tabla 3. Grandes productoras de fibra óptica en
Europa según capacidad, 1988 (km/año)

Empresa	Capacidad estimada (km/año)	País	Licencia Corning
Optical Fibers	250.000	UK	Sí
STC	20.000	UK	No
GEC	20.000	UK	No
Pirelli General	25.000	UK	No
CLTO (CGL)	25.000	Francia	Sí
Industria de Fibra Óptica	55.000	Francia	Sí
AEG	10.000	RFA	No
Standard Elektrik Lorenz	15.000	RFA	No
Philips Communication Industries	5.000	RFA	No
Siecor	80.000	RFA	Sí
Wacker-Sumitomo	100.000	RFA	No
Fibre Ottiche Sud[45]	75.000	Italia	Sí
Philips	60.000	Holanda	Sí

[44] United States International Trade Commission 1988, 10-5; *JEI Report*, 25-47, 1987, 50; United States Congress. Senate. Committee on Finance. Subcommittee on International Trade 1986, 190.

[45] Fibre Ottiche era una empresa conjunta de Pirelli y Sirti (United States International Trade Commission 1988, 10-27).

NKT	20.000	Dinamarca	No
L. M. Ericsson	15.000	Suecia	No
Nokia	15.000	Finlandia	No
Cabloptic	4.000	Suiza	No
Total	794.000		

Fuente: Elaboración a partir de United States International
Trade Commission (1988), 10-16.

El enfoque de Corning Glass sobre las peculiaridades culturales difería sensiblemente del practicado, al menos en algún momento, por otras grandes compañías, como AT&T. CGW se caracterizaba por el mantenimiento de un bajo perfil público para evitar una sensación de dominio, recurso a personal autóctono para subrayar el entorno local y creación de una identidad predominantemente europea[46].

4. Dependencia tecnológica, multinacionales y desarrollo regional

Con un socio tecnológico de las características señaladas se embarcó Telefónica para montar una fábrica de fibra óptica en España. Un protocolo dio vía libre al estudio de la viabilidad de una empresa conjunta con una participación minoritaria de Telefónica en la inversión –35% frente al 65% de Corning–. Los proyectos conjugaban la absoluta especialidad de la producción en la tecnología más avanzada –Outside Vapour deposition (OVD)– con la elevada cualificación del empleo –un centenar de puestos de trabajo–. Una factoría modular tendría capacidad para producir en cantidades crecientes hasta los 100.000 km anuales de fibra monomodo con destino al mercado interior y a la exportación[47].

---

[46]   AT&T, ajena a la diferencia de valores respecto a su socio Olivetti, hubo de rectificar e imitó a CGW (Huber y Glick 1993, 315). En vez de una empresa conjunta y un amplio y duradero acuerdo, la alianza AT&T-Olivetti cuajó como una serie de contratos de suministro renovados periódicamente entre los socios. Para profundizar en este caso, véase Doz y Hamel 1995, 13 y Calvo 2020, 15.

[47]   Solana Madariaga (1986), 7; *Electronics*, 59, 1986, 232; *Le Monde*, 29 de abril de 1985. La participación de Telefónica se fijaba en 1.050 millones ptas; las inversiones previstas en 1.500 millones ptas. y las ventas en 1088 1006 en 18.300 millones ptas., un 30-40% en el mercado exterior. Estaban previstas ayudas financieras del Centro para el Desarrollo Tecnológico e Industrial (CDTI) y como empresa acogida a la ZUR (*LACA*, 30 de enero de 1985). Variantes en las cifras: capacidad de producción de 85.500 km, ampliables a 110.000 transcurrido un decenio (Telefónica, *Memoria,* 1989, 19 y 178). La OVD consiste

El acuerdo de intenciones entre Telefónica y CGW se completó con un segundo, en condiciones muy ventajosas para la multinacional, para crear una nueva empresa con el nombre de TELCOR y con un convenio que implicaba transferencia de tecnología de última generación, compromisos de exportación y recompra de un tercio de la capacidad instalada y localización en España de la I+D en esa gama. Un poco ulterior fue la elección de Asturias para ubicar la producción (Roche 1992, 410; Noam 1992, 256)[48].

En contra de las previsiones, los planes de fabricación no culminaron en ninguna realización concreta sin que exista unanimidad en los motivos. Diversos testimonios culpan del fracaso al retroceso de la demanda de fibra óptica en el mercado nacional o al exceso de capacidad y alguno añade los reparos de la administración comunitaria. Uno más en liza cargaba no tanto contra la caída de la demanda de fibra sino más bien contra el descenso de los precios en unas condiciones cambiantes del mercado[49]. Pese al fiasco, todavía en 1994, Corning recogía entre sus filiales a TELCOR, en la que declaraba una participación del 47,29% a través de Corning Investments Inc. de Delaware (Corning Incorporated 1994)[50].

Dos aspectos relacionados con la elección de Asturias como emplazamiento, una constante en los sucesivos proyectos, merecen atención. En juego están las vías de salida a la grave situación de declive económico propio de la región. Un diagnóstico de la situación lo ofrecía el socialista Pedro de Silva, cuando todavía no era presidente de la comunidad autónoma, al resumir en cuatro rasgos el proceso de la región: «La creciente especialización económica, la progresiva publificación, la profundidad de los desequilibrios y la

en una hidrólisis de llama, en la que el SiCl4 reacciona con el oxígeno para producir sílice (SiO2) y HCl.

[48] Proyecto de una unidad de investigación de apoyo a la fabricación y proyectos coordinados con CGL en fibra (*LACA*, 28 de mayo de 1986; Dyer y Gross 2001, 243). Técnicos españoles en electrónica consideraron las condiciones excesivamente ventajosas debido a que entre subvenciones, *royalties*, compras de maquinaria y pagos por transferencia de tecnología la empresa norteamericana se instalaba en España sin apenas realizar inversiones. Además, la empresa conjunta ofrecía a Corning la garantía de un socio seguro como Telefónica y de un mercado cautivo en la práctica (*Diario de Burgos: de avisos y noticias*, 25 de abril de 1985, 24). TELCOR fue calificada de «engine venture» por el director general de Electrónica e informática (González Sabat) (Comisiones 9, *Diario de sesiones del Senado*, 5 de noviembre de 1986, 11).

[49] *New York Times*, 22 de junio de 1987; United States International Trade Commission 1988, 7/8.

[50] Ciertos autores incluyen TELCOR entre las empresas conjuntas formadas con éxito en otros cuatro países europeos –Italia, Francia, UK y Alemania occidental (Chaffee 2012, 139).

persistente decadencia» (Silva 1982)[51]. Se impone, por tanto, hablar una vez más de política industrial.

España disponía de instrumentos heredados, que incentivaban la localización productiva, a la vez que impulsaban las sociedades de desarrollo regional y el sistema de planes provinciales y comarcales modificado. En la primera mitad de la década de los ochenta, puso en marcha mecanismos de incentivación e instrumentos de promoción de diversa índole, dentro de las políticas de ajuste para solucionar el declive y la profunda crisis industrial. El fundamental fue la Ley 27/1984 de reconversión y reindustrialización de los sectores maduros de la economía[52].

Junto al nivel nacional de decisión, la política regional europea, enraizada en el Tratado de Roma, constitutivo de la Comunidad Económica Europea en 1957, contaba desde 1968 con la Dirección General de Política Regional de la Comisión Europea. Los avances en esa vía culminaron un septenio después, con la creación del Fondo Europeo de Desarrollo Regional (FEDER). En 1988, en respuesta a la incorporación de tres naciones del sur de Europa –Grecia (1981), España y Portugal (1986)–, los Fondos Estructurales, dotados con un presupuesto de 64.000 millones de ecus, se integraron en una política de cohesión, que priorizaba las regiones más atrasadas y la orientación estratégica de las inversiones.

En ese marco se inscriben los nuevos instrumentos sobre los que se asentó la política regional, a saber, Fondo de Compensación Interterritorial (FCI), FEDER y el nuevo sistema de incentivos regionales. También las medidas puntuales y limitadas temporalmente de mediados de la década de 1980, promovidas desde el gobierno en los sectores maduros de la industria con el objetivo de paliar los impactos territoriales más acusados de la crisis y de las políticas de ajuste industrial. Entre esas medidas destacó la creación de las Zonas de Urgente Reindustrialización (ZUR). Un balance de los dieciocho primeros meses de actividad arrojaba inversiones por 162.000 millones de pe-

---

[51] García Delgado (1978) responsabilizaba a los empresarios de la grave situación de deterioro regional. Mario Bango calificaba de «Principado del INI» a Asturias, a cuya economía atribuía cinco rasgos: región en declive, sometida a la reconversión siderúrgica y naval, fuertemente dependiente del sector público, amenazada por las secuelas del ingreso en la CEE, con marcados desequilibrios interiores y, finalmente, con una inoperancia privada (*El País*, 26 de agosto de 1986). Muy recientemente, se ha cuestionado la visión de Asturias como territorio desindustrializado al subrayar que la aparición de actividades transformadoras en torno a la metalurgia/carbón alentó las economías externas, que generaron un entorno clusterizado, capaz de poner coto al declive de los grandes sectores hegemónicos y desbordar sus mercados tradicionales (Antuña 2022, pp. 124-135).

[52] La política regional en 1989 1990, 11.

setas, con 11.164 puestos de trabajo ofertados, que implicaban subvenciones por 27.400 millones de pesetas[53].

En Asturias, estas políticas vinieron a reforzar las herramientas preexistentes, entre ellas el Polo de Desarrollo, creado en 1971 y a punto de expirar a finales de la década. De nuevo cuño pero de idéntico final anunciado era la ZUR de Asturias, que abarcaba diecinueve municipios de la zona central y las cuencas mineras. La Ley de Incentivos Regionales dio paso, desde mediados de 1988, a una Zona de Promoción Económica (ZPE) y a la calificación de Asturias como Zona Industrial en Declive (ZID). La ZPE abarcaba la mayor parte del territorio regional con un tipo máximo de subvenciones del 40% mientras que la ZID actuaba en un total de once municipios mineros y servía de canal para conceder subvenciones de hasta el 45% (Vázquez y Hernández 1991, 23-24). Dichos mecanismos de incentivación e instrumentos de promoción se doblaron con la actuación de entidades públicas no estatales. La configuración del estado de las autonomías, con la subsiguiente descentralización de competencias, alentó la creación de organismos impulsores del desarrollo de las respectivas comunidades. Las Agencias de Desarrollo Regional (AdDR), surgidas en el arranque de la década de 1980, dieron pie a los gobiernos autonómicos a participar en el establecimiento, aplicación y gestión de medidas encaminadas a sentar las bases para el futuro crecimiento económico de la región[54].

---

[53] Las ZUR tenían una duración de año y medio, prorrogable por idéntico periodo de tiempo (*Balance de actuación de las zonas de urgente reindustrialización (ZUR)*, DSC, 202, 26 de noviembre de 1987, 7.381-7.382). En 1987, las inversiones alcanzaban 103.794 millones de pesetas y los puestos de trabajo creados 7.350, es decir, el 41% y el 37,9% de los proyectos aprobados, respectivamente, con un volumen de subvenciones de 42.032 millones de pesetas. En término comparativo, recordemos que la subvención concedida hasta 1988 por la Administración central a AT&T en la creación de AT&T Microelectrónica de España ascendía a 3.280 millones de pesetas (Asamblea de Madrid, *Diario de Sesiones*, 242, 14 de octubre de 1988, 4.774).

[54] A finales de la década de 1990 existían en España nueve AdDR en otras tantas comunidades autónomas: Andalucía, Aragón, Asturias, Cataluña, Galicia, Madrid, Murcia; País Vasco y Valencia (Argüelles 1997, 128). En 1989, la inversión subvencionable y el empleo creado en Asturias –2% del total español– se situaban por debajo del porcentaje del peso de la economía asturiana en el conjunto nacional. Las ayudas a la inversión concedidas en el Principado totalizaron unos 2.900 millones, el 1,4% de las concedidas en España, con un porcentaje sobre el total de la inversión del 16,7%, cuatro puntos porcentuales por debajo de la media española. La ratio de inversión por empleo en Asturias, –20,6 millones–, igualaba prácticamente a la nacional, con una elevación respecto al nivel medio correspondiente a la etapa de vigencia de la ZUR. Asturias superaba al conjunto de España en porcentaje de expedientes aprobados respecto a los presentados (Vázquez y Hernández 1991, 24).

El gobierno autonómico de Asturias fomentó instrumentos y mecanismos para ayudar e incentivar la inversión con resultados dispares[55]. El Instituto de Fomento Regional (IFR) ejerció una extensa y diversificada tarea de promoción industrial, a la vez que diversas actuaciones tanto directamente como en colaboración con otros organismos. Destaca la promoción de suelo industrial, junto con la Sociedad de Gestión y Promoción de Suelo (SOGEPSA), visible en la creación de cinco polígonos industriales[56]. La Sociedad Regional de Promoción (SRP), en cuyo capital social el Principado y la Caja de Ahorros de Asturias participaban con un 51 y un 32,9%, respectivamente, inició sus actividades en 1985 con un ritmo vigoroso, que se desaceleró de forma notable en adelante[57].

Veamos ahora la imposición por Corning Glass de la localización precisa de la fábrica de fibra óptica en Asturias y sus consecuencias, decidida tras una gira por España. Asturias, Barcelona, Málaga y Valencia[58] rivalizaban en la lista de zonas que los técnicos de Corning consideraban más idóneas para la

---

[55] Dentro del Programa de Actuaciones Urgentes (PAUR), Asturias avaló la concesión de créditos a las PME para realizar nuevas inversiones con un límite de riesgo a asumir de 200 millones de pesetas en el ejercicio 1987 (Ley 15/1986, de 30 de diciembre, de Presupuestos Generales del Principado de Asturias para el ejercicio de 1987, *BOE*, 50, 27 de febrero de 1987, 5.890). En el ejercicio siguiente, la suma por ese mismo concepto se duplicó con holgura –500 millones de pesetas– y se vio acrecentada por otros 1.000 millones de pesetas para operaciones de crédito con destino directo y específico a inversiones en la reindustrialización (Ley 7/1987, de 30 de diciembre, de Presupuestos Generales del Principado de Asturias para el ejercicio de 1988, *BOE*, 55, 4 de marzo de 1988, 6.878-6.899).

[56] El detalle revela hasta nueve actuaciones a nivel regional y nacional: convenios con instituciones económicas; coordinación de planes sectoriales regionales; información, formación y prestación de servicios a las empresas; bolsa de subcontratación; gestión de incentivos económicos y programas comunitarios; asesoramiento tecnológico, colaboración con la Fundación para el Fomento de la Investigación Científica y Tecnológica (FICYT) y participación en el Plan Regional de Investigación (*El País*, 26 de agosto de 1986; Vázquez y Hernández (1991), 24); polígonos industriales: Riaño (Langreo), Mieres, Las Arobias (Avilés), Silvota (Llanera) y Mora (Gijón), junto a los que planeaba el Plan Regional de Suelo Industrial para el cuatrienio 1990-1993.

[57] Castells et al. 1994, 31.

[58] La planta de producción de fibra óptica pensaba instalarse en el malagueño polígono industrial de Guadalhorce, con una inversión que oscilaba entre 20 y 30 millones de dólares. El proyecto, que debía estar terminado antes de final del año, preveía entre 70-80 puestos do trabajo directos, para titulados superiores en su mitad. No parecía fundada la noticia difundida sobre la relación entre la implantación en España de esta fábrica de fibra óptica y la firma de los acuerdos del Comité de Control de las Exportaciones (COCOM) de alta tecnología de doble uso (*Boletín Oficial de las Cortes Generales*, Senado, 29 de marzo de 1985, 5.566).

factoría[59]. En común tenían la característica de zonas costeras pero divergían en las ventajas comparativas que, dentro de una gama diversa, podían ofrecer a la multinacional e inclinar la balanza a favor de una concreta. En términos comparativos, recordemos que en la decisión de ubicar su futura factoría, la multinacional alemana Nixdorf Computer AG, con una docena de años de presencia en España, consideraba distintas alternativas en varias provincias españolas, si bien, las condiciones de infraestructura, comunicaciones y mano de obra cualificada existentes, así como el apoyo de las instituciones regionales propiciaban escoger una zona próxima a Tudela, en la que estaban instaladas Sanyo y la emblemática Piher, fabricantes de componentes electrónicos[60]. Es sabido que la multinacional de la informática barajó otras alternativas y finalmente se decantó en 1981 por Toledo para ubicar la fábrica de ordenadores. Seguía así los pasos de IBM, la líder mundial afincada en Valencia[61].

Resulta de interés detenerse en el caso frustrado de la primera candidata a albergar la producción de fibra óptica, desconocido aunque de amplias implicaciones.

Por lo general, los gobernantes extranjeros confiaban plenamente en el dinamismo económico y cultural de Cataluña, sus capacidades y las innumerables oportunidades de inversión y exportación, así como el deseo mayoritario de las empresas catalanas de integrarse en la CEE sin arredrarse ante la competencia industrial (Prat y Sánchez 2017)[62].

Los especialistas niegan consistencia a las políticas industriales de la Generalitat de Catalunya durante las cuatro décadas transcurridas desde su restablecimiento como institución de autogobierno. La fuerza que por más tiempo la presidió, el catalanismo conservador de Convergència Democràtica de Ca-

---

[59] La prensa madrileña señalaba que la multinacional estadounidense consideraba que Barcelona ofrecía mejores condiciones que ningún otro enclave para albergar el nuevo establecimiento, mientras que Telefónica se inclinaba por Asturias. la candidatura catalana se barajó también durante las negociaciones para la implantación de AT&T, pero Telefónica impuso su criterio favorable a los alrededores de Madrid (*La Vanguardia*, 17 de marzo de 1986, 36).

[60] *El País,* 19 de diciembre de 1979. En sus orígenes (1949), Piher fabricaba componentes para aparatos de radio para autoabastecimiento en unas instalaciones provisionales hasta que el aumento de la plantilla (una treintena de trabajadores en total) forzó el traslado a una nueva planta. Superar el confinamiento de la empresa al mercado nacional exigía un enfoque innovador, centrado en la producción de bienes protegidos por el Estado y en el abaratamiento de la mano de obra. Piher apostó por invertir en I+D para competir en el mercado mundial. En el primer semestre de 1973, exportó un 70% más que en el año anterior (Calvo 2016a, 60-85 y 2018, 39-40).

[61] *ABC*, 21 de octubre de 2013; proyecto de fábrica en Alcalá de Henares: *El País*, 9 de mayo de 1979; posible alternativa Barcelona-Madrid: Cabana (1987), 29-30.

[62] Citado con permiso del autor y la autora.

talunya, tendió a confundir sus intereses personales con los del país (Catalan 2019, 157-198; Escorsa 1986, 163)[63]. Al iniciarse el decenio de 1980, planteaba la trilogía productividad-innovación tecnológica-exportaciones competitivas. Frente a la crisis y el paro enarbolaba la bandera de la inversión pública y la privada mediante medidas destinadas a subvencionar de forma discrecional a empresas en crisis de las que se beneficiaban las grandes empresas[64].

Curiosamente, en 1984, Jordi Pujol reclamaba para Cataluña no la reindustrialización al estilo de la prevista en la ley del gobierno central, es decir, centrada en áreas geográficas muy limitadas y como consecuencia de la reconversión de un único sector industrial. Propugnaba que la zona de urgente reindustrialización en Cataluña siguiera siendo más localizada y más multisectorial, no limitada a ayudar a reindustrializar algunos territorios o sectores, como el textil[65].

La política industrial se desmarcó del intervencionismo propugnado por el Gobierno de la nación, que, como sabemos, gravitaba en delimitar y potenciar sectores y actividades con futuro. En cambio, viró hacia una política industrial autocalificada de «moderna», consistente en la consecución de un marco idóneo al desarrollo con facilidad de las decisiones de inversión privada y no en los recursos asignados desde la Administración central. El propio Pujol reconocía una actitud de rechazo a las multinacionales cuando se refería a una «época en que nos hicimos la ilusión de que podríamos prescindir de ellas, pero eso es imposible»[66]. Algo semejante recalcaba Pasqual Maragall al señalar que desde el gobierno autonómico no «se hizo todo lo que se debía hacer en este asunto» porque «entonces la Generalitat aún respiraba aires de "multinacionales, no"». Con el tiempo, desde la *conselleria* de industria

---

[63] Las líneas maestras de esta política ya estaban trazadas desde el comienzo de la transición (Pujol, 1976).

[64] *Diari de sessions del Parlament de Catalunya (DSPC)*, pleno del Parlament, 73, 24 de septiembre de 1981, 1976.

[65] *DSPC*, sesión plenaria, 2.1, 29 de mayo de 1984, 14.

[66] En 1986, ya dentro del mercado, el Patronato abrió una delegación en Bruselas (Fundació Jaume Bofill 1989, 131). En un estudio conjunto sobre la reconversión, Joan Hortalà, del ala liberal de Esquerra Republicana de Cataluña (ERC), señalaba la excepcionalidad de Cataluña, que, por su estructura económica, quedó fuera de las grandes reconversiones de los ochenta, centradas fundamentalmente, pero no solo, en la siderurgia y los astilleros (Hortalà y Puig, 1984, 501-509). ERC venía propugnando una racionalización de la inversión pública, el fomento de la privada, el apoyo a la operatividad productiva y un conjunto de reformas administrativas (*Los Sitios de Gerona*, 15 de diciembre de 1979). Hortalà tildaba la política del gobierno central de tardía e inadecuada a la estructura industrial catalana (*Ekonomiaz*, 3-4, 1986, 163).

de la Generalitat de Cataluña, Joan Hortalà potenció las herramientas institucionales y financieras de la política industrial: la subdirección general de desarrollo empresarial, el centro de información y desarrollo empresarial (CIDEM), el Patronat Català Pro-Europa (1982) y la Sociedad catalana de capital riesgo, SA. La primera tenía como finalidad promover el progreso industrial mediante la mejora tecnológica, en busca del aumento de la productividad. El CIDEM fue creado por Ley 5/1985, de 16 de abril (*BOE*, 183, 1 de agosto de 1985, 24.523-24.524). Al Patronat Català Pro-Europa se le encomendó la misión de preparar la entrada en el mercado europeo, tarea que llevó a cabo a través de estudios de los problemas, información a los empresarios y planteamiento de posibles soluciones. La tercera se constituyó con un capital escriturado de 500 millones de pesetas y quedó integrada por la Administración autonómica a través del CIDEM y las cuatro cajas catalanas participantes. La nueva sociedad debía impulsar iniciativas con incorporación tecnológica (*El País*, 27 de febrero de 1986).

Por otra parte, la ZUR del cinturón industrial de Barcelona acordada con la Generalitat de Cataluña no llegó a ser declarada hasta 1985. Esta medida aportaba soluciones potenciales a la crisis de empleo provocada por los planes de reconversión y al esfuerzo inversor. Sus objetivos abarcaban cuatro ámbitos: paliar los efectos de los planes de reconversión mediante la creación de puestos de trabajo; acrecentar la eficacia y oportunidad en la inversión; completar las actuaciones de fomento con un mayor alcance territorial y optimizar el uso de las infraestructuras[67]. La ZUR atrajo empresas tecnológicas, entre ellas Sanyo y Sharp en el sector electrónico e informático, a la vez que sirvió de acicate a nuevas inversiones en empresas de implantación anterior.

---

[67] *La Nueva España*, 23 de abril de 1986, 6. Parece oportuno señalar que las implicaciones de este asunto forman parte de un secreto bien guardado. Barcelona era todavía la capital industrial de España, que orientaba su producción a un mercado protegido por aranceles pero a punto de auparse al segundo nivel de la jerarquía urbana europea, encabezada por París y Londres. Maragall reiteraba la propuesta de un acuerdo de coordinación con la Generalitat sobre promoción industrial, con el objetivo de atraer empresas (*La Vanguardia*, 20 de junio de 1986, 35). El Gobierno de Jordi Pujol ponía trabas al desarrollo institucional del área metropolitana de Barcelona (Gomà y Subirats 2001, 69). La declaración de ZUR de Cataluña –11 municipios, tres polígonos públicos y tres áreas calificadas como zona industrial– quedó por debajo de las pretensiones de los promotores, que incluían 34 y 28 municipios, respectivamente (*BOE*, 148, de 21 de junio de 1985, 19.263-19.265; Conejos y Puig 1992, 76-84); recogido por la prensa (*El País*, 9 de mayo de 1985). En cuanto a la oferta del suelo industrial, la Generalitat y el Gobierno central coincidieron pronto en la necesidad de un análisis de las ayudas de las administraciones pública y local (*La Vanguardia*, 9 de diciembre de 1984).

Digamos para entender mejor la envergadura de esta IED y de sumo interés para contrastar con las grandes teorías de la internacionalización, el proceso de inversión que acostumbran a seguir las empresas japonesas se prologa comparativamente más que en el caso de las empresas occidentales. Aquellas realizan con bastante frecuencia pequeñas inversiones iniciales en su actividad principal y amplían sus operaciones si esta inversión da buenos resultados. Posteriormente, se diversifican en nuevas áreas de negocio mediante la entrada en el mercado extranjero. Las occidentales tienden a preferir las grandes inversiones vinculadas a una expectativa de retorno rápido de las inversiones (Glowik 2016, 37-38).

El proyecto de la multinacional japonesa Sharp Co., dedicada principalmente a I+D, venta y *marketing* de productos de la electrónica de consumo, sistemas de información y componentes electrónicos, se plasmó en la creación, a mediados de 1986, de una filial con el nombre de Sharp Electrónica España. Según las previsiones a cinco años efectuadas por Sharp, la planta empezaría a fabricar unos 4.000 televisores mensuales e iría aumentando la cifra hasta llegar a los 18.000 televisores al mes en 1990. En un planteamiento diversificador, estaba prevista, además, la fabricación de aparatos de alta fidelidad durante el primer quinquenio y no se descartaban artículos de mayor valor tecnológico a continuación. La inversión *greenfield* de Sharp en su nueva fábrica de Sant Cugat del Vallés, inaugurada a inicios de octubre de 1987, se elevó a 2.300 millones de ptas. La planta, con una nómina inicial de 250 personas, se destinó a fabricar fundamentalmente televisores si bien más tarde diversificó la producción con aparatos de fax para el mercado europeo. Sharp Electrónica España amplió la planta con una nueva cadena de producción de pantallas de cristal líquido LCD, que supuso la inversión aproximada de 2,5 millones de € en dos años. Ya entrado el milenio, con más de 15 millones de aparatos, la empresa cedió los activos productivos al grupo Nortia[68].

---

[68] Generalitat de Catalunya, Departament de la Presidència 2002; *La Vanguardia*, 2 de octubre de 1987; *Consumer Goods Europe*, 458-461, 2001, 85; *Política exterior*, 8, 41-42, 1994, 213; *Época*, 9 de junio de 1986. Las primeras cifras de inversión y empleo apuntaban a 3.710 millones, un 60,78% en capital fijo y el resto en capital circulante, y una plantilla de 190 trabajadores. Alberto Faus fue presidente de la filial española (*El País*, 28 de mayo de 1986). En 2008, la matriz Sharp mantenía su fabricación de productos de electrónica de consumo en Sharp Electronics Ltd., Middlesex, Reino Unido, y, fuera de Europa y Japón, en China, Taiwán, Malasia, Indonesia, Filipinas y Estados Unidos, donde, a través de Sharp Laboratories of America, Inc., también estableció actividades locales de investigación y desarrollo (Glowik 2016, 37-38).

Otros grandes proyectos utilizaban mecanismos específicos sin integrarse dentro de los planes de las ZUR, entre ellos los proyectos con socios tecnológicos de diversa procedencia y orientación – Olivetti y las multinacionales estadounidenses Kelsey Hayes[69] y Hewlett Packard (HP) (Tabla 2) (Escorsa 1986, 158; Fundació Jaume Bofill 1989, 143)[70].

En cuanto a la primera, conviene recordar que se estaba gestando uno de los primeros grupos de alcance europeo en el terreno de la electrónica. En este marco, la multinacional italiana Olivetti elaboraba una estrategia de expansión en España mediante un *holding* industrial de la electrónica y la informática que suponía la creación de nuevas empresas, entre ellas *joint ventures* en sectores nuevos para la empresa, y la adquisición de otras[71].

La presencia de Olivetti en Cataluña se remontaba a la creación de una filial en Barcelona –Hispano Olivetti– a comienzos de 1929, años antes de su incipiente expansión europea –Bélgica y Francia– y latinoamericana – Brasil y a Argentina– y, ni qué decir tiene, de su entrada en el Reino Unido, primero en asociación con el capital local en una empresa conjunta comercial en 1947, después dotada de un establecimiento industrial (Renzi 2008, 18). España vio la primera experiencia industrial de internacionalización de la casa matriz, financiada con capital mayoritario catalán (De Witt 2005, 58 y 62; González 2011, 30-31). Tras comprar una pequeña empresa local –La Rápida– que producía máquinas de escribir y coser, empezó a producir en un modesto edificio

---

[69] En 1985, la Empresa Nacional de Innovación (ENISA), del INI se asoció a Kelsey Hayes (grupo Fruahaufe) en una empresa conjunta, con un capital de 1.000 millones de pesetas, 35% aportados por ENISA, mediante una inversión *greenfield* de unos 3.000 millones de pesetas en una fábrica para producir llantas y accesorios de aluminio en la localidad catalana de Sant Joan Despí (*El País*, 19 de junio y 5 de septiembre de 1985; *El Periódico de Catalunya*, 14 de junio de 1985 y *Cinco Días*, 19 de julio de1985).

[70] Los sesudos ejecutivos de HP antepusieron los campos de golf y las conexiones rápidas con Barcelona y su aeropuerto a las ventajas que ofrecía Sabadell en la informática con su Centre de Càlcul y el Logic Control (*El Día de Sabadell*, 18 de abril de 2019). La Generalitat priorizaba ayudas y avales a proyectos industriales ubicados en determinadas zonas del interior de Cataluña, no incluidas en el decreto regulador de zona de urgente reindustrialización (ZUR) de Barcelona (*El País*, 5 de septiembre de 1985). Hacia finales de 1985, las ZUR de Cataluña contabilizaban 379 proyectos, de los cuales 41 estaban a la espera de la aprobación del Banco de Crédito Industrial. De estos últimos, los 29 primeros suponía un máximo de inversión de 8.300 millones de pesetas y la creación de 1.114 nuevos puestos de trabajo (*El País*, 7 de noviembre de 1985). Jordi Pujol atribuyó a la ZUR catalana resultados superiores a la madrileña, pese a la extremada concentración de grandes proyectos, incluido el de la AT&T (*Diari de sessions del Parlament de Catalunya*, 3, 22 de junio de 1988, sesión plenaria, 2, 60).

[71] Joan Majó fue nombrado presidente a mediados de 1987 (*La Vanguardia*, 11 de julio de 1987).

con unas cuantas máquinas importadas y de fabricación propia. Aspecto de enorme importancia, la capacidad tecnológica se completó con la aportación de conocimiento procedente de la matriz. Esta transferencia directa tomó la forma de llegada de los primeros técnicos e instructores, entre ellos Ermanno Franchetto, experto en los sistemas de producción y control de vanguardia, cuya implantación impulsó en los talleres[72].

De la precariedad Hispano Olivetti pasó a consolidar su producción con la construcción de una fábrica en 1942, en los tiempos terribles del franquismo sanguinario[73]. Desde entonces, aumentó la producción. Entre 1968 y 1971, se vio inmersa en una compleja racionalización y concentración de la matriz Olivetti, que representó la primera operación de articulación estructural del sistema industrial hacia unidades autónomas, centradas estratégicamente en una única línea de productos. Los portátiles se produjeron en centros separados geográficamente: la turinesa Aglié y Barcelona. Ambas unidades siguieron abasteciendo el mercado europeo pero con una distribución de los volúmenes igualmente diferenciada. Asimismo, la segunda ciudad se especializó en máquinas portátiles de alta gama, las Semistandards, y de productos manuales de escritura estándar, la Línea 98, para el mercado español. Por su parte, la planta de Glasgow se centró en la escritura eléctrica, sucesivamente con la nueva Lettera 36 y la Lexicon 82 en la segunda mitad de la década de 1970 (De Witt 2005, 124). Sin embargo, la pérdida de competitividad por aumento de los costes llevó en 1980 a transferir toda la actividad de producción a un proveedor europeo de bajo coste, que fue identificado como UNIS, una empresa yugoslava con buena tecnología mecánica. Mientras que esta

---

[72] Máquinas importadas: una fresadora universal Brown & Sharps, adquirida en EE. UU. en 1908, una rectificadora Wunderli procedente de Suiza; de fabricación propia: un taladrador múltiple; sistemas de producción: fundición inyectada de aleaciones ligeras, fabricación de la tornillería con máquinas automáticas de marcas líderes, templado parcial con aparato de alta frecuencia, hornos para el secado de barnices de canal con transporte en cadena y para las operaciones de control (Hispano Olivetti 1954, 23-24); característica: reducido coste de la materia prima. Franchetto (1965, 20-27) es el autor de un artículo destacado sobre la máquina de cálculo. Muestra de la apuesta internacional, si bien tiznada por la voluntad de reafirmar su autoridad, en 1945, Adriano Olivetti trató sin éxito de llevar a cabo una acción de transferencia de conocimiento: trasladar a España como jefe de taller de la planta de Barcelona a uno de los directivos principales –el ingeniero Gino Martinoli, introductor en la Necchi de la división del trabajo y la cadena de montaje– (Archivio Storico Olivetti).

[73] Durante la Guerra civil abasteció a la administración, como prueban diversas piezas del Archivo Histórico Nacional, una de las cuales deja un interrogante sobre la procedencia de las máquinas: ¿realmente se importaron unidades Hispano Olivetti o eran simplemente Olivetti? (Correspondencia varia referente a la importación de máquinas de escribir Hispano Olivetti, FC-PRESID_GOB_ADQUISICIONES, 197, Exp.28, 1938-1939).

deslocalización sufrió retrasos, la devaluación del peso en 1982 convirtió en competitivas las portátiles producidas en México, que se reorientaron al mercado europeo (De Witt 2005, 175-177)[74]. La plantilla de Barcelona sufrió una sangría constante que le hizo perder un cuarto sobrado de su plantilla de 750 trabajadores en tan solo dos años.

Hacia finales de 1984, tuvo lugar una doble operación de diversificación y afianzamiento de las capacidades de la empresa. Olivetti se estrenó en la fabricación de ordenadores personales M-24 en su factoría barcelonesa, el grueso de los mismos destinados a la exportación. Simultáneamente, decidió crear un Centro de I+D para proyectar nuevos equipos de escritura electrónica e informática de gran consumo[75].

Pasados unos años, tres razones coincidieron para preparar el cambio de ubicación de la histórica fábrica barcelonesa. La empresa vio la necesidad de unas instalaciones modernas para lograr el cambio tecnológico a las máquinas de escribir eléctricas y a los ordenadores. A esta razón se añadía otra de tipo corporativo-urbanístico, a saber, el proyecto de Parc Tecnològic del Vallès (PTV) y la voluntad del Ayuntamiento de abrir la zona donde estaba ubicada hasta el mar. La filial de la multinacional italiana se trasladó al PTV en 1992. La historia no tuvo éxito porque cuatro años después Olivetti decidió dejar la fábrica con una plantilla de 180 trabajadores tras una larga etapa de presencia industrial en el mercado español. Para empezar, la filial sirvió de nuevo de pedestal para deslocalizar la producción de ordenadores a otras empresas del grupo. El 1994 planteó un plan de viabilidad para la planta, que pasó a fabricar teléfonos multimedia con videotex, más allá de la gama de impresoras (*Ara*, 16 de noviembre de 2014). Elemento importante fue el centro de investigación en el Parque Tecnológico del Vallés (CICYT 1990, 330).

---

[74] La producción de máquinas de escribir manuales se trasladaron a San Paolo desde 1979 y la de portátiles se concentró en la fábrica de Ciudad de México de 1982 a 1984. En 1980, se abrió una nueva fábrica en Singapur para satisfacer la demanda de producción de calculadoras para todo el grupo (Berta y Onida 2011, 26).

[75] *El País*, 20 de diciembre de 1984. Dos protocolos formalizaron la inversión de 15 millones de dólares (unos 2.300 millones de pesetas) en la nueva factoría de ordenadores personales de Cerdanyola (Barcelona): un convenio entre la matriz y el Ministerio de Industria por el cual podría acogerse a las ayudas previstas en el Plan Energético e Informático Nacional; un segundo entre Hispano Olivetti y la Corporación Metropolitana de Barcelona para ceder los terrenos de la nueva planta (*El País*, 30 de enero de 1985). Hispano Olivetti facturó 29.757 millones de pesetas en 1986 – 21,9% más que el año anterior– destinadas primordialmente (84,63%) al mercado nacional; en 1986 Hispano Olivetti vendió 13.456 ordenadores personales, con un incremento del 107,5% respecto al año anterior (*El País*, 20 de marzo de 1987).

En cuanto al otro gran proyecto con socios tecnológicos de diversa procedencia y orientación, hacia finales de 1984 Hewlett Packard dio el visto bueno a abrir en España una fábrica de elementos periféricos, equipos de instrumentación y registros gráficos de ordenadores. Daba así preferencia a España sobre varias naciones europeas aspirantes, entre ellas Holanda e Italia, país este por el que apostaría más tarde. La multinacional –de modesta cuna pero inventora de la impresión láser, el chorro de tinta, el microprocesador RISC y la entrada en sistemas abiertos con el UNIX– afianzaba su penetración del mercado español en el que ya contaba con trece años de antigüedad (Uriz 2005, 81 y 83)[76]. Hewlett Packard Española, S. A. abastecía de diversos productos a las administraciones públicas. La expansión de HP en España avanzó desde el estadio comercial hasta el de fabricación y de *marketing*, ingeniería e I+D. HP Española siguió una trayectoria a veces divergente por completo respecto al conjunto del sector. En 1994-1995 la filial amplió las instalaciones destinadas a producir impresoras e incrementó su plantilla en un 34% cuando el empleo del sector informático en España disminuyó un 5,56% respecto al año anterior[77].

La multinacional, rectificando a la baja los datos adelantados por la administración española, cifró la inversión en unos 2.000 millones, escalonadamente en cinco años, y la producción prevista en 12.000 millones anuales, el grueso destinado al mercado exterior[78].

Hewlett Packard, después de descartar la alternativa de Navarra, tomó la decisión de instalarse en Cataluña, independiente pero paralela a la elección

[76] El primer producto de Hewlett Packard fue el Model 200A, un oscilador de audio, la primera máquina de diseño propio y bajo coste, capaz de generar altas frecuencias de radio. En 1964, las ventas de productos de computación de HP no aportaban nada a sus ventas totales 125 millones de dólares pero al cabo de treinta años alcanzaron los 20 mil millones de dólares, cerca de 78% del negocio anual de la empresa (Packard 2007). Hewlett Packard decidió crear en Bérgamo un maxi polo internacional de investigación en aplicaciones de Internet, con especial atención al sector de la telefonía celular y los servicios a estaciones móviles. A Bérgamo se le asignaron competencias e infraestructuras de investigación en dependencia directa del centro *hub* de Helsinki (Sgro 2020, 150). Los valores fundacionales –las «Reglas del Garaje»– incluían el respeto por el individuo, la contribución a los clientes y a la comunidad, la integridad sin concesiones, trabajo en equipo e innovación (Hewlett Packard 2000, 15).

[77] *Boletín oficial de la provincia de Santander*, XXXVII, 73, 18 de junio de 1973; *Hoja oficial de la provincia de Barcelona*, LII, 2.043, 15 de mayo de 1978; *Computerworld*, 28 de abril de 1995. Se especializó en la gama de impresoras de gran formato como centro mundial de desarrollo, producción y distribución: *Expansión*, 4 de febrero de 1995.

[78] La prensa señalaba la enorme diferencia respecto a la envergadura del proyecto de AT&T en Madrid (*La Vanguardia*, 4 de noviembre de 1984).

de Madrid por la AT&T, a lo largo de 1984, si bien algunas «maniobras diversivas» pretendieron ocultarlo para evitar la especulación inmobiliaria[79]. Todo parece indicar que las autoridades españolas se inclinaron por esa ubicación a título de compensación por la instalación de AT&T en Madrid. HP empezó a producir *plotters* o trazadores gráficos a mediados de 1985 en tres cadenas de montaje instaladas en locales alquilados de Terrassa antes de construir la fábrica propia de Sant Cugat en Silicón Vallés, que se convirtió en el centro de definición y diseño de las impresoras de inyección de tinta de gran formato para el mercado mundial[80]. Merece la pena señalar que estamos en presencia de un caso de transferencia inversa, concepto que indica el intercambio intrainstitucional de conocimientos técnicos o tecnología e información desde filiales internacionales (países anfitriones) a las sedes de las empresas (países de origen) (Ambos 2018; Mansfield 1984, 127-154)[81].

En una evaluación de conjunto, la política industrial catalana consistente en atraer a empresas multinacionales ha tenido limitaciones. En lo que parece haber tenido éxito es en la configuración de una red de subcontratistas locales de multinacionales implantadas. Barcelona desempeñó un importante papel en ese aspecto ya que no solo aparece como un lugar preferido para la localización de plantas de IED sino también para subcontratar fabricación[82].

Nada hay de gratuito en la anterior exposición, que nos sitúa en el tema central. Las exigencias de Corning and Glass indujeron al gobierno del Principado de Asturias a promover un parque tecnológico en la localidad de Llanera, cercana a Oviedo, que exigió una inversión de 2.066 millones de pese-

---

[79] *La Vanguardia*, 9 de noviembre de 1984; Hewlett Packard exploró la viabilidad de instalar la fábrica de periféricos en Navarra (*Cinco Días*, 19 de enero de 1985; *Diario 16* 19 de enero de 1985).

[80] *La Vanguardia*, 11 de enero de 1986. La tercera cadena estaba destinada a trazadores de alto rendimiento y gran formato de papel, del modelo denominado *draftmaster*, el más avanzado de Hewlett Packard (*La Vanguardia*, 14 de septiembre de 1987). La entrada de multinacionales en el país servía de pedestal a la ampliación de la IED. Juan Soto, director de HP, hizo una loa de las multinacionales como factores de progreso para el país (*Diario de Burgos*, 1 de marzo de 1986). En el cambio de milenio, el pujante mercado de consumo de Hewlett-Packard incluyó ordenadores domésticos, portátiles, PDA, dispositivos de almacenamiento personal, impresoras de inyección de tinta y consumibles, escáneres, cámaras digitales e impresoras fotográficas; preveía una expansión por los mercados clave de Europa, Asia y América Latina (Hewlett-Packard (2000), 15).

[81] El término «transferencia inversa» (reverse transfer) fue acuñado por Yamin (1995) y reutilizado por Hakanson y Nobel (2001). Una modalidad de transferencia, que ejemplifica General Motors, se da entre filiales –horizontales.

[82] Holl, Pardo y Rama 2012, 1.335-1.355; Comunicación escrita de Ruth Rama, 6 de abril de 2022.

tas, el grueso de aportación autonómica y el resto de fondos europeos, y echó a andar en 1991[83].

Nuestro relato subraya un factor sustancial: el papel motor de las multinacionales, que se conjugaba con la política industrial si bien no siempre en el *tempo* conveniente. Lo asumían los gobiernos regionales, que competían entre si en una auténtica carrera por encauzar hacia su molino el potencial de innovación inherente a esas empresas o, en otro de los símiles utilizados, por no perder el tren de la innovación. Por su parte, nos remite a las claves de la llegada de esas empresas a un territorio concreto[84]. Muy ligado con lo anterior aparece el coste de oportunidad de las decisiones tomadas: las subvenciones concedidas restaban presupuesto para poder favorecer a otras empresas. Pero en el caso de las ZUR, la selección de las beneficiarias era el Consejo de ministros, en su papel de elemento sancionador de las ayudas, y no el gobierno regional[85].

5. La ofensiva del capital multinacional europeo: Siemens y Tefosa

Una vez el proyecto de TELCOR en vía muerta, Telefónica no cejó en su empeño de producir fibra óptica sin abandonar la fórmula de un socio tecnológico y dirigió sus miras a AT&T, antes descartada a causa de la ya reseñada diversificación de socios tecnológicos, con un plan idéntico de producto y localización[86]. Pero la multinacional norteamericana hizo caso omiso, ajena a las condiciones favorables existentes entre ambas empresas, inmersas en el proyecto para fabricar chips que conocemos (Calvo 2017, 51-62). La estrategia dio entonces un vuelco geográfico. A finales de 1987, Telefónica acordó con la japonesa Sumitomo Electric Industries Ltd. la constitución de una *joint*

---

[83]   La teoría atribuye a los parques tecnológicos la condición de factor de atracción de empresas con un efecto difusor de actividad en áreas más distantes (Mella 2000, 630-638); véase Ondategui (2001) para una visión de conjunto.

[84]   En otro ejemplo de comunidad autónoma –Aragón–, la oposición socialista señalaba que las nuevas tecnologías reclamaban empresas bien dispuestas, importantes tareas de relaciones públicas, buenas conexiones políticas e infraestructuras a punto (Pregunta n.º 25/91, relativa al parque tecnológico de Aragón, *Diario de Sesiones de las Cortes de Aragón,* 009 de Plenos. III Legislatura, 1991-1993).

[85]   Comparecencia del Sr. Consejero de Economía, Informe sobre la AT&T de Tres Cantos, *Diario de Sesiones de la Comunidad de Madrid,* 242, 14 de octubre de 1988, 4.775.

[86]   De Silva (Izquierda Unida), Pleno de la Junta general, II Legislatura, *Diario de sesiones del Principado de Asturias (DSdPdA),* 2, 20 de julio de 1987 (*El País,* 8 de octubre de 1988).

venture para producir fibra óptica, controlada por capital nipón. Una y otra estaban implicadas en su condición de aspirante a beneficiarse del potencial de crecimiento en Europa en el caso de la japonesa y como cliente de ese nuevo material necesario para la modernización de la extensa red en el de Telefónica –cerca de los 12.000 km hasta 1990–. Ambas dieron pasos en la negociación de un acuerdo a la vez que en la definición del plan general de empresa y, en particular, de lo relativo a cuantificar el tamaño del mercado interior y de exportación. En el primer aspecto pesaba la categoría de la operadora española como cliente primordial y la eventualidad de diversificar la producción por inclusión de nuevos clientes como RENFE y las empresas eléctricas[87].

Debido sin duda al carácter estratégico de la fibra óptica, el empeño por ser la primera empresa española en fabricar ese material y accesorios exteriores para telecomunicaciones fue culminado con algún cambio de protagonistas respecto a los planes iniciales[88].

El primero fue la autoexclusión de Telefónica, ya fuera de los planteamientos de *holding* industrial pero que, con toda probabilidad, asumió un papel de puente para garantizar la continuidad de los proyectos. Cuando había transcurrido un trienio después del fracaso de TELCOR e igualmente en continuidad con aquella iniciativa en cuanto a emplazamiento –no en cuanto a inversión– una alianza entre la multinacional alemana Siemens con una empresa española –el grupo General Cable– y una entidad pública –la SRP del Principado de Asturias, brazo operativo del IFR, como sabemos– despejaba

---

[87] Un quinquenio después de su desmantelamiento, AT&T, firmemente partidaria de la fibra óptica como material de futuro, cifraba en más de 100 mil millones de dólares la inversión en el cableado de EE. EU. durante el cuarto de siglo siguiente. En esa «killer technology» se jugaba la que sus directivos identificaban como batalla de AT&T *versus* Japan Inc., ya que sería la sustituta de las redes coaxiales de cable en la televisión por cable y teléfono (*New York Times*, 8 de noviembre de 1988). Cabe recordar el papel de AT&T como proveedora de la fibra óptica en el cable Las Palmas-Santa Cruz de Tenerife (*ACE*, 9 de mayo de 1984). Sumitomo, muy dada a diversificar sus mercados, estaba controlada por un grupo de grandes empresas japonesas de los sectores industrial (NEC Corp.), financiero (Sumitomo Bank, Industrial Bank of Japan) y de seguros (Sumitomo Life, Dai Ichi-Mitsui Life, Nippon Life Insurance) (*El País*, 4 de noviembre de 1987). En su país de origen, Sumitomo, al igual que Fujikura, aparecía como beneficiaria potencial de sublicencias de Furukawa Electric Co, derivadas de una licencia otorgada por Corning en 1977 (86/405/EEC: Commission Decision of 14 July 1986, *Official Journal L 236*, 22/8/1986). Los contactos de Sumitomo con el mercado español se remontaban cuando menos a los planes de financiación de la siderurgia española en 1970 (*Diario de Burgos: de avisos y noticias*, 4 de noviembre de 1970).

[88] La CTNE contemplaba instalar 30.000 kilómetros de fibra óptica a lo largo de unos 2.800 kilómetros de la geografía española en su plan cuadrienal de inversiones de 1985-1988 (*El País*, 25 de enero de 1985).

el camino a una nueva sociedad para producir fibra óptica[89]. Por lo demás, el acuerdo dejaba abierto un portillo a la entrada del INI con una participación del 5-10% a través de la Empresa Nacional de Investigación (Enisa). Corning Glass Works recuperó su rol de socio tecnológico y accionista por medio de Siecor GMBH en la empresa conjunta con Siemens, veterana candidata a abrir una planta de producción en España[90].

La nueva empresa se constituyó a finales de 1989 con el nombre de Tecnologías de la Fibra Óptica (Tefosa) según un esquema de integración vertical con el objetivo de desarrollar actividad en el terreno de los cables, en particular I+D, fabricación, comercialización de fibra óptica y fabricación de equipos y accesorios[91]. Su campo abarcaba no solo la fibra óptica sino lo relacionado con la electricidad, la electrónica y las técnicas y procesos de la información y la telecomunicación. La composición del primer órgano corporativo, muy acorde con la estructura de poder en la empresa, congregó personas con saberes técnicos, gerenciales y económicos[92]. Los 850 millones de pesetas de capital social fueron aportados a través de sus filiales Siecor y RXS por Siemens AG como socio mayoritario (58,1%), por Cables de Co-

[89] En calidad de presidente de la CTNE, Solana comunicó a las autoridades asturianas que no albergaba duda alguna sobre la ubicación de la empresa de fibra óptica en Asturias (Junta del Principado de Asturias (JGPA), Pleno, *DSdPdA*, 8, 16 de noviembre de 1987). Más tarde, el gobierno asturiano encomendó a Solana la tarea de buscar empresas de tecnología avanzada para su instalación en el Principado (*Hoja del Lunes*, 1 de julio de 1991).

[90] Principales cifras del plan: 2.000 millones de pesetas de inversión, un centenar de nuevos puestos de trabajo de alta cualificación y producción anual de 70.000 kilómetros de fibra óptica, un quinto para la exportación (*El País*, 31 de julio de 1989). Siemens planeó adquirir la planta cántabra de Standard Eléctrica y convertirla en una fábrica de fibra óptica.

[91] *Expansión*, 12 de diciembre de 1989; *La Nueva España*. 4 de noviembre de 1989, 18; *Diario 16*, 7 de noviembre de 1989.

[92] Registro Mercantil de Oviedo (RMO), tomo 508, libro 329, folio 24, inscripción primera. Comenzó su actividad en noviembre de 1989 y, posteriormente, redujo su capital a 10 millones (RMO, tomo 957, libro 625, hoja 4.652). Siemens AG Munchen ordenó al Banco Central dos pagos a Tefosa por 100,512 y 22,95 millones de ptas. procedentes de Siecor y RXS, respectivamente (RMO, tomo 957, libro 625, hoja 4.652). Detallamos la composición del primer consejo de administración: Siecor Geselschaft fur Lichtwellwnbleiter Nit Beschränter Haftung (Siecor) estaba representada por el gerente técnico Wulf-Dieter Seiffert (presidente); Cables de Comunicaciones por el ingeniero zaragozano José Manuel Landeira Fariña (vicepresidente), y por el abogado barcelonés Juan Ribalta Aguilera (secretario no consejero). Las vocalías recayeron en Hugo Schroers (gerente comercial administrativo), Helmut von Deimling (director comercial administrativo), el director técnico Gabriel Marín García, el empleado Ángel Rodríguez García, el director técnico Manuel Navarro Marco, el economista José Luis San Miguel Cela (SRP) y en el gerente técnico Manfred Heier de RXS Schumptechnik-Garnituren Geselschaft Nit BE-Beschränter Haftung (RXS). Más tarde, José L. San Miguel Cela ocupó la presidencia del Consejo de Administración, en representación de la SRP (RMO, tomo 1.711, hoja AS10.914).

municaciones (31,9%), filial del Grupo Español General Cable, y por la SRP (10%). En calidad de socio tecnológico, Siemens AG aportaba el *know how* de sus dos filiales señaladas en la doble vertiente de fibra y componentes, respectivamente[93]. Los planes cuajaron en un proyecto de fábrica y una previsión de inversión de 2.500 millones, escasa para las aspiraciones de Siemens, dispuesta a duplicar la cantidad. Algo se torció porque Siemens AG se mostró reticente a continuar con el proyecto, a diferencia de los socios, dispuestos a proseguir el plan[94]. Finalmente, decidió abandonar el proyecto por razones nunca reveladas pero que algunos atribuyeron a dos de distinto orden, a saber, la evolución futura en el mercado mundial de fibra óptica y la vaguedad de Telefónica como cliente primordial en la definición de los contratos. En definitiva, Siemens optó por otras localizaciones. En 1999, en el momento de venderla a Corning, la sección de cables de comunicaciones de Siemens comprendía dos plantas en Alemania y otras tres más, localizadas en Italia, Francia y Turquía[95].

Indagar en los motivos del nuevo revés exige hablar de política industrial en sus diversos niveles de planificación y ejecución, como también de estrategia de las multinacionales en su expansión mundial. El gobierno asturiano llevó a cabo estudios para inversiones extranjeras, en general, y para la asociación con Siecor, en particular. Hacia finales de 1989, contactó en Nueva York con inversores norteamericanos para presentar la imagen y las posibilidades de Asturias, llegando a ofrecer el parque industrial para localizar las actividades[96].

Resulta conveniente conocer las implicaciones de la intervención de las multinacionales en el tejido productivo español para determinar lo excepcio-

---

[93] *La Nueva España*. 4, 7 y 11 de noviembre de 1989; *Diario 16*, 7 de noviembre de 1989; *Expansión de la actualidad económica diaria*, 7 de noviembre de 1989. Contabilización de la inversión de 85 millones de ptas. de la SPR en la empresa (Sociedad Regional de Promoción, *Libro de Actas*, 24 de julio de 1989 –cortesía de Ángeles Silverio–). Con la disminución del capital a 10 millones, Siecor y RXS mantenían la mayoría (581 acciones) mientras que las restantes se repartían entre los socios españoles Cables de Comunicaciones (319) y SRP (100) (RMO, tomo, hoja AS10.914).

[94] Ubicación prevista en el Parque Tecnológico de Asturias (*ABC*, 7 de noviembre de 1989). Finalmente, la inversión se fijó en 2.100 millones de pesetas, mientras que la capacidad de producción inicial –70.000 kilómetros de fibra óptica– y el empleo no sufrieron alteraciones (*El País*, 8 de octubre de 1988, 7 de noviembre de 1989 y 5 de junio de 1990). Los intentos de la Generalitat de Cataluña por instalarla en el Parque Tecnológico de Barcelona resultaron infructuosos.

[95] *Fiber Optics Online*, 8 de diciembre de 1999; *Photonics Spectra*, 24, 1990, 7-12, 51.

[96] Junta General del Principado de Asturias, II Legislatura, pleno, *DSdPdA*, 119, 25 de julio de 1990.

nal o habitual del caso. El anuncio de la llegada de Siemens a Asturias coincidió temporalmente con el del emplazamiento de una fábrica de siliconas y plásticos de la multinacional norteamericana General Electric (GE) en España[97]. Esta empresa presenta el caso, sin duda mejor documentado, de la voluntad de las autoridades asturianas para atraer inversiones y de las exigencias de las multinacionales. La norteamericana consideró instalarse en Asturias por las ventajas económicas y la oportunidad del momento en que tenía lugar: al atractivo de la subvención como zona ZUR se unía la circunstancia de que GE barajaba ampliar sus instalaciones de Holanda y frente a las alternativas de otros países europeos, entre ellos Irlanda, país que rivalizaba con España como destino de IED[98]. El primer contacto de GE con el mercado asturiano ocurrió en 1985, cuando impulsaba un proyecto de polímeros y, con asesoría de la consultora Foster Wheeler, recorrió todas las zonas ZUR de España. Un año más tarde, resolvió ejecutar el proyecto como ampliación de su fábrica en Holanda. La vuelta a la opción española se relacionó con la fabricación de siliconas. Tras descartar diversas zonas candidatas y, más en concreto, Huelva, la favorita, quedaron como aspirantes Murcia y Asturias. En 1988, en un giro en la decisión empresarial General Electric decidió sumar el de polímeros al primer proyecto de las siliconas, triplicando las previsiones de inversión iniciales– unos 60.000 millones de pesetas– e incrementando las expectativas de creación de empleo. Altos representantes de la matriz GE y de sus filiales en Holanda y España forjaron un acuerdo total con el consejo de economía del gobierno regional sobre las condiciones del emplazamiento –localidad, tamaño del suelo industrial, urbanización, zona de seguridad y disponibilidad del mismo–[99].

La administración asturiana se hizo cargo de urbanizar y costear tanto los suministros básicos como la formación de personal –técnicos altamente cualificados y de grado medio– en el extranjero –EE. EU. y Holanda– durante el

---

[97] General Electric producía en Nueva York emisores, detectores, LED infrarrojos y detectores de fotodarlington, una combinación integrada de fotodiodo y transistor (*International Fiber Optics & Communications,* febrero 1986, 56).

[98] De hecho, hasta 1995, la IED per cápita en España superaba a la irlandesa (Barry 2004, 12).

[99] El terreno elegido se situaba en el valle de Tamón, próximo al puerto gijonés de El Musel, a Avilés y a la nueva acería de Ensidesa (*Hoja del Lunes,* 15 de agosto de 1988). Debía contar con una extensa zona de seguridad de 470 ha., un terreno anejo de 70 ha. La GE se mostró preocupada por la necesidad de expropiar una cuarentena de viviendas y de desalojar a los ocupantes, a lo que se añadía la aversión del público hacia las plantas químicas (JGPA, II Legislatura, Comisión de Industria, Energía y Comercio, *DSdPdA,* 048, 25 de octubre de 1988).

decenio de ejecución del proyecto. La asignación de terrenos a la planta química implicó negociar aspectos impositivos con los municipios del territorio en busca de tasas decrecientes. Fue preciso apalabrar con el gobierno el suministro de componentes –cumeno– y gestionar con ENSIDESA la autorización para la salida al mar de los residuos. El desacuerdo del equipo técnico de General Electric por la región de emplazamiento –Asturias o Murcia– obligó a la máxima autoridad de la empresa a desplazarse para tomar una decisión con conocimiento directo de los lugares.

Un proyecto de estas características no podía por menos que requerir la intervención estatal. GE mantuvo al menos dos contactos con los ministros de Industria y de Economía, solicitando información sobre el porcentaje de subvención, que, sujeta a la ley de incentivos, iba a destinar el Gobierno. Ambos ministros pusieron un 30% como techo máximo, con independencia del lugar escogido, y dieron especial relieve a la opción Asturias por el impacto positivo sobre el desempleo y la oportunidad de diversificar una estructura muy escorada a industrias tradicionales[100].

Los vientos parecían hinchar las velas del bajel asturiano. Al estudio *in situ* de los lugares susceptibles de construir la fábrica –Cartagena y Asturias– les suceden una última reunión con el gobierno de la segunda comunidad previa a la decisión final, nueva visita a los terrenos de la futura planta y canto en favor de Asturias. Pero resurgen las vacilaciones a propósito del terreno poblado, la compañía no presenta criterios uniformes y la decisión sufre un retraso leve. Para ella la cultura industrial de la región brinda elementos positivos pero se inclina por las zonas más agrícolas con una cultura industrial en ciernes, en un reto claro a las economías de aglomeración (Krugman 1991, 483-499; Glaeser 2010; Chisholm 1990, 137-164).

En definitiva, las dos regiones en liza satisfacen los requisitos de GE, que fía la decisión a la idoneidad de la ubicación. Finalmente, antes de entrevistarse con las autoridades nacionales competentes para hacer pública su decisión, la multinacional transmite al gobierno del Principado que se han decantado por Murcia como emplazamiento. En la medida habían pesado la superioridad de la región en diversos aspectos: amplia disponibilidad y mayor adecuación de terrenos, inmediatez en el inicio del proyecto y fácil acceso a uno de los materiales necesarios –el fenol de la empresa Repsol. En definitiva, la decisión aparecía determinada por la abundancia de factores físicos, la

---

[100] La prensa aireó un supuesto apoyo de un miembro muy destacado del gobierno –el vicepresidente Alfonso Guerra– a la opción asturiana.

disponibilidad de uno de los componentes, las posibles sinergias e, incluso, el muy apreciable ahorro en inversión[101].

Lecciones no menos sugestivas ofrece el análisis desde la perspectiva de la opción ganadora. Por un lado, el gobierno de Murcia apostó por drenar inversiones que incorporasen las nuevas tecnologías. Por otro lado, el mercado impuso estrategias empresariales que obstaculizaron los planes de General Electric[102].

Empecemos por la implicación institucional. La comunidad autónoma de Murcia donó a la GE para su factoría una finca que había adquirido en 1990 por 1.500 millones de pesetas, un hecho que partió en dos al PSOE, por entonces al frente del gobierno regional. Adicionalmente, la multinacional se benefició de una media de seis millones de euros anuales en ayudas del gobierno regional. A ellas se añadieron las muy cuantiosas subvenciones estatales emanadas de la Ley de Incentivos Regionales, destinadas a favorecer la creación o renovación del tejido industrial en ciudades castigadas por la crisis a inicios del decenio de 1990[103].

Veamos la actuación de la GE. Para empezar, centró sus exigencias en la disponibilidad de terrenos apropiados a las necesidades de la empresa y disponibles en el momento requerido. Las aludidas necesidades de suelo sufrieron variaciones al ampliarse el primer proyecto inversor y cambiar el emplazamiento, con implicaciones sobre los dos núcleos de población de la zona – Los Beatos y Los Camachos – y el riesgo de conflictividad social, también presente en la opción asturiana. La GE fue concretando sus exigencias al paso que se estudiaba el suelo industrial –entonces el de Casa Grande–, el impacto ambiental y las infraestructuras, y se delimitaba el polígono completo. La

---

[101] JGPA, II Legislatura, Comisión de Industria, Energía y Comercio, *DSdPdA*, 48, 25 de octubre de 1988. Diversas ingenierías asesoraron a GE además de la consultora; Carlos Solchaga, ministro de Economía y Hacienda, subrayó la espectacularidad de la inversión de la multinacional en Cartagena junto al papel de palanca de un desarrollo extraordinario de la formación de capital fijo, de la productividad y de la capacidad exportadora (*DSCD,* 142, 25 de octubre de 1988, 8.266).

[102] Comparecencia (1992). Un conjunto de acontecimientos mundiales repercutieron con fuerza sobre el mercado petroquímico y el proyecto se tambaleó. El frenazo de China tras los episodios sangrientos de Tiananmen, la profundización de la crisis del tercer mundo y la incertidumbre respecto al futuro económico en el extinto bloque comunista (*La Opinión*, 20 de octubre de 1990).

[103] En breve, opción de terrenos, subvenciones y ayudas rondaban la quinta parte de la inversión total (*El Confidencial,* 11 de mayo de 2007). La Comisión Europea no desbarató la intención de las autoridades españolas de conceder una subvención de 152 millones de euros a GE Plastics SL para una nueva fábrica de policarbonato en Cartagena (European Commission, IP/01/1286, Bruselas, 19 de septiembre de 2001).

multinacional hubo de dirimir de forma reservada con el grupo Ferrovial las fuertes diferencias respecto a las exigencias planteadas inicialmente[104].

Circunstancias de mercado habían inclinado a General Electric a reformular su proyecto, sin modificar su dimensión, calendario total y perfil de la inversión a lo largo de los años. Las peticiones al gobierno iban en consonancia. En definitiva, el proceso de decisión del emplazamiento por General Electric responde, objetivamente y en última instancia, al modelo de Alfred Weber. Del mismo modo que otras multinacionales buscaban la proximidad a las materias primas, GE primó el seguro acceso a una de ellas –el fenol– ofrecida por Repsol[105].

Lejos de tratarse de un caso aislado, otros proyectos significativos se vieron pospuestos por los inversionistas debido a circunstancias de mercado[106]. Como a tantas otras, el síndrome de la inevitabilidad del declive y la sumisión de regiones y territorios a la lógica implacable de las tendencias productivas a nivel mundial acorralaban a Asturias, receptora de la inversión.

Esta coyuntura podía dar una respuesta de relanzamiento o de liquidación. Parafraseado a Castells, cabía intentar una estrategia de desarrollo basada en la capacidad productiva del trabajo y en una fuerte identidad regional como ventaja comparativa. Tal estrategia debía aprovechar la experiencia industrial acumulada, vertiéndola en una industria bien conectada con los servicios, tecnológicamente avanzada y apoyada en una sólida base de I+D, generadora de

---

[104] Tras sopesar diversas opciones, en octubre de 1988, General Electric eligió los terrenos de Los Camachos en Cartagena, cuyo Ayuntamiento inició gestiones directas para adquirir fincas de los propietarios, que se organizaron en *lobby*; meses después, ya en 1989, el gobierno regional acordó con el Ayuntamiento de Cartagena asumir la gestión de la compra; a inicios de julio General Electric notificó al gobierno autonómico su elección de Las Victorias (Casa Grande) como emplazamiento. Durante su visita a Murcia, el presidente de la multinacional, Jack Welch –el empresario que reinventó la empresa– comunicó su propósito de ampliar la inversión en 100.000 millones de pesetas y, en consecuencia, la necesidad de más terreno – 50 hectáreas. Cumplir el compromiso con General Electric implicaba habilitar otro polígono industrial en Los Camachos, suficiente para albergar nuevas inversiones, y reservar allí suelo urbanizado; suponía, además, ceder terrenos en el polígono de El Palmar destinados al Centro de Nuevas Tecnologías (Intervención del presidente del Consejo de Gobierno (Collado Mena), *Diario Sesiones Asamblea Regional de Murcia,* 3 de febrero de 1992, 1.153).

[105] Un modelo tosco y no exento de «mecanicismo» (Cuervo, 1978, 132) pero apto para describir las decisiones de ubicación de las plantas en ciertas ramas concretas; potenciales sobrecostes permanentes en la cuenta de resultados a lo largo del ciclo de vida de la planta convierten estas decisiones claves en el largo plazo; véase Anderson (2012) y Alonso (1964).

[106] Intervención del secretario de estado de Economía (Pérez Fernández), Comisión de Economía, comercio y hacienda, *DSCD*, 186, 11 de diciembre de 1990, 5.682.

trabajo altamente cualificado y de productos de alto valor añadido. Dos piezas institucionales debían culminar este entramado: redes de empresas regionales y organismos descentralizados de los que extraer asesoramiento comercial y tecnológico e información[107]. Evidentemente, en un proceso de integración y de globalización rampante cabía también la intervención exterior. Junto a Corning Glass, habían escogido Asturias otras empresas de la Tercera Revolución Industrial, si bien se observaba un nivel de ocupación bajo para el espacio industrial ofertado. De hecho, Asturias recibió una proporción del total de inversiones extranjeras inferior a su dimensión territorial y demográfica (Castells et al. 1994, 31; *El País*, 26 de agosto de 1986)[108].

En diversos planes inversores, el gobierno del Principado entabló sucesivamente contactos y negociaciones sin resultado alguno. Los proyectos de Suzuki entre 1987 y 1990 reflejan una cierta actitud de las multinacionales, sellada en no pocas ocasiones por las exigencias sin contrapartida. La secuencia comprende unos primeros escarceos de Suzuki en torno a la posibilidad de ampliar la fábrica de motocicletas de Gijón pero sin compromisos[109], la posibilidad de un estudio, la consideración de un traslado, la inversión, la petición de un informe con la oferta del gobierno y gestiones de Suzuki con el ayuntamiento de Gijón. El gobierno del Principado no ocultaba la gran incertidumbre que entrañaban las conversaciones, por otra parte muy fluidas: indecisión de la japonesa, falta de información precisa sobre los posibles avances en la inversión, sensación de impotencia a la espera de un planteamiento de posibilidades y de la decisión final y hermetismo ante la opinión pública impuesto por la propia multinacional para evitar costes de imagen en forma de

---

[107] Síntesis del brillante y precioso artículo de Castells (1994), antiguo director del programa de investigación Estrategias de Reindustrialización de Asturias (ERA). El síndrome parece pesar sobre Asturias. La industria de Asturias compartía con la española cinco debilidades principales, que identificaba un diagnóstico reciente: pronunciada atomización empresarial, baja intensidad tecnológica junto a reducido peso del sector industrial, escasa orientación al mercado exterior y pérdida gradual de competitividad (Gobierno del Principado de Asturias 2019, 10).

[108] Estas empresas de la Tercera Revolución Industrial, entre ellas Vesubius y Datotec, presentaban una alternativa para una región de industria pesada, anticuada, sobrecargada de personal y de pobre rendimiento (*El País*, 30 de agosto de 1986).

[109] La entrada de Suzuki Motor España se llevó a cabo de forma gradual: primero controló la fábrica de motocicletas en 1987 y al año siguiente la totalidad del capital. Una síntesis de los orígenes y evolución de la fábrica desde la construcción de maquinaria y herramientas como Avello y Cía SL hasta la producción de motos bajo la denominación de Avello y Agusta (Calvo 2020, 26-27); véase también para algunos aspectos García y Flores (2000). La que en día fue principal planta europea en la gama de dos ruedas amagó sucesivas veces con dejar el Principado y cerró en 2013 por deslocalización a Asia.

falsas expectativas. En el fondo, el gobierno regional reconocía su impotencia por considerar que en la decisión empresarial intervenía una serie de elementos –mercado, situación de la economía en general– que escapaban a los que la comunidad podía ofrecer, limitados primordialmente a suelo industrial en Gijón y subvenciones[110]. El control de los tiempos también se le escapaba. En definitiva, Suzuki aparecía como «el exponente y el reflejo de la imposibilidad de cuadrar las cosas» y de avanzar en la decisión empresarial[111]. Las nuevas instalaciones fabriles del polígono gijonés de Porceyo no se abrieron hasta 1993 en sustitución de la planta histórica (*El País*, 7 de agosto de 2005).

En otros casos, los movimientos de empresas de gran talla (Du Pont, Euro Metals y Thyssen-Krupp) indujeron al gobierno autonómico a pensar en un cambio de tendencia por aumento de la inversión y el inicio de la apuesta por Asturias. Un grupo de representantes del gobierno autónomo y empresarios de la región se trasladó a EE. EU. para captar inversiones, cerrar acuerdos empresariales de colaboración y abrir mercados a las fábricas asturianas.

Una de las empresas contactadas fue la tejana Euro Metals Processing, que proyectaba abrir una fábrica de piezas para el sector aeronáutico con destino al mercado europeo y norteamericano. Un encuentro de las dos partes en Asturias permitió precisar los medios materiales –emplazamiento de la fábrica en el valle minero de Langreo y naves industriales adecuadas– y financieros –mecanismos de captación de subvenciones, cifradas en el 45% de la inversión total, por tratarse de una ZID–. El acicate de un 30% de subvención en una inversión de 12.539 millones ponía a Euro Metals en la senda del gigante de la industria química Du Pont de Nemours en su entrada en Asturias. El gobierno de esta región se comprometió a ofrecer hasta tres emplazamientos alternativos y a fomentar la participación de socios locales en el proyecto (*El País*, 14 de mayo de 1990 y 22 de noviembre de 1989; *La Nueva España*, 30 de diciembre de 1989, 59). Todo quedó en humo, hasta el punto que ni

---

[110] Intervención de la consejera de Industria, comercio y turismo (Fernández Felgueroso), Junta General del Principado de Asturias (JGPA), Pleno, *DSdPdA*, 119, 25 de julio de 1990. Algunas voces anteponían la redefinición del papel del sector público estatal, en busca de mayor dinamismo, empuje y compromiso con el futuro de la región, a abocar recursos del estado en forma de cuantiosas inversiones, especialmente en la siderurgia, y en ayudas financieras. En el caso de la fibra óptica, reclamaban medidas de atracción y una necesaria continuidad en la confluencia de esfuerzos en favor de la implantación de industrias de alta tecnología en Asturias, capaces de modificar el perfil industrial de la región (De Silva Cienfuegos-Jovellanos (Izquierda Unida), Pleno, JGPA, *DSdPdA*, 2, 20 de julio de 1987).

[111] JGPA, II Legislatura, 183, 14 de noviembre de 1990.

siquiera la decena de empresas participadas por la SRP llegaron a crear un solo empleo[112].

Una aleccionadora discusión en la Junta General del Principado de Asturias reconocía la existencia de factores que echaban por tierra los planes aparentes de las multinacionales por invertir en Asturias. Además de razones particulares, como había ocurrido en el caso de General Electric con los terrenos y la proximidad de industria petroquímica, el debate hacía aflorar una lista miscelánea que incluía la cortedad de incentivos regionales (CDS), las deficientes infraestructuras de comunicaciones, negada por el gobierno regional para GE, y la inestabilidad sociolaboral de la región (Alianza Popular). La consejera competente rechazaba que el conjunto de proyectos se hubiera visto frustrado y limitaba el fracaso al de GE ya que Siemens iba a dar continuidad al primitivo proyecto de Corning Glass[113]. En contradicción con el parecer mayoritario de los analistas, antes mencionado, atribuía la espantada de esta a un litigio internacional sobre la tecnología en que se vio envuelta, pleito que dio lugar a una sentencia del tribunal europeo[114].

No existe unanimidad en la valoración de los resultados finales en el conjunto de la economía asturiana. Los optimistas señalan que la renovación de la estructura industrial en la década de 1990 fue fruto de una nueva oleada de inversiones de multinacionales europeas, japonesas y estadounidenses,

[112] Junta General del Principado de Asturias, II Legislatura, Pleno, *DSdPdA*, 119, 25 de julio de 1990. Presente en España desde dos decenios antes, en 1981 Du Pont convirtió la oficina en filial –Du Pont Ibérica–. Du Pont proyectaba una inversión mínima de 108.000 millones de pesetas, con una subvención de 32.000 millones y con una capacidad de generación de un millar de empleos directos (Vázquez y Hernández 1991, 34). La planta asturiana de 1990 en el valle de Tamón llegó a ser la instalación productiva y de servicios más moderna de la matriz en Europa. A partir de 1990, invirtió 580 millones de euros en inmovilizado material de un complejo con cuatro centros de producción, además de un centro de servicios, que controlaba la contabilidad del grupo en Europa (Du Pont de Nemours & CO, *Informe*, s. a., 209).

[113] JGPA, Comisión de Industria, Energía y Comercio, *DSCD*, 048, 25 de octubre de 1988. Cartagena también adolecía de infraestructuras deficientes, según reconocía el CDS (Comisiones, *DSCD*, 354, 25 de octubre de 1988, 12.156). Los entendidos sitúan en la accesibilidad geográfica y el desarrollo de las conexiones externas un eterno estrangulamiento y un problema para las empresas asturianas unido a un freno a la localización industrial (Vázquez y Lomba (2000), 6).

[114] JGPA, Comisión de Industria, Energía y Comercio, *DSCD*, 048, 25 de octubre de 1988. A juicio de la Comisión Europea, si Corning participaba en tres empresas conjuntas de idéntica actividad empresarial y situadas en tres Estados miembros, podría ocasionar un reparto de mercado entre las tres mediante una coordinación de las decisiones –producción, ventas y fijación de precios– y por intercambio de información competitiva sensible. La Comisión objetó determinadas disposiciones específicas insertas en los acuerdos e inició un procedimiento con el fin de establecer la posible existencia de una infracción de acuerdos relativa a licencias de patente para la fabricación y venta de fibras ópticas y cables ópticos: 6/405/EEC (Commission Decision of 14 July 1986, *Official Journal L 236*, 22/08/1986).

atraídas por el ingreso de España en la CEE y por los apoyos públicos. A ellas se sumaron las inversiones de capital asturiano en la modernización del aparato productivo de un conjunto de empresas industriales (Idepa 2014, 20). La pervivencia de las deficiencias en el largo plazo arroja dudas sobre los resultados. Cabe preguntarse una vez más si había alternativas. El lejano ejemplo de Corea en el sector que analizamos aquí apunta a una respuesta afirmativa. Ajenas al entreguismo ibérico, en el país asiático instituciones públicas de investigación contribuyeron a fortalecer la capacidad de negociación de empresas locales en la adquisición de tecnología extranjera crecientemente sofisticada en condiciones favorables. Cuando en 1977 Corning Glass rechazó transferir tecnología a Corea, la alianza de dos grandes productores locales de cable de cobre con una institución pública dio lugar a un proyecto conjunto de I+D. Transcurridos siete años, cable óptico desarrollado en Corea fue probado con éxito en una ruta de corta distancia (Kim 2003, 14 y 24).

La observación microeconómica arroja algunos matices. Siemens decidió paralizar –«congelar» en la terminología del gobierno regional– el proyecto de Tefosa, sin abandonarlo, ante la incertidumbre del mercado. El consejo de administración decidió reducir el capital y el socio tecnológico, el más escéptico pese a su mayor implicación inicial, sufragó los crecidos gastos que se habían ocasionado, en especial por el sofisticado diseño de la fábrica. Tefosa sobrevivió a la reducción de capital y los otros dos socios recibieron autorización para buscar un socio tecnológico diferente, tarea que se hacía complicada debido al control de las patentes por Corning. Los socios españoles acordaron mantenerse en la expectativa y demorar la puesta en marcha durante un bienio como máximo, a la espera de reemprender el negocio en ese intervalo con un nuevo socio tecnológico. Por su parte, el gobierno regional dio amparo a empresas autóctonas de tecnología punta[115].

En realidad, el gobierno autonómico siguió un planteamiento múltiple con las empresas. Las creadas para evaluar un proyecto que finalmente se había revelado inviable fueron liquidadas. Por su parte, empresas que, por razones varias, no lograron los resultados apetecidos se liquidaban o se vendían al promotor principal siempre que resultaba posible. En determinadas circunstancias, las inversiones continuaron y no faltaron empresas que consiguieran empezar a funcionar[116].

---

[115] Junta General del Principado de Asturias, II Legislatura, pleno, *DSdPdA*, 119, 25 de julio de 1990.

[116] Intervención del director del IFR, JGPA, pleno, *DSdPdA*, 119, 25 de julio de 1990. El deterioro económico de la región y una crisis industrial que había cercenado 30.000 puestos de

Pese al golpe de Siemens, los socios nacionales de Tefosa, lejos de abandonar el proyecto, se empeñaron en buscar un nuevo socio tecnológico. Por cierto, si la fortísima concentración del mercado ya determinaba la elección, las dos recientes tentativas frustradas reducían drásticamente el margen de maniobra. La sola opción viable era la japonesa Sumitomo Electric Industries Ltd., con una fuerte tradición de alianzas internacionales, mercado estadounidense incluido[117]. En consecuencia, las gestiones del grupo español General Cable y de la Sociedad Regional de Promoción se orientaron hacia aquella empresa, contrincante formidable de Corning Glass y atenta al mercado español, como sabemos[118]. Pero sobre la industria de fibra óptica en España se cernía una especie de maldición.

6. Conclusiones

Este capítulo indaga en la interrelación entre la pauta de expansión de las empresas multinacionales y la política industrial aplicada en España por distintas entidades públicas contra la crisis en las dos últimas décadas del siglo XX. Se inscribe en un contexto de profundo y acelerado cambio tecnológico, acompañado de un intenso proceso de globalización. La investigación pone de relieve que la estrategia de entrada de las multinacionales obedece a un conjunto de parámetros y, en ocasiones, advierte de la utilidad de no olvidar viejos y sencillos modelos de equilibrio parcial, de raíces a lo Marshall. Un ejemplo de ello lo ofrece la decisión de GE de emplazar la fábrica fuera de las zonas tradicionales de concentración manufacturera. En el diseño de las políticas industriales de los países receptores un elemento fundamental fue el recurso a las multinacionales. La primacía tecnológica y el dominio de los resortes financieros convirtieron a estas empresas en factores fundamentales para afrontar los retos que planteaba la sociedad de esos años. Esa primacía y ese poderío pusieron en manos de las multinacionales la llave de lo que podían haber sido soluciones a la profunda crisis que se cebaba sobre las economías industriales. Contra ese fortín se estrellaron las políticas pú-

---

trabajo empujaron a UGT y CCOO a convocar una huelga general en Asturias (*ABC*, 23 de octubre de 1991).

[117] A partir de los años 80, Sumitomo Electric Industries creó *joint ventures* en EE.UU. con varias empresas (National Research Council 1990); en 1988 creó la filial europea Sumitomo Electric Europe SA.

[118] *La Vanguardia*, 8 de junio de 1990.

blicas. En esta ocasión ni siquiera se consiguieron logros tangibles a corto y medio plazo, salvo si se da la razón a algunos revisionistas que reivindican la aparición de un entorno clusterizado, pertrechado para poner freno al declive de los grandes sectores hegemónicos y desbordar sus mercados tradicionales (Antuña 2022, 124-135). En general, los resultados finales dejaron sin resolver problemas estructurales que, todavía hoy, atenazan la economía y la sociedad españolas. Sin embargo, la experiencia internacional (Corea) pone en evidencia que existían caminos para superar esos inconvenientes y conseguir algunos éxitos.

Anexo 1. Comparación de la fibra óptica y diversos *media*

Media	Alcance	Ancho de banda	Pérdidas	Inmunidad EMI/RFI*	Seguridad	Coste	Comentarios
Fibra óptica	2-10km	>100Mhz-km	Alta	Excelente	Muy buena	Alto	Costes decrecientes rápidamente
Línea telefónica	-	50kHz	Alta	Pobre	Pobre	Bajo	Base instalada de bajo coste
Cable plano multi-conductor	<100m	<10Mhz	Alta	Pobre	Correcto	Alto	Blindaje disponible
Cable de par trenzado	<1200m	<100Mhz	Alta	Muy buena	Correcto	Bajo	Barato, alcance limitado
Twinaxial cable	<1km	<200Mhz	50-100 dB/km	Correcto	Correcto	Alto	Impedancia controlada; compatible con 802
Cable coaxial	<2km		6,5-60 dB/km	Correcto	Correcto	de bajo a muy alto	compatible con 802
Infrarrojo	300m	<20Mhz	Alta	Bueno	Correcto	Alto; potencialmente bajo	
Microondas	<50km	>100Mhz	1r	Pobre	Correcto	Bajo	(Espacio libre) línea de visión; sujeto a dispersión; pérdida de enlace dependiente del tamaño de la antena

* EMI (ElectroMagnetic Interference) o RFI (Radio Frequency Interference)

Fuente: Elaboración a partir de *International Fiber Optics & Communications*, febrero de 1986, 27.

Referencias

Aditi, P. S. 2012. «Submarine Optical Cables as a Key Component in Undersea Tele-communications: A Review», *International Journal of Application or Innovation in Engineering & Management* 1, n.º 4, diciembre: 79-83.

Albella, José M. 1988. *Optoelectrónica y comunicación óptica*. Madrid: CSIC.

Alonso, William. 1964. «Teoría de la localización». En *Análisis regional. Textos escogidos*, editado por Needleman, L. Madrid: Tecnos, 303-329.

Alonso, William. 1989. «Cuestiones regionales e integración europea». En *Política Regional en la Europa de los años 90*. Madrid: Ministerio de Economía y Hacienda, 246-247.

Álvaro, Adoración y Puig, Nuria. 2015. «La huella del capital extranjero en España: un análisis comparado». *Revista de Historia Industrial* 58: 249-285.

Álvaro, Adoración y Puig, Nuria. 2016. «The Long-term Impact of Foreign MNEs in Spain: New Insights into an Old Topic», *Journal of Evolutionary Studies in Business* 2: 14-39.

Ambos, Tina C. 2018. «Reverse knowledge transfer». En *The Palgrave Encyclopedia of Strategic Management*, editado por Augier, Mie y Teece, David, 1.475-1476. Londres: Palgrave Macmillan.

Anderson, William P. 2012. *Economic Geography*. Londres: Routledge.

Antuña, Guillermo. (2022). «Un paso al frente: el sector metalmecánico asturiano ante la reconversión industrial, 1978-2000». *Investigaciones de Historia Económica – Economic History Research* n.º 18: 124-135.

Argüelles, Margarita. 1997. *Los incentivos como instrumento de política regional en las comunidades de Asturias, Cantabria y Galicia*. Oviedo: Universidad de Oviedo.

Barry, Frank. 2004. «Export platform FDI: the Irish experience». *European Investment Bank Papers*, 9 (2): 8-37.

Berta, Giuseppe y Onida, Fabrizio. 2011. «Old and New Italian Multinational Firms». *Bank of Italy Economic History Working Paper* n.º 15, October: 1-59.

Bidault, Francis. 2012. *Managing Joint Innovation: How to balance trust and control in strategic alliances*. Nueva York: Macmillan.

Blanco-Vázquez, Carlos. 1990. «Desarrollo de cables de fibra óptica en Alcatel-Standard Electrica». *Dyna*, mayo, vol. 65, n.º 4: 25-27.

Boucher, Didier. 1986. *Fiber Optics Industry in Europe*. Boston MA: Information Gatekeepers Inc.

Bucher, Eliane. 2010. *Next Generation Connectivity: A review of broadband Internet transitions and policy from around the world.* Cambridge MA: Berkman Center.

Buckley, Peter J. y Casson, Mark C. 1976. *The Future of the Multinational Enterprise.* Londres: Macmillan.

Buesa, Mikel y Molero, José. 1986. *La intervención estatal en la remodelación del sistema productivo español.* Madrid: Facultad de CCEE y Empresariales.

Cabana, Francesc. 1987. *Nixdorf Computer: los primeros veinte años en España (1967-1987).* Barcelona: Nixdorf Computer.

Calvo, Ángel. 2020. «Política industrial, multinacionales y desarrollo regional en España. La IED en la industria de la fibra óptica a finales del siglo xx». *Biblio3W Revista Bibliográfica de Geografía y Ciencias Sociales.* Vol. XXV, 1-36.

Calvo, Ángel. 2016a. *Historia de Telefónica: 1976-2000. Las telecomunicaciones en la España democrática.* Barcelona: Ariel/Fundación Telefónica,

Calvo, Ángel. 2016b. «Innovating in Hard Time. Spanish Firms under Pressure in the Cold War». *Harvard Deusto Business Research*, V, n.º 1: 60-85.

Calvo, Ángel. 2017. «Multinacionales, Estado y empresa semipública en la industria de tecnología avanzada durante la década de 1980». *Investigaciones de Historia Económica, Journal of the Spanish Economic History Association*, 13, n.º 1: 51-62.

Calvo, Ángel. 2018. «Economy and politics in the embargo of high technology during the Cold War. The case of a semiperipheral country (Spain)». *International Journal of Humanities and Social Science,* 8, n.º 5: 25-44.

Cantoni, Virginio et al. 2011. *Storia delle telecomunicazioni*, Vol. 1, Florencia: Firenze University Press.

Castells, Manuel. 1986. *Nuevas tecnologías, economía y sociedad en España*, 1, Madrid: Alianza.

Castells, Manuel. 1994. «El síndrome de Asturias», *El País*, 16 de agosto.

Castells, Manuel et al. 1994. *Estrategias para la reindustrialización de Asturias.* Oviedo: Principado de Asturias.

Catalan, Jordi. 2019. «La industrialización de Cataluña, 1685-2018». En *Políticas industriales en España*, editado por García Ruiz, J. L. et al., 157-198. Madrid: Ediciones Paraninfo.

Chisholm, Michael. 1990. «The locations needs of modern firms». En *Regions in Recession and Resurgence.* Londres. Unwin Hyman, 137-164.

CICYT, 1990. *Centros de investigación en España. Plan nacional de I+D.* Madrid: Ministerio de Educación, 330.

Commission of the European Communities. 1991. *Employment and social aspects of electronic media and advanced telecommunications services*. Luxemburgo: Office for Official Publications of the European Communities.

Comparecencia (1992) del Consejo de Gobierno para informar sobre lo relacionado con la adquisición de terrenos, en el municipio de Cartagena, para la instalación de General Electric, III Legislatura, 30, Diario de Sesiones de la Asamblea Regional de Murcia, 3 de febrero.

Corning Inc. 2006. *International Directory of Company Histories*. Farmington Hills Michigan: Thomson Gale.

Corning Incorporated. 2000. *Annual Report 2000*, Corning.

Corning Incorporated. 2000. *Annual report 1994*, Securities and Exchange Commission, Form 10-K, Commission file number 1-3247.

Crandall, Robert W. y Flamm, Kenneth. 1989. *Changing the Rules: Technological Change, International Competition, and Regulation in Communications*. Washington: Brookings Institution Press.

Cuervo, Álvaro. 1978. «Entrevista». En *Asturias: una crisis permanente*, Juan de Lillo. Salinas: Ayalga Ediciones, 127-153.

Chaffee, C. David. 2012. *The Rewiring of America The Fiber Optics Revolution*. Orlando Fl: Academic Press.

De la Dehesa, Guillermo. 2004. «Deslocalización y externalización». *El País*, 19 de junio, 72.

De Witt, Giovanni. 2005. *Le fabbriche ed il mondo: l'Olivetti industriale nella competizione globale, 1950-90*. Milán: Franco Angeli.

Doz, Yves L. y Hamel, Gary. 1995. «The use of alliances in implementing technology strategies». En *Managing strategic innovation and change*, editado por Tushman, M. L. y Anderson, P., 556-580. Nueva York: Oxford University Press.

Dunning, John H. y Lundan, Sarianna M. 2008. *Multinational Enterprises and the Global Economy*. Cheltenham: Edward Elgar.

Dyer, Davis y Gross, Daniel. 2001. *The Generations of Corning: The Life and Times of a Global Corporation*. Nueva York: Oxford University Press.

Ericsson. 1995. *Annual report*. Estocolmo: Ericsson.

Elion, Glenn R. y Elion, Herbert A. 1978. *Fiber Optics in Communications Systems*. Nueva York: Marcel Dekker, 213.

Franchetto, Ermanno. 1965. «La macchina da calcolo dal progetto all'attrezzaggio». *Notizie Olivetti*, 62, n.º 69: 20-27.

Fundació Jaume Bofill. 1989. *Catalunya 77-78. Societat, Economia, Política, Cultura*. Barcelona: Publicacions de la Fundació Jaume Bofill-Edicions de la Magrana.

Gambhir, Ankit. 2013. «Merits and demerits of optical fiber communication». *International Journal of Research in Engineering & Applied Sciences* 3, n.º 3: 99-104.

García, Paz y Flores, José M. 2000. *Gijón, la ciudad de vapor. Historia de la industria y el comercio*. Gijón: Biblioteca Gijonesa del Siglo XX.

García Delgado, José L. 1978. *La economía asturiana ante la Autonomía Regional, Historia General de Asturias*, tomo 12, Gijón: Silverio Cañada.

Generalitat de Catalunya, Departament de la Presidència. 2002. *Actuacions més destacades del Govern de la Generalitat de Catalunya*, Número 1, Barcelona: Oficina de Comunicació del Govern.

Glaeser, Edward L. 2010. *Agglomeration Economics*. Chicago: The University of Chicago Press.

Gobierno del Principado de Asturias. 2019. *Estrategia Industrial para Asturias*. IDEPA: Llanera, 10.

Gomà, Ricard y Subirats, Joan. 2001. *Govern i polítiques públiques a Catalunya (1980-2000): Autonomia i benestar*. Barcelona: Universitat Autònoma de Barcelona.

González, Arnau. 2011. *Cataluña bajo vigilancia: El consulado italiano y el fascio de Barcelona (1930-1943)*. Valencia: Universitat de València.

Graham, Edward M. y Krugman, Paul R. 1993. «The Surge in Foreign Direct Investment in the 1980s». En *Foreign Direct Investment*, editado por Froot K. A., 13-36. Chicago: University of Chicago Press.

Grimes, Seamus y Collins, Patrick. 2009. «The contribution of the overseas ICT sector to expanding R&D investment in Ireland». *Irish Geography* 42, n.º 1: 45-67.

Hakanson, Lars y Nobel, Robert. 2001. Organizational characteristics and reverse knowledge transfer. *Management International Review*, 41: 395-420. https://www.scielo.br/scielo.php?script=sci_arttext&pid=S180 7-76922017000100305

Hérisson, Pierre. 2001. *Rapport d'information No 273 fait au nom de la commission des Affaires économiques*. Sénat de la France, 26 de marzo.

Hernández, Exequiel y Guillén, Mauro F. 2018. «What's theoretically novel about emerging market multinationals». *Journal of International Business Studies*, 49, n.º 1. 24–33.

Hewlett Packard. 2000. *Annual report,* 15. Hill, Roy. 1974. «Corning Glass reshapes its international operations», *International management*, 10-01, n.º 29 (10): 32.

Hispano Olivetti (1954): *25 años: 1929-1954.* Barcelona: Seix y Barral Hnos.

Holl, Adelheid; Pardo, Rafael y Rama, Ruth. 2012. «Comparing Outsourcing Patterns in Domestic and FDI Manufacturing Plants. Empirical Evidence from Spain». *European Planning Studies* vol. 20, n.º 8: agosto: 1.335-1.355.

Huber, George P. y Glick, William H. *Organizational Change and Redesign: Ideas and Insights for Improving Performance.* Nueva York: Oxford University Press.

Hufbauer, Gary C. (ed.). 1990. *Europe 1992: An American Perspective.* Washington: Brookings Institution.

IGI Consulting. 1998. *Repeatered Submarine Fiber Optics Systems.*, Boston MA: IGI, 35-37.

Information Gatekeepers Inc. 1994. *Fiber Optics Broadband ISDN.* Boston MA: IGI.

Information Gatekeepers. 1991. *Papers Presented at the Ninth Annual European Fibre Optic Communications and Local Area Network Conference/Efoc/Lan 91/Eln-91/E9912Pr*, Vol. 2, Boston MA: IGI.

Information Gatekeepers. 1987. *Fiber Optic ISDN/Broadband Field Trials.* Boston MA: IGI.

Jensen, Nathan M. 2006. *States and the Multinational Corporation: A Political Economy of Direct Foreign Investment.* Princeton N.J.: Princeton University Press.

Johansson, Ulf y Lundstrom, Gunnar. 1980. «Developments in Fibre Optics within the Ericsson Group». *Ericsson Review*, 3, n.º 7: 74-79.

Kim, Linsu. 2003. *Technology Transfer & Intellectual Property Rights. The Korean Experience.* Ginebra: International Centre for Trade and Sustainable Development.

Klein, Naomi. 2000. *No Logo: Taking Aim at the Brand Bullies.* Nueva York: Picador.

Kline, Pat y Moretti, Enrico. 2014. «People, Places and Public Policy: Some Simple Welfare Economics of Local Economic Development Programs». *Annual Review of Economics* vol. 6: 629-662.

Krugman, Paul. 1992. «Motivos y dificultades en la política industrial». En *Política industrial, teoría y práctica*, coordinado por Martín, C., 21-46. Madrid: Economistas Libros.

Krugman, Paul. 1991. «Increasing Returns and Economic Geography». *The Journal of Political Economy*, 99, n.º 3: 483-499.

Lipsey, Robert E. 2002. «Home and Host Country Effects of FDI». *NBER Working Paper,* 9, n.º 293, National Bureau of Economic Research.

Mccarthy, James M. [sa]. *Interior Competitiveness of the Fiber Optics Industry.* Boston MA: Information Gatekeepers Inc.

Mansfield, Edwin. 1984. «R&D and innovation: some empirical findings». En *R&D, Patents, and Productivity*, editado por Griliches, Zvi., 127-154. Chicago y Londres: The University Chicago Press y NBER.

Mella, José M. 2000. «Parques tecnológicos y entorno territorial: la experiencia española». *Comercio Exterior*, septiembre: 630-638.

Mishra, Arvind K. 2013. «Evolution of Optical Fiber Technologies Application Notes». *Sterlite Tech,* mayo: 1-7.

Moncalvo, Agostino y Tosco, Federico. 1983. «European field trials and early applications in telephony». IEEE, 1 (3): 398–403.

Munier, John H. 1976. *A Perspective of the Role of Research, Development, and Engineering in the Corning Glass Works: The First Hundred Years.* Nueva York: Corning Glass Works.

National Research Council. 1990. *Learning the R&D System: Industrial R&D in Japan and the United States.* Washington: National Academy.

Noam, Eli M. 1992. *Telecommunications in Europe.* Nueva York-Oxford: Oxford University Press.

Ondategui, Julio C. 2001. *Los parques científicos y tecnológicos en España: retos y oportunidades.* Madrid: Comunidad de Madrid.

Onida, Fabrizio (a cuidado de). 1987. *Strategie multinazionali: imprese, ambiente, opportunità.* Vol. 1, Milán: Edizioni del Sole 24 Ore.

Packard, David. 2008. *El estilo HP: cómo Bill Hewlett y yo creamos nuestra empresa.* Bilbao: Deusto.

Porter, Michael E. 1983 *Cases in Competitive Strategy.* Nueva York: The Free Press.

Prat, Marc y Sánchez, Esther M. 2017. «Crisis industrial, inversión exterior y terciarización. La influencia del capital extranjero en la transformación de la economía catalana, 1973-1986», *XII Congreso Internacional de la Asociación Española de Historia Económica*, Salamanca.

Pujol, Jordi. 1976. *Una Política industrial per a Catalunya.* Barcelona: Cambra Oficial de Comerç, Indústria i Navegació de Barcelona.

RACE common functional specifications issue. 1991. Luxemburgo: Office for Official Publications of the European Communities.

Renzi, Emilio. 2008. *Comunità concreta. Le opere e il pensiero di Adriano Olivetti.* Turín: Guida Editori.

Roche, Edward M. 1992. *Managing Information Technology in Multinational Corporations.* Nueva York: Macmillan.

Rodrik, Dani. 2006 «Goodbye Washington consensus, hello Washington confusion? A review of the World Bank's economic growth in the 1990s: Learning from a decade of reform». *Journal of Economic Literature* 44, n.° 4: 973–987.

Sánchez, Esther. 2011 «Un siglo de vidrio francés: Saint Gobain en España, de 1905 a la actualidad». *Investigaciones de Historia Económica* 7: 395–407.

Servicio de defensa de la competencia. 2004. *Informe Draka/Alcatel*, n.° 04039.

Sgro, Valentina. 2020. *A Century of Italian American Economics: The American Chamber of Commerce in Italy (1915-2015).* Cambridge: Cambridge Scholars Publishing.

Silva, Pedro de. 1982. *Asturias, realidad y proyecto.* Gijón: Noega.

Solana Madariaga, Luis. 1985. «La Cia. Telefónica Nacional de España impulsora de la industria colateral», *Jornadas internacionales sobre nuevas tecnologías en la empresa*, Madrid: 5-8 de marzo: *La Vanguardia*, 24 de febrero de 1985.

Solana Madariaga, Luis. 1986. «Comparecencia del señor Presidente de la Compañía Telefónica Nacional de España». *Diario de sesiones del senado*, 14 de febrero, 1-7.

Standard Eléctrica. 1983. *Memoria 1983.* Madrid: Standard Eléctrica.

Stiglitz, Joseph. 2002. *Globalization and Its Discontents.* Nueva York: Norton and Company.

Strange, Roger. 2003. *Japanese Manufacturing Investment in Europe: Its Impact on the UK economy.* Londres: Routledge.

Strange, Susan. 1996. *The Retreat of the State: The Diffusion of Power in the World Economy.* Cambridge: Cambridge University Press.

UNCTAD. 2006. *World Investment Report 2006. FDI from Developing and Transition Economies: Implications for Development.* Nueva York-Ginebra: United Nations.

United States. Office of International Marketing. 1976. *Business Equipment and Systems.* Vol. 57, Washington: Office of International Marketing.

Uriz, Javier. 2005. *Homo valens: naturaleza, origen y gestión del valor en la empresa.* Madrid-Buenos Aires: Ediciones Díaz de Santos.

U. S. Congress. Senate. Committee on Finance. 1986. *Intellectual Property Rights: Hearing Before the Subcommittee on International Trade of the Committee on Finance, United States Senate,* May 14, Washington: U.S. Government Printing Office.

U. S. Department of Commerce. 1994. *U. S. Industrial Outlook, 1994*, St. Paul, MN: JIST Works.

U.S. Industrial Outlook. 1985. Washington: U.S. Department of Commerce, Industry and Trade Administration, 29-4.

U.S. International Trade Commission. 1988. *U.S. global competitiveness: optical fibers, technology and equipment.* Washington: U.S. International Trade Commission.

Vázquez, Juan A. y Hernández, Manuel. 1991. *La industria asturiana: ¿podemos pasar la página del declive?* Doumentos de trabajo, Universidad de Oviedo, Doc. 038: 1-46.

Vázquez, Juan A. y Lomba, Ramiro. 2000. «La industria asturiana, un sector en transformación», *Economía Industrial*, V-VI: 335/336, 1-12.

VV. AA. 1990. *La políica regional en 198. Informe anual 1989.* Madrid: Impresores.

Wilkins, Mira. 1970. *The Maturing of Multinational Enterprise: American Business Abroad from 1914 to 1970.* Harvard: Harvard University Press.

Winzer, Peter J.; Neilson, David T. y Chraplyvy, Andrew R. 2018. «Fiber-optic transmission and networking: the previous 20 and the next 20 years». *Optics Express* 26, n.º 18: 24.190-24.239.

Woodward, Douglas P. y Nigh, Douglas W. 1998. *Foreign Ownership and the Consequences of Direct Investment in the United States: Beyond Us and Them.* Westport-Londres: Quorum Books.

Yamin, Mo. 1995. «Determinants of reverse transfer: The experience of UK multinationals». En *New challenges for European and International Business*, proceedings of the 21st annual EIBA conference, Urbino: Schiattarella.

II. La industria de las telecomunicaciones en ebullición: de la conmutación electromecánica a la electrónica

1. Tecnología de las multinacionales: la reconversión de la industria de equipo de telecomunicaciones en España a partir de la década de 1980

1. Introducción

En la última década del siglo xx se desencadenó una megatendencia sobre el medio ambiente, la economía, la sociedad y la vida de los ciudadanos a escala local y global (Nasbitt 1982). Un rápido y notable cambio tecnológico hizo que las telecomunicaciones pasaran de ser una industria monolítica basada en líneas de cobre a una industria de servicios polifacética, como señalaba el European Monitoring Center of Change. Junto con la convergencia de las telecomunicaciones y los ordenadores, el colosal y rápido cambio tecnológico impulsó la desregulación y liberalización del sector, como un amplio proceso (Mayer-Schönberger y Strasser 1999, 561-588) con concreciones particulares por grandes áreas en la fabricación y el servicio. Al mismo tiempo, este cambio actuó como catalizador de profundas transformaciones en la industria de equipos de telecomunicaciones.

Las alteraciones desafiaron a los monopolios estatales, fuertemente arraigados durante décadas en muchos países y, a veces, como en Francia, incrustados en departamentos ministeriales. Uno tras otro fueron liberalizados y se convirtieron en empresas telefónicas privadas. Esto ocurrió, en los casos más significativos, con el pionero Post Office, el Bundespost alemán y el PTT francés, para formar British Telecom, Deutsche Telekom y France Telecom, respectivamente (Sapir 1988, 232-233; Eliassen y Sjovaag (ed.) 1999). Junto con esto, la ruptura de la industria de equipos de telecomunicaciones (IEquiptel) integrada verticalmente *de facto* destruyó el equilibrio existente en ese sector. Más cerca del núcleo de la problemática, el cambio tecnológico provocado por la microelectrónica, los equipos de conmutación digital, la fibra óptica, la comunicación inalámbrica, los satélites y la transmisión de datos impulsaron a la vez profundas transformaciones en la IEquipTel. En este sector se produjeron cambios significativos en el tamaño, la estructura y el número de empresas previamente establecidas (Olley y Pakes 1996, 1.263-1.297). Dicho esto, la primera hipótesis sugiere que, dentro de este cambio global, la reestructuración fue generalizada y que, por otro lado, se produjeron disparidades en los patrones de respuesta (Kornelakis 2015, 885-902), cuyos factores deben ser dilucidados. Las claves podrían encontrarse en la articulación entre las prácticas de las operadoras de servicios y la industria de equipos, las políticas industriales de los estados nacionales y las acciones de otros actores. La tecnología digital y las crecientes tendencias de normalización y desregulación permitieron la integración horizontal transfronteriza entre proveedores, clientes y otros participantes de la industria. En consecuencia, las configuraciones de recursos de los productores también cambiaron, ya que el nivel general de dispersión se redujo de forma limitada y el nivel de especialización aumentó de manera espectacular (Ghoshal y Bartlett 1990, 614-615).

En el ámbito mundial, un acontecimiento concreto acabó por desestabilizar la industria de las telecomunicaciones. Tras un largo periodo de intentos infructuosos, el desmembramiento de American Telephone and Telegraph (AT&T) hizo añicos la división del mercado internacional en pie desde los años veinte, por la que la gigantesca empresa dominaba el mercado nacional de EE.UU. e IT&T se volcaba en el extranjero. AT&T se dividió en siete operadoras regionales independientes que mantuvieron el nombre del sistema Bell (Bell Regional Operating Companies, BROCs o *baby* Bells (Forester 1987, 88) y se orientaron al mercado interior. Por su parte, como propietaria de la marca, la histórica AT&T, ahora con el nombre de AT&T Technology y de tamaño más reducido, conservó el potencial de innovación a través de los Laboratorios Bell y se orientó hacia el mercado exterior, el europeo en particular.

En sustancia, lo que ocurrió en el lado de la oferta fue una fragmentación del mercado interior de Estados Unidos y el surgimiento de un nuevo competidor mundial[1].

Las BROC resultantes del desmantelamiento legal de AT&T socavaron la estabilidad del mercado al diversificar sus proveedores más allá de Western

---

[1]   Henck et al. 1988 abogan por definir el desmantelamiento de AT&T como una evolución gradual.

Electric, el tradicional brazo manufacturero de AT&T. A partir de mediados de la década de 1980, los años decisivos de esta historia, se inició una carrera competitiva para llenar los vacíos dejados por algunas empresas en su empeño por crear grandes conglomerados. AT&T se movió con rapidez y eficacia (una estrategia llamada «rabifante» por su velocidad de conejo y su tamaño de elefante) para convertirse en un competidor global, en un claro desafío a las posiciones de los fabricantes en Europa.

Con el surgimiento de nuevos contrincantes, pero también de nuevos campos de acción (*BIT*, noviembre de 1985, 40-46), el antiguo vínculo entre la operadora de servicios de cada país y el productor de equipos se rompió y la integración vertical entre el servicio y la industria se escindió. Los mercados dejaron de obedecer a las lógicas locales y exigieron soluciones globales. El conjunto del sector sufrió un doble proceso de desinversión llevado a cabo por algunas empresas y de concentración en su estructura global, supuestamente para salvaguardar la organización oligopólica de la industria (European Commission 1997, 39; Crandall y Flamm (eds.) 1989; Feldstein 2007, 420)[2].

Las formulaciones de esa gran transformación varían sin afectar al fondo de los hechos. Como señalaba un destacado dirigente empresarial, nada menos que presidente de la European Roundtable of Industrialists (ERT) –empeñada, como sabemos, en fortalecer y desarrollar las capacidades competitivas de Europa–, la competencia mundial y el desarrollo tecnológico estaban transformando las empresas y la sociedad, en Europa y en todo el mundo (Stone 1989, 90)[3].

---

[2] Los debates candentes llegaron antes de la ruptura de AT&T (Agnew y Romeo 1981, 273-288). En su influyente informe al presidente Valéry Giscard d'Estaing, Nora y Minc (1978) acuñaron una nueva palabra –«télématique» (télécommunication + informatique)– y propusieron como piedra angular la estrategia de la «boda» de la informática y las tecnologías de la comunicación. En España, el presidente Felipe González encargó unos años más tarde al prestigioso sociólogo Manuel Castells (1986) un estudio similar, que inspiró la actitud socialista de presionar a las multinacionales para negociar la reestructuración industrial.

[3] La ERT, creada a mediados de 1983 en Ámsterdam, estaba formada por medio centenar de empresarios europeos que trabajaban a nivel nacional y europeo para reforzar la competitividad de la economía europea, por entonces carente de dinamismo e innovación en comparación con las de Japón y Estados Unidos. En el Reino Unido, un sector del Parlamento reconocía la necesidad inapelable de la reestructuración ya que, en numerosas ocasiones, las estrategias adoptadas por los gobiernos habían resultado poco interesantes y de escaso éxito e incluso desastrosas. En un sector clave como el de semiconductores tan solo el 6,89% de la producción mundial total, que ascendía a 29.000 millones de dólares, correspondía a Europa occidental en su conjunto, 62,06% a Estados Unidos y el resto a Japón (HC Deb 15 May 1985 vol 79. cc328-423).

Ese fue el caso de IT&T, una de las protagonistas de esta historia. En el trasfondo de las profundas tendencias identificadas, *shocks* externos –la presión del rápido y profundo cambio tecnológico– y deficiencias internas –una inadecuada estrategia de organización e innovación y un débil desarrollo financiero– combinaron sus efectos para empujarla a la reestructuración. Esta multinacional buscó una tremenda diversificación de las áreas de negocio y se desprendió del grueso de sus plantas de equipos dispersas en Europa, siendo las más importantes Standard Elektrik Lorenz (SEL) en Alemania, IT&T Austria GmbH, FACE en Italia, Bell Telephone Manufacturing Company (BTM) en Bélgica y Standard Eléctrica (en adelante, SESA) en España[4].

Nuestra investigación debería dilucidar la magnitud de la tarea. En el marco de los grandes organismos, concretamente el recién señalado *lobby* ERT, surgió un clima de estímulo a la industria desde las altas esferas de las multinacionales europeas.

De manera muy crucial, en los estratos más altos del poder político de algunos países europeos, Francia en particular, brotó un espíritu de confrontación con el dominio de las multinacionales estadounidenses, junto con la conciencia de la necesidad de un frente europeo de autoridades supranacionales, gobiernos de los estados nacionales y administraciones de los PTT para contrarrestar las ambiciones de AT&T e IBM (Nora y Minc 1978).

Dos alternativas políticas estaban en juego: la integración de los principales clientes de la industria de equipos en una estrategia global bajo la hegemonía de Estados Unidos o la creación de un eje central en Europa (Quatrepoint 1986, 8). En Europa, pese a los desafíos comunes planteados por la integración y la liberalización del mercado, el comportamiento de las operadoras de telecomunicaciones sugiere una variedad de modos de ajuste y vías de privatización (Eurofound 2003; Edwards 2001; Kornelakis 2015, 885-902).

Las políticas industriales y tecnológicas aplicadas en los estados nacionales dieron lugar a diferencias notables entre países, a la vez que fomentaron contrastes en la configuración de la industria en el contexto de la integración del mercado europeo y el aumento de la competencia internacional (Batt y Darbishire 1997, 59-79; Baskoy 2008; Thatcher 1999, 199)[5]. Así, el italiano

---

4	IT&T consideraba claramente a SEL como una empresa alemana por su capacidad de fabricación y su investigación independiente (Ziegler 1997, 84); SESA insistía en su independencia jurídica y su adscripción a la legislación española.

5	A principios de la década de 1980, Michalet (1981, 61-75) propuso un enfoque multidimensional integral que tomaba en cuenta la dimensión comercial, la tecnología y la producción financiera. La introducción de consideraciones tomadas de la teoría de la economía indus-

implicó la apertura de un gran mercado a las empresas del país y el aumento del grado de concentración en las industrias intensivas en capital. Sin embargo, Italia no alcanzó el grupo de cabeza en las industrias dominadas por las tecnologías de la información (Brambilla y Colli 2016, 112-113; Balbi y Fari 2014, 235-258) y en 1980-1987 fracasó la reestructuración de la industria nacional (Llerena, Matt y Trenti 2000, 226). Las experiencias belga y alemana apuntan en esta dirección de patrones diferentes (Batt y Darbishire 1997, 59-79; Baskoy 2008; Thatcher 1999, 199). ¿Qué ocurrió en España?

2. España: un buen caso de estudio en un sector complejo

Conviene presentar el perfil del país seleccionado, empezando por las peculiaridades y similitudes con los países de su entorno en varios ámbitos políticos y económicos. España compartió un escenario de recesión a principios de los años ochenta, al tiempo que mostraba una tendencia incesante a la liberalización del mercado. En cuanto a su singularidad, el primer rasgo se refiere a su creciente integración en el mercado mundial a pesar de no pertenecer al grupo de las grandes potencias junto con su tardía incorporación al mercado común europeo como miembro de pleno derecho tras un periodo de aspirante. Esto constituye un punto destacado, ya que el plan de reestructuración industrial fomentado y supervisado por el Estado nación y basado en parte en la financiación pública podría no haberse producido como miembro de pleno derecho de la Comunidad Económica Europea (CEE) porque la cuestión era competencia de la Comisión Europea.

La segunda consideración atañe al propio modelo productivo de baja tecnología de España, excesivamente vinculado a factores de crecimiento inestables, mano de obra barata, modestas aportaciones de capital y baja productividad total de los factores. De hecho, era un perfil incompatible con la integración en el mercado único europeo y que requería una reconversión desde el ángulo de la estructura (Becattini, Bellandi y De Propris 2009, 343; Kaldor y Selchow 2015, 120).

El tercer punto de partida se refiere a la condición de España como país en transición de un régimen dictatorial a una democracia de corte occidental con gobiernos proactivos en política industrial, interesados en atraer inversiones

---

trial permite definir una nueva interpretación de la especialización internacional en términos de competitividad.

generadoras de puestos de trabajo, con presupuestos, competencias y estructuras de decisión propias. Según una línea de pensamiento, el advenimiento de la democracia marcó el paso a un nuevo sistema de desarrollo orientado hacia el exterior, que, a su vez, se consideró un requisito previo para la reactivación sostenida del crecimiento tras la globalización (Ethier 1997, 2). Supuso la irrupción de nuevos socios antes excluidos –partidos políticos y sindicatos influyentes con poder de negociación–[6].

El caso español muestra deficiencias significativas: el país carecía de cuadros capaces de afrontar los enormes desafíos industriales de la época, a diferencia de Francia (una parte esencial de este estudio), que contaba con líderes de la industria bien formados en las escuelas de élite.

En definitiva, todas las cuestiones definen una pauta de reconversión de la industria de equipos de telecomunicaciones compleja, negociada y casi totalmente consensuada aunque no exenta de conflictos. Cabe destacar como hecho idiosincrático que el monopolio en el servicio telefónico se mantuvo intacto durante varios años mediante una política pactada con la CEE, con evidentes implicaciones para la industria de las telecomunicaciones. Ello supuso que la semipública Compañía Telefónica Nacional de España (CTNE) conservara parte de las prerrogativas –elección de tecnología, por ejemplo– que el Estado le había cedido desde su fundación por parte de IT&T en 1924, y que no perdería hasta la tardía liberalización, como se sabe un proceso con desfase temporal negociado en relación con el conjunto de Europa y de aplicación gradual[7].

Existen algunas razones adicionales para considerar el caso de España. Seis líderes mundiales del sector y todas las grandes empresas, junto con compañías locales de nicho de tamaño y tecnología significativos tenían pre-

---

[6] OECD (1993, 27-28). Cabe señalar que en la década de 1980 la CEE aún no había adoptado la directiva sobre los comités de empresa europeos, que favoreció el resurgimiento de las relaciones laborales transnacionales en la década de 1990 (Erne 2008, 134).

[7] La liberalización comenzó a mediados de los años 80 y culminó en 1998 con la apertura del servicio de telefonía fija a la competencia. Europa actuó de motor del cambio, pero fue un objetivo ajeno al sector –el control de la inflación– lo que llevó al gobierno a acelerar la reforma. Entre 1987 y 1993, mientras las autoridades europeas impulsaban la liberalización, el gobierno socialista dio prioridad a recuperar el control de la política de telecomunicaciones, modernizar el servicio y universalizar el acceso a la telefonía vocal fija. Posteriormente, entre 1993 y 1996, el Ejecutivo trató de utilizar políticamente la liberalización como incentivo para reducir los precios de las telecomunicaciones y contener la inflación cerca de la exigencia del Tratado de Maastricht. Finalmente, en el corto intervalo de 1996 a 1998, el gobierno de derechas del PP aceleró la liberalización y estableció el nuevo marco regulatorio (Calzada y Costas 2016, 3-55).

sencia comercial en España, entre ellas IT&T con su histórica SESA (1926). Como principal proveedora del monopolio CTNE, SESA era una de las más significativas del grupo de unidades manufactureras orientadas al mercado interior en Europa (Linvill 1984, 83), con cuotas y peso variables en los mercados internos, hecho con potenciales implicaciones para las modalidades de reestructuración. Su relevancia en el grupo se veía acrecentada por su capacidad de crear conocimiento en un centro de investigación propio y de transferirlo a la matriz y al resto. El tamaño del mercado de SESA se vio muy incrementado por la amplia presencia y la relativa facilidad de penetración en América Latina[8].

La singularidad del caso radica también en la estructura del mercado nacional de telecomunicaciones, dominado por el monopolio semipúblico de la CTNE con una participación minoritaria en la filial de IT&T SESA – fabricante del equipo de telecomunicaciones–, y, por lo tanto, un actor importante, aunque supeditado en última instancia a decisiones gubernamentales, como herramienta de la política económica de las autoridades españolas por su disponibilidad de recursos financieros no sometidos a los presupuestos del Estado. En este ámbito de la diferenciación de la estructura del sector, la integración parcial de la CTNE en SESA estableció un vínculo industria-servicio en el mercado nacional de las telecomunicaciones y brindó a la operadora un importante papel en la industria de equipos.

Por imposición institucional externa, la CTNE pasó de ser el motor de la industria con su *holding* industrial a sustituir la integración vertical por la horizontal, buscando un lugar en el mercado global como operador de redes. Este objetivo se convirtió en una palanca para socavar las posiciones del monopolio frente a las instituciones europeas.

En general, el sector español representaba el polo de I+D más importante del país y era altamente competitivo. De ahí el carácter exportador de las empresas, localizadas geográficamente en Madrid y con un alto grado de clusterización (Canalejo 1993; Rama y Holl 2009, 182-204)[9]. Por tomar un país algo similar a España, dentro de diferencias notables, en Italia no fue la

---

8   En 1970, SESA ocupaba el tercer lugar entre las mayores unidades de fabricación de IT&T de Europa (Estados Unidos. Congreso 1971, 81). A pesar de actuar en un mercado nacional más pequeño que el de los grandes países europeos, las filiales españolas del grupo IT&T representaban en 1985 el 4,83% de las ventas del grupo (Standard Eléctrica S.A. 1987, 24) y preveían un crecimiento proporcionalmente superior al del resto del grupo.

9   Miguel Canalejo, ingeniero industrial, pertenecía a la tercera generación de directivos de SESA ya en la época de Alcatel.

homóloga de SESA, es decir, FACE (IT&T) quien lideró el mercado nacional de equipos de conmutación, sino el campeón nacional SIT-Siemens, un fabricante integrado verticalmente que abastecía a más de la mitad del mercado italiano. Además, el «polo italiano» para fomentar la conmutación digital bajo la alianza de FACE y FATME, filial de Ericsson, fracasó (Helg y Ranci 1988, 51; Llerena, Matt y Trenti 2000, 223 y 226; Edquist, Hommen y Tsipouri 2000, 226).

Otro rasgo importante de la estrategia de la empresa estudiada se refiere a la forma específica de cambio tecnológico, es decir, la adopción gradual de la tecnología digital, frente a alternativas más rápidas y contundentes.

La última razón para elegir España gira en torno a la relevancia y riqueza de las fuentes disponibles que abarcan la acción de diversos actores, comenzando por los gubernamentales y continuando con la compañía telefónica monopolista y los sindicales.

A pesar de todas estas peculiaridades, los estudiosos no han prestado suficiente atención al caso español, a despecho del potencial explicativo que ofrece. Sin duda, debido a su extraordinario impacto en la economía y la sociedad españolas, los investigadores en ciencias sociales han dado prioridad a la reestructuración industrial de la década de 1980, dejando algunas áreas sin cubrir, un vacío que pide ser llenado. Los hechos estratégicos relevantes en España se han dejado de lado, en primer lugar, porque la narración histórica ha girado principalmente entorno a los países centrales, de los que esta nación quedó excluida, y en los principales acontecimientos de la reestructuración industrial masiva en España, en especial la siderurgia y la industria naval, como sabemos (Sáez y Díaz Morlán 2009; Valdaliso 2003, 52-67)[10].

¿Qué aporta el caso de este país no central al análisis de la evolución de las grandes empresas multinacionales y la reestructuración de la IEquiptel? Este capítulo trata de contribuir al conocimiento general de la evolución de los grandes negocios, las empresas de alta tecnología y la reestructuración de la industria de las telecomunicaciones a través del caso del «conglomerado cada vez más reducido de IT&T» (NYT, 12 de enero de 2011) y de Alcatel.

Otra cuestión clave se refiere a los actores: ¿cómo se combinan las políticas del Gobierno que representa los intereses del Estado nación, las multi-

---

[10] Para un texto clásico sobre el debate de la política industrial, véase Johnson (1904); para un argumento convincente sobre la política industrial en los Estados Unidos, véase Cohen y DeLong (2016), 103. A diferencia de otras antiguas filiales de IT&T, SESA ya cuenta con algunos estudios, como Chakravarthy (1996, 529-539) desde el punto de vista de la gestión y Kippenberger (1998, 37-40) para los cambios corporativos en general.

nacionales que tratan de imponer sus estrategias y las reivindicaciones de los trabajadores?

En definitiva, la investigación trata de esclarecer las estrategias de las multinacionales, las herramientas utilizadas para imponerlas y las formas de respuesta de otros actores. En este sentido, y tomando a España como caso de estudio, intenta articular claramente el margen de maniobra que le queda a la política industrial del Estado nación en un contexto de crisis estructural del sector, de intensa liberalización y creciente competencia internacional, de integración del mercado europeo y de cambio en la división internacional del trabajo.

Las multinacionales moldearon en profundidad la globalización de la economía, que a pesar de su alcance universal, toleró discrepancias en los procesos de reestructuración global (Ruigrok y van Tulder 1995; Fitzgerald 2016, 440)[11]. Ello lleva a una cuestión clave, reflejada por partida doble en el reverdecido debate sobre sobre los campeones industriales europeos (Maincent y Navarro 2006) y el de la globalización, de hecho, la fuerza más profunda que comenzó a actuar a la cabeza del sistema económico mundial (Friedman y Jones 2011, 1-8; Fitzgerald 2016; Boon 2017, 511-535). Por otro lado, esto enlaza con la avivada discusión sobre la política industrial en general (Berglof 2016, 335-340; Pryce 2012; Cirillo, Guarascio y Pianta 2014; Aghion et al. 2012) y también sobre el desequilibrio económico de los países (Kinossian 2017, 1-11; Bartlett y Prica 2016, 1-30). Desde un punto de vista metodológico, algunos reclaman enfoques a nivel de planta (Kim; Lee y Shin 2021, 1-9) y a nivel regional, como en el caso de la industria de defensa militar alemana, para captar mejor las divergencias en los procesos de reestructuración global (Elsner 1993, 1.254-1.262).

Sobre el trasfondo de las controversias y con ánimo de tomar posición en ellas, esta investigación trata de colmar una laguna en la narrativa histórica, que se ha centrado sustancialmente en los grandes acontecimientos de la reestructuración industrial en España y se ha preocupado menos por otros

---

[11]   Entronca con los debates de los años ochenta acerca de la relación entre gobiernos y multinacionales, reflejados por Poynter (2013); también se aproxima a Colli y Piscitello (2014, 487-508), que analizan la interacción entre las operadoras de telecomunicaciones tradicionales y su Administración de origen, reivindicando el papel de los gobiernos como estrategas orientados a objetivos. La cesión de soberanía por parte del Estado nación a las instituciones y los mercados junto con la adquisición de nuevas esferas de control para fomentar la «competitividad nacional» e influir en el ritmo de la globalización es motivo de controversia (Cable 1995, 23-53).

acontecimientos estratégicos relevantes[12]. Uno de ellos corresponde a la reestructuración de Standard Eléctrica, fabricante de equipos de telecomunicaciones y filial de la multinacional IT&T en su más amplio contexto societario y de mercado[13].

El capítulo consta de seis secciones principales, en las que se exponen las razones de España como un buen estudio de caso para arrojar luz en un sector muy difícil y se examina el desarrollo de la política y la trayectoria de ajuste a través de la transformación gradual de SESA, la filial española de las multinacionales IT&T y Alcatel posteriormente.

Sobre todo, a propósito de la complejidad, las secciones debaten las interrelaciones entre los diferentes niveles de cambios (tecnología, personal y propiedad/estructura) y las motivaciones/estrategias de los actores. La narración se basa en fuentes primarias, en primer lugar las actas del consejo de administración de la operadora líder, así como varios documentos públicos y privados, en particular los de la propia Alcatel-SESA, denominación que tomó SESA tras su inserción en la nueva multinacional Alcatel[14].

Antes de proseguir, parece oportuno llamar la atención sobre algunas consideraciones preliminares relacionadas con los criterios, la cronología y las características de la industria analizada.

Empezando por los criterios, ¿por qué un estudio de caso? Este enfoque metodológico es oportuno porque, como se ha dicho, las pautas de reestructuración del mercado y sus consecuencias difieren según los países. Además, la creciente interdependencia económica mundial parece dar lugar a comparaciones internacionales como consecuencia metodológica esencial (Eliassen y Sjovaag, ed. 1999). Seguimos con otra consideración genérica, que define

---

[12] Para un texto clásico sobre la política industrial, para un argumento convincente sobre la política industrial en los Estados Unidos y para un llamamiento a una nueva política industrial en los países avanzados, véanse respectivamente Johnson (1984), Cohen y DeLong (2016, 103) y Pryce (2012).

[13] Conviene categorizar el caso de IT&T como el de una multinacional con dilatada presencia industrial en España, para diferenciarlo de otros dos tipos de multinacionales –sin actividad industrial aunque con ventas en el país y sin apenas presencia ninguna en el mercado español (Intervención de Pedro María García, director de la Actualidad Electrónica, Congreso de los diputados, 24 de octubre de 1984, 229, 7.201).

[14] También destacan las fuentes parlamentarias, tanto españolas como extranjeras. Por lo general, la prensa recibió la información directamente de los interlocutores, por lo que sus datos pueden considerarse fiables. Sin embargo, algunos de ellos tuvieron que ser aclarados, como ocurrió, por ejemplo, cuando UGT se vio obligada a enmendar las cifras erróneas proporcionadas por la prensa (Nota de prensa de UGT Metal a todos los medios de comunicación, 16 de noviembre de 1983, Archivo de la Fundación Largo Caballero (AFLC).

la naturaleza compleja de la reestructuración institucional y técnica en las telecomunicaciones (Mansell et al. 1990, 51-66). Desde el punto de vista de la reestructuración organizativa, se trata del marco analítico *chandleriano* de la transición de una empresa multifuncional multiunidad a una empresa multidivisional que separaba la estrategia de la operación y, en consecuencia, de la centralización y la división por la función, a la división por característica del producto (Chandler 1975, 251-252; Chandler, 1990).

La cronología revela una concentración de hechos durante la década de los ochenta a diferentes niveles (desmantelamiento de AT&T, tecnología digital, reestructuración de la industria, entrada de España en el mercado común, creación de la nueva multinacional Alcatel), lo que la convierte en un punto de inflexión en las estrategias empresariales y las políticas industriales en Europa. Por otra parte, la cronología apunta a la incorporación de España a procesos tardíos como el italiano, cuyas empresas han sido estudiadas por Colli y Vasta (2010).

En cuanto a los rasgos de TEquipI, el más general obedece al fuerte impacto que la incertidumbre de la demanda tiene en su evolución. Destaca, en particular, su aguda sensibilidad a los impactos de las innovaciones tecnológicas y la consiguiente rápida obsolescencia de los productos por el desequilibrio entre el elevado coste de las mismas, más el adicional de los cambios normativos posteriores, y el largo tiempo de recuperación (Thatcher 1999, 58)[15]. A ello se añade del lado de la demanda la dependencia tecnológica a largo plazo que las operadoras desarrollan sobre un sistema. También se tiene en cuenta el papel crucial que desempeña el tamaño entre las empresas competidoras debido a la demanda cíclica, así como la intensidad tecnológica, de I+D y de capital, y las elevadas barreras de acceso al mercado (Department of Commerce 1986, 53)[16].

La estructura de la industria sufrió cambios profundos entre los años 1970-1990. Los desarrollos tecnológicos en marcha desde la década de 1970 habían aumentado la sofisticación de los bienes de telecomunicación a la vez que provocaban dramáticas caídas de costes en términos reales y cambios en la estructura de costes. Su explicación radica en la caída del coste unitario de los equipos de conmutación —el corazón del sistema moderno de teleco-

---

[15] El ciclo de vida de la tecnología digital acortaba unos dos decenios el de la electromecánica (Hendry y Eccles 1992, 135).

[16] Las empresas deben combinar la innovación rápida con la solidez financiera para resistir la intensa competencia en un entorno de fuertes caídas de precios y dependencia de las subvenciones estatales a la investigación (Baskoy 2008, 148).

municaciones (Linvill 1984, 83)– inducida en parte por el creciente impacto del *software* y la digitalización[17]. En 1970, el *software*, componente principal de los gastos de I+D, se elevaba a la quinta parte de los gastos de desarrollo totales, mientras al *hardware* le correspondía el 80%. A mediados de los años ochenta, cuando los sistemas de conmutación dependían cada vez más de los programas informáticos, con sus elevados costes de desarrollo, la necesidad de aumentar drásticamente la cuota de mercado y, por tanto, de buscar el crecimiento a escala internacional, se convirtió en algo fundamental. Los fabricantes se enfrentaron al doble reto de innovar obligatoriamente en productos basados en la electrónica y la tecnología de la información altamente integradas y, en ese caso, de ajustarse a un descenso de la demanda de empleo en la fabricación de equipos totalmente digitales. El desarrollo de estos sistemas elevó los costes de I+D de la industria de equipos y las inversiones de los fabricantes de todo el mundo. En el decenio siguiente, la proporción del gasto se invirtió en favor del desarrollo de *software*, que absorbió las cuatro quintas partes de los gastos de desarrollo[18]. De suma importancia, la inversión cada vez mayor en I+D, tal como preveían las especificidades de la industria antes mencionadas, provocó el alza de las ya de por sí altas barreras de entrada en la industria (Commission of the European Communities 1990, 28–30; Grupp y Schnöring 1992, 46-66). Nació una división internacional del trabajo según la cual las empresas europeas se centraban en las telecomunicaciones, mientras que las japonesas ponían mayor énfasis en otros campos, como el de la electrónica audiovisual, punto de partida para acceder a las telecomunicaciones (Commission of the European Communities 1992, 13; Schmoch y Schnöring 1994, 397-413). Tan solo en algunos segmentos del mercado (periféricos) tuvo lugar una apertura del oligopolio a nuevas empresas, algunas de las cuales se auparían al centro de la industria de equipo, como fue el caso de Nokia, llamada a un papel estelar (Maculan 1992, 85).

---

[17] Los equipos de telecomunicaciones comprenden tres tipos de productos: la conmutación, ya sea pública o privada; las transmisiones, para generar y recibir señales, y los cables de soporte (cuando son necesarios); los terminales, para enviar y recibir comunicaciones de voz, datos, texto o imágenes (Sutton 2001, 137; BIPE 1991, 12-19). La conmutación, que constituye el grueso del mercado de equipos de telecomunicaciones, representó en 1989 el 17% de las ventas del sector en Estados Unidos y casi la mitad de la producción europea (Sutton 2001, 137).

[18] En ese momento, el *software* para operar un sistema de conmutación pública comprendía aproximadamente 1 millón de instrucciones programadas (Commission of the European Communities (1987, 90).

A su vez, las imperiosas necesidades de I+D empujaron a estos fabricantes de equipos de telecomunicaciones a una reestructuración con el objetivo de captar economías de escala en I+D y producción y de facilitar el acceso a diferentes mercados geográficos, bajo aguda competencia. Los ingredientes potenciales para el mantenimiento de la estructura oligopólica parecen, por tanto, existir en la idiosincrasia del sector.

Tabla 1. Equipos de telecomunicaciones en Europa: principales indicadores (millones de ECU)

	Consumo aparente	Exportaciones netas	Producción
1980	12.734	1.142	14.176
1981	14.113	1.692	15.805
1982	15.136	1.851	16.987
1983	16.302	1.851	18.153
1984	18.250	1.745	19.995
1985	20.184	1.570	21.754
1986	20.307	1.241	21.548
1987	21.555	1.029	22.584
1988	22.848	91	22.939
1989	23.229	110	23.339
1990	25.532	296	25.828

Fuente: Eurostrategies ESTEL, Eurostat (Comext).

Europa compartió con otras zonas las dificultades de la reestructuración mundial de la industria de equipos de telecomunicaciones (Tabla 1). La falta de estándares internacionales para los equipos clave se sumó a la fragmentación en mercados de Estados nación distintos y autoabastecidos, característica del ya mencionado monopsonio a nivel de país. A favor de la complejidad, los Estados nación conservaron la capacidad de interferir en las opciones tecnológicas de las operadoras de servicios a través de barreras no arancelarias, como su control sobre la aprobación de los productos. Los fabricantes tendieron a adoptar una estrategia de integración multivariada: a través de tipologías de equipos basadas en la adscripción de cada mercado nacional a algunos productores relativamente grandes y diversificados; como parte de grupos matrices multinacionales en busca de diferentes beneficios y vinculados con los PTT en algunos países; finalmente, por la ya mencionada integración lejana en la cadena de valor con los proveedores de componentes (Ghoshal y Bartlett 1990, 614-615; (Pontarollo 1994, 88; Carr 1998)[19].

Para seguir con las peculiaridades europeas, el aumento de los costes de desarrollo, la confusión sobre las normas y la desaceleración de las tasas de crecimiento fomentaron la tendencia a la consolidación. En la década de 1980, mientras que el valor de la producción solo aumentó un 1,8% y las exportaciones netas sufrieron una importante contracción, el consumo aparente (producción+importaciones/exportaciones) se duplicó con creces debido al aumento de las importaciones (Tabla 1)[20]. Esta hemorragia de la industria europea es lo que la IT&T, inquieta por el futuro de sus activos industriales en el continente en esa zona, pretendía detener (Eurostrategies ESTEL, Eurostat (Comext)[21]. La estrategia encajaba con la presión para abrir los mercados y la

---

[19] Los beneficios incluían compartir los elevados costes de desarrollo de productos con otros países, lograr la transferencia de tecnología más fácilmente y reducir el costo de la inversión de capital (European Commission 1997, 97). Ciertos países, como Francia, practicaban una política de «compra nacional» (Department of Commerce 1986, 51-52). Había dos grandes grupos de proveedores, el principal de los cuales estaba formado por especialistas en telecomunicaciones, cuya actividad dominante era la producción de equipos. Estos, a su vez, eran más bien generalistas dentro del sector de los equipos de telecomunicaciones (Alcatel, Ericsson e Italtel, a los que se añadieron AT&T y Northern Telecom a nivel mundial). El segundo gran grupo estaba formado por generalistas de la electrónica (Siemens, Bosch y Philips) (BIPE 1991, 12/23). Uno de los objetivos de la CEE fue la armonización de los equipos de telecomunicación, que, combinada con la liberalización, habría de beneficiar a los usuarios al reducir las tarifas y ampliar la oferta de servicios. La liberalización debía vincularse a la competitividad, asociada a una asignación eficiente de los recursos (Commission of the European Communities 1992, 1; Nihoul 1998/99, 2). La creación del Mercado Común en la Comunidad Europea afectó de lleno a las empresas. Philips se vio forzada a integrar las actividades de producción en todos los países europeos. Este esfuerzo tuvo consecuencias para su filial australiana, que, en lugar de transformarse en un centro regional de Philips con el apoyo de su matriz, como se pretendía en la década de 1960, fue absorbida al abordar los cambios en la política comercial australiana y el aumento de las importaciones japonesas. La producción y el empleo en Philips Australia se redujeron drásticamente durante la década de 1970 (Eng 2017, 217-238).

[20] https://ec.europa.eu/eurostat/data/database.

[21] El mercado europeo de equipos de telecomunicaciones se cifraba en 14.370 millones de dólares en 1984, 13.900 millones en 1987 y 25.000 cinco años después (AHCIET, 40-45, 1990, 53; desglose de ventas por empresas en 1984: IT&T 21,2%; Siemens 16,9%; CGE (Francia) 14%; Ericsson 12,4%; G.E.C. (Reino Unido) 6,3% y otros 29,2%. Desglose regional de las ventas de equipos de telecomunicaciones de IT&T en 1984: Europa 65%; Asia 18%; América del Norte 10%; América Latina 4%; África, Pacífico Sur 3% (New York Times, 27 de junio de 1986) (Anexo 1). Los analistas pronosticaban la reducción de fabricantes de equipo a dos o tres (New Scientist, 23 de octubre de 1980, 239). La creación del mercado único europeo hacía prever fuertes sacudidas en muchas industrias porque, como señalaba el ya citado dirigente de la ERI, «simplemente no hay espacio en Europa para seis o siete fábricas de telecomunicaciones» (Stone 1989, 90-95).

especialización transversal entre los proveedores de los Estados nación que fomentan las élites políticas de la UE en una amplia gama de actividades. Nos encontramos en el núcleo del tema principal[22].

Nuestro planteamiento inicial exige abordar el problema desde una de las fracciones nacionales. Sin dejar de reconocer el papel clave que han desempeñado las actuaciones de IT&T en el inicio de la reconversión, conviene en primer lugar esbozar el marco en el que se desenvuelven en la práctica, es decir, los entornos del Estado nación, que pueden influir en sus estrategias y decisiones.

3. El marco estatal de la estrategia de las multinacionales: la política industrial proactiva en la nueva España democrática de corte occidental

La década que arranca en los años ochenta presenta también un elemento de continuidad con el predominio de los servicios de voz en la telefonía, ante los grandes cambios de la telefonía móvil[23]. Esa década pletórica de transformaciones tuvo su continuidad con matices propios en las siguientes.

En cuanto a aspectos más específicos, informes cualificados situaban a las tecnologías de la información y la comunicación como eje de las estructuras productivas de las sociedades industriales avanzadas y les atribuían una tasa de crecimiento superior al nivel general de la industria manufacturera[24].

---

[22] Se fomentó la especialización cruzada en telecomunicaciones, ferrocarriles, generación de energía, equipos médicos y transporte urbano (*Foundations for the future of European industry*, Amsterdam meeting, 1 de junio de 1983).

[23] Al final de la década, los servicios de voz representaban alrededor del 90% de los ingresos de las operadoras (Council of Europe 1990, 15).

[24] *BIT*, julio-agosto de 1981, 10-11. A mediados de la década de 1980, las telecomunicaciones aportaban a la facturación mundial en el sector de las TIC 390.000 millones de ECUs –76,92% de servicios (estimada) y 23,07% de equipo–; la informática 170.000 millones de ECUs –29,41% de servicios y 79,48 restantes de equipo–; la electrónica de consumo 105.000 millones de ECU –47,61% en servicios y el resto en equipo–. y los componentes de equipo 30 mil millones de ECU (International Labour Organisation 1991, 20). En 1990, el mercado comunitario de las telecomunicaciones se cifraba en 116.000 millones de ECUs y se componía de una fracción mayoritaria, los servicios de telecomunicaciones –90.000 millones– y los equipos de telecomunicación, con un volumen de negocios de 26 mil millones de ECUs y una tasa de crecimiento interanual del 7,8% en el quinquenio anterior (Commission of the European Communities 1992, 5).

Por otro lado, parece importante subrayar los rasgos más sobresalientes de la industria de alta tecnología de equipos de telecomunicaciones, empezando por su carácter estratégico y de «*general purpose technology*» con efectos sobre la totalidad del sistema económico, que incitaba a una postura intervencionista del estado, como agente de la política industrial, demandante directo de equipos y fuente de financiación de la I+D. En esencia, la industria de alta tecnología se refiere a aquella que se encuentra en las fronteras científicas y tecnológicas del mundo, debido a su intenso esfuerzo científico y tecnológico y a la gran velocidad de innovación o aplicación de nuevas tecnologías basadas en la ciencia a los productos y/o procesos de producción (Patrick 1986, 6-8). La industria a que nos referimos se compone de varios tipos principales de productos, que pueden a reducirse tres: equipos de conmutación, de transmisión y aparatos de abonado o terminales (Arpege Group 1994, 2)[25]. Pues bien, entre 1989-1995, mientras que la conmutación crecía por debajo del 6% y los terminales el 8,3%, porcentajes intermedios del 7,7% medio, los datos y teléfonos móviles lo hacían al 14,4 y 16,9%, respectivamente (European Communities 1992).

De suma importancia para el presente estudio, la estructura de costes de la industria de equipo de telecomunicación arrojaba el predominio claro de los materiales tanto en el equipo de conmutación como en los terminales telefónicos (Gráfico 1), traducido en una intensidad tecnológica y de capital. Por su parte, existían economías de escala a corto plazo en la fabricación de centralitas y de aparatos telefónicos[26].

---

[25] El cambio radical de la red telefónica fue el resultado de avances diversos: rápida digitalización de las redes gracias a la introducción de la transmisión digital y la conmutación temporal; la evolución de las redes de telefonía hacia redes de multiservicios de telecomunicaciones gracias a la generalización del control de programa almacenado, en una combinación de las técnicas de la conmutación telefónica con las de la informática; la introducción de la señalización por canal semáforo CCITT No. 7, que condujo a las nuevas estructuras de red y, por último, la importancia del *software* (Jacob y Penn, 1995, [3]. La competitividad de la industria de equipos de telecomunicaciones depende fuertemente de la disponibilidad de componentes electrónicos, clave para el diseño y la producción de cualquier equipo de telecomunicaciones y a la vez uno de los principales clientes de la industria de *software* (Commission of the European Communities 1992, 5).

[26] WS Atkins Management Consultants (1988, 149 y 156). La introducción de la electrónica hizo caer de forma notable los costes laborales, de forma que en fechas relativamente tempranas los costes unitarios del equipo de conmutación se redujeron a menos de la mitad y el trabajo necesario mermó hasta la tercera y cuarta parte (Doz 1979, 82-84).

Gráfico 1. Estructura de costes de la industria de equipo de telecomunicación (%)

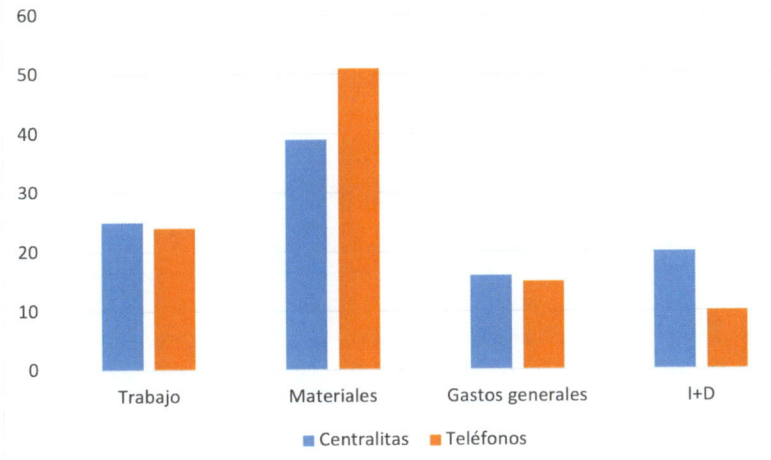

Fuente: Elaboración a partir de Atkins (1988), 149.

Al iniciarse la década de 1980, en todo el mundo dominaban los sistemas electromecánicos de conmutación. Europa iba rezagada respecto a EE. UU. en la adopción de la conmutación electrónica o digital. Esta situación afectaba a la totalidad de países, si bien existían diferencias en el seno de Europa; Bélgica y RU eran lo más avanzados con cifras de 7 y 5% en medio de una tónica general de 1 al 3% (*New Scientist*, 23 de octubre de 1980, 235). Respecto a los sistemas de conmutación digital, existían quince en todo el mundo, originarios de diez países[27]. La mayoría pertenecía a siete países de Europa, zona que además participaba en el desarrollo del Sistema 12 de IT&T según un

[27] He aquí la lista completa (System X, UK), E-10 de CIT-Alcatel (Francia); MT/Thomson CSF (Francia); AXE de Ericsson (Suecia); Proteo/SIT Siemens (Italia); System 12 de ITT (multinacional); ESS de Western Electric (USA), DMS de Northern Telecom (Canadá); ITS de TRW Vidar (USA); System Century/Stromberg Carlsson (USA); EAX de GTE (USA); PRXD de Philips (Holanda); IFS de Hasler/Siemens Ibis y STR (Suiza); EWSD de Siemens (Alemania) y NEAX (Japón) (*New Scientist*, 23 de octubre de 1980, 239). Años después la lista de sistemas digitales comprendía, aparte de los sistemas europeos, los estadounidenses GTD 5, 4 ESS y 5 ESS, EAX Domestic de ATT; el GTD 5 EAX International de Siemens; los indios C DOT RAX, C DOT MAX y C DOT DSS de la india C DOT; los coreanos TDX 1 de Samsung-Goldstar y TDX 10 de Daewoo-Otelco; los japoneses Fetex 150 de Fujitsu, HDX 10 y D 60/70 de Hitachi– OKI y NEAX 61 de NEC; el DX 200 de la finesa Telenokia; el DMS 10 y DMS 100/200 de Northem Telecom (Canada); el SI 2000 de la yugoslava Iskra y el Tropico de la brasileña Elebra, señalado en otro lugar (Fischman y Jorstad 1990, I-2). Griset y Fridenson (2013) hablan de «convergencia» entre los sistemas E 10 y 12, lo que, en definitiva, contribuía a reforzar los equipos de ingenieros en las filiales.

esquema colaborativo. El coste de desarrollo de los sistemas de conmutación digital se cifraba en 7 billones de dólares en Europa –1,4 billones el Sistema X– frente a los 2,5 billones en EE.UU. Los sistemas europeos variaban según la eficiencia, en una escala en que los primeros puestos los ocupaban Alcatel y Siemens. Las centrales del tipo E-10 de Alcatel se beneficiaron de inversiones masivas de la DGT francesa y se adueñaron de la quinta parte del mercado mundial de centrales digitales (WS Atkins Management Consultants 1988, 146). La penetración en mercados ajenos obedeció a esquemas relativamente complejos. Las vías de acceso fueron el comercio mundial y la inversión directa por medio de participaciones minoritarias en empresas locales[28].

En cuanto a la estructura de mercado, y refiriéndonos más a Europa, existía una relación comercial *sui géneris* entre demanda y oferta –cliente y proveedor–, caracterizada por la fuerte dependencia y el reducido margen de libertad entre las operadoras telefónicas y los grandes grupos del sector, causante de los eternos problemas de suministro en esta industria. Como sabemos, el servicio telefónico era prestado por los monopolios estatales o PTT –los llamados dinosaurios– que concertaban sus pedidos de equipos de telecomunicación con un restringido grupo de proveedores nacionales. La industria autóctona o de las empresas filiales de multinacionales implantadas en cada país dominaba el mercado en la Europa de los monopolios públicos. En la región el mercado se abrió al menos a una casa extranjera pero los fabricantes autóctonos retuvieron una posición dominante en su respectivo mercado interior (WS Atkins Management Consultants 1988, 139)[29].

---

[28] Ya en 1979, la francesa CIT emprendió la fabricación de centrales E10 Five según las normas vigentes en EE.UU. a través de su filial Telecommunications Switching Systems. En 1983, CIT construyó (Reston, Virginia) e instaló las primeras centrales E-10 Five –versión controlada por programa almacenado del sistema E10 (Chapuis y Joel 2003, 347)– y enseguida decidió fabricarlas en serie. En 1981, adquirió el 25% de Lynch Communications Systems, al cabo de tres años ampliada hasta el 42%, especializada en la producción de centrales digitales según el estándar USA. En 1984, CIT adquirió el 20% de Sonitrol, especializada en la producción de equipos de control y televigilancia, con el objetivo de utilizar su red de distribución para comercializar la PABX de Telic, filial de CIT-Alcatel (Marseille (dir.) 1992; *Le Point*, 311-319, 1978, 115). Un estudio de la London Business School (Grindley, 1987, 151) fijaba en un 10% el precio añadido que debían pagar los abonados de British Telecom por la elección de subsidiar el sistema X en lugar de adoptar el E-10 francés. Cálculos atribuían a la reestructuración de la industria ahorros en I+D y gastos generales que podrían representar economías de escala en torno al 10%. Grindley señalaba que los elevados costes ocultos de la contratación pública doblaban el coste aparente del sistema X.

[29] En 1986, Alemania era el principal mercado de centralitas digitales, con 26,9 millones instaladas, seguida de Francia, Reino Unido, Italia y Bélgica. En Francia, las ventajas de los proveedores autóctonos frente a los extranjeros estribaban en los carteles o clubes de fa-

Gráfico 2. Cuota de mercado de centralitas digitales en Europa.

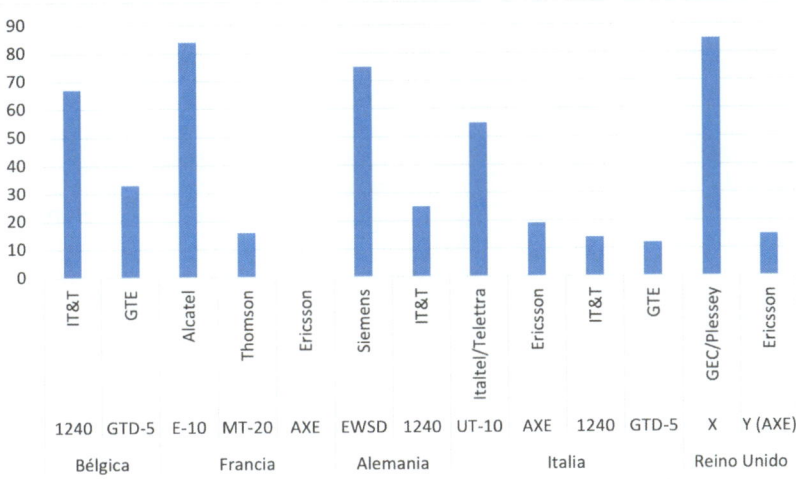

Fuente: Smidt y Weber (2013), 81.

Así sucedió en Alemania con los sistemas digitales EWS-D y 12 de Siemens y SEL (IT&T) o en Francia con los E10/E12 de CIT-Alcatel-Thomson y AXE de CGTE. La estructura de mercado más anómala por abierta era la italiana (Helg y Ranci 1988, 1-82), con cuatro sistemas distintos y el predomio claro del UT-10 de Italtel/Telettra. España, país con monopolio semipúblico, siguió esta tendencia con una adaptación del Sistema 12 de IT&T – la central digital de media y gran capacidad 1240– y con el AXE de Ericsson. Por su parte, Suecia representa la fidelidad al proveedor histórico y el predominio absoluto del AXE de Ericsson (100%) (Gráfico 2 y Tabla 2).

bricantes de equipos de telefonía y telegrafía (SOCOTEL) y de datos (SOTOLEC), participados por el gobierno y con sus cuotas asociadas; el apoyo de los PTT para obtener la aprobación técnica; proyectos conjuntos de desarrollo con el Centre National d'Études en Télécommunications (CNET), el centro técnico de la DGT; desarme arancelario para las importaciones; política gubernamental y apoyo positivo de los PTT a las exportaciones y política implícita de los PTT para «comprar francés», sin cerrar por ello la puerta a productores extranjeros (*Inteltrade*, 15 de noviembre de 1978, 2).

Tabla 2. Estructura geográfica del mercado europeo de centrales digitales

	Sistema	Tecnología	Cuota de mercado nacional (%)	Fabricante	Empresa
Bélgica	1240	IT&T	67	BTM	Alcatel NV
	GTD-5	GTE	33	ATEA	NTB (Siemens/GTE)
Francia	E-10	Alcatel	84	Alcatel	
	MT-20	Thomson	16	CGCT-Alcatel	
	AXE	Ericsson	0	Matra/Ericsson	Ericsson
Alemania	EWSD	Siemens	75	Siemens/Telenorma/DeTeWe	
	1240	IT&T	25	SEL	Alcatel NV
Italia	UT-10	Italtel/Telettra	55	Italtel/Telettra	
	AXE	Ericsson	19	FATME	
	1240	IT&T	14	FACE	Alcatel NV
	GTD-5	GTE	12	GTE	NTB (Siemens/GTE)
Reino Unido	X	GEC/Plessey	85	GEC/Plessey	
	Y (AXE)	Ericsson	15	Thorn/Ericsson	

Fuente: Smidt y Weber (2013), 81.

Por lo que atañe a los aparatos telefónicos, en la CE, los principales fabricantes coincidían en sustancia con las empresas dedicadas a equipos de conmutación. Se trataba de SAPhilips (filial de Philips NV de Holanda), BTM y ATEA (Bélgica); Alcatel, Matra Communication (Francia); Siemens, Telenorma (Alemania); Italtel, Marconi Italiana (Italia); Plessey, GEC y STC (Reino Unido). Las que no integraban la conmutación eran Matra Communication (fabricante de equipos PABX y de instalaciones de clientes) y Marconi Italiana (filial de GEC) y STC, fabricante de una extensa gama de productos de telecomunicaciones. Tradicionalmente, la industria autóctona se parapetó de la competencia en los PTT. Los monopolios públicos tenían la prerrogativa de establecer especificaciones, utilizar el proceso de aprobación o simplemente excluir a los competidores para apoyar a los productores nacionales (WS Atkins Management Consultants 1988, 153).

En resumidas cuentas, en ausencia aún de normas supranacionales, los proveedores nacionales ajustaron el equipo a patrones nacionales y, por ello, erigieron una «barrera no arancelaria» contra empresas extranjeras, poco proclives a ingentes inversiones para producir el equipo según el estándar nacional sin garantía de conseguir cuotas de mercado suficientes para recuperar los elevados gastos de desarrollo (Thatcher 1999, 58)[30].

A propósito de la distribución geográfica, la producción y el consumo mundiales de equipos de telecomunicaciones se concentraban en siete países desarrollados, siendo Japón y Estados Unidos (y sus empresas multinacionales) los principales productores (BIPE 1991, 12/20)[31]. La evolución de esta industria tendió a ser impulsada por la creciente demanda de nuevos y mejores servicios y se vio afectada por un entorno regulador cambiante (Brown 1994, 3)[32].

4. El desarrollo de políticas industriales en España

España inició la reconversión industrial con un notable desfase temporal respecto al conjunto de países industrializados de la OCDE, sumidos ya desde 1974 en políticas de ajuste en sectores azotados por la crisis. La reestructu-

---

[30] La UE daba en el clavo al señalar el choque entre el elevadísimo coste de desarrollo de una nueva familia de conmutadores de división de tiempo –entre 700 y 1.300 millones de dólares–, la enorme cuantía de las ventas necesarias para lograr un rendimiento razonable de los costes de desarrollo –14.000 millones de dólares– y lo exiguo del tamaño de los mercados nacionales – 7.200 millones el británico, 10.900 el francés y 11.700 el alemán–. Dicho sea de paso, señalar la reserva del mercado a un campeón nacional y la realización de las compras de equipos sin las ventajas de la competencia no parece que fuera un obstáculo a la consecución de rendimientos razonables de la inversión en nuevas centrales (Commission of the European Communities 1983, 36).

[31] En 1990, la producción mundial de equipos de comunicación aumentó a 64.000 millones de dólares, desde casi 38.000 millones de dólares siete años antes (Butcher 1991, 2-11).

[32] Se esperaba que segmentos como las comunicaciones móviles y espaciales, así como la transmisión óptica y algunas comunicaciones empresariales, impulsaran la demanda total de equipos de telecomunicaciones en un 7,7% en términos reales hasta 1992 (BIPE 1991, 12-19).

ración industrial se llevó a cabo en dos fases sucesivas durante la incipiente etapa democrática que sepultó la sangrienta dictadura de Franco (Hamann 2012)[33]. En la primera, entre mediados de 1977 y finales de 1980, visiblemente supeditada al consenso político y a la paz laboral, prevalecieron tímidas reestructuraciones sectoriales, concesión de subvenciones y nacionalización de las empresas en crisis. El despliegue de planes de reconversión sectorial y la renuncia a las medidas de reestructuración empresa a empresa encarnaron la política de la segunda etapa (Marín 2006, 61-62). En definitiva, los planes de reconversión sectorial aprobados, prácticamente inaplicados, adolecían de una notable cortedad para resolver los graves problemas de la industria española.

Al formar gobierno en 1982, los socialistas concibieron un programa de expansión a base de inversión como motor de la economía con la prioridad en la creación de empleo. Asimismo, aspiraba a convertir la empresa pública saneada gerencial y financieramente en plataforma de creación de puestos de trabajo y logro de un desarrollo estable y como vía de absorción de mano de obra empleada en actividades obsoletas (sobrante de la reconversión). Finalmente, se mostraba abierto a la colaboración con el capital privado (Recio y Roca, en Glyn 2001, 174)[34].

Al reto de la revolución tecnológica y de su incuestionable peso en el incremento de la competitividad y en la modernización productiva el programa respondía con una decidida voluntad política de acometer el desarrollo en España de la electrónica, informática y telecomunicaciones, así como el control de sus efectos. Se trataba de prestar apoyo selectivo a los segmentos del mercado con posibilidades de crear una industria nacional competitiva en un contexto de liberalización de los mercados, auspiciada por las grandes instituciones internacionales y plasmada en la quiebra de los monopolios[35].

---

[33] La política de la Unión del Centro Democrático (UCD) para el consenso con los partidos de oposición dio lugar a los Pactos de Moncloa (octubre de 1977) en una tentativa de hacer frente a la catastrófica situación económica. Chocantes en el contexto de los gobiernos centristas de la UCD, las nacionalizaciones sirvieron a los intereses de los accionistas mayoritarios y de las instituciones financieras, amenazadas por considerables reclamaciones pendientes. Solana Madariaga (1981, 5), entonces diputado por el PSOE, atribuía a los gobiernos conservadores en la primera transición española un «mariposeo» de la economía industrial del país. Para un ejemplo de reestructuración financiera con despidos en AEG-Telefunken, véase Le Monde, 11 de marzo de 1983.

[34] Esta idea de la industria como palanca para el desarrollo (Maurov, 1981) fue inspirada por Mitterrand, pero estaba vinculada a la socialdemocracia nórdica en su abandono de las nacionalizaciones. Sobre las políticas de Francia, véase Holton (1986, 67-80) y Zysman (1977).

[35] La competencia aumentó con el desmembramiento del gigantesco entramado de AT&T (Bell System) y la consiguiente aparición de las compañías regionales (Feldstein 2007, 420).

Gráfico 3. Gasto del Gobierno en España, 1982-1995 (% PIB)

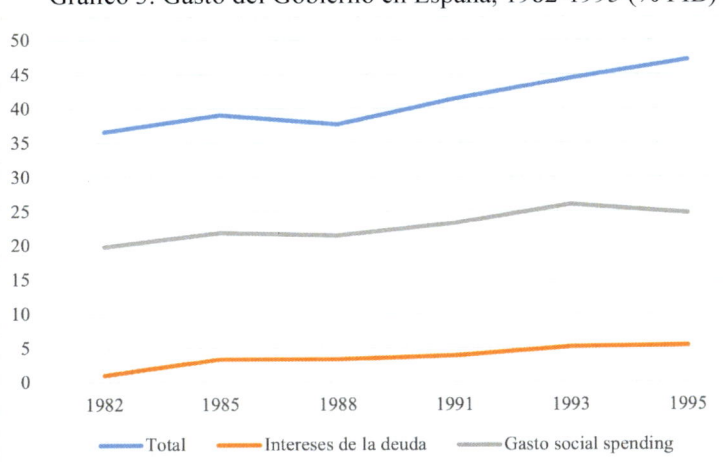

Fuente: Calculado a partir de INE, *Contabilidad Nacional de España*.

Aleccionado por el fracaso cosechado en Francia por Mitterrand, el gobierno español rechazó con parecido acento las políticas expansivas y las nacionalizaciones. Cierto que el gasto público se incrementó en casi diez puntos de porcentaje sobre el PNB (Gráfico 3) –del 37,6 al 47,1%–, pero el Gobierno se volcó preferentemente en corregir los desequilibrios internos y externos, reconvertir la industria y hacer de España un país competitivo para incorporarlo a la UEE con posibilidades de éxito[36].

Las líneas maestras de la reconversión propuestas por el ministro de Industria, Carlos Solchaga, se plasmaron en el *Libro Blanco de la reindustrialización* de 1983. Ya en su prólogo explicitaba claramente la necesidad imperiosa de acometer el proceso de reconversión industrial evitando un ajuste salvaje, basado en la supervivencia de los más fuertes y apostando por una intervención que ordenara el salvamento de aquellas partes del tejido industrial que, sometidas a los ajustes necesarios, pudiesen sobrevivir en una próxima incorporación a la CEE[37]. No olvidemos en este punto que la CEE tenía como

El ya presidente de Telefónica Luis Solana Madariaga (1983, 32) se refería al relevo del componente ideológico por el de la racionalidad y la eficacia.

[36] Los intereses de la deuda se multiplicaron por cinco puntos porcentuales y el gasto social creció en casi cinco puntos (Recio y Roca, en Glyn 2001, 193).

[37] El enfoque sectorial o específico de la reestructuración estuvo determinado por el exceso de capacidad, los fallos del mercado y los procesos de producción ineficientes en sectores enteros (Aranzadi 1992, 11); véase asimismo Círculo de Empresarios (1984, 304). Según el análisis de un especialista, el *Libro Blanco* propugnaba reordenar, redimensionar la enver-

horizonte una Europa abierta e innovadora cuya industria asumía el papel de principal motor del crecimiento económico en el futuro inmediato, objetivo inalcanzable sin un clima de negocios sumamente mejorado para desarrollar y aplicar nuevas tecnologías creadoras de riqueza (CEE 1983)[38].

En 1984, los sectores enfrentados en el seno del Gobierno por la reconversión industrial pactaron el modo y la velocidad con que debía aplicarse la misma. El compromiso se situaba en un punto intermedio entre el ajuste duro, auspiciado por los ministros económicos, y el ajuste flexible sin despidos respaldado por una parte de la dirección del partido y por la UGT[39].

Una ley (1984) recogió la «nueva» política económica sobre la reestructuración o reconversión industrial con el objetivo de reducir el acuciante exceso de capacidad en la industria y de proporcionar fondos públicos a cambio de ajuste. Como resultado, muchas empresas en varios sectores industriales no tardaron en recuperar de nuevo la rentabilidad (Catalan 1999, 365-366)[40].

La inflación había descendido hasta el 7%, pero seguía superando a la de los países vecinos. La intensidad del ajuste industrial significó una gran sangría de puestos de trabajo y, finalmente, la crisis dejó enquistado el problema del paro. El desempleo llegó a afectar al 22% de la población activa; solo cuando el crecimiento fue superior al 3% se produjo aumento neto de empleo. Un rasgo de nuestra economía que ha seguido vigente hasta hoy (Sudrià 2012).

El grupo de industrias en que estaba incluido el sector de equipo de telecomunicación presentó ligeras discrepancias en materia de empleo respecto al conjunto de sectores industriales. Este conjunto exhibió por lo general tasas de crecimiento del empleo negativas en el nefasto trienio 1992-1994 –acorde con la profundidad de la crisis de esos años que desembocó en la desaparición de AHV o de algunos astilleros–. Las tasas de crecimiento del empleo en el

---

gadura y empleo de los sectores en crisis y sanear financieramente las empresas para dar paso a inversiones productivas (Fernández Castro 1985, 405). El presidente Felipe González atribuía a la reconversión industrial un papel fundamental para entrar en Europa, a la vez que señalaba que España debía dejar de ser definitivamente «un país débil» en la escena internacional (*El País*, 3 de diciembre de 1983; EEC 1983). Desde una perspectiva comparada, Italia tenía como objetivo promover la innovación tecnológica y el desarrollo de productos y procesos mediante prestamos a bajo interés (Nelson 1993, 253).

[38]   Véase Román (1997) para el conjunto.

[39]   División en el gobierno entre Solchaga y Boyer, por un lado, y Enrique Barón y Alfonso Guerra, por otro (Navarro 1990, 85).

[40]   Como reconocía M. A. Fernández Ordóñez, dentro de la política reformista de los gobiernos socialistas, la reforma del mercado de trabajo fue trascendental porque introdujo el despido libre a través de la contratación temporal (Iglesias 2010).

sector estudiado fueron positivas en la segunda mitad, excepto la correspondiente a 1996. El empleo en el sector de tecnología avanzada –material y equipo eléctrico, electrónico y óptico– cayó a menos de la mitad (Banco de España 2000, 110).

El Instituto Nacional de Industria (INI) recibió poco antes de finalizar 1984 autorización del Gobierno para proceder a las primeras desinversiones, que afectaron a dos empresas (Aranzadi 1989, 258-261)[41]. A partir de 1985, el Instituto privatizó diversas empresas (SEAT, SECOINSA, etc.) con el consiguiente recorte cercano a un 30% del empleo[42].

El programa del PSOE para las elecciones de 1986 abogaba en sus nuevas orientaciones por un sector público en actividades básicas, servicios públicos y sectores estratégicos con el objetivo fundamental de consolidar un conjunto empresarial viable, garante de la competitividad ante la entrada en la CEE. Promovía la reducción de pérdidas a corto plazo mediante el saneamiento financiero, la modernización de instalaciones a través de la innovación y la desconcentración de las decisiones mediante creación de grupos empresariales homogéneos o subholdings[43].

Incorporarse a Europa significó para España que no podría actuar libre de rendición de cuentas a órganos supranacionales. En 1987 se concluyeron varios planes sectoriales de reestructuración y reindustrialización iniciados un trienio antes, que englobaban la industria del cobre, siderurgia, sistemas de automatización electrónica, componentes electrónicos y textiles[44].

Según un balance de 1993, el gobierno había llevado a cabo una política industrial en tres niveles. Comprendía actuaciones normativas orientadas a modificar el marco institucional –leyes de industria y de ordenación del sector petrolero y la ley de ordenación del sistema eléctrico en trámite–, programas de promoción industrial de carácter horizontal –no discriminatorios entre sec-

---

[41] Para mayor precisión, Soler Almirall y Textil Tarazona.

[42] Una postura crítica con la política de reconversión industrial, en Benton (1990, 171); algunos la tachan de neoliberal «concebida para estabilizar la economía mediante la reducción de la inflación y de las pérdidas del sector público» (Montero 2010).

[43] Fernández Marugán, coordinador del programa socialista de 1986 y del sector guerrista, reconocía que el paro era el principal problema con el que se enfrentaba la sociedad española (El País, 26 de noviembre de 1988). Un breve recorrido por los hechos fundamentales de esta etapa (Cinco Días, 20 de junio de 2008); sobre las telecomunicaciones, véase Clifton et al. (ed.) 2014, 133).

[44] La modernización del aparato productivo español entrañó una reestructuración industrial para ponerlo al día, según el líder socialista Felipe González (Bitar y Lowenthal 2015, 371). Para una referencia institucional internacional, véase OCDE (1988, 33).

tores industriales sin homogeneidad estricta desde el punto de vista sectorial– y políticas sectoriales[45].

En las telecomunicaciones, los acontecimientos más significativos fueron las reestructuraciones del grupo industrial de IT&T, del grupo electrónico público del INI y del holding industrial de CTNE. Digamos una vez más, esta operadora de monopolio semipúblico utilizó su considerable poder de compra (cimentado en recursos financieros sustanciales que no dependían del presupuesto estatal) para dos fines industriales paralelos y complementarios. En primer lugar, se esforzó por canalizar inversiones hacia los sectores españoles con capacidad de arrastre y, por otro lado, promovió proyectos de producción conjunta que implicaban la exportación de capital[46].

Esta parte de la estrategia se proponía acceder a las tecnologías más avanzadas en las telecomunicaciones, la microelectrónica, la fibra óptica y la informática por medio de alianzas con los líderes mundiales de los sectores afectados. En consecuencia, se firmaron acuerdos con AT&T para microelectrónica y con Fujitsu para ordenadores (Calvo 2017, 51-62; *New York Times*, 5 de diciembre de 1985)[47]. En general, encajaban dentro del alcance de los planes elaborados por el gobierno, que proporcionaba recursos y apoyo. CTNE se convirtió en un instrumento de política económica que aspiraba a hacer competitivas a las empresas españolas para que pudieran operar en mercados abiertos, asumiendo así parte del papel del Estado en una especie de ministerio de Industria *bis* (*ACE*, 23 de febrero de 1983).

5. Cambios tecnológicos y ajuste de la mano de obra

A lo largo de los años, IT&T se convirtió en un conglomerado con dificultades tecnológicas, sobredimensionado desde un punto de vista legal y financiero pero con una estructura técnica y comercial insuficiente (Suard 2002;

---

[45] *El País*, 24 de junio de 1993.

[46] Luis Solana Madariaga, conversación con el autor, Madrid, 8 de marzo de 2016; Calvo (2016). Conviene no olvidar, sin embargo, que en Francia, por ejemplo, los PTT fueron autorizados a crear compañías financieras, un mecanismo fuertemente impulsor del sector: en la década de 1970, la proporción de las telecomunicaciones en la inversión nacional pasó del 2% a casi el 5%; los créditos de funcionamiento se multiplicaron por cinco y las inversiones por doce (*Le Monde*, 12 de enero de 1984). Solana atribuyó al plan cuatrienal de Telefónica la misión de definir la demanda (*BIT*, junio de 1983, 33).

[47] AT&T reconocía la apuesta de las empresas multinacionales por entrar en los mercados europeos (*AT&T Annual Report*, 1986).

Zanfei 1992, 83-105). Desde los últimos meses de 1985, IT&T se veía inmersa en una verdadera constelación de problemas, que comprendían caídas del dividendo y del precio de las acciones; anónimos y actividades de topo; prensa hostil; la ira de los tradicionales accionistas leales; escepticismo de analistas financieros; posibles fusiones y presencia de tiburones camuflados, por no hablar de propuestas para liquidar la empresa. A pesar de la emoción, el efecto acumulativo tuvo que ser debilitante y distraer del negocio real de funcionamiento de IT&T. Nada más empezar 1985, la multinacional anunció desinversiones de compañías por valor de 1,7 mil millones de dólares. El talón de Aquiles de IT&T estaba en los 10.000 millones de dólares de activos en el extranjero, expuestos a acciones legales y extrajudiciales. Esa extrema vulnerabilidad no resultaba lo suficiente atractiva para un liquidador experto (Araskog 1999, 122, 125, 155 y 156).

En 1973, IT&T contaba con más de 250 empresas asociadas y divisiones en 68 países que empleaban a más de 400.000 personas y operaban en equipos y operaciones de telecomunicaciones y otras seis grandes áreas: productos industriales y de consumo, servicios de consumo, servicios financieros y empresariales, procesamiento de alimentos y servicios, recursos naturales y sistemas espaciales de defensa electrónica (United States. Congress 1973, 209). Entre 1982 y 1984, los ingresos por operaciones del principal negocio europeo de IT&T cayeron drásticamente desde el 9,01% de unas ventas de 7.020 millones de dólares hasta el 7,32% de unas ventas de 5.280 millones. Esa reducción de las ganancias se debió a las pérdidas de divisas, los problemas en su negocio de seguros, los nuevos costes de puesta en marcha de los productos, los mayores gastos de investigación, desarrollo y reestructuración y, precisamente, la competencia severa en equipos de telecomunicación. A pesar del descenso, IT&T trató de mejorar las filiales europeas, realizó algunos cambios estructurales importantes y concibió planes para vender participaciones minoritarias en varias empresas para recaudar dinero, reforzar su valor y abrirlas más ampliamente para contratos gubernamentales poniendo parcialmente la propiedad en manos de los ciudadanos locales. IT&T anunció que invertiría 4.800 millones de dólares en investigación e inversión de capital en Europa en los cinco años siguientes. Más de 2.000 millones de dólares se destinaban a la República Federal Alemana, principalmente para aumentar el desarrollo tecnológico en microelectrónica, comunicaciones y componentes de vehículos de motor (*New York Times*, 17 de enero y 29 de abril de 1985).

Los gerentes de conglomerados estaban descubriendo que podían obtener rendimientos mayores vendiendo activos improductivos y devolviendo los ingresos a los inversionistas o utilizando el efectivo en un grupo más restringido de negocios en crecimiento.

En la estricta política de cartera de IT&T como conglomerado muy heterogéneo en el que las telecomunicaciones eran solo un segmento de la industria entre muchos otros estribarían las auténticas razones de la venta a CGE-Alcatel y no en las necesidades de coordinar sus diversos sistemas (United Nations Conference on Trade and Development 2000, 22)[48].

El notable cambio tecnológico acaecido desde la segunda mitad de la década de los setenta provocó en el mercado mundial de equipos de telecomunicación exceso de empleo directo dedicado hasta el momento a la fabricación de elementos y subconjuntos intensivos en mano de obra. Los fabricantes de estos equipos de telecomunicación se enfrentaban al doble inconveniente de la inexcusable innovación en producto a base de electrónica de alta integración y del reajuste del empleo a las demandas muy inferiores de personal en la fabricación de equipos de conmutación de nuevo tipo (Commission of the European Communities 1990, 28–30).

La industria europea de las telecomunicaciones se vio afectada por el aumento de los costes de desarrollo, la confusión sobre las normas y la desaceleración de las tasas de crecimiento.

Gráfico 4. Principales fabricantes españoles de equipo de telecomunicación. Facturación (millones ptas. corrientes)

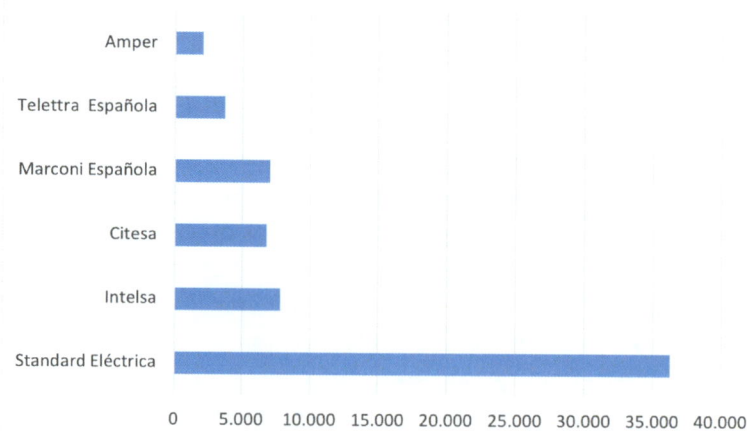

Fuente: Elaboración propia a partir de *BIT*, julio-agosto de 1981, 15.

[48] En 1997, IT&T vendió algo más de la mitad de su participación en Alcatel, una parte de ella a un fondo de inversiones (Ramu 1999, 116).

Tabla 3. La industria de equipo de telecomunicación
en España: principales fabricantes, 1980

Empresa	Facturación (millones ptas. corrientes)	Plantilla	I+D (% sobre facturación)	Suministro a CTNE (% total)
Standard Eléctrica	36.284	17.044	3,25	73*
Intelsa	7.800	3.200	0,13	74
Citesa	6.776	3.100		
Marconi Española	7.003	3.064		
Telettra Española	3.700	1.340	2,80	76
Amper	2.083	869	10,00	53
Total	63.646	28.617	–	-

* Incluye % de Citesa y Marconi Española.
Fuente: Elaboración propia a partir de *BIT*, julio-agosto de 1981, 15.

Por lo que se refiere a España, la industria de equipos de comunicaciones comprendía una treintena de empresas, que empleaban aproximadamente 33.000 personas. He aquí una industria fuertemente concentrada ya que las cinco primeras empresas del sector acaparaban el 89% de la producción total y el 88% de la mano de obra (Gráfico 4 y Tabla 3) (*BIT*, julio-agosto de 1981, 10-11). En su mayoría eran filiales de empresas extranjeras, origen que afectaba también a las licencias bajo las que muchas pequeñas casas fabricaban. CTNE mantenía una participación accionarial importante en Standard Eléctrica –SESA–, Citesa, Intelsa, Telettra Española y Cables de Comunicaciones, proveedores de equipos de la empresa operadora de servicios públicos; a su vez, la operadora era el principal cliente de las empresas. Los fabricantes españoles tenían una presencia en el mercado internacional con ventas que representaban casi el 8% de la producción de la industria hacia 1980 (U.S. Department of Commerce 1977, 95).

El grupo de IT&T en España se componía de tres empresas: Standard Eléctrica, Marconi Española y CITESA, fabricantes de equipos de telefonía y comunicaciones en general con tecnología de origen estadounidense en varias plantas de Madrid, Cantabria en la costa norte y Málaga en el sur. Iban destinados prioritariamente al mercado interior, en especial al estado español. SESA era sin duda la más relevante por el tamaño de la empresa y por la posición aplastante en el mercado interior de equipo[49]. Por su volumen de ventas,

[49] El grueso del capital de SESA estaba en manos de IT&T (65%), mientras el resto se lo repartían CTNE (20%), la luxemburguesa SOLIMO (10%) y diversos inversores privados (5%)

27.000 millones de pesetas en 1975, SESA ocupaba la decimocuarta posición entre las empresas de España y por su volumen de exportaciones la vigésimo segunda. Las cifras escondían mal las dificultades. Si bien ese año las ventas aumentaron un 9% en términos monetarios, en términos reales, descontada la tasa de inflación, habían disminuido. Ese indicio preocupante se complicó a continuación con un ciclo de conflictividad e inestabilidad laboral que jalonaría todos esos años y situaría la empresa a la avanzadilla del movimiento obrero en España.

Si nos situamos en el arranque de la segunda mitad de la década de 1970, SESA se encontró con un cambio en la tendencia declinante de la actividad industrial del mercado interior, compensada por el dinamismo de las exportaciones. En 1977, se esmeró en presentar una cara risueña adornando su imagen con el incremento de las exportaciones (57%) dentro de unas ventas y unos beneficios que superaban en un 19% y 27%, respectivamente, los del ejercicio anterior. En un mercado interno lejos todavía de la saturación, la empresa mantenía sus previsiones de inversión, en buena medida encaminada a potenciar la ya importante investigación tecnológica, en busca de efectos multiplicadores sobre el empleo, y a reducir los riesgos inflacionarios. Fue asimismo el año en que entró en pleno funcionamiento la fábrica de ferritas de Toledo, la tercera planta europea en su especialidad, que abastecía el mercado nacional y exportaba a los de Hispanoamérica y Europa[50].

De hecho, los años finales de la década no estuvieron exentos de dificultades; en 1979 saltó la alarma de las pérdidas en Marconi y al año siguiente sucedió lo propio con las otras dos empresas del grupo IT&T, como veremos. Por si fuera poco, el cambio tecnológico hacía asomar la obsolescencia de numerosos productos y empezaban a sonar los primeros compases de la liberali-

---

(*El País*, 16 de mayo de 1978). Standard Eléctrica aprovechó presuntas irregularidades financieras de sociedades radicadas en América para reivindicar su independencia respecto a la matriz IT&T (*El País*, 18 de mayo 1978).

[50] *El País*, 8 de mayo de 1976. La tasa de penetración del teléfono en España –principal componente de demanda de Standard Eléctrica gracias a sus contratos con Telefónica– era solamente de 24/100 habitantes, diez puntos por debajo de la media de los países de la CEE; la I+D había alcanzado los 1.100 millones de pesetas en 1977 (*El País*, 24 de junio de 1978). Bélgica, Francia, Alemania e Italia eran los principales clientes de ferritas (*El País*, 20 de octubre de 1977). Mayor precisión en 1987: ventas de Alcatel-Standard por 68.277 millones de pesetas, inversión anual de 1.006 millones en activo fijo, gastos laborales totales de 25.998 y unos beneficios antes de costes de reestructuración de 10.283 millones, pero pérdidas netas de 7.569 millones (*SESA, Memoria anual* 1987, 5). Según la *Enciclopedia Británica*, la ferrita es un material de tipo cerámico útil en muchos dispositivos electrónicos debido a sus propiedades magnéticas.

zación del mercado de equipos. Telefónica, cliente principal, repitámoslo una vez más, manejaba datos que revelaban una SESA apegada a la tecnología tradicional, con precios no competitivos –17,5% superiores a los corrientes en el mercado nacional– y pérdida de liderazgo frente a otras casas del grupo IT&T, cuadro amenazador para los intereses de la operadora[51].

El año 1981 aparece en los anales de la empresa como depresivo, debido al desequilibrio entre capacidades productivas y falta de demanda que se arrastraba desde 1976 y a excesivos costes financieros (SESA, *Memoria*, 1981, 1, 4 y 5). Más en detalle, los males comprendían la caída de la actividad productiva en un 3%, graves pérdidas (1.543 millones de ptas.) y enorme volumen de la carga financiera (3.419 millones de ptas.), superior a la del ejercicio anterior en un 31%. A su vez, el descenso de la actividad productiva obedecía a la práctica estabilización de las inversiones de las entidades explotadoras de telecomunicaciones, en particular la CTNE, así como por cambios en la estructura de las inversiones, con descenso del suministro de equipos procedentes del sector industrial, junto al impacto del cambio tecnológico[52].

De ahí arrancó la necesidad de un plan de reordenación industrial de SESA en sus aspectos financieros, laborales y tecnológicos, basado en la contribución equilibrada de todos los implicados (SESA, *Memoria*, 1981, 5).

Ya conocemos la sensibilidad del sector a los impactos de las innovaciones tecnológicas y la consiguiente rápida obsolescencia de los productos. Siendo importante la cronología, vamos a examinar con cierto detenimiento las posiciones de partida de los protagonistas. Todos los indicios apuntan a una ofensiva general lanzada por IT&T para lidiar con la digitalización que condenaba su tecnología electromecánica a la caducidad y parte de su fuerza laboral al desempleo[53].

En la negociación de los convenios colectivos, momento clave para los protagonistas, el grupo IT&T lanzó una oferta de exiguas alzas salariales, por debajo de las expectativas de los sindicatos más influyentes, es decir, Comisiones Obreras (CCOO) y la Unión General de Trabajadores (UGT). Los analistas más finos

---

[51] *El País,* 1 de noviembre de 1983.

[52] No obstante, SESA consideraba razonable el nivel de endeudamiento (crédito bancario de 16.515 millones de ptas., frente a 18.577 de recursos propios) (SESA, *Memoria*, 1981, p. 5).

[53] La doctrina oficial estadounidense achacaba la movilidad laboral a los avances económicos y tecnológicos. Cierres de fábricas, recortes de producción o eliminación de un trabajo en particular ocasionaron 1,3 millones de cambios de empleo. La tasa de desempleo de los trabajadores desplazados –14% en 1988– superaba con creces la tasa nacional de paro y más de la cuarta parte de los que encontraron nuevos empleos a tiempo completo vieron caer sus haberes por encima de un 20 por ciento (Economic Report 1990, 163).

de las centrales obreras no llegaban a ver claro en los motivos aunque sí advertían en IT&T prisas por enmendar inversiones erróneas de los últimos años, causantes del deterioro de la estructura financiera y de pérdidas cuantiosas[54].

Si la negociación de los convenios fue una piedra de toque, SESA no tardó en anunciar una sustancial reestructuración de instalaciones y de plantillas, motivada por un ejercicio «muy desfavorable» achacable a los fuertes desajustes entre la oferta y la demanda, causa del sobredimensionamiento –unos 3.700 trabajadores ociosos, el 20% de las plantillas– y a las fuertes cargas financieras[55]. Como señalaba Luis Solana desde su escaño en el Congreso, el presidente de IT&T, en medio de una crisis mundial del sector, se desplazó a España espantado de la inacción del gobierno y del absentismo de la CTNE, que él motejaba de «liberalismo». La Intelsa de Ericsson presentó un expediente ante el exceso de jornada laboral y de personal[56].

[54]   En su característico tono vibrante, el por entonces diputado socialista y miembro de UGT Luis Solana barajaba varias razones de la actitud de IT&T (desinterés de la multinacional por España y la búsqueda de una deslocalización de la producción; deseo de irritar a las centrales sindicales y desviar las presiones hacia la CTNE, dando lugar a más pedidos y mejores precios, estrategia ya ensayada infructuosamente; búsqueda del apoyo del Gobierno para reducir la plantilla de IT&T según una secuencia choque laboral-laudo-expediente de crisis, con externalización de los costes). A través de Solana la UGT reclamaba un triple plan de consolidación de las estructuras de capital, de incorporación de las tecnologías de punta del grupo, con el reparto de trabajo por áreas geográficas, de incorporación de nuevos productos y desarrollo de investigaciones, medido todo en disminución de *royalties*. El objetivo era una negociación salarial dentro de una banda general y mantenimiento en lo posible del empleo mediante un reparto equitativo del impacto económico y laboral de la innovación (*El País*, 22 de enero de 1981).

[55]   La reducción de las inversiones de Telefónica como efecto de una disminución de la demanda pendía como espada de Damocles sobre SESA y agravaba los planes de reducción de plantilla de Standard Eléctrica concebidos desde la cúspide de IT&T (*El País*, 18 de septiembre de 1981).

[56]   Solana Madariaga (1981). Solana apuntaba la posibilidad de que el grupo IT&T en España albergara la esperanza de que el Gobierno le costease una regulación de empleo del orden de 3.000 trabajadores. Resulta inexplicable el silencio del gobierno ante las cuatro preguntas que formuló Solana en el Congreso, que, reseñadas textualmente, eran las siguientes: 1. ¿Presentó o comentó el Presidente de IT&T al Ministro de Industria algún plan de esta multinacional para sus filiales en España?; 2. Si presentó algún plan o lo comentó, ¿solicitó o dio por sentado algún apoyo del Estado?; 3. Si lo solicitó o lo consideró, ¿podría el Gobierno hacer público el plan o los comentarios comunicados por el Presidente de IT&T al Ministro de Industria?; 4. Si no hizo presentación de ningún plan ni lo comentó, ¿de qué hablaron el presidente de IT&T y el Ministro de Industria? Así finalizaba Solana su escrito: «Señor Araskog, usted me regaló una corbata con las siglas IT&T repetidas en colores elegantes; yo prometo regalarle otra corbata con repetidos colores rojos y amarillos si nos ayuda a despertar a este Gobierno de su siesta quinquenal y si se anima a apostar por la electrónica en España. Ya sé que es usted un tipo racional y que estos envites le dejan frío –como debe ser, supongo–, pero no crea que toda España es como el Gobierno; somos

Queda meridianamente claro que entre una primera toma de contacto del presidente de IT&T, Rand Araskog, calificada de «cortesía», y una segunda visita de contenidos, la multinacional norteamericana diseñó su plan de reestructuración de SESA[57]. En esa segunda estancia en España, el alto ejecutivo mantuvo reuniones con los directivos de su filial y se entrevistó con representantes del gobierno al máximo nivel –el presidente Felipe González y el ministro de Industria– y con el presidente de CTNE[58].

A la constatación sin reservas de la crisis de la empresa, el Plan de reordenación industrial aprobado el 20 de julio de 1982 pretendía resolver las estrecheces de financiación, nivel de demanda, costes y mercado de trabajo. Según sus términos, SESA veía reforzada su estructura financiera por varias vías: acceso a un crédito oficial por 4.000 millones de ptas., aportación de 3.062,5 millones de pesetas por los accionistas a la recapitalización, una segunda ampliación de capital de 6.125 mp y renuncia al reparto de dividendos por los accionistas. Los costes se veían aliviados por partida doble mediante la reducción en más de la mitad de los cánones que correspondían a IT&T por asistencia técnica y por absorción por CTNE de un mínimo de 300 empleados anuales durante cuatro años. La superación del desequilibrio entre capacidades y demanda se fiaba a la fijación de pedidos de CTNE a SESA, cifrados en 630.000 líneas telefónicas anuales en 1982-1984 (SESA, *Memoria* 1982, 6).

SESA se acogió repetidamente a las posibilidades que ofrecía la legislación en las situaciones críticas de las empresas. En 1982, SESA formuló dos expedientes de regulación de empleo. El primero consistió en ceses definitivos de

muchos más los que alimentamos la esperanza, aunque usted no los haya visitado estos días; lo siento. Pero vamos a ver si a pesar de unos y de otros llegamos a tiempo. Aún».

[57] El viaje de Araskog tuvo lugar poco después del anuncio a la prensa internacional (*Financial Times*) de un posible desgajamiento de la sección de comunicaciones de IT&T a la que se destinaban inversiones cercanas a los 150 millones de dólares anuales, para convertirla en empresa independiente e incluso llegar a algún acuerdo con otras compañías internacionales del sector (*El País*, 8 de enero de 1982).

[58] *El País*, 21 de enero de 1983. Resultaba verosímil suponer que IT&T había comunicado al ministro de Industria sus planes a corto y largo plazo sobre sus filiales en España: Pregunta formulada por el Diputado don Luis Solana Madariaga, del grupo parlamentario socialista del Congreso, relativa a visita del Presidente de IT&T a España (*BOCG*, 2647-1, 9 de diciembre de 1981, 5.495); Pregunta del Diputado don Santiago Carrillo Solares, del Grupo Parlamentario Mixto, relativa a situación en Standard Eléctrica, S.A., (Congreso de los diputados, 2 de marzo de 1983, 233). Araskog se entrevistó posteriormente con el presidente de Telefónica, Luis Solana. En junio de 1983, Felipe González volvió a coincidir con Araskog en Nueva York bajo el patrocinio de Rockefeller, poco después que este visitase España de regreso de una cumbre de la Comisión Trilateral.

contrato mediante bajas voluntarias por prejubilación a los cincuenta y ocho años, indemnizadas o por trasvase a CTNE. Fue asumido por la Administración y consensuado con la representación obrera de la empresa. El segundo expediente se diferenció del anterior en dos aspectos: tomó la forma de suspensión temporal y parcial de contratos –seis meses y 1.300 trabajadores– y no contó con el respaldo de la representación de los trabajadores. En otras palabras, las posiciones se habían endurecido notablemente y se auguraba una etapa complicada. A lo largo de 1982, la plantilla de SESA se había reducido en un total de 1.700 personas[59].

A primeros de 1983, Standard Eléctrica empezó a tramitar un nuevo expediente, esta vez con suspensión temporal de 1.213 contratos durante veinticuatro meses[60]. Para desterrar cualquier aproximación simplista a problemas complejos, recogemos algunos detalles, a modo de ejemplo, de las implicaciones que representaba la tramitación de un ERE. Con la presentación del nuevo expediente, la Dirección General de Empleo (DGE) celebró reuniones con la empresa y los sindicatos previas a la finalización del periodo de consultas. A ellas asistieron el director general de Electrónica e Informática del ministerio de Industria y Energía y un representante de la CTNE. Al no haber alcanzado una salida pactada diferente a la planteada por la empresa, la DGE, aceptó los planteamientos de la empresa –situación de excedente real de plantilla– y resolvió una medida de carácter temporal. Los principios en los que se basó fueron el menor coste posible para los trabajadores, el reparto equitativo de estos costes de la crisis entre los trabajadores de la empresa y la subordinación a la solución del futuro defendida por el ministerio de Trabajo y Seguridad Social, a saber, un acuerdo entre empresa y trabajadores con jubilaciones anticipadas, bajas incentivadas y absorción parcial por otras empresas de los excedentes laborales. Por Resolución de 25 de febrero la DGE redujo a 1.170

---

[59] El segundo contó con el pláceme del gobierno, que desestimó el contrainforme sindical que denunciaba la falsedad de la situación de crisis y rechazando el recurso de alzada basado en defectos de forma: Pregunta del Diputado don Santiago Carrillo Solares, del Grupo Parlamentario Mixto, relativa a situación en Standard Eléctrica, S.A. (Congreso de los diputados, 2 de marzo de 1983, 233; *ABC,* 22 de septiembre de 1982). UGT acusaba a IT&T de presionar a la Administración con los expedientes de regulación de empleo presentados en Standard, Marconi y CITESA en las negociaciones de carácter secreto que mantenían. Para el sindicato, la dureza de IT&T a la hora de negociar con los comités de empresa indicaba que utilizaba presuntamente los expedientes de regulación de empleo como arma y condición absoluta para tratar cualquier tema (*El País,* 1 de abril de 1982).

[60] El 28 de enero, SESA comunicó a la Dirección General de Empleo del ministerio de Trabajo y Seguridad Social el inicio del periodo de consultas previo a la presentación del expediente de regulación: Pregunta del Diputado don Santiago Carrillo Solares, del Grupo Parlamentario Mixto, relativa a situación en Standard Eléctrica, S.A. (Congreso de los Diputados, 2 de marzo de 1983, 468).

trabajadores la suspensión de relaciones laborales de los 1.213 trabajadores propuestos por la empresa y a seis meses la duración, en lugar de veinticuatro meses solicitados. Los trabajadores afectados debían ser obligatoriamente diferentes a los implicados por suspensiones anteriores. La Resolución contemplaba la imposición de un complemento del subsidio de desempleo a cargo de la empresa, equivalente a la totalidad del salario y con carácter coyuntural para evitar ahogar económicamente a la empresa. La Resolución incluía una invitación a la patronal para poner en práctica de manera inmediata las propuestas alternativas realizadas por los trabajadores; el compromiso de reemplazar las bajas producidas en la empresa mediante la reincorporación de personal incluido en el expediente. Por último, la Resolución emplazaba a las partes a negociar las medidas encaminadas a corregir de una manera definitiva los desequilibrios de personal existentes[61].

En la esfera política, la izquierda parlamentaria se mostraba clarividente en la percepción de una remodelación de plantillas a medio plazo, fundamentalmente por la negativa inicial de las distintas empresas a negociar su periodificación y salidas alternativas para utilizar al máximo la capacidad productiva de los equipos y de las plantillas. Standard Eléctrica representaba el auténtico paradigma de empresas que seguían la doble estrategia de buscar drásticas reducciones de empleo, anticipándose incluso a los efectos negativos reales del cambio tecnológico, y de hacer recaer sobre las arcas públicas los costes de dichas reducciones y de los planes industriales anejos[62].

Pero volvamos a las posiciones de salida de los protagonistas en los siguientes episodios a punto de desencadenarse, según el esquema que se ha trazado en el primer apartado de estas páginas.

Desde el gobierno, los responsables de la política industrial, situados en el ala liberal del PSOE, se oponían a una planificación centralizada de la reindustrialización y a destinar recursos públicos para subvencionar empresas o sectores dudosamente rentables. En ese sentido, cuestionaba la atribución al Estado de la elección de los sectores y actividades de éxito en el futuro sin un ajuste industrial flexible en los sectores en crisis y una reducción general del

---

[61]   Contestación formulada por el Gobierno a la pregunta del Diputado don Santiago Carrillo Solares, del Grupo Parlamentario Mixto, relativa a situación en Standard Eléctrica, S.A. (Congreso de los Diputados, 2 de marzo de 1983, 469).

[62]   Pregunta del Diputado don Santiago Carrillo Solares, del Grupo Parlamentario Mixto, relativa a situación en Standard Eléctrica, S.A. (Congreso de los diputados, 2 de marzo de 1983, 233).

proteccionismo[63]. El máximo responsable del área, Solchaga, amparaba una política de reindustrialización tendente a una movilización de recursos productivos desde determinados sectores profundamente afectados por la crisis, como el siderúrgico y el naval, hacia otros con porvenir, entre ellos el de la electrónica, la alimentación o el de material de defensa. El gobierno, con Solchaga al mando, propugnaba dejar de dar prioridad al saneamiento financiero y al ajuste del empleo en los sectores en declive para reorientar los recursos públicos y privados hacia la creación de empleos alternativos. La nueva política de reindustrialización incluía un conjunto de medidas de cobertura, cuyos rasgos más salientes comprendían medidas financieras, medidas de cobertura regional y diseño del perfil tecnológico de los sectores en crisis y de la contribución de las tecnologías importadas así como su coste, principalmente cuando existieran multinacionales implicadas en los planes de reconversión. En este sentido, se proclamaba la necesidad de profundizar y revisar los planes de reconversión en marcha para las empresas de componentes electrónicos, aquejados hasta entonces de fuertes deficiencias[64].

En las entrevistas de las autoridades españolas con representantes de IT&T, la actitud fue de respaldo a la continuidad de la multinacional en España, en su condición de eje de la industria de la telefonía. En ellas se hizo palpable la voluntad de dicha empresa en colaborar con la política del Gobierno, especialmente en el fomento de las exportaciones españolas hacia América Latina y otros países, y la preocupación del Gobierno sobre la situación del empleo en el Grupo IT&T de España[65].

---

[63]   Ministerio de Industria y Energía (1983); Solchaga (1997, 57); *El País,* 9 de 6 de 1983. El portavoz del grupo mixto en el Congreso de los diputados afeó al Gobierno la falta de política de I+D y le conminó a presentar con carácter urgente un proyecto de Ley sobre reindustrialización que incluyese la política de reconversión, de desarrollo tecnológico y de promoción industrial (*Boletín Oficial de las Cortes Generales (BOCG)*, 3 de agosto de 1983).

[64]   La canalización de recursos financieros hacia la incentivación de nuevos proyectos de inversión con futuro se llevaría a cabo con cobertura social suficiente para hacer viable el ajuste, es decir, a través de los fondos de promoción de empleo, con el respaldo del sistema bancario cuya misión fundamental era la gestión activa del colectivo afectado por la reconversión, con un objetivo básico: el de su reinserción en el sistema productivo. Solchaga desglosaba tres fases en el proceso de actuación concreta: la fase de análisis de los planes de viabilidad; la toma de decisiones y tramitación de las ayudas y, en tercer lugar, la fase de gestión y seguimiento de los planes: Acta taquigráfica de la sesión celebrada por la comisión de Industria, obras públicas y servicios el martes, día 22 de febrero de 1983, con asistencia del señor Ministro de industria y Energía (Solchaga Catalán, 13-15).

[65]   Contestación del Gobierno a la pregunta formulada por don Santiago Carrillo Solares, del Grupo Parlamentario Mixto, sobre situación de Standard Eléctrica, S. A. (*BOCG*, 20, 11 de abril de 1983, 468). Política del gobierno: Acta taquigráfica de la sesión celebrada por la

Desde el terreno empresarial, IT&T estaba ya lejos de su etapa de gloria y su imagen había sido dañada por comportamientos poco éticos para hablar con suavidad[66]. En una apuesta estratégica, IT&T optó por el ESS (sistema de conmutación electrónica, por sus siglas en inglés) 12 (Sistema 12), la serie más versátil de la que formaba parte el Sistema 1240 y que fue retirada de los mercados de EE. UU. debido a problemas en el *software* y en su adaptación al entorno doméstico (Chapuis y Joel 2003, 570. Dicha tecnología fue diseñada para responder a los requisitos del futurista Network 2000, explotaba la estructura modular y tenía una capacidad de hasta 100.000 líneas (Viswanathan y Bhatnagar 2015). Pese al gran esfuerzo financiero dedicado –unos 1.000 millones de dólares invertidos–, una serie de problemas obstaculizaron su implantación en el mercado mundial. El proyecto sufrió retrasos debido a una serie de barreras técnicas insalvables, sobre todo por dificultades en la adaptación del *software* a los estándares USA –RDSI, encaminamientos según mínimo coste– y de homologación en Europa. IT&T interpretó de forma errónea la estructura del mercado de la conmutación digital en EE. UU., dominado por los competidores. No pocos achacaron los problemas a la fragmentación del desarrollo de esa tecnología entre la casa madre de EE. UU. y las distintas filiales de IT&T en Europa, con el consiguiente fracaso a la hora de integrar sus conocimientos y recursos técnicos dispersos (Bartlett y Ghoshal 2002, 13)[67].

Después de concentrar el empeño en EE. UU., IT&T decidió coordinar los esfuerzos europeos desde el Centro Internacional de Telecomunicaciones (CCI) en Bruselas. La multinacional atravesaba por serias contrariedades en su sección europea de conmutación (Gambardella y Malerba 1999, 142)[68]. La

comisión de Industria, obras públicas y servicios el 22 de febrero de 1983, con asistencia del señor ministro de Industria y Energía (Solchaga Catalán, 14).

[66] El órgano de prensa del PSOE en el exilio, apoyándose en la campaña de prensa norteamericana contra el monopolio, tachaba a la IT&T de «empresa multinacional monstruosa» por su implicación en actuaciones contra el Gobierno de Allende en Chile, en abusos por su tamaño gigantesco y en sobornos a funcionarios públicos (*Le Socialiste*, 18 de mayo de 1972, 5-6).

[67] En 1986, el Sistema 12 había sido homologado en diversos países, entre ellos Noruega, Bélgica, Suiza, República Federal de Alemania o Italia. IT&T firmó acuerdos en 21 países para el suministro de 12,5 millones de líneas telefónicas, de las que se habían entregado 1,3 millones hasta septiembre de dicho año. Interesantes precisiones sobre la adaptación al mercado noruego según el consabido esquema colaborativo y adopción del Sistema 12 en Noruega los ofrece Christensen (2006, 288).

[68] En manera alguna estaba libre de errores en España. Muestra de diversidad: en Francia el primer sistema de conmutación electrónica operacional (1968) se instaló bajo los auspicios del CNET con el nombre de RITA (Réseau Intégré de Transmission Automatique pour

más alta autoridad de Standard Eléctrica reconoció la difícil situación del grupo IT&T en España y se vio obligada a desmentir los temores a un abandono del país[69].

Analicemos los argumentos en el arranque de la década de 1980 que hagan más comprensible el carácter de la reconversión de la empresa. Para empezar por el más de conjunto, el ejecutivo de SESA achacaba la difícil situación por la que atravesaba la empresa a la evolución tecnológica y a la caída de la demanda por parte de Telefónica, como consecuencia de la crisis económica. Por lo demás, tenía la convicción de que fuerzas sociales y económicas del país aceptaban la «idea de una industria fuertemente dinámica, sometida a las leyes inexorables del mercado y llamada, por tanto, a una continua transformación». Desde este punto de partida, abogaba por un proceso gradual, aun a sabiendas de obligadas concesiones, que habrían de ser temporales y asumidas hasta sus últimas consecuencias por todos los implicados en una atmósfera de consenso. En este horizonte aparecía con claridad la necesidad de una flexibilización moderada de plantillas en la industria por resultar aún inalcanzable una más completa debido a su elevado coste social y político. El dirigente sabía que, en general, causas de la situación, nivel de gravedad y

Application Militaire): el progreso en FSS se aceleró (Das 2003, 5). Las centrales debían ser modificadas para adaptarlas a las peculiaridades nacionales –cantidad diferente de dígitos en sus números de teléfono y diferentes esquemas de llamada, entre muchas otras características diferentes– (*New York Times*, 27 de junio de 1986). El coste de adaptar el Sistema 12 al mercado norteamericano ascendió a 200 millones de dólares (Fransman (1995, 80). En 1985, AT&T y Northern Telecom –presente en EE. UU. mucho antes del desmembramiento de AT&T y favorecida por el hecho de que el sistema telefónico canadiense era prácticamente idéntico al estadounidense– detentaban el 41,95 y el 45% del mercado estadounidense de centrales, respectivamente (*New York Times*, 27 de junio de 1986; *BIT*, marzo de 1986, 11; *Business Week*, 2.797-2.805, 1983); detalles sobre el proceso de creación (Hendry y Eccles 1992). El cese del desarrollo del Sistema 12 en EE. UU. para concentrar esfuerzos en Europa provocaron la deslocalización de un centenar de los 1.200 puestos de trabajo suspendidos en las fábricas de IT&T en Raleigh, Delaware, Ohio; Shelton, CONN. y Cape Cañaveral, FLA; la empresa admitió un posible traslado de los empleados a Europa (*New York Times*, 14 de febrero de 1986). La expatriación de mano de obra entrañaba transferencia de conocimiento. Un estudio sobre las razones esgrimidas por las empresas italianas a la hora de relocalizar parte de su producción en el exterior, referido a los años 2001-2003, sitúa la búsqueda de factores de producción (mano de obra y materias primas) a bajo costo en primer lugar – más de la mitad de empresas– seguida de la mayor proximidad a los mercados –12%– y de la reducción de los precios –24%– a través de una reducción en los costes de transporte o de una mejor combinación de factores productivos (Castellani 2007, 469).

69   Comparecencia Manuel Márquez Balín, presidente de Standard Eléctrica para informar sobre los planes de inversiones a medio plazo en el sector de las comunicaciones (Congreso de los diputados, Sesión del 2 de enero de 1982; *El País*, 3 de febrero de 1982).

posibilidades de recuperación muy diversas dificultaban cualquier política de reconversión eficaz. España añadía a esta dificultad la ausencia de tradición competitiva, herencia del intervencionismo y el proteccionismo de etapas anteriores[70].

SESA se presentaba como una superviviente de las crisis y quiebras bancarias propias de la economía española posdictatorial gracias a los contratos privilegiados de suministro de CTNE, que le proporcionaba un 73% de los beneficios. En esta situación, el estancamiento de las ventas en el mercado interior y la debilidad de las exportaciones pintaban un cuadro sombrío que se completó con las pérdidas mencionadas. La inmediatez de la entrada de España en la CEE había colocado a SESA en un mercado ferozmente competitivo.

En un ejercicio de investigación participativa realizado por la cúpula, SESA pudo poner el dedo en la llaga al descubrir una serie de problemas. En lo fundamental, sobraba énfasis en la preocupación por encajar las personalidades en la empresa y faltaba una auténtica estrategia. Por otra parte, había adoptado el sistema descentralizado de IT&T, que concedía autonomía presupuestaria a las filiales respaldada por proyecciones mecánicas de resultados y no por un análisis serio del mercado. SESA debía transitar por el camino del aumento de la productividad que le garantizase el dominio del mercado español, aumento de la cuota internacional de mercado y reducción de la dependencia respecto a CTNE a través de la diversificación (Kippenberger 1998, 37-40; Palmer y Tunstall 1990, 152)[71].

El proceso complejo en torno a SESA comenzó a mediados de 1983. El Gobierno consideraba el problema de IT&T como puramente tecnológico, debido a su dependencia de equipos de telecomunicaciones algo obsoletos. En consecuencia, rechazó el proyecto de reconversión que la multinacional le presentó en junio de 1983 por considerarlo escasamente favorable a los intereses de España. Por su parte, pidió a la multinacional una participación más amplia en planes de reestructuración, pero se mostró tolerante con los ajustes de personal[72]. Administración e IT&T entablaron negociaciones sobre el plan, en el que se contemplaba la reducción de 6.500 empleos, para explorar vías

---

[70] *El País*, 22 de febrero de 1981.

[71] La empresa diversificó su base de ingresos: la cuota de Telefónica en los ingresos cayó del 73% en 1984 a menos de la mitad en 1994 (Chakravarthy 1996, 532).

[72] *ABC*, 30 de septiembre de 1983.

de salida[73]. La Administración se inclinaba por apoyar propuestas de la multinacional a cambio de unos principios de respeto a la innovación tecnológica en el país, fomento de las exportaciones, sustitución de importaciones, mayor diversificación de productos y diversas contrapartidas pertinentes. Frente a ello, Standard Eléctrica seguía con su visión negativa –sobredimensionamiento de la plantilla– y escasa capacidad de creación de puestos de trabajo –medio millar–[74].

En el nuevo plan presentado, IT&T introducía una serie de modificaciones en la cuantía del excedente y en la forma de llevar adelante el proceso. Así, rebajaba el excedente laboral fijado anteriormente a 2.800 trabajadores, incorporaba un programa para evitar traumas sociales y preveía crear 2.100 empleos en la fabricación de productos de alta tecnología para la exportación[75].

El Ejecutivo designó una comisión negociadora del plan sobre el futuro de las empresas españolas de IT&T, presidida por el director general de Electrónica e Informática. Pero las disensiones en su seno sobre los planes para la multinacional retrasaron el inicio de las negociaciones.

Las centrales sindicales mayoritarias –CCOO y UGT– hacían recaer en la sección española de IT&T la responsabilidad de frenar el ritmo de destrucción de puestos de trabajo, consecuencia de la reestructuración del grupo, con un programa de empleos alternativos, paralelos a las inversiones de la CTNE y de las ayudas estatales. Ambos sindicatos abogaban por vías no traumáticas de ajustar la plantilla a las necesidades reales de producción, entre ellas la reducción de jornada, factible por el aumento de la productividad y la rentabilidad de los productos de telecomunicación, jubilaciones anticipadas voluntarias más bajas incentivadas y, sobre todo, trasvase de personal a la CTNE. Dichas medidas debían completarse con el aumento de las exportaciones y la diversificación en productos[76].

---

[73]   El País, 28 de septiembre de 1983; ABC, 30 de septiembre de 1983. Se creó un grupo de trabajo para la posterior negociación del nuevo plan (El País, 13 de noviembre de 1983).

[74]   El País, 30 de septiembre de 1983.

[75]   La estimación de exportaciones para 1986 pasó de 8.700 millones de pesetas a 22.200; por otra parte, el mantenimiento de 1.000 puestos de trabajo en el año 1986 se confiaba a un incremento de la demanda de la CTNE (El País, 13 de noviembre de 1983).

[76]   Los proyectos de IT&T suponían la desaparición de más de 6.000 puestos de trabajo. A juicio de CC OO, IT&T perseguía tres objetivos: asegurar la demanda de la CTNE, limitar la diversificación de productos y doblegar a los sindicatos en sus propuestas de despidos (El País, 30 de septiembre de 1983). En la «vía obrera» a la diversificación, CCOO reclamaba ampliar la gama de productos en campos diferentes a la telecomunicación y un trato para las filiales españolas similar al concedido a las alemanas y belgas. UGT insistía en una po-

A caballo entre los últimos días de 1983 y primeros del año siguiente, se sucedieron dos propuestas, con un cambio sustancial entre las mismas a juicio de la parte sindical, UGT en la ocasión, que añadieron nuevos desgarros[77].

Las discusiones dejaron paso a la actividad legislativa, plasmada en el Real Decreto de reconversión 1.380/1984. Las empresas afectadas no fueron las tres del grupo sino dos –SESA y Marconi Española– al quedar descartada CITESA, ya integrada en SESA[78]. El argumento central de la reconversión reposaba en la situación del mercado mundial ya señalada, a lo que se añadía el descenso en la demanda interna y exterior de los productos que fabricaban. El objetivo radicaba en garantizar la viabilidad de las empresas desde el punto de vista industrial y financiero así como en recuperar las cuotas de mercado en los nuevos equipos de conmutación electrónica y en garantizar el máximo posible de empleo, edulcorada expresión del redimensionamiento de las empresas.

El Plan se obligaba a mejorar las condiciones de competitividad mediante la reordenación que en sus aspectos técnicos suponía la introducción de nuevas tecnologías, en los financieros la realización de nuevas inversiones y en los sociales la generación de nuevos empleos. Se trataba de fabricar nuevos productos destinados fundamentalmente a la exportación con el fin de crear puestos de trabajo alternativos y mejorar la balanza comercial española[79].

Después de un proceso complejo, la primera etapa de la reestructuración de las filiales españolas de IT&T llegó con el acuerdo multipartito de 1984, que combinaba los compromisos de todos los diferentes actores involucra-

---

lítica agresiva de sustitución de importaciones en la rama de la electrónica, apoyada por la exigencia de contrapartidas a IT&T por parte de CTNE (*El País,* 12 de septiembre de 1983).

[77] Las modificaciones introducidas en la última propuesta de acuerdo presentada por la Administración se referían a incentivos para jubilaciones anticipadas y para los trabajadores que pasasen de SESA a la operadora. UGT se negaba a admitir que las indemnizaciones a los trabajadores que se acogiesen a la jubilación anticipada a los 55 años se cobrasen al cumplir los 60 como proponía la nueva redacción de la propuesta (*El País*, 20 de 1 de 1984). Los representantes de los trabajadores en las tres empresas de IT&T en España adoptaron medidas de presión para formar parte de la comisión tripartita –Administración, CTNE e IT&T– encargada de elaborar el futuro plan estratégico e industrial de IT&T en España (*ABC*, 23 de junio de 1983).

[78] La absorción de CITESA fue aprobada en noviembre de 1982 y se ejecutó una vez resueltos pormenores de distinto tipo (SESA, *Memoria* 1982, 6).

[79] Inversiones por un valor mínimo total de 9.700 millones de pesetas en 1984-1986; nuevos empleos: 350 en 1984, 1.050 en 1985, 1.750 en 1986 y 350 en 1987; situar las exportaciones en 1984, 1985 y 1986, respectivamente, en 12.000, 18.000 y 26.500 millones de pesetas (*BOE*, 177, 25 de 7 de 1984, 21.876-21.877). Plan aprobado por la Comisión Delegada del Gobierno para Asuntos Económicos, en su reunión de primeros de junio de 1984.

dos. Dentro de una reestructuración más integral de su presencia internacional, IT&T acordó reubicar a 2.000 trabajadores estadounidenses en España; CTNE crearía 1.000 empleos; el gobierno promovería actividades de I+D en la empresa y le otorgaría beneficios fiscales; los sindicatos consentían en despidos y bajas voluntarias.[80]

En las difíciles y complejas negociaciones sobre el futuro de SESA, IT&T y CTNE pasaron a centrar su preocupación por la cuestión de las ganancias y el precio del Sistema 1240. La revisión de acuerdos anteriores posibilitó concretar un programa de entregas de SESA a CTNE, así como nuevos precios de equipos de conmutación y subsidios de CTNE para SESA. IT&T acordó crear empleos (700 durante 1985) reubicando parte de la producción de otras empresas del grupo en tres plantas españolas. El plan comenzaría con la construcción de una nueva planta para terminales telefónicos en la fábrica de SESA en Villaverde (Madrid), que alcanzaría la plena capacidad de producción y la integración en un plazo muy corto de tiempo (a principios de 1986). En la segunda fase, una fuerza de trabajo reubicada aumentaría tanto la fábrica de conmutación en Madrid como la de cable en Cantabria.[81]

Telefónica y Standard Eléctrica limaron sus diferencias con un acuerdo amplio por el que la primera otorgó a la segunda la calificación técnica provisional del Sistema 12– las centrales digitales más avanzadas–, cerrando las dudas planteadas por el funcionamiento de dicho sistema de conmutación con nuevos suministros y abriendo nuevas posibilidades a la exportación y al saneamiento financiero de la empresa. Telefónica se comprometía a comprar a

---

[80]   El acuerdo incluyó términos que afecaban el futuro de Marconi. IT&T acordó invertir 49.000 millones de pesetas en España durante cinco años y emplear 2.250 nuevos puestos de trabajo a fabricar productos de alta tecnología para la exportación (*El País*, 24 de septiembre de 1984). El plan fue aprobado por referéndum y aceptado solo por uno de los sindicatos (UGT) (*UGT-Metal*, marzo de 1983).

[81]   *LACA*, 19 de diciembre de 1984, 27 de marzo de 1985 y 30 de enero de 1985. SESA firmó un contrato (en el marco de la política industrial socialista) con US Digital Equipment Corporation de los Estados Unidos para la fabricación de terminales de ordenador (*El País*, 18 de mayo de 1985). Como indicador de los intentos de reestructurar el control oligopólico a nivel mundial, la multinacional Siemens planeaba adquirir la fábrica de cables de SESA y pasarla a la fibra óptica para diversificar el suministro de cable y reducir la cuota de mercado de IT&T (*LACA*, 4 de octubre de 1985). Según una información, al cabo de dos años, Siemens llegó incluso a poner sus miras en la compra de Standard Eléctrica (Antonio de Luna Aguado, Agrupación Parlamentaria del Partido Liberal, *Boletín Oficial de las Cortes Generales*, 1.357, Senado, 3.541). La fábrica cántabra de cable se convirtió en reducto en tecnología del cobre hasta 1999, año inicial de una mayor inversión en fibra óptica (Canalejo 2020, 56).

Standard Eléctrica 200.000 líneas del Sistema 12 en dos años y 253.000 del sistema electromecánico Pentaconta como promedio anual. Ambas acordaron colaborar en los mercados de exportación de forma que Telefónica Internacional se convertía en canal de comercialización de la producción de SESA, incluido el Sistema 12, con todo lo que suponía de red de relaciones con empresas de telecomunicaciones y organismos supranacionales[82]. No podemos pasar por alto la superioridad numérica de la tecnología electromecánica en la demanda. La razón primordial de esta opción estribaba en las complementariedades e imposiciones de las opciones tecnológicas previas. Frente a los retos de la reducción de costes de explotación y de la mejora de la calidad, Telefónica puso a punto un dispositivo que se acoplaba a las centrales automáticas PC-1000 y ARF, en realidad un puro remedio ante la falta de alternativas y de recorrido corto[83]. Fundamental para el presente estudio, el apego a la que podría considerarse tecnología desfasada, más intensiva en trabajo, dio

[82] SESA participó, nótese, junto a Telefónica, en el desarrollo de la conmutación más avanzada, las centrales del Sistema 12 de IT&T, y en concreto de sus aplicaciones rurales en uno de los seis centros de diseño de IT&T en el mundo (Calvo 2016, 196; *ABC*, 30 de septiembre de 1982; Wisdom 1987, 161). El desarrollo del Sistema 12 estuvo precedido por una serie de investigaciones en conmutación numérica, algunas de las cuales resultaron fallidas, como muestra el ejemplo del sistema I0AX, desarrollado por Standard Eléctrica en Madrid (Calvo 2014, 324). El Sistema 12, cuyo lanzamiento fue considerado un hito, representaba el 60% de la producción de Standard Eléctrica, que había suministrado a Telefónica 10 centrales, con un total ligeramente superior a 85.000 líneas telefónicas, cobradas tan solo en una quinta parte. La calificación técnica provisional permitiría a Standard Eléctrica recibir los restantes 3.000 millones de pesetas, proseguir con el programa se suministros y cobrar atrasos por unos 7.500 millones de pesetas (*El País*, 2 de octubre de 1986). El Sistema 12 fue un instrumento de penetración en los mercados internacionales. En 1981, SESA cerró el primer contrato de exportación de centrales de ese tipo para Venezuela, mientras que exportaba una treintena de centrales PC-1000 a Latinoamérica, Argelia e Irak (SESA, *Memoria*, 1981, p. 11). En 1983, SESA firmó un acuerdo con la asociada en Argentina para suministrarle 50.000 líneas con una ampliación hasta alcanzar las 132.000; presentó ofertas en Argelia por un total de 250.000 líneas equivalentes y en Uruguay por 200.000. Asimismo, continuó los contactos comerciales con la Administración telefónica marroquí para conseguir instalar una central piloto en el país vecino (SESA, *Memoria anual*, 1983, 30). En 1985 finalizaron la mayoría de las pruebas de calificación técnica, sin tráfico real, de la central digital de media y gran capacidad (Sistema 1240) (Calvo 2020, 1-13). En 1987, SESA obtuvo de Telefónica la calificación técnica de toda la gama de centrales digitales del sistema 12 de las que vendió 99 con 177.760 líneas (SESA, *Memoria anual*, 1987 7).

[83] Se trataba del registrador electrónico MORE, de extrema utilidad para la facturación detallada gracias a la marcación multifrecuencia desde terminales de los usuarios, el registro detallado de llamadas y la ampliación de la numeración (Calvo 2020, 1-13). Había que resolver problemas urgentes y la necesidad de las facturas detalladas, en una situación en que las centrales electromecánicas tenían un final anunciado pero se trataba de alargar la vida de los equipos, por un lado, y de recuperar la inversión en poco tiempo, por otro (Entrevistas del autor a Luis Lada, 22 de mayo y 17 de junio de 2013).

base material a los compromisos de CTNE con el mantenimiento del empleo, muy acordes con los programas del gobierno socialista y con las aspiraciones de los sindicatos.

6. Cambios en la propiedad y nuevas formas de organización

Debido a su amplitud, complejidad y duración, sumadas a la diversidad de actores, las negociaciones para implementar el plan bien podrían describirse como ‹tortuosas», un término utilizado por los medios de comunicación cuando AT&T y CTNE crearon AT&T Microelectrónica de España (Calvo 2017, 51-62). Las divisiones dentro del gobierno y las discrepancias puntuales entre los sindicatos españoles, junto con los cambios en los interlocutores extranjeros (IT&T y CGE) y en las estrategias de los actores, prolongaron las discusiones e impidieron el acuerdo en torno a Standard Eléctrica, la joya de la corona de IT&T en España.

CTNE había dado neto apoyo al proyecto de consorcio europeo EUROTEL en el que se comprometió a tomar parte en el 7% con una inversión de 40.000 millones de pesetas y elaboró el estudio de viabilidad de su participación. Por su parte, el Gobierno español, favorable al principio, mostró –y mantuvo– sus reticencias debido a la fuerte inversión financiera exigida en la operación, estimada en 300 millones de dólares en capital. Tras varias reuniones con los bancos del entorno de la compañía se logró un esbozo de la ingeniería financiera inherente a la operación. Pero el Gobierno y la operadora variaron su postura inicial para sumirse en el escepticismo, matizado por cierta expectación frente a la reacción de la CGE, que revisó su estrategia[84].

La modificación de la postura inicial de CTNE obedeció en parte a cambios de los acuerdos en varios aspectos. En cuanto al grado de implicación en el *holding* europeo de telecomunicaciones EUROTEL, la CGE anunció que reducía su participación al 60% de la cuota y se reservaba el derecho a com-

---

[84] El primer ministro francés Jacques Chirac presionó a Telefónica para que participase en el consorcio CGE-IT&T (Palmer y Tunstall 1990), 151; *El País*, 6 de noviembre de 1986). Felipe González aprobó la inversión después de una larga entrevista con Luis Solana (Araskog 1999, 192). Las reticencias a la entrada de CTNE en EUROTEL debido a la elevada inversión que implicaba emanaban primordialmente de Solchaga, ministro de Economía, quien, junto con Joan Majó, siguió de cerca las negociaciones; el esquema de financiación reposaba en un crédito de los bancos destinado a crear un fondo de inversiones en el que participarían las entidades bancarias del entorno de la CTNE; un sector de la operadora española se oponía a la participación por juzgarla cara e ineficaz.

prar el 10% hasta llegar al porcentaje pactado, compromiso que daba a CTNE un 10% de ese total y a IT&T el 30% restante. Si bien oficialmente CTNE ratificó su interés en el proyecto, condicionaba la participación al cumplimiento de tres puntos básicos. Para empezar por el carácter, buscaba un proyecto con dimensión europea y no solo francesa, condición no cumplida con la inclusión en el proyecto de la Société Générale de Belgique (SGB) con un 10% de la cuota correspondiente a CGE. En segundo lugar, la aquiescencia de CTNE llevaba aparejada la venta a EUROTEL del 21% de las acciones en manos de la filial de IT&T Standard Eléctrica, así como de su participación en Marconi. Por último, CTNE exhibía su condición diferencial de operadora –Alcatel, del grupo CGE, era industrial y la SGB belga exclusivamente financiera– para reclamar un peso específico superior al que le correspondería por su mera participación accionarial. La nueva postura de CTNE hizo variar la estrategia de los negociadores franceses, que buscaron acuerdos en sucesivas reuniones en España. La tercera alteración sustancial de los planteamientos de los acuerdos iniciales atañía a la decisión del gobierno conservador francés de destituir al presidente de CGE-Alcatel así como a la decisión de reprivatizar el consorcio de telecomunicaciones[85].

---

[85] *TNYT*, 3 de julio de 1986; *Économie et politique*, 378-389, 1986, 44; *Le Monde,* 27 de diciembre de 1986; *El País*, 4 de septiembre de 1986; *Worldwide Report telecommunications policy, research, and development national technical information service,* National Technical Information Service. La prensa financiera señalaba que IT&T vendía su negocio mundial de telecomunicaciones por menos de la mitad de su valor (*Fortune*, 21 de julio de 1986); pendientes de negociar quedaban algunos aspectos globales de la operación, como era el de la financiación de los costes de reestructuración de EUROTEL. A los 600 millones de dólares, según el plan de viabilidad elaborado, había que añadir otros 250 millones de dólares incluidos en una partida de complementos. CGE asumiría mil millones de dólares de las deudas de IT&T (*New York Times*, 21 de agosto de 1986). La participación de la SGB estaba auspiciada por el antiguo comisario europeo Étienne Davignon, impulsor a partir de las doce mayores empresas europeas –the Big Twelve– de una estrategia común para el desarrollo de la industria de la información y candidato a CEO de la empresa. La destitución afectó a George Pébereau, firmante del acuerdo de fusión de CGE con IT&T. La nacionalización apartó a los empleadores tradicionales y exaltó a las nuevas élites empresariales de las *grandes écoles*, concebidas por Napoleón para dotar al país de gerentes eficientes y bien formados (Barsoux y Löscher 1991). A juicio de Pébereau, la manera de resistir a la ofensiva del gigante estadounidense AT&T, hasta hacía poco confinado a su mercado interior, pasaba por las alianzas industriales y comerciales (JPRS 82808, *West Europe Report*, n.ª 2098, 7 de febrero de 1983, 54). Pébereau fue sustituido por Pierre Suard, representante de un capitalismo oligárquico controlado por la élite del sector público (Cohen 2004; Araskog 1999, 199; Pébereau 2005, 96-104; *New York Times*, 18 de febrero de 1982). Pébereau habló de «oportunidad histórica» en el ascenso de Francia y Europa al liderazgo en la industria de las telecomunicaciones hasta el final del siglo. Suard consideraba la operación una cuestión de estrategia industrial en un momento en que CGE disponía de liquidez para mantener la actividad y los colosales costes de investigación exigían aumentar la cuota de

Altos representantes de la dirección de CTNE negociaron en París con la empresa francesa. Mientras tanto, Luis Solana manifestaba en Madrid ante una delegación de eurodiputados la oposición de CTNE a aceptar que fuese la empresa francesa la beneficiada por la operación[86]. Evidentemente, el liderazgo lo ostentaba CGE, afianzada en el mercado desde que en 1983 absorbiera la sección de telecomunicaciones de Thomson y ansiosa por entrar en el mercado estadounidense, que se abrió después del desmembramiento de AT&T (Marseille (dir.) 1992). La reorganización de CGE y Thomson, los dos grupos nacionalizados líderes en la industria electrónica, ahondaba el objetivo de racionalizar las actividades de las empresas estatales y canalizar los recursos humanos y financieros hacia el desarrollo de nuevos productos, en especial en el campo de las telecomunicaciones (Commission of the European Communities 1985, 46-47)[87]. El llamado «segundo Yalta de la electrónica» convirtió a CIT-Alcatel en el nuevo campeón nacional de las telecomunicaciones; CGE escaló a quinto fabricante mundial de equipos telefónicos (Hulsink 2012, 261; Pederson 2000, 29). La industria telefónica en Francia se había concentrado anteriormente cuando Thomson se hizo cargo de la filial francesa de IT&T Le Matériel Téléphonique (LMT) y la Société des Téléphones Ericsson (Chapuis y Joel Jr. 2003, 327)[88].

La CGE consideró inaceptables las condiciones de CTNE para los intereses de los accionistas, negó a la operadora carácter especial dentro del

---

mercado, aspecto destacado por los teóricos. Los norteamericanos, por su parte, consideraron solo los aspectos financieros (New York Times, 25 de agosto de 1986). Siemens, marginada de la transacción CGÉ-IT&T como Northern Telecom, recelaba de la posible entrada de CTNE.

[86] El País, 29 de octubre de 1986.

[87] Thomson, un revoltijo desconcertante de divisiones a cuyo frente estaba el otrora socialista radical Alain Gómez, descendiente de un republicano español, perdió 275 millones de dólares en 1982; vendió negocios atrasados para concentrarse en cuatro campos de la electrónica: bienes de consumo, sistemas militares, equipos médicos y componentes electrónicos. Las pérdidas se redujeron a 4 millones de dólares en 1983 sobre unas ventas de 7.200 millones de dólares (Fortune, 9 de diciembre de 1985).

[88] IT&T hubo de negar que la venta de LMT fuese resultado del deseo de IT&T de retirarse de Francia y estuvo sujeta a varios requisitos, entre ellos, la adopción por los PTT de las centrales Metaconta en la expansión masiva del servicio en Francia, así como la aclaración de la posición de la filial francesa de IT&T, la CGCT. El acuerdo se inscribía en el marco de un programa de «francificación» de la industria francesa en el suministro de equipos para la modernización de la industria telefónica francesa (IT&T YIELDS TO GOF PRESSURE TO SELL ONE OF ITS FRENCH SUBSIDIARIES1976 May Wikeleaks, 4, 1976PARIS12951_b 4).

grupo por su condición única de tal y, en definitiva, la excluyó[89]. No hubo un bloqueo absoluto de las negociaciones pese a todo. Luis Solana y Pierre Suard, presidentes de la CTNE y de la CGT, formaron sendas comisiones mixtas de trabajo con sede en París y Madrid. Divididas las funciones de cada cual, la de la capital francesa se encargaba de analizar los aspectos organizativos de EUROTEL, mientras que a la comisión madrileña le competía estudiar la posición del grupo IT&T en España (*El País*, 17 de septiembre de 1986)[90].

Evidentemente, el centro clave de decisión estaba en Francia y no en Madrid, por más que SESA fuera una pieza importante del grupo IT&T, porque francesa era la líder de la operación. Entre finales de 1986, fecha del acuerdo IT&T/CGÉ, y la primera mitad de 1987, un aguerrido grupo de negociadores encabezado por Pierre Suard alumbró el holding Alcatel NV como sociedad acogida al derecho holandés, domiciliada en Amsterdam y con sede en Bruselas, el 35% de cuyas actividades se desarrollaban en Francia y el resto en Alemania. IT&T cedió a las exigencias francesas de elevar su participación en la *joint venture* del 30 al 37%, con la consiguiente disminución de la aportación gala de 1,8 a 1,5 miles de millones de dólares, y de dejar abierta la puerta a una *joint venture* entre CIT y AT&T (Marseille (dir.) 1992; *Network World*, 3, 22, 1986). En el obligado nuevo reparto de participaciones de la nueva empresa, IT&T se adjudicó el 37% y el *holding* paneuropeo EUROTEL –ahora sin Telefónica– el restante 63%, distribuido entre CGE –55,6%–, la Societé Genérale de Belgique –5,7%– y el Crédit Lyonnais –1,7% (Noam 1992, 157; European Commission 1997,

---

89 *ABC*, 8 de enero de 1987, 23. CGE señaló que no había lugar para Telefónica (*La Vanguardia*, 8 de enero de 1987).

90 El gobierno español encomendó a tres directores generales seguir de cerca el asunto y la CTNE se mantuvo en contacto permanente con la parte francesa. La cúpula de la CTNE subrayaba el cambio sustancial que significaba para España pasar «de ser un país que necesitó de IT&T para crear su Telefónica a ser un país que tiene que comprar IT&T porque está en crisis» no sin expresar su pesimismo ante la postura de los franceses no sin sentar como principio primordial la voluntad de no morder el anzuelo de integrarse en la futura segunda empresa del mundo de telecomunicaciones ni de ceder al «señuelo del "show" frente a la realidad del empleo, de la tecnología, del peso de Telefónica» (Comparecencia del presidente de la compañía telefónica nacional de España (don Luis Solana Madariaga), *Diario de Sesiones del Senado*, 23 de octubre de 1986; *El País*, 17 de septiembre de 1986). Alcatel ofreció fabricar algunos de sus nuevos productos en las filiales de IT&T en España, sin que la contraoferta convenciera a la parte española (*El País*, 8 de enero de 1987; Beaujolin-Bellet e Issaverdens 2006).

107)[91]. Standard Telephones and Cables, una exfilial británica de IT&T y otros nombres asociados con las negociaciones internacionales, entre otros la británica Plessey y la italiana STET, quedaron fuera del acuerdo y del grupo Alcatel, que sí incluyó Cables de Lyon (Baskoy 2008, 155; *New York Times,* 3 de julio de 1986).

Culminaba de esta guisa el paso del llamado colbertismo galo *high-tech* a un capitalismo de mercados financieros con una doble operación, es decir, la compra de los activos de telecomunicaciones de IT&T en Europa por la CGE y, a continuación, la fusión de los mismos con la división de telecomunicaciones del grupo Alcatel, compuesto por CIT Alcatel y Thomson Télécommunications, filiales de la CGE y de Thomson. CGE transfería a las filiales europeas de IT&T recién adquiridas el negocio de la conmutación hasta el momento centralizado en CIT, a la vez que conseguía las necesarias economías de escala y se beneficiaba de los avances de IT&T en la tecnología digital. En otras palabras, la historia daba un vuelco: la división industrial de la norteamericana Western Electric que originó el gigante integrado IT&T pasaba a fortalecer la posición mundial de la multinacional europea Alcatel (Chandler 1999, 236-237; Kumps et al. 1989; Gambardella y Malerba 1999, 142; Cohen 2004; Hulsink 2012, 261)[92].

El coste de la operación ascendió a 902 millones de dólares por los activos en el sector, el grueso de los cuales fue abonado en metálico por la CGE,

---

[91] Las negociaciones francesas con IT&T, que estaban exentas de la ley de nacionalizaciones debido a la intensa participación del capital extranjero, buscaron mantener vínculos tecnológicos, industriales y comerciales sin abandonar el programa de nacionalización (Mauroy 1981). Acuerdo en la Reunión FIOM-FEM de coordinación IT&T-CGE, Ginebra, 7 octubre de 1986; los expertos establecían en 1986 que una empresa industrial de telecomunicación debía tener como mínimo del 7 al 8% del mercado mundial, o, si se prefiere, la fracción francesa del 5% más un 2-3% de exportación (Longuet 1995, 228. 3). Curiosamente, en noviembre de 1986 IT&T aceptaba fijar en 35% su participación en la empresa conjunta y transferir Valtec, la pionera fabricante de fibra óptica para cables con sede en Massachusetts, así como ciertas actividades de componentes eléctricos en Europa, con un valor combinado de 65 millones de dólares (*Los Angeles Times*, 4 de noviembre de 1986). Debido a su complejidad, las negociaciones de IT&T-CGE se han convertido en un caso de libro de texto (Weiss 1993, 269-300); sobre la elección de los socios como una estrategia de riesgo compartido, ver Pébereau (2005, 96–104). Suard declinó precisar quién había tomado la iniciativa originalmente en la fusión («Interview with CGE Chief Suard». *JPRS-TTP-86-029*, 15 de diciembre de 1986, 61).

[92] ALCATEL: Alsacienne de Constructions Atomiques, de Télécommunications et d'Électroniquo; CIT: Compagnio Induotriollo doo Télóoommunioationo. La pronoa ooñaló quo ol colbertismo se estaba tambaleando (*Libération*, 18 de abril de 1995); sobre el fracaso del colbertismo *high-tech* y las políticas industriales, véase Thibault (2008). Suard insistía en las economías de escala y relativizaba la importancia del Sistema 12 («Interview with CGE Chief Suard», *JPRS-TTP-86-029*, 15 de diciembre de 1986, 61).

más 350 millones correspondientes a la deuda interna. La CGE planeaba una pronta ampliación de capital, condicionada por una posible mejora del mercado financiero de París, la salida a las principales bolsas de Europa y EE. UU, así como la privatización de la CGE en busca de equiparase a sus competidores en un mercado abierto.

Alcatel emprendió una tarea de unificación y armonización del complejo conglomerado heredado de IT&T con medidas inmediatas de contenido simbólico como la elección del nombre y el uso del ECU, precursor del Euro, en la contabilidad, el presupuesto y la planificación. Tarea fundamental fue garantizar la necesaria cohesión del grupo por encima de las peculiaridades tradicionalmente cultivadas en las filiales (Calvo (2014)[93]. En conjunto, Alcatel NV afianzó su naturaleza de multinacional y quedó formada por seis filiales grandes, otras veintiuna con asentamientos industriales en diferentes regiones, treinta empresas conjuntas con fabricantes locales y ciento veinte unidades de venta. A través de la filial Alcatel Trade International la matriz se aseguraba la posibilidad de identificar oportunidades en países en los que carecía de establecimientos industriales. Según el esquema de *reverse transfer*, una red de representantes de esta filial proporcionaba información a la matriz sobre las soluciones óptimas para el control del mercado y coordinación de las actividades internacionales de las filiales industriales (Canalejo 2020, 42; *Project and Trade Finance* 135-140, 1994).

En materia de expansión internacional, la entrada de las filiales en nuevos mercados estaba sujeta a la disponibilidad de productos y recursos, así como al cumplimiento de determinadas condiciones y directrices, agrupadas en un proceso denominado *sourcing*. SESA concentró sus recursos en países en los que podría tener ventajas competitivas, sobre la base de la presencia histórica, los lazos culturales, las relaciones gubernamentales y la compatibilidad de los productos. A ello añadió el tamaño del mercado potencial del país en cuestión (alta demanda, baja proporción de líneas por habitante), junto con la capacidad de encontrar recursos financieros para financiar a los nuevos clientes. El producto fundamental sobre el que basar la internacionalización fueron las centrales digitales del Sistema 12, un

---

[93] CGE inspiró el nombre de Alcatel frente al de Teleglobal (Araskog (1999, 221). El mundo de los negocios mostraba una Alcatel empeñada en superar a AT&T en equipos de teléfonos con un rosario de adquisiciones pero muy lastrada por su excesiva dependencia de France Telecom y Deutsche Telekom para la mayoría de los beneficios (*Business Week*, 3.418-3.421, 1995, 69).

producto estratégico para el cliente, atractivo y con capacidad de generar ingresos a largo plazo. Los países elegidos fueron dos asiáticos –China e Indonesia–, uno latinoamericano –Brasil–, uno europeo –Polonia– y uno norteafricano –Argelia–. Lazos culturales tradicionales con España decidieron asimismo la inclinación por mercados más pequeños en Latinoamérica. La homogeneidad de planteamientos no se tradujo en resultados uniformes. Los éxitos del acceso al mercado chino, brasileño y polaco contrastaron con los modestos resultados del indonesio y argelino[94].

China se convirtió en un pilar fundamental de la estrategia internacional de SESA hasta el punto de superar a Telefónica como su mayor cliente de conmutación. La expansión en el gigante asiático siguió un esquema gradualista, una versión modificada de la propuesta por la escuela nórdica de la internacionalización. SESA mantuvo contactos incipientes en la República Popular China desde 1986 y, tras más de dos años de negociación, firmó el primer contrato por valor de 11,5 millones de dólares, al que le siguieron entre 1988 y 1992 otros por 25 millones de líneas en trece provincias, que reunían más de la mitad de la población. La salida al mercado chino consistió en exportaciones directas de productos fabricados en España y vendidos a operadoras de diferentes provincias chinas. El servicio postventa exigió un centro de operaciones en Hong Kong con dos funciones esenciales, a saber, satisfacer con rapidez las necesidades de los clientes y optimizar el uso de los recursos locales[95]. A partir de 1993, los importadores chinos hicieron varios pedidos para entregas escalonadas –1993 a 1995 y 1995 a 1998– de 8,14 millones de líneas. En uno de los casos –2 millones de líneas por valor de 300 millones de dólares–, la financiación corrió a cargo de la casa madre. A la implantación comercial y de servicios en China le siguió la implantación industrial mediante la asociación con dos fabricantes locales – con Meshian, para producir equipos de transmisión en Chengdu y con WPT (Wuhart Power Telecommunications) para fuentes de alimentación inteligentes con destino a centrales de telecomunicaciones en la capital de Wuhan– (Canalejo 2020, 42-43; Project and Trade Finance 1994); *Cambio 16*, 1.015-1.018, 1991, 16-33; Guillén, García-Canal y Llaneza 2012, 36).

---

[94] Conviene recordar la implantación de SESA en Latinoamérica a través de asociadas, como era el caso de la mexicana IDETEL (SESA. *Memoria*, 1987 32).

[95] La penetración en el mercado chino se llevó a cabo, a veces, mediante alianzas con socios chinos, como ocurrió en 1993 con la forjada por Alcatel España alianza para el suministro de equipos de telecomunicaciones (Guillén y García-Canal 2007, 23-34).

En Polonia, el país con gran mercado potencial y líder en la apertura a la economía de mercado, Alcatel SESA buscaba consolidar su presencia y construir una plataforma industrial y comercial de penetración en el este de Europa, en especial en la antigua URSS. En 1990, se asoció a dos empresas polacas y creó una empresa conjunta –Alcatel Setel– para la fabricación del Sistema 12 en Varsovia (*El País*, 24 de setiembre de 1990). Alcatel Setel comenzó a fabricar equipos de conmutación S12 en 1992, con una cifra inicial de 600.000 líneas anuales, que esperaba aumentar hasta un millón en el plazo de cuatro o cinco años. Por entonces, CIT, la filial francesa de Alcatel NV, dio vida a otra empresa conjunta (Alcatel CIT-Polska) en la que se reservó la mayoría accionarial (55%), mientras que las empresas polacas se repartían el resto –Teletra (30%) y Elektrim (15%). Traducido en tecnología el mercado polaco de Alcatel quedó repartido entre el Sistema 12 de SESA y el Sistema E10 de Alcatel CIT, el primero de mayor envergadura (1 millón de líneas frente a las 350.000 de CIT a principios de 1993) y con una mayor red comercial en Polonia. Insatisfecho por la situación, el gobierno pidió que solo se comercializara un sistema digital de Alcatel NV en el futuro. A mediados de 1992, la multinacional francesa decidió concentrar todas las actividades de Alcatel en Polonia en una única empresa –Alcatel Polska–. SESA –y no CIT– asumió la propiedad y la gestión de Alcatel Polska, que se encargó de comercializar el Sistema 12 (Canalejo 2020, 42-43; *Computerworld* 27 de julio de 1992)[96].

En lo tocante a I+D, a cada unidad de I+D de Alcatel se le asignaron los recursos y el mandato de perseguir una tecnología específica y bien definida o una tarea de desarrollo, frente a la situación anterior en la que la mayoría de ellas desarrollaban toda la gama de productos para sus mercados locales (Ghoshal y Bartlett 1990, 614-615).

La presencia en la mayoría de los países europeos permitió a Alcatel centrar sus esfuerzos en racionalizar la gama de productos en lugar de sus operaciones de ventas y marketing. En 1995, la fabricante parecía haber culminado su racionalización al conseguir una familia única de centrales en toda Europa, la serie Alcatel 4.000, apropiada para cada mercado geográfico. Sin embargo,

---

[96] SESA (51%), (PT, 34% y Elektrim, 15%). Stan Scrdakowsky, un ingeniero polaco al servicio de SESA desde 1953 y director técnico en la época de IT&T, fue nombrado director general. Según matizan Radosevic y Sadowski (2007, 89), Alcatel Polska S.A. quedó formada por Alcatel Teletra, Alcatel CIT Polska, Alcatel Setel Polska y PZT Telecom.

la tozuda realidad mostraba desajustes derivados de la coexistencia de productos nuevos y antiguos en dicha serie 4.000[97].

Tras su creación Alcatel aplicó medidas que supusieron el despido de unos 35.000 trabajadores. De gran importancia para entender lo que vamos a explicar para España, el Consejo Mundial de Alcatel (IT&T) se reunió en dos ocasiones sucesivas –en 1986 y 1987–. La principal preocupación fue estrechar los contactos entre los representantes de los trabajadores y mejorar la información sobre las medidas propuestas (Rüb 2002, 32).

En España, Alcatel tenía ante si el problema inmediato de sus filiales y en especial el de Marconi, a la que reservaba un futuro en el sector público español. Debía resolver también el exceso de plantilla en SESA, estimado en algo menos de la mitad de los 14.000 empleos existentes (*ABC*, 8 de enero de 1987, 23). Más delante veremos que Marconi fue vendida y SESA recapitalizada con 100 millones de ecus a cambio de un programa de incremento de pedidos y un plan de reducción de plantillas en varios miles aprobado por el gobierno[98].

Con la adquisición de SESA a finales de 1986, Alcatel NV fortaleció su posición en la industria de conmutación y pasó de representar una cuarta parte del total a más de un tercio. Vale la pena recordar que SESA era la filial más grande fuera de Francia, tenía una de las mayores cuotas de mercado de las filiales en la CEE y prometía un crecimiento proporcionalmente más alto que el resto del grupo[99].

La industria global de equipos de telecomunicaciones se caracterizaba entonces por la extraordinaria concentración del suministro o, en otras palabras, por el control oligopólico del mercado, que también estaba fragmentado por productos. En 1980, las cuatro compañías principales (AT&T, IT&T, Siemens

---

[97] Alcatel tenía diferentes familias de PBX en varios países; en España coexistían las centrales de los sistemas 12 y 100 de IT&T y las Opus 300 y 4000 de Thomson (European Commission 1997, 115 y 119).

[98] La empresa presentó la venta de Marconi, en situación límite y con amenazas sobre el conjunto del grupo, con un coste de desinversión de 10.740 millones de pesetas, como una solución no traumática desde el punto de vista social (Alcatel Standard Eléctrica 1987, 6 y 1991, 8). El sindicato CCOO equiparó la venta de SESA a Alcatel con el desmantelamiento progresivo de la industria electrónica y con la reestructuración del sector de las telecomunicaciones, al hacerla coincidir con el inicio de un largo periodo de reestructuraciones y ajustes de plantilla y de externalización de actividades (CCOO 2008, 17). En el reajuste de plantillas, las cifras muestran una tendencia al reforzamiento de los titulares superiores en el conjunto a costa sobre todo de los llamados técnicos.

[99] En 1985, se preveía un aumento de 2,8 puntos porcentuales en cinco años para el 4,3% del mercado de Alcatel y resultados cercanos a la rentabilidad para 1988 (Araskog 1999, 221; *El País*, 23 de junio de 1987).

y Ericsson) dominaban más de la mitad del mercado global de telecomunicaciones. Siete años más tarde, esta concentración había disminuido ya que la participación de las compañías líderes ahora representaba menos de un tercio del mercado y aparecieron nuevos fabricantes. Además, la composición del grupo líder había cambiado significativamente. Alcatel NV reemplazó a IT&T en la segunda posición detrás de AT&T y NEC relegó a Ericsson (cuarto en 1980) a una posición más baja, mientras que Siemens se mantuvo en tercer lugar (Edquist, Hommen y Tsipouri 2000, 213)[100].

Tabla 4. Concentración del suministro de equipos de telecomunicación, 1989 (%)

Mercado total	Mundo	CE
5 empresas más grandes	35,7	54,4
10 empresas más grandes	46,7	70,5
20 empresas más grandes	57,6	81,8

Fuente: Elaboración propia a partir de Eurostrategies ESTEL, Eurostat (Comext).

En 1989, el control del mercado por parte de unos pocos proveedores fue más pronunciado en Europa que en el resto del mundo. Las diez empresas más grandes representaron el 46,7% del comercio mundial en el sector (con una tendencia al alza), mientras que su participación en el mercado europeo alcanzó el 70,5%. Es más, si reducimos a cinco ese grupo de las empresas más grandes se sitúan en casi quince puntos porcentuales por encima de su participación en el mercado mundial (Tabla 4). En ese mismo año, Alcatel NV alcanzó la primera posición por ventas en el *ranking* europeo de empresas de equipos de telecomunicaciones, como se muestra en el Gráfico 5. En un contexto general de pugnas por mayores participaciones en un sector en expansión, ciertas compañías prefirieron diversificarse en grandes conglomerados, algo que IT&T hizo con notable éxito durante algún tiempo (Eurostrategies ESTEL, Eurostat (Comext)[101].

---

[100] En 1987, los sistemas digitales E-10 y 12 de Alcatel ocupaban la cuarta posición, con el 11,7% del mercado mundial, tras por el 5-ESS de AT&T, el DMS-1 de Northern Telecom y el AXE de Ericsson, y por delante de otros grandes, como los de NEC, Plessey, GTE, Fujitsu, GEC y Siemens (ASM International 1989, 384(. Como ejemplo de movimientos en el mercado, Nokia, que se especializó en la transmisión, aspiraba a entrar en el sector de conmutación a través de un acuerdo de fabricación entre su filial Telefeeno (Nokia y la estatal TEBVA al 50%) y CIT-Alcatel (*Le Monde diplomatique*, octubre de 1977, 25).

[101] Intensificación del oligopolio mundial (Smidt y Weber 2013, 81). En 1970, la red tentacular de IT&T abarcaba 331 filiales, de las cuales más de un tercio eran europeas (United States. Congress. House. 1970 41).

Gráfico 5. Principales empresas de equipos de telecomunicaciones, ventas en 1989 (millones ecus)

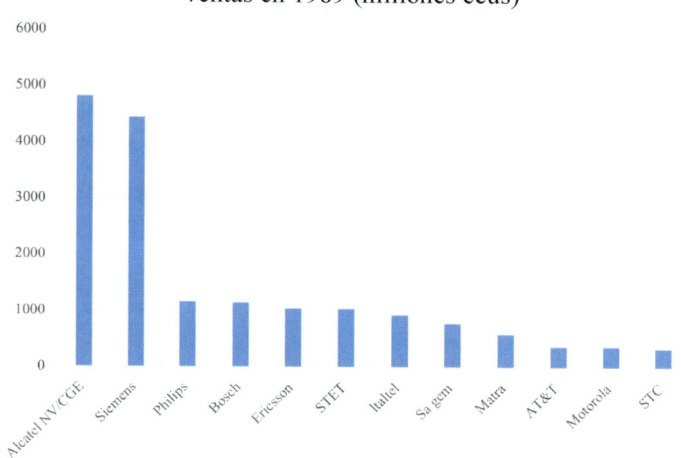

Fuente: Elaboración a partir de Eurostrategies ESTEL, Eurostat (Comext).

Esa estructura de oligopolio se vio claramente reforzada por nuevos episodios de copetición por el afianzamiento en el mercado. Para afrontar el imperativo del tamaño de mercado adecuado a los elevados costes del desarrollo de las nuevas tecnologías y otros, las empresas buscaron alianzas y *joint ventures*, estrategia plasmada en diez ocasiones durante tan solo tres años. En ello abunda un caso de fusión –CGE (CIT-Alcatel) con Thomson Alcatel–, dos *joint ventures* –Siemens y GTE, AT&T y Philips para crear APT con el objetivo de adaptar el ESS-5 al mercado europeo– y tres adquisiciones –de activos de IT&T en Europa por CGE, de la Compagnie Générale des Constructions Téléphoniques (CGCT) por Ericsson y del 27,5% de STC por Northern Telecom–. Varios casos más no llegaron a ser culminados o quedaban pendientes de resolver: la adquisición de CGCT por AT&T-Philips a través de la francesa Societé Anonyme de Télécommunications (SAT) (Teece 1998, 501; *Techmonitor*, 1 de marzo de 1987), la licitación de GEC por Plessey, bloqueada por el gobierno británico (*New York Times*, 5 de diciembre de 1985), a la que siguieron los planes de fusión de ambas; la fusión fallida pese a los buenos presagios de Italtel/Teletra para formar Telit, que arrastró la anunciada empresa conjunta entre Telit y Ericsson (*La Repubblica*, 24 de febrero de 1990). En algún caso, el resultado fue la eliminación del mercado de un sistema de conmutación, como sucedió con la central PRXD de Philips, que abandonó el desarrollo de este equipo. En contrapartida, las tentativas que atañían a GEC y Plessey no interrumpieron la colaboración para la fabricación del Sistema X^{102}. Éxitos y fracasos traducían una tendencia avasalladora hacia la concentración. Poco antes de cerrarse la década de 1980, GEC y Plessey habían unido sus fuerzas para crear GPT; Siemens se había fusionado con GEC y adquirido Rolm, una filial de IBM productora de centrales automáticas, APT (Philips/AT&T) se había convertido en AT&T-Networks International e Italtel había forjado una alianza con AT&T (Council of Europe 1990, 17)^{103}.

Asegurar el futuro requería resolver la situación en España, que reflejaba los problemas generales del sector. El primer plan fracasado para SESA dio paso a un segundo plan más draconiano bajo los auspicios de Alcatel NV^{104}. La multinacional centró sus esfuerzos en reestructurar y modernizar el grupo en España en busca de la rentabilidad a corto plazo y la competitividad en un horizonte más dilatado. El gobierno, a través del jefe de Industria, y CGE, a través de su presidente y máximo representante de Alcatel NV, sostuvieron negociaciones tensas en marzo de 1987 para abordar el futuro de SESA. Los objetivos incluían llegar a un consenso sobre el número de

---

[102] WS Atkins Management Consultants 1988, 149; *New Scientist*, 23 de octubre de 1980, 207 y 239; *Problèmes Économiques*, 2.156-2.165, 1990, 25. Otras alianzas no eran tan evidentes: Telefónica cooperaba con la organización técnico-comercial de Northern Telecom (NT) en vistas a la implantación de la citada red. Northern Telecom España carecía de planta de producción en el país si bien tenía un equipo técnico de apoyo a las ventas. Suministraba los equipos utilizados para la transmisión de datos en la red UNO de Telefónica con un sistema basado en los equipos multimedia de banda ancha de la familia Magellan, el DPN-100. Los otros dos productos de la familia Magellan eran el Concorde y el Gateway (*Network World*, 11, 8, 1994).

[103] La *joint venture* de AT&T y Philips permitía a AT&T comercializar sus equipos de conmutación a través de la red de distribución de la holandesa en todo el mundo, salvo en Irlanda y Corea del Sur, donde ya estaba implantada, y Taiwan, país muy receptivo de la tecnología estadounidense (Iwens 1984, 10). Rolm, fundada en California en 1969, estaba especializada en cuadros computerizados para las comunicaciones en centralitas privadas o PBX (*New York Times*, 14 de diciembre de 1988). Gobiernos europeos, como el francés, coincidían con los líderes de grandes empresas al señalar que las dificultades que afrontaba la industria electrónica europea reclamaban estrategias de alianza o una fuerte cooperación entre competidores europeos, especialmente en el campo de la investigación y el desarrollo (Réponse du ministère de l'Industrie, *Journal Officiel*, Sénat, 28 de noviembre de 1991, 2.645).

[104] *Le Monde*, 2 de junio de 1987. Alcatel NV hizo patente su control de SESA con la ocupación de puestos en el consejo de administración, como lo muestra la entrada de Philippe Gluntz, videpresidente de Alcatel y de Bernardo Jeux, formado en la Escuela Politécnica de Grenoble y con una amplia carrera de dos decenios al servicio de la francesa CGE en diversos países en que esta gran empresa estaba implantada. Específicamente, en el segundo ejemplo supuso transferencia de capacidades por expatriación de personal (SESA. Memoria 1987, 32).

compras, aumentar los precios acordados y garantizar un volumen fijo de adquisiciones[105].

Un nuevo *impasse* sobrevino cuando CGE-Alcatel bloqueó el plan cuatrienal de la Administración (1987-1991), respaldado por UGT y CTNE, que preveía reducir el excedente de 3.700 empleados mediante ceses voluntarios y jubilaciones, sin recurrir a despidos.

Después de casi un año de negociaciones, Pierre Suard, partidario de los despidos debido a su coste inferior, acordó finalmente diferentes fórmulas para reducir los excedentes en SESA. CGE-Alcatel aceptó jubilaciones anticipadas y despidos voluntarios (casi 2.600 en 1991 y al menos 1.000, respectivamente). El gobierno y la propia empresa pecharían conjuntamente con la financiación del coste, evaluado en más de 50.000 millones de pesetas.

Algunos días después, las aguas se enturbiaron. UGT sugirió incluir en el plan de viabilidad el acuerdo salarial y los ajustes de personal para los años venideros, mientras que CTNE y SESA mantuvieron sus posiciones encontradas. El resto de las condiciones permanecieron intactas, incluidas las compras de CTNE. Por su parte, el ministerio de Industria estimularía la I+D con unos 4.000 millones de pesetas[106].

En realidad, el verdadero obstáculo para la reconversión de SESA residía en su alto coste económico, compartido a partes iguales entre la compañía y el gobierno. La cantidad, ya de por sí notable, podría aumentar considerablemente debido a la inflación y, de hecho, los sindicatos la estimaron en 80.000 millones. Alcatel consideró que el gasto inmediato de unos 15.000 millones era excesivo y que, además, no garantizaría la viabilidad de su filial, que de hecho se consideró en los cálculos de la Comisión mixta de seguimiento[107].

---

[105] *El País*, 30 de marzo de 1987 y 2 de abril de 1987; *Boletín Oficial de las Cortes Generales*, 1.357, Senado, 88, 1987, 3.541. CTNE acordó aumentar sus compras a 32.000 millones de pesetas, una cantidad que luego elevó nuevamente a 50.000 millones. Esta demanda de equipos de telecomunicaciones beneficiaría a SESA, Intelsa y Telettra en el mercado interno, pero podría dañar las exportaciones de la primera; la filial de Amper y AT&T-Philips también negoció su participación en el nuevo mercado (*El País*, 5 de octubre de 1987).

[106] UGT pidió un aumento salarial durante tres años y consideró la jubilación anticipada como la única forma de reducir el excedente de casi 2.500 empleados; CCOO canceló una convocatoria de huelga en protesta contra las reducciones de personal y la demora en el plan de viabilidad (*El País*, 9 de abril de 1987).

[107] Alcatel, inicialmente dispuesta a inyectar en Standard 10.000 millones de pesetas, se negaba a sufragar el tratamiento de los excedentes sin asegurar previamente la viabilidad del negocio y tampoco se deducía la intención de desinvertir en Standard (Antonio de Luna Aguado, Agrupación Parlamentaria del Partido Liberal, *Boletín Oficial de las Cortes Generales*, 27 de mayo de 1987, 1.357, Senado, 3.541).

Una vez superados diversos obstáculos, los cuatro interlocutores (Alcatel NV, CTNE, UGT, y los ministerios de Trabajo e Industria) firmaron un acuerdo en 1987 cuyos distintos extremos fueron ratificados con posterioridad por la Comisión delegada del gobierno. De vigencia cuatrienal, contemplaba un conjunto de actuaciones en los ámbitos industrial, financiero, tributario y laboral, por no hablar de otras relacionadas con la demanda interna y exterior. La multinacional presentó los acuerdos de reestructuración firmados en abril dentro de plan de reconversión industrial 1987-1991 como un auténtico plan estratégico para lograr el triple objetivo de asegurar el cumplimiento de los objetivos empresariales, a la vez que consolidar el liderazgo nacional y la competitividad internacional.

Retomando aspectos del ya señalado acuerdo de 1982, Alcatel y la CTNE se obligaban a llevar a cabo una ampliación de capital de hasta 14.000 y 3.720 millones de pesetas respectivamente. Los accionistas renunciaban además durante los dos primeros años de vigencia del acuerdo a repartir dividendos, que debían ser capitalizados. CTNE incrementaría el volumen de pedidos a SESA en una cuantía que superaba los 32.000 millones de pesetas de las previsiones anteriores. SESA seguiría beneficiándose de las vigentes bonificaciones fiscales y Alcatel NV renunciaría a la mitad de los *royalties*, esta vez tan solo en el bienio 1987-1989. El plan pretendía garantizar la viabilidad futura de SESA y el mantenimiento de una plantilla objetivo de 7.700 trabajadores al final de 1991. El ajuste del empleo a las previsiones de la demanda se combinaba con un completo sistema de cobertura para los excedentes. Por último, Alcatel NV y el Gobierno español revalidaron su resolución de consensuar un futuro plan de viabilidad de Marconi Española[108].

Un aspecto no desdeñable se refiere a la reestructuración organizativa. La imperiosa diversificación y el crecimiento horizontal fuera de las telecomuni-

---

[108] Alcatel Standard Eléctrica (1987, 6; *BOCG*, Senado, 88, 30 abril 1987, 3.541-3.542). En el debate del Congreso de los diputados se señalaba que Alcatel, al igual que Intelsa, receptoras de cuantiosas ayudas del Estado, estaba subcontratando obras sin dejar de acogerse a esos beneficios de la reconversión. Por otra parte, las fuertes inversiones de Telefónica en esos momentos permitían augurar abundancia de actividad fabril en un futuro inmediato. El ministro de Trabajo y seguridad social –Chaves– justificaba el plan de reestructuración, que buscaba fundamentalmente la rentabilidad de la empresa, que pasaba en esos momentos por la reestructuración de plantillas por suspensión de contratos de trabajo durante un año (*Diario de Sesiones del Congreso de los Diputados*, 128, Intervenciones, 29 de junio de 1988, 7.549). La práctica continuó en momentos de intensificación de trabajos como sucedió a las puertas de 1992, cuando en Madrid y Sevilla se contrataron trabajadores a destajo (Sentencia de TS, Sala 4ª, de lo Social, 30 de Abril de 1994).

caciones y la electromecánica desembocaron en una práctica de creación de secciones especializadas.

En el arranque de la década de 1980, SESA constaba de tres direcciones, a saber, una general, otra de divisiones operativas y la tercera de departamentos, en consonancia con la empresa multidivisional a la que se ha aludido (Chandler 1975, 251-252; Chandler, 1990)[109].

En 1983, tras la absorción de CITESA, SESA creó la división de tecnologías de la información, que abarcaba los tres grandes grupos de sistemas de comunicaciones (de voz, de texto y datos) de forma independiente y en proyectos de sistemas integrados de comunicaciones de la empresa. En la faceta de los equipos de comunicación los productos principales fueron las centralitas telefónicas privadas, los intercomunicadores, los equipos busca personas yotros dispositivos electrónicos –los UNIMAT–, con clientela en la banca y organismos de seguridad del estado. Dentro de los sistemas de texto, lanzó una impresora electrónica. El área de datos del mercado informático produjo terminales inteligentes, fondos de pantalla de controladores, terminales multifunción y un sistema de proceso de datos distribuidos[110].

Sin esperar mucho (1984) a esta división le siguió la unidad Productos Industriales y Servicios, una baza que podía exhibir para contrarrestar la imagen de empresa liquidadora de puestos de trabajo. De ahí nacieron al cabo de dos años las secciones de servicios y de electrónica industrial, que obtuvo contratos de Digital Equipment Corporation, Teves, IBM, Toshiba e IT&T. En 1989, la sección de electrónica industrial proporcionaba ocupación a 638 trabajadores, muchos de ellos excedentes del plan de reestructuración[111].

---

[109] Divisiones operativas: conmutación, sistemas electrónicos, cables e instalaciones; departamentos: mercado de exportación, mercado nacional, información y relaciones exteriores, relaciones industriales, diversificación, calidad, técnico, Sonelec e I+D, ingenierías, fabricación e instalaciones (SESA, *Memoria*, 1981, p. 3). Sonelec fue el gran proyecto de instalación en Argelia de una planta completa en la modalidad de producto en mano, conseguido por SESA en un contienda internacional (Calvo 2014, 275-283).

[110] UNIMAT 4021 y 4041; impresora electrónica ITT3000; controladores 3280; terminales multifunción ITT3290 y de proceso de datos distribuidos ITT-3480. En 1983, la división de tecnología de la información alcanzó unas ventas superiores a los 1.100 millones de pesetas (SESA, Memoria anual *1983*, 26).

[111] Mediante aprovechamiento del conocimiento adquirido en el proyecto con Teves, la sección de electrónica industrial invirtió 1 billón de pesetas en 1992-1993 en un nuevo producto para la identificación de los vehículos y en electrónica de potencia o de corrientes fuertes, un componente creciente de costos de los equipos, con un porcentaje cercano al

En la nueva etapa, calificada de histórica por la propia empresa, SESA se reestructuró en siete grupos operativos y divisiones, nueve departamentos funcionales, una subdirección financiera-intervención general y una tesorería general (SESA Memoria 1987, 3)[112].

Alcatel tenía tres problemas bastante espinosos: la situación de las antiguas filiales de IT&T en España; el rendimiento del Sistema 12 y las actividades de los sistemas empresariales en los Estados Unidos (*Électronique Actualités*, 30 de octubre de 1987). Tras adquirir los activos de IT&T en España, Alcatel NV pugnó por integrar a todas las empresas, incluyendo a SESA, en una sociedad financiera denominada Alcatel España, con la misión de canalizar inversiones en el país. Además, planeó sacar Alcatel NV en todas las bolsas de valores europeas, incluída la española. Siguiendo el planteamiento general indicado anteriormente, la multinacional ideó un plan a corto plazo para unificar sus tecnologías de conmutación: E 10 y MT 25, mucho menos avanzadas, desarrolladas por CGE, y el sistema digital 12, heredado de las unidades de I+D de IT&T en todo el mundo[113].

La integración y la compatibilidad deberían ser logradas en una secuencia que empezaría por los componentes, seguiría por las tarjetas y el *software* y finalizaría con los dos sistemas, para evitar la duplicación y, obviamente, para asegurar el suministro a los clientes.

Idéntica índole gradual pensaba aplicar Alcatel NV a la segregación –dos o tres años– de SESA en varias unidades por áreas de actividad para lograr

5% de los costos (Chakravarthy 1996, 534). En 1993, la sección fue designada centro de excelencia de toda la empresa en Alcatel.

[112] Grupos operativos y divisiones: Informática y Comunicaciones, Empresas de Servicios, Redes Públicas, Transmisión y Radio, Cables, Planta Externa y Electrónica Industrial; departamentos funcionales: dirección técnica, desarrollo corporativo, administración, calidad, industria, información y relaciones exteriores, legal.

[113] Los ingenieros fiaban la compatibilidad de los sistemas al desarrollo de módulos comunes susceptibles de hacer la gama homogénea (*Journal officiel de la République française*, 26 de enero de 1988, 40). En cifras de finales de 1981, el balance de la penetración en Francia de los dos sistemas seleccionados por la Administración de PTT arrojaba 2.150 líneas del E 10A; 2.785 del E 10B y 2.010 de MT 25 y el número de centros: 167, 200 y 158, respectivamente. El número de líneas se considera más significativo que el volumen de ventas, que depende del respectivo nivel de precios en los diferentes países. Aproximadamente 12 millones de líneas electrónicas o líneas equivalentes de diseño francés estaban en cartera o en servicio en 40 países (incluyendo Francia), casi la mitad del total global. Al Sistema E 10 correspondían casi 8,2 millones de líneas o líneas equivalentes en servicio en veintiséis países, incluyendo Francia, en un total de 236 centrales–; el sistema MT de Thomson contaba con unos 3,5 millones de líneas o líneas equivalentes en pedidos en 15 países incluyendo a Francia, con un total de 235 centrales. Del total, los pedidos de exportación representaban cerca del 40% (Réponse du ministre des PTT, Sénat, Séance 26 janvier 1982, 4.096).

flexibilidad a la hora de competir en sus respectivos mercados. El plan por el que se convertiría en matriz de estas sociedades debía empezar por la planta exterior y extenderse sucesivamente a las de mayor importancia para la empresa –terminales, ofimática y conmutación y transmisión–. La de mayor envergadura, dedicada a la fabricación de aparatos telefónicos bajo el nombre de Alcatel-CITESA, tendría como núcleo la planta de Málaga en el sur. La multinacional pretendía poner coto a la amenaza de pérdida de sus existentes cuotas debido a la anunciada liberalización de los equipos y a la apertura del mercado. Una vez constituida la nueva empresa, Standard debía suscribir una sustanciosa ampliación de capital y readaptar la capacidad de ventas y las redes comerciales[114]. Alcatel se proponía un plan industrial cuyo objetivo final estribaba en consolidar la estructura industrial de la empresa con cinco fábricas y 6.000 personas en el área de fabricación antes de finalizar el Plan de reconversión e inversión de 1.996 millones de ptas. El primer eje pasaba por la reorganización de la producción por líneas de productos, a imitación de Alcatel NV, para reducir el tamaño de las unidades y lograr mayor competitividad, mayor flexibilidad y mejor servicio al cliente. Esta orientación alumbró unidades independientes, entre las que se encontraba FYCSA, constituida por transformación del departamento de formación. Esta empresa creció a base de la cartera de clientes externos al grupo Alcatel SESA, de manera que la mitad de las grandes empresas españolas utilizaron los servicios de formación y consultoría de FYCSA en 1987 (SESA, *Memoria*, 1987 17-18).

La segunda línea maestra reposaba en la especialización de Villaverde I en conmutación, Villaverde III en electrónica industrial, terminales en Málaga –con un interludio de unos dos años en que también se fabricarían en Toledo centrales del Sistema 12– y transmisión y radio en Toledo. En tercer lugar, el plan preveía introducir modernas técnicas que comprendían la fabricación integrada por ordenador en Villaverde, la fabricación flexible y la robotización. Cerraba la lista un programa de calidad total que aunaba la satisfacción de las necesidades de los clientes y la competitividad[115].

---

[114] Previsiones de Alcatel-CITESA: plantilla entorno a las 1.500 personas y capacidad de producción de dos millones de teléfonos anuales; facturación y ampliación de capital de unos 16.000 y 3.000 millones de pesetas, respectivamente; Alcatel-REYSSA: capital social de 250 millones de pesetas, suscrito en su totalidad por esa compañía; facturación, unos 1.700 millones de pesetas (*El País*, 2 de mayo de 1988 y 24 de octubre de 1988).

[115] Alcatel Standard Eléctrica (1987, 13-15). En Toledo se aplicaron mejoras en la fabricación de circuitos a través de la adecuación de las instalaciones fijas de la planta; se instaló un robot de soldadura en Villaverde, donde continuó la fabricación de monitores para DEC y se empezó a producir controladores de alta tecnología para ordenadores.

Esa dilatada reconversión, orientada en su etapa final a la venta y racionalización de actividades marginales, abrió las compuertas de su negocio principal a la norteamericana AT&T, su mayor competidora. Segregación de activos con creación de una nueva filial unida a una ampliación de capital se repetía con ligeras variantes en las áreas de equipos de oficina y de instalaciones de infraestructura para servicios telefónicos y eléctricos. En el primer caso, el nacimiento de Alcatel-IBERTEL, dedicada al diseño, fabricación, venta, instalación y mantenimiento de equipos y sistemas de oficinas, descansaba en dos pilares[116]: IBERTEL, base de la implantación de CGE en España antes de la compra de IT&T-Europa, y Téléphonie Industrielle et Commerciale (Telic), proveedor de equipos. SESA se reservaba el 90% de la nueva empresa y el restante quedaba para la francesa Telic. Para acabar, la más pequeña de las nuevas empresas, Redes y Servicios, SA (Alcatel-REYSSA), era la encargada de agrupar las actividades de la división de planta exterior de Alcatel Standard Eléctrica[117].

[116] Resulta de interés trazar al esquema comercial de Alcatel IBERTEL, S.A., que se presentaba como única importadora autorizada de determinados aparatos telefónicos y de sus componentes electrónicos (Sentencia 126/2000, de 16 de mayo, *BOE*, 147, 20 de junio de 2000); fabricaba diversos modelos, entre ellos el minisistema Centralita para PYMES Alcatel 312, Alcatel 500 y Alcatel 550 (*Computerworld*, 9 de diciembre de 1994); actuaba en España como agencia de obtención de certificados de aceptación para equipos del grupo, por ejemplo de la centralita privada digital modelo 4200E-M homologado para la RDSI paneuropea, fabricada por Alcatel Business Systems en Francia (*BOE*, 269, 7 de noviembre de 1996, 33.896-33.897); centralitas y otros equipos fabricados por Alcatel Bell Telephone en Bélgica eran homologados a instancia de Ibertel. Los objetivos eran concentrar la producción de equipos de transmisión en Toledo y prácticamente todas las grandes plantas del Sistema digital 12 en Villaverde (Madrid); proporcionar una ampliación de capital en Alcatel-Ibertel hasta alcanzar los 2.500 millones de pesetas, una facturación de unos 8.000 millones de pesetas y empleo para 600 personas en la fábrica de Madrid, así como lograr para REYSSA un capital social en la región de 250 millones de pesetas (*El País*, 2 de mayo de 1988 y 13 de septiembre de 1988; *ABC*, 5 de octubre de 1988, 82). A finales de 1987, la plantilla de la fábrica de Toledo se componía de 1.097 personas –191 mujeres y 906 hombres– cuya edad media era de 42 años. Alcatel-Standard preveía un 20% de crecimiento anual hasta 1992 (*El Día de Toledo*, 20 de diciembre de 1987). Con el cambio en el modelo territorial, las entidades públicas no estatales (comunidades autónomas) se unieron al estado para financiar la inversión en la nueva fábrica de teléfonos móviles ALCATEL-CITESA en el Parque Tecnológico de Málaga (Andalucía), inaugurada a finales de octubre de 1995 (*El Diario 1*, 26 de octubre de 1997; *Database*, 19, 2-3, 1996, 23). ALCATEL-CITESA implantó el sistema de trabajo por objetivos (S.T.O.), básicamente una modalidad de promoción y de incentivos salariales vinculados a objetivos cumplidos y a comportamiento personal (Sección Sindical de CCOO de Alcatel Citesa a la Dirección provincial de Trabajo de Málaga, 7 de julio de 1997).

[117] Se preveía una ampliación de capital de 2.000 millones de pesetas en Alcatel-IBERTEL hasta alcanzar los 2.500, facturación de unos 8.000 millones de pesetas y plantilla de 600 personas en la fábrica de Madrid; capital social de REYSSA situado en tomo a los 250 millones

La tríada española de Alcatel (CITESA, IBERTEL y REYSSA) adquirió una estructura organizativa similar a la de la matriz, basada en unidades separadas divididas por áreas de actividad. La multinacional francesa había encontrado la forma de competir de manera más efectiva y, a través de Alcatel-CITESA, lanzó un plan de inversión quinquenal por valor de 2.500 millones de pesetas para dotarse de un centro de producción y otro de diseño, planificación y distribución[118]. La reestructuración del grupo de empresas españolas de Alcatel se completó con una pieza clave final: la adquisición de la participación minoritaria pero sustancial de CTNE en SESA, a la que ya se ha aludido.

Alcatel SESA actuó de forma coordinada con todas las fábricas de la matriz. De acuerdo con el plan previsto, emprendió la automatización de las plantas, el recurso a la fabricación integrada por ordenador en entornos CIM (Computer Integrated Manufacturing) en Villaverde y Toledo, así como a instalaciones para el montaje de superficie en Villaverde, Toledo y Málaga (Alcatel SESA *Memoria anual*, 1987 14).

Alcatel Standard Eléctrica calificó el ejercicio de 1989 como excepcional por las ventas –suministro de 1.082.00 líneas digitales y 268.000 analógicas (frente a 523.100 y 374.200 en 1988)– la organización –descentralización de la gestión de negocios– y la inversión de 10.969 millones de ptas. en I+D[119]. Al año siguiente, las ventas empezaron a declinar, arrastradas por el descenso de los pedidos de Telefónica, principal cliente, aunque con una caída atemperada por el aumento de las exportaciones (Gráfico 6). Las secciones de redes públicas de conmutación y de transmisión y radio fueron los puntales de la producción en esos años (Tabla 5).

---

de pesetas (*El País*, 2 de mayo de 1988 y 13/9/1988; *ABC*, 5 de octubre de 1988, 82); Alcatel-CITESA se propuso integrar la plantilla preexistente –1.150 trabajadores– y sumarse a la reconversión del grupo (*ABC*, 10/11/1989). Izquierda Unida-Convocatoria por Andalucía denunció el incumplimiento de los compromisos sobre empleo e I+D contraídos en el plan de reconversión (*Boletín Oficial del Parlamento Andaluz*, 27/9/1991, 3.877). Con el cambio de modelo territorial entidades públicas no estatales – Administración autonómica– se sumaron al Estado en la financiación de la inversión en la nueva fábrica de ALCATEL-CITESA en Andalucía. La planta de CITESA, inaugurada en 1995, producía anualmente 1.300.000 terminales y realizó ventas por 173.000 millones de pesetas en 1994, de los que 107.000 provinieron de exportaciones; contaba con laboratorios de diseño mecánico asistido por ordenador, de diseño topológico de plata y telefonometría, electroacústica, electrónico y de radiofrecuencia (*Computerworld*, 10 de noviembre de 1995; *Acuerdos Junta de Andalucía-Alcatel*, 1993; *ABC*, 27 de octubre de 1995). Ejemplo de rotación de capital humano, el ingeniero industrial Miguel Iraburu Elizondo desembarcó en la gerencia general de Alcatel Citesa procedente de la planta madrileña de SWF-Autoelectric S.A.

[118] *El País*, 24 de octubre de 1988; *ABC*, 5 de octubre de 1988.

[119] Alcatel Citesa y Alcatel Sistemas (Alcatel Standard Eléctrica 1989, 6-7).

Gráfico 6. Ventas de SESA/Alcatel-SESA por clientes
(millones de pesetas corrientes)

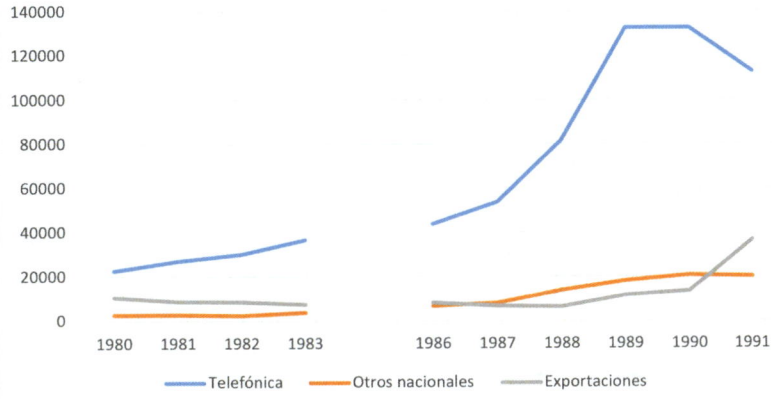

Fuente: Elaboración propia a partir de Standard Eléctrica/
Alcatel SESA, *Memoria(s) Anual(es)*.

Tabla 5. Composición de las ventas de Alcatel-
SESA por grupos operativos y divisiones

	190	1986	1987	1988	1989	1990	1991
Redes públicas conmutación	62,86	36,66	31,94	38,35	45,35	47,81	58,75
Transmisión y radio	9,67	17,83	19,47	25,62	27,35	33,66	29,57
Informática y comunicaciones	0,00	28,66	29,24	0,00	0,00	0,00	0,00
Cables	12,11	12,51	13,34	13,00	12,85	12,15	7,37
Electrónica industrial	0,00	3,73	5,29	3,93	5,89	6,37	4,28
Audiocomunicaciones	0,00	0,00	0,00	14,90	8,42	0,00	0,00
Ofimática	0,00	0,00	0,00	2,68	0,00	0,00	0,00
Otros	15,36	0,61	0,71	1,51	0,15	0,00	0,03
Total	100	100	100	100	100	100	100

Fuente: Elaboración propia a partir de Alcatel Standard
Eléctrica, *Memoria(s) Anual(es)*.

Conclusión

Tanto en la metodología como en el contenido, este trabajo es una aportación a los historiadores económicos y empresariales interesados en el cambio tecnológico y las limitaciones institucionales que acompañan y a veces condicionan las opciones técnicas. A diferencia de otras investigaciones, destaca por tener en cuenta las políticas industriales, especialmente su aplicación, que puede resultar difícil de diseñar.

El trabajo se apoya en un enfoque metodológico que utiliza casos concretos para explicar fenómenos globales poniendo en relación a varios actores. La utilización de España como caso de estudio ha proporcionado elementos clave para analizar el desarrollo de la gran empresa en un sector de alta tecnología, el papel de los grandes protagonistas, la acción de las multinacionales que consiguieron mantener un oligopolio en el proceso y la reestructuración del sector TEquipI con especial insistencia en la elaboración de la política de reestructuración. En un contexto de cambio tecnológico acelerado, SESA ofrece un intento de transición controlada de la oferta, apoyada por los demás agentes implicados, con el fin de atenuar los efectos negativos sobre el territorio y el empleo.

A lo largo de los años ochenta, auténticas turbulencias normativas y tecnológicas pusieron patas arriba el mundo de las telecomunicaciones, reconfigurándose a escala mundial el oligopolio de la industria de equipos, con excepción de la apertura en algunos segmentos del mercado (periféricos). La piedra angular la puso el campeón nacional francés CGE, de propiedad pública, en un momento de su recorrido desde la nacionalización en 1982 hasta su vuelta a la esfera privada cinco años más tarde.

¿Por qué y cómo consiguieron las multinacionales mantener la estructura oligopolística del sector en medio de un proceso de cambio radical? La explicación principal radica en un intento de los Estados nacionales de convertir una parte del sector de propiedad pública nacional europea en un líder capaz de adquirir activos de una multinacional estadounidense. Este movimiento, unido a las consecuencias geográficas del traslado del centro de toma de decisiones a Europa, dejó intacta la estructura de oligopolio e incluso la reforzó, principalmente mediante el uso de todos los poderes del Estado y la incorporación de nuevos activos al sector para permitirle escalar posiciones en la clasificación mundial. La parte nacional francesa lideró la transformación, cerrando cualquier posibilidad de mantener algún tipo de integración vertical entre servicio e la industria y limitando a los competidores potenciales. El nuevo gigante mundial que ahora era Alcatel centró sus estrategias en la reconversión de los activos nacionales para mantener y ampliar los mercados tradicionales.

En este sentido, España desempeña un papel subordinado en el mercado mundial en el que pretendía competir, pero también ofrece un ejemplo esclarecedor de los diversos factores que subyacen a la evolución global de las grandes empresas, así como una vía de ajuste (Kornelakis, 2015, 885-902).

En definitiva, el caso español aporta una serie de características importantes al análisis de la remodelación y reestructuración en el oligopolio del sector TEquipI. Para empezar por la cuestión fundamental, añade una mayor complejidad y elementos distintivos. En términos más generales, las pruebas exigen deshechar cualquier visión simplificada o unidireccional de los fenómenos en favor de la sutileza y el matiz. Las estrategias de las multinacionales variaron a lo largo del tiempo, al igual que las políticas gubernamentales y las posturas sindicales en medio de un considerable descontento.

El desarrollo de su política industrial como parte de un proceso de integración en la CEE retrasado permitió al Estado español ejercer una mayor autonomía, que a su vez se vio moderada en cierta medida por la transferencia de competencias del gobierno central a las comunidades autónomas. Sin embargo, en última instancia, la plena integración en la CEE equiparó al país con los demás miembros, sometiéndolo a políticas de desintegración vertical que fueron significativas en el sector (por ejemplo, la desinversión de Telefónica en SESA). Por su parte, los factores de continuidad actuaron a través del mantenimiento de barreras de entrada no fiscales –la homologación de equipos por el Gobierno– y la intervención del Estado nación en las negociaciones de reestructuración industrial, como ocurrió en la etapa de Alcatel tras la entrada de España en la CEE.

El caso español ilustra la motivación de las respuestas de reestructuración a la integración europea y la liberalización, así como las idiosincrasias que surgieron en las pautas de ajuste. Arroja luz sobre el contraste entre el alcance nacional de la CEE y la política industrial del gobierno español, el intervencionismo de la CTNE, la acción sindical y el alcance global de la postura de IT&T y Alcatel. Esto apunta al margen de maniobra dentro del propio programa político para encontrar soluciones alternativas y continuidades en las políticas industriales en el marco de programas políticos opuestos en los que, si acaso, solo cambian los agentes.

Entre las competencias transferidas por el Estado a la CTNE figuraban la financiación parcial de los costes de reestructuración, la estabilización de la demanda y la asunción del excedente de empleo del proceso de reestructuración. A pesar de los límites impuestos por la transferencia histórica de una parte de sus competencias, el Estado seguía desempeñando un papel importante. Obstaculizó la entrada de la CTNE en el consorcio EUROTEL y, por tanto, su capacidad de actuación en la configuración de la siguiente fase del TEquipI. Exigió negociaciones tripartitas como condición para la concesión de subvenciones y ayudas y nombró un comité para abordar el futuro de las filiales españolas. En definitiva, actuó como estratega orientado a objetivos, en consonancia con Colli, Mariotti y Piscitello (2014, 487-508) y su análisis de la interrelación entre los operadores tradicionales de telecomunicaciones y el Gobierno. La política industrial se combinó con la política aplicada por la operadora de red, que actuó como un monopolio semipúblico durante varios años precisamente porque el Estado-nación tenía margen de maniobra para llegar a acuerdos con la CEE, lo que dio lugar a claras implicaciones para la industria de las telecomunicaciones. Así, la CTNE respaldaba al Estado al tiempo que utilizaba su poder de compra para intervenir en el mercado de equipos con independencia del presupuesto del Estado o de cualquier otro organismo estatal, a diferencia de los PTT europeos. Por último, hay que señalar la importancia del marco político y la implicación no siempre unánime de los sindicatos CCOO y UGT, que actuaron como grupos de presión legítimos en un país con una democracia nueva, aún frágil y que todavía no contaba con la larga trayectoria de otras naciones.

España, cada vez más integrada en la economía mundial, desempeñó un papel importante y distintivo en la remodelación del oligopolio por razones históricas, concretamente por la notable y extensa presencia de IT&T en el territorio a través de su filial SESA. Dado el fuerte predominio de SESA como proveedor de CTNE y sus perspectivas en el creciente mercado latinoamericano, el futuro del sector en un mercado global fuertemente competitivo se jugó en gran medida en España. SESA fue una pieza destacada en la creación de Alcatel y en los cambios que se produjeron en el sector y apoyó su carácter oligopolístico. Sin embargo, cuando la monopolística CTNE, cliente y accionista minoritario de SESA, se excluyó del consorcio paneuropeo EUROTEL, origen del campeón europeo Alcatel, vio debilitado su poder de decisión sobre la política específica de reestructuración de SESA. ¿Qué había cambiado en las telecomunicaciones a finales de los años ochenta? Dentro de un panorama mixto de continuidades y cambios, hubo continuidad en la liberalización de las telecomunicaciones a escala mundial y en la reestructuración de la industria de equipos, con un énfasis en el aumento de la concentración.

En España, el monopolio semipúblico CTNE siguió siendo el principal cliente de equipos de telecomunicaciones. Sin embargo, pasó de ser un motor de industrialización a través de su anterior *holding* industrial a seguir una estrategia de expansión internacional. Como elemento de continuidad, cuando la presión exterior de las grandes instituciones obligó a la empresa a desinvertir en la industria, su internacionalización como operadora de red amplió su potencial de aprovisionamiento y logró alcanzar precios y condiciones de entrega equiparables a los ofrecidos por las empresas fabricantes en las que participaba.

La evolución de la industria estuvo muy marcada por la incertidumbre de la demanda, que se mantuvo alta en 1987-1991 con el plan cuatrienal y posteriormente descendió. La competencia se intensificó: Alcatel-SESA se vio obligada a compartir el suministro de equipos de transmisión, conmutación y radio con varios proveedores. En estas circunstancias, la empresa diversificó su clientela tradicional reforzando el papel de algunas secciones o grupos operativos, por ejemplo con las redes públicas de conmutación. De hecho, la estructura de mercado de Alcatel-SESA cambió en estos años de gran demanda. En una clara tendencia de sustitución, la cuota de Telefónica en las ventas totales cayó ocho puntos porcentuales, que fueron exactamente los que se ganaron en exportaciones, según los informes anuales de la compañía. Por lo tanto, en términos de relación entre continuidad y complejidad, la sustitución de clientes no socavó el oligopolio porque la empresa cubrió el declive de su principal comprador con demanda extranjera.

La telefonía móvil tardaría unos años en convertirse en un instrumento del servicio universal. En las fases avanzadas del desarrollo de la tecnología –es decir, la tercera generación, 3G o UMTS– Telefónica actuaría como un operador agresivo al participar en subastas en varios países europeos. Por último, la rápida obsolescencia de la tecnología digital, que puede acortar el ciclo electromecánico en unas dos décadas, añadió una razón más a la inacabada reestructuración del sector.

La supervivencia del oligopolio en el sector TEquipI en medio de la creciente liberalización del mercado se debió a complejas estrategias empresariales –adquisiciones, empresas conjuntas, fusiones y diversificación– así como a las intervenciones de los Estados nacionales y otros agentes. Desde el punto de vista español, la reestructuración del sector fue el resultado de la compleja interacción y el peso desigual de múltiples actores, a saber, las multinacionales IT&T/Alcatel y la UE en el escenario exterior y el Estado español, las comunidades autónomas de España y sus sindicatos recientemente legalizados en el escenario nacional.

Al final, el vínculo en España entre el operador monopolista histórico y los proveedores nacionales de equipos se debilitó pero no se destruyó porque el Estado nación conservó una influencia sobre los mercados liberalizados a través de su política industrial y de ciertas barreras no arancelarias ya mencionadas que favorecían a los fabricantes ya establecidos en el país. En un principio, SESA adoptó una transición tecnológica gradual basada en una estrategia orientada a la inversión y trató de mitigar los conflictos laborales derivados de los recortes de personal, objetivo que no se consiguió. Posteriormente, la presión de su empresa matriz obligó a SESA a endurecer su postura y acelerar la transición. Como ilustra el caso de SESA, la reestructuración de la industria de equipos de telecomunicaciones tuvo el carácter de una reorganización interna que no debilitó el oligopolio. Ninguno de los agentes implicados cuestionó la validez de la estructura del mercado.

En resumen, SESA personifica una reestructuración compleja, a largo plazo, negociada y casi consensuada de la industria de las telecomunicaciones, que no se parecía al «estilo *bulldozer*» perseguido por Alcatel Bell Telephone en Bélgica, por ejemplo. Sin embargo, el proceso de reestructuración de SESA no estuvo exento de conflictos. También resultó muy costoso para el erario público y, a la larga, no tuvo éxito. Una vez en el ámbito de Alcatel, la reestructuración aúna la continuidad de las formas y la centralización de las grandes decisiones, sin dejar apenas lugar a rasgos nacionales específicos.

Conviene hacer una última consideración antes de concluir. El eje del análisis corresponde aquí a un alto el fuego temporal. Alcatel no tardaría en imponer un cambio de estrategia consistente en fabricar sin fábrica, lo que provocó cierres de plantas, despidos masivos y deslocalización de la actividad. Al final, nada pudo evitar que fuera engullida por Nokia.

La evolución de la industria mundial de las telecomunicaciones y el papel desempeñado por el principal objeto de esta investigación apoyan la idea de una industria caracterizada por un cambio de agentes dentro de la supervivencia del oligopolio.

Anexos

Anexo 1. Desglose regional de las ventas de equipos de telecomunicaciones de ITT, 1984 (%)

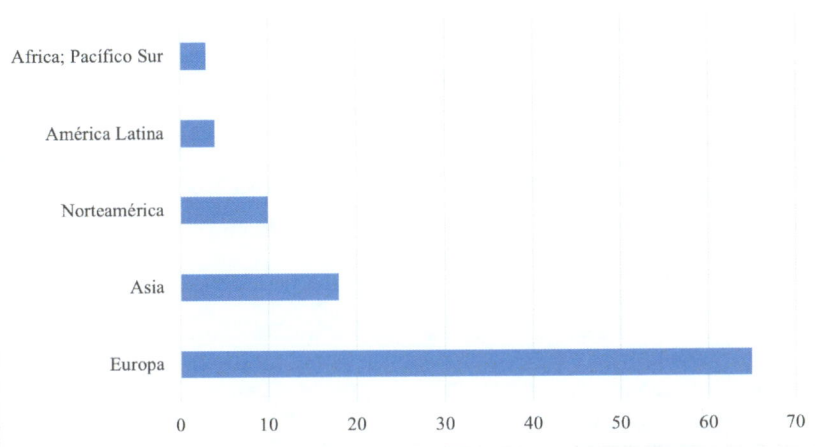

Fuente: Elaboración a partir de *New York Times*, 27 de junio de 1986.

Fuentes

Archives de l'Assemblée Nationale, Francia.

Archives Nationales, Francia.

Archives du Sénat, Francia.

Archivo del Congreso de los Diputados, Madrid.

Comisión Nacional del Mercado de Valores (CNMV), Madrid.

Telefónica, Madrid.

Hemeroteca

ABC, España.

AHCIET, *Revista de telecomunicaciones*, España.

Computer Business Review

Computerworld

El País, España.
La Repubblica, Italia.
Le Monde, Italia.
Libération, Francia.
New York Times

Referencias

Aghion, Philippe; Dewatripont, Mathias; Du, Luosha ; Harrison, Ann y Legros, Patrick. 2012. «Industrial Policy and Competition». *NBER Working Paper*, n°. 18048.

Agnew, Carson E. y Romeo, Anthony A. 1981. «Restructuring the US telecommunications industry: Impact on innovation». *Telecommunications Policy*, 5, n°.4: December: 273-288.

Alcatel. 1998. *Alcatel 1000 S12*. París: Alcatel.

Alcatel-Lucent. *Submission to Commerce Commission Discussion Paper on Next Generation Networks*. febrero de 2009.

Alcatel SESA. 1991. *Memoria Anual 1991*. Madrid: Alcatel SESA.

Anonym. 2012. *Diversification Strategies of Nokia*. Munich: GRIN Verlag.

Aranzadi, Claudio. 1992. La estrecha relación entre el progreso y la innovación. *Desarrollo Tecnológico*. N°.1: 6-11.

Aranzadi, Claudio. 1989. «La política de desinversiones en el INI». *Papeles de economía Española*. N°.38: 258-261.

Araskog, Rand V. 1999. *The ITT Wars: An Insider's View of Hostile Takeovers*. Washington: Beard Books.

Arpege Group. 1994. *Network Management: Concepts and tools*. Londres: Chapman and Hall.

ASM International. 1989. *Electronic Materials Handbook: Packaging*. Materials Park OH: ASM International.

Ballarín, Eduard y Boudeguer, R. M. 2000. «The Internationalization of Alcatel Standard Eléctrica S.A.» *IESE*, DG-1117-E, 1/1995.

Balbi, Gabriele, Fari, Simone y Richeri, Giuseppe. 2014. «Telecommunications Italian Style. The shaping of the constitutive choices (1850-1914)». *History of Technology*, 32, 235-258.

Banco de España. 2000. *Resultados anuales de las empresas no financieras 1990-1997*. Madrid: Central de Balances del Banco de España.

Bartlett, Christopher A. y Ghoshal, Sumantra S. 1989. Managing Across Borders: The Transnational Solution. Cambridge MA: Harvard Business School Press.

Bartlett, Will y Prica, Ivana. 2016. «Interdependence between Core and Peripheries of the European Economy: Secular Stagnation and Growth in the Western Balkans». *LEQS Paper* No. *104/2016,* febrero: 1-25.

Barsoux, Jean-Louis y Löscher, Peter. 1991. «The Making of a French Manager». *Harvard Business Review,* July-August, 58-67.

Baskoy, Tuna. 2008. *The Political Economy of European Union Competition Policy: A Case Study of the Telecommunications Industry*. Nueva York: Routledge.

Batt, Rosemary y Darbishire, Owen. 1997. «Institutional determinants of deregulation and restructuring in telecommunications: Britain, Germany, and United States compared». *International Contributions to Labour Studies*. N°.7: 59-79.

Beaujolin-Bellet, Rachel e Issaverdens, Olivier. 2006. *Restructuration de la direction industrielle du site d'Alcatel Business System à Illkirch Graffenstaden, Alsace, France*. Reims: MIRE.

Becattini, Giacomo, Bellandi, Marco y De Propris, Lisa. 2009. *A Handbook of Industrial Districts*. Cheltenham: Edward Elgar.

Bellas, C. J. et al. 1994. *Foreign privatization in Poland*. Varsovia: Center for Social & Economic Research.

Benton, L. A. 1990. *Invisible Factories: The Informal Economy and Industrial Development*. Nueva York: SUNY Press.

Berglof, Erik. 2016. «European Industrial Policy – Tapping the Full Growth Potential of the EU». *Intereconomics*. 51, 16: 335-340.

BIPE. 1991. *Electronic engineering*. Bruselas: BIPE.

Bitar, Sergio y Lowenthal, Abraham F. 2015. *Democratic Transitions: Conversations with World Leaders*. Baltimore: JHU Press.

Boon, Marten. 2017. «Business Enterprise and Globalization: Towards a Transnational Business History». *Business History Review* 91, Special Issue 3: 511-535.

Brambilla, Carlo and Andrea Colli. 2016. «Big Business performance in Twentieth-Century Italy». En *Serp. 279*, Cassis, Youssef, Colli, Andrea y Schröter, Harm G. 110-113.

Brenner, Robert. 2003. *The Boom and the Bubble: The US in the World Economy*. Londres-Nueva York: Verso.

Bresciani, Stefano y Ferraris, Aliberto. 2012. *Imprese multinazionali. Innovazione e scelte localizzative*. Santarcangelo di Romagna: Maggioli Editore.

Brown, Lori H.1994. *Telecommunications Equipment*. Washington: Office of Industries.

Burnier, Michel. 2002. «La empresa sin fábricas, entrevista de Michel Le Doaré, responsable sindical de Alcatel». *TERMINAL*, 87, primavera/verano, 5-7.

Butcher, Arona. 1991. *Global Competitiveness of U.S. Advanced-technology Manufacturing Industries: Communications Technology and Equipment*. Washington: U.S. International Trade Commission.

Cable, Vincent. 1995. «The Diminished Nation-State: A Study in the Loss of Economic Power». *Daedalus*, 124, n°.2: 23-53.

Calvo, Ángel. 2020. «Local R&D Capacity Building Strategies in the Two Decades Prior to the Great Recession of 2008: The Case of ICTs in Spain». *European Journal of Business and Management Research*, Vvol. 5, Issue 2, 1-13.

Calvo, Ángel. 2016. «Innovar en tiempos difíciles. Empresas bajo presión en la Guerra Fría». En Calvo, Ángel (2016): 3-55.

Calvo, Ángel. 2017. «Multinacionales, Estado y empresa semipública en la industria de tecnología avanzada durante la década de 1980». *Investigaciones de Historia Económica - Economic History Research*, 13, n°.1: 51-62.

Calvo, Ángel. 2014. Telecomunicaciones y el nuevo mundo digital en España. *La aportación de Standard Eléctrica*. Madrid: Planeta-Fundación Telefónica.

Calzada, Joan y Costas, Antón. «Economía política de la liberalización: ideas, intereses y estrategias». En «Innovar en tiempos difíciles. Empresas bajo presión en la Guerra Fría». *Harvard Deusto Business Research*, 5, n°.1, Calvo, Ángel (2016): 3-55.

Canalejo, Miguel. 2020. «Una multinacional dentro de otra multinacional, SESA (1984-2000)». En *Internacionalización de las industrias de telecomunicación*, Naeve, Ingemar et al., 38-57, Madrid: Foro Histórico Telecomunicaciones, COIT-AEIT.

Canalejo, Miguel. 1995. «Innovación organizativa en Alcatel Standard Eléctrica S.A.» *V Congreso Nacional de ACEDE*, vol. 1. Madrid: San Lorenzo de El Escorial, septiembre, 205-216.

Canalejo, Miguel. 2005. «Una lección de cambio cultural: Alcatel». En *Homo valens: naturaleza, origen y gestión del valor en la empresa*, Uriz, Javier. 51-60, Madrid-Buenos Aires: Ediciones Díaz de Santos.

Canalejo, Miguel. «La contribución de las operadoras de telecomunicaciones al desarrollo económico y social de España». *La Noche de las Telecomunicaciones*. 13 de noviembre, Pamplona, 2008.

Carr, Robert et al. 1998. *Telecommunications Equipment: U.S. Performance in Selected Major Markets, Staff Research Study*. Washington: DIANE Publishing.

Cassis, Youssef, Colli, Andrea y Schröter, Harm G. 2016. *The Performance of European Business in the Twentieth Century*. Oxford: Oxford University Press.

Castellani, D. 2007. «L'internazionalizzazione della produzione in Italia: caratteristiche delle imprese ed effetti sul sistema económico». *L'Industria*, 3, julio-septiembre: 467-493.

CCOO. 2008. *Las políticas sectoriales y su repercusión en la reorganización del sector eTIC*. 1 de diciembre, 25.

CEE. 1983. *Foundations for the future of European industry*. Ámsterdam meeting, junio 1.

Chakravarthy, Bala. 1996. «The Process of Transformation: In Search of Nirvana». *European Management Journal*, 14, 6, December, 529-539.

Chandler, Alfred D. 1990. *Scale and Scope*. Cambridge MA: Cambridge University Press.

Chandler, Alfred D. Jr.; Amatori, Franco y Hikino, Takashi. 1999. *Big Business and the Wealth of Nations*. Cambridge MA: Cambridge University Press.

Chapuis, Robert J. y Joel, Amos E. 2003. *100 Years of Telephone Switching*. Ámsterdam: IOS Press.

Christensen, Sverre A. 2006. *Switching Relations. The rise and fall of the Norwegian telecom industry*. Oslo: BI Norwegian School of Management, Oecon Series of Dissertations 2/2006.

Círculo de Empresarios. 1984. «La reconversión industrial: un posible análisis». *Papeles de Economía Española*, 21, 291-310.

Cirillo, Valeria, Guarascio, Dario y Pianta, Mario. 2014. *Will Europe's industry survive the crisis? Competitiveness, employment and the need for an industrial policy*. Urbino: Università degli Studi.

Cisco Systems. 2001. *Annual report pursuant to section 13 or 15,d) of the securities exchange act of 1934 for the fiscal year ended july 30 2011*. Commission file number 0-18225.

Clifton, Judith, Pierre Lanthier y Schröter, Harm (ed.). 2014. *The Economic and Social Regulation of Public Utilities: An International History*. Londres: Routledge.

Cohen, Stephen y DeLong, J. Bradford 2016. *Concrete Economics: The Hamilton Approach to Economic Growth and Policy*. Brighton, MA: Harvard Business Review.

Colli, Andrea, Mariotti, Sergio y Piscitello, Lucia. 2014. «Governments as strategists in designing global players: The case of European utilities». *Journal of European Public Policy*, 21, n°.4: 487-508.

Comisión de Regulación de Telecomunicaciones. 2000. *El sector de las Telecomunicaciones en Colombia, en la década de los 90s*. Bogotá: CRT.

Commission of the European Communities. 1992. «The European telecommunications equipment industry. The state of play, issues at stake and proposals for action». SEC, 92, 1.049 final, Bruselas, 15 July.

Commission of the European Communities. 1990. *Green Paper on the Development of the Common Market for Telecom Equipment*. Boston: Information Gatekeepers.

Commission of the European Communities. 1985. *Social Europe. Supplement on new technologies and social change*. Luxemburgo: Office for Official Publications of the European Communities.

Commission of the European Communities. 1983. *Prospects for the development of new policies: Research and development, energy and new technologies*. Luxemburgo: Office for Official Publications of the European Communities.

Council of Europe. 1990. *Documents*. Estrasburgo: Council of Europe.

Crandall, Robert W. y Flamm, Kenneth (eds.) 1989. *Changing the Rules: Technological Change, International Competition, and Regulation in Communications*. Washington: Brookings Institution Press.

Dangeard, Frank. 2011. *Décision de crise dans l'entreprise (La): 12 histoires de gouvernance*. París: Odile Jacob.

Darmon, Jacques. 2010. «Modalités et portée de la sortie du téléphone de Thomson». *Entreprises et histoire*, 61, 4, 108-112.

Dataquest. 1990. *European semiconductor application markets, 1987-1992*. San José: Dataquest.

De la Fuente, Juan M. y Galán, José I. 2000. «La gran empresa española: estrategia, propiedad y organización». *Dirección y Organización*, 23, 99-100.

Dörrenbächer, Christoph. 2000. «Between global market constraints and national dependencies: the internationalization of the world's leading telecommunications equipment suppliers». *Transnational Corporations*, 9, n°.3: 1-32.

Doz, Yves L. 1979. *Government Control and Multinational Strategic Management: Power Systems and Telecommunications Equipment*. Nueva York: Praeger.

Durán, Juan J. 1994. «La actividad exterior de la empresa española». *Economistas*, 60, 109-112.

Economic Report of the President Transmitted to the Congress February 1990. 1990. Washington: U.S. Government Printing Office.

Edquist, Charles; Hommen, Lief y Tsipouri, Lena. 2000. *Public technology procurement and innovation*. Nowell, MA: Springer.

Edwards, Tony. 2001. «The consequences of corporate restructuring for employees and unions». *Eurofound*, 27 April. https://www.eurofound.europa.eu/publications/article/2002/restructuring-and-job-cuts-in-the-telecoms-sector

Eliassen, Kjell A. y Sjovaag, Marit (ed.) 1999. *European telecommunications liberalisation*. New York: Routledge.

Elsner, Wolfram. 1993. «Industrial Defense Conversion: Guiding the Market at the Regional Level: The Case of the State of Bremen, Germany». *Journal of Economic Issues*, 27, 4: 1254-1262.

Emiroğlu, Ulaş. 2003. «Catch-up with Generative State: Lessons from Chinese Telecom Equipment Industry» STOS-WS-15/03. Ankara: METU-STPS.

Erne, Roland. 2008. *European Unions: Labor's Quest for a Transnational Democracy*. Ithaca-Londres: Cornell University Press.

Espina, Álvaro. 1995. *Hacia una estrategia española de competitividad.* Madrid: Fundación Argentaria.

Estudios de Política Exterior. 1995. «Los FAD en 1994 se adaptan a Helsinki». *Política Exterior*, 9, 46, agosto-septiembre: 184-186.

Ethier, Diane. 1997. *Economic Adjustment in New Democracies: Lessons from Southern Europe*. Houndsmills: Macmillan.

Eurofound. 2003. *EMCC dossier on industrial restructuring*. Bruselas: Eurofound. https://www.eurofound.europa.eu/observatories/emcc/articles/business-working-conditions/emcc-dossier-on-industrial-restructuring

European Commission. 1997. *1996 Single Market Review*. Luxemburgo: Office for Official Publications of the European Communities.

European Communities. 1992. *Panorama of EC industry Statistical supplement 1992. Latest information on manufacturing and service industries in the European Community*. Office for Official Publications of the European Communities, Luxemburgo.

Fainboim, Israel y Rodríguez, Carlos J. 2004. *Colombia: Desarrollo Económico Reciente en Infraestructura (REDI). Balanceando las necesidades sociales y productivas de Infraestructura*. Documento del Banco Mundial, 1 de septiembre.

Fanjul, Enrique. 2003. «Relaciones comerciales: España en la China de la reforma». *Revista CIDOB d'Afers Internacionals*, 63, 151-166.

Feldstein, Martin. 2007. *American Economic Policy in the 1980s*. Chicago: University of Chicago Press.

Fernández Castro, Joaquín. 1985. «Una aproximación sociológica a la reconversión industrial». *Papeles de Economía Española*, 22, 403-424.

Fischman, Kurt y Jorstad, Norman D. 1990. *Digital SPC switching technology. Foreign technology assessment*. IDA paper p-2498, Institute for Defense Analyses, diciembre.

Fitzgerald, Robert. 2015. *The Rise of the Global Company: Multinationals and the Making of the Modern World*. Cambridge MA: Cambridge University Press.

Forester, Tom. 1987. *High-tech Society: The Story of the Information Technology Revolution*. Cambridge MA: MIT Press.

Fransman, Martin. 1995. *Japan's Computer and Communications Industry: The Evolution of Industrial Giants and Global Competitiveness*. Oxford: Oxford University Press.

Friedman, Walter, A. y *Geoffrey Jones*. 2011. «*Business* History: Time for Debate». Business *History Review* 85, 11 May: 1-8.

Froehlich, Fritz E. y Kent, Allen. 1990. *The Froehlich/Kent Encyclopedia of Telecommunications*. Nueva York: CRC Press.

Funk, Jeffrey. 2002. *Global Competition Between and Within Standards: The Case of Mobile Phones*. Houndsmille: Palgrave.

Galgoczi, Béla, Keune, Maarten y Watt, Andrew. 2008. *Jobs on the Move: An Analytical Approach to Relocation and Its Impact on Employment*. Bruselas: Peter Lang.

Gazier, Bernard y Bruggeman, Frédéric. (eds.) 2008. *Restructuring Work and Employment in Europe: Managing Change in an Era of Globalisation*. Cheltenham: Edward Elgar.

Ghoshal, Sumantra y Bartlett, Christopher A. 1990. «The Multinational Corporation As an Interorganizational Network». *The Academy of Management Review*, 15, 4: 603-625.

Grignon, Francis. 2004. *Délocalisations: pour un néo-colbertisme européen*. Rapport d'information nº. 374 fait au nom de la commission des Affaires économiques, 23 de junio.

Grindley, Peter C. 1987. «System X: The Failure of Procurement». *Working Paper Series*, nº. 29, agosto.

Griset, Pascal y Fridenson, Patrick. 2013. *Entreprises de haute technologie, État et souveraineté depuis 1945*. París: Institut de la gestion publique et du développement économique.

Grupp, Hariolf y Schnöring, Thomas. 1992. «Research and development in telecommunications: National systems under pressure». *Telecommunications Policy* 16, Issue 1, January–February: 46-66.

Guillén, Mauro F.; García-Canal, Esteban y Llaneza, Ana. 2012. «La presencia de las empresas españolas en el exterior». *Panorama social*, 16, 33-52.

Guillén, Mauro F. y García-Canal, Esteban. 2007. La expansión internacional de la empresa española: una nueva base de datos sistemática. *ICE, Revista de Economía*, 839: 23-34.

Hamann, Kerstin. 2012. *The Politics of Industrial Relations: Labor Unions in Spain*. Nueva York: Routledge.

Helg, Rodolfo y Ranci, Pippo. 1988. «Economías de escala y la integración de la economía europea: el caso de Italia». *Economic Papers*, 69, octubre, 1-82.

Hendry, John y Eccles, Tony. 1992. *European Cases in Strategic Management*. Edimburgo: Chapman and Hall.

Henck, Fred W. et al. 1988. *A Slippery Slope: The Long Road to the Breakup of AT&T*. Westport CT: Greenwood Press.

Holton, Richard. 1986. «Industrial Politics in France: Nationalisation Under Mitterrand». *West European* Politics, 9, n°.1: 67-80.

Hooley, Margot L. 1998. «Telecommunications in Colombia». En *Telecommunications in Latin America.* Noam, Eli. 99-114. Nueva York: Oxford University Press.

Hulsink, Willem. 2012. *Privatisation and Liberalisation in European Telecommunications: Comparing Britain, the Netherlands and France*. Londres: Routledge.

Iglesias, María Antonia. 2010. *La memoria recuperada: Lo que nunca han contado Felipe González y los dirigentes socialistas*. Madrid: Aguilar.

IGI Consulting. 1996. *ATM Product Directory.* Boston: Information Gatekeepers.

International Labour Organisation. 1991. *Consequences of Technological Developments in the Postal and Telecommunications Services, Together with an Examination of the Conditions Governing Participation in Decision-making Concerning the Introduction and Utilisation of New Technologies*. Joint Committee for Postal and Telecommunications Services, Ginebra.

ITU. 2003. *The evolution to 3G mobile - Status report*. ITU, Ginebra.

Iwens, Jean-Luc. 1984. *Évolution récente de 3 sociétés: ATT. CIT_Alcatel, Ericsson.* Bruselas: GRESEA.

Jacob, Jean-Baptiste y Penn, Corentin. 1995. *Commutation téléphonique. Autocommutateurs des reseaux publics.* París: Techniques de l'ingénieur.

Johnson, Chalmers. 1984. *The Industrial Policy Debate.* San Francisco CA: ICS Press.

Kaldor, Mary; Selchow, Sabine y Murray-Leach, Tamsin. 2015. *Subterranean Politics in Europe.* Nueva York: Palgrave Macmillan.

Kaynaket, Erdener et al. 2014. *Multinational Strategic Management: An Integrative Entrepreneurial Context-Specific Process.* Londres/Nueva York: Routledge.

Kim, Minho; Munseob, Lee y Yongseok, Shin. 2021. «The Plant-Level View of an Industrial Policy: The Korean Heavy Industry Drive of 1973». *NBER, Working Paper* 29, 252, September, 1-9.

Kinossian, Nadir. 2017. «Planning strategies and practices in non-core regions: a critical response». *European Planning Studies,* 3, 1-11.

Kippenberger, T. 1998. «A different approach to change in Spain: the case of Alcatel Standard Eléctrica SA (ASESA)». *The Antidote,* 3, n°.4: 37-40.

Kirby, Peadar y Carmody, Padraig. 2013. *The Legacy of Ireland's Economic Expansion: Geographies of the Celtic Tiger.* Londres-Nueva York: Routledge.

Kornelakis, Andreas. 2015. «European market integration and the political economy of corporate adjustment: OTE and Telecom Italia, 1949-2009». *Business History,* 57, n°.6: 885-902.

Laffitte, Pierre y Trégouët, René. 2001. *Les conséquences de l'évolution scientifique et technique dans le secteur des télécommunications.* Rapport n°, 159, 20 de diciembre.

Leckey, Andrew. 2002. *The Best Business Stories of the Year.* Nueva York: Vinage Books.

Linvill, John G. 1984. *The Competitive Status of the U.S. Electronics Industry: A Study of the Influences of Technology in Determining International Industrial Competitive Advantage.* Washington: National Academies.

Llerena, Patrick; Matt, Mireille and Trenti, Stefania. 2000. «Public technology procurement: The case of digital switching systems in Italy». En *Public technology procurement and innovation,* Edquist, Charles, Hommen, Leif y Tsipouri, Lena. Nueva York: Springer.

Longuet, Gérard. 1995. *L'espoir industriel.* París: Éditions France-Empire.

Lüthje, Boy et al. 2013. *From Silicon Valley to Shenzhen: Global Production and Work in the IT Industry.* Lanham: Rowman & Littlefield.

Maculan, A. M. 1992. «As novas estratégias tecnológicas das multinacionais do setor das telecomunicações». *Brazilian Journal of Political Economy*, 12, n°.3: 71-90.

Maincent, Emmanuelle and Navarro, Lluis. 2006. «A Policy for Industrial Champions: From picking winners to fostering excellence and the growth of firms», *DG Enterprise and Industry*. Bruselas: European Commission.

Majó i Cruzate, Joan. 1997. *Chips, cables y poder: la clase dominante en el siglo XXI.* Barcelona: Planeta.

Malsan, Sylvie. 2001. *Filles d'Alcatel: histoire d'une reconversion industrielle.* Toulouse: Octarès.

Mansell, Robin et al. 1990. «European Integration and Telecommunications: Restructuring Markets and Institutions». *Prometheus,* 8, n°.1: 51-66.

Marginson, Paul y Meardi, Guglielmo. 2009. *Multinational companies and collective bargaining.* Dublín: European Foundation for the Improvement of Living and Working Conditions.

Maricourt, Thierry. 2006. *Ils ont bossé– et puis après?: Alcatel-Illkirch, entreprise high-tech et restructurations.* París: Syllepse.

Marseille, Jacques. (dir.) 1992. *Alcatel Alsthom. Histoire de la Compagnie Générale d'Electricité.* París: Larousse.

Mauroy, Pierre. 1981. *Discours à l'Assemblée nationale.* 8 de julio.

Mayer-Schönberger, Viktor y Strasser, Mathias. 1999. «A Closer Look at Telecom Deregulation: The European Advantage». *Harvard Journal of Law and Technology* 12, 3, Summer, 561-588.

Méndez-Manjón, Carmen. 1998. *Repercusiones de las autopistas de la información en el entorno radio-televisivo.* Tesis doctoral. Universidad Complutense de Madrid.

Michalet, Charles-Albert. 1981. «Une nouvelle approche de la spécialisation internationale». *Revue d'Économie Industrielle*, 17, 61-75.

Micron Electronics. 1998. *Quarterly report pursuant to section 13 or 15,d) of the securities exchange act of 1934, for the quarterly period ended february 26.* Commission File Number 1-10658.

Ministerio de Comercio y Turismo. 1995. «Los créditos FAD 1977-1994». *Boletín Económico del ICE*, 2.446, 7-18.

Monitoring Innovative Restructuring in Europe. 2006. julio.

Monopolies and Mergers Commission. 1994. *Alcatel Cable SA and STC Limited: a report on the proposed acquisition by Alcatel Cable SA of STC Limited; presented to Parliament by the Secretary of State for Trade and Industry by Command of Her Majesty*. 1 de febrero, Londres: HMSO.

Mytelka, Lynn Krieger. 1999. *Innovation and Competitiveness in Developing Countries*. París: OECD Publishing.

Nasbitt, John. 1982. *Megatrends: Ten New Directions Transforming Our Lives*. Nueva York: Warner Books.

Nelson, Richard R. 1993. *National Innovation Systems: A Comparative Analysis*. Oxford: Oxford University Press.

Nihoul, Paul. 1998/99. «Convergence in European telecommunications: a case study on the relationship between regulation and competition (law)». *International Journal of Communications Law and Policy* 2, Winter, 1-33.

Noam, Eli. 1992. *Telecommunications in Europe*. Nueva York: Oxford University Press.

Nokia, 1995. *Annual Report 1995*.

Nora, Simon y *Minc*, Alain. *1978. L'informatisation de la société. Rapport à M. le Président de la République [The computerization of the society. Report to the President of the Republic]*. París: Seuil.

OECD. 1988. *Industrial Policy Developments in OECD Countries: Annual Review*. París: OECD.

OECD. 1993. *Regional industrial restructuring: report on the Maastricht seminar*. París: OECD.

OECD. 2000. *OECD Reviews of Regulatory Reform OECD Reviews of Regulatory Reform: Regulatory Reform in Spain 2000*. París: OECD Publishing.

OECD. 2001. *Innovative Clusters Drivers of National Innovation Systems: Drivers of National Innovation Systems*. París: OECD Publishing.

OECD. 2002. *Competition and regulation issues in telecommunications*. París: Directorate for financial, fiscal and enterprise affairs competition committee.

Oficina Económica y Comercial de la Embajada de España en Bogotá. 2005. *El sector de las Telecomunicaciones en Colombia*. Bogotá: ECECEEB.

O'Keefe, Thomas A. 1996. *Latin American Trade Agreements*. Nueva York: Transnational Publishers.

Olley, George S. y Pakes, Ariel. 1996. «The Dynamics of Productivity in the Telecommunications Equipment Industry». *Econometrica*, 64, n°.6: 1.263-1.297.

Osorio, Manuel. 1998. «Estrategia de inversión en telecomunicaciones en el mercado brasileño». *La Revista de Telecomunicaciones de Alcatel*, 2° semestre, 95-99.

OTA Advisory Group. 1993. *U. S. Telecommunications Services in Europe.* Washington: DIANE Publishing.

Pacheco, José L. 1991. «Calidad total y grupos de desarrollo. Una experiencia en Alcatel Standard Eléctrica». *Economía Industrial*, 278, 179-184.

Palmer, Michael B., y Jeremy Tunstall. *Liberating Communications: Policy-making in France and Britain*. Londres: Basil Blackwell, 1990.

Patrick, Hugh. 1986. «Japanese high technology industrial policy in comparative context»., *Working paper*, n°.1. Center on Japanese Economy and Business: Columbia University.

Pébereau, Georges. 2005. «L'Amérique, la France, les reseaux». *Flux*, 60-61, 96-104.

Plunkett, Jack W. 2007. *Plunkett's Outsourcing And Offshoring Industry Almanac 2008.* Houston TX: Plunkett Research.

Poynter, Thomas A. 2013. Multinational *Enterprises and* Government *Intervention*. Abingdon, Oxon: Routledge.

Pojomovsky, Nora y Gómez, Elena. 2006. *Nunca olvides esto...: los mejores consejos de grandes directivos españoles*. Pozuelo de Alarcón: ESIC Editorial.

Pontarollo, Enzo. 1994. «Procurement and market structure in the telecommunications industry: A European survey». *European Journal of Purchasing & Supply Management*, 1, n°.2: 88-97.

Pryce, Vicky. 2012. *Britain needs a fourth generation industrial policy*. Londres: CentreForum.

Quatrepoint, Jean-Michel. 1986. «Les enjeux internationaux de la privatisation de la CGCT». *Le Monde diplomatique*, Décembre, 8.

Quatrepoint, Jean-Michel. 2015. *Alstom, scandale d'État*. París: Fayard.

Radosevic, Slavo y Sadowski, Bert M. 2007. *International Industrial Networks and Industrial Restructuring in Central and Eastern Europe.* Dordrecht: Kluwert.

Rama, Ruth y Holl, Adelheid. 2009. «Networking and R&D in domestic and FDI plants in Spanish electronics clusters». *International Journal of Strategic Business Alliances*, 1, n°.2: 182-204.

Ramu, S. Shiva. 1999. *Restructuring and Break-ups: Corporate Growth Through Divestitures, Splits, Spin-Offs and Swaps.* Nueva Delhi: Response Books.

Recio, Alberto, y Roca, Jordi. 2001. En *Social Democracy in Neoliberal Times: The Left and Economic Policy Since 1980*, Glyn, Andrew. Oxford: Oxford University Press.

Ripoll, Fabrice. 2004. «Cherbourg, ville-arsenal en crise». *Norois*, 190, 67-84.

Rodríguez-Ruiz, Óscar. 2014. «The history of human resource management in Spain: an autocratic legacy beyond the waves of rational and normative control». *Management & Organizational History*, 9, 12 de febrero, 256-271.

Roldán, José. 2013. *PEGASO. Del paternalismo a la Desregulación. Las relaciones laborales entre 1954 y 1994*. Madrid: Autor-editor.

Rüb, Stefan. 2002. «World Works Councils and Other Forms of Global Employee Representation in Transnational Undertakings. A survey». *Arbeitspapier 55*, 1-59.

Rugman, Alan y D'Cruz, Joseph R. 2003. *Multinationals as Flagship Firms: Regional Business Networks*. Oxford: Oxford University Press.

Ruigrok, Winfried y van Tulder, Rob. 1995. *The Logic of International Restructuring: The Management of Dependencies in Rival Industrial Complexes*. Londres: Routledge.

Sáez, Miguel Ángel y Díaz Morlán, Pablo. 2009. *El puerto del acero: Historia de la siderurgia de Sagunto (1900-1984)*. Madrid: Marcial Pons.

Sanmina-SCI. 2002. *Annual report pursuant to section 13 or 15,d) of the securities exchange act of 1934, for the fiscal year ended September 28*.

Sapir, André. 1988. International Trade in Telecommunications Services. En *Issues in US-EC Trade Relation*, editado por Baldwin, Robert E. et al., 231-246. Chicago Press: University of Chicago Press.

Schipke, Alfred y Taylor, Alan M. 2012. *The Economics of Transformation: Theory and Practice in the New Market Economies,* Londres: Springer.

Schmoch, Ulrich y Schnöring, Thomas. 1994. «Technological strategies of telecommunications equipment manufacturers: A patent analysis». *Telecommunications Policy*. 18, 5, julio, 397-413.

Smidt, Marc de y Weber, Egbert. 2013. *The Corporate Firm in a Changing World Economy: Case Studies in the Geography of Enterprise*. Londres-Nueva York: Routledge.

Solchaga, Carlos. 1997. *El final de la edad dorada*. Madrid: Taurus.

Solana Madariaga, Luis. 1983a. «Empresa pública, Empresa privada: debate en revisión». *BIT*, julio, 33-34.

Solana Madariaga, Luis. 1981b. «Electrónica y telecomunicaciones, ¿alguien sabe a dónde vamos?». *BIT,* marzo-abril, 5.

Solana Madariaga, Luis. 1981. «Y Araskog vino a España». *El País,* 11 de octubre.

Stone, Nan. 1989. «The Globalization of Europe: an Interview with Wisse Dekker». *Harvard Business Review*, 3, mayo–junio: 90-95.

Stroux, Sigrid. 2004. *US and EC Oligopoly Control*. La Haya: Kluwer Law International.

Suard, Pierre. 2002. *L'Envol Saboté d'Alcatel Alsthom*. París: Éditions France Empire.

Suard, Pierre. 1993. «Strategy for telecommunications equipment suppliers». *Electrical Communication*, 66, 210.

Suárez, David y Álvarez, Ignacio. 2011. *CEO Succession Study. España 2004-2010. Radiografía del relevo del Consejero Delegado*. Madrid: Booz & Company.

Sudrià, Carles. 2012. «El ajuste económico de la transición». *El País*, 12 de febrero.

Sutton, John. 2001. *Technology and Market Structure: Theory and History*. Cambridge: MIT Press.

Teece, David J. 1998. *Economic Performance and the Theory of the Firm*. vol. 1. Cheltenham: Edward Elgar.

Thatcher, Mark. 1999*The Politics of Telecommunications: National Institutions*. Oxford: Oxford University Press.

Thibault, Guillaume. 2008. *Quelle stratégie industrielle pour la France face à la mondialisation?* París: Éditions TECHNIP.

Trappman, Vera. 2013. *Fallen heroes in global capitalism: Workers and the Restructuring of the Polish Steel Industry.* Nueva York: MacMillan.

Tribunal de Defensa de la Competencia. 1997. *Informe expediente de concentración económica 26/97*, 10/28.

United Nations Conference on Trade and Development. 2000. *Transnational corporations*. Vol. 9, 3, diciembre.

United Nations Conference on Trade and Development. 1997. *World Investment Report 1997 Transnational Corporations, Market Structure and Competition Policy.* Nueva York y Ginebra: United Nations.

United States Congress. 1990. *Telecommunications Opportunities in Eastern Europe: Hearing Before the Subcommittee on Telecommunications and Finance of the Committee on Energy and Commerce*. Vol. 4. Washington: U.S. Government Printing Office.

United States. Congress. 1973. *Multinational Corporations; a Compendium of Papers Submitted to the Subcommittee on International Trade*. Washington: Senate. Finance.

United States. Congress. House. 1970. *Hearings before the antitrust subcommittee, ITT*. Washington: Government Printing Office.

Uriz, Javier. 2001. «La era "Post-Recursos Humanos". Análisis de una encrucijada». *RRHH Magazine*, 28 de febrero, 1.

Vagadia, Bharat. 2011. *Strategic Outsourcing: The Alchemy to Business Transformation in a Globally Converged World*. Londres: Springer.

Valdaliso, José María. 2003. «Crisis y reconversión de la industria de construcción naval en el País Vasco». *Ekonomiaz*, cuarto trimestre, n°.54: 52-67.

Verbeke, Alain. 2013. *International Business Strategy*. Cambridge: Cambridge University Press.

Visscher, Klaasjan, Lenferink Desie y Van Looy, Bart. 2001. *The development of ADSL at Alcatel, Case description. Confidential*. Université Catholique de Louvain.

Weiss, Stephen E. 1993. «Analysis of Complex Negotiations in International Business: The RBC Perspective». *Organization Science*, 4, 2, May, 269-300.

Wisdom, G. J. 1987. «Transferencia de la tecnología de programación del núcleo genérico del Sistema 12». *Comunicaciones Eléctricas*, 61, n°.2: 160-165.

WS Atkins Management Consultants. 1988. *The 'cost of non-Europe' in Public Sector Procurement*. Luxemburgo: Office for Official Publication of the European Communities.

Zanfei, Antonello. 1992. «Changing Competitive Behaviour in the Telecommunications Industry». *Revue d'Économie Industrielle*, 62, n°.1: 83-105.

Ziegler, Nicholas. 1997. *Governing Ideas: Strategies for Innovation in France and Germany*. Ithaca-Londres: Cornell University Press.

Zysman, John. 1977. *Political Strategies for Industrial Order: State, Market, and Industry in France*. Berkeley: University of California Press.

2. Dependencia tecnológica y atraso económico: Citesa

1. Introducción

En España, el impulso a la producción de equipos telefónicos precedió al lanzamiento de los planes generales de desarrollo y fue el fruto de los incentivos del franquismo a la localización industrial. Más en concreto, fue el resultado de la actuación combinada del plan Málaga y del Patronato pro industrialización –Patronato de Desarrollo Socio-Económico e Industrialización de la provincia de Málaga–, creado en 1959 para potenciar la implantación de industrias a través de ayudas financieras y subvenciones a fondo perdido[1]. Dicha acción combinada cuajó en varias empresas de ramos diferentes, entre ellas la textil Intelhorce, la embotelladora de Butano y la norteamericana de la industria química Amoníaco Español (Sánchez 2003, 321)[2].

Actividades tan diversas no pueden ocultar que la provincia de Málaga se distinguió por la aparición de una especialización productiva bisectorial, compuesta por el turismo y las telecomunicaciones. La llamada «industria limpia» enarbola los nombres de SECOINSA, Fujitsu, Siemens, Hughes Microelectrónica, Isofoton, SECOTON y la Compañía Internacional de Teleco-

---

[1] Patronato de Desarrollo Socio-Económico e Industrialización de la Provincia de Málaga (1973); véase el contexto en Sánchez Picón (coord.) (2013).

[2] Intelhorce fue motejada de «tiovivo que ha mareado constantemente a Málaga, un tiovivo de la tensión entre el sector público y privado» y su fábrica de «catedral industrial de Málaga» (*Sur*, 31 de julio de 2017): Intervención del representante del grupo parlamentario centrista, *DSPA* 5, I Legislatura, 1 de marzo de 1983, 170. En realidad, fue un paradigma del esplendoroso fango del franquismo en el terreno industrial, con privatizaciones y operaciones especulativas y fraudulentas (De Mateo y Heredia 2012, p. 109).

municación y Electrónica S.A. (CITESA, en adelante Citesa), protagonista de este capítulo[3].

La problemática tiene como marco los cinco planes económicos sucesivos con los que contó Andalucía durante el periodo autonómico. Incluyen el Plan Económico para Andalucía (1984-1986); el Programa Andaluz de Desarrollo Económico (1987-1990); el Plan Andaluz de Desarrollo Económico (1991-1994); el Plan Económico Andalucía Horizonte 2000 (1998-2000) y el Plan Económico Andalucía Siglo XXI (2002-2005) (Rodero 2006, 41-46).

El mérito fundamental de este estudio reside en analizar la trayectoria de una empresa perteneciente a un sector al que los historiadores económicos y de la empresa han dedicado una atención menor en comparación a la prestada a procesos industriales agregados o a episodios similares que acaecieron en la siderurgia y en la industria naval[4].

En los años y el sector concernidos sobresalen las reestructuraciones de la división electrónica del INI, del gigante estadounidense IT&T y del *holding* industrial de Telefónica, así como la integración de empresas privadas y públicas para crear una industria sólida de defensa con el exótico nombre de Indra. Todos ellos merecen una atención específica por sus peculiaridades y algunos han sido ya abordados[5] (Calvo 2020a, 1-36; Calvo 2020b; Calvo 2021; Calvo 2023). El caso de Citesa es uno de los de menor magnitud por envergadura de empleo y producción.

---

[3] *Diario de sesiones del Parlamento de Andalucía (DSPA)*, 9 de abril de 1986, 119, I Legislatura, 5.806. La implantación de Hughes Microelectrónica, una actuación *greenfield*, fue posible mediante el acuerdo alcanzado entre esta empresa y el Gobierno español, que incluía la concesión de importantes ayudas (Respuesta escrita del ministerio de Obras Públicas y Transportes a la pregunta escrita Senado, 684/010260 del grupo parlamentario socialista, *Boletín Oficial de las Cortes Generales (BOCG)*, Senado, 1 de marzo de 1993). Índole distinta tuvo la fórmula usada por Siemens, que consistió en la adquisición en 1974 de una empresa electrónica preexistente, a saber, la pionera en Málaga Central Técnica Científica, creada por el alemán Th. Schnade y especializada en condensadores (De Mateo y Heredia 2012, 86-87; *Sur*, 5 noviembre 2011).

[4] Una lista de aportaciones centrales de historiadores económicos sobre España, sin pretensiones de exhaustividad, incluye a: Díaz-Morlán y Sáez-García (2017a, 38–50); Díaz Morlán y Sáez García (2017b); Díaz-Morlán (2009, 547-568); Díaz Morlán, Escudero y Sáez (2008, 161-188); Valdaliso (2003, 52-67); Fernández de Pinedo (2003, 28-51); Navarro (2005, 167-184) y (1989). Carácter agregado tiene, por ejemplo, el estudio de Valdaliso (2010, 194-221). Sí ha merecido atención el sector de las TIC (Tecnologías de la Información y la Comunicación) en España con un enfoque interdisciplinar por parte de un restringido grupo de estudiosos, entre los que sobresalen López (2016, 159-180); López y Molero (2005); López, Pueyo y Zlatanova (2002, 81-96).

[5] Calvo (2019a); Calvo (2019b); Calvo (2019c); Calvo (2019d).

Desde el punto de vista metodológico, el capítulo pretende sumarse al esfuerzo por ilustrar la interacción entre las estrategias de inversión de las multinacionales y la política llevada a cabo por el estado nación en el país de acogida[6]. Dentro de este marco de yuxtaposición multinacionales Estados nación, introduce un matiz significativo ya que amplía el interlocutor local –el gobierno del Estado nación– con otros nuevos –el gobierno autonómico y los sindicatos (Nygaard y Dahlstrom 1992, 3-13)–. El estudio se ciñe a la comprensión del proceso de remodelación mundial de la industria de las telecomunicaciones en las dos décadas finales del siglo veinte y los primeros años del nuevo milenio. El periodo comprende la transición de una industria basada en la vinculación estrecha, por no decir integración estricta, entre monopolio del servicio telefónico e industria nacional de equipo de telecomunicaciones. El estudio se estructura en cuatro apartados principales, que abordan sucesivamente los orígenes y evolución de Citesa, la crisis y la reestructuración, la empresa ante la globalización de los mercados y las estrategias adoptadas ante el mercado global.

2. Orígenes y evolución de Citesa

Citesa fue impulsada por la inversión nacional y extranjera, con la colaboración de la industria, el Estado y la banca. El capital de 250 millones de pesetas fue aportado en su mitad por IT&T, en la quinta parte por Standard Eléctrica (SESA), en el 15% por Marconi Española, incorporada al INI, en el 10% por CTNE y en el 5% restante por los bancos Hispano Americano y Urquijo, parte del núcleo financiero inicial de CTNE. La estructura accionarial varió al cabo de un tiempo, al adquirir CTNE en 1968 10% de las acciones de Citesa al tipo del 125%; en 1971, el control de la empresa pasó a manos del grupo integrado en Intelsa, una filial de la multinacional sueca Ericsson[7]. Al iniciarse la década de 1980, en la composición del capital de Citesa predo-

---

[6] El debate arranca de la aportación pionera del especialista político Joseph Nye (1974) sobre las multinacionales y se prolonga hasta nuestros días con diagnósticos como «*retreat of the state*» (Strange 1996) o «outsourcing of sovereignty» (Cohen 2007). Strange se apoya para sus asertos en el ejemplo clásico de las telecomunicaciones como expresión del proceso por el que la autoridad se ha desplazado masivamente de los gobiernos de los estados a las empresas.

[7] Para la trayectoria de Citesa, véase Calvo (2011, 145-174); Calvo (2012, 43-72); Calvo (2014, 267-268); Cerón (2018, 363-390).

minaba SESA con un 56%, seguida por la CTNE (31%) y completada por un grupo de accionistas en el que predominaban los bancos[8].

Lo apuntado incita a remachar que Citesa pertenecía al grupo de IT&T en España, compuesto por otras dos empresas que cubrían especialidades diferentes de la industria de equipo de telecomunicación, conforme a una estrategia de división de plantas. Se trataba de Standard Eléctrica y Marconi Española, fabricantes de equipos de telefonía y comunicaciones en general[9]. Su producción, basada en tecnología de origen estadounidense, iba destinada prioritariamente al mercado interior y, muy en especial, a Telefónica. Hacia 1981, Citesa producía el 11% de la industria de equipos de telecomunicación en España, un porcentaje que quedaba muy alejado del 61% de SESA (U.S. Department of Commerce 1984, 2).

El periplo industrial de Citesa arrancó en 1964, fecha en la que echó a andar en Málaga la nueva fábrica de aparatos telefónicos, que venía a romper con «un panorama plano en las telecomunicaciones de Málaga», al decir de uno de los protagonistas. La elección del emplazamiento de la fábrica se debió a dos razones: la primera de ellas, la existencia del puerto como punto de salida de las exportaciones y la segunda de carácter sentimental[10]. La razón de su capacidad –750.000 aparatos anuales– obedecía, por un lado, a las necesidades del mercado interior y, por otro, a la apuesta por el exterior (Sánchez 2003, 321 332)[11]. Su producción por hora alcanzaba mil piezas según el sistema en cadena, sometidas a control automático, y a dos centenares de aparatos[12].

---

[8]   *ABC*, 29 de septiembre de 1982; pequeñas variantes en las cifras para el 31 de diciembre de 1981: Standard Eléctrica el 55%, Telefónica el 12%, Marconi Española el 15% (Intervención del presidente de Citesa, Audio de la sesión de la Comisión de Transportes y Comunicaciones Comisión de Transportes, Turismo y Comunicaciones, Congreso de los diputados, 2 de febrero de 1982).

[9]   Comúnmente se le calificaba de IT&T Business System Group (*Información comercial española*, 525-529, 1977, 193).

[10]   Alusión a los lazos del entonces director general con Málaga (Méndez 2000, 56-57); sobre la fábrica, véase García de Castro (1964).

[11]   Aspecto importante para aportar evidencias sobre la dependencia extranjera, se recurrió a equipo avanzado de procedencia mayoritaria (76%) extranjera al igual que las materias primas; *know how* adquirido en parte en EEUU (Sánchez 2003, 324-325).

[12]   *La Opinión de Málaga*, 2002. La noticia de la creación de la nueva fábrica contó con una difusión internacional (*International Commerce*, 14 de diciembre de 1964, 1; *Spanish Newsletter*, 31 de diciembre de 1964, 8). La fábrica era una nave-taller longitudinal de altura única con una entreplanta lateral mínima, un cuerpo de oficinas, un depósito de agua y una torre de refrigeración. El espacio interior diáfano de la nave-taller se resolvía mediante una estructura de pilares compuestos empresillados que sustentaban vigas trianguladas de

A ello siguieron años de empuje entre 1969-1972 y de crisis en la mitad de la década. En términos comparativos, Citesa se situaba en el rango de la recién nombrada Marconi Española y ligeramente por debajo de empresas de otros sectores, como Cristalería Española, Solvay o la Sociedad Metalúrgica Duro Felguera (Ministerio de Industria y Energía 1976, 16).

En definitiva, Citesa distribuía su producción en los centros de Madrid y Málaga, los que se añadían establecimientos alquilados. Además de las fábricas, contaba con una división comercial para vender terminales de datos y de textos importados de EE. UU. y Europa, resultado de la estrategia de IT&T de importar productos cuya demanda no alcanzaba el volumen suficiente como para fabricarlos en España (*ABC*, 29 de septiembre de 1982).

En los inicios, Citesa era en sustancia una fábrica con una integración fabril que completaba la integración vertical derivada de la vinculación estrecha con la operadora monopolista del servicio de teléfonos. La integración con el mercado llevaba consigo una disminución de costes de transacción y de las estructuras comerciales. La empresa contaba además con un departamento de I+D o Ingeniería de Desarrollo, rimbombante nombre para una sección que, en la práctica, se encargaba de elaborar la documentación de los aparatos que se iban a fabricar, transponiendo y traduciendo la documentación original de los equipos, procedentes por lo general de la filial de IT&T en Bélgica[13].

En realidad, en los inicios la ingeniería de desarrollo se mantuvo en la planta de Standard Eléctrica en Madrid, con la que se coordinaba un corresponsal en Málaga para garantizar el buen funcionamiento de la I+D. Málaga tan solo disponía de un laboratorio de electroacústica y medidas telefonométricas, creado por Lorenzo Martínez, necesario para controlar los equipos de medida y ciertas características técnicas de los teléfonos fabricados. Hacia 1967 y en el marco de una reorganización de la I+D, IT&T desdobló

sección constante (García de Castro y Mexia 1964, 132-137). Algunas fuentes secundarias (Instituto Internacional San Telmo, 1992, 2) atribuyen la creación de Citesa a la influencia de la filial alemana de IT&T Standard Electric Lorenz, extremo que no se ha podido documentar con fuentes primarias. Citesa aplicaba las tablas y métodos propios de la Organización Científica del Trabajo, como revela la anécdota de un cronometrador, quien descubrió cómo el tiempo de un paso estaba calculado según la talla media del estadounidense (*Cuadernos para el Diálogo*, 3 de abril de 1976, 46-48). Para una reconstrucción del papel de Citesa en el movimiento obrero y sindical andaluz, véase, entre otros, los trabajos de Martínez (coord.) (2005) y Villalba; Ruiz y Ortega (2004, 427-446).

[13] Al decir de uno de los protagonistas, Citesa no ofertaba teléfonos: había un departamento comercial y prácticamente una gestión de venta; no había vendedores porque Telefónica era la cliente y los interlocutores eran técnicos o comerciales; el único inconveniente era un problema de planificación de fàbrica, tener a tiempo los materiales (Casado 2012).

las responsabilidades en audiocomunicaciones entre una sección europea y otra mundial, radicadas en Bruselas y en Nueva York, respectivamente. Tras visitar los establecimientos en España, los directores de I+D para Europa y para el resto del mundo decidieron trasladar a Málaga la I+D de audiocomunicaciones y ponerla bajo la dirección de Lorenzo Martínez, procedente del taller de ensamble, del que era jefe. Ahí arranca la creación del propiamente dicho departamento de I+D en la fábrica de Málaga, indispensable, junto con el tamaño, para el acceso a los convenios universidad-empresa del Plan Nacional o a los programas de I+D de la CE, generalmente con varios países participantes. Ambas circunstancias –tamaño e I+D– coincidían en la más tardía Alcatel Citesa, a diferencia de lo que ocurría en otras grandes empresas, que, como Siemens, practicaron una estrategia de fábrica enclave e incorporaron tarde la I+D localizada en la región y establecieron conexiones con la Universidad (Méndez 2000, 56-57; Martínez 2008; Jordá 1991, 141 y 143)[14]. Los expertos alinean a Alcatel Citesa entre las filiales de multinacionales que ceñían su actividad innovadora a adaptar o desarrollar investigaciones básicas realizadas en la sede central del grupo. A esta categoría pertenecían las actividades de desarrollo tecnológico, ingeniería y diseño de teléfonos (Ruiz 2005, 76).

La fábrica de Málaga creció por incorporación de nuevas secciones, entre las que destaca el laboratorio de diseño electrónico y el departamento de *marketing*, el primero de ellos fundamental para dotar a la fábrica de recursos técnicos a bordo que le dieran cierta autonomía y le quitaran vulnerabilidad incluso frente a otra compañía del grupo para evitar el desplazamiento de la fabricación. Hacia 1980 se empezaron a externalizar algunas actividades según el modelo de *outsourcing*, que afectó a los talleres de prensa, plástico y utillaje[15]. Además de la actividad productiva, tenía una pequeña función

---

[14] Por tamaño, medido por el beneficio, Citesa ocupaba el centro de la lista de las cien mayores compañías andaluzas, muy por delante de Hughes Microelectrónica (*ABC*, 1 de junio de 1998). Los directores de I+D para Europa y para el resto del mundo eran Keith Preece y Frank Palen, respectivamente; técnicos de Citesa desarrollaron la centralita Pentomat, fabricada y montada por la empresa (Calvo 2016, 152; *Economista: Revista Semanal Científica e Independiente*, 1976, 30; Compañía Internacional de Telecomunicación y Electrónica (1976); constancia de exportaciones a Latinoamérica: *Hispano Americano,* 1973, 17; *Economista: Revista Semanal Científica e Independiente*, vol. 84, 1972, 2.812).

[15] Citesa exhibía con orgullo esa integración por la que solo compraba la materia prima y fabricaba hasta los tornillos; la ingeniería de diseño electrónico fue creada por José Antonio Maestre con el nombre de laboratorio de electrónica (Lorenzo Martínez) o de laboratorio de diseño electrónico (Méndez s.a. 69; Casado, 2012); el departamento de *marketing* fue obra de Lorenzo Martínez (Casado 2012); años antes existía una estructura comercial con una gerencia de exportación, al frente de la cual estuvo Alfredo Remón, futuro director de *marketing* (*Momento,* 1969, IX).

de reventa con ánimo de explorar el mercado para las tecnologías futuras, es decir, los equipos utilizados directamente por el usuario final, tales como terminales de datos, teleimpresores, facsímiles, intercomunicadores y busca personas[16].

Con el tiempo se impuso una determinada división entre lo que se podría definir como productos de red y productos de usuarios. La configuración de los primeros, lo básico de un país, recaía directamente sobre el Estado. Citesa tenía como misión abastecer a ese segmento de los usuarios finales como contrapunto al subsector de red, que el Estado confiaba tradicionalmente a SESA[17].

Concebida para fabricar exclusivamente material telefónico para la exportación, Citesa pronto varió su orientación, hasta el punto que, en la primera mitad de la década de 1970, un mercado internacional casi plano tuvo como compensación cierto dinamismo de las ventas en el interior (Anexo 3) (Calvo 2014, 267-268)[18].

Una vez que la CTNE decidió ampliar su abastecimiento de terminales y equipos a segundos proveedores, Citesa vendía PABXs, las llamadas centralitas telefónicas, a clientes finales, en parte comercializadas a través de Cosesa y otras directamente, estas destinadas a agencias oficiales, ministerios y servicios de la administración. La exportación la hacían directamente bien utilizando agentes propios, compañías subsidiarias de IT&T o los propios servicios comerciales.

Citesa basaba su especialización primordial desde sus inicios en los equipos de conmutación e instalación de equipos periféricos para Telefónica, fundamentalmente centralitas de barras y diversas variedades de aparatos telefónicos, desde los muy sencillos y tradicionales hasta los más complejos. El modelo Heraldo, un salto de modernidad importante en España que desplazó a los clásicos de baquelita, respondió a los requerimientos de Telefónica para

---

[16] Participación de estos segmentos: teléfonos representaban un 70%; centralitas un 25% y actividades menores el 5% restante (Intervención del presidente de Citesa, Audio de la sesión de la Comisión de Transportes y Comunicaciones Comisión de Transportes, Turismo y Comunicaciones, Congreso de los diputados, 2 de febrero de 1982).

[17] Intervención de Palomares, Grupo comunista, Audio de la sesión de la Comisión de Transportes y Comunicaciones Comisión de Transportes, Turismo y Comunicaciones, Congreso de los diputados, 2 de febrero de 1982.

[18] Citesa obtuvo la carta de exportador en 1969 (BOE, 99, 25 de abril de 1969, 6.198). En ese mismo año, participó en el suministro de terminales telefónicos a Venezuela, en el marco de un vasto programa de entregas para el Plan Quinquenal de ese país (Momento, 1969, ıx).

el futuro, de la misma manera que otros modelos fueron diseñados a petición de diversas administraciones telefónicas europeas.

El modelo original lo fabricó en Stuttgart Standard Electric Lorenz, si bien pronto fue copiado en Amberes por Bell Telephone Manufacturing Co., una y otra filiales de IT&T. Telefónica tomó dicho modelo como referencia. Resulta de interés referirse al esquema colaborativo del ciclo del producto. Citesa desplegó esfuerzos de captación de conocimiento por vía directa. A finales de 1961, destacó ingenieros de telecomunicaciones a Amberes para una estancia de varios meses con objeto de estudiar la fabricación y efectuar el control de calidad, así como de comprobar el funcionamiento de un laboratorio de telefonometría similar al proyectado en Málaga. Las herramientas para este primer modelo Heraldo se fabricaron en Holanda y España. Para comprobar que el diseño era correcto, mientras se estaba construyendo la nueva fábrica en Málaga, se completaron 20.000 aparatos en Madrid, en la sede madrileña de la calle Ramírez de Prado. Muestra del crecimiento de la década de 1960, la producción del modelo Heraldo, el aparato básico, se multiplicó por 2,57 en tan solo dos años, los de 1965 y 1967 (Gruger y Holst 1963, 230; De Mateo y Heredia 2012, 82)[19].

Uno de los terminales más emblemáticos, el Teide, fue diseñado completamente por los técnicos de Citesa juntamente con el departamento de desarrollo de Telefónica, que actuaba de guía. El modelo Góndola consistía en una copia del Trimline, fabricado por Western Electric para AT&T, que hacia 1965 lo comercializó en EE.UU. Citesa, a petición del CTNE, fabricó este aparato para la red española desde 1970 y lo exportó a más de medio centenar de países. Resulta de interés el proceso de adopción por la CTNE: conocimiento *in situ* del modelo (1968), petición de la CTNE a Citesa de adaptarse a sus especificaciones, transferencia de la información de fabricación, preparación de la información de ingeniería y diseño, construcción de herramientas y fabricación en España (1970)[20]. En el departamento de I+D de

---

[19] El modelo original del Heraldo se llamó *Assistent* y en Bélgica *Assistant* (Iraburu 2019. Blog Lorenzo Martínez, 29 de febrero de 2008). Una rápida reestructuración –«*bulldozer*»– dio a Bell TMC la perspectiva de mantener una posición de liderazgo en las centrales telefónicas dentro de Alcatel (*Le Soir*, 18 de febrero de 1989). Según los pactos, un porcentaje de las ventas de cada empresa se transfería a la IT&T para I+D. Esto permitía a cualquier empresa del grupo tener toda la información de fabricación y fabricar un producto siempre y cuando los planes de negocio mostraran la oportunidad de que el producto existiera en el nuevo país.

[20] Clark y Ryecart (1997, 13) dan como fecha de creación el año 1965. El modelo góndola se convirtió en el primer teléfono extranjero homologado en Japón (*Telecommunication Journal*, 49, 1982, 298; *La Vanguardia*, 19 de mayo de 1982). El diseño fue realizado por Henry Dreyfuss Associates y debido a su extraordinaria calidad se ganó ser expuesto en el Museo

Citesa en Málaga se hacía el diseño de modelos como el Domo o los teléfonos de monedas, destinados a Telefónica o a Iberoamérica. Citesa fabricó los aparatos Forma en sus diferentes versiones a partir de un diseño de Interisa y desarrolló toda la gama de teléfonos públicos, así como las primeras generaciones de inalámbricos analógicos CT0 y del estándar europeo digital DECT (Digital European Cordless Telecommunication)[21].

Ya como Alcatel Citesa, desde muy temprano la matriz Alcatel parecía reservarle un puesto en la conquista de mercados europeos a partir de nichos específicos. Alcatel negoció a través de la unidad española aliarse con la multinacional británica Amstrad PLC en una empresa conjunta para la fabricación de una gama de teléfonos destinados inicialmente al mercado nacional a través de la red comercial y luego a toda Europa. La planta Citesa Alcatel en Málaga albergaría la producción de dispositivos inalámbricos y móviles, que aumentaría hasta decenas de miles de unidades. La británica Amstrad PLC, que contaba con una extensísima red de distribución, adquirió Indescomp, especializada en videojuegos, y en 1983 la transformó en su filial Amstrad España (Dataquest 1990, 9; *European Communities* 1996, 45; *Computer Busines Review*, 15 de febrero de 1989; *Practical Computing*, 10, 1987, 19; *El País*, 30 de enero de 1987)[22].

de Arte Moderno de Nueva York. Su diseño mecánico era muy complicado: circuito impreso situado en el microteléfono flexible, soldadura de sus componentes por ola, «gancho conmutador», a base de resortes que había que ajustar, requiriendo precisión y tiempo. Una aportación de Citesa: sustitución de la pequeña lámpara incandescente que iluminaba el disco y se alimentaba por un transformador conectado a la red eléctrica, por un LED (diodo luminoso) alimentado por la corriente de la línea telefónica (48 V). Citesa preparó la especificación del LED y se encomendó a un fabricante, quien aceptó el pedido y diseñó el LED solicitado. AT&T, posteriormente, equipó con un LED los aparatos producidos en USA. Posteriormente se rediseñó el aparato, pasando casi toda la circuitería a la base y eliminando el circuito impreso flexible (Luis Méndez, Comunicación personal al autor, 3 de agosto de 2020).

21 *BIT*, agosto-septiembre de 2009. Finalizada la fabricación del Heraldo y del Teide, se diseñaron y produjeron nuevos modelos, entre ellos el Marbella, Ibiza y Venturer (López 2008, 12). Los DECT debían ser aptos para funcionar en la banda de frecuencias 1880-1900 MHz y estar disponibles en la Comunidad Europea. Además, debían proporcionar con tecnología inalámbrica aplicaciones para los usuarios residenciales que se interconectarían a la RDSI/ PSTN y para empresas con un acceso de red pública a un teléfono. Una aplicación específica debería proporcionar un medio de radio para extender las redes públicas y privadas a las instalaciones de los usuarios. Finalmente, debía permitir la explotación simultánea de dos o más sistemas independientes en la misma zona geográfica (Council Recommendation of 3 June 1991 on the coordinated introduction of digital European cordless telecommunications (DECT) into the Community, 91/288/EEC).

22 José Luis Domínguez, fundador de Indescomp (Investigación y desarrollo de computadoras) y consejero internacional en el Board Meeting de Amstrad Plc., ofrece detalles de gran

Parece oportuno detenerse un tanto en estas últimas tecnologías. Citesa incorporó en 1989 a su oferta comercial los teléfonos sin hilo CTO, diseñados y fabricados por una compañía de la República Popular China. A partir de esta plataforma comercial, fue adquiriendo las capacidades necesarias para el desarrollo de la tecnología e integrando gradualmente la fabricación en Málaga. Por su parte, la llegada al mercado de los primeros terminales digitales inalámbricos DECT –llamados en otros países como el Reino Unido CT2 (Carr et al. 2001, 342)– destinados al uso residencial se remonta a 1996 y hasta el año siguiente no dio lugar a ventas significativas. Los analistas pensaban que la fuerte inversión necesaria para desarrollar la tecnología DECT levantaría una barrera a la entrada de las compañías asiáticas en Europa durante un tiempo. No obstante, no solo las compañías asiáticas estuvieron presentes en el mercado residencial de esa gama ya desde su nacimiento sino que la mayoría de las empresas europeas del sector empezaron a poner su marca a productos fabricados en dicha zona. La causa del cambio residió precisamente en la necesidad de recuperar con rapidez la continua inversión realizada por las compañías de circuitos integrados que desarrollaron la tecnología básica para el DECT (Philips, entre ellas). Debido a ello, facilitaron el acceso a las compañías asiáticas a esos componentes e incluso al *know how* para el diseño de los productos. En estas circunstancias, Alcatel Citesa decidió posponer la producción de teléfonos digitales DECT para el sector residencial ya que con el precio resultante de su fabricación local se hacía imposible competir en el mercado (Alcatel Citesa SA 1999, 7-8)[23].

interés. En sus inicios, Indescomp distribuía productos de Amstrad, pero también de competidores de Amstrad. Los videojuegos desempeñaron un papel central en las negociaciones con Amstrad (*Amstrad.ES Forum*, 7 de octubre de 2005). En su autobiografía, Alan Sugar, el patrón de Amstrad, alude a su actuación en España y al papel desempeñado por Domínguez y su empresa Indescom. La prensa española señaló un acuerdo entre Amstrad PLC, Amstrad España y la estadounidense Telequest para fabricar en España televídeos y teléfonos (*ABC*, 26 de enero de 1988).

[23] La producción de circuitos integrados en Taiwán, por ejemplo, había crecido de forma impresionante en los años anteriores (United States. Bureau of International Commerce 1974, 110). Para entonces, la industria taiwanesa de las TIC había atravesado por tres etapas distintas –embrionaria (1978 a 1985), de crecimiento (1986-1989) y de conmoción (1990 a 1992)– (Lee y Pecht 1997, 31). De acuerdo con el plan de viabilidad, la fábrica de Málaga en 1996 tenía que haber fabricado 470.000 terminales DECT en exclusiva para toda Europa pero solo se alcanzó el 16% de esa cifra (Intervención del portavoz del g.p. Izquierda Unida-Convocatoria por Andalucía (R. Rodríguez Bermúdez), *DSPA*, 81, III Legislatura, 13 de octubre de 1992, 4.075).

3. Crisis y reestructuración de Citesa

Más allá del arranque de la trayectoria industrial, los años comprendidos entre el final de la década de 1970 y el inicio de la siguiente proporcionaron indicaciones de diferente signo dentro de una tónica general de crisis, como se observa en el caso de Standard Eléctrica. Las ventas totales de Citesa cayeron en 36 millones de pesetas desde los 6.086 de 1978, hasta quedar reducidos a 6.050 en 1979 (435 millones exportados a Argelia, país en el que la empresa compartía liderazgo con SESA en terminales de teléfonos) pero crecieron en 1.163 en 1981 (con exportaciones de 1.335). La plantilla pasó de 3.413 a finales de 1978 a 3.301 al año siguiente y a 2.500 en 1981 (Anexo 2 y 3)[24]. En las pérdidas presentadas en 1980 –unos ochocientos millones de pesetas– se parapetó Citesa para poner en evidencia lo absurdo de aferrarse a alguna de sus secciones, que competían abiertamente con SESA, y la necesidad de reestructurarse en sus actividades y dimensiones[25].

---

[24] Calvo (2014), *passim*; U.S. Department of Commerce (1982), 4; *Información comercial española: Boletín semanal,* 1979, 410; *El País,* 25 de noviembre de 1982; *BIT,* junio-julio de 1980, 31. La prensa clandestina informa de movilizaciones obreras en Citesa desde al menos los inicios de 1973, esta vez en solidaridad con Intelhorce (*Estrella Roja,* 7 de enero de 1973). En 1974, la huelga afectó a los centros de Madrid y Málaga y en ella la revisión del convenio colectivo tuvo suma importancia (*Villaverde Obrero. Boletín de las CCOO de Villaverde,* 2, 1974, 4; *Expresión Obrera,* diciembre de 1974, 1 y 8; *Nuestra Clase,* 21, octubre de 1974). Tres años después, en 1978, el personal se declaró en huelga contra la ruptura de las negociaciones del convenio y por la subida lineal de salarios, diferenciando entre las diversas categorías: *El País,* 3 de mayo y 10 de mayo de 1978; en ese mismo años tuvo lugar una huelga de solidaridad en el establecimiento de Citesa de Barcelona (*Unió,* 1 de enero de 1978, 13); en 1981 tuvieron lugar movilizaciones por el desbloqueo del convenio colectivo en una situación calificada por Citesa de sobredimensionamiento de plantillas (*El País,* 24 de enero de 1981; *ABC,* 25 de junio de 1981). UGT denunciaba la actitud dura y provocativa –triste en palabras de Luis Solana, futuro presidente de CTNE– con una baja oferta de subidas salariales (*El País,* 1 de abril, 2 de marzo y 25 de enero de 1982). Parece indiscutible que el nuevo movimiento obrero se fraguó en buena medida en la industria de tecnología avanzada, incluida en el ramo del metal, y, más en concreto, en Standard Eléctrica y Citesa. En el establecimiento de esta última en Málaga, UGT y CCOO estaban igualadas en número de representantes (*Boletín de la Unión Provincial de CCOO de Toledo,* febrero de 1978; «Standard Eléctrica S.A. El reajuste salarial». *Metal,* febrero-marzo de 1966, 9).

[25] *El País,* 25 de junio de 1981; Comparecencia de don Carlos Tiana Viají, presidente de la Compañía Internacional de Telecomunicación y Electrónica, Sociedad Anónima (CITESA), para informar sobre los planes de inversiones a medio plazo en el sector de las comunicaciones, (211/000573), 22 de mayo de 1981. Aquí subyace un debate entre IT&T, CTNE y los sindicatos por la práctica contable de la multinacional. En efecto, un documento de la CTNE revelaba que el 4% de *royalties* sobre cuentas que Citesa – y también SESA– abonaba a IT&T eran contabilizados como coste de ventas (*El País,* 1 y 17 de noviembre de 1983).

En este contexto, algunos datos apuntan a un crecimiento de Citesa, como son diversas ampliaciones llevadas a cabo en la fábrica sita en el malagueño Parque Tecnológico de Andalucía (PTA). Estas ampliaciones afectaron a su superficie ocupada, su plantilla y su capacidad de producción, que se multiplicaron respectivamente por 2,6 desde 10.000 m^2, por 5,37 desde 465.000 teléfonos y por 5,36 desde 405 empleados (Alcatel Citesa SA 1999, 2; Bennetts 1994, 164)[26]. Pero en 1982, IT&T revelaba claramente sus planes de integración, que tendría lugar el 20 de julio y llevarían consigo cerrar el establecimiento de Antonio López (Madrid) y trasladar el grueso de la actividad de este a Toledo. A una parte del personal se le ofrecía incorporarse a Toledo sin tocar las condiciones laborales que tenían y al resto esperar los resultados de las negociaciones del grupo IT&T[27].

Tras cuatro meses de negociaciones sobre un expediente de empleo presentado por Standard Eléctrica, IT&T rompió las conversaciones con el anuncio de sendos expedientes de rescisión de contrato en el conjunto del grupo en España – SESA, Marconi y Citesa–[28]. Por su parte, las instancias oficiales ya hablaban sin tapujos de inversiones por reconversión (Ministerio de Industria y Energía 1982, 114).

Citesa adolecía de una estructura de capital extremadamente frágil, en la que la relación entre deuda bancaria y fondos propios rondaba el 77/23. Los créditos sumaban unos 2.500 millones de pesetas y se repartían entre medio centenar de bancos que incluían todos los importantes. Uno de los principales objetivos de la empresa en el futuro inmediato radicaba en reforzar esta estructura financiera con el objeto de distribuir las cargas financieras, gravosas para la cuenta de resultados[29].

---

[26] En 1976, año del contrato con Nigeria a realizar en cinco años y por valor superior a 26 millones de dólares, a Citesa se le atribuía presencia en más de medio centenar de países con sus productos (*Economista: Revista Semanal Científica e Independiente*, 88, 1976, 53).

[27] Los interlocutores obreros eran conscientes del poder de la multinacional IT&T y de la posibilidad de que usara la amenaza de cesar su actividad en España («Hoja informativa de sección sindical de Comisiones obreras de Standard Eléctrica», Madrid, 31 de agosto de 1982, 4 y 20). Los talleres mecánicos de Citesa, así como los de Toledo, iban a ser desmantelados y solo subsistirían los de Villaverde.

[28] Los expedientes afectaban a 2.700, 1.400 y 400 trabajadores, respectivamente (González 1982, 8-10). En julio de 1982, el gobierno concedió al grupo IT&T en España 4.600 millones de pesetas de crédito oficial, sujeto a compromisos de inversión, entre otros. El anuncio de expediente de regulación de plantilla, que afectaría a 700 obreros, provocó movilizaciones (*El País*, 2 de marzo de 1982).

[29] Frente a informaciones de la prensa, la empresa rechazaba denegación de avales ni denegación de prórrogas (Intervención del presidente de Citesa, Audio de la sesión de la Comi-

En 1983, SESA absorbió a Citesa, que en esos momentos mantenía el nivel de empleo de dos años antes y 7.213 millones de ptas. en ventas, el 18,8% de ellos en el exterior (Anexo 3)[30]. La operación respondía a la lógica de la racionalización de las entonces asociadas a IT&T por vía de la integración de las especialidades productivas y eliminación de costes operativos y laborales. La fábrica de Málaga se trocó en la división de Audiocomunicaciones de SESA y la de Madrid no tardó en cerrar y trasladarse a la planta histórica de Ramírez de Prado, que también acogió al grueso de la plantilla. La racionalización del sistema productivo propuesta por SESA implicaba que Citesa quedaba integrada en la filial de IT&T. SESA debería hacer frente al coste de reestructuración de Citesa mediante bajas voluntarias y retiros anticipados, entre otras medidas[31].

El hecho central de la industria de las telecomunicaciones en España de finales de la década de 1980 e inicios de la siguiente tuvo lugar cuando la empresa francesa del sector energético Compagnie Générale d'Électricité (CGE) creó Alcatel NV a partir de las filiales europeas de la multinacional norteamericana IT&T. Entonces surgió Alcatel Standard Eléctrica S.A., que ulteriormente pasó a denominarse Alcatel España S.A. (Calvo 2020, 81-94; Todd 2019. Desde el punto de vista organizativo, Alcatel sustituyó la estructura que había heredado de IT&T, basada en áreas geográficas, por otra basada en líneas de producto. Las fábricas de Málaga y Madrid se insertaron, pues, en el nuevo Business System Group. En el arranque de la década de 1990, Alcatel España S.A estaba formada por las siguientes sociedades: Alcatel Standard Eléctrica S.A., Formación y Consultoría S.A., Alcatel Cable Contracting S.A., Alcatel Citesa S.A., Alcatel Ibertel S.A., Alcatel Espacio S.A. y Alcatel Sistemas de Información S.A.[32]

sión de transportes, turismo y comunicaciones, Congreso de los diputados, 2 de febrero de 1982).

[30] Clientes más importantes en 1982: Telefónica con el 60% aproximadamente y otros clientes nacionales con el 21,5; el 18,5% iba a la exportación (Intervención del presidente de Citesa, Audio de la sesión de la Comisión de transportes, turismo y comunicaciones, Congreso de los diputados, 2 de febrero de 1982).

[31] Manuel Márquez Balín†, Madrid, 18 de julio de 1983; la plantilla restante se integró en Villaverde (López (2008), 9; *La Vanguardia*, 25 de noviembre de 1982; *ABC*, 29 de septiembre de 1982; *Network World*, 14 de diciembre de 1987, 5). El capital social de Standard Eléctrica quedó fijado en más de 12.335 millones de pesetas (*El País*, 25 de noviembre y 29 de septiembre de 1982). Se sabía que SESA recurría con cierta frecuencia a otras empresas hermanas del grupo IT&T para abastecer a Telefónica de nuevos productos importados, como los equipos de medición AUTRAX para la gestión de sistemas telefónicos completos (*El País*, 1 de noviembre de 1983).

[32] Tribunal Supremo. Sala de lo Contencioso, Madrid, Sección 2, 15/12/2008. De la importancia del cobre en la fase anterior hablan, por ejemplo, los avisos a Citesa por parte de IT&T

Citesa se enfrentaba a diversos factores simultáneos que acarreaban cambios sustanciales en las fábricas. El primero se refiere al implacable cambio tecnológico, mencionado en otro lugar, que aceleraba, automatizaba y reducía el requerimiento de mano de obra, a la vez que alteraba la composición de materiales necesarios. A ello se añadía la aplicación de la informática en el área de diseño con sistemas AutoCAD, que provocaban un excedente de delineantes y otros técnicos, y a las oficinas (López 2008, 10; González 1982, 8-10).

En el profundo y rápido cambio tecnológico gravita un hilo conductor primordial de nuestro relato. La digitalización de los equipos redujo las necesidades de personal y, por ende, ocasionó excedentes de mano de obra a la vez que exigió recursos humanos, técnicos y fabriles diferentes. Así, por cada dieciséis horas necesarias para fabricar una centralita electromecánica se necesitaban tres para fabricar una electrónica[33].

La crisis que arrastraban sectores básicos de la industria impuso un planteamiento específico y la adopción de medidas de reconversión industrial, con el fin de lograr la racionalización de los procesos productivos y su adecuación a las exigencias del desarrollo económico y tecnológico y a las condiciones del mercado. El Gobierno impulsó un marco normativo, que, de forma gradual, estableció medidas que incluían ventajas fiscales, financieras y laborales[34].

El marco general de la política industrial del Gobierno en su faceta de promoción horizontal lo estableció el ministerio de Industria, Comercio y Turismo al promover diferentes programas de ayudas (Plan de Actuación Tecnológico Industrial –(PATI)–, Plan de Calidad, Plan de Internacionalización

–más tarde implicada en la conspiración contra el presidente socialista– sobre la posible alteración de los precios con el triunfo de Allende en Chile (United States. Congress. Senate 1973, 301).

[33] Intervención del presidente de Citesa, Audio de la sesión de la Comisión de Transportes y Comunicaciones Comisión de Transportes, Turismo y Comunicaciones, Congreso de los diputados, 2 de febrero de 1982; Alcatel Citesa S.A. (1999), 2.

[34] Real Decreto-ley 9/1981, de 5 de junio, sobre medidas para la reconversión industrial, *BOE*, 138, 10 de junio de 1981, 13.115-13.117; fue recogido en la prensa (*El País*, 13 de mayo de 1981) y sustituido por la Ley 21/1982, de 9 de junio, sobre medidas para la reconversión industrial (vigente hasta el 31 de Diciembre de 1982) (*BOE*, 169, 16 de julio de 1982, 19.293). En opinión de uno de sus principales artífices, la reconversión tuvo como base un «sistema de privatizaciones pragmático» cuyo funcionamiento se encajó inicialmente dentro de los procesos que marcaba el ministerio de Industria. El sistema de privatizaciones definía que las empresas que no eran viables debían ser cerradas, pero otras que tenían oportunidad de serlo necesitaban formar parte de un grupo (SEPI, Sala de prensa, 26 de noviembre de 2018).

de Apoyo a la Empresa Española, Plan de Diseño Industrial, entre otros). El PATI tenía como objetivo el impulso de la innovación tecnológica de las empresas, mediante subvenciones y ayudas a los proyectos de I+D, sirviendo de marco diversos planes específicos, entre ellos el Plan Electrónico e Informático Nacional (PEIN III), cuyo objeto esencial era estimular el desarrollo en el campo de las tecnologías de la información. Por su parte, el Centro para el Desarrollo Tecnológico Industrial (CDTI), trataba de estimular el desarrollo tecnológico en la industria por medio de créditos preferenciales. Además, se pusieron en marcha tres planes, que, trataban de potenciar el desarrollo en las áreas de *software*, robótica y automática y microelectrónica con fondos nacionales y de la Comisión Europea[35].

A partir del marco normativo recién señalado, aunque sin ser nombrada específicamente, dada su pertenencia a SESA, Citesa quedó incluida en el conflictivo plan de reconversión industrial del grupo IT&T en España por un acuerdo entre los principales implicados, es decir, el Estado, los sindicatos y la empresa. Tenía un doble objetivo de mercado y empleo: recuperar las cuotas de mercado en los nuevos productos de conmutación electrónica y asegurar la mayor parte posible de puestos de trabajo[36]. La aplicación del plan trajo consigo los expedientes de regulación de empleo y un goteo de bajas en la plantilla mediante bajas indemnizadas y algunas prejubilaciones soportadas por la Seguridad Social[37].

En 1988, Citesa estaba sumida abiertamente en un proceso denominado de reordenación empresarial[38]. A mediados del año siguiente, la multinacional

---

[35] Respuesta escrita del Ministerio de Obras Públicas y Transportes a la pregunta escrita Senado 684/010260 del Grupo Socialista sobre la existencia de un plan de viabilidad a medio y largo plazo de la planta fabril de Fujitsu España, S. A. en Málaga, *BOCG*, Senado, 1 de marzo de 1993.

[36] Real Decreto 1.380/1984, de 20 de junio, por el que se declara en reconversión al grupo de Empresas IT&T España (Standard Eléctrica, S. A., y Marconi Española, Sociedad Anónima); para mayor detalle, véase Calvo (2020, 81-94). Algunos autores (Benton, 1990, 171) incluyen directamente a Citesa como empresa en reconversión según el mencionado Real Decreto.

[37] Uno de los dos sindicatos mayoritarios –CCOO– se opuso al acuerdo propuesto por la Administración, por considerarlo inviable si no había garantías ciertas de la demanda de CTNE y porque significaba un reforzamiento económico del grupo IT&T sobre las espaldas de la Administración y de los trabajadores, debido a incrementos fortísimos de productividad y a los despidos. Una de las reivindicaciones incidía en la equiparación salarial y de condiciones de trabajo de Citesa a las de SESA (Federación del Metal de CCOO, Secciones de CCOO del grupo IT&T, Madrid, 12 de enero de 1984).

[38] Admisión a trámite de la solicitud de comparecencia del Sr. Consejero de Fomento y Trabajo ante la Comisión de Economía, Industria y Energía, con el fin de que presente informe, se co-

Alcatel decidió segregar Alcatel Citesa del grupo Alcatel-Standard Eléctrica, S A., para crear una factoría dedicada al diseño, fabricación y venta de una amplia gama de productos con el objetivo de responder de manera competitiva a la liberalización del mercado con una infraestructura productiva y un grado de especialización adecuados[39]. Para llevar a cabo el proyecto la multinacional francesa firmó, esta vez con los sindicatos en contra, un plan en el que los actores implicados adquirían una serie de compromisos, que quedaban sometidos a la vigilancia de una comisión de seguimiento con una composición plural. La empresa se comprometió a presentar un plan industrial que contemplaba diversificar la producción con la incorporación de nuevos productos y mantener una plantilla de un millar de trabajadores en Málaga a finales de 1991. Este plan incluía el compromiso de compra de productos por parte de Telefónica, de subvenciones, bonificaciones y exenciones por parte del Estado.

En el marco del Plan de reconversión del sector el Gobierno abogaba por mantener y consolidar la base industrial existente en la filial de Málaga del Grupo Alcatel mediante medidas continuistas de promoción y consolidación de diversos productos. Al mismo tiempo, empujaba a la empresa por el camino de medidas tendentes a asegurar su competitividad, la modernización de los productos la garantía del empleo[40]. Según la apreciación de observadores externos, el Gobierno central se atuvo al acuerdo, desembolsando más de 20.000 millones de dinero público en concepto de subvenciones, bonificaciones y exenciones. Lo propio hizo en parte Telefónica, contribuyendo a los importantes beneficios para el grupo Alcatel Citesa. Sin embargo, a pocos

nozca y se debata en la reunión acerca de la situación por la que atraviesan los trabajadores de CITESA, ubicada en Málaga, y presentada por el Ilmo. Sr. D. Andrés Cuevas González y cinco Diputados más, del grupo parlamentario Izquierda Unida-Convocatoria por Andalucía (*Boletín Oficial del Parlamento de Andalucía (BOPA)*, 213, 14 de junio de 1988, 6.553).

[39] Aun con un acento puesto en la especialización en el ramo de la audiotelefonía, la producción prevista incluía aparatos de distinto tipo –telefónicos fijos, de previo pago, vía hilo, de sistema telepunto y de radio celular–, sistemas múltiples, sistemas de voz y datos, así como equipos periféricos y centralitas de baja capacidad (Proposición no de Ley relativa a la situación laboral y económica de Alcatel-Citesa, presentada por el Grupo Izquierda Unida-Convocatoria por Andalucía, *BOPA*, 102, 27 de septiembre de 1991, 3.878).

[40] Conviene destacar la respuesta evasiva del Gobierno, por boca del ministro de Industria Aranzadi, a la pregunta sobre las medidas para garantizar el cumplimiento de los acuerdos entre la CTNE y CITESA: «CITESA es un fabricante de equipos de telecomunicaciones y, por tanto, suministrador de Telefónica de España, S. A. Esta empresa es una sociedad privada, con participación del Estado, cuya gestión de compras la llevan a cabo sus órganos administrativos para conseguir una mejor rentabilidad» (*Diario de Sesiones del Senado*, 66, 7 de mayo de 1991, 3.604-3.605).

meses de finalizar el plazo señalado, la empresa había faltado a sus promesas, al menos en parte, si bien había logrado diversificar la producción con una fuerte inversión. Pero la fabricación de nuevos productos relacionados con las centrales digitales chocó con la caída transitoria de la demanda, que reclamó un expediente de regulación de empleo[41]. La planta de Málaga, arrollada por la globalización, se convirtió en un centro de ensamble del material importado directamente del suroeste asiático, fundamentalmente de Taiwán, e incluso de etiquetado de dichos productos. La factoría de Málaga sufrió un desmantelamiento progresivo y continuo, que alimentó la subcontratación de producción en el exterior y, con ello, el trabajo precario, la economía sumergida y las relaciones laborales desreguladas[42]. El departamento de I+D, trascendental para la empresa, corrió parecida suerte ya que fue dividido y su personal – 67 técnicos y administrativos– reducido a la mitad, asolado por la baja cartera de pedidos que le impedía absorber los elevados costos y amenazaba con encarecer los productos que fabricaba. En otras palabras, una parte pasó directamente a ingeniería de fabricación y el resto a ingeniería de desarrollo. A esta medida de la dirección en España, la casa madre Alcatel impuso desde París la segregación de la I+D, que pasó a depender directamente de Francia. Sin técnicos ni medios para su desarrollo, la factoría de Málaga se vio abocada a un destino poco halagüeño. Alcatel no tardó en anunciar a las centrales sindicales el objetivo de reducir la plantilla en 200 trabajadores y dejar de fabricar terminales telefónicos. Sobre Citesa planeaba la amenaza de ser reducida a un mero centro de embalaje de productos importados desde Taiwán, de convertirse en un departamento comercial para la venta en Europa de productos telefónicos importados en su totalidad o bien en una mezcla de ambos[43].

[41] *Diario de Sesiones del Senado*, 66, 7 de mayo de 1991, 3.604-3.605; la plantilla alcanzaba 74 empleados menos que la cifra comprometida y 331 trabajadores se encontraban en expediente de desempleo (*BOPA*, 102, 27 de septiembre de 1991, 3.878). La oposición de derechas en el parlamento andaluz reconocía el esfuerzo realizado –inversión superior a 9.000 millones de pesetas en el plan de bajas en cuatro años en Málaga– y los logros –conversión en líder mundial de algunos productos–, a la vez que llegaba a reclamar que el gobierno autonómico pechase con el coste de la I+D (Intervención del portavoz del grupo parlamentario popular de Andalucía (Gutiérrez de Ravé), *DSPA*, 81, III Legislatura, 13 de octubre de 1992, 4.071).

[42] En 1991, la oposición denunciaba el escaso control de las bajas incentivadas y las regulaciones de empleo, soportadas con dinero público, a la vez que los incentivos de Alcatel a las subcontrataciones y, con ellas, la economía sumergida (*Diario de Sesiones del Senado*, 66, 7 de mayo de 1991, 3.604-3.605).

[43] Pregunta de Andrés Cuevas González, Grupo Mixto, 29 de abril de 1991, Archivo de las Cortes Generales, Senado; Intervención del representante del Grupo de Izquierda Unida-Convocatoria por Andalucía, *DSPA*, 81, III Legislatura, 13 de octubre de 1992, 4.066-

En definitiva, la crisis de Citesa se agravó tras su absorción por Alcatel NV para crear Alcatel Citesa y la prórroga de la reconversión del Grupo hasta 1991 en las cláusulas y condiciones de la anterior[44]. El nuevo acuerdo que ampliaba el plan anterior llamado «Reajuste del Plan de Reconversión» amparaba dos planes de rentas que afectaban a los mayores de cincuenta años. Como consecuencia, salidas masivas de personal, cifradas en 1.400 trabajadores en un decenio, dejaron una Citesa teóricamente reestructurada y con una plantilla ligeramente superior a los tres centenares de personas.

4. Citesa ante la globalización de los mercados

Vayamos a las raíces y al relato del proceso. Los males de Alcatel Citesa estribaban en instalaciones y equipo inapropiados, una pesada estructura de personal y una falta de recursos financieros para afrontar la inaplazable reconversión. Esta empresa encaró la situación crítica con una estrategia basada en aprovechar las posibilidades comerciales, técnicas e industriales que le ofrecía el grupo empresarial de Alcatel, la demanda y el nuevo marco del mercado único europeo. La mencionada estrategia cobró forma en el Plan de viabilidad de 1993-1998 al que se llegó de manera gradual (Alcatel Citesa 1999).

En el último trimestre de 1991, la empresa planteó un expediente de regulación de empleo e inició un periodo de consultas para reducir 234 puestos de trabajo. La empresa, la parte obrera –trabajadores, comité de empresa y sindicatos– y la administración autonómica como mediadora negociaron salidas a

---

4.074. A la crisis por la que atravesaba desde hacía tiempo Alcatel-Citesa en la provincia de Málaga se añadía la debilidad y la fragilidad del sector industrial, visible en la desaparición en quince años de cincuenta empresas del sector del metal con una destrucción importante de empleo y de riqueza (Intervención del representante del Grupo de Izquierda Unida-Convocatoria por Andalucía, *DSPA*, 81, III Legislatura, 13 de octubre de 1992. 4.066-4.074). Aquí hay un debate importante. El portavoz del Grupo parlamentario andalucista eximía de responsabilidad de la grave situación a Citesa y culpaba a la demanda. Según el mismo, Telefónica adjudicó a Interisa, participada por un exdirector general de Telefónica, un contrato de más de medio millón de teléfonos anuales durante varios años, cifrado en unos 18.000 millones de pesetas. Interisa, empresa no fabricante, debería actuar simplemente de intermediaria y subcontratar con empresas radicadas en España, o, en el peor de los casos, comprar en Extremo Oriente los productos solicitados, sin generar puestos de trabajo ni valor añadido para la economía española (Intervención del portavoz del Grupo parlamentario andalucista, *DSPA*, 81, III Legislatura, 13 de octubre de 1992, 4.070).

[44] El alto directivo de SESA Márquez Balín (2016, 94) apuntaba que no sería justo señalar a Alcatel como gran culpable.

la situación. De esa fase negociadora emanó un acuerdo genérico que contemplaba la reducción del señalado volumen de empleo con carácter voluntario. El acuerdo, firmado ante la Consejería de Trabajo el 3 de diciembre de 1992, implicaba indemnizaciones, jubilaciones anticipadas para los trabajadores a partir de 55 años y traslados voluntarios. Sin embargo, la empresa, acosada por las pérdidas, presentó un plan de viabilidad con el doble compromiso de asegurar el mantenimiento de la plantilla y de impulsar un proyecto industrial nuevo. La segunda vertiente del compromiso suponía la fabricación de una línea de productos relacionados con la telefonía inalámbrica, con tecnología avanzada y una gran demanda. La actividad debía localizarse en el Parque Tecnológico de Andalucía y el plan descrito requeriría unas inversiones de diez mil millones de pesetas, el grueso de los cuales –el 60%– se destinarían a I+D, para desarrollo de este producto. Tras varias reuniones de la empresa con el gobierno andaluz –las consejerías de Economía y de Trabajo– se estudió y se propuso la ayuda de la Junta de Andalucía a la implementación de este proyecto, sujeta a la compatibilidad con las normas de la competencia establecidas por la Comunidad Económica Europea. Las ayudas tendrían carácter complementario con los incentivos regionales procedentes del Gobierno central. Por su parte, la empresa aseguraba el mantenimiento de los puestos de trabajo y la instalación de la fábrica moderna en el Parque Tecnológico de Andalucía[45].

Una parte del esfuerzo inversor recayó sobre Alcatel Citesa, que aportó recursos propios. La autofinanciación se triplicó con creces entre 1993-1998, pasando de 1.009,4 millones de ptas. corrientes a 3.350,3.

Citesa se benefició de subvenciones de organismos oficiales del poder central y del regional, si bien es cierto que entre las cantidades concedidas y las finalmente aprobadas hubo diferencias notables. Las sumas finales de las subvenciones aprobadas fueron de 1.594.250 millones de ptas. procedentes del

[45] La oposición de izquierda criticó al Gobierno autónomo la ausencia de un diseño, en el marco de la política general, de políticas adecuadas de intervención y de interlocución con las multinacionales (Comparecencia del Consejero de Trabajo para informar sobre los planes de reducción de plantilla por la empresa de Alcatel Citesa y de la ejecución del acuerdo adoptado por el parlamento de Andalucía en sesión plenaria el 13 de octubre de 1992, relativo a la viabilidad y mantenimiento de empleo en Alcatel Citesa, *Diario de sesiones de comisiones*, Fondo Documental Núm. 74, III Legislatura, 19 de mayo de 1993, 4). Las ayudas iban destinadas al inicio de la obra civil, la fabricación del nuevo teléfono inalámbrico digital en una cantidad de 300.000 unidades al año y el mantenimiento del nivel de empleo durante diez años: Alcatel Citesa (1999), 3; Alcatel Citesa, Diario 1 (Canal Sur TV), Efemérides del 9 de junio, consultado en http://blogs.canalsur.es/documentacionyarchivo/malaga-la-fabrica-de-telefonos-de-alcatel-citesa-en-martiricos/

ministerio de Industria y Energía y de 1.553.075 de la Junta de Andalucía. En cuanto a la composición, las cuatro quintas partes de la cantidad del ministerio se destinaron a activos tangibles y el resto a I+D, mientras que la Junta de Andalucía reforzó más aún los porcentajes de los activos tangibles (Alcatel Citesa 1999b, 2). A ello cabe añadir la condonación de pagos de impuestos por un monto total de 53,96 millones de ptas. entre 1993 y 1996, que se desglosaban en un 83,02% para trasmisiones patrimoniales, 6,94% para compra de terreno y el resto para aumentos de capital. Entre 1994-1996, el Centro para el Desarrollo Tecnológico Industrial (CDTI) concedió a Citesa préstamos a largo plazo para la financiación parcial de proyectos de I+D por valor de 504,9 millones de ptas. Finalmente, en 1994, el Instituto de Fomento de Andalucía concedió préstamos a Citesa por 50 millones de ptas., destinados a financiar dos proyectos específicos (Autoscam y Clarm)[46].

A lo señalado sobre subvenciones oficiales se ha de añadir que una parte del esfuerzo financiero de la ejecución del plan de viabilidad recayó sobre otras espaldas. La matriz Alcatel España concedió a su filial 2.720 millones de ptas. en 1992, y, de otro lado, esta obtuvo préstamos bancarios por 2.819 millones de ptas.

A todas luces, la empresa adolecía de una estructura financiera de extremada debilidad, situación que el plan de viabilidad pretendía corregir. Avances serios en esta dirección fueron la aportación de 7.095 millones de ptas. que realizaron los accionistas en 1993, la ampliación de capital de 200 millones de ptas. tres años más tarde y el incremento de las reservas con la inyección de beneficios no distribuidos (Alcatel Citesa l999b, 6).

Pese al optimismo que exhibía la empresa, algunas cifras de la estructura financiera llevan cuando menos a incitar a la reflexión. La primera sorpresa radica en el descenso del capital social –3.005 millones de ptas. en 1992 a 1.220 en 1998– y el pequeño incremento del inmovilizado material neto –2.669 millones de ptas. frente a 2.673–. Parece lógico que la reserva de reestructuración sufriera una reducción drástica –2.151 millones de ptas en 1992 y 289 en 1998–. El porcentaje de activos sobre ventas disminuyó de 113,8 a 70,6 y el del capital circulante, en disminución (de 1.951 a 1.323

---

[46] Alcatel Citesa (1999), 4; CDTI, «Noticias», junio de 1994, 5. Entre 1994-1996, el Ministerio de Industria y Energía concedió a Citesa un total de 296.678.074 ptas. en concepto de subvenciones por las inversiones realizadas en proyectos específicos de I+D sobre tecnologías GSM, TPV, DEC y CTO. El CDTI financió los proyectos siguientes: Sistema de multiprocesadores en paralelo para control de terminales telefónicos; Sistema multilínea según el estándar europeo digital Digital European Cordless Telecommunication (DECT) (CDTI. «Noticias», junio de 1994, 5).

millones de ptas. en 1992-1998) sobre ventas pasó de 16,3% a 9,4%. La drástica reducción de los gastos de reestructuración pesó con fuerza en la estructura de costes de Alcatel Citesa que sufrió un cambio enorme e implicó el incremento del porcentaje de los costes de producción. No obstante, en 1998 la estructura de costes presentaba una mejora sensible ya que la relación entre los costes de producción y unas ventas en aumento había disminuido (Alcatel Citesa 1999, 16).

Citesa presumió de haber cumplido con los tres objetivos fundamentales del plan industrial del periodo 1993/1994, a saber, construcción de una nueva factoría, adquisición del equipamiento necesario para la fabricación de equipos de radiofrecuencia –en especial de la anteriormente mencionada tecnología DECT– y modernización de los equipos y métodos de fabricación. Las cifras así parecen avalarlo, sobre todo en el gasto de I+D, que se multiplicó por ocho, si bien menos en el personal de I+D, que se mantuvo relativamente estable entre 1993-1998. Entre estos años Alcatel Citesa invirtió en I+D cerca de 4.000 millones de pesetas con una distribución anual y por línea de proyectos que recoge el Gráfico 1.

Gráfico 1. Gasto de I+D en Alcatel Citesa, 1993-1998 (millones de ptas. corrientes)

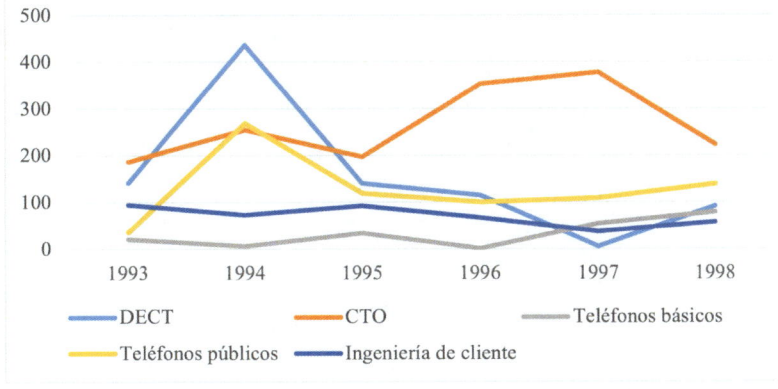

Fuente: Elaboración a partir de Alcatel Citesa (1999), 13.

Tabla 1. Personal de I+D en Alcatel Citesa, 1993-1998

Número						
	1993	1994	1995	1996	1997	1998
Titulados superiores	17	20	19	19	17	18
Titulados medios	14	14	14	14	14	14
Técnicos	11	11	11	11	11	11
Administrativos	1	1	1	1	1	1
Total	43	46	45	45	43	44

Porcentaje					
39,53	43,48	42,22	42,22	39,53	40,91
32,56	30,43	31,11	31,11	32,56	31,82
27,82	25,30	26,05	26,05	27,82	26,89
2,33	2,17	2,22	2,22	2,33	2,27
100	100	100	100	100	100

Fuente: Elaboración a partir de Alcatel Citesa (1999), 13.

Siguiendo un esquema cooperativo, desde los comienzos de la gestación del estándar DECT Alcatel Citesa participó activamente en los organismos europeos que definieron y desarrollaron los estándares de esa tecnología en la EFTA (European Free Trade Association) y en el ETSI, que elaboró las normas paneuropeas. Alcatel Citesa desarrolló las tecnologías requeridas para los productos DECT durante los años 1993 y 1994 en colaboración con los laboratorios de investigación de Alcatel España en Madrid. Además, llevó a cabo más de medio centenar de proyectos tecnológicos en colaboración con la Universidad de Málaga con un coste total superior a los noventa millones de pesetas (Alcatel Citesa 1999, 4). El Gráfico 2 ilustra un comportamiento poco sostenido de las inversiones en el periodo 1993-1998. Los activos tangibles crecieron entre 1993-1995 para desplomarse a continuación, mientras que la I+D y otros intangibles cayeron incluso antes. El esfuerzo inversor en I+D y otros intangibles representó las cuatro quintas partes del total correspondiente a los años 1993-1995.

Gráfico 2. Inversiones de Alcatel Citesa, millones de ptas. corrientes

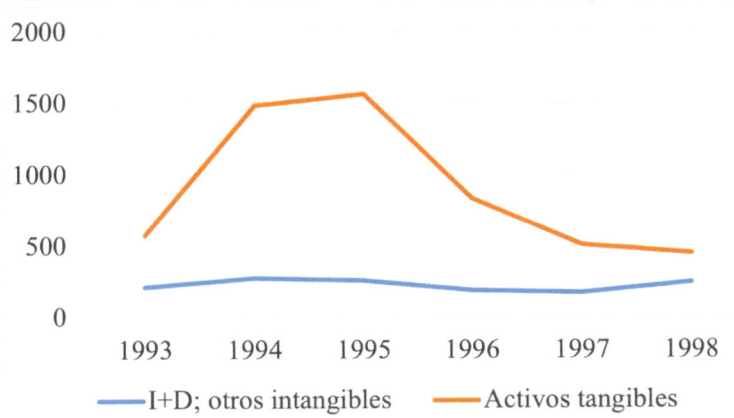

Fuente: Elaboración a partir de Informes de auditoría,
Arthur Andersen, 24 de febrero de 1999, 2.

Citesa conjugó una concentración en las actividades de fabricación clave –ensamblaje de componentes en placas de circuito impreso y montaje final de aparatos y su prueba final– con la externalización de las no específicas para la fabricación y cuyo volumen no justificaba la producción interna –fabricación de placas de circuito impreso, inyección de piezas de plástico o la reparación de aparatos. Llevar a cabo las actividades externalizadas con garantía de calidad y el control de la producción final exigió establecer acuerdos con proveedores preferentes–. Con la inversión en activos fijos realizada entre mediados de 1993 y finales de 1998, cifrada en más de cinco mil millones de pesetas, la empresa se vio dotada de los equipos e instalaciones y maquinaria necesarios para la producción de equipos terminales telefónicos de alta tecnología[47].

---

[47] A subrayar la referencia oficial a la inversión en maquinaria de Citesa en la fábrica de Málaga – cerca de 3.500 millones de pesetas (Ministerio de Industria y Energía 1994, 144). Destacaban: sistemas de diseño mecánico en 3D (Proengineer) y de diseño topológico de circuitos impresos con ayuda por ordenador (Menthor graphics); laboratorios de electrónica, radio frecuencia, telefonometría y electroacústica; cámaras de Faraday y de bajo ruido; célula Getel para medidas de radiaciones electromagnéticas; ordenador personal en la totalidad de los puestos de trabajo; red de área local y red de Internet. Tras las inversiones industriales del plan, la fábrica de Alcatel Citesa contaba al final de 1998 con el equipamiento básico siguiente: almacén automático para gestión de componentes; ensambles de placas de circuito impreso; cuatro líneas de componentes miniatura con una capacidad para 360 millones de componentes por año y máquina de soldadura por ola en atmósfera inerte; horno de refusión atmósfera inerte; máquinas automáticas para inserción de componentes convencionales con una capacidad anual para 105 millones de componentes; equipos de prueba estructural integrados en las líneas de montaje; líneas de montaje para ensamble

Gráfico 3. Composición del capital fijo de la fábrica de Málaga, 1998 (millones ptas.)

- Terrenos y solares
- Edificios industriales
- Otras construcciones
- Maquinaria e instalaciones
- Otras inversiones de equipo

Fuente: Elaboración a partir de Junta de Andalucía, Consejería
de Economía y Hacienda, Málaga, 1998.

Gáfico 4. Composición de la producción anual de Alcatel Citesa (millones de ptas.)

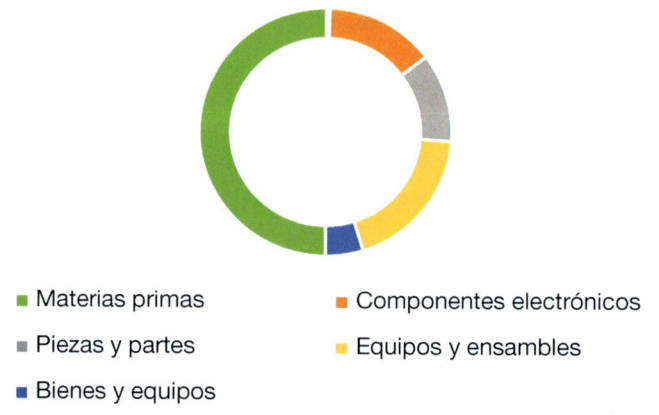

- Materias primas
- Componentes electrónicos
- Piezas y partes
- Equipos y ensambles
- Bienes y equipos

Fuente: Elaboración a partir de Junta de Andalucía, Consejería
de Economía y Hacienda, Málaga, 1998.

final de aparatos; automática para teléfonos con capacidad de 1,5 millones de aparatos anuales, para teléfonos públicos (150.000), automática para terminales DECT (250.000) y para estaciones base DECT (275.000); equipos de prueba automáticos y nuevo sistema informático de gestión de la fabricación SAP puesto en operación en enero de 1999 (Alcatel Citesa 1999, 6-7). La nueva fábrica para la filial Citesa tenía una capacidad de producción anual de 1,3 millones de terminales y realizó ventas por valor de 173.000 millones de pesetas en 1994, de los que el grueso correspondió a exportaciones (Anexo 2 y Anexo 3) (*Computerworld*, 10 de noviembre de 1995).

Más allá de este pronóstico de tono triunfalista, interesa ver las bases de su sistema productivo a través del análisis de diversas variables relativas a la fábrica de Málaga en 1998 (Junta de Andalucía, Consejería de Economía y Hacienda, Málaga, 1998). En la estructura de capital fijo la partida predominante estaba formada por la maquinaria e instalaciones con casi la mitad sobre un total de 1.331,955 millones de ptas. Si le sumamos otras inversiones de equipo, la cifra se elevaba a casi el 70% del total. Terrenos y solares tenían un porcentaje de 14,44% y edificios industriales más otras construcciones el 15,85%. Las cifras de producción muestran un panorama poco risueño. La planta de Málaga producía por un valor anual estimado de 6.896 millones de ptas., que se componía mayoritariamente de equipos, bienes y ensambles (47,71%), componentes electrónicos (28,28%), piezas y partes (23,13%) (Gráfico 4). En la producción de terminales telefónicos predominaba la maquinaria de origen nacional, que alcanzaba los cuatro quintos del total.

Si hablamos del coste de producción de Alcatel Citesa (millones de ptas.), los abastecimientos (61,62%) y los gastos de personal (16,11%) rebasaban las tres cuartas partes del total. Otros gastos de explotación (15,70%), dotaciones de amortizaciones del inmovilizado (4,05%) y variación de las provisiones de tráfico (2,52%) constituían el resto. La producción de la planta de Málaga tenía como destino mayoritario el propio Grupo Alcatel con más de la mitad de las ventas (casa madre el 44,89% y Alcatel España el 6,61%), porcentaje seguido a distancia por los clientes exteriores al grupo (24,50%) y las administraciones públicas (23,94%) (Alcatel Citesa, Intervención, 1999).

En materia de resultados del plan de viabilidad, las cifras de ventas se multiplicaron por 1,7 y pasaron de 1.124 miles de unidades en 1994 a 1.909 cinco años después. A lo largo del quinquenio, tuvo lugar un deslizamiento progresivo hacia el mercado exterior de manera que en 1998 el peso de las ventas en el mercado interior y las realizadas en el extranjero se había igualado. Un desglose de las ventas muestra el predominio claro de los teléfonos básicos, muy por encima de los públicos y terminales inalámbricos DECT pero, especialmente, de los teléfonos inalámbricos analógicos CTO, una de las apuestas fuertes de la compañía (Gráfico 5).

Gráfico 5. Ventas de Alcatel Citesa, 1994-1998 (miles unidades)

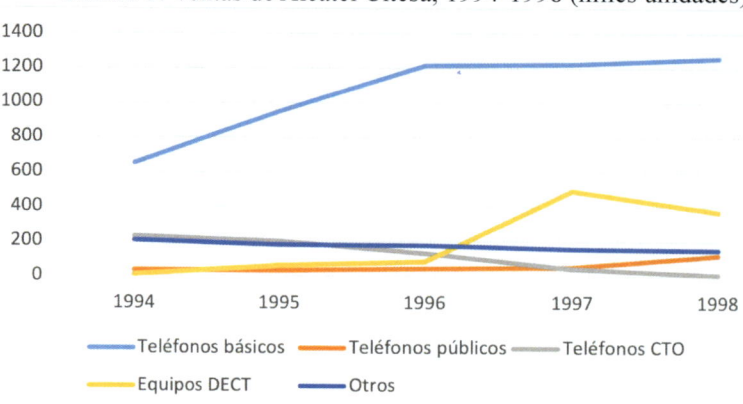

Fuente: Elaboración a partir de Alcatel Citesa (1999), 12.

La matriz Alcatel NV forjó un plan de deslocalización por el que confinaba en Málaga la fabricación de un producto clave –las centralitas–. La planta de Málaga se convertía asimismo en fabricante de una serie de equipos destinados a los clientes de Alcatel en el conjunto de Europa. Comprendían centralitas de baja capacidad y aparatos telefónicos de diversa gama. Alcatel incumplió el compromiso al excluir por completo productos claves como teléfonos básicos y parte de las centralitas (Comité de empresa de Alcatel Citesa 1992, 2).

Durante los años del plan de viabilidad la plantilla de Alcatel Citesa se mantuvo relativamente estable en cuanto a su número y a su composición. Tan solo resultó notable el aumento del peso de los titulados medios (Cuadro 1 y Anexo 4).

Alcatel Citesa fabricó para Telefónica el teléfono regular de monedas autónomo (TRMA), especialmente indicado para un uso intensivo y que empezó a comercializarse en 1991. Idéntica fórmula se aplicó en la adjudicación a Alcatel Citesa y Abecomsa de la fabricación del producto Punto de Conexión de Red con Módulo de Telemedida (PCR-T/M). Alcatel Citesa, junto con Amper Telemática, asumió la fabricación del aparato Forma 1, sujeta a contrato[48].

---

[48] El PCR o terminal de acceso era un dispositivo electrónico con una misión de concentración o distribución, similar a la del actual PTR (Calvo 2016, 220-221). Por el servicio que prestaban esos teléfonos se les consideraba como elemento básico de comunicación, sujeto a regulación (*BOE*, 165, 11 de julio de 1981, 15.874-15.875). El teléfono regular de monedas (TRM) fue diseñado de forma conjunta por SESA y CITESA (SESA, *Memoria*, 1981, p. 11).

Citesa había estado presente desde el origen en un mercado de teléfonos profesionales con los Sistemas Satai de Telefónica. Ese mercado profesional se alimentaba también con los teléfonos con cordón, asociados a centralitas, fabricados y comercializados con marca Alcatel. Citesa se vio obligada a competir con otras fábricas del grupo, entre ellas la de Illkirch. Málaga encontró un balón de oxígeno con la asignación de la fabricación de los teléfonos U.A., gama de la que llegó a fabricar varios cientos de miles al año. Pero los planes de Alcatel pasaban por la centralización. La multinacional puso en marcha en 1991 un proyecto para concentrar en una única fábrica toda la producción de teléfonos básicos dispersa por Europa (López 2008, 12).

Ya sabemos que Citesa lideró dentro del grupo Alcatel el despegue de los teléfonos inalámbricos, tanto en la tecnología analógica CT0 como en la tecnología DECT, esta desarrollada por Citesa, Alcatel Standard de Madrid y Alcatel SEL de Alemania. En este tipo de terminales telefónicos Citesa actuó de manera combinada entre departamentos de la empresa –*marketing*, ingeniería y compras– y empresas extranjeras. Estas diseñaron modelos con las especificaciones técnicas a la medida del cliente de Telefónica y Citesa consiguió homologar el primer teléfono inalámbrico que se certificaba en España (Anexo 1) (Testimonio, José Luis Casado, julio de 2008; Casado 2012)[49].

Alcatel Citesa incluyó en el plan de viabilidad un programa de teléfonos inalámbricos con desarrollo y fabricación en Málaga. Como resultado de este programa se produjeron y comercializaron tres familias de teléfonos inalámbricos –T4000, Evolution y Eole–, caracterizadas por tener diseños originales y una calidad y prestaciones superiores a los provenientes de países asiáticos. Sin embargo, algunos éxitos comerciales tales como el suministro a grandes operadoras –Telefónica y France Telecom– y un reconocimiento general de calidad en el mercado no se tradujeron en una rentabilidad positiva. La razón fundamental no residía en la liberalización del mercado sino en la conversión de los teléfonos CTO en productos de consumo en los cuales el factor decisorio, el precio, y en menor medida una estética atractiva inmediata y factores tales como la calidad la tecnología las funciones de cierta sofisticación etcétera no son consideradas por el comprador si el producto supera la barrera de entrada del precio.

Por ello en este tipo de mercado la industria europea no pudo competir con compañías asiáticas, asentadas en países de muy bajo coste de mano de obra

---

[49] Certificado de aceptación al teléfono sin cordón marca Alcatel, modelo Delta II, fabricado en Taiwán por la empresa productora de equipos de comunicación Sampo Corporation, en un caso claro de outsourcing (*BOE*, 299, 14 de diciembre de 1990, 37.306).

(China continental, Malasia e Indonesia), y que se beneficiaban de economías de escala propiciadas por el acceso al mercado estadounidense. Más aún, una parte importante de los componentes y piezas de estos teléfonos carecían de altas exigencias de calidad y podían ser adquiridos a precio muy competitivo en el mercado asiático.

Pese a su liderazgo en esta gama de productos, al iniciarse la década de 1990, la casa madre empezó a centralizar la decisión de negocio en París con la consiguiente absorción de la responsabilidad de *marketing* de las filiales, entre ellas la de Citesa. A partir de 1997, Alcatel Citesa cesó de fabricar los teléfonos CTO en Málaga encargando su fabricación a una empresa china. En consecuencia, dejaron de aplicarse subvenciones públicas a las actividades de desarrollo relacionadas con esta línea de producto que fueron financiadas en su totalidad por fondos propios de Alcatel Citesa (Alcatel Citesa 1999, 10).

Como sabemos, el plan de viabilidad contemplaba además la fabricación de otros tipos de equipos –convencionales y teléfonos públicos de monedas– (Alcatel Citesa 1999, 7-10). Pese a previsiones de una venta constante de 400.000 teléfonos anuales, la apertura de los mercados dejaba lugar en el mercado español a una fuerte demanda de un teléfono básico fiable y de calidad. Por otra parte, surgió la oportunidad de incluir en el teléfono básico los elementos necesarios para un fácil acceso a los servicios telefónicos adicionales que las operadoras, entre ellas Telefónica, comenzaron a ofrecer. Bajo la dirección de Telefónica y en colaboración con dos proveedores tradicionales de esta, Alcatel Citesa desarrolló y fabricó el teléfono Forma en tres versiones –Forma 1, Forma multiservicio y Forma multiservicio v2– junto a versiones destinadas a algunos mercados sudamericanos de Telefónica. Esta estrategia permitió alcanzar una producción estable superior a 1,2 millones de unidades durante los tres últimos años del plan duplicándose prácticamente la cifra de ventas en 1998 con respecto a las de 1993. A partir de 1999 Telefónica cambió el modelo Forma por el Domo, que incluía mayores prestaciones, y encomendó parte de su producción a Alcatel Citesa. Por las mismas fechas la sociedad matriz decidió transferir a Alcatel Citesa la fabricación del terminal digital modelo U.A. (terminales dedicados de centralitas) que incorporaba nuevas prestaciones[50].

---

[50] Nuevas prestaciones del terminal digital modelo U.A.: identificación, manos libres, recepción amplificable, mensajería, indicación de fecha y hora, información relativa al estado de la llamada (Alcatel Citesa 1999, 7-10).

Suerte muy diferente les cupo a los teléfonos públicos de monedas. Las previsiones iniciales –producción constante de unas 25.000 unidades a lo largo de los cinco años del plan– chocaron con una importante demanda de ese equipo por su potencial utilización como proveedor de servicios de valor añadido. Telefónica adoptó una estrategia específica para desarrollar este tipo de mercado contando con Alcatel Citesa como socio tecnológico e industrial exclusivo. Esta estrategia se basaba en un sistema de gestión cooperativa del servicio telefónico de pago previo con reparto de funciones. Telefónica proveía la red, su filial Cabitel explotaba y mantenía el servicio y el cliente, normalmente un establecimiento público, facilitaba el emplazamiento y llevaba a cabo la recaudación. Como resultado, las ventas se duplicaron entre 1993 y 1998 y el modelo de explotación del servicio se trasladó a otros mercados que introdujeron esa gama de producto. Así sucedió en varios países –Hungría, Portugal y Chile– y numerosos operadores del servicio telefónico en países sudamericanos – Brasil, Argentina y Perú– realizaron peticiones concretas. Dato probatorio de esta tendencia expansiva del mercado, en 1999 Alcatel Citesa tenía presupuestada una venta de unidades de teléfonos públicos tres veces superior a la prevista en el plan original. Cerramos nuestra referencia al plan de viabilidad con el compromiso adquirido de fabricar equipos de acceso radio fija basados en cobertura móvil, en régimen temporal y de subcontratación para otra división española del grupo Alcatel (Alcatel Citesa 1999, 7-10).

5. El mercado global: exportaciones y alianzas

La mención de las exportaciones reclama, cuando menos, referirse a los mecanismos o canales de estas. Para lograrlo, utilizamos la información aportada por un testimonio sobre las exportaciones de aparatos telefónicos a Japón, en cuyo mercado Citesa fue la primera empresa extranjera en acceder. En primer lugar y para intervenir en el debate sobre la internacionalización, se trata de exportaciones sin oficina o delegación comercial en el país de destino de los productos. La elaboración de la información nos ha permitido descomponer el proceso de penetración en el mercado japonés de un producto concreto de Citesa, los aparatos telefónicos (Cuadro 2).

Cuadro 2. El ciclo de las exportaciones de equipos: Citesa en Japón

Fases	Lugar de la acción	Entidad/sección implicada	Contenido
1 (1981)	Berlín	*Marketing* de Citesa	Situación mercado japonés
2	Málaga	Dirección de Citesa	Recepción información
3	Málaga	Dirección de Citesa	Decisión de intentar la entrada en Japón
4	Málaga	Ventas de Citesa	Envío del ingeniero de ventas a Japón para recabar más información
5	Tokio	Oficina de IT&T	Implicación en el asunto
6	Málaga	Ventas de Citesa	Consecución de las especificaciones japonesas
7	Málaga	Ventas de Citesa	Contacto con un posible distribuidor (SUN)
8	Málaga	Ventas de Citesa	Informe de ventas a Citesa
9	Málaga	I+D de Citesa	Estudio de especificaciones; realización de pruebas y modelos
10	Málaga	I+D de Citesa	Test necesarios; superación
11	Harlow	Standard Tele-communication Laboratories	Pruebas; positivas
12	Málaga	*Marketing* de Citesa	Preacuerdo con el distribuidor (cantidades, precios, garantías)
13	Tokio	*Marketing* de Citesa/SUN	Concreción de aspectos con el distribuidor
14	Málaga	(Ventas de Citesa)	Preparación de muestras e información para la homologación y envío a Japón.
15	Japón	oficina de IT&T	Cooperación con el distribuidor en gestiones administrativas; rápida obtención de la homologación
16	Málaga	Ventas de Citesa	Primeros envíos durante un año y entrada de otros competidores; rebaja de precios

17	Japón	Distribuidor	Petición a CITESA de algunos cambios de características en el modelo
18	Japón	Ventas/distribuidor	Fijación de los cambios con técnicos de SUN
19	Málaga	I+D	Realización de cambios
20	Málaga	Ventas	Inicio de los envíos
21	Japón	Distribuidor	Información sobre desajustes en el producto y posibles correcciones realizadas por sus técnicos en Japón
22	Málaga	Fábrica	Aplicación de cambios a la producción
23	Málaga	(Ventas/*Marketing*)	Solicitud de muestras del producto reajustado y comprobación
24	Málaga	(Ventas/*Marketing*)	Subcontrata con el distribuidor de reajustar aparatos en Japón, cargando los costes a Citesa (menos de 1 dólar por unidad)
25	Málaga	Ventas	Aclaraciones sobre factura costes de ajustes de aparatos
26	Málaga	Ingeniería Industrial de Citesa	Estudio de costes de ajustes
27 (mayo de 1984)	Tokio, Japón	SUN/Ventas/*Marketing*	Discusión con SUN: comparación de cálculos, aclaración de malentendidos y admisión de error por SUN

Fuente: Elaboración a partir de Lorenzo Martínez,
Testimonio, 18 de septiembre de 2008.

Los aparatos de previo pago de Citesa fueron exportados por primera vez a Estados Unidos en 1986. En Europa, un testimonio permite trazar los canales puestos a contribución para acceder al mercado en Hungría. Citesa facturaba a Alcatel Hungría, que, a su vez, vendía a la operadora Matáv y daba soporte local. El proceso fue el siguiente: Alcatel Hungría se entera de la licitación de la operadora húngara Matáv Hungarian Telecommunications Company Ltd.; transmisión de la noticia al director de exportación de Citesa; inicio de la participación del equipo de I+D[51] (departamento de Sistemas, Ingeniería de Sistemas y desarrollo SW) y la sección comercial; adaptación a los requisitos de Matav (del producto a la red húngara y del validador de Azkoyen a las monedas del país, elevando la gama y el poder de discriminación); recurso a la embajada de España en Atenas para conseguir un juego de monedas fraudulentas; transferencia de conocimiento a personal de Matav; curso de formación y pruebas de aceptación del validador con un ingeniero y una inspectora de la compañía húngara (Rafael Vertedor, Testimonio, 9 de diciembre de 2007).

La exportación a Australia empezó en 1982, tan solo un año después de que se recibieran las primeras informaciones sobre la demanda australiana de aparatos telefónicos tipo Góndola. Las copias de este modelo fabricadas en Taiwan y Hong Kong, de mala calidad pero a precios bajos, hundieron el mercado de Citesa Australia[52].

Exportar significaba algo más que el simple hecho de vender productos. Cuando Citesa firmó un contrato de venta de centrales electrónicas del Sistema 12 a Teléfonos de México se comprometió a crear un centro de formación, mantenimiento y reparaciones. Recalcamos, un establecimiento educativo con servicio posventa y no una oficina de ventas. Comportamientos generales del sector en años posteriores y un testimonio específico para el caso autorizan a pensar que era una práctica habitual como elemento de marcada competitividad[53].

---

[51] El departamento de I+D de ingeniería de *software* de Alcatel Citesa en Málaga programaba el código que gobernaba las funciones de un teléfono y diseñaba los modelos para el mercado interior, es decir, Telefónica, y para la exportación, predominantemente a Iberoamérica (*BIT*, 174, abril-mayo, 2009, 11).

[52] El circuito fue el siguiente: reunión mantenida en STL (Harlow), transmisión de información por Standard Telephones & Cables de Sydney, contactos de Citesa con STC Sydney y con IT&T en España e IT&T en Nueva York; asignación de la fabricación a Málaga y viaje a Sydney para negociar con Australian Telecom; reuniones con Australian Telecom en Sydney y en Melbourne; logro del pedido e inicio de las entregas en 1982; problemas de calidad; viaje a Sydney en 1983; estudio del problema en Sydney, Harlow (STL), Málaga y laboratorios del fabricante de CMOS (IT&T Intermetall, Friburgo); descubrimiento de la causa en Málaga; estancia en Málaga de un inspector chileno de STC Sydney (Lorenzo Martínez, Testimonio, 15 de septiembre de 2008); de la asistencia posventa habla otro protagonista al referirse a «viajes de trabajo que hice para Citesa» (Rafael Vertedor, Testimonio, 30 de diciembre de 2007).

[53] Manuel Márquez Balín, Comunicación personal, 5 de junio de 2017; *BIT*, junio-julio de 1980, 31. En la industria asiática de las telecomunicaciones, el soporte técnico y el mantenimiento del hardware normalmente eran proporcionados por los grandes proveedores de equipos de telecomunicaciones, entre ellos Alcatel-Lucent (Emerging Strategy 2008, 3).

Así, pues, consideramos la exportación solo una vertiente de la presencia de una empresa en el mercado mundial. Veamos ahora si hubo otras modalidades de penetración. Al abandonar la organización propia de IT&T, basada en áreas geográficas, y adoptar la basada en «líneas de producto», la fábrica de Málaga quedó encuadrada en el Business System Group. Al compás de la estructuración de la pirámide de decisión financiera en París, Alcatel implantó un sistema de *reporting* propio[54].

La estrategia de Alcatel llevó a Citesa a la internacionalización de su actividad. Tras sellar una alianza en 1999 con el fabricante de componentes electrónicos Thomson Multimedia, esta empresa tomó el control de Alcatel Citesa, a través de Otalec. A comienzos del año siguiente Alcatel constituyó una *joint venture* a partes iguales con Thomson Multimedia bajo el nombre de Atlinks, a la que aportó sus activos de telefonía, entre otros, su fábrica de Málaga. El nacimiento de Atlinks obedecía a la voluntad de competir en el mercado de la comunicación digital en Internet, último peldaño de la fusión de los negocios de telefonía fija, terminales de Internet, módems ADSL y digitales para el cable de las socias[55]. Ya entonces, se habían alcanzado unas ventas anuales de 84 millones de euros, de los cuales, el 65,6% estaba destinado a exportación. Transcurrido un año, Atlinks repitió la fórmula con una empresa complementaria y una de las líderes del sector, la multinacional francesa A Novo, bien aleccionada por el éxito de la conversión de la recién adquirida fábrica de TRT-Philips en Brive, con la misión de diversificar y optimizar la capacidad de producción de la planta de Málaga. La actuación en la fábrica de TRT-Philips mostró a A Novo el camino para transformar una planta de producción en otra de servicios industrializados, mantenimiento de infraestructuras y tecnología para nuevos productos (*L'Express*, 19 de febrero de 2002)[56].

[54] En materia contable y financiera, Málaga siguió funcionando como una división de SESA, cuya contabilidad se consolidó en Madrid y el informe a la matriz Alcatel se trasladó de Bruselas a París. En cuanto a tesorería, totalmente centralizada en SESA, la necesidad de recursos financieros como las posiciones de liquidez generadas en Málaga eran diariamente gestionadas por la tesorería central mediante transferencias automáticas en uno u otro sentido hasta dejar el saldo matinal del banco en cero (Testimonio de Ángel López Esteve, abril de 2008).

[55] CNMC, N/030, 11 de noviembre de 1999; *El País*, 26 de febrero de 2000. Atlinks se adelantó en la difusión de las centralitas DECT en Europa (Méndez sd., 66).

[56] Además de Málaga, A Novo adquirió una fábrica en Milán. En 1998, se embarcó en un proceso de expansión internacional con diversas adquisiciones, entre las que se cuenta la participación de 74% en la española Sadelta, especializada en el negocio de teléfonos móviles y con dos filiales, Tecnosoporte, afincada en Barcelona, y Coretel, con sede en

En efecto, A Novo se comprometió a prolongar la producción de teléfonos fijos en la planta de Málaga y, a la vez, a diversificarla, incorporando el mantenimiento y reparación de los teléfonos GSM y descodificadores[57]. Ello significaba mantener los niveles de actividad en dicha planta, a saber, 287.000 centralitas anuales, un elevado volumen de teléfonos fijos, en particular 980.000 del modelo Domo, y 60.000 teléfonos públicos, destinados al mercado interior y al sudamericano en el primer caso y al mercado sudamericano en el segundo. Según los pactos, al cabo de dos años la totalidad del capital pasaría A Novo, que sería la propietaria de la fábrica de Málaga y asumiría la plantilla, a excepción de 50 asalariados, integrados a la estructura de Atlinks España y dedicados a actividades comerciales y de desarrollo. Ambos socios reafirmaban el objetivo de la presencia en el mercado interior y el sudamericano. En una cláusula adicional del contrato, las partes se obligaban a no competir entre ellas durante siete años[58]. Atlinks cedió, pues, la planta de producción a A Novo, presente en el país como accionista mayoritario de la recién constituida A Novo Comlink España S.A., que integraría parcialmente la plantilla existente[59]. Atlinks, gestionada por Thomson Multimedia y ya un

Valencia, de las que poseía el 100 y el 50%, respectivamente. Esta adquisición permitió a A Novo construir una sociedad con Airtel, la futura filial española de Vodafone (A Novo 2000-2001, 5). Sadelta empezó su actividad en unos locales de Barcelona y después se trasladó al Parque Tecnológico del Vallés, pionero de los parques tecnológicos de España (Bennetts 1994, 7-9; *La Vanguardia*, 25 de noviembre de 1982). En 1997, Thomson se centró en la fabricación y montaje de componentes clave y productos de consumo hasta alcanzar el 98% de las ventas. El deterioro significativo de los resultados operativos y la situación financiera en la década de 1990 obligó a una recapitalización por parte del Estado francés, a través de TSA, la antigua Thomson SA. Varias iniciativas de reestructuración y reingeniería permitieron recuperar la rentabilidad. A mediados del año 2000, Thomson desplegó una estrategia de reposicionamiento incorporando nuevos segmentos de la industria del video al mercado tradicional de la electrónica de consumo (US Securities and Exchange Commission, file number 0-3003, 2003, 23).

[57] El acuerdo contemplaba el mantenimiento de las actividades de I+D y de producción durante diez años y una plantilla mínima de 304 trabajadores (Presidente del comité de empresa de A Novo Comlinks España a M. Chaves, presidente de la Junta de Andalucía, 8 de abril de 2005).

[58] Asociación Atlinks-A Novo, Colombes, 1 de diciembre de 2001; *L'Atelier*, 13 de noviembre de 2000. A Novo estaba implantada en catorce países y se dedicaba a video y telecomunicación, dinero electrónico y tecnologías de la información. Según lo acordado, Alcatel tenía la opción de vender su participación del 50% en Atlinks a partir de octubre de 2002. Por acuerdo de febrero entre las socias, Thomson debía abonar 68 millones de euros en efectivo a cambio de la participación de Alcatel en Atlinks (Thomson Group, *Annual Report 2005*, 132).

[59] Rafael Márquez Gallo, Málaga, 24 de enero de 2001, A la atención del Comité de empresa de Atlinks España. En enero de 2001, el grupo A Novo creó A Novo Comlink en la que adquirió una participación accionarial del 33%, duplicada al año siguiente y llevada hasta

líder mundial en telefonía residencial e Internet, retuvo las fases iniciales y finales del proceso de producción, es decir, el diseño y la comercialización de los productos (Testimonio de Ángel López Esteve, abril de 2008). La planta de Málaga comenzó a procesar teléfonos Philips (GSM y residenciales) hacia mediados de 2001[60].

La actividad se incrementó en 2002 con la fabricación de teléfonos móviles en forma de subcontrata para la vecina Vitelcom. La plantilla de A Novo creció con la contratación de trabajadores temporales, en su mayoría cedidos por empresas de trabajo eventual, entre ellas Adecco y ADPG. Sin embargo, la actividad de Vitelcom no se mantuvo y A Novo Comlink España se quedó con una plantilla de 291 trabajadores con contratos fijos, 92 con contrato temporal de A Novo y un centenar de cedidos por ADPG[61].

Durante el periodo en que Alcatel mantuvo una participación en el capital de A Novo a través de Atlinks, la fábrica de Málaga tuvo garantizado por un contrato bianual un volumen de trabajo y A Novo cerró con beneficios. Finalizado el periodo transitorio, Alcatel cesó la fabricación en Málaga de los teléfonos U.A. y DECT, que deslocalizó a otras de sus plantas en Francia. Desarmada por no haber respondido al mercado con la presteza suficiente, la fábrica de Málaga se vio abocada a una nueva reestructuración y, con ella, a un adelgazamiento de la plantilla a través de un ERE en tres fases. Para financiarlo, vendió la fábrica del PTA a A Novo y se trasladó a unas instalaciones de menor tamaño en régimen de alquiler. Atlinks se escindió en dos sociedades mercantiles diferentes y finalmente se convirtió en Thomson España, que diseñó, produjo y comercializó los modelos del teléfono clásico. Su mercado era el mercado nacional y el de exportación –Suecia, Australia, Estados Unidos y Japón, además de numerosos países de Europa e Hispanoamérica–. Contaba con oficinas comerciales en Madrid y en Chile (*La Última Milla*, 2, enero 2006, 5)[62].

---

el control total (A Novo 2000-2001, 26). A Novo Comlink España, surgió de la transferencia de activos de Atlinks España y de la combinación de todas sus actividades españolas de servicios (A Novo 2000-2001, 38).

[60] Tan solo medio año después de iniciar la actividad de reparación, A Novo Comlinks ya realizaba reparaciones en 150.000 unidades al año y aspiraba a lograr un contrato de Telefónica Móviles (A Novo 2000-2001, 26).

[61] Presidente del comité de empresa de A Novo Comlinks España a M. Chaves, presidente de la Junta de Andalucía, 8 de abril de 2005.

[62] En 1988 se había creado Thomson Telecom España SA, que se dedicaba a la importación, fabricación, venta, exportación, instalación y mantenimiento de equipos, sistemas y acce-

A mediados de 2007, la planta de teléfonos de A Novo en Málaga fabricó para Thomson España la última partida de teléfonos Domo y se especializó en el mantenimiento y reparación de terminales de telefonía fija y móvil, así como de otros aparatos electrónicos[63].

Conclusión

La implantación en España desde antiguo de importantes multinacionales de las tecnologías avanzadas convirtió a este país en un campo de batalla de la recomposición mundial de dicho sector que siguió a la desmembramiento de la multinacional norteamericana AT&T y a la liberalización del mercado. Este estudio ha indagado en la comprensión del proceso de conformación global de la industria de las telecomunicaciones en las dos décadas finales del siglo XX y los primeros años del nuevo milenio. El periodo abarca la transición de una industria basada en la estrecha vinculación, cuando no estricta integración, entre el monopolio del servicio telefónico y la industria nacional de equipos de telecomunicaciones. En este estudio, el componente territorial y los factores de localización cobran gran importancia. El caso de Citesa ilustra el cambio de estrategia de algunas multinacionales, que pasaron a centralizar las principales opciones de mercado y a asignar funciones específicas a las filiales, lejos de la autonomía relativa característica de la era IT&T. Dependencia tecnológica y dependencia empresarial en una transición de mercado cautivo a la competencia forzaron alianzas, fusiones e internacionalización, sobre todo en América Latina, en busca de economías de escala. Por último, las condiciones cambiantes de las distintas fracciones del mercado mundial condujeron a la externalización en la industria de las telecomunicaciones. La estrategia de las multinacionales, regida por los principios de un mercado globalizado, imponía sus prioridades por encima de las peculiariades del

sorios de telecomunicación, electrónica e informática (Registro mercantil de Málaga, hoja MA-3.647, tomo 1633, folio 69, 18/11/1988).

63 El ERE contemplaba el despido en septiembre de 2005 de todos los mayores de 55 años, que pasarían a jubilación parcial a los 60 años, hasta los 65 en que se alcanzaba la jubilación definitiva (Testimonio de Ángel López Esteve, abril de 2008). El mercado de los teléfonos con el estándar DECT en Europa pasó de más de seis millones de unidades en 1998 a 11 millones en 2000. Atlinks fabricaba teléfonos, terminales de Internet y módems para Alcatel, Thomson, General Electric y RCA; realizaba la mitad de sus ventas en los EE. UU. y el 30% en Europa (*Les Échos*, 30 de junio de 2000). Los aparatos electrónicos diversos comprendían ordenadores de sobremesa y portátiles, videoconsolas y decodificadores de televisión (*Sur*, 17 de enero de 2010).

mercado nacional y de la política industrial de los estados nación. Empresas significativas para el tejido industrial de una región o de un país, que habían absorbido cuantiosos recursos financieros, fueron reducidas a unidades con escasa capacidad de generación de valor añadido, arrolladas por los vientos de las reconversiones y la deslocalización.

Anexo 1. Los teléfonos inalámbricos

Citesa no tenía las competencias necesarias para la tecnología inalámbrica. Debido a ello, llevó a cabo una exploración de aparatos sin hilos disponibles en los «cuatro dragones» del este de Asia. Tras visitas de estudio en Japón, Hong-Kong, Taiwán y Corea, se seleccionó un aparato de la compañía tai-wanesa Sampo Corp., una de las pocas grandes proveedoras de componentes (Palacios 2008, 102), con la que se llegó a un acuerdo de suministro de tipo ODM (Original Design Manufacturing). Este convenio, acorde con la estra-tegia de penetración en Europa, significaba la contratación externa del diseño y la fabricación de un equipo siguiendo las especificaciones y los niveles de calidad del cliente. Los acuerdos contemplaban la transferencia de tecnología de fabricación desde Sampo a Citesa para llevar a cabo un cierto nivel de ensamble local en Málaga. El resultado fue el teléfono Telyco Delta, el pri-mer teléfono fijo sin hilos homologado en España y que se vendió a Telyco, compañía comercial de Telefónica. En su segunda faceta, el plan llevó a crear un equipo para desarrollar internamente los productos. Ingenieros de nueva incorporación expertos en tecnología de radiofrecuencia se unieron a los téc-nicos de diseño electrónico y de SW existentes en la empresa. Este grupo llegó a liderar en Alcatel el desarrollo de los teléfonos inalámbricos de tecno-logía analógica CT0. No sucedió lo mismo con los teléfonos DECT, rama que acabó siendo centralizada en Francia. Desde el punto de vista económico, el éxito del negocio de los teléfonos sin hilos no llegó hasta que la fabricación se hizo íntegramente en China. Resultaba inviable llevar a cabo ensambles locales sin tener ni los costes ni el mercado necesarios para competir con las fábricas chinas de ámbito global (Casado 2012).

Anexo 2

Producción de aparatos telefónicos en Citesa (miles)

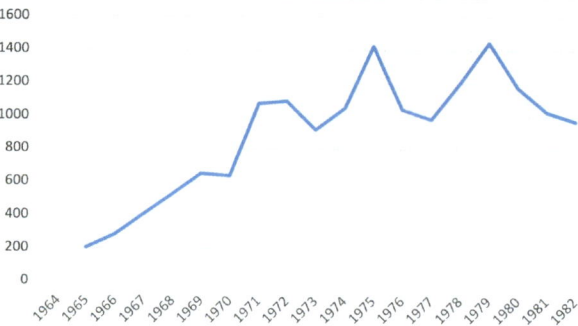

Anexo 3

Citesa: Venta en el mercado nacional y en el exterior (millones de ptas. corrientes)

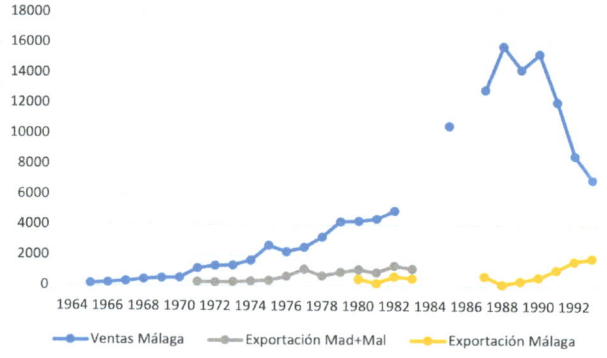

Evolución de empleo en Citesa

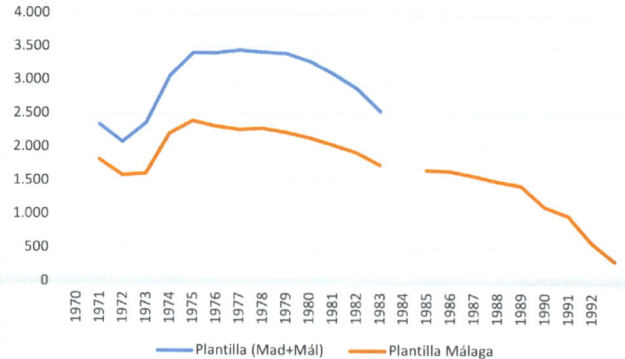

Anexo 4

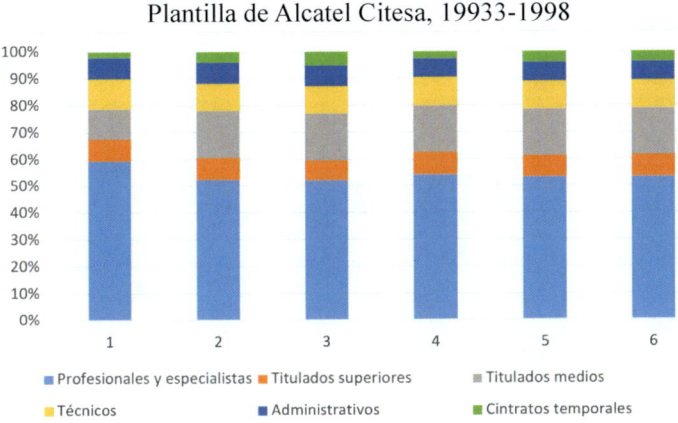

Plantilla de Alcatel Citesa, 19933-1998

Fuente: Elaboración a partir de Alcatel Citesa (1999), 12.

Fuente oral

Luis Méndez, Comunicación personal al autor, 3 de agosto de 2020.

Procedencia de fuentes

Ángel López Esteve, Testimonio, 2008.
Archivo de Comisiones Obreras, Fundación Primero de Mayo.
Congreso de los Diputados, España.
Parlamento de Andalucía.
Rafael Vertedor, Testimonio, 2007.
Thomson Group.

Hemeroteca

ABC, España.
Cuadernos para el diálogo, España.
Economista: Revista Semanal Científica e Independiente, España.

El País, España.

Información comercial española: Boletín semanal, España.

La Vanguardia, España.

Les Échos, Francia.

Villaverde Obrero. Boletín de las CCOO de Villaverde.

Referencias

Alcatel Citesa. 1999a. *Memoria que formula Alcatel Citesa SA. Sobre el desarrollo del Plan de Viabilidad de 1993-1998*. Málaga, 16 de marzo.

Alcatel Citesa. 1999b. *Informe sobre el cumplimiento de las condiciones establecidas en los expedientes de concesión de incentivos*. Málaga, 6 de marzo.

A Novo. 2000-2001. *Document of reference*.

Bennetts, F. 1994. *Science Park Networks. A Report to the European Commission.* Vol. 2, Cambridge MA: Segal Quince Wicksteed Limited.

Benton, Lauren A. 1990. *Invisible Factories: The Informal Economy and Industrial Development in Spain*. Nueva York: State University of New York Press.

Calvo, Ángel. 2011. «Telecomunicaciones y spillovers. La industria de equipo telefónico en España entre el mercado cautivo y la liberalización, 1953-1963». *Revista de Historia Industrial*, 45, 145-174.

Calvo, Ángel. 2012. «La liberalización en la industria de equipo de telecomunicación en España, 1963-1973». *Investigaciones de Historia Económica*. 8-3, 43-72.

Calvo, Ángel. 2014. *Telecomunicaciones y el nuevo mundo digital en España. La aportación de Standard Eléctrica*. Barcelona: Ariel.

Calvo, Ángel. 2016. *Historia de Telefónica: 1976-2000. Las telecomunicaciones en la España democrática*. Barcelona: Ariel/Fundación Telefónica.

Calvo, Ángel. 2019a. «World telecommunications equipment industry from the National champions to outsourcing: the case of ALCATEL». *The International Journal of Business Management and Technology*. Vol. 3, 6°.: 130-152.

Calvo, Ángel. 2019b. «Consolidation and rationalization of the public companies in Spain: the information and communication technologies (ICT) holding». *Journal of Evolutionary Studies in Business*, 4(1), 142-179.

Calvo, Ángel. 2019c. «The emergence of global companies in the high-tech industry of defense: the case of Indra in Spain, 1993-2007». *Eurasian Journal of Social Sciences,* vol. 7(2), 29-47.

Calvo, Ángel. 2019d. «Tecnología, empresa y política en la industria española de la electrónica, las telecomunicaciones y la defensa: Marconi Española». *Quaderns d'Història de l'Enginyeria*. Vol. XVII, 75-110.

Calvo, Ángel. 2020a. «Política industrial, multinacionales y desarrollo regional en España. La IED en la industria de la fibra óptica a finales del siglo XX». *Biblio3W, Revista Bibliográfica de Geografía y Ciencias Sociales*. Vol. XXV, n°. 1.288, 1-36.

Calvo, Ángel. 2020b. «Domestic market and internationalisation in the telecommunications equipment industry: Telettra Española at the end of the 20th century». *Storia economica*, Año XXIII, 2020b, 1, 203-228.

Calvo, Ángel. 2020c. «La reconversión en la industria de equipos de telecomunicación entre finales de la década de 1980 e inicios del siglo XXI. El caso de Alcatel-SESA». *Investigaciones de Historia Económica* 16, n°.2: 81-94. https://doi.org/10.33231/j.ihe.2020.01.005

Calvo, Ángel. 2021. «Japanese ICT multinationals in Southern Europe by the end of the twentieth century: Fujitsu in Spain». *Journal of the Knowledge Economy*, 12 de marzo. https://rdcu.be/cgGcw

Calvo, Ángel. 2023. «Firm restructuring in the telecommunications equipment industry: the case of IT&T in Spain towards the end of the XXth century» (Bussiness History, November: 1-36).

Carr, Joseph J. et al. 2001. *Understanding Telephone Electronics.* Boston: Newnes.

Casado, José L. 2102. *Testimonios y memorias de citesianos. José Luis Casado habla de Citesa.* http://citesa.blogspot.com/2012/01/testimonios-y-memorias-de-citesianos.html?m=1

Cerón, Cristian. 2018. «La modernización en la industria de equipo telefónico en España durante el segundo franquismo. CITESA 1965-1975». *Memoria y civilización. Anuario de historia*, 21, 363-390. http://dadun.unav.edu/bitstream/10171/56081/1/25721-75908-2-PB.pdf

Clark, Paul y Ryecart, Guy. 1997. *The Phone: An Appreciation.* Ringwood, Victoria: Viking.

Cohen, Stephen D. 2007. «Multinational Corporations versus the Nation-State: Has Sovereignty Been Outsourced?» En *Multinational Corporations and Foreign Direct Investment: Avoiding Simplicity, Embracing Complexity.* New York: Oxford Academic.

De Mateo, Elías y Heredia, Víctor. 2012. *Málaga Tecnológica.* Málaga: Fundación Málaga.

Díaz-Morlán, Pablo. 2009. «The restructuring of the Spanish integrated steel industry in the European panorama (1971–86): a lost opportunity». *Business History* 51, 547-568.

Díaz-Morlán, Pablo y Sáez-García, Miguel Á. 2017a. «State aid for the restructuring of the Spanish steel industry from a European perspective (1975–1988)». *Investigaciones de Historia Económica*. 13, n°1.: 38-50.

Díaz-Morlán, Pablo y Sáez-García, Miguel. 2017b. «Lecciones de la historia reciente de la siderurgia española». *XII Congreso de la AEHE*. Sesión coordinada por J. L. García Ruiz y J. Mª Valdaliso, Salamanca, 20 y 21 de abril.

Díaz-Morlán, Pablo; Escudero, Antonio y Sáez, Miguel Á. 2008. «El desmantelamiento de la siderurgia integral del Mediterráneo español (1977-1984)». *Revista de Historia Industrial* 38, XVII, n°.3: 161-188.

Dirección General de Industrias. 1975. *La industria en el Perú*. Lima: Oficina de Planeamiento y Promoción.

Emerging Strategy. 2008. *Telecommunications Network Maintenance Services. Key Trends in Asia*, Emerging Strategy, Washington, octubre.

Fernández de Pinedo, Emiliano. 2003. «Desarrollo, crisis y reconversión de la siderurgia española a través de una empresa vizcaína, AHV (1929-1996)». *Ekonomiaz* 54, 28-51.

García de Castro, Rafael. 1964. *Factoría de C.I.T.E.S.A. en Málaga*. Madrid: Patronato Juan de la Cierva de Investigación Técnica.

García de Castro, Rafael y Mexia, Ricardo. 1964. «Factoría de C.I.T.E.S.A. en Málaga». *Informes de la Construcción* 166, diciembre, 132-137.

González, Juan. 1982. «Empleo en Standard: Historia de un martirio». *BIT*, marzo, 8-10.

Instituto Internacional San Telmo. 1992. *Alcatel Citesa. Historia de la compañía*. Sevilla: Instituto Internacional San Telmo.

Iraburu, Miguel. «CITESA». 2019. Comunicación escrita al autor, 13 de noviembre.

Jensen, Nathan M. 2006. *Nation-States and the Multinational Corporation: A Political Economy of Foreign Direct Investment*. Princeton: Princeton University Press.

Jordá, Rosa M. 1991. «Transformaciones Recientes de la Economía Andaluza». *Revista de Estudios Andaluces* 16, 138-149.

La Opinión de Málaga. 2002. «Citesa, el nacimiento de un gigante». *La Opinión*, Málaga.

Lee, Chung-shing y Pecht, Michael G. 1997. *Electronics Industry in Taiwan*. Boca Ratón FL: CRC.

López, Santiago. 2016. «Economía y política del cambio tecnológico». En *Historia de Telefónica: 1976-2000. Las telecomunicaciones en la España democrática.* Calvo, Ángel, 159-180, Barcelona: Ariel/Fundación Telefónica..

López, Santiago y Molero, José. 2005. «Innovación e internacionalización en las empresas españolas de componentes para telecomunicaciones un estudio de caso». En *La empresa multinacional española. Estrategias y ventajas competitivas.* Durán, Juan J. (coord.), 197-226, Madrid: Minerva Ediciones.

López, Santiago; Pueyo, Ana y Zlatanova, Goritza. 2002. «Colaboración bajo incertidumbre: la formación de un grupo tecnológico en el sector de las telecomunicaciones». *Economía Industrial* 346, 81-96.

Márquez Balín, Manuel. 2016. *Mi Historia.* CreateSpace Independent Publishing Platform, [s.l.].

Martínez, Alfonso (coord.) 2005. *La conquista de la libertad. Historia de las Comisiones Obreras de Andalucía (1962-2000).* Cádiz: Fundación de Estudios Sindicales-Archivo Histórico de CC.OO.-A.

Martínez, Lorenzo. 2008. «Comentario al artículo de J. L. Casado "Citesa no era solo una fábrica"». Blog, 24 de febrero. Citesa.blogspot.com/2008

Méndez, Félix. *Equipos terminales utilizados en España hasta final del siglo xx.* Vol. 2, Félix Méndez, mimeo (cortesía del autor).

Méndez, Luis. 2000. «Las Telecomunicaciones en Málaga en el siglo xxi». *BIT*, noviembre – diciembre, 56-57.

Ministerio de Industria y Energía. 1994. *Informe sobre la industria española.* Vol. 2. Madrid: Secretaría General Técnica.

Ministerio de Industria y Energía. 1982. *Informe anual sobre la industria española.* Madrid: Ministerio de Industria y Energía.

Ministerio de Industria y Energía. 1976. *Las 500 grandes empresas industriales españolas en 1974.* Madrid: Servicio de Publicaciones.

Navarro, Mikel. 2005. «La larga marcha de la siderurgia española hacia la competitividad». *Economía Industrial* 355-356, 167-184.

Navarro, Mikel. 1989. *Crisis y reconversión de la siderurgia española, 1978-1988.* Pasajes: Junta del Puerto de Pasajes y Ministerio de Obras Públicas y Urbanismo.

Nye, Joseph S. 1974. «Multinational Corporations in World Politics». *Foreign Affairs* 53, n°1: 153-175.

Nygaard, Arne y Dahlstrom, Robert. 1992. «Multinational company strategy and host country policy». *Scandinavian Journal of Management*, Vol. 8, 1, 3-13.

Palacios, Juan J. (ed.) 2008. *Multinational Corporations and the Emerging Network Economy in Asia and the Pacific*. Londres: Routledge.

Patronato de Desarrollo Socio-Económico e Industrialización de la Provincia de Málaga. 1973. *El Desarrollo económico y social de Málaga*, Málaga: Patronato.

Rodero, Adolfo. 2006. «La planificación económica en Andalucía». *Revista de Estudios Regionales* 75, I, 41-46.

Ruiz, Francisca. 2005. *I+D y Territorio*. Sevilla: Junta de Andalucía.

Sánchez, Fernando H. 2003. «Aproximación a la implantación de CITESA en Málaga (1961-1964)». *Isla de Arriarán: Revista cultural y científica* 1.133-6.293, n°.22: 321-332.

Sánchez Picón, Andrés. (coord.). 2013. *Industrialización y desarrollo económico en Andalucía*. Sevilla: Centro de Estudios Andaluces.

Todd, Daniel. 2019. *Routledge Revivals: The World Electronics Industry (1990)*. Abingdon: Routledge.

United States. Bureau of International Commerce. 1974. *Electronic Components*. Vol. 57. Washington: U.S. Government Printing Office.

U.S. Department of Commerce. 1984. *Telecommunications Equipment, Spain*. Vol. 61. Washington: International Trade Administration.

U.S. Department of Commerce. 1982. *Communications Equipment, Algeria*. Vol. 61. Washington. International Trade Administration.

Valdaliso, Jesús M. 2010. «Treinta años de cambios en las empresas vascas: un estudio exploratorio y descriptivo». *Ekonomiaz: Revista vasca de economía*, 25, 194-221.

Valdaliso, Jesús M. 2003. «Crisis y reconversión de la industria de construcción naval en el País Vasco». *Ekonomiaz*, 4 trimestre: 52-67.

Villalba, Mª José; Ruiz, Mª Carmen y Ortega, Emilio. 2004. «Comisiones Obreras en Málaga, 1960-1997». *Baetica*, 26, 427-446.

VVAA. 1973. *10 años de CITESA en Málaga: del 19 al 21 de noviembre 1973: ciclo de conferencias, exposiciones, concurso de fotografía y pintura* [s.n.].

3. De los campeones nacionales al *outsourcing*: Alcatel-SESA

1. Introducción

El cambio tecnológico y la liberalización, a los que se ha hecho referencia en otros capítulos, causaron cambios en profundidad en las telecomunicaciones de todo el mundo, que se vieron abocadas a una aguda competencia. En la industria europea de equipos de telecomunicaciones –un sector *high tech*– una defensa de los campeones nacionales, responsable del desarrollo y comercialización de innovaciones de alta tecnología (Hulsink 2012)[1], dio paso

---

[1] Las innovaciones primordiales fueron la digitalización que provoca una estandarización cada vez más uniforme de la producción electrónica y los avances en las telecomunicaciones que permiten interconectar instalaciones en tiempo real dispersas en escalas geográficas cada vez más grandes (Carroué 2004-2005, 131-136; Mouline y Hafsi 2008, 27-37). La pauta del campeón nacional, uno de los ocho modelos de difusión de las TIC del siglo xx, se caracteriza por «la creación de una industria informática nacional fuertemente protegida y preferida a través de la política y acción del gobierno». Los restantes modelos de difusión contemplados eran los siguientes: Government-supported/private-sector-driven; Corporate diffusion; Industry-driven; Asian private-sector-driven; Planned economy: public policy; Application diffusion and Technology-standards diffusion (Cortada 2009 y 2016). Cuatro etapas en la historia de la subcontratación: diferenciación, movilización, legitimación y simbiosis (Sarma y Sun 2017, 587-617). Para un marco general, ver Berglof (2016, 335-340) y Cirillo, Guarascio y Pianta (2014); específicamente sobre las telecomunicaciones véase OECD (2002); Baskoy (2008); Commission of the European Communities (1992), (1990) y (1983); Crandall y Flamm (eds.) (1989); Griset y Fridenson (2013). Para el caso francés: Heidenreich (2012, 278-279); para un panorama general sobre la revolución de la información, véase Forester (1987); para el marco internacional de las empresas, véase Hamilton y Webster (2012).

a una estrategia de *outsourcing*[2], basada en empresas sin fábricas (*fab–less*)[3].

Las polémicas empiezan por la definición de los términos. Las primeras controversias relativas al contenido se centraron en la valoración del impacto del fenómeno. Así, un informe fijaba en un 84% los efectivos asalariados de la industria deslocalizables, correspondientes al 81% del valor añadido del sector (Arthuis 1993, 150)[4]. Tales apreciaciones fueron tachadas de exorbitadas por quienes intentaron rebajar la intensidad del debate limitando el alcance del fenómeno, mientras que otros las relativizaron. Las cifras desnudas arrojan un cuadro concluyente del alcance de la deslocalización. El número de casos de deslocalización entre 2003-2006 representa el 10% del total y el anunciado recorte de empleo el 8% (Eurofound 2008, 15 y 27)[5].

[2]   Se entiende por *outsourcing* la contratación con un proveedor de servicios para la gestión y realización de un trabajo, por un coste, lapso temporal y nivel de servicio determinados (Oshri et al. 2009, 8) o como un «proceso específico que permite a las empresas –en particular las de logística, tecnologías de la información, relaciones públicas, servicios económicos y jurídicos y gestión de instalaciones– separar las actividades subordinadas de su estructura interna y transferirlas a un sujeto externo especializado en la actividad u operación empresarial concreta (subcontratista)» (EEIP, A.S. Praga). El *outsourcing*, uno de los nueve modelos empresariales de activos ligeros (*asset-light*), permite a las empresas aumentar su competitividad al centrarse en sus principales actividades de negocios (Maly y Palter 2002, 1). La subcontratación o Electronic Manufacturing Services (EMS) arrojó en 2003 cifras de mercado global anual de más de 70.000 millones de dólares, de los cuales el 23% provenía de los seis grupos más grandes (Carroué 2004-2005, 131-136; *BCG Perspectives*, 30 de septiembre de 2014; *ComputerWorld*, 19 de abril de 1996).

[3]   Algunos han considerado el *fab-less* el tercer dogma asesino de la industria, junto a los de la sociedad postindustrial y la nueva economía (*Le Nouvel Économiste*, 30 de enero de 2013); otros lo entendieron como una opción económica razonable en momentos de transformación radical de la industria (*La Libre Belgique,* 31 de agosto de 2001).

[4]   Existen diversas definiciones prevalecientes en el debate europeo: «La reubicación, a veces también denominada deslocalización, significa el cierre o la reducción de las actividades de una empresa en el mercado interior tras el cambio de partes de la cadena de producción en el extranjero», entendido por lo general como fuera de la UE (EP, 2006, 3, 5); Comité Económico y Social Europeo: «La deslocalización se produce cuando una actividad comercial se suspende total o parcialmente, se reabre en el extranjero mediante inversión directa)». Los sindicatos europeos: traslado de «las actividades económicas hacia sitios extranjeros, incluido el cierre de sitios nacionales o la reducción de sus actividades» (Galgóczi et al. 2005). Asesores de la Oficina de Política Económica: «reubicación de actividades económicas hacia sitios extranjeros, el cierre de actividades en el país» (BEPA 2006, 36; Comisión Europea, DG Empresa). Entre todas, retenemos la siguiente: transferencia de producción y de otras actividades manufactureras a lugares fuera del país de origen (European Techno-Economic Policy Support 2007, 4).

[5]   Al año 2005 le corresponde la cifra más alta de casos (1.049) y al 2004 el porcentaje más elevado (12%). Según el impacto del *offshoring*, medido en pérdidas de empleo en 2005,

Sin embargo, la virulencia con que el *outsourcing*, *offshoring*, deslocalización y subcontratación fueron realmente percibidos atrajo el interés mediático e impulsó el debate académico y político[6]; por su parte, este se ha prolongado hasta nuestros días[7].

Los científicos sociales han dedicado en publicaciones y encuentros internacionales una atención muy particular a esos fenómenos[8]. Tras la Burbuja tecnológica, el debate académico se centró en gran medida sobre el papel desempeñado por las multinacionales, con visiones discrepantes (*New York*

cabe dividir los países europeos en tres grandes grupos. El primero (Portugal 54,7; Austria 29,6; Dinamarca 28,8; Eslovaquia 25,2; Eslovenia 24 e Irlanda 23,6) arrojaba un porcentaje superior al 20% por dicha causa; un segundo grupo de países presentaba un porcentaje entre el 10 y el 20% (Finlandia 15.9; Italia 15.7 y Bélgica 10.9), mientras que a un tercer grupo, el más mayoritario, le correspondía un porcentaje inferior al 10% (Alemania 7,2; Hungría 5,7; Suecia 5,4; Francia 4,6; Reino Unido 3,4; España 2,3; Polonia 2,2; República Checa 0,9 y Holanda 0,7; Chipre, Estonia y Malta 0) (Storrie 2006, 41-43). En los EE. UU. las empresas con ventas anuales superiores a 80 millones de dólares aumentaron la subcontratación en un 26% en 1997, hasta 85.000 millones de dólares. La tecnología de la información fue la actividad más dinámica de la subcontratación, representando casi la tercera parte de los gastos totales de subcontratación (OECD 2000, 15).

[6] En EE. UU., el punto álgido de la atención prestada al *outsourcing* en 2004 revela una conexión con el ciclo electoral. Las menciones al término en los cuatro periódicos principales se dispararon después del lanzamiento del informe del presidente y luego volvieron a aumentar justo antes de las elecciones presidenciales. El *outsourcing* rebrotó en el debate público dos veces más, coincidiendo con una propuesta política del senador Kerry sobre la problemática y con una irrupción del economista Paul Samuelson (2004, 135-146; Mankiw y Swagel 2006, 5). En la controversia intervino asimismo el economista Jagdish Bhagwati (2004, 93-114).

[7] En su más rabiosa actualidad, el debate político ha ampliado la tradicional división en mercados por costes laborales al *dumping* social y fiscal que nutre la movilidad de las empresas dentro de Europa (European Parliament, «The impact of delocalisation on workers and regions», Strasbourg, 30 de mayo de 2018): establecimiento en un país extranjero (reubicación pura), agrupación en el extranjero de actividades de servicios repartidas en varios sitios en Francia (reubicación difusa) y localización en el extranjero de actividades localizables en Francia (no localización) (Jean-François Lécole, Travaux de la commission des finances, Sénat de la France, 9 mars 2005). Una obra de referencia: Atkinson (2004). Dentro de la UE se distinguen dos tipos de reubicación: interna (transferencia de actividad comercial a otro Estado miembro) o externa (a países no pertenecientes a la UE) (CESE 2005).

[8] Estudios generales de economía evolucionista yuxtaponen la deslocalización a la desintegración vertical, al *outsourcing* y a la desconglomeración (Dosi et al. 2013). La economía institucional y evolutiva prefirió el término de «corporación hueca», definido como una entidad empresarial sin ninguna competencia técnica básica que utiliza mecanismos contractuales para vincular mercados particulares (Dosi 2000, 283; Casson 1996, 520; Teece 1998, 206). Otras aportaciones desde este enfoque, relativo al *software* y contraposición de las estrategias de despidos colectivos o deslocalización (Niosi y Tschang 2009, 269-294, Coucke et al. 2007, 161-182). Entre los congresos, destacan: «Delocalisation of Labour Intensive Industries», Cracovia, Polonia, abril de 2007 y 2nd Central European Regional Science, Nový Smokovec, Eslovaquia, octubre de 2007.

Times), 19 de junio de 2005)[9]. Para unos, estas, en su nueva estrategia global, claramente diferenciada de la tradicional, «desempeñaron un papel destacado, ya que su alcance global les permite coordinar la producción y la distribución en muchos países y cambiar las actividades de acuerdo con las condiciones cambiantes de la demanda y los costes» (OECD 2007, 7; Andreff 2009, 5-34). En aspectos concretos, como en el influjo sobre la desigualdad del salario, otros restaban importancia a la contribución de las multinacionales al *outsourcing* (Slaughter 2000, 449-472)[10].

En contraste con la copiosa bibliografía producida por los científicos sociales en general, los historiadores de la empresa se han acercado con timidez al fenómeno, que, no obstante, ha sido incluido recientemente en la agenda de investigación para el futuro[11].

En este capítulo se examinan desde la perspectiva empresarial nuevos episodios de la reorganización de la estructura oligopólica de la industria europea de equipos de telecomunicaciones (el sector) en la década de 1990 y los primeros años del nuevo milenio. La multinacional francesa Alcatel, en sus diversas de-

[9]   Para algunos, el *outsourcing* refuerza una anterior triple segmentación funcional, técnica y social, hasta entonces realizada internamente, dentro de un proceso que cambia la dimensión territorial al desplazar las escalas nacionales o continentales preexistentes a una escala verdaderamente mundial (Carroué et al. 2005, 234). El debate sobre política industrial de los años 80 quedaba muy lejano (Johnson 1984)

[10]   Aproximación desde la gestión, centrada en un estudio de caso –un fabricante de equipos de telecomunicaciones que subcontrata una serie de actividades a proveedores (McIvor 2003, 380-394).

[11]   Un trabajo interdisciplinar sobre el marco general de las telecomunicaciones: Griset y Fridenson (2013). Ekberg y Lange (2014, 69-81) reconocen el carácter *side-lined* de la problemática en una serie de debates; Schniederjans et al. (2006, 14) señalan que el *outsourcing* es un «recodo en el río», no un hecho importante de la *business history*. Autores reputados se refieren a la desintegración para ahorrar costes fijos y variables, la desverticalización y la descentralización (Amatori y Colli 2013); Keneley (2013, 255-277) asimila *offshoring* a internacionalización. El componente geográfico (India) desde la Bussiness History (Roy 2018). Reconociendo las deficiencias, Wilson et al. (2016, 294) abogan por una agenda que incluya estudios de las prácticas pasadas con respecto a la subcontratación, la propiedad extranjera, la seguridad y la corrupción, así como más trabajos sobre el rendimiento. The Annual Meeting of the Business History Conference –Cartagena de Indias, Colombia, 14-16 de marzo de 2019– tenía como objetivo concentrarse en «las agendas de investigación de la historia de los negocios que permiten una comprensión matizada de los fenómenos de la globalización y la desglobalización». Algunos especialistas sostienen que los campos de la iniciativa empresarial, los negocios internacionales y la estrategia no han abarcado la investigación orientada a la historia en la misma medida que otros campos dentro de los estudios de negocios y gestión (Perchard et al. 2014). Una etapa muy temprana de la externalización ha sido investigada a nivel sectorial –la empresa de ingeniería de EE. UU.– por Pinney (2002, 620-626) y a nivel de empresa industrial –Steam Ship Company (más tarde Ocean Transport & Trading), una de las principales empresas navieras del Reino Unido– por Petersson (2018, 88-123).

nominaciones de Alcatel NV, CGE Alcatel Alsthom, Alcatel Alsthom y Alcatel-Lucent, se presenta en su vasta implantación geográfica, gama de productos y estilos de *management* como un magnífico exponente de las transformaciones ocurridas a escala mundial. Desde el punto de vista metodológico, el caso se utiliza como artefacto para ratificar que una comprensión correcta del ajuste en la economía mundial requiere dilucidar cómo se reestructuraron las grandes empresas[12]. En su vertiente de estudio de caso dentro de la perspectiva empresarial sigue a Petersson (2018, 88-123) y a Daviet (2000).

Alcatel NV cuenta con importantes estudios que cubren el periodo aquí analizado, si bien lagunas persistentes en aspectos de su trayectoria brindan la oportunidad de nuevas investigaciones (Miller 1990; Marseille (dir.) 1992; Gibson 1995 y Malsan 2001)[13].

El capítulo está basado en fuentes de las empresas, en documentos parlamentarios de diversos países, en documentos judiciales y en un trabajo minucioso de hemeroteca[14]. El texto se compone de tres apartados principales, precedidos por una introducción y acabados en unas conclusiones. El primero traza una panorámica general de la evolución del sector y los dos siguientes se refieren al estudio de caso, abordando la globalización y sus efectos desde la perspectiva de la mencionada multinacional en dos de sus etapas sucesivas (Alcatel y Alcatel-Lucent).

3. La industria de equipos de telecomunicación y Alcatel: la reestructuración clásica

Tras sucesivas reestructuraciones en la década de 1980, la industria de equipos de telecomunicaciones continuó con el proceso de concentración, empu-

---

[12] A esta conclusión llega Hancké (2002, 158) a partir de los casos de empresas ya citadas.

[13] A ellas se añade las obras testimoniales, como la del ex CEO Pierre Suard (2002). Aun con honrosas excepciones (Mouline y Hafsi, 2008, 27-37), choca la rareza de la emblemática Alcatel en ejercicios sobre la reestructuración empresarial en Francia, que sí recurren a Renault, Électricité de France y Moulinex, pionera en las deslocalizaciones (Hancké 2002, 158). Por lo general, las filiales nacionales carecen de bibliografía, si bien existen notables monografías de algunas plantas, entre ellas Illkirch (Beaujolin-Bellet e Issaverdens 2006) y Colfontaine (Issaverdens y Naedenoen 2006).

[14] Destacados especialistas a partir de una investigación desde EE. UU. (Baumol et al. 2003, 30) avalan la precisión notable de los análisis de los periodistas sobre los casos de reducción de personal. Las fuentes judiciales se revelan como un instrumento de primer orden para el conocimiento de la transferencia de tecnología.

jada por el cambio tecnológico (Cooke 2015). A mediados de la década de 1990, las diez empresas más importantes de EE. UU., Europa y Japón sumaban más del 60% del mercado mundial[15]. En el subsector de la conmutación, en particular, la concentración era más fuerte ya que cuatro grandes compañías controlaban más de las tres cuartas partes del total. Alcatel encabezaba la lista con el 28% de la cuota, que, al cabo de tres años, había crecido dos puntos porcentuales (Information Gatekeepers 1995, 146-147). Lejos de detenerse, el afianzamiento de la estructura oligopólica del sector prosiguió en lo sucesivo. Los fabricantes de equipos se vieron seriamente afectados por las políticas de compra muy estrictas de las operadoras de servicio. El excepcional dinamismo de las TIC dejó de ir parejo con un crecimiento en valor de similar magnitud. Este bajo crecimiento en valor condujo a la progresiva consolidación entre operadoras, principales clientes de los industriales, y de sus subcontratistas, que, en espiral fatídica, se vieron arrastrados a nuevas reestructuraciones, especialmente por la vía de fusiones y adquisiciones (Faure et al. 2007).

Lejos de la uniformidad, las fracciones nacionales de ese mercado mundial presentan notables peculiaridades. Así, por ejemplo, en Francia, que había realizado durante la década de 1970 una gran reestructuración de la industria de equipos, se intentó eliminar del mercado interior proveedores extranjeros (Ericsson y filiales no locales de IT&T) y crear a través de Thomson un segundo proveedor nativo (Sutton 2001, 143). Más determinante fue la irrupción de un nuevo actor con proyección sobre todo el mundo. Como se señala en otro lugar, un consorcio internacional liderado por la pública Compagnie Générale d'Électricité (CGE) francesa adquirió en 1986 una participación mayoritaria –55,6% mientras que IT&T tenía el 37% y el resto pasó a la Société Générale de Bélgica y al banco francés Crédit Lyonnais– de la división de equipos telefónicos propiedad de IT&T en varios países europeos.

CGE utilizó su control en la nueva compañía y la combinó con su propia filial Alcatel CIT para formar Alcatel NV, la segunda compañía de telecomunicaciones más grande del mundo y el futuro centro de la estrategia de CGE

---

[15] El grupo incluía AT&T-Lucent, Motorola, NEC, Nortel, Nokia, Fujitsu, Bosch, Siemens, Alcatel y Ericsson, las tres últimas con una fuerte implantación en el mercado norteamericano (Dörrenbächer 2000, 13; Carr et al. 1998, 3-2). En 1997, Alcatel tenía el 4% de la infraestructura mundial de telefonía móvil y el 2,5 de terminales, cifra que dos años después había subido al 4,2%, siempre a la zaga de los grandes del sector –Nokia, Motorola y Ericsson (Funk 2002, 8); en 2001, su cuota del mercado europeo de terminales –140 millones– era del 10%.

como compañía privatizada. La empresa quedó compuesta por cinco principales filiales –Alcatel CIT en Francia, Alcatel-Bélgica, Alcatel Standard Elektrik Lorenz (SEL) en Alemania, considerada la joya de la corona en Europa, Alcatel FACE (Fabbrica Apparecchiature per Comunicazioni Elettriche) en Italia y Alcatel SESA en España.

Como se recoge en otro lugar, Alcatel NV tendió a racionalizar y modernizar desde muy temprano el variopinto conjunto de empresas resultantes de la adquisición de los activos de IT&T. La primerísima actuación consistió en reagrupar todas las actividades de Business Systems en EE. UU., excepto Friden Alcatel, junto a la fusión entre Telic Alcatel y Alcatel Électronique en Francia, con potenciales repercusiones sobre España por la implicación de Telic. A ambas se añadió la adquisición de Dial, que daría a Alcatel el 15% del mercado italiano de la empresa, así como la desinversión de Sesa (sic) y la francesa GSI[16].

Una parte de la práctica inicial consistió en desinversiones, recortes de empleo y alianzas estratégicas, que completaron la ya mencionada práctica de fusiones y adquisiciones. En la primera modalidad –venta a Nokia – se vio implicada una sección de electrónica de ocio y componentes de Standard Elektrik Lorenz SEL (Tabla 2), que arrastraba pérdidas. Lo relevante es que se trataba de una operación de desinversión de carácter estratégico porque, al año siguiente, SEL se incorporó al Consorcio European Cellular Radio 900 (ERC 900), una alianza industrial con AEG y Nokia –ahora reforzada en su carrera por una acentuada diversificación– para desarrollar, fabricar y comercializar conjuntamente el sistema telefónico móvil digital paneuropeo de segunda generación GSM (Groupe Spécial Mobile) (Fletcher 2013, 65; Anonym 2012, 2; *Network World*, 23 de enero de 1989)[17]. La modalidad de

---

16 Sesa (Francia) desarrollaba sistemas de conmutación de paquetes, base del desarrollo de la red de transmisión de datos Transpac (European Commission (1997), 107).

17 El recorte en SEL, participante destacada en el desarrollo del sistema 12, afectó al 5,25% de un total de 21.600 empleos sin que hubiese despidos (*Computer Business Review*, 25 de enero de 1993). Nokia era en 1995 el segundo fabricante mundial de teléfonos móviles con ventas en 120 países y líder en Europa, así como de proveedor líder mundial de redes GSM/DCS celulares (Nokia 1995, 2). En 2002, el 69% de los abonados a la telefonía móvil en el mundo utilizaba el standard GSM, CDMA el 13%, TDMA el 10% y PDC el 3% (ITU 2003) Para el desarrollo de las primeras instalaciones en 1991, el consorcio ECR900 planeaba superar 300 millones de marcos alemanes en gastos y emplear a 400 personas. Alcatel, Nokia y AEG participaban en los gastos en una proporción de 50/35/15% (*JPRS Report*, 31 de marzo de 1988, 27). Al no requerir una tecnología uniforme, el acuerdo del consorcio ECR900 dejaba libre el desarrollo de diferentes componentes del sistema con la garantía de la compatibilidad y la intercambiabilidad de las piezas de diferentes fabricantes. Para las licitaciones se presentó Motorola como no fabricante (que empleaba componentes del

recortes de empleo afectó a la fábrica de Alcatel CIT de Querqueville, en el área metropolitana de Cherbourg (Tabla 1), considerada uno de los dos pivotes de la producción de centrales digitales, si bien enfrentados a una feroz competencia, suprimió más de dos centenares de puestos de trabajo. Las autoridades manifestaban una actitud de apoyo pero dejaban claro que el mantenimiento del empleo implicaba necesariamente la conquista de los mercados de exportación. Asimismo, reconocían un efecto estabilizador sobre la carga de las fábricas francesas al mantenimiento de las dos líneas de productos de conmutación digital, E 10/MT y Sistema 12. En otras plantas, Eu y Cherburgo para mayor precisión, Alcatel CIT se mostraba más proclive a aumentar la competitividad mediante la simplificación de determinados servicios corporativos que a imponer recortes de empleo[18]. Así, pues, la estrategia no aparece ni homogénea ni perfectamente definida desde el principio, algo realmente digno de destacar.

Entre 1980 y 1990 el negocio de telecomunicaciones del grupo Alcatel creció sustancialmente a través de una estrategia múltiple de adquisiciones, *joint ventures* y fusiones[19]. La posición de la empresa se vio reforzada por el aumento de su participación hasta el 61,5% a través de la consolidación interna de dos importantes filiales, la Compagnie Financière Alcatel y Alsthom.

En la década de 1990, Alcatel sufrió importantes alteraciones. Pese a que el ritmo de las adquisiciones se redujo, Alcatel, rebautizada como Alcatel Alsthom Compagnie Générale d'Electricité y conocida comúnmente como Alcatel Alsthom, compró el 30% de la participación de IT&T en Alcatel N V y el 7 por ciento de Alcatel.

sistema adquiridos a terceros) y como proveedores Ericsson/Orbitel, Ericsson/Matra/Ascom Hasler, Philips/Bosch/Siemens, Bosch/Philips, Matra-Ericsson, Orbitel/Matra/Ericsson, Orbitel (Racal/Plessey) (90/446/EEC: Commission Decision of 27 July, Konsortium ECR 900, *Official Journal of the European Communities*, L 228, 22 de agosto de 1990, 31-34).

[18] Réponse du ministère de l'Industrie, *Journal Officiel du Sénat (JOdD)*, 14/4/1988, 513. En 1985-1986, fueron vendidas acciones de Electro-financiera y de la planta en Vitry Tecafiltres, y cedidas la fábrica de calderas de Tamaris y el establecimiento de Dalmas (Archives Nationales de la France, 20000487/18, Dossier 1).

[19] ALCATEL creció desde 9.000 a 27.600 millones de dólares anuales; adquisiciones: 15 compañías de energía, transporte y comunicaciones durante 1989; más de 35 compañías de 1987 a 1991; *joint ventures*: North American Intermagnetics General Corp., Ferro Corp. y Exide Electronics; fusiones: la filial de energía y transporte de CGE en Alsthom con la División de Sistemas de Potencia de General Electric Company del Reino Unido formaron GEC Alsthom N.V. (Dörrenbächer y Wortmann 1994, 202). En estos años, nuevas centrales y líneas son instaladas en el mercado latinoamericano, a veces con el respaldo de crédito francés (U.S. Department of Commerce 1989, 20, 38 y 49).

Alcatel propició la internacionalización mediante acuerdos de suministro, que representaron el 77% de sus operaciones de acercamiento, porcentaje superior a los de Ericsson (52%), Nokia (44%) y Nortel (42%). Si consideramos el origen sectorial de los aliados de Alcatel y Lucent Technologies en materia de acuerdos tecnológicos, de 1996 a 2005, Alcatel estableció 193 alianzas y realizó 22 adquisiciones, cifras que para Lucent Technologies fueron de 55 y 40, respectivamente. Estas acciones estratégicas estuvieron en el centro de los ajustes que estas empresas llevaron a cabo para tener en cuenta los cambios en su estructura industrial (Mouline y Hafsi 2008, 28 y 30).

A partir de mediados del decenio de 1990, Alcatel apostó por los mercados de telecomunicaciones de gran crecimiento, entre ellos las redes de datos de Internet y los teléfonos móviles. En respuesta a la naturaleza cambiante de la demanda de los operadores nacionales tradicionales, desplazó el centro de su desarrollo estratégico desde los productos hacia los programas informáticos, sistemas y servicios para convertirse en un proveedor de soluciones completas[20]. Alcatel se sumó a la tendencia general de diversificación de la producción según una forma de integración horizontal, que originó un grupo diversificado en las áreas de la energía, transmisión (cables eléctricos y de fibra óptica) y telecomunicaciones, sin olvidar el espacio y la defensa (Tabla 1). Destacaba, además, como grupo global, compuesto de ocho divisiones regionales con total responsabilidad sobre sus resultados operativos y de cuatro grandes zonas a nivel internacional (Dörrenbächer 2000, 13)[21].

Alcatel NV centralizaba las decisiones sobre la expansión internacional de las filiales. La empresa matriz les autorizaba a desarrollar nuevos mercados cuando tenían los productos y recursos para hacerlo, siempre que cumplieran con ciertas condiciones y siguieran determinadas pautas, agrupadas en un proceso de *sourcing*. Alcatel NV, tras estudiar la situación del mercado propuesto por una filial, sus puntos fuertes y débiles junto a los de los competidores, concedía a una filial el derecho (y a partir de entonces también la

---

[20] Soluciones desde la concepción, el diseño, la fabricación y la instalación hasta la ingeniería financiera (Mtar 2001, 112-116).

[21] Protagonistas de los procesos de cambio señalan que, al iniciarse la década de 1990, Alcatel empezó a centralizar la decisión de negocio en París con la consiguiente absorción de la responsabilidad de *marketing* de las filiales, entre ellas la de Citesa, pese a su liderazgo en teléfonos inalámbricos, como se ha visto en otro capítulo (Testimonio, José Luis Casado, 29 de agosto de 2008). En 1995, Alcatel fue calificado de «mastodonte en riesgo» (*Le Temps*, 12 de octubre de 1999), o mamut del pasado (Quatrepoint, 2015), pero también de «fleuron du capitalisme français» (*Les Échos*, 30 de julio de 2008) y «the Lucent of Europe» (*Bloomberg News*, 12 de octubre de 1998).

obligación) de «desarrollar» –o entrar– en un mercado específico (Canalejo 2020, 42).

Tabla 1. Visión selectiva del sistema mundial de Alcatel

Matriz o filial	Plantas	Localización	Especialidad
ALCATEL CIT*	Querqueville (Cherbourg)	Francia	Centrales digitales e 10 y mt
ALCATEL CIT	Annecy	Francia	Grabado de semi-conductores
ALCATEL CIT	Amilly	Centre-Val de Loire, Francia	Electrónica
ALCATEL CIT	Colombes	Hauts-de-Seine, Francia	Equipos telefónicos
TELIC	St Nicolas d'Aliermont	Alta Normandía, Francia	Telefonía
ALCATEL, WOERTH	Woerth	Alsacia, Francia	
ALCATEL CABLE	Dinard	Bretaña, Francia	
ALCATEL	Tourlaville	Manche, Francia	Equipos para transmisiones por microondas para telefonía móvil
ALCATEL	Brest Laval (Mayenne) Coutances Saintes Conflans-Sainte-Honorine (Yvelines) Illkirch Rennes Lannion	Francia	Brest: equipo telefónico (centrales de conmutación privadas y de empresa basadas en ip

Matriz o filial	Plantas	Localización	Especialidad
ALCATEL ÎLE-DE FRANCE	Massy Vélizy (Yvelines) Meudon Colombes Marcoussis Villarceaux	Francia	
ALCATEL	Eu (Normandía)	Francia	Integración y prueba de soluciones electrónicas para equipos de telecomunicaciones
ALCATEL	Optronics	Francia	Componentes ópticos
ALCATEL LUCENT	Grenoble Châteaudun L'Isle-d'Abeau (2)	Francia	
ALCATEL BUSINESS SYSTEM	Gundershoffen (Estrasburgo)	Francia	
ALCATEL CABLES	Lyon y otras 29 plantas (Calais, Douvrin, etc.)	Francia	Cables
ALCATEL CABLES	Greenwich (RU)		
ALCATEL SEL AG	Berlín Nuremberg Mannheim	Alemania	
ALCATEL SEL AG	Gunzenhausen	Alemania	Sistemas de transmisión de datos y conmutación de voz

Matriz o filial	Plantas	Localización	Especialidad
ALCATEL SEL AG	Stuttgart Altena Bochum Bonndorf Esslingen Geroldsgün Hambourg Landshut Mannheim Pforzheim Straubing Ziemtesha-usen	Alemania	
ALCATEL SEL AG FILIALES DEHLOFF ELEC-TRONIC SEL SOFTWARE SEL BUSINESS SYSTEMS EXPORT SEL FINANZ CTM COMPUTER-TECHNIK MULLER SEL SEÑALIZA-CIÓN SEL TELECOMMU-NICATIONS	Stuttgart Berlín Stuttgart Berlín Konstanz España Malta	Alemania	
ALCATEL LUCENT	Hilversum	Netherland	
ALCATEL BELL	Colfontaine	Bélgica	Telecomunicaciones
ALCATEL BELL	Geel	Bélgica	Producción de centrales
ALCATEL BELL	Gante	Bélgica	Circuitos impresos
ALCATEL BELL	Namur		Centro de investigación

Matriz o filial	Plantas	Localiza-ción	Especialidad
ALCATEL BELL SPACE	Hoboken	Bélgica	Equipo electróni-co espacial
ALCATEL ETCA	Charleroi	Bélgica	Equipo electró-nico espacial; tele-comunicaciones
ALCATEL CABLE SUISSE	Cortaillod	Suiza	Fibra óptica
ALCATEL CABLE SUISSE	Cossonay	Suiza	Cables, telecomu-nicaciones, distri-bución de material electrotécnico
ALCATEL CABLE SUISSE	Breitenbach	Suiza	Cables, telecomu-nicaciones, distri-bución de material electrotécnico
ALCATEL SESA		España	Equipos de con-mutación, cables, transmisiones
ALCATEL DATA NETWORKS (*joint venture* de SPRINT CORP. Y ALCATEL AL 49/51%)	Ashburn	EE. UU.	Productos asyn-chronous transfer mode (atm)
OPTRONICS	Gatineau	Canadá	Fábrica de senso-res de fibra óptica bragg (fbg)
OPTRONICS	Livingston	Escocia	
OPTRONICS	Kanata, Ontario	Canadá	I+d
OPTRONICS	Shannon Cork Blanchardstown Ci-tywest (Dublín)	Irlanda Irlanda Irlanda Irlanda	Componentes para la transmisión en fibra óptica

Matriz o filial	Plantas	Localización	Especialidad
OPTRONICS	Bandon	Irlanda	Desarrollo de *software* hlr
ALCATEL	Plano Longview	Texas, EE. UU.	Planta de montaje
ALCATEL NETWORK SYSTEMS	Raleigh	Carolina del Norte, EE. UU.	Equipos para telecomunicaciones de banda ancha y redes de datos
ALCATEL	Chantilly	Virginia, EE. UU.	Centro técnico y de *marketing*
ALCATEL	Nogales	Arizona	Planta de montaje
ALCATEL	Claremont N. C.	California, EE. UU.	Fibra óptica
ALCATEL	México	México	Planta de montaje
ALCATEL	Richardson	Texas	Aparatos de telecomunicación
ALCATEL NETWORK SYSTEMS	Bethesda	Maryland	Equipo terminal digital de alta capacidad
ALCATEL LUCENT (Western Electric en 1956)	Merrimack Valley, North Andover	Massachussets, EE. UU.	Bobinas para teléfonos y luego equipos de red de fibra óptica para telefonía y otros sectores de telecomunicaciones
ALCATEL	Clinton, N.C.	EE. UU.	Equipo de telecomunicaciones
ALCATEL	Aguadilla	Puerto Rico	Equipo de telecomunicaciones
ALCATEL CABLES	Port Botany	Australia	Cables

*Véase Anexo para mayor precisión.
Fuente: Elaboración a partir del texto.

Alcatel finalizó el año 1989 con una tesorería boyante –reforzada por ayudas del Estado francés destinadas a la investigación– que toleró pagos a IT&T por la recompra de acciones y abundantes fondos aplicados al redespliegue militar. Sin embargo, Alcatel CIT decidió abandonar la fabricación de equipos para el grabado de semiconductores en Annecy (Haute-Savoie) y recortar empleos[22]. A partir básicamente de 1992, ya no pudieron mantenerse tres plantas industriales de esta filial fragmentando su producción como había sucedido hasta entonces. La batalla por la competitividad reclamaba mejorar la productividad del orden de 8 a 10% anual y efectuar importantes inversiones. A ese envite respondió el anuncio del cierre de Amilly con un doble plan de actuación industrial (cesión parcial de la actividad a un subcontratista de la electrónica con el mantenimiento por Alcatel CIT del volumen de la actividad durante tres años y continuidad de un 58% de los 300 empleados) y un plan social (Tabla 2)[23].

4. La globalización y sus efectos: la era Tchuruk en Alcatel

Hasta 2006, Alcatel aprovechó muchas de sus ventajas comerciales en todo el mundo mediante el uso de agentes y consultores externos[24]. Dentro de las transformaciones de la década, el año 1995 marca un giro importante en Alcatel, entonces vigésimo tercera entre las multinacionales por activos, inmediatamente después de FIAT, Siemens y Sony. El índice de multinacionalidad, es decir, el promedio de la relación entre activos, ventas y empleo en el extranjero respecto al total, la situaba en la trigésima posición, a enorme distancia de la líder Nestlé pero inmediatamente por delante de Coca-Cola[25].

---

[22] Question 34,202 de Mme. Jacquaint Muguette (representante comunista, Seine-Saint-Denis, *JOAN*, 21 de octubre de 1991, 4.333).

[23] Incluía trasvase de empleo a Lannion y ayudas a la reclasificación y la formación (Réponse du ministre de l'Industrie et du Commerce Extérieur, *Journal Officiel de l'Assemblée Nationale (JOAN)*, 27 de julio de 1992, 3.402); para un marco general, véase Butcher et al. (1991); para Alcatel CIT (Iwens 1984).

[24] Se demostró la vulnerabilidad de este modelo comercial por su propensión a la corrupción, ya que los consultores se utilizaban repetidamente como canales para el pago de sobornos sea a funcionarios extranjeros o a ejecutivos de empresas privadas para lograr o mantener negocios en muchos países (SEC 2010-58, 27 de diciembre de 2010).

[25] Por detrás de Total, Rhône-Poulenc y General Electric, por ejemplo (United Nations Conference on Trade and Development 1997, 29). Alcatel se considera una multinacional típica, frente a la estructura de red de France Télécom (Rugman y D'Cruz 2003, 125).

Alcatel estaba embarcada en adquisiciones de empresas –Telettra[26], STC y Kable de AEG– pero arrastraba una situación de pérdidas por 5.200 millones de dólares. Un relevo en la cúpula aupó a la dirección a Serge Tchuruk, *polytechnicien* y antiguo dirigente del sector energético[27]. Frente a la estrategia precedente, Alcatel reorientó su actividad con el objetivo de abandonar la política de conglomerado y de recentrarse en las telecomunicaciones, que por entonces representaban el 40% de la cifra de negocios (*New York Times*, 6 de octubre de 1995 y 29 de marzo de 1996)[28].

Vale la pena volver a insistir que la reestructuración emprendida a partir de 1995 obedecía al comportamiento opuesto del valor añadido industrial, tendente a disminuir, y del valor intangible, tal como la I+D, tendente a aumentar sin cesar[29]. Con el cambio en la alta dirección varió completamente el diagrama de la empresa, cuya actividad comercial estaba gestionada hasta el momento por las cinco principales filiales ya citadas. Sobreimpuesta a las empresas legales, se formó una organización de la matriz con un cierto número de divisiones de

[26] Los directivos de Alcatel esperaban que la adquisición de Telettra, junto a la de la unidad Rockwell –ambas implicadas en el desarrollo de sistemas de transmisión síncrona– permitiera a Alcatel y a las empresas adquiridas racionalizar sus respectivos programas de investigación y suprimir el solapamiento de esfuerzos (*International Herald Tribune*, October 7, 1991, 18).

[27] Tchuruk, procedente del sector del petróleo y con fama de cirujano de empresas, era ajeno a un sector de ciclo de producto extremadamente corto como el de las telecomunicaciones (*Bloomberg News*, 12 de octubre de 1998; *Libération,* 8 de octubre de 2013). Tchuruk pertenece al equipo de grandes gestores de los noventa –Messier, John Welch (expresidente de General Electric) y Chris Gent (primer ejecutivo de Vodafone), entre otros (*Cinco Días*, 27 de junio de 2002). John Welch –no un patricio sino «hambriento de poder, sediento de dinero»– encabezó ese movimiento de despidos masivos y cierres de fábricas que otras empresas siguieron (Gelles 2022, 3 y 94), un estilo captado por el economista Milton Friedman en su frase de The Times Magazine «la responsabilidad social de las empresas es aumentar sus beneficios». A la llegada de Tchuruk en 1995, vendió unidades ajenas a las telecomunicaciones, desde viñedos a revistas, con el objetivo de posicionarse en las batallas de telecomunicaciones.

[28] La Comisión de las Comunidades Europeas juzgó que la concentración Alcatel/AEG Kabel no daba lugar a una posición dominante de esta empresa en el mercado comunitario ya que representaría una cuota del 18% sobre el total y existían otros competidores potentes (BICC, Pirelli y Siemens); por ello, dio el Placet a la absorción de Kabel, filial de AEG (Case No IV/M.165 –Alcatel/AEG Kabel, Document 391M0165, 18.12.1991). Al parecer, la Comisión estaba esperando un caso claro para introducir el concepto de dominio oligopólico en virtud del Reglamento de concentraciones (Stroux 2004, 204). Alcatel, rendida a las sinergias, buscaba nuevos activos para adquirir, especialmente la gigante francesa de la electrónica, defensa y medios de comunicación Thomson S.A. (*NYT*, 29 de marzo de 1996; Beaujolin-Bellet e Issaverdens 2006).

[29] *Libération*, 8 de octubre 2013; visión del giro estratégico de Tchuruk desde Italia (*La Repubblica*, 28 de junio y 1 de noviembre de 2001). Al final de la década de 1990, los costes de reestructuración de Alcatel representaban en torno al 5% de las ventas (Alcatel, *Annual report for the fiscal year ended December 31*, Form 20-F, 1-11,130, 2002, 1).

negocio, por un lado, y de áreas geográficas por el otro, y todas las actividades legales se adscribieron a las actividades y gestión del área[30].

La reestructuración de Alcatel propiamente dicha se inició debido a la combinación letal de *shocks* exógenos provocados por la llegada de tecnologías menos intensivas en trabajo y por opciones estratégicas. La especificidad de las coyunturas propias de las distintas economías en que estaban inmersas y otros factores impusieron cronologías y tempos diferentes[31].

En un ejercicio hasta ahora inédito, complementario del de laTabla 1, en la Tabla 2 se sistematiza una copiosa información dispersa sobre los diversos tipos de reestructuración llevados a cabo por Alcatel a lo largo de una veintena de años[32]. El ejercicio tiene valor por si mismo debido a una penuria de datos agregados, proporcionados por las grandes organismos internacionales –Eurostat, por ejemplo– solamente a partir del final de periodo aquí analizado. De su análisis se desprende la división en dos grandes fases y un periodo de transición, que pasamos a considerar.

En una primera fase, inmediatamente anterior al estallido de la burbuja tecnológica, las medidas trajeron consigo cierres y recortes de plantilla, junto a algunos episodios de deslocalización y *outsourcing* (Tabla 2).

Si cuantificamos los casos, entre 1986-2000, hubo nueve recortes de plantilla, tres ventas o cesiones; diez cierres; nueve deslocalizaciones (tres dentro del país y dos mixtas); cuatro casos de despido; un caso de conversión empresarial y, finalmente, otro de reestructuraciones y filialización o conversión de secciones operativas en filiales.

En una amplísima mayoría de ocasiones, las medidas no se tomaron de forma aislada sino asociadas a otras. Así sucedió en cuatro de los nueve casos de

---

[30] Las cuatro zonas: Norteamérica, Asia Pacífico, Europa Norte y Europa Sur (España, Portugal y Andorra); divisiones de negocio: comunicaciones fijas, comunicaciones inalámbricas, comunicaciones convergentes, grupo de negocio de empresas y grupo de negocio de servicios (Observatorio industrial de electrónica, tecnologías de la información y telecomunicaciones 2008, 25).

[31] Por ejemplo, la alemana Alcatel SEL registró en 1991 resultados 'excepcionales' en las exportaciones y los beneficios debido a la fuerte demanda en infraestructuras de la antigua RDA. La reconstrucción de la red telefónica abría buenas perspectivas para el futuro (*Les Échos*, 14 de mayo de 1992).

[32] Superan con holgura los recogidos por el European Restructuring Monitor, dedicado expresamente a esa tarea. Relación sucinta de fuentes consultadas para la elaboración de la Tabla 2 (Parlamentarias: Réponse du ministre de l'Industrie et PTT, *JOAN,* 24/2/1997, 971; Question 554 de M. Gremetz Maxime (communiste-Somme), *JOAN,* 30 de junio de 1997, 2.243. Prensa: *The Washington Post*, 23 de abril de 1999; *Dallas Business Journal*, 3 de octubre de 2001: *BBC News*, 10 de julio de 2001).

recortes de plantilla, en dos de los tres de venta o cesión, en seis de los diez de cierre, en seis de los nueve de deslocalización y en la mitad de los de despido. Cabe insistir en la existencia de una deslocalización a plantas de fuera del país, con tres zonas preferenciales, que reunían las características de bajos costes laborales y *dumping* social y fiscal: Europa del Este –Rumania y Hungría–, un país del Mediterráneo Oriental – Turquía – y Asia –China[33]–.

Dos hechos particulares son dignos de mención. La fábrica belga de Colfontaine, una región deprimida, ofrece un ejemplo de discrepancias intraempresariales en la apreciación de las soluciones a la crisis, en la ocasión entre la sede central de París, partidaria del cierre, y la dirección local de la planta, más propensa a la continuidad. Una segunda lección se refiere a la inestabilidad de la propiedad y a la validez relativa de las decisiones empresariales (Issaverdens y Naedenoen 2006; Gazier y Bruggeman (eds.) 2008, 188-189)[34].

El espigueo y sistematización de la información dispersa proporciona puntualmente algunas claves sobre los hechos que analizamos. Respecto a las causas, presenta a Alcatel CIT sumida desde 1995 en un deterioro de sus resultados y sin perspectiva de superar su situación de déficit en un futuro inmediato (Réponse du ministère de l'Industrie, *JOdD,* 14 de abril de 1988, 513 y 24 de febrero de1997, 971). La planta de Saint Nicolas d'Aliermont, en la Alta Normandía, sufría la competencia de terminales telefónicos fabricados en Asia y fácilmente accesibles al gran público (*Les Échos,* 12 de junio de 1991). Otra causa aducida, recortes drásticos en la ocasión, se refiere al hundimiento persistente de las ventas de equipos de telecomunicación, simple peripecia de la desaceleración de la economía en su conjunto[35]. Algunas gamas

---

[33] Los analistas atribuyen el número creciente de empresas extranjeras de las telecomunicaciones implantadas en China a tres razones principales: el enorme tamaño del mercado potencial, la dotación de recursos humanos relativamente baratos y el fuerte apoyo del gobierno chino, en forma de tipos impositivos bajos a las empresas extranjeras, especialmente a las de alta tecnología (Li y Li, 2009, 2).

[34] Una de las afectadas –la empresa conjunta de Alcatel y Sprint Alcatel Data Networks– desarrollaba productos ATM, una solución avanzada para las redes de datos de alta velocidad operadas por universidades y grandes empresas a la que Alcatel hizo una contribución significativa. Sprint, tercera por tamaño entre las compañías de larga distancia de EE. UU., aportaba una pequeña filial de fabricación e instalación de redes de conmutación de paquetes de datos y Alcatel una similar y más pequeña (OTA Advisory Group 1993, 78; *NYT,* 4 de febrero de 1993; *Washington Business Journal,* 14 de julio de 1997).

[35] La distribución de 2.800 despidos: un 28,57% en Plano; 25% en Raleigh, casi la mitad de la plantilla; una cuarta parte de los 400 en Virginia y 32,14% en el resto del país (*BBC News,* 10 de julio de 2001). En un guiño a los accionistas, Alcatel incrementó un 14% el dividendo en 1999 (*Le Temps,* 12 de marzo de 1999; *Network World,* 16, nº.11, 15 de marzo de 1999:6; IGI Consulting 1996, 35).

de equipo de telecomunicación atravesaron por situaciones especiales. El bajo nivel de gastos de capital en 1991 y la primera mitad de 1992 y la saturación relativa acentuaron la competencia en el mercado de las telecomunicaciones de empresas. Los menores precios y la consiguiente erosión de los márgenes en el sector auguraban malos tiempos[36].

Uno de los subsectores, el mercado de cable óptico, se distinguió hasta el año 2000 por un fuerte crecimiento y la realización de importantes inversiones. En lo sucesivo, la crisis de las TIC reveló un considerable exceso de capacidad en este tipo de equipos.

Alcatel Cable France registró una disminución del 60% de su facturación y tuvo que emprender un plan de salvaguarda del empleo. A optoelectrónica fue destinada en 2001 la planta de Illkirch, en sustitución de tecnología móvil de segunda generación (GSM), cuyo despliegue internacional Alcatel había respaldado con entusiasmo junto a otros fabricantes de equipos (Siemens y Nokia). Pero al año siguiente, las ventas de Alcatel Optronics se desplomaron estrepitosamente. Las formaciones en curso fueron congeladas y parte de la mano de obra «convertida» volvió de nuevo a la producción de terminales. La incertidumbre obligó a encontrar un nuevo proyecto industrial para Illkirch. Pese a la contención de la caída a partir de 2004, la competencia y la presión ejercida por las operadoras de telefonía causaron una fuerte erosión de los precios (30% entre 2004 y 2005). Cierto que la peculiar estructura del mercado de optoelectrónica, en buena medida un mercado cautivo, presentaba algún cobijo sin llegar a estar a cubierto[37].

Respecto al mecanismo seguido para facilitar la cesión de fábricas, la vía escogida era la conversión en filiales, como hizo Alcatel CIT en Saintes y Coutances, que totalizaban unas 300 personas (*L'Usine Nouvelle*, 20 de abril

---

[36] La demanda de la operadora France Télécom, básicamente de grandes centrales, no repercutía en la empresa. Debían afectar a 745 personas entre agosto de 1992 y abril de 1993, 65 de las cuales en Colombes (Réponse du ministre des PTT, Assemblée Nationale, *Journal Officiel*, 24/08/1992, 3.927). Alcatel Business Systems buscó aligerar su estructura y reducir sus costes de producción con supresiones de empleo.

[37] Réponse du ministère attributaire, *Journal Officiel*, Assemblée Nationale, *N* 3/5/2005, 4,680; CEPAL (2001), 192; *L'Usine Nouvelle*, 2/5/2002. Alcatel y Drakka fusionaron sus respectivos negocios de cables y sistemas de telecomunicaciones de fibra óptica en todo el mundo así como los derechos de propiedad intelectual en una empresa de nueva creación –NEWCO–. Drakka, titular del 50,1% del capital, se reservó el control exclusivo sobre la gestión y estrategia del negocio. Drakka Com Tech se vio forzada a formular un plan de salvaguarda del empleo hasta octubre de 2004. Alcatel Optronics solo vendía el 18% a los clientes externos (USA 10%, Asia 5% y Europa 3%).

de 2000). Por lo general, la cesión de plantas fue una solución pasajera, como sucedió con la de Tourlaville (Manche) en 2001[38].

Otro tipo de actuación se refiere a los llamados planes sociales que acompañaban a los procesos de reestructuración, la intervención de los sindicatos y las autoridades locales, así como el destino de los trabajadores afectados por diversas medidas[39]. Tras el cierre de Alcatel Cable en Dinard, entre el 35-43% de los despedidos no habían encontrado trabajo dos años después[40]. En Conflans se aplicó un plan de protección del empleo y de recolocación externa. Alcatel Cable fue obligada a reincorporar a 170 exempleados de dicha localidad despedidos en 2002 y 2003. Alcatel CIT intentó consensuar con los sindicatos medidas de distribución de tiempo de trabajo con tres orientaciones: reducción de jornada, retiros voluntarios a partir de cincuenta y dos años y jubilación anticipada[41].

---

[38] La finalización de los contratos en exclusiva entre Alcatel-Lucent y Sanmina hizo volver a la situación de los inicios. Después de cerrar las instalaciones de Grenoble, Châteaudun y dos de la isla de Abeau, al finalizar a finales de 2006 el contrato exclusivo con Sanmina por Tourlaville, la producción fue trasladada parcialmente a Hungría y Tailandia (*L'Usine Nouvelle*, 30 de octubre de 2001). Ante la posibilidad de cierre total o parcial del establecimiento, un representante político de la región pedía la mediación del gobierno para ayudar a la empresa a buscar nuevos clientes y conservar puestos de trabajo locales (Jean-Pierre Godefroy, Question orale 0046S, Representante de Manche – SOC, *Journal Officiel du Sénat*, 27/09/2007, 1.689). Otras adquisiciones de Sanmina en 1999: activos netos del subsistema electromecánico de Châteaudun – inventarios, equipos y plantilla– así como pasivo de Nortel Networks Co. por un precio de compra aproximado de 14,2 millones de dólares (US Securities and Exchange Commission, Commission, 0-21.272, 1 de enero de 2000, 8). Las deslocalizaciones sucesivas de la misma empresa fueron calificadas de nomadismo industrial (Audition de M. Jean-Claude Karpeles, Sénat, Commission des finances, 22 de marzo de 2005).

[39] En Claremont N. C., los despedidos –aproximadamente el 21% del empleo total– se beneficiarían de indemnización por despido, asistencia de colocación laboral y prestaciones médicas (*Dallas Business Journal*, 3 de octubre de 2001; *BBC News*, 10 de julio de 2001).

[40] Question 554 de M. Gremetz Maxime (communiste-Somme), Assemblée Nationale, *Journal Officiel*, 30 de junio de 1997, 2.243; Question 8,722, representante de Leyzour Félix, comunista (Côtes d'Armor), Assemblée Nationale, *Journal Officiel*, 12 de enero de 1998, 149; *Le Parisien*, 10 de noviembre de 2004; Réponse du Ministère attributaire, *Journal Officiel*, 3 de agosto de 2004, 6. Tampoco abundan los datos sobre el precio de algunas operaciones y las empresas involucradas. Entre las excepciones, Alcatel cedió Saft por 390 millones de euros a Doughty Hanson & Co, empresa de gestión de fondos independiente con oficinas en siete ciudades europeas (Londres, Estocolmo, Frankfurt, Múnich, París: Praga y Milán) y dos estadounidenses (Nueva York y Chicago): United States Securities and Exchange Commission, Report for the month of January, 2004. Saft, líder en baterías industriales y especializadas, dispersaba su producción en 14 plantas distribuidas en ocho países, que empleaban a 4.000 personas (*EE Times*, 20 de octubre de 2003).

[41] Réponse du ministre de l'Industrie et PTT, Assemblée Nationale, *Journal Officiel*, 24 de febrero de 1997, 971.

Tabla 2. Lista selectiva de operaciones de Alcatel

Empresa	Año	Sección	Operación	Empresa destinataria
ALCATEL CIT (Conflans-Saint-Honorine)	1986-1988	Terminales telefónicos	Anuncio de supresiones de empleos y de cierre en 1988; deslocalización a La Ville-du-Bois (Essonne)	ALCATEL
ALCATEL CIT	1977-1984	Terminales telefónicos	Recorte de empleo	ALCATEL
STANDARD ELEKTRIK LORENZ	1987	Electrónica de ocio y componentes	Venta	Nokia
ALCATEL CIT (Saintes)	1984-2000		Reestructuraciones y filialización	ALCATEL
ALCATEL (Christian Roving)	1988	Circuitos de alta gama para aerolíneas	Deslocalización; desvinculación administrativa y cesión	Bolt, Beraenek & Newmann (USA)
ALCATEL CIT (Annecy)	1989	Equipos para el grabado de semiconductores	Cierre de la sección y eliminación de 135 empleos	ALCATEL
ALCATEL BUSINESS SYSTEMS	1992 1993	Sistemas	Recortes de empleo	ALCATEL
ALCATEL CIT Amilly	1992		Anuncio del cierre (300 empleados); deslocalización; cesión parcial de la actividad a un subcontratista	ALCATEL

Empresa	Año	Sección	Operación	Empresa destinataria
ALCATEL	1992	Laboratorios de investigación	Deslocalización	China
ALCATEL TELIC, St Nicolas d'Aciermont		Equipos de telefonía	Cierre	Reestructuración interna
ALCATEL, Woerth		Especializada en la producción de minitel	Cierre	Reestructuración interna
ALCATEL BUSINESS SYSTEM, Gundershoffen	1995	Terminales de radiomensajería	Cesión de 222 asalariados	Infö Réalité, futura Infö-Industrie
ALCATEL Colfontaine	1995		Primera reestructuración: 60 despidos y reorganización de la empresa	
ALCATEL SEL AG STUTTGART (Berlín, Nuremberg y Mannheim)			Reducciones de Empleo	ALCATEL
ALCATEL CABLES SUISSE		Cables, las telecomunicaciones y la distribución de material electrotécnico	Reducciones de empleo	ALCATEL
ALCATEL CABLE Dinard	1997		Cierre, despido de la plantilla y deslocalización por traslado de la producción	Filial ALCATEL en España

Empresa	Año	Sección	Operación	Empresa destinataria
ALCATEL DATA NETWORKS, Ashburn			Recorte de puestos de trabajo	ALCATEL
ALCATEL Colfontaine	1997		Anuncio de cierres y reubicaciones en Francia, China y Türkiye; cierre y cesiones sucesivas	Micron Custom Manufacturing Services (USA); Punch; Valoric, que la reflotó
ALCATEL CIT COLOMBES (Hauts- de-Seine)	1997		Anuncio de cierre, despidos (227) y deslocalización a Vélizy	ALCATEL
ALCATEL CIT Lannion	1997		Anuncio de despidos (398)	
ALCATEL CIT Ormes (Loiret)	1997		Despidos (491)	
ALCATEL NETWORK SYSTEMS, Bethesda	1997		Anuncio del traslado de la mayoría de los 150 empleados a Raleigh	ALCATEL
ALCATEL (Colfontaine)	1997			Micron Custom Manufacturing Services

Empresa	Año	Sección	Operación	Empresa destinataria
ALCATEL, Texas, California, Puerto Rico y Carolina del Norte	1999		Recorte de empleo; traslado parcial de los efectivos de Raleigh a Arizona y México	ALCATEL
ALCATEL CABLES	2000	Cables	Conversión empresa	Nexans
ALCATEL	2000		Planes de deslocalizar en Rumania, Hungría y China	Solectron y Flextronics
TOURLAVILLE	2001	Equipos para la telefonía móvil	Cesión	Sanmina
SAINTES (Charente Maritime)	2001		Cesión	Groupe Métal Découpe
ILLKIRCH	2001	Terminales gsm	Reconversión de la sección optoelectrónica; plan de cierre de secciones de $software$ de diseño planar y MEMs	ALCATEL
ALCATEL Nozay		Componentes activos	Cierre y deslocalización	ALCATEL
ALCATEL, Gante y Hoboken	2001		Negociaciones con subcontratistas	

Empresa	Año	Sección	Operación	Empresa destinataria
ALCATEL GEEL (ALCATEL-Lucent, Bélgica)	2001	Centrales	Deslocalización de la producción en Gunzenhausen (Alemania); énfasis en productos de acceso a la banda ancha	ALCATEL-Lucent
ALCATEL, Laval	2002	Terminales telefónicos	Cesión	Sanmina
ALCATEL, Coutances (Manche)	2002		Cesión	Sanmina
MADDALONI Y FROSINONE (MF)	2002		Venta y cesión; nueva empresa (MFcomponenti)	Cesión a CST
ALCATEL OPTRONICS (Gatineau, Canadá)	2002	Sensores de fibra óptica bragg (fbg)	Cierre y traslado a Livingston, Escocia; traslado de la sección de I+D y delegación comercial a Kanata, Ontario	ALCATEL
ALCATEL OPTRONICS, Lannion	2002		Empleo a tiempo parcial y recorte de la plantilla: jubilación anticipada	ALCATEL
ALCATEL OPTRONICS (Irlanda)	2002		Recorte de plantilla; venta	Avanex (USA); creación de Avanex Francia

Empresa	Año	Sección	Operación	Empresa destinataria
ALCATEL OPTRONICS (Shannon y Cork, Irlanda)			Recortes de más de la mitad de los 160 empleados; cierre del centro logístico en Shannon	
ALCATEL Bandon	2002	Unidad de desarrollo de *software* hlr	Cierre	
ALCATEL Cherburgo (Francia)	2002	Sistemas de ensamblaje y prueba para aplicaciones en las bandas de frecuencias 1,5 y 38 ghz	Venta	Sanmina-SCI
ALCATEL Gunzenhausen (Alemania)	2002	Sistemas de transmisión de datos y conmutación de voz	Venta	Sanmina-SCI
ALCATEL Space Dinamarca	2003	Productos informáticos, electrónicos y ópticos	Quiebra/Cierre	
ALCATEL Brest[42]	2004	Centrales privadas y de empresa basadas en ip	Cesión	Sanmina
ALCATEL Saft	2004		Cesión	Doughty Hanson & Co

[42] Brest, uno de polos de investigación y de formación, junto a los de Rennes y Lannion, formaba la *filière* electrónica-telecomunicaciones de la región de la Bretaña (Boyer 2009) Cuando en 2001 Flextronics se hizo cargo de la planta de Alcatel en Laval, significativamente, los empleados de Flextronics en Monceau-les-Luneville fueron despedidos (*Lutte Ouvrière*, 175.515, marzo de 2002). Debate en el Senado francés por las amenazas de deslocalización en Flextronic (Sénat de la France, Séance, 11 de octubre de 2001).

Empresa	Año	Sección	Operación	Empresa destinataria
Geel (ALCATEL-Lucent, Bélgica)	2004	Producción de placas adsl	Reducción de 46 puestos de trabajo y subcontratación de otros 30 en las secciones no productivas	-
Rieti y Battipaglia	2004		Anuncio de cesión	
ALCATEL: Île-de France Massy Vélizy Meudon Colombes Marcoussis Villarceaux	2006		Planes de cierre y deslocalización (2.000 personas)	ALCATEL: Vélizy et Villarceaux (près de Monthléry)
Geel (ALCATEL-Lucent, Bélgica)	2007		Venta	Tbp Electronics B.V. (Holanda)

Fuente: Elaboración a partir del texto y nota.

En el cambio de década, el estallido de la burbuja punto com propinó un golpe mortal al crecimiento económico, con efectos negativos sobre el empleo, a la vez que forzó a las industrias del sector TIC a reestructurarse (OECD 2007, 68)[43]. La industria mundial de las telecomunicaciones no se estabilizó hasta 2004 e inició una senda de crecimiento modesto en 2005 y 2006, como muestra el aumento de los gastos de capital de las operadoras y la creciente demanda de servicios de telecomunicaciones (United States Securities and Exchange Commission. Fiscal year ended September 30, 2006).

Gráfico 1. Costes medios en la industria en un grupo de países (en dólares/hora)

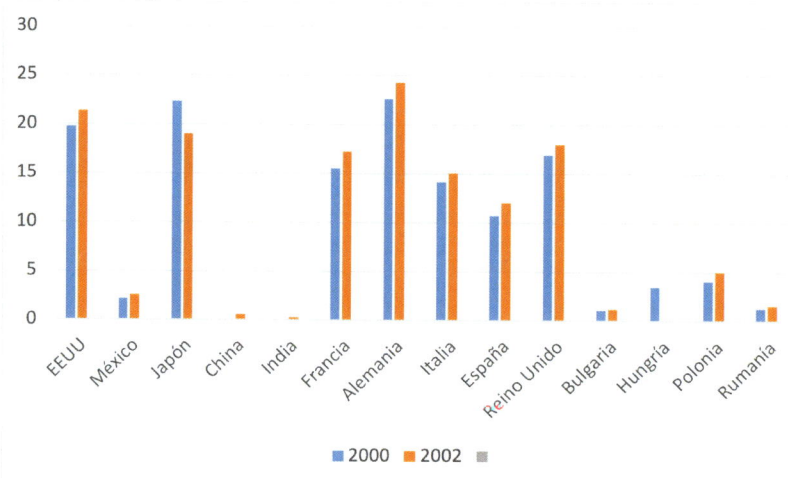

Fuente: Elaboración a partir de U.S. Department of Labor,
Bureau of Labor Statistics, May 2004, IXIS CIB.

A nivel individual, las empresas mostraron perfiles diferentes, como una observación de diversos casos certifica. Algunas mantuvieron los niveles de

---

[43] Veamos el comportamiento de dos grandes multinacionales. Entre 2001-2008, Ericsson redujo significativamente los puestos de trabajo (30% en todo el mundo y 52% en Suecia), siendo la reducción de costes y la racionalización los principios rectores de sus decisiones. La producción se externalizó en gran medida en el extranjero, aunque una parte relativamente grande permaneció en Suecia al servicio del mercado nacional (Eurofound 2009, 37-38). Siemens anunció la supresión de 6.500 puestos de trabajo para 2003; Lucent y Nortel pronto verían sus plantillas reducidas respectivamente a 43.000 y 50.000. Un fenómeno clásico de desaceleración de la demanda en una madurez del mercado se combinó con una retroalimentación desproporcionada de la economía financiera a la economía real (Laffitte y Trégouët 2001). El desplome de la industria de telecomunicaciones provocó aproximadamente un cuarto de la disminución del crecimiento económico entre la primera mitad de 2000 y la de 2001 (Brenner 2003), 295.

empleo con algunos cambios de actividades entre países y mucha reestructuración dentro de los países. Otras multinacionales sufrieron importantes pérdidas de empleo, lo que reflejó la incapacidad de las mismas para adaptarse a las cambiantes condiciones del mercado, en lugar de una tendencia general a la disminución del empleo en las grandes empresas. La mayoría de las multinacionales transfirieron al menos parte de su producción fuera de la UE-15 a los nuevos Estados miembros para contener o reducir los costes de producción. Otro importante grupo de multinacionales ubicó sus instalaciones de producción en zonas asiáticas. Los bajos costes de la mano de obra fueron el principal factor que influyó en las decisiones de localización, aunque otros factores también desempeñaron un papel importante, entre ellos la disponibilidad de mano de obra debidamente cualificada (Eurofound 2009, 9-10).

En ese escenario general se inscribe la segunda fase de la reestructuración de Alcatel (2001-2004)[44]. Con 56.000 empleados distribuidos en 130 países, dividía la actividad en tres áreas: comunicaciones fijas, comunicaciones y comunicaciones privadas móviles (para la industria y el sector público). La sección principal por mano de obra y ventas era la de redes, con clara ventaja respecto a óptica, negocios, espacio y componentes (Anexo 2) (Alcatel 2003, 126; Beaujolin-Bellet e Issaverdens 2006)[45].

En cuanto a la distribución geográfica de la mano de obra, Francia presentaba la máxima concentración de efectivos (casi la mitad de un total de 76.900 en el año 2000), seguida de Alemania, Bélgica e Italia. España ocupaba el último lugar de estos cinco países (Anexo 3).

De acuerdo con el análisis de la Tabla 2, en los años 2001-2008, posteriores a la burbuja punto com, predominaron las cesiones o ventas –once casos–, la inmensa mayoría de los cuales se tomaron como medida exclusiva y tuvieron como *partenaire* principal la multinacional norteamericana Sanmina. Cuantitativamente, siguen en importancia los cierres –cinco, tres de ellos asociados a

---

[44] Alcatel pensaba reestructurarse centrándose en sus áreas principales de negocio de redes, óptica y espacio, equivalentes al 80% del negocio. Esta reestructuración –sin recortes de empleos y con principal énfasis en Europa– implicaba tres elementos: vender su actividad de distribución empresarial; lanzar en 2001 al mercado Nexans, compañía de cable y componentes, y reducir la división de terminales a una base de costos mínimos (*EE Times*, 6 de enero de 2001; Saint-Étienne 2013, 87). La salida de Nexans a bolsa ha sido considerada como uno de los hitos en la historia de Alcatel (*Les Échos*, 15 de abril de 2015).

[45] Ante los resultados trimestrales de 2002, fueron anunciados «planes de acción complementaria», descentralizados, filial por filial y en función de la fuerza en sus mercados –alrededor de la mitad del capital de la empresa en manos de accionistas franceses; el 40% de la actividad llevado a cabo en Europa y el 20% en los EE. UU. (Audition de M. Serge Tchuruk, président directeur général d'Alcatel, Sénat de la France, 26 de junio de 2002).

deslocalización–, seguidos por los recortes de plantilla –cuatro casos, en su totalidad asociados a otras medidas; deslocalización, modalidad que suma cinco casos, uno de ellos fuera del país (UE)–. Finalmente, dos casos se refieren específicamente a subcontratación, por igual parcial y total, estrategia ya ensayada en la etapa anterior en Alcatel Business System, que cedió 222 asalariados de la fábrica de terminales de radiomensajería de Gundershoffen, cercana a Estrasburgo, a Info Réalité, futura Info-Industrie (Suard 2002; Suard 1993, 210; *Les Échos,* 15 de julio de 1997). Nos llamaríamos a engaño si pensáramos que una cantidad menor de casos en algún año significa menor intensidad de las diversas medidas de reestructuración. Así, Alcatel recortó en EE. UU. más de 7.000 empleos en tan solo el año 2001, como se ha visto antes[46].

En el segmento de mercado particular de la industria de cable óptico, al que ya se ha hecho referencia, Alcatel aplicó en Optronics, filial especializada en componentes ópticos, un plan de reconversión industrial (*industrial redeployment plan*), un concepto muy a lo Giscard D'Estaing, que conllevaba cierre de varias plantas, relocalización de empleo y despido de un cuarto de su mano de obra en todas las fábricas hasta dejarla en 1.350 empleados. Las plantas de Irlanda sufrieron los efectos del desplome del mercado y de las escasas perspectivas de rebrote de la demanda (Tabla 2). El plan abarcaba el cierre y reubicación de actividades en la fábrica de sensores de fibra óptica Bragg (FBG) en Gatineau, Canadá, y el traslado a la planta situada en Livingston, Escocia. La sección de I+D junto con una presencia comercial se mantendrían en Canadá, basándose en sus instalaciones de Kanata, Ontario. El plan se reproduciría en el caso de la planta de montaje del amplificador de fibra óptica (OFA) y de subsistema de interfaz óptico (OIF) de Illkirch, que sería trasladada a la planta francesa de componentes activos de Nozay. La planta de Illkirch había sido objeto de una actuación con resultados considerados significativos en términos de reducción de costes, control de inventarios y congelación de gastos de capital. En Nozay, al igual que en Lannion, Alcatel Optronics recurriría al empleo a tiempo parcial y a la jubilación anticipada, entre otras soluciones para reducir la plantilla. La compañía también tenía la intención de desprenderse de sus actividades de *software* de diseño planar y MEMs[47].

---

[46] Alcatel Data Networks en Ashburn, sede central de Plano en Texas, y en las plantas de California, Puerto Rico y Raleigh en Carolina del Norte. En general, los especialistas han prestado escaso interés a las plantas de Alcatel fuera de Europa.

[47] Industrial Redeployment Plan, París, 5 de junio de 2002; *Electronics Weekly*, 6 de junio de 2002; *EE Times*, 6 de junio de 2002. En 1996, Alcatel aseguró a las autoridades francesas,

A caballo entre las dos fases, Alcatel fue orientándose a la desinversión en su vertiente de fabricante. El ensayo de la saga tuvo como escenario precisamente EE. UU.: en 2000 y 2001, fueron vendidas a la proveedora de *electronics manufacturing services* (EMS) Sanmina-SCI las fábricas de Carolina del Norte y Richardson. Muy importante, las transacciones incluyeron sendos contratos plurianuales de suministro y el traspaso de empleados[48]. Esta práctica se extendió a continuación a Europa con idénticos protagonistas. En 2002 fueron vendidas dos plantas a Sanmina-SCI, fortalecida con recientes acuerdos con los gigantes IBM y HP para subcontratar la fabricación de ordenadores personales[49].

En definitiva, la reestructuración del grupo bajo la égida de S. Tchuruk emuló los principios del modelo *fab-less*, basado en la externalización de la actividad productiva, caros a la industria electrónica estadounidense y, más en concreto, las prácticas de Cisco, auténtica pionera y rival de Alcatel (Burnier 2002, 5-7; Leckey 2002, 225; Cisco Systems 2011)[50]. A escala mundial, el

inquietas por el futuro de Lannion, que la fábrica, con 320 empleados, era absolutamente esencial para el grupo y su sostenibilidad estaba garantizada. El Ministerio de Industria proclamaba sus afanes por la defensa y el desarrollo de la actividad industrial y el empleo (*Réponse du ministère de l'Industrie, Journal Officiel du Sénat de la France*: 1 de febrero de 1996, 208). Los planes eran generalmente negociados con los sindicatos. Estudios con diferentes enfoques sobre la reconversión desde el punto de vista obrero en Maricourt (2006) y Malsan (2001). La adquisición de Innovative Fibers Inc. en el año 2000 y de Kymata Ltd. en 2001 dio como resultado las filiales canadiense y británica de Alcatel Optronics. Dos empresas alsacianas de electrónica, Asteel Développement y Oristano, alquilaron de Illkirch 130 y 60 empleados respectivamente; al final de 2004, la planta de Illkirch empleaba 1.100 personas que trabajaban en I+D y servicios (Alcatel 2008, 25).

[48] El precio de compra se fijó por los activos netos adquiridos, incluidos inventarios: Sanmina-SCI (2002), 80 y 83. Sanmina-SCI competía con otras compañías similares, entre ellas Micron Technology, Inc. Como cabecera de un grupo de filiales – Micron Semiconductor, Inc., Micron Custom Manufacturing Services, Inc., and Micron Computer, Inc.–, su especialización era el diseño, desarrollo, fabricación y comercialización de productos semiconductores para memorias, principalmente de DRAM (Micron Electronics 1998, 10). En 2008, Sanmina-SCI tenía 54.397 empleados y fábricas en 18 países de los cinco continentes; además de Alcatel, entre sus socios figuraban HP, EchoStar, IBM, Philips y Nokia (Plunkett 2008). La subcontratación (EMS) ascendió en 2001 a unos 178.000 millones de dólares con un crecimiento anual medio del 25% desde 1998 (Carroué 2004-2005, 131-136; *ComputerWorld*, 19 de abril de 1996).

[49] La Comisión Europea no puso objeciones a la operación (Case N°. COMP/M.2734 – SANMINA-SCI CORPORATION/Alcatel, *Official Journal of the European Communities*, C 54, 1/3/2002, 9). En Alcatel-CIT los 1.450 empleados se redujeron a 665 en 1990 y a 300 cuando cerró sus puertas seis años después (*Electronics Production*, 7 de abril de 2008: Ripoll 2004, 67-84); la alemana estaba especializada en sistemas de transmisión de datos y conmutación de voz (*RedesTelecom*, 25 de enero de 2002).

[50] Entre la multitud de empresas tecnológicas que adoptaron la estrategia de la externalización de actividades destacan NEC, IBM, Hewlett-Packard (HP), Cisco, Ericsson, Siemens, Sony y Microsoft. Ericsson practicó con Flextronics esta estrategia de externalización, al

fenómeno no era nuevo sino que databa al menos de la década de 1960 y se había desarrollado en tres oleadas sucesivas[51].

Alcatel cerró multitud de fábricas en Europa pero solo externalizó la mitad de la producción por motivos diversos. En ocasiones, la existencia de una normativa difícil de eludir –disfrazada como razones sociales– aconsejó salvaguardar producción propia. Su estrategia de mantener actividades con un valor añadido elevado así lo determinó, si bien tampoco sistemáticamente. Una razón importante consistió en la necesidad de responder de forma adecuada a la demanda de determinados productos en los mercados nacionales[52].

contrario que Samsung (Lüthje et al. 2013 133); Saint-Étienne (2013, 87). Así pues, la práctica fomentó una boyante industria de la subcontratación. En esta categoría predominaban las norteamericanas –Plexus, Jabil Circuit, Solectron y Sanmina SCI– y las asiáticas –Flextronics (Singapur), China Electronics, Daeduck de Corea y la tailandesa Delta Electronics-; en Canadá, figuraba Celestica y en Europa las finesas Aspocomp y Elcoteq, junto a la austriaca AT&S (Galgoczi, Keune y Watt 2008, 152; Alcatel 2008, 9; Vagadia 2011, 63). De menor importancia era Micron Technology, Inc. Resulta significativo que Tchuruk tratase de quitar hierro a la expresión *fab-less* ante los representantes políticos del país. Sin embargo, no ocultó que la miniaturización conllevaba una rápida disminución del peso de la electrónica en relación a la unidad de cifra de negocios. Ericsson practicó con Flextronics esta estrategia de externalización, al contrario que Samsung (Lüthje et al. 2013, 133; Saint-Étienne 2013, 87). Alcatel denunció a Cisco por apropiación indebida de secretos de fabricación: Alcatel USA, Inc. v. Cisco Systems, Inc., U.S. (District Court for the Eastern District of Texas – December 17, 2002).

[51] La estrategia defensiva de mercado ocasionó una primera ola de deslocalizaciones hacia el sudeste asiático entre 1965 y 1980, coincidente con el comienzo de una fase ascendente de la participación del comercio mundial en el PIB. En una segunda oleada, en los años ochenta, las áreas de inversión se ampliaron a nuevos países emergentes con bajos sueldos y a las áreas del entorno de las grandes potencias económicas, a la vez su «taller» y potencialmente importadoras. Por último, la mejora tecnológica gradual de algunos de estos países y la aparición de los gigantes económicos ofrecieron además de una tercera ola de traslados, nuevas oportunidades de trasladar o reubicar los servicios (Grignon 2004). A título de ejemplo, la irrupción de la India en el *outsourcing* y el cambio del papel del país (Niosi y Tschang 2009, 269-294).

[52] En el año 2000, Alcatel planeaba deslocalizar en Rumanía, Hungría y China con Solectron y Flextronics (*L'Usine Nouvelle*, 20 de abril de 2000). En Italia, la planta de Rieti o Cittaducale, incorporada a Alcatel en el momento de la absorción de Telettra en 1990, estaba especializada en fibra óptica y transmisión por radio, el fortín de Telettra (Bresciani y Ferraris 2012, 207-208). La venta de los establecimientos de Maddaloni y Frosinone (MF) en 2002 a un grupo financiero encabezado por el profesor R. A. Cenciarini dio lugar a MFcomponenti, cuya reorganización comenzó con la cesión inmediata de la planta de Frosinone a CST de la familia Botti (*Caserta News*, 1 de marzo de 2008). Battipaglia había recibido subvenciones de la Unión Europea (Parliamentary questions, Answer given by Mr Špidla on behalf of the Commission E-3537/2009, 1 de septiembre de 2009; Interrogazione 3-01233 sullo stabilimento di Rieti dell'Alcatel, Senato della Repubblica, 19 de febrero do 2004). Tchuruk anunció que solo se quedaría con doce fábricas, si bien después redujo la cifra de cierres a 50 (27 en Europa y el resto en EE. UU.) con 13.500 asalariados (*01net.com*, 29 de junio de 2001); efectivamente, se mantuvieron algunas, especialmente en Francia,

Todas las plantas de fabricación de móviles pasaron a manos del grupo indio Singapur Flextronics International y las de componentes a Thomson Multimedia, Sammina y Thales, tradicionales competidores (Observatorio industrial de electrónica, tecnologías de la información y telecomunicaciones 2008, 25)[53].

Alcatel entendía la reestructuración como uno de los tres factores primordiales de su fortaleza competitiva, al mismo título que su liderazgo en el mercado europeo y la densidad de su red de distribución. El carácter multinacional de esa empresa impuso estrategias incomprensibles en una perspectiva de Estado nación. Alcatel deslizó gradualmente su IED desde las adquisiciones a las empresas conjuntas y desde Europa Occidental a Europa del Este y Asia,

sede de la casa madre, e Italia, considerada estratégica (Jacques 2006). El centro de investigación y desarrollo de Nozay en París suprimió puestos de trabajo de ingenieros de desarrollo de *software* del teléfono (Question écrite 8,582 de Mme Marie-France Beaufils (Indre-et-Loire – CRC), *Journal Officiel du Sénat,* 24 de julio de 2003, 2.345). Respecto a la región parisiense, destaca la importancia de las funciones de I+D y la alta cualificación de los empleos y su concentración en las zonas periféricas (Guieysse 1986, 134). Alcatel trasladó parcialmente sus laboratorios de investigación a China, localización que, junto con la India, resultaba atractiva por la sencilla razón de que existía mano de obra cualificada y de que el coste de un investigador era diez veces menor que en Francia (Sénat de la France, 5 de junio de 2008; Li y Li, 2009, 2). La representante de la Union pour un Mouvement Populaire (Essonne) subrayaba que ninguna de las operaciones de la empresa escapaban a los reajustes, incluidas las relacionadas con la innovación y la investigación y el desarrollo (Question 919 de Mme Kosciusko-Morizet Nathalie, *JOAN,* 19 de octubre de 2004, 8.005). En ese momento se cuestionaba la deslocalización de la I+D hacia China, que el gobierno vinculaba a la toma de control de Shanghai Bell por Alcatel y cifraba en el 10% el personal de I+D del grupo. Esta presencia en China, donde Alcatel vendía cinco millones mensuales de terminales, era considerada por el gobierno esencial para una empresa global y requisito previo para arrebatar cuota de mercado a los muy agresivos competidores chinos y tener acceso a la financiación china para proyectos. El gobierno insistía en el predominio neto de la participación de Francia en la I+D de Alcatel: con un 40% de su fuerza de trabajo en investigación y desarrollo frente a un 10% de facturación en el país («Réponse du ministre délégué à l'industrie», *JOAN,* 19 de octubre de 2004, 8.005). Respecto a las ventajas de localización, un indicador del año 2004 situaba la India como principal lugar y España en el puesto veintidós, por encima de Türkiye, Israel e Irlanda, en una lista de los 25 destinos más atractivos (A.T. Kearney's 2004 Offshore location Attractiveness Index. Making Offshore Décisions, mayo de 2004, 16). Alcatel teorizaba sobre la concentración de la I+D como factor de flexibilidad (*Les Échos,* 25 de enero de 2006).

53 Las plantas de fabricación de teléfonos móviles en Alsacia y Mayenne vendidas sumaban 1.660 empleados (*Znet,* 3 de octubre de 2001). Las principales desinversiones de Thales afectaron en 1983 a las telecomunicaciones civiles (acuerdo con CGE) y en 1987 al sector médico (cedido a General Electric). La fusión en 1987 de las actividades de semiconductores con IRI-Finmeccanica dio a luz a SGS-Thomson. Para los cambios en Thomson, véase Fridenson (1992, 26-41) y Darmon (2010, 108-112). En 1987, Thales recuperó la situación financiera por la reorientación de la cartera a la electrónica profesional y de defensa (Thales, *Rapport annuel 2007,* 6).

movimiento geográfico que se aplicó a la apertura de filiales. Para afianzar su posición con el acceso a nuevos mercados, forjó alianzas estratégicas con socios locales, ya creando empresas conjuntas o adquiriendo las de estos. El movimiento tuvo como objetivo el logro de vías de penetración por medio primordialmente de la fabricación de centrales. En la gama de equipos PBX que, no obstante, contribuyó menos que la conmutación pública al desarrollo internacional de Alcatel, se concretó así: adquisición de National Telecom (fabricante de pequeñas centrales PBX) en el Reino Unido; un protocolo con Siemens para redes heterogéneas; apertura de filiales en el este de Europa y norte de África –Checoslovaquia y Túnez–; una *joint venture* con una empresa yugoslava (que servía casi la mitad de su mercado nacional) y un acuerdo con un fabricante y una filial de la operadora nacional en Hungría[54]. En un solo año, el de 1992, Alcatel abrió filiales en Bulgaria, Kazajstán, Polonia, Rusia, Eslovaquia y la República Checa. La multinacional estableció una estructura jerárquica de centros de investigación con responsabilidades de grado diverso. Concentró su núcleo PBXR & Din en los laboratorios principales, localizados en Francia y Alemania, formó una red secundaria de laboratorios dispersos en diversos países y mantuvo núcleos muy pequeños en casi todos los países para satisfacer las exigencias específicas de los respectivos mercados interiores[55]. Ejemplo posterior de entrada en Latinoamérica como inversor fue la integración en la Empresa Metropolitana de Comunicaciones (Metrotel), un consorcio mixto formado por Alcatel Bell Telephone de Bélgica, el Área Metropolitana de Barranquilla, Telecom, Tele Cartagena y el Banco de Colombia a través de su filial Colcorp (Tejada 1996, 143)[56].

---

[54] Gestión de redes en Noruega, aplicaciones PBX en Austria, terminales en Francia y terminales inalámbricos en España. Alcatel además mantenía equipos muy pequeños en casi todos los países para la adaptación de los productos (European Commission 1997, 52-53 y 119). En Europa, Alcatel fraguó alianzas, por ejemplo con VEB Kombinat Nachrichtenelektronik en Alemania, con Videoton en Hungría y con varios socios locales en Yugoslavia (*Computer Business Review*, 22 de abril de 1990).

[55] No sin algunos sobresaltos ocasionados por el CoCom, el Comité de control de las exportaciones (Calvo, 2016, 60-85), Alcatel accedió a los territorios de la antigua URSS –Rusia, Bielorrusia (con MPOVT en 1998), Georgia, Armenia y Ucrania– por medio de contratos de suministro y *joint ventures* (Alcatel, *Annual Report 2005*, 29); en Rusia, competía con NEC, Siemens e IskraTel en equipos de conmutación de alta calidad, que lograron la homologación como producto nacional: OCDE (2002), 306.

[56] Estrictamente hablando los convenios se firmaron entre Telecom y UT Alcatel, Alcatel Bell y Alcatel ASESA y afectaban a tres departamentos y cincuenta y seis localidades, 2 y 45; y 12 y 280, respectivamente (Comisión de Regulación de Telecomunicaciones 2000, 201; *El Tiempo*, 7 de abril de 1995). La concesión del Área Metropolitana de Barranquilla otorgada a Metrotel por un término de dos decenios en calidad de instaladora, operadora y mantene-

A iniciativa de la Empresa Nacional de Telecomunicaciones (Telecom), Alcatel Standard Eléctrica SA presentó propuesta para el desarrollo de programas de telefonía local y rural, propuesta que fue seleccionada. Para llevarla a cabo, en septiembre de 1993, forjó un convenio de asociación con la Telecom, que fue trasvasado dos años después al consorcio conformado con Alcatel SESA Technical Services S.A. y Telealca SA. La duración del contrato estaba determinada por la obtención de una TIR del 12% en dólares sobre la inversión realizada a fin de permitir al asociado recuperar el desembolso por concepto de la inversión. En la distribución de riesgos sobre ingresos del contrato, el riesgo máximo para la asociada era del 10% y para Telecom del 90%. Según el plan de negocios, el socio se obligó a realizar una aportación de equipos por una suma de 265.347.509 de dólares, mientras que el aporte de Telecom se cifraba en unos 30 millones de dólares, procedente de un crédito FAD del gobierno español destinado a la adquisición de equipo a Alcatel SESA, a través de un contrato de suministro. Por tanto, esta operación de exportación, propia de la internacionalización, dio lugar a órganos corporativos temporales que implicaban al cliente (Tribunal Arbitral 2002)[57].

dora de 100 mil líneas con tecnología Alcatel Bell Telephone Co., es decir, el sistema 12 (*El Tiempo*, 16 de julio de 1999).

[57] Análisis en Cortés y Paredes (2013, 56-57). Noam (1998, 110) describe la finalidad de los contratos sin entrar en la problemática de los mismos. Alcatel SESA y Telecom debieron establecer un comité, encargado de desarrollar y coordinar los aspectos operacionales, técnicos, comerciales y de procedimientos para dar soluciones efectivas en la prestación del servicio a los usuarios (Sentencia 2004-01542, 20 de junio de 2013, Consejo de Estado, Sala de lo Contencioso administrativo, sección cuarta). El contrato con Alcatel fue uno de los quince que Telecom firmó entre 1993 y 1998 con multinacionales, entre ellas Siemens, Alcatel, Ericsson, NEC, Itochu y Nortel, y que la llevaron a la ruina debido a la notable desigualdad del riesgo máximo compartido. El firmado con Alcatel SESA correspondía a la «primera generación de contratos», orientada al aumento de la teledensidad del país en particular en zonas rurales. Como resultado de la ejecución de los contratos suscritos por Telecom, a noviembre de 2003, se instalaron 1.631.626 nuevas líneas y los Asociados recibieron la suma 1.189,4 millones de dólares, cuantía que dejó espacio para reclamaciones (*Tiempo*, 28 de agosto de 1993; *Semana*, 15 de junio de 2003; Consejo Nacional de Política Económica y Social República de Colombia, Departamento Nacional de Planeación de Hacienda y Crédito Público Ministerio de Comunicaciones, DNP, DIE-STEL, Bogotá, 2 de febrero de 2004; Herrera 2008, 169-170). Los contratos fueron calificados de «el peor negocio de la historia» ya que la suma impuesta a Telecom como pago equivalía a la ayuda estadounidense del Plan Colombia para dos años o, en otro supuesto, a una suma que multiplicaba por diez la ayuda gubernamental de emergencia a los cafeteros en un año (*Semana*, 20 de agosto de 2001). Nortel se arrogaba el título de «líder en la implementación de acuerdos de riesgo compartido en Colombia» (Canadian Centre for Policy Alternatives, 1 de octubre de 2004), años antes de que la china Huawei acabara con su brillante trayectoria.

Los cierres de fábricas y la externalización se conjugaron con la adquisición de empresas, según estrategias cambiantes y, como se ha visto, ya ensayadas. En 1998, Alcatel se situó en el cuarto puesto del mercado mundial de equipos de telecomunicaciones con unas ventas de 19.600 millones de dólares, un 17% más, por detrás de Lucent, Ericsson y Motorola (Migaud 2000, 25-30).

A partir de 1998, Alcatel, sustancialmente orientada a la tecnología de voz, se embarcó en esa estrategia, capaz de afrontar la convergencia en torno al Internet Protocol (IP) –el centro de excelencia era Alcatel Bell– y de brindar una oferta global (OCDE 2001, 117). El grupo adoptó la estrategia de «perlas», que privilegiaba la adquisición de *start-ups*. Dentro de sus planes de expansión por Estados Unidos, Alcatel Alsthom SA se hizo por unos 4.400 millones de dólares con DSC Communications Corp. (Plano, Texas), con la intención de reforzar el negocio en sistemas de conmutación digital y gestión de redes, talón de Aquiles de la compañía. Sin embargo, las previsiones se torcieron y los clientes clave de Alcatel, entre ellos Deutsche Telekom y France Telecom, redujeron sus pedidos en un 37%, con la consiguiente caída del valor de sus acciones, ante la gran indignación de los inversores en DSC, que interpusieron demandas por deficiente información sobre el comportamiento del precio de las acciones. La compra de DSC desmanteló la estrategia de perlas, a la vez que sellaba la voluntad de acelerar su reposicionamiento en el mercado de datos para las redes de las operadoras y de buscar su equilibrio en el mercado americano[58]. La apuesta norteamericana de Alcatel continuó con la captura de presas tecnológicas como Packet Engines, Xylan, Assured Access y Genesys, que le brindaron la posibilidad de ofrecer una amplia gama de *routers* (*L'Usine Nouvelle*, 2.723, 2 de marzo de 2000; Mtar 2001, 112-116)[59]. Las tres primeras, compradas con el objetivo de aumentar las ventas

---

[58] *Bloomberg News*, 12 de octubre y 4 de junio de 1998; *Los Angeles Times*, 5 de junio de 1998; *PRNews*, 2 de noviembre de 1998.

[59] El mercado mundial de los *routers* (enrutadores) estaba dominado con holgura por los fabricantes americanos, con Cisco a la cabeza (70%), muy por delante de IBM y Fujitsu. El acceso a la banda ancha actuó como motor de crecimiento para Alcatel, que se convirtió en líder mundial en ADSL y sistemas de transmisión (SDH, SONET y DWDM) (ver Glosario de términos). Las dos empresas conjuntas creadas con la empresa pública Thomson Multimedia mejoraron la posición de Alcatel en el mercado de los terminales. La oferta de Alcatel para las redes de área local fue el resultado de la adquisición de Xylan, principalmente en el mercado de las comunicaciones corporativas. Alcatel apostó fuertemente por la ISDN (Integrated Services Digital Network, capaz de ofrecer voz, video, datos y otros servicios) de banda ancha por su potencial de futuro (Migaud 2000, 25-30). Thomson Multimedia, controlada por la empresa pública Thomson S.A. se dedicaba principalmente al sector de

en el área de Internet de 150 millones de euros a 1 billón en tan solo un año, costaron 2,7 billones de dólares. La adquisición de Internet Devices y Genesys Telecommunications Laboratories para auparse al liderazgo en el mercado norteamericano de integración de redes de voz y datos elevó el total de la inversión en ese segmento a 5.000 millones de dólares. Para ser integrada en esta última Alcatel adquirió Telera, especializada en la transmisión de voz a través de Internet, una operación posible gracias a la fuerte liquidez de la compradora. Estados Unidos se había convertido en el primer mercado de Alcatel en el campo de las telecomunicaciones con una facturación de 3 billones de dólares y un crecimiento anual estimado del 12%[60]. En Asia, Alcatel adquirió en 2002 el control de Shanghai Bell, desde diez años antes el mayor fabricante de equipos de telecomunicaciones en China y con casi la mitad del mercado chino de conmutación digital en sus manos[61].

A primeros de 2000, las actividades de telecomunicaciones del grupo se reorganizaron en torno a tres segmentos principales –redes, Internet y óptica y empresas y consumidores– con volumen de negocios dispares –44,6 millones de francos franceses, 32 millones y 20,9, respectivamente–.

Los efectos de la crisis de 2001 se prolongaron. Sin ánimo de centrarnos en ellos, cabe tener presente que Alcatel CIT, como es sabido la principal filial francesa del grupo y cuya plantilla ascendía a 7.200 personas, también pechó con los efectos de la crisis. Su receta para sortearla se llamó Plan 2004 de reequilibrio de recursos entre las actividades de telefonía fija y ópticas en declive y el negocio móvil en crecimiento, objeto de un acuerdo con las organizaciones sindicales mayoritarias en la empresa[62].

---

los productos electrónicos de consumo, como los descodificadores, los módems y los productos de los estudios de radiodifusión televisiva, como las cámaras y los mezcladores. La Comisión Europea no se opuso a la operación de *joint venture* (Case No COMP/M.2048 – Alcatel/Thomson Multimedia/JV Notification of 26.09.2000 pursuant to Article 4 of Council Regulation (EEC) No4064/89).

[60] *Silicon Valley Business Journal*, 12 de agosto de 2002; *Computerworld*, 11 y 18 de febrero de 2000; Telera costó 136 millones de $ en acciones: *La Libre Belgique,* 30 de mayo de 2002.

[61] Shanghai Bell Telephone Equipment Manufacturing Co. (1983) fue la primera empresa conjunta extranjera, creada mediante un acuerdo de transferencia de tecnología entre el gobierno belga y el chino, el Ministerio de Correos y Telecomunicaciones (MPT), Bell Telephone Manufacturing Company (BTM), IT&T y la Sociedad Industrial de Correos y Telecomunicaciones (PTIC) (Emiroğlu 2003, 5-6); algunos matices (Alcatel, *Annual Report 2005,* 30-31).

[62] Réponse du ministre délégué à l'industrie, *JOAN,* 19 de octubre de 2004, 8.005.

La lógica de las empresas en Europa obedecía a la situación del mercado mundial y, en particular, de una de sus porciones mayores. Al menos en
una parte del mercado mundial –EE. UU.– la revitalización de la demanda de
los operadores de telecomunicaciones, impulsada por la intensificación en la
captura de nuevos abonados, repercutió en los proveedores de equipos. Para
mantener su competitividad, los operadores necesitaban ampliar los servicios
mediante actualizaciones de la red y oferta de precios atractivos, lo que dicta-
ba la necesidad de una infraestructura de red de bajo coste[63].

5. Alcatel-Lucent: nuevo giro estratégico

Lo sucedido con la creación de Alcatel –más tarde confirmado en la absorción
de esta por Nokia– se repitió en 2006 con la fusión al 60/40% de Alcatel y
Lucent Technologies Inc., que fue bendecida por la Comisión Europea[64]. Un
quinquenio después de un primer intento fallido, el acuerdo dio origen con
la denominación de Alcatel-Lucent al segundo mayor proveedor mundial de
redes de telecomunicaciones y equipos móviles después de la ya citada Cisco
Systems Inc[65]. El mercado norteamericano resultaba tentador por su avanzada

---

[63] Además, los operadores se esforzaban por hacer converger varias redes de superposición
(Bonenfant y Leopold 2006, 102-108).

[64] Ambas totalizaban un volumen de negocios mundial por encima de 5.000 millones de euros
(Alcatel: 13.135 millones de euros; Lucent: 7.588.742 euros). En la mayoría de los mercados afectados el aumento de la cuota de mercado rondaba [0-10%] (a nivel de Europa, el
Oriente Medio y África (EMEA) (Anexo 4). El volumen de negocios comunitario de cada una
de ellas superaba los 250 millones de euros, pero su volumen de negocios comunitario total
en un mismo Estado miembro no superaba los dos tercios. Por lo tanto, la operación tenía
una dimensión comunitaria (Case No COMP/M.4214 –Alcatel/LUCENT TECHNOLOGIES,
REGULATION (EC) n°. 139/2004, Merger procedure, Bruselas, 24 de julio de 2006, 2). Las
circunstancias que habían cambiado en 2006 incluían la necesidad de fusionarse para competir con los fabricantes chinos y otros líderes de la industria, debido a la intensificación de
la competencia en la industria de las telecomunicaciones móviles e Internet. En segundo
lugar, la alta dirección de Lucent pudo superar sus temores con respecto a su participación
en el poder dentro de la nueva empresa fusionada. No obstante, Alcatel y Lucent expre-
saron su preocupación por las perspectivas de propuesta en general y la compatibilidad
cultural entre las dos empresas en particular (Nordick on line). La adquisición de Alcatel
por Nokia obedeció al lema «The right time, the right solutions, the right companies» (Alcatel-Lucent S.A., Commission File No. 001-11130).

[65] En sentido estricto, Alcatel-Lucent se formó el 2 de abril de 2006 tras el Acuerdo y Plan de
Fusión entre Lucent y una filial de Alcatel por el que esta absorbió a Lucent y se convirtió
en una filial absoluta de Alcatel (United States Securities and Exchange Commission. 2006.
Form 10-K for the fiscal year ended September 30, 2).

tecnología, la relativa escasez de la penetración china y la estabilidad de los precios (Études & Analyses 2008, 1-31).

La presencia en un centenar largo de países, un equipo experimentado de servicios globales en la industria de las telecomunicaciones y una de las mayores organizaciones de investigación, tecnología e innovación daban a Alcatel-Lucent, junto a los Bell-Labs, un alcance nítidamente global[66].

La fusión ocurría en el marco de un mercado cambiante cuyos factores fundamentales eran de muy diversa índole. Se trataba de la presión sobre el precio de los productos debido a la aparición de nuevos proveedores –los chinos Huawei Technologies y ZTE–; la disminución del número de operadoras de Telecomunicaciones; el cambio en el diseño de las redes de Telecomunicaciones de la tecnología tradicional de conmutación de circuitos a los sistemas IP y la preferencia por dispositivos híbridos que soportan ambos tipos de redes (*TechNewsWorld,* 12 de septiembre de 2006).

Nada más presentarse ante la opinión pública, la compañía anunció recortes masivos de empleo –unos 9.000– en todo el mundo. Alcatel-Lucent registró una pérdida neta de 615 millones de euros en el último trimestre de 2006, frente al beneficio de 381 millones de euros realizado en 2005, resultados atribuidos genéricamente a la incertidumbre del cliente y a los retos de los reguladores. Esas graves pérdidas y una fuerte caída en las ventas en el último trimestre de 2006 llevaron a revisar al alza la cifra de recortes de personal hasta situarla en unos 13.000, más del 15% del total. En análisis más finos, Alcatel vinculó las reducciones de personal no solo a la fusión de 2006 sino también a la adquisición de las actividades de telefonía móvil de

---

[66] US Securities and Exchange Commission, Alcatel, 333-133.919, 4 de agosto de 2006; *The Wall Street Journal*, 23 de mayo de 2001. Implicaciones de la fusión de Alcatel y Lucent Technologies: Alcatel y Lucent, esta un símbolo de los años 90, habían concebido el acuerdo abortado de 2001 como una fusión de 22,8 billones de dólares entre pares pero fracasó por la indefinición del control que le correspondería a Alcatel (*NYT*, 30 de mayo de 2001); tras el fiasco, Alcatel tentó a Lucent Technologies para comprarle la división de fibra óptica (*Expansión*, 27 de abril de 2001). El dúo Alcatel-Lucent/Bell Labs era el proveedor líder mundial de tecnologías y conocimientos especializados xDSL, de tecnologías GPON FTTH y de CDMA/EV-DO, con una cuota de mercado mundial de más del 46% en 2007. Había desplegado sistemas comerciales de tercera generación (UMTS/HSPA y CDMA/EV-DO) para más de setenta operadoras en todo el mundo y proporcionado equipos y tecnología en más de 80 despliegues de FTTx en el 90% de las principales economías de banda ancha, incluyendo más de veinte operadores nacionales y más de sesenta municipios y servicios públicos. Colaboraba con más de veinticinco operadoras de Telecomunicaciones principales y competidoras en las transformaciones de red IP de extremo a extremo, entre muchos otros proyectos de transformación; había proporcionado plataformas en Australia y Nueva Zelanda en las que se entregaban más de 300 Terabytes diarios de datos (equivalentes a 60 millones de canciones), (Alcatel-Lucent 2009, 2).

tercera generación (UMTS) de Nortel, sin olvidar la adaptación del modelo de negocio impuesto por las necesidades de rápida evolución de sus clientes y el ajuste de algunas actividades a las perspectivas de mercado. Una mayor competencia en el sector, menores precios y saturación del mercado de la telefonía configuraban un futuro incierto para la empresa, que fue deslizándose hacia el abismo[67].

Esa lógica y especialmente la redefinición de la cartera de productos explicaban las razones de extender la reducción de empleos a la I+D. El anuncio ante los sindicatos de la decisión de concentrar la inversión en I+D en los EE. UU. y Asia se tradujo inmediatamente en la congelación de la contratación en Europa Occidental. La centralización de las estructuras financieras, de la cadena de suministro y de los sistemas de información engrosaría los recortes de empleo (Tabla 3)[68].

Tabla 3. Restructuración de Alcatel-Lucent en un grupo de países, 2007

País	Bélgica	Alemania	Holanda	Irlanda	España	Francia
Empleo en el país	1.844	5.000	700	260	1.250	12.500
Recorte de empleo en el país	140	770	140-180	70	310	1.468-1.500
% plantilla afectada	7.6	15.4	20	25.71	24.8	12

Fuente: Elaboración a partir de *European Restructuring Monitor Quarterly,* 1, spring 2007, 12-13.

[67] Así se analizaba la situación en un informe a los sindicatos franceses (*European Restructuring Monitor Quarterly*, 1, spring 2007, 10). Reveses acumulados por el grupo durante varios años: caída del 60% en el mercado de valores; división por dos de los negocios y empleos; falta de clarificación estratégica; proceso de fusión caótico; salidas masivas de ejecutivos, entre otros (*L'Observateur*, 1 de agosto de 2008). A ello se sumaron conflictos de gestión y culturales cruzados, que desembocaron en la dimisión del equipo directivo, compuesto por Patricia Russo y S. Tchuruk como CEO y Chairman, respectivamente. Las funciones ejecutivas de ambos cargos se entendían de manera diferente en la cultura empresarial francesa y norteamericana; Russo no dominaba el francés, algo imperdonable para el entorno galo (UKEssays 2018); *The New York Times* (30 de julio de 2008) habló de un «trans-Atlantic culture clash».

[68] *European Restructuring Monitor Quarterly,* 1, spring 2007; Alcatel: comunicato del Coordinamento nazionale: Action day, 15 de febrero de 2007. Paradójicamente, los especialistas presentaban a Alcatel-Lucent como una campeona de la gestión de la diversidad y de la variedad de modelos, firme defensora de que «las iniciativas de diversidad más eficaces surgen de las bases de la empresa» (Verbeke 2013, 43).

La Tabla 3 muestra la incidencia asimétrica de la reestructuración de plantillas en varios países europeos. En términos absolutos, la cifra más alta de supresión de puestos de trabajo corresponde a Francia pero en porcentajes se llevaban la palma España e Irlanda, países por lo demás muy distintos en cuanto a presencia de la empresa. Es evidente que la racionalidad económica así como la búsqueda de una reducción de costes y las economías de escala se impuso pero algo tuvieron que ver las peculiaridades del marco regulatorio, de la cultura de empresa o de la estructura del mercado nacional, por no hablar de la desigual fuerza con que golpeó la crisis a los diferentes subsectores. La tardía regulación europea de las relaciones sociales en la industria afectaba por igual a los países miembros pero algunas leyes protectoras del empleo –la ley Renault de 1997 en Bélgica, por ejemplo, que obligaba a procedimientos de información y concertación con sanciones– eran exclusivas de algunos.

Los ajustes de empleo formaban parte de un plan global de reducción de costes de 1.700 millones de euros en tres años. Con este método la compañía pretendía resolver duplicaciones en puestos de trabajo y racionalizaciones en la cartera de productos y soluciones, así como esfuerzos de eficiencia de costos en curso. El enfrentamiento estaba servido. Los sindicatos no reconocían la mala situación económica aducida como argumento por la empresa y atribuían a la fusión un subterfugio para aumentar los recortes de puestos de trabajo y deslocalizar la actividad a los países de bajos costes. Por ello, decidieron emprender acciones legales contra la empresa y exigieron información urgente y detallada sobre el plan de reestructuración[69].

Alcatel-Lucent mantuvo la estrategia de cesiones de plantas, empleados y activos de fabricación incluidos, como el caso de la belga de Geel pone en evidencia. Alcatel-Lucent se comprometió a mantener la actividad durante al menos tres años y a considerar a Geel TBP en sus planes de innovación en producto y en las instalaciones de producción piloto y de industrialización,

---

[69] *European Restructuring Monitor Quarterly,* 1, spring 2007, 10; Alcatel: comunicato del Coordinamento nazionale: Action day, 15 de febrero de 2007; diecisiete centrales sindicales de ocho países con centros del grupo Alcatel-Lucent impulsaron una campaña para pedir a los altos directivos de la empresa –Russo y Tchuruk– la renuncia a sus «paracaídas de oro» (bono de salida). La petición estaba respaldada por 5.969 firmas, el grueso de ellas procedente de Francia (3.198) y de Alemania (1.024), seguidas a distancia por Italia (761), Bélgica (365), España (350) y USA (271) (Secretarías Nacionales de FIM-CISL-UIL FIOM-CGIL UILM Coordinación Nacional de Alcatel Lucent Italia, 17 de septiembre de 2008).

incluso para la transferencia de tecnología a otras plantas de mayor enverga-dura[70].

La estrategia *fab-less* no representaba, pues, una política del pasado, en abierta contradicción con las declaraciones de la dirección de Alcatel en una reunión del European Committee for Information and Dialogue, un ente de diálogo social[71].

Gráfico 2. Evolución del empleo en la industria de
equipo de telecomunicación de la CEE

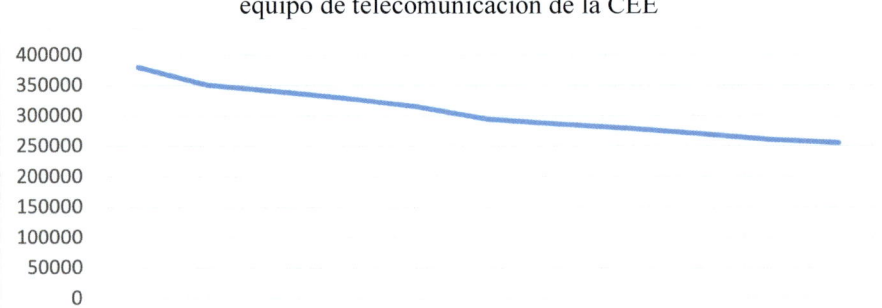

Fuente: Elaboración a partir de Eurostrategies ESTEL, Eurostat (Comext)

Una de las consecuencias más flagrantes de la reestructuración del sector fue la caída del empleo, que afectó al conjunto de la CEE (Gráfico 2). Para-lelamente, la productividad siguió una senda de ascenso en el conjunto de países de la CEE (Gráfico 3).

---

[70] *EE Times,* 2 de agosto de 2007; *Telecompaper*, 7 de febrero de 2007. Previamente, Al-catel-Lucent no había incluido las plantas belgas de Anvers y Geel en la restructuración. Alcatel era líder mundial en ADSL, especialidad que representaba el 65% de los ingresos de Alcatel Bell. La mitad de las líneas vendidas por Alcatel se fabricaban en Bélgica (*La Libre Belgique*, 30 de abril de 2003).

[71] Alcatel: comunicato del Coordinamento nazionale: Action day, 15 de febrero de 2007. Los sindicatos priorizaban el modo de abordar la movilidad geográfica y respondieron de diver-sas maneras a las amenazas de relocalización (Marginson y Meardi 2009, 26). Rudi Tho-maes, director general de Alcatel Bélgica, teorizaba que la movilidad del personal era un factor constante en la empresa y la versatilidad de las personas el activo más importante (*La Libre Belgique*, 3 de diciembre de 2001).

Gráfico 3. Evolución de la productividad en la industria de equipo de telecomunicación de la CEE

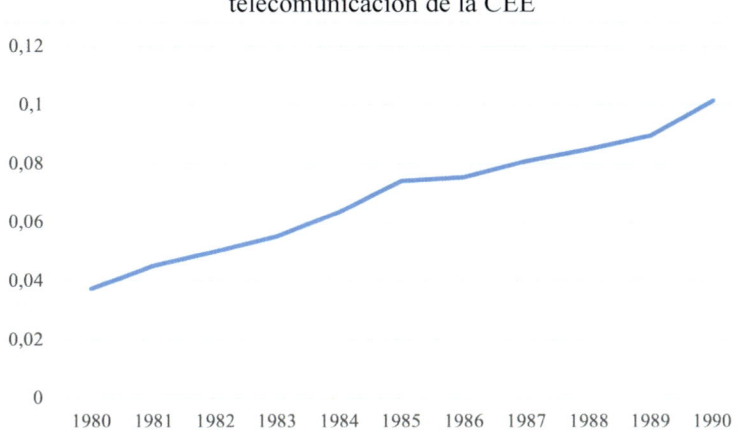

Fuente: Elaboración a partir de Eurostrategies ESTEL, Eurostat (Comext)

6. Conclusión

Este capítulo tiene como objetivo analizar uno de los aspectos más trascendentales de la economía actual –la tercerización– a partir de un estudio de caso en el que la vertiente narrativa cobra importancia capital. Ante la penuria de estudios de historia de la empresa, el capítulo reivindica la validez plena de un relato que recabe y sistematice la copiosa información dispersa. El capítulo ha indagado en algunos de los ejes del funcionamiento de la economía mundial durante los últimos años del siglo xx y los primeros del nuevo milenio. Más en concreto, se ha ocupado de dilucidar qué revelan los orígenes del *outsourcing* sobre los mecanismos de la economía mundial, la incidencia del comportamiento cíclico y el papel desempeñado por los agentes, con las multinacionales al frente y en el marco de una creciente movilidad de los factores de producción y cambio.

Las páginas abordan un ciclo largo de reestructuración de la industria de equipos de telecomunicación que llega hasta nuestros días. En un plano general, la evidencia aportada avala la complejidad del proceso de transformación de esa industria. En un primer nivel muy básico y en el marco de una penuria de datos agregados, el estudio aporta precisiones a la cronología de la reestructuración y del *outsourcing*, distinguiendo entre una fase inicial de reestructuración clásica y, dentro de ella, una primerísima reestructuración, y una ligada a la globalización. Se ha identificado asimismo una transición entre las dos fases, en la que Alcatel fue orientándose a la externalización de su producción. Episodios de deslocalización intraempresarial pero también de cesión completa o parcial de la actividad a un subcontratista se dan antes de la etapa divisoria ente las grandes etapas. Una tarea importante ha consistido en reconstruir de todas piezas el sistema productivo de Alcatel y la diversidad de formas de reestructuración de la empresa.

La investigación llevada a cabo confirma el estudio de la gran empresa multinacional como un instrumento eficaz para entender la remodelación de la industria de equipos de Telecomunicaciones. El caso de la multinacional francesa Alcatel, ejemplo por excelencia de empresa global por la amplitud de su implantación, la variedad de sus productos y la diversidad de las culturas empresariales, ha mostrado las características básicas de ese proceso, que implicó en sustancia el paso de la integración vertical a la externalización de la producción y de los campeones nacionales a las empresas globales.

La evidencia aportada aquí no dibuja una trayectoria lineal de este proceso; más bien revela posibles alternativas contempladas por los agentes y correcciones a las políticas emprendidas. De la misma forma, parece negar a la estrategia adoptada una homogeneidad y una perfecta definición desde el principio. Alcatel conjuga el *outsourcing* con desinversiones pero también con adquisiciones de empresas, alianzas estratégicas con socios locales, ya creando empresas conjuntas o adquiriendo las de estos. Por otra parte, esa transición de los mercados cautivos al *outsourcing* que se ha anunciado en el planteamiento inicial tolera asimismo la pervivencia de los primeros, como prueba el hecho que alguna de las filiales de Alcatel abastezca primordialmente a empresas dentro del propio grupo.

Tratándose de un proceso general, el estudio revela diferencias de impacto entre países, sea debido al papel desempeñado por alguno en el conjunto del grupo Alcatel –caso de Francia, sede central, y de Italia, considerada estratégica–, por la importancia de los productos de un determinado país para el conjunto o a la posición de los gobiernos y de los sindicatos.

Anexo 1. Organigrama de Alcatel CIT, hacia 1994

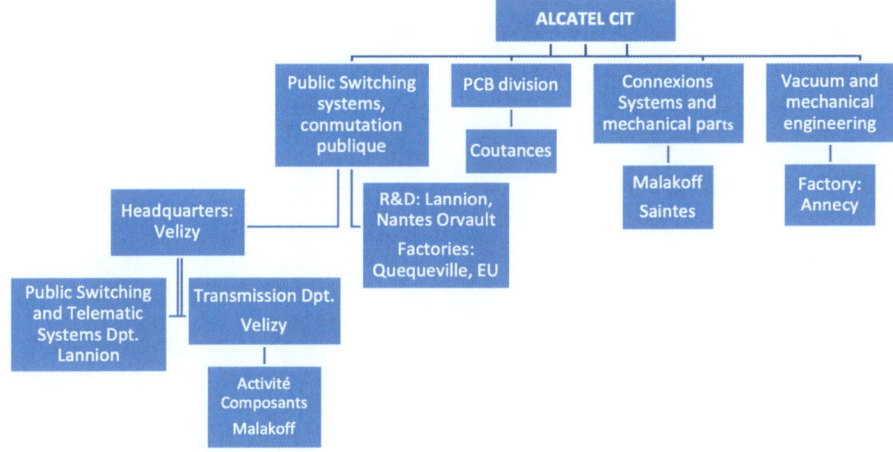

Fuente: Elaboración propia a partir de Wedgwood (2013), 26.

Anexo 2.

Alcatel: distribución de la mano de obra y las ventas por secciones, 2000 (%)

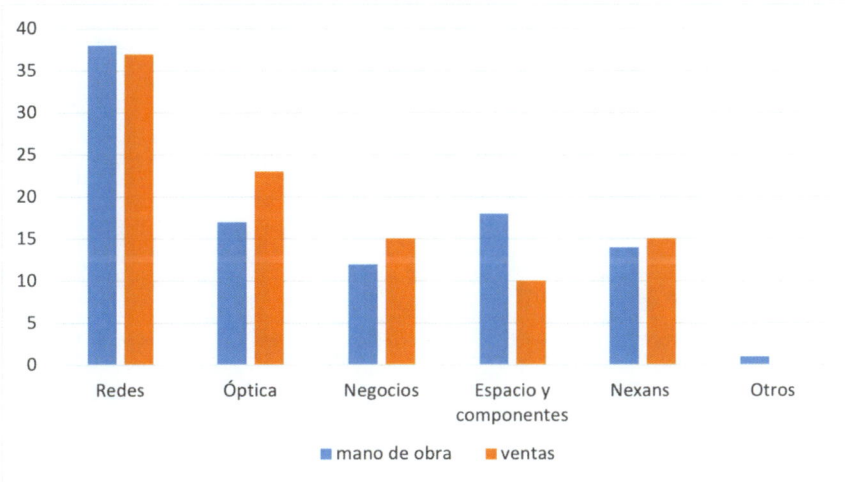

Fuente: Elaboración a partir de Alcatel (2008), p. 26.

Anexo 3

Alcatel: distribución geográfica de la mano de obra por países, 2000-2003

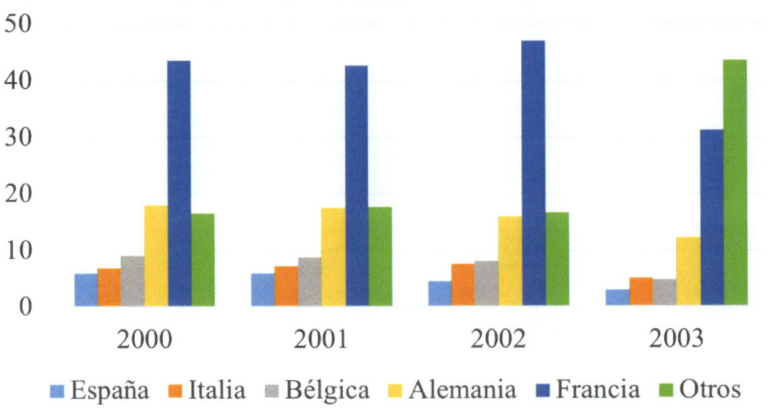

Fuente: Elaboración a partir de Alcatel (2008, 26).

Anexo 4

Mercado de Alcatel en el equipo de conmutación y *enrutamiento*
(% del valor máximo), 2004

	Equipo S/R	Conmutadores ATM/MPLS	Conmuta-dores TDM	OCS
Alcatel	[10-20]	[25-35]	[20-30]	[20-30]
Lucent	[0-10]	[0-10]	[0-10]	[20-30]
Cisco	[40-50]	[0-10]	0	0
Nortel	[10-20]	[40-50]	[0-10]	0
Juniper	[10-20]	0	0	0
Ericsson/ Marconi	0	[0-10]	[10-20]	[10-20]
Siemens	0	0	[60-70]	0
Ericsson	0	0	[0-10]	0
Huawei	0	0	0	[0-10]
Sycamore	0	0	0	[0-10]
Ciena	0	0	0	[0-10]

Fuente: Elaboración a partir de Case No COMP/M.4214 –
Alcatel/Lucent Technologies, Regulation (EC) No 139/2004,
Merger procedure, Bruselas, 24 de julio de 2006, 12.

Glosario

ADSL (Asymmetric Digital Subscriber Line): una nueva tecnología de módem que convertía las líneas telefónicas de par trenzado existentes en vías de acceso para comunicaciones de alta velocidad de vario tipo.

ADM (add-drop multiplexores) son dispositivos de agregación de antigua generación que acumulan los datos de una red de acceso a un flujo de datos mayor (para su transporte posterior a la red central) y viceversa.

Ancho de banda es una medida de la capacidad del canal de comunicación para transportar y encaminar la información a través de una red.

ATM: conmutadores que permitían una transmisión de voz y datos a alta velocidad y capacidades de calidad de servicio. A principios de los años noventa, las redes basadas en ATM empezaron a ser sustituidas por redes de transporte basadas en IP/Ethernet.

Dispositivos de borde óptico (optical edge devices, OED) son dispositivos de agregación de nueva generación que superan al ADM por la posibilidad de interconectar y mapear el tráfico de datos nativos, como Ethernet, ATM, etc., con los estándares de transmisión tradicionales.

SONET (Synchronous Optical Network o Red Óptica Síncrona) es el estándar principal en América del Norte, mientras que SDH (Synchronous Digital Hierarchy o Jerarquía Digital Síncrona) lo es en regiones fuera de América del Norte, incluyendo Europa.

WDM (o DWDM, Dense wavelength division multiplexers) facilita el transporte de datos a través de múltiples longitudes de onda en un solo cable de fibra óptica entre dos puntos, utilizando una tecnología láser.

Fuentes primarias

Archives de l'Assemblée Nationale, Francia.
Archives Nationales, Francia.
Archives du Sénat, Francia.
Archivo del Congreso de los Diputados, Madrid.
Telefónica, Madrid.

Hemeroteca

ABC, España.
AHCIET, Revista de Telecomunicaciones, España.
BBC News
Computer Business Review
Computerworld
Electronics Production
El País, España.
La Libre Belgique, Bélgica.
La Repubblica, Italia.
Le Monde, Francia.
Libération, Francia.
New York Times, USA.
The Washington Post, USA.
Dallas Business Journal, USA.

Referencias

Alcatel. 2008. *Sustainable development report 2004.*
Alcatel. 1998. Alcatel 1000 S12. París: Alcatel.
Alcatel-Lucent. 2009. *Submission to Commerce Commission Discussion Paper on Next Generation Networks,* febrero.
Alcatel Optronics. 2001. *Financial report* 2001, Alcatel.
Alcatel SESA. 1991. *Memoria Anual 1991.* Madrid: Alcatel SESA.
Amatori, Franco y Colli, Andrea. 2013. *Business History: Complexities and Comparisons.* Londres: Routledge.
Andreff, Wladimir. 2009. «Outsourcing in the new strategy of multinational companies: foreign investment, international subcontracting and production relocation». *Papeles de Europa,* 18, 5-34.
Anonym. 2012. *Diversification Strategies of Nokia.* Munich: GRIN Verlag.
Arthuis, Jean. 1993. *Rapport d'information sur l'incidence économique et fiscale des délocalisations hors du territoire national des activités industrielles et de service, Rapport à la commission des Finances du Sénat,* 337, 4 de junio.

Atkinson, Robert D. 2004. *Understanding the Offshoring Challenge*. Washington: Progressive Policy Institute.

Baskoy, Tuna. 2008. *The Political Economy of European Union Competition Policy: A Case Study of the Telecommunications Industry*. Nueva York: Routledge.

Beaujolin-Bellet, Rachel y Issaverdens, Olivier. 2006. *Restructuration de la direction industrielle du site d'Alcatel Business System à Illkirch-Graffenstaden (Alsace, France)*. Reims: MIRE.

Baumol, William A. et al. 2003. *Downsizing in America: Reality, Causes, and Consequences*. Nueva York: Russell Sage Foundation Press.

Bhagwati, Jagdish, Panagariya, Arvind y Srinivasan, T.N. 2004. «The Muddles over Outsourcing», *Journal of Economic Perspectives,* vol. 18, n°.4: 93-114.

Brenner, Robert. 2003. *The Boom and the Bubble: The US in the World Economy*. Londres-Nueva York: Verso.

Bresciani, Stefano y Ferraris, Alberto. 2012. *Imprese multinazionali. Innovazione e scelte localizzative*. Santarcangelo di Romagna: Maggioli Editore.

Burnier, Michel. 2002. «La empresa sin fábricas, entrevista de Michel Le Doaré, responsable sindical de Alcatel», *TERMINAL*, 87, 5-7.

Butcher, Arona et al. 1991. *Global Competitiveness of U.S. Advanced-technology Manufacturing Industries: Communications Technology and Equipment*. Washington: U.S. International Trade Commission.

Calvo, *Ángel.* 2016. «Innovar en tiempos difíciles. Empresas bajo presión en la Guerra Fría», *Harvard Deusto Business Research*, 5, n°.: 60-85.

Calvo, *Ángel.* 2017. «Multinacionales, Estado y empresa semipública en la industria de tecnología avanzada durante la década de 1980», *Investigaciones de Historia Económica – Economic History Research*, 13, n°.1:51-62.

Calvo, *Ángel.* 2019. «World Telecommunications equipment industry from the National champions to outsourcing: the case of Alcatel», *The International Journal of Business Management and Technology*, vol. 3, Issue 6, November–December, 130-152. http://www.theijbmt.com/archive/0930/557514347.pdf

Canalejo, Miguel. 2020. «Internacionalización de las industrias de Telecomunicación». En *Internacionalización de las industrias de Telecomunicación*, Naeve, I. et al., Madrid: Foro Histórico Telecomunicaciones, COIT-AEIT.

Carr, Robert. 1998. *Telecommunications equipment: U.S. performance in selected major markets*, Office of Industries U.S. International Trade Commission, Publication 3150, December.

Carroué, Laurent. 2004-2005. «Le mythe des entreprises sans usine: les sous-traitants de l'électronique en pleine mondialisation. *Cahiers Nantais* 62-63, 131-136.

Carroué, Laurent et al. *2005. La mondialisation: Genèse, acteurs et enjeux.* Rosny-sous-Bois: Bréal.

Casson, Mark. 1996. *The Theory of the Firm*. Cheltenham: Edward Elgar.

Cirillo, Valeria, Guarascio, Dario y Pianta, Mario. 2014. *Will Europe's industry survive the crisis? Competitiveness, employment and the need for an industrial policy.* Urbino: Università degli Studi.

Cisco Systems. 2001. *Annual report pursuant to section 13 or 15,d) of the securities exchange act of 1934 for the fiscal year ended july 30 2011,* Commission file 0-18225.

Clifton, Judith; Pierre Lanthier y Schröter, Harm (ed.). 2014. *The Economic and Social Regulation of Public Utilities: An International History*. Londres: Routledge.

Colli, Andrea, Mariotti, Sergio y Piscitello, Lucia. 2014. «Governments as strategists in designing global players: The case of European utilities». *Journal of European Public Policy,* 21, 4, 487-508.

Comisión de Regulación de Telecomunicaciones. 2000. *El sector de las Telecomunicaciones en Colombia, en la década de los 90s*. Bogotá: CRT.

Commission of the European Communities. 1992. «The European Telecommunications equipment industry. The state of play, issues at stake and proposals for action». SEC, 92, 1.049 final, Bruselas, 15 de julio.

Commission of the European Communities. 1990. *Green Paper on the Development of the Common Market for Telecom Equipment*. Boston MA: Information Gatekeepers.

Commission of the European Communities. 1983. *Prospects for the development of new policies: Research and development, energy and new technologies.* Luxemburgo: Office for Official Publications of the European Communities.

Cortada, James W. 2009. *How Societies Embrace Information Technology: Lessons for Management and the Rest of Us*. Hoboken NJ: Wiley.

Cortada, James W. 2016. *The Computer in the United States: From Laboratory to Market, 1930-60.* Abingdon: Routledge.

Cortés, Claudia J. y Paredes, Juan C. 2013. *Análisis jurisprudencial de decisiones arbitrales en materia contencioso administrativa*. Bogotá: Universidad de la Sabana.

Cooke, Philip. 2015. *Towards Global Localization*. Londres: Routledge.

Coucke, Kristien et al. 2007. «Employee layoff under different modes of restructuring: exit, downsizing or relocation». *Industrial and Corporate Change*, vol. 16, Issue 2, 1 abril, 161–182.

Crandall, Robert W. y Flamm, Kenneth (eds.) 1989. *Changing the Rules: Technological Change, International Competition, and Regulation in Communications.* Washington: Brookings Institution Press.

Darmon, Jacques. 2010. «Modalités et portée de la sortie du téléphone de Thomson». *Entreprises et histoire*, 61, n°.4 : 108-112.

Daviet, Sylvie. 2000. «Émergence et structuration d'une multinationale européenne du semi-conducteur: le cas de ST Microelectronics». *Annales de Géographie*, 612, 132-151.

Dörrenbächer, Chistoph. 2000. «Between global market constraints and national dependencies: the internationalization of the world's leading Telecommunications equipment suppliers». *Transnational Corporations,* 9, 3, UNCTAD.

Dörrenbächer, Chistoph y Wortmann, Michael. 1994. «Multinational companies in the EU and European Works Councils», *Intereconomics, Nomos Verlagsgesellschaft*, Baden-Baden, vol. 29, 4, 199-206.

Dosi, Giovanni. 2000. *Innovation, Organization and Economic Dynamics: Selected Essays*, Cheltenham: Edward Elgar.

Ekberg, Espen y Lange, Even. 2014. «Business history and economic globalisation». *Business History*, vol. 56, Issue 1, 69-81.

Emiroğlu, Ulaş. 2003. «Catch-up with Generative State: Lessons from Chinese Telecom Equipment Industry». STPS-WP_15/03, Ankara: METU-STPS.

Eurofound. 2008. *Report 2007. Restructuring and employment in the EU: The impact of globalisation.* Dublín: European Restructuring Monitor.

Eurofound. 2009. *ERM case studies: Employment impact of relocation of multinational companies across the EU.* Dublín: European Restructuring Monitor.

European Commission, 1997. *1996 Single Market Review.* Luxemburgo: Office for Official Publications of the European Communities.

European Communities. 1992. *Panorama of EC industry Statistical supplement 1992. Latest information on manufacturing and service industries in the European Community.* Luxemburgo: Office for Official Publications of the European Communities.

European Techno-Economic Policy Support. 2007. *Delocalisation of EU Industry. Delocalisation and the challenge of structural adjustment. A review of policy options*. Bruselas: The Network for European Techno-Economic Policy Support ETEPS AISBL.

Forester, Tom. 1987. *High-tech Society: The Story of the Information Technology Revolution*. Cambridge MA: MIT Press.

Fridenson, Patrick. 1992. «De la diversification au recentrage: le groupe Thomson (1976-1989)». *Entreprises et histoire*, abril, 26-41.

Funk, Jeffrey L. 2002. *Global Competition Between and Within Standards: The Case of Mobile Phones*. Houndsmille: Palgrave.

Galgoczi, Béla, Keune, Maarten y Watt, Andrew. 2008. *Jobs on the Move: An Analytical Approach to Relocation and Its Impact on Employment.* Bruselas: Peter Lang.

Gazier, Bernard y Bruggeman, Frédéric. (eds.). 2008. *Restructuring Work and Employment in Europe: Managing Change in an Era of Globalisation.* Cheltenham: Edward Elgar.

Gelles, David. 2022. *The Man Who Broke Capitalism*. Nueva York: Simon and Schuster.

Gibson, Stuart. 1995. *Alcatel Alsthom: a strategic analysis.* Nueva York: Northern Business Information.

Grignon, Francis. 2004. *Délocalisations: pour un néo-colbertisme européen*, Rapport d'information No 374 fait au nom de la Commission des Affaires économiques, 23 de junio.

Griset, Pascal y Fridenson, Patrick. 2013 *Entreprises de haute technologie, État et souveraineté depuis 1945*. París: Institut de la gestion publique et du développement économique.

Guieysse, Jean A. 1986. «L'industrialisation en Île-de-France depuis 1965». *Villes en parallèle*, n°.11: 134-161.

Hamilton, Leslie y Webster, Philip. 2012. *The International Business Environment.* Oxford: OUP.

Hancké, Bob. 2002. *Large Firms and Institutional Change: Industrial Renewal and Economic Restructuring in France*. Nueva York: Oxford University Press.

Heidenreich, Martin. 2012. *Innovation and Institutional Embeddedness of Multinational Companies*. Cheltenham: Edward Elgar.

Herrera, Hernán. 2008. «Innovación e incumbent failure: una ilustración en la industria de las Telecomunicaciones en Colombia». *Cuadernos de Administración*, vol. 21, 37, enero-junio, 161-183.

Hulsink, Willem. 2012. *Privatisation and Liberalisation in European Telecommunications: Comparing Britain, the Netherlands and France*. Londres: Routledge.

IGI Consulting. 1996. *ATM Product Directory.* Boston MA: Information Gatekeepers.

Information Gatekeepers. 1995. *China Telecom 2000Switching Market and Opportunities in China.* Vol. 3, Boston MA: Information Gatekeepers.

ITU. 2003. *The evolution to 3G mobile – Status report.* Ginebra: ITU.

Iwens, Jean-Luc. 1984. *Évolution récente de 3 sociétés: ATT. CIT_Alcatel, Ericsson.* Bruselas: GRESEA.

Johnson, Chalmers. 1984. *The Industrial Policy Debate.* San Francisco CA: ICS Press.

Keneley, Monica. 2013. «Does Organizational Heritage Matter in the Development of Offshore Markets? The Case of Australian Life Insurers». *Business History Review*, vol. 87, n.º 2, Summer, 255-277.

Kirby, Peadar y Carmody, Padraig. 2013. *The Legacy of Ireland's Economic Expansion: Geographies of the Celtic Tiger.* Londres-Nueva York: Routledge.

Laffitte, Pierre y Trégouët, René. 2001. *Les conséquences de l'évolution scientifique et technique dans le secteur des télécommunications,* Rapport No 159, 20 de diciembre.

Leckey, Andrew. 2002. *The Best Business Stories of the Year.* Nueva York: Vintage Books.

Li, Jizhen y Li, Xing. 2009. *Cultural Differences and Process Adaption in International R&D Project Management: The Case of Alcatel-Lucent China Research Technology Center.* Aalborg: Institut for Historie, Internationale Studier og Samfundsforhold.

Faure, Pascal et al. 2007. *Rapport d'étape du groupe de travail sur les perspectives du secteur des télécommunications en France et en Europe,* 16 de abril.

Lüthje, Boy et al. 2013. *From Silicon Valley to Shenzhen: Global Production and Work in the IT Industry.* Lanham: Rowman & Littlefield.

Malsan, Sylvie. 2001. *Filles d'Alcatel: histoire d'une reconversion industrielle.* Toulouse: Octarès.

Maly, Jiri y Palter, Robert N. 2002. «Restating the value of capital light». *McKinsey on Finance*, vol. 5, 1-5.

Mankiw, N. Gregory y Swagel, Phillip L. 2006. «The Politics and Economics of Offshore Outsourcing», *NBER Working Paper* N°. 12398, julio. https://ssrn.com/abstract=921564

Marginson, Paul y Meardi, Guglielmo. 2009. *Multinational companies and collective bargaining.* Dublín: Eurofound.

Maricourt, Thierry. 2006. *Ils ont bossé– et puis après?: Alcatel-Illkirch, entreprise high-tech et restructurations.* París: Syllepse.

Marseille, Jacques. (dir.) 1992. *Alcatel Alsthom. Histoire de la Compagnie Générale d'Électricité.* París: Larousse.

McIvor, Ronan. 2003. «Outsourcing: Insights from the Telecommunications industry». *Supply Chain Management*, 8(4), octubre, 380-394.

Micron Electronics. 1998. *Quarterly report pursuant to section 13 or 15,d) of the securities exchange act of 1934, for the quarterly period ended February 26*, 1-10658.

Migaud, Didier. 2000. *Rapport*, Assemblée Nationale, onzième législature, 2.624, 12 de octubre.

Miller, Michael. 1990. *CGE Alcatel: a strategic analysis.* Nueva York: Northern Business Information.

Mouline, Aziz y Hafsi, Taieb. 2008. «Adaptation stratégique et mondialisation: Le cas d'Alcatel-Lucent Technologies». *Gestion*, 1, vol. 33, 27-37.

Mtar, Monia. 2001. *French multinationals' international strategy. National Identity Under the Effect of Globalisation.* Coventry: The University of Warwick.

Niosi, Jorge y Tschang, F. Ted. 2009. «The strategies of Chinese and Indian software multinationals: implications for internationalization theory», *Industrial and Corporate Change*, vol. 18, n°.2: 269-294.

Noam, Eli M. 1998. *Telecommunications in Latin America.* Nueva York-Oxford: Oxford University Press.

Nokia. 1995. *Annual Report 1995.*

Nordick, Bill. «Alcatel-Lucent Merger Failure: A Critical Analysis», *Research Methodology,* https://research-methodology.net/Alcatel-lucent-merger-failure-a-critical-analysis/

Observatorio industrial de electrónica, tecnologías de la información y Telecomunicaciones. 2008. *Las políticas sectoriales y su repercusión en la reorganización del sector eTIC.* Madrid: CCOO.

OECD. 2000. *The service economy.* París: OECD.

OECD. 2002. *Competition and regulation issues in Telecommunications.* París: Directorate for financial, fiscal and enterprise affairs competition committee.

OECD. 2007a. *Staying Competitive in the Global Economy. Moving up the value chain.* París: OECD.

OECD. 2007b. *Reviews of Regional Innovation Globalisation and Regional Economies. Can OECD Regions Compete in Global Industries?* París: OECD.

Oshri, Ilan et al. 2009. *The Handbook of Global Outsourcing and Offshoring.* Nueva York: Palgrave.

OTA Advisory Group. 1993. *U. S. Telecommunications Services in Europe.* Darby PA: DIANE.

Perchard, Andrew et al. 2014. *Clio in the business school: historical approaches in strategy, international business, entrepreneurship and quantitative research.* Rotterdam: 30th EGOS Colloquium.

Petersson, Niels P. 2018. «Managing a 'People Business' in Times of Uncertainty: Human Resources Strategy at Ocean Transport & Trading in the 1970s», *Enterprise & Society,* vol. 19, Issue 1, marzo, 88-123.

Pinney, Benjamin W. 2002. «Projects, Management, and Protean Times: Engineering Enterprise in the United States, 1870–1960», *Enterprise & Society*, vol. 3, Issue 4, diciembre, 620-626.

Plunkett, Jack W. 2007. *Plunkett's Outsourcing And Offshoring Industry Almanac 2008.* Houston TX: Plunkett Research.

Quatrepoint, Jean-Michel. 2015. *Alstom, scandale d'État.* París: Fayard.

Ripoll, Fabrice. 2004. «Cherbourg, ville-arsenal en crise». *Norois*, 190, 67-84.

Roy, Tirthankar. 2018. *A Business History of India: Enterprise and the Emergence of Capitalism from 1700.* Cambridge: Cambridge University Press.

Rugman, Alan y D'Cruz, Joseph R. 2003. *Multinationals as Flagship Firms: Regional Business Networks.* Oxford: Oxford University Press.

Saint-Étienne, Christian. 2013. *France: état d'urgence: Une stratégie pour demain.* París: Odile Jacob.

Samuelson, Paul A. 2004. «Where Ricardo and Mill Rebut and Confirm Arguments of Mainstream Economists Supporting Globalization», *Journal of Economic Perspectives*, vol. 18, 3, Summer, 135-146.

Sanmina-SCI. 2002. *Annual report pursuant to section 13 or 15,d) of the securities exchange act of 1934, for the fiscal year ended September 28.*

Sarma, Sunny Li y Sun, Sumita. 2017. «The genesis of fabless business model: Institutional entrepreneurs in an adaptive ecosystem», *Asia Pacific Journal of Management*, vol. 34, n°.3: 587-617.

Schniederjans, Marc J. et al. 2006. *Outsourcing and insourcing in an international context*. M. E. Armonk NJ: Sharpe.

Slaughter, Matthew J. 2000. «Production Transfer Within Multinational Enterprises and American Wages». *Journal of International Economics*, abril, 449-472.

Storrie, Donald. 2006. *ERM Report 2006 – Restructuring and employment in the EU: Concepts, measurement and evidence*. Dublín: ERM.

Stroux, Sigrid. 2004. *US and EC Oligopoly Control.* La Haya: Kluwer Law International.

Suard, Pierre. 2002. *L'Envol Saboté d'Alcatel Alsthom*. París: Éditions France Empire.

Suard, Pierre. 1993. «Strategy for Telecommunications equipment suppliers». *Electrical Communication*, 66, 210.

Sutton, John. 2001. *Technology and Market Structure: Theory and History*. Cambridge MA: MIT Press.

Szapiro, Marina y De Souza, Honorio. 2000. «Technological Capability in the Telecommunications Industry in Brazil: Development and Impacts of the Structural Reform in the 90s». *4th International Conference on Technology Policy and Innovation,* Curitiba, August 28-31.

Tan, Felix B. 2008. *Global information technologies: concepts, methodologies, tools and* applications, vol. 3. Hershey: IGI Global.

Teece, David J. 1998. *Economic Performance and the Theory of the Firm*. Cheltenham: Edward Elgar.

Tejada, María Teresa. 1996. *Las Telecomunicaciones y su evolución en Colombia.* Bogotá: Tercer Mundo.

Tribunal Arbitral de Empresa Nacional de Telecomunicaciones (Telecom). 2002. vs. Alcatel España S.A. Sucursal Colombia, Alcatel SESA Technical Services S.A. y Telealca S.A., Bogotá, D.C., 21 de mayo.

UK Essays. 2018. «The Alcatel Lucent Merger What went wrong? ». noviembre, https://www.ukessays.com/essays/management/the-Alcatel-lucent-merger-what-went-wrong-management-essay.php?vref=1.

United Nations Conference on Trade and Development. 1997. *World Investment Report 1997. Transnational Corporations, Market Structure and Competition Policy.* Nueva York y Ginebra: United Nations.

U.S. Department of Commerce. 1989. *A Guide to Telecommunications Markets in Latin America*, vol. 61. Washington: U.S. Department of Commerce, International Trade Administration.

Vagadia, Bharat. 2011. *Strategic Outsourcing: The Alchemy to Business Transformation in a Globally Converged World.* Londres: Springer.

Verbeke, Alain. 2013. *International Business Strategy.* Cambridge: CUP.

Wedgwood, C. G. 2013. *European Electronics Directory 1994: Systems and Applications.* Londres: Elsevier.

Wilson, John et al. ed. 2016. *The Routledge Companion to Business History*. Abingdon Ox: Routledge.

III. TELECOMUNICACIONES, ELECTRÓNICA E INFORMÁTICA EN LA ERA DIGITAL

1. Una apuesta tecnológica autóctona en un mercado oligopólico: Amper, 1980-2003

1. Introducción

Se cuentan por decenas las obras que analizan el auge y caída de las empresas, preferentemente las multinacionales, sean las de un sector concreto o tomadas individualmente[1]. Por su parte, desde sus orígenes, la historia económica ha prestado atención sostenida a averiguar las razones del auge y declive de las naciones[2]. El debate académico y su corolario de orientación para los responsables políticos tienen plena vigencia hoy en día no solamente para los países en desarrollo sino también para aquellos otros económicamente avanzados pero tecnológicamente dependientes y, por tanto, lastrados en su crecimiento por tal carencia, caso de España[3]. En definitiva, de nuevo nos situamos en el meollo del debate sobre la intersección entre tecnología, competitividad y papel de las multinacionales en la economía mundial[4].

Por lo que se refiere a España, predominantemente receptora de tecnología, como detalla otro capítulo de esta obra, algunos especialistas han explorado el comportamiento de la empresa industrial del país en esos espacios comprendidos entre el Estado nación y las multinacionales y en un contexto

---

[1]   Tres obras claves: Fox (1987); Temin y Galambos (1987); Toninelli (ed.) (2000). Para el conjunto del capítulo, véase Calvo (2020b), 1-53.

[2]   Dos obras significativas, un tanto separadas en el tiempo: son Landes (1969); Olson (1982).

[3]   Hoekman y Javorcik (2006) recogen a satisfacción la polémica.

[4]   De acuerdo con las consideraciones de Dunning (2013, 131) en su clasificación de un conjunto de países avanzados, España sería un país con una comunidad científica de baja intensidad, con un tamaño de mercado medio, con nivel de precios bajo y con baja cota de estímulo para maximizar la I+D local.

de creciente integración económica, de rápida transición a economías abiertas sometidos y de globalización. Pues bien, estos estudios han marginado en buena medida las empresas de telecomunicaciones (Binda 2005, 117-154 y 2019, 335-365)[5].

Con el propósito de profundizar y mejorar la comprensión de la problemática, este capítulo explora las vías de supervivencia de una empresa de la industria de las telecomunicaciones, surgida a partir de tecnología autóctona, en un contexto de creciente liberalización e integración del mercado, a la vez que de competencia oligopólica entre los proveedores[6]. Metodológicamente, presenta un enfoque de estudio de caso, centrado en la peripecia de Amper, no muy conocida en su conjunto aunque sí repetidamente señalada en hechos aislados. El relato está trabado por un trabajo sistemático de hemeroteca y a partir de la Comisión Nacional del Mercado de Valores (CNMV), remedo de las Actas del Consejo de Administración, no disponibles hasta el momento. La exploración más profunda de la trayectoria se basa en fuentes variadas, entre las que sobresalen las propias de Amper. El texto se estructura en cuatro grandes apartados, que incluyen los factores de la expansión de Amper, la asociación estratégica con multinacionales, la internacionalización de la empresa en sus diversas facetas y las desinversiones y segregaciones.

Parecen pertinentes unas puntualizaciones preliminares. La primera atañe a la idiosincrasia del sector de las TICs, compuesto por dos subsectores económicos diferentes e interrelacionados: la prestación de servicios y la oferta de productos industriales. Uno y otro se hallaban en constante cambio debido a la incesante transformación de la prestación de servicios, impulsada por la liberalización del mercado, los cambios en la tecnología de las redes y la demanda de nuevos servicios. La profundidad y virulencia del cambio tecnológico, unida a la globalización, empujaron a los fabricantes a una nueva frontera en que la cadena de valor –la *filière*, en terminología preferida por otros– se amplió enormemente, al englobar todo el equipo, soluciones y dispositivos relacionados con las telecomunicaciones. A los característicos

---

[5]   La problemática se enmarca en el debate más amplio sobre el papel de las multinacionales, recogido por Puig y Álvaro-Moya (2016). En un ámbito más amplio, el sector de las Tecnologías de la Información y la Comunicación (TICs), sí existen estudios, entre los que destacan los de Holl y Rama (2019); Molero y Rama (2013). 73-83; Rama, Ferguson y Melero (2003) y Suárez-Villa y Rama (1996).

[6]   En el plano microeconómico, la competitividad radica en la capacidad de las empresas para producir de manera constante y rentable bienes sujetos a los requisitos de un mercado abierto en términos de precio y calidad (European Communities. European Commission 2003, 1-2).

de una red telefónica, como en los primeros días, se añadió una gama mucho más amplia con dispositivos más sofisticados y características más integradas (Lera 2000, 413-437; Pasadilla y Low (eds.) 2016, 481-482)[7]. El subsector que nos ocupa pertenece a la industria de alta tecnología, el conjunto de expansión más rápida dentro de la industria en general. En este contexto, conviene tener presente que Amper desplegaba su actividad en un entorno altamente competitivo, que requería importantes recursos humanos, materiales, técnicos y financieros. La adjudicación de nuevos proyectos y contratos exigía como factores clave experiencia y recursos materiales, técnicos y financieros, así como el conocimiento de cada mercado local. Existía un riesgo de perder nuevas oportunidades o de verse forzado a aceptar proyectos con una rentabilidad inferior a la obtenida en el pasado. Por otra parte, la estrategia innovadora de Amper se dirigía al diseño de soluciones tecnológicas diferenciadoras que la exponían a riesgos inherentes al cambio rápido y constante de las tecnologías aplicadas, en constante perfeccionamiento y de creciente complejidad (Amper 2018, 21).

La segunda aclaración alude al contexto de rápido e intenso cambio tecnológico como telón de fondo de lo narrado. Más específicamente, nos referimos a la transición de la electromecánica a la electrónica, *general purpose technology* ahorradora de mano de obra y de costes en general, y, como consecuencia, a una obsolescencia acelerada de los productos (World Institute for Development Economics Research 2002, 84).

En un recorrido sucinto, Amper centra su sobrado medio siglo de historia en siete hitos que comprenden desde su creación como Amper Radio S.L. hasta la reciente toma de participación mayoritaria en Proes Consultores, S.A. (https://www.grupoAmper.com/; CNMV, 285.799, 9/1/2020). Desde el punto de vista sectorial, uno de los hitos de Amper es su conversión en una empresa especializada en la defensa y la seguridad (United States Committee on Governmental Affairs 1991, 203; Fabrie 1987).

Los efectos positivos de la demanda de la operadora monopolista semipública Compañía Telefónica Nacional de España (CTNE) en productos variados se plasmaron en la creación –Telettra España, Citesa, Intelsa y Marconi Española S. A. (MESA)– o integración –Amper Radio– de una serie de empresas especializadas. Todas son piezas claves del grupo industrial de CTNE, que, añadidas a la histórica Standard Eléctrica de la multinacional

---

[7]   Además de las telecomunicaciones, la cadena de la electrónica incluía una decena de sectores, entre ellos los componentes electrónicos, las industrias de *software* y la electrónica de consumo y profesional (Bruce, Cunard y Director 2014, 513).

norteamericana IT&T, finalizarían por consolidar el sector de equipos de telecomunicación en España. A más largo plazo, sin embargo, el grupo español de IT&T no escapó a la reconversión impuesta por el importante cambio tecnológico en la fabricación de equipos telefónicos, el exceso de mano de obra y la difícil adaptación de una parte de la misma a las exigencias de los nuevos procesos de fabricación con alto contenido tecnológico, propios de la electrónica de alta integración (Calvo 2014, 124 y 142; Standard Eléctrica 1983 y 1987)[8].

2. La solución autóctona: de la independencia a la integración vertical

La protagonista de este relato fue fundada en 1956 con el nombre de Amper Radio S.L. por el ingeniero de telecomunicaciones Antonio Peral con el propósito de fabricar dispositivos de intercomunicación a muy corta distancia, porteros automáticos para mayor precisión. La nueva empresa fue creciendo en tamaño, cambió de naturaleza jurídica al adoptar el nombre de Amper S.A. y, en pocos años, se convirtió en instrumento para conquistar el único gran cliente del mercado español de telecomunicaciones de la época, la operadora monopolista CTNE, que acabó comprando la empresa y encomendarle funciones cruciales (CTNE 1983, 56; CTNE 1986, 36; Calvo 2014, 242-243; Torres 2017; Foro Histórico de las Telecomunicaciones)[9].

Al cumplirse el tercer quinquenio de su creación, Amper Radio S.L. perdió su condición de empresa familiar para convertirse en una sociedad anónima con el nombre de Amper S.A. El cambio de nombre se acompañaba de la ampliación del objeto social con un amplio abanico de actividades –producción, comercialización y gestión– en campos diversos – equipos, componentes y sistemas de telecomunicación y electrónica–, simiente de su futura estructura corporativa[10].

A poco de finalizar los años 70, Amper S.A. se afianzó como gran empresa al sobrepasar el medio millar de trabajadores (*La Vanguardia*, 18 de

---

[8]   Ley 27/1984, de 26 de julio, sobre reconversión y reindustrialización.

[9]   Algunos protagonistas (Juan Mulet Melià, Conversación con el autor, 16 de mayo de 2013) consideran a Peral una persona que «nació en un momento equivocado y en un país equivocado».

[10] Abarcaban la producción, comercialización y gestión en campos diferentes –sistemas, equipos y componentes de telecomunicación y electrónica– (Fundesco 1991, 438; Grupo Amper 2002, 44).

mayo de 1977, 6). En la razón de salvaguardar una casa con una excepcional capacidad tecnológica y cuya supervivencia estaba amenazada se escudó Telefónica en 1983 para adquirir Amper S. A., que emprendió una profunda reestructuración (CTNE 1983, 56; Fundesco 1991, 438; Velázquez-Gaztelu 1995, 13.625)[11].

Conviene anunciar desde ahora que matriz y filial mantuvieron una relación marcada por las prioridades cambiantes que impuso la primera. Con todo, un pequeño pero significativo resquicio permitió a la segunda negociar aspectos determinados, entre ellos uno de relieve –las prioridades en productos– y otro de interés –los plazos del contrato de abastecimiento– como se verá. En el contexto de su propósito de racionalizar el grupo, a veces no coincidentes con los gubernamentales, la CTNE reservaba a Amper un puesto destacado como cabeza de su grupo industrial y pieza clave de un grupo fundamentalmente español (CTNE 1986, 36).

Efectivamente, con la reestructuración emprendida por la operadora monopolista Amper se situó en cabeza de un grupo diversificado de empresas de electrónica y equipos terminales, activo también en las telecomunicaciones públicas (CTNE 1987, 32)[12]. La CTNE la propulsó con una capitalización, un plan de compras espectacular y una capacitación tecnológica con trasvase de I+D propia.

Amper basó su estrategia de crecimiento en tres palancas esenciales. La primera consistió en la salida al mercado de capitales. Dos años después de dar acceso al cuarteto de los grandes bancos – Español de Crédito (Banesto), Central, Bilbao e Hispano– logró una inusitada expansión tras sacar un 68% de sus acciones a cotización en bolsa (*El País*, 7 de octubre de 1983; Amper 2018, 21)[13]. En los tres primeros años que siguieron a la adquisición por CTNE, Amper consiguió revertir una situación de pérdidas cuantiosas y, a la vez, lograr tanto un elevado beneficio bruto como una voluminosa factura-

---

[11] Según atestigua uno de los protagonistas, los acuerdos iniciales de la CTNE con Standard Eléctrica, en los que Telettra, Cables de Comunicaciones e Intelsa se incorporaban como proveedores, no contemplaban una filial para la fabricación de terminales. Amper se sumó como proveedor de estos aparatos, gama en la que había crecido de forma importante (Luis Lada, Entrevistas con el autor, 22 de mayo de 2013 y 17 de junio de 2013). Banegas (inédito) subraya la irrelevancia de Amper en ese momento, cuestionando así la excepcional capacidad tecnológica de Amper esgrimida por la CTNE como razón para adquirirla.

[12] La modernización dio prioridad a las centralitas de pequeña potencia y a los terminales (Jesús Banegas, Comunicación personal con el autor, 27 de mayo de 2020); véase Calvo (2019a, 113-150) para Marconi Española.

[13] En 1984, Amper tenía un capital de 3.400 millones de ptas. y una plantilla de 987 empleados (CTNE 1985, 48).

ción. La segunda palanca de la estrategia de crecimiento consistió en adquisiciones de empresas, fórmula muy al uso, que conjugaba rapidez, baratura y menor riesgo y se concretó en la compra de Telefonía y Datos y Elasa[14]. La tercera palanca estribó en el papel que le encomendó el Ministerio de Industria y Energía (MINER) al convertirla en eje de la respuesta industrial española para concentrar las actividades del disperso sector electrónico-informático en un grupo de telecomunicaciones civiles y militares.

En cuanto a tamaño relativo, Amper representaba en torno al 5% de las ventas del *holding* industrial de la CTNE, muy alejado de las grandes –SECOINSA, Intelsa, Sintel y Telettra Española–. Al final de la década de 1980, Amper se situaba en el puesto noventa y siete –cola de león– de las cien grandes compañías mundiales de teléfonos. La lista la encabezaba el cuarteto de NTT, AT&T, British Telecommunications y GTE, «titanes» con un control oligopólico en el mercado de equipo de telecomunicación[15].

Precisamente, ese momento marcó la aparición de problemas en letal mezcla de rampantes costes de reestructuración de las filiales castigadas por la crisis y de reducción de los compromisos de Telefónica con la empresa, con el consiguiente descenso del volumen de facturación así como de los beneficios consolidados del grupo. La operadora monopolista de redes mantenía un elevado volumen de compras de equipos, pese a una política de expansión orientada a diversificar los mercados, visible en varias alianzas internacionales, así como en la compra de activos de MESA, señaladas en otro apartado[16].

---

[14]   Pérdidas: 655 millones de ptas.; beneficio bruto: casi 1.000 millones y facturación: más de 9.000 millones de pesetas (*El País,* 6 de julio de 1987). En 1977, Radio Industria Bilbaína, a la que Telefónica había ubicado en un polígono industrial en las inmediaciones de Zaragoza, cambió su nombre por el de Electrónica Aragonesa S.A. (Elasa) (*El Periódico de Aragón,* 26 de junio de 2003). En 1985, su sección de ingeniería y desarrollo comprendía una treintena de personas, un 6,3% de la plantilla, mientras que los gastos de desarrollo alcanzaron un 2,6% sobre la cifra de ventas. Elasa colaboraba estrechamente con el Centro de Investigación y Desarrollo de Telefónica, especialmente en la realización de equipos ECO (equipo de cobro opcional) y CCM (control a distancia de teléfonos de monedas) (Electrónica Aragonesa S.A., *Memoria 1985,* 5 y 16).

[15]   Las ventas de NTT multiplicaban por 258 las de Amper (U.S. Department of Commerce 1990, 1-2). El desarrollo del temporizador de tres minutos para Telefónica, un adelanto que la operadora explotó con asiduidad, dio a Amper fortaleza económica y un gran impulso. Un matiz sobre el carácter genuino de la tecnología de Amper: fabricó terminales telefónicos de marcación con falso teclado usando un chip encargado a Texas Instruments, dada la escasa capacidad de fabricantes españoles (Piher y Fagor) (Juan Mulet Melià, Conversación con el autor, 16 de mayo de 2013; Torres 2017).

[16]   El 71% a la facturación de Amper provenía de Telefónica en 1988.

Esta fase de dificultades lleva el sello de la reordenación de las telecomunicaciones en su conjunto bajo las formas de concentración y reestructuraciones, en las que el sector público desempeñó un papel destacado. Los actores fueron el Gobierno, el Instituto Nacional de Industria (INI) con su *miniholding* electrónico Inisel, otras dos empresas del sector público – MESA, antigua filial de IT&T al borde de la quiebra, y Pesa Electrónica, fabricante de equipos de televisión profesional y proveedor del Ejército–[17]. El objetivo consistía en lograr un mínimo grado de especialización y de dimensión crítica en las empresas del sector a través de un proceso de colaboración industrial entre varias instancias.

Dentro de ese objetivo de reordenar e integrar los activos del sector público dispersos, en los días finales de 1988, Telefónica y el INI sellaron un protocolo de acuerdo, mientras que el MINER se ofrecía como catalizador de las propuestas de la empresa semipública. Por otra parte, el ministerio competente pretendía ampliar el acuerdo de integración a otros fabricantes de productos complementarios, entre los que descollaban como candidatas idóneas Ceselsa, empresa de electrónica, base de la futura Indra, y Abengoa, casa madre de la empresa de electrónica profesional Sainco. Una iniciativa semejante no estaba exenta de dificultades ya que requería conjugar el impulso institucional y el control y planificación de la demanda[18].

Sin duda, la necesidad de buscar una salida a MESA abonó la creación del grupo público de telecomunicaciones civiles y militares nucleado en torno a Amper. Según los planes, la reestructuración marcaría el punto de partida

---

[17]   En 1982, el consumo aparente del sector electrónico se situaba en el 2,2% del PIB español (439.000 millones de pesetas). El PEIN pretendía incrementarlo en un 65,8% en pesetas constantes de dicho año, hasta situarlo en el equivalente del 3,1% del PIB (Ministerio de Industria y Energía 1983, 12). El MINER había autorizado la constitución en EE. UU. de una filial de Piher Electrónica (PE) partir de tres empresas públicas –Experiencias Industriales SA, Equipos Electrónicos SA y Empresa Nacional de Óptica– y un capital inicial de 280.000 dólares, a suscribir íntegramente por PE. Fue inscrita con el nombre de Pesa América como sociedad instrumental para la comercialización de los productos de su matriz (MINER, Extracto del Expediente para el Consejo de Ministros, 1 de agosto de 1984, Archivo de SEPI).

[18]   *El País*, 27 de mayo de 1989. En opinión de Banegas (1989), no compartida de forma unánime, España, desde hacía tiempo en la órbita de los países desarrollados –homologado por la convergencia de sus modelos industriales, la organización oligopólica de la industria de alta tecnología, la planificación de la demanda como exigencia previa al desarrollo tecnológico–, contaba con mercado y recursos financieros y profesionales para desarrollar un grupo industrial en el sector de las telecomunicaciones. Medios especializados recogían la incertidumbre del momento (*Anuario Cip: 1991-1992*, 1992, 54).

para configurar el nuevo grupo de telecomunicaciones y articularlo en torno a una nueva filial, previsiblemente bajo la razón social de Amper Defensa[19].

El protocolo entre Telefónica y el INI obligaba a Amper a absorber la cartera de pedidos y la plantilla de MESA, Pesa Electrónica y la sección de telecomunicaciones civiles y militares de Inisel. En esa coyuntura, Amper aspiraba a lograr la mitad del gasto previsto por el ministerio de Defensa para el cuatrienio 1988-1991, cifrado en 53.500 millones de pesetas. De inmediato, el Gobierno reforzó la formación del nuevo grupo de telecomunicaciones liderado por Amper con ayudas destinadas a financiar la reestructuración de MESA[20].

Precisamente, ya en 1989, en su plan de viabilidad Amper preveía integrar MESA con la sección de comunicaciones militares de Inisel en una filial mediante un intercambio del 10% propio por acciones de la nueva empresa. La plantilla de la filial estaría formada por la suma de los trabajadores de MESA absorbidos por Amper y otro centenar crecido procedente de Inisel[21]. Bajo el nombre de Amper Programas de Electrónica y Comunicaciones (en adelante, Amper Programas), fue creada, repitámoslo, a partir de un acuerdo entre Inisel y Amper propiciado por el MINER con el objetivo de abastecer primordialmente al Ministerio de Defensa. La concentración del grueso de las actividades industriales relacionadas con las telecomunicaciones en el Grupo Amper, fortalecido por la creación de la nueva filial, buscaba un hueco en las telecomunicaciones para defensa. El organismo competente, ahora con el nombre de Ministerio de Industria, Comercio y Turismo (MICYT), se comprometió a mantener su respaldo al Grupo Amper dentro de los programas horizontales de apoyo a la industria. Para ello destinó a proyectos de dicho Grupo Amper durante el trienio un 17% del presupuesto de subvenciones del Plan Electrónico e Informático Nacional (PEIN), en sustancia un programa de subsidios al desarrollo tecnológico de las empresas (Castells 1986)[22]. Sin em-

---

[19] Cuantía de las inversiones estimadas: unos 2.000 millones de pesetas (*El País*, 30 de enero de 1989).

[20] Cartera de pedidos a absorber: 1.000 millones de pesetas; activos humanos: casi medio millar de trabajadores; volumen de facturación de Pesa Electrónica: en torno a 4.000 millones de pesetas; ayudas: 2.800 millones de pesetas (*El País*, 30 de diciembre de 1988, 20 de enero de 1989 y 3 de diciembre de 1994).

[21] En los ejercicios de 1990 y 1991, se esperaba que el reflotamiento de Marconi causara pérdidas de 1.000 y 700 millones de pesetas respectivamente. Pesa seguiría funcionando como sociedad anónima, con personalidad jurídica propia. En el plan, la nueva filial contemplaba el umbral de rentabilidad – beneficios de 500 millones de ptas en 1992– a tres años (*El País*, 12 de enero de 1989).

[22] El plan reunía la definición de objetivos, exposición de políticas y asunción de compromisos (Ministerio de Industria y Energía 1983, 9). Una de las medidas previstas aludía, sin nom-

bargo, Amper Programas encajó las restricciones presupuestarias de la Defensa, que, por lo demás, afectaban a la industria de defensa de todos los países y a todas las empresas proveedoras[23].

Por supuesto, la ejecución de los planes dependía en gran manera de la actuación de Telefónica. Ahora bien, durante el ejercicio de 1989, la operadora redujo en una quinta parte sus compras a Amper, que vio disminuir sus beneficios en un 43% respecto a los del mismo periodo del año anterior cifrados en 1.178 millones. Su peso en la facturación de esta – las «muletas» de Telefónica– bajó veintiún puntos porcentuales hasta situarse en el 50%, anticipo de unas previsiones que apuntaban a un nuevo descenso del 12,1%[24]. La contracción en la gama básica de terminales ponía a Amper en una autocalificada «dificultad transitoria», cuya salida pendía de la culminación de la liberalización en este subsector en su vertiente administrativa. Telefónica priorizaba desprenderse de su *stock* antes de abordar nuevas compras y Amper encontraba dificultades para aprovechar su red de comercialización para vender en un mercado abierto.

En el fondo, la esencia de las relaciones entre Telefónica y Amper radicaba en armonizar dos aspectos primordiales para los intereses de ambas: el tipo de productos y la duración de los contratos. La clave estaba en afianzar la gama de productos de telecomunicaciones no liberalizados, entre otros, telefonía pública, transmisión de datos, sistemas de mantenimiento y equipos de tarificación. El contrato tendría vigencia anual, si bien Amper buscaba garantizar también unas previsiones de demanda bianuales –1991 y 1992– sin olvidar «actuaciones especiales» encaminadas a salvar el ejercicio anual[25].

---

brarla, a Amper: «Se tomarán con capital público o privado las medidas necesarias para asegurar la continuidad de la producción y la investigación en el seno de la única empresa española por capital y por tecnología existente en el sector de equipos para telefonía» (Ministerio de Industria y Energía 1983, 70).

[23] Amper Programas se creó con un capital social de 1.234 millones de pesetas en una especialización que abarcaba, entre otros, radioteléfonos, sistemas de comunicación tácticos, de combate y estratégicos; los directivos del Grupo se lamentaban de la nula consecución de contratos significativos del ministerio, que planteó la propia viabilidad de la empresa, condenada a la quiebra sin una regulación de empleo (*El País,* 21 de enero de 1991).

[24] El peso de Telefónica en la facturación de Amper cayó desde el 71% en 1988 al 50%– y las previsiones apuntaban a un nuevo descenso hasta situarse en el 37,9%.

[25] En coincidencia con el plan operativo vigente en Amper, las compras de Telefónica durante 1989 estaban cuantificadas en 11.600 millones. Sin ampliación de las compras previstas a Amper durante los dos meses finales de ese año, los beneficios de esta empresa caerían en una cuantía aproximada de 800 millones de pesetas, frente a los 2.500 registrados en 1988 y a los 2.000 millones anunciados el mes de abril. Amper justificó la rescisión de contratos

Finalmente, las largas negociaciones entre Telefónica y Amper culminaron en un acuerdo marco con medidas urgentes, que establecía las líneas básicas de cooperación e identificaba nuevas áreas de negocio abiertas a Amper. En el primer aspecto, el acuerdo consideraba la colaboración de Amper con el grupo de empresas de Telefónica. Al mismo tiempo, pretendía favorecer las estrategias de Amper y, nada despreciable, su política de planificación, dentro de «un contexto competitivo en calidad, precio y plazos de entrega»[26].

En su ejecución el plan pactado, que fijaba en unos 8.000 millones de pesetas en 1990 la cuantía de compras a Amper S.A., tropezó con dificultades. Los pedidos de la operadora para el primer semestre no alcanzaban ni un tercio, con efectos negativos para el volumen total de facturación y beneficios de la compañía matriz[27].

Sin embargo, Telefónica, en un momento en que a dúo con el INI pretendía asegurarse su preeminencia en el capital de Amper, no se arredró ante la caída de beneficios y amplió significativamente su participación en esta. Por su parte, el INI realizó diversos movimientos hasta conseguir aproximarse a la posición patrimonial de Telefónica. El primero consistió en aportar activos de la filial Pesa y de la sección de telecomunicaciones civiles y militares, equivalentes al 6,87% del capital de Amper. El segundo lo llevó a cabo mediante la adquisición de títulos equivalentes al 1,5% de Amper, aprovechando la caída de cotización, y el tercero implicó la inversión de 1.500 millones de pesetas en obligaciones[28].

A los protagonistas de los procesos de concentración apadrinados por el Gobierno y mencionados hasta aquí conviene añadir otras casas del sector, codiciadas por Amper. La lista incluye Control (TYC) y Page Ibérica y Telecomunicación, dedicadas a la fabricación de equipos de radio y al montaje de sistemas de telecomunicaciones civiles y militares, respectivamente. En ellas tenían participaciones sustanciales dos entidades del núcleo bancario propietario de Amper –Banesto y Banco Bilbao de Vizcaya (BBV)– junto al Banco de Crédito Industrial (BCI). La operación permitiría además clarificar las car-

---

temporales por la política de compras de Telefónica (*El País*, 26 de octubre y 8 de noviembre de 1989).

[26] Telefónica, *Actas del Comité ejecutivo (ACE)*, 10 de enero de 1990; *El País*, 23 de noviembre de 1989.

[27] *El País*, 8 de noviembre de 1989 y 29 de enero de 1990.

[28] En 1991 el INI tenía una participación del 9,89% en Amper, de las más bajas junto con las de DEFEX y Midsco: *Grupo INI 1991*, 128; el porcentaje difiere con el que ofrecen fuentes externas (*El País*, 29 de septiembre y 26 de agosto de 1989).

teras de participaciones de los tres bancos en esta industria porque implicaba canjear sus títulos en Page y TYC por títulos de la autocartera de Amper[29]. Profundizando en la integración dentro del sector y haciendo oídos sordos a otras ofertas, Banesto efectuó una operación dineraria y de canje de acciones, consistente en vender a Amper su participación en Page Ibérica por una suma de 1.200 millones de pesetas, la mitad pagada en acciones propias de la compradora. Esta operación la aupó a la cuarta posición como accionista de Amper, con una participación del 3,5% del capital[30].

3. El desenlace foráneo: la alianza con multinacionales

En viva divergencia con la vía nacional seguida por esas sociedades, otras siguieron derroteros distintos. Uno de los claves fue la consabida asociación estratégica con multinacionales, que se convertían en socias tecnológicas y titulares de acciones. En esa dirección avanzó Amper con una estrategia calificada de reestructuración jurídico-financiera, que comprendía restructuración, soluciones financieras, desinversiones y recorte de personal en una sección y varias filiales. Amper ideaba conciliar la estructura jurídica del grupo con las nuevas exigencias de la ley del Mercado de Valores, propensa a la consolidación de resultados. El éxito dependía de la capacidad de integrar todas las participaciones financieras de su casi veintena de filiales con un valor de 30.000 millones de pesetas en un *holding* y fundirse en él como miembro (Anexo 1)[31].

Amper se movía en un escenario en el que su doble condición de productora de componentes y equipos la empujaba a crear estructuras de gestión muy flexibles (en estrella, con autonomía y descentralizadas) y a forjar múltiples alianzas. Para empezar, la formidable diversificación del grupo reclamaba un esfuerzo de racionalización para ajustarse a la mengua del peso

---

[29] La participación conjunta de Banesto, BBV, Santander, Central e Hispano Americano sumaba el 15% del capital de Amper, idéntico porcentaje que Telefónica, y mayor que el del INI, que aspiraba a situarse en torno al 10% del capital de la empresa (*El País*, 14 de noviembre de 1989).

[30] *El País*, 19 de noviembre de 1989; otras multinacionales habían realizado ofertas de mayor cuantía a Banesto Elerco.

[31] *ABC*, 24 de mayo de 1993. Amper accedió a los diez valores del segmento especial del mercado continuo procedentes de la bolsa tradicional, que empezó a funcionar en abril de 2000 y cuya capitalización representaba la décima parte de la correspondiente al total de las bolsas españolas (*Boletín Económico*, Banco de España, mayo de 2000, 9).

específico de la matriz en el Grupo[32]. Escapar a los números rojos demandaba ajustes en varias áreas, a saber, la división de telemática y Amper Programas, previa venta del 49% a una multinacional –la candidata era Thomson– como opción preferida. En 1990 la primera mutó en filial a partir de Olamtel con el nombre de Amper Telemática, al entender de los críticos una operación de ingeniería jurídica para suprimir puestos de trabajo. Por su parte, la nueva empresa y Amper Cosesa iniciarían un proceso de concentración de actividades, acompañado de otro ajuste de personal. En el capítulo de ventas la búsqueda de plusvalías hacía incluir los activos de la filial Télétechnique y diversos inmuebles[33].

Para captar mejor las grandes transformaciones parece oportuno precisar la dimensión del Grupo Amper. En 1989, sus activos totales alcanzaban 53.000 millones de pesetas, su volumen de negocio 40.000 millones de pesetas, sus beneficios antes de impuestos por encima de 3.000 millones y su plantilla 5.187 trabajadores. Esta, en franca disminución, se distribuía en tres centros de trabajo, situados en Madrid y en dos localidades al sur de la Comunidad autónoma –San Fernando de Henares y Getafe–. En ellos se fabricaban terminales, destinados a Telefónica en un porcentaje elevado aunque declinante, como sabemos[34].

Si vamos a los hechos, los primeros años de la década de 1990 mostraron una empresa asomada al abismo. En 1990, las pérdidas volvieron a cebarse en el Grupo, que las achacó a la política económica aplicada por el Gobierno socialista en detrimento de la industria española, a los altos tipos de interés y a la incidencia negativa de un hecho coyuntural –la guerra del Golfo– sobre la demanda. En Amper Telemática empezó a aparecer la amenaza de un recorte de empleo,

---

[32] *El País*, 29 de mayo y 28 de junio de 1990. La cúpula directiva hacía hincapié en este cambio de naturaleza en la empresa, que, en su nueva estructura duplicaría su volumen de ventas («Amper ha dejado de ser ya la empresa de terminales que dio origen a todo el grupo») (*El País*, 28 de enero de 1990). Tan solo dos años antes, Amper homologó el terminal modelo Teide 5/1613 (analógico, manos libres, con visualizador y salida para cascos telefónicos), un producto al gusto de la CTNE (*BOE*, 256, 25 de octubre de 1988, 30.752).

[33] Cosesa, constituida en 1966, instaló en sus veintidós primeros años de existencia el 75% de las centralitas privadas existentes en España; cifras significativas hacia 1988: facturación de 6.943 millones de pesetas, pérdidas de 251 millones de pesetas, red comercial de 20 delegaciones provinciales y plantilla de 426 personas (*El País*, 20 de agosto de 1988). A finales de 1990, los trabajadores de la línea de negocio de telemática fueron absorbidos por Amper Telemática S.A. con el reconocimiento de su antigüedad (STS, Tribunal Supremo – Sala Cuarta, 29 de abril de 1998).

[34] *El País*, 28 de junio y 25 de mayo de 1990. Amper pertenecería al grupo de industrias calificadas de tractoras, un escalón por debajo de las de cabecera, representadas por EADS-CASA (Abad 2010, 287).

mientras que en Amper Programas y Télétechnique se concretaba en desinversión por venta inmediata de casi la mitad o en su totalidad, respectivamente[35].

Los años 1991-1993 estuvieron dominados por suspensiones de pagos y de contratos, planes de viabilidad y regulaciones de empleo en las filiales del Grupo Amper. La secuencia empezó con Amper Programas y se propagó al resto[36].

En Amper Telemática y Amper Cosesa, las medidas de ajuste laboral se completaron con las financieras y estas, a su vez, con planes de viabilidad de contenido industrial, organizativo, comercial y laboral. En conjunto buscaban cimentar la supervivencia de ambas sociedades y culminaron en una solicitud de declaración de suspensión de pagos[37]. Sendas operaciones de aumento de fondos propios por ampliación del capital, previa reducción del capital social a cero, y de la prima de emisión le permitieron recuperar su nivel de capital social previo. Los excedentes patrimoniales de las dos filiales, unidos a las medidas de reconversión pendientes y a los acuerdos con los acreedores, permitirían sentar las bases para encarar un futuro risueño. Al mismo tiempo, el grupo saldría reforzado al disminuir los resultados negativos de estas sociedades en el consolidado del grupo y al desaparecer las fuertes exigencias de financiación de ambas[38].

La reestructuración industrial prosiguió durante 1993 especialmente en Telemática, con la remodelación de la plantilla, la reorganización industrial y el saneamiento de activos, con pérdidas importantes (Ernst & Young 1994, 2). En la sección de defensa, Amper decidió desprenderse de una participación de Amper Programas amarrando, eso sí, la mayoría. Con este fin cerró un acuerdo por el que Thomson tomaría en sucesivas fases hasta el 49% de la filial. En la primera la multinacional francesa obtuvo el 15% mediante la suscripción de la quinta parte de la ampliación de capital por 2.498 millones de ptas.[39].

---

[35] Las pérdidas alcanzaron 1.156 millones de pesetas. En un alegato nacionalista, el presidente de Amper acusaba al Gobierno de desmantelar la base industrial del país, acuciado por la retirada masiva de empresarios en 1990, el control abrumador de sociedades por capital extranjero y la intervención de inversores foráneos en la mitad crecida de la producción (*El País*, 28 de junio de 1991).

[36] Respuesta escrita del ministro Virgilio Zapatero, Madrid, 8/1992, Congreso de los diputados, 5/1992, 303; CNMV, Otros hechos relevantes, 340, 12 de junio de 1991 y 562, 12 de noviembre de 1991.

[37] CNMV, 2.636, 23 de noviembre de 1993; Ernst & Young (1994), 33.

[38] CNMV, 2.566, 15 de noviembre de 1993 y 2.632, 19 de noviembre de 1993.

[39] CNMV, 1950, 11 de mayo de 1993. De la dependencia estrecha de esta filial con la demanda oficial habla un contrato firmado en 1997 para la integración de los diferentes subsiste-

La restructuración trajo consigo cambios en la dimensión de la empresa, medida por la capitalización bursátil. Al crecimiento espectacular de los primeros siete años de la década de 1990 sucedió un desplome de idénticas características y una leve recuperación a comienzos del siglo XXI. A su vez, la restructuración aportó novedades en la composición de las actividades del Grupo Amper. Lo ocurrido entre 1992 y 2000 evidencia la evaporación de la sección de audiovisual proporcionada por Pesa, la caída drástica de las comunicaciones públicas debido a la finalización de contratos en el exterior y a la cesión de la sección especializada (Elasa) así como la irrupción modesta de la integración de sistemas (Gráfico 1).

Gráfico 1. Ventas del Grupo Amper por por actividades,
1992-2000 (millones ptas. corrientes)

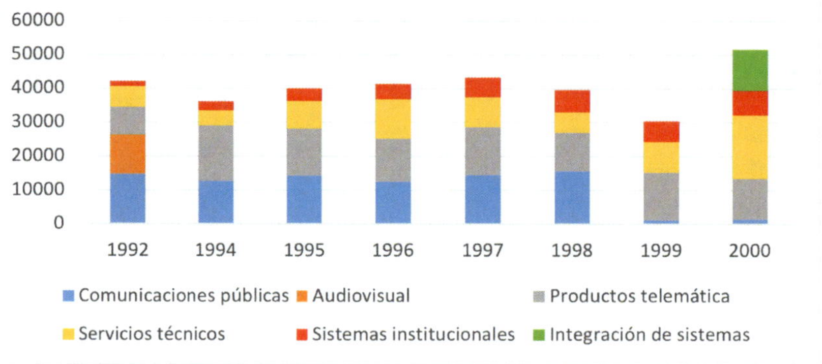

Fuente: Elaboración a partir de Grupo Amper, *Memoria(s) anual(es)*.

La restructuración dejó a la vez plantillas menguadas e importantes alteraciones en la composición de las mismas. El Gráfico 2 muestra a las claras el drástico desplome del número de obreros. La mano de obra más cualificada, representada por los titulados superiores, se duplicó con holgura al ganar casi once puntos porcentuales a partir del 7,26% en el conjunto.

mas que compondrían la red básica de área del ejército de tierra (CNMV, 8.174, 7 de enero de 1997).

Gráfico 2. Ventas del grupo Amper (miles de euros)

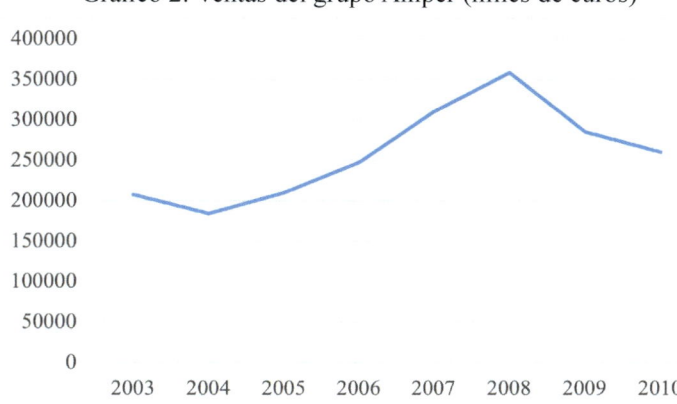

Fuente: Elaboración a partir de Grupo Amper, *Memoria(s) anual(es)*.

Por su parte, la productividad del Grupo Amper creció a lo largo de la década de 1990, con la sola excepción de 1999, y recuperó la senda anterior en el año 2000. Expresada en ventas por empleado, un indicador aceptado por lo común, los 10,5 millones de ptas. de 1991 se multiplicaron por 1,74 en 1994 y casi se triplicaron en 1997. Tras la señalada caída de 1999, drástica por lo demás, remontaron con vigor de inmediato y alcanzaron una cifra que triplicaba con generosidad la de 1991.

Sin duda, algo tuvo que ver el descenso del personal excedente y el incremento del capital humano recién señalado (Gráfico 2), junto al aumento de la intensidad en I+D, medida en inversión por empleado, realidad apuntada más arriba.

No menos importancia adquirieron los cambios en la composición del capital. Amper tenía dos accionistas principales –la operadora Telefónica y la fabricante de equipo y proveedora de sistemas Indra–. En posiciones secundarias se encontraba un grupo de once entidades bancarias y de ahorro, tanto nacionales como extranjeras, junto a un variado grupo de instituciones, entre ellas las de crédito, fondos e inversores, así como particulares. Pese a algún amago de movimientos, la participación de Telefónica en el capital social de Amper S.A. no varió respecto al tradicional 15,35% (Tabla 1). La entrada de Indra tuvo como objetivo primordial el acceso a la caja de Amper, que se había engrosado con la venta de su filial Amper Elasa a Siemens, hasta alcanzar el saldo de 18.000 millones de pesetas. En contrapartida, la situación patrimonial de Indra en aquel momento no era muy boyante. Pese a los desmentidos, Indra concibió en algún momento la fusión con Amper para hacer en España un grupo potente en telecomunicaciones y electrónica civil y militar[40].

Tabla 1. Principales accionistas de Amper S. A. (% del capital)

	1993	1995	1996	1997	1999	2000	2003
Telefónica de España	15,35	15,35	15	15	12,2	6,1	6,1
Indra Sistemas	9,89	9,4	9,4	9,4	–	–	–
Lucent Technologies					12,2	12,2	
Amper S. A.					2,73	2,96	2,17
Union Bank of Switzerland						2,81	
Skandinavisca Enskilda Banken					2,35		
Tecnocom							12,2
Arlington Capital Investors						7,00	5,8
Argentaria	1,63						
Deutsche Auslandskassenverein	1,51						
Concepción Guevara Sojo	1,48						
Westdeutsche Genossenshafts	1,19						
Dresdner Bank	1,18				1,50		
D. G. Bank Bayern	1,14						
Boston Safe Deposit & Trust	0,95						
Commerzbank	0,91						
Chase Manhatan Bank		2,3	1,74	1,41			
Antonio de la Fuente Guevara		1,58	1,58	1,58	1,58	1,47	
Brown Brothers Harriman		3,24	1,53				
Banco Santander			1,29				
Les Fils Dreyfus et Cie.			1,22				
The Bank of New York			1,2				
Banco de Vizcaya			0,81				
Renta 4			0,79				

---

[40] CNMV, 6.613, 5 de diciembre de 1996; el Consejo de Administración de Amper del 24 de abril de 1996 valoró positivamente la nota hecha pública por Indra ocho días antes (CNMV, 6.842, 26 de abril de 1996); de los movimientos de Indra por Amper se habló en sede parlamentaria (*Diario de Sesiones del Congreso de los Diputados*, Comisiones, 445, Comisión de Infraestructuras y Medio Ambiente, 7 de marzo de 1995, 13.623-13.627). A juicio de algunos protagonistas, la fusión Amper/Indra quizás hubiera merecido la pena (José Luis Adanero, Comunicación personal con el autor, 27 de mayo de 2020).

Manuel Armijo Alonso	1,55					
Agepasa	1,32					
Morgan Guarantee Trust Co.	1,23					
Growth Fund of Spain	1,15					
A. B. Asesores Bursátiles		3,14				
Robert Fleming		1,98				
Morgan Stanley Bank		1,28				
Ahorro Corporación Financiera		1,09				
Caja Madrid		0,92				
Crédit Lyonnais		0,91				
Skandinavisca Enskilda Banken			2,35			
Bak Leu			2,21	1,30		
State Street Bank			1,35	1,34		
Bankers Trust			1,35			
Société Générale			1,32			
Macquerel SIMCAV S. A.				1,50		
Cedel Bank				1,34		

Fuente: Elaboración a partir de Amper, *Memoria(s) anual(es)*.

En contraste con esta estabilidad relativa, Amper modificó de forma notable su base accionarial en varios aspectos a lo largo de los años 90. Sin lugar a dudas, el más destacado consistió en la desinversión escalonada de Telefónica –el abandono del «doble anillo»– que la situó primero en un 12,2% del capital de la compañía y en un modesto 6,1% en el año 2000 (Tabla 1). El segundo hecho trascendental se refiere a un acuerdo de colaboración estratégica y asociación que puso en manos del gigante industrial norteamericano Lucent Technologies, heredero del sistema Bell, el 12,2% del capital de Amper, S.A. y, al año siguiente, le catapultó a la posición de principal accionista desbancando a Telefónica[41]. Este movimiento de retirada en la cúspide permitió al

---

[41] La adquisición de las acciones de Amper S.A. costó a Lucent Technologies 6.811 millones de pesetas (CNMV, 14.880, 1 de diciembre de 1998). Esta empresa surgió en 1995 cuando AT&T, una vez desmembrada, se desprendió de la parte de fabricación de equipos y del área de operaciones informáticas, de reciente adquisición a NCR (National Research Council 2006, 15; Lazonick 2011, 64-65). Por su parte, Telefónica reconoció a Lucent Technologies como uno de los proveedores globales preferentes de sistemas de telecomunicaciones. Con la expresión «doble anillo» Luis Solana aludía al holding industrial de Telefónica, inviable desde la integración de España en la CEE y reemplazado en parte por la posibilidad

capital extranjero escalar posiciones hasta lograr ligeramente por encima de los dos tercios del capital total en ese año 2000[42]. En el 2003, la empresa norteamericana fue desplazada por Tecnocom Telecomunicaciones y Energía, la multinacional española y líder en el sector TIC (Anexo 2). Por su parte, Telefónica se situó como segundo accionista principal pero no tardó en desprenderse de un porcentaje del capital de Amper S.A. en dos tramos sucesivos del 2,11% y del 7%[43].

4. Estrategias de crecimiento en contextos competitivos: la internacionalización en sus diversas facetas

A ciencia cierta, la participación del capital extranjero, creciente, en el accionariado de Amper ya es un aspecto de la internacionalización, particularidad que la propia empresa consideraba como uno de los jalones de su trayectoria. Veamos hasta qué punto el caso de Amper encaja con una de las corrientes predominantes en la teoría de la internacionalización de las empresas. La ya mencionada escuela de Upsala preconiza una expansión gradual, a partir del establecimiento de delegaciones comerciales en países cercanos psicológicamente –ya que no geográficamente– por compartir historia o cultura hasta la inversión directa.

Abordar la internacionalización con tecnología propia que protagonizó Amper reclama recordar sin cesar el papel primordial de Telefónica en este

---

de comprar a proveedores externos en condiciones ventajosas por el aumento del volumen debido a la expansión internacional de la operadora.

[42] En el año 2000, Telefónica S.A. vendió el 6,1% del capital social de Amper S.A. a Arlington Capital Investors Limited, entidad gestora de los fondos de inversión European Strategic Investors Holdings y European Renaissance Fund, con la consiguiente reducción de la participación a la mitad (CNMV, 20.666, 11 de febrero de 2000).

[43] A partir de una filial industrial en Madrid, se expandió sectorial y geográficamente por el conjunto de España, Portugal, América Latina (Chile, Colombia, México, Perú, Brasil, Paraguay y República Dominicana) y EEUU (Miami). Tecnocom se convirtió en el mayor mantenedor de redes de telecomunicaciones en Perú y creó con Motorola la *joint venture* TM Data de Brasil, que comenzó a prestar servicios en Sao Paulo (CNMV, 34.747, 23 de abril de 2002; 11.615, 15 de noviembre de 2001 y 11.405, 26 de diciembre de 2001). Motorola y Amper acordaron colaborar en el desarrollo de redes con infraestructura de fibra óptica y cable (*El País*, 22 de abril de 1999). La transición a la nueva economía, el precio de sus acciones y su red externa daban a Amper muchos atractivos para ser cortejada por diversas empresas –«un pez rodeado de múltiples anzuelos»– entre ellas Dragados. Desmentidos de Amper a la CNMV sobre ofertas detalladas procedentes de empresas nacionales y extranjeras (CNMV, 26.548, 1 de febrero de 2001; *El País*, 21 de enero de 2001).

proceso y también en su empeño de informar a Amper sobre la evolución de las operadoras y la aparición de cadenas mundiales de valor añadido.

En sustancia, Amper presenta un caso peculiar. En un principio, el Grupo Amper debió de contar en exclusiva con algún pequeño establecimiento comercial. Todo apunta a una primera oficina europea en París hacia 1989, simultáneo con una inversión exterior, es decir, la entrada del Grupo en la francesa Télétechnique. Al año siguiente, Amper estrenó oficina en la ciudad de México, seguramente en coincidencia con la firma del contrato con la operadora Telmex y vinculada al proyecto de la expansión del Intelligent Payphone Business en ese país, América Central y la Región Andina. He aquí, pues, dos modalidades diferentes: la inversión en una empresa ya existente y la actuación como consecuencia de actividad exportadora[44]. En una variante de oficina comercial con rango corporativo, Amper promovió el consorcio latinoamericano Ematel (Empresas Asociadas de Telecomunicación), grupo de empresas nacionales para potenciar las ventas en la región, dominada tradicionalmente por el trío de grandes multinacionales – Siemens, Ericsson e IT&T– que abastecían a unos buenos tres cuartos del mercado[45].

Transitamos por el terreno de la exportación, uno de los indicadores usados por los teóricos para determinar la internacionalización de una empresa. La necesidad de quebrar las servidumbres de la tremenda dependencia de Amper respecto a su principal cliente –las «muletas de Telefónica»– y las exigencias de la apertura del mercado empujaron a una creciente salida al exterior. El Gráfico 3 recoge algunos pormenores de esta orientación en el conjunto del Grupo Amper y muestra que no tuvo un comportamiento estable en las dos variables de comercio interior y exterior. La línea de tendencia del primero tiende a caer mientras que la del segundo presenta un comportamiento al alza, con un papel de sustitución en algún momento[46].

---

[44] El contrato con Telmex ascendía a 15 millones de dólares. Las Memorias de Amper son avaras en información sobre la creación de esas oficinas en el exterior; una fuente sustitoria son las biografías del personal. En 1993 la partida de resultados extraordinarios no refleja gastos por delegaciones (*Informe de gestión*, 1).

[45] Adanero et al. (2006), 530. En Latinoamérica, el suministro de equipo de telecomunicaciones estaba dominado por las grandes multinacionales, tres de las cuales tenían cuotas similares –Ericsson (28%), Siemens (25%) e IT&T (24%)– y otras dos participaciones más reducidas –GTE (8%) y NEC (6%). Entre 1981-1983, las cinco mayores empresas españolas o afincadas en España –SESA, Citesa, Telettra Española, Intelsa y Sintel– habían exportado por 631 millones de ptas. a la región, cifra equivalente al 4% del total (Torres 1983/84, 13-14).

[46] *El País*, 2 de febrero de 1984.

Gráfico 3. Mercado del grupo Amper, 1992-2001 (millones ptas. corrientes)

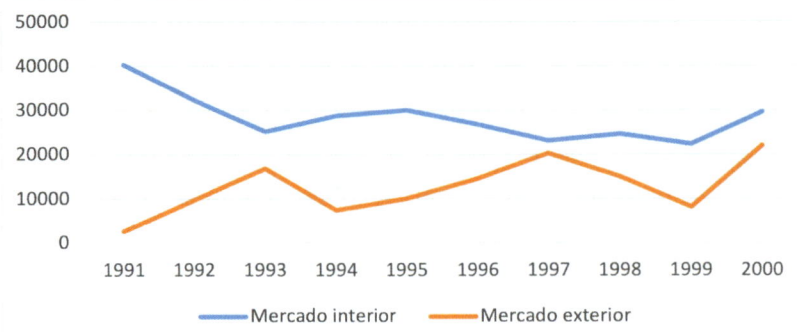

Fuente: Elaboración a partir de Amper, *Memoria*
2001, 1 y Ernst & Young (1994), 32.

Por lo general, la salida al mercado exterior goza de connotaciones positivas pero conviene desmitificarla, al menos en cierto sentido, y ver la incidencia real en las empresas. Un episodio, referido a una operación de Amper Programas, ilustra la pretendida competitividad y excelencia. Como venía haciendo desde años antes, esta empresa contrató la importación de módulos para control de vuelo de misiles por un valor añadido de 100 millones de pesetas y un coeficiente de rendimiento del 100%. En un plazo preestablecido, la mercancía importada sufría un proceso de transformación – montaje, pruebas y ajustes– antes de su reexportación a EE. UU. En definitiva, se trataba de tareas de subcontratación a realizar en España, que se caracterizaban por su bajo contenido tecnológico y su valor añadido escaso, cifrado en la quinta parte del valor del producto importado, repuesto aparte[47].

Telefónica encabezaba la distribución de las ventas por clientes, con porcentajes ligeramente oscilantes, si bien por debajo de la mitad, participación nada desdeñable pero muy alejada de cifras que rondaban las tres cuartas par-

---

[47] El propio mecanismo de la exportación reviste cierto interés. A mediados de 1996 Amper Programas obtuvo la autorización para realizar la operación y un aval bancario con el fin de garantizar aspectos como el IVA; al cabo de unos dos meses, importó los módulos desde Texas. La empresa española debía abonar el importe de la factura FOB Texas (157.000 $) y cubrir el seguro del 3% del valor FOB de la mercancía, contratar con una compañía aérea el transporte (434 $) y pagar la parte del flete por cruce del espacio aéreo nacional (15.271 pesetas). Se exigía licencia de exportación y certificado internacional de importación del cliente y, una vez realizada la exportación, el agente de aduanas representante de la empresa solicitaba la cancelación del documento único administrativo de importación junto a la devolución de la garantía depositada en su día (Billón y Sánchez 1999, 61-62).

tes hacia 1994. Con el objeto de compensar la finalización de contratos de telefonía pública con varios países, Amper reorientó la actividad internacional reforzando la presencia en mercados estratégicos, entre ellos Latinoamérica[48]. Al inicio del nuevo milenio, el mercado interior era el principal destino de las ventas del Grupo Amper, con una holgada mitad. La Unión Europea y los países de la OCDE ocupaban posiciones muy modestas en esta distribución geográfica de las ventas.

Este cuadro reclama ser completado a partir del análisis de Amper como empresa madre. A las funciones acordes con su condición de cabeza del grupo, la matriz sumaba la actividad de exportación de las empresas del grupo por medio de la división internacional. La primera se refiere al neto predominio de las exportaciones (80,33%) en la facturación total en 1993. Dentro de ese predominio, destacaba una fuerte concentración ya que casi las tres cuartas partes del total tenían como destino el continente americano, geográficamente remoto pero psicológicamente cercano, en la terminología de la escuela de Upsala. En otras palabras, la proximidad geográfica representada por Europa no era un factor decisivo, como muestra su parco porcentaje de participación en el total (7%)[49]. Al cabo de cuatro años, el ya abultado predominio de las exportaciones de Amper S. A. en el negocio total resultaba abrumador (94,74%). A su vez, la diversificación geográfica se había robustecido por la fuerte irrupción del mercado australiano, que pasó a ocupar la segunda posición en el destino de las exportaciones con el 41,38% sobre el total de las mismas, es decir, unos cinco puntos porcentuales por debajo del continente americano y a gran distancia del 6,13% de Asia y del 5,12% de Europa. No resulta muy arduo atribuir tal cambio a la creación de Amper Australia PTY Ltd. en 1997, sin duda un efecto colateral de la penetración comercial en el país (*Telecommunications Directory*, vols. 1-2 2007, 1.092).

Para volver al Grupo Amper, como indicador añadido de la internacionalización, la distribución geográfica del personal muestra el predominio claro del afincado en España. Presumiblemente, en un principio el Grupo tan solo debió de mantener un número escaso de personal en el extranjero, muy congruente con las ya citadas escasas oficinas comerciales. El arranque fuerte de la internacionalización impuso un aumento significativo del personal, que en 1997 rozaba el 8% de los 1.387 asentados en España.

---

[48] Amper S. A., *Informe de gestión 1998*.

[49] Amper 1993, 29.

Otro exponente de la internacionalización lo representa la cesión de licencias, escasamente documentado pese a su existencia relativamente temprana. A este renglón pertenece la fabricación en Francia de equipos con licencia Amper ya en 1976 y un contrato de licencia temporal con el grupo mexicano Sistemas Integrales de Comunicación por el que Amper cedía a este la fabricación de 100.000 unidades del teléfono Versafón, de diseño y fabricación propios[50].

En sus planes de expansión de índole, volumen y geografía distintos, Amper adoptó la estrategia de la inversión extranjera directa (IED), modalidad por la que Amper creó Elektronik en la ciudad renana de Dusseldorf (Ernst & Young 1997; Telecommunications Directory, vols. 1-2 2007, 1.092)[51]. Asimismo, tenía participaciones minoritarias en diversas compañías, a veces con discretos resultados: en Amper Prodata con la multinacional Prodata, líder europeo en medios de pago electrónicos para establecimientos comerciales, y en Ingecom, una empresa de ingeniería de servicios[52].

En Latinoamérica, Amper concluyó un acuerdo para comprar el 20% de la compañía Telefónica Hispanoamericana de Puerto Rico (THdPR), fabricante de aparatos telefónicos para Puerto Rico Telephone Company. La operación se efectuó por medio de la redistribución del accionariado español de la sociedad, es decir, la banca y Telefónica, que cedían un 10% cada una. Con la inversión la empresa española conseguía una puerta de acceso al mercado estadounidense de la telecomunicación desde Puerto Rico, estado asociado de la Unión. Al mismo tiempo, Amper se convertía en el socio industrial del cliente telefónico de Puerto Rico y establecía una base industrial en EE. UU. La transferencia tecnológica desde España siguió diversos canales, entre ellos el conocimiento y el diseño de producto[53].

---

[50] *BIT*, abril 1979, 8-12. El contrato con Sistemas Integrales de Comunicación suponía en el primer año un volumen de negocio de unos 320 millones de pesetas (más de dos millones de dólares) (*El País*, 2 de febrero de 1984).

[51] El capital social de la empresa se cifraba en 4.186 millones de pesetas a finales de 1997.

[52] *El País*, 6 de julio de 1987. Participación en Amper Prodata y en Ingecom: 44% y 40%, respectivamente. La inversión ascendió a 300 mil dólares (unos 38 millones de pesetas).

[53] *El País*, 6 de julio de 1987. THdPR era una empresa auxiliar con un proyecto industrial a base de tecnología española dedicada a la fabricación de componentes y con ambición de reinventarse en el futuro como fabricante de aparatos telefónicos, acorde con la senda perseguida por Telefónica. La asistencia técnica y el *know-how* provenía de Elasa (Calvo 2016, 251). Técnicos de THdPR recibieron instrucción en la sección de ingeniería y desarrollo de Elasa para la puesta en marcha paulatina de una factoría similar a la de la casa española, adaptada a las necesidades locales. Asimismo, Elasa diseñó para la citada empresa un prototipo de nuevo horno de secado más económico tanto en su realización como en su

En esta faceta de internacionalización por IED, Amper S.A. participó de forma paritaria con el madrileño BEE de Desarrollo e Inversión en la sociedad conjunta Amper Technologies S.A. cuya gestión asumió (Ernst & Young 1997)[54]. Amper firmó un contrato millonario para el suministro de seis sistemas de gestión de red y varios miles de aparatos de uso público a la compañía telefónica australiana Telstra, la histórica Telecom Australia por entonces en vías de privatización. El contrato incluía la formación técnica del personal de Telstra y la opción de un pedido adicional. Todo autoriza a afirmar que la perspectiva de un contrato suculento con la operadora principal de Australia aconsejó a Amper realizar una inversión *greenfield* que facilitara la adjudicación. Por su parte, la capacitación de personal *in situ* exigía una mínima infraestructura local. La creación de una nueva filial, ya avanzada la década de 1990, parecía la solución idónea para amarrar el contrato, reducir los costes operativos inherentes a la venta de equipo, ajustarse a los requisitos del mercado local y garantizar la continuidad de suministro en el futuro (Michael 2009, 176; *El País,* 13 de mayo de 1997; *Telecompaper,* 17 de abril de 1997). Testimonios directos de los hechos (Banegas, inédito; Banegas 2023, 167-168) explican la adjudicación del concurso por un triple motivo: agilidad de Amper en su respuesta y hábil propuesta económica de precios del *hardware* y *software* y sus aranceles, seriedad e independencia del equipo profesional de la operadora junto al brillante quehacer comercial y elevada capacidad tecnológica[55].

Por razones obvias, producción resultante de la IED y comercialización se encadenaban. Un acuerdo con la multinacional Mannesmann, el decimosexto grupo industrial de la RFA, abría la posibilidad de fabricación y comercialización conjunta de diversos productos en el mercado nacional y latinoamericano, zona esta última en la que la multinacional alemana estaba ya implantada (Argentina y un *holding* en Brasil). Entre los productos apa-

consumo de energía. A su vez, Elasa analizó de forma exhaustiva la situación de cuatro centenares de aparatos telefónicos que había de sentar las bases para redimensionar los almacenes de repuesto en la proyectada fábrica de reparación de teléfonos (Electrónica Aragonesa S.A. 1985, 11).

[54] El capital social de la empresa se cifraba en 4.186, millones de pesetas a finales de 1997.

[55] Discrepancias en las cantidades de aparatos y en el coste según las fuentes: 38.000 teléfonos y 11.310 millones de pesetas (*El País*); 25.000 teléfonos públicos y 7.500 millones de pesetas (*Telecompaper*). Telstra vendió más de 10 millones de tarjetas telefónicas inteligentes y suministró 35.000 teléfonos públicos de la marca Amper (Matthew L. James, Science, Technology, Environment and Resources Group, Australian Parliament, 16 de febrero de 1999).

recían los componentes electrónicos para estaciones de servicio de Campsa mecanizadas[56].

Capítulo aparte merecen las alianzas internacionales. En Europa, Amper perseguía un acceso indirecto al mercado, a través de acuerdos específicos y alianzas con otras empresas o grupos fuertemente implantados. En este proceder se encuadran las negociaciones con Olivetti para organizar la distribución de diversos productos mediante un acuerdo OEM (Original Equipment Manufacturing). La compañía española se alió al 49/51% con la multinacional italiana en la fugaz empresa conjunta Olamtel, que, con un capital social de 5 millones de pesetas, se dedicó por breve tiempo a la comercialización de productos de las telecomunicaciones privadas a través de la red comercial de Olivetti (*Diario de esiones de la Asamblea de Madrid*, 957, 2/1995. 20.878-20.891). El acuerdo planeaba utilizar la extensa red comercial de Olivetti en la comercialización del magnetógrafo de lectura y grabación de documentos bancarios de Amper (*La Repubblica,* 20 de octubre de 1987)[57].

En último término, las bazas de mayor alcance se jugaban en el mercado mundial. Los efectos del cataclismo provocado en EE. UU. por la salida de AT&T de su espacio estadounidense y su irrupción en el mercado mundial como consecuencia del desmantelamiento del monopolio en 1984 llegaron hasta España. AT&T se propuso entrar en el mercado internacional a través de alianzas estratégicas en forma de empresas conjuntas, que le proporcionaran un acceso inmediato, experiencia en el país y formas de funcionamiento arraigadas que eliminaban los altos costes de empezar desde cero. AT&T pugnó por disputar una cuota de mercado en Europa, sobre todo para su central telefónica digital (ESS-5) una vez adaptada a las condiciones técnicas de la red española. Para ser competitiva en el mercado interior Amper dependía de AT&T, única con capacidad tecnológica suficiente para realizar adaptaciones técnicas que permitieran aligerar las prestaciones de los equipos para disminuir sus precios. En ese contexto, AT&T negoció con la CTNE la entrada de Amper S.A. como tercer socio industrial (en competencia con Alcatel Standard Eléctrica e Intelsa LM Ericsson) en su filial europea AT&T-Network Systems, recientemente reorganizada tras la entrada de Philips NV. Vale la

---

[56] Amper veía una oportunidad de comercializar productos, entre ellos el magnetógrafo de lectura y grabación de documentos bancarios y los expendedores automáticos de billetes en los parquímetros (*El País,* 6 de julio de 1987).

[57] AT&T se negó a aportar recursos necesarios para las modificaciones pertinentes (Banegas inédito). La bibliografía italiana recoge el episodio (Cominotti y Mariotti 1989, 130 y 171; CER 1988).

pena resaltar que el movimiento coincidía con la voluntad manifestada por Italtel, el fabricante italiano de equipos de telecomunicación, de comprar la quinta parte del capital de dicha filial. En realidad, se trataba de encontrar una vía de participación en el proyecto global, incluidos los pactos en mercados internacionales firmados entre AT&T, Philips e Italtel (United States Senate 1985, 137; *El País*, 6 de marzo de 1989)[58].

Dentro de su estrategia de alianzas, en 1988 Amper se asoció a AT&T, con más propiedad AT&T Philips Telecommunications, en la empresa conjunta APT España en posición minoritaria, exactamente al 51/49%[59]. El emplazamiento escogido para la fábrica era Tres Cantos, en refuerzo del que se presentaba como uno de enclaves de alta tecnología más importante de Europa dentro del clúster madrileño. APT invertiría 25.000 millones de pesetas y crearía unos 800 empleos a partir de 1992. No obstante, el inicio de la producción se fijaba en 1991, año en que fabricaría la primera central telefónica digital española. A partir de entonces, APT produciría medio millón anual de líneas digitales, el grueso para Telefónica, volumen que permitió el afianzamiento de Amper (Banegas (inédito); Banegas 2023, 140-142; *El País*, 9 y 10 de marzo de 1989)[60]. Aquella alianza aportó a Amper dos elementos cruciales: un aumento notable en la dimensión, medida en volumen de ventas y en plantilla, y, en segundo lugar, un incremento considerable de su capacidad tecnológica. Como colofón obtuvo una elevada plusvalía de su inversión a la hora de vender su participación.

[58] Una valoración realizada por Amper sobre la base de los acuerdos recientes entre AT&T-NS y el grupo público de telecomunicaciones de Italia STET fijaba la inversión de Telefónica en AT&T-NS en 12.000 millones de pesetas (*El País*, 3 de julio de 1989). Intelsa se integró en Telettra (Intervención de Salvador Sánchez Terán, Congreso de los Diputados, sesión de la comisión, 2 de febrero de 1982).

[59] No está de más señalar que la alianza entre Philips y AT&T significaba una operación de concentración a la que no se opuso la European Commission, Case N° IV/M.651– AT&T-Philips. Revelaba tres hechos fundamentales. Por un lado, mostraba que AT&T buscaba saltar las barreras proteccionistas y acceder al mercado europeo de equipos de telecomunicaciones. Además, este acuerdo indicaba la continuidad de los esfuerzos conjuntos en el ámbito de las telecomunicaciones internacionales. Finalmente, ilustraba la tendencia de Estados Unidos hacia un entorno más liberal para las inversiones en el extranjero (Hudson 1983, 591-592).

[60] De las valoraciones de Amper e Inisel se encargaba Arthur Young (*El País*, 20 de abril de 1989). La asociación con AT&T tuvo lugar el mismo año en que Nokia adquirió la sección de informática de Ericsson (Mytelka 1991, 170). Para el clúster madrileño, véase Rama, Ferguson y Melero (2003, 71–88). Los protagonistas otorgan a esta alianza un aumento extraordinario de las ventas y la plantilla, a la vez que acceso a un nivel tecnológico inédito hasta entonces (Banegas 2023, 142).

Amper consideraba de vital importancia entrar en la telefonía móvil, negocio incipiente pero de gran futuro. Descartada la viabilidad de un desarrollo propio, la fórmula ideal, calcada de Telefónica, consistía en asociarse a un líder tecnológico, proveedor de equipo, y ofrecer su capacidad en el mercado de las infraestructuras de móviles para realizar el despliegue de instalaciones, logística, etc. en las redes. Con estas premisas y las perspectivas de un mercado fuerte y en expansión como el español bajo el acicate de una segunda licencia a Airtel, pudo vencer las resistencias iniciales de Motorola[61] y con la multinacional participó, eso sí, en posición minoritaria del 35%, en una empresa con el nombre de Telcel. Se trataba de una alianza industrial con un proveedor tecnológico, que incluía un plan de inversión con el objetivo de disputar el mercado abierto a Ericsson, líder absoluto en conmutación y en telefonía móvil de primera generación. Yendo a los resultados, sucesivamente Telcel triunfó en la segunda generación de telefonía móvil analógica y mantuvo el liderazgo largo tiempo en la primera digital con el GSM, que abrió el mercado a la competencia. Telcel aportó continuos e importantes recursos económicos sin los cuales el Grupo Amper difícilmente hubiera superado su crisis industrial. Junto al éxito económico directo, Amper logró rendimientos indirectos –económicos y tecnológicos– al conseguir en exclusiva la instalación de las infraestructuras de todos los nuevos despliegues[62]. Con los años,

[61]   Motorola se anticipó a Sony en el anuncio de la fabricación en España de equipos de radio en el estándar GSM. Motorola no tenía rival en precio de los terminales (40.000 ptas., frente a 139.150 ptas. de los CM-R 111 de Sony y 49.900 del N 100 de Nokia) y compartía la concesión de gratuidad de conexión con otras compañías (Panasonic y Sony). Se preveía que los abonados a la telefonía móvil en España se triplicaran en un quinquenio, hasta alcanzar la cifra de 1,2 millones. Motorola atravesaba por una expansión en el mercado chino (*Expansión*, 4 y 17 de enero de 1995).

[62]   Junto a Universal Data Systems y Nipon Motorola, Telcel formaba el trio de filiales de Motorola sin el nombre de la marca de la multinacional en cabeza (Walsh 1995, 1.183). Las negociaciones no progresaron hasta que Banegas y su equipo no lograron que Motorola admitiera la superioridad del potencial del mercado de España frente a Austria (Banegas inédito, 14; European Commission 1987, 41; Ignacio Menéndez de Luarca, Comunicación personal al autor, 4 de junio de 2020). Motorola y Ericsson prestaban servicios de radio móvil por los estándares TAV y TMA, respectivamente, en las áreas de Madrid y Barcelona. Telcel, con una modesta cifra de un millar de empleados, aportó unos ingresos de 16.900 millones de pesetas durante el ejercicio fiscal de 1992. Organigrama de Telcel: David Hughes, presidente; Jesús Banegas, vicepresidente; Ignacio Camarero, director general, sustituto de Jaime Martorell por incorporación de este al cargo de vicepresidente de Motorola para América; Juan del Puerto, director financiero; José R. Puente, director comercial y Ricardo de Mariano, director de recursos humanos. Martorell ejemplifica la aportación de cualificación por algunos altos directivos, en su calidad de ingeniero de telecomunicaciones por la Universidad de Santa Clara (California), empleado durante catorce años en diversas empresas estadounidenses del sector electrónico y exalto directivo (director general de *marketing*, ventas

creó un Centro de desarrollo y formación en Madrid, una inversión aproximada de 1.000 millones de pesetas, con la misión de investigar en la infraestructura celular para la telefonía rural española. El Centro albergaba un laboratorio de desarrollo y pruebas de *software* para centrales de conmutación y equipamiento radio de telefonía celular; allí se llevaba a cabo el control de calidad *software* y las tareas de formación del personal interno y técnico de Telefónica (*Computerworld*, 9 de abril de 1993).

La creación de Telcel fue relativamente simultánea con la ya señalada primera oficina de Amper en Europa. Tiempo después, como ya se ha apuntado, Amper Programas sirvió de cabeza de puente para el aterrizaje de Thomson CSF, rebautizada como Thales, que se convirtió en el socio multinacional del negocio dedicado a las comunicaciones de defensa. Sería poco sensato minusvalorar hechos como el apuntado, ya que parte del capital de Thales fue intercambiada con Alcatel por las acciones de la Société Franco-Américaine de Constructions Atomiques (Framatome) en su poder, rescatadas posteriormente por el Estado con destino a la industria nuclear (OCDE 2001, 115)[63]. Amper tenía acuerdos de comercialización con varias empresas –Exelvisión para fabricar y comercializar el videotex de este nombre a través de El Corte Inglés y con Parcon Suecia para ordenadores portátiles. Entre los proyectos inmediatos se encontraban, además de alguno ya señalado, la participación en MESA, entonces a la espera de un socio extranjero, y la entrada en México y China (*El País*, 6 de julio de 1987).

Amper persistió en su búsqueda de alianzas estratégicas que se plasmaran en cruces de participaciones accionariales con otras compañías extranjeras como vía de diversificar riesgos y mejorar su posición competitiva en el mercado único europeo (CNMV, 243, 10 de mayo de 1991). Entre otras posibles opciones existentes, Ericsson se situaba como predilecta para tomar una participación por cesión de algún socio. En la carrera se interpuso casi a última hora AT&T, bien situada por su alianza con Amper en la empresa conjunta AT&T Network Systems. La pugna se enmarañó cuando Telefónica pactó vender su participación en Amper a las multinacionales Matra y AT&T, una

---

y centros de diseño) de AT&T Microelectrónica (*Computerworld*, 17 de septiembre de 1993: *PCWEEK*, 16 de septiembre de 1993).

[63] En el marco del PEIN, Thomson se encontraba entre las candidatas a participar en acciones de promoción industrial impulsadas por el Gobierno, concretamente en el desarrollo y fabricación de condensadores de tántalo (Ministerio de Industria y Energía 1983, 28). Conviene recordar que Framatome (1995) era una de las empresas líderes del sector de equipo mecánico pesado y de precisión en Francia.

operación que contaba con el respaldo del MINER y no cerraba las puertas a las pretensiones de Ericsson, si bien las complicaba por la entrada de una nueva pretendiente. La multinacional sueca sumaba un liderazgo en equipos de conmutación y en sistemas electrónicos para la defensa, ramo en el que disponía de una filial en España. La presencia de dos socios podía impedir a cualquiera de ellos rebasar el 25% del capital en una hipotética ampliación, prevista inicialmente para permitir al socio único llegar a tener hasta una tercera parte del capital de Amper[64]. El desenlace final podría ser la entrada de Ericsson en Amper Programas como opción que no descartaba otras posibles[65].

Decididamente, había sonado la hora de las multinacionales y la diana era Amper Programas en cuyo accionariado, como sabemos, Thomson CSF había protagonizado una entrada minoritaria en 1993. Por un acuerdo de colaboración a mediados del año siguiente y una posterior aceleración del calendario pretendía elevar su participación hasta un 49% cuando el Gobierno autorizó una nueva inversión de mil millones de pesetas en Amper Programas. En 1995, alcanzó el 39% con desembolso de 400 millones de ptas., la mitad con destino al capital social y la otra mitad para financiar la adquisición de acciones por parte de la matriz Amper (*Expansión*, 4 de enero de 1995; *El País*, 4 de enero de 1995)[66]. En marzo de 1996, alcanzó el porcentaje planeado

[64] Ericsson (1991), 4; Ericsson España (1990), 37. El valor en Bolsa de dicha participación rozaba los 3.200 millones de pesetas (*El País*, 10 de mayo de 1991). Matra y Motorola competían en el segmento de las telecomunicaciones móviles (*Expansión*, 15 de octubre de 1991). La prensa económica destacaba las posiciones contrapuestas dentro del gobierno entre Industria –alianza AT&T/Amper– y Transportes –opción Alcatel como salida europea –, por un lado, y Telefónica –desinversión en activos industriales para financiar la internacionalización como operadora de redes (*Expansión*, 9 de noviembre de 1990).

[65] Claudio Aranzadi y Cándido Velázquez mostraron su aquiescencia con la opción AT&T, si bien Telefónica subrayó su oposición a vender su participación del 15% (*El País,* 11 de mayo de 1991). Curiosamente, Ericsson no figuraba entre los socios potenciales de Amper señalados por algunos medios, que sí incluían además de Siemens, AT&T, Northern Telecom y Philips, dos empresas francesas (Bull y Spie-Batignolles) y sendas norteamericana (Digital Equipment Co.), suiza (Hasler-Ascom), italiana (Olivetti), sueca (Pargon) y belga (Prodata) (Management Europe 1988, 102).

[66] Restructuraciones del consejo de administración de Amper Programas: nombramiento de Eugenio Vela Sastre, en sustitución del fundador y presidente Antonio López, como vicepresidente y consejero delegado el 16 de noviembre de 1994 (CNMV, 4.431, 4 de abril de 1995); entrada de Jesús Banegas como presidente, en sustitución del efímero Eugenio Vela como resultado del pacto entre Telefónica y Teneo, y de Guillaume Dehollain –antiguo delegado del ministerio francés de la Defensa en Thomson (*Air et cosmos*, 1.004 1.106, 1086, 12), como vicepresidente y nombramiento de cuatro delegados por Amper y tres por Thomson (*Expansión*, 1 y 4 de enero de 1995). Más tarde, poco antes de finalizar el año 1998, Telefónica nombró presidente de la matriz a Arturo Baldasano (*El País*, 2 de febrero de 1998).

inicialmente por adquisición de una décima parte de las acciones (CNMV, 6.466, 29 de marzo de 1996).

También se pusieron en el blanco otras dos filiales, que, como se ha visto, habían atravesado por turbulencias: Amper Telemática y Amper Cosesa, en suspensión de pagos y recién salida de la suspensión, respectivamente[67].

En realidad, la vía nacional se agotó con esta reestructuración del grupo electrónico español, que escondía una operación más ambiciosa: la venta de Amper y su integración en un mayor conglomerado empresarial para aliviar definitivamente las pérdidas cuantiosas. Con el ajuste y la reestructuración de la plantilla el Grupo Amper esperaba poner coto a años de pérdidas y recuperar beneficios en 1994. De hecho, en ese año las ventas alcanzaron los 40.000 millones de ptas., un 30% más que las del año anterior, la quinta parte correspondientes a exportaciones (*Expansión*, 2 de febrero de 1995).

A mediados de 1994, quedó aprobado un plan de futuro que tenía como objetivos primordiales garantizar la viabilidad del Grupo, reducir el endeudamiento financiero y maximizar a medio plazo el valor para los accionistas (CNMV, 6.842, 26 de abril de 1996).

Una de las piezas del mencionado Plan radicaba en la culminación de un acuerdo de venta con una multinacional. Siemens era la mejor situada de las dos en liza con las que la dirección de Amper y representantes del MINER habían entablado negociaciones. Junto al gigante alemán de la electrónica competía, si bien con menor vigor, la canadiense Northern Telecom, notoria por sus tentativas de invertir en España y aspirante a hacerse un hueco en ese mercado mediante la asociación con alguna empresa local, para lo que contaba con Amper. Una vez encarada la solución Siemens, el principal obstáculo para cerrar la operación residía en cuantificar la deuda exacta de Amper, crucial para determinar el valor del grupo y fijar el precio a pagar[68].

---

[67] Amper Cosesa presentó suspensión de pagos en noviembre; la aprobación del convenio con los acreedores –quita mínima del 55% y una moratoria de pago– permitió levantar la suspensión de pagos (*El País*, 14 de junio de 1994).

[68] En esa misma dirección apuntaba la reciente adquisición de la mitad de su filial española en poder de la constructora Agroman (*Expansión*, 17 de julio de 1991). Amper subcontrató a Northern Telecom, Ltd. la fabricación en Galway (Irlanda) de un terminal telefónico marca Amper. Se trataba de un teléfono analógico, multifrecuencia, con visualizador, memorización automática, llamada en espera y marcación abreviada; fue homologado junto con otro de la marca Northern Telecom (*BOE*, 238, 4 de octubre de 1991, 32.357). Los mayores accionistas de Amper eran por entonces Telefónica, con el 15%, y el INI, con el 9,5%. El capital restante estaba muy repartido y buena parte del mismo se encontraba en Bolsa, lo cual le obligaría a lanzar una OPA.

Bajo los auspicios del MINER, hacia mediados de 1996, Siemens, a través de su filial española, y Amper lograron un acuerdo de intenciones con el objetivo de desarrollar conjuntamente actividades en telecomunicaciones mediante la implicación de filiales. Le siguió la alianza, plasmada en un acuerdo básico que atañía a tres filiales de Amper, a saber, Elasa, Datos y Telemática (CNMV, 7.587, 4 de octubre de 1996).

El pacto tuvo implicaciones para cada uno de los firmantes. En el lado de la parte compradora, Siemens adquiría el grueso de acciones de Elasa –80%– y el porcentaje restante quedaba a disposición de comprador y vendedor, a través de opciones ejercitables en un breve espacio de tiempo. Por el acuerdo de intenciones, Siemens convertiría Elasa en su centro mundial de competencia para telefonía pública. En segundo lugar, Siemens compraba el 10% menos una acción de Amper Datos y dejaba abierta la puerta a ampliar su participación sin rebasar el 30% del capital hasta finales de 1997 estrictamente, fecha en la que Amper podría recomprar el 10% de la filial (*Europe*, 6.865-6.883, 1996, 17; *Computerworld*, 5 de julio de 1996)[69]. Adicionalmente, Siemens protegía su posición a través del derecho a impedir las operaciones minoritarias cruzadas, en el caso de que un competidor internacional adquiriese una posición relevante en el accionariado o en la gestión de Amper S.A. Por lo que se refiere a la parte vendedora, el Grupo Amper reduciría su tamaño y fortalecería su estructura financiera por eliminación del endeudamiento gracias al ingreso cercano a los 14.000 millones de ptas., una situación idónea para emprender nuevas inversiones productivas en las telecomunicaciones.

En la tercera adquisición, la alemana compraba las secciones de telemática de Amper Telemática, decisión sujeta a la pronta resolución de las reclamaciones judiciales derivadas del expediente de regulación de empleo de 1992. Para cerrar la operación Siemens debía integrar sus actividades de telecomunicaciones en España en una sociedad de nueva creación con el nombre de Siemens Telecomunicaciones S.A. El precio quedaba determinado por el valor contable neto de los activos y pasivos que se transferían. Por otra parte, Amper se reservaba una opción de compra de hasta un 34% de esta compañía al valor contable, a ejercitar antes de acabar el año 1997 (CNMV, 6.864, 1 de

---

[69] Los precios de las acciones vendidas a Siemens se desglosan así: el 80% de las acciones de Elasa: 12.966 millones de ptas.; las opciones ejercitables: 3.241 millones de ptas. más intereses; el 10% menos una acción de Amper Datos: 957 millones de ptas. (CNMV, 6.864, 1 de mayo de 1996). Por interés fiscal de Amper se estipuló que la compraventa se haría en dos fases consecutivas y que durante varios años el grupo Amper tendría la exclusividad de las ventas internacionales (Banegas, inédito).

mayo de 1996). Los aspectos pendientes de resolver se referían sustancialmente a cuestiones legales y pertinentes cautelas, dada la trascendencia del acuerdo para ambas compañías. A finales de 1996 se hizo efectivo el acuerdo de intenciones firmado entre Amper y Siemens el año anterior en los términos establecidos de porcentajes de capital y precio (CNMV, 6.613, 24 de abril de 1996; *El País*, 3 de noviembre de 1996).

Como previsto, al entrar Siemens en el capital, las filiales de Amper –Amper Elasa Amper Telemática– quedaron incorporadas a su organigrama y pasaron a operar con la marca de la alemana como cabecera –Siemens Elasa y Siemens Telecomunicaciones S. A.– (Amper S. A. 1997, 5 y 25)[70].

El proceso de concentración en Siemens prosiguió con matices a lo largo de 1998 por sucesivas cesiones y el consiguiente adelgazamiento de Amper S. A. A comienzos del año, esta vendió la sección de terminales telefónicos y PABX de pequeña y mediana capacidad a Siemens además de la quinta parte de sus acciones de Siemens Elasa S.A. a Siemens AG[71]. A poco de acabar el año, Amper asumió las actividades de exportación de sistemas de telefonía de uso público a diversos países, entre ellos Australia y Venezuela (Amper, *Informe de gestión 1999*, 2) y recompró a Siemens el 10% de la filial Amper Datos transferido en 1996 (Ernst & Young 1997)[72].

En los momentos anteriores a las desinversiones de 1996-1998, el Grupo Amper presentaba una estructura de enorme sencillez, ya que su organigrama tan solo recogía tres sociedades llamadas dependientes, dos de ellas comerciales –Telecomunicaciones Amper Argentina y Amper International, con sedes en Buenos Aires y Jersey– y una industrial –Teléfonos de los Urales (Telur)–, empresa conjunta en la que tuvo un papel decisivo en la doble faceta de socio tecnológico y capitalista minoritario en la lógica del *holding* industrial de la CTNE durante el mandato de Luis Solana. La fórmula consistió en fabricar en la URSS teléfonos de diseño y desarrollo propios –el modelo

---

[70] En 2004, la planta de Siemens cercana a Zaragoza, con una plantilla de 363 personas y especializada en la producción de teléfonos públicos, fabricaba antenas avanzadas para infraestructuras de telefonía móvil (*El Periódico*, 6 de agosto de 2004).

[71] El 20% de las acciones de Siemens Elasa S.A. fueron vendidas a Siemens AG por 3.386.522.431 ptas., con plusvalías de unos 2.500 millones de ptas. (CNMV, 14.400, 1 de diciembre de 1998).

[72] El precio de venta de la sección se fijó en 770 millones de pesetas, igual al valor contable de los activos y pasivos que se transferían a Siemens (CNMV, 11.140, 2 de febrero de 1998; 11.098, 6 de febrero de 1998). Los productos de Elasa se exportaban desde el departamento internacional del Grupo Amper pese a las reticencias iniciales de Siemens a aceptar esa práctica temporal (Banegas inédito).

Tarsis– a los que se incorporaban componentes de origen local. Sin arredrarse ante las dificultades financieras, Amper se propuso anticiparse a otras multinacionales en el mercado de la URSS. En realidad se trataba de la participación como agente ejecutor –socio minoritario o, al menos, gestor– de varios proyectos soviéticos de mayor alcance en las telecomunicaciones. El conjunto abarcaba el aumento y diversificación de la producción de equipo – teléfonos públicos y centralitas telefónicas privadas– así como componentes –circuitos impresos– en la fábrica de Telur ampliada y en una nueva factoría, respectivamente (Calvo 2016, 253-254; Campbell 2019; *El País*, 4 de junio de 1988; *BIT*, enero de 1990, 16-17)[73].

En múltiples aspectos, y así lo reconoce de hecho la historia oficial de Amper, el año 1996 marca un jalón en la internacionalización. Precisamente, la expansión exterior por lanzamiento de nuevos productos y servicios auguraba unas perspectivas favorables y expectativas de beneficios en la mayoría de las empresas del grupo (Amper S.A., *Memoria 1996*, 5). La división internacional de Amper se engrosó con una nueva empresa industrial en Perú, país en el que ya estaba implantada –Telecomunicaciones Amper Perú– mientras que Telecomunicaciones Amper Argentina alcanzó la categoría de empresa industrial[74].

Más adelante, en 1998, Amper mantenía una presencia internacional con nueve unidades a las que calificaba de delegaciones en el exterior. Once países engrosaban la lista antes mencionada, dos de ellos en Europa –Portugal y Croacia– cinco en Latinoamérica –Chile, Colombia, Cuba, Venezuela y Bra-

---

[73] Participación del 44% en Telur, cuyo capital ascendía a 5,6 millones de rublos (Amper, *Informe de gestión 1996*, 6). Detalles interesantes sobre las negociaciones en Banegas (inédito). Aspecto poco resaltado, Luis Solana intentó incorporar al proyecto de invertir en la URSS a las grandes del sector: Standard Eléctrica, Ericsson, Telettra y Amper (Banegas 2023, 142). Junto a la transferencia tecnológica directa, cabe destacar la transferencia de conocimiento: técnicos de Amper peritaron las instalaciones preexistentes en Perm; utilización de la experiencia previa como «trader» en la URSS de un ejecutivo de Amper y trabajos de identificación de minerales exportables en los Urales por geólogos de la Facultad de Ciencias Geológicas de la Universidad de Madrid (Banegas 2023, pp. 146-147).

[74] Telecomunicaciones Amper Perú, propiedad al 100%, tenía un capital de 95.000 nuevos soles (Amper, *Informe de gestión 1996*, 6). Amper Perú figuraba en tercera posición entre las TIC peruanas (Instituto Nacional de Estadística e Informática 2000, 55). Amper destacaba entre los proveedores de terminales telefónicos para la Compañía Peruana de Teléfonos (CPT), la célebre y controvertida apuesta de Telefónica por Latinoamérica en 1994. Los terminales suministrados a esta operadora al año siguiente duplicaban con holgura la cantidad vendida a Alcatel Citesa España o Internacional Ibérica de Control y Telefonía, creada en 1980 tras la absorción de Internacional Ibérica de Control por Internacional Ibérica de Telefonía (*BOE*, 20 de agosto de 1980, 21.118); el valor FOB se elevaba a 2,0328 millones de dólares, cifra inferior a la de sus rivales (CPT, *Actas,* 23/1995).

sil– y cuatro en Asia –India, China, Malasia y Singapur–. La presencia exterior se completaba con una alianza tecnológica, Amper Technology Ventures, de vida efímera, con domicilio social en Madrid y oficina principal en California (Grupo Amper, *Informe de gestión 1998*, 9)[75]. Al año siguiente se sumó Hemisferio Norte S.A., orientada al desarrollo de proyectos y participación en empresas de las TIC[76].

A lo largo del tiempo, las delegaciones en el exterior fueron cambiando su perfil. Hasta el año 2000, la estrategia de IED de Amper cuajó en casi una decena de filiales, la mayoría en varios países latinoamericanos –Amper Perú, Telecomunicaciones Amper Argentina, Amper do Brasil, Amper Centroamericana S.A. de C.V., Amper Telecommunications de Puerto Rico y Amper Guatemala S.A. DCV– y las restantes dispersas en tres continentes –Amper Australia, Telur y una Société à Responsabilité Limitée à Associé Unique (SARLAAU) en Marruecos–[77].

El Grupo Amper hizo de la expansión internacional su factor clave, que se combinaba con otros, algunos ya mencionados. Se trata de la ampliación de la oferta de productos y servicios y la extensión geográfica de los mercados, junto a la apuesta por líneas de negocio estratégicas en su afianzamiento como líder del sector español de equipos y sistemas de telecomunicación. Esa diversificación descansaba en el desarrollo de productos propios por un incremento de las inversiones, y en el acceso a productos ajenos, fruto de alianzas estratégicas con empresas líderes. Una mayor disponibilidad de bienes y servicios estratégicos –sistemas de comunicaciones y control e integraciones de sistemas de acceso a las comunicaciones tácticas– dio al grupo instrumentos para consolidar su presencia en los mercados internacionales, entre ellos Colombia y Brasil (Szapiro y De Souza 2000, 28-31). Se trata de una estrategia inclusiva, que aspiraba a aprovechar la ampliación de la cadena de valor tanto

---

[75] En 1998 el presidente era Rafael Posada Díaz-Crespo mientras que Anthony Leone reunía tres cargos cruciales –vicepresidente, tesorero y secretario (State of Delaware Office of the Secretary of State, 17 de septiembre de 1998); al año siguiente figuraba un director (Jaime Martorell) (Amper Technology Ventures, Inc. C2120711, 9/18/1998; Application by foreign Corporation to transact business in Florida, 24 de agosto de 1999).

[76] La inversión total invertida ascendió a 8.692.451.387 pesetas, aportación a una ampliación de capital (CNMV, 19.913, 1 de diciembre de 1999).

[77] En Argentina, por ejemplo, Amper figuraba entre los fabricantes locales de equipos de telecomunicación, junto a Ericsson, Alcatel CIT, NEC y Siemens (U.S. Department of Commerce 1984, 7). Con los años, Amper estaba presente en El Salvador, Venezuela, Colombia, Costa Rica, Ecuador, Honduras, Nicaragua y Panamá (*El Comercio*, 21/2012; Amper 2000, 4).

en el mercado interior como, más específicamente, junto a los clientes institucionales y nuevos operadores de telecomunicaciones[78].

Está en juego un punto central, es decir, la capacidad tecnológica y, en suma, la I+D de Amper, una de sus insignias[79]. La empresa efectuaba investigación en un departamento propio, que combinaba con alianzas tecnológicas, por ejemplo, la forjada en 1988 con AT&T y Philips en la empresa conjunta ATP España. Sin duda, con el adelgazamiento de su tamaño fue perdiendo capacidad de inversión en I+D a la vez que se fue deteriorando la relación entre inversión y gastos destinados a I+D y ventas hasta el punto que esa relación cayó casi ocho puntos porcentuales en el periodo 1993-2000. Sin embargo, una lectura más minuciosa de los datos revela una tendencia creciente de los titulados superiores en la composición del empleo en el Grupo Amper (Gráfico 2) y un comportamiento de la I+D respecto al personal empleado en el departamento. Ahora bien, se observan oscilaciones ya que en un año concreto –1996– las actividades de I+D recibieron sumas superiores a las del año anterior aunque la plantilla no alcanzaba dicho nivel –106 millones de ptas. más y 95 menos, respectivamente– mientras que en 1998 el gasto y la inversión bajaron a 1.583 millones de ptas. y el personal a 184.

La búsqueda de las claves de la trayectoria empresarial invita a intentar mejorar este breve cuadro con una aproximación particular a partir de Medidata. Esta filial fundamentó su naturaleza de proveedor estratégico en el mercado de telecomunicaciones en su capacidad de respuesta a los desafíos de los nuevos servicios de valor añadido en una cadena de valor ampliada con la incorporación de soluciones de convergencia de datos y una amplia y diversificada oferta, sobre todo en el terreno de la integración voz-datos e Internet. En este contexto, Medidata continuaba expandiéndose en mercados a veces muy pujantes como proveedora de bienes industriales y prestadora de servicios –gestión, finanzas y *utilities*–. En una de sus puntas de lanza, la filial continuó invirtiendo en nuevas tecnologías, como gerenciamiento de datos, telefonía por Internet (Internet Protocol, IP) y continuidad de negocios, seguridad e identidad y servicios preventivos de valor agregado en *datacenters*, para citar algunos.

En esa senda de crecimiento, en el 2000, Medidata aportaba un cuarto del negocio total del Grupo Amper, porcentaje que aumentó hasta un tercio al año

---

[78] Las líneas estratégicas incluían los sistemas de acceso a redes de comunicaciones militares tácticas de acceso rápido, entre otras (Amper S.A., *Memoria 1997*).

[79] En 1979, Amper subrayaba que siempre había utilizado tecnología propia sin pagar un céntimo por *royalties* (*BIT*, abril de 1979, 8).

siguiente antes de caer a la quinta parte de su nivel inicial en 2002 y 2003, respectivamente, en medio de la crisis de las empresas tecnológicas. Tomando en conjunto el ascenso y la caída, entre 2000 y 2005, las ventas de Medidata pasaron de 7.304 millones de ptas. a 11.620, es decir, se multiplicaron por 1,59. Esta progresión descansó mayoritariamente en los productos con un 61% de las ventas totales, por tanto, a gran distancia de los servicios. Desde el punto de vista geográfico, su mercado, tradicionalmente centrado en Brasil, se ensanchó a partir de 2005 por la penetración en España a través de la nueva Amper Medidata, resultado de calcar en el mercado español el mismo modelo de Brasil.

Amper Medidata nació con un triple objetivo en las facetas de proyecto, producto y estrategia. El primero consistía en erigirse en un centro de excelencia en IP, movilidad, almacenamiento y seguridad de red para para la totalidad de actividades y empresas del Grupo Amper. Sus dos objetivos restantes perseguían nuevos desarrollos –líneas con tecnologías de Internet dirigidas a los clientes del grupo– junto a prospección –nuevas oportunidades de negocio (*Valor Económico*, 25 de noviembre de 2004, B4)[80]. Superada la crisis internacional de las punto com, Medidata, cuya cartera se incrementó en 2004 en un 38% respecto al año anterior, aspiraba a aprovechar las nuevas oportunidades inherentes a las perspectivas económicas y políticas del país. En particular, con proceder selectivo iba en busca de clientes de alto potencial de compra y modernización de sus infraestructuras. Junto al sector de telecomunicaciones brasileñas, esta empresa ponía su mirada en las nuevas tecnologías con aplicaciones específicas para diferentes sectores de actividad. También estaba haciendo especial hincapié en otros mercados como el financiero.

Pasemos de los resultados a los medios. En parte logró sus propósitos utilizando a las filiales o subfiliales para su expansión. Así sucedió cuando Pesa Electrónica, cabecera del Grupo Pesa, golpeada por la recesión en el mercado nacional, recurrió a varias filiales en EE.EU. como instrumento de penetración en el mercado norteamericano. Esta empresa presentó la oferta de compra del 81% del Grupo Chyron, un líder mundial en sistemas de edición, dibujo elec-

---

[80] Amper Medidata sobresalía por su capital humano –podía movilizar hasta 2.000 ingenieros y expertos en soluciones IP– y la diversidad de las especializaciones que presentaba, en consonancia con la variedad de su oferta de productos y servicios, los principales de los cuales eran comunicaciones IP, gestión y operación de redes y sistemas y almacenamiento y seguridad. Ya en sus primeros momentos, se adjudicó proyectos en grandes infraestructuras –aeropuertos de Madrid y Albacete–, con diversas instituciones – ministerios de Seguridad y Defensa y Parlamento Vasco– e Ibermutua, colaboradora con la Seguridad Social (Grupo Amper, *Memoria 2004*; Amper, *Resultados 2003*, marzo 2004, 7).

trónico y de generadores completando la actividad de Pesa. Poco después, en la primavera de 1993 para mayor precisión, otra de sus filiales al 100%, Pesa Inc., adquirió la norteamericana Micro Communications Inc.[81] En ese año, el Grupo Pesa, con un capital de 1.238 millones de ptas. y unas pérdidas de 1.315 millones de ptas., reunía hasta siete sociedades clasificadas como dependientes y asociadas, cuatro de ellas participadas al ciento por ciento (Anexo 1).

La puesta de filiales o subfiliales al servicio de la expansión o la adquisición de empresas lo ejerció Amper de forma reiterada a través de Amper Servicios. La matriz absorbió en su totalidad la brasileña Telinst Telecomunicaçoes Ltd., especializada en la instalación e ingeniería de redes de telecomunicaciones. Rebautizada como Amper do Brasil Telecomunicaçoes Ltd., tenía la misión de aportar una base de operaciones para suministrar equipos y servicios al mercado brasileño, empezando por la operadora Compañía Riograndense de Telecomunicaciones (Ernst & Young 1997; *Telecompaper*, 20 de agosto de 1997)[82]. El proceder se repitió en 1999 con la absorción de tres filiales de nueva creación ahora en distintas latitudes, una de ellas –Amper Guatemala SACV– con el 99% y un 1% de SA de Finanzas y Telecomunicaciones y otras dos –Amper Centroamérica SA en El Salvador y Amper Télécommunications, la ya menciomnada SARLAAU en Marruecos– con la compra de la totalidad de las acciones (Anexo 1) (Grupo Amper 1999, 5).

En orden cronológico, idéntico papel instrumental desempeñó Hemisferio Norte S.A. en operaciones con modalidades diversas a lo largo del ejercicio 2000 (CNMV, 19.913, 1 de diciembre de 1999), que engrosaron el grupo de filiales o participadas en el extranjero con cuatro empresas. Amper utilizó el *green-field investment* para crear en solitario Hemisferio Sul Participaçoes Ltda. Esta y Hemisferio Norte fueron utilizadas en la faceta de *mergers and acquisitions* para llevar a cabo una suscripción y dos compras. En detalle, Hemisferio Norte S.A. participó en la compra en su totalidad de Dominio Diez S.A. y, junto a Hemisferio Sul Participaçoes Ltda, intervino en la adquisición escalonada en dos tramos del 51% de Medidata Informática S.A. (Anexo 1) (Grupo Amper 2000, 3-4)[83].

---

[81] Precios de compra en dólares de Micro Communications Inc.: 1,5 millones y del 81% del Grupo Chyron: 10 millones (Ernst&Young 1994, 22; CNMV, 528, 18 de octubre de 1991).

[82] Adquisición de Telinst Telecomunicaçoes Ltd. por unos 400.000 dólares (Ernst & Young 1997).

[83] Al iniciarse el año 2000, Amper selló un acuerdo de intenciones para adquirir una participación accionarial del 40% en Medidata con opción para convertirse en mayoritaria (Grupo Amper, *Informe de gestión 1999,* 5). Las ventas de Medidata superaron los 55 millones de

5. Una reordenación incesante: desinversiones y segregaciones en Amper

Ya conocemos la nueva frontera a la que el cambio tecnológico y la globalización empujaron a los fabricantes de equipo con la extraordinaria ampliación de la cadena de valor. Por la misma razón que el nuevo escenario reclamaba la adopción de estructuras flexibles, imponía extremar la racionalización de la estructura en un horizonte de incertidumbre en el conjunto del sector[84].

En sentido opuesto a las absorciones, una de las facetas de la reordenación en la década de 1990 se plasmó con una corriente de repliegue por la vía de desinversiones y segregaciones sucesivas. Mediado el año 1992, Amper vendió a AT&T Network Systems International BV (Holanda) en dos tramos casi idénticos su participación del 49% en la filial española de esta empresa. La venta garantizaba la continuidad del negocio de instalación y asistencia técnica que Amper Servicios mantenía con AT&T Network Systems España. Los recursos generados – resultados extraordinarios positivos de 2.246 millones de ptas.– debían cubrir las tres cuartas partes de los gastos de reestructuración de Amper Telemática y Amper Programas, en los que estaban implicados casi medio centenar de personas en el ejercicio[85]. En 1993, Amper se desprendió del 23,53% que poseía en la compañía portorriqueña Telefónica Hispanoamericana e hizo lo propio con su filial Télétechnique en favor de Sogestel (CNMV, 243, 15 de noviembre de 1993)[86].

Las desinversiones siguieron con la venta de Pesa Electrónica S.A. en su totalidad a un conjunto estadounidense de inversores liderado por Percival Hudgins & Company, una operación que sufrió retrasos por causas que varia-

---

dólares en 1999; además de Telefónica, la empresa brasileña contaba con grandes empresas internacionales entre su clientela principal (CNMV, 20.574, 3 de febrero de 2000 y 6.499, 10 de marzo de 2000).

[84] En los años 90, el valor añadido bruto al coste de los factores de las empresas de material y equipo electrónico creció de forma moderada respecto al año anterior; como excepción, en 1992, el crecimiento fue negativo y en 1994, hubo un crecimiento elevado; esas empresas aparecen agrupadas con sus homólogas eléctricas y ópticas (Banco de España 2002, 54).

[85] Precio del 49% en AT&T Network Systems España: 4.410 millones de pesetas; recursos generados: resultados extraordinarios positivos de 2.246 millones de ptas. (CNMV, 1.061, 23 de julio de 1992; 1950, 11 de mayo de 1993).

[86] Amper, que acababa de comprar un 49% de Télétechnique al Grupo Spie por el importe simbólico de un franco francés, debía responder de los créditos y avales concedidos a la empresa vendida hasta ese momento, monto que sería reemplazado en el pasivo de Télétechnique por un crédito de 10 millones de francos a favor de Amper, avalado por Sogestel (CNMV, 449, 6 de agosto de 1991).

ban dependiente de la fuente –según la empresa por pequeños problemas jurídicos y según los sindicatos por escasa solvencia del comprador[87]–. A poco de finalizar la década de 1990, Amper Technology Ventures, creada por Amper algo más de un año antes y vendida en su mitad poco después, echó el cierre (Grupo Amper 1998, 5 y 1999, 5).

Amper observaba los cambios acelerados de la estructura y forma de hacer negocio, caracterizados por la externalización de funciones o tareas hasta entonces consideradas una parte esencial del mismo y la dedicación creciente de recursos a los clientes. La empresa veía cómo el desmantelamiento de los monopolios históricos, la desregulación del sector y el avance tecnológico permitían añadir servicios especializados prestados por operadoras noveles y nuevas soluciones de valor añadido (Amper 2000, 1-2).

El Grupo Amper había adoptado a finales de 1990 una estructura organizativa basada en empresas especializadas por familias de productos (telefonía inalámbrica, telefonía pública, terminales básicos, sistemas de gestión de red, etcétera) y por funciones horizontales (fabricación, instalación y, en cierta medida, la comercialización) agrupadas en divisiones. Esta estructura parecía adecuada en su momento para responder al reto de la competencia y exigencias del mercado, así como sus adaptaciones a lo largo de la década de 1980. Las nuevas necesidades de los clientes, basadas en soluciones integradas ágiles y eficaces con un creciente valor añadido potencial, la hicieron totalmente inadecuada (Amper 2000, 1-2).

La amplitud de la reestructuración bien merece detenernos en su planteamiento y desarrollo. Amper S. A. buscaba una respuesta eficaz a las exigencias del mercado, como empresa integradora de soluciones globales de alto valor añadido para los clientes, y una vía para dar un vuelco al deterioro de los resultados en el ejercicio 1999 y recuperar la senda del crecimiento. En el nuevo modelo la empresa matriz debía ejercer de centro corporativo, que agrupara la mayor parte de sus recursos en dos áreas operativas nucleadoras – Tecnologías y Soluciones –, a la vez que asumiera las funciones de definición como estrategia y control de los negocios. Los recursos restantes debían trasvasarse a las empresas operativas con el objetivo de simplificar el modelo

---

[87] Application by foreign Corporation to transact business in Florida, 24 de agosto de 1999; Application for withdrawal, 7 de diciembre de 1999. Los despedidos de Amper Telemática realizaron un encierro en la factoría para reclamar su puesto de trabajo. La Comunidad de Madrid, por presiones de los trabajadores y mediación forzada del alcalde de Getafe, reclamó un plan de viabilidad para la empresa y prometió créditos de 600 millones en ayudas (*El País*, 4 de julio y 3 de agosto de 1994).

de gestión, ahorrar costes, acelerar la llegada de las decisiones al cliente e incrementar la creación de valor para el accionista.

En tales criterios de suprema eficacia para la clientela y de generación de valor para el accionista se basó para concentrar en una empresa todas las actividades del grupo, tradicionalmente encuadradas en el campo de las telecomunicaciones civiles alrededor de Cosesa. Convertida de sección especializada en unidad con entidad jurídica propia – filialización–, la nueva empresa, bajo la denominación de Amper Soluciones, asumía la tarea de reorganizarse de forma descentralizada con el fin de cumplir sus cometidos y alcanzar los acuerdos tecnológicos y estratégicos pertinentes. La táctica consistía en que la matriz Amper S.A. cediera en su totalidad a Amper Soluciones S.A. las participaciones accionariales de su casi una docena de filiales, dos de ellas locales –Amper Datos S.A. y Amper Servicios S.A.– y el resto fruto de la IED. El plan culminaba con una profundización de la internacionalización mediante el reajuste de la infraestructura exterior por cierre de las unidades activas –agencias, delegaciones y sucursales tanto de la matriz como de Amper Servicios S. A.– y remodelación del conjunto según el instrumento jurídico más conforme a la legislación del país en cuestión. Otras funciones consistían en garantizar soluciones de redes llave en mano a las grandes operadoras en el mercado interior y en el latinoamericano, así como lograr capacidades para prestar servicios de datos a las grandes empresas y clientes corporativos. Desde el punto de vista organizativo debía agrupar los recursos operativos en torno a tres áreas de mercado –operaciones y *marketing* y tecnología– y relacionarlas estrechamente entre sí. En ellas tres deberían confluir los recursos disponibles en Cosesa y Servicios y los de la propia matriz, así como los de las filiales y participadas en el exterior. Finalmente, parecía necesario adoptar una gestión homogénea en los negocios o empresas no instrumentales, ajenas al área de soluciones y que fundamentaban la creación de valor tanto en su singularidad como en acuerdos tecnológicos o estratégicos con otras empresas (Amper 2000, 3).

En su segunda plasmación, la transformación de las secciones en filiales desembocaba en una nueva unidad jurídicamente independiente –Amper Tecnologías– a partir de la antigua Amper Telemática y mediante concentración de la totalidad de las participaciones accionariales de Amper S.A. en Amper Programas, Amper Sistemas S.A., Amper Ibersegur S.A. y Telecomunicaciones Celulares S.A. La actuación iba de nuevo encaminada al logro de sinergias y a la realización de inversiones estratégicas de contenido tecnológico, capaces de acrecentar el valor de la participación accionarial por asunción de la gestión y forja de alianzas estratégicas. En este contexto, a Amper Programas se le encomendaba la tarea de centrarse en negocios con un alto potencial de crecimiento y de aprovechar oportunidades emanadas de la nueva unidad en inversiones estratégicas a medio y largo plazo con opciones de ser integradas en la cartera de esta. Todas las operaciones señaladas debían llevarse a cabo a un precio coincidente con el valor en libros de las participaciones accionariales en los estados financieros de las sociedades transmitentes a último día de 1999 (Amper 2000, 1-2).

La caída de las ventas de terminales telefónicos y teléfonos públicos que sobrevino en 1998 como efecto lógico –al menos en parte– de los acuerdos con Siemens obligó al Grupo Amper a redoblar esfuerzos en la refocalización de los negocios. A ello contribuían las filiales con sus resultados récord y el importante crecimiento de la facturación. En ese año, Amper y Siemens Elasa prorrogaron por un trienio el acuerdo de comercialización que otorgaba a Amper la prerrogativa de vender los productos fabricados por la segunda, en particular teléfonos públicos, en determinados mercados exteriores y en un área geográfica más reducida. Además de reforzar la posición internacional, Amper impulsó la optimización de los recursos, que se resolvió por la reducción de la plantilla en España en un 25,6% y la mengua de los gastos de personal y generales en el 11%, como recoge el Informe de gestión de 1998.

Amper estaba empeñada en afianzar su estrategia de diversificación de productos y servicios con nuevas líneas de negocio que le permitieran dar prioridad a los clientes corporativos sin menoscabo de los operadores tradicionales. Al mismo tiempo, pretendía ofrecer una completa gama de *outsourcing* de soluciones a ambos tipos de clientes. Nos referimos a movimientos en la tan repetida cadena de valor. En ese momento, Latinoamérica ocupaba una parte integral de la actividad del grupo y, a medio plazo, presentaba un elevado potencial de aportación constante a la cuenta de explotación. Por otra parte, Amper pretendía contrarrestar la desinversión de Telefónica con la reafirmación de su papel como uno de los proveedores preferentes en una amplia gama de servicios. Amper concebía este objetivo de crecimiento como una ampliación del grupo con una lista significativa de nuevas empresas y actividades, tales como redes Internet Protocol (IP), servicios de Internet e integración de voz y datos (Amper S.A., *Memoria 1999*, 5)

Respecto a filiales y, por consiguiente, a segmentos de actividad, la recién creada Amper Soluciones planeaba una reordenación orientada a capturar el potencial de crecimiento a partir de tres pilares básicos relacionados con las nuevas oportunidades, la eficiencia y la organización. La también nueva Amper Tecnologías propugnaba un crecimiento agresivo orientado a capturar en plenitud el potencial de valor del negocio a través de nuevos sectores, áreas geográficas y plataformas. En cuanto a filiales en el exterior, Medidata debía consolidar su liderazgo no solo en Brasil sino también en otros mercados clave de Latinoamérica[88].

Ya en el nuevo milenio, se reanudó el repliegue como resultado del estallido de la burbuja tecnológica. Amper Ibersegur fue vendida por 8,25 millones de euros a un consorcio inversor liderado por Catalana d'Iniciatives[89]. Las exiguas perspectivas de relanzamiento económico en América Latina se conjugaron con la deficitaria situación de las filiales en la zona para cesar de forma ordenada la actividad de Amper. En 2002, procurando minimizar costes, echaron el cerrojo las filiales y delegaciones de Amper Soluciones en cinco países –Brasil, Guatemala, Colombia, El Salvador y Venezuela–. Sobrevivieron las de Perú y Chile no sin una reducción al mínimo del personal propio e intentando mantener los beneficios[90]. Ese proceso se llevó adelante de manera paulatina con el objetivo de minimizar los costes de ejecución. Como fruto, Amper se consolidó como un «grupo multivendedor, multicliente y multitecnología, orientado a suministrar productos y servicios en la vanguardia de las soluciones tecnológicas y estructurado con criterios de clientela y de mercados en torno a tres grandes divisiones operativas –Amper Tecnologías, Amper Soluciones y Medidata (Brasil)– (Amper, *Memoria 2001*, 4-5).

En 2003, Amper dio por ultimada una etapa importante en la reestructuración del Grupo, que supuso el punto de inflexión hacia una nueva fase basada en el liderazgo en las comunicaciones militares y los sistemas para la seguridad y la defensa. Amper vislumbró en ese ámbito nuevas oportunidades de crecimiento, de negocio y de exportación de su tecnología.

Amper S.A. perduró como cabecera de un grupo fuertemente diversificado de las TIC, sin grandes variaciones en su denominación y objeto social desde su constitución en 1971. Agrupaba sociedades en el subsector de electrónica

---

[88] Los pilares abarcaban organización y procesos de soporte; oportunidad de crecimiento, negocios actuales y nuevas oportunidades; eficiencia en costes, rentabilidad y competitividad (Amper S.A., *Memoria 2000*, 5). Amper Tecnologías se especializó en los mercados de defensa, Seguridad, Sector Público y Networking (Amper, *Memoria 2003,* 12).

[89] La plusvalía fue de 3,7 millones de euros (Grupo Amper 2004, 18).

[90] Nombres de las afectadas: Amper Centroamérica SA de Capital Variable (El Salvador), Amper Guatemala, S.A., Desarrollo de Soluciones Específicas, C. A. (Venezuela) y Amper Sucursal en Colombia (Grupo Amper, *Memoria del ejercicio anual 2002*; Intervención de Enrique Used, Junta de accionistas de Amper, 25 de junio de 2002).

y *software* y su especialización mayor estribaba en el desarrollo y empleo de soluciones tecnológicas a gusto del cliente.

Antes de concluir, parece oportuno un epílogo. En años recientes, el Grupo Amper no ha escapado a la reestructuración, a las pérdidas contables y al adelgazamiento en operaciones con cierto sabor a paraíso fiscal[91]. Amper se componía de tres grandes verticales de negocio, a saber, Amper Telecom y Seguridad, Amper Industrial y Amper Integración, correspondientes, respectivamente, a las antiguas España Telecom, Amper Industrial y Amper Latinoamérica. Completaba el organigrama un Centro de excelencia de ingeniería y desarrollo, trasversal a las tres verticales de negocio. Geográficamente, el Grupo Amper desarrolla su actividad en España, Latinoamérica y Pacífico Sur a través de diecinueve centros operativos en nueve países. El Grupo Amper contaba con relaciones a largo plazo con grandes clientes, si bien desde el ejercicio 2016, las ventas se habían atomizado hasta el punto de que no constaba ningún cliente significativo. Grupo Navantia, Endesa, Telefónica, Orange Espagne, S.A.U. y Metro de Madrid eran los cinco primeros clientes, todos españoles, y sumaban en torno a la cuarta parte de las ventas. Amper se caracterizaba por la elevada concentración de proveedores. Respecto a la I+D, Amper siguió exhibiendo como seña de identidad su capacidad de generar y desarrollar con su propia tecnología productos y servicios competitivos en los mercados nacionales e internacionales. Abonaba su estrategia de reactivación de la I+D la creación en 2018 como socio único de Amper Robotics S.L. Dicha unidad estaba enfocada primordialmente al desarrollo de tecnología aplicada a la cartera tecnológica y, a través de su sociedad Nervión, a la industrial. Tal solemne proclama no ocultaba recortes en el desarrollo y fomento de una política de actividades de I+D+i, hasta tal punto que en los ejercicios 2016-2017 el Grupo no destinó recursos a las actividades de I+D. Las líneas prioritarias del Plan Estratégico 2018-2020 comprendían proyectos de Robótica/Tecnología aplicada al sector industrial/renovables, Big Data

[91] En 2013, pérdidas de 58 millones de euros y un patrimonio neto negativo impusieron a Amper la reestructuración del capital y la refinanciación con entidades financieras. En 2014-2015, se desprendió de participaciones en Amper Programas de Electrónica y Comunicaciones (51% del capital social) y en su filial venezolana. La primera fue vendida a Thales España por 5 millones de euros y la segunda a Ertona Business, S.A., con un beneficio de 2,855 millones de euros. Las filiales del Grupo, AST Telecom LLC (American Samoa) y Bluesky Samoa Ltced. (Samoa) se asociaron a inversores en las Islas Cook para tomar una participación mayoritaria (60%) en la operadora local Telecom Cook Islands Ltd., mediante la filial Teleraro Ltd. por un precio de 15,975 millones de euros, transacción financiada por entidades de la región.

aplicada a redes, diseño de consolas inteligentes de comunicación y seguridad medioambiental con nuevas soluciones para control de emisiones[92].

6. Conclusión

La investigación ha puesto en evidencia las estrategias, alianzas, inversiones y expansión exterior del Grupo Amper entre 1980 y 2003 a partir de fuentes primarias y de hemeroteca. El interés del caso radica en la naturaleza de Amper como empresa española con tecnología propia en un tiempo particularmente problemático. El caso ilustra el carácter cambiante de las relaciones, señaladas en el debate teórico, entre los servicios y la industria dentro del sector de las telecomunicaciones, a la vez que aporta claves de la transición de la economía industrial a la de servicios. Asimismo, arroja luz sobre la incidencia de la transformación del subsector de servicios en la industria como resultado de una combinación de factores –cambio tecnológico, liberalización del mercado y diversificación de la demanda de nuevos servicios–.

El capítulo ha permitido seguir el recorrido de Amper desde su condición de empresa familiar a una compleja organización multinacional de las TIC especializada en la defensa y la seguridad. Se trata, por tanto, de una pieza en la configuración de la industria española de defensa y en el paso de una situación de dependencia del mercado exterior a una condición de país exportador. La supervivencia de Amper fue posible gracias a las estrategias inclusivas y a la combinación de desarrollo de tecnología propia y recurso a la tecnología externa mediante el logro de alianzas con líderes tecnológicos. La evidencia presentada deja poco espacio a dudas sobre el papel crucial de Amper en numerosas operaciones que se llevaron a cabo en la industria de las telecomunicaciones desde las décadas de 1980 y 1990.

El estudio de caso muestra que los pilares fundamentales de la supervivencia de Amper radicaron en una serie compleja de factores, cuya lista comprende una apuesta por tecnología autóctona, asociación con la poderosa CTNE, reestructuraciones, internacionalización, alianzas estratégicas con multinacionales y adelgazamiento corporativo.

---

[92] En el ejercicio 2014, el Grupo Cisco Systems, Inc. concentraba en solitario casi la mitad del volumen total de compras del Grupo (Amper 2018, 48-49, 51 y 79; Amper, *Informe de gestión 2019,* 4-5). La plantilla total del Grupo Amper al final del ejercicio 2018 se cifraba en 1.151, con un predominio aplastante de personal masculino (Amper, *Memoria Anual 2018,* 65 y 68).

El final del trayecto deja a la primitiva fabricante de porteros automáticos y a continuación multinacional de las telecomunicaciones transmutada en una ingeniería de diseño de soluciones, integración de equipos y puesta en funcionamiento de complejos sistemas (Amper, *Memoria 2005*, 15).

Anexo 1. Composición del Grupo Amper, 1993 y 2002

Grupo Amper, 1993

Compañías	Participación %	Capital millones ptas.	Beneficios millones ptas.
Amper Elasa	100	300	928
Amper Datos	100	500	296
Amper Servicios	100		-97
Amper Sistemas	100		
Amper Telemática	100	600	5518
Amper Cosesa	100		
Amper Ibersegur	100	200	-217
Samp[93]	100	1.017	
I.T.C.	41		
Safitel	100	500	
Amper Internacional	100	1.061	
Grupo Pesa	99	1.238	
Pesa International	100	22	
Pesa Inc.	100	21	
Pesa Switching	100	-1.135	
Pesa Mycro Com.	100		
Chyron Inc.	69		
Aurora System P.	69		
CMX Products	69		

[93] No hay constancia de una afirmación de un representante del Grupo Popular, que señalaba a Samp (Sociedad Anónima de Mediación y Promoción) como receptora de todas o la gran mayoría de las propiedades de Amper (*Diario de Sesiones del Congreso de los Diputados, Comisiones*, 445, Comisión de Infraestructuras y Medio Ambiente, 7 de marzo de 1996, 13.623-13.627). Registralmente, Samp aparece vinculada a Amper S. A. y a la Sociedad Anónima de Finanzas y Telecomunicación (SAFITEL) (Registro Mercantil, Acto 000385683, 13 de octubre de 2003).

Amper Programas	89,5	1.000	-883
Telur	44	6	435
Telcel	35	200	1.256

Fuente: Elaboración a partir de Amper, *Memoria(s) anual(es).*

Grupo Amper, 2002

Compañías	Participación %	Capital (miles €)	Beneficios (miles €)
Dependientes			
Amper Soluciones	100	6.928	-6.576
Visual Plan	51	120	-1
Grupo STC	51	1000	105
I.T.P.	51	60	197
Amper Perú	100	463	-91
Amper Tecnologías	100	1.503	2.382
Amper Programas			
Amper Sistemas			
Amper Ibersegur			
Samp			
Safitel			
Hemisferio Norte	100	58.298	1.002
Amper Brasil	100	9.656	-10.323
Amper Centroamérica	100	327	-81
Amper Guatemala	100	283	268
Amper Argentina	100	15	-4
Amper Marruecos	100	194	420
Hemisferio Sul	100	26.685	248
Medidata	75	5.657	4.685
Syscraft	75	11	-17
Unishop Informática	75	-	-
X.C.	75	559	1.169
Obis Inversiones	100	1.353	158
Dominio Díez	100	15	-

Amper Australia	100		
Asociadas indirectas			
Telcel	35	1.202	6.592
Bucle 21	21,16	5	-1.574
Telur	31	-	-
Telma Auditex	24,23	8	1
Finaves	6,25	2.885	-296
Marco Polo	4,38		

Fuente: Elaboración a partir de GRUPO AMPER,
Memoria del ejercicio anual 2002, 67

Anexo 2. Los orígenes de Tecnocom

Tecnocom se autodefine como una empresa española líder en el campo de las TIC, que ofrece a sus clientes una completa gama de servicios en las ramas de la consultoría, externalización, integración de aplicaciones, mantenimiento y gestión de redes. Su facturación proforma se cifra en 450 millones de euros, cotiza en Bolsa desde 1987 y cuenta entre sus clientes con una veintena larga de las empresas que forman el IBEX 35. Los orígenes de Tecnocom se remontan a la creación de IB-MEI S.A., fabricante de motores eléctricos para electrodomésticos, que en 1967 mutó su nombre por el de Corporación IB-MEI S.A. A raíz de su salida a Bolsa y tras un fuerte crecimiento de los recursos propios, inició un importante proceso de expansión y diversificación en distintos sectores.

A finales de 1988, tras importantes inversiones en la toma de participaciones en distintas sociedades, se transformó en sociedad de cartera mediante una escisión de activos y pasivos ligados a la fabricación de motores. En 1993 el objeto social de la Corporación IB-MEI lo constituía la promoción y participación en empresas y sociedades industriales comerciales inmobiliarias de servicios y de cualquier otro tipo. IB-MEI S.A. controlaba un grupo de sociedades compuesto por Nuova IB-MEI S.A., ZERTAN Electrónica, Talleres Goyama e Irena. Otras empresas gestionadas conjuntamente con diversos socios o participadas eran Micromotor, en suspensión de pagos, Seinsa, Sedma, Inversiones Móstoles, Zabalburu y Ambiente 2000. A su vez, Seinsa tenía participaciones en Inversiones Tres Cantos, Centromar, Prolur, Gesinder, Gesilur y Gestión y promoción inmobiliaria Molinar. Entre los negocios tecnológicos de Tecnocom destacaba la creación de una compañía en Miami desde donde habían comenzado a trabajar con un importante fabricante de equipos para la instalación de redes en América Latina (Corporación IB-MEI *1993*, 1-2).

Tecnocom se adjudicó importantes contratos de instalaciones en Latinoamérica, entre ellos las de la red de telecomunicación para navegación aérea en Centroamérica y las nuevas estaciones celulares de Telefónica en Puerto Rico, así como la verificación de la calidad de la red de Telefónica de Argentina y el mantenimiento de la red de telefonía celular en Guatemala (CNMV, 6.616, 5/4/2000; 6.857, 4/5/2000; 6.633, 11/4/2000 y 6.601, 1/3/2000). De la etapa de Corporación IB-Mei data un principio de acuerdo con Motorola para desarrollar en Brasil un sistema bidireccional de transmisión de datos por radio, como primer peldaño para la constitución de una empresa conjunta con planes de inversión en las dos principales ciudades del país (CNMV, 21.261, 23/3/2000). Tecnocom culminó los planes de su antecesora con la creación al 50% de una empresa de telecomunicaciones en Turquía, a través de una *joint venture* con la empresa local Iletisim Hizmetleri A.S. En tan solo dos años, sucesivos planes estratégicos permitieron la consolidación internacional en su especialidad de instalación de redes de telefonía móvil y transmisión de datos vía radio con filiales en América y Europa (CNMV, 6.578, 27/3/2000; 21.239, 21/03/2000).

Fuentes primarias

Comisión Nacional del Mercado de Valores (CNMV).
CTNE/Telefónica, Libros de Actas del Comité Ejecutivo.
CTNE/Telefónica, Libros de Actas del Consejo de administración.
Compañía Peruana de Teléfonos, Libros de Actas.
Registro Mercantil de Madrid

Fuentes orales

Jesús Banegas, Comunicación personal con el autor, 27 de mayo de 2020.
José Luis Adanero, Comunicación personal con el autor, 27 de mayo de 2020.
Juan Mulet Melià, Conversación con el autor, 16 de mayo de 2013.
Luis Lada, Entrevista con el autor, 22 de mayo de 2013 y 17 de junio 2013.

Referencias

Abad, Luis. 2010. *Estrategias de innovación industrial y desarrollo económico en las ciudades intermedias de España*. Madrid: Fundación BBVA.

Adanero, José L. et al. 2006. *Crónicas y testimonios de las telecomunicaciones españolas*. Madrid: COIT.

Amper S. A. 1997. *Memoria del ejercicio anual 1996*. Madrid: Amper

Amper S.A. 1998. *Memorial anual del ejercicio 1997*. Madrid: Amper.

Amper. 2000. *Informe del Consejo de Administración sobre la reestructuración societaria del grupo Amper.* 16 de febrero. Madrid: Amper.

Amper. 2000. *Reinventando Amper*. Madrid: I.E.A.F.

Amper. 2000. *Informe de gestión 1996*. Madrid: Amper.

Amper. 2018. *Folleto de emisión,* CNMV, 10.899, 14 de junio.

Banco de España. 2002. *Central de Balances. Resultados anuales de las empresas no financieras 2001.* Madrid: Banco de España.

Banegas, Jesús. 1989. «¿La gran ocasión?». *El País*, 21 de octubre.

Banegas, Jesús. [s.f.]. *Memorias Profesionales*. Manuscrito inédito (cortesía de Jesús Banegas).

Billón, Margarita y Sánchez, Paloma. 1999. *Ejercicios prácticos de comercio exterior.* Madrid: AKAL.

Binda, Verónica. 2005. «Entre el Estado y las multinacionales: la empresa industrial española en los años de integración a la CEE. *Revista de Historia Industrial*, 28, 117-154.

Bruce, Robert R.; Cunard, Jeffrey P. y Director, Mark D. 2014. *From Telecommunications to Electronic Services: A Global Spectrum of Definitions, Boundary Lines, and Structures.* Washington: Butterworth-Heinemann.

Calvo, Ángel. 2014. *Telecomunicaciones y el nuevo mundo digital en España. La aportación de Standard Eléctrica.* Barcelona: Ariel-Fundación Telefónica.

Calvo, Ángel. 2019a. «Tecnología y Empresa en la Industria Española de la Electrónica, las Telecomunicaciones y la Defensa: MARCONI ESPAÑOLA». *Quaderns d'Història de l'Enginyeria*, xvii, 113-150.

Calvo, Ángel. 2019b. «The emergence of global companies in the high-tech industry of defense: the case of Indra in Spain, 1993-2007». *Eurasian Journal of Social Sciences*, 7(1), 29-47.

Calvo, Ángel. 2020a. «Política industrial, multinacionales y desarrollo regional en España. La IED en la industria de la fibra óptica». *Biblio3W Revista Bibliográfica de Geografía y Ciencias Sociales,* XXV, n°.1.288, 20 de febrero: 1-36.

Calvo, Ángel. 2020b. «De empresa familiar a multinacional de las TIC: Amper 1976-2003». *DT-AEHE* n° 2009, septiembre, 1-53.

Campbell, Robert W. 2019. *Soviet And Post-Soviet Telecommunications: An Industry Under Reform.* Nueva York: Routledge.

Castells, Manuel. 1986. *Nuevas tecnologias, economia y sociedad en España.* Vol. 1. Madrid: Alianza.

CER. 1988. «L'attività innovativa in Italia: i brevetti nell'industria». Report 6, CNEL.

Cominotti, Ruggero y Mariotti, Sergio. 1989. *Italia multinazionale: gli investimenti esteri in Italia e dell'Italia verso i paesi esteri: il rapporto R&P al CNEL.* Milán: Il Sole.

Corporación IB-MEI. 1993. *Memoria del ejercicio 1993.* Madrid: Arthur Andersen, 1-2.

CTNE. 1983. *Memoria: Ejercicio Social 1983.*

CTNE. 1984. *Memoria: Ejercicio Social 1984.*

CTNE. 1987. *Memoria 1987.*

Dunning, John H. 2013. *Multinationals, Technology & Competitiveness.* Londres-Nueva York: Routledge.

Electrónica Aragonesa S.A. 1985. *Memoria 1985.*

Ericsson España. 1990. *Informe anual 1990.* Madrid: Ericsson España.

Ernst & Young. , 1997. *Informe de Auditoría de cuentas anuales 1993.* Madrid: Amper.

Foro Histórico de las Telecomunicaciones [sa.]. «Peral Hernández, Antonio», *Personajes españoles.* Madrid: Foro Histórico de las Telecomunicaciones.

Fabrie, Robert. 1987. *World Support Base, Spain.* Washington: National Defense University.

Fox, Loren. 2003. *Enron: The Rise and Fall.* Hoboken: John Wiley and Sons.

Framatome. 1995. *Framatome: an industrial and business success story.* París: Albin Michel.

FUNDESCO. 1991. *La Industria de las tecnologías de la información (1985-1990): España en el contexto mundial.* Madrid: Fundesco.

Grupo Amper. 2000. *Memoria del ejercicio anual 2000.*

Grupo Amper. 2004. *Amper resultados 2003,* marzo.

Hoekman, Bernard M. y Javorcik, Beata S. 2006. *Global Integration and Technology Transfer.* Washington: World Bank Publications.

Holl, Adelheid y Rama, Ruth. 2019. «Local cooperation for innovation in ICT–Domestic groups with collaborations for innovation abroad and foreign subsidiaries», *Sience and Public Policy,* vol. 46, nº. 4: 599-610.

Hudson, Edward P. 1983. «Telecommunications –Joint Ventures– The Significance of the AT&T-Philips Joint Venture». *Georgia Journal of International & Comparative Law*, Vol. 13, No. 2: 591-601.

Instituto Nacional de Estadística e Informática. 2000. *Perú, estadísticas de tecnología de la información y comunicación.* Lima: INEeI.

Landes, David S. 1969. *The Unbound Prometheus.* Cambridge: Cambridge University Press.

Lazonick, William. 2011. «The rise and demise of Lucent Technologies». *Business History Conference.* Vol. 9, 1-66.

Lera, Emilio. 2000. «Changing relations between manufacturing and service provision in a more competitive telecom environment». *Telecommunications Policy* 24, 5, junio, 413-437.

López, Santiago; Pueyo, Ana y Zlatánova, Goritza. 2002. «Colaboración bajo incertidumbre: la formación de un grupo tecnológico en el sector de las telecomunicaciones» *Economía industrial* 346, nº.4: 81-107.

López, Santiago y Molero, José. 2005. «Innovación e internacionalización en las empresas españolas de componentes para telecomunicaciones: un estudio de caso». En *La empresa multinacional española. Estrategias y ventajas competitivas*, coordinado por Durán, Juan J., 197-226, Madrid: Minerva Ediciones.

Management Europe. 1988. *Business International, S.A.* Ginebra: Management Europe.

Michael, Katina. 2009. *Innovative Automatic Identification and Location-Based Services: From Bar Codes to Chip Implants: From Bar Codes to Chip Implants.* Hershey PA: IGI Global.

Ministerio de Industria y Energía. 1983. *Plan electrónico e informático nacional. Programa económico a medio plazo 1983-1986.* Madrid: Archivo del SEPI.

Molero, José y Rama, Ruth. 2013. «La internacionalización de las empresas españolas del sector TIC: marco general y experiencias de éxito». *Economistas* 137, 73-83.

Mytelka, Lynn Krieger. 1991. *Strategic Partnerships: States, Firms, and International Competition.* Londres: Printer Publishers.

OCDE. 2001. *Études économiques de l'OCDE: France.* París: OCDE.

Olson, Mancur. 2008. *The Rise and Decline of Nations: Economic Growth, Stagflation, and Social Rigidities.* New Haven CT: Yale University Press.

Rama, Ruth, Ferguson, Deron y Melero, Ana. 2003. «Subcontracting Networks in Industrial Districts: The Electronics Industries of Madrid». *Regional Studies,* Vol. 37, 1, 71–88.

Standard Eléctrica. 1983. *Plan de reordenación industrial del Grupo ITT,* Fundación LC, 1.718.

Standard Eléctrica. 1987. *Reajuste del Plan de reconversión,* Fundación LC, 1.718.

Suárez-Villa, Luis y Rama, Ruth. 1996. «Outsourcing, R&D and the pattern of intra-metropolitan location: the electronics industries of Madrid». *Urban Studies,* 33, 1.155-1.197.

Temin, Peter y Galambos, Luis. 1987. *The Fall of the Bell System: A Study in Prices and Politics.* Cambridge MA: Cambridge University Press.

Toninelli, Pier A. 2000. *The Rise and Fall of State-Owned Enterprise in the Western World.* Cambridge MA: Cambridge University Press.

Torres, Eugenio. 2017. *Cien empresarios madrileños,* Madrid: Cid.

Torres, Ramón. 1983/84. «Telecomunicaciones en Iberoamérica. La oportunidad española». *Revista T,* 1, 4-21.

United States Committee on Governmental Affairs. 1991. *Trade in conventional weapons: the international arms bazaar: hearing before the Permanent Subcommittee on Investigations of the Committee on Governmental Affairs.* Washington: G.P.O.

U.S. Department of Commerce. 1984. *Telecommunications Equipment, Argentina.* Vol. 61. Washington: U.S. Department of Commerce.

U.S. Department of Commerce. 1990. *U.S. Telecommunications in a Global Economy: Competitiveness at a Crossroads: a Report from the Secretary of Commerce to the Congress and the President of the United States.* Washington: U.S. Department of Commerce.

United States Senate. 1985. *Long-distance Competition: Hearing Before the Subcommittee on Communications of the Committee on Commerce, Science, and Transportation.* Septiembre, 5 y 11.

Velázquez-Gaztelu, Cándido. 1995. Intervención. *Diario de Sesiones del Congreso de los Diputados*, 445, Comisión de Infraestructuras y Medio Ambiente, 7 de marzo, 13.625.

Walsh, Elizabeth. 1995. *The Corporate Directory of US Public Companies 1995.* San Mateo CA: Walker`s.

World Institute For Development Economics Research. *Governing Globalization: Issues and Institutions.* Oxford: Oxford University Press.

Zhu, Huani y Pasadilla, Gloria O. 2002. «Manufacturing of Telecommunications Equipment». En *Services In Global Value Chains: Manufacturing-related Services*, editado por Pasadilla, Gloria O. y Patrick Low, 481-531. New Jersey NJ: World Scientific.

2. Estrategias de supervivencia entre dos crisis: Amper, una multinacional de las TIC

1. Introducción

Este capítulo examina el comportamiento de un sector oligopólico a través del caso de una empresa multinacional de tamaño mediano, perteneciente a la industria de equipo de telecomunicación. Se trata de un ejemplo de interés por su contraste con una situación general durante el periodo seleccionado –la primera década del nuevo milenio– marcada por el predominio claro del pequeño tamaño en las empresas del planeta, por un lado, y el de las grandes empresas en los negocios multinacionales. En este sentido, es una aportación al debate sobre la incidencia de las limitaciones de recursos y del tamaño en la internacionalización de las pequeñas y medianas empresas (pymes) (Kalinic y Forza 2012; Kuo y Li 2003; Urata y Kawai 2000), consideradas como tales según el criterio económico (Buckley, 1989, 89-100). Interviene, asimismo, en la polémica sobre las ventajas para adaptarse a los mercados y al cambio tecnológico en general (Chen y Hambrick, 1995)[1]. De forma más precisa, es un intento de revitalizar el debate en el contexto más actual de la globalización (Acs y Yeung 1999; Lohrmann 2013)[2].

---

[1] Una revista tan emblemática como *Small Business Economics* parece más interesada por temas como las redes, la productividad y los ecosistemas.

[2] Por economía globalizada se entiende aquella en que los costes de transporte y comunicación serían casi nulos y en que las barreras creadas por las diferentes jurisdicciones nacionales (estados nacionales u organizaciones económicas regionales) habrían desaparecido (Wolf 2001, 178-190). Tres procesos relacionados con la globalización se combinan para dificultar a diversos países la satisfacción de sus necesidades de defensa y seguridad. Se trata del aumento del coste de las armas, la competencia entre las principales empresas

En la faceta particular de la internacionalización basada en la inversión extranjera directa (IED) es una aportación al «cómo» y «por qué» de la IED de las pymes defendidos por las teorías tradicionales. La manera incluye principalmente la teoría de la IED vertical y horizontal basada en la organización industrial (Caves) y el modelo de innovación gradualista (Johanson y Vahlne). La causa comprende principalmente las teorías de la ventaja monopolística basada en la competencia imperfecta (Hymer), del ciclo de vida del producto (Vernon), del comercio y la inversión acorde con la ventaja comparativa marginal (Kojima) y de la internalización basada en el coste de transacción (Buckley y Casson) o en el paradigma ecléctico (Ownership, Location Internalization: OLI) de Dunning[3].

La empresa que analizamos se desenvuelve en un marco general caracterizado por las fluctuaciones de las condiciones del mercado durante el decenio comprendido entre 1995 y 2005. El sector de las telecomunicaciones realizó fuertes inversiones hasta el año 2000, pero a renglón seguido las operadoras de larga distancia, inmersas en la crisis de las punto com, redujeron drásticamente sus gastos de capital y sus inversiones. Los fabricantes de equipos telefónicos recortaron los gastos de capital de forma más agresiva y tuvieron que reducir su actividad (OECD 2007, 71-72)[4].

En 2008, la situación económica global sufrió un deterioro generalizado y el impacto negativo prosiguió en la mayor parte de los países desarrollados a lo largo de 2009, año en el que se desató «la peor desaceleración mundial de la historia reciente» anterior a la pandemia de la Covid-19, según la calificó el Fondo Monetario Internacional (2010, 1).

Los distintos sectores acusaron de forma diferente los efectos de la crisis. La tasa de crecimiento de las ventas netas se redujo en el conjunto de sectores mientras que aumentó en los de baja intensidad de I+D, primordialmente debido a los altos precios del petróleo en 2008 que favorecieron a las industrias

multinacionales de armamento y, por último, la internacionalización de las cadenas de suministro de componentes (Devore 2013, 532-572). Criterios económicos se refieren a los considerados por el Bolton Report de 1971: cuota de mercado no lo suficientemente grande como para influir en los precios, independencia y control del negocio y *management* personalizado de los propietarios sin apenas delegación en la elección de la estrategia y en la toma de decisiones (Pu y Zheng 2015, 99).

3   Revisión de la bibliografía realizada por Pu y Zheng (2015, 99). Las pautas incluyen estrategias como las desinversiones, de gran importancia pero mal conocidas y, por tanto, de gran interés (Moschieri y Mair 2008, 399-422). En el paradigma OLI, siglas inglesas de Propiedad-Lugar-Internalización, el éxito de la IED debe cumplir esas tres condiciones.

4   En conjunto, el sector de las telecomunicaciones alcanzó por primera vez en 2005 unos ingresos de mil millones de dólares (OECD 2003, 7-8).

relacionadas con el crudo. Un grado extremo de esta tendencia lo presentó el sector de alta intensidad de I+D de la UE, donde las ventas netas crecieron a una tasa inferior a la mitad de la lograda por sus homólogos estadounidenses. La capitalización del mercado se redujo de forma más marcada en el último periodo (agosto de 2008 – agosto de 2009) y con grados diferentes según la intensidad de I+D. El mayor impacto lo acusaron las empresas de los sectores de intensidad media-alta en el caso de la UE y de intensidad media-baja en el caso de EE.UU. Las empresas de los sectores de alta intensidad de I+D parecen menos afectadas en el grupo de los EE.UU (European Communities 2009, 39).

En cuanto a la incidencia de la crisis en la I+D, tema de sumo interés en este estudio, la inversión empresarial en I+D siguió creciendo en 2008, si bien a un ritmo menor que el año anterior (6,9 en lugar de 9%). El número de empresas que aumentaron su inversión en I+D en 2008 fue similar en la UE y fuera de esta. Tomando las cien empresas más importantes, tan solo cincuenta y cinco aumentaron su I+D por encima del 5% y en veintisiete disminuyó. La intensidad de la I+D siguió aumentando gradualmente en todo el mundo, ya que las inversiones en capital fijo crecieron más rápidamente que las ventas netas. Las empresas de la UE exhibieron el mayor crecimiento en inversiones de capital fijo[5].

Durante el segundo semestre de 2009, se empezó a vislumbrar algunos signos de recuperación, en modo alguno generalizada al conjunto de las economías mundiales. En España, la caída del PIB en casi un 3,6%, el mayor descenso en el último medio siglo, junto a medidas de contención del gasto público y a los subsiguientes recortes presupuestarios, tuvo repercusiones negativas sobre el conjunto de las empresas y del sector TIC, en particular. Según los datos de la Asociación de Empresas de Electrónica, Tecnologías de la Información y Telecomunicaciones de España, la caída de las inversiones durante el ejercicio en el subsector de las industrias de telecomunicaciones al que pertenece Amper contribuyó a un descenso de la facturación del 24% (Amper 2009, 20).

En esos años turbulentos tuvieron lugar cambios notables en el *ranking* mundial. Si nos situamos en 2009, al final de periodo aquí analizado, al grupo de cabeza de las diez mayores empresas de tecnología de la información se habían aupado la estadounidense Hewlett-Packard y la japonesa Toshiba. En

---

[5]   El Scoreboard define la intensidad de I+D como la relación entre la I+D y las ventas netas (European Communities 2009, 16).

ese grupo tan solo figuraba una de las mayores empresas de equipo de telecomunicación (NEC) y otra de la lista de las grandes del sector de la electrónica (Ericsson) del año 2000. En su componente geográfico, la lista estaba integrada mayoritariamente por empresas chinas (Hoyt 2001, 3-4; OECD 2010, 58-59).

En este contexto, el capítulo se estructura en tres grandes apartados. El primero analiza las estrategias de crecimiento en entornos liberalizados, el segundo se refiere a las alianzas estratégicas y acuerdos alcanzados y el tercero a la acumulación de capacidades tecnológicas en busca de incrementar la competitividad. Las fuentes utilizadas son en sustancia las de la empresa estudiada y, en la faceta oficial, las de la Comisión Nacional del Mercado de Valores (CNMV).

2. Estrategias de crecimiento en entornos liberalizados

Conviene añadir al marco esbozado que tampoco había cambiado la estructura oligopólica del sector. Sin embargo, uno de los aspectos que sí había variado sustancialmente respecto a la generalidad de la etapa anterior se refería al entorno institucional inmediato ya que el sector había alcanzado una liberalización plena.

Ya en la fase de salida de la nefasta burbuja de las punto com, en 2004, Amper triplicó el resultado neto, al mismo tiempo que saneó la actividad y se especializó al desprenderse de algunas áreas fuera del núcleo central.

La estructura accionarial sufrió una serie de cambios relevantes por la salida de algunos socios tradicionales en un contexto de alza del volumen negociado y del precio de los títulos. Fruto de estos movimientos, Telefónica recuperó el lugar preponderante entre el grupo de accionistas. En 2008, la Caja de Ahorros de Castilla-La Mancha (CCM) y una nueva agrupación en la que figuraba el *holding* familiar Naropa Capital alcanzaron sendas participaciones del 9,1% de Amper[6]. Al término cronológico de nuestro estudio, el accionista mayoritario había pasado a ser la CCM, seguida por Telefónica, mientras que casi la mitad de las acciones –47,2%– se negociaban en Bolsa.

---

[6]   *El Economista*, 17 de junio de 2008; *CincoDías*, 27 de febrero de 2008. Naropa Capital, nombre con fuertes resonancias budistas, fue creada por la familia del vallisoletano Fernández Fermoselle a partir de la venta de una empresa inmobiliaria (Salgado 2012).

Tabla 1. Adquisiciones de participaciones societarias

Empresa	Activo o participación adquirida	Vendedora	% adquirido	Año	Precio (millones €)	Observaciones
Amper	EPICOM, SA		100	2005		
Amper	Landata Ingeniería, SA	Landata Ingeniería, SA	100	2006	75 millones €	Al contado: 58 millones
Hemisferio Norte, SA	participación adicional de Medidata Informática	Medidata Informática	13,96	2006	19.942.739,32 reales	
Amper	Sociedad Telecomunicación e Instalaciones (Telcar)	Telcar	100	2006	23,5	
Amper	FEDETEC		100	2007		
Amper	Knosos, S.L	Knosos, S.L	100	2007		

Fuente: Elaboración a partir de Amper, *Memoria(s) anual(es)* y CNMV.

De forma inmediata, Amper empezó a actuar en dos frentes, el primero de los cuales consistía en el control de gastos, en concreto, salarios, con el objetivo de adecuar las principales partidas de los costes al tamaño de la empresa. En segundo lugar, Amper pretendía volver a alcanzar una dimensión empresarial similar a la existente antes de la severa crisis de 2001, por medio de una política de crecimiento orgánico (nuevos contratos, incremento de ventas, optimización fiscal y financiera) y corporativo mediante adquisición selectiva (Tabla 1) (Amper, *Memoria 2004*)[7].

En su conjunto, el Grupo Amper adoptó estrategias de índole distinta. La clave consistía en concentrarse y crecer en negocios atractivos a largo plazo, siempre que le permitieran lograr posiciones de liderazgo. De esta manera, su objetivo era consolidarse como uno de los líderes nacionales y europeos en el dominio de los sistemas de comunicaciones, de mando y control civiles y militares, optimizar las sinergias en el sector de integración de sistemas y tecnologías de la información y adaptarse al sector de operadores de telecomunicación entrando en aquellas actividades rentables y de alto valor añadido.

Si consideramos unidades del grupo, Amper Programas introdujo sus productos en el exigente mercado suizo de defensa, fruto de potenciar su faceta exportadora, y Amper Sistemas presentó su solución tecnológica para vigilancia de fronteras en los mercados de todo el mundo (Anexo 2)[8].

La estrategia de crecimiento no tardó en plasmarse en la creación de una nueva empresa en asociación con Medidata Brasil al 86 y 14%, que culminaba dos movimientos previos de entrada para controlar la brasileña. Como señalamos en el capítulo anterior, se llamó Amper Medidata y nacía como centro de excelencia en tecnologías IP, movilidad, almacenamiento y seguridad en comunicaciones (CNMV, 6.499, 10/03/2000; *Computing*, 22 de febrero de 2005). Poco después reforzó el área de integración de sistemas con la adquisición de Telecomunicación e Instalaciones (Telcar) y Landata[9].

Volviendo a la matriz, diversos movimientos de integración y desinversión respondieron a la estrategia de consolidar y potenciar su liderazgo en el

---

[7]　Amper situaba sus perspectivas en la duplicación de su volumen de negocios en los dos años siguientes (Amper 2004a, 3).

[8]　Algunos autores señalan el comienzo de la nueva etapa coercitiva de la globalización (Rosiere y Jones 2012, 227-228).

[9]　Amper Medidata modificó el artículo 2º de los Estatutos Sociales, incorporando el diseño, la fabricación, la comercialización e instalación de equipos y sistemas informáticos, do pro cesamiento electrónico de voz y datos, instalaciones eléctricas y la prestación de servicios de consultoría, asistencia y mantenimiento técnico (*Boletín Oficial del Registro Mercantil (BORME)*, 227, 26 de noviembre de 2010, 37.160.

área de seguridad y defensa. En la modalidad de concentración, algunos no llegaron a ser culminados. Debido a notables discrepancias sobre la estructura final de la operación, Amper desistió del acuerdo de intenciones sellado al iniciarse 2004 con Page Ibérica S.A. por el que las firmantes se comprometían a integrar sus actividades (*CincoDías*, 1 de junio de 2004)[10]. Amper adquiría el capital de Page en su totalidad mediante el pago del valor de las acciones de esta, compuesto por una combinación de efectivo y acciones de nueva emisión, asumiendo una deuda financiera[11].

En la misma faceta de concentración se inscribía la adquisición de participaciones sociales de Tecnobit, S.L. por un precio total de 5.640.382,25 €, suma pagadera en efectivo –3,13 € por participación– y en acciones de dicha sociedad de nueva emisión[12]. Otro eje de la estrategia del Grupo Amper pasó por fortalecer su posición en el área de integración de redes convergentes de voz, datos y video. Ejemplo destacado fue la adquisición de Landata Ingeniería, una de las principales ingenierías de redes de comunicación en el mercado español, perteneciente al Grupo Landata. Amper financió por entero

---

[10] Page, fundada en 1965, era cabecera de un grupo empresarial dedicado a la investigación, desarrollo, fabricación, comercialización e ingeniería de sistemas de comunicaciones y equipos electrónicos en los segmentos aeroportuario, de seguridad y defensa. Page estaba especializada primordialmente en productos de comunicaciones para clientes públicos y privados, entre ellos AENA y las Fuerzas Armadas. En 2002 sus ventas ascendieron a 46 millones de euros, el EBITDA a 4,2 m y el beneficio neto a 2,8 m. En ese año, el endeudamiento financiero neto se redujo un 70% y, al año siguiente, la compañía, con una situación financiera saneada –endeudamiento financiero neto igual a cero– y una cartera de productos muy diversificada, experimentó un importante crecimiento en todas sus magnitudes financieras (CNMV, Hechos relevantes, 47.163, 30/1/2004; 15.910 26/02/2004).

[11] El valor de las acciones de Page se fijó en 37 millones de euros, el pago en efectivo en unos 24,8 millones de euros y acciones de nueva emisión y la deuda financiera neta en 7,4 millones de euros. Se estimaba que la operación generaría para Amper 26 millones de euros. Los accionistas de Page suscribirían una ampliación de capital representativa del 10% del capital social de Amper (CNMV, 50.140, 31/5/2004).

[12] El compromiso, firmado a finales de 2003 y novado a continuación, fijaba las participaciones sociales de Tecnobit, S.L. representativas del 28,87% de su capital social (CNMV, 47.163, 30/1/2004). Creada en 1985, Tecnobit comenzó desarrollando la transmisión de mensajes secretos para el ministerio de Defensa y se situó entre las mayores y más vanguardistas compañías de la electrónica y la aviónica profesional de Europa. Tras la suspensión de pagos de Eurotrónica, absorbió parte de los contratos que esta tenía en el proyecto del Eurofigther. En 1998, un cambio de propietarios abrió el camino a absorciones – Sidocor y Elco Sistemas, procedente de la antigua Ceselsa– con el objetivo de aumentar la capacidad tecnológica y acceder a programas de mayor calado. La española CASA, British Aerospace y la alemana Daimler Benz eran los principales clientes de los sistemas desarrollados por la empresa, que tenía 132 trabajadores, en su totalidad ingenieros industriales, de telecomunicaciones y técnicos superiores(*El Mundo*, 4 de junio de 2000). *Eurotrónica* suministró equipos de la marca Raytheon (*Economista*, 1972, 3.090).

la transacción mediante un crédito puente de 61 millones de euros, concedido por el HSBC Bank. La integración del Grupo Landata dentro del Grupo Amper significó un salto en cuanto a tamaño, solidez y posibilidades de desarrollo adicional del segmento en el que estaban presentes ambos grupos (CNMV, 73.975, 18/12/2006)[13].

Propia de Amper fue igualmente la estrategia de fortalecer su posición en el diseño e implantación de redes y sistemas de seguridad y comunicaciones críticas (Homeland Security). En esta área Amper tenía como principales clientes a los servicios de emergencias, vigilancia de fronteras, bomberos, brigadas forestales y emergencias sanitarias.

En septiembre de 2007 adquirió el capital total de la Knosos, S.L., pequeña y dinámica empresa especializada en el diseño, fabricación y mantenimiento de equipos con tecnología propia en el campo de los sistemas de navegación, localización GPS y unidades de transmisión de datos, sistemas de acceso a información remota para las fuerzas de Seguridad y plataformas de gestión de la información en movilidad, mediante uso de PDA. Los objetivos consistían en optimizar las prestaciones de los complejos sistemas de Amper y reducir los riesgos de su integración. La absorción de Knosos permitía a Amper comenzar, de forma inmediata, la exportación del catálogo de Knosos a través de la red comercial internacional de Amper Homeland Security y, por otra parte, desarrollar las complementariedades de ambas empresas en los mercados internacionales, a los que Knosos había comenzado a incorporarse[14].

---

[13] Amper compró en su totalidad a la Corporación IBV Landata Ingeniería S. A., propietaria, a su vez, del 80,1% de Landata Comunicaciones de Empresa (Ericsson España el 19,9% restante), la totalidad de Landata Ingeniería de Seguridad y el 60% de Lanaccess Telecom SA (Presentación sobre la operación, CNMV, 71.302 5/10/2006). Landata diseñaba, implantaba y mantenía las soluciones integrales de comunicaciones (voz, datos, video, etc.), tanto en el segmento de operadores de telecomunicaciones como en el de empresas e instituciones (usuarios finales). El Grupo Landata tenía una facturación consolidada en 2005 de 84,9M€ y un EBITDA de 9,2 M€; en 2005, el 67,7% de las ventas correspondía a productos, el 20,6% a servicios y el 11,7% a mantenimiento. Landata Ingeniería se especializó en la integración de soluciones de redes de datos y se centró en el desarrollo de Redes IP, Redes digitales de acceso y transporte, Redes HFC, Cabeceras de video y video walls, proyectos llave en mano y consultoría de redes.

[14] Con una facturación en 2006 de 6,8 millones de euros y un EBITDA de 1,6 millones. El precio acordado ascendía a un máximo de 16,38 millones de euros (al contado 6,02 millones de euros; importe aplazado y variable: 10,36 millones de euros, condicionado al cumplimiento de diversos). Redes móviles TETRA/TETRAPOL, INMARSAT y GPRS; composición de la clientela de Knosos (¾ Ministerio Interior –Dirección General de Tráfico y Guardia Civil «Frontex»-) y ¾ Servicios Públicos y Emergencias (Policías locales, Ambulancias). La empresa tenía una plantilla de unas 40 personas, en su mayoría –aproximadamente el 70%–

Ya hacia el final del periodo estudiado, Amper marcaba una línea de continuidad con los objetivos estratégicos principales de la etapa inmediatamente posterior a la crisis. Se trataba de una continuidad matizada porque perseguía un crecimiento orgánico con una meta concreta –duplicar tamaño–: una internacionalización selectiva centrada en unidades de negocio con alto potencial de crecimiento y adquisiciones corporativas (CNMV, 23.585 30/5/2007)[15]. Casi de inmediato, si bien remachaba su prioridad por el ajuste de estructura y control de costes, manifestaba su voluntad de impulsar el crecimiento y rentabilidad a largo plazo, reforzando los ejes de innovación e internacionalización. Por la primera protegía márgenes y ganaba cuota de mercado en un entorno crecientemente competitivo. La segunda, además de compensar la caída en el mercado nacional, servía de aliciente al forzar al máximo el nivel de excelencia global en productos y servicios (Grupo Amper, *Informe Anual 2009*, 11).

En el nuevo plan estratégico de 2007 Amper volcó sus esfuerzos en ingeniería y soluciones integrales de comunicaciones civiles y militares, siempre con el norte de unos substanciales objetivos de crecimiento y rentabilidad. Esta estrategia de «foco» llevaba aparejados importantes esfuerzos de innovación e internacionalización (Amper, *Informe anual 2009*, 11). Durante 2007 Amper Programas abrió dos establecimientos con la finalidad de intervenir en los proyectos aeronáuticos más importantes que se anunciaban en España: los helicópteros de Eurocopter en Albacete y los de Airbus en el clúster Aerópolis de Sevilla. La empresa planeaba dedicarse al desarrollo de los sistemas de aviónica para estas aeronaves con la colaboración de las administraciones estatales, autonómicas y de la Unión Europea. En su arranque, el centro de Sevilla, ubicado en instalaciones ajenas, era de no muy elevada cualificación pero Amper albergaba la intención de dotarlo de una sección de I+D y convertirlo en el centro logístico de Thales en el Sur de Europa[16].

técnicos jóvenes y de elevada cualificación. Primer contrato: suministro de un sistema móvil de localización al Departamento de Policía de París (CNMV, 83.671, 6/9/2007).

[15] En sus líneas básicas, el Plan Estratégico (2005-07) del Grupo Amper perseguía el crecimiento –crecimiento orgánico del volumen de negocio con una tasa media anual sostenida de 10%– el aumento de la rentabilidad, incremento del margen bruto de explotación (EBITDA/Ventas) del 8,8% en 2004 al 10% en 2007, multiplicar al menos por 1,5 el resultado ordinario actual y continuar con la optimización del circulante y con la generación de excedente financiero (Grupo Amper, *Información Económica y Financiera del Grupo*, 2005, 115-116).

[16] Helicópteros de Eurocopter (Tigre, NH-90 y helicópteros civiles; aviones A400 y supertankers; localización (Parque Científico y Tecnológico de Albacete y Aerópolis, Parque Tecnológico Aerospacial de Andalucía (Amper, *Informe 2007*, 24; *Cinco Días*, 1 de sep-

En una reafirmación de su perfil, en 2010, Amper se definía como una multinacional española de dilatada trayectoria, especializada en el diseño e implementación de soluciones en el sector de las TIC y, más específicamente, en actividades de defensa, comunicaciones y seguridad[17].

Amper simplificó su estructura corporativa con una reformulación de los elementos de su modelo de negocio plasmada en el plan estratégico 2011/2013, que giraba en torno a los ejes de la internacionalización, la eficiencia y la innovación, como vías para recuperar la rentabilidad.

Gráfico 1. Ventas del Grupo Amper, 2003-2010 (miles €)

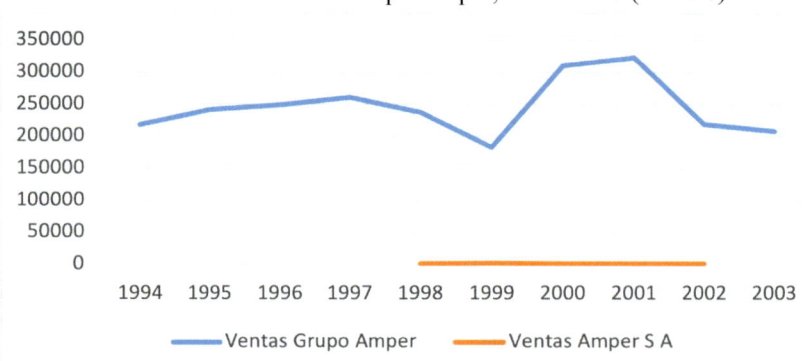

Fuente: Elaboración a partir de Amper, *Memoria(s) anual(es)* e *Informe(s) anual(es)* y CNMV.

tiembre de 2007; *ABC*, 22 de mayo de 2007). Amper forjó un acuerdo con la empresa andaluza Prevención de Riesgos y Calidad (Prescal) por el que ocuparía espacios cedidos por la empresa andaluza en Aerópolis (Sevilla) en su centro de ingeniería y mantenimiento de equipos de aviónica del A400M. Prescal pretendía afianzar su posición como empresa tractora en el mercado aeronáutico andaluz. Amper debía trabajar en principio en tres líneas fundamentales (prestar apoyo a la planta (Final Assembly Line) del A400M en las pruebas e instalación de los equipos suministrados por Thales; desarrollar la ingeniería de sistemas con EADS-CASA y, finalmente, ofrecer a las empresas servicios de I+D relacionados con la aviónica y electrónica para nuevos equipos). El departamento de I+D+I debía estar compuesto de ingenieros y técnicos, fundamentalmente de las Universidades de Cádiz y Sevilla, que se formarían durante un año en la empresa Thales (Burdeos), en el marco de un importante programa de transferencia tecnológica (*Andalucía*, 13 de julio de 2007; *Aeronáutica Andaluza*, 5, octubre-diciembre de 2007, 45). Con la planta ya abierta, piezas fundamentales se fabricaban en el extranjero, como sucedía con el juego de alas de Airbus (Reino Unido), el fuselaje (Airbus Francia) y de los conjuntos de la cola para el primer aparato (Europa Press, 4 de mayo de 2007).

[17] El plan estratégico preveía un incremento del peso de las ventas internacionales desde un 35% en 2010 al 70% hasta iniciar 2013 (Amper, *Informe anual 2010*, 14 y 25).

Tras una caída subsiguiente a la primera reestructuración, las ventas del Grupo Amper en términos corrientes crecieron hasta 2008 y declinaron después (Gráfico 1). Sus principales clientes eran el sector público, con un porcentaje en torno al 44% del volumen de ventas en 2003-2005, seguido de Telefónica con un tercio aproximado, del sector privado con un porcentaje medio de 21% y del resto de operadoras de telecomunicaciones. Por destinos geográficos, las ventas se realizaban mayoritariamente en el mercado interior (72,4% en 2003) pero las exportaciones mostraron un mayor dinamismo, de forma que en 2005-2006 alcanzaban una media del 38%[18]. De forma más decidida, si cabe, Amper apostó por los mercados exteriores y por la internacionalización como elemento conductor y motor de su crecimiento. El Gráfico 2 muestra a las claras el papel sustitutorio de las exportaciones, primordialmente dirigidas a Latinoamérica[19].

Gráfico 2. Distribución de los mercados de Amper por zonas geográficas, 2004-2010 (%)

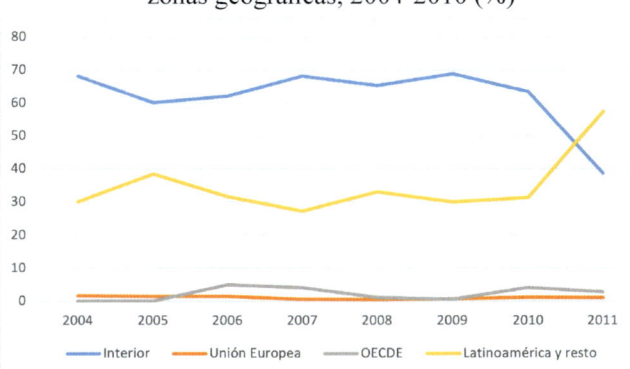

Fuente: Elaboración a partir de Amper, *Memorias* e *Informes anuales*, 2004-2011.

Un hito en la internacionalización que cierra el periodo estudiado es la adquisición del 85% de la empresa norteamericana eLandia y su integración

---

[18] Exportaciones (31% en 2009; 37% en 2010 (Amper, *Informe anual 2010*, 18).

[19] Si tomamos algunas unidades por separado, IRS Brasil aportaba en 2009 la cuarta parte de los ingresos totales del grupo, porcentaje muy similar al de IRS España (Grupo Amper, *Informe Anual 2009*, 20). La exportación contribuye al crecimiento de las ventas, a la vez que brinda ventajas adicionales: diversificación de la base de clientes con reducción de la dependencia de unos pocos importantes; oportunidad de igualar las fluctuaciones de la demanda relacionadas con el ciclo comercial regional; oportunidades a la especialización de productos, poco probable en el mercado local estrecho y obtención de experiencia a través de la red de contactos y socios (Recklies 2001).

en Medidata, que engrosó Amper en Latinoamérica con 3.000 nuevos clientes industriales, entre ellos dieciséis grandes operadoras de telecomunicaciones, y proporcionó una plataforma del negocio (Amper, *Informe anual 2010,* 14). En 2010, la alta dirección de Amper remachaba: «Nuestro objetivo no es ser una Compañía Internacional, sino una verdadera Multinacional» (Amper, *Informe anual 2010,* 12)[20].

3. Estrategia de crecimiento: alianzas estratégicas y acuerdos alcanzados

Vistos los objetivos, vayamos a los medios de lograrlos. La estrategia de crecimiento de Amper se completaba con alianzas estratégicas con terceros, fueran de carácter temporal, orientadas a un objetivo muy concreto, o a más largo plazo. Amper había forjado desde muy temprano una cultura de pactos. A ella contribuyeron acuerdos como los cerrados entre finales de 1975 y 1978 con los PTTs franceses para el suministro de contestadores telefónicos. En lo esencial, consistían en una cesión de licencia con *royalty* del 4,5% para fabricar los equipos en las instalaciones de la Compagnie de Signaux et d'Entreprises Électriques (CSEE) y en el suministro inicial de equipos completos y de piezas o subconjuntos cuando la firma abordase la fabricación en la planta industrial[21].

[20] En 2010 Amper tenía su sede central en Madrid y contaba con una red de subsedes por áreas (la de defensa en Getafe; la de comunicaciones y seguridad en Tres Cantos y en Getafe), de centros de trabajo (la de defensa en Albacete y Sevilla) y de delegaciones (el área de comunicaciones y seguridad dispersas en ocho ciudades españolas de la península y las islas–Algeciras, Oviedo, Barcelona, Bilbao, Palma de Mallorca, Valencia y varias en Sevilla, además de una en Getafe (Epicom). En América Latina, las sedes del área de comunicaciones y seguridad se localizaban en veinticuatro ciudades de catorce países –Miami; Buenos Aires (Argentina), Río de Janeiro, Belo Horizonte, Porto Alegre, Sao Paulo, Brasilia y Barueri (Brasil); Bogotá, Medellín y Cali (Colombia); San José (Costa Rica); Quito y Guayaquil (Ecuador); San Salvador (El Salvador); Ciudad de Guatemala (Guatemala); Tegucigalpa (Honduras); México (México); Managua (Nicaragua); Ciudad de Panamá (Panamá); Santo Domingo (República Dominicana); Trinidad y Tobago (Trinidad); Caracas y Maracaibo (Venezuela)– (Amper, *Informe anual 2010,* 60-62). En 2011, el Grupo contaba con sedes centrales en Madrid, Sao Paulo y Miami y con treinta y ocho oficinas en veintidós países (Amper, *Informe Anual 2012,* 8).

[21] Amper ganó el concurso con el modelo CM-52, segunda generación del equipo CM-5 suministrado a CTNE, y al cabo de dos años renovó otro contrato para el suministro de una nueva versión, el CM-60 (Rico, César, «Notas». Comunicación al autor, 25 de junio de 2020). CSEE sería calificada de oficina de estudios gigante, con medio millar de ingenieros altamente cualificados (*Les Échos,* 10 de septiembre de 1991).

Durante 2005 Amper llegó a un acuerdo con Motorola para considerar en los proyectos de regadíos la tecnología IRRINET. Esta tecnología de tipo «customizada», es decir, diseñada o adaptada a la medida de cada cliente, fue especialmente desarrollada para regadíos y consistía en incorporar unas estaciones remotas PLC de bajo consumo con unidades concentradoras y SCADA personalizable. Existía un mercado en expansión para este tipo de sistemas cuya demanda de prestaciones no era muy elevada (Amper *Memoria,* 2005, 33)[22].

En el área de control y gestión de fronteras no reguladas Amper lideró un consorcio compuesto por quince empresas españolas y extranjeras (entre ellas Telvent, Boeing, GMV e Isdefe) y veinticinco organismos de investigación, con el fin de llevar a cabo el proyecto cuatrienal INTEGRA, rama del Programa nacional CENIT y destinado a desarrollar herramientas de ayuda para el control de fronteras no reguladas y para la toma de decisiones en situaciones de crisis[23].

Junto a INTEGRA, los proyectos de investigación más relevantes en España y Europa en los que participaba Amper eran GLOBE, TECAMIS+, IDS3D, Wolf y Sintonía. GLOBE, destinado a definir el futuro sistema de gestión de fronteras de la Unión Europea y subvencionado dentro del programa europeo FP7, estaba dotado con 1,1 millones de euros. Amper lideró los trabajos correspondientes a las fronteras no reguladas.

Amper lideraba el proyecto de I+D TECAMIS+ que trabajaba en un desarrollo de arquitectura modular para aprovechar las funcionalidades de Internet. El proyecto, subvencionado en un 11% y con financiación pública del 50%, se incluyó dentro del Plan Avanza auspiciado por el ministerio de Industria[24].

En la modalidad de consorcio, Amper colaboró con la Universidad Politécnica de Valencia y un grupo de empresas europeas en el desarrollo del

---

[22] Motorola publicitaba su IRRInet M como una plataforma de gestión total del agua con una unidad terminal remota de campo flexible de radio o celular inalámbrica capaz de un control avanzado.

[23] INTEGRA contaba con un presupuesto global de 28,4 millones de euros, subvencionado en su mitad por el Programa CENIT. Las herramientas con las que se trabajaba presentaban simulaciones de diferentes escenarios que servían para automatizar los procesos de decisión (Amper, *Informe Anual 2009,* 55). El Consejo de Ministros autorizó una subvención (Amper, *Memoria 2008*, 2). Abengoa reivindicaba el liderazgo de Telvent en el proyecto INTEGRA para la gestión de la migración, seleccionado dentro del programa CENIT. Amper Sistemas S.A. se benefició de ayudas para el proyecto Sistema de vigilancia de fronteras terrestres dentro del Programa-Investigación y Desarrollo de la Sociedad de la Información (Resolución de 2 de marzo de 2005, de la Dirección General para el Desarrollo de la Sociedad de la Información, *BOE*, 84, 8 de abril de 2005, 12.283).

[24] TECAMIS+ implicaba una inversión de 8 millones de euros durante tres años (Amper, *Informe 2009*, 55).

programa MARIUS, financiado por la Unión Europea dentro del Programa Europeo de Seguridad y encaminado a definir y diseñar un sistema europeo para la integración de sensores y para la fusión de datos en una plataforma aeroembarcada cuya finalidad era la gestión de crisis. En este proyecto europeo Amper aportaba el sistema de mando y control (Amper, *Memoria 2006*, 27).

En la esfera de la integración de Telefonía IP y las Plataformas de Comunicaciones Unificadas y Colaboración en España, Amper se alió con Microsoft para comercializar soluciones de los centros de contactos tras obtener la certificación de Voice Partner. Amper elaboró un plan de negocio y de capacitación técnica a lo largo de un año y con implicación de todos los departamentos de la unidad. Simultáneamente, construyó la oferta de servicios relacionados con la plataforma de comunicaciones unificadas de Microsoft (*El Economista*, 5 de abril 2006).

Amper selló un acuerdo de colaboración con la compañía británica Detica para desarrollar un proyecto de Seguridad Lógica en Telefónica. La primera fase consistió en una prueba piloto de un detector de anomalías de red (Amper. *Informe Anual 2009*, 4-5).

Un acuerdo estratégico con la operadora dio paso a un primer contrato para la venta en Sudamérica de los equipos personales de criptografía para GSM (670E). Estos equipos toleraban cualquier tipo de terminal GSM y proporcionaban un grado de confidencialidad muy elevado (Amper, *Memoria 2007*).

Ejemplo de alianzas lo ofrece la cerrada con Chertoff Group, compañía de asesoramiento en seguridad y gestión de riesgos liderada por un antiguo funcionario de la administración Bush. El acuerdo tenía como objetivo el desarrollo conjunto de negocios y la ejecución de proyectos en el dominio de la seguridad interior –control de fronteras, centros de emergencia 112 y protección de infraestructuras críticas– en Estados Unidos y en otros mercados internacionales. Además, Chertoff Group debía ayudar a Amper S.A. a establecer asociaciones con empresas estadounidenses líderes con el fin de perseguir oportunidades de negocio específicas en los diferentes programas de seguridad establecidos a nivel federal y estatal. Como parte del acuerdo, Chertoff Group debía tomar una participación del 0,59% de Amper S.A., que podía proceder de la autocartera de libre disposición de la sociedad[25].

---

[25] Amper S.A. pretendía superar los 200 millones de euros de contratación en el mercado internacional de Homeland Security en los tres años sucesivos (CNMV, 115.970, 9/11/2009; Amper, *Informe anual*, 2009, 45; *El Economista*, 10 de noviembre de 2009). Chertoff Group validó la tecnología de seguridad al aliarse con Amper (Amper, *Informe Anual 2009*, 12). El

Junto a medio centenar de organismos de investigación y empresas (Indra, Sener, Aernova, Cesa, Aries Complex o Insa, entre otras), Amper desarrolló tecnologías aplicables a los aviones no tripulados o drones en el marco del proyecto Sintonia (Sistemas No Tripulados Orientados al Nulo Impacto Ambiental) y del programa Cenit-E del Ministerio de Industria, financiado por el CDTI. A Amper le correspondían labores de coordinación y de investigación de fórmulas para optimizar la transmisión de los datos de los sensores en las naves y de soluciones para realizar el lanzamiento y la recuperación del avión no tripulado de manera automática y segura (*Cinco Días*, 15 de septiembre de 2010).

Amper y eLandia, proveedor líder de productos y servicios, concertaron una alianza regional para aprovechar las fortalezas de ambas y competir en toda América Latina como uno de los mayores proveedores regionales de productos de información y telecomunicaciones junto con capacidades y operaciones. Para ello utilizaron sus respectivas filiales Medidata y Desca Holdings, este un proveedor de infraestructura de redes e integración de sistemas en EE. UU. y en trece países de América Latina. Amper y eLandia se comprometían también a hacer un esfuerzo conjunto de ventas orientado a clientes regionales y multinacionales en América Latina. La alianza también apoyaba los esfuerzos de ventas de la cartera completa de productos de Amper en sus tres divisiones de negocios (Defensa, Seguridad Nacional y Telecomunicaciones) en toda la región de América Latina. Para eLandia, la alianza también debía apoyar la expansión de su negocio de educación llevada a cabo a través de CTT en Brasil[26]. Por otro acuerdo específico, la empresa norteamericana con sede en Delaware le transfería el control de las licencias de sus filiales en el Servicio Inalámbrico Avanzado a Amper (Federal Communications Commission 2010; eLandia International Inc. 2010).

Acorde con la estrategia de incorporación de nuevas zonas geográficas, en 2010, Amper negoció con diferentes empresas de la India en la doble dirección de abordar proyectos conjuntos y de optimizar los productos tec-

---

acuerdo contemplaba la posibilidad de que Chertoff ayudase a Amper a establecer asociaciones con el fin de establecer programas de seguridad tanto en los estados como en el ámbito federal (*Cinco Días*, 10 de noviembre de 2009). El mercado bursátil premió el acuerdo con alzas superiores al 8% en la cotización de los títulos de Amper (*El Periódico*, 10 de noviembre de 2009).

[26] Desca Holdings, con sede en Miami, Florida, actuaba en Argentina, Colombia, Costa Rica, Ecuador, El Salvador, Guatemala, Honduras, México, Nicaragua, Trinidad y Tobago, Panamá, Perú, y Venezuela (EX-10.1 2 DEX101.HTM Strategic alliance agreement, 24 de mayo de 2010).

nológicos propios. A esta categoría pertenecía un acuerdo con un socio local –Mistral Solutions– con el doble objetivo de introducir sus productos de emergencias y movilidad en la India a cambio de reducir el coste de producción de la industria local mediante soluciones tecnológicas avanzadas. Amper transfería a su socia *know how* sobre sus soluciones *hardware* de emergencia y movilidad (El *Economista*, 26 de mayo de 2011). El acuerdo, cierto, firmado en 2011, obedecía a un innovador esquema de compartición de costes que permitía a la compañía india la distribución exclusiva de los productos de seguridad de Amper en la región así como el rediseño y puesta en producción de esa gama de productos de Amper a escala mundial (Amper, *Informe 2011*, 36-37; Amper, *Informe anual 2010*, 27)[27].

Según esquemas colaborativos de carácter transversal, Amper desarrolló el proyecto I-3D conjuntamente con dos entidades de características muy dispares como eran la Universidad Politécnica de Madrid y la consultora empresarial Novagenia Information Technologies. El proyecto, financiado por el Gobierno, tenía como finalidad el desarrollo de un portal en tres dimensiones para identificación y seguimiento en entornos controlados[28].

Hasta en cuatro ocasiones se asoció Amper con empresas nacionales e internacionales para participar en concursos entre 2003 y 2005 con opciones de éxito. En dos ocasiones lo llevó a cabo como matriz y en las dos restantes a través de las filiales Amper Programas y Amper Medidata. En la primera modalidad formó sendas Uniones Temporales de Empresas con Telefónica para suministrar a AENA y la segunda con Ofiteco y SICE para el mantenimiento y conservación de la red automática Cuenca Hidrográfica del Ebro. En la modalidad de actuación a través de las filiales, Amper Programas y Amper Medidata se aliaron con Cisco y Sun, Thales Communications AG e Hitachi Data Systems para para cumplir con los compromisos de los contratos con Telefónica en São Paulo, el ejército suizo y la Companhia de Processamento

---

[27] Se introdujo el nemesis EMS (Emergency Management System). Mistral Solutions, con sede en Bangalore (India), estaba muy centrada en el diseño, desarrollo y fabricación de soluciones *hardware* y *software* en las áreas de defensa, seguridad y espacio, destinadas a empresas de diferentes países, Estados Unidos incluido (*ComputerWorld*, 27 de mayo de 2011; *Infodefensa*, 27 de mayo de 2011).

[28] Con financiación dentro del subprograma Avanza I+D del Ministerio de Industria Turismo y Comercio, se trataba de un desarrollo tecnológico que permitiera la generación de escenarios virtuales en tiempo real en espacios específicos como infraestructuras refinerías puertos áreas de seguridad a partir de datos provenientes de cámaras fijas desplegadas en el área a controlar y de otros sistemas de vigilancia (Amper, *Informe anual 2010*, 40). Actividad CNAE de Novagenia Information Technologies (6209 – Otros servicios relacionados con las tecnologías de la información y la informática).

de Dados do Estado de São Paulo (Prodesp)[29] (Anexo 2). Para finalizar una larga lista, no siempre fácil de documentar, Amper logró multitud de contratos con clientes significados del sector servicios[30].

Amper colaboró con la fundación COTEC Europa y empresas españolas, italianas y portuguesas en un proyecto pionero cuyo objetivo era el desarrollo de sistemas tecnológicos para mejorar la seguridad marítima y medioambiental así como la interoperabilidad de las agencias que actuaban en el Mediterráneo.

A la estrategia adoptada por el Grupo se añaden las ya señaladas desinversiones, llevadas a cabo por lo general después de un importante saneamiento financiero y una adecuación de la plantilla a la situación del entorno competitivo (Tabla 2)[31]. Ya en 2003, Amper Soluciones había vendido a Intelsis sus Servicios de Red, unidad que venía representando aproximadamente el 40% de sus ventas y la mitad de su plantilla. Amper Soluciones abandonaba así las actividades directamente relacionadas con la externalización de trabajos de planta interna y externa para la red fija de las operadoras de telecomunicación. Tras esta operación, la empresa mantenía sus unidades de negocio de proyectos especiales, productos, servicios de radio y servicios profesionales. En lo sucesivo, la filial pensaba centrarse en la línea de negocios de productos, a través de su oferta en el área de acceso a las redes, que cubría tanto los terminales y equipos de los usuarios finales como los equipos de acceso propiamente dicho. En el campo de los servicios, su oferta se centraría en la ingeniería e instalación de sistemas radio de tipo celular o de cualquier otra tecnología (LMDS, PDH, SDH, etc.)[32].

---

[29] Hitachi Data Systems era una empresa conjunta de Hitachi Ltd. y Electronic Data System que pugnaba por competir con Amdahl (*ComputerWorld*, 8 de mayo de 1989).

[30] MUFACE, Tesorería General de la Seguridad Social, Instituciones Penitenciarias, universidades como las de Cartagena, Cádiz, Complutense de Madrid; cadenas de hoteles como Westin y gestores inmobiliarios como Richard Ellis. Permítasenos algunas precisiones disponibles. En el ejemplo de la Universidad de Barcelona, la definición de un «marco de excelencia» para el uso de las TIC en el ámbito universitario implicó el diseño e implantación de un modelo de red colaborativa de investigación con las más altas prestaciones tecnológicas. En el de la Seguridad Social, Amper renovó las redes de telefonía con tecnología Aastra en 460 sedes y un total de 14.000 teléfonos, implantó los sistemas de gestión y tarificación y desplegó sistemas de telefonía IP en 300 sedes con 1.200 teléfonos IP con conexión a Next Generation Network (*Informe Anual 2009,* 80-81).

[31] Las desinversiones comprenden la enajenación y venta de activos, instalaciones, líneas de productos, filiales, divisiones y unidades de negocio de la empresa matriz (Moschieri y Mair 2008, 399-422; Borga, Ibarlucea-Flores y Sztajerowska 2020, 1).

[32] La empresa ofrecía un abanico de productos avanzados (ADSL, WiFi, etc.) para las operadoras de las redes fijas y móviles. Las ventas a último día de marzo de 2004 alcanzaban

A mediados de 2004, realizó una nueva desinversión: la venta de Ibersegur dedicada al desarrollo, fabricación y venta de sistemas de gestión de *parking* y de parquímetros, que supuso la salida definitiva del Grupo Amper del negocio. Antes de finalizar el año, Amper Soluciones, SA vendió a la sociedad inversora española American Pacific S.A. su participación en el Grupo STC, Sistemas, Telecomunicación y Control S.A., dedicado a la gestión de proyectos de radioenlaces de alta y baja capacidad. Con posterioridad esta operación, Amper Soluciones, filial dedicada a las operadoras de telecomunicación en España, mantenía sus cuatro unidades de negocio de proyectos especiales, productos, servicios de radio y servicios profesionales. En adelante, pasó a centrarse en los nichos con mejores perspectivas de futuro en el mercado de telecomunicaciones[33].

9,45 millones de euros, cifra que representaba una caída del 17% respecto al año anterior, debida a la venta de la unidad de servicios de red y al cierre de la actividad en Perú. En contrapartida, el notable impulso en las actividades estratégicas (proyectos especiales, productos, servicios de radio y servicios profesionales) colmó con creces las expectativas de ventas. Las ventas homogéneas, sin el efecto de la venta de la unidad de servicios de red, se situaban en 9,45 millones de euros, un 28% más que los 7,37 millones de euros del mismo periodo del año anterior.

[33] Dicha venta aportó una importante plusvalía. American Pacific, S.A. se proponía introducirse en el mercado de Telecomunicaciones y se revelaba altamente cualificada para relanzar las actividades del Grupo STC. A finales de 2003, alcanzó una cifra de negocio de 8,39 millones de euros (CNMV, 50.621, 11/6/2004). Amper Ibersegur contribuía al negocio del Grupo Amper, a cierre del primer semestre del 2003, con unas ventas de 5,67 millones de euros y con un resultado atribuible de 0,39 millones de euros (CNMV, 50.122, 28/5/2004, 3).

Tabla 2. Desinversiones del Grupo Amper

Empresa	Activo o participación vendida	Empresa compradora	Año	Precio millones €	Observaciones
Amper Soluciones	Servicios de Red	Intelsis	2003	2,7	
Amper Tecnologías	Ibersegur	Societat Catalana d'Iniciatives	2003	8,25	
Amper Soluciones	Grupo STC, Sistemas, Telecomunicación y Control, SA	American Pacific, SA	2004	0,75	American Pacific (gestión de proyectos de radioenlaces de alta y baja capacidad)
	Networking para pymes	-	2003	-	Cierre para centrarse en grandes empresas (AENA)

Fuente: Elaboración a partir de Amper, *Memoria(s) e Informes anual(es)*

4. La pugna por la competitividad: las capacidades tecnológicas

Difícilmente hubiera podido mantener Amper su competitividad internacional sin cuidar el desarrollo tecnológico, más allá de los acuerdos estratégicos con líderes tecnológicos. Desde la misma acta fundacional de Amper, la I+D figuraba como componente esencial de la razón de ser de la empresa y, a lo largo de su trayectoria, había ido reafirmando esa faceta distintiva. En 2010 Amper ocupaba la quinta posición en el *ranking* de empresas españolas por inversión en investigación, desarrollo e innovación (I+D+i) (Amper, *Informe 2010,* 40)[34]. Dentro de los planes estratégicos, objetivos como el aumento de la rentabilidad entrañaban la adopción de medidas concretas, que, de una u otra manera, atañían a la I+D. Forzando enormemente las cifras, Amper presumía de dedicar un 12,1% de su facturación a invertir en tecnología susceptible de incorporar I+D. El objetivo de esta elevada intensidad tecnológica apuntaba al logro del liderazgo y a la excelencia en los mercados en los que estaba presente (Amper, *Memoria 2005,* 13; Amper, *Informe 2006,* 27).

[34] Las *Memorias* e *Informes* anuales presentan una serie de inconvenientes para profundizar en aspectos relativos a la I+D. Entre ellos destacan por su frecuencia la incongruencia de los datos, la discontinuidad y la falta de homogeneidad de los conceptos utilizados a lo largo de los años. Por ejemplo, solo recogen pagos de inmovilizaciones en dos años (2004-2005: 1,12 y 3,65 millones de euros) y no establecen diferencia entre inmateriales y materiales. Por tanto, tan solo podemos deducir que Amper recurría a compras de bienes inmateriales pero no podemos precisar el tipo. Una variable que permite aproximarse a la I+D, queda recogida unas veces como activos intangibles, otras como inmovilizado inmaterial y unas terceras recibe el calificativo de inmovilizado intangible; en ocasiones señala la I+D y en otras la I+D+i. Resultados de la actividad de I+D, como bienes y derechos inmateriales o propiedad industrial solo se recogen esporádicamente (1,68 y 27,55 millones de euros en 2003; 1,81 en 2006). El activo intangible entre 2004-2010 se multiplicó por 6,3 con tres etapas diferenciadas (2004-2006 por encima de la línea de tendencia; 2006-2008 por debajo y 2009-2011 por encima o muy pegado a la tendencia (Anexo 3).

Gráfico 3. La intensidad de I+D en Amper (I+D/ventas netas)

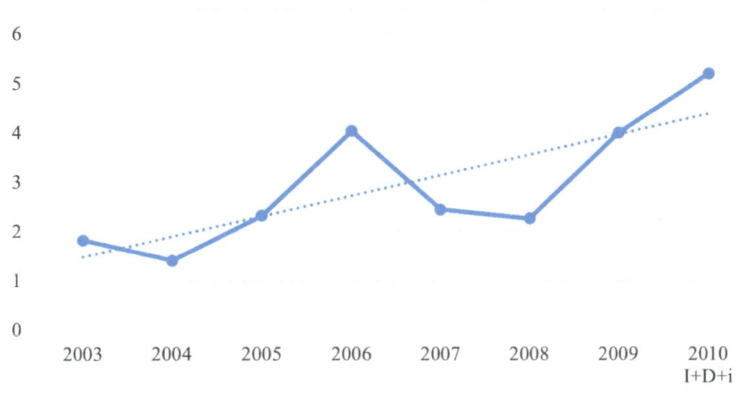

Fuente: Elaboración a partir de Amper, *Memoria(s)* e *Informes anuales*

Vistos en conjunto, los años 2003-2010 se caracterizaron por una tendencia creciente a la inversión en I+D, con disparidades que situaron el punto más bajo en 2004 y el más alto en el año final (Gráfico 3). Si consideramos los activos intangibles, un indicador de la I+D, la composición de los años conocidos arroja un claro predominio del esfuerzo en desarrollo, con porcentajes de 67,92 y 83,81% en 2004-2005 y un más modesto 46,42% en 2006, debido a la aparición de la propiedad industrial. El peso de las aplicaciones informáticas fue de menor cuantía, con un porcentaje medio del 20,89% sobre el total del esfuerzo inversor de 2004-2006[35].

Durante el año 2007, con 7,61 millones de euros destinados a inversiones y gastos de I+D+i y un equipo humano de 98 personas, Amper finalizó el primer desarrollo operativo del nuevo sistema de gestión de crisis, que le permitiría reforzar la competitividad en este mercado (Amper, *Informe Anual 2007*, 21)[36].

La apuesta por la innovación en 2008 fue reconocida en el *ranking* EU Industrial R&D Investment Score-board, elaborado por la Comisión Europea y encabezado por Nokia en las TIC, que situaba a Amper como la quinta

---

[35] Las inversiones de 2005 ascendieron a 3.047 miles de euros, de los cuales 1.508 miles de euros procedían de desarrollos internos y 1.539 miles de euros de adquisiciones individuales (Deloitte, *Información económica y financiera del Grupo Amper*, 2005, 56).

[36] Se consideran NEC (Network Enabled Capabilities) los instrumentos encaminados a obtener capacidades adicionales para el desarrollo de operaciones militares por medio del uso de las tecnologías de la información las comunicaciones (Fundación Círculo de Tecnologías para la Defensa y la Seguridad 2009, 143-145).

empresa española por inversión en I+D+i en relación con su número de empleados y la octava en relación con sus ingresos. Telefónica encabezaba en España la lista de las TIC y ocupaba el puesto 40 en la lista mundial, mientras que Indra Sistemas figuraba en el 103[37].

En 2009, Amper invirtió 12,65 millones de euros en I+D+i –el 4% de la facturación–, área a la que se dedicaron más de 150 personas. Amper logró soluciones punteras para sistemas de mando y control, gestión de emergencias, protección de fronteras y criptosistemas.

Dentro de la tendencia general, cabe destacar que la intensidad varió sustancialmente según las filiales o secciones del Grupo. En seguridad y defensa el porcentaje de facturación susceptible de incorporar I+D llegó a moverse en torno al 20% de la cifra de negocio (Amper, *Memoria 2005*, 13). En 2004 y 2005 Amper Programas destinó a I+D+i 7,9 y 8 millones de euros, respectivamente, con una participación en las ventas del año superior al 14% y al 13%. El grueso de estos recursos se asignó al desarrollo de equipos y productos de nueva generación en el ámbito de los sistemas CIS, a la búsqueda de una posición puntera en un campo en el que la compañía basaba su estrategia de desarrollo para los años venideros[38]. Durante el ejercicio 2006, Homeland Security destinó a I+D 1,1 millones de euros (un 4,3% sobre la cifra de ventas) y una plantilla de doce personas. Desde el principio de 2006 consiguió financiación pública, por un importe de 1,5 millones de euros, para desarrollar proyectos I+D+i. Más específicamente, la sección de Criptosistemas enfocó su actividad bajo la doble perspectiva de la venta de equipos nacionales de tecnología propia, a los que se añadieron otros no nacionales (OTAN), y del desarrollo de actividades de I+D+i bajo contrato. Estas actividades representaban un 30% del total de las ventas del ejercicio. Especial relieve cobraba la realización de prototipos de nuevos cifradores IP[39].

---

[37] Repsol YPF figuraba en el puesto 183, Iberdrola en el 206, Acciona en el 213, Zeltia en el 242, Fagor Electrodomésticos en el 247 y Amper en el 646 (European Communities 2009, 76; Amper. *Informe* 2008, 12).

[38] Deloitte, *Información Económica y Financiera del Grupo*, 2004, 115-116; Amper, *Memoria 2004*, 17 y *Memoria 2005*, 28.

[39] Destacaron los proyectos «Fusión de datos multisensor» para la Comunidad Autónoma de Madrid dentro del Plan Madrid Innova y «Nueva Arquitectura C4 para Fronteras más Abierta y Portable» financiado con fondos PROFIT (Amper, *Memoria 2006*, 32). Homelad Security preparaba el lanzamiento comercial de uno de los criptos IP más rápido del mercado mundial y tenía a punto un cripto personal capaz de conectarse a cualquier teléfono GSM de última generación. A los nuevos cifradores IP se destinaron 2,3 millones de euros y una plantilla de 20 personas.

Como muestra de capacidad tecnológica, Amper se dotó de instrumentos transversales de I+D. Así, creó la unidad de innovación con el cometido de asegurar la gestión y transferencia del conocimiento entre las diferentes unidades, la promoción y coordinación de las actividades de ingeniería e iniciativas de I+D+i y el mantenimiento y la mejora de las competencias tecnológicas. A finales de 2006, la unidad contaba con 267 empleados, el 23% de la plantilla total, que se dedicaban al desarrollo de productos propios y a la ejecución de contratos de alta tecnología (Amper, *Memoria 2006*, 16).

En 2007 Amper dio un paso importante en la configuración de sus capacidades tecnológicas propias con la puesta en marcha del Amper.Lab, un centro NEC de experimentación en red muy sofisticado que combinaba equipos reales y escenarios virtuales para el análisis de situaciones y escenarios de operaciones. Por medio de la simulación virtual de las capacidades de los sistemas y equipos se comprobaba su eficacia y se programaban los cambios necesarios previos al diseño e implantación definitivos. Amper.Lab estaba conformado para operar en conexión con la red de veintinueve centros similares dispersos por el planeta, palanca de su rendimiento operativo y su capacidad de dar respuesta a las necesidades concretas de los clientes. La experimentación de soluciones de defensa y comunicaciones encontró en él un medio clave de avance. El Amper.Lab mostró su eficacia en el ahorro de costes. Durante 2009, el centro puso en marcha el demostrador de los sistemas de información y vetrónica para un nuevo vehículo táctico– (Amper, *Memoria 2007*, 24; Amper, *Informe 2010*, 43)[40].

A esos instrumentos transversales de I+D Amper añadió una red de centros de excelencia, dedicados a la I+D de soluciones en defensa, comunicaciones y seguridad, publicitados como los tres ejes estratégicos de Amper –internacionalización, eficiencia e innovación. Los centros se localizaban en las dos mayores ciudades españolas –Madrid y Barcelona– en una ciudad asiática y en otra latinoamericana –Bangalore y Bogotá, respectivamente (Amper, *Informe Anual 2012*, 23)[41].

La segunda fuente de acumulación de capacidad técnica estribaba en la adquisición de bienes intangibles, una realidad señalada pero insuficientemente documentada. Sabemos, por ejemplo, que en dos años (2004-2005) se efectuaron pagos de inmovilizaciones inmateriales, un concepto correspon-

---

[40] El demostrador permite la operación conjunta de los sistemas del vehículo con los sistemas reales en operación en el Ejército de Tierra (Amper, *Informe Anual 2009*, 54-55).

[41] Obviamente, el centro de Bangalore se relacionaba estrechamente con el mencionado acuerdo con Mistral Solutions (*ComputerWorld*, 27 de mayo de 2011).

diente en parte a I+D. Conocemos, asimismo, que en 2005 las adquisiciones individuales ascendieron a la mitad del total de 3.047 miles de euros[42].

Gráfico 4. Composición de la plantilla de Amper por categorías profesionales, 2003-2006 (%)

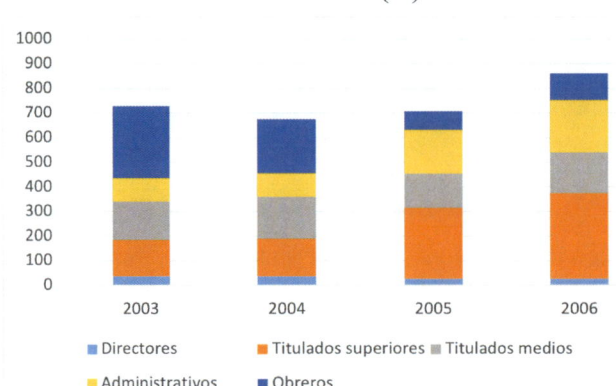

Fuente: Elaboración a partir de Amper, *Memoria(s)* e *Informe(s) anual(es)*.

La acumulación de capacidad técnica emanaba en tercer lugar del alto nivel de cualificación de la mano de obra.

Entre 2003-2011, la plantilla se multiplicó por 2,6. En tan solo los cuatro primeros años de ese periodo, los ajustes de empleo, las desinversiones y las adquisiciones contribuyeron a dar un vuelco a la situación del empleo en la empresa. En 2006, casi el 60% de la plantilla eran titulados, un 40% de los cuales lo eran de grado superior, casi el doble que en 2003, justo la otra cara del espejo de lo sucedido con los obreros. Una parte menos significativa de la capacidad técnica la representaban los directores, que pasaron del 5% al 3% (Gráfico 4). Esta faceta de Amper era el resultado en parte de aplicar una contratación selectiva. A lo largo del trienio 2003-2005, más de las tres cuartas partes de los nuevos contratados eran especialistas en alta tecnología, mientras que casi la mitad de los recién incorporados eran ingenieros y titulados superiores y el 31% ingenieros técnicos y titulados medios (Amper, *Memoria 2005*, 13).

---

[42] Hay referencias a subcontrataciones (10,2 y 29,76 millones de euros) en 2004-2005, sin más precisión (Deloitte, *Información Económica y Financiera del Grupo Amper. Cuentas anuales*, 2005, 72). En el programa INTEGRA la Universidad Politécnica de Madrid participaba como subcontratada de Amper cooperando en la tarea definida como *Investigación en Tecnologías para ayuda en la ejecución y toma de decisiones en sistemas C4ISR (Command, Control, Communications, Computers, Intelligence, Surveillance and Reconnaissance)*.

Fuera ya del periodo de estudio, en 2011, la plantilla estaba formada por profesionales con experiencia en el sector y cualificados –el 54% tenían titulación universitaria y el 37% titulación de especialistas técnicos–. La contratación selectiva, junto a una renovación generacional intensa y constante, se tradujo en un rejuvenecimiento del personal. En 2005, la media de edad de la plantilla de Amper era de 41 años. Tres años después, un poco más de la mitad de la plantilla no llegaba a los 40 años, el 28% se situaban entre los 40 y los 50 años y el 19% restante estaban en la franja de edad superior a los cincuenta años (Amper, *Memoria 2008*, 56). Al cabo de tres años, la media de edad era de 38 años y tres cuartas partes no llegaban a 45 años; cuatro quintas partes eran varones. Según la distribución geográfica, la mayoría estaban empleados en 14 países extranjeros (59,43%), entre los que destacaba por su mayor volumen Samoa, Brasil, Colombia, Venezuela y México, que sumaban casi el 43%[43].

Gráfico 5. Productividad de Amper (ventas/plantilla, millones de euros)

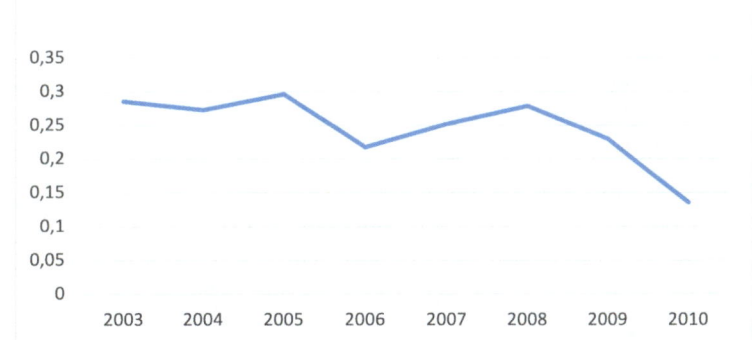

Fuente: Elaboración a partir de Amper, *Memoria(s)* e *Informe(s) anual(es)*.

Estos datos llevarían de forma natural a constatar resultados positivos en una de las variables decisivas en la configuración de una empresa de éxito. Sin embargo, el Gráfico 5 nos dice que no fue exactamente así, al menos en los años finales del periodo en estudio, como muestran esa primera caída de 2006, justo el año considerado como la gran trasformación de la empresa, y la incontestable de 2009. Otras dos variables significativas –ingresos por empleado y beneficio neto por empleado– tuvieron un mal comportamiento. Finalmente, a lo largo de los años 2004-2010, solo en dos (2007 y 2008)

---

[43] En 2011, dedicó 210 profesionales a la I+D+i (Amper, *Informe 2011*, 61).

mejoró la productividad del activo y en tres (2005, 2007 y 2008) creció la rentabilidad sobre activos. Desde otro punto de vista, en 2007-2010 el Free Cash Flow (FCF) medio se cifró en -0,48 millones de euros, y el crecimiento medio anual del -10,72%, según los analistas una muestra de la incapacidad de la empresa para generar dinero con su negocio[44].

Sin duda, la explicación, al menos en parte, estriba en otras cifras que Amper presenta, modificando ligeramente el criterio anterior, que muestran una descualificación de la mano de obra. En la composición de la plantilla por funciones de 2010, la ingeniería había perdido fuelle (34%), mientras que las operaciones se situaron casi a la altura del año 2003 (38%), algo sin duda relacionado con la apertura de plantas de ensamblaje en Sevilla y Albacete[45]. La descualificación tiene su reflejo en la caída, cierto, leve, de los gastos salariales por empleado. Desde otro lado, la rentabilidad del salario medida por la ratio ingresos/gastos de personal sufrió descenso.

Conclusión

Este capítulo señala el indiscutible impacto de las crisis en las empresas, que se vieron obligadas a aplicar estrategias de supervivencia. A su vez, revela que una parte de las soluciones a las crisis vino precisamente de esas situaciones que acompañaron a la llegada de la globalización.

La investigación se ha centrado en un estudio de caso de una empresa de las TIC en España, caracterizada por su independencia tecnológica. Durante los años 2001 a 2003, como consecuencia del estallido de la burbuja tecnológica, Amper atravesó una profunda crisis, que obligó a una reestructuración y supuso una reducción importante en su tamaño. En ese escenario mundial desfavorable, sin embargo, Amper logró paliar los efectos de la difícil coyuntura económica y su cifra de negocio en España se redujo un 12,8% con respecto a la del ejercicio anterior (*Informe Anual 2009*, 20; Amper, *Memoria 2007*, 14). En 2003, Amper comenzó a recuperarse y en 2004

---

[44] El FCF, suma de dinero en efectivo que genera un negocio después de pagar todos los gastos e inversiones de capital, se considera uno de los indicadores más significativos y menos manipulable para determinar la evolución real de los resultados de una empresa, de acuerdo con el servicio de análisis financiero WallueStreet en 2020.

[45] Sorprende la falta de información sobre el empleo y otros aspectos en estas plantas. La inversión realizada en Sevilla alcanzó 284 millones de euros (Europa Press, 4 de mayo de 2007). En Albacete Eurocopter empleaba a 450 personas (Cortes de Castilla-La Mancha, *Diario de sesiones*, VII Legislatura, 34, 12 de marzo de 2009, 4).

dio por cerrado el periodo de ajuste e, incluso, señalaba nuevas altas en la empresa, centradas en cuadros con perfiles técnicos altamente cualificados y orientados hacia la integración de sistemas, la actividad que más valor añadido aportaba. Desde 2003 hasta 2006, ventas y resultados volvieron al crecimiento. A finales del 2006, Amper se planteó la necesidad de abordar un proceso de cambio profundo, para superar definitivamente la herencia de los años difíciles y situar a la compañía en condiciones de afrontar los retos de un mercado crecientemente complejo y competitivo. Curiosamente, la reestructuración de 2008, que afectó a medio centenar de personas, parecía más bien orientada a corregir ineficiencias (Amper, *Memoria 2004,* 12)[46].

Un largo periodo de crecimiento combinado con sucesivas restructuraciones hizo de Amper una empresa especializada en la defensa y la seguridad. En el tránsito perdió su carácter de empresa familiar fundamentada en un nicho de mercado para convertirse en una multinacional. El objeto social de Amper, sin apenas variación desde su constitución en 1971, abarcaba una amplia variedad de actividades centradas en los sistemas y equipos de telecomunicación y electrónica y sus componentes –investigación, desarrollo, fabricación, reparación, comercialización, ingeniería, instalación y mantenimiento–, así como un conjunto relacionado con bienes muebles e inmuebles y valores[47].

En suma, el modelo de empresa con tecnología propia e internacionalizada representado por Amper cosechó logros irrefutables. Amper fundó su apuesta estratégica en tres principios básicos: reafirmación de la estrategia enfocada, hincapié en los factores diferenciales para conquistar nuevos segmentos de negocio o ámbitos geográficos, máxima eficiencia operativa, junto a una esmerada gestión financiera. Ello suponía implicar a toda la organización en un proceso de cambio cultural, plasmado en una única visión de compromiso con el cliente, innovación tecnológica y búsqueda de la excelencia. Se dirigía a los accionistas con expresiones como deberes cumplidos y estrategia acertada (Amper *Memoria 2008,* 11).

Pese al tono triunfalista de la empresa, algunas cifras hablan de vuelta atrás, desajustes y logros incumplidos. No obstante, los analistas continuaban

---

[46] El grueso de las personas afectadas por la reestructuración –40– pertenecía a la unidad de IRS y las restantes a la estructura corporativa. La reestructuración se llevó a efecto a través de un programa de bajas incentivadas y de amortización de puestos de trabajo. En total, las indemnizaciones laborales no recurrentes alcanzaron la cifra de 5,4 millones de euros (Amper, *Memoria 2008*, 58).

[47] Grupo Amper, *Memoria consolidada del ejercicio anual 2004*, 76.

insistiendo en su clara vocación internacional y su compromiso fuerte con la ingeniería innovadora y excelente, según WallueStreet en 2020.

Anexo 1. El grupo Landata

Landata Comunicaciones de Empresa prestaba servicios de instalación, reposición, mantenimiento y actualización para los clientes de la Red Ibercom de Telefónica (redes de voz, aplicaciones corporativas convergentes de voz-datos, sistemas de *call centers*, soluciones de movilidad y servicios de soporte). Contrato de exclusividad con Ericsson para suministros a Telefónica (renovado en 2006 y con validez hasta diciembre de 2007). Lanaccess enfocaba su actividad principalmente al desarrollo de soluciones específicas (HW y SW) de transmisión y tratamiento de vídeo digital. Asimismo, desarrollaba sus productos y soluciones ligadas principalmente a aplicaciones de vigilancia/seguridad. Ingresos en 2005: 3,9 millones de euros; EBITDA (Earnings Before Interest Taxes Depreciation and Amortization): 1,4 millones de euros. Composición de las ventas: productos (35,9%); clientes: BBVA, Fichet, VSK, Securitas, etc.; servicios y mantenimiento: (13%): BBVA, T-Systems, Unilever y La Caixa, entre otros. Cerca del 80% de los ingresos estaban ligados a un producto maduro (OnSafe), con *upgrade* previsto para 2007 dirigido a una base de más extensa. Otros productos (Postes SOS, Fiber Gate Swith) ligados a infraestructuras. Soluciones multiestándar de alto rendimiento y adaptables a las exigencias del cliente. El Plan de negocio preveía un ritmo de crecimiento de las ventas del 10,8% anual y una paulatina mejora de la rentabilidad a consecuencia del mayor peso de las actividades de servicios y mantenimientos así como del apalancamiento operativo. La inversión proyectada en CAPEX rondaba los 1,2 millones de euros anuales.

Anexo 2. Contratos y proyectos del Grupo Amper

Empresa	Cliente	Año	Producto o servicio	Precio millones €	Observaciones
	Confederación Hidrográfica del Ebro	2003	Nueva red de comunicaciones Tetra		
Amper	Presa de Itoiz	2003	Sistema de Gestión de Emergencias		
Amper	Regantes del Campo de Cartagena	2003	Ampliación del sistema de telecontrol		
Unión Temporal de Empresas	AENA-Navegación Aérea	2003	Red Nacional de Datos de Navegación Aérea, fase 4		Ute con telefónica
Amper Programas	Ejército suizo	2004	Sistemas de información para el mando y control (programa FIS HE)		Asociada con thales communications ag
Amper Programas	Ejército de tierra	2004	Red Básica de Área: nueva versión	Poco más de 21	
Amper Medidata	ONO	2005	Consultoría/integración de servicios multimedia		Dentro de la migración a su nueva red ip
Amper Programas	AENA	2005	*Hardware* y *software* para análisis de datos en tierra GBAS		Facilitar la navegación aérea basada en satélite

Empresa	Cliente	Año	Producto o servicio	Precio millones €	Observaciones
Amper Sistemas	Abarán (Murcia)	2005	Sistema de control de con tecnología punta MOS-CAD (Motorola)		
Amper Sistemas	ENDESA	2005	Suministro de 400 estaciones repetidoras, 1.500 terminales de radio PMR y equipamiento auxiliar		Prestar servicio de comunicaciones en diferentes puntos
Amper	Gobierno de Estonia	2005	Sistema de vigilancia de fronteras		Planes de invertir 150 millones de euros en 7 años
Amper Medidata	Compañía de Procesamiento de Datos del Estado São Paulo (Prodesp)	2005	Implementación del subsistema Lighting 9980 V		En asociación con Hitachi data systems
Amper	Ejército del Aire	2005	Mantenimiento de instrumentos de navegación aérea	3	Instrumentos: señalización, comunicaciones y electrónica de aparatos
Amper	Serbia y Montenegro	2005	Sistema para vigilancia de fronteras	2,4	Sistema c4isr
Amper	AENA	2005	Red multiservicio de telecomunicaciones	más de 15	Nuevo entorno aeroportuario de barcelona

Empresa	Cliente	Año	Producto o servicio	Precio millones €	Observaciones
Amper	Agencia de Reconstrucción (Belgrado) UE	2005	Sistema táctico de vigilancia de fronteras terrestres	2,4	Contra la entrada de ilegales (Programa europeaid)
Amper Medidata	Ibermutuamur	2005	Equipos para integrar las redes de voz y datos		Equipos Cisco, call manager y Cisco unity
Amper	Oficina Europea de Patentes y Marcas	2005	Sistema de cableado estructurado		
Amper Medidata	Telefónica en São Paulo	2005	Despliegue de de la red WiFi		Asociada a Cisco y sun
Amper Medidata	Telefónica	2005	Proyecto de Redes Metro Ethernet, expansión del Backbone y red ATM IP		Metro ethernet (Cisco)
Amper Medidata	Grupo Telmex (Embratel)	2005	Suministro de solución de consolidación		Para servidores sun microsystems
Amper Medidata	Telefónica	2005	Suministro de la Red IP a los organismos del Estado de Sao Paulo		Estabecimientos cívicos, educativos, fiscales etc.
Amper Medidata	(Brasil)	2005	Proyectos de readecuación de redes regionales y expansión del Backbone de IP		

Empresa	Cliente	Año	Producto o servicio	Precio millones €	Observaciones
Amper Medidata	Petrobrás	2005	Red de datos para el nuevo edificio		Interconexión de redes de edificios centrales y expansión de otras
Amper Medidata	Banco Nacional del Desarrollo	2005	Red de datos para la sede		
Amper Medidata	Telemar	2005	Servidores SUN para sistemas de mediación y facturación		
Amper Medidata	Telemar	2005	Sistema de Back Up corporativo Sto-ragetek		
Amper Medidata	Unibanco	2005	Sistema de almacenamiento de última generación Tagma		Sistemas de datos Hitachi
Amper Medidata	Citibank	2005	Red de datos para interconexión		Con telefonía ip
Amper Programas	Ejército de Tierra Armada	2006	Equipos de radiocomunicaciones		
Amper	Unidad Militar de Emergencia	2006	Sistema de comunicaciones móviles		

Empresa	Cliente	Año	Producto o servicio	Precio millones €	Observaciones
Amper	AENA	2006	Sistemas de radio ayuda a la navegación aérea		Destaca un sistema dvor-dme (aeropuerto de Huesca)
Amper	AENA	2006	Sistemas DME		Aeropuerto de Palma de Mallorca
Amper Programas	Armada	2006	Nuevo sistema ILS-DME		Aeropuerto de Fuerteventura
Amper	AENA	2006	Sistema avanzado para supervisar por satélite señales de navegación		Aeropuerto de málaga; carácter experimental
Amper Programas	Ejército de Tierra	2006	Equipos radio		De nueva generación pr4g v3
Amper Programas	Ejército del Aire	2006	Modernización de las comunicaciones y sistemas de navegación		Mirage f1
Amper	Gobierno de Murcia	2006	Servicios informáticos	1,4	Proyecto copicor: primera fase
Amper	Ejército suizo	2006	Sistema de Mando y Control (SMyC) (C2IS): actualizac ión	12,6	

Empresa	Cliente	Año	Producto o servicio	Precio millones €	Observaciones
Amper Programas		2006	SMyC: versión definitiva	superior a 43	
Amper Sistemas	MINTRA (Comunidad de Madrid)	2006	Sistema de radiocomunicaciones «trunking»	3,2	Para el metro norte y metro este
Amper	Metro de Madrid	2006	Redes de comunicaciones de línea y estaciones		Línea 3
Amper	Confederaciones Hidrográficas del Guadiana y del Ebro	2006	Ampliación, soporte logístico y mantenimiento		Sistemas de radiocomunicaciones tetra
Amper	Metro de Madrid	2007	Sistemas de comunicaciones en Grupo Cerrado de Usuario		Estación de canal
Amper	Ministerio del Interior	2007	Diversos	2,6	
Amper	Guardia Civil	2007	Mantenimiento y repuestos del SIVE (Sistema Integral de Vigilancia Exterior)		
Amper	AENA		Suministro e instalación de la red TETRA	1,8	Aeropuerto de barcelona

Empresa	Cliente	Año	Producto o servicio	Precio millones €	Observaciones
Amper Sistemas	Endesa	2007	Despliegue de red IP TETRA en sustitución de su red analógica		Asociada a Motorola; en Cataluña y otras partes de España
Amper	Guardia Civil	2007	Sistema de Vigilancia Costera		Valencia y Alicante
Amper	Defensa	2007	Radios de combate	180	Radios pr4g (Anexo 4)
Amper Programas	Eurocopter España	2007	Comunicaciones	9,1	Tácticas –vhf (helicópteros tigre had)
Amper	Empresas privadas españolas, entidades públicas españolas e internacionales*	2007	Sistemas de gestión de crisis y sistemas de comunicaciones radio digitales		Radio digitales (tetra)
Amper	Ministerio de Defensa	2007	Desarrollo de un equipo cripto		Especificaciones otan (ikms)
Amper		2007	Equipos de criptografía		Equipos personales 670e para gsm
Amper	AENA	2008	Red multiservicio		Aeropuerto de ibiza
Amper (IRS)	Companhia Siderúrgica Nacional (Brasil)	2008	Nueva estructura de Seguridad de Red		Implantación

Empresa	Cliente	Año	Producto o servicio	Precio millones €	Observaciones
Amper (IRS)	Telesp	2008	Expansión del backbone IP y corporativo		
Amper (IRS)	Euskaltel	2008	Renovación de la plataforma de provisión de servicios de datos sobre cable		Cablemodems
Amper	Ejército suizo	2008	Ampliación del contrato para el suministro del SMyC		Sistema fis he
Amper	Banco Santander	2008	Instalación de redes IP multiservicio; provisión de infraestructuras		
Amper	Guardia Civil	2008	Proyecto piloto de sistema		Sistema de gestión de crisis sigecra
Amper	UME	2008	Suministro y puesta en explotación		Estaciones mérida y león
Amper	Ejército de Tierra	2008	Equipos de radio de nueva generación		Equipos pr4g-v3: producción de más de 1.200 Unidades

Empresa	Cliente	Año	Producto o servicio	Precio millones €	Observaciones
Amper	Ejército de Tierra	2008	Radioteléfonos ligeros; vehículos equipados con estaciones		Radioteléfonos pnr-500: más de 5.000 Y 200 Vehículos para 50 configuraciones diferentes
Amper	Junta de Extremadura; Servicio Extremeño de Salud	2008	Desarrollo de la red corporativa de telefonía		Telefonía ip
Amper (Homeland Security)	Policía Local de Elche	2009	Refuerzo de infraestructuras de comunicación		
Amper	policía local de Vitoria; policía local de Telde	2009	Implantación de los centros de control de emergencias		
Amper	Cuenca Hidrográfica del Ebro	2009	Mantenimiento/conservación de la red automática	13	Ute en asociación con ofiteco y sice
Amper	AENA	2009	Despliegue de las infraestructuras de comunicación digital de radio		Aeropuerto de alicante
Amper	Banco Santander	2009	Instalación del cableado del nuevo CPD		Ciudad financiera banco Santander

Empresa	Cliente	Año	Producto o servicio	Precio millones €	Observaciones
Amper	Unión Europea	2009	Estudio sobre viabilidad de creación de un sistema de gestión de fronteras		Proyecto globe, con subvención de la ue dentro de su programa fp7
Amper	Puesto fronterizo de Tarifa (Cádiz)	2009	Instalación del sistema de identificación automático de matriculas		Sistema siam; primero de la serie
Amper	AENA	2009	Puesta en marcha de una red de comunicaciones		Red pionera:integraba los servicios de la instalación
Amper	Fuerzas de seguridad del Estado	2009	Inicio de desarrollo del proyecto Tecamis		Para elaborar una nueva arquitectura modular
Amper	México	2009	Soluciones de comunicación y gestión de emergencias		Proyecto «ciudad segura», líder en el ámbito de la seguridad de las grandes capitales
Amper	Guardia Civil (Cádiz)	2009	Dos estaciones sensoras fijas del SIVE		1.500 Km de costa española contaban con tecnología de Amper
Amper	Comunidad Valenciana	2009	Sistemas de localización en aviones		Destinados a la lucha contra el fuego

Empresa	Cliente	Año	Producto o servicio	Precio millones €	Observaciones
Amper Homeland Security		2009	Finalización del despliegue del SIVE de Levante		Sistema innovador de gestión de crisis (nemesis)
Amper	Desembocadura del Guadalquivir y en Cádiz	2009	Ampliaciones en las dos zonas		Tecnología c4isr del nemesis
Amper	AENA	2009	Sistemas de radio ayudas a la navegación (equipos DVOR)		Aeropuertos de málaga, tenerife sur, san javier y lasso (gran canaria)
Amper	Feria BcnRail (Barcelona)	2009	Soluciones tecnológicas para el transporte		
Amper	Telefónica	2009	Desarrollo de un proyecto de Seguridad Lógica: primera fase		Asociada a la británica detica; prueba piloto de un detector de anomalías de red
Amper	Metro de Río de Janeiro	2009	Sustitución y ampliación de su red de comunicaciones		
Amper	Telefónica de Chile Telefónica de Venezuela	2010	Equipos para la recepción de televisión satelital		Antenas y lnbs: televisión satelital direct to home en latinoamérica

Empresa	Cliente	Año	Producto o servicio	Precio millones €	Observaciones
Amper	Servicio de salud Castilla la Mancha; Extremadura	2010	Despliegue de redes de telefonía IP		
Amper	Emergencias del Estado	2010	Tecnología IP del centro de operación compleja; ampliación de capacidad del sistema de radiocomunicaciones digitales		
Amper	Emergencias, Maule (Chile)	2010	Centro Piloto de Gestión de Emergencia		Analizar la eficacia de un número único para emergencias
Amper	Ayuntamiento de Elche	2010	Sistema de comunicaciones seguras (policía local)		
Amper	Ejército de Tierra	2010	Sistemas de mando y control		Sistemas de nueva generación
Amper	Metro de Madrid	2010	Nuevo sistema de comunicaciones móviles	3,8	Sistema digital radio tetra
Amper	Autoridad portuaria de Gijón	2010	Red de radiocomunicaciones digitales	0,367	Mejorar atención y coordinación durante emergencias

Empresa	Cliente	Año	Producto o servicio	Precio millones €	Observaciones
Amper	Servicio de asistencia médica de urgencia (Charente Maritime, Francia)	2010	Sistema tecnológico para integrar los sistemas de comunicaciones		Modernización y potenciación de los sistemas de gestión de emergencias y comunicaciones
Amper	Instituto Tecnológico La Marañosa	2010	Servicios de telefonía IP sobre de banda estrecha		Ministerio de defensa; Tipo pr4g compatible con redes tácticas
Amper	Ejército del Aire	2010	Sistemas para protección y seguridad en misiones internacionales (sensores desatendidos)		Detección, identificación y clasificación de posibles intrusiones
Amper Medidata	Telebras	2010	Soluciones de integración de la red IP	más de 10	Plan nacional de banda ancha
Amper	Gobierno de México	2010	Suministro de plataformas de integración de las comunicaciones para la integración automática de voz y datos		Dentro del proyecto méxico ciudad segura
Amper	Flight Technologies (Brasil)	2010	Suministro de equipos y tareas de gestión para drones		Operaciones espías y de control de fronteras

Empresa	Cliente	Año	Producto o servicio	Precio millones €	Observaciones
	Fuerzas Armadas Emiratos Á. U.		Sistema de mando y control	92	

*ENDESA, AENA, Gobierno Vasco, Red Tetrapol, Policía y Guardia Civil, comunidades autónomas y ayuntamientos; policía (París), sistemas de emergencia para bomberos (Francia); Centros de Control 911 (Mendoza, Argentina).

Fuente: Elaboración a partir de CNMV y Amper, *Memoria(s) anual(es)*.

Anexo 3. Composición del activo intangible de Amper (miles de euros)

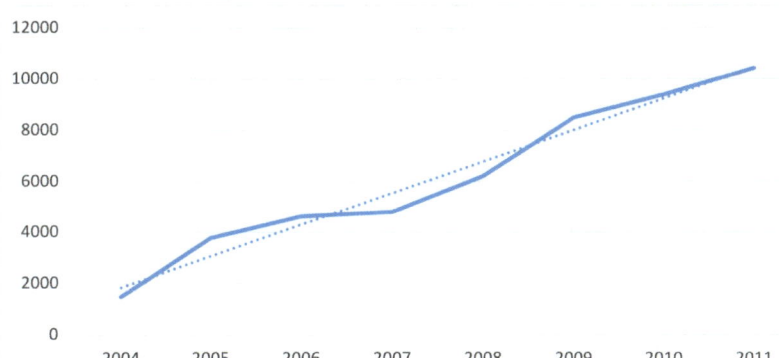

Anexo 4. El Ejército de tierra como cliente de Amper

El Ejército de Tierra comenzó en el año 1992 a sustituir los equipos de radio portátiles y los instalados en los vehículos por un radioteléfono de nueva generación que permitía mayor seguridad en las comunicaciones. El sistema seleccionado fue la radio PR4G de la empresa Amper. Desde entonces, se adquirieron equipos de las versiones 1, 2 y 3, si bien las dos primeras se modernizaron. La versión 3 estaba en dotación de numerosas unidades y vehículos del Ejército de Tierra y con la nueva adquisición se pretendía completar la dotación de aquellas unidades carentes de ellos, a fin de garantizar la comunicación entre unidades y unificar y optimizar los medios radio. El Acuerdo suponía la adquisición de radioteléfonos tácticos de la familia PR4G, así como de los accesorios necesarios para su funcionamiento, antenas, bastidores, cableado, etcétera (CNMV, Madrid, 10 de Septiembre de 2007).

Referencias

Acs, Zoltan J. y Yeung, Bernard. 1999. *Small and medium-sized enterprises in the global economy*. Ann Arbor: University of Michigan Press.

Amper. 2004. *Información sobre la evolución y perspectivas de su negocio*. CNMV, 50.122, 28 de mayo.

Borga, Maria; Ibarlucea-Flores, Perla y Sztajerowska, Monica. 2020. *Divestments by multinational enterprises*, OECD, enero.

Buckley, Peter J. «Foreign direct investment by small and medium sized enterprises: The theoretical background». *Small Business Economics*, 1, 89-100.

Devore, Marc R. 1989. «Arms production in the Global Village: Options for Adapting to Defence-Industrial Globalization». *Security Studies*, vol. 22, 532-572.

Elandia International Inc. 2010. *Annual report for the fiscal year ending Friday,* December 31.

Fondo Monetario Internacional. 2010. *Perspectivas de la economía mundial, Washington: Fondo Monetario Internacional.*

Fundación Círculo de Tecnologías para la Defensa y la Seguridad. 2009. *Retos y oportunidades tras 25 años de colaboración: Fuerzas Armadas, Fuerzas y Cuerpos de Seguridad del Estado, Empresas y Universidades ante el siglo XXI.* Madrid: Fundación Círculo de Tecnologías para la Defensa y la Seguridad.

Hoyt, Kenneth S. 2001. *Technology Hits the wall: The Top 50 Telecommunications Equipment Suppliers in 2000.* Boston MAS: Information Gatekeepers Inc.

Kalinic, Igor y Forza, Cipriano. 2012. «Rapid internationalization of traditional SMEs: Between gradualist models and born globals». *International Business Review* 21, n°.4: 694-707.

Kuo, Hsien C. y Li, Yang. 2003. «A dynamic decision model of SMEs' FDI». *Small Business Economics* 20, n°.3: 219-231.

Lohrmann, Christoph. 2013. *Globalization and its opportunities for small– and medium-sized enterprises.* Munich: Grin.

OECD. 2003. *OECD Communications Outlook: 2003.* París: OECD.

OECD. 2007. *Communications Outlook 2007.* París: OECD.

OECD. 2010. *OECD Information Technology Outlook 2010.* París: OECD.

Pu, Hualin y Zheng, Yongdan. 2015. «The FDI of Small– and Middle-Sized Enterprises: A Literature Review». *Technology and Investment* 6: 63-70.

Recklies, Dagmar. 2001. «Small and Medium-Sized Enterprises and Globalization». *The Manager.org,* octubre.

Rosiere, Stéphane y Jones, Reece. 2012. «Teichopolitics: Re-considering Globalisation Through the Role of Walls and Fences», *Geopolitics* 17, n°.1: 217-234. DOI: 10.1080/14650045.2011.574653

Salgado, Jesús. 2012. *Hasta que la herencia nos separe: Conflictos, pasiones y vendettas.* Madrid: La Esfera de los Libros.

Urata, Shujiro y Kawai, Hiroki. 2000. «The determinants of the location of foreign direct investment by Japanese small and medium-sized enterprises». *Small Business Economics* 15, n°.2: 79-103.

Wolf, Martin. 2001. «Will the Nation-State Survive Globalization?». *Foreign Affairs*, enero/febrero, 178-190.

3. Diversificación de los socios tecnológicos. Tecnología japonesa en la informática española: Fujitsu

1. Introducción

Una corriente actual cuestiona la historia construida a escala global y se pregunta por qué, a veces, tiene sentido que dos fábricas en diferentes países se mantengan como empresas conjuntas dado que las grandes empresas eran líderes (Graham y Krugman 1993, 28)[1]. ¿Qué puede aportar el enfoque a nivel de la empresa a la investigación relativa a las políticas del país anfitrión con respecto a las empresas multinacionales extranjeras?[2] ¿Cómo funciona en la práctica el ensamblaje de culturas empresariales tan dispares, como la japonesa y la de un país del sur de Europa?; ¿en qué medida el comportamiento de Fujitsu Ltd. en España confirma o modifica la tendencia seguida por la multinacional en las filiales extranjeras?; ¿cuáles son los factores determinantes de la ubicación de la actividad de I+D de las empresas multinacionales en el extranjero (Kumar 2001) y las fases de la evolución de la capacidad de las filiales de I+D (Lagerström; Schweizer y Jakobsson 2019, 35-53)? ¿En qué sentido el patrón de asignación de la I+D a la filial española anticipa la respuesta futura al reto de formular estrategias tecnológicas y gestionar redes de

---

[1] Entre una infinidad, una de las respuestas a la expansión de la IED en los años ochenta apunta a la abolición global de los controles de capital (Ghauri y Oxelheim 2003, 20-21). Desde esos años, las multinacionales han pretendido relajar las reglamentaciones mundiales en beneficio de sus operaciones internacionales (Rodrik 2011, 96). Diversos aspectos han sido tratados en Calvo (2021).

[2] Años atrás, Blomström y Kokko (1997, 33) adujeron la necesidad de realizar investigaciones sobre cuestiones relacionadas con las políticas de los países receptores respecto de las empresas multinacionales extranjeras.

laboratorios y alianzas de I+D cada vez más difusas y diversas en el contexto de instituciones nacionales dispares (Yue 2005, 317-337)[3].

A diferencia de las «inversiones de cartera» en valores, la bibliografía sobre la IED y las empresas multinacionales o leviatanes aumentó poderosamente desde el periodo posterior a la Segunda Guerra Mundial[4]. No obstante, muchos estudiosos descontentos con los logros obtenidos admiten que el consenso se limita al reconocimiento de la creciente importancia de la IED y del número cada vez mayor de multinacionales, que no puede ser ignorado. Como señalan, tenemos un conocimiento acumulativo todavía inadecuado sobre la IED y las multinacionales y conclusiones generalizadas que pueden ser defendidas como duraderas y precisas frente a la heterogeneidad de las empresas y los países (Cohen 2007, 24-25)[5]. Un número no desdeñable de personas que reconocen la importancia de la IED y las EMN en la economía mundial insisten en las lagunas en la investigación sobre el tema y señalan los factores que determinan las pautas de la IED como una de las cuestiones generales más significativas[6]. No faltan quienes se preguntan sobre las consecuencias de las diferentes instituciones políticas sobre la IED (Jensen 2006).

Los modelos tradicionales consideran que el crecimiento de la inversión es una función de los cambios en el capital social y la depreciación, que a su vez depende de diversas variables, como el costo del capital y la producción.

---

[3] Los académicos (Strach y Everett 2006, 55-69) proponen que las empresas japonesas aplican los mismos métodos de prácticas de gestión de los conocimientos en el extranjero que en el país cuando los consideran apropiados para la transferencia a un entorno extranjero. La capacidad de investigación y desarrollo de las filiales evoluciona en cuatro fases: identificar en el país receptor una oportunidad que desencadene la creación de capacidades locales de I+D; lograr apoyo de diversas fuentes y recursos; reunir recursos para crear capacidades y, por último, aprovechar las capacidades (Lagerström; Schweizer y Jakobsson 2019, 35-53). Li y Yue (2005, 320) indican cuatro categorías de configuración de la I+D en un país receptor: I+D concentrada; investigación dispersa y desarrollo concentrado; investigación concentrada y desarrollo disperso e I+D dispersa.

[4] He aquí algunas obras esenciales, comenzando con Mira Wilkins (1970) y continuando con Buckley y Casson (1976) así como con Chandler y Mazlish (2005) y terminando con Dunning y Lundan (2008).

[5] Las multinacionales tejieron una red mundial que operaba con ciento setenta millares de filiales y en 1990 generaba más de 5,5 trillones de dólares de ventas, cifra superior a la correspondiente a las exportaciones mundiales de bienes (Beltz 1995, 63). Como hemos apuntado páginas atrás, los críticos niegan a la creciente entrada de IED los estímulos económicos previstos para los países en desarrollo (Stiglitz 2002; Rodrik 2011, 973-987; Chang 2010); otros acusan abiertamente a la IED de explotar recursos y mano de obra barata, alimentar tensiones y apoyar regímenes represivos (Klein 2000; Aid 2004).

[6] Blonigen (2006, 1); Lipsey (2002) afirma que los estudios microeconómicos sobre los efectos de las entradas de IED en el crecimiento económico no son concluyentes, ya que no permiten afirmar que haya repercusiones universales de la IED en el crecimiento.

Para algunos estudiosos, la incertidumbre acerca de las condiciones económicas futuras y los beneficios previstos desempeñan un papel fundamental en el impulso de la inversión, mientras que las condiciones de financiación siguen siendo un determinante importante. Por una parte, el modelo del acelerador describe la inversión como una función del crecimiento de la producción. En el modelo neoclásico, depende de manera positiva de la producción pero de manera negativa del coste del capital para el usuario. El entorno financiero, las barreras a la inversión vinculadas al entorno institucional, laboral y empresarial son otras variables consideradas (European Commission 2017). La bibliografía más actual reconoce las imperfecciones de los mercados de bienes y factores como la principal explicación de la IED. Al tiempo, afirma que una bibliografía pequeña pero creciente admite como plausibles los efectos de las imperfecciones de los mercados de capital (Veeramani et al. 2020, 185-217).

En ese contexto, una característica importante del debate se centra en las relaciones entre las empresas multinacionales y los países anfitriones y, más concretamente, en la posición estratégica bilateral de dichas relaciones (Nygaard y Dahlstrom 1992, 3-13). Algunos expertos cuestionan la eficacia a largo plazo de los incentivos que utilizan los países para atraer proyectos y aumentar su atractivo (Young 2004).

Si consideramos una fracción de la IED, la de las multinacionales japonesas en Europa, la corriente tradicional plantea tres cuestiones principales: la elección del lugar dada la asimetría de la economía de la UE; la decisión sobre el método de inversión y la forma en que las multinacionales japonesas abordan sus empresas desde una perspectiva paneuropea (Ando 2005, 6).

Teniendo esto en cuenta, el presente capítulo tiene por objeto proporcionar material para colmar esas lagunas, enlazando con un capítulo de la historia de las empresas japonesas en Europa, que operan principalmente bajo la forma de filiales y son consideradas por algunos como defensivas frente al proteccionismo y por otros como creativas (Pearce y Papanastassiou 1996; Sachwald 1995, 39). Más en detalle, se proporcionan algunos antecedentes sobre una fracción de la IED mundial hacia finales del siglo xx –la IED japonesa en España– y las razones de la implantación de las multinacionales japonesas altamente competitivas de TIC (Tecnologías de la Información y la Comunicación)[7] en ese país del sur de Europa con un perfil similar al de Ir-

---

[7] Los orígenes y la evolución de la industria informática han merecido durante mucho tiempo la atención de los especialistas, de manera que se ha generado una bibliografía verdaderamente voluminosa sobre este tema. La búsqueda de «informática, historia» en Internet

landa como destino de la IED[8]. Sin embargo, en algunas ocasiones, España es excluida de las observaciones sobre la IED, posiblemente debido a su tardía integración en la Comunidad Europea, pero esta circunstancia precisa añade elementos al interés de estudiarla (Boutellier et al. 2008, 43).

Cabe señalar que la economía española estaba experimentando una fuerte internacionalización en la que las multinacionales presentes en el país desempeñaban un papel importante. Esto supuso un cambio profundo ya que no solo aparecieron nuevas multinacionales sino que las ya establecidas cambiaron el modo de competir buscando una mayor integración con su grupo y reduciendo el nivel de localización (Jarillo y Martínez 1990, 258).

El capítulo aborda con un enfoque cualitativo un estudio de caso sobre la creación y evolución de la empresa Fujitsu España en sus distintas denominaciones como alianza estratégica de capital[9]. La metodología de investigación combina fuentes cualitativas y cuantitativas de diversa procedencia y naturaleza,

arroja la asombrosa cifra de 2,54 millones de resultados, por lo que un mínimo de prudencia aconseja renunciar a un estado de la cuestión. Señalamos tres importantes obras: Cortada (1983), Ceruzzi (2003) y Campbell-Kelly (2004). La industria electrónica japonesa es una de las más productivas de la economía de esa nación, motivo primordial de la potencia exportadora de los fabricantes japoneses de electrónica: U.S. Congress, U.S. Office of Technology Assessment (1983, 5).

[8] España (7,61%) figuraba entre Australia (8%) y Holanda (10,14%) en los coeficientes medios de la IED respecto de la formación bruta de capital fijo en los años 1970-1995 (Lipsey 2002, 39). El volumen de IED japonesa en España nunca superó el 2,1% del total de Europa Occidental entre 1996 y 2005 (JETRO, 1995-2020 Japan External Trade Organization. https://www.jetro.go.jp/en/reports/statistics.html). En Irlanda, la inversión extranjera en I+D en el sector de las tecnologías de la información y la comunicación en los últimos años representa una etapa nueva en la evolución de las filiales de TIC, que han pasado de dedicarse a la industria manufacturera a participar cada vez más en actividades de mayor valor añadido (Grimes y Collins 2009, 42:1, 45-67).

[9] Una alianza estratégica de capital entre al menos dos empresas se caracteriza por la aportación de recursos y capacidades en determinados porcentajes a una nueva empresa conjunta con el fin de lograr una ventaja competitiva (Hitt et al. 2012). La teoría de la internacionalización formulada por la escuela de Uppsala (Johanson y Weidershiem-Paul 1975), pronto perfeccionada por Johanson y Vahlne (1977, 23-32), se basa en algunos estudios de casos de la industria. Mohannak (2011, 1-15) ofrece un estudio de caso sobre Fujitsu Ltd. Burgenmeier y Mucchielli (2012) y Aaron (1999), por ejemplo, utilizan la metodología del enfoque del estudio de casos, que se beneficia de su mayor capacidad para poner mejor de relieve las dimensiones políticas de las decisiones de inversión interna, pero adolece de defectos por el tamaño reducido de la muestra; los criterios de la IED incluyen el país receptor, la magnitud de la empresa y la inversión, la condición de proveedor o fabricante final, el mercado de productos, la politización de la inversión (Aaron 1999, 7-8). Otro ejemplo, Nygaard y Dahlstrom (1992, 3-13) utilizan la industria petrolera noruega para considerar la posición estratégica bilateral como marco desde el que evaluar las relaciones entre las empresas multinacionales y el país anfitrión. Para estrategias de multinacionales, véase Bucheli y Salvaj (2014).

algunas de ellas de extraordinaria relevancia por su valor intrínseco y la dificultad de acceso para los especialistas. Entre ellas destacan las procedentes de la operadora monopolista Telefónica. La histórica Compañía Telefónica Nacional de España fundada en 1924 por el gigante estadounidense IT&T y rescatada por el capital nacional a principios del periodo posterior a la Segunda Guerra Mundial bajo la dictadura de Franco.

El texto se estructura en cinco secciones principales, que esbozan el marco general de la inversión extranjera japonesa en Europa y abordan las circunstancias de la creación de Fujitsu España, la profundización de las relaciones entre la IED y las multinacionales en España y la reestructuración de esta empresa en sus aspectos organizativos, laborales y corporativos[10].

2. El marco general: la inversión extranjera japonesa en Europa y Fujitsu

Las tendencias de la inversión extranjera directa mundial plantean dos cuestiones generales (los países industrializados impulsan el crecimiento de la IED en 1998; la caída de la IED de los países en desarrollo debido a las caídas en algunas partes de Asia); dos relativas a las fusiones y adquisiciones (crecimiento continuo de las transfronterizas y cambios en los sistemas y condiciones que las fomentan); dos específicas del Japón (recuperación de las salidas de IED japonesa en el ejercicio económico de 1999; aumento de los ingresos de extranjeros)[11].

El núcleo del capítulo se inscribe en el marco del ascenso del Japón a posiciones de liderazgo mundial, de acuerdo con el impulso estatal de la sociedad de la información[12].

Buigues y Jacquemin (1992, 39-101) ponen de relieve que el Japón basó su principal estrategia de acceso a los mercados internacionales en las exportaciones, al tiempo que señalan que la IED y las exportaciones del Japón, al igual que las de los Estados Unidos, a la CEE demostraron ser fuertemente complementarias a nivel sectorial.

---

[10]   Calvo 2008, 455-473. Se mantiene el nombre de Fujitsu España para diferenciarlo de Fujitsu Spain, una de las dos filiales creadas a raíz de la segregación de Fujitsu ICL España.

[11]   Japan External Trade Organization 2000, 1-27.

[12]   Una tarea central recayó en el Japan Computer Usage Development Institute (JACUDI), que colocó la información en el centro de su proyecto de sociedad y la cooperación internacional en un lugar destacado (representaba el 5% del total) (Nora y Minc 1978, 178).

A lo largo de la segunda mitad de los años noventa, las inversiones extranjeras japonesas en la industria europea dieron un predominio del Reino Unido, acompañado de una tendencia al alza de Holanda y, en menor medida, de Suecia, así como una sustitución de Suiza por Francia. Como nuevo país favorable a la IED, junto con otros países europeos, España desempeñó un papel bastante modesto en la inversión extranjera japonesa, muy similar al de Italia en términos comparativos y, en parte, un sustituto (Anexo 1)[13]. La estabilidad política alcanzada por España, los bajos salarios, el crecimiento de los mercados, el nivel de vida y la adhesión a la CEE contribuyeron de manera significativa al aumento del número de empresas japonesas establecidas en el país durante el decenio de 1980[14].

Aunque deben considerarse las diferencias en el clima de inversión de cada país, la diferencia en la forma de avance de las empresas filiales japonesas en Europa puede explicarse en cierta medida por el tipo de industrias implantadas en el país. En España, el predominio de las industrias de maquinaria de transporte, piezas de esta y productos metálicos coincidió con un reducido porcentaje de empresas de propiedad exclusiva y un alto porcentaje de empresas mixtas, participación de capital y adquisición de empresas. Lo mismo ocurría en Francia con los productos alimenticios. En el Reino Unido y Alemania, el predominio de las industrias de maquinaria de precisión, maquinaria y piezas electrónicas/eléctricas y mecanizado en general coincidió con un alto porcentaje de empresas de propiedad exclusiva afiliadas en Europa[15].

---

[13]   Japan External Trade Organization 1996-2016. El grupo que buscó con asiduidad y de manera proactiva atraer la IED incluyó al Reino Unido, Irlanda, los países del Benelux y España. Otro conjunto diverso (Portugal, Grecia, Francia, los países escandinavos y los nuevos miembros de la UE de Europa del Este) que tradicionalmente no fue bien recibido por la IED se convirtió en «propicio para la IED». Un tercer grupo siguió siendo más bien «poco amistoso» para atraer la IED (Alemania e Italia) (Ghauri y Oxelheim 2003, 20-21). Para un panorama muy reciente de la economía japonesa, véase Ito y Hoshi (2020).

[14]   Díaz, Kawamura y González-Torre 1999, 115-120. Un ejemplo en el sector electrónico fue Omron Electronics –nueva denominación de Carlo Gavazzi Omron S. A. desde la venta de la participación de Carlo Gavazzi a Omron Tateisi Electrocnics– que tenía su sede corporativa en Ámsterdam y su principal centro industrial en Kyoto (laboratorio de I+D y la filial Tateisi Electronics); sus asociadas estaban implantadas en las dos grandes capiales europeas (París y Londres), Centroeuropa (Dusseldorf, Viena, Bruselas, Baar y Copenhague), norte de Europa (Lillehammer, Huddinge y Espoo) y sur de Europa (Madrid, Atenas y Milán) (Wedgwood 2013, 150). En 1988, buscaba solar para construir cuo nuevas oficinas en Cataluña (La Vanguardia, 1 de mayo de 1988, p. 66).

[15]   Predominio de las industrias de maquinaria de precisión y general, maquinaria y piezas electrónicas/eléctricas (Status 1992, 13-14).

Para retomar el caso empírico específico de la electrónica, Fujitsu Ltd. globalizó rápidamente sus operaciones y se convirtió en la segunda mayor empresa informática del mundo mediante una estrategia tentacular que combinaba adquisiciones, participaciones en el capital y alianzas con fabricantes locales de ordenadores de todo el mundo[16].

En su proceso de globalización, la empresa matriz Fujitsu Ltd. siguió de cerca el patrón de los fabricantes de electrónica japoneses al establecer una filial de ventas en el extranjero. Fujitsu California inició este proceso en 1968 dentro de Fujitsu Ltd. En la década de 1970, se añadieron cuatro empresas a su creciente lista de sucursales de ventas y producción en el extranjero, entre ellas Fujitsu España S.A. (en adelante FESA)[17]. Así, Fujitsu Ltd. asimiló el patrón de internacionalización de una filial del sur de Europa con el de otras tres filiales del sudeste asiático.

En una muestra de 204 empresas, Fujitsu Ltd. tenía el 18,36% de los subcontratistas por el principal grupo empresarial vertical y el número de filiales manufactureras de la empresa principal en el sudeste asiático (cinco subcontratistas) y Europa/América del Norte (cuatro subcontratistas)[18]. La evolución del número de filiales japonesas en Europa describe una línea de ascenso constante con un punto de aceleración a finales de los años ochenta y una ligera inflexión hacia el comienzo del siguiente (Anexo 2).

Conocemos el perfil, el estado, las motivaciones y los propósitos del progreso en Europa y las razones para determinar la dirección del progreso, así como el problema de la ubicación. En cuanto a su perfil, las filiales japonesas establecidas en Europa se caracterizaban por una escala media; un promedio de algo más de trescientos empleados –Portugal y la industria de la maquinaria de transporte tenían el mayor número medio de empleados –; un capital medio de casi 2,9 millones de dólares y el predominio de la propiedad absoluta en las empresas. La motivación cada vez más poderosa tenía que ver con la estrategia de la globalización y las condiciones de distribución geográficamente favorables. Por su parte, en la atracción de las inversiones extranjeras, los gobiernos u organizaciones de los países anfitriones reclamaban como prioridad la creación de oportunidades de empleo (76,8% de los casos), muy por delante de la segunda reclamación, la

---

[16] Egan y McKiernan 1994, 52; *InfoWorld* 5, 14, 4 de abril de 1983. 35.

[17] Fujitsu Singapore Ltd., FACOM Korea Ltd. y FACOM Philippines Inc. formaban el resto (Chandler y Mazlish 2005, 122).

[18] Belderbos 1997, 210.

transferencia de la tecnología más reciente (37%). Por regiones, en el sur de Europa, el aumento de la relación exportación-importación ocupó el primer lugar con un alto porcentaje del 64,5%, seguido por el 58,1% de la creación de oportunidades de empleo.

La respuesta a la unificación del mercado de la CE consistió en promover la producción y la localización de la gestión y el establecimiento de empresas integrales. En cuanto a la situación de la gestión de las filiales japonesas en Europa, la mitad creciente de las empresas gozaba de buena salud, aunque era difícil obtener un beneficio inmediato al inicio de las operaciones. El grueso de los beneficios se destinaba a la reinversión en fábricas e instalaciones; las relaciones entre el trabajo y la gestión eran buenas pero no estaban exentas de problemas debido al absentismo, las horas extraordinarias y las vacaciones[19].

En el emplazamiento de la producción se observaron mejoras constantes, que se reflejaron en un aumento significativo del índice de adquisición de piezas locales por las industrias manufactureras y de montaje, a menudo a través de subcontratistas locales, un salto significativo en el índice de adquisición de acciones locales por empresas de propiedad exclusiva. Por otra parte, había aumentado el acceso al empleo local para los puestos de dirección y la transferencia de autoridad. El sistema de localización de I+D había avanzado, en respuesta a las necesidades de productos locales, intensificando la competencia tecnológica. Por último, en lo que respecta a la penetración en la sociedad local y los elementos para evitar la fricción de la inversión, se había mejorado constantemente la creación de vínculos estrechos con la industria local, al tiempo que se hacía vital una mayor localización de la producción y la gestión[20].

En este contexto, Fujitsu Ltd. gozaba de una sólida implantación en el mercado mundial a la vez que estaba inmersa en lo que la empresa definía como un proceso de personalización, es decir, la transición de las unidades centrales de las empresas e instituciones públicas a las computadoras per-

---

[19] Status 1992, 6-10 y 15-37.

[20] Status 1992, 40-59. Algunos autores consideran que las filiales fomentan el flujo de conocimientos desde la sede de la multinacional a las empresas del país anfitrión de las sucursales. La difusión de los conocimientos se correlaciona positivamente con la fuerza, pero no con las capacidades de clase mundial que tienen tanto la capacidad de absorción para aprender de las partes extranjeras como la motivación, así como la disponibilidad de inventores de satélites que han patentado previamente con la casa matriz (por lo que tienen conocimientos de la sede) o con otras empresas locales, por lo que tienen redes sociales locales más fuertes (Blit 2019, 1-43).

sonales[21]. Según una valoración correspondiente a un periodo ligeramente posterior, Fujitsu ocupaba una posición media entre las mayores empresas multinacionales no financieras en cuanto a activos en el extranjero –en la posición 59– y rezagada por el índice de transnacionalidad –en la posición 85–[22].

Por otro lado, pasaba de lo global a lo local, de vuelta de la mencionada pugna por los mercados maduros y emergentes[23].

La naturaleza particular de los productos básicos de su gama –telecomunicaciones y semiconductores– que requieren pocos cambios para los diferentes mercados, impuso un sesgo y permitió el florecimiento de las inversiones. A mediados de los años ochenta, el crecimiento de Fujitsu en el extranjero se desaceleró y comenzó a reevaluar la estrategia de inversión en las filiales extranjeras y a sustituirla por asociaciones más pequeñas con empresas occidentales[24].

[21] Fujitsu tenía 62.071 empleados, ventas netas de 4.782.099 dólares y unos activos totales de 5.046.008 dólares (Fujitsu Sales Prospector 1986, 1-2). Una breve nota sobre los EE.UU., los fabricantes de computadoras y periféricos acentúan la asignación de recursos al diseño industrial y a la ingeniería de factores humanos; la facilidad de uso era vital para vender sistemas informáticos a nuevos clientes (U.S. Congress, U.S. Office of Technology Assessment 1983, 5).

[22] El índice de transnacionalidad equivale al promedio de los activos en el extranjero sobre los activos totales, las ventas en el extranjero sobre las ventas totales y el empleo en el extranjero sobre el empleo total (United Nations 1999, 77; Dunning y Lundan 2008, 4 y 61).

[23] Michael E.C. Ely, Entrevistado por: Charles Stuart Kennedy, The Association for Diplomatic Studies and Training Foreign Affairs Oral History Project, 9 de marzo de 1993.

[24] Fujitsu America Inc., con sede en California, se convirtió en la mayor filial de la empresa en el extranjero y Fujitsu Microelectronics Inc. (1979), una antigua agencia de ventas y luego filial de chips de los Estados Unidos, se convirtió en el mayor proveedor de matrices de puertas del Silicon Valley, una especie de chip avanzado que podía personalizarse para dar inteligencia a casi cualquier dispositivo electrónico. Tras el fiasco de Fairchild, en 1987 Fujitsu compró Intellistor, un fabricante estadounidense (Colorado) de varios dispositivos de memoria para ordenadores, y lo convirtió en su centro de I+D (Schlender y Alpert 1991, 78-84). Fujitsu reagrupó la División de Microsistemas Profesionales de su filial estadounidense, el fabricante de semiconductores Fujitsu Microelectronics Inc. en una nueva filial de Fujitsu America bajo el nombre de Fujitsu Microelectronics of America (*ComputerWorld*, 19, 241, 7 de junio de 1985, 101). Fujitsu Microelectronics ofrece un caso de adaptación de las técnicas de gestión japonesas a los Estados Unidos. Para prestar atención a uno de los protagonistas, la mayor diferencia entre los EE.UU. y Japón fue que en el primer país la dirección tuvo que definir su trabajo y sus variaciones, mientras que en Japón había una dirección clara, aunque el ingeniero debía ser capaz de interpretar con precisión los deseos del personal directivo superior (Fujii, Shigeru oral history, Entrevista, 1 de noviembre de 2012, Museo de Historia de la Computación). Esta es una observación a la que hay que referirse cuando se habla de la estructura de la dirección en España.

En cualquier caso, Fujitsu superó en agresividad en sus incursiones europeas a las restantes compañías japonesas, excepto a Hitachi. Fujitsu consolidó su presencia europea país por país, a menudo a través de socios locales, para construir una red de actividades totalmente integrada que abarcara toda la cadena de valor. Fujitsu distribuía su fabricación en Europa en tres plantas, que empleaban a más de tres cuartas partes de los 3.400 puestos de trabajo. En Eire, Fujitsu Microelectronics fabricaba componentes y Fujitsu Isotec producía componentes de impresoras para exportar a la planta de FESA algunos pequeños ordenadores y equipos de telecomunicaciones, lo que naturalmente nos lleva a nuestra descripción del caso. De hecho, en 1979 se inició la producción local en España, donde se especializó tempranamente en la gama de terminales bancarios de pequeña escala y terminales de reserva de plazas para empresas de transporte, comprometiéndose a seguir desarrollando la capacidad de producción de la empresa en el futuro. Este es un hito que debe ser narrado en sus distintos pasos (Young y Hamill 1992, 71; Strange 2002, 250)[25].

3. La inversión extranjera directa y el capital local: Fujitsu España (1983)

Conviene recordar cosas sabidas. Casi desde su nacimiento, la Compañía Telefónica Nacional de España (CTNE) se abastecía de equipos de Standard Eléctrica, una filial española de IT&T en la que tenía una participación minoritaria. Para asegurar un suministro cada vez más voluminoso y diverso, creó su propio *holding* industrial, asociándose en repetidas ocasiones con los líderes tecnológicos de las respectivas gamas de producción, incluyendo AT&T. Una de estas grandes apuestas tecnológicas supuso un cambio notable no solo de protagonistas sino también de área geoestratégica. La confluencia de inte-

---

[25] La numerosa clientela internacional del FACOM de Fujitsu incluía la operadora española CTNE, que compró un FACOM M-190, así como otros, entre ellos una empresa de datos y la Bolsa (Fujitsu Ltd, *Annual Report 1980*, 18). Al igual que Furukawa, Fuji y Yasakawa, Fujitsu pertenecía a las empresas de electrónica del Dai-Ichi Kangyo keiretsu (DKB); este era uno de los seis principales grupos empresariales horizontales de Japón (Mitsui, Sumitomo, Mitsubishi, Fuyo, Dai Ichi Kangyo, DKB y Sanwa), que poseía casi un tercio de los activos del sector privado en ese país (Belderbos 1997, 103). Un *keiretsu* es un grupo o red de empresas (Shimizu 1995, 85). Keiretsu representaba menos del 0,1% de todas las empresas del Japón, pero el 78% del valor de todas las acciones de los mercados de valores de Tokio; las filiales de *keiretsu* representaban alrededor del 68% de las inversiones japonesas en empresas de alta tecnología de los Estados Unidos y la Unión Europea desde finales de 1989 (Kim 2018).

reses entre la japonesa Fujitsu Ltd. y la CTNE dio lugar en 1983 a la nueva Fujitsu España S. A. Desde finales de la década de 1970, Fujitsu Ltd. se había esforzado por establecerse con éxito en mercados maduros –los Estados Unidos– y emergentes –Asia y España–[26].

Desde estas bases, Fujitsu Ltd. intentó entrar con sus grandes ordenadores en Europa y América Latina. Por su parte, la CTNE confió en la tecnología de Fujitsu en el sistema de transmisión de datos por conmutación de paquetes desarrollado por esta empresa en su propio departamento, conocido como TESYS[27].

En comparación con su área geográfica, España estaba entre los países con una industria inmadura. Sin embargo, como es sabido, era atractiva para el capital extranjero: en 1981-1986, este país recibió un promedio anual de 2.051 millones de dólares de IED, una cantidad muy inferior a la del Reino Unido pero cercana al nivel de Francia. La adhesión a la CEE en 1986 impulsó la entrada de inversiones, de modo que el promedio de 1991 quintuplicó el de 1981-1986[28].

Desde el punto de vista de la regulación en el campo aquí estudiado, en la segunda mitad de los años 70, el Ministerio de Industria previó un impuesto extraordinariamente alto –hasta el 200%– que hizo prohibitiva la introducción

[26] Fujitsu, al igual que Hitachi, vendía con enormes descuentos de hasta el 70%, inalcanzables para las casas americanas potencialmente competidoras, como Cray (Michael E.C. Ely, Entrevistado por Charles Stuart Kennedy, The Association for Diplomatic Studies and Training Foreign Affairs Oral History Project, 9 de marzo de 1993).

[27] CTNE, *Memoria, Balance Social 1984-1985*, 155; Calvo 2014, 209 y 399); entrevista con Teófilo J. del Pozo. La CTNE utilizaba desde 1976 Infonet, servicio informático público creado por la North American Computer Sciences e introducido en los Estados Unidos y Europa; consumo y facturación de Infonet: de 43 millones de pesetas en 1977 a 575 en 1982 y de 24 millones de pesetas a 28 millones; oferta de uso de Infonet en buenas condiciones de ENTEL a la CTNE (Acta del Comité Ejecutivo (ACE), 14 de diciembre de 1983). Las estimaciones para la década de 1970 situaban a la informática como la tercera industria del mundo, después del petróleo y el automóvil; su tasa de crecimiento prevista para Europa era de alrededor del 20% anual para esa década, porcentaje que se situaba entre el más bajo de los Estados Unidos y el más alto del Japón (EU Commission 1973, 21). Más del 90% de los ordenadores instalados en Europa se basaban en tecnología estadounidense y alrededor del 60% del mercado europeo estaba en manos de una sola empresa, no europea (IBM), posición dominante que le permitía dictar el ritmo del comercio de la innovación y el modelo de mercado, precios y normas (Comisión de la UE 1973, 1).

[28] En 1986-1991, la relación entre las entradas de IED y la formación bruta de capital interno en España ascendió al 9,2%, cifra cercana a la de Australia o Grecia y superior a la de las grandes potencias europeas. El número de filiales extranjeras en España en 1987 representó el 7,6% del total de los países desarrollados (UNCTAD 1993, 20; 43 y 251). Para una posición muy reciente en el debate sobre los efectos positivos de la IED en el crecimiento de España, véase Bajo-Rubio (2020, 1-16).

de productos informáticos sin certificado de fabricación nacional. Esta barrera privilegiaba la producción procedente de las fábricas de las multinacionales instaladas en España. Algunas empresas pugnaron por obtener la autorización del Gobierno para instalarse en el territorio nacional. Las más diligentes en aspirar a la condición de fabricante nacional fueron IBM, la empresa que dominó por sí sola la infancia de la industria informática con su plataforma System/360, y Univac (Corsino y Giuri 2018)[29]. Entre otras del sector de las TIC, AT&T, Corning Glass, Ericsson y Hewlett Packard buscaron las ventajas de la localización ofrecida en España. Varias empresas japonesas, incluida Fujitsu, tampoco se quedaron atrás en la forja de acuerdos[30].

El interés de Japón por invertir en España se remontaba a años atrás, aunque se acentuó a partir de finales de los años 70, siempre como destino secundario de la IED japonesa. En 1980, esta categoría de inversión internacional equivalía al 26,50%, 20% y 11,82% de los niveles de Francia, Alemania y el Reino Unido, respectivamente. Incluso países más pequeños como Bélgica y los Países Bajos superaron a España como geografías de destino de la IED japonesa, lo que no ocurrió con otro país del sur de Europa: Italia (Hollerman y Myers 1996, 89).

España desempeñó un papel importante en el proceso por el cual Fujitsu Ltd. adquirió una dimensión verdaderamente relevante en toda Europa. En 1981, a través de la intermediación de las Cajas de Ahorros Postales japonesas, cliente de Fujitsu, un acuerdo de colaboración entre La Caixa y Fujitsu convirtió a SECOINSA-Fujitsu en el proveedor del nuevo cajero automático. Dos años más tarde, con la instalación del primer cajero automático, Fujitsu comenzó la sustitución gradual de las unidades IBM hasta que todos los cajeros automáticos comenzaron a ofrecer servicios de tarjetas y libretas en 1986. A partir de 1984, se prestó especial atención a los nuevos terminales y computadoras de la serie M, y en 1987 se introdujeron nuevos productos de Fujitsu. Posteriormente, los cajeros automáticos de Fujitsu fueron utilizados por La Caixa durante largo tiempo[31].

---

[29] La planta de IBM estaba situada en la ciudad oriental de Valencia (*El País*, 10 de julio de 1977); significativamente, el texto referido se titulaba «La autarquía informática imposible». Para el contexto general, véase Barceló (2008).

[30] Ministerio de Industria y Energía 1984, 74. Japón protagonizó el primer desembarco de empresas multinacionales asiáticas en España desde el decenio de 1970, al que siguieron los surcoreanos en los decenios de 1980 y 1990 (Beltrán 2009, 25)

[31] Los nuevos productos de Fujitsu: cajeros automáticos y terminales de mostrador (Maixé-Altés 2012, 288; Batiz-Lazo y Efthymiou 2016, 110-111). Fujitsu España acordó con el Banco Popular Español extender a otras instituciones financieras la tecnología y las aplicaciones

Fujitsu formó parte de una delegación de empresas japonesas que en 1982 participó en un encuentro empresarial España-Japón, organizado por la Asociación para el Progreso de la Dirección. Reunió a la empresa pública y privada española, los bancos españoles y japoneses, la representación oficial japonesa en España, la Organización de Comercio Exterior de Japón (Japan External Trade Organization, JETRO), los representantes en España de las Empresas de Comercio Exterior, y al gobierno español[32].

Una cuarentena de plantas de empresas japonesas de las más variadas ramas se instalaron en suelo hispano a finales de los años ochenta. Sin embargo, debido principalmente a los factores internos –pobres resultados económicos del país– el crecimiento de la IED japonesa en la década de 1990 se desaceleró (Ando 2005, 2).

Las inversiones japonesas se encontraban dispersas por toda España, con la rara y sorprendente excepción del País Vasco, potencialmente atractivo por su alta industrialización. Este patrón de ubicación se debió al predominio de plantas de empresas conjuntas con empresas japonesas que a menudo adquirían las operaciones existentes – la planta de Nissan Motor Ibérica en Barcelona, considerada junto a Dusseldorf la plataforma industrial de Japón en Europa (Fundació Jaume Bofill 1989, 143). En cambio, la inversión industrial japonesa en España se centró en tres sectores principales: la electrónica, los vehículos y los productos químicos, los dos primeros de los cuales se concentraron en Cataluña, la mejor plataforma para la exportación (Morris

---

informáticas utilizadas en este banco, que contaba con una red de más de 2.000 sucursales y estaba presente a través de otros canales, como los cajeros automáticos. Estas soluciones cubrían todo el ciclo de negocio de una institución financiera, desde la informática de negocio desarrollada hasta la solución de sucursal desarrollada por Fujitsu España (CNMV, 19 de julio de 1998). En 2001, la actividad de los cajeros automáticos representaba la mitad de la producción de la fábrica (*ComputerWorld*, 22 de junio de 2001). Se añadieron nuevos productos y soluciones a la cartera: Fujitsu ICL España lanzó sus nuevos discos duros Hornet, más resistentes que las familias anteriores, y acordó con Microsoft el desarrollo de la Intranet corporativa de la Federación Española de Fútbol (*Empresa Exterior*, 1 de marzo de 2002; *Control de Publicidad*, 1 de julio de 2002). El gobierno regional de las Islas Canarias adjudicó a Fujitsu ICL España el suministro, instalación y posterior mantenimiento de un subsistema de almacenamiento en disco F6497L y el arrendamiento y mantenimiento del producto de *software* GSM/TDMF (*BOC*, 4 de enero de 2002, 63).

[32] La inversión japonesa en España alcanzó los 173 millones de dólares; con esta cifra, equivalente al 0,5% del total de la inversión japonesa, España ocupaba la séptima posición europea después de las grandes potencias –Inglaterra, Alemania y Francia– e incluso de países pequeños, de la talla de Holanda y Bélgica. Del total de esta inversión, 123 millones de dólares se destinaron a la industria, siendo la cifra más importante de Europa; las empresas japonesas que participaron en la delegación (Mitsui, The Industrial Bank of Japan y Sanno Institute of Bussiness Administration) (*ABC*, 28 de febrero de 1982).

(ed.) 2002, 202)[33]. En 1986, el valor estimado de la producción y el empleo en los servicios de telecomunicaciones y electrónica en España ascendía a 543.275 millones de pesetas, de los cuales tres cuartas partes correspondían a los servicios de telefonía fija; el 14,5% y el 13,3% del total otorgaban a los ordenadores una modesta participación en la producción y el empleo, respectivamente (Gráfico 1). La productividad de los distintos tipos de servicios de valor añadido era muy similar[34].

[33] Sucursales japonesas en España que producían componentes electrónicos en 1991: Eunasa Nakagawa Europe (1987, Nakagawa Electric Industry: 50%) productor de temporizadores y motores giratorios para microondas y refrigeradores; Eurotron (1978, Sanyo 100%) para piezas y componentes de CTV; Reprografía Ibérica (1987) para piezas y componentes de PPC y equipos de oficina; JS España para conectores y terminales (Strange 2002, 250). Sanyo, en la electrónica de consumo, fue pionera en las empresas japonesas que establecieron operaciones desde Japón en el mercado catalán (1969), pero hubo que esperar hasta mediados del siglo xx para que un gran número de empresas japonesas comenzaran a establecer operaciones allí. Mediado el decenio de 1980, había margen para ampliar la nómina de empresas niponas en España. Sanyo, en colaboración con el grupo español Aznarez, consiguió dos de las tres adjudicaciones concedidas por el gobierno para fabricar vídeos en España. A una cuarta adjudicación, aspiraban las japonesas Hitachi y Sharp y la francesa Thomson. La multinacional alemana Grundig consiguió la tercera adjudicación y empezó a fabricar en el país (*El País*, 12 de mayo de 1985). El origen del grupo industrial electrónico Aznárez, que fabricaba en Huesca y Tudela y comercializaba desde 1962 productos japoneses en España, se remontaba a un taller familiar establecido en Zaragoza en 1933. En 1963 empezó a fabricar los productos Sanyo y seis años después adquirió un paquete accionarial del 37% del capital. Los recursos propios de la firma alcanzaban los 3.500 millones de pesetas y su plantilla los 1.030 trabajadores, mientras que la facturación en 1982 superaba los 10.000 millones de pesetas (*El País*, 9 de febrero de 1983 y 9 de onoro de 1985).

[34] Entre 1982 y 1987, en España el empleo en la informática se multiplicó por 1,4 (Commission of the European Communities 1991, 40-41).

Gráfico 1. Valor estimado de la producción y el empleo en los servicios de
telecomunicaciones y electrónica en España, 1986
(millones de ptas. y número de puestos de trabajo)

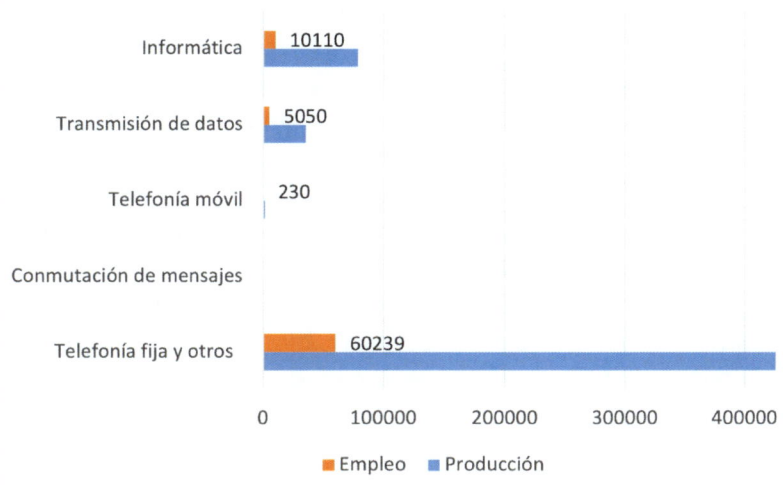

Fuente: Elaboración propia a partir de Commission of
the European Communities 1991, 40-41.

En ese arranque de la segunda mitad de la década de 1980, la enorme ventaja que ofrecía el mercado español respecto a otros países europeos estribaba en el hecho que España apenas tenía electrónica doméstica que proteger. Los grandes nombres de la industria japonesa, como Honda, Sony, Nissan, Suzuki, Yamaha y Matushita (National Panasonic) habían movido sus piezas en los últimos años en España, a la que un observador veía en el futuro cercano como la «California de Europa» (*JPRS*, abril de 1987, 14-15).

El espacio económico en el que se integró España no presentaba una situación brillante. La incapacidad de alcanzar el tamaño crítico suficiente para aprovechar las economías de escala entorpeció a las empresas europeas competir en igualdad de condiciones con las estadounidenses y las japonesas, quedando relegadas a un segundo lugar en el mercado. En realidad, pagaron muy caro la protección de la que gozaban los gobiernos europeos, que en los decenios de 1960 y 1970 habían promovido campeones nacionales en lugar de grupos paneuropeos. Competir efectivamente exigió a no pocas empresas europeas forjar alianzas con fabricantes extranjeros, como fue el caso de Siemens y el campeón nacional británico ICL (International Computers Ltd.) con

Fujitsu, preludio de un proceso de absorción, como veremos (Commission of the European Communities 1990, 49)[35].

Una pieza importante del proyecto de alianza estratégica de capital en España fue la Sociedad Española de Comunicaciones e Informática S.A. (SECOINSA). Era propiedad de CTNE y del público Instituto Nacional de Industria (INI), y una auténtica rareza dentro del muy modesto sector informático español[36]. CTNE decidió adquirir la participación mayoritaria del INI –69,1% del capital– y reorientar la fábrica de Málaga a la producción de ordenadores, dejando de lado el montaje. El plan preveía la integración de la línea de grandes ordenadores de Fujitsu en la nueva empresa, la transferencia real de tecnología en sus múltiples aspectos –fabricación, ingeniería de sistemas, know-how y formación de personal– el fomento de las exportaciones y la respuesta global a la demanda existente en informática, ofimática y telemática[37]. CTNE podría presumir de una posición de vanguardia tecnológica basada en tres pilares diferentes, a saber, la tecnología de EE.UU. con AT&T, la japo-

---

[35] Bull se asoció con NEC y Honeywell como Olivetti lo hizo con AT&T (Fletcher 2013, 60). La alianza de Fujitsu con International Computers Ltd (ICL) buscaba un «ataque agresivo» a los mercados de IBM. El Facom de Fujitsu presentó una alternativa económica compatible con IBM. Además, ICL planeaba proporcionar sus productos de conectividad con los de IBM (*New York Times*, 8 de octubre de 1981) y desarrolló la familia System-4, perfectamente comparable a la IBM 360 (Coopey (ed.) 2004, 312). Vale la pena recordar las alianzas conjuntas, como el consorcio de la Fábrica de Software EUREKA (ESF), establecido bajo el paraguas del programa EUREKA; ICL se integró con otras trece empresas, universidades e institutos de investigación. La estrategia del consorcio ICL consistía en la unión de las fuerzas europeas en el ámbito de la producción de programas informáticos para crear la base tecnológica; entrañaba tres objetivos conjuntos: definir y promover la norma, apoyar el desarrollo tecnológico y preparar el conocimiento del mercado de las nuevas tecnologías. ICL siguió tres líneas estratégicas principales para la ingeniería de *software* en 1987: un programa de mejora de la ingeniería, el proyecto ALVEY/IPSE2.5 y la necesidad de una fuerte presencia en un proyecto europeo crítico para lograr una integración rentable de los componentes de los entornos avanzados. La estrategia tenía por objeto mejorar la productividad de los procesos y el control de calidad de los sistemas de *software* suministrados (Thomas et al. 1990, 317).

[36] SECOINSA vendió el 40% de su producción al sector público (*Diario de Sesiones del Congreso (DSC)*, 215, 18 de febrero de 1982, 12.697).

[37] En 1986, el capital social de la nueva Fujitsu España era de 6.000 millones de pesetas, de los cuales Telefónica poseía el 40% (Telefónica, *Memoria 1985*, p. 39). El proyecto de instalación de telefonía pública multiacceso de Fujitsu, considerado el más idóneo, sufrió retrasos y, una vez finalizado el desarrollo conjunto CTNE-Telettra, se replanteó y se decidió limitar la compra a Fujitsu de lo que ya se había importado (*ACE*, 11 de mayo de 1983). La pauta de transferencia de tecnología parece coherente con la identificada en el debate teórico (Strach y Everett 2006, 55-68), que equipara los métodos de las prácticas de gestión del conocimiento de las empresas japonesas en el extranjero y en el país de origen. Sobre la telemática, véase Arroyo (1980).

nesa con Fujitsu y la europea con Ericsson[38]. Por su parte, Fujitsu garantizó el intercambio y la asistencia tecnológica para poner nuevos productos avanzados al alcance de la filial. La estructura accionarial de SECOINSA sufriría un cambio por el traspaso de la participación del INI a CTNE y la entrada de Fujitsu a través de un aumento de capital para sanearla financieramente e iniciar un cambio en su gestión[39].

El protocolo firmado en 1984 en Tokio convirtió a Fujitsu en socio tecnológico y a SECOINSA en el eje para desarrollar en España la tecnología de la informática y la telemática. El acuerdo estableció los criterios para establecer el valor patrimonial de SECOINSA.

En aquel momento, el panorama internacional se dirigía hacia una confluencia de las grandes empresas IBM, AT&T y Fujitsu no sin algún conflicto. La dureza de las negociaciones con Fujitsu no auguraba una solución rápida o fácil, ya que los japoneses desconfiaban del sector público y exigían al INI la salida anticipada de SECOINSA. La aproximación de criterios en la valoración de las acciones allanó los obstáculos y retrasó la fijación definitiva del valor por parte de un consultor independiente[40]. Sin esperar esta eventualidad, la CTNE compró su participación en SECOINSA al INI y se convirtió en propietaria del 92,86% del capital social de la empresa. Fujitsu (7,1%) y Piher (0,04%) se repartieron el resto. Esa pequeña participación engrosaría la del operador en un futuro próximo. Según la fórmula básica, el INI retuvo la cartera de clientes y las patentes adquiridas de Digipower, así como su participación en dos empresas –Telesincro e Isel[41].

---

[38] *LACA*, 28 de noviembre y 19 de diciembre de 1984.

[39] El INI y la CTNE participarían en una ampliación de capital de 6.200,5 millones de pesetas en una proporción del 74,52 y el 25,48% respectivamente, pero no así Fujitsu o Piher, una pequeña empresa local de electrónica (Telefónica, *Libros de Actas del consejo de administración (LACA)*, 28 de septiembre de 1983; *El País*, 8 de julio de 1983). Esta forma de entrada se diferenciaba claramente del habitual predominio de la propiedad absoluta en las empresas, lo que socavaba la posición de los actores locales.

[40] Hubo discrepancias en la valoración de los paquetes de acciones de Telesincro, ISEL y Digi Power, que el INI iba a recomprar; apoyo de la casa real japonesa a las negociaciones, manifestado en una visita oficial a España (*LACA*, 6 de marzo de 1985).

[41] Precio de 1.199.037 de las acciones adquiridas: 2.234 millones de pesetas. Es importante recordar un hecho frecuentemente repetido, a saber, la lucha de las comunidades autónomas para atraer la instalación de industrias a su territorio. Desde una perspectiva localista, la Dirección General de Electrónica e Informática del Ministerio de Industria y Energía, dirigida por el catalán Joan Majó, sería acusada de asentar la industria informática nacional en Cataluña, impulsando a Telesincro, filial de SECOINSA. Se mencionaba como apoyo al hecho de que Telesincro fabricara 1.500 impresoras para SECOINSA, producto sin salida en el mercado nacional o extranjero y que permitía el pleno empleo en Telesincro (Pregunta

El acuerdo eliminó el principal obstáculo puesto por Fujitsu, que elaboró una propuesta marco aceptable, aunque considerada insuficiente por el momento[42]. A continuación, en 1985, CTNE y Fujitsu acordaron concentrar FESA y SECOINSA en una empresa conjunta con el objetivo de fabricar grandes ordenadores en España, incluyendo productos electrónicos, transmisión de datos y automatización de oficinas tanto para el mercado doméstico como para el internacional. Como síntoma de progreso en la negociación, Fujitsu casi había completado la gama de productos que iba a fabricar en España y programó una visita a España de su presidente, Takuma Yamamoto[43]. Finalmente, el Consejo de Ministros aprobó el 9 de mayo la fusión de SECOINSA y Fujitsu en la nueva Fujitsu España, autorizando la inversión de 1.434 millones de ptas., con una participación del 40% por parte de la CTNE.

En este punto, es necesario llamar la atención sobre un asunto relacionado con el comportamiento de Telefónica, como sabemos el único proveedor de electrónica TESYS. En contraste con el esquema teórico de cuatro fases (Lagerström; Schweizer y Jakobsson, 2019, 35-53), cuando Telefónica aún estaba en negociaciones con Fujitsu para su integración en SECOINSA decidió reforzar la gama movilizando parcialmente sus propios recursos. Basándose en Telefonía y Datos, una filial destinada a completar la actividad de otra filial en la reparación de dispositivos de abonado, Telefónica reforzó el clúster de Madrid con una inversión de 866 millones de pesetas en una nueva fábrica de equipos telemáticos y telefónicos situada en las proximidades de la capital (Getafe) para beneficiarse como zona ZUR (Zona de reindustrialización urgente), subvencionada con dinero público. La base tecnológica estaría en un equipo en desarrollo en EE.UU., en colaboración con el área tecnológica de Telefónica, y la producción se orientaría sobre todo a la exportación[44].

---

número 18.033 sobre la situación de la fábrica de SECOINSA en Málaga y su futura producción en relación con Andalucía, *DSPA*, 22 de enero de 1983).

[42] *LACA*, 27 de marzo de 1985. El valor de los fondos propios de SECOINSA, ajustado a los criterios del acuerdo inicial de marzo de 1985 y fijado en 3.235 millones de pesetas, superó en 300 millones de pesetas las primeras estimaciones del INI (*El País*, 26 de julio de 1985).

[43] *LACA*, 30 de abril y 29 de mayo de 1985; Yamamoto 1992, 69; *Spanish Economic News Service*, 2.059-2.081, 1986. Firma de acuerdos en Tokio el 25 de abril (*ALCAC*, 30 de abril de 1985); en España, Takuma Yamamoto fue recibido por las más altas autoridades del país (*ALCAC*, 29 de enero de 1986; *ABC*, 11 de febrero de 1986, 20).

[44] Telefonía y Datos promovió los nuevos desarrollos en la comunicación de datos, empezando por el sistema de «datos de voz», ideal para extensiones de centrales telefónicas analógicas; capital inicial de 2.000 millones de pesetas aportado íntegramente por Telefónica y posterior participación de entidades financieras; empleo de 300 personas (*LACA*, 30 de enero y 27 de marzo de 1985).

El sistema TESYS estaba disponible o cerca de ser implantado en redes de muchos países europeos, norteafricanos y asiáticos. Sin embargo, el desarrollo del *hardware* esperaría hasta que las actividades de investigación y desarrollo de Telefónica se consolidaran. Cuando la orientación tecnológica precisa de la empresa ya estaba definida, la sección de I+D desarrolló el TESYS-B, un equipo de segunda generación con gran capacidad de conmutación y el *software* correspondiente a la primera entrega, programado para 1990[45].

Tan solo dos años después de atacar el mercado español, Fujitsu, líder de informática en Japón, apuntaba alto. El plan quinquenal iniciado en 1986 tenía como objetivo convertir a FESA en la segunda empresa de la industria informática española[46]. Bajo el estímulo del plan de negocios desarrollado entre los socios Fujitsu y Telefónica, la nueva filial emprendió un ambicioso programa de expansión con un contenido integrado verticalmente a través de una fuerte inversión en I+D, fabricación y comercialización. Entre los ejercicios 1986 y 1989, FESA invirtió un total de 4.976 millones de pesetas. Como primer resultado, las ventas se duplicaron en el trienio, en un momento en el que el sector atravesaba una etapa de importante crecimiento[47].

4. La IED y las multinacionales en España: un análisis cualitativo

Es hora de retomar algunos de los temas descritos para profundizar en ellos. El primero se refiere a las razones del atractivo de España para la inversión directa japonesa, considerada una de las cuestiones generales más significativas planteadas por los estudiosos (Blonigen, 2006, 1; Lipsey, 2002).

A España se le consideraba un país de industria inmadura en su zona geográfica. Aún con todo, el país resultaba atractivo para el capital extranjero

---

[45] El TESYS-B alcanzó los 60.000 paquetes por segundo y 300.000 circuitos virtuales (*LACA*, 25 de marzo de 1992). Para el quinquenio 1987-91 se esperaban unas ventas de 18.000 millones de pesetas en los cinco continentes (Telefónica, *Informe anual*, 1989, 31).

[46] Para 1987, FESA pretendía aumentar las ventas en España en un 25% con respecto a 1986, hasta 22.300 millones de pesetas (171,5 millones de dólares), a la vez que alcanzar un volumen de negocio de 25.000 millones de pesetas en 1989 (*JPRS*, abril 1987, 14-15).

[47] Expediente de regulación de empleo de la empresa Fujitsu España SA, 15 de junio de 1990 a 26 de febrero de 1993. Las ventas de las diez mayores empresas de ordenadores aumentaron en más de un 30% en 1985; España ocupaba el sexto lugar en Europa en el submercado de microprocesadores profesionales, de los cuales 52.000 se vendieron en 1985 (Commission of the European Communities 1987, 92). Los ejercicios fiscales comenzaron y terminaron en abril.

porque ofrecía ayudas públicas bajo diversas formas, incentivos laborales y fiscales, así como política industrial, de acuerdo con el debate teórico sobre los determinantes de la IED (Kumar, 2001). Una fuente japonesa –boletín de JETRO– decía que España buscaba reconstruir su sistema industrial sobre una base de alta tecnología y atraer inversiones extranjeras combinadas con transferencias de tecnología (*Spanish Economic News Service* 38, 1-51, 8).

Gráfico 2. Factores de localización de las empresas japonesas en cinco países europeos, 1992

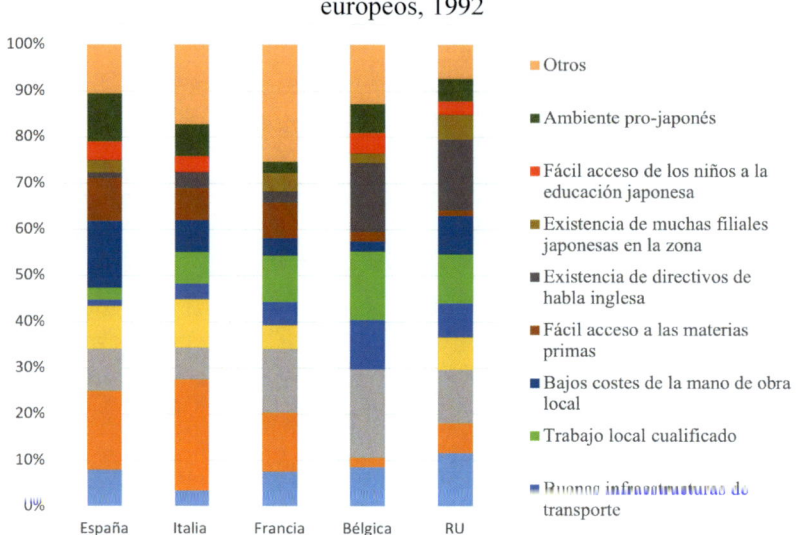

Fuente: Elaboración propia a partir de Status 1992.

Pero no bastan las apreciaciones generales para lograr el perfil adecuado. Si pasamos a un marco más preciso a nivel de empresa, en una muestra muy significativa que comprende setenta y seis casos, las razones económicas por las que las empresas japonesas eligieron España prevalecieron con el 79,41% del total conocido. Predominó el gran tamaño del mercado nacional, con 13 casos del total, seguido de las buenas infraestructuras (8), la existencia de industrias afines (industrias auxiliares) (7), las condiciones de distribución geográficamente favorables (7) y el fácil acceso a las materias primas (7). Algo menos representativas fueron la mayor calidad del trabajo local en la zona de operaciones (2) y la abundancia de filiales japonesas que avanzaban en la esfera de la fabricación (2). Las razones culturales representaron el 20,59%, desglosado en el entorno projaponés (8 casos), los escasos problemas para la educación infantil debido a la existencia de escuelas japonesas (3) y la posibilidad de emplear a directivos de habla inglesa (1). En términos comparativos, las razones económicas por las que las empresas japonesas eligieron España fueron cuantitativamente menores que en Italia y Francia y mayores que en Bélgica y el Reino Unido, por ejemplo. Al igual que en España, el gran tamaño del mercado interno fue la principal razón en Italia y Francia, mientras que el trabajo local cualificado y las condiciones de distribución geográficamente favorables fueron importantes en Bélgica y el Reino Unido (Gráfico 2) (Status 1992, 19)[48].

Una problemática importante se refiere al impacto de la acción de la multinacional en el país receptor, una de las cuestiones más debatidas (Bajo-Rubio, 2020, 1-16) aunque no suficientemente aclarada en los estudios sobre las interacciones entre las multinacionales y la IED, como ya se ha mencionado (Blonigen, 2006; Lipsey, 2002).

Las tendencias de los gastos en investigación y desarrollo de las cincuenta principales empresas parecen bastante estables en el año 2000 y la proporción de los ingresos destinados a la I+D de 20 de las 25 principales empresas de TI se situó en un promedio de alrededor del 7%. Los gastos de algunas empresas en relación con los ingresos disminuyeron ligeramente entre 1994 y 1998, como en el caso de Fujitsu, mientras que otras mostraron grandes incrementos[49].

En cuanto a la clasificación en el mundo de la investigación y el desarrollo, Fujitsu, junto con Hitachi y NEC, figuraba entre los diez principales solicitantes en función de su número total de patentes en los años ochenta y noventa, pero cayó en la década de 2000, a diferencia de otros cuatro solicitantes japoneses –Canon, Toshiba, Ricoh y Sony– que aparecían constantemente entre los diez principales en cada una de estas tres décadas (World Intellectual Property Organization 2015, 10).

Si consideramos la IED en I+D, la participación de filiales extranjeras en I+D empresarial en 2003 situó a España entre los países que estaban muy por encima de la media. El grupo incluía tres grandes economías occidentales (Reino Unido, Francia y Alemania), varios países occidentales desarrollados

---

[48] La ayuda de la Administración española a Fujitsu no fue solo directa, sino también indirecta, como por ejemplo la creación de varias especialidades tecnológicas en la Universidad de Málaga para satisfacer las demandas de mano de obra cualificada (*DSC*, Comisiones, 601, 16 de febrero de 1993, 18.103).

[49] Los gastos en proporción a los ingresos disminuyeron del 10,5 al 7,8% (OECD 2000, 42-43).

(Suecia e Italia) y un conjunto de naciones con rasgos muy diferentes (United Nations Conference on Trade and Development 1993, 125).

Ya en el tema central de nuestro estudio, FESA fue popularmente apodada el «hermano mayor» – una terminología extraída de las cofradías religiosas de Semana Santa– de la Málaga tecnológica debido al peso de su producción, inversiones y empleo en la economía andaluza.

En los años 1979/1984 tuvo lugar un vertiginoso crecimiento de las ventas y un aumento de la cartera de clientes institucionales. A Telefónica se sumaron el ministerio de Hacienda con un gran contrato junto a UNIVAC, el INEM, el ministerio de Sanidad, el Instituto Nacional de la Seguridad Social y la diputación de Málaga para la administración del hospital civil. SECOINSA creó asímismo el banco de datos de la Costa del Sol para la gestión hotelera así como el del teléfono turístico andaluz. También destacó el impulso de la proyección exterior, visible, por ejemplo, en los acuerdos de colaboración firmados a finales de 1980 con la empresa francesa CIII-Honeywell-Bull para la fabricación de terminales Questar bajo licencia. Los clientes locales incluso la escuela de turismo, se equiparon con ordenadores SECOINSA ofreciendo como incentivo cursos de informática[50].

A mediados de los años 80, la empresa atravesaba buenos momentos en cuanto a capital social, plantilla, I+D y facturación. Sus planes incluían la ampliación de la fábrica de Málaga para consolidarse como punta de lanza en los mercados europeos, nutrida también por una filial más pequeña de la multinacional en Irlanda[51].

SECOINSA tenía en la dependencia tecnológica su talón de Aquiles, ya que se veía obligada a importar el grueso de componentes de alta tecnología que montaba en sus productos. A mediados de la década de 1980, el 72% de las materias primas y componentes eran importados. Se adquirían más de 2,5 millones de estos, en especial a Fujitsu pero también a Intel, uno de los mayores fabricantes mundiales de semiconductores que suministraba los micropro-

---

[50]   Fracasó en el intento de hacerse con el macrocontrato para el equipamiento informático del campeonato mundial de fútbol España 82 (Mateo y Heredia 2012, 130-134).

[51]   Tenía un capital social de 6.000 millones de pesetas, una plantilla creciente y más de una quinta parte de ella dedicada a la I+D. Su facturación se situaba en torno a los 18.000 millones de pesetas, con un incremento del 20% respecto al año anterior (Strange 2002, 250). El gigante de la electrónica japonesa predicaba una «apuesta seria» por parte de la industria española (*El País*, 18 de diciembre de 1986). Evolución de las ventas en los últimos años: 1977, 192 millones de pesetas; 1978, 1.072; 1979, 2.293; 1980, 3.128; 1981, 3.223 y 1984, 9.434; en 1984 obtuvo por primera vez beneficios por una cuantía de 52 millones de ptas. En 1985, la planta de Málaga contaba con una plantilla de 226 personas, que se incrementó en los dos años siguientes a 246 y 413.

cesadores 80286 y 80386 para los equipos TESYS. Se adquirían materiales a Hitachi, Texas Instruments y NEC. Las tarjetas de los circuitos integrados las producían dos empresas catalanas, Elbasa[52] y Primo, que fabricaba bobinas pequeñas y llegó a establecer una fábrica en el Parque Tecnológico de Andalucía (PTA), mientras que la también catalana Lam suministró mini transformadores y mini bobinas. La aportación andaluza se redujo a los productos de nulo nivel tecnológico y escaso valor añadido, como los embalajes[53].

En el ejercicio económico 1987/1988 la planta de Málaga permitió cambiar la escala de producción con el inicio de la producción de impresoras a gran escala, al tiempo que se innovaba en producto. A pesar de los planes iniciales de renunciar al montaje, FESA montó cabezales de impresión y otros componentes críticos de la impresora fabricados en Dublín y enviados a España por Fujitsu Isotec, una filial de Fujitsu. Por lo tanto, aquí funciona una de las formas del modelo de empresa multinacional de Birkinshaw como un sistema de mercado interno[54].

Tal estatus como una empresa de fabricación en lugar de una empresa de montaje de productos hizo de FESA una rareza en la industria informática española. En una lista de 40 empresas de *hardware* en España, ocupó el sexto lugar con el 4,6% de las ventas totales en 1988, muy por detrás de los líderes del mercado de larga trayectoria –IBM, Nixdorf[55], Olivetti, Unisyx y NCR–.

---

[52] Electrónica Básica, S. A. con instalaciones en Barcelona, dedicadas a la fabricación de circuitos impresos, con arreglo a los planes de expansión aprobados por la Dirección General de Industrias Siderometalúrgicas y Navales en 1975 (*BOE*, 43, 18 de febrero de 1976, 3.478).

[53] Mateo y Heredia 2012, 130-134 y testimonio personal de José Estrada en las páginas 321-322 de dicha obra. Para una descripción del PTA dirigida a los inversores extranjeros, véase Romera (1991, 90-107).

[54] Birkinshaw 2000; Fujitsu España 1987/1988, 2-3; Business International Corporation (1989, 83); Egan y McKiernan 1994, 201. Fujitsu Isotec, en el suburbio dublinés de Blanchardstown, cerró en 2002. Años más tarde, la Investigación, el Desarrollo Tecnológico y la Innovación de Andalucía mostraron una tendencia positiva, especialmente en el gasto regional en I+D en el sector empresarial (BERD), pasando del 5,2% del gasto regional total en I+D en 2002 al 6,4% en 2004, y en el gasto empresarial en innovación del 6,2% al 9,5% en el mismo periodo (García; Gayo & del Pozo 2006, 6).

[55] Cabana (1987, 31-32) hace arrancar los orígenes de Nixdorf en España de Wanderer. Los orígenes de Nixdorf Computer, S. A. se remontan a una sociedad creada en Barcelona en 1967. En marzo de 1973 trasladó su domicilio a Madrid ahora bajo la denominación de Nixdorf Computer, S. A., que sustituyó en septiembre de 1990 por la de Siemens Nixdorf Sistemas de Información, S. A. (*Boletín Oficial de las Cortes Generales*, 20 de junio de 1997, 93, 21-22). Nixdorf Computer España, S. A. tenía como presidente del consejo de administración a Günter G. Gronke, a Antonio Roca Puig como secretario y a Francisco Robert como director; su red de oficinas comerciales abarcaba a cuatro ciudades –Barcelona, Madrid, Zaragoza y Valencia (*Hoja oficial de la provincia de Barcelona*, 1.652, 26 de

Algunos años después y considerando los ingresos totales, se mantuvo en el mismo lugar con el 5,6% del total, mientras que IBM iba a la cabeza con el 54,81[56].

Tabla 1. Inversión, producción, empleo y productividad
en Fujitsu España, 1986-1990

	1980	1981	1982	1986	1987	1988	1989
Inversiones				843	1.113	2.344	1.490
Producción	445	1.000	2.000	4.915	6.033	13.042	18.436
Personal	122			290	334	519	729
Productividad	3,64			16,94	18,06	25,12	25,28

Nota: Inversiones, producción y productividad en millones
de pesetas; personal: número de trabajadores.
Fuente: Elaboración propia a partir de Fujitsu España (1987/1988, 23) y *Boletín Oficial de la Junta de Andalucía (BOJA)*, 73, 31 de agosto de 1990, 7.213.

En esta etapa de la expansión conviene tener presentes las alianzas estratégicas. Fujitsu España acordó cooperar con Intertechnique, especializada en la aeronáutica espacial, la telemedida y la informática, con objeto de ofrecer un servicio de soporte a los clientes del Sistema Operativo PICK en el mercado interior. En su segunda vertiente, el acuerdo contemplaba la creación de una nueva empresa de informática con partici

---

octubre de 1970, 21. y 1.664, 18 de enero de 1971, 28). Las ventas de Nixdorf en España rondaban los 117.000 millones de pesetas en 1985 (*El País*, 19 de marzo de 1986). La filial española Nixdorf Computer S. A. fabricaba la centralita telefónica privada digital (modelos 8818-3000) en Toledo (España); junto con su homóloga, fabricada por Nixdorf Computer A. G. en Paderborn (República Federal Alemana), fue homologada en España (*BOE*, 158, 2 de julio de 1988, 20.668); el ejemplo ofrece una muestra de la estrategia de penetración de la multinacional en el mercado español.

[56] Fujitsu España 1987/1988, 2-3; Fujitsu España, *Plan de viabilidad*, 1993; *Expansión*, 27 de noviembre de 1994. IBM (39,84%), Nixdorf (6,31%), Olivetti (6,29%), Unisyx (5,34%) y NCR (4,75%) del total de las ventas en 1988 (445.400 millones de ptas) (*Mercado*, 341, 15 de abril de 1988, 62). En 1987, Fujitsu decidió fabricar en Europa ordenadores de gama media –nicho de Nixdorf–, incluidos miniordenadores e incluso ordenadores personales con diseño propio de Málaga. Fujitsu España introdujo en el mercado español dos series de ordenadores, la K y la Senda, diseñadas íntegramente con ingenieros locales y producidas en España (*AFP Sciences*, 5 de marzo de 1987, 36; Servicio Español de Noticias Económicas, 2.105-2.127, 1987). Siemens se hizo cargo de Nixdorf y dio nacimiento al mayor fabricante de ordenadores de Europa (*Expansión*, 22 de enero de 1990, 54). Siemens Francia formó el IN2 Groupe Siemens a partir del IN2 y la empresa de ordenadores Leanord, adquirida en noviembre de 1987. IN2 Groupe Siemens pensaba seguir ofreciendo sus sistemas de *picking* y ordenadores personales al mercado francés (*Computer Business Review*, 1 de febrero de 1990).

pación de Intertechnique y capital español. Con el nombre de IN2, tenía por finalidad distribuir dos gamas de productos IBER y el resto de productos de Intertechnique (*Elektor Spanish 1987*, 2, 83, 1987).

Gráfico 3. Composición de la plantilla de Fujitsu España, 1987-1990 (%)

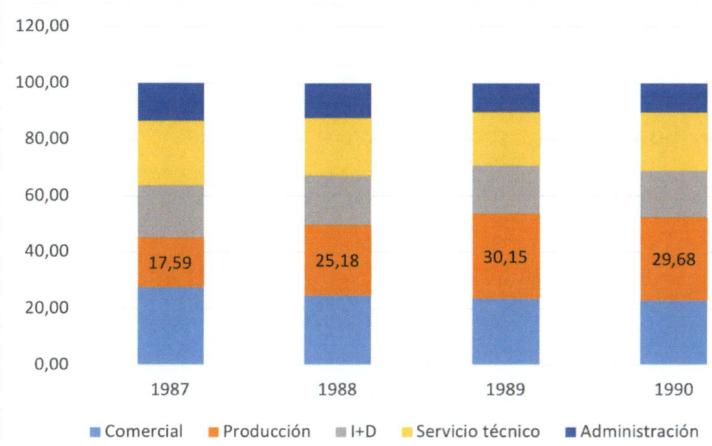

Fuente: Elaboración propia a partir de Fujitsu España,
Memoria(s) anual(es) 1987-1990.

Al crecimiento de Fujitsu España le acompañó una transformación de las estructuras de producción, que se hizo evidente en los cambios de la composición de la fuerza de trabajo. El personal de producción se multiplicó por 1,53 entre 1987 y 1990 principalmente a expensas del departamento comercial. De casi trescientas personas, el 75% tenía títulos universitarios y más de la mitad eran ingenieros, licenciados y técnicos de nivel medio, mientras que los oficiales y especialistas y los técnicos no cualificados representaban el 17,42 y el 3,27%, respectivamente[57]. Más importante aún, a finales del decenio de 1980, FESA mostró una tendencia al alza en sus diversas variables de inversión, producción y productividad (Tabla 1).

Uno de los objetivos de la creación de empresas mixtas con las multinacionales estribó en el logro de su propia tecnología. Idéntico era el objetivo de los poderes públicos para cubrir las actividades y planes de expansión de

---

[57] Tendencia opuesta de las variables: el número de empleados aumentó del 17,59% al 29,68%; el del departamento comercial pasó del 27,63% al 22,86% (Fujitsu España, *Plan de viabilidad*, 1990).

nuevas empresas: sacudirse la dependencia tecnológica. ¿Qué pasó en la realidad y por qué?

Fujitsu Ltd. decidió fabricar en España productos para Europa basados en tecnología japonesa adaptada al mercado europeo. En 1988, FESA creó un centro de I+D en su planta de Málaga para las telecomunicaciones y el procesamiento de datos, encargado de equilibrar la necesidad de ampliar las áreas de mercado y la gama de nuevos productos con el cumplimiento puntual de los plazos de entrega requeridos. Los 320 millones de pesetas invertidos en la nueva planta mejoraron significativamente las instalaciones técnicas y permitieron ampliar el laboratorio de electrónica y CAD, el centro informático y el taller de maquinaria[58].

La estrategia de internacionalización a partir de las empresas conjuntas mencionadas anteriormente se completó con la descentralización corporativa de la I+D. La empresa tenía una intensidad de I+D (es decir, el gasto en I+D dividido por las ventas) del 7%[59]. Tal estrategia se anticipó en dos años a las primeras instalaciones de Fujitsu Ltd. en el Reino Unido y por lo tanto, antes de abrir las primeras sucursales en Alemania y Francia, para promover la investigación avanzada en tecnología de la información, telecomunicaciones e informática[60].

[58] La nueva planta tenía 3.700 metros^2 dedicados a esta actividad. El laboratorio de I+D+i llegó a contar con cerca de 100 personas, en su mayoría jóvenes ingenieros de telecomunicaciones procedentes principalmente de la escuela superior de Madrid (De Mateo y Heredia 2012, 137-144; Fujitsu España, *Feasibility Plan*). El diseño y la construcción de la fábrica siguieron un esquema de colaboración con división de funciones; fueron llevadas a cabo por dos filiales del INI, mientras que ingenieros japoneses coordinaron el trabajo y lo supervisaron en detalle. La fábrica estaba equipada con tecnología muy avanzada, incluyendo sistemas de control de polvo y dispositivos de seguridad. Se trataba de sistemas de origen japonés que se readaptaron al mercado local. También se fabricaron impresoras matriciales en grandes series a un costo competitivo y barato, muchas de las cuales se vendieron en Europa. La velocidad de producción era de una unidad/20 segundos y cuatro líneas en 16 horas (José Estrada, Entrevista con el autor, 22 de julio de 2020). La empresa privilegió la contratación de mano de obra local, dentro de un entorno caracterizado por la presencia de empresas, homólogas o de otros sectores. La rotación de la mano de obra se mantuvo baja para que la empresa pudiera retener el talento y hacer rentable el aprendizaje (Gustavo Hylander, Entrevistado por el autor, 4 de agosto de 2020). En cuanto a actividad de diffusion, el Centro publicó una revista técnica (Cuadernos de divulgación técnica); en 1986, Fujitsu España organizó los encuentros con entidades financieras sobre Adecuación de las nuevas tecnologías de la información (NTI) al sector financiero.

[59] Fujitsu España 1987/1988, 5 y 23. La intensidad de la investigación y el desarrollo en Fujitsu Ltd. aumentó en más de dos puntos porcentuales hasta 1996, desde el 9,2 de 1992 (Fujitou Ltd. 1006, 40).

[60] En 2001, se fusionaron para formar Fujitsu Laboratories of Europe Limited (Egan y McKiernan 1994, 201). En términos comparativos, solo menos del 3% de las patentes que Toyota

Una cuestión importante atañe al plan estratégico de la empresa matriz con respecto a la filial. La sede central japonesa determinó la línea de productos que se fabricaría en Málaga. Mientras tanto, el grupo de investigación y desarrollo de Málaga diseñó productos, específicamente pequeños ordenadores de las series 10 y 20. Cuando se diseñaron nuevos productos, la maquinaria necesaria fue definida desde la sede y vino de Japón (José Estrada, Entrevista con el autor, 22 de julio de 2020). Por otra parte, Fujitsu España subcontrató tareas de baja cualificación a empresas nacionales. Así ocurrió con la producción de la pieza mecánica y las planchas, que se confiaron a la empresa catalana Motek, casa dedicada a la electrónica profesional y de aplicaciones industriales e informáticas en el mercado nacional. La transferencia de conocimientos funcionó en dos direcciones: los ingenieros españoles se formaban en Japón y sus homólogos japoneses hacían lo mismo en España por periodos de hasta dos años.

En el marco de un «Acuerdo de Colaboración para el desarrollo del subsector andaluz de la electrónica, la informática y las telecomunicaciones», Fujitsu España expresó su intención de seguir promoviendo sus productos y actividades de investigación y desarrollo en Málaga[61].

La empresa se había estrenado en España fabricando módems, impresoras y piezas de ordenador. Tras sucesivas reorientaciones de la producción en la fábrica de Málaga a lo largo de cuarenta años, se dedicó a la producción de radios, automóviles y cajeros automáticos. El cambio de tipología de los productos no es anecdótico ya que supone, en primer lugar, una alteración en la tarea encomendada por Telefónica a la empresa y, en segundo lugar, contra todos los optimistas, una pérdida de contenido tecnológico, dado el tipo de producto predominante[62].

Motor Corporation había registrado en todo el mundo estaban en los EE.UU. y menos del 1% en Europa. El grueso de las patentes (96,6%) corresponde a la actividad de I+D llevada a cabo en los laboratorios de I+D del país de origen.

[61] *Boletín Oficial de la Junta de Andalucía,* 73, 31 de agosto de 1990.

[62] *La Opinión de Málaga,* 23 de septiembre de 2017; *Diario de Sesiones del Parlamento de Andalucía (DSPA)*, 22 de enero de 1983. La perspectiva de la Exposición Universal de 1992 (Expo'92) perfilaba un horizonte apasionante. En 1988, Fujitsu se convirtió en empresa asociada a esta Exposición con una aportación de 400 millones de pesetas. El vicepresidente y consejero delegado de la multinacional en España señaló la posibilidad de instalarse definitivamente en el pabellón que Fujitsu construiría para la Expo'92 y lo consideró un escaparate de propaganda de primera magnitud para sus proyecciones en 3-D de Imax con gafas de la casa (*ABC*, 12 de julio de 1990; *Expo Hemeroteca*, 2 de diciembre de 1988). Sin dejar de considerar la importancia de las exposiciones internacionales como instrumento de difusión de las nuevas tecnologías, es importante tener en cuenta sus limitaciones. A veces, incluso

Su estrategia de centrar la I+D en proyectos de diseño de *hardware* resultó ser inadecuada debido al cambio de orientación del mercado hacia el *software* y los servicios, que dio lugar a pérdidas extraordinarias de 1.346 millones de pesetas. La situación económica se vio agravada por una cierta infrautilización de la capacidad en este ámbito debido a la imposibilidad de emprender nuevos proyectos de inversión a largo plazo en ausencia de un flujo de caja positivo (Fujitsu España 1992).

A través de la I+D, la FESA desempeñó un papel principal en un proceso de internacionalización después de convertir la división en una unidad plenamente operativa. A finales de 1991, en el contexto de una reestructuración orgánica que siguió a un periodo de dificultades –inundaciones y descenso de ventas– la Junta de Andalucía y Fujitsu decidieron convertir el centro de I+D en una sociedad anónima, Ingeniería e Integración Avanzadas, S.A. (Ingenia), que se instaló en el Parque Tecnológico de Andalucía[63]. Se trataba de la conversión habitual de una sección de la empresa en una unidad independiente de capital mixto, dedicada al diseño, asesoramiento, aplicación y mantenimiento de sistemas informáticos. El sector público participó a través del Instituto Andaluz de Fomento (IFA) y la Empresa Municipal de Iniciativas y Actividades

---

se habla de mediocridad y desencanto, sentimientos que dejó la participación de los Estados Unidos de América en la Exposición de Tsukuba [Japón] de 1985 en la que participó Fujitsu (Henry Gosho, Entrevistado por G. Lewis Schmidt, The Association for Diplomatic Studies and Training Foreign Affairs Oral History Project, Biblioteca del Congreso, 4 de enero de 1989).

[63] En la concepción de la empresa, el aglutinamiento de la masa gris sobrante de Fujitsu España y las gestiones con las instituciones tuvo un papel destacado el ingeniero de telecomunicaciones Felipe Romera (Soria, 1954), como recoge su aportación en De Mateo y Heredia (2012, 331-344): Ingenia era propiedad en un 40% de Fujitsu Ltd (Fujitsu Ltd, *Annual Report*, 2000, p. 48). El consejero de Economía y Hacienda de la Junta de Andalucía describió la operación como «reconversión de los activos de investigación» de Fujitsu España (Comparecencia para informar sobre la situación actual y las perspectivas de futuro del Parque Tecnológico de Andalucía, Parlamento de Andalucía, *Diario de Sesiones de Comisiones*, Comisión del Parque Tecnológico, III Legislatura, Fondos Documentales, 28 de octubre de 1993, 3-17). Transferencia al PTA (*La Opinión de Málaga*, 23 de septiembre de 2017). Los ingenieros de I+D de SECOINSA que desarrollaron el sistema TESYS transfirieron parte de sus conocimientos a la Universidad de Málaga. Dos ingenieros crearon el sistema MICROMEC, un microordenador para desarrollar proyectos industriales y educativos; permitió realizar proyectos desde la Universidad con empresas industriales locales, introducir microprocesadores en la educación universitaria y desarrollar numerosos proyectos de fin de carrera. También desarrollaron un subproducto de la tecnología TESYS llamado SECOM, una extensión de la cual fue diseñada por la pública SADIEL para funcionar como un télex (Romera (s. f.), 6 y 21).

Empresariales de Málaga (MCIBAM)[64]. Después de su primera andadura, en 1996 llegó la crisis, a la que Ingenia respondió con planes de expansión interna y externa[65]. Por un lado, abrió dos nuevas sucursales –en Barcelona y Sevilla, sucesivamente– y, por otro, dio el salto internacional con iniciativas en Oriente Medio, Marruecos y México, entre otros países. Con el tiempo, Ingenia se expandió a América Latina y se convirtió en una empresa con cientos de clientes para los que desarrolló herramientas de comunicación, sistemas de gestión informática, auditorías y un sinfín de aplicaciones[66].

FESA dependía estrechamente de la demanda de Telefónica, pero también de diversos tipos de ayudas y subvenciones públicas, en general, y de los organismos regionales, en particular[67]. En cuanto a las ayudas públicas, en 1990, al inicio de la crisis internacional, después de haber ayudado a la empresa du-

---

[64] A mediados de los años 80, el Ayuntamiento de Málaga creó el MCIBAM, más conocido como Promálaga, para fomentar y generar nuevas actividades en la provincia (José Estrada Fernández, Entrevistado por el autor, 18 de mayo de 2011).

[65] Ingenia se esforzó en llevar Internet a Málaga a través del PTA, donde instaló la primera infraestructura de comunicaciones por fibra óptica con tecnología de la norteamericana Cray. También desarrolló la primera banca electrónica de Unicaja con la marca Univía. Otras empresas con participación del grupo: Ingenia Advanced Training (formación), Vingenia (tecnología aplicada a la salud), Aretne (e-business) y PTEC (Plataforma Tecnológica) (*Sur*, 20 de diciembre de 2009; *Tiempo de hoy*, 974-978, 2001, 57). En el debate parlamentario afloró la alarma provocada por la actitud de otras empresas que, como Alcatel-Citesa, segregaron el departamento de I+D y lo hicieron directamente dependiente de Francia (Parlamento de Andalucía: *DSPA*, III Legislatura, 19 de mayo de 1993, Fondos Documentales, 9).

[66] La entrada en Marruecos se debió a la proximidad y a las oportunidades de desarrollo tecnológico, mientras que la del Oriente Medio fue una consecuencia, ya que un agente de desarrollo de negocios se puso en contacto con Ingenia, y la de México se debió a las referencias que tenía en las soluciones de *e-Learning*. Como consecuencia de todas ellas, se produjo el gran salto hacia América Latina (Chile en 2011 y Perú en 2012), descartando a Brasil (José Blanco Arjona, Comunicación personal al autor, 19 de julio de 2020). Históricamente, Fujitsu, junto con Cisco, fue el único de los diez principales fabricantes de equipos de telecomunicaciones en el mundo que no tenía actividades de producción local en Brasil, a pesar de que comercializaba sus productos (Cepal 2005, 113).

[67] Andalucía estaba dotada de diversos instrumentos y mecanismos para promover y desarrollar la actividad económica, entre ellos la Sociedad para la Promoción y Reconversión Económica de Andalucía, SOPREA), el Instituto de Fomento de Andalucía (IFA) con funciones de promoción, coordinación y financiación, y el Parque Tecnológico de Andalucía. El PTA se inspiró en los modelos de tecnópolis avanzadas de California y Niza, estudiados *in situ* por altos representantes de la Junta. Un estudio encargado a la consultora japonesa Technova apuntaba a centrarse en las TIC y llegaba a la conclusión de que la Costa del Sol, la zona turística por excelencia, ofrecía una ubicación ideal para el PTA; se estimaba la inversión en 30.000 millones de pesetas (*La Opinión de Málaga*, 27 de febrero de 2008). La Sociedad Andaluza para el Desarrollo de las Tecnologías de la Información y la Electrónica (SADIEL), fundada en 1984, se encargó de la investigación y el desarrollo de nuevos productos electrónicos e informáticos (*BOJDA*, 73, 31 1990, 7.213; Romera (s. f.), 16 y 21).

rante siete años por considerarla un pilar del desarrollo de las tecnologías de la información, la electrónica y las telecomunicaciones, el gobierno autonómico andaluz rescindió el acuerdo que preveía una subvención de unos cuatrocientos cincuenta millones de pesetas, junto con compromisos de compra.

Los cambios negativos en uno y otro concepto no podían sino provocar serios retrocesos en el progreso de la empresa. En los años noventa, Telefónica liberó sus participaciones en los proveedores industriales, en parte para cumplir con la recomendación de concentrarse en las empresas de explotación de redes que la Comisión Europea llevó a cabo en octubre de 1990, y también como resultado del cambio de estrategia. Uno por uno fue desgranando las cuentas de un rosario. En 1991, Telefónica se desprendió de la participación del 40% del capital de FESA, operación que puso fin a la empresa conjunta con Fujitsu Ltd. Ambas partes reconocieron la divergencia en sus actividades básicas sin cortar sus relaciones o, en el caso de Telefónica, su condición de cliente de servicios, licencias y productos de Fujitsu[68].

La crisis general en el sector de la tecnología de la información provocó pérdidas considerables –7.598 millones de pesetas– debido a la reducción de su producción en un 40,6%, una caída del 25% en las ventas con respecto al año anterior y, por consiguiente, en los ingresos, así como en la cartera de pedidos. El desplome de las ventas se debió principalmente a causas exógenas y, por tanto, imprevistas, entre las que se encuentran la disminución de la demanda de Telefónica y las exportaciones a las filiales de Fujitsu en Europa. Lo más importante es que el desglose muestra una reducción selectiva de las ventas que afectó principalmente a las actividades con mayor peso en el margen de explotación porque requerían mayores recursos en términos de personal, sistemas, ventas, soporte central y gestión técnica. Este mayor impacto en el margen bruto y en los resultados fue fruto de la imposibilidad de ajustar la estructura a la velocidad de la caída de las ventas (Fujitsu España, *Plan de viabilidad* 1993)[69]. En la segunda mitad del año, la empresa redujo su plantilla de 784 empleados en un 17,85% por medio de jubilaciones. FESA fue eliminada de un contrato para el suministro de equipos informáticos a la Seguridad Social por valor de 1.500 millones de pesetas. El concurso fue

---

[68] Cantidad desembolsada por Fujitsu Ltd: 3.200 millones de pesetas (Calvo 2016, 259; Comisión Nacional del Mercado de Valores, 486, 20/9/1991; Fujitsu España, *Plan de viabilidad*, 1003).

[69] Fujitsu redujo su producción de 17.076 millones de pesetas en 1989 a 10.140 millones de pesetas al año siguiente.

adjudicado a la británica ICL, filial también de la multinacional asiática desde 1990 tras años de alianza tecnológica (Anexo 3) (*ABC*, 22 febrero de 1991).

En realidad, estamos tratando con causas complejas de la crisis: las encontramos en la salida de Telefónica, la disminución del volumen de pedidos, la aparición de nuevos productos más competitivos que los producidos por la fábrica de Málaga y el derrumbe de los precios en un mercado con renovación acelerada con equipos láser[70].

Para empeorar las cosas, las Administraciones tendían a contener los gastos, los márgenes de otras empresas se reducían debido a una competencia muy agresiva y, muy posiblemente, a la amenaza de devaluación de la moneda española.

El año fiscal de 1991 significó un punto de inflexión para la empresa. FESA fue dimensionada para un nivel de actividad mucho más alto de lo que era apropiado en ese momento como resultado de una combinación de hechos. La razón principal estribó en la disminución de las expectativas de crecimiento del mercado de las TIC después de un periodo de prosperidad y los márgenes de producto en el mercado. La lista también incluía tanto la recesión en el mercado europeo al que se dirigían sus exportaciones como el cambio de socios con la salida de Telefónica y la toma de la totalidad de las acciones por parte de Fujitsu.

Dado que la empresa renunció desde el principio a la estrategia de reducción traumática y seca a favor de una progresiva, esto significó una prolongación de las pérdidas durante un periodo de tiempo importante. Como en muchos otros casos, la crisis dio lugar a una reconversión con el fin de recuperar la rentabilidad[71].

5. La reestructuración de Fujitsu España

FESA llevó a cabo una reestructuración en las facetas organizativa y laboral. Con los cambios introducidos en la primera se abrió paso una estructura de

---

[70] Mientras se imponían las impresoras láser en el mercado, la planta de Málaga fabricaba principalmente impresoras matriciales, que representaban nada menos que el 70% de su capacidad de producción. Por su parte, la estrategia de I+D de la empresa, basada en el *hardware*, perdió contenido en este periodo, en beneficio del *software* y los servicios (Grupo Socialista, *DSC*, 601, Comisiones, IV Legislatura, 16 de febrero de 1993).

[71] *DSC*, Commission for Social Policy, 52, Series A, IV Legislature, 30 de noviembre de 1994, 1.308.

apoyo a la gestión, con un comité ejecutivo compuesto por tres miembros, así como un asistente del director general (Tabla 2). El objetivo fundamental era acercar a los responsables de cada área de negocio a las verdaderas necesidades de los clientes por medio de una organización más ágil en su respuesta a los problemas de los clientes, más clara en cuanto a las responsabilidades y más eficaz. Se estableció la separación entre las unidades de negocio –elementos para diferenciar las distintas unidades de la empresa con responsabilidad sobre los clientes en los distintos mercados– y el resto de las funciones agrupadas en distintos departamentos con la misión de apoyar a las divisiones de gestión clave de la empresa. Una característica relevante fue la movilidad funcional de las carreras de los directivos de alto nivel mediante una rotación por las diversas funciones y unidades para darles la oportunidad de desarrollar sus habilidades y calificarlos para la administración general[72].

En el terreno laboral, la empresa redujo su plantilla durante los años 1991 y 1992 mediante despidos voluntarios. A finales del año anterior se inició el plazo de consulta previo a la presentación de un plan de regulación de empleo, que implicaba la extinción de las relaciones laborales por causas económicas en los diferentes centros de trabajo. La falta de acuerdo del periodo de consulta dio lugar a la presentación del propio plan[73].

A nadie se le ocultaba la gravedad de la situación que atravesaba la empresa y sus repercusiones en la economía andaluza, dada la condición de líder del sector de la electrónica, básico en la estructura productiva de Málaga y en el futuro del desarrollo del Parque Tecnológico de Andalucía[74].

Fujitsu presentó a la directiva un plan de viabilidad para el futuro de la empresa, que se basaba en dos ejes principales. El primero consistía en fomentar la producción en Málaga de impresoras matriciales ya obsoletas durante un primer bienio, comenzando con una ligera disminución previa. Gradualmente, introducirían algunos nuevos productos fundamentales –terminales banca-

---

[72] Hideo Mita, Interview, *ComputerWorld*, 6 mayo de 1994; Nalbantian y Guzzo (2009, 1-10); Gustavo Hylander, entrevistado por el autor, 4 de agosto de 2020; José Estrada, entrevistado por el autor, 22 de julio de 2020.

[73] La restante mano de obra excedentaria inicialmente contemplada había causado baja en la empresa al haberse acogido al sistema de bajas voluntarias incentivadas que se había pactado con los representantes de los trabajadores en noviembre de 1992 (Ministro de Trabajo y Seguridad Social (Martínez Noval), *DSC*, Comisiones, IV Legislatura No. 601, 16 de febrero de 1993).

[74] Pregunta oral número 171/93, relativa a las actuaciones del gobierno andaluz en relación al plan a corto y medio plazo de la multinacional Fujitsu con la factoría de Málaga, Rodríguez Bermúdez, *DSPA*, III Legislatura, 24 de noviembre de 1993, 6.684-6.697.

rios y de recepción de dinero a dos de ellos– transformándolos en un producto con mayor capacidad de servicio, así como instrumentos para procesar todos los documentos bancarios. Finalmente, se incorporaría el ensamblaje de ordenadores de Fujitsu. Las diferentes medidas supondrían la reducción de ciento cuarenta puestos de trabajo. Los trabajadores respondieron con la petición a la Administración de un plan de formación, que fue aceptado por el Gobierno regional, propenso a mantener el mayor número posible de empleos. Por su parte, la empresa reaccionó, entonces, con el anuncio de incentivos[75].

El plan de viabilidad chocó con la dura realidad de las enormes pérdidas de 1992-1993 (4.300 millones de pesetas), el doble de la cantidad prevista, y hubo que aplazarlo un año. El estado general de la sede central no ayudó. Los números rojos del Grupo Fujitsu alcanzaron niveles históricos al superar los 16.000 millones de yenes en su último año. Otras empresas japonesas corrieron una suerte similar, por lo que algunos pensaron en una crisis estructural de la industria informática en Japón. Los analistas atribuyeron la razón principal de estos malos resultados a la reducción de la demanda derivada de la crisis económica que comenzó en los Estados Unidos y que se apoderó de Japón y Europa, así como a la reforma de la estructura empresarial[76]. En 1993, FESA tuvo ventas de 22.400 millones de pesetas pero las pérdidas se mantuvieron en niveles altos. Fujitsu Limited aprobó a principios de abril un aumento de capital con un doble objetivo. El primero era permitir la reestructuración y corroborar la intención de la empresa de permanecer en el mercado español con actividades comerciales e industriales, desmontando los rumores de abandono del país, alimentados quizás por una supuesta práctica poco ortodoxa de Fujitsu Limited dirigida a concentrar las pérdidas en FESA (Hideo Mita, Interview, *ComputerWorld*, 6 de mayo de 1994)[77].

---

[75] Consejero de trabajo, DSPA, III Legislatura, 24 de noviembre de 1993, 6.684-6.697.

[76] Pérdidas y aumento de capital de 5.890 y 8.000 millones de pesetas, respectivamente. Fuerte reducción de la demanda después de las Olimpiadas y la Expo'92, que contribuyó a la pérdida de margen bruto (Hideo Mita, CEO de Fujitsu España, *ComputerWorld*, 10 de septiembre de 1993). La comparación del valor añadido por empresa entre las de participación extranjera mayoritaria y el resto arroja un valor medio mucho más elevado para las primeras, en especial cuando se excluyen los sectores de la energía, el transporte y las comunicaciones. A su vez, este resultado se repite a nivel sectorial, hecho que se explica por el mayor tamaño de las plantas de producción de las empresas con participación extranjera mayoritaria o por la mayor eficiencia en los procesos productivos involucrados (Ortega 1992, 134).

[77] En el Parlamento de Andalucía un grupo a la izquierda del Partido Socialista presentó una Propuesta no de Ley relativa al plan de viabilidad tripartita en Fujitsu. Haciéndose eco de las acusaciones de los sindicatos, el Grupo Parlamentario Socialista señaló que Fujitsu Ltd.

En la vía de enfrentarse a las dificultades aprendemos algo sustancial para entender el funcionamiento de la empresa en particular en los mercados. Los altos costes financieros no fueron el único obstáculo en salvar. La empresa matriz Fujitsu Ltd. aceptó un plan de cuatro años para renovar progresivamente la gama de productos de la fábrica de Málaga. Lo interesante es que, si bien el plan se puso en marcha definitivamente, la multinacional cedió a FESA algunos mercados hasta el momento fuera del área de esta última para mantener una carga de trabajo mínima. El esfuerzo especial en todas las áreas que había llevado al desarrollo de ordenadores totalmente nacionales en la fábrica de Malaga se estrelló con la enorme velocidad de la innovación tecnológica, lo que interrumpió la continuidad[78].

Los planes de Fujitsu Ltd. se concretaron en su aspiración al liderazgo mundial en materia de TIC a partir de 1994, cuando se propuso mejorar el negocio de los sistemas abiertos, fortalecer las ventas de ordenadores personales, reforzar el negocio de los programas informáticos y los servicios, localizar nuevos mercados multimedia y aumentar la producción de dispositivos electrónicos[79].

En ese año, un crecimiento del 11% y un aumento de las ventas en el 6% llevó a FESA a reducir las pérdidas en un 80%, sin perspectivas todavía de un retorno seguro a los beneficios de inmediato. Con el aumento de las ventas, concentrado en la sección de informática, hasta alcanzar los 24.658 millones de pesetas mejoró el margen de beneficios en un 6% respecto al año anterior. Para cumplir los objetivos de crecimiento, FESA no tuvo ningún tipo de inyección de capital de la casa madre. La empresa consiguió reducir significativamente los gastos operativos y financieros. Para aplicar el plan de viabilidad de la planta de Málaga, negoció con la casa matriz japonesa la introducción de un producto de consumo masivo adecuado para su producción en grandes series y con potencial de creación de empleo. A este plan, FESA pretendía

podría haber concentrado las pérdidas en Fujitsu España manteniendo los altos costes de producción causados por la compra de componentes a precios más altos que los de la competencia (*Diario de Sesiones*, iv Legislatura, 30 de noviembre de 1994, 1.307-1.308).

[78] Fujitsu (*Annual Report*, 1995, 1) consideraba que la creación de redes, los sistemas abiertos, el ajuste de derechos y los multimedia eran las palabras clave y las tecnologías que simbolizaban el mundo de las computadoras y las comunicaciones, así como de la sociedad de la información avanzada.

[79] El presidente de Fujitsu Ltd. señaló una demanda particularmente fuerte de terminales de trabajo y ordenadores personales, impulsada por las tendencias hacia los sistemas abiertos y el «rightsizing», como también era el caso de los semiconductores, encabezados por los productos de memoria (Fujitsu Ltd, *Annual Report*, marzo de 1995).

destinar unos 4.000 millones de pesetas[80]. Todo ello se sumó a la política de alianzas estratégicas. Con el fin de unificar su oferta en Europa, Fujitsu acordó con la empresa informática Metrologie Ibérica comercializar sus productos en España (discos duros de mayor capacidad y mejor tiempo de acceso), que eran compatibles con otros sistemas[81].

6. Fusión para competir: Fujitsu-ICL España

Antes de avanzar, parece pertinente aclarar la estructura del mercado, especialmente en lo que respecta al papel del fabricante de ordenadores ICL[82]. Al tomar el control de la mayoría del capital de ICL en 1990, Fujitsu Ltd se fijó el objetivo de encontrar un hueco importante en el mercado europeo –el segundo en importancia tras el japonés– mediante tácticas de acercamiento a los clientes. Para ello, ICL dividió su negocio en tres unidades. En la unidad de Tecnología, centrada casi por completo en la microinformática, era necesario proporcionar productos de calidad al resto de unidades, así como disponer de sus propios canales de venta y telecompra indirectos. La unidad de Servicios

[80] El Grupo Fujitsu alcanzó unas ventas totales de 36.600 millones de dólares, lo que equivale a un aumento del 4% con respecto al año anterior. El crecimiento de las ventas de ordenadores fue del 109% sobre un volumen de 2.094 millones de pesetas durante 1993. La reducción de los gastos de explotación se situó en el 6%, alcanzando los 8.389 millones de pesetas, y dio lugar a un resultado de explotación prácticamente equilibrado, frente a los más de 1.500 millones de pérdidas de explotación del año anterior. Los gastos financieros pasaron de 2.000 millones de pesetas en 1993 a 859 millones en el siguiente. Ello se debió principalmente a una ganancia de capital en 1994, a la reducción de los tipos de interés en 1993 y a la mejora de la gestión del capital circulante (Fujitsu Ltd, *Annual Report*, marzo de 1995; *ComputerWorld*, 9 de junio de 1995).

[81] *Expansión,* 13 de enero de 1994. Metrologie Ibérica se orientó a la sustitución de sucursales y oficinas con representantes, así como a la creación de una línea telefónica gratuita para atender a todos sus clientes en España y Portugal. Dos meses antes había firmado contratos de distribución con Compaq e IBM y buscaba ampliar su mercado de PCs con ICL (*ComputerWorld*, 23 de septiembre de 1994).

[82] ICL, constituida en 1968 por la fusión de English Electric Computers e International Computers and Tabulators, era el noveno mayor fabricante de unidades de ordenadores centrales del mundo, la quinta mayor empresa de ordenadores de Europa occidental y la más lucrativa, con unos beneficios de explotación de 234,6 millones de dólares y unas ventas de 2.610 millones de dólares en 1989. Representaba una quinta parte del mercado británico de ordenadores y entre el 5 y el 10% del mercado de Europa Occidental (*New York Times*, 31 de julio de 1990). ICL comenzó a desarrollar la serie 2900 desde su inicio, al darse cuenta de que en el futuro necesitaría una gama de máquinas para reemplazar las heredadas –1900, Sistema 4 y 4100–, incompatibles en casi todos los aspectos, y racionalizar el costo de mantenimiento de tres líneas de producción (Buckle 1978, 5).

reunía todo lo relacionado con la atención al cliente, el mantenimiento, la consultoría y la subcontratación. La tercera unidad, la de Integración de Sistemas, se centraba en diferentes mercados verticales, definidos por la realidad de cada país. En España, por ejemplo, tales mercados serían la banca y la Administración pública y no existía el riesgo de una división en tres empresas diferentes, como en otros países europeos, sino más bien la perspectiva de una reestructuración en esas tres áreas[83].

Tabla 2. Estructura de gestión de Fujitsu España y Fujitsu
Spain: ciudadanía de los altos ejecutivos

Anterior dirección	
Gerentes japoneses	Directivos españoles
directores (3)	presidente
	vicepresidentes (2)
Gestión reestructurada	
Gerentes japoneses	Directivos españoles
vicepresidente y director general	presidente sin funciones ejecutivas
director de administración	
CEO	
Hacia 1991	
Gerentes japoneses	Directivos españoles
vicepresidente y director general	presidente (sin funciones ejecutivas)
director de administración	–
CEO	altos ejecutivos (6/7)
Hacia 2001	
Gerentes japoneses	Directivos españoles
vicepresidente y CEO	presidente

Fuente: Elaboración propia a partir del texto

[83] Fujitsu Ltd. *Annual report 1998*, 11; *ComputerWorld*, 8 de julio de 1994. Los principales países y regiones pertenecen a segmentos geográficos, excepto el Japón: Europa (Reino Unido, España, Suecia, Alemania, Finlandia y Holanda); las Américas (Estados Unidos, Canadá); otros (China, Tailandia, Vietnam, Malasia, Filipinas, Singapur, Taiwán y Australia) (Fujitsu Ltd., *Annual report,* 1999, 45). A partir del modelo de gestión de la calidad definido por P. Crosby en 1987, Fujitsu ICL España fue evolucionando hasta la autoevaluación según el modelo EFQM, pasado por la certificación según las normas ISO 9000 (Pájaro 1999, 50-52).

La peculiaridad de España jugó un papel en la política de fusiones. A diferencia de lo que ocurría en toda Europa, donde Fujitsu actuaba en numerosos lugares a través de ICL, en España ICL y Fujitsu España mantenían cuotas de mercado separadas, una situación no exenta de rigideces e incomodidades.

Al dividir sus actividades en tres áreas de negocio independientes ICL buscaba unificar recursos y seleccionar mercados en cada división, posibilitando la redefinición de la compañía en la misma línea que otros proveedores. A comienzos de 1995 se creó ICL Sorbus mediante la fusión de los negocios de la compañía norteamericana Sorbus e ICL Customer Service Europe. Hasta el momento, Sorbus era una iniciativa conjunta de ICL y Bell Atlantic Business Systems al 51/49%, focalizada en servicios relacionados con plataformas no suministradas por ICL, mientras que ICL Customer Service, con más de tres años de antigüedad, se concentraba en plataformas suministradas por la propia compañía. Nacía así una organización independiente en el suministro de servicios dentro del mercado informático y en el entorno multifabricante. ICL Sorbus tenía como misión ofrecer su catálogo de servicios agrupado en cuatro grandes familias. La primera de ellas, relativa al centro de proceso de datos, contaba con un grupo de expertos que soportaba los CPDs de IBM, Digital e ICL (*Computerworld*, 2 de junio de 1995).

ICL estaba presente en España desde 1976 a través de ICL Computers, dedicada a la comercialización de *hardware* y ordenadores personales fabricados y distribuidos en Europa. A continuación creó ICL Sorbus España, especializada en la prestación de servicios informáticos a nivel mundial.

Fujitsu España tejió una importante red de distribución en todo el territorio nacional, compuesta por treinta y tres delegaciones comerciales y de mantenimiento, así como por concesionarios y distribuidores. La adopción de otro tipo de acciones dependía de la sede en Tokio, pero era plausible pensar en la posibilidad de otro modelo de operación en España (Tabla 2) (*ComputerWorld*, 10 de marzo de 1995)[84]. FESA actuó en el ámbito de las unidades centrales y en la

---

[84] La experiencia en SECOINSA demostró a Fujitsu Ltd. que las alianzas no son una panacea; hubo desarmonía en las relaciones y en la gestión debido a la confrontación del *ringi-sho* japonés (decisión consensuada) con la capacidad y el mérito en el caso español (Shenkar y Luo 2008, 420). Fujitsu España provenía de una cultura empresarial y una filosofía de negocios que dejaba a los socios españoles el máximo nivel de representatividad (el presidente de SECOINSA y bajo su mando dos vicepresidentes, representantes del INI y de CTNE, junto con un director general). En el siguiente nivel, Fujitsu Ltd colocó tres directores japoneses, dos de ellos residentes en Japón, y el tercero de forma permanente en España, el enlace individual de Fujitsu sobre el terreno (McFatridge 1977, 18). Una vez constituida, Fujitsu España mantuvo sin funciones ejecutivas a un español como presidente, que durante un tiempo compatibilizó su posición con la gestión financiera general de Telefónica.

oferta de soluciones integradas, campos en los que ICL carecía de experiencia. En otras palabras, podría haber espacio para la acción en esa área sin que ICL España se convirtiera necesariamente en una división de FESA (Hideo Mita, Interview, *ComputerWorld*, 10 de septiembre de 1993)[85].

Desde principios de 1995, Fujitsu Ltd. planeó la vía mejor de llevar a cabo una integración sin choques, traumatismos importantes o ajustes. La salida a una situación considerada ilógica se hizo esperar, pero llegó con la formación de Fujitsu-ICL España. Esta empresa nació con una estructura de capital dominada por Fujitsu Ltd y un 20% restante aportado por ICL PLC, obligada a suscribir íntegramente una ampliación de capital por valor de 2.000 millones de pesetas. Con esta fusión de sus empresas en España, Fujitsu e ICL PLC buscaban reforzar la competitividad, mejorando la eficiencia de la organización y aprovechando las sinergias. Fujitsu-lCL España, impulsada hasta la cuarta posición en la industria informática en España, aspiraba a facturar 42.500 millones de pesetas en 1996 con una plantilla de 1.140 empleados y a superar las ventas en años posteriores[86].

Posteriormente, los representantes de la empresa matriz Fujitsu Ltd. accedieron a los más altos cargos ejecutivos. Se trataba de Shigeji Tomio, antiguo responsable de los mercados informáticos de Europa y Estados Unidos, Hiroaki Eguchi como vicepresidente y director general, y Kazuo Sakakura, antiguo ayudante de la presidencia de Fujitsu España, director del departamento comercial para Europa y América de Fujitsu y director de administración en España; fue nombrado vicepresidente en 2006. En 1991, la empresa matriz ocupaba la vicepresidencia y el cargo de director general en una sola persona, mientras que el presidente y seis de los siete altos ejecutivos eran españoles (Whiteside 2012, 895; *DealerWorld*, 1 de septiembre de 1996 y 1 de enero de 2002; *BORME*, Registro Mercantil de Madrid, T 17829, F 30, S 8, HM 307271, I/A 65 (26.01.07). El cuartel general tuvo sumo cuidado en controlar el departamento de asuntos generales y relaciones exteriores de Fujitsu España, vital en su papel de enlace entre la dirección japonesa y la realidad española (*ComputerWorld*, 15 de abril de 1994). El nombramiento de cargos en las sucursales y divisiones internacionales fue una práctica de Fujitsu en los distintos países; en 1990, Yasushi Nakamura y Atsushi Iwakata fueron director y gerente de Fujitsu América (San José, CL) y Fujitsu Europa (Uxbridge, Reino Unido), respectivamente (Carr 2012, 407).

85   En 1995, ICL rechazó comentar las especulaciones sobre la posibilidad de que ICL España fuera absorbida en breve por Fujitsu España y se reafirmó en el mantenimiento de buenas relaciones (*Computer Business Review*, November 8, 1995).

86   En cuanto a la ilógica o poco realista presencia de dos empresas del grupo Fujitsu Ltd, la dirección japonesa consideró que las actividades no se superponían totalmente, especialmente en las áreas de servicios y productos, sino que tenían campos de acción diferentes (*ComputerWorld*, 13 de septiembre de 1996). Fujitsu España entabló negociaciones con los sindicatos para que la regulación de empleo alcanzara el 9,9% de una plantilla de unos 1.400 trabajadores (*El País*, 9 de septiembre de 1996; 1 de octubre de 1996). En 1998 se firmó un convenio colectivo de Fujitsu ICL España: *BOE*, 144, 17 de junio de 1998; posteriormente, abrió una nueva sede en las cercanías de Madrid (*ABC*, 16 de julio de 2001). En

Fujitsu ICL España continuó con la producción en Málaga de impresoras, ordenadores y equipos para sistemas bancarios[87]. En contra de las previsiones y pese al supuesto buen funcionamiento de las sinergias, Fujitsu-ICL terminó el año 1996/1997 con una facturación menor –42.500 millones de pesetas– y con pérdidas de 1.300 millones. Sin embargo, en el siguiente ejercicio logró invertir la situación y obtener más beneficios[88].

A comienzo de 2002, en medio de la caída de las empresas punto com con nuevas pérdidas que empujaron a Fujitsu a recortar el 10% de la fuerza de trabajo, se introdujo en el campo del ensamblaje de dispositivos electrónicos para automóviles y placas de circuitos impresos (PCB). Por su parte, las secciones de ventas y servicios de Fujitsu habían avanzado hacia un modelo de proveedor de soluciones, logrando beneficios en el área de la integración de sistemas.

Finalmente, a pesar de las previsiones anteriores, en el marco de una reestructuración global, Fujitsu Ltd. reorganizó su actividad en España mediante la separación de las unidades de fabricación y venta, lo que dividiría a Fujitsu ICL España en dos empresas independientes, filiales al completo y denominadas Fujitsu Manufacturing Spain y Fujitsu Spain. Su objetivo era mejorar la competitividad, la eficiencia y la capacidad de respuesta de ambas, de modo que cada una de ellas se centrara en sus respectivos campos de especialización y competencias. En este diseño, Fujitsu Spain se encargó de englobar el Servicio de Atención al Cliente de Fujitsu y otras filiales, así como de proporcionar soluciones y servicios que incorporaran nuevos servicios de subcontratación. Se encomendó a Fujitsu Manufacturing Spain la misión de concentrarse en la reducción de los plazos de entrega y los costes y en la mejora de la calidad. Esta rama industrial debía aprovechar su experiencia y conocimientos en dispositivos electrónicos para el automóvil, cajeros

septiembre de 1998, el Banco Popular y Fujitsu ICL España lanzaron la banca electrónica del Banco por Internet (CNMV, 19 de julio de 1998).

[87] Fujitsu España fabricaba en Málaga impresoras para la matriz y para fuera del grupo (Gustavo Hylander, entrevistado por el autor, 4 de agosto de 2020). Fujitsu ICL España acordó con Fujitsu Siemens Computers, una empresa conjunta al cincuenta por ciento entre Fujitsu Ltd y Siemens AG, convertirse en el principal proveedor de plataformas informáticas en Europa, transfiriéndole su unidad de negocio de venta de plataformas basada en el canal. Aunque esta instalación se destinó inicialmente a la producción de ordenadores personales, el objetivo era fabricar posteriormente los servidores, lo que supuso duplicar la producción de la fábrica hasta las 80.000 unidades (*Channel Partner,* 14 de enero de 2000).

[88] *ComputerWorld*, 4 de julio de 1997; *New York Times*, 21 de agosto de 2001. En el año fiscal 1997/1998, Fujitsu alcanzó 44.400 millones de pesetas y un beneficio neto de 600 millones de pesetas (*PCWorld*, 1 de diciembre de 1998).

automáticos y conjuntos de placas de circuitos impresos con el fin de prestar servicios de producción electrónica (Electronic Manufacturing Service) y tener una base sólida en Europa para competir en el mercado de la electrónica del automóvil.

La reestructuración garantizó la relación entre ambas empresas, ya que Fujitsu Manufacturing Spain, ubicada en Málaga, se especializaría en la producción de cajeros automáticos, dispositivos eléctricos para la industria automotriz y PCB para abastecer a la nueva empresa de ventas y servicios, Fujitsu Spain, con sede en Madrid[89].

Fujitsu logró estar presente en todo el mercado español, con la consiguiente capacidad de prestar servicios a los clientes dondequiera que estuvieran. Así, Fujitsu mantuvo una enorme red de cajeros automáticos en España, desde los que también operó con empresas globales presentes en otros países europeos y en América Latina[90].

6. Conclusión

Esta investigación ha abordado la internacionalización de la TIC japonesa Fujitsu Ltd a través de fusiones y adquisiciones y alianzas desde la perspectiva de una de sus filiales europeas –Fujitsu España– primero como empresa conjunta con la operadora monopolista Telefónica y luego como filial única. Ha analizado de forma descriptiva las razones de la implantación de las multinacionales TIC japonesas en España a finales del siglo xx como una fracción de la IED mundial a través de la creación y evolución de la empresa Fujitsu España. La evidencia empírica ha demostrado que es imposible concebir la relación IED/multinacional sin tener en cuenta la implicación de las diversas instituciones políticas o culturales, ya sean transnacionales, estatales o regionales (Estado nación, Unión Europea, empresa, sindicatos), en sus diferentes niveles de influencia.

---

[89] *ComputerWorld*, 19 de abril de 2002; *Channel Partner*, 22 de abril de 2002. En 2001, los destinos más importantes eran los Estados Unidos, China, Sudáfrica y el Reino Unido (*ComputerWorld*, 30 de septiembre de 2002 y 22 de junio de 2001). Véase para el marco más general (Valdaliso 2018, 1-26).

[90] Entrevista con Ángeles Delgado, directora general de Fujitsu España (*Executive excellence*, 95, 2012, 40-43).

Además, para comprender mejor la importancia de la descripción del caso, el capítulo ha contribuido al conocimiento general con un marco de los determinantes de la IED empresarial japonesa.

Por otra parte, la empresa hace un guiño a las nuevas orientaciones en España hacia una mayor flexibilidad/movilidad de la mano de obra y la liberalización de la economía. En este sentido, planeó la ampliación de la fábrica de Málaga en la Costa del Sol bajo las nuevas orientaciones de España hacia una mayor liberalización en 1996. También es evidente que la preocupación de los poderes públicos españoles por el empleo se antepone a las cuestiones de soberanía nacional. El estudio de caso tiene un rasgo distintivo, ya que la tecnología predominante en España no era japonesa. En este sentido, además, no se trata de una alianza con el líder tecnológico (IBM) sino con un socio tecnológico que aspiraba a ocupar los primeros puestos en la escena mundial.

La actuación de Fujitsu Ltd en España altera la tendencia a sustituir la estrategia de inversión en las filiales extranjeras por asociaciones más pequeñas con empresas occidentales. En este sentido, la multinacional japonesa mantuvo e incluso incrementó el nivel de compromiso en el país, en el sentido de algunas teorías de internacionalización (escuela de Uppsala). Cabe destacar que Fujitsu España representa más bien una reafirmación de una inversión anterior que un caso de primera inversión. Por lo tanto, el conocimiento del mercado que propugna el modelo de Uppsala ya se ha logrado a través de la experiencia en ese mercado específico.

En cuanto a la ubicación geográfica de los centros de I+D, Fujitsu España cumple con la tipología de Li y Yue (2005, 320) de esquema policéntrico descentralizado y concentrado en el país receptor, más cercano a los mercados de productos. Contrariamente a la tendencia evolutiva de la investigación y el desarrollo en China, por ejemplo, las estrategias de configuración de la I+D de Fujitsu en España muestran una trayectoria fija de investigación y desarrollo concentrada. Sin embargo, la estabilidad iba unida a las alteraciones en la estructura corporativa, ya que el centro especializado de I+D se convirtió en una unidad jurídica independiente (Ingenia) bajo la forma de una empresa conjunta.

En cuanto a la acumulación de capacidades, la evidencia empírica apunta a la movilidad funcional de las carreras de los directivos de alto nivel mediante una rotación a través de diversas funciones y unidades. A su vez, apoya la movilidad geográfica del personal sobre la base de una pauta de intercambio en una doble dirección entre la empresa matriz y la filial.

Un aspecto relacionado con la cuestión clave de la repercusión de la IED en el país receptor requiere una explicación más detallada. Desde el país anfitrión, el estudio arroja luz, en esencia, sobre la dependencia tecnológica y económica de España, dependencia que el socio no reduce en lo más mínimo.

Cerramos el capítulo –y el libro, en realidad– con la certeza de haber palpado uno de los males de un modelo de crecimiento dual basado en el turismo+tecnología avanzada y en la asociación con multinacionales extranjeras.

Fuentes primarias

Computer History Museum, Oral history

Congreso de los Diputados, España

Fujitsu Ltd.

Gustavo Hylander, Entrevistado por el autor, 4 de agosto de 2020.

José Estrada, Entrevista con el autor, 22 de julio de 2020.

Library of Congress, The Association for Diplomatic Studies and Training Foreign Affairs Oral History Project

Parlamento de Andalucía

Telefónica de España

Telefónica Internacional

Teófilo J. del Pozo Entrevista con el autor.

Hemeroteca

ABC

Boletín Oficial de la Junta de Andalucía (BOJA)

ComputerWorld

El País

La Opinión de Málaga

Silicon Newsletters

The Telegraph

Referencias

Aaron, Carl. 1999. *The Political Economy of Japanese Foreign Direct Investment in the US and the UK: Multinationals, Subnational Regions and the Investment Location Decision*. Houndmills: Macmillan Press.

Aid, Christian. 2004. *Behind the Mask: The Real Face of Corporate Social Responsibility*. Londres: Christian Aid.

Amatori, Franco y Colli, Andrea. 2013. *Business History: Complexities and Comparisons*. Londres: Routledge.

Ando, Ken-ichi. 2005. *Japanese Multinationals in Europe: A Comparison of the Automobile and Pharmaceutical Industries*. Aldershot: Edward Elgar.

Antonietti, Roberto; Bronzini, Raffaello y Cainelli, Giulio. 2015. «Inward greenfield FDI and innovation». *Economia e Politica Industriale* 42: 93–116.

Arroyo, Luis. 1980. *Del bit a la telemática: introducción a los ordenadores*. Madrid: Alhambra.

Bajo-Rubio, Óscar. 2020. «The role of foreign direct investment in growth: Spain, 1964-2013». *GLO Discussion Paper Series, Global Labor Organization*, nº 676: 1-16.

Barceló, Miquel. 2008. *Una historia de la informática*. Barcelona: UOC.

Batiz-Lazo, Bernardo y Efthymiou, Leonidas. 2016. *The Book of Payments: Historical and Contemporary Views on the Cashless Society*. Londres: Palgrave-Macmillan.

Belderbos, René A. 1997. *Japanese Electronics Multinationals and Strategic Trade Policies*. Oxford: Clarendon Press.

Beltrán, Joaquín. 2009. «Comunidades asiáticas en España». *Revista CIDOB d'Afers Internacionals 92*, enero: 15-37.

Beltz, Cynthia A. (ed.) 1995. *The Foreign Investment Debate: Opening Markets Abroad Or Closing Markets at Home?* Washington: American Enterprise Institute.

Birkinshaw, Julian. 2000. *Entrepreneurship in the global firm*. Londres: Sage.

Blit, Joel. 2018. «Foreign R&D Satellites as a Medium for the International Diffusion of Knowledge». *Canadian Journal of Economics* 51, 4, November: 1118-1150. https://ssrn.com/abstract=3199206 or http://dx.doi.org/10.2139/ssrn.3199206.

Blomström, Magnus y Kokko, Ari. 1997. «How Foreign Investment Affects Host Countries». *Policy research working paper, The World Bank*. 1.745, marzo: 1-41.

Blonigen, Bruce A. 2006. «Foreign Direct Investment Behavior of Multinational Corporations». *NBER Reporter: Research Summary*, Winter: 11-14.

Boutellier, Roman et al. 2008. *Managing Global Innovation: Uncovering the Secrets of Future Competitiveness.* Berlín: Springer.

Bucheli, Marcelo y Salvaj, Erika. 2014. «Adaptation Strategies of Multinational Corporations, State-Owned Enterprises, and Domestic Business Groups to Economic and Political Transitions: A Network Analysis of the Chilean Telecommunications». *Past Working Papers* 15, Universidad del Desarrollo, School of Business and Economics.

Buckle, John K. 1978. *The origins of the 2900 series.* Londres: The Macmillan Press Ltd.

Buckley, Peter J. y Casson, Mark. 1976. *The Future of the Multinational Enterprise.* Londres: Macmillan.

Buigues, Pierre y Jacquemin, Alexis. 1992. «Inversión extranjera directa y exportaciones en el Mercado Común; aspectos teóricos, empíricos y de política económica». *Moneda y Crédito* 194: 39-101.

Burgenmeier, Beat y Mucchielli, Jean-Louis. 2012. *Multinationals and Europe 1992: Strategies for the Future.* Abingdon: Routledge.

Business International Corporation. 1989. *Gaining a competitive edge in the new Europe: strategic responses of non-European companies to 1992.* Nueva York: Business International Corporation.

Calvo, Ángel. 2008. «State, firms and technology. The rise of multinational telecommunications companies: ITT and the Compañía Telefónica Nacional de España, 1924–1945». *Business History* 50, 4: 455-473.

Calvo, Ángel. 2014. *Telecomunicaciones y el nuevo mundo digital en España: La aportación de Standard Eléctrica.* Barcelona: Ariel/Fundación Telefónica.

Calvo, Ángel. 2016. *Historia de Telefónica: 1976-2000. Las telecomunicaciones en la España democrática.* Barcelona: Ariel/Fundación Telefónica.

Calvo, Ángel. 2021. «Japanese ICT multinationals in Southern Europe by the end of the twentieth century: Fujitsu in Spain». *Journal of the Knowledge Economy* 12, marzo: https://rdcu.be/cgGcw

Cámara de Cuentas de Andalucía 2013. *Fiscalización de regularidad de la Sociedad para la Promoción y Reconversión Económica de Andalucía (SOPREA) y de los fondos sin personalidad jurídica en los que interviene.* Ejercicio 2010 (OE 10/2011), Sevilla, marzo.

Campbell-Kelly, Martin. 2004. *Computer: a history of the information machine*. Boulder CO: Westview.

Cepal, 2005. *La inversión extranjera en América Latina y el Caribe*. Santiago de Chile: Naciones Unidas.

Ceruzzi, Paul E. 2003. *A history of modern computing*. Cambridge MA: MIT Press.

Chandler, Alfred D. Jr y Mazlish. Bruce. 2005. *Leviathans: Multinational Corporations and the New Global History*. Nueva York: Cambridge University Press.

Chang, Ha-Joon. 2010. *23 Things They Don't Tell You About Capitalism*. Londres: Penguin Books.

Child, John et al. 2005. *Cooperative Strategy*. Oxford: Oxford University Press.

Cohen, Stephen D. 2007. *Multinational Corporations and Foreign Direct Investment: Avoiding Simplicity, Embracing Complexity*. Oxford: Oxford University Press.

Colin, Egan y McKiernan, Peter. 1994. *Inside Fortress Europe: Strategies for the Single Market*. Londres: Economist Intelligence Unit.

Commission of the European Communities. 1987. *Social Europe*. nº 2/87. Luxemburgo: Office for Official Publications of the European Communities.

Commission of the European Communities. 1990. *Panorama of EC Industry*. Luxemburgo: Office for Official Publications of the European Communities.

Commission of the European Communities. 1991. *Employment and social aspects of electronic media and advanced telecommunications services*. Luxemburgo: Office for Official Publications of the European Communities.

Coopey, Richard. (ed.) 2004. *Information Technology Policy: An International History*. Nueva York: OUP.

Corsino, Marco y Giuri, Paola. 2018. «Computer Industry». En *The Palgrave Encyclopedia of Strategic Management*, editado por Mie Augier y David J. Teece. Londres: Palgrave Macmillan.

Cortada, James W. 1983. *An annotated bibliography on the history of data processing*. Westport CONN: Greenwood Press.

De Mateo, Elías y Heredia, Víctor Manuel. 2012. *Málaga Tecnológica*. Málaga: Fundación Málaga.

Díaz, Adenso, Yayoi Kawamura y González-Torre, Pilar. 1999. «Cultural practices in the Spanish subsidiaries of Japanese companies». *Industrial Management & Data System*. Vol. 99, nº. 3: 115-120. https://doi.org/10.1108/02635579910250439

Dunning, John H.; Lundan, Sarianna M. 2008. *Multinational Enterprises and the Global Economy*. Cheltenham: Edward Elgar.

Egan, C. y McKiernan, Peter. 1994. *Inside Fortress Europe: Strategies for the Single Market*. Munich: Addison-Wesley Longmann.

EU Commission. 1973. *Community policy on data processing. Communication of the Commission to the Council*. SEC (73) 4300 final, 21 November.

European Commission. 2017. *Investment in the EU Member States*. Institutional Paper 062, October.

Fletcher, Andrew E. 2013. *The European Electronics Industry Towards 1992: A Profile of Market Leaders*. Oxford: Elsevier.

Fujitsu España, *1987/1988. Annual report*.

Fujitsu España, *1992. Annual report*.

Fujitsu Ltd. *1996. Annual report*.

Fujitsu Ltd. *2000. Annual report*.

Fundació Jaume Bofill. 1989. *Catalunya 77-78. Societat, Economia, Política, Cultura*, Barcelona: Publicacions de la Fundació Jaume Bofill-Edicions de la Magrana.

García, Eva, Elena Gayo, y Luis del Pozo. 2006. *RIP-Watch analysis of the regional dimensions of investment in research case study regional report: Andalusia (Spain)*. Madrid: IDETRA.

Ghauri, Pervez N. y Oxelheim, Lars. 2003. *European Union and the Race for Foreign Direct Investment in Europe*. Amsterdam; Elsevier

Graham, Edward M. y Krugman, Paul R. 1993. «The Surge in Foreign Direct Investment in the 1980s». En *Foreign Direct Investment*, editado por Kenneth A. Froot, 13-36, Chicago: University of Chicago Press.

Grimes, Seamus y Collins, Patrick. 2009. «The contribution of the overseas ICT sector to expanding R&D investment in Ireland». *Irish Geography*, 2: 1: 45-67.

Hitt, Michael A. et al. 2012. *Strategic Management: Concepts and Cases: Competitiveness and Globalization*. Andover: Cengage Learning.

Hollerman, Leon y Myers, Ramon H. 1996. *The Effect of Japanese Investment on the World Economy: A Six-Country Study, 1970–1991*. Stanford CL: Hoover Press.

Ito, Takatoshi y Hoshi, Takeo. 2020. *The Japanese Economy*. Cambridge MA: MIT Press.

Japan External Trade Organization, 1996-2016. *Reports and Statistics (on-line). Japan's Outward and Inward Foreign Direct Investment, 1996-2016*. Minato-Tokio: JETRO. https://www.jetro.go.jp/en/reports/statistics.html.

Japan External Trade Organization. 2000. *JETRO White Paper on Foreign Direct Investment 2000*. Minato-Tokio: JETRO. https://www.jetro.go.jp/ext_images/en/reports/white_paper/invest2000.pdf

Jarillo, J. Carlos y Martínez, Jon I. 1990. «Different roles for subsidiaries: The case of multinational corporations in Spain». *Strategic Management Journal* 11, n.° 7: 501-512.

Jensen, Nathan M. 2006. *States and the Multinational Corporation: A Political Economy of Direct Foreign Investment*. Princeton NJ: Princeton University Press.

Johanson, Jan y Vahlne, Jan-Erik. 1977. «The internationalizationprocess of the firm: A model of knowledge development and increasing foreign market commitments». *Journal of International Business Studies* 8, n.° 1: 23-32.

Johanson, Jan y Weidershiem-Paul, Finn. 1975. «The internationalization of the firm. Four Swedish cases». *Journal of Management Studies* 12, n.° 3: 305-322.

Kim, Young-Chan. 2018. *Japanese Inward Investment in UK Car Manufacturing*. Abingdon: Routledge.

Klein, Naomi. 2000. *No Logo: Taking Aim at the Brand Bullies*. Nueva York: Picador.

Kumar Nagesh. 2001. «Determinants of location of overseas R&D activity of multinational enterprises: the case of U.S. and Japanese corporations». *Research Policy* 30, n.° 1: 159-174.

Lagerström, Katarina; Schweizer, Roger y Jakobsson, Johan. 2019. «Building R&D capability in subsidiaries - conceptualization of a process perspective». *Multinational Business Review* 27, 1: 35-53.

Li, Jiatao y Yue, Deborah R. 2005. «Managing Global Research and Development in China: Patterns of R&D Configuration and Evolution». *Technology Analysis and Strategic Management* 17, 3, septiembre: 317–337.

Lipsey, Robert E. 2002. «Home and Host Country Effects of FDI». *NBER Working Paper* 9, 293, National Bureau of Economic Research.

Lipsey, Robert E. 2000. «Interpreting Developed Countries' Foreign Direct Investment». *NBER Working Paper* 7, 810, National Bureau of Economic Research.

McFatridge, Joe. 1977. *Fujitsu in Spain: technology and tradition*. Tokio: Sophia University.

Maixé-Altés, Joan C. 2012. *Innovació i compromis social: 60 anys d'informatització i creixement, 1950-2011*. Barcelona: Caixa d'Estalvis i Pensions de Barcelona.

Ministerio de Industria y Energía. 1984. *Informe sobre la industria española*. Madrid: Secretaría General Técnica.

Morris, Jonathan (ed.). 2002. *Japan and the Global Economy: Issues and Trends in the 1990s*. Londres y Nueva York: Routledge.

Nalbantian, Haig R. y Guzzo, Richard A. 2009. «Making Mobility Matter». *Harvard Business Review*, marzo: 1-10.

Nora, Simon y Minc, Alain. 1978. *L'informatisation de la société. Rapport à M. le Président de la République*. París: Seuil.

Nygaard, Arne y Dahlstrom, Robert. 1992. «Multinational company strategy and host country policy». *Scandinavian Journal of Management* 8, n.º1, diciembre: 3-13.

Ortega, Eloísa. 1992. *La inversión extranjera directa en España (1986-1990)*. Madrid: Banco de España.

Pájaro, Senén J. 1999. «La gestión del conocimiento, factor clave». *Qualitas hodie*, nº.50: 50-52.

Pearce, Robert D. y Papanastassiou, Marina. 1996. *The Technological Competitiveness of Japanese Multinationals: The European Dimension*. Ann Arbor MI: University of Michigan Press.

Rodrik, Dani. 2011. *The Globalization Paradox: Democracy and the Future of the World Economy*. Nueva York y Londres: W. W. Norton & Company.

Rodrik, Dani. 2006. «Goodbye Washington consensus, hello Washington confusion? A review of the World Bank's economic growth in the 1990s: Learning from a decade of reform». *Journal of Economic Literature* 44, n°.4. 973-987.

Romera, Felipe. 1991. «Profit Through the Silicon Cycle: The Next Ten Years Andalucia Technology Park». *Dataquest's European Semiconductor Industry Conference*, Marbella, 90-107.

Romera, Felipe. [s. f.]. *Una aproximación histórica y apasionada al sistema de innovación andaluz desde el parque tecnológico de Andalucía*. Sevilla: Academia Andaluza de Ciencia Regional.

Sachwald, Frédérique. 1995. *Japanese Firms in Europe*. Luxemburgo: Harwood.

Secretaría General Técnica. 1977. *La Informática en España 1976*. Madrid: Servicio central de publicaciones.

Shenkar, Oded y Luo, Yadong. 2008. *International Business*. Thousand Oaks CA: SAGE.

Shimizu, Ikko. 1995. *The Dark Side of Japanese Business: Three «industry Novels»*. Nueva York: Sharpe.

Schlender, Brenton R. y Alpert, Mark. 1991. «How Fujitsu will tackle the giants». *Fortune* 124, 7, enero: 78-84.

Strach, Pavel y Everett, André M. 2006. «Knowledge transfer within Japanese multi-nationals: Building a theory». *Journal of Knowledge Management* 10, n.º 1, enero: 55-68. 10.1108/13673270610650102

Status of Japanese-affiliated manufacturing operations in Europe. 1992. *JPRS Report, reproduced by U.S. Department of Commerce.* Springfield VA: Technical information service.

Stiglitz, Joseph E. 2002. *Globalization and Its Discontents.* Nueva York: Norton and Company.

Strange, Roger. 2002. *Japanese Manufacturing Investment in Europe: Its Impact on the UK Economy.* Londres y Nueva York: Routledge.

Thomas, Richard et al. 1990. «ESF-A European Programme for Evolutionary Introduction of Software Factories». *ICL Technical Journal* 7, 2, noviembre: 307-318.

Turner, Louis. 2010. *Industrial Collaboration with Japan.* Londres: Routledge.

United Nations Conference on Trade and Development. 1993. *World investment Report 1993.* Nueva York: United Nations.

United Nations. 1999. *World Investment Report 1999. Foreign Direct Investment and the Challenge of Development.* Nueva York y Ginebra: United Nations.

U.S. Congress, U.S. 1983. *Office of Technology Assessment, International Competitiveness in Electronics.* Washington DC: Government Printing Office.

Valdaliso, José Mª. 2018. «Accounting for the resilience of the machine tool industry in Spain, c. 1960-2015». *Business History* 62, n.º 1: 1-26.

Veeramani, Siv et al. 2019. «Financial theories of foreign direct investment: a review of literature». *Journal of Industrial and Business Economics* 47: 185–217.

Wedgwood, C.G. 2013. *European Electronics Directory 1994: Systems and Applications.* Kidlington: Elsevier.

Whiteside, R. M. 2012. *Major Companies of Europe 1991-1992. Vol. 1: Major Companies of the Continental European Community.* Londres: Springer.

Wilkins, Mira. 1970. *The Emergence of Multinational Enterprise: American Business Abroad from the Colonial Era to 1914.* Cambridge MA: Harvard University Press.

World Intellectual Property Organization. 2015. *World Intellectual Property Indicators 2015.* Ginebra: WIPO.

Yan, Aimin y Luo, Yadong. 2016. *International Joint Ventures: Theory and Practice: Theory and Practice.* Abingdon: Routledge.

Young, Stephen (ed.). 2004. *Multinationals and Public Policy.* Cheltenham: Edward Elgar.

Young, Stephen y Hamill, James. 1992. *Europe and the multinationals: issues and responses for the 1990s.* Aldershot: Edward Elgar.

Anexo 1. Inversión industrial extranjera del Japón por países de destino ($)

País	1996	1997	1998	1999	2000
Alemania	4.217	5.412	4.711	3.431	4.130
Reino Unido	20.320	28.796	24.801	17.999	21.765
Francia	1.515	2.788	3.061	3.019	3.071
Holanda	8.440	8.106	9.283	17.482	16.667
Italia	474	696	708	695	642
Bélgica y Luxemburgo	6.033	4.372	4.244	3.404	3.932
Suiza	2.967	2.479	2.208	1.102	978
Suecia	122	103	128	55	1.433
España	964	928	974	932	1.131

Fuente: Elaboración propia a partir de Japan External
Trade Organization (1996-2016).

Anexo 2. Filiales de empresas industriales japonesas en Europa (número)

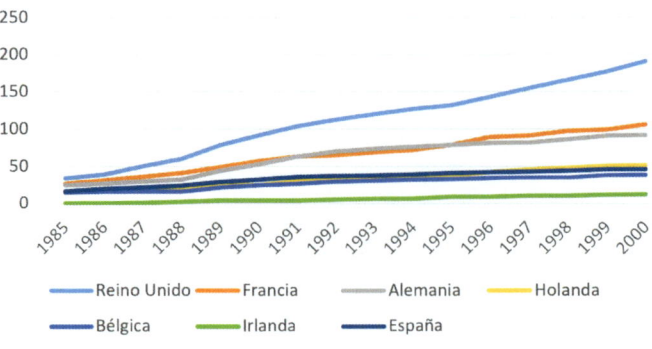

Fuente: Elaboración a partir de Jetro 2006, 3

Anexo 3. ICL, el gigante británico de la informática

ICL, el gigante británico de la informática, vivió su edad de oro en el decenio de 1970 y entró en años turbulentos a continuación, coincidiendo con la llegada de un producto competitivo de la relevancia del ordenador personal compatible de IBM y la consiguiente demanda de menores costes en la industria informática británica. En 1980, sus ventas en el extranjero fueron seis veces superiores a las de 1973 y ofreció una gama de productos más completa y competitiva. El valor de su clientela mundial superó los 2.000 millones de libras esterlinas en 80 países, junto con el de IBM, el mayor de todos los fabricantes de ordenadores, fuera de los Estados Unidos y el Japón. Sin embargo, la compañía sufrió una fuerte caída en sus beneficios a mediados de los 80. En 1980, una dramática caída en la demanda mundial de ordenadores, sobre todo los de gran tamaño, golpeó a ICL, así como a muchos otros fabricantes de ordenadores. ICL tomó medidas enérgicas para contener los costes, incluyendo el 10% de los despidos anunciados y una propuesta a los sindicatos para un aumento salarial nulo en 1981: Ministro de Industria y Tecnología de la Información (Sr. Kenneth Baker), House of Commons, Deb, 6 de abril de 1981, vol 2 cc, 746-758. El gobierno británico acudió al rescate de la LCI en la crisis financiera con una garantía de préstamo, que le permitió mantenerse independiente. A pesar de los esfuerzos de la italiana Olivetti y la holandesa Philips por llegar a un pacto, ICL cambió la dirección de la asociación y aceptó acceder a las tecnologías de LSI de Fujitsu. Combinadas con la capacidad CAD interna, permitieron a ICL diseñar y fabricar las computadoras de la serie 39 y vender computadoras personales también en 1984 (Silicon Newsletters, 18 de agosto de 2017). Child et al. (2005, 408), tras integrarse en la «familia» de Fujitsu, ICL mantuvo la identidad y fue tratada como un socio en lugar de una filial; finalmente, la marca desapareció para ser engullida por la casa madre (*The Telegraph*, 21 de junio de 2001).

Anexo 4. Fujitsu Ltd.: distribución geográfica de las ventas

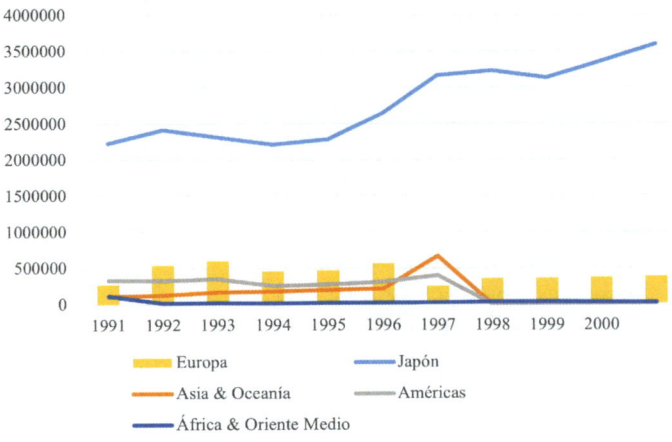

Fuente: Elaboración a partir de Fujitsu, *Annual Reports*.

IV. Resúmenes y abstracts

I. Los fundamentos: materiales y componentes

1. Los componentes de la Tercera Revolución Industrial: AT&T Microelectrónica de España[1]

En este capítulo se examina una de las dos iniciativas empresariales más destacadas en la tecnología de los semiconductores: AT&T Microelectrónica de España. Se trata de una de las realizaciones estrella impulsadas por la operadora monopolista CTNE en la década de 1980, fruto de la cooperación con una líder del sector: la multinacional norteamericana AT&T. En el contexto de la convergencia entre informática y electrónica, la feroz competencia entre numerosos gobiernos europeos por atraerse al mismo socio añadió nuevos elementos al acuerdo. A su vez, la iniciativa entraña una apuesta por el acceso a los componentes básicos, crucial para la competencia y el progreso en las TIC en su calidad de núcleo de las telecomunicaciones, los ordenadores, los bienes de consumo y otros sistemas electrónicos. Si se considera el país de origen, estamos ante una inversión horizontal o producción en el extranjero de la misma línea de productos que en casa y desde el punto de vista del país receptor, se trata de la suma de sustitución de importaciones, aumento de exportación e inversión con iniciativa mixta público-privada condicionada por

---

[1] Versión preliminar 2017. «Multinacionales, Estado y empresa semipública en la industria de tecnología avanzada durante la década de 1980». *Investigaciones de Historia Económica - Economic History Research (IHE-EHR)*, 13, 1: 51-62

la condición mixta de la empresa concernida. La transferencia de tecnología resulta ser de índole vertical por implicar un movimiento desde un país avanzado a otro más atrasado. El capítulo se basa en fuentes primarias de diversa procedencia y naturaleza (CTNE, Congreso de los Diputados, Archivo SEPI (INI), Archivo Margaret Thatcher, NATO Archives y Securities Exchange Commission, USA), junto a fuente oral y una extensa bibliografía secundaria.

Abstract

This chapter examines one of the two most prominent business ventures in semiconductor technology: AT&T Microelectrónica de España. It is one of the star achievements of the monopoly operator CTNE in the 1980s, the result of cooperation with a leader in the sector: the US multinational AT&T. In the context of the convergence between IT and electronics, the fierce competition between many European governments to attract the same partner added new elements to the agreement. At the same time, the initiative entails a commitment to access to basic components, crucial for competition and progress in ICT as the core of telecommunications, computers, consumer goods and other electronic systems. From the point of view of the country of origin, it is a horizontal investment or production abroad of the same product line as at home, and from the point of view of the host country, it is the sum of import substitution, export growth and mixed public-private initiative investment conditioned by the mixed status of the company concerned. Technology transfer turns out to be vertical in nature as it involves a movement from an advanced country to a more backward one. The chapter is based on primary sources of various origins and nature (CTNE, Congress of Deputies, SEPI Archive (INI), Margaret Thatcher Archive, NATO Archives and Securities Exchange Commission, USA), together with oral sources and an extensive secondary bibliography.

2. Los componentes. Alianzas internacionales por la autosuficiencia en la electrónica: la paneuropea European Silicon Structures[2]

Este capítulo se centra en una de las alianzas forjadas en Europa, muy desviada de las prácticas de la mayoría por involucrar a una empresa con socios

---

[2]   Versión preliminar publicada en: 2016. «Strategic Alliances in the European Industries of the Third Industrial Revolution». *Journal of Evolutionary Studies in Business*. Vol. 2, nº1: 235-265. https://raco.cat/index.php/JESB/article/view/311908

exclusivamente europeos. Adopta la perspectiva de un país periférico (España) en la economía global y del estatus especial de al menos uno de los socios en un monopolio. Por último, el capítulo sigue la metodología del estudio de caso, que pretende profundizar en la complejidad de los procesos y los fenómenos en cuestión. La investigación responde a la necesidad de un enfoque alternativo para el análisis de la industria, especialmente importante para las industrias de base tecnológica y las industrias de alta tecnología más turbulentas. La primera parte examina la creación de European Silicon Structures como alianza estratégica en la industria europea de semiconductores. Las partes segunda y tercera examinan el caso de España y el papel de la demanda con el ejemplo de Telefónica. Las conclusiones se presentan en la sección final.

Abstract

This chapter focuses on one of the alliances forged in Europe, which deviates from mainstream practice by involving a company with exclusively European partners. It adopts the perspective of a peripheral country (Spain) in the global economy and the special status of at least one of the partners in a monopoly. Finally, the chapter follows the case study methodology, which aims to delve into the complexity of the processes and phenomena in question. The research responds to the need for an alternative approach to industry analysis, especially important for technology-based industries and the more turbulent high-tech industries. The first part examines the creation of European Silicon Structures as a strategic alliance in the European semiconductor industry. The second and third parts examine the case of Spain and the role of demand with the example of Telefónica.

3. La tecnología avanzada en el sector público: la división electrónica del INI[3]

Este capítulo aborda un sector estratégico en los primeros años del nuevo milenio, cuyos resultados ya se han presentado parcialmente. Se estructura en cuatro grandes apartados, que incluyen la introducción, una presentación

---

[3] Versión preliminar 2019. «Consolidation and rationalization of the public companies in Spain: the information and communication technologies (ICT) holding». *Journal of Evolutionary Studies in Business*. Vol. 2, n°1: 142-179.

del sector público de las tecnologías de la información y la comunicación, la reestructuración del sector público de las TIC y el nacimiento del grupo Inisel, llamado a jugar un importante papel en el futuro por su protagonismo en la creación de la empresa tecnológica Indra. El capítulo, de carácter predominantemente descriptivo, combina la historia industrial con la gestión estratégica, y metodológicamente es un estudio de caso que utiliza fuentes primarias de origen público y privado junto con informes y estudios de grandes organizaciones internacionales.

Abstract

This chapter addresses a strategic sector in the first years of the new millennium, the results of which have already been partially presented. It is structured in four main sections, which include the introduction, a presentation of the public ICT sector, the restructuring of the public ICT sector and the birth of the Inisel group, which will play an important role in the future due to its leading role in the creation of the technology company Indra. The chapter, predominantly descriptive in nature, combines industrial history with strategic management, and methodologically it is a case study that uses primary sources of public and private origin together with reports and studies by large international organisations.

4. Los materiales de la Tercera Revolución Industrial: la fibra óptica en España[4]

Este capítulo aborda la creación y evolución de las empresas mixtas relacionadas con la fibra óptica en España en el marco preciso de un amplio debate teórico sobre el alcance de la IED en ese país en la segunda mitad del siglo XX. El estudio se basa fundamentalmente en fuentes cualitativas y cuantitativas de diverso origen y naturaleza, algunas de ellas de extraordinaria relevancia por su valor intrínseco y dificultad de acceso para los investigadores. Entre ellas se encuentran las de la Compañía Telefónica Nacional de España, junto con las de instituciones nacionales, regionales e internacionales. El texto se estructura en cuatro grandes apartados, que describen sucesiva-

---

4   Versión preliminar publicada en: Calvo, Ángel. 2020. «Política industrial, multinacionales y desarrollo regional en España. La IED en la industria de la fibra óptica a finales del siglo XX». *Biblio3W Revista Bibliográfica de Geografía y Ciencias Sociales*. Vol. XXV, 1-36.

mente la revolución de la fibra óptica y su extensión mundial, la estrategia de expansión de las multinacionales en España, la dependencia tecnológica de las multinacionales en este país y la alternativa del capital multinacional europeo.

Abstract

This chapter explores the creation and evolution of fibre optic joint ventures in Spain within the precise framework of a broad theoretical debate on the extent of FDI in Spain in the second half of the twentieth century. The study is based fundamentally on qualitative and quantitative sources of diverse origin and nature, some of them of extraordinary relevance due to their intrinsic value and difficulty of access for researchers. Among them are those of the Compañía Telefónica Nacional de España, together with those of national, regional and international institutions. The text is structured in four main sections, which successively describe the fibre optic revolution and its worldwide extension, the expansion strategy of multinationals in Spain, the technological dependence of multinationals in this country and the alternative of European multinational capital.

II. La industria de las telecomunicaciones en ebullición: de la conmutación electromecánica a la electrónica

1. Tecnología de las multinacionales: la reconversión de la industria de equipo de telecomunicaciones en España a partir de la década de 1980: Standard Eléctrica[5]

Los avances tecnológicos provocados por la microelectrónica, la informática y la fibra óptica despejaron el camino a la poderosa ola mundial de desregulación de las telecomunicaciones en la última década del siglo xx. A su vez, activaron profundas transformaciones en la industria de equipos de telecomunicaciones. El vínculo tradicional entre operadores y productores de equipos se rompió y la integración vertical entre el servicio y la industria se fragmen-

---

[5] Versión preliminar en: 2024. «Corporate restructuring in the telecommunications equipment industry: the case of Spain in the late XXth century». *Business History*, Calvo, Ángel, November, 1-36.

tó. Como consecuencia, se requería una reestructuración que preservara el carácter oligopólico del mercado. El capítulo examina la trayectoria de reconversión en la mencionada industria española durante la segunda mitad de la década de 1980 y los inicios del siglo XXI. Analiza la compleja interacción entre múltiples protagonistas en la configuración de la nueva industria global en el entorno de la creciente integración de España a la economía mundial, de la división internacional del trabajo y del aumento de la competencia internacional.

Abstract

The technological advances brought about by microelectronics, computing and fibre optics paved the way for the powerful global wave of telecommunications deregulation in the last decade of the 20th century. At the same time, they triggered profound transformations in the telecommunications equipment industry. The traditional link between operators and equipment producers was broken and the vertical integration between service and industry fragmented. As a result, restructuring was required to preserve the oligopolistic nature of the market. The chapter examines the trajectory of reconversion in the aforementioned Spanish industry during the second half of the 1980s and the beginning of the 21st century. It analyses the complex interaction between multiple actors in the configuration of the new global industry in the context of Spain's growing integration into the world economy, the international division of labour and increased international competition.

2. Dependencia tecnológica y atraso económico: Citesa[6]

Este capítulo investiga las complejas relaciones entre la expansión de las multinacionales y el nacionalismo económico en el sur de Europa durante un periodo de crisis industrial, creciente integración económica e intenso cambio tecnológico, todo ello en medio de una notable alteración del marco regulador. El documento se centra en el proceso de reestructuración global de la industria de las telecomunicaciones en las dos últimas décadas del siglo XX y

---

[6] Versión preliminar en: Calvo, Ángel. 2020. «Technological dependence, captive market and outsourcing in the Spanish telecommunications equipment industry». *International Journal of Social Research*, 46, n°.4: pp. 1-25. https://escipub.com/Articles/IJSR/IJSR-2020-05-1606.pdf

los primeros años del nuevo milenio. El período abarca la transición de una industria basada en la estrecha vinculación, si no la estricta integración, entre el monopolio del servicio telefónico y la industria nacional de equipos de telecomunicaciones. Metodológicamente, se basa en un estudio de caso –el de la Compañía Internacional de Telecomunicaciones y Electrónica– en un enfoque interdisciplinario y en fuentes variadas. El capítulo revela los factores que han llevado a la transformación de una empresa integrada verticalmente en otra que externalizó su producción antes de verse envuelta en la economía globalizada. También destaca el papel de los mercados internacionales y, más concretamente, del mercado latinoamericano.

Abstract

This chapter investigates the complex relationships between multinational expansion and economic nationalism in southern Europe during a period of industrial crisis, growing economic integration and intense technological change, all in the midst of a significantly altered regulatory framework. The paper focuses on the process of global restructuring of the telecommunications industry in the last two decades of the 20th century and the early years of the new millennium. The period covers the transition from an industry based on close linkage, if not strict integration, between the telephone service monopoly and the domestic telecommunications equipment industry. Methodologically, it is based on a case study – that of the International Telecommunications and Electronics Company – an interdisciplinary approach and a variety of sources. The chapter reveals the factors that have led to the transformation of a vertically integrated company into one that outsourced its production before becoming involved in the globalised economy. It also highlights the role of international markets and, more specifically, the Latin American market.

3. De los campeones nacionales al outsourcing: Alcatel-SESA[7]

En las dos últimas décadas del siglo xx, las telecomunicaciones mundiales experimentaron grandes cambios. Las fracciones nacionales de ese mercado

---

[7] Una versión preliminar fue publicada en Calvo, Ángel 2019. «World telecommunications equipment industry from the National champions to outsourcing: the case of ALCATEL». *The International Journal of Business Management and Technology*, 3, n°.6, November–December, 130-152. http://www.theijbmt.com/archive/0930/557514347.pdf

mundial presentan notables peculiaridades. Este capítulo se refiere a los nuevos episodios de la reorganización de la estructura oligopólica de la industria europea de equipos de telecomunicaciones durante los años 90 y los primeros años del nuevo milenio desde la perspectiva de Alcatel. La multinacional francesa aporta un magnífico ejemplo de las transformaciones que se han producido a escala mundial. Metodológicamente, el caso sirve de artefacto para comprobar que una comprensión cabal del ajuste en la economía mundial requiere dilucidar cómo se reestructuraron las empresas multinacionales. El capítulo se basa en las fuentes de las empresas afectadas, en informes de grandes organizaciones internacionales, en documentos parlamentarios de varios países y en una minuciosa hemeroteca.

Abstract

In the last two decades of the twentieth century, world telecommunications underwent major changes. The national fractions of that world market present remarkable peculiarities, with differing features according to the countries. This chapter concerns new episodes of the reorganization of the oligopolistic structure of the European telecommunications equipment industry during the 1990s and the first years of the new millennium from the perspective of Alcatel. The French multinational brings a superb example of the transformations that have taken place on a global scale. Methodologically, the case serves as an artifact to verify that a thorough understanding of the adjustment in the world economy requires elucidating how multinational companies were restructured. The chapter relies on the sources of the companies concerned, on reports from large international organizations, on parliamentary documents from various countries and on a meticulous newspaper archive.

III. La pugna por la independencia tecnológica

1. Una apuesta tecnológica autóctona en un mercado oligopólico: Amper, 1980-2003[8]

El capítulo explora las pautas de supervivencia de una empresa de las telecomunicaciones con tecnología de base autóctona en un contexto de creciente liberalización e integración del mercado, que, no obstante, mantenía su estructura oligopólica. En cuanto a la metodología, prima lo narrativo, ya que relata la peripecia de Amper, no muy conocida en su conjunto aunque sí repetidamente señalada en hechos aislados. Ese relato, minucioso en ocasiones, está trabado por la prensa y la CNMV, remedo de las Actas del Consejo de Administración, inaccesibles hasta el momento. El análisis de la trayectoria se basa en fuentes variadas, entre las que sobresalen las de la propia Amper. El capítulo se estructura en cuatro grandes apartados, que incluyen los factores de la expansión de Amper, la internacionalización de la empresa en sus diversas facetas, la asociación corporativa con multinacionales y las desinversiones y segregaciones.

Abstract

The chapter addresses the patterns of survival of a telecommunication company with indigenously based technology in a context of increasing market liberalization and integration, which nevertheless maintains its oligopolistic structure. As for the methodology, the narrative prevails, since it describes the vicissitudes of Amper, which are not well known as a whole, although they have been repeatedly pointed out in isolated events. This account, which is sometimes detailed, is blocked by the press and the CNMV, imitating the Minutes of the Board of Directors, which are not available at present. The analysis of the trajectory is based on various sources, among which Amper's own stand out. The chapter is structured in four main sections, which include

---

8   Versiones preliminares publicadas en Calvo, Ángel 2020. «Tecnología autóctona y oligopolio en el sector de las telecomunicaciones: Amper 1980-2003». *Revista de Historia Industrial* 29, n°.79:165-202. https://www.researchgate.net/publication/343016348_Tecnologia_autoctona_y_oligopolio_en_el_sector_de_las_telecomunicaciones_Amper_1980-2003; 2020, September 11; «Survival Strategies in the Spanish ICT Sector: Amper between Two Crises». *International Journal of Emerging Trends in Social Sciences*, 9, n°1:1-20. https://doi.org/ https://doi.org/10.20448/2001.91.1.20.

the factors of Amper's expansion, the internationalisation of the company in its various facets, corporate partnership with multinationals and divestments and segregations.

2. Estrategias de supervivencia entre dos crisis: Amper, una multinacional de las TIC[9]

Este capítulo tiene como objetivo estudiar el comportamiento de un sector oligopólico a través del caso de una empresa multinacional de tamaño mediano, perteneciente a la industria de equipo de telecomunicación, en una época de crisis. Su interés radica en el contraste con una situación general durante la primera década del nuevo milenio, sellada por el predominio numérico del pequeño tamaño en las empresas del planeta, por un lado, y el peso determinante de las grandes empresas multinacionales. En este sentido, pretende realizar una aportación al debate sobre la incidencia de las limitaciones de recursos y del tamaño en la internacionalización de las pequeñas y medianas empresas (pymes) (Kalinic y Forza, 2012; Kuo y Li, 2003; Urata y Kawai, 2000), consideradas como tales según el criterio económico (Buckley, 1989, pp. 89-100). Asimismo, pretende intervenir en la polémica sobre las pautas para adaptarse a los mercados y al cambio tecnológico en general (Chen y Hambrick, 1995) en su pugna por la supervivencia. En la faceta particular de la internacionalización basada en la inversión extranjera directa (IED) busca ahondar en las pautas y las razones de la IED de las pymes defendidas por las teorías tradicionales. La manera incluye principalmente la teoría de la IED vertical y horizontal basada en la organización industrial (Caves) y el modelo de internacionalización gradualista (Johanson y Vahlne). La causa comprende principalmente las teorías de la ventaja monopolística basada en la competencia imperfecta (Hymer), del ciclo de vida del producto (Vernon), así como del comercio y la inversión basada en la ventaja comparativa marginal (Kojima). En el mismo ámbito, incluye la internalización basada en el coste de transacción (Buckley y Casson) y en el modelo OLI (Dunning).

---

[9]   Versión preliminar publicada en Calvo, Angel 2020. «Survival Strategies in the Spanish ICT Sector: Amper between Two Crises». *International Journal of Emerging Trends in Social Sciences*. Vol. 9, nº1: 1-20.

Abstract

This chapter aims to study the performance of an oligopolistic sector through the case of a medium-sized multinational company, belonging to the telecommunications equipment industry, in a time of crisis. Its interest lies in the contrast with a general situation during the first decade of the new millennium, sealed by the numerical predominance of the small size in the companies of the planet, on the one hand, and the determining weight of the big multinational companies. In this sense, it aims to make a contribution to the debate on the impact of resource and size constraints on the internationalization of small and medium-sized enterprises (SMEs) (Kalinic and Forza, 2012; Kuo and Li, 2003; Urata and Kawai, 2000), considered as such according to the economic criterion (Buckley, 1989, pp. 89-100). It also seeks to intervene in the controversy over patterns of adaptation to markets and technological change in general (Chen and Hambrick, 1995) in their struggle for survival. In the particular facet of internationalization based on foreign direct investment (FDI), it seeks to delve into the patterns and reasons for SME FDI defended by traditional theories. The way includes mainly the theory of vertical and horizontal FDI based on industrial organization (Caves) and the gradualist internationalization model (Johanson and Vahlne). The cause comprises mainly the theories of monopolistic advantage based on imperfect competition (Hymer), the product life cycle (Vernon), as well as trade and investment based on marginal comparative advantage (Kojima). In the same area, it includes internalisation based on transaction cost (Buckley and Casson) and the OLI model (Dunning).

3. Diversificación de los socios tecnológicos. Tecnología japonesa en la informática española: Fujitsu[10]

Este capítulo se inscribe en el interminable debate de la relación entre la IED y las empresas multinacionales, que a su vez conecta con la polémica sobre el crecimiento económico y la globalización. Trata de una fracción de la IED global hacia finales del siglo xx –la IED japonesa en España– y las razones

---

[10] Versión preliminar publicada en Calvo, Ángel 2022. «Japanese ICT multinationals in Southern Europe by the end of the twentieth century: Fujitsu in Spain». *Journal of the Knowledge Economy*, 12 de marzo, 1.341–1.373. https://rdcu.be/cgGcw. Quiero dar las gracias a Gustavo Hylander, José Blanco, José Estrada y Teófilo J. del Pozo; agradezco asimismo la intermediación de la Sra. Sara Nadal (Fundació Bancària «La Caixa»).

de la entrada de las multinacionales japonesas de las TIC en ese país del sur de Europa. Aborda la creación y evolución de la empresa Fujitsu España y se basa fundamentalmente en fuentes cualitativas y cuantitativas de diversa procedencia y naturaleza. La investigación se estructura en cuatro grandes apartados, en los que se expone el marco general de la inversión extranjera japonesa en Europa, y se abordan sucesivamente las circunstancias de la creación de Fujitsu España (1983), así como la reestructuración de esta empresa en sus aspectos organizativos, laborales y corporativos.

Abstract

This article is rooted in the endless debate of the relationship between FDI and multinational companies, which in turn connects with the controversy about economic growth and globalization. It deals with a global FDI's fraction towards the end of the twentieth century –the Japanese FDI in Spain– and the reasons for the entry of the Japanese ICT multinationals into that southern European country. It addresses the company Fujitsu España creation and evolution and is based essentially on qualitative and quantitative sources of diverse provenance and nature. The research is structured in four main sections, which outline the general framework of Japanese foreign investment in Europe, and successively addresses the circumstances in the creation of Fujitsu Spain (1983), as well as the restructuring of this company in its organisational, labour and corporate issues.